A SELECT LIBRARY

OF THE

NICENE AND POST-NICENE FATHERS

OF

THE CHRISTIAN CHURCH.

EDITED BY

PHILIP SCHAFF, D.D., LL.D.,

PROFESSOR IN THE UNION THEOLOGICAL SEMINARY, NEW YORK,
IN CONNECTION WITH A NUMBER OF PATRISTIC SCHOLARS OF EUROPE AND AMERICA.

VOLUME I

THE CONFESSIONS AND LETTERS OF ST. AUGUSTIN,

WITH A SKETCH OF HIS LIFE AND WORK.

T&T CLARK
EDINBURGH

WM. B. EERDMANS PUBLISHING COMPANY
GRAND RAPIDS, MICHIGAN

British Library Cataloguing in Publication Data

Nicene & Post-Nicene Fathers. — 1st series
1. Fathers of the church
I. Title   II. Schaff, Philip
230′.11   BR60.A62

T&T Clark ISBN 0 567 09390 5

Eerdmans ISBN 0-8028-8098-3

Reprinted, March 1994

PHOTOLITHOPRINTED BY EERDMANS PRINTING COMPANY
GRAND RAPIDS, MICHIGAN, UNITED STATES OF AMERICA

PREFACE.

ENCOURAGED by the assured co-operation of competent Patristic scholars of Great Britain and the United States, I have undertaken the general editorship of a SELECT LIBRARY OF THE NICENE AND POST-NICENE FATHERS OF THE CHRISTIAN CHURCH. It is to embrace in about twenty-five large volumes the most important works of the Greek Fathers from Eusebius to Photius, and of the Latin Fathers from Ambrose to Gregory the Great.

The series opens with St. Augustin, the greatest and most influential of all the Christian Fathers. Protestants and Catholics are equally interested in his writings, and most of all in his *Confessions*, which are contained in this volume. They will be followed by the works of St. Chrysostom, and the Church History of Eusebius.

A few words are necessary to define the object of this Library, and its relation to similar collections.

My purpose is to furnish ministers and intelligent laymen who have no access to the original texts, or are not sufficiently familiar with ecclesiastical Greek and Latin, with a complete apparatus for the study of ancient Christianity. Whatever may be the estimate we put upon the opinions of the Fathers, their historical value is beyond all dispute. They are to this day and will continue to be the chief authorities for the doctrines and usages of the Greek and Roman Churches, and the sources for the knowledge of ancient Christianity down to the age of Charlemagne. But very few can afford to buy, or are able to use such collections as Migne's Greek Patrology, which embraces 167 quarto volumes, and Migne's Latin Patrology which embraces 222 volumes.

The three leaders of the now historic Anglo-Catholic movement of Oxford, Drs. PUSEY, NEWMAN, and KEBLE, began, in 1837, the publication of "*A Library of Fathers of the Holy Catholic Church, anterior to the Division of the East and West. Translated by Members of the English Church,*" Oxford (John Henry Parker) and London (J. G. F. & J. Rivington). It is dedicated to "William Lord Archbishop of Canterbury, Primate of all England." The editors were aided by a number of able classical and ecclesiastical scholars. Dr. Pusey, the chief editor and proprietor, and Dr. Keble died in the communion of the church of their fathers to which they were loyally attached; Dr. Newman alone remains, though no more an Anglican, but a Cardinal of the Church of Rome. His connection with the enterprise ceased with his secession (1845).

The Oxford Library was undertaken not so much for an historical, as for an apologetic and dogmatic purpose. It was to furnish authentic proof for the supposed or real agreement of the Anglo-Catholic school with the faith and practice of the ancient church before the Greek schism. The selection was made accordingly. The series embraces 48 vols. It is very valuable as far as it goes, but incomplete and unequal. Volume followed volume as it happened to get ready. An undue proportion is given to exegetical works; six volumes are taken up with Augustin's Commentary on the Psalms, six with Gregory's Commentary on Job, sixteen with Commentaries of Chrysostom; while many of the most important doctrinal, ethical, and historical works of the Fathers, as Eusebius, Basil, the two Gregorys, Theodoret, Maximus Confessor, John of Damascus, Hilary, Jerome, Leo the Great, were never reached.

In 1866, Mr. T. Clark, Lord Provost of Edinburgh, and an Elder in the Free Church of Scotland, who has done more than any publisher for the introduction of German and other foreign theological literature to the English reading community, began to issue the valuable "*Ante-Nicene Christian Library*," edited by Rev. ALEXANDER ROBERTS, D. D., and JAMES DONALDSON, LL. D., which was completed in 1872 in 24 volumes, and is now being republished, by arrangement with Mr. Clark, in America in 8 volumes under the editorship of Bishop A. CLEVELAND COXE, D. D. (1884–1886). Mr. Clark, in 1871, undertook also the publication of a translation of select works of St. AUGUSTIN under the editorial care of Rev. MARCUS DODS, D. D., of Glasgow, which was completed in 15 volumes. The projected translation of CHRYSOSTOM was abandoned from want of encouragement.

Thus Episcopal divines of England, and Presbyterian divines of Scotland have prepared the way for our American enterprise, and made it possible.

We must also briefly mention a similar collection which was prepared by Roman Catholic scholars of Germany in the interest of their Church, namely the *Bibliothek der Kirchenväter. Auswahl der vorzüglichsten patristischen Werke in deutscher Uebersetzung, herausgegeben unter der Oberleitung von Dr. Valentin Thalhofer (Domdekan und Prof. der Theol. in Eichstätt*, formerly Professor in Munich). Kempten., Köselsche Buchhandlung. 1869–1886. Published in over 400 small numbers, three or four of which make a volume. An alphabetical Index vol. is now in course of preparation by Ulrich Uhle (Nos. 405 sqq.). The series was begun in 1869 by Dr. Fr. X. Reithmayr, Prof. of Theol. in Munich, who died in 1872. It embraces select writings of most of the Fathers. Seven volumes are devoted to Letters of the Popes from Linus to Pelagius II. (A. D. 67–590).

"The Christian Literature Company," who republish Clark's "Ante-Nicene Library," asked me to undertake the editorship of a Nicene and Post-Nicene Library to complete the scheme. Satisfactory arrangements have been made with Mr. Clark and with Mr. Walter Smith, representing Dr. Pusey's heirs, for the use of their translations, as far as our plan will permit. Without such a preliminary arrangement I would not have considered the proposal for a moment.

I have invited surviving authors of older translations to revise and edit their work for the American series, and I am happy to state that I received favorable replies. Some of them are among the list of contributors, others (including Cardinal Newman) have, at least, expressed a kindly interest in the enterprise, and wish it success.

The Nicene and Post-Nicene Library will be more complete and more systematic as well as much cheaper than any which has yet appeared in the English language. By omitting the voluminous Patristic commentaries on the Old Testament we shall gain room for more important and interesting works not embraced in the Oxford or Edinburgh series; and by condensing three or more of these volumes into one, and counting upon a large number of subscribers, the publishers think themselves justified in offering the Library on terms which are exceedingly liberal, considering the great expense and risk. It will be published in the same handsome style as   their Ante-Nicene Library.

May the blessing of the Great Head of the Church accompany and crown this work.

PHILIP SCHAFF.

New York, *October*, 1886.

CONTENTS.

PROLEGOMENA.

ST. AUGUSTIN'S LIFE AND WORK.

FROM SCHAFF'S CHURCH HISTORY, REVISED EDITION.

NEW YORK 1884. VOL. III. 988–1028.

Revised and enlarged with additions to literature till 1886.

CHAPTER I.—*Literature.*

I. SOURCES.

AUGUSTIN'S Works. S. AURELII AUGUSTINI *Hipponensis episcopi Opera* . . . *Post Lovaniensium theologorum recensionem* [which appeared at Antwerp in 1577 in 11 vols.], *castigatus* [referring to tomus primus, etc.] *denuo ad MSS. codd. Gallicanos*, etc. *Opera et studio monachorum ordinis S. Benedicti e congregatione S. Mauri* [Fr. Delfau, Th. Blampin, P. Coustant, and Cl. Guesnié]. Paris, 1679–1700, 11 tom. in 8 fol. vols. The same edition reprinted, with additions, at Antwerp, 1700–1703, 12 parts in 9 fol.; and at Venice, 1729–'34, in 11 tom. in 8 fol. (this edition is not to be confounded with another Venice edition of 1756–'69 in 18 vols. 4to, which is full of printing errors); also at Bassano, 1807, in 18 vols.; by *Gaume fratres*, Paris, 1836–'39, in 11 tom. in 22 parts (a very elegant edition); and lastly by *J. P. Migne*, Petit-Montrouge, 1841–'49, in 12. tom. ("Patrol. Lat." tom. xxxii.–xlvii.). Migne's edition gives, in a supplementary volume (tom. xii.), the valuable *Notitia literaria de vita, scriptis et editionibus Aug.* from SCHÖNEMANN'S "Bibliotheca historico-literaria Patrum Lat." vol. ii. Lips. 1794, the *Vindiciæ Augustinianæ* of Cardinal NORIS (NORISIUS), and the writings of Augustin first published by Fontanini and Angelo Mai. So far the most complete and convenient edition.

But a thoroughly reliable critical edition of Augustin is still a desideratum and will be issued before long by a number of scholars under the direction of the Imperial Academy of Vienna in the "Corpus Scriptorum ecclesiasticorum Latinorum."

On the controversies relating to the merits of the Bened. edition, which was sharply criticized by Richard Simon, and the Jesuits, but is still the best and defended by the Benedictines, see the supplementary volume of Migne, xii. p. 40 sqq., and THUILLIER: *Histoire de la nouvelle éd. de S. Aug. par les PP. Bénédictins*, Par. 1736.

The first printed edition of Augustin appeared at Basle, 1489–'95; another, in 1509, in 11 vols.; then the edition of Erasmus published by Frobenius, Bas. 1528–'29, in 10 vols., fol.; the *Editio Lovaniensis*, of sixteen divines of Louvain, Antw. 1577, in 11 vols. and often reprinted at Paris, Geneva, and Cologne.

Several works of Augustin have been often separately edited, especially the *Confessions* and the *City of God*. Compare a full list of the editions down to 1794 in SCHÖNEMANN'S *Bibliotheca*, vol. ii. p. 73 sqq.; for later editions see BRUNET, *Manuel du libraire*, Paris 1860, tom. I. vol. 557–567. Since then WILLIAM BRIGHT (Prof. of Ecclesiast. Hist. at Oxford) has published the Latin text of *Select Anti-Pelagian Treatises of St. Aug. and the Acts of the Second Council of Orange.* Oxford (Clarendon Press) 1880. With a valuable Introduction of 68 pages.

English translations of select works of Augustin are found in the "Oxford Library of the Fathers," ed. by Drs. Pusey, Keble, and Newman, viz.: The *Confessions*, vol. i., 1838, 4th ed., 1853; *Sermons on the N. T.*, vol. xvi., 1844, and vol. xx. 1845; *Short Treatises*, vol. xxii., 1847; *Exposition of the Psalms*, vols. xxiv., xxv., xxx., xxxii., xxxvii., xxxix., 1847, 1849, 1850, 1853, 1854; *Homilies on John*, vols. xxvi. and xxix., 1848 and 1849. Another translation by Marcus Dods and others, Edinb. (T. & T. Clark), 1871–'76, 15 vols., containing the *City of God*, the *Anti-Donatist*, the *Anti-Pelagian*, the *Anti-Manichaean* writings, *Letters, On the Trinity, On Christian Doctrine, the Euchiridion, On Catechising, On Faith and the Creed*, Commentaries on *the Sermon on the Mount*, and *the Harmony of the Gospels*, Lectures on *John*, and *Confessions*. There are several separate translations and editions of the *Confessions*: the first by Sir Tobias Matthews (a Roman Catholic), 1624, said, by Dr. Pusey, to be very inaccurate and subservient to Romanism; a second by Rev. W. Watts, D. D., 1631, 1650; a third by Abr. Woodhead (only the first 9 books). Dr. Pusey, in the first vol. of the Oxford Library of the Fathers, 1838 (new ed. 1883), republished the translation of Watts, with improvements and explanatory notes, mostly borrowed from Dubois's Latin ed. Dr. Shedd's edition, Andover, 1860, is a reprint of Watts (as republished in Boston in 1843), preceded by a thoughtful introduction, pp. v.–xxxvi. H. DE ROMESTIN translated minor doctrinal tracts in *Saint Augustin.* Oxford 1885.

German translations of select writings of Aug. in the Kempten *Bibliothek der Kirchenväter,* 1871–79, 8 vols. There are also separate translations and editions of the *Confessions* (by Silbert, 5th ed., Vienna, 1861; by Kautz, Arnsberg, 1840; by Gröninger, 4th ed., Münster, 1859; by Wilden, Schaffhausen, 1865; by Rapp, 7th ed., Gotha, 1878), of the *Enchiridion,* the *Meditations,* and the *City of God* (*Die Stadt Gottes,* by Silbert, Vienna, 1827, 2 vols.).

French translations, *Les Confessions,* by Dubois, Paris, 1688, 1715, 1758, 1776, and by Janet, Paris, 1857; a new translation with a preface by Abbé de la Mennais, Paris, 1822, 2 vols.; another by L. Moreau, Paris, 1854. *La Cité de Dieu,* by Emile Saisset, Paris, 1855, with introd. and notes, 4 vols.; older translations by Raoul de Præsles, Abbeville, 1486; Savetier, Par. 1531; P. Lombert, Par. 1675, and 1701; Abbé Goujet, Par. 1736 and 1764, reprinted at Bourges 1818; L. Moreau, with the Latin text, Par. 1846, 3 vols. *Les Soliloques,* by Pélissier, Paris, 1853. *Les Lettres,* by Poujoulat, Paris, 1858, 4 vols. *Le Manuel,* by d'Avenel, Rennes, 1861.

II. BIOGRAPHIES.

POSSIDIUS (Calamensis episcopus, a pupil and friend of Aug.): *Vita Augustini* (brief, but authentic, written 432, two years after his death, in tom. x. Append. 257–280, ed. Bened., and in nearly all other editions).

BENEDICTINI EDITORES: *Vita Augustini ex ejus potissimum scriptis concinnata,* in 8 books (very elaborate and extensive), in tom. xi. 1–492, ed. Bened. (in Migne's reprint, tom. i. col. 66–578).

The biographies of Aug. by TILLEMONT (*Mém.* tom. xiii.); ELLIES DUPIN (in "Nouvelle bibliothèque des auteurs ecclésiastiques," tom. ii. and iii.); P. BAYLE (in his "Dictionnaire historique et critique," art. Augustin); REMI CEILLIER (in "Histoire générale des auteurs sacrés et ecclés.," vol. xi. and xii.); CAVE (in "Lives of the Fathers," vol. ii.); KLOTH (*Der heil Aug.,* Aachen, 1840, 2 vols.); BÖHRINGER (*Kirchengeschichte in Biographien,* vol. i. P. iii. p. 99 sqq., revised ed. Leipzig, 1877–'78, 2 parts); POUJOULAT (*Histoire de S. Aug.* Par. 1843 and 1852, 2 vols.; the same in German by *Fr. Hurter,* Schaffh. 1847, 2 vols.); EISENBARTH (Stuttg. 1853); C. BINDEMANN (*Der heil. Aug.* Berlin, 1844, '55, '69, 3 vols., the best work in German); EDW. L. CUTTS (*St. Augustin,* London, 1880); E. DE PRESSENSÉ (in Smith and Wace, "Dictionary of Christ. Biogr." I. 216–225); PH. SCHAFF (*St. Augustin,* Berlin, 1854; English ed. New York and London, 1854, revised and enlarged in *St. Augustin, Melanchthon and Neander; three biographies,* New York, and London, 1886, pp. 1–106). On Monnica see BRAUNE: *Monnica und Augustin.* Grimma, 1846.

III. SPECIAL TREATISES ON THE SYSTEM OF AUGUSTIN.

(1) The *Theology* of Augustin. The Church Histories of NEANDER, BAUR, HASE (his large work, 1885, vol. I. 514 sqq.), and the Doctrine Histories of NEANDER, GIESELER, BAUR, HAGENBACH, SHEDD, NITZSCH, SCHWANE, BACH, HARNACK (in preparation, first vol., 1886).

The voluminous literature on the Pelagian controversy embraces works of G. J. VOSS, GARNIER, JANSEN (died 1638; *Augustinus,* 1640, 3 vols.; he read Aug. twenty times and revived his system in the R. Cath. Church, but was condemned by the Pope), Cardinal NORIS (*Historia Pelagiana,* Florence, 1673), WALCH (*Ketzergeschichte,* vols. IV. and V., 1768 and 1770), WIGGERS (*Augustinismus und Pelagianismus,* 1821 and 1833), BERSOT (*Doctr. de St. Aug. sur la liberté et la Providence,* Paris, 1843), JACOBI (*Lehre des Pelagius,* 1842), JUL. MÜLLER (*Lehre von der Sünde,* 5th ed. 1866, Engl. transl. by Urwick, 1868), MOZLEY (*Augustinian Doctrine of Predestination,* London, 1855, very able), W. BRIGHT (Introduction to his ed. of the Anti-Pelag. writings of Aug. Oxford 1880), and others. See SCHAFF, vol. III. 783–785.

VAN GOENS: *De Aur. August. apologeta, sec. l. de Civitate Dei.* Amstel. 1838.

NIRSCHL (Rom. Cath.). *Ursprung und Wesen des Bösen nach der Lehre des heil. Augustin.* 1854.

F. RIBBECK: *Donatus und Augustinus, oder der erste entscheidende Kampf zwischen Separatismus und Kirche.* Elberfeld, 1858, 2 vols.

FR. NITZSCH: *Augustin's Lehre vom Wunder.* Berlin, 1865.

GANGAUF: *Des heil. August. Lehre von Gott dem dreieinigen.* Augsburg, 1866. EMIL FEUERLEIN: *Ueber die Stellung Augustin's in der Kirchen = und Kulturgeschichte,* in Sybel's "Histor. Zeitschrift" for 1869, vol. XI. 270–313. NAVILLE: *Saint Augustin, Etude sur le développement de sa pensée.* Genève, 1872. ERNST: *Die Werke und Tugenden der Ungläubigen nach Augustin.* Freiburg, 1872. AUG. DORNER (son of Is. A. D.): *Augustinus, sein theol. System und seine religionsphilosophische Anschauung.* Berlin, 1873 (comp. his art. in Herzog's "Encycl." 2d ed. I. 781–795, abridged in Schaff-Herzog I. 174 sqq.). CH. H. COLLETT: *St. Aug., a Sketch of his Life and Writings as affecting the controversy with Rome.* London, 1883. H. REUTER (Prof. of Church

History in Göttingen) : *Augustinische Studien,* in Brieger's "Zeitschrift für Kirchengeschichte," for 1880–'86 (several articles on Aug.'s doctrine of the church, of predestination, the kingdom of God, etc.,—very valuable).

(2) The *Philosophy* of Augustin is discussed in the larger Histories of Philosophy by BRUCKER, TENNEMANN, RIXNER, H. RITTER (vol. vi. pp. 153–443), ERDMANN (*Grundriss der Gesch. der Philos.* I. 231 sqq.), UEBERWEG (*Hist. of Philos.,* transl. by Morris, New York, vol. I. 333–346); PRANTL (*Geschichte der Logik im Abendlande,* Leipzig, 1853, I. 665–672); HUBER (*Philosophie der Kirchenväter,* München, 1859), and in the following special works :

THEOD. GANGAUF : *Metaphysische Psychologie des heil. Augustinus.* 1ste Abtheilung, Augsburg, 1852. T. THÉRY : *Le génie philosophique et littéraire de saint Augustin.* Par. 1861. Abbé FLOTTES : *Études sur saint Aug., son génie, son âme, sa philosophie.* Montpèllier, 1861. NOURRISSON : *La philosophie de saint Augustin (ouvrage couronné par l'Institut de France),* deuxiéme éd. Par. 1866, 2 vols. REINKENS : *Geschichtsphilosophie des Aug.* Schaffhausen, 1866. FERRAZ : *De la psychologie de S. Augustin,* 2d ed. Paris, 1869. SCHÜTZ : *Augustinum non esse ontologum.* Monast. 1867. A. F. HEWITT : *The Problems of the Age, with Studies in St. Augustin.* New York, 1868. G. LOESCHE : *De Augustino Plotinizante.* Jenae, 1880 (68 pages).

(3) On Aug. as a Latin author see BÄHR : *Geschichte der röm Literatur,* Suppl. II. EBERT : *Geschichte der latein. Literatur* (Leipzig, 1874, I. 203 sqq.). VILLEMAIN : *Tableau de l'éloquence chrétienne au IV* siècle (Paris, 1849).

CHAPTER II.—*A Sketch of the Life of St. Augustin.*

It is a venturesome and delicate undertaking to write one's own life, even though that life be a masterpiece of nature and the grace of God, and therefore most worthy to be described. Of all autobiographies none has so happily avoided the reef of vanity and self-praise, and none has won so much esteem and love through its honesty and humility as that of St. Augustin.

The "Confessions," which he wrote in the forty-fourth year of his life, still burning in the ardor of his first love, are full of the fire and unction of the Holy Spirit. They are a sublime composition, in which Augustin, like David in the fifty-first Psalm, confesses to God, in view of his own and of succeeding generations, without reserve the sins of his youth ; and they are at the same time a hymn of praise to the grace of God, which led him out of darkness into light, and called him to service in the kingdom of Christ.[1] Here we see the great church teacher of all times "prostrate in the dust, conversing with God, basking in his love ; his readers hovering before him only as a shadow." He puts away from himself all honor, all greatness, all merit, and lays them gratefully at the feet of the All-merciful. The reader feels on every hand that Christianity is no dream nor illusion, but truth and life, and he is carried along in adoration of the wonderful grace of God.

AURELIUS AUGUSTINUS, born on the 13th of November, 354,[2] at Tagaste, an unimportant village of the fertile province of Numidia in North Africa, not far from Hippo Regius, inherited from his heathen father, Patricius,[3] a passionate sensibility, from his Christian mother, Monnica (one of the noblest women in the history of Christianity, of a highly intellectual and spiritual cast, of fervent piety, most tender affection, and all-conquering love), the deep yearning towards God so grandly expressed in his sentence : "Thou hast made us for Thyself, and our heart is restless till it rests in Thee."[4] This yearning, and his reverence for the sweet and holy name of Jesus, though crowded into the background, attended him in his studies at the schools of Madaura and Carthage, on his journeys to Rome and Milan, and on his tedious wanderings through the labyrinth of carnal pleasures, Manichæan mock-wisdom, Academic skepticism, and Platonic idealism ; till at last the prayers of his mother, the sermons of Ambrose, the biography

---

[1] Augustin himself says of his *Confessions : " Confessionum mearum libri tredecim et de malis et de bonis meis Deum laudant justum et bonum, atque in eum excitant humanum intellectum et affectum." Retract.* l. ii. c. 6. He refers to his *Confessions* also in his *Epistola ad Darium, Ep.* CCXXXI. cap. 5 ; and in his *De dono perseverantiæ,* cap. 20 (53).

[2] He died, according to the Chronicle of his friend and pupil Prosper Aquitanus, the 28th of August, 430 (in the third month of the siege of Hippo by the Vandals) ; according to his biographer Possidius he lived seventy-six years. The day of his birth Augustin states himself, *De vita beata,* § 6 (tom. i. 300) : " *Idibus Novembris mihi natalis dies erat."*

[3] He received baptism shortly before his death.

[4] *Conf.* i. 1 : " *Fecisti nos ad Te, et inquietum est cor nostrum, donec requiescat in Te."* In all his aberrations, which we would hardly know, if it were not from his own free confession, he never sunk to anything mean, but remained, like Paul in his Jewish fanaticism, a noble intellect and an honorable character, with burning love for the true and the good.

of St. Anthony, and, above all, the Epistles of Paul, as so many instruments in the hand of the Holy Spirit, wrought in the man of three and thirty years that wonderful change which made him an incalculable blessing to the whole Christian world, and brought even the sins and errors of his youth into the service of the truth.[1]

A son of so many prayers and tears could not be lost, and the faithful mother who travailed with him in spirit with greater pain than her body had in bringing him into the world,[2] was permitted, for the encouragement of future mothers, to receive shortly before her death an answer to her prayers and expectations, and was able to leave this world with joy without revisiting her earthly home. For Monnica died on a homeward journey, in Ostia at the mouth of the Tiber, in her fifty-sixth year, in the arms of her son, after enjoying with him a glorious conversation that soared above the confines of space and time, and was a foretaste of the eternal Sabbath-rest of the saints. If those moments, he says, could be prolonged for ever, they would more than suffice for his happiness in heaven. She regretted not to die in a foreign land, because she was not far from God, who would raise her up at the last day. "Bury my body anywhere," was her last request, "and trouble not yourselves for it; only this one thing I ask, that you remember me at the altar of my God, wherever you may be."[3] Augustin, in his *Confessions*, has erected to Monnica a noble monument that can never perish.

If ever there was a thorough and fruitful conversion, next to that of Paul on the way to Damascus, it was that of Augustin, when, in a garden of the Villa Cassiciacum, not far from Milan, in September of the year 386, amidst the most violent struggles of mind and heart—the birth-throes of the new life—he heard that divine voice of a child: "Take, read!" and he "put on the Lord Jesus Christ" (Rom. xiii. 14). It is a touching lamentation of his: "I have loved Thee late, Thou Beauty, so old and so new; I have loved Thee late! And lo! Thou wast within, but I was without, and was seeking Thee there. And into Thy fair creation I plunged myself in my ugliness; for Thou wast with me, and I was not with Thee! Those things kept me away from Thee, which had not been, except they had been in Thee! Thou didst call, and didst cry aloud, and break through my deafness. Thou didst glimmer, Thou didst shine, and didst drive away my blindness. Thou didst breathe, and I drew breath, and breathed in Thee. I tasted Thee, and I hunger and thirst. Thou didst touch me, and I burn for Thy peace. If I, with all that is within me, may once live in Thee, then shall pain and trouble forsake me; entirely filled with Thee, all shall be life to me."

He received baptism from Ambrose in Milan on Easter Sunday, 387, in company with his friend and fellow-convert Alypius, and his natural son Adeodatus (*given by God*). It impressed the divine seal upon the inward transformation. He broke radically with the world; abandoned the brilliant and lucrative vocation of a teacher of rhetoric, which he had followed in Rome and Milan; sold his goods for the benefit of the poor; and thenceforth devoted his rare gifts exclusively to the service of Christ, and to that service he continued faithful to his latest breath. After the death of his mother, whom he revered and loved with the most tender affection, he went a second time to Rome for several months, and wrote books in defence of true Christianity against false philosophy and against the Manichæan heresy. Returning to Africa, he spent three years, with his friends Alypius and Evodius, on an estate in his native Tagaste, in contemplative and literary retirement.

Then, in 391, he was chosen presbyter against his will, by the voice of the people, which, as

---

[1] For particulars respecting the course of Augustin's life, see my work above cited, and other monographs. Comp. also the fine remarks of Dr. BAUR in his posthumous *Lectures on Doctrine-History* (1866), vol. i. Part ii. p. 26 sqq. He compares the development of Augustin with the course of Christianity from the beginning to his time, aud draws a parallel between Augustin and Origen.

[2] Conf. ix. c. 8: "*Quæ me parturivit et carne, ut in hanc temporalem, et corde, ut in æternam lucem nascerer.*" L. v. 9: "*Non enim satis eloquor, quid erga me habebat animi, et quanto majore sollicitudine me parturiebat spiritu, quam carne pepererat.*" In *De dono persev.* c. 20, he ascribes his conversion under God "to the faithful and daily tears" of his mother.

[3] Conf. l. ix. c. 11: "*Tantum illud vos rogo, ut ad Domini altare memineritis mei, ubi fueritis.*" This must be explained from the already prevailing custom of offering prayers for the dead, which, however, had rather the form of thanksgiving for the mercy of God shown to them, than the later form of intercession for them.

in the similar cases of Cyprian and Ambrose, proved to be the voice of God, in the Numidian maritime city of Hippo Regius (now Bona) ; and in 395 he was elected bishop in the same city. For eight and thirty years, until his death, he labored in this place, and made it the intellectual centre of Western Christendom.[1]

His outward mode of life was extremely simple, and mildly ascetic. He lived with his clergy in one house in an apostolic community of goods, and made this house a seminary of theology, out of which ten bishops and many lower clergy went forth. Females, even his sister, were excluded from his house, and could see him only in the presence of others. But he founded religious societies of women ; and over one of these his sister, a saintly widow, presided.[2] He once said in a sermon, that he had nowhere found better men, and he had nowhere found worse, than in monasteries. Combining, as he did, the clerical life with the monastic, he became unwittingly the founder of the Augustinian order, which gave the reformer Luther to the world. He wore the black dress of the Eastern cœnobites, with a cowl and a leathern girdle. He lived almost entirely on vegetables, and seasoned the common meal with reading or free conversation, in which it was a rule that the character of an absent person should never be touched. He had this couplet engraved on the table :

> *" Quisquis amat dictis absentum rodere vitam,*
> *Hanc mensam vetitam noverit esse sibi."*

He often preached five days in succession, sometimes twice a day, and set it as the object of his preaching, that all might live with him, and he with all, in Christ. Wherever he went in Africa, he was begged to preach the word of salvation.[3] He faithfully administered the external affairs connected with his office, though he found his chief delight in comtemplation. He was specially devoted to the poor, and, like Ambrose, upon exigency, caused the church vessels to be melted down to redeem prisoners. But he refused legacies by which injustice was done to natural heirs, and commended the bishop Aurelius of Carthage for giving back unasked some property which a man had bequeathed to the church, when his wife unexpectedly bore him children.

Augustin's labors extended far beyond his little diocese. He was the intellectual head of the North African and the entire Western church of his time. He took active interest in all theological and ecclesiastical questions. He was the champion of the orthodox doctrine against Manichæan, Donatist, and Pelagian. In him was concentrated the whole polemic power of the catholic church of the time against heresy and schism ; and in him it won the victory over them.

In his last years he took a critical review of his literary productions, and gave them a thorough sifting in his Retractations. His latest controversial works, against the Semi-Pelagians, written in a gentle spirit, date from the same period. He bore the duties of his office alone till his seventy-second year, when his people unanimously elected his friend Heraclius to be his assistant.

The evening of his life was troubled by increasing infirmities of body and by the unspeakable wretchedness which the barbarian Vandals spread over his country in their victorious invasion,

---

1 He is still known among the inhabitants of the place as " the great Christian " (Rumi Kebir). GIBBON (ch. xxxiii. ad ann. 430) thus describes the place which became so famous through Augustin : " The maritime colony of *Hippo*, about two hundred miles westward of Carthage, had formerly acquired the distinguishing epithet of *Regius*, from the residence of the Numidian kings ; and some remains of trade and populousness still adhere to the modern city, which is known in Europe by the corrupted name of Bona." Sallust mentions Hippo once in his history of the Jugurthine War. A part of the wealth with which Sallust built and beautified his splendid mansion and gardens in Rome, was extorted from this and other towns of North Africa while governor of Numidia. Since the French conquest of Algiers Hippo Regius was rebuilt under the name of Bona and is now one of the finest towns in North Africa, numbering over 10,000 inhabitants, French, Moors, and Jews.

2 He mentions a sister, " *soror mea, sancta proposita* " [*monasterii*], without naming her, *Epist.* 211, n. 4 (ed. Bened.), alias *Ep.* 109. He also had a brother by the name of Navigius.

3 Possidius says, in his *Vita Aug.* : " *Cæterum episcopatu suscepto multo instantius ac ferventius, majore auctoritate, non in una tantum regione, sed ubicunque rogatus venisset, verbum salutis alacriter, ac suaviter pullulante atque crescente Domini ecclesia, prædicavit.*"

destroying cities, villages, and churches, without mercy, and even besieging the fortified city of Hippo.[1] Yet he faithfully persevered in his work. The last ten days of his life he spent in close retirement, in prayers and tears and repeated reading of the penitential Psalms, which he had caused to be written on the wall over his bed, that he might have them always before his eyes. Thus with an act of penitence he closed his life. In the midst of the terrors of the siege and the despair of his people he could not suspect what abundant seed he had sown for the future.

In the third month of the siege of Hippo, on the 28th of August, 430, in the seventy-sixth year of his age, in full possession of his faculties, and in the presence of many friends and pupils, he past gently and peacefully into that eternity to which he had so long aspired. " O how wonderful," wrote he in his *Meditations*,[2] " how beautiful and lovely are the dwellings of Thy house, Almighty God ! I burn with longing to behold Thy beauty in Thy bridal-chamber. . . . O Jerusalem, holy city of God, dear bride of Christ, my heart loves thee, my soul has already long sighed for thy beauty ! . . . The King of kings Himself is in the midst of thee, and His children are within thy walls. There are the hymning choirs of angels, the fellowship of heavenly citizens. There is the wedding-feast of all who from this sad earthly pilgrimage have reached thy joys. There is the far-seeing choir of the prophets ; there the company of the twelve apostles ; there the triumphant army of innumerable martyrs and holy confessors. Full and perfect love there reigns, for God is all in all. They love and praise, they praise and love Him evermore. . . . Blessed, perfectly and forever blessed, shall I too be, if, when my poor body shall be dissolved, . . . I may stand before my King and God, and see Him in His glory, as He Himself hath deigned to promise : ' Father, I will that they also whom Thou hast given Me be with Me where I am ; that they may behold My glory which I had with Thee before the world was.' " This aspiration after the heavenly Jerusalem found grand expression in the hymn *De gloria et gaudiis Paradisi :*

> " *Ad perennis vitæ fontem mens sativit arida.*"

It is incorporated in the *Meditations* of Augustin, and the ideas originated in part with him, but were not brought into poetical form till long afterwards by Peter Damiani.[3]

He left no will, for in his voluntary poverty he had no earthly property to dispose of, except his library ; this he bequeathed to the church, and it was fortunately preserved from the depredations of the Arian barbarians.[4]

Soon after his death Hippo was taken and destroyed by the Vandals.[5] Africa was lost to the Romans. A few decades later the whole West-Roman empire fell in ruins. The culmination of the African church was the beginning of its decline. But the work of Augustin could not perish. His ideas fell like living seed into the soil of Europe, and produced abundant fruits in nations and countries of which he had never heard.[6]

---

[1] Possidius, c. 28, gives a vivid picture of the ravages of the Vandals, which have become proverbial. Comp. also Gibbon, ch. xxxiii.

[2] I freely combine several passages.

[3] Comp. *Opera*, tom. vi. p. 117 (Append.) ; Daniel: *Thesaurus hymnol.* i. 116 sqq., and iv. 203 sq., and Mone : *Lat. Hymner,* i. 422 sqq., Mone ascribes the poem to an unknown writer of the sixth century, but Trench (*Sacred Latin Poetry*, 2d ed., 315) and others attribute it to Cardinal Peter Damiani, the friend of Pope Hildebrand (d. 1072). Augustin wrote his poetry in prose.

[4] Possidius says, *Vita,* c. 31 : " *Testamentum nullum fecit, quia unde faceret, pauper Dei non habuit. Ecclesiæ bibliothecam omnesque codices diligenter posteris custodiendos semper jubebat.*"

[5] The inhabitants escaped to the sea. There appears no bishop of Hippo after Augustin. In the seventh century the old city was utterly destroyed by the Arabians, but two miles from it Bona was built of its ruins. Comp. Tillemont, xiii. 945, and Gibbon, ch. xxxiii. Gibbon says, that Bona, " in the sixteenth century, contained about three hundred families of industrious, but turbulent manufacturers. The adjacent territory is renowned for a pure air, a fertile soil, and plenty of exquisite fruits." Since the French conquest of Algiers, Bona was rebuilt in 1832, and is gradually assuming a French aspect. It is now one of the finest towns in Algeria, the key to the province of Constantine, has a public garden, several schools, considerable commerce, and a population of over ten thousand of French, Moors, and Jews, the great majority of whom are foreigners. The relics of St. Augustin have been recently transferred from Pavia to Bona. See the letters of abbé Sibour to Poujoulat *sur la translation de la relique de saint Augustin de Pavie à Hippone,* in POUJOULAT's *Histoire de saint Augustin,* tom. i. p. 413 sqq.

[6] Even in Africa Augustin's spirit reappeared from time to time notwithstanding the barbarian confusion, as a light in darkness, first in VIGILIUS, bishop of Thapsus, who, at the close of the fifth century, ably defended the orthodox doctrine of the Trinity and the person of Christ, and to whom the authorship of the so-called Athanasian Creed has sometimes been ascribed; in FULGENTIUS,

CHAPTER III.—*Estimate of St. Augustin.*

Augustin, the man with upturned eye, with pen in the left hand, and a burning heart in the right (as he is usually represented), is a philosophical and theological genius of the first order, towering like a pyramid above his age, and looking down commandingly upon succeeding centuries. He had a mind uncommonly fertile and deep, bold and soaring; and with it, what is better, a heart full of Christian love and humility. He stands of right by the side of the greatest philosophers of antiquity and of modern times. We meet him alike on the broad highways and the narrow footpaths, on the giddy Alpine heights and in the awful depths of speculation, wherever philosophical thinkers before him or after him have trod. As a theologian he is *facile princeps*, at least surpassed by no church father, schoolman, or reformer. With royal munificence he scattered ideas in passing, which have set in mighty motion other lands and later times. He combined the creative power of Tertullian with the churchly spirit of Cyprian, the speculative intellect of the Greek church with the practical tact of the Latin. He was a Christian philosopher and a philosophical theologian to the full. It was his need and his delight to wrestle again and again with the hardest problems of thought, and to comprehend to the utmost the divinely revealed matter of the faith.[1] He always asserted, indeed, the primacy of faith, according to his maxim: *Fides præcedit intellectum;* appealing, with theologians before him, to the well known passage of Isaiah vii. 9 (in the LXX.): "*Nisi credideritis, non intelligetis.*"[2] But to him faith itself was an acting of reason, and from faith to knowledge, therefore, there was a necessary transition.[3] He constantly looked below the surface to the hidden motives of actions and to the universal laws of diverse events. The Metaphysician and the Christian believer coalesced in him. His *meditatio* passes with the utmost ease into *oratio*, and his *oratio* into *meditatio*. With profundity he combined an equal clearness and sharpness of thought. He was an extremely skilful and a successful dialectician, inexhaustible in arguments and in answers to the objections of his adversaries.

He has enriched Latin literature with a greater store of beautiful, original, and pregnant proverbial sayings, than any classic author, or any other teacher of the church.[4]

---

bishop of Ruspe, one of the chief opponents of Semi-Pelagianism, and the later Arianism, who with sixty catholic bishops of Africa was banished for several years by the Arian Vandals to the island of Sardinia, and who was called the Augustin of the sixth century (died 533); and in FACUNDUS OF HERMIANE (died 570), and FULGENTIUS FERRANDUS, and LIBERATUS, two deacons of Carthage, who took a prominent part in the Three Chapter controversy.

[1] Or, as he wrote to a friend about the year 410, *Epist.* 120, c. 1, § 2 (tom. ii. p. 347, ed. Bened. Venet.; in older ed., *Ep.* 122): "*Ut quod credis intelligas . . . non ut fidem respuas, sed ea quæ fidei firmitate jam tenes, etiam rationis luce conspicias.*" He continues, ibid. c. 3: "*Absit namque, ut hoc in nobis Deus oderit, in quo nos reliquis animalibus excellentiores creavit. Absit, inquam, ut ideo credamus, ne rationem accipiamus vel quæramus; cum etiam credere non possemus, nisi rationales animas haberemus.*" In one of his earliest works, *Contra Academ.* l. iii. c. 20, § 43, he says of himself: "*Ita sum affectus, ut quid sit verum non credendo solum, sed etiam intelligendo apprehendere impatienter desiderem.*"

[2] Ἐὰν μὴ πιστεύσητε, οὐδὲ μὴ συνῆτε. But the proper translation of the Hebrew is: "If ye will not believe [in me, בְּ for כְּ], surely ye shall not be established (or, not remain)."

[3] Comp. *De præd. sanct.* cap. 2, § 5 (tom. x. p. 792): "*Ipsum credere nihil aliud est quam cum assensione cogitare. Non enim omnis qui cogitat, credit, cum ideo cogitant, plerique ne credant; sed cogitat omnis qui credit, et credendo cogitat et cogitando credit. Fides si non cogitetur, nulla est.*" *Ep.* 120, cap. 1, § 3 (tom. ii. 347), and *Ep.* 137, c. 4, § 15 (tom. ii. 408): "*Intellectui fides aditum aperit, infidelitas claudit.*" Augustin's view of faith and knowledge is discussed at large by GANGAUF, *Metaphysische Psychologie des heil. Augustinus*, i. pp. 31–76, and by NOURRISSON, *La philosophie de saint Augustin*, tom. ii. 282–290.

[4] Prosper Aquitanus collected in the year 450 or 451 from the works of Augustin 392 sentences (see the Appendix to the tenth vol. of the Bened. ed. p. 223 sqq., and in Migne's ed. of Prosper Aquitanus, col. 427–496), with reference to theological purport and the Pelagian controversies. We recall some of the best which he has omitted:

"*Novum Testamentum in Vetere latet, Vetus in Novo patet.*"
"*Distingue tempora, et concordabit Scriptura.*"
"*Cor nostrum inquietum est, donec requiescat in Te.*"
"*Da quod jubes, et jube quod vis.*"
"*Non vincit nisi veritas, victoria veritatis est caritas.*"
"*Ubi amor, ibi trinitas.*"
"*Fides præcedit intellectum.*"
"*Deo servire vera libertas est.*"
"*Nulla infelicitas frangit, quem felicitas nulla corrumpit.*"

The famous maxim of ecclesiastical harmony: "*In necessariis unitas, in dubiis* (or, *non necessariis*) *libertas, in omnibus* (*in utrisque*) *caritas,*"—which is often ascribed to Augustin, dates in this form not from him, but from a much later period. Dr. LUCKE

He had a creative and decisive hand in almost every dogma of the Latin church, completing some, and advancing others. The centre of his system is the FREE REDEEMING GRACE OF GOD IN CHRIST, OPERATING THROUGH THE ACTUAL, HISTORICAL CHURCH. He is evangelical or Pauline in his doctrine of sin and grace, but catholic (that is, old-catholic, not Roman Catholic) in his doctrine of the church. The Pauline element comes forward mainly in the Pelagian controversy, the catholic-churchly in the Donatist; but each is modified by the other.

Dr. Baur incorrectly makes *freedom* the fundamental idea of the Augustinian system. But this much better suits the Pelagian; while Augustin started (like Calvin and Schleiermacher) from the idea of the absolute *dependence* of man upon God. He changed his idea of freedom during the Pelagian controversy. Baur draws an ingenious and suggestive comparison between Augustin and Origen, the two greatest intellects among the church fathers. "There is no church teacher of the ancient period," says he,[1] "who, in intellect and in grandeur and consistency of view, can more justly be placed by the side of Origen than Augustin; none who, with all the difference in individuality and in mode of thought, so closely resembles him. How far both towered above their times, is most clearly manifest in the very fact that they alone, of all the theologians of the first six centuries, became the creators of distinct systems, each proceeding from a definite idea, and each completely carried out; and this fact proves also how much the one system has that is analogous to the other. The one system, like the other, is founded upon the idea of *freedom;* in both there is a specific act, by which the entire development of human life is determined; and in both this is an act which lies far outside of the temporal consciousness of the individual; with this difference alone, that in one system the act belongs to each separate individual himself, and only falls outside of his temporal life and consciousness; in the other, it lies within the sphere of the temporal history of man, but is only the act of one individual. If in the system of Origen nothing gives greater offence than the idea of the pre-existence and fall of souls, which seems to adopt heathen ideas into the Christian faith, there is in the system of Augustin the same overleaping of individual life and consciousness, in order to explain from an act in the past the present sinful condition of man; but the pagan Platonic point of view is exchanged for one taken from the Old Testament. . . . What therefore essentially distinguishes the system of Augustin from that of Origen, is only this: the fall of Adam is substituted for the pre-temporal fall of souls, and what in Origen still wears a heathen garb, puts on in Augustin a purely Old Testament form."

The learning of Augustin was not equal to his genius, nor as extensive as that of Origen and Eusebius, but still considerable for his time, and superior to that of any of the Latin fathers, with the single exception of Jerome. He had received in the schools of Madaura and Carthage the usual philosophical and rhetorical preparation for the forum, which stood him in good stead also in theology. He was familiar with Latin literature, and was by no means blind to the excellencies of the classics, though he placed them far below the higher beauty of the Holy Scriptures. The *Hortensius* of Cicero (a lost work) inspired him during his university course with enthusiasm for philosophy and for the knowledge of truth for its own sake; the study of Platonic and Neo-Platonic works (in the Latin version of the rhetorician Victorinus) kindled in him an incredible fire;[2] though in both he missed the holy name of Jesus and the cardinal virtues of love and humility, and found in them only beautiful ideals without power to conform

---

(in a special treatise on the antiquity of the author, the original form, etc., of this sentence, Göttingen, 1850) traces the authorship to RUPERT MELDENIUS, an irenical German theologian of the seventeenth century. Baxter, also, who lived during the intense conflict of English Puritanism and Episcopacy, and grew weary of the "fury of theologians," adopted a similar sentiment. The sentence is held by many who differ widely in the definition of what is "necessary" and what is "doubtful." The meaning of "charity in all things" is above doubt, and a moral duty of every Christian, though practically violated by too many in all denominations.

[1] *Vorlesungen über die christl. Dogmengeschichte*, vol. I. P. II. p. 30 sq.

[2] *Adv. Academicos,* l. ii. c. 2, § 5: "*Etiam mihi ipsi de me incredibile incendium concitarunt.*" And in several passages of the *Civitas Dei* (viii. 3–12; xxii. 27) he speaks very favourably of Plato, and also of Aristotle, and thus broke the way for the high authority of the Aristotelian philosophy with the scholastics of the middle age.

him to them. His City of God, his book on heresies, and other writings, show an extensive knowledge of ancient philosophy, poetry, and history, sacred and secular. He refers to the most distinguished persons of Greece and Rome; he often alludes to Pythagoras, Plato, Aristotle, Plotin, Porphyry, Cicero, Seneca, Horace, Vergil, to the earlier Greek and Latin fathers, to Eastern and Western heretics. But his knowledge of Greek literature was mostly derived from Latin translations. With the Greek language, as he himself frankly and modestly confesses, he had, in comparison with Jerome, but a superficial acquaintance.[1] Hebrew he did not understand at all. Hence, with all his extraordinary familiarity with the Latin Bible, he made many mistakes in exposition. He was rather a thinker than a scholar, and depended mainly on his own resources, which were always abundant.

NOTES.—We note some of the most intelligent and appreciative estimates of Augustin. ERASMUS (*Ep. dedicat. ad Alfons. archiep. Tolet.* 1529) says, with an ingenious play upon the name Aurelius Augustinus: "*Quid habet orbis christianus hoc scriptore magis aureum vel augustius? ut ipsa vocabula nequaquam fortuito, sed numinis providentia videantur indita viro. Auro sapientiæ nihil pretiosius: fulgore eloquentiæ cum sapientia conjunctæ nihil mirabilius. . . . Non arbitror alium esse doctorem, in quem opulentus ille ac benignus Spiritus dotes suas omnes largius effuderit, quam in Augustinum.*" The great philosopher LEIBNITZ (*Præfat. ad Theodic.* § 34) calls him "*virum sane magnum et ingenii stupendi,*" and "*vastissimo ingenio præditum.*" Dr. BAUR, without sympathy with his views, speaks enthusiastically of the man and his genius. Among other things he says (*Vorlesungen über Dogmengeschichte,* i. i. p. 61): "There is scarcely another theological author so fertile and withal so able as Augustin. His scholarship was not equal to his intellect; yet even that is sometimes set too low, when it is asserted that he had no acquaintance at all with the Greek language; for this is incorrect, though he had attained no great proficiency in Greek." C. BINDEMANN (a Lutheran divine) begins his thorough monograph (vol. i. preface) with the well-deserved eulogium: "St. Augustin is one of the greatest personages in the church. He is second in importance to none of the teachers who have wrought most in the church since the apostolic time; and it can well be said that among the church fathers the first place is due to him, and in the time of the Reformation a Luther alone, for fulness and depth of thought and grandeur of character, may stand by his side. He is the summit of the development of the mediæval Western church; from him descended the mysticism, no less than the scholasticism, of the middle age; he was one of the strongest pillars of the Roman Catholicism, and from his works, next to the Holy Scriptures, especially the Epistles of Paul, the leaders of the Reformation drew most of that conviction by which a new age was introduced." STAUDENMAIER, a Roman Catholic theologian, counts Augustin among those minds in which an hundred others dwell (*Scotus Erigena,* i. p. 274). The Roman Catholic philosophers A. GÜNTHER and TH. GANGAUF, put him on an equality with the greatest philosophers, and discern in him a providential personage endowed by the Spirit of God for the instruction of all ages. A striking characterization is that of the Old Catholic Dr. HUBER (in his instructive work: *Die Philosophie der Kirchenväter,* Munich, 1859, p. 312 sq.): "Augustin is a unique phenomenon in Christian history. No one of the other fathers has left so luminous traces of his existence. Though we find among them many rich and powerful minds, yet we find in none the forces of personal character,

---

[1] It is sometimes asserted that he had no knowledge at all of the Greek. So Gibbon, for example, says (ch. xxxiii.): "The superficial learning of Augustin was confined to the Latin language." But this is a mistake. In his youth he had a great aversion to the glorious language of Hellas because he had a bad teacher and was forced to it (*Conf.* i. 14). He read the writings of Plato in a Latin translation (vii. 9). But after his baptism, during his second residence in Rome, he resumed the study of Greek with greater zest, for the sake of his biblical studies. In Hippo he had, while presbyter, good opportunity to advance in it, since his bishop, Aurelius, a native Greek, understood his mother tongue much better than the Latin. In his books he occasionally makes reference to the Greek. In his work *Contra Jul.* i. c. 6 § 21 (tom. x. 510), he corrects the Pelagian Julian in a translation from Chrysostom, quoting the original. "*Ego ipsa verba Græca quæ a Joanne dicta sunt ponam:* διὰ τοῦτο καὶ τὰ παιδία βαπτίζομεν, καίτοι ἁμαρτήματα οὐκ ἔχοντα, *quod est Latine: Ideo et infantes baptizamus, quamvis peccata non habentes.*" Julian had freely rendered this: "*cum non sint coinquinati peccato,*" and had drawn the inference: "*Sanctus Joannes Constantinopolitanus* [John Chrysostom] *negat esse in parvulis originale peccatum.*" Augustin helps himself out of the pinch by arbitrarily supplying *propria* to ἁμαρτήματα, so that the idea of sin inherited from another is not excluded. The Greek fathers, however, did not consider hereditary corruption to be proper sin or guilt at all, but only defect, weakness, or disease. In the *City of God,* lib. xix. c. 23, he quotes a passage from Porphyry's ἐκ λογίων φιλοσοφία, and in book xviii. 23, he explains the Greek monogram ἰχθύς. He gives the derivation of several Greek words, and correctly distinguishes between such synonyms as γεννάω and τίκτω, εὐχή and προσευχή, πνοή and πνεῦμα. It is probable that he read Plotin, and the Panarion of Epiphanius or the summary of it, in Greek (while the Church History of Eusebius he knew only in the translation of Rufinus). But in his exegetical and other works he very rarely consults the Septuagint or Greek Testament, and was content with the very imperfect *Itala,* or the improved version of Jerome (the *Vulgate*). The Benedictine editors overestimate his knowledge of Greek. He himself frankly confesses that he knew very little of it. *De Trinit.* l. iii. Proœm. ("*Græcæ linguæ non sit nobis tantus habitus, ut talium rerum libris legendis et intelligendis ullo modo reperiamur idonei*"), and *Contra literas Petiliani* (written in 400), l. ii. c. 38 ("*Et ego quidem Græcæ linguæ perparum assecutus sum, et prope nihil*"). On the philosophical learning of Augustin may be compared NOURRISSON, *l. c.* ii. p. 92 sqq.

mind, heart, and will, so largely developed and so harmoniously working. No one surpasses him in wealth of perceptions and dialectical sharpness of thoughts, in depth and fervour of religious sensibility, in greatness of aims and energy of action. He therefore also marks the culmination of the patristic age, and has been elevated by the acknowledgment of succeeding times as the first and the universal church father.—His whole character reminds us in many respects of Paul, with whom he has also in common the experience of being called from manifold errors to the service of the gospel, and like whom he could boast that he had laboured in it more abundantly than all the others. And as Paul among the Apostles pre-eminently determined the development of Christianity, and became, more than all others, the expression of the Christian mind, to which men ever afterwards return, as often as in the life of the church that mind becomes turbid, to draw from him, as the purest fountain, a fresh understanding of the gospel doctrine,—so has Augustin turned the Christian nations since his time for the most part into his paths, and become pre-eminently their trainer and teacher, in the study of whom they always gain a renewal and deepening of their Christian consciousness. Not the middle age alone, but the Reformation also, was ruled by him, and whatever to this day boasts of the Christian spirit, is connected at least in part with Augustin." VILLEMAIN, in his able and eloquent *"Tableau de l'éloquence Chrétienne au IVᵉ siècle"* (Paris, 1849, p. 373), commences his sketch of Augustin as follows: *"Nous arrivons a l'homme le plus étonnant de l'Eglise latine, à celui qui portat le plus d'imagination dans la théologie, le plus d'éloquence et même sensibilité dans la scholastique ; ce fut saint Augustin. Donnez-lui un autre siècle, placez-le dans meilleure civilisation ; et jamais homme n'aura paru doué d'un génie plus vaste et plus facile. Métaphysique, histoire, antiquités, science des moers, connaissance des arts, Augustin avait tout embrassé. Il écrit sur la musique comme sur le libre arbitre ; il explique le phénomène intellectual la de mémoire, comme il raisonne sur la décadence de l'empire romain. Son esprit subtil et vigoureux a souvent consumé dans des problèmes mystiques une force de sagacité qui suffirait aux plus sublimes conceptions."* FRÉDÉRIC OZANAM, in his *"La civilisation au cinquième siècle"* (translated by A. C. Glyn, 1868, Vol. I. p. 272), counts Augustin among the three or four great metaphysicians of modern times, and says that his task was "to clear the two roads open to Christian philosophy and to inaugurate its two methods of mysticism and dogmatism." NOURRISSON, whose work on Augustin is clothed with the authority of the Institute of France, assigns to him the first rank among the masters of human thought, alongside of Plato and Leibnitz, Thomas Aquinas and Bossuet. *"Si une critique toujours respectueuse, mais d'une inviolable sincérité, est une des formes les plus hautes de l'admiration, j'estime, au contraire, n'avoir fait qu'exalter ce grand coeur, ce psychologue consolant et ému, ce métaphysicien subtil et sublime, en un mot, cet attachant et poétique génie, dont la place reste marquée, au premier rang, parmi les maîtres de la pensée humaine, à côté de Platon et de Descartes, d'Aristote et de saint Thomas, de Leibnitz et de Bossuet."* (*La philosophie de saint Augustin,* Par. 1866, tom. i. p. vii.) PRESSENSÉ (in art. *Aug.*, in Smith & Wace, *Dict. of Christ. Biography*, I. 222): "Aug. still claims the honour of having brought out in all its light the fundamental doctrine of Christianity ; despite the errors of his system, he has opened to the church the path of every progress and of every reform, by stating with the utmost vigour the scheme of free salvation which he had learnt in the school of St. Paul." Among English and American writers, Dr. SHEDD, in the Introduction to his edition of the *Confessions* (1860), has furnished a truthful and forcible description of the mind and heart of St. Augustin. I add the striking judgment of the octogenarian historian Dr. KARL HASE (*Kirschengeschichte auf der Grundlage akademischer Vorlesungen*, Leipzig 1885, vol. I. 522): "The full significance of Augustin as an author can be measured only from the consideration of the fact that in the middle ages both scholasticism and mysticism lived of his riches, and that afterwards Luther and Calvin drew out of his fulness. We find in him both the sharp understanding which makes salvation depend on the clearly defined dogma of the church, and the loving absorption of the heart in God which scarcely needs any more the aid of the church. His writings reflect all kinds of Christian thoughts, which lie a thousand years apart and appear to be contradictions. How were they possible in so systematic a thinker? Just as much as they were possible in Christianity, of which he was a microcosm. From the dogmatic abyss of his hardest and most illiberal doctrines arise such liberal sentences as these: 'Him I shall not condemn in whom I find any thing of Christ;' 'Let us not forget that in the very enemies are concealed the future citizens.' "

CHAPTER IV.—*The Writings of St. Augustin.*

The numerous writings of Augustin, the composition of which extended through four and forty years, are a mine of Christian knowledge, and experience. They abound in lofty ideas, noble sentiments, devout effusions, clear statements of truth, strong arguments against error, and passages of fervid eloquence and undying beauty, but also in innumerable repetitions, fanciful opinions, and playful conjectures of his uncommonly fertile brain.[1]

---

[1] ELLIES DUPIN (*Bibliothèque ecclésiastique*, tom. iii. 1ʳᵉ partie, p. 818) and NOURRISSON (*l. c.* tom. ii. p. 449) apply to Augustin the term *magnus opinator*, which Cicero used of himself. There is, however, this important difference that Augustin, along with his many opinions on speculative questions in philosophy and theology, had very positive convictions in all essential doctrines, while Cicero was a mere eclectic in philosophy.

His style is full of life and vigour and ingenious plays on words, but deficient in simplicity, purity and elegance, and by no means free from the vices of a degenerate rhetoric, wearisome prolixity, and from that *vagabunda loquacitas*, with which his adroit opponent, Julian of Eclanum, charged him. He would rather, as he said, be blamed by grammarians, than not understood by the people; and he bestowed little care upon his style, though he many a time rises in lofty poetic flight. He made no point of literary renown, but, impelled by love to God and to the church, he wrote from the fulness of his mind and heart.[1] The writings before his conversion, a treatise on the Beautiful (*De Pulchro et Apto*), the orations and eulogies which he delivered as rhetorician at Carthage, Rome, and Milan, are lost. The professor of eloquence, the heathen philosopher, the Manichæan heretic, the sceptic and free thinker, are known to us only from his regrets and recantations in the *Confessions* and other works. His literary career for us commences in his pious retreat at Cassiciacum where he prepared himself for a public profession of his faith. He appears first, in the works composed at Cassiciacum, Rome, and near Tagaste, as a Christian philosopher, after his ordination to the priesthood as a theologian. Yet even in his theological works he everywhere manifests the metaphysical and speculative bent of his mind. He never abandoned or depreciated reason, he only subordinated it to faith and made it subservient to the defence of revealed truth. Faith is the pioneer of reason, and discovers the territory which reason explores.

The following is a classified view of his most important works.[2]

I. AUTOBIOGRAPHICAL works. To these belong the *Confessions* and the *Retractations;* the former acknowledging his sins, the latter retracting his theoretical errors. In the one he subjects his life, in the other his writings, to close criticism; and these productions therefore furnish the best standard for judging of his entire labours.[3]

The *Confessions* are the most profitable, at least the most edifying, product of his pen; indeed, we may say, the most edifying book in all the patristic literature. They were accordingly the most read even during his lifetime,[4] and they have been the most frequently published since.[5] A more sincere and more earnest book was never written. The historical part, to the tenth book, is one of the devotional classics of all creeds, and second in popularity only to the "Imitation of Christ," by Thomas a Kempis, and Bunyan's "Pilgrim's Progress." Certainly no autobiography is superior to it in true humility, spiritual depth, and universal interest. Augustin records his own experience, as a heathen sensualist, a Manichæan heretic, an anxious inquirer, a sincere penitent, and a grateful convert. He finds a response in every human soul that struggles through the temptations of nature and the labyrinth of error to the knowledge of

---

1 He was not "intoxicated with the exuberance of his own verbosity," as a modern English statesman (Lord Beaconsfield) charged his equally distinguished rival (Mr. Gladstone) in Parliament.

2 In his *Retractations*, he himself reviews ninety-three of his works (embracing two hundred and thirty-two books, see ii. 67), in chronological order; in the first book those which he wrote while a layman and presbyter, in the second those which he wrote when a bishop. See also the extended chronological index in SCHÖNEMANN's *Biblioth. historico-literaria Patrum Latinorum*, vol. ii. (Lips. 1794), p. 340 sqq. (reprinted in the supplemental volume, xii., of Migne's ed. of the *Opera*, p. 24 sqq.); and other systematic and alphabetical lists in the eleventh volume of the Bened. ed. (p. 494 sqq., ed. Venet.), and in Migne, tom. xi.

3 For this reason the Benedictine editors have placed the *Retractations* and the *Confessions* at the head of his works.

4 He himself says of them, *Retract.* l. ii. c. 6: "*Multis fratribus eos* [*Confessionum libros tredecim*] *multum placuisse et placere scio.*" Comp. *De donon perseverantiæ*, c. 20: "*Quid autem meorum opusculorum frequentius et delectabilius innotescere potuit quam libri Confessionum mearum?*" Comp. *Ep.* 231 *Dario comiti.*

5 SCHÖNNEMANN (in the supplemental volume of Migne's ed. of Augustin, p. 134 sqq.) cites a multitude of separate editions of the *Confessions* in Latin, Italian, Spanish, Portuguese, French, English, and German, from A. D. 1475 to 1776. Since that time several new editions have been added. One of the best Latin editions is that of Karl von Raumer (Stuttgart, 1856), who used to read the *Confessions* with his students at Erlangen once a week for many years. In his preface he draws a comparison between them and Rousseau's *Confessions* and Hamann's *Gedanken über meinen Lebenslauf.* English and German translations are noticed above in the Lit. Dr. Shedd (in his ed., Pref. p. xxvii) calls the *Confessions* the best commentary yet written upon the seventh and eighth chapters of Romans. "That quickening of the human spirit, which puts it again into vital and sensitive relations to the holy and eternal; that illumination of the mind, whereby it is enabled to perceive with clearness the real nature of truth and righteousness; that empowering of the will, to the conflict of victory—the entire process of restoring the Divine image in the soul of man—is delineated in this book, with a vividness and reality never exceeded by the uninspired mind." . . . "It is the life of God in the soul of a strong man, rushing and rippling with the freedom of the life of nature. He who watches can almost see the growth; he who listens can hear the perpetual motion; and he who is in sympathy will be swept along."

truth and the beauty of holiness, and after many sighs and tears finds rest and peace in the arms of a merciful Saviour. The style is not free from the faults of an artificial rhetoric, involved periods and far-fetched paronomasias; but these defects are more than atoned for by passages of unfading beauty, the devout spirit and psalm-like tone of the book. It is the incense of a sacred mysticism of the heart which rises to the throne on high. The wisdom of some parts of the *Confessions* may be doubted.[1] The world would never have known Augustin's sins, if he had not told them; nor were they of such a nature as to destroy his respectability in the best heathen society of his age; but we must all the more admire his honesty and humility.

Rousseau's "Confessions," and Goethe's "Truth and Fiction," may be compared with Augustin's *Confessions* as works of rare genius and of absorbing psychological interest, but they are written in a radically different spirit, and by attempting to exalt human nature in its unsanctified state, they tend as much to expose its vanity and weakness, as the work of the bishop of Hippo, being written with a single eye to the glory of God, raises man from the dust of repentance to a new and imperishable life of the Spirit.[2]

Augustin composed the *Confessions* about the year 397, ten years after his conversion. The first nine books contain, in the form of a continuous prayer and confession before God, a general sketch of his earlier life, of his conversion, and of his return to Africa in the thirty-fourth year of his age. The salient points in these books are the engaging history of his conversion in Milan, and the story of the last days of his noble mother in Ostia, spent as it were at the very gate of heaven and in full assurance of a blessed reunion at the throne of glory. The last three books and a part of the tenth are devoted to speculative philosophy; they treat, partly in tacit opposition to Manichæism, of the metaphysical questions of the possibility of knowing God, and the nature of time and space; and they give an interpretation of the Mosaic cosmogony in the style of the typical allegorical exegesis usual with the fathers, but foreign to our age; they are therefore of little value to the general reader, except as showing that even abstract metaphysical subjects may be devotionally treated.

The *Retractations* were produced in the evening of his life (427 and 428), when, mindful of the proverb: "In the multitude of words there wanteth not transgression,"[3] and remembering that we must give account for every idle word,[4] he judged himself, that he might not be judged.[5] He revised in chronological order the numerous works he had written before and during his episcopate, and retracted or corrected whatever in them seemed to his riper knowledge false or obscure, or not fully agreed with the orthodox catholic faith. Some of his changes were reactionary and no improvements, especially those on the freedom of the will, and on religious toleration. In all essential points, nevertheless, his theological system remained the same from his conversion to this time. The *Retractations* give beautiful evidence of his love of truth, his conscientiousness, and his humility.[6]

To this same class should be added the *Letters* of Augustin, of which the Benedictine editors, in their second volume, give two hundred and seventy (including letters *to* Augustin) in chronological order from A. D. 386 to A. D. 429. These letters treat, sometimes very minutely,

---

[1] We mean his sexual sins. He kept a concubine for sixteen years, the mother of his only child, Adeodatus, and after her separation he formed for a short time a similar connection in Milan; but in both cases he was faithful. *Conf.* IV. 2 (*unam habebam . . . servans tori fidem*"); VI. 15. Erasmus thought very leniently of this sin as contrasted with the conduct of the priests and abbots of his time. Augustin himself repented deeply of it, and devoted his life to celibacy.

[2] NOURRISSON (l. c. tom. i. p. 19) calls the *Confessions* "*cet ouvrage unique, souvent imité, toujours parodié, où il s'accuse, se condamne et s'humilie, prière ardente, récit entraînant, métaphysique incomparable, histoire de tout un monde qui se reflète dans l'histoire d'une âme.*" Comp. also an article on the *Confessions* in "The Contemporary Review" for June, 1867, pp. 133–160.

[3] Prov. x. 19. This verse (*ex multiloquio non effugies peccatum*) the Semi-Pelagian Gennadius (*De viris illustr. sub Aug.*) applies against Augustin in excuse for his erroneous doctrines of freedom and predestination.

[4] Matt. xii. 36.

[5] 1 Cor. xi. 31. Comp. his Prologus to the two books of *Retractationes*.

[6] J. MORELL MACKENZIE (in W. Smith's *Dictionary of Greek and Roman Biography and Mythology*, vol. i. p. 422) happily calls the *Retractations* of Augustin "one of the noblest sacrifices ever laid upon the altar of truth by a majestic intellect acting in obedience to the purest conscientiousness."

of all the important questions of his time, and give us an insight of his cares, his official fidelity, his large heart, and his effort to become, like Paul, all things to all men.

When the questions of friends and pupils accumulated, he answered them in special works; and in this way he produced various collections of *Quæstiones* and *Responsiones*, dogmatical, exegetical, and miscellaneous (A. D. 390, 397, &c.).

II. PHILOSOPHICAL treatises, in dialogue; almost all composed in his earlier life; either during his residence on the country-seat Cassiciacum in the vicinity of Milan, where he spent half a year before his baptism in instructive and stimulating conversation, in a sort of academy or Christian Platonic banquet with Monnica, his son Adeodatus, his brother Navigius, his friend Alypius, and some cousins and pupils; or during his second residence in Rome; or soon after his return to Africa.[1]

To this class belong the works; *Contra Academicos libri tres* (386), in which he combats the skepticism and probabilism of the New Academy,—the doctrine that man can never reach the truth, but can at best attain only probability; *De vita beata* (386), in which he makes true blessedness to consist in the perfect knowledge of God; *De ordine,*—on the relation of evil to the divine order of the world[2] (386); *Soliloquia* (387), communings with his own soul concerning God, the highest good, the knowledge of truth, and immortality; *De immortalitate animæ* (387), a continuation of the *Soliloquies; De quantitate animæ* (387), discussing sundry questions of the size, the origin, the incorporeity of the soul; *De musica libri vi* (387–389); *De magistro* (389), in which, in a dialogue with his son Adeodatus, a pious and promising, but precocious youth, who died soon after his return to Africa (389), he treats on the importance and virtue of the word of God, and on Christ as the infallible Master.[3] To these may be added the later work, *De anima et ejus origine* (419). Other philosophical works on grammar, dialectics (or *ars bene disputandi*), rhetoric, geometry, and arithmetic, are lost.[4]

These works exhibit as yet little that is specifically Christian and churchly; but they show a Platonism seized and consecrated by the spirit of Christianity, full of high thoughts, ideal views, and discriminating argument. They were designed to present the different stages of human thought by which he himself had reached the knowledge of the truth, and to serve others as steps to the sanctuary. They form an elementary introduction to his theology. He afterwards, in his *Retractations*, withdrew many things contained in them, like the Platonic view of the pre-

---

[1] In tom. i. of the ed. Bened., immediately after the *Retractationes* and *Confessiones*, and at the close of the volume. On these philosophical writings, see BRUCKER: *Historia critica philosophiæ*, Lips. 1766, tom. iii. pp. 485-507; H. RITTER: *Geschichte der Philosophie*, vol. vi. p. 153 sqq.; UEBERWEG, *History of Philosophy*, I. 333-346 (Am. ed.); ERDMANN, *Grundriss der Geschichte der Philosophie*, I. 231-240; BINDEMANN, *l. c.* I. 282 sqq.; HUBER, *l. c.* I. 242 sqq.; GANGAUF, *l. c.* p. 25 sqq., and NOURRISSON, *l. c.* ch. i. and ii. Nourrisson makes the just remark (i. p. 53): "*Si la philosophie est la recherché de la verité, jamais sans doute il ne s'est rencontré une âme plus philosophe que celle de saint Augustin. Car jamais âme n'a supporté avec plus d' impatience les anxiétés du doute et n'a fait plus d'efforts pour dissiper les fantômes de l'erreur.*"

[2] Or on the question: "*Utrum omnia bona et mala divinæ providentiæ ordo contineat?*" Comp. *Retract.* i. 3.

[3] Augustin, in his *Confessions* (l. ix. c. 6), expresses himself in this touching way about this son of his illicit love: "We took with us [on returning from the country to Milan to receive the sacrament of baptism] also the boy Adeodatus, the son of my carnal sin. Thou hadst formed him well. He was but just fifteen years old, and he was superior in mind to many grave and learned men. I acknowledge Thy gifts, O Lord, my God, who createst all, and who canst reform our deformities; for I had no part in that boy but sin. And when we brought him up in Thy nurture, Thou, only Thou, didst prompt us to it; I acknowledge Thy gifts. There is my book entitled, *De magistro;* he speaks with me there. Thou knowest that all things there put into his mouth were in his mind when he was sixteen years of age. That maturity of mind was a terror to me; and who but Thou is the artificer of such wonders? Soon Thou didst take his life from the earth; and I think more quietly of him now, fearing no more for his boyhood, nor his youth, nor his whole life. We took him to ourselves as one of the same age in Thy grace, to be trained in Thy nurture; and we were baptised together; and all trouble about the past fled from us." He refers to him also in *De vita beata,* § 6: "There was also with us, in age the youngest of all, but whose talents, if affection deceives me not, promise something great, my son Adeodatus." In the same book (§ 18), he mentions an answer of his: "He is truly chaste who waits on God, and keeps himself to Him only."

[4] The books on grammar, dialectics, rhetoric, and the ten Categories of Aristotle, in the Appendix to the first volume of the Bened. ed., are spurious. For the genuine works of Augustin on these subjects were written in a different form (the dialogue) and for a higher purpose, and were lost in his own day. Comp. *Retract.* i. c. 6. In spite of this, PRANTL (*Geschichte der Logik in Abendlande,* pp. 665-674, cited by HUBER, *l. c.* p. 240) has advocated the genuineness of the *Principia dialecticæ,* and HUBER inclines to agree. GANGAUF, *l. c.* p. 5, and NOURRISSON, i. p. 37, consider them spurious.

existence of the soul, and the Platonic idea that the acquisition of knowledge is a recollection or excavation of the knowledge hidden in the mind.[1] The philosopher in him afterwards yielded more and more to the theologian, and his views became more positive and empirical, though in some cases narrower also and more exclusive. Yet he could never cease to philosophise, and even his later works, especially *De Trinitate*, and *De Civitate Dei*, are full of profound specula-tions. Before his conversion he followed a particular system of philosophy, first the Manichæan, then the Platonic ; after his conversion he embraced the Christian philosophy, which is based on the divine revelation of the Scriptures, and is the handmaid of theology and religion ; but at the same time he prepared the way for the catholic ecclesiastical philosophy, which rests on the authority of the church, and became complete in the scholasticism of the middle age.

In the history of philosophy he deserves a place in the highest rank, and has done greater service to the science of sciences than any other father, Clement of Alexandria and Origen not excepted. He attacked and refuted the pagan philosophy as pantheistic or dualistic at heart ; he shook the superstitions of astrology and magic ; he expelled from philosophy the doctrine of emanation, and the idea that God is the soul of the world ; he substantially advanced psychology ; he solved the question of the origin and the nature of evil more nearly than any of his predecessors, and as nearly as most of his successors ; he was the first to investigate thoroughly the relation of divine omnipotence and omniscience to human freedom, and to construct a theodicy ; in short, he is properly the founder of a Christian philosophy, and not only divided with Aristotle the empire of the mediæval scholasticism, but furnished also living germs for new systems of philoso-phy, and will always be consulted in the speculative discussions of Christian doctrines.

The philosophical opinions of Augustin are ably and clearly summed up by Ueberweg as follows : [2]

" Against the skepticism of the Academics Augustin urges that man needs the knowledge of truth for his hap-piness, that it is not enough merely to inquire and to doubt, and he finds a foundation for all our knowledge, a foundation invulnerable against every doubt, in the consciousness we have of our sensations, feelings, our willing, and thinking, in short, of all our psychical processes. From the undeniable existence and possession by man of some truth, he concludes to the existence of God as the truth *per se ;* but our conviction of the existence of the material world he regards as only an irresistible belief. Combating heathen religion and philosophy, Augustin defends the doctrines and institutions peculiar to Christianity, and maintains, in particular, against the Neo-Platoniste, whom he rates most highly among all the ancient philosophers, the Christian theses that salvation is to be found in Christ alone, that divine worship is due to no other being beside the triune God, since he created all things himself, and did not commission inferior beings, gods, demons, or angels to create the material world ; that the soul with its body will rise again to eternal salvation or damnation, but will not return periodically to renewed life upon the earth; that the soul does not exist before the body, and that the latter is not the prison of the former, but that the soul begins to exist at the same time with the body; that the world both had a beginning and is perishable, and that only God and the souls of angels and men are eternal.—Against the dualism of the Manichæans, who regarded good and evil as equally primitive, and represented a portion of the divine substance as having entered into the region of evil, in order to war against and conquer it, Augustin defends the monism of the good principle, or of the purely spiritual God, explaining evil as a mere negation or privation, and seeking to show from the finiteness of the things in the world, and from their differing degrees of perfection, that the evils in the world are necessary, and not in contradiction with the idea of creation ; he also defends in opposition to Manichæism, and Gnosticism in general, the Catholic doctrine of the essential harmony between the Old and New Testaments. Against the Donatists, Augustin maintains the unity of the Church. In opposition to Pelagius and the Pelagians, he asserts that divine grace is not conditioned on human worthiness, and maintains the doctrine of absolute predestination, or, that from the mass of men who, through the disobedience of Adam (in whom all mankind were present potentially), have sunk into corruption and sin, some are chosen by the free election of God to be monuments of his grace, and are brought to believe and be saved, while the greater number, as monuments of his justice, are left to eternal damnation."

---

[1] Ἡ μάθησις οὐκ ἄλλο τι ἢ ἀνάμνησις. On this Plato, in the Phædo, as is well known, rests his doctrine of pre-existence. Augustin was at first in favor of the idea, *Solil.* ii. 20, n. 35 ; afterwards he rejected it, *Retract.* i. 4, § 4 ; but after all he assumes in his anthro-pology a sort of unconscious, yet responsible, pre-existence of the whole human *race* in Adam as its organic head, and hence taught a universal fall in Adam's fall.

[2] *History of Philosophy*, vol. i. 333 sq., translated by Prof. Geo. S. Morris.

III. Apologetic works against Pagans and Jews. Among these the twenty-two books, *De Civitate Dei*, are still well worth reading. They form the deepest and richest apologetic work of antiquity; begun in 413, after the occupation of Rome by the Gothic king Alaric, finished in 426, and often separately published. They condense his entire theory of the world and of man, and are the first attempt at a comprehensive philosophy of universal history under the dualistic view of two antagonistic currents or organized forces, a kingdom of this world which is doomed to final destruction, and a kingdom of God which will last forever.[1]

This work has controlled catholic historiography ever since, and received the official approval of Pope Leo XIII., who, in his famous Encyclical *Immortale Dei* (Nov. 1, 1885), incidentally alludes to it in these words: "Augustin, in his work, *De Civitate Dei*, set forth so clearly the efficacy of Christian wisdom and the way in which it is bound up with the well-being of civil society, that he seems not only to have pleaded the cause of the Christians at his own time, but to have triumphantly refuted the calumnies against Christianity for all time."

From the Protestant point of view Augustin erred in identifying the kingdom of God with the visible Catholic Church, which is only a part of it.

IV. Religious-Theological works of a general nature (in part anti-Manichæan): *De utilitate credendi*, against the Gnostic exaltation of knowledge (392); *De fide et symbolo*, a discourse which, though only presbyter, he delivered on the Apostles' Creed before the council at Hippo at the request of the bishops in 393; *De doctrina Christiana iv libri* (397; the fourth book added in 426), a compend of exegetical theology for instruction in the interpretation of the Scriptures according to the analogy of the faith; *De catechizandis rudibus* likewise for catechetical purposes (400); *Enchiridon*, or *De fide, spe et caritate*, a brief compend of the doctrine of faith and morals, which he wrote in 421, or later, at the request of Laurentius; hence also called *Manuale ad Laurentium*.[2]

V. Polemic-Theological works. These are the most copious sources of the history of Christian doctrine in the patristic age. The heresies collectively are reviewed in the book *De hæresibus ad Quodvultdeum*, written between 428 and 430 to a friend and deacon in Carthage, and give a survey of eighty-eight heresies, from the Simonians to the Pelagians.[3] In the work *De vera religione* (390), Augustin proposed to show that the true religion is to be found not with the heretics and schismatics, but only in the catholic church of that time.

The other controversial works are directed against the particular heresies of Manichæism, Donatism, Arianism, Pelagianism and Semi-Pelagianism. Augustin, with all the firmness of his convictions, was free from personal antipathy, and used the pen of controversy in the genuine Christian spirit, *fortiter in re, suaviter in modo*. He understood Paul's ἀληθεύειν ἐν ἀγάπῃ, and forms in this respect a pleasing contrast to Jerome, who had by nature no more fiery temperament than he, but was less able to control it. "Let those," he very beautifully says to the Manichæans, "burn with hatred against you, who do not know how much pains it costs to find the truth, how hard it is to guard against error;—but I, who after so great and long wavering came to know the truth, must bear myself towards you with the same patience which my fellow-believers showed towards me while I was wandering in blind madness in your opinions."[4]

---

[1] In the Bened. ed. tom. vii. Comp. *Retract.* ii. 43, and *Ch. Hist.* III. § 12. The *City of God* and the *Confessions* are the only writings of Augustin which Gibbon thought worth while to read (chap. xxxiii.). Huber (*l. c.* p. 315) says: "Augustin's philosophy of history, as he presents it in his *Civitas Dei*, has remained to this hour the standard philosophy of history for the church orthodoxy, the bounds of which this orthodoxy, unable to perceive in the motions of the modern spirit the fresh morning air of a higher day of history, is scarcely able to transcend." Nourrisson devotes a special chapter to the consideration of the two cities of Augustin, the City of the World and the City of God (tom. ii. 43–88). Compare also the Introduction to Saisset's *Traduction de la Cité de Dieu*, Par. 1855, and Reinken's (old Cath. Bishop), *Geschichtsphilosophie des heil. Aug.* 1866. Engl. translation of the *City of God* by Dr. Marcus Dods, Edinburgh, 1872, 2 vols., and in the second vol. of this *Library of the Nicene and Post-Nicene Fathers*.

[2] Separately edited by Krabinger, Tübingen, 1861.

[3] This work is also incorporated in the *Corpus hæreseologicum* of Fr. Oehler, tom. i. pp. 192–225.

[4] *Contra Epist. Manichæi quam vocant fundamenti*, l. i. 2.

1. The ANTI-MANICHÆAN works date mostly from his earlier life, and in time and matter follow immediately upon his philosophical writings.[1] In them he afterwards found most to retract, because he advocated the freedom of the will against the Manichæan fatalism. The most important are: *De moribus ecclesiæ catholicæ, et de moribus Manichæorum*, two books (written during his second residence in Rome, 388); *De vera religione* (390); *Unde malum, et de libero arbitrio*, usually simply *De libero arbitrio*, in three books, against the Manichæan doctrine of evil as a substance, and as having its seat in matter instead of free will (begun in 388, finished in 395); *De Genesi contra Manichæos*, a defence of the biblical doctrine of creation (389); *De duabus animabus*, against the psychological dualism of the Manichæans (392); *Disputatio contra Fortunatum* (a triumphant refutation of this Manichæan priest of Hippo in August, 392); *Contra Epistolam Manichæi quam vocant fundamenti* (397); *Contra Faustum Manichæum*, in thirty-three books (400–404); *De natura boni* (404), &c.

These works treat of the origin of evil; of free will; of the harmony of the Old and New Testaments, and of revelation and nature; of creation out of nothing, in opposition to dualism and hylozoism; of the supremacy of faith over knowledge; of the authority of the Scriptures and the Church; of the true and the false asceticism, and other disputed points; and they are the chief source of our knowledge of the Manichæan Gnosticism and of the arguments against it.

Having himself belonged for nine years to this sect, Augustin was the better fitted for the task of refuting it, as Paul was peculiarly prepared for the confutation of the Pharisaic Judaism. His doctrine of the nature of evil is particularly valuable. He has triumphantly demonstrated for all time, that evil is not a corporeal thing, nor in any way substantial, but a product of the free will of the creature, a perversion of substance in itself good, a corruption of the nature created by God.

2. Against the PRISCILLIANISTS, a sect in Spain built on Manichæan principles, are directed the book *Ad Paulum Orosium contra Priscillianistas et Origenistas* (411);[2] the book *Contra mendacium*, addressed to Consentius (420); and in part the 190th Epistle (alias Ep. 157), to the Bishop Optatus, on the origin of the soul (418), and two other letters, in which he refutes erroneous views on the nature of the soul, the limitation of future punishment, and the lawfulness of fraud for supposed good purposes.

3. The ANTI-DONATISTIC works, composed between the years 393 and 420, argue against separatism, and contain Augustin's doctrine of the church and church-discipline, and of the sacraments. To these belong: *Psalmus contra partem Donati* (A. D. 393), a polemic popular song without regular metre, intended to offset the songs of the Donatists; *Contra epistolam Parmeniani*, written in 400 against the Carthaginian bishop of the Donatists, the successor of Donatus; *De baptismo contra Donastistas*, in favor of the validity of heretical baptism (400); *Contra literas Petiliani* (about 400), against the view of Cyprian and the Donatists, that the efficacy of the sacraments depends on the personal worthiness and the ecclesiastical status of the officiating priest; *Ad Catholicos Epistola contra Donatistas*, or *De unitate ecclesiæ* (402); *Contra Cresconium grammaticum Donastistam* (406); *Breviculus Collationis cum Donatistis*, a short account of the three days' religious conference with the Donatists (411); *De correctione Donatistarum* (417); *Contra Gaudentium, Donat. Episcopum*, the last anti-Donatistic work (420).[3]

These works are the chief patristic authority of the Roman Catholic doctrine of the Church and against the sects. They are thoroughly Romanizing in spirit and aim, and least satisfactory to Protestant readers. Augustin defended in his later years even the principle of forcible

---

[1] The earliest anti-Manichæan writings (*De libero arbitrio; De moribus eccl. cath. et de Moribus Manich.*) are in tom. i. ed. Bened.; the latter in tom. viii.

[2] Tom. viii. p. 611 sqq.

[3] All these in tom. ix. Comp. *Church Hist.* III. §§ 69 and 70.

coërcion and persecution against heretics and schismatics by a false exegesis of the words in the parable " Compel them to come in "(Luke xiv. 23). The result of persecution was that both Catholics and Donatists in North Africa were overwhelmed in ruin first by the barbarous Vandals, who were Arian heretics, and afterwards by the Mohammedan conquerors.

4. The ANTI-ARIAN works have to do with the deity of Christ and of the Holy Spirit, and with the Holy Trinity. By far the most important of these are the fifteen books *De Trinitate* (400–416);—the most profound and discriminating production of the ancient church on the Trinity, in no respect inferior to the kindred works of Athanasius and the two Gregories, and for centuries final to the dogma.[1] This may also be counted among the positive didactic works, for it is not directly controversial. The *Collatio cum Maximino Ariano*, an obscure babbler, belongs to the year 428.

5. The numerous ANTI-PELAGIAN works of Augustin are his most influential and most valuable, at least for Protestants. They were written between the years 412 and 429. In them Augustin, in his intellectual and spiritual prime, develops his system of anthropology and soteriology, and most nearly approaches the position of Evangelical Protestantism: *On the Guilt and the Remission of Sins,* and *Infant Baptism* (412); *On the Spirit and the Letter* (413); *On Nature and Grace* (415); *On the Acts of Pelagius* (417); *On the Grace of Christ, and Original Sin* (418); *On Marriage and Concupiscence* (419); *On Grace and Free Will* (426); *On Discipline and Grace* (427); *Against Julian of Eclanum* (two large works, written between 421 and 429, the second unfinished, and hence called *Opus imperfectum*); *On the Predestination of the Saints* (428); *On the Gift of Perseverance* (429); &c.[2]

These anti-Pelagian writings contain what is technically called the Augustinian system of theology, which was substantially adopted by the Lutheran Church, yet without the decree of reprobation, and in a more rigorous logical form by the Calvinistic Confessions. The system gives all glory to God, does full justice to the sovereignty of divine grace, effectually humbles and yet elevates and fortifies man, and furnishes the strongest stimulus to gratitude and the firmest foundation of comfort. It makes all bright and lovely in the circle of the elect. But it is gloomy and repulsive in its negative aspect towards the non-elect. It teaches a universal damnation and only a partial redemption, and confines the offer of salvation to the minority of the elect; it ignores the general benevolence of God to all his creatures; it weakens or perverts the passages which clearly teach that " God would have all men to be saved "; it suspends their eternal fate upon one single act of disobedience; it assumes an unconscious, and yet responsible pre-existence of Adam's posterity and their participation in his sin and guilt; it reflects upon the wisdom of God in creating countless millions of beings with the eternal foreknowledge of their everlasting misery; and it does violence to the sense of individual responsibility for accepting or rejecting the gospel-offer of salvation. And yet this Augustinian system, especially in its severest Calvinistic form, has promoted civil and religious liberty, and trained the most virtuous, independent, and heroic types of Christians, as the Huguenots, the Puritans, the Covenanters, and the Pilgrim Fathers. It is still a mighty moral power, and will not lose its hold upon earnest characters until some great theological genius produces from the inexhaustible mine of the Scriptures a more satisfactory solution of the awful problem which the universal reign of sin and death presents to the thinking mind.

In Augustin the anti-Pelagian system was checked and moderated by his churchly and sacramental views, and we cannot understand him without keeping both in view. The same apparent contradiction we find in Luther, but he broke entirely with the sacerdotal system of

---

[1] Tom. viii. ed. Bened. p. 749 sqq. Comp. *Ch. Hist.* III. § 131. The work was stolen from him by some impatient friends before revision, and before the completion of the twelfth book, so that he became much discouraged, and could only be moved to finish it by urgent entreaties.

[2] *Opera*, tom. x., in two parts, with an Appendix. The same in Migne. W. Bright, of Oxford, has published *Select Anti-Pelagian Treatises of St. Aug.*, in Latin, 1880. On the Pelagian controversy comp. *Ch. Hist.* III. §§ 146–160.

Rome, and made the doctrine of justification by faith the chief article of his creed, which Augustin never could have done. Calvin was more logical than either, and went back beyond justification and Adam's fall, yea, beyond time itself, to the eternal counsel of God which preordains, directs and controls the whole history of mankind to a certain end, the triumph of his mercy and justice.

VI. Exegetical works. The best of these are: *De Genesi ad literam* (The Genesis word for word), in twelve books, an extended exposition of the first three chapters of Genesis, particularly the history of the creation literally interpreted, though with many mystical and allegorical interpretations also (written between 401 and 415);[1] *Enarrationes in Psalmos* (mostly sermons);[2] hundred and twenty-four Homilies on the Gospel of John (416 and 417);[3] ten Homilies on the First Epistle of John (417); the Exposition of the Sermon on the Mount (393); the Harmony of the Gospels (*De consensu evangelistarum*, 400); the Epistle to the Galatians (394); and an unfinished commentary on the Epistle to the Romans.[4]

Augustin deals more in lively, profound, and edifying thoughts on the Scriptures than in proper grammatical and historical exposition, for which neither he nor his readers had the necessary linguistic knowledge, disposition, or taste. He grounded his theology less upon exegesis than upon his Christian and churchly mind saturated with Scriptural truths. He excels in spiritual insight, and is suggestive even when he misses the natural meaning.

VII. Ethical and Ascetic works. Among these belong three hundred and ninety-six *Sermones* (mostly very short) *de Scripturis* (on texts of Scripture), *de tempore* (festival sermons), *de sanctis* (in memory of apostles, martyrs, and saints), and *de diversis* (on various occasions), some of them dictated by Augustin, some taken down by hearers.[5] Also various moral treatises: *De continentia* (395); *De mendaico* (395), against deception (not to be confounded with the similar work already mentioned *Contra mendacium*, against the fraud-theory of the Priscillianists, written in 420); *De agone Christiano* (396); *De opere monachorum*, against monastic idleness (400); *De bono conjugali adv. Jovinianum* (400); *De virginitate* (401); *De fide et operibus* (413); *De adulterinis conjugiis*, on 1 Cor. vii. 10 sqq. (419); *De bono viduitatis* (418); *De patientia* (418); *De cura pro mortuis gerenda*, to Paulinus of Nola (421); *De utilitate jejunii*; *De diligendo Deo*; *Meditationes*;[6] &c.

As we survey this enormous literary labor, augmented by many other treatises and letters now lost, and as we consider his episcopal labors, his many journeys, and his adjudications of controversies among the faithful, which often robbed him of whole days, we must be really astounded at the fidelity, exuberance, energy, and perseverance of this father of the church. Surely, such a life was worth the living.

---

[1] Tom. iii. 117–324. Not to be confounded with two other books on Genesis, in which he defends the biblical doctrine of creation against the Manichæans. In this exegetical work he aimed, as he says, *Retract.* ii. c. 24, to interpret Genesis " *non secundum allegoricas significationes, sed secundum rerum gestarum proprietatem.*" The work is more original and spirited than the *Hexaëmeron* of Basil or of Ambrose.

[2] Tom. iv., the whole volume. The English translation of the Com. on the Psalms occupies six volumes of the Oxford Library of the Fathers.

[3] Tom. iii. 289–824. Translated in Clark's ed. of Augustin's works.

[4] All in tom. iii. Translated in part.

[5] Tom. v. contains beside these a multitude (317) of doubtful and spurious sermons, likewise divided into four classes. To these must be added recently discovered sermons, edited from manuscripts in Florence, Monte Cassino, etc., by M. Denis (1792), O. F. Frangipane (1820), A. L. Caillau (Paris, 1836), and Angelo Mai (in the *Nova Bibliotheca Patrum*).

[6] Most of them in tom. vi. ed. Bened. On the *scripta deperdita, dubia et spuria* of Augustin, see the index by Schönemann, *l. c.* p. 50 sqq., and in the supplemental volume of Migne's edition, pp. 34–40. The so-called *Meditations* of Augustin (German translation by August Krohne, Stuttgart, 1854) are a later compilation by the abbot of Fescamp in France, at the close of the twelfth century, from the writings of Augustin, Gregory the Great, Anselm, and others.

CHAPTER V.—*The Influence of St. Augustin upon Posterity, and his Relation to Catholicism and Protestantism.*

In conclusion we must add some observations respecting the influence of Augustin on the Church and the world since his time, and his position with reference to the great antagonism of Catholicism and Protestantism. All the church fathers are, indeed, the common inheritance of both parties; but no other of them has produced so permanent effects on both, and no other stands in so high regard with both, as Augustin. Upon the Greek Church alone has he exercised little or no influence; for this Church stopped with the undeveloped synergistic anthropology of the previous age, and rejects most decidedly, as a Latin heresy, the doctrine of the *double* procession of the Holy Spirit (the *Filioque*) for which Augustin is chiefly responsible.[1]

1. Augustin, in the first place, contributed much to the development of the doctrinal basis which Catholicism and Protestantism hold *in common* against such radical heresies of antiquity as Manichæism, Arianism, and Pelagianism. In all these great intellectual conflicts he was in general the champion of the cause of Christian truth against dangerous errors. Through his influence the canon of Holy Scripture (including, indeed, the Old Testament Apocrypha) was fixed in its present form by the councils of Hippo (393) and Carthage (397). He conquered the Manichæan dualism, hylozoism, and fatalism, and saved the biblical idea of God and of creation, and the biblical doctrine of the nature of sin and its origin in the free will of man. He developed the Nicene dogma of the Trinity, in opposition to tritheism on the one hand, and Sabellianism on the other, but also with the doubtful addition of the *Filioque*, and in opposition to the Greek, gave it the form in which it has ever since prevailed in the West. In this form the dogma received classical expression from his school in the falsely so called Athanasian Creed, which is not recognized by the Greek Church, and which better deserves the name of the Augustinian Creed.

In Christology, on the contrary, he added nothing new, and he died shortly before the great Christological conflicts opened, which reached their œcumenical settlement at the council of Chalcedon, twenty years after his death. Yet he anticipated Leo in giving currency in the West to the important formula: "Two natures in one person."[2]

2. Augustin is also the principal theological creator of the *Latin-Catholic* system as distinct from the Greek Catholicism on the one hand, and from evangelical Protestantism on the other. He ruled the entire theology of the middle age, and became the father of scholasticism in virtue of his dialectic mind, and the father of mysticism in virtue of his devout heart, without being responsible for the excesses of either system. For scholasticism thought to comprehend the divine with the understanding, and lost itself at last in empty dialectics; and mysticism

---

[1] The church fathers of the first six centuries are certainly far more Catholic than Protestant, and laid the doctrinal foundation of the orthodox Greek and Roman churches. But it betrays a contracted, slavish, and mechanical view of history, when Roman Catholic divines claim the fathers as their exclusive property; forgetting that they taught many things which are as inconsistent with the papal as with the Protestant Creed, and that they knew nothing of certain dogmas which are essential to Romanism (such as the infallibility of the pope, the seven sacraments, transubstantiation, purgatory, indulgences, auricular confession, the immaculate conception of the Virgin Mary, etc.). "I recollect well," says Dr. NEWMAN, the former intellectual leader of Oxford Tractarianism (in his Letter to Dr. Pusey on his *Eirenicon*, 1866, p. 5), "what an outcast I seemed to myself, when I took down from the shelves of my library the volumes of St. Athanasius or St. Basil, and set myself to study them; and how, on the contrary, when at length I was brought into Catholic communion, I kissed them with delight, with a feeling that in them I had more than all that I had lost, and, as though I were directly addressing the glorious saints, who bequeathed them to the Church, I said to the inanimate pages, 'You are now mine, and I am yours, beyond any mistake.'" With the same right the Jews might lay exclusive claim to the writings of Moses and the prophets. The fathers were living men, representing the onward progress and conflicts of Christianity in their time, unfolding and defending great truths, but not unmixed with many errors and imperfections which subsequent times have corrected. Those are the true children of the fathers who, standing on the foundation of Christ and the apostles, and, kissing the New Testament rather than any human writings, follow them only as far as they followed Christ, and who carry forward their work in the onward march of evangelical catholic Christianity.

[2] He was summoned to the council of Ephesus, which condemned Nestorianism in 431, but died a year before it met. He prevailed upon the Gallic monk, Leporius, to retract Nestorianism. His Christology is in many points defective and obscure. Comp. DORNER's *History of Christology*, ii. pp. 88–98 (Germ. ed.). Jerome did still less for this department of doctrine.

endeavoured to grasp the divine with feeling, and easily strayed into misty sentimentalism; Augustin sought to apprehend the divine with the united power of mind and heart, of bold thought and humble faith.[1] Anselm, Bernard of Clairvaux, Thomas Aquinas, and Bonaventura, are his nearest of kin in this respect. Even now, since the Catholic Church has become a Roman Church, he enjoys greater consideration in it than Ambrose, Hilary, Jerome, or Gregory the Great. All this cannot possibly be explained without an interior affinity.[2]

His very conversion, in which, besides the Scriptures, the personal intercourse of the hierarchical Ambrose and the life of the ascetic Anthony had great influence, was a transition not from heathenism to Christianity (for he was already a Manichæan Christian), but from heresy to the historical, orthodox, episcopally organized church, as, for the time, the sole authorized vehicle of the apostolic Christianity in conflict with those sects and parties which more or less assailed the foundations of the Gospel. It was, indeed, a full and unconditional surrender of his mind and heart to God, but it was at the same time a submission of his private judgment to the authority of the church which led him to the faith of the gospel.[3] In the same spirit he embraced the ascetic life, without which, according to the Catholic principle, no high religion is possible. He did not indeed enter a cloister, like Luther, whose conversion in Erfurt was likewise essentially catholic, but he lived in his house in the simplicity of a monk, and made and kept the vow of voluntary poverty and celibacy.[4]

He adopted Cyprian's doctrine of the church, and completed it in the conflict with Donatism by transferring the predicates of unity, holiness, universality, exclusiveness, and maternity, directly to the actual church of the time, which, with a firm episcopal organization, an unbroken succession, and the Apostles' Creed, triumphantly withstood the eighty or the hundred opposing sects in the heretical catalogue of the day, and had its visible centre in Rome. In this church he had found rescue from the shipwreck of his life, the home of true Christianity, firm ground for his thinking, satisfaction for his heart, and a commensurate field for the wide range of his powers.[5] The predicate of infallibility alone he does not plainly bring forward; he assumes a progressive correction of earlier councils by later; and in the Pelagian controversy he asserts the same independence towards pope Zosimus, which Cyprian before him had shown towards pope Stephen in the controversy on heretical baptism, with the advantage of having the right on his side, so that Zosimus found himself compelled to yield to the African church. But after

---

[1] WIGGER's (*Pragmat. Darstellung des Augustinismus und Pelagianismus*, i. p. 27) finds the most peculiar and remarkable point of Augustin's character in his singular union of intellect and imagination, scholasticism and mysticism, in which neither can be said to predominate. So also HUBER, *l. c.* p. 313.

[2] NOURRISSON, the able expounder of the philosophy of Augustin, says (*l. c.* tom. i. p. iv): "*Je ne crois pas, qu'excepté saint Paul, aucun homme ait contribué davantage, par sa parole comme par ses écrits, à organiser, à interpréter, à répandre le christianisme; et, après saint Paul, nul apparemment, non pas même le glorieux, l'invincible Athanase, n'a travaillé d'une manière aussi puissante à fonder l'unité catholique.*"

[3] We recall his famous anti-Manichæan dictum: "*Ego evangelio non crederem, nisi me catholicæ ecclesiæ commoveret auctoritas.*" The Protestant would reverse this maxim, and ground his faith in the church on his faith in Christ and in the gospel. So with the well-known maxim of Irenæus: "*Ubi ecclesia, ibi Spiritus Dei, et ubi Spiritus Dei, ibi ecclesia.*" According to the spirit of Protestantism it would be said conversely: "Where the Spirit of God is, there is the church, and where the church is, there is the Spirit of God."

[4] According to genuine Christian principles it would have been far more noble, if he had married the African woman with whom he had lived in illicit intercourse for thirteen years, who was always faithful to him, as he was to her, and had borne him his beloved and highly gifted Adeodatus; instead of casting her off, and, as he for a while intended, choosing another for the partner of his life, whose excellences were more numerous. The superiority of the evangelical Protestant morality over the Catholic asceticism is here palpable. But with the prevailing spirit of his age he would hardly have enjoyed so great regard, nor accomplished so much good if he had been married. Celibacy was the bridge from the heathen degradation of marriage to the evangelical Christian exaltation and sanctification of the family life.

[5] On Augustin's doctrine of the church, see *Ch. Hist.* III. § 71, and especially the thorough account by R. ROTHE: *Anfänge der christl. Kirche und ihrer Verfassung*, vol. i. (1837), pp. 679–711. "Augustin," says he, "decidedly adopted Cyprian's conception [of the church] in all essential points. And once adopting it, he penetrated it in its whole depth with his wonderfully powerful and exuberant soul, and, by means of his own clear, logical mind, gave it the perfect and rigorous system which perhaps it still lacked" (p. 679 sqq.). "Augustin's conception of the doctrine of the church was about standard for succeeding times" (p. 685). See also an able article of Prof. Reuter, of Göttingen, on Augustin's views concerning episcopacy, tradition, infallibility, in Brieger's "*Zeitschrift für Hist. Theol.*" for 1885 (Bk. VIII. pp. 126–187).

the condemnation of the Pelagian errors by the Roman see (418), he declared that "the case is finished, if only the error were also finished."[1]

He was the first to give a clear and fixed definition of the sacrament, as a visible sign of invisible grace, resting on divine appointment; but he knows nothing of the number seven; this was a much later enactment. In the doctrine of baptism he is entirely Catholic, though in logical contradiction with his dogma of predestination; he maintained the necessity of baptism for salvation on the ground of John iii. 5 and Mark xvi. 16, and derived from it the horrible dogma of the eternal damnation of all unbaptized infants, though he reduced their condition to a mere absence of bliss, without actual suffering.[2] In the doctrine of the holy communion he stands, like his predecessors, Tertullian and Cyprian, nearer to the Calvinistic than any other theory of a spiritual presence and fruition of Christ's body and blood. He certainly can not be quoted in favor of transubstantiation. He was the chief authority of Ratramnus and Berengar in their opposition to this dogma.

He contributed to promote, at least in his later writings, the Catholic faith of miracles,[3] and the worship of Mary;[4] though he exempts the Virgin only from actual sin, not from original, and, with all his reverence for her, never calls her "mother of God."[5]

At first an advocate of religious liberty and of purely spiritual methods of opposing error, he afterwards asserted the fatal principle of forcible coërcion, and lent the great weight of his authority to the system of civil persecution, at the bloody fruits of which in the middle age he himself would have shuddered; for he was always at heart a man of love and gentleness, and personally acted on the glorious principle: "Nothing conquers but truth, and the victory of truth is love."[6]

Thus even truly great and good men have unintentionally, through mistaken zeal, become the authors of incalculable mischief.

3. But, on the other hand, Augustin is, of all the fathers, nearest to *evangelical Protestantism*, and may be called, in respect of his doctrine of sin and grace, the first forerunner of the Reformation. The Lutheran and Reformed churches have ever conceded to him, without scruple, the cognomen of Saint, and claimed him as one of the most enlightened witnesses of the truth and most striking examples of the marvellous power of divine grace in the transformation of a sinner. It is worthy of mark, that his Pauline doctrines, which are most nearly

---

[1] Hence the famous word: "*Roma locuta est, eausa finita est,*" which is often quoted as an argument for the modern Vatican dogma of papal infallibility. But it is not found in this form, though we may admit that it is an epigrammatic condensation of sentences of Augustin. The nearest approach to it is in his *Sermo CXXXI.* cap. 10, § 10 (Tom. VII. 645): "*Iam enim de hac causa duo concilia missa sunt ad sedem apostolicam* (Rome), *inde etiam rescripta venerunt. Causa finita est, utinam aliquando error finiatur.*" Comp. Reuter, *l. c.* p. 157.

[2] Respecting Augustin's doctrine of baptism, see the thorough discussion in W. WALL's *History of Infant Baptism*, vol. i. p. 173 sqq. (Oxford ed. of 1862). His view of the slight condemnation of all unbaptized children contains the germ of the scholastic fancy of the *limbus infantum* and the *pœna damni*, as distinct from the lower regions of hell and the *pœna sensus.*

[3] In his former writings he expressed a truly philosophical view concerning miracles (*De vera relig.* c. 25, § 47; c. 50, § 98; *De utilit. credendi*, c. 16, § 34; *De peccat. meritis et remiss.* l. ii. c. 32, § 52, and *De civit. Dei*, xxii. c. 8); but in his *Retract.* l. i. c. 14, § 5, he corrects or modifies a former remark in his book *De utilit. credendi*, stating that he did not mean to deny the continuance of miracles altogether, but only such great miracles as occurred at the time of Christ ("*quia non tanta nec omnia, non quia nulla fiunt*"). See *Ch. Hist.* III. §§ 87 and 88, and the instructive monograph of the younger NITZSCH: *Augustinus' Lehre vom Wunder*, Berlin, 1865 (97 pp.).

[4] See *Ch. Hist.* III. §§ 81 and 82.

[5] Comp. *Tract. in Evang. Joannis*, viii. c. 9, where he says: "*Cur ergo ait matri filius; Quid mihi et tibi est, mulier? nondum venit hora mea* (John ii. 4). *Dominus noster Jesus Christus et Deus erat et homo: secundum quod Deus erat, matrem non habebat; secundum quod homo erat, habebat. Mater ergo* [Maria] *erat carnis, mater humanitatis, mater infirmitatis quam suscepit propter nos.*" This strict separation of the Godhead from the manhood of Jesus in his birth from the Virgin would have exposed Augustin in the East to the suspicion of Nestorianism. But he died a year before the council of Ephesus, at which Nestorius was condemned.

[6] See *Ch. Hist.* III. § 27, p. 144 sq. He changed his view partly from his experience that the Donatists, in his own diocese, were converted to the catholic unity "*timore legum imperialium*," and were afterwards perfectly good Catholics. He adduces also a misinterpretation of Luke xiv. 23, and Prov. ix. 9: "*Da sapienti occasionem et sapientior erit.*" *Ep. 93, ad Vincentium Rogatistam*, § 17 (tom. ii. p. 237 sq. ed. Bened.). But he expressly discouraged the infliction of death on heretics, and adjured the proconsul Donatus Ep. 100, by Jesus Christ, not to repay the Donatists in kind. "*Corrigi eos cupimus, non necari.*"

akin to Protestantism, are the later and more mature parts of his system, and that just these found great acceptance with the laity. The Pelagian controversy, in which he developed his anthropology, marks the culmination of his theological and ecclesiastical career, and his latest writings were directed against the Pelagian Julian and the Semi-Pelagians in Gaul, who were brought to his notice by two friendly laymen, Prosper and Hilary. These anti-Pelagian works have wrought mightily, it is most true, upon the Catholic church, and have held in check the Pelagianizing tendencies of the hierarchical and monastic system, but they have never passed into its blood and marrow. They waited for a favourable future, and nourished in silence an opposition to the prevailing system.

In the middle age the better sects, which attempted to simplify, purify, and spiritualize the reigning Christianity by return to the Holy Scriptures, and the Reformers before the Reformation, such as Wiclif, Hus, Wessel, resorted most, after the apostle Paul, to the bishop of Hippo as the representative of the doctrine of free grace.

The Reformers were led by his writings into a deeper understanding of Paul, and so prepared for their great vocation. No church teacher did so much to mould Luther and Calvin; none furnished them so powerful weapons against the dominant Pelagianism and formalism; none is so often quoted by them with esteem and love.[1]

All the Reformers in the outset, Melanchthon and Zwingle among them, adopted his denial of free will and his doctrine of predestination, and sometimes even went beyond him into the abyss of supralapsarianism, to cut out the last roots of human merit and boasting. In this point Augustin holds the same relation to the Catholic church, as Luther to the Lutheran; that is, he is a heretic of unimpeachable authority, who is more admired than censured even in his extravagances; yet his doctrine of predestination was *indirectly* condemned by the pope in Jansenism, as Luther's view was rejected as Calvinism by the Formula of Concord.[2] For Jansenism was nothing but a revival of Augustinianism in the bosom of the Roman Catholic church.[3]

---

[1] LUTHER pronounced upon the church fathers (with whom, however, excepting Augustin, he was but slightly acquainted) very condemnatory judgments, even upon Basil, Chrysostom, and Jerome (for Jerome he had a downright antipathy, on account of his advocacy of fasts, virginity, and monkery); he was at times dissatisfied even with Augustin, because he after all did not find in him his *sola fide*, his *articulus stantis vel cadentis ecclesiæ*, and says of him: "Augustin often erred; he cannot be trusted. Though he was good and holy, yet he, as well as other fathers, was wanting in the true faith." But this cursory utterance is overborne by numerous commendations; and all such judgments of Luther must be taken *cum grano salis*. He calls Augustin the most pious, grave, and sincere of the fathers, and the patron of divines, who taught a pure doctrine and submitted it in Christian humility to the Holy Scriptures, etc., and he thinks, if he had lived in the sixteenth century, he would have been a Protestant (*si hoc seculo viveret, nobiscum sentiret*), while Jerome would have gone with Rome. Compare his singular but striking judgments on the fathers in *Lutheri Colloquia*, ed. H. E. Bindseil, 1863, tom. iii. 149, and many other places. GANGAUF, a Roman Catholic (a pupil of the philosopher Günther), concedes (*l. c.* p. 28, note 13) that Luther and Calvin built their doctrinal system mainly on Augustin, but, as he correctly thinks, with only partial right. NOURRISSON, likewise a Roman Catholic, derives Protestantism from a corrupted (!) Augustinianism, and very superficially makes Lutheranism and Calvinism essentially to consist in the denial of the freedom of the will, which was only one of the questions of the Reformation. "*On ne saurait le méconnaître, de l'Augustinianisme corrompu, mais enfin de l'Augustinianisme procède le Protestantisme. Car, sans parler de Wiclif et de Huss, qui, nourris de saint Augustin, soutiennent, avec le réalisme platonicien, la doctrine de la prédestination: Luther et Calvin ne font guère autre chose, dans leurs principaux ouvrages, que cultiver des semences d'Augustinianisme*" (*l. c.* ii. p. 176). But the Reformation is far more, of course, than a repristination of an old controversy; it is a new creation, and marks the epoch of modern Christianity which is different both from the mediæval and from ancient or patristic Christianity.

[2] It is well known that LUTHER, as late as 1526, in his work, *De servo arbitrio*, against Erasmus, which he never retracted, proceeded upon the most rigorous notion of the divine omnipotence, wholly denied the freedom of the will, declared it a mere lie (*merum mendacium*), pronounced the calls of the Scriptures to repentance a divine irony, and based eternal salvation and eternal perdition upon the secret will of God; in all this he almost exceeded Calvin. See particulars in the books on doctrine-history; the inaugural dissertation of JUL. MÜLLER: *Lutheri de prædestinatione et libero arbitrio doctrina*, Gött. 1832; and a historical treatise on predestination by CARL BECK in the "*Studien und Kritiken*" for 1847. We add, as a curiosity, the opinion of GIBBON (ch. xxxiii.), who, however, had a very limited and superficial knowledge of Augustin: "The rigid system of Christianity which he framed or restored, has been entertained, with public applause, and secret reluctance, by the Latin church. The church of Rome has canonized Augustin, and reprobated Calvin. Yet as the *real* difference between them is invisible even to a theological microscope, the Molinists are oppressed by the authority of the saint, and the Jansenists are disgraced by their resemblance to the heretic. In the mean while the Protestant Arminians stand aloof, and deride the mutual perplexity of the disputants. Perhaps a reasoner, still more independent, may smile in *his* turn when he peruses an Arminian commentary on the Epistle to the Romans." NOURRISSON (ii. 179), from his Roman stand-point, likewise makes Lutheranism to consist "*essentiellement dans la question du libre arbitre.*" But the principle of Lutheranism, and of Protestantism generally, is the supremacy of the Holy Scriptures as a rule of faith, and salvation by free grace through faith in Christ.

[3] On the mighty influence of Augustin in the seventeenth century in France, especially on the noble Jansenists, see the works on Jansenism, and also NOURRISSON, *l. c.* tom. ii. pp. 186–276.

The excess of Augustin and the Reformers in this direction is due to the earnestness and energy of their sense of sin and grace. The Pelagian looseness could never beget a reformer. It was only the unshaken conviction of man's own inability, of unconditional dependence on God, and of the almighty power of his grace to give us strength for every good work, which could do this. He who would give others the conviction that he has a divine vocation for the church and for mankind, must himself be penetrated with the faith of an eternal, unalterable decree of God, and must cling to it in the darkest hours.

In great men, and only in great men, great opposites and apparently antagonistic truths live together. Small minds cannot hold them. The catholic, churchly, sacramental, and sacerdotal system stands in conflict with the evangelical Protestant Christianity of subjective, personal experience. The doctrine of universal baptismal regeneration, in particular, which presupposes a universal call (at least within the church), can on principles of logic hardly be united with the doctrine of an absolute predestination, which limits the decree of redemption to a portion of the baptized. Augustin supposes, on the one hand, that every baptized person, through the inward operation of the Holy Ghost, which accompanies the outward act of the sacrament, receives the forgiveness of sins, and is translated from the state of nature into the state of grace, and thus, *qua baptizatus*, is also a child of God and an heir of eternal life; and yet, on the other hand, he makes all these benefits dependent on the absolute will of God, who saves only a certain number out of the "mass of perdition," and preserves these to the end. Regeneration and election, with him, do not, as with Calvin, coincide. The former may exist without the latter, but the latter cannot exist without the former. Augustin assumes that many are actually born into the kingdom of grace only to perish again; Calvin holds that in the case of the non-elect baptism is an unmeaning ceremony; the one putting the delusion in the inward effect, the other in the outward form. The sacramental, churchly system throws the main stress upon the baptismal regeneration, to the injury of the eternal election; the Calvinistic or Puritan system sacrifices the virtue of the sacrament to the election; the Lutheran and high Anglican systems seek a middle ground, without being able to give a satisfactory theological solution of the problem. The Anglican Church, however, allows the two opposite views, and sanctions the one in the baptismal service of the Book of Common Prayer, the other in her Thirty-nine Articles, and other standards, as interpreted by the low church or evangelical party in a moderately Calvinistic sense.

It was an evident ordering of God, that Augustin's theology, like the Latin Bible of Jerome, appeared just in that transitional period of history, in which the old civilization was passing away before the flood of barbarism, and a new order of things, under the guidance of the Christian religion, was in preparation. The church, with her strong, imposing organization and her firm system of doctrine, must save Christianity amidst the chaotic turmoil of the great migration, and must become a training-school for the barbarian nations of the middle age.[1]

In this process of training, next to the Holy Scriptures, the scholarship of JEROME and the theology and fertile ideas of AUGUSTIN were the most important intellectual agents.

---

[1] GUIZOT, the Protestant historian and statesman, very correctly says in his *Histoire générale de la civilisation en Europe* Deuxième lecon, p. 45 sq. ed. Bruxelles, 1850): "*S'il n'eût pas été une église, je ne sais ce qui en serait avenu au milieu de la chute de l'empire romain. . . . Si le christianisme n'eût été comme dans les premiers temps, qu'une croyance, un sentiment, une conviction individuelle, on peut croire qu'il aurait succombé au milieu de la dissolution de l'empire et de l'invasion des barbares. Il a succombé plus tard, en Asie et dans tous le nord de l'Afrique, sous une invasion de même nature, sous l'invasion des barbares musulmans; il a succombé alors, quoiqu'il fût à l'état d'institution, d'église constituée. A bien plus forte raison le même fait aurait pu arriver au moment de la chute de l'empire romain. Il n'y avait alors aucun des moyens par lesquels aujourd'hui les influences morales s'établissent ou résistent indépendamment des institutions, aucun des moyens par lesquels une pure vérité, une pure idée acquiert un grand empire sur les esprits, gouverne les actions, détermine des événemens. Rien de semblable n'existait au IV⁰ siècle, pour donner aux idées, aux sentiments personels, une pareille autorité. Il est clair qu'il fallait une société fortement organisée, fortement gouvernée, pour lutter contre un pareil désastre, pour sortir victorieuse d'un tel ouragan. Je ne crois pas trop dire en affirmant qu'à la fin du IV⁰ et au commencement du V⁰ siècle, c'est l'église chrétienne qui a sauvé le christianisme; c'est l'église avec ses institutions, ses magistrats, son pouvoir, qui s'est défendue vigoureusement contre la dissolution intérieure de l'empire, contre la barbarie, qui a conquis les barbares, qui est devenue le lien, le moyen, le principe de civilisation entre le monde romain et le monde barbare.*"

Augustin was held in so universal esteem that he could exert influence in all directions, and even in his excesses gave no offence. He was sufficiently catholic for the principle of church authority, and yet at the same time so free and evangelical that he modified its hierarchical and sacramental character, reacted against its tendencies to outward, mechanical ritualism, and kept alive a deep consciousness of sin and grace, and a spirit of fervent and truly Christian piety, until that spirit grew strong enough to break the shell of hierarchical tutelage, and enter a new stage of its development. No other father could have acted more beneficently on the Catholicism of the middle age, and more successfully provided for the evangelical Reformation than St. Augustin, the worthy successor of Paul, and the precursor of Luther and Calvin.

He had lived at the time of the Reformation, he would in all probability have taken the lead of the evangelical movement against the prevailing Pelagianism of the Roman Church, though he would not have gone so far as Luther or Calvin. For we must not forget that, notwithstanding their strong affinity, there is an important difference between Catholicism and Romanism or Popery. They sustain a similar relation to each other as the Judaism of the Old Testament dispensation, which looked to, and prepared the way for, Christianity, and the Judaism after the crucifixion and after the destruction of Jerusalem, which is antagonistic to Christianity. Catholicism covers the entire ancient and mediæval history of the church, and includes the Pauline, Augustinian, or evangelical tendencies which increased with the corruptions of the papacy and the growing sense of the necessity of a "*reformatio in capite et membris.*" Romanism proper dates from the council of Trent, which gave it symbolical expression and anathematized the doctrines of the Reformation. Catholicism is the strength of Romanism, Romanism is the weakness of Catholicism. Catholicism produced Jansenism, Popery condemned it. Popery never forgets and never learns anything, and can allow no change in doctrine (except by way of addition), without sacrificing its fundamental principle of infallibility, and thus committing suicide. But Catholicism may ultimately burst the chains of Popery which have so long kept it confined, and may assume new life and vigour.

Such a personage as Augustin, still holding a mediating place between the two great divisions of Christendom, revered alike by both, and of equal influence with both, is furthermore a welcome pledge of the elevating prospect of a future reconciliation of Catholicism and Protestantism in a higher unity, conserving all the truths, losing all the errors, forgiving all the sins, forgetting all the enmities of both. After all, the contradiction between authority and freedom, the objective and the subjective, the churchly and the personal, the organic and the individual, the sacramental and the experimental in religion, is not absolute, but relative and temporary, and arises not so much from the nature of things, as from the deficiencies of man's knowledge and piety in this world. These elements admit of an ultimate harmony in the perfect state of the church, corresponding to the union of the divine and human natures, which transcends the limits of finite thought and logical comprehension, and is yet completely realized in the person of Christ. They are in fact united in the theological system of St. Paul, who had the highest view of the church, as the mystical "body of Christ," and "the pillar and ground of the truth," and who was at the same time the great champion of evangelical freedom, individual responsibility, and personal union of the believer with his Saviour. WE BELIEVE IN AND HOPE FOR ONE HOLY CATHOLIC APOSTOLIC CHURCH, ONE COMMUNION OF SAINTS, ONE FLOCK, ONE SHEPHERD. The more the different churches become truly Christian, the nearer they draw to Christ, and the more they labor for His kingdom which rises above them all, the nearer will they come to one another. For Christ is the common head and vital centre of all believers, and the divine harmony of all discordant human sects and creeds. IN CHRIST, says Pascal, one of the greatest and noblest disciples of Augustin, IN CHRIST ALL CONTRADICTIONS ARE SOLVED.

CHIEF EVENTS IN THE LIFE OF ST. AUGUSTIN,

(AS GIVEN, NEARLY, IN THE BENEDICTINE EDITION).

A.D.

354. Augustin born at Tagaste, Nov. 13; his parents, Patricius and Monnica; shortly afterwards enrolled among the Catechumens.

370. Returns home from studying Rhetoric at Madaura, after an idle childhood, and from idleness falls into dissipation and sin.

371. Patricius dies; Augustin supported at Carthage by his mother, and his friend Romanianus; forms an illicit connection.

372. Birth of his son Adeodatus.

373. Cicero's *Hortensius* awakens in him a strong desire for true wisdom.

374. He falls into the Manichæan heresy, and seduces several of his acquaintances into it. His mother's earnest prayers for him; she is assured of his recovery.

376. Teaches Grammar at Tagaste; but soon returns to Carthage to teach Rhetoric—gains a prize.

379. Is recovered from study of Astrology—writes his books *De pulchro et apto*.

382. Discovers the Manichæans to be in error, but falls into scepticism. Goes to Rome to teach Rhetoric.

385. Removes to Milan; his errors gradually removed through the teaching of Ambrose, but he is held back by the flesh; becomes again a Catechumen.

386. Studies St. Paul; converted through a voice from heaven; gives up his profession; writes against the Academics; prepares for Baptism.

387. Is baptized by Bishop Ambrose, with his son

A.D.

Adeodatus. Death of his mother, Monnica, in her fifty-sixth year, at Ostia.

388. Aug. revisits Rome, and then returns to Africa. Adeodatus, full of promise, dies.

389. Aug. against his will ordained Presbyter at Hippo by Valerius, its Bishop.

392. Writes against the Manichæans.

394. Writes against the Donatists.

395. Ordained Assistant Bishop to Valerius, toward the end of the year.

396. Death of Bishop Valerius. Augustin elected his successor.

397. Aug. writes the *Confessions*, and the *De Tinitate* against the Arians.

398. Is present at the fourth Council of Carthage.

402. Refutes the Epistle of Petilianus, a Donatist.

404. Applies to Cæcilianus for protection against the savageness of the Donatists.

408. Writes *De urbis Romæ obsidione*.

411. Takes a prominent part in a conference between the Catholic Bishops and the Donatists.

413. Begins the composition of his great work *De Civitate Dei*, completed in 426.

417. Writes *De gestis Palæstinæ synodi circa Pelagium*.

420. Writes against the Priscillianists.

424. Writes against the Semipelagians.

426. Appoints Heraclius his successor.

428. Writes the *Retractations*.

429. Answers the Epistles of Prosper and Hilary.

430. Dies Aug. 28, in the third month of the siege of Hippo by the Vandals.

THE CONFESSIONS

OF

ST. AUGUSTIN

TRANSLATED AND ANNOTATED BY

J. G. PILKINGTON, M.A.,

VICAR OF ST. MARK'S, WEST HACKNEY; AND SOMETIME CLERICAL SECRETARY OF THE
BISHOP OF LONDON'S FUND.

"Thou hast formed us for Thyself, and our hearts are restless till they
find rest in Thee."—*Confessions*, i. 1.

"The joy of the solemn service of Thy house constraineth to tears,
when it is read of Thy younger son [Luke xv. 24] 'that he was
dead, and is alive again; he was lost, and is found.'"—*Ibid*. viii. 6.

27

TRANSLATOR'S PREFACE.

"If St. Augustin," says Nourrisson,[1] "had left nothing but his *Confessions* and the *City of God*, one could readily understand the respectful sympathy that surrounds his memory. How, indeed, could one fail to admire in the *City of God* the flight of genius, and in the *Confessions*, what is better still, the effusions of a great soul?" It may be safely predicted, that while the mind of man yearns for knowledge, and his heart seeks rest, the *Confessions* will retain that foremost place in the world's literature which it has secured by its sublime outpourings of devotion and profound philosophical spirit. There is in the book a wonderful combination of childlike piety and intellectual power. Desjardins' idea,[2] that, while in Augustin's other works we see the philosopher or the controversialist, here we see the man, is only to be accepted as a comparative statement of Augustin's attitude in the *Confessions*; for philosophy and piety are in many of his reflections as it were molten into one homogeneous whole. In his highest intellectual flights we find the breathings of faith and love, and, amid the profoundest expressions of penitential sorrow, gleams of his metaphysical genius appear.

It may, indeed, be from the man's showing himself so little, as distinguished from the philosopher, that some readers are a little disappointed in the book. They have expected to meet with a copiousness of biographic details, and have found, commingled with such as are given, long disquisitions on Manichæanism, Time, Creation, and Memory. To avoid such disappointment we must ascertain the author's design. The book is emphatically *not* an autobiography. There is in it an outline of the author's life up to his mother's death; but only so much of detail is given as may subserve his main purpose. That purpose is clearly explained in the fourth section of his Tenth Book. It was that the impenitent on reading it might not say, "I cannot," and "sleep in despair," but rather that, looking to that God who had raised the writer from his low estate of pride and sin to be a pillar of the Church, he might take courage, and "awake in the sweetness of His grace, by which he that is weak is made strong;" and that those no longer in sin might rejoice and praise God as they heard of the past lusts of him who was now freed from them.[3] This, his design of encouraging penitence and stimulating praise, is referred to in his *Retractations*,[4] and in his *Letter to Darius*.[5]

These two main ideas are embodied in the very meaning of the title of the book, the word *confession* having, as Augustin constantly urges, two meanings. In his exposition of the Psalms we read: "Confession is understood in two senses, of our *sins*, and of God's *praise*. Confession of our sins is well known, so well known to all the people, that whenever they hear the name of confession in the lessons, whether it is said in praise or of sin, they beat their breasts."[6] Again: "Confession of sin all know, but confession of praise few attend to."[7] "The former but showeth the wound to the physician, the latter giveth thanks for health."[8] He would therefore have his hearers make the sacrifice of praise their ideal, since, in the City of God, even in the New Jerusalem, there will be no longer confession of sin, but there will be confession of praise.[9] It is not surprising, that with this view of confession he should hinge on the incidents of his life such considerations as tend to elevate the mind and heart of the reader. When, for example, he speaks of his youthful sins,[10] he diverges into a disquisition on the motives to sin; when his friend dies,[11] he moralizes on death; and—to give one example of a reverse process—his profound psychological review of memory[12] recalls his former sin (which at times haunts him in his dreams), and leads up to devout reflections on God's power to cleanse from sin. This undertone of penitence and praise which pervades the *Confessions* in all its episodes, like the golden threads which run through the texture of an Eastern garment, presents one of its peculiar charms.

It would not be right to overlook a charge that has been brought against the book by Lord Byron. He says, "Augustin in his fine *Confessions* makes the reader envy his transgressions." Nothing could be more reckless or

---

[1] *Philosophie de St. Augustin*, Preface.   [2] *Essai sur les Conf. de St. Aug.* p. 5.   [3] *Confessions*, x. sec. 4.
[4] See the passage quoted immediately after this Preface.   [5] *Ep.* ccxxxi. sec. 6.
[6] *Enarr. in Ps.* cxli. sec. 19 : see also *in Ps.* cxvii. sec. 1, xxix. sec. 19, xciv. sec. 4, and xxix. sec. 19.
[7] *Enarr. in Ps.* cxxxvii. sec. 2.   [8] *Enarr. in Ps.* cx. sec. 2.   [9] *In Ps.* xliv. sec. 33, xcix. sec. 16.
[10] Book ii. secs. 6-18.   [11] Book iv. secs. 11-15.   [12] Book x. secs. 41, 42.

further from the truth than this charge. There is here no dwelling on his sin, or painting it so as to satisfy a prurient imagination. As we have already remarked, Augustin's manner is not to go into detail further than to find a position from which to "edify" the reader, and he treats this episode in his life with his characteristic delicacy and reticence. His sin was dead; and he had carried it to its burial with tears of repentance. And when, ten years after his baptism, he sets himself, at the request of some, to a consideration of what he then was at the moment of making his confessions,[1] he refers hardly at all to this sin of his youth; and such allusions as he does make are of the most casual kind. Instead of enlarging upon it, he treats it as past, and only speaks of temptation and sin as they are common to all men. Many of the French writers on the *Confessions*[2] institute a comparison in this matter between the confessions of Augustin and those of Rousseau. Pressensé[3] draws attention to the delicacy and reserve which characterise the one, and the arrogant defiance of God and man manifested in the other. The confessions of the one he speaks of as "*un grand acte de repentir et d'amour;*" and eloquently says, "In it he seems, like the Magdalen, to have spread his box of perfumes at the foot of the Saviour; from his stricken heart there exhales the incense most agreeable to God—the homage of true penitence." The other he truly describes as uttering "a cry of triumph in the very midst of his sin, and robing his shame in a royal purple." Well may Desjardins[4] express surprise at a book of such foulness coming from a genius so great; and perhaps his solution of the enigma is not far from the truth, when he attributes it to an overweening vanity and egotism.[5]

It is right to point out, in connection with this part of our subject, that in regard to some at least of Augustin's self-accusations,[6] there may be a little of that pious exaggeration of his sinfulness which, as Lord Macaulay points out in his essays on Bunyan,[7] frequently characterises deep penitence. But however this may be, justice requires us to remember, in considering his transgression, that from his very childhood he had been surrounded by a condition of civilisation presenting manifold temptations. Carthage, where he spent a large part of his life, had become, since its restoration and colonization under Augustus Cæsar, an "exceeding great city," in wealth and importance next to Rome.[8] "African Paganism," says Pressensé,[9] "was half Asiatic; the ancient worship of nature, the adoration of Astarte, had full licence in the city of Carthage; Dido had become a mythological being, whom this dissolute city had made its protecting divinity, and it is easy to recognise in her the great goddess of Phœnicia under a new name." The luxury of the period is described by Jerome and Tertullian, when they denounce the custom of painting the face and tiring the head, and the prodigality that would give 25,000 golden crowns for a veil, immense revenues for a pair of ear-rings, and the value of a forest or an island for a head-dress.[10] And Jerome, in one of his epistles, gives an illustration of the Church's relation to the Pagan world at that time, when he represents an old priest of Jupiter with his grand-daughter, a catechumen, on his knee, who responds to his caresses by singing canticles.[11] It was a time when we can imagine one of Augustin's parents going to the Colosseum, and enjoying the lasciviousness of its displays, and its gladiatorial shows, with their contempt of human life; while the other carefully shunned such scenes, as being under the ban of the teachers of the Church.[12] It was an age in which there was action and reaction between religion and philosophy; but in which the power of Christianity was so great in its influences on Paganism, that some received the Christian Scriptures only to embody in their phraseology the ideas of heathenism. Of this last point Manichæanism presents an illustration. Now all these influences left their mark on Augustin. In his youth he plunged deep into the pleasures of his day; and we know how he endeavoured to find in Manichæanism a solution of those speculations which haunted his subtle and inquiring mind. Augustin at this time, then, is not to be taken as a type of what Christianity produced. He is to a great extent the outgrowth of the Pagan influences of the time. Considerations such as these may enable us to judge of his early sin more justly than if we measured it by our own privileges and opportunities.

The style of Augustin is sometimes criticised as not having the refinement of Virgil, Horace, or Cicero. But it should be remembered that he wrote in a time of national decay; and further, as Desjardins has remarked in the introduction to his essay, he had *no time* "to cut his phrases." From the period of his conversion to that of his death, he was constantly engaged in controversy with this or that heresy; and if he did not write with classical accuracy, he so inspired the language with his genius, and moulded it by his fire,[13] that it appears almost to pulsate with the throbbings of his brain. He seems likewise to have despised *mere* elegance, for in his *Confessions*,[14] when

---

[1] Book x. sec. 4.

[2] In addition to those referred to, there is one at the beginning of vol. ii. of Saint-Marc Girardin's *Essais de Littérature et de Morale*, devoted to this subject. It has some good points in it, but has much of that sentimentality so often found in French criticisms.

[3] *Le Christianisme au Quatrième Siècle*, p. 269.   [4] *Essai sur les Conf.*, etc. p. 12.

[5] He concludes: "*La folie de son orgueil, voilà le mot de l'énigme, ou l'énigme n'en a pas.*"—*Ibid.* p. 13.

[6] Compare *Confessions*, ii. sec. 2, and iii. sec. 1, with iv. sec. 2.

[7] In vol. i. of his *Crit. and Hist. Essays*, and also in his *Miscellaneous Writings*.   [8] Herodian *Hist.* vii. 6.

[9] *Le Christianisme*, etc. as above, p. 274.   [10] Quoted by Nourrisson, *Philosophie*, etc. ii. 436.   [11] *Ibid.* ii. 434, 435.

[12] See *Confessions*, iii. sec. 2, note, and vi. sec. 13, note.

[13] See Poujoulat, *Lettres de St. Augustin*, Introd. p. 12, who compares the language of the time to Ezekiel's Valley of Dry Bones, and says Augustin inspired it with life.

[14] *Confessions*, v. sec. 10.

speaking of the style of Faustus, he says, "What profit to me was the elegance of my cup-bearer, since he offered me not the more precious draught for which I thirsted?" In this connection the remarks of Collenges [1] are worthy of note. He says, when anticipating objections that might be made to his own style: "It was the last of my study; my opinion always was what Augustin calls *diligens negligentia* was the best diligence as to that; while I was yet a very young man I had learned out of him that it was no solecism in a preacher to use *ossum* for *os*, for (saith he) an iron key is better than one made of gold if it will better open the door, for that is all the use of the key. I had learned out of Hierom that a gaudry of phrases and words in a pulpit is but *signum insipientiæ*. The words of a preacher, saith he, ought *pungere, non palpare*, to prick the heart, not to smooth and coax. The work of anorator is too precarious for a minister of the gospel. Gregory observed that our Saviour had not styled us the *sugar* but the *salt* of the earth, and Augustin observeth, that through Cyprian in one epistle showed much of a florid orator, to show he could do it, yet he never would do so any more, to show he would not."

There are several features in the *Confessions* deserving of remark, as being of special interest to the philosopher, the historian or the divine.

1. Chiefest amongst these is the intense desire for knowledge and the love of truth which characterised Augustin. This was noticeable before his conversion in his hungering after such knowledge as Manichæanism and the philosophy of the time could afford. [2] It is none the less observable in that better time, when, in his quiet retreat at Cassiciacum, he sought to strengthen the foundations of his faith, and resolved to give himself up to the acquisition of divine knowledge. [3] It was seen, too, in the many conflicts in which he was engaged with Donatists, Manichæans, Arians, and Pelagians, and in his earnest study of the deep things of God. This love of knowledge is perhaps conveyed in the beautiful legend quoted by Nourisson, [4] of the monk wrapped in spirit, who expressed astonishment at not seeing Augustin among the elect in heaven. "He is higher up," he was answered, "he is standing before the Holy Trinity disputing thereon for all eternity."

While from the time of his conversion we find him holding on to the fundamental doctrines of the faith with the tenacity of one who had experienced the hollowness of the teachings of philosophy, [5] this passion for truth led him to handle most freely subjects of speculation in things non-essential. [6] But whether viewed as a controversialist, a student of Scripture, or a bishop of the Church of God, he ever manifests those qualities of mind and heart that gained for him not only the affection of the Church, but the esteem of his unorthodox opponents. To quote Guizot's discriminating words, there was in him "*ce mélange de passion et de douceur, d'autorité et de sympathie, d'étendue d'esprit et de rigueur logique, qui lui donnait un si rare pouvoir.*" [7]

2. It is to this eager desire for truth in his many-sided mind that we owe those trains of thought that read like forecasts of modern opinion. We have called attention to some such anticipations of modern thought as they recur in the notes throughout the book; but the speculations on Memory, Time, and Creation, which occupy so large a space in Books Ten and Eleven, deserve more particular notice. The French essayists have entered very fully into these questions. M. Saisset, in his admirable introduction to the *De Civitate Dei*, [8] reviews Augustin's theories as to the mysterious problems connected with the idea of Creation. He says, that in his subtle analysis of Time, and in his attempt at reconciling "the eternity of creative action with the dependence of things created, . . . he has touched with a bold and delicate hand one of the deepest mysteries of the human mind, and that to all his glorious titles he has added another, that of an ingenious psychologist and an eminent metaphysician." Desjardins likewise commends the depth of Augustin's speculations as to Time, [9] and maintains that no one's teaching as to Creation has shown more clearness, boldness, and vigor—avoiding the perils of dualism on the one hand, and atheism on the other. [10] In his remarks on Augustin's disquisitions on the phenomena of Memory, his praise is of a more qualified character. He compares his theories with those of Malebranche, and, while recognising the practical and animated character of his descriptions, thinks him obscure in his delineation of the *manner in which* absent realities reproduce themselves on the memory. [11]

We have had occasion in the notes to refer to the *Unseen Universe*. The authors of this powerful "Apologia" for Christianity propose it chiefly as an antidote to the materialistic disbelief in the immortality of the soul amongst scientific men, which has resulted in this age from the recent advance in physical science; just as in the last century English deism had its rise in a similar influence. It is curious, in connection with this part of our subject, to note

---

1 *The Intercourses of Divine Love betwixt Christ and His Church*, Preface (1683).

2 See *Confessions*, iv. sec. 1, note.   3 *Ibid*. ix. sec. 7, note, and compare x. sec. 55, note.

4 *Philosophie*, etc. as above, i. 320.   5 See *Confessions*, xiii. sec. 33, note.   6 *Ibid*. xi. sec. 3, note 4.

7 *Histoire de la Civilisation en France*, i. 203 (1829). Guizot is speaking of Augustin's attitude in the Pelagian controversy.

8 A portion of this introduction will be found translated in Appendix ii. of M. Saisset's *Essay on Religious Philosophy* (Clark).

9 *Essai*, etc. as before, p. 129.   10 *Essai*, etc. p. 130.

11 *Ibid*. pp. 120-123. Nourrisson's criticism of Augustin's views on Memory may well be compared with that of Desjardins. He speaks of the powerful originality of Augustin—who is ingenious as well as new—and says some of his disquisitions are "the most admirable which have inspired psychological observation." And further, one does not meet in all the books of St. Augustin any philosophical theories which have greater depth than that on Memory."—*Philosophie*, etc. as above, i. 133.

that in leading up to the conclusion at which he arrives, M. Saisset quotes a passage from the *City of God*,[1] which contains an adumbration of the theory of the above work in regard to the eternity of the invisible universe.[2] Verily, the saying of the wise man is true: "The thing that hath been, it is that which shall be; and that which is done, is that which shall be done: and there is no new thing under the sun."[3]

3. We have already, in a previous paragraph, briefly adverted to the influence Christianity aud Paganism had one on the other. The history of Christianity has been a steady advance on Paganism and Pagan philosophy; but it can hardly be denied that in this advance there has been an absorption—and in some periods in no small degree—of some of their elements. As these matters have been examined in the notes, we need not do more than refer the reader to the Index of Subjects for the evidence to be obtained in this respect from the *Confessions* on such matters as Baptism, False Miracles, and Prayers for the Dead.

4. There is one feature in the *Confessions* which we should not like to pass unnoticed. A reference to the *Retractations*[4] will show that Augustin highly appreciated the spiritual use to which the book might be put in the edification of the brethren. We believe that it will prove most useful in this way; and spiritual benefit will accrue in proportion to the steadiness of its use. We would venture to suggest that Book X., from section 37 to the end, may be profitably used as a manual of self-examination. We have pointed out in a note, that in his comment on the 8th Psalm he makes our Lord's three temptations to be types of all the temptations to which man can be subjected; and makes them correspond in their order, as given by St. Matthew, to "the Lust of the Flesh, the Lust of the Eyes, and the Pride of Life," mentioned by St. John.[5] Under each of these heads we have, in this part of the *Confessions*, a most severe examination of conscience; and the impression is deepened by his allegorically likening the three divisions of temptation to the beasts of the field, the fish of the sea, and the birds of the air.[6] We have already remarked, in adverting to allegorical interpretation,[7] that where "the strict use of the history is not disregarded," to use Augustin's expression, allegorizing, by way of spiritual meditation, may be profitable. Those who employ it with this idea will find their interpretations greatly aided, and made more systematic, by realizing Augustin's methods here and in the last two books of the *Confessions*,—as when he makes the sea to represent the wicked world, and the fruitful earth the Church.[8]

It only remains to call attention to the principles on which this translation and its annotations have been made. The text of the Benedictine edition has been followed; but the head-lines of the chapters are taken from the edition of Bruder, as being the more definite and full. After carefully translating the whole of the book, it has been compared, line by line, with the translation of Watts[9] (one of the most nervous translations of the seventeenth century), and that of Dr. Pusey, which is confessedly founded upon that of Watts. Reference has also been made, in the case of obscure passages, to the French translation of Du Bois, and the English translation of the first Ten Books alluded to in the note on Bk. ix. ch. 12. The references to Scripture are in the words of the Authorized Version wherever the sense will bear it; and whenever noteworthy variations from our version occur, they are indicated by references to the old Italic version, or to the Vulgate. In some cases, where Augustin has clearly referred to the LXX. in order to amend his version thereby, such variations are indicated.[10] The annotations are, for the most part, such as have been derived from the translator's own reading. Two exceptions, however, must be made. Out of upwards of four hundred notes, some forty are taken from the annotations in Pusey and Watts, but in every case these have been indicated by the initials E. B. P. or W. W. Dr. Pusey's annotations (which will be found chiefly in the earlier part of this work) consist almost entirely of quotations from other works of Augustin. These annotations are very copious, and Dr. Pusey explains that he resorted to this method "partly because this plan of illustrating St. Augustin out of himself had been already adopted by M. Du Bois in his Latin edition . . . and it seemed a pity not to use valuable materials ready collected to one's hand. The far greater part of these illustrations are taken from that edition." It seemed the most proper course, in using such notes of Du Bois as appeared suitable for this edition, to take them from Dr. Pusey's edition, and, as above stated, to indicate their source by his initials. A Textual Index has been added, for the first time, to this edition, and both it and the Index of Subjects have been prepared with the greatest possible care.

J. G. P.

St. Mark's Vicarage, West Hackney, 1876.

---

[1] Book xii. chap. 15.
[2] This position is accepted by Leibnitz in his *Essais de Théodicée*. See also M. Saisset, as above, ii. 196–8 (Essay by the translator).
[3] Eccles. i. 9. [4] Quoted immediately after this preface. [5] 1 John ii. 16.
[6] See *Confessions*, v. sec. 4, note, and x. sec. 41, note. [7] See *ibid.* vi. sec. 5, note.
[8] See *Confessions*, xiii. sec. 20, note 3, and sec. 21, note 1.
[9] "St. Augustin's *Confessions* translated, and with some marginal notes illustrated by William Watts, Rector of St. Alban's, Wood St. (1631)."
[10] For whatever our idea may be as to the extent of his knowledge of Greek, it is beyond dispute that he frequently had recourse to the Greek of the Old and New Testament with this view. See Nourrisson, *Philosophie*, etc. ii. p. 96.

THE OPINION OF ST. AUGUSTIN

CONCERNING HIS

CONFESSIONS, AS EMBODIED IN HIS *RETRACTATIONS*, II. 6

---

1. "THE Thirteen Books of my *Confessions* whether they refer to my evil or good, praise the just and good God, and stimulate the heart and mind of man to approach unto Him. And, as far as pertaineth unto me, they wrought this in me when they were written, and this they work when they are read. What some think of them they may have seen, but that they have given much pleasure, and do give pleasure, to many brethren I know. From the First to the Tenth they have been written of myself; in the remaining three, of the Sacred Scriptures, from the text, 'In the beginning God created the heaven and the earth,' even to the rest of the Sabbath (Gen. i. 1, ii. 2)."

2. "In the Fourth Book, when I acknowledged the distress of my mind at the death of a friend, saying, that our soul, though one, had been in some manner made out of two ; and therefore, I say, perchance was I afraid to die lest he should die wholly whom I had so much loved (chap. vi.) ;—this seems to me as if it were a light declamation rather than a grave confession, although this folly may in some sort be tempered by that 'perchance' which follows. And in the Thirteenth Book (chap. xxxii.) what I said, viz. : that the 'firmament was made between the spiritual upper waters, and the corporeal lower waters,' was said without due consideration ; but the thing is very obscure."

[In *Ep. ad Darium, Ep.* ccxxxi. c. 6, written A. D. 429, Augustin says: "Accept, my son, the books containing my *Confessions* which you desired to have. In these behold me that you may not praise me more than I deserve ; there believe what is said of me, not by others, but by myself; there mark me, and see what I have been in myself, by myself; and if anything in me please you, join me in praising Him to whom, and not to myself, I desired praise to be given. For 'He hath made us, and not we ourselves' (Ps. l. 3). Indeed, we had destroyed ourselves, but He who made us has made us anew (*qui fecit, refecit*). When, however, you find me in these books, pray for me that I may not fail, but be perfected (*ne deficiam, sed perficiar*). Pray, my son, pray. I feel what I say ; I know what I ask."—P. S.]

[*De Dono Perseverantiæ,* c. 20 (53) : "Which of my smaller works could be more widely known or give greater pleasure than my *Confessions?* And although I published them before the Pelagian heresy had come into existence, certainly in them I said to my God, and said it frequently, 'Give what Thou commandest, and command what Thou willest' (*Conf.* x. 19, 31, 37). Which words of mine, Pelagius at Rome, when they were mentioned in his presence by a certain brother and fellow-bishop of mine, could not bear. . . . Moreover in those same books . . . I showed that I was granted to the faithful and daily tears of my mother, that I should not perish. There certainly I declared that God by His grace converted the will of men to the true faith, not only when they had been turned away from it, but even when they were opposed to it."—P. S.]

CONTENTS OF THE CONFESSIONS.

BOOK FIRST.

COMMENCING WITH THE INVOCATION OF GOD, AUGUSTIN RELATES IN DETAIL THE BEGINNING OF HIS LIFE, HIS INFANCY AND BOYHOOD UP TO HIS FIFTEENTH YEAR; AT WHICH AGE HE ACKNOWLEDGES THAT HE WAS MORE INCLINED TO ALL YOUTHFUL PLEASURES AND VICES THAN TO THE STUDY OF LETTERS.

BOOK SECOND.

HE ADVANCES TO PUBERTY, AND INDEED TO THE EARLY PART OF THE SIXTEENTH YEAR OF HIS AGE, IN WHICH, HAVING ABANDONED HIS STUDIES, HE INDULGED IN LUSTFUL PLEASURES, AND, WITH HIS COMPANIONS, COMMITTED THEFT.

BOOK THIRD.

OF THE SEVENTEENTH, EIGHTEENTH, AND NINETEENTH YEARS OF HIS AGE, PASSED AT CARTHAGE,
WHEN, HAVING COMPLETED HIS COURSE OF STUDIES, HE IS CAUGHT IN THE SNARES OF A LI-
CENTIOUS PASSION, AND FALLS INTO THE SNARES OF THE MANICHÆANS.

BOOK FOURTH.

THEN FOLLOWS A PERIOD OF NINE YEARS FROM THE NINETEENTH YEAR OF HIS AGE, DURING WHICH,
HAVING LOST A FRIEND, HE FOLLOWED THE MANICHÆANS—AND WROTE BOOKS ON THE FAIR AND
FIT, AND PUBLISHED A WORK ON THE LIBERAL ARTS, AND THE CATEGORIES OF ARISTOTLE.

BOOK FIFTH.

HE DESCRIBES THE TWENTY-NINTH YEAR OF HIS AGE, IN WHICH, HAVING DISCOVERED THE FALLA-
CIES OF THE MANICHÆANS, HE PROFESSED RHETORIC AT ROME AND MILAN. HAVING HEARD
AMBROSE, HE BEGINS TO COME TO HIMSELF.

BOOK SIXTH.

ATTAINING HIS THIRTIETH YEAR, HE, UNDER THE ADMONITION OF THE DISCOURSES OF AMBROSE,
DISCOVERED MORE AND MORE THE TRUTH OF THE CATHOLIC DOCTRINE, AND DELIBERATES AS
TO THE BETTER REGULATION OF HIS LIFE.

BOOK SEVENTH.

HE RECALLS THE BEGINNING OF HIS YOUTH, *i. e.* THE THIRTY-FIRST YEAR OF HIS AGE, IN WHICH VERY GRAVE ERRORS AS TO THE NATURE OF GOD, AND THE ORIGIN OF EVIL, BEING DISTINGUISHED, AND THE SACRED BOOKS MORE ACCURATELY KNOWN, HE AT LENGTH ARRIVES AT A CLEAR KNOWLEDGE OF GOD, NOT YET RIGHTLY APPREHENDING JESUS CHRIST.

BOOK EIGHTH.

HE FINALLY DESCRIBES THE THIRTY-SECOND YEAR OF HIS AGE, THE MOST MEMORABLE OF HIS WHOLE LIFE, IN WHICH, BEING INSTRUCTED BY SIMPLICIANUS CONCERNING THE CONVERSION OF OTHERS, AND THE MANNER OF ACTING, HE IS, AFTER A SEVERE STRUGGLE, RENEWED IN HIS WHOLE MIND, AND IS CONVERTED UNTO GOD.

BOOK NINTH.

HE SPEAKS OF HIS DESIGN OF FORSAKING THE PROFESSION OF RHETORIC; OF THE DEATH OF HIS FRIENDS, NEBRIDIUS AND VERECUNDUS; OF HAVING RECEIVED BAPTISM IN THE THIRTY-THIRD YEAR OF HIS AGE; AND OF THE VIRTUES AND DEATH OF HIS MOTHER MONICA.

BOOK TENTH.

HAVING MANIFESTED WHAT HE WAS AND WHAT HE IS, HE SHOWS THE GREAT FRUIT OF HIS CONFESSION; AND BEING ABOUT TO EXAMINE BY WHAT METHOD GOD AND THE HAPPY LIFE MAY BE FOUND, HE ENLARGES ON THE NATURE AND POWER OF MEMORY. THEN HE EXAMINES HIS OWN ACTS, THOUGHTS, AND AFFECTIONS, VIEWED UNDER THE THREEFOLD DIVISION OF TEMPTATION; AND COMMEMORATES THE LORD, THE ONE MEDIATOR OF GOD AND MEN.

BOOK ELEVENTH.

THE DESIGN OF HIS CONFESSIONS BEING DECLARED, HE SEEKS FROM GOD THE KNOWLEDGE OF THE HOLY SCRIPTURES, AND BEGINS TO EXPOUND THE WORDS OF GENESIS I. I, CONCERNING THE CREATION OF THE WORLD. THE QUESTIONS OF RASH DISPUTERS BEING REFUTED, "WHAT DID GOD BEFORE HE CREATED THE WORLD?" THAT HE MIGHT THE BETTER OVERCOME HIS OPPONENTS, HE ADDS A COPIOUS DISQUISITION CONCERNING TIME.

BOOK TWELFTH.

HE CONTINUES HIS EXPLANATION OF THE FIRST CHAPTER OF GENESIS ACCORDING TO THE SEPTUAGINT, AND BY ITS ASSISTANCE HE ARGUES, ESPECIALLY CONCERNING THE DOUBLE HEAVEN, AND THE FORMLESS MATTER OUT OF WHICH THE WHOLE WORLD MAY HAVE BEEN CREATED; AFTERWARDS OF THE INTER-PRETATIONS OF OTHERS NOT DISALLOWED, AND SETS FORTH AT GREAT LENGTH THE SENSE OF THE HOLY SCRIPTURE.

BOOK THIRTEENTH.

OF THE GOODNESS OF GOD EXPLAINED IN THE CREATION OF THINGS, AND OF THE TRINITY AS FOUND IN THE FIRST WORDS OF GENESIS. THE STORY CONCERNING THE ORIGIN OF THE WORLD (GEN. I.) IS ALLEGORICALLY EXPLAINED, AND HE APPLIES IT TO THOSE THINGS WHICH GOD WORKS FOR SANCTIFIED AND BLESSED MAN. FINALLY, HE MAKES AN END OF THIS WORK, HAVING IMPLORED ETERNAL REST FROM GOD.

THE THIRTEEN BOOKS

OF THE

CONFESSIONS OF ST. AUR. AUGUSTIN,

BISHOP OF HIPPO.

BOOK I.

COMMENCING WITH THE INVOCATION OF GOD, AUGUSTIN RELATES IN DETAIL THE BEGINNING OF HIS LIFE, HIS INFANCY AND BOYHOOD, UP TO HIS FIFTEENTH YEAR; AT WHICH AGE HE ACKNOWLEDGES THAT HE WAS MORE INCLINED TO ALL YOUTHFUL PLEASURES AND VICES THAN TO THE STUDY OF LETTERS.

CHAP. I.—HE PROCLAIMS THE GREATNESS OF GOD, WHOM HE DESIRES TO SEEK AND INVOKE, BEING AWAKENED BY HIM.

1. GREAT art Thou, O Lord, and greatly to be praised; great is Thy power, and of Thy wisdom there is no end.[1] And man, being a part of Thy creation, desires to praise Thee,—man, who bears about with him his mortality, the witness of his sin, even the witness that Thou "resistest the proud,"[2]—yet man, this part of Thy creation, desires to praise Thee.[3] Thou movest us to delight in praising Thee; for Thou hast formed us for Thyself, and our hearts are restless till they find rest in Thee.[4] Lord, teach me to know and understand which of these should be first, to call on Thee, or to praise Thee; and likewise to know Thee, or to call upon Thee. But who is there that calls upon Thee without knowing Thee? For he that knows Thee not may call upon Thee as other than Thou art. Or perhaps we call on Thee that we may know Thee. "But how shall they call on Him in whom they have not believed? or how shall they believe without a preacher?"[5] And those who seek the Lord shall praise Him.[6] For those who seek shall find Him,[7] and those who find Him shall praise Him. Let me seek Thee, Lord, in calling on Thee, and call on Thee in believing in Thee; for Thou hast been preached unto us. O Lord, my faith calls on Thee,—that faith which Thou hast imparted to me, which Thou hast breathed into me through the incarnation of Thy Son, through the ministry of Thy preacher.[8]

CHAP. II.—THAT THE GOD WHOM WE INVOKE IS IN US, AND WE IN HIM.

2. And how shall I call upon my God—my God and my Lord? For when I call on Him I ask Him to come into me. And what place is there in me into which my God can come—into which God can come, even He who made heaven and earth? Is there anything in me, O Lord my God, that can contain Thee? Do indeed the very heaven and the earth, which Thou hast made, and in which Thou hast made me,

---

[1] Ps. cxlv. 3, and cxlvii. 5.
[2] Jas. iv. 6, and 1 Pet. v. 5.
[3] Augustin begins with praise, and the whole book vibrates with praise. He says elsewhere (*in Ps*. cxlix.), that "as a new song fits not well an old man's lips, he should sing a new song who is a new creature and is living a new life;" and so from the time of his new birth, the "new song" of praise went up from him, and that "not of the lip only," but (*ibid*. cxlviii.) *conscientia lingua vita*.
[4] And the rest which the Christian has here is but an earnest of the more perfect rest hereafter, when, as Augustin says (*De Gen. ad. Lit*. xii. 26), "all virtue will be to love what one sees, and the highest felicity to have what one loves." [Watts, followed by Pusey, and Shedd, missed the paronomasia of the Latin: " cor nostrum *inquietum* est donec *requiescat* in Te," by translating: " our heart is *restless*, until it *repose* in Thee." It is the finest sentence in the whole book, and furnishes one of the best arguments for Christianity as the only religion which leads to that rest in God.—P. S.]

[5] Rom. x. 14.
[6] Ps. xxii. 26.
[7] Matt. vii. 7.
[8] That is, Ambrose, Bishop of Milan, who was instrumental in his conversion (vi. sec. 1; viii. sec. 28, etc.). "Before conversion," as Leighton observes on 1 Pet. ii. 1, 2, "wit or eloquence may draw a man to the word, and possibly prove a happy bait to catch him (as St. Augustin reports of his hearing St. Ambrose), but, once born again, then it is the milk itself that he desires for itself."

45

contain Thee? Or, as nothing could exist without Thee, doth whatever exists contain Thee? Why, then, do I ask Thee to come into me, since I indeed exist, and could not exist if Thou wert not in me? Because I am not yet in hell, though Thou art even there; for "if I go down into hell Thou art there."[1] I could not therefore exist, could not exist at all, O my God, unless Thou wert in me. Or should I not rather say, that I could not exist unless I were in Thee from whom are all things, by whom are all things, in whom are all things?[2] Even so, Lord; even so. Where do I call Thee to, since Thou art in me, or whence canst Thou come into me? For where outside heaven and earth can I go that from thence my God may come into me who has said, I fill heaven and earth"?[3]

CHAP. III.—EVERYWHERE GOD WHOLLY FILLETH ALL THINGS, BUT NEITHER HEAVEN NOR EARTH CONTAINETH HIM.

3. Since, then, Thou fillest heaven and earth, do they contain Thee? Or, as they contain Thee not, dost Thou fill them, and yet there remains something over? And where dost Thou pour forth that which remaineth of Thee when the heaven and earth are filled? Or, indeed, is there no need that Thou who containest all things shouldest be contained of any, since those things which Thou fillest Thou fillest by containing them? For the vessels which Thou fillest do not sustain Thee, since should they even be broken Thou wilt not be poured forth. And when Thou art poured forth on us,[4] Thou art not cast down, but we are uplifted; nor art Thou dissipated, but we are drawn together. But, as Thou fillest all things, dost Thou fill them with Thy whole self, or, as even all things cannot altogether contain Thee, do they contain a part, and do all at once contain the same part? Or has each its own proper part—the greater more, the smaller less? Is, then, one part of Thee greater, another less? Or is it that Thou art wholly everywhere whilst nothing altogether contains Thee?[5]

CHAP. IV.—THE MAJESTY OF GOD IS SUPREME, AND HIS VIRTUES INEXPLICABLE.

4. What, then, art Thou, O my God—what, I ask, but the Lord God? For who is Lord but the Lord? or who is God save our God?[6] Most high, most excellent, most potent, most omnipotent; most piteous and most just; most hidden and most near; most beauteous and most strong, stable, yet contained of none; unchangeable, yet changing all things; never new, never old; making all things new, yet bringing old age upon the proud and they know it not; always working, yet ever at rest; gathering, yet needing nothing; sustaining, pervading, and protecting; creating, nourishing, and developing; seeking, and yet possessing all things. Thou lovest, and burnest not; art jealous, yet free from care; repentest, and hast no sorrow; art angry, yet serene; changest Thy ways, leaving unchanged Thy plans; recoverest what Thou findest, having yet never lost; art never in want, whilst Thou rejoicest in gain; never covetous, though requiring usury.[7] That Thou mayest owe, more than enough is given to Thee;[8] yet who hath anything that is not Thine? Thou payest debts while owing nothing; and when Thou forgivest debts, losest nothing. Yet, O my God, my life, my holy joy, what is this that I have said? And what saith any man when He speaks of Thee? Yet woe to them that keep silence, seeing that even they who say most are as the dumb.[9]

CHAP. V.—HE SEEKS REST IN GOD, AND PARDON OF HIS SINS.

5. Oh! how shall I find rest in Thee? Who will send Thee into my heart to inebriate it, so that I may forget my woes, and embrace Thee, my only good? What art Thou to me? Have compassion on me, that I may speak. What am I to Thee that Thou demandest my love, and unless I give it Thee art angry, and threatenest me with great sorrows? Is it, then, a light sorrow not to love Thee? Alas! alas! tell me of Thy compassion, O Lord my God, what Thou art to me. "Say unto my soul, I am thy salvation."[10] So speak that I may hear. Behold, Lord, the ears of my heart are before Thee; open Thou them, and "say unto my soul, I am thy salvation." When I hear, may I run and lay hold on Thee. Hide not Thy face from me. Let me die, lest I die, if only I may see Thy face.[11]

6. Cramped is the dwelling of my soul; do Thou expand it, that Thou mayest enter in. It is in ruins, restore Thou it. There is that about it which must offend Thine eyes; I confess and

---

[1] Ps. cxxxix. 8.
[2] Rom. xi. 36,
[3] Jer. xxiii. 24.
[4] Acts ii. 18.
[5] In this section, and constantly throughout the *Confessions*, he adverts to the materialistic views concerning God held by the Manichæans. See also sec. 10; iii. sec. 12; iv. sec. 31, etc. etc.
[6] Ps. xviii. 31.

[7] Matt. xxv. 27.
[8] *Supererogatur tibi, ut debeas.*
[9] "As it is impossible for mortal, imperfect, and perishable man to comprehend the immortal, perfect and eternal, we cannot expect that he should be able to express in praise the fulness of God's attributes. The Talmud relates of a rabbi, who did not consider the terms, 'the great, mighty, and fearful God,' which occur in the daily prayer, as being sufficient, but added some more attributes—'What!' exclaimed another rabbi who was present, 'imaginest thou to be able to exhaust the praise of God? Thy praise is blasphemy. Thou hadst better be quiet.' Hence the Psalmist's exclamation, after finding that the praises of God were inexhaustible: לך דומיה תהלה, 'Silence is praise to Thee.'"—BRESLAU.
[10] Ps. xxxv. 3.
[11] *Moriar ne moriar, ut eam videam.* See Ex. xxxiii. 20.

know it, but who will cleanse it? or to whom shall I cry but to Thee? Cleanse me from my secret sins,[1] O Lord, and keep Thy servant from those of other men. I believe, and therefore do I speak;[2] Lord, Thou knowest. Have I not confessed my transgressions unto Thee, O my God; and Thou hast put away the iniquity of my heart?[3] I do not contend in judgment with Thee,[4] who art the Truth; and I would not deceive myself, lest my iniquity lie against itself.[5] I do not, therefore, contend in judgment with Thee, for "if Thou, Lord, shouldest mark iniquities, O Lord, who shall stand?"[6]

CHAP. VI.—HE DESCRIBES HIS INFANCY, AND LAUDS THE PROTECTION AND ETERNAL PROVIDENCE OF GOD.

7. Still suffer me to speak before Thy mercy—me, "dust and ashes."[7] Suffer me to speak, for, behold, it is Thy mercy I address, and not derisive man. Yet perhaps even Thou deridest me; but when Thou art turned to me Thou wilt have compassion on me.[8] For what do I wish to say, O Lord my God, but that I know not whence I came hither into this—shall I call it dying life or living death? Yet, as I have heard from my parents, from whose substance Thou didst form me,—for I myself cannot remember it,—Thy merciful comforts sustained me. Thus it was that the comforts of a woman's milk entertained me; for neither my mother nor my nurses filled their own breasts, but Thou by them didst give me the nourishment of infancy according to Thy ordinance and that bounty of Thine which underlieth all things. For Thou didst cause me not to want more than Thou gavest, and those who nourished me willingly to give me what Thou gavest them. For they, by an instinctive affection, were anxious to give me what Thou hadst abundantly supplied. It was, in truth, good for them that my good should come from them, though, indeed, it was not from them, but by them; for from Thee, O God, are all good things, and from my God is all my safety.[9] This is what I have since discovered, as Thou hast declared Thyself to me by the

blessings both within me and without me which Thou hast bestowed upon me. For at that time I knew how to suck, to be satisfied when comfortable, and to cry when in pain—nothing beyond.

8. Afterwards I began to laugh,—at first in sleep, then when waking. For this I have heard mentioned of myself, and I believe it (though I cannot remember it), for we see the same in other infants. And now little by little I realized where I was, and wished to tell my wishes to those who might satisfy them, but I could not; for my wants were within me, while they were without, and could not by any faculty of theirs enter into my soul. So I cast about limbs and voice, making the few and feeble signs I could, like, though indeed not much like, unto what I wished; and when I was not satisfied—either not being understood, or because it would have been injurious to me—I grew indignant that my elders were not subject unto me, and that those on whom I had no claim did not wait on me, and avenged myself on them by tears. That infants are such I have been able to learn by watching them; and they, though unknowing, have better shown me that I was such an one than my nurses who knew it.

9. And, behold, my infancy died long ago, and I live. But Thou, O Lord, who ever livest, and in whom nothing dies (since before the world was, and indeed before all that can be called "before," Thou existest, and art the God and Lord of all Thy creatures; and with Thee fixedly abide the causes of all unstable things, the unchanging sources of all things changeable, and the eternal reasons of all things unreasoning and temporal), tell me, Thy suppliant, O God; tell, O merciful One, Thy miserable servant[10]—tell me whether my infancy succeeded another age of mine which had at that time perished. ·Was it that which I passed in my mother's womb? For of that something has been made known to me, and I have myself seen women with child. And what, O God, my joy, preceded that life? Was I, indeed, anywhere, or anybody? For no one can tell me these things, neither father nor mother, nor the experience of others, nor my own memory. Dost Thou laugh at me for asking such things, and command me to praise and confess Thee for what I know?

10. I give thanks to Thee, Lord of heaven and earth, giving praise to Thee for that my first being and infancy, of which I have no memory; for Thou hast granted to man that from others he should come to conclusions as to himself, and that he should believe many things concerning himself on the authority of feeble women. Even then I had life and being; and

---

[1] Ps. xix. 12, 13. "Be it that sin may never see the light, that it may be like a child born and buried in the womb; yet as that child is a man, a true man, there closeted in that hidden frame of nature, so sin is truly sin, though it never gets out beyond the womb which did conceive and enliven it."—SEDGWICK.
[2] Ps. cxvi. 10.
[3] Ps. xxxii. 5.
[4] Job ix. 3.
[5] Ps. xxvi. 12, *Vulg.* "The danger of ignorance is not less than its guilt. For of all evils a secret evil is most to be deprecated, of all enemies a concealed enemy is the worst. Better the precipice than the pitfall; better the tortures of curable disease than the painlessness of mortification; and so, whatever your soul's guilt and danger, better to be aware of it. However alarming, however distressing self-knowledge may be, better *that* than the tremendous evils of self-ignorance."—CAIRD.
[6] Ps. cxxx. 3.
[7] Gen. xviii. 27.
[8] Jer. xii. 15.
[9] Prov. xxi. 31.

[10] "Mercy," says Binning, "hath but its name from misery, and is no other thing than to lay another's misery to heart."

as my infancy closed I was already seeking for signs by which my feelings might be made known to others. Whence could such a creature come but from Thee, O Lord? Or shall any man be skilful enough to fashion himself? Or is there any other vein by which being and life runs into us save this, that "Thou, O Lord, hast made us,"[1] with whom being and life are one, because Thou Thyself art being and life in the highest? Thou art the highest, "Thou changest not,"[2] neither in Thee doth this present day come to an end, though it doth end in Thee, since in Thee all such things are; for they would have no way of passing away unless Thou sustainedst them. And since "Thy years shall have no end,"[3] Thy years are an ever present day. And how many of ours and our fathers' days have passed through this Thy day, and received from it their measure and fashion of being, and others yet to come shall so receive and pass away! "But Thou art the same;"[4] and all the things of to-morrow and the days yet to come, and all of yesterday and the days that are past, Thou wilt do to-day, Thou hast done to-day. What is it to me if any understand not? Let him still rejoice and say, "What is this?"[5] Let him rejoice even so, and rather love to discover in failing to discover, than in discovering not to discover Thee.

CHAP. VII.—HE SHOWS BY EXAMPLE THAT EVEN INFANCY IS PRONE TO SIN.

11. Hearken, O God! Alas for the sins of men! Man saith this, and Thou dost compassionate him; for Thou didst create him, but didst not create the sin that is in him. Who bringeth to my remembrance the sin of my infancy? For before Thee none is free from sin, not even the infant which has lived but a day upon the earth. Who bringeth this to my remembrance? Doth not each little one, in whom I behold that which I do not remember of myself? In what, then, did I sin? Is it that I cried for the breast? If I should now so cry,—not indeed for the breast, but for the food suitable to my years,—I should be most justly laughed at and rebuked. What I then did de-

served rebuke; but as I could not understand those who rebuked me, neither custom nor reason suffered me to be rebuked. For as we grow we root out and cast from us such habits. I have not seen any one who is wise, when "purging"[6] anything cast away the good. Or was it good, even for a time, to strive to get by crying that which, if given, would be hurtful—to be bitterly indignant that those who were free and its elders, and those to whom it owed its being, besides many others wiser than it, who would not give way to the nod of its good pleasure, were not subject unto it—to endeavour to harm, by struggling as much as it could, because those commands were not obeyed which only could have been obeyed to its hurt? Then, in the weakness of the infant's limbs, and not in its will, lies its innocency. I myself have seen and known an infant to be jealous though it could not speak. It became pale, and cast bitter looks on its foster-brother. Who is ignorant of this? Mothers and nurses tell us that they appease these things by I know not what remedies; and may this be taken for innocence, that when the fountain of milk is flowing fresh and abundant, one who has need should not be allowed to share it, though needing that nourishment to sustain life? Yet we look leniently on these things, not because they are not faults, nor because the faults are small, but because they will vanish as age increases. For although you may allow these things now, you could not bear them with equanimity if found in an older person.

12. Thou, therefore, O Lord my God, who gavest life to the infant, and a frame which, as we see, Thou hast endowed with senses, compacted with limbs, beautified with form, and, for its general good and safety, hast introduced all vital energies—Thou commandest me to praise Thee for these things, "to give thanks unto the Lord, and to sing praise unto Thy name, O Most High;"[7] for Thou art a God omnipotent and good, though Thou hadst done nought but these things, which none other can do but Thou, who alone madest all things, O Thou most fair, who madest all things fair, and orderest all according to Thy law. This period, then, of my life, O Lord, of which I have no remembrance, which I believe on the word of others, and which I guess from other infants, it chagrins me—true though the guess be—to reckon in this life of mine which I lead in this world; inasmuch as, in the darkness of my forgetfulness, it is like to that which I passed in my mother's womb. But if "I was shapen in iniquity, and in sin did my mother conceive

---

[1] Ps. c. 3.
[2] Mal. iii. 6.
[3] Ps. cii. 27.
[4] Ibid.
[5] Ex. xvi. 15. This is one of the alternative translations put against " it is manna " in the margin of the authorized version. It is the literal significance of the Hebrew, and is so translated in most of the old English versions. Augustin indicates thereby the attitude of faith. Many things we are called on to believe (to use the illustration of Locke) which are above reason, but none that are contrary to reason. We are but as children in relation to God, and may therefore only expect to know " parts of His ways." Even in the difficulties of Scripture he sees the goodness of God. " God," he says, " has in Scripture clothed His mysteries with clouds, that man's love of truth might be inflamed by the difficulty of finding them out. For if they were only such as were readily understood, truth would not be eagerly sought, nor would it give pleasure when found."—De Ver. Relig. c. 17.

[6] John xv. 2.
[7] Ps. xcii. 1.

me," [1] where, I pray thee, O my God, where, Lord, or when was I, Thy servant, innocent? But behold, I pass by that time, for what have I to do with that, the memories of which I cannot recall?

CHAP. VIII.—THAT WHEN A BOY HE LEARNED TO SPEAK, NOT BY ANY SET METHOD, BUT FROM THE ACTS AND WORDS OF HIS PARENTS.

13. Did I not, then, growing out of the state of infancy, come to boyhood, or rather did it not come to me, and succeed to infancy? Nor did my infancy depart (for whither went it?); and yet it did no longer abide, for I was no longer an infant that could not speak, but a chattering boy. I remember this, and I afterwards observed how I first learned to speak, for my elders did not teach me words in any set method, as they did letters afterwards; but I myself, when I was unable to say all I wished and to whomsoever I desired, by means of the whimperings and broken utterances and various motions of my limbs, which I used to enforce my wishes, repeated the sounds in my memory by the mind, O my God, which Thou gavest me. When they called anything by name, and moved the body towards it while they spoke, I saw and gathered that the thing they wished to point out was called by the name they then uttered; and that they did mean this was made plain by the motion of the body, even by the natural language of all nations expressed by the countenance, glance of the eye, movement of other members, and by the sound of the voice indicating the affections of the mind, as it seeks, possesses, rejects, or avoids. So it was that by frequently hearing words, in duly placed sentences, I gradually gathered what things they were the signs of; and having formed my mouth to the utterance of these signs, I thereby expressed my will.[2] Thus I exchanged with those about me the signs by which we express our wishes, and advanced deeper into the stormy fellowship of human life, depending the while on the authority of parents, and the beck of elders.

CHAP. IX.—CONCERNING THE HATRED OF LEARNING, THE LOVE OF PLAY, AND THE FEAR OF BEING WHIPPED NOTICEABLE IN BOYS: AND OF THE FOLLY OF OUR ELDERS AND MASTERS.

14. O my God! what miseries and mockeries did I then experience, when obedience to my teachers was set before me as proper to my boyhood, that I might flourish in this world, and distinguish myself in the science of speech, which should get me honour amongst men, and deceitful riches! After that I was put to school to get learning, of which I (worthless as I was) knew not what use there was; and yet, if slow to learn, I was flogged! For this was deemed praiseworthy by our forefathers; and many before us, passing the same course, had appointed beforehand for us these troublesome ways by which we were compelled to pass, multiplying labour and sorrow upon the sons of Adam. But we found, O Lord, men praying to Thee, and we learned from them to conceive of Thee, according to our ability, to be some Great One, who was able (though not visible to our senses) to hear and help us. For as a boy I began to pray to Thee, my "help" and my "refuge," [3] and in invoking Thee broke the bands of my tongue, and entreated Thee though little, with no little earnestness, that I might not be beaten at school. And when Thou heardedst me not, giving me not over to folly thereby,[4] my elders, yea, and my own parents too, who wished me no ill, laughed at my stripes, my then great and grievous ill.

15. Is there any one, Lord, with so high a spirit, cleaving to Thee with so strong an affection—for even a kind of obtuseness may do that much—but is there, I say, any one who, by cleaving devoutly to Thee, is endowed with so great a courage that he can esteem lightly those racks and hooks, and varied tortures of the same sort, against which, throughout the whole world, men supplicate Thee with great fear, deriding those who most bitterly fear them, just as our parents derided the torments with which our masters punished us when we were boys? For we were no less afraid of our pains, nor did we pray less to Thee to avoid them; and yet we sinned, in writing, or reading, or reflecting upon our lessons less than was required of us. For we wanted not, O Lord, memory or capacity,—of which, by Thy will, we possessed enough for our age,—but we delighted only in play; and we were punished for this by those who were doing the same things themselves. But the idleness of our elders they call business, whilst boys who do the like are punished by those same elders, and yet neither boys nor men find any pity. For will any one of good sense approve of my being whipped because, as a boy, I played ball, and so was hindered from learning quickly those lessons by means of which, as a man, I should play more unbecomingly? And did he by whom I was beaten do other than this, who, when he was overcome in any little controversy with a co-tutor, was more tormented by anger and envy than I when beaten by a playfellow in a match at ball?

---

[1] Ps. li. 5.
[2] See some interesting remarks on this subject in Whately's *Logic*, Int. sec. 5.

[3] Ps. ix. 9, and xlvi. 1, and xlviii. 3.
[4] Ps. xxii. 2, *Vulg.*

CHAP. X.—THROUGH A LOVE OF BALL-PLAYING AND SHOWS, HE NEGLECTS HIS STUDIES AND THE INJUNCTIONS OF HIS PARENTS.

16. And yet I erred, O Lord God, the Creator and Disposer of all things in Nature,—but of sin the Disposer only,—I erred, O Lord my God, in doing contrary to the wishes of my parents and of those masters; for this learning which they (no matter for what motive) wished me to acquire, I might have put to good account afterwards. For I disobeyed them not because I had chosen a better way, but from a fondness for play, loving the honour of victory in the matches, and to have my ears tickled with lying fables, in order that they might itch the more furiously—the same curiosity beaming more and more in my eyes for the shows and sports of my elders. Yet those who give these entertainments are held in such high repute, that almost all desire the same for their children, whom they are still willing should be beaten, if so be these same games keep them from the studies by which they desire them to arrive at being the givers of them. Look down upon these things, O Lord, with compassion, and deliver us who now call upon Thee; deliver those also who do not call upon Thee, that they may call upon Thee, and that Thou mayest deliver them.

CHAP. XI.—SEIZED BY DISEASE, HIS MOTHER BEING TROUBLED, HE EARNESTLY DEMANDS BAPTISM, WHICH ON RECOVERY IS POSTPONED —HIS FATHER NOT AS YET BELIEVING IN CHRIST.

17. Even as a boy I had heard of eternal life promised to us through the humility of the Lord our God condescending to our pride, and I was signed with the sign of the cross, and was seasoned with His salt [1] even from the womb of my mother, who greatly trusted in Thee. Thou sawest, O Lord, how at one time, while yet a boy, being suddenly seized with pains in the stomach, and being at the point of death—Thou sawest, O my God, for even then Thou wast my keeper, with what emotion of mind and with what faith I solicited from the piety of my mother, and of Thy Church, the mother of us all, the baptism of Thy Christ, my Lord and my God. On which, the mother of my flesh being much troubled,—since she, with a heart pure in Thy faith, travailed in birth [2] more lovingly for my eternal salvation,—would, had I not quickly recovered, have without delay provided for my initiation and washing by Thy life-giving sacraments, confessing Thee, O Lord Jesus, for the remission of sins. So my cleansing was deferred, as if I must needs, should I live, be further polluted; because, indeed, the guilt contracted by sin would, after baptism, be greater and more perilous. [3] Thus I at that time believed with my mother and the whole house, except my father; yet he did not overcome the influence of my mother's piety in me so as to prevent my believing in Christ, as he had not yet believed in Him. For she was desirous that Thou, O my God, shouldst be my Father rather than he; and in this Thou didst aid her to overcome her husband, to whom, though the better of the two, she yielded obedience, because in this she yielded obedience to Thee, who dost so command.

18. I beseech Thee, my God, I would gladly know, if it be Thy will, to what end my baptism was then deferred? Was it for my good that the reins were slackened, as it were, upon me for me to sin? Or were they not slackened? If not, whence comes it that it is still dinned into our ears on all sides, "Let him alone, let him act as he likes, for he is not yet baptized"? But as regards bodily health, no one exclaims, "Let him be more seriously wounded, for he is not yet cured!" How much better, then, had it been for me to have been cured at once; and then, by my own and my friends' diligence, my soul's restored health had been kept safe in Thy keeping, who gavest it! Better, in truth. But how numerous and great waves of temptation appeared to hang over me after my childhood! These were foreseen by my mother; and she preferred that the unformed clay should be exposed to them rather than the image itself.

CHAP. XII.—BEING COMPELLED, HE GAVE HIS ATTENTION TO LEARNING; BUT FULLY ACKNOWLEDGES THAT THIS WAS THE WORK OF GOD.

19. But in this my childhood (which was far less dreaded for me than youth) I had no love of learning, and hated to be forced to it, yet was I forced to it notwithstanding; and this was well done towards me, but I did not well, for I would not have learned had I not been compelled. For no man doth well against his will, even if that which he doth be well. Neither did they who forced me do well, but

---

[1] "A rite in the Western churches, on admission as a catechumen, previous to baptism, denoting the purity and uncorruptedness and discretion required of Christians. See S. Aug. *De Catechiz. rudib.* c. 26; Concil. Carth. 3, can. 5; and Liturgies in *Assem. Cod. Liturg.* t. i."—E. B. P. See also vi. 1, note, below.

[2] Gal. iv. 19.

[3] Baptism was in those days frequently (and for similar reasons to the above) postponed till the hour of death approached. The doctors of the Church endeavoured to discourage this, and persons baptized on a sick-bed ("clinically") were, if they recovered, looked on with suspicion. The Emperor Constantine was not baptized till the close of his life, and he is censured by Dr. Newman (*Arians,* iii. sec. 1) for presuming to speak of questions which divided the Arians and the Orthodox as "unimportant," while he himself was both unbaptized and uninstructed. On the postponing of baptism with a view to unrestrained enjoyment of the world, and on the severity of the early Church towards sins committed after baptism, see Kaye's *Tertullian,* pp. 234-241.

the good that was done to me came from Thee, my God. For they considered not in what way I should employ what they forced me to learn, unless to satisfy the inordinate desires of a rich beggary and a shameful glory. But Thou, by whom the very hairs of our heads are numbered,[1] didst use for my good the error of all who pressed me to learn; and my own error in willing not to learn, didst Thou make use of for my punishment—of which I, being so small a boy and so great a sinner, was not unworthy. Thus by the instrumentality of those who did not well didst Thou well for me; and by my own sin didst Thou justly punish me. For it is even as Thou hast appointed, that every inordinate affection should bring its own punishment.[2]

CHAP. XIII.—HE DELIGHTED IN LATIN STUDIES AND THE EMPTY FABLES OF THE POETS, BUT HATED THE ELEMENTS OF LITERATURE AND THE GREEK LANGUAGE.

20. But what was the cause of my dislike of Greek literature, which I studied from my boyhood, I cannot even now understand. For the Latin I loved exceedingly—not what our first masters, but what the grammarians teach; for those primary lessons of reading, writing, and ciphering, I considered no less of a burden and a punishment than Greek. Yet whence was this unless from the sin and vanity of this life? for I was "but flesh, a wind that passeth away and cometh not again."[3] For those primary lessons were better, assuredly, because more certain; seeing that by their agency I acquired, and still retain, the power of reading what I find written, and writing myself what I will; whilst in the others I was compelled to learn about the wanderings of a certain Æneas, oblivious of my own, and to weep for Dido dead, because she slew herself for love; while at the same time I brooked with dry eyes my wretched self dying far from Thee, in the midst of those things, O God, my life.

21. For what can be more wretched than the wretch who pities not himself shedding tears over the death of Dido for love of Æneas, but shedding no tears over his own death in not loving Thee, O God, light of my heart, and bread of the inner mouth of my soul, and the power that weddest my mind with my innermost thoughts? I did not love Thee, and committed fornication against Thee; and those around me thus sinning cried, "Well done! Well done!" For the friendship of this world is fornication against Thee;[4] and "Well done!

Well done!" is cried until one feels ashamed not to be such a man. And for this I shed no tears, though I wept for Dido, who sought death at the sword's point,[5] myself the while seeking the lowest of Thy creatures—having forsaken Thee—earth tending to the earth; and if forbidden to read these things, how grieved would I feel that I was not permitted to read what grieved me. This sort of madness is considered a more honourable and more fruitful learning than that by which I learned to read and write.

22. But now, O my God, cry unto my soul; and let Thy Truth say unto me, "It is not so; it is not so; better much was that first teaching." For behold, I would rather forget the wanderings of Æneas, and all such things, than how to write and read. But it is true that over the entrance of the grammar school there hangs a vail;[6] but this is not so much a sign of the majesty of the mystery, as of a covering for error. Let not them exclaim against me of whom I am no longer in fear, whilst I confess to Thee, my God, that which my soul desires, and acquiesce in reprehending my evil ways, that I may love Thy good ways. Neither let those cry out against me who buy or sell grammar-learning. For if I ask them whether it be true, as the poet says, that Æneas once came to Carthage, the unlearned will reply that they do not know, the learned will deny it to be true. But if I ask with what letters the name Æneas is written, all who have learnt this will answer truly, in accordance with the conventional understanding men have arrived at as to these signs. Again, if I should ask which, if forgotten, would cause the greatest inconvenience in our life, reading and writing, or these poetical fictions, who does not see what every one would answer who had not entirely forgotten himself? I erred, then, when as a boy I preferred those vain studies to those more profitable ones, or rather loved the one and hated the other. "One and one are two, two and two are four," this was then in truth a hateful song to me; while the wooden horse full of armed men, and the burning of Troy, and the "spectral image" of Creusa[7] were a most pleasant spectacle of vanity.

CHAP. XIV.—WHY HE DESPISED GREEK LITERATURE, AND EASILY LEARNED LATIN.

23. But why, then, did I dislike Greek learn-

---

[1] Matt. x. 30.
[2] See note, v. sec. 2, below.
[3] Ps. lxxviii. 39, and Jas. iv. 14.
[4] Jas. iv. 4.

[5] Æneïd, vi. 457.
[6] "The 'vail' was an emblem of honour, used in places of worship, and subsequently in courts of law, emperors' palaces, and even private house. See Du Fresne and Hoffman sub v. That between the vestibule, or proscholium, and the school itself, besides being a mark of dignity, may, as St. Augustin perhaps implies, have been intended to denote the hidden mysteries taught therein, and that the mass of mankind were not fit hearers of truth."—E. B. P.
[7] Æneïd, ii. 772.

ing, which was full of like tales?[1] For Homer also was skilled in inventing similar stories, and is most sweetly vain, yet was he disagreeable to me as a boy. I believe Virgil, indeed, would be the same to Grecian children, if compelled to learn him, as I was Homer. The difficulty, in truth, the difficulty of learning a foreign language mingled as it were with gall all the sweetness of those fabulous Grecian stories. For not a single word of it did I understand, and to make me do so, they vehemently urged me with cruel threatenings and punishments. There was a time also when (as an infant) I knew no Latin; but this I acquired without any fear or tormenting, by merely taking notice, amid the blandishments of my nurses, the jests of those who smiled on me, and the sportiveness of those who toyed with me. I learnt all this, indeed, without being urged by any pressure of punishment, for my own heart urged me to bring forth its own conceptions, which I could not do unless by learning words, not of those who taught me, but of those who talked to me; into whose ears, also, I brought forth whatever I discerned. From this it is sufficiently clear that a free curiosity hath more influence in our learning these things than a necessity full of fear. But this last restrains the overflowings of that freedom, through Thy laws, O God,—Thy laws, from the ferule of the schoolmaster to the trials of the martyr, being effective to mingle for us a salutary bitter, calling us back to Thyself from the pernicious delights which allure us from Thee.

CHAP. XV.—HE ENTREATS GOD, THAT WHATEVER USEFUL THINGS HE LEARNED AS A BOY MAY BE DEDICATED TO HIM.

24. Hear my prayer, O Lord; let not my soul faint under Thy discipline, nor let me faint in confessing unto Thee Thy mercies, whereby Thou hast saved me from all my most mischievous ways, that Thou mightest become sweet to me beyond all the seductions which I used to follow; and that I may love Thee entirely, and grasp Thy hand with my whole heart, and that Thou mayest deliver me from every temptation, even unto the end. For lo, O Lord, my King and my God, for Thy service be whatever useful thing I learnt as a boy—for Thy service

what I speak, and write, and count. For when I learned vain things, Thou didst grant me Thy discipline; and my sin in taking delight in those vanities, Thou hast forgiven me. I learned, indeed, in them many useful words; but these may be learned in things not vain, and that is the safe way for youths to walk in.

CHAP. XVI.—HE DISAPPROVES OF THE MODE OF EDUCATING YOUTH, AND HE POINTS OUT WHY WICKEDNESS IS ATTRIBUTED TO THE GODS BY THE POETS.

25. But woe unto thee, thou stream of human custom! Who shall stay thy course? How long shall it be before thou art dried up? How long wilt thou carry down the sons of Eve into that huge and formidable ocean, which even they who are embarked on the cross (*lignum*) can scarce pass over?[2] Do I not read in thee of Jove the thunderer and adulterer? And the two verily he could not be; but it was that, while the fictitious thunder served as a cloak, he might have warrant to imitate real adultery. Yet which of our gowned masters can lend a temperate ear to a man of his school who cries out and says: "These were Homer's fictions; he transfers things human to the gods. I could have wished him to transfer divine things to us."[3] But it would have been more true had he said: "These are, indeed, his fictions, but he attributed divine attributes to sinful men, that crimes might not be accounted crimes, and that whosoever committed any might appear to imitate the celestial gods and not abandoned men."

26. And yet, thou stream of hell, into thee are cast the sons of men, with rewards for learning these things; and much is made of it when this is going on in the forum in the sight of laws which grant a salary over and above the rewards. And thou beatest against thy rocks and roarest, saying, "Hence words are learnt; hence eloquence is to be attained, most necessary to persuade people to your way of thinking, and to unfold your opinions." So, in truth, we should never have understood these words, "golden shower," "bosom," "intrigue," "highest heavens," and other words written in the same place, unless Terence had introduced a good-for-nothing youth upon the stage, setting up Jove as his example of lewdness:—

> "Viewing a picture, where the tale was drawn,
> Of Jove's descending in a golden shower
> To Danaë's bosom . . . with a woman to intrigue."

And see how he excites himself to lust, as if by celestial authority, when he says:—

---

[1] Exaggerated statements have been made as to Augustin's deficiency in the knowledge of Greek. In this place it is clear that he simply alludes to a repugnance to learn a foreign language that has often been seen in boys since his day. It would seem equally clear from Bk. vii. sec. 13 (see also *De Trin.* iii. sec. 1), that when he could get a translation of a Greek book, he preferred it to one in the original language. Perhaps in this, again, he is not altogether singular. It is difficult to decide the exact extent of his knowledge, but those familiar with his writings can scarcely fail to be satisfied that he had a sufficient acquaintance with the language to correct his Italic version by the Greek Testament and the LXX., and that he was quite alive to the importance of such knowledge in an interpreter of Scripture. See also *Con. Faust.* xi. 2–4; and *De Doctr. Christ.* ii. 11–15.

[2] So in Tract. II. on John, he has: "The sea has to be crossed, and dost thou despise *the wood?*" explaining it to mean the cross of Christ. And again: "Thou art not at all able to walk in the sea, be carried by a ship—be carried by *the wood*—believe on the Crucified," etc.

[3] Cic. *Tusc.* i. 26.

> " Great Jove,
> Who shakes the highest heavens with his thunder,
> And I, poor mortal man, not do the same!
> I did it, and with all my heart I did it." [1]

Not one whit more easily are the words learnt for this vileness, but by their means is the vileness perpetrated with more confidence. I do not blame the words, they being, as it were, choice and precious vessels, but the wine of error which was drunk in them to us by inebriated teachers; and unless we drank, we were beaten, without liberty of appeal to any sober judge. And yet, O my God,—in whose presence I can now with security recall this,—did I, unhappy one, learn these things willingly, and with delight, and for this was I called a boy of good promise. [2]

CHAP. XVII.—HE CONTINUES ON THE UNHAPPY METHOD OF TRAINING YOUTH IN LITERARY SUBJECTS.

27. Bear with me, my God, while I speak a little of those talents Thou hast bestowed upon me, and on what follies I wasted them. For a lesson sufficiently disquieting to my soul was given me, in hope of praise, and fear of shame or stripes, to speak the words of Juno, as she raged and sorrowed that she could not

> " Latium bar
> From all approaches of the Dardan king," [3]

which I had heard Juno never uttered. Yet were we compelled to stray in the footsteps of these poetic fictions, and to turn that into prose which the poet had said in verse. And his speaking was most applauded in whom, according to the reputation of the persons delineated, the passions of anger and sorrow were most strikingly reproduced, and clothed in the most suitable language. But what is it to me, O my true Life, my God, that my declaiming was applauded above that of many who were my contemporaries and fellow-students? Behold, is not all this smoke and wind? Was there nothing else, too, on which I could exercise my wit and tongue? Thy praise, Lord, Thy praises might have supported the tendrils of my heart by Thy Scriptures; so had it not been dragged away by these empty trifles, a shameful prey of [4] the fowls of the air. For there is more than one way in which men sacrifice to the fallen angels.

CHAP. XVIII.—MEN DESIRE TO OBSERVE THE RULES OF LEARNING, BUT NEGLECT THE ETERNAL RULES OF EVERLASTING SAFETY.

28. But what matter of surprise is it that I was thus carried towards vanity, and went forth from Thee, O my God, when men were proposed to me to imitate, who, should they in relating any acts of theirs—not in themselves evil—be guilty of a barbarism or solecism, when censured for it became confounded; but when they made a full and ornate oration, in well-chosen words, concerning their own licentiousness, and were applauded for it, they boasted? Thou seest this, O Lord, and keepest silence, "long-suffering, and plenteous in mercy and truth," [5] as Thou art. Wilt Thou keep silence for ever? And even now Thou drawest out of this vast deep the soul that seeketh Thee and thirsteth after Thy delights, whose "heart said unto Thee," I have sought Thy face, "Thy face, Lord, will I seek." [6] For I was far from Thy face, through my darkened [7] affections. For it is not by our feet, nor by change of place, that we either turn from Thee or return to Thee. Or, indeed, did that younger son look out for horses, or chariots, or ships, or fly away with visible wings, or journey by the motion of his limbs, that he might, in a far country, prodigally waste all that Thou gavest him when he set out? A kind Father when Thou gavest, and kinder still when he returned destitute! [8] So, then, in wanton, that is to say, in darkened affections, lies distance from Thy face.

29. Behold, O Lord God, and behold patiently, as Thou art wont to do, how diligently the sons of men observe the conventional rules of letters and syllables, received from those who spoke prior to them, and yet neglect the eternal rules of everlasting salvation received from Thee, insomuch that he who practises or teaches the hereditary rules of pronunciation, if, contrary to grammatical usage, he should say, without aspirating the first letter, a *uman* being, will offend men more than if, in opposition to Thy commandments, he, a human being, were to hate a human being. As if, indeed, any man should feel that an enemy could be more destructive to him than that hatred with which he is excited against him, or that he could destroy more utterly him whom he persecutes than he destroys his own soul by his enmity. And of a truth, there is no science of letters more innate than the writing of conscience—that he is doing unto another what he himself would not suffer. How mysterious art Thou, who in silence "dwellest on high," [9] Thou God, the only great, who by an unwearied law dealest out the punishment of blindness to illicit desires! When a man seeking for the reputation of eloquence stands before a human judge while

---

[1] Terence, *Eunuch.* Act 3, scene 6 (Colman).
[2] Until very recently, the *Eunuchus* was recited at "the play" of at least one of our public schools. See *De Civ. Dei*, ii. secs. 7, 8, where Augustin again alludes to this matter.
[3] *Æneid*, i. 36–75 (Kennedy).
[4] See note on v. 4, below.

[5] Ps. lxxxvi. 15.
[6] Ps. xxvii. 8.
[7] Rom. i. 21.
[8] Luke xv. 11–32.
[9] Isa. xxxiii. 5.

a thronging multitude surrounds him, inveighs against his enemy with the most fierce hatred, he takes most vigilant heed that his tongue slips not into grammatical error, but takes no heed lest through the fury of his spirit he cut off a man from his fellow-men.[1]

30. These were the customs in the midst of which I, unhappy boy, was cast, and on that arena it was that I was more fearful of perpetrating a barbarism than, having done so, of envying those who had not. These things I declare and confess unto Thee, my God, for which I was applauded by them whom I then thought it my whole duty to please, for I did not perceive the gulf of infamy wherein I was cast away from Thine eyes.[2] For in Thine eyes what was more infamous than I was already, displeasing even those like myself, deceiving with innumerable lies both tutor, and masters, and parents, from love of play, a desire to see frivolous spectacles, and a stage-stuck restlessness, to imitate them? Pilferings I committed from my parents' cellar and table, either enslaved by gluttony, or that I might have something to give to boys who sold me their play, who, though they sold it, liked it as well as I. In this play, likewise, I often sought dishonest victories, I myself being conquered by the vain desire of pre-eminence. And what could I so little endure, or, if I detected it, censured I so violently, as the very things I did to others, and, when myself detected I was censured, preferred rather to quarrel than to yield? Is this the innocence of childhood? Nay, Lord, nay, Lord; I entreat Thy mercy, O my God. For these same sins, as we grow older, are transferred from governors and masters, from nuts, and balls, and sparrows, to magistrates and kings, to gold, and lands, and slaves, just as the rod is succeeded by more severe chastisements. It

was, then, the stature of childhood that Thou, O our King, didst approve of as an emblem of humility when Thou saidst: "Of such is the kingdom of heaven."[3]

31. But yet, O Lord, to Thee, most excellent and most good, Thou Architect and Governor of the universe, thanks had been due unto Thee, our God, even hadst Thou willed that I should not survive my boyhood. For I existed even then; I lived, and felt, and was solicitous about my own well-being,—a trace of that most mysterious unity[4] from whence I had my being; I kept watch by my inner sense over the wholeness of my senses, and in these insignificant pursuits, and also in my thoughts on things insignificant, I learnt to take pleasure in truth. I was averse to being deceived, I had a vigorous memory, was provided with the power of speech, was softened by friendship, shunned sorrow, meanness, ignorance. In such a being what was not wonderful and praiseworthy? But all these are gifts of my God; I did not give them to myself; and they are good, and all these constitute myself. Good, then, is He that made me, and He is my God; and before Him will I rejoice exceedingly for every good gift which, as a boy, I had. For in this lay my sin, that not in Him, but in His creatures—myself and the rest—I sought for pleasures, honours, and truths, falling thereby into sorrows, troubles, and errors. Thanks be to Thee, my joy, my pride, my confidence, my God—thanks be to Thee for Thy gifts; but preserve Thou them to me. For thus wilt Thou preserve me; and those things which Thou hast given me shall be developed and perfected, and I myself shall be with Thee, for from Thee is my being.

---

[1] Literally, "takes care not by a slip of the tongue to say *inter hominibus*, but takes no care lest *hominem auferat ex hominibus*."
[2] Ps. xxxi. 22.

[3] Matt. xix. 14. See i. sec. 11, note 3, above.
[4] " To be is no other than to be one. In as far, therefore, as anything attains unity, in so far it ' is.' For unity worketh congruity and harmony, whereby things composite are in so far as they are; for things uncompounded are in themselves, because they are one; but things compounded imitate unity by the harmony of their parts, and, so far as they attain to unity, they are. Wherefore order and rule secure being, disorder tends to not being."—AUG. *De Morib. Manich.* c. 6.

BOOK II.

HE ADVANCES TO PUBERTY, AND INDEED TO THE EARLY PART OF THE SIXTEENTH YEAR OF HIS AGE, IN WHICH, HAVING ABANDONED HIS STUDIES, HE INDULGED IN LUSTFUL PLEASURES, AND, WITH HIS COMPANIONS, COMMITTED THEFT.

CHAP. I.—HE DEPLORES THE WICKEDNESS OF HIS YOUTH.

1. I WILL now call to mind my past foulness, and the carnal corruptions of my soul, not because I love them, but that I may love Thee, O my God. For love of Thy love do I it, recalling, in the very bitterness of my remembrance, my most vicious ways, that Thou mayest grow sweet to me,—Thou sweetness without deception! Thou sweetness happy and assured!—and re-collecting myself out of that my dissipation, in which I was torn to pieces, while, turned away from Thee the One, I lost myself among many vanities. For I even longed in my youth formerly to be satisfied with worldly things, and I dared to grow wild again with various and shadowy loves; my form consumed away,[1] and I became corrupt in Thine eyes, pleasing myself, and eager to please in the eyes of men.

CHAP. II.—STRICKEN WITH EXCEEDING GRIEF, HE REMEMBERS THE DISSOLUTE PASSIONS IN WHICH, IN HIS SIXTEENTH YEAR, HE USED TO INDULGE.

2. But what was it that I delighted in save to love and to be beloved? But I held it not in moderation, mind to mind, the bright path of friendship, but out of the dark concupiscence of the flesh and the effervescence of youth exhalations came forth which obscured and overcast my heart, so that I was unable to discern pure affection from unholy desire. Both boiled confusedly within me, and dragged away my unstable youth into the rough places of unchaste desires, and plunged me into a gulf of infamy. Thy anger had overshadowed me, and I knew it not. I was become deaf by the rattling of the chains of my mortality, the punishment for my soul's pride; and I wandered farther from Thee, and Thou didst "suffer"[2] me; and I was tossed to and fro, and wasted, and poured out, and boiled over in my fornications, and Thou

didst hold Thy peace, O Thou my tardy joy! Thou then didst hold Thy peace, and I wandered still farther from Thee, into more and more barren seed-plots of sorrows, with proud dejection and restless lassitude.

3. Oh for one to have regulated my disorder, and turned to my profit the fleeting beauties of the things around me, and fixed a bound to their sweetness, so that the tides of my youth might have spent themselves upon the conjugal shore, if so be they could not be tranquillized and satisfied within the object of a family, as Thy law appoints, O Lord,—who thus formest the offspring of our death, being able also with a tender hand to blunt the thorns which were excluded from Thy paradise! For Thy omnipotency is not far from us even when we are far from Thee, else in truth ought I more vigilantly to have given heed to the voice from the clouds: "Nevertheless, such shall have trouble in the flesh, but I spare you;"[3] and, "It is good for a man not to touch a woman;"[4] and, "He that is unmarried careth for the things that belong to the Lord, how he may please the Lord; but he that is married careth for the things that are of the world, how he may please his wife."[5] I should, therefore, have listened more attentively to these words, and, being severed "for the kingdom of heaven's sake,"[6] I would with greater happiness have expected Thy embraces.

4. But I, poor fool, seethed as does the sea, and, forsaking Thee, followed the violent course of my own stream, and exceeded all Thy limitations; nor did I escape Thy scourges.[7] For what mortal can do so? But Thou wert always by me, mercifully angry, and dashing with the bitterest vexations all my illicit pleasures, in order that I might seek pleasures free from vexation. But where I could meet with such except in Thee, O Lord, I could not find,—except in Thee, who teachest by sorrow,[8] and

---

[1] Ps. xxxix. 11.
[2] Matt. xvii. 17.

[3] 1 Cor. vii. 28.
[4] 1 Cor. vii. 1.
[5] 1 Cor. vii. 32, 33.
[6] Matt. xix. 12.
[7] Isa. x. 26.
[8] Deut. xxxii. 39.

woundest us to heal us, and killest us that we may not die from Thee.[1] Where was I, and how far was I exiled from the delights of Thy house, in that sixteenth year of the age of my flesh, when the madness of lust—to the which human shamelessness granteth full freedom, although forbidden by Thy laws—held complete sway over me, and I resigned myself entirely to it? Those about me meanwhile took no care to save me from ruin by marriage, their sole care being that I should learn to make a powerful speech, and become a persuasive orator.

CHAP. III.—CONCERNING HIS FATHER, A FREEMAN OF THAGASTE, THE ASSISTER OF HIS SON'S STUDIES, AND ON THE ADMONITIONS OF HIS MOTHER ON THE PRESERVATION OF CHASTITY.

5. And for that year my studies were intermitted, while after my return from Madaura[2] (a neighbouring city, whither I had begun to go in order to learn grammar and rhetoric), the expenses for a further residence at Carthage were provided for me; and that was rather by the determination than the means of my father, who was but a poor freeman of Thagaste. To whom do I narrate this? Not unto Thee, my God; but before Thee unto my own kind, even to that small part of the human race who may chance to light upon these my writings. And to what end? That I and all who read the same may reflect out of what depths we are to cry unto Thee.[3] For what cometh nearer to Thine ears than a confessing heart and a life of faith? For who did not extol and praise my father, in that he went even beyond his means to supply his son with all the necessaries for a far journey for the sake of his studies? For many far richer citizens did not the like for their children. But yet this same father did not trouble himself how I grew towards Thee, nor how chaste I was, so long as I was skilful in speaking—however barren I was to Thy tilling, O God, who art the sole true and good Lord of my heart, which is Thy field.

6. But while, in that sixteenth year of my age, I resided with my parents, having holiday from school for a time (this idleness being imposed upon me by my parents' necessitous circumstances), the thorns of lust grew rank over my head, and there was no hand to pluck them out. Moreover when my father,

seeing me at the baths, perceived that I was becoming a man, and was stirred with a restless youthfulness, he, as if from this anticipating future descendants, joyfully told it to my mother; rejoicing in that intoxication wherein the world so often forgets Thee, its Creator, and falls in love with Thy creature instead of Thee, from the invisible wine of its own perversity turning and bowing down to the most infamous things. But in my mother's breast Thou hadst even now begun Thy temple, and the commencement of Thy holy habitation, whereas my father was only a catechumen as yet, and that but recently. She then started up with a pious fear and trembling; and, although I had not yet been baptized,[4] she feared those crooked ways in which they walk who turn their back to Thee, and not their face.[5]

7. Woe is me! and dare I affirm that Thou heldest Thy peace, O my God, while I strayed farther from Thee? Didst Thou then hold Thy peace to me? And whose words were they but Thine which by my mother, Thy faithful handmaid, Thou pouredst into my ears, none of which sank into my heart to make me do it? For she desired, and I remember privately warned me, with great solicitude, "not to commit fornication; but above all things never to defile another man's wife." These appeared to me but womanish counsels, which I should blush to obey. But they were Thine, and I knew it not, and I thought that Thou heldest Thy peace, and that it was she who spoke, through whom Thou heldest not Thy peace to me, and in her person wast despised by me, her son, "the son of Thy handmaid, Thy servant."[6] But this I knew not; and rushed on headlong with such blindness, that amongst my equals I was ashamed to be less shameless, when I heard them pluming themselves upon their disgraceful acts, yea, and glorying all the more in proportion to the greatness of their baseness; and I took pleasure in doing it, not for the pleasure's sake only, but for the praise. What is worthy of dispraise but vice? But I made myself out worse than I was, in order that I might not be dispraised; and when in anything I had not sinned as the abandoned ones, I would affirm that I had done what I had not, that I might not appear abject for being more innocent, or of less esteem for being more chaste.

8. Behold with what companions I walked the streets of Babylon, in whose filth I was rolled, as if in cinnamon and precious ointments. And that I might cleave the more tena-

[1] Ps. xciii. 20, *Vulg.* "Lit. 'Formest trouble in or as a precept.' Thou makest to us a precept out of trouble, so that trouble itself shall be a precept to us, *i.e.* hast willed so to discipline and instruct those Thy sons, that they should not be without fear, lest they should love something else, and forget Thee, their true good."—S. AUG. *ad loc.*—E. B. P.
[2] "Formerly an episcopal city; now a small village. At this time the inhabitants were heathen. St. Augustin calls them 'his fathers,' in a letter persuading them to embrace the gospel.—*Ep.* 232."—E. B. P.
[3] Ps. cxxx. 1.
[4] *Nondum fideli*, not having rehearsed the articles of the Christian faith at baptism. See i. sec. 17, note, above; and below, sec. 1, note.
[5] Jer. ii. 27.
[6] Ps. cxvi. 16.

ciously to its very centre, my invisible enemy trod me down, and seduced me, I being easily seduced. Nor did the mother of my flesh, although she herself had ere this fled " out of the midst of Babylon," [1]—progressing, however, but slowly in the skirts of it,—in counselling me to chastity, so bear in mind what she had been told about me by her husband as to restrain in the limits of conjugal affection (if it could not be cut away to the quick) what she knew to be destructive in the present and dangerous in the future. But she took no heed of this, for she was afraid lest a wife should prove a hindrance and a clog to my hopes. Not those hopes of the future world, which my mother had in Thee; but the hope of learning, which both my parents were too anxious that I should acquire,— he, because he had little or no thought of Thee, and but vain thoughts for me—she, because she calculated that those usual courses of learning would not only be no drawback, but rather a furtherance towards my attaining Thee. For thus I conjecture, recalling as well as I can the dispositions of my parents. The reins, meantime, were slackened towards me beyond the restraint of due severity, that I might play, yea, even to dissoluteness, in whatsoever I fancied. And in all there was a mist, shutting out from my sight the brightness of Thy truth, O my God; and my iniquity displayed itself as from very " fatness." [2]

CHAP. IV.—HE COMMITS THEFT WITH HIS COMPANIONS, NOT URGED ON BY POVERTY, BUT FROM A CERTAIN DISTASTE OF WELL-DOING.

9. Theft is punished by Thy law, O Lord, and by the law written in men's hearts, which iniquity itself cannot blot out. For what thief will suffer a thief? Even a rich thief will not suffer him who is driven to it by want. Yet had L a desire to commit robbery, and did so, compelled neither by hunger, nor poverty, but through a distaste for well-doing, and a lustiness of iniquity. For I pilfered that of which I had already sufficient, and much better. Nor did I desire to enjoy what I pilfered, but the theft and sin itself. There was a pear-tree close to our vineyard, heavily laden with fruit, which was tempting neither for its colour nor its flavour. To shake and rob this some of us wanton young fellows went, late one night (having, according to our disgraceful habit, prolonged our games in the streets until then), and carried away great loads, not to eat ourselves, but to fling to the very swine, having only eaten some of them; and to do this pleased us all the more because it was not permitted. Behold my heart, O my God; behold my heart, which Thou hadst pity upon when in the bottomless pit. Behold, now, let my heart tell Thee what it was seeking there, that I should be gratuitously wanton, having no inducement to evil but the evil itself. It was foul, and I loved it. I loved to perish. I loved my own error—not that for which I erred, but the error itself. Base soul, falling from Thy firmament to utter destruction—not seeking aught through the shame but the shame itself!

CHAP. V.—CONCERNING THE MOTIVES TO SIN, WHICH ARE NOT IN THE LOVE OF EVIL, BUT IN THE DESIRE OF OBTAINING THE PROPERTY OF OTHERS.

10. There is a desirableness in all beautiful bodies, and in gold, and silver, and all things; and in bodily contact sympathy is powerful, and each other sense hath his proper adaptation of body. Worldly honour hath also its glory, and the power of command, and of overcoming; whence proceeds also the desire for revenge. And yet to acquire all these, we must not depart from Thee, O Lord, nor deviate from Thy law. The life which we live here hath also its peculiar attractiveness, through a certain measure of comeliness of its own, and harmony with all things here below. The friendships of men also are endeared by a sweet bond, in the oneness of many souls. On account of all these, and such as these, is sin committed; while through an inordinate preference for these goods of a lower kind, the better and higher are neglected,—even Thou, our Lord God, Thy truth, and Thy law. For these meaner things have their delights, but not like unto my God, who hath created all things; for in Him doth the righteous delight, and He is the sweetness of the upright in heart. [3]

11. When, therefore, we inquire why a crime was committed, we do not believe it, unless it appear that there might have been the wish to obtain some of those which we designated meaner things, or else a fear of losing them. For truly they are beautiful and comely, although in comparison with those higher and celestial goods they be abject and contemptible. A man hath murdered another; what was his motive? He desired his wife or his estate; or would steal to support himself; or he was afraid of losing something of the kind by him; or, being injured, he was burning to be revenged. Would he commit murder without a motive, taking delight simply in the act of murder? Who would credit it? For as for that savage and brutal man, of whom it is declared that he was gratuitously wicked and cruel, there is yet

[1] Jer. li. 6.
[2] Ps. lxxiii. 7.
[3] Ps. lxiv. 10.

a motive assigned. "Lest through idleness," he says, "hand or heart should grow inactive."[1] And to what purpose? Why, even that, having once got possession of the city through that practice of wickedness, he might attain unto honours, empire, and wealth, and be exempt from the fear of the laws, and his difficult circumstances from the needs of his family, and the consciousness of his own wickedness. So it seems that even Catiline himself loved not his own villanies, but something else, which gave him the motive for committing them.

CHAP. VI.—WHY HE DELIGHTED IN THAT THEFT, WHEN ALL THINGS WHICH UNDER THE APPEARANCE OF GOOD INVITE TO VICE ARE TRUE AND PERFECT IN GOD ALONE.

12. What was it, then, that I, miserable one, so doted on in thee, thou theft of mine, thou deed of darkness, in that sixteenth year of my age? Beautiful thou wert not, since thou wert theft. But art thou anything, that so I may argue the case with thee? Those pears that we stole were fair to the sight, because they were Thy creation, Thou fairest[2] of all, Creator of all, Thou good God—God, the highest good, and my true good. Those pears truly were pleasant to the sight; but it was not for them that my miserable soul lusted, for I had abundance of better, but those I plucked simply that I might steal. For, having plucked them, I threw them away, my sole gratification in them being my own sin, which I was pleased to enjoy. For if any of these pears entered my mouth, the sweetener of it was my sin in eating it. And now, O Lord my God, I ask what it was in that theft of mine that caused me such delight; and behold it hath no beauty in it—not such, I mean, as exists in justice and wisdom; nor such as is in the mind, memory, senses, and animal life of man; nor yet such as is the glory and beauty of the stars in their courses; or the earth, or the sea, teeming with incipient life, to replace, as it is born, that which decayeth; nor, indeed, that false and shadowy beauty which pertaineth to deceptive vices.

13. For thus doth pride imitate high estate, whereas Thou alone art God, high above all. And what does ambition seek but honours and renown, whereas Thou alone art to be honoured above all, and renowned for evermore? The cruelty of the powerful wishes to be feared; but who is to be feared but God only,[3] out of whose power what can be forced away or withdrawn—when, or where, or whither, or by whom? The enticements of the wanton would fain be deemed love; and yet is naught more enticing than Thy charity, nor is aught loved more healthfully than that, Thy truth, bright and beautiful above all. Curiosity affects a desire for knowledge, whereas it is Thou who supremely knowest all things. Yea, ignorance and foolishness themselves are concealed under the names of ingenuousness and harmlessness, because nothing can be found more ingenuous than Thou; and what is more harmless, since it is a sinner's own works by which he is harmed?[4] And sloth seems to long for rest; but what sure rest is there besides the Lord? Luxury would fain be called plenty and abundance; but Thou art the fulness and unfailing plenteousness of unfading joys. Prodigality presents a shadow of liberality; but Thou art the most lavish giver of all good. Covetousness desires to possess much; and Thou art the Possessor of all things. Envy contends for excellence; but what so excellent as Thou? Anger seeks revenge; who avenges more justly than Thou? Fear starts at unwonted and sudden chances which threaten things beloved, and is wary for their security; but what can happen that is unwonted or sudden to Thee? or who can deprive Thee of what Thou lovest? or where is there unshaken security save with Thee? Grief languishes for things lost in which desire had delighted itself, even because it would have nothing taken from it, as nothing can be from Thee.

14. Thus doth the soul commit fornication when she turns away from Thee, and seeks without Thee what she cannot find pure and untainted until she returns to Thee. Thus all pervertedly imitate Thee who separate themselves far from Thee[4] and raise themselves up against Thee. But even by thus imitating Thee they acknowledge Thee to be the Creator of all nature, and so that there is no place whither they can altogether retire from Thee.[5] What, then, was it that I loved in that theft? And wherein did I, even corruptedly and pervertedly, imitate my Lord? Did I wish, if only by artifice, to act contrary to Thy law, because by power I could not, so that, being a captive, I might imitate an imperfect liberty by doing with impunity things which I was not allowed to do, in obscured likeness of Thy omnipotency?[6] Behold this servant of Thine, fleeing from his Lord, and following a shadow![7] O rottenness! O monstrosity of life and profundity of death!

---

[1] Sallust, *De Bello Catil.* c. 9.
[2] Ps. xlv. 2.
[3] Ps. lxxvi. 7.

[4] Ps. vii. 15.
[5] Ps. cxxxix. 7, 8.
[6] "For even souls, in their very sins, strive after nothing else but some kind of likeness of God, in a proud and preposterous, and, so to say, slavish liberty. So neither could our first parents have been persuaded to sin unless it had been said, 'Ye shall be as gods.'"—AUG. *De Trin.* xi. 5.
[7] Jonah i. and iv.

Could I like that which was unlawful only because it was unlawful?

CHAP. VII.—HE GIVES THANKS TO GOD FOR THE REMISSION OF HIS SINS, AND REMINDS EVERY ONE THAT THE SUPREME GOD MAY HAVE PRESERVED US FROM GREATER SINS.

15. "What shall I render unto the Lord,"[1] that whilst my memory recalls these things my soul is not appalled at them? I will love Thee, O Lord, and thank Thee, and confess unto Thy name,[2] because Thou hast put away from me these so wicked and nefarious acts of mine. To Thy grace I attribute it, and to Thy mercy, that Thou hast melted away my sin as it were ice. To Thy grace also I attribute whatsoever of evil I have not committed; for what might I not have committed, loving as I did the sin for the sin's sake? Yea, all I confess to have been pardoned me, both those which I committed by my own perverseness, and those which, by Thy guidance, I committed not. Where is he who, reflecting upon his own infirmity, dares to ascribe his chastity and innocency to his own strength, so that he should love Thee the less, as if he had been in less need of Thy mercy, whereby Thou dost forgive the transgressions of those that turn to Thee? For whosoever, called by Thee, obeyed Thy voice, and shunned those things which he reads me recalling and confessing of myself, let him not despise me, who, being sick, was healed by that same Physician[3] by whose aid it was that he was not sick, or rather was less sick. And for this let him love Thee as much, yea, all the more, since by whom he sees me to have been restored from so great a feebleness of sin, by Him he sees himself from a like feebleness to have been preserved.

CHAP. VIII.—IN HIS THEFT HE LOVED THE COMPANY OF HIS FELLOW-SINNERS.

16. "What fruit had I then,"[4] wretched one, in those things which, when I remember them, cause me shame—above all in that theft, which I loved only for the theft's sake? And as the theft itself was nothing, all the more wretched was I who loved it. Yet by myself alone I would not have done it—I recall what my heart was—alone I could not have done it. I loved, then, in it the companionship of my accomplices with whom I did it. I did not, therefore, love the theft alone—yea, rather, it was that alone that I loved, for the companionship was nothing. What is the fact? Who is it that can teach me, but He who illumineth mine heart and searcheth out the dark corners thereof? What is it that hath come into my mind to inquire about, to discuss, and to reflect upon? For had I at that time loved the pears I stole, and wished to enjoy them, I might have done so alone, if I could have been satisfied with the mere commission of the theft by which my pleasure was secured; nor needed I have provoked that itching of my own passions, by the encouragement of accomplices. But as my enjoyment was not in those pears, it was in the crime itself, which the company of my fellow-sinners produced.

CHAP. IX.—IT WAS A PLEASURE TO HIM ALSO TO LAUGH WHEN SERIOUSLY DECEIVING OTHERS.

17. By what feelings, then, was I animated? For it was in truth too shameful; and woe was me who had it. But still what was it? "Who can understand his errors?"[5] We laughed, because our hearts were tickled at the thought of deceiving those who little imagined what we were doing, and would have vehemently disapproved of it. Yet, again, why did I so rejoice in this, that I did it not alone? Is it that no one readily laughs alone? No one does so readily; but yet sometimes, when men are alone by themselves, nobody being by, a fit of laughter overcomes them when anything very droll presents itself to their senses or mind. Yet alone I would not have done it—alone I could not at all have done it. Behold, my God, the lively recollection of my soul is laid bare before Thee—alone I had not committed that theft, wherein what I stole pleased me not, but rather the act of stealing; nor to have done it alone would I have liked so well, neither would I have done it. O Friendship too unfriendly! thou mysterious seducer of the soul, thou greediness to do mischief out of mirth and wantonness, thou craving for others' loss, without desire for my own profit or revenge; but when they say, "Let us go, let us do it," we are ashamed not to be shameless.

CHAP. X.—WITH GOD THERE IS TRUE REST AND LIFE UNCHANGING.

18. Who can unravel that twisted and tangled knottiness? It is foul. I hate to reflect on it. I hate to look on it. But thee do I long for, O righteousness and innocency, fair and comely to all virtuous eyes, and of a satisfaction that never palls! With thee is perfect rest, and life unchanging. He who enters into thee enters into the joy of his Lord,[6] and shall have no fear, and shall do excellently in the most Excellent. I sank away from Thee, O my God, and I wandered too far from Thee, my stay, in my youth, and became to myself an unfruitful land.

---

[1] Ps. cxvi. 12.
[2] Rev. iii. 5.
[3] Luke iv. 23.
[4] Rom. vi. 21.
[5] Ps. xix. 12.
[6] Matt. xxv. 21.

BOOK III.

OF THE SEVENTEENTH, EIGHTEENTH, AND NINETEENTH YEARS OF HIS AGE, PASSED AT CARTHAGE, WHEN, HAVING COMPLETED HIS COURSE OF STUDIES, HE IS CAUGHT IN THE SNARES OF A LICENTIOUS PASSION, AND FALLS INTO THE ERRORS OF THE MANICHÆANS.

CHAP. I.—DELUDED BY AN INSANE LOVE, HE, THOUGH FOUL AND DISHONOURABLE, DESIRES TO BE THOUGHT ELEGANT AND URBANE.

1. To Carthage I came, where a cauldron of unholy loves bubbled up all around me. I loved not as yet, yet I loved to love; and, with a hidden want, I abhorred myself that I wanted not. I searched about for something to love, in love with loving, and hating security, and a way not beset with snares. For within me I had a dearth of that inward food, Thyself, my God, though that dearth caused me no hunger; but I remained without all desire for incorruptible food, not because I was already filled thereby, but the more empty I was the more I loathed it. For this reason my soul was far from well, and, full of ulcers, it miserably cast itself forth, craving to be excited by contact with objects of sense. Yet, had these no soul, they would not surely inspire love. To love and to be loved was sweet to me, and all the more when I succeeded in enjoying the person I loved. I befouled, therefore, the spring of friendship with the filth of concupiscence, and I dimmed its lustre with the hell of lustfulness; and yet, foul and dishonourable as I was, I craved, through an excess of vanity, to be thought elegant and urbane. I fell precipitately, then, into the love in which I longed to be ensnared. My God, my mercy, with how much bitterness didst Thou, out of Thy infinite goodness, besprinkle for me that sweetness! For I was both beloved, and secretly arrived at the bond of enjoying; and was joyfully bound with troublesome ties, that I might be scourged with the burning iron rods of jealousy, suspicion, fear, anger, and strife.

CHAP. II.—IN PUBLIC SPECTACLES HE IS MOVED BY AN EMPTY COMPASSION. HE IS ATTACKED BY A TROUBLESOME SPIRITUAL DISEASE.

2. Stage-plays also drew me away, full of representations of my miseries and of fuel to my fire.[1] Why does man like to be made sad when viewing doleful and tragical scenes, which yet he himself would by no means suffer? And yet he wishes, as a spectator, to experience from them a sense of grief, and in this very grief his pleasure consists. What is this but wretched insanity? For a man is more affected with these actions, the less free he is from such affections. Howsoever, when he suffers in his own person, it is the custom to style it "misery;" but when he compassionates others, then it is styled "mercy."[2] But what kind of mercy is it that arises from fictitious and scenic passions? The hearer is not expected to relieve, but merely invited to grieve; and the more he grieves, the more he applauds the actor of these fictions. And if the misfortunes of the characters (whether of olden times or merely imaginary) be so represented as not to touch the feelings of the spectator, he goes away disgusted and censorious; but if his feelings be touched, he sits it out attentively, and sheds tears of joy.

3. Are sorrows, then, also loved? Surely all men desire to rejoice? Or, as man wishes to be miserable, is he, nevertheless, glad to be merciful, which, because it cannot exist without passion, for this cause alone are passions loved? This also is from that vein of friendship. But whither does it go? Whither does it flow? Wherefore runs it into that torrent of pitch,[3] seething forth those huge tides of loathsome lusts into which it is changed and transformed, being of its own will cast away and corrupted from its celestial clearness? Shall, then, mercy be repudiated? By no means. Let us, therefore, love sorrows sometimes. But beware of uncleanness, O my soul, under the protection of my God, the God of our fathers, who is to be praised and exalted above all for ever,[4] beware of uncleanness. For I have not now ceased to have compassion; but then in the theatres I sympathized with lovers when they sinfully enjoyed one another, although this was

---

[1] The early Fathers strongly reprobated stage-plays, and those who went to them were excluded from baptism. This is not to be wondered at, when we learn that "even the laws of Rome prohibited actors from being enrolled as citizens" (*De Civ. Dei*, ii. 14), and that they were accounted infamous (Tertullian, *De Spectac.* sec. xxii.). See also Tertullian, *De Pudicitia*, c. vii.

[2] See i. 9, note, above.
[3] An allusion, probably, as Watts suggests, to the sea of Sodom, which, according to Tacitus (*Hist.* book v.), throws up bitumen "at stated seasons of the year." Tacitus likewise alludes to its pestiferous odour, and to its being deadly to birds and fish. See also Gen. xiv. 3, 10.
[4] Song of the Three Holy Children, verse 3.

done fictitiously in the play. And when they lost one another, I grieved with them, as if pitying them, and yet had delight in both. But now-a-days I feel much more pity for him that delighteth in his wickedness, than for him who is counted as enduring hardships by failing to obtain some pernicious pleasure, and the loss of some miserable felicity. This, surely, is the truer mercy, but grief hath no delight in it. For though he that condoles with the unhappy be approved for his office of charity, yet would he who had real compassion rather there were nothing for him to grieve about. For if good-will be ill-willed (which it cannot), then can he who is truly and sincerely commiserating wish that there should be some unhappy ones, that he might commiserate them. Some grief may then be justified, none loved. For thus dost Thou, O Lord God, who lovest souls far more purely than do we, and art more incorruptibly compassionate, although Thou art wounded by no sorrow. "And who is sufficient for these things?"[1]

4. But I, wretched one, then loved to grieve, and sought out what to grieve at, as when, in another man's misery, though feigned and counterfeited, that delivery of the actor best pleased me, and attracted me the most powerfully, which moved me to tears. What marvel was it that an unhappy sheep, straying from Thy flock, and impatient of Thy care, I became infected with a foul disease? And hence came my love of griefs—not such as should probe me too deeply, for I loved not to suffer such things as I loved to look upon, but such as, when hearing their fictions, should lightly affect the surface; upon which, like as with empoisoned nails, followed burning, swelling, putrefaction, and horrible corruption. Such was my life! But was it life, O my God?

CHAP. III.—NOT EVEN WHEN AT CHURCH DOES HE SUPPRESS HIS DESIRES. IN THE SCHOOL OF RHETORIC HE ABHORS THE ACTS OF THE SUBVERTERS.

5. And Thy faithful mercy hovered over me afar. Upon what unseemly iniquities did I wear myself out, following a sacrilegious curiosity, that, having deserted Thee, it might drag me into the treacherous abyss, and the beguiling obedience of devils, unto whom I immolated my wicked deeds, and in all which Thou didst scourge me! I dared, even while Thy solemn rites were being celebrated within the walls of Thy church, to desire, and to plan a business sufficient to procure me the fruits of death; for which Thou chastisedst me with grievous punishments, but nothing in compari-

son with my fault, O Thou my greatest mercy, my God, my refuge from those terrible hurts, among which I wandered with presumptuous neck, receding farther from Thee, loving my own ways, and not Thine—loving a vagrant liberty.

6. Those studies, also, which were accounted honourable, were directed towards the courts of law; to excel in which, the more crafty I was, the more I should be praised. Such is the blindness of men, that they even glory in their blindness. And now I was head in the School of Rhetoric, whereat I rejoiced proudly, and became inflated with arrogance, though more sedate, O Lord, as Thou knowest, and altogether removed from the subvertings of those "subverters"[2] (for this stupid and diabolical name was held to be the very brand of gallantry) amongst whom I lived, with an impudent shamefacedness that I was not even as they were. And with them I was, and at times I was delighted with their friendship whose acts I ever abhorred, that is, their "subverting," wherewith they insolently attacked the modesty of strangers, which they disturbed by uncalled for jeers, gratifying thereby their mischievous mirth. Nothing can more nearly resemble the actions of devils than these. By what name, therefore, could they be more truly called than "subverters"?—being themselves subverted first, and altogether perverted—being secretly mocked at and seduced by the deceiving spirits, in what they themselves delight to jeer at and deceive others.

CHAP. IV.—IN THE NINETEENTH YEAR OF HIS AGE (HIS FATHER HAVING DIED TWO YEARS BEFORE) HE IS LED BY THE "HORTENSIUS" OF CICERO TO "PHILOSOPHY," TO GOD, AND A BETTER MODE OF THINKING.

7. Among such as these, at that unstable period of my life, I studied books of eloquence, wherein I was eager to be eminent from a damnable and inflated purpose, even a delight in human vanity. In the ordinary course of study, I lighted upon a certain book of Cicero, whose language, though not his heart, almost all admire. This book of his contains an exhortation to philosophy, and is called *Hortensius*. This book, in truth, changed my affections, and turned my prayers to Thyself, O Lord, and made me have other hopes and desires. Worthless suddenly became every vain hope to me; and, with an incredible warmth of heart, I

---

[1] 2 Cor. ii. 16.

[2] *Eversores.* "These for their boldness were like our 'Roarers,' and for their jeering like the worser sort of those that would be called 'The Wits.'"—W. W. "This appears to have been a name which a pestilent and savage set of persons gave themselves, licentious alike in speech and action. Augustin names them again, *De Vera Relig.* c. 40; *Ep.* 185 *ad Bonifac.* c. 4; and below, v. c. 12; whence they seemed to have consisted mainly of Carthaginian students, whose savage life is mentioned again, *ib.* c. 8."—E. B. P.

yearned for an immortality of wisdom,[1] and began now to arise[2] that I might return to Thee. Not, then, to improve my language—which I appeared to be purchasing with my mother's means, in that my nineteenth year, my father having died two years before—not to improve my language did I have recourse to that book; nor did it persuade me by its style, but its matter.

8. How ardent was I then, my God, how ardent to fly from earthly things to Thee! Nor did I know how Thou wouldst deal with me. For with Thee is wisdom. In Greek the love of wisdom is called "philosophy,"[3] with which that book inflamed me. There be some who seduce through philosophy, under a great, and alluring, and honourable name colouring and adorning their own errors. And almost all who in that and former times were such, are in that book censured and pointed out. There is also disclosed that most salutary admonition of Thy Spirit, by Thy good and pious servant: "Beware lest any man spoil you through philosophy and vain deceit, after the tradition of men, after the rudiments of the world, and not after Christ: for in Him dwelleth all the fulness of the Godhead bodily."[4] And since at that time (as Thou, O Light of my heart, knowest) the words of the apostle were unknown to me, I was delighted with that exhortation, in so far only as I was thereby stimulated, and enkindled, and inflamed to love, seek, obtain, hold, and embrace, not this or that sect, but wisdom itself, whatever it were; and this alone checked me thus ardent, that the name of Christ was not in it. For this name, according to Thy mercy, O Lord, this name of my Saviour Thy Son, had my tender heart piously drunk in, deeply treasured even with my mother's milk; and whatsoever was without that name, though never so erudite, polished, and truthful, took not complete hold of me.

CHAP. V.—HE REJECTS THE SACRED SCRIPTURES AS TOO SIMPLE, AND AS NOT TO BE COMPARED WITH THE DIGNITY OF TULLY.

9. I resolved, therefore, to direct my mind to the Holy Scriptures, that I might see what they were. And behold, I perceive something not comprehended by the proud, not disclosed to children, but lowly as you approach, sublime as you advance, and veiled in mysteries; and I was not of the number of those who could enter into it, or bend my neck to follow its steps. For not as when now I speak did I feel when I turned towards those Scriptures,[5] but they appeared to me to be unworthy to be compared with the dignity of Tully; for my inflated pride shunned their style, nor could the sharpness of my wit pierce their inner meaning.[6] Yet, truly, were they such as would develope in little ones; but I scorned to be a little one, and, swollen with pride, I looked upon myself as a great one.

CHAP. VI.—DECEIVED BY HIS OWN FAULT, HE FALLS INTO THE ERRORS OF THE MANICHÆANS, WHO GLORIED IN THE TRUE KNOWLEDGE OF GOD AND IN A THOROUGH EXAMINATION OF THINGS.

10. Therefore I fell among men proudly raving, very carnal, and voluble, in whose mouths were the snares of the devil—the birdlime being composed of a mixture of the syllables of Thy name, and of our Lord Jesus Christ, and of the Paraclete, the Holy Ghost, the Comforter.[7] These names departed not out of their mouths, but so far forth as the sound only and the clatter of the tongue, for the heart was empty of truth. Still they cried, "Truth, Truth," and spoke much about it to me, "yet was it not in them;"[8] but they spake falsely not of Thee only—who, verily, art the Truth—but also of these elements of this world, Thy

---

[1] Up to the time of Cicero the Romans employed the term *sapientia* for φιλοσοφία (Monboddo's Ancient Metaphys. i. 5). It is interesting to watch the effect of the philosophy in which they had been trained on the writings of some of the Fathers. Even Justin Martyr, the first after the "Apostolic," has traces of this influence. See the account of his search for "wisdom," and conversion, in his *Dialogue with Trypho*, ii. and iii.
[2] Luke xv. 18.
[3] See above, note 1.
[4] Col. ii. 8, 9.

[5] In connection with the opinion Augustin formed of the Scriptures before and after his conversion, it is interesting to recall Fénélon's glowing description of the literary merit of the Bible. The whole passage might well be quoted did space permit:—" L'Ecriture surpasse en naïveté, en vivacité, en grandeur, tous les écrivains de Rome et de la Grèce. Jamais Homère même n'a approché de la sublimité de Moïse dans ses cantiques. . . . Jamais nulle ode Grecque ou Latine n'a pu atteindre à la hauteur des Psaumes. . . . Jamais Homerè ni aucun autre poëte n'a égalé Isaïe peignant la majesté de Dieu. . . . Tantôt ce prophète à toute la douceur et toute la tendresse d'une églogue, dans les riantes peintures qu'il fait de la paix ; tantôt il s'élève jusqu' à laisser loin au-dessous de lui. Mais qu'y a-t-il, dans l'antiquité profane, de comparable au tendre Jérémie, déplorant les maux de son peuple ; ou à Nahum, voyant de loin, en esprit, tomber la superbe Ninive sous les efforts d'une armée innombrable ? On croit voir cette armée, ou croit entendre le bruit des armes et des chariots ; tout est dépeint d'une manière vive qui saisit l'imagination ; il laisse Homère loin derrière lui. . . . Enfin, il y a autant de différence entre les poëtes profanes et les prophètes, qu'il y en a entre le véritable enthousiasme et le faux."—*Sur l' Éloq. de la Chaire*, Dial. iii.
[6] That is probably the "spiritual" meaning on which Ambrose (vi. 6, below) laid so much emphasis. How different is the attitude of mind indicated in xi. 3 from the spiritual pride which beset him at this period of his life! When converted he became a little child, and ever looked to God as a Father, from whom he must receive both light and strength. He speaks, on Ps. cxlvi., of the Scriptures, which were plain to "the little ones," being obscured to the mocking spirit of the Manichæans. See also below, iii. 14, note.
[7] So, in Book xxii. sec. 13 of his reply to Faustus, he charges them with "professing to believe the New Testament in order to entrap the unwary ;" and again, in sec. 15, he says : "They claim the impious liberty of holding and teaching, that whatever they deem favourable to their heresy was said by Christ and the apostles ; while they have the profane boldness to say, that whatever in the same writings is unfavourable to them is a spurious interpolation." They professed to believe in the doctrine of the Trinity, but affirmed (*ibid.* xx. 6) "that the Father dwells in a secret light, the power of the Son in the sun, and His wisdom in the moon, and the Holy Spirit in the air." It was this employment of the phraseology of Scripture to convey doctrines utterly unscriptural that rendered their teaching such a snare to the unwary. See also below, v. 12, note.
[8] 1 John ii. 4.

creatures. And I, in truth, should have passed by philosophers, even when speaking truth concerning them, for love of Thee, my Father, supremely good, beauty of all things beautiful! O Truth, Truth! how inwardly even then did the marrow of my soul pant after Thee, when they frequently, and in a multiplicity of ways, and in numerous and huge books, sounded out Thy name to me, though it was but a voice![1] And these were the dishes in which to me, hungering for Thee, they, instead of Thee, served up the sun and moon, Thy beauteous works— but yet Thy works, not Thyself, nay, nor Thy first works. For before these corporeal works are Thy spiritual ones, celestial and shining though they be. But I hungered and thirsted not even after those first works of Thine, but after Thee Thyself, the Truth, " with whom is no variableness, neither shadow of turning;"[2] yet they still served up to me in those dishes glowing phantasies, than which better were it to love this very sun (which, at least, is true to our sight), than those illusions which deceive the mind through the eye. And yet, because I supposed them to be Thee, I fed upon them; not with avidity, for Thou didst not taste to my mouth as Thou art, for Thou wast not these empty fictions; neither was I nourished by them, but the rather exhausted. Food in our sleep appears like our food awake; yet the sleepers are not nourished by it, for they are asleep. But those things were not in any way like unto Thee as Thou hast now spoken unto me, in that those were corporeal phantasies, false bodies, than which these true bodies, whether celestial or terrestrial, which we perceive with our fleshly sight, are much more certain. These things the very beasts and birds perceive as well as we, and they are more certain than when we imagine them. And again, we do with more certainty imagine them, than by them conceive of other greater and infinite bodies which have no existence. With such empty husks was I then fed, and was not fed. But Thou, my Love, in looking for whom I fail[3] that I may be strong, art neither those bodies that we see, although in heaven, nor art Thou those which we see not there; for Thou hast created them, nor dost Thou reckon them

amongst Thy greatest works. How far, then, art Thou from those phantasies of mine, phantasies of bodies which are not at all, than which the images of those bodies which are, are more certain, and still more certain the bodies themselves, which yet Thou art not; nay, nor yet the soul, which is the life of the bodies. Better, then, and more certain is the life of bodies than the bodies themselves. But Thou art the life of souls, the life of lives, having life in Thyself; and Thou changest not, O Life of my soul.

11. Where, then, wert Thou then to me, and how far from me? Far, indeed, was I wandering away from Thee, being even shut out from the very husks of the swine, whom with husks I fed.[4] For how much better, then, are the fables of the grammarians and poets than these snares! For verses, and poems, and Medea flying, are more profitable truly than these men's five elements, variously painted, to answer to the five caves of darkness,[5] none of which exist, and which slay the believer. For verses and poems I can turn into[6] true food, but the " Medea flying," though I sang, I maintained it not; though I heard it sung, I believed it not; but those things I did believe. Woe, woe, by what steps was I dragged down "to the depths of hell!"[7]—toiling and turmoiling through want of Truth, when I sought after Thee, my God,—to Thee I confess it, who hadst mercy on me when I had not yet confessed,—sought after Thee not according to the understanding of the mind, in which Thou desiredst that I should excel the beasts, but according to the sense of the flesh! Thou wert more inward to me than my most inward part; and higher than my highest. I came upon that bold woman, who "is simple, and knoweth nothing,"[8] the enigma of Solomon, sitting "at the door of the house on a seat," and saying, "Stolen waters are sweet, and bread eaten in secret is pleasant."[9] This woman seduced me, because she found my soul beyond its portals, dwelling in the eye of my flesh, and thinking on such food as through it I had devoured.

CHAP. VII.—HE ATTACKS THE DOCTRINE OF THE MANICHÆANS CONCERNING EVIL, GOD, AND THE RIGHTEOUSNESS OF THE PATRIARCHS.

12. For I was ignorant as to that which really is, and was, as it were, violently moved to give

---

[1] There was something peculiarly enthralling to an ardent mind like Augustin's in the Manichæan system. That system was kindred in many ways to modern Rationalism. Reason was exalted at the expense of faith. Nothing was received on mere authority, and the disciple's inner consciousness was the touchstone of truth. The result of this is well pointed out by Augustin (Con. Faust, xxxii. sec. 19) : " Your design, clearly, is to deprive Scripture of all authority, and to make every man's mind the judge what passage of Scripture he is to approve of, and what to disapprove of. This is not to be subject to Scripture in matters of faith, but to make Scripture subject to you. Instead of making the high authority of Scripture the reason of approval, every man makes his approval the reason for thinking a passage correct." Compare also Con. Faust, xi. sec. 2, and xxxii. sec. 16.
[2] Jas. i. 17.
[3] Ps. lxix. 3.

[4] Luke xv. 16; and see below, vi. sec. 3, note.
[5] See below, xii. sec. 6, note.
[6] " Of this passage St. Augustin is probably speaking when he says, ' Praises bestowed on bread in simplicity of heart, let him (Petilian) defame, if he will, by the ludicrous title of poisoning and corrupting frenzy.' Augustin meant in mockery, that by verses he could get his bread; his calumniator seems to have twisted the word to signify a love-potion.—Con. Lit. Petiliani, iii. 16."—E. B. P.
[7] Prov. ix. 18.
[8] Prov. ix. 13.
[9] Prov. ix. 14, 17.

my support to foolish deceivers, when they asked me, "Whence is evil?"[1]—and, "Is God limited by a bodily shape, and has He hairs and nails?"—and, "Are they to be esteemed righteous who had many wives at once, and did kill men, and sacrificed living creatures?"[2] At which things I, in my ignorance, was much disturbed, and, retreating from the truth, I appeared to myself to be going towards it; because as yet I knew not that evil was naught but a privation of good, until in the end it ceases altogether to be; which how should I see, the sight of whose eyes saw no further than bodies, and of my mind no further than a phantasm? And I knew not God to be a Spirit,[3] not one who hath parts extended in length and breadth, nor whose being was bulk; for every bulk is less in a part than in the whole, and, if it be infinite, it must be less in such part as is limited by a certain space than in its infinity; and cannot be wholly everywhere, as Spirit, as God is. And what that should be in us, by which we were like unto God, and might rightly in Scripture be said to be after "the image of God,"[4] I was entirely ignorant.

13. Nor had I knowledge of that true inner righteousness, which doth not judge according to custom, but out of the most perfect law of God Almighty, by which the manners of places and times were adapted to those places and times—being itself the while the same always and everywhere, not one thing in one place, and another in another; according to which Abraham, and Isaac, and Jacob, and Moses, and David, and all those commended by the mouth of God were righteous,[5] but were judged unrighteous by foolish men, judging out of man's judgment,[6] and gauging by the petty standard of their own manners the manners of the whole human race. Like as if in an armoury, one knowing not what were adapted to the several members should put greaves on his head, or boot himself with a helmet, and then complain because they would not fit. Or as if, on some day when in the afternoon business was forbidden, one were to fume at not being allowed to sell as it was lawful to him in the forenoon. Or when in some house he sees a

servant take something in his hand which the butler is not permitted to touch, or something done behind a stable which would be prohibited in the dining-room, and should be indignant that in one house, and one family, the same thing is not distributed everywhere to all. Such are they who cannot endure to hear something to have been lawful for righteous men in former times which is not so now; or that God, for certain temporal reasons, commanded them one thing, and these another, but both obeying the same righteousness; though they see, in one man, one day, and one house, different things to be fit for different members, and a thing which was formerly lawful after a time unlawful —that permitted or commanded in one corner, which done in another is justly prohibited and punished. Is justice, then, various and changeable? Nay, but the times over which she presides are not all alike, because they are times.[7] But men, whose days upon the earth are few,[8] because by their own perception they cannot harmonize the causes of former ages and other nations, of which they had no experience, with these of which they have experience, though in one and the same body, day, or family, they can readily see what is suitable for each member, season, part, and person—to the one they take exception, to the other they submit.

14. These things I then knew not, nor observed. They met my eyes on every side, and I saw them not. I composed poems, in which it was not permitted me to place every foot everywhere, but in one metre one way, and in another another, nor even in any one verse the same foot in all places. Yet the art itself by which I composed had not different principles for these different cases, but comprised all in one. Still I saw not how that righteousness, which good and holy men submitted to, far more excellently and sublimely comprehended in one all those things which God commanded,

---

[1] The strange mixture of the pensive philosophy of Persia with Gnosticism and Christianity, propounded by Manichæus, attempted to solve this question, which was "the great object of heretical inquiry" (Mansel's *Gnostics*, lec. i.). It was Augustin's desire for knowledge concerning it that united him to this sect, and which also led him to forsake it, when he found therein nothing but empty fables (*De Lib. Arb.* i. sec. 4). Manichæus taught that evil and good were primeval, and had independent existences. Augustin, on the other hand, maintains that it was not possible for evil so to exist (*De Civ. Dei*, xi. sec. 22), but, as he here states, evil is "a privation of good." The evil will has a *causa deficiens*, but not a *causa efficiens* (*ibid.* xii. 6), as is exemplified in the fall of the angels.

[2] 1 Kings xviii. 40.
[3] John iv. 24.
[4] Gen. i. 27; see vi. sec. 4, note.
[5] Heb. xi. 8-40.
[6] 1 Cor. iv. 3.

[7] The law of the development of revelation implied in the above passage is one to which Augustin frequently resorts in confutation of objections such as those to which he refers in the previous and following sections. It may likewise be effectively used when similar objections are raised by modern sceptics. In the Rabbinical books there is a tradition of the wanderings of the children of Israel, that not only did their clothes not wax old (Deut. xxix. 5) during those forty years, but that they *grew* with their growth. The written word is as it were the swaddling-clothes of the holy child Jesus; and as the revelation concerning Him—the Word Incarnate—grew, did the written word grow. God spoke in sundry parts [πολυμέρως] and in divers manners unto the fathers by the prophets (Heb. i. 1); but when the "fulness of the time was come" (Gal. iv. 4), He completed the revelation in His Son. Our Lord indicates this principle when He speaks of divorce in Matt. xix. 8. "Moses," he says, "because of the hardness of your hearts suffered you to put away your wives; but from the beginning it was not so." (See *Con. Faust.* xix. 26, 29.) When objections, then, as to obsolete ritual usages, or the sins committed by Old Testament worthies are urged, the answer is plain: the ritual has become obsolete, because only intended for the infancy of revelation, and the sins, while recorded in, are not approved by Scripture, and those who committed them will be judged according to the measure of revelation they received. See also *De Ver. Relig.* xvii.; *in Ps.* lxxiii. 1, liv. 22; *Con. Faust.* xxii. 25; Trench, *Hulsean Lecs.* iv., v. (1845); and Candlish's *Reason and Revelation*, pp. 58-75.
[8] Job xiv. 1.

and in no part varied, though in varying times it did not prescribe all things at once, but distributed and enjoined what was proper for each. And I, being blind, blamed those pious fathers, not only for making use of present things as God commanded and inspired them to do, but also for foreshowing things to come as God was revealing them.[1]

CHAP. VIII.—HE ARGUES AGAINST THE SAME AS TO THE REASON OF OFFENCES.

15. Can it at any time or place be an unrighteous thing for a man to love God with all his heart, with all his soul, and with all his mind, and his neighbour as himself?[2] Therefore those offences which are contrary to nature are everywhere and at all times to be held in detestation and punished; such were those of the Sodomites, which should all nations commit, they should all be held guilty of the same crime by the divine law, which hath not so made men that they should in that way abuse one another. For even that fellowship which should be between God and us is violated, when that same nature of which He is author is polluted by the perversity of lust. But those offences which are contrary to the customs of men are to be avoided according to the customs severally prevailing; so that an agreement made, and confirmed by custom or law of any city or nation, may not be violated at the lawless pleasure of any, whether citizen or stranger. For any part which is not consistent with its whole is unseemly. But when God commands anything contrary to the customs or compacts of any nation to be done, though it were never done by them before, it is to be done; and if intermitted it is to be restored, and, if never established, to be established. For if it be lawful for a king, in the state over which he reigns, to command that which neither he himself nor any one before him had commanded, and to obey him cannot be held to be inimical to the public interest,—nay, it were so if he were not obeyed (for obedience to princes is a general compact of human society),—how much more, then, ought we unhesitatingly to obey God, the Governor of all His creatures! For as among the authorities of human society the greater authority is obeyed before the lesser, so must God above all.

16. So also in deeds of violence, where there is a desire to harm, whether by contumely or injury; and both of these either by reason of revenge, as one enemy against another; or to obtain some advantage over another, as the highwayman to the traveller; or for the avoiding of some evil, as with him who is in fear of another; or through envy, as the unfortunate man to one who is happy; or as he that is prosperous in anything to him who he fears will become equal to himself, or whose equality he grieves at; or for the mere pleasure in another's pains, as the spectators of gladiators, or the deriders and mockers of others. These be the chief iniquities which spring forth from the lust of the flesh, of the eye, and of power, whether singly, or two together, or all at once. And so do men live in opposition to the three and seven, that psaltery "of ten strings,"[3] Thy ten commandments, O God most high and most sweet. But what foul offences can there be against Thee who canst not be defiled? Or what deeds of violence against thee who canst not be harmed? But Thou avengest that which men perpetrate against themselves, seeing also that when they sin against Thee, they do wickedly against their own souls; and iniquity gives itself the lie,[4] either by corrupting or perverting their nature, which Thou hast made and ordained, or by an immoderate use of things permitted, or in "burning" in things forbidden to that use which is against nature;[5] or when convicted, raging with heart and voice against Thee, kicking against the pricks;[6] or when, breaking through the pale of human society, they audaciously rejoice in private combinations or divisions, according as they have been pleased or offended. And these things are done whenever Thou art forsaken, O Fountain of Life, who art the only and true Creator and Ruler of the universe, and by a self-willed pride any one false thing is selected therefrom and loved. So, then, by a humble piety we return to Thee; and thou purgest us from our evil customs, and art merciful unto the sins of those who confess unto Thee, and dost "hear the groaning of the prisoner,"[7] and dost loosen us from those fetters which we have forged for ourselves, if we lift not up against Thee the horns of a false liberty,—

---

[1] Here, as at the end of sec. 17, he alludes to the typical and allegorical character of Old Testament histories. Though he does not with Origen go so far as to disparage the letter of Scripture (see *De Civ. Dei*, xiii. 21), but upholds it, he constantly employs the allegorical principle. He (alluding to the patriarchs) goes so far, indeed, as to say (*Con. Faust.* xxii. 24), that "not only the speech but the life of these men was prophetic; and the whole kingdom of the Hebrews was like a great prophet;" and again: "We may discover a prophecy of the coming of Christ and of the Church both in what they said and what they did." This method of interpretation he first learned from Ambrose. See note on "the letter killeth," etc. (below, vi. sec. 6), for the danger attending it. On the general subject, reference may also be made to his *in Ps.* cxxxvi. 3; *Serm.* 2; *De Tentat. Abr.* sec. 7; and *De Civ. Dei*, xvii. 3.
[2] Deut. vi. 5, and Matt. xxii. 37-39.

[3] Ps. cxliv. 9. "St. Augustin (*Quæst. in Exod.* ii. qu. 71) mentions the two modes of dividing the ten commandments into three and seven, or four and six, and gives what appear to have been his own private reasons for preferring the first. Both commonly existed in his day, but the Anglican mode appears to have been the most usual. It occurs in Origen, Greg. Naz., Jerome, Ambrose, Chrys. St. Augustin alludes to his division again, *Serm.* 8, 9, *de x. Chordis*, and sec. 33 on this psalm : ' To the first commandment there belong three strings, because God is trine. To the other, *i. e.*, the love of our neighbour, seven strings. These let us join to those three, which belong to the love of God, if we would on the psaltery of ten strings sing a new song.' "—E. B. P.
[4] Ps. xxvii. 12, *Vulg.*
[5] Rom. i. 24-29.
[6] Acts ix. 5.
[7] Ps. cii. 20.

losing all through craving more, by loving more our own private good than Thee, the good of all.

CHAP. IX.—THAT THE JUDGMENT OF GOD AND MEN, AS TO HUMAN ACTS OF VIOLENCE, IS DIFFERENT.

17. But amidst these offences of infamy and violence, and so many iniquities, are the sins of men who are, on the whole, making progress; which, by those who judge rightly, and after the rule of perfection, are censured, yet commended withal, upon the hope of bearing fruit, like as in the green blade of the growing corn. And there are some which resemble offences of infamy or violence, and yet are not sins, because they neither offend Thee, our Lord God, nor social custom : when, for example, things suitable for the times are provided for the use of life, and we are uncertain whether it be out of a lust of having ; or when acts are punished by constituted authority for the sake of correction, and we are uncertain whether it be out of a lust of hurting. Many a deed, then, which in the sight of men is disapproved, is approved by Thy testimony ; and many a one who is praised by men is, Thou being witness, condemned ; because frequently the view of the deed, and the mind of the doer, and the hidden exigency of the period, severally vary. But when Thou unexpectedly commandest an unusual and unthought-of thing—yea, even if Thou hast formerly forbidden it, and still for the time keepest secret the reason of Thy command, and it even be contrary to the ordinance of some society of men, who doubts but it is to be done, inasmuch as that society is righteous which serves Thee?[1] But blessed are they who know Thy commands ! For all things were done by them who served Thee either to exhibit something necessary at the time, or to foreshow things to come. [2]

CHAP. X.—HE REPROVES THE TRIFLINGS OF THE MANICHÆANS AS TO THE FRUITS OF THE EARTH.

18. These things being ignorant of, I de-

rided those holy servants and prophets of Thine. And what did I gain by deriding them but to be derided by Thee, being insensibly, and little by little, led on to those follies, as to credit that a fig-tree wept when it was plucked, and that the mother-tree shed milky tears ? Which fig notwithstanding, plucked not by his own but another's wickedness, had some "saint"[3] eaten and mingled with his entrails, he should breathe out of it angels ; yea, in his prayers he shall assuredly groan and sigh forth particles of God, which particles of the most high and true God should have remained bound in that fig unless they had been set free by the teeth and belly of some "elect saint" ! [4] And I, miserable one, believed that more mercy was to be shown to the fruits of the earth than unto men, for whom they were created ; for if a hungry man—who was not a Manichæan—should beg for any, that morsel which should be given him would appear, as it were, condemned to capital punishment. [5]

CHAP. XI.—HE REFERS TO THE TEARS, AND THE MEMORABLE DREAM CONCERNING HER SON, GRANTED BY GOD TO HIS MOTHER.

19. And Thou sendedst Thine hand from above,[6] and drewest my soul out of that profound darkness, when my mother, Thy faithful one, wept to thee on my behalf more than mothers are wont to weep the bodily deaths of their children. For she saw that I was dead by that faith and spirit which she had from Thee, and Thou heardest her, O Lord. Thou heardest her, and despisedst not her tears, when, pouring down, they watered the earth[7] under her eyes in every place where she prayed ; yea, Thou heardest her. For whence was that dream with which Thou consoledst her, so that she permitted me to live with her, and to have my meals at the same table in the house, which she had begun to avoid, hating and detesting the blasphemies of my error ? For she saw herself standing on a certain wooden rule,[8] and a bright youth advancing towards her, joyous and smiling

---

[1] The Manichæans, like the deistical writers of the last century, attacked the spoiling of the Egyptians, the slaughter of the Canaanites, and such episodes. Referring to the former, Augustin says (*Con. Faust.* xxii. 71), " Then, as for Faustus' objection to the spoiling of the Egyptians, he knows not what he says. In this Moses not only did not sin, but it would have been sin not to do it. It was by the command of God, who, from His knowledge both of the actions and of the hearts of men, can decide upon what every one should be made to suffer, and through whose agency. The people at that time were still carnal, and engrossed with earthly affection ; while the Egyptians were in open rebellion against God, for they used the gold, God's creature, in the service of idols, to the dishonour of the Creator, and they had grievously oppressed strangers by making them work without pay. Thus the Egyptians deserved the punishment, and the Israelites were suitably employed in inflicting it." For an exhaustive vindication of the conduct of the children of Israel as the agents of God in punishing the Canaanites, see *Graves on the Pentateuch*, Part iii. lecture 1. See also *De Civ. Dei*, i. 26 ; and *Quæst. in Jos.* 8, 16, etc.
[2] See note on sec. 14, above.

[3] *i. e.* Manichæan saint.
[4] According to this extraordinary system, it was the privilege of the "elect" to set free in eating such parts of the divine substance as were imprisoned in the vegetable creation (*Con. Faust.* xxxi. 5). They did not marry or work in the fields, and led an ascetic life, the "hearers" or catechumens being privileged to provide them with food. The "elect" passed immediately on dying into the realm of light, while, as a reward for their service, the souls of the "hearers" after death transmigrated into plants (from which they might be most readily freed), or into the "elect," so as, in their turn, to pass away into the realm of light. See *Con. Faust.* v. 10, xx. 23 ; and *in Ps.* cxl.
[5] Augustin frequently alludes to their conduct to the poor, in refusing to give them bread or the fruits of the earth, lest in eating they should defile the portion of God contained therein. But to avoid the odium of their conduct, they would inconsequently give money whereby food might be bought. See *in Ps.* cxl. sec. 12 ; and *De Mor. Manich.* 36, 37, and 53.
[6] Ps. cxliv. 7.
[7] He alludes here to that devout manner of the Eastern ancients, who used to lie flat on their faces in prayer.—W. W.
[8] Symbolical of the rule of faith. See viii. sec. 30, below.

upon her, whilst she was grieving and bowed down with sorrow. But he having inquired of her the cause of her sorrow and daily weeping (he wishing to teach, as is their wont, and not to be taught), and she answering that it was my perdition she was lamenting, he bade her rest contented, and told her to behold and see "that where she was, there was I also." And when she looked she saw me standing near her on the same rule. Whence was this, unless that Thine ears were inclined towards her heart? O Thou Good Omnipotent, who so carest for every one of us as if Thou caredst for him only, and so for all as if they were but one!

20. Whence was this, also, that when she had narrated this vision to me, and I tried to put this construction on it, "That she rather should not despair of being some day what I was," she immediately, without hesitation, replied, "No; for it was not told me that 'where he is, there shalt thou be,' but 'where thou art, there shall he be'"? I confess to Thee, O Lord, that, to the best of my remembrance (and I have oft spoken of this), Thy answer through my watchful mother—that she was not disquieted by the speciousness of my false interpretation, and saw in a moment what was to be seen, and which I myself had not in truth perceived before she spake—even then moved me more than the dream itself, by which the happiness to that pious woman, to be realized so long after, was, for the alleviation of her present anxiety, so long before predicted. For nearly nine years passed in which I wallowed in the slime of that deep pit and the darkness of falsehood, striving often to rise, but being all the more heavily dashed down. But yet that chaste, pious, and sober widow (such as Thou lovest), now more buoyed up with hope, though no whit less zealous in her weeping and mourning, desisted not, at all the hours of her supplications, to bewail my case unto Thee. And her prayers entered into Thy presence,[1] and yet Thou didst still suffer me to be involved and re-involved in that darkness.

1 Ps. lxxxviii. 1.

CHAP. XII.—THE EXCELLENT ANSWER OF THE BISHOP WHEN REFERRED TO BY HIS MOTHER AS TO THE CONVERSION OF HER SON.

21. And meanwhile Thou grantedst her another answer, which I recall; for much I pass over, hastening on to those things which the more strongly impel me to confess unto Thee, and much I do not remember. Thou didst grant her then another answer, by a priest of Thine, a certain bishop, reared in Thy Church and well versed in Thy books. He, when this woman had entreated that he would vouchsafe to have some talk with me, refute my errors, unteach me evil things, and teach me good (for this he was in the habit of doing when he found people fitted to receive it), refused, very prudently, as I afterwards came to see. For he answered that I was still unteachable, being inflated with the novelty of that heresy, and that I had already perplexed divers inexperienced persons with vexatious questions,[2] as she had informed him. "But leave him alone for a time," saith he, "only pray God for him; he will of himself, by reading, discover what that error is, and how great its impiety." He disclosed to her at the same time how he himself, when a little one, had, by his misguided mother, been given over to the Manichæans, and had not only read, but even written out almost all their books, and had come to see (without argument or proof from any one) how much that sect was to be shunned, and had shunned it. Which when he had said, and she would not be satisfied, but repeated more earnestly her entreaties, shedding copious tears, that he would see and discourse with me, he, a little vexed at her importunity, exclaimed, "Go thy way, and God bless thee, for it is not possible that the son of these tears should perish." Which answer (as she often mentioned in her conversations with me) she accepted as though it were a voice from heaven.

2 We can easily understand that Augustin's dialectic skill would render him a formidable opponent, while, with the zeal of a neophyte, he urged those difficulties of Scripture (*De Agon. Christ.* iv.) which the Manichæans knew so well how to employ. In an interesting passage (*De Duab. Anim. con. Manich.* ix.) he tells us that his victories over "inexperienced persons" stimulated him to fresh conquests, and thus kept him bound longer than he would otherwise have been in the chains of this heresy.

BOOK IV.

THEN FOLLOWS A PERIOD OF NINE YEARS FROM THE NINETEENTH YEAR OF HIS AGE, DURING WHICH HAVING LOST A FRIEND, HE FOLLOWED THE MANICHÆANS—AND WROTE BOOKS ON THE FAIR AND FIT, AND PUBLISHED A WORK ON THE LIBERAL ARTS, AND THE CATEGORIES OF ARISTOTLE.

CHAP. I.—CONCERNING THAT MOST UNHAPPY TIME IN WHICH HE, BEING DECEIVED, DECEIVED OTHERS; AND CONCERNING THE MOCKERS OF HIS CONFESSION.

1. DURING this space of nine years, then, from my nineteenth to my eight and twentieth year, we went on seduced and seducing, deceived and deceiving, in divers lusts; publicly, by sciences which they style "liberal"—secretly, with a falsity called religion. Here proud, there superstitious, everywhere vain! Here, striving after the emptiness of popular fame, even to theatrical applauses, and poetic contests, and strifes for grassy garlands, and the follies of shows and the intemperance of desire. There, seeking to be purged from these our corruptions by carrying food to those who were called "elect" and "holy," out of which, in the laboratory of their stomachs, they should make for us angels and gods, by whom we might be delivered.[1] These things did I follow eagerly, and practise with my friends—by me and with me deceived. Let the arrogant, and such as have not been yet savingly cast down and stricken by Thee, O my God, laugh at me; but notwithstanding I would confess to Thee mine own shame in Thy praise. Bear with me, I beseech Thee, and give me grace to retrace in my present remembrance the circlings of my past errors, and to "offer to Thee the sacrifice of thanksgiving."[2] For what am I to myself without Thee, but a guide to mine own downfall? Or what am I even at the best, but one sucking Thy milk,[3] and feeding upon Thee, the meat that perisheth not?[4] But what kind of man is any man, seeing that he is but a man? Let, then, the strong and the mighty laugh at us, but let us who are "poor and needy"[5] confess unto Thee.

CHAP. II.—HE TEACHES RHETORIC, THE ONLY THING HE LOVED, AND SCORNS THE SOOTHSAYER, WHO PROMISED HIM VICTORY.

2. In those years I taught the art of rhetoric, and, overcome by cupidity, put to sale a loquacity by which to overcome. Yet I preferred—Lord, Thou knowest—to have honest scholars (as they are esteemed); and these I, without artifice, taught artifices, not to be put in practise against the life of the guiltless, though sometimes for the life of the guilty. And Thou, O God, from afar sawest me stumbling in that slippery path, and amid much smoke[6] sending out some flashes of fidelity, which I exhibited in that my guidance of such as loved vanity and sought after leasing,[7] I being their companion. In those years I had one (whom I knew not in what is called lawful wedlock, but whom my wayward passion, void of understanding, had discovered), yet one only, remaining faithful even to her; in whom I found out truly by my own experience what difference there is between the restraints of the marriage bonds, contracted for the sake of issue, and the compact of a lustful love, where children are born against the parents' will, although, being born, they compel love.

3. I remember, too, that when I decided to compete for a theatrical prize, a soothsayer demanded of me what I would give him to win; but I, detesting and abominating such foul mysteries, answered, "That if the garland were of imperishable gold, I would not suffer a fly to be destroyed to secure it for me." For he was to slay certain living creatures in his sacrifices, and by those honours to invite the devils to give me their support. But this ill thing I also refused,

---

[1] Augustin tells us that he went not beyond the rank of a "hearer," because he found the Manichæan teachers readier in refuting others than in establishing their own views, and seems only to have looked for some esoteric doctrine to have been disclosed to him under their materialistic teaching as to God—viz. that He was an unmeasured Light that extended all ways but one, infinitely (*Serm.* iv. sec. 5.)—rather than to have really accepted it.—*De Util. Cred. Præf.* See also iii. sec. 18, notes 1 and 2, above.
[2] Ps. cxvi. 17.
[3] 1 Pet. ii. 2.
[4] John vi. 27.

[5] Ps. lxxiv. 21.
[6] Isa. xlii. 3, and Matt. xii. 20.
[7] Ps. iv. 2.

not out of a pure love[1] for Thee, O God of my heart ; for I knew not how to love Thee, knowing not how to conceive aught beyond corporeal brightness.[2] And doth not a soul, sighing after such-like fictions, commit fornication against Thee, trust in false things,[3] and nourish the wind?[4] But I would not, forsooth, have sacrifices offered to devils on my behalf, though I myself was offering sacrifices to them by that superstition. For what else is nourishing the wind but nourishing them, that is, by our wanderings to become their enjoyment and derision?

CHAP. III.—NOT EVEN THE MOST EXPERIENCED MEN COULD PERSUADE HIM OF THE VANITY OF ASTROLOGY, TO WHICH HE WAS DEVOTED.

4. Those impostors, then, whom they designate Mathematicians, I consulted without hesitation, because they used no sacrifices, and invoked the aid of no spirit for their divinations, which art Christian and true piety fitly rejects and condemns.[5] For good it is to confess unto Thee, and to say, " Be merciful unto me, heal my soul, for I have sinned against Thee ;"[6] and not to abuse Thy goodness for a license to sin, but to remember the words of the Lord, " Behold, thou art made whole ; sin no more, lest a worse thing come unto thee."[7] All of which salutary advice they endeavour to destroy when they say, " The cause of thy sin is inevitably determined in heaven ;" and, " This did Venus, or Saturn, or Mars ;" in order that man, forsooth, flesh and blood, and proud corruption, may be blameless, while the Creator and Ordainer of heaven and stars is to bear the blame. And who is this but Thee, our God, the sweetness and well-spring of righteousness, who renderest " to every man according to his deeds,"[8] and despisest not " a broken and a contrite heart ! "[9]

5. There was in those days a wise man, very skilful in medicine, and much renowned therein, who had with his own proconsular hand put the Agonistic garland upon my distempered head, not, though, as a physician ;[10] for this disease Thou alone healest, who resistest the proud, and givest grace to the humble.[11] But didst Thou fail me even by that old man, or forbear from healing my soul? For when I had become more familiar with him, and hung assiduously and fixedly on his conversation (for though couched in simple language, it was replete with vivacity, life, and earnestness), when he had perceived from my discourse that I was given to books of the horoscope-casters, he, in a kind and fatherly manner, advised me to throw them away, and not vainly bestow the care and labour necessary for useful things upon these vanities ; saying that he himself in his earlier years had studied that art with a view to gaining his living

---

[1] " He alone is truly pure who waiteth on God, and keepeth himself to Him alone" (Aug. *De Vita Beata*, sec. 18). " Whoso seeketh God is pure, because the soul hath in God her legitimate husband. Whosoever seeketh of God anything besides God, doth not love God purely. If a wife loved her husband because he is rich, she is not pure, for she loveth not her husband but the gold of her husband" (Aug. *Serm.* 137). " Whoso seeks from God any other reward but God, and for it would serve God, esteems what he wishes to receive more than Him from whom he would receive it. What, then? hath God no reward? None, save Himself. The reward of God is God Himself. This it loveth ; if it love aught beside, it is no pure love. You depart from the immortal flame, you will be chilled, corrupted. Do not depart ; it will be thy corruption, will be fornication in thee" (Aug. *in Ps.* lxxii. sec. 32). " The pure fear of the Lord (Ps. xix. 9) is that wherewith the Church, the more ardently she loveth her Husband, the more diligently she avoids offending Him, and therefore love, when perfected, casteth not out this fear, but it remaineth for ever and ever" (Aug. *in loc.*). " Under the name of pure fear is signified that will whereby we must needs be averse from sin, and avoid sin, not through the constant anxiety of infirmity, but through the tranquillity of affection" (*De Civ. Dei*, xiv. sec. 65).—E. B. P.

[2] See note on sec. 9, below.

[3] " Indisputably we must take care, lest the mind, believing that which it does not see, feign to itself something which is not, and hope for and love that which is false. For in that case it will not be charity out of a pure heart, and of a good conscience, and of faith unfeigned, which is the end of the commandment" (*De Trin.* viii. sec. 6). And again (*Confessions*, i. 1): " For who can call on Thee, not knowing Thee? For he that knoweth Thee not may call on Thee as other than Thou art."

[4] Hosea xii. 1.

[5] Augustin classes the votaries of both wizards and astrologers (*De Doctr. Christ.* ii. 23; and *De Civ. Dei*, x. 9; compare also Justin Martyr, *Apol.* ii. c. 5) as alike " deluded and imposed on by the false angels, to whom the lowest part of the world has been put in subjection by the law of God's providence ;" and he says, "All arts of this sort are either nullities, or are part of a guilty superstition springing out of a baleful fellowship between men and devils, and are to be utterly repudiated and avoided by the Christian, as the covenants of a false and treacherous friendship." It is remarkable that though these arts were strongly denounced in the Pentateuch, the Jews—acquiring them from the surrounding Gentile nations—have embedded them deeply in their oral law, said also to be given by Moses (*e. g.* in *Moed Katon* 28, and *Shabbath* 156), prosperity comes from the influence of the stars ; in *Shabbath* 61 it is a question whether the influence of the stars or a charm has been effective; and in *Sanhedrin* 17 magic is one of the qualifications for the Sanhedrin). It might have been expected that the Christians, if only from that reaction against Judaism which shows itself in Origen's disparagement of the letter of the Old Testament Scriptures (see *De Princip.* iv. 15, 16), would have shrunk from such strange arts. But the influx of pagans, who had practised them, into the Christian Church appears gradually to have leavened it in no slight degree. This is not only true of the Valentinians (see Kaye's *Clement of Alex.* vi.) and other heretics, but the influence of these contacts is seen even in the writings of the " orthodox." Those who can read between the lines will find no slight trace of this (after separating what they would conceive to be true from what is manifestly false) in the story told by Zonaras, in his *Annals*, of the controversy between the Rabbis and Sylvester, Bishop of Rome, before Constantine. The Jews were worsted in argument, and evidently thought an appeal to miracles might, from the Emperor's education, bring him over to their side. An ox is brought forth. The Jewish wonder-worker whispers a mystic name into its ear, and it falls dead ; but Sylvester, according to the story, is quite equal to the occasion, and restores the animal to life again by uttering the name of the Redeemer. It may have been that the cessation of miracles may have gradually led unstable professors of Christianity to invent miracles; and, as Bishop Kaye observes (*Tertullian*, p. 95), " the success of the first attempts naturally encouraged others to practise similar impositions on the credulity of mankind." As to the time of the cessation of miracles, comparison may be profitably made of the views of Kaye, in the early part of c. ii. of his *Tertullian*, and of Blunt, in his *Right Use of the Early Fathers*, series ii. lecture 6.

[6] Ps. xli. 4.

[7] John v. 14.

[8] Rom. ii. 6, and Matt. xvi. 27.

[9] Ps. li. 17.

[10] This physician was Vindicianus, the " acute old man " mentioned in vii. sec. 8, below, and again in *Ep.* 138, as " the most eminent physician of his day." Augustin's disease, however, could not be reached by his remedies. We are irresistibly reminded of the words of our great poet :—
" Canst thou minister to a mind diseased ;
Pluck from the memory a rooted sorrow;
Raze out the written troubles of the brain ;
And, with some sweet oblivious antidote,
Cleanse the stuff'd bosom of that perilous stuff
Which weighs upon the heart ! "—*Macbeth*, act. v. scene 3.

[11] 1 Pet. v. 5, and Jas. iv. 6.

by following it as a profession, and that, as he had understood Hippocrates, he would soon have understood this, and yet he had given it up, and followed medicine, for no other reason than that he discovered it to be utterly false, and he, being a man of character, would not gain his living by beguiling people. "But thou," saith he, "who hast rhetoric to support thyself by, so that thou followest this of free will, not of necessity—all the more, then, oughtest thou to give me credit herein, who laboured to attain it so perfectly, as I wished to gain my living by it alone." When I asked him to account for so many true things being foretold by it, he answered me (as he could) "that the force of chance, diffused throughout the whole order of nature, brought this about. For if when a man by accident opens the leaves of some poet, who sang and intended something far different, a verse oftentimes fell out wondrously apposite to the present business, it were not to be wondered at," he continued, "if out of the soul of man, by some higher instinct, not knowing what goes on within itself, an answer should be given by chance, not art, which should coincide with the business and actions of the questioner."

6. And thus truly, either by or through him, Thou didst look after me. And Thou didst delineate in my memory what I might afterwards search out for myself. But at that time neither he, nor my most dear Nebridius, a youth most good and most circumspect, who scoffed at that whole stock of divination, could persuade me to forsake it, the authority of the authors influencing me still more; and as yet I had lighted upon no certain proof—such as I sought—whereby it might without doubt appear that what had been truly foretold by those consulted was by accident or chance, not by the art of the star-gazers.

CHAP. IV.—SORELY DISTRESSED BY WEEPING AT THE DEATH OF HIS FRIEND, HE PROVIDES CONSOLATION FOR HIMSELF.

7. In those years, when I first began to teach rhetoric in my native town, I had acquired a very dear friend, from association in our studies, of mine own age, and, like myself, just rising up into the flower of youth. He had grown up with me from childhood, and we had been both school-fellows and play-fellows. But he was not then my friend, nor, indeed, afterwards, as true friendship is; for true it is not but in such as Thou bindest together, cleaving unto Thee by that love which is shed abroad in our hearts by the Holy Ghost, which is given unto us.[1] But yet it was too sweet, being ripened by the

fervour of similar studies. For, from the true faith (which he, as a youth, had not soundly and thoroughly become master of), I had turned him aside towards those superstitious and pernicious fables which my mother mourned in me. With me this man's mind now erred, nor could my soul exist without him. But behold, Thou wert close behind Thy fugitives—at once God of vengeance[2] and Fountain of mercies, who turnest us to Thyself by wondrous means. Thou removedst that man from this life when he had scarce completed one whole year of my friendship, sweet to me above all the sweetness of that my life.

8. "Who can show forth all Thy praise"[3] which he hath experienced in himself alone? What was it that Thou didst then, O my God, and how unsearchable are the depths of Thy judgments![4] For when, sore sick of a fever, he long lay unconscious in a death-sweat, and all despaired of his recovery, he was baptized without his knowledge;[5] myself meanwhile little caring, presuming that his soul would retain rather what it had imbibed from me, than what was done to his unconscious body. Far different, however, was it, for he was revived and restored. Straightway, as soon as I could talk to him (which I could as soon as he was able, for I never left him, and we hung too much upon each other), I attempted to jest with him, as if he also would jest with me at that baptism which he had received when mind and senses were in abeyance, but had now learnt that he had received. But he shuddered at me, as if I were his enemy; and, with a remarkable and unexpected freedom, admonished me, if I desired to continue his friend, to desist from speaking to him in such a way. I, confounded and confused, concealed all my emotions, till he should get well, and his health be strong enough to allow me to deal with him as I wished. But he was withdrawn from my frenzy, that with Thee he might be preserved for my comfort. A few days after, during my absence, he had a return of the fever, and died.

9. At this sorrow my heart was utterly darkened, and whatever I looked upon was death. My native country was a torture to me, and my father's house a wondrous unhappiness; and whatsoever I had participated in with him, wanting him, turned into a frightful torture. Mine eyes sought him everywhere, but he was not granted them; and I hated all places because he was not in them; nor could they now say to me, "Behold, he is coming," as they did when he was alive and absent. I

[1] Rom. v. 5.

[2] Ps. xciv. 1.
[3] Ps. cvi. 2.
[4] Ps. xxxvi. 6, and Rom. xi. 33.
[5] See i. sec. 17, note 3, above.

became a great puzzle to myself, and asked my soul why she was so sad, and why she so exceedingly disquieted me ;[1] but she knew not what to answer me. And if I said, "Hope thou in God,"[2] she very properly obeyed me not; because that most dear friend whom she had lost was, being man, both truer and better than that phantasm[3] she was bid to hope in. Naught but tears were sweet to me, and they succeeded my friend in the dearest of my affections.

CHAP. V.—WHY WEEPING IS PLEASANT TO THE WRETCHED.

10. And now, O Lord, these things are passed away, and time hath healed my wound. May I learn from Thee, who art Truth, and apply the ear of my heart unto Thy mouth, that Thou mayest tell me why weeping should be so sweet to the unhappy.[4] Hast Thou—although present everywhere—cast away far from Thee our misery? And Thou abidest in Thyself, but we are disquieted with divers trials; and yet, unless we wept in Thine ears, there would be no hope for us remaining. Whence, then, is it that such sweet fruit is plucked from the bitterness of life, from groans, tears, sighs, and lamentations? Is it the hope that Thou hearest us that sweetens it? This is true of prayer, for therein is a desire to approach unto Thee. But is it also in grief for a thing lost, and the sorrow with which I was then overwhelmed? For I had neither hope of his coming to life again, nor did I seek this with my tears; but I grieved and wept only, for I was miserable, and had lost my joy. Or is weeping a bitter thing, and for distaste of the things which aforetime we enjoyed before, and even then, when we are loathing them, does it cause us pleasure?

CHAP. VI.—HIS FRIEND BEING SNATCHED AWAY BY DEATH, HE IMAGINES THAT HE REMAINS ONLY AS HALF.

11. But why do I speak of these things?

For this is not the time to question, but rather to confess unto Thee. Miserable I was, and miserable is every soul fettered by the friendship of perishable things—he is torn to pieces when he loses them, and then is sensible of the misery which he had before ever he lost them. Thus was it at that time with me; I wept most bitterly, and found rest in bitterness. Thus was I miserable, and that life of misery I accounted dearer than my friend. For though I would willingly have changed it, yet I was even more unwilling to lose it than him ; yea, I knew not whether I was willing to lose it even for him, as is handed down to us (if not an invention) of Pylades and Orestes, that they would gladly have died one for another, or both together, it being worse than death to them not to live together. But there had sprung up in me some kind of feeling, too, contrary to this, for both exceedingly wearisome was it to me to live, and dreadful to die. I suppose, the more I loved him, so much the more did I hate and fear, as a most cruel enemy, that death which had robbed me of him ; and I imagined it would suddenly annihilate all men, as it had power over him. Thus, I remember, it was with me. Behold my heart, O my God! Behold and look into me, for I remember it well, O my Hope! who cleansest me from the uncleanness of such affections, directing mine eyes towards Thee, and plucking my feet out of the net.[5] For I was astonished that other mortals lived, since he whom I loved, as if he would never die, was dead ; and I wondered still more that I, who was to him a second self, could live when he was dead. Well did one say of his friend, "Thou half of my soul,"[6] for I felt that my soul and his soul were but one soul in two bodies ;[7] and, consequently, my life was a horror to me, because I would not live in half. And therefore, perchance, was I afraid to die, lest he should die wholly[8] whom I had so greatly loved.

CHAP. VII.—TROUBLED BY RESTLESSNESS AND GRIEF, HE LEAVES HIS COUNTRY A SECOND TIME FOR CARTHAGE.

12. O madness, which knowest not how to love men as men should be loved! O foolish man that I then was, enduring with so much impatience the lot of man! So I fretted, sighed, wept, tormented myself, and took neither rest nor advice. For I bore about with me a rent and polluted soul, impatient of being borne by me, and where to repose it I found not. Not

---

[1] Ps. xlii. 5.
[2] Ibid.
[3] The mind may rest in theories and abstractions, but the heart craves a being that it can love ; and Archbishop Whately has shown in one of his essays that the idol worship of every age had doubtless its origin in the craving of mind and heart for an embodiment of the object of worship. "Show us the Father, and it sufficeth us," says Philip (John xiv. 8), and he expresses the longing of the soul; and when the Lord replies, "He that hath seen Me hath seen the Father," He reveals to us God's satisfaction of human wants in the incarnation of His Son. Augustin's heart was now thrown in upon itself, and his view of God gave him no consolation. It satisfied his mind, perhaps, in a measure, to think of God as a "corporeal brightness" (see iii. 12; iv. 3, 12, 31; v. 19, etc.) when free from trouble, but it could not satisfy him now. He had yet to learn of Him who is the very image of God—who by His divine power raised the dead to life again, while, with perfect human sympathy, He could "weep with those that wept,"—the "Son of Man" (not of a man, He being miraculously born, but of the race of men [ανθρώπου]), i. e. the Son of Mankind. See also viii. sec. 27, note, below.
[4] For so it has ever been found to be :—
       "Est quaedam flere voluptas ;
    Expletur lacrymis egeriturque dolor."
            —OVID, Trist. iv. 3, 38.

[5] Ps. xxv. 15.
[6] Horace, Carm. i. ode 3.
[7] Ovid, Trist. iv. eleg. iv. 72.
[8] Augustin's reference to this passage in his Retractations is quoted at the beginning of the book. He might have gone further than to describe his words here as declamatio levis, since the conclusion is not logical.

in pleasant groves, not in sport or song, not in fragrant spots, nor in magnificent banquetings, nor in the pleasures of the bed and the couch, nor, finally, in books and songs did it find repose. All things looked terrible, even the very light itself; and whatsoever was not what he was, was repulsive and hateful, except groans and tears, for in those alone found I a little repose. But when my soul was withdrawn from them, a heavy burden of misery weighed me down. To Thee, O Lord, should it have been raised, for Thee to lighten and avert it.[1] This I knew, but was neither willing nor able; all the more since, in my thoughts of Thee, Thou wert not any solid or substantial thing to me. For Thou wert not Thyself, but an empty phantasm,[2] and my error was my god. If I attempted to discharge my burden thereon, that it might find rest, it sank into emptiness, and came rushing down again upon me, and I remained to myself an unhappy spot, where I could neither stay nor depart from. For whither could my heart fly from my heart? Whither could I fly from mine own self? Whither not follow myself? And yet fled I from my country; for so should my eyes look less for him where they were not accustomed to see him. And thus I left the town of Thagaste, and came to Carthage.

CHAP. VIII.—THAT HIS GRIEF CEASED BY TIME, AND THE CONSOLATION OF FRIENDS.

13. Times lose no time, nor do they idly roll through our senses. They work strange operations on the mind.[3] Behold, they came and went from day to day, and by coming and going they disseminated in my mind other ideas and other remembrances, and by little and little patched me up again with the former kind of delights, unto which that sorrow of mine yielded. But yet there succeeded, not certainly other sorrows, yet the causes of other sorrows.[4] For whence had that former sorrow so easily penetrated to the quick, but that I had poured out my soul upon the dust, in loving one who must die as if he were never to die? But what revived and refreshed me especially was the consolations of other friends,[5] with

whom I did love what instead of Thee I loved. And this was a monstrous fable and protracted lie, by whose adulterous contact our soul, which lay itching in our ears, was being polluted. But that fable would not die to me so oft as any of my friends died. There were other things in them which did more lay hold of my mind,—to discourse and jest with them; to indulge in an interchange of kindnesses; to read together pleasant books; together to trifle, and together to be earnest; to differ at times without ill-humour, as a man would do with his own self; and even by the infrequency of these differences to give zest to our more frequent consentings; sometimes teaching, sometimes being taught; longing for the absent with impatience, and welcoming the coming with joy. These and similar expressions, emanating from the hearts of those who loved and were beloved in return, by the countenance, the tongue, the eyes, and a thousand pleasing movements, were so much fuel to melt our souls together, and out of many to make but one.

CHAP. IX.—THAT THE LOVE OF A HUMAN BEING, HOWEVER CONSTANT IN LOVING AND RETURNING LOVE, PERISHES; WHILE HE WHO LOVES GOD NEVER LOSES A FRIEND.

14. This is it that is loved in friends; and so loved that a man's conscience accuses itself if he love not him by whom he is beloved, or love not again him that loves him, expecting nothing from him but indications of his love. Hence that mourning if one die, and gloom of sorrow, that steeping of the heart in tears, all sweetness turned into bitterness, and upon the loss of the life of the dying, the death of the living. Blessed be he who loveth Thee, and his friend in Thee, and his enemy for Thy sake. For he alone loses none dear to him to whom all are dear in Him who cannot be lost. And who is this but our God, the God that created heaven and earth,[6] and filleth them,[7] because by filling them He created them?[8] None loseth Thee but he who leaveth Thee. And he who leaveth Thee, whither goeth he, or whither fleeth he, but from Thee well pleased to Thee angry? For where doth not he find Thy law in his own punishment? "And Thy law is the truth,"[9] and truth Thou.[10]

CHAP. X.—THAT ALL THINGS EXIST THAT THEY MAY PERISH, AND THAT WE ARE NOT SAFE UNLESS GOD WATCHES OVER US.

15. "Turn us again, O Lord God of Hosts,

---

[1] "The great and merciful Architect of His Church, whom not only the philosophers have styled, but the Scripture itself calls τεχνίτης (an artist or artificer), employs not on us the hammer and chisel with an intent to wound or mangle us, but only to square and fashion our hard and stubborn hearts into such *lively stones* as may both grace and strengthen His heavenly structure."—BOYLE.

[2] See iii. 9; iv. 3, 12, 31; v. 19.

[3] As Seneca has it: "Quod ratio non quit, sæpe sanabit mora" (*Agam.* 130).

[4] See iv. cc. 1, 10, 12, and vi. c. 16.

[5] "Friendship," says Lord Bacon, in his essay thereon,—the sentiment being perhaps suggested by Cicero's "Secundas res splendidiores facit amicitia et adversas partiens communicansque leviores" (*De Amicit.* 6),—"redoubleth joys, and cutteth griefs in halves." Augustin appears to have been eminently open to influences of this kind. In his *De Duab. Anim. con. Manich.* (c. ix.) he tells us that friendship was one of the bonds that kept him in the ranks of the Manichæans; and here we find that, aided by time and weeping, it restored him in his great grief. See also v. sec. 19, and vi. sec 26, below.

[6] Gen. i. 1.
[7] Jer. xxiii. 24.
[8] See i. 2, 3, above.
[9] Ps. cxix. 142, and John xvii. 17.
[10] John xiv. 6.

cause Thy face to shine; and we shall be saved."[1] For whithersoever the soul of man turns itself, unless towards Thee, it is affixed to sorrows,[2] yea, though it is affixed to beauteous things without Thee and without itself. And yet they were not unless they were from Thee. They rise and set; and by rising, they begin as it were to be; and they grow, that they may become perfect; and when perfect, they wax old and perish; and all wax not old, but all perish. Therefore when they rise and tend to be, the more rapidly they grow that they may be, so much the more they hasten not to be. This is the way of them.[3] Thus much hast Thou given them, because they are parts of things, which exist not all at the same time, but by departing and succeeding they together make up the universe, of which they are parts. And even thus is our speech accomplished by signs emitting a sound; but this, again, is not perfected unless one word pass away when it has sounded its part, in order that another may succeed it. Let my soul praise Thee out of all these things, O God, the Creator of all; but let not my soul be affixed to these things by the glue of love, through the senses of the body. For they go whither they were to go, that they might no longer be; and they rend her with pestilent desires, because she longs to be, and yet loves to rest in what she loves. But in these things no place is to be found; they stay not—they flee; and who is he that is able to follow them with the senses of the flesh? Or who can grasp them, even when they are near? For tardy is the sense of the flesh, because it is the sense of the flesh, and its boundary is itself. It sufficeth for that for which it was made, but it is not sufficient to stay things running their course from their appointed starting-place to the end appointed. For in Thy word, by which they were created, they hear the fiat, "Hence and hitherto."

---

[1] Ps. lxxx. 19.

[2] See iv. cc. 1, 12, and vi. c. 16, below.

[3] It is interesting in connection with the above passages to note what Augustin says elsewhere as to the *origin* of the law of death in the sin of our first parents. In his *De Gen. ad Lit.* (vi. 25) he speaks thus of their condition in the garden, and the provision made for the maintenance of their life: " Aliud est *non posse mori*, sicut quasdam naturas immortales creavit Deus; aliud est autem *posse non mori*, secundum quem modum primus creatus est homo immortalis." Adam, he goes on to say, was *able to avert death*, by partaking of the tree of life. He enlarges on this doctrine in Book xiii. *De Civ. Dei.* He says (sec. 20): " Our first parents decayed not with years, nor drew nearer to death—a condition secured to them in God's marvellous grace by the tree of life, which grew along with the forbidden tree in the midst of Paradise." Again (sec. 19) he says: " Why do the philosophers find that absurd which the Christian faith preaches, namely, that our first parents were so created, that, if they had not sinned, they would not have been dismissed from their bodies by any death, but would have been endowed with immortality as the reward of their obedience, and would have lived eternally with their bodies?" That this was the doctrine of the early Church has been fully shown by Bishop Bull in his *State of Man before the Fall*, vol. ii. Theophilus of Antioch was of opinion (*Ad Autolyc.* c. 24) that Adam might have gone on from strength to strength, until at last he " would have been taken up into heaven." See also on this subject Dean Buckland's *Sermon on Death;* and Delitzsch, *Bibl. Psychol.* vi. secs. 1 and 2.

CHAP. XI.—THAT PORTIONS OF THE WORLD ARE NOT TO BE LOVED; BUT THAT GOD, THEIR AUTHOR, IS IMMUTABLE, AND HIS WORD ETERNAL.

16. Be not foolish, O my soul, and deaden not the ear of thine heart with the tumult of thy folly. Hearken thou also. The word itself invokes thee to return; and there is the place of rest imperturbable, where love is not abandoned if itself abandoneth not. Behold, these things pass away, that others may succeed them, and so this lower universe be made complete in all its parts. But do I depart anywhere, saith the word of God? There fix thy habitation. There commit whatsoever thou hast thence, O my soul; at all events now thou art tired out with deceits. Commit to truth whatsoever thou hast from the truth, and nothing shalt thou lose; and thy decay shall flourish again, and all thy diseases be healed,[4] and thy perishable parts shall be re-formed and renovated, and drawn together to thee; nor shall they put thee down where themselves descend, but they shall abide with thee, and continue for ever before God, who abideth and continueth for ever.[5]

17. Why, then, be perverse and follow thy flesh? Rather let it be converted and follow thee. Whatever by her thou feelest, is but in part; and the whole, of which these are portions, thou art ignorant of, and yet they delight thee. But had the sense of thy flesh been capable of comprehending the whole, and not itself also, for thy punishment, been justly limited to a portion of the whole, thou wouldest that whatsoever existeth at the present time should pass away, that so the whole might please thee more.[6] For what we speak, also by the same sense of the flesh thou hearest; and yet wouldest not thou that the syllables should stay, but fly away, that others may come, and the whole[7] be heard. Thus it is always, when any single thing is composed of many, all of which exist not together, all together would delight more than they do simply could all be perceived at once. But far better than these is He who made all; and He is our God, and He passeth not away, for there is nothing to succeed Him. If bodies please thee, praise God for them, and turn back thy love upon their Creator, lest in those things which please thee thou displease.

CHAP. XII.—LOVE IS NOT CONDEMNED, BUT LOVE IN GOD, IN WHOM THERE IS REST THROUGH JESUS CHRIST, IS TO BE PREFERRED.

18. If souls please thee, let them be loved in God; for they also are mutable, but in Him

[4] Ps. ciii. 3.

[5] 1 Pet. i. 23.

[6] See xiii. sec. 22, below.

[7] A similar illustration occurs in sec. 15, above.

are they firmly established, else would they pass, and pass away. In Him, then, let them be beloved ; and draw unto Him along with thee as many souls as thou canst, and say to them, "Him let us love, Him let us love ; He created these, nor is He far off. For He did not create them, and then depart ; but they are of Him, and in Him. Behold, there is He wherever truth is known. He is within the very heart, but yet hath the heart wandered from Him. Return to your heart,[1] O ye transgressors,[2] and cleave fast unto Him that made you. Stand with Him, and you shall stand fast. Rest in Him, and you shall be at rest. Whither go ye in rugged paths ? Whither go ye ? The good that you love is from Him ; and as it has respect unto Him it is both good and pleasant, and justly shall it be embittered,[3] because whatsoever cometh from Him is unjustly loved if He be forsaken for it. Why, then, will ye wander farther and farther in these difficult and toilsome ways ? There is no rest where ye seek it. Seek what ye seek ; but it is not there where ye seek. Ye seek a blessed life in the land of death ; it is not there. For could a blessed life be where life itself is not ? "

19. But our very Life descended hither, and bore our death, and slew it, out of the abundance of His own life ; and thundering He called loudly to us to return hence to Him into that secret place whence He came forth to us— first into the Virgin's womb, where the human creature was married to Him,—our mortal flesh, that it might not be for ever mortal,—and thence "as a bridegroom coming out of his chamber, rejoicing as a strong man to run a race."[4] For He tarried not, but ran crying out by words, deeds, death, life, descent, ascension, crying aloud to us to return to Him. And He departed from our sight, that we might return to our heart, and there find Him. For He departed, and behold, He is here. He would not be long with us, yet left us not ; for He departed thither, whence He never departed, because "the world was made by Him."[5]

And in this world He was, and into this world He came to save sinners,[6] unto whom my soul doth confess, that He may heal it, for it hath sinned against Him.[7] O ye sons of men, how long so slow of heart ?[8] Even now, after the Life is descended to you, will ye not ascend and live ?[9] But whither ascend ye, when ye are on high, and set your mouth against the heavens ?[10] Descend that ye may ascend,[11] and ascend to God. For ye have fallen by "ascending against Him." Tell them this, that they may weep in the valley of tears,[12] and so draw them with thee to God, because it is by His Spirit that thou speakest thus unto them, if thou speakest burning with the fire of love.

CHAP. XIII.—LOVE ORIGINATES FROM GRACE AND BEAUTY ENTICING US.

20. These things I knew not at that time, and I loved these lower beauties, and I was sinking to the very depths ; and I said to my friends, "Do we love anything but the beautiful ? What, then, is the beautiful ? And what is beauty ? What is it that allures and unites us to the things we love ; for unless there were a grace and beauty in them, they could by no means attract us to them ?" And I marked and perceived that in bodies themselves there was a beauty from their forming a kind of whole, and another from mutual fitness, as one part of the body with its whole, or a shoe with a foot, and so on. And this consideration sprang up in my mind out of the recesses of my heart, and I wrote books (two or three, I think) "on the fair and fit." Thou knowest, O Lord, for it has escaped me ; for I have them not, but they have strayed from me, I know not how.

CHAP. XIV.—CONCERNING THE BOOKS WHICH HE WROTE "ON THE FAIR AND FIT," DEDICATED TO HIERIUS.

21. But what was it that prompted me, O Lord my God, to dedicate these books to Hierius, an orator of Rome, whom I knew not by

---

[1] Augustin is never weary of pointing out that there is a *lex occulta* (*in Ps.* lvii. sec. 1), a law written on the heart, which cries to those who have forsaken the written law, "Return to your hearts, ye transgressors." In like manner he interprets (*De Serm. Dom. in Mon.* ii. sec. 11) "Enter into thy closet," of the heart of man. The door is the gate of the senses through which carnal thoughts enter into the mind. We are to shut the door, because the devil (*in Ps.* cxli. 3) *si clausum invenerit transit.* In sec. 16, above, the figure is changed, and we are to fear lest these objects of sense render us "deaf in the ear of our heart" with the tumult of our folly. Men will not, he says, go back into their hearts, because the heart is full of sin, and they fear the reproaches of conscience, just (*in Ps.* xxxiii. 5) "as those are unwilling to enter their houses who have troublesome wives." These outer things, which too often draw us away from Him, God intends should lift us up to Him who is better than they, though they could all be ours at once, since He made them all ; and "woe," he says (*De Lib. Arb.* ii. 16), "to them who love the indications of Thee rather than Thee, and remember not what these indicated."

[2] Isa. lvi. 8.
[3] See iv. cc. 1, 10, above, and vi. c. 16, below.
[4] Ps. xix. 5.
[5] John i. 10.

[6] 1 Tim. i. 15.
[7] Ps. xli. 4.
[8] Luke xxiv. 25.
[9] " The Son of God," says Augustin in another place, "became a son of man, that the sons of men might be made sons of God." He put off the *form* of God—that by which He manifested His divine glory in heaven—and put on the " form of a servant" (Phil. ii. 6, 7), that as the outshining [ἀπαύγασμα] of the Father's glory (Heb. i. 3) He might draw us to Himself. He descended and emptied Himself of His dignity that we might ascend, giving an example for all time (*in Ps.* xxxiii. sec. 4) ; for, "lest man should disdain to imitate a humble man, God humbled Himself, so that the pride of the human race might not disdain *to walk in the footsteps of God.*" See also v. sec. 5, note, below.
[10] Ps. lxxiii. 9.
[11] " There is something in humility which, strangely enough, exalts the heart, and something in pride which debases it. This seems, indeed, to be contradictory, that loftiness should debase and lowliness exalt. But pious humility enables us to submit to what is above us ; and nothing is more exalted above us than God ; and therefore humility, by making us subject to God, exalts us."—*De Civ. Dei,* xiv. sec. 13.
[12] Ps. lxxxiv. 6.

sight, but loved the man for the fame of his learning, for which he was renowned, and some words of his which I had heard, and which had pleased me? But the more did he please me in that he pleased others, who highly extolled him, astonished that a native of Syria, instructed first in Greek eloquence, should afterwards become a wonderful Latin orator, and one so well versed in studies pertaining unto wisdom. Thus a man is commended and loved when absent. Doth this love enter into the heart of the hearer from the mouth of the commender? Not so. But through one who loveth is another inflamed. For hence he is loved who is commended when the commender is believed to praise him with an unfeigned heart; that is, when he that loves him praises him.

22. Thus, then, loved I men upon the judgment of men, not upon Thine, O my God, in which no man is deceived. But yet why not as the renowned charioteer, as the huntsman,[1] known far and wide by a vulgar popularity— but far otherwise, and seriously, and so as I would desire to be myself commended? For I would not that they should commend and love me as actors are,—although I myself did commend and love them,—but I would prefer being unknown than so known, and even being hated than so loved. Where now are these influences of such various and divers kinds of loves distributed in one soul? What is it that I am in love with in another, which, if I did not hate, I should not detest and repel from myself, seeing we are equally men? For it does not follow that because a good horse is loved by him who would not, though he might, be that horse, the same should therefore be affirmed by an actor, who partakes of our nature. Do I then love in a man that which I, who am a man, hate to be? Man himself is a great deep, whose very hairs Thou numberest, O Lord, and they fall not to the ground without Thee.[2] And yet are the hairs of his head more readily numbered than are his affections and the movements of his heart.

23. But that orator was of the kind that I so loved as I wished myself to be such a one; and I erred through an inflated pride, and was "carried about with every wind,"[3] but yet was piloted by Thee, though very secretly. And whence know I, and whence confidently confess I unto Thee that I loved him more because of the love of those who praised him, than for the very things for which they praised him? Because had he been upraised, and these self-same men had dispraised him, and with dispraise and scorn told the same things of him, I should never have

been so inflamed and provoked to love him. And yet the things had not been different, nor he himself different, but only the affections of the narrators. See where lieth the impotent soul that is not yet sustained by the solidity of truth! Just as the blasts of tongues blow from the breasts of conjecturers, so is it tossed this way and that, driven forward and backward, and the light is obscured to it and the truth not perceived. And behold it is before us. And to me it was a great matter that my style and studies should be known to that man; the which if he approved, I were the more stimulated, but if he disapproved, this vain heart of mine, void of Thy solidity, had been offended. And yet that "fair and fit," about which I wrote to him, I reflected on with pleasure, and contemplated it, and admired it, though none joined me in doing so.

CHAP. XV.—WHILE WRITING, BEING BLINDED BY CORPOREAL IMAGES, HE FAILED TO RECOGNISE THE SPIRITUAL NATURE OF GOD.

24. But not yet did I perceive the hinge on which this impotent matter turned in Thy wisdom, O Thou Omnipotent, "who alone doest great wonders;"[4] and my mind ranged through corporeal forms, and I defined and distinguished as "fair," that which is so in itself, and "fit," that which is beautiful as it corresponds to some other thing; and this I supported by corporeal examples. And I turned my attention to the nature of the mind, but the false opinions which I entertained of spiritual things prevented me from seeing the truth. Yet the very power of truth forced itself on my gaze, and I turned away my throbbing soul from incorporeal substance, to lineaments, and colours, and bulky magnitudes. And not being able to perceive these in the mind, I thought I could not perceive my mind. And whereas in virtue I loved peace, and in viciousness I hated discord, in the former I distinguished unity, but in the latter a kind of division. And in that unity I conceived the rational soul and the nature of truth and of the chief good[5] to consist. But

[1] See vi. sec. 13, below.
[2] Matt. x. 29, 30.
[3] Eph. iv. 14.

[4] Ps. cxxxvi. 4.
[5] Augustin tells us (*De Civ. Dei*, xix. 1) that Varro, in his lost book *De Philosophia*, gives two hundred and eighty-eight different opinions as regards the chief good, and shows us how readily they may be reduced in number. Now, as then, philosophers ask the same questions. We have our hedonists, whose "good" is their own pleasure and happiness; our materialists, who would seek the common good of all; and our intuitionists, who aim at following the dictates of conscience. When the pretensions of these various schools are examined without prejudice, the conclusion is forced upon us that we must have recourse to Revelation for a reconcilement of the difficulties of the various systems; and that the philosophers, to employ Davidson's happy illustration (*Prophecies*, Introd.), forgetting that their faded taper has been insensibly kindled by gospel light, are attempting now, as in Augustin's time (*ibid.* sec. 4), "to fabricate for themselves a happiness in this life based upon a virtue as deceitful as it is proud." Christianity gives the golden key to the attainment of happiness, when it declares that "godliness is profitable for all things, having the promise of the life which now is, and of that which is to come" (1 Tim. iv. 8). It was a saying

in this division I, unfortunate one, imagined there was I know not what substance of irrational life, and the nature of the chief evil, which should not be a substance only, but real life also, and yet not emanating from Thee, O my God, from whom are all things. And yet the first I called a Monad, as if it had been a soul without sex,[1] but the other a Duad,—anger in deeds of violence, in deeds of passion, lust, —not knowing of what I talked. For I had not known or learned that neither was evil a substance, nor our soul that chief and unchangeable good.

25. For even as it is in the case of deeds of violence, if that emotion of the soul from whence the stimulus comes be depraved, and carry itself insolently and mutinously; and in acts of passion, if that affection of the soul whereby carnal pleasures are imbibed is unrestrained,—so do errors and false opinions contaminate the life, if the reasonable soul itself be depraved, as it was at that time in me, who was ignorant that it must be enlightened by another light that it may be partaker of truth, seeing that itself is not that nature of truth. "For Thou wilt light my candle; the Lord my God will enlighten my darkness;[2] and "of His fulness have all we received,"[3] for "that was the true Light which lighted every man that cometh into the world;"[4] for in Thee there is "no variableness, neither shadow of turning."[5]

26. But I pressed towards Thee, and was repelled by Thee that I might taste of death, for Thou "resistest the proud."[6] But what

prouder than for me, with a marvellous madness, to assert myself to be that by nature which Thou art? For whereas I was mutable,—so much being clear to me, for my very longing to become wise arose from the wish from worse to become better,—yet chose I rather to think Thee mutable, than myself not to be that which Thou art. Therefore was I repelled by Thee, and Thou resistedst my changeable stiffneckedness; and I imagined corporeal forms, and, being flesh, I accused flesh, and, being "a wind that passeth away,"[7] I returned not to Thee, but went wandering and wandering on towards those things that have no being, neither in Thee, nor in me, nor in the body. Neither were they created for me by Thy truth, but conceived by my vain conceit out of corporeal things. And I used to ask Thy faithful little ones, my fellowcitizens,—from whom I unconsciously stood exiled,—I used flippantly and foolishly to ask, "Why, then, doth the soul which God created err?" But I would not permit any one to ask me, "Why, then, doth God err?" And I contended that Thy immutable substance erred of constraint, rather than admit that my mutable substance had gone astray of free will, and erred as a punishment.[8]

27. I was about six or seven and twenty years of age when I wrote those volumes—meditating upon corporeal fictions, which clamoured in the ears of my heart. These I directed, O sweet

---

[7] Ps. lxxviii. 39.

[8] It may assist those unacquainted with Augustin's writings to understand the last three sections, if we set before them a brief view of the Manichæan speculations as to the good and evil principles, and the nature of the human soul:—(1) The Manichæans believed that there were two principles or substances, one good and the other evil, and that both were eternal and opposed one to the other. The good principle they called God, and the evil, matter or Hyle (*Con. Faust.* xxi. 1, 2). Faustus, in his argument with Augustin, admits that they sometimes called the evil nature "God," but simply as a conventional usage. Augustin says thereon (*ibid.* sec. 4): "Faustus glibly defends himself by saying, 'We speak not of two gods, but of God and Hyle;' but when you ask for the meaning of Hyle, you find that it is in fact another god. If the Manichæans gave the name of Hyle, as the ancients did, to the unformed matter which is susceptible of bodily forms, we should not accuse them of making two gods. But it is pure folly and madness to give to matter the power of forming bodies, or to deny that what has this power is God." Augustin alludes in the above passage to the Platonic theory of matter, which, as the late Dean Mansel has shown us (*Gnostic Heresies, Basilides,* etc.), resulted after his time in Pantheism, and which was entirely opposed to the dualism of Manichæus. It is to this "power of forming bodies" claimed for matter, then, that Augustin alludes in our text (sec. 24) as "not only a substance but real life also." (2) The human soul the Manichæans declared to be of the same nature as God, though not created by Him—it having originated in the intermingling of part of His being with the evil principle, in the conflict between the kingdoms of light and darkness (*in Ps.* cxl. sec. 10). Augustin says to Faustus: "You generally call your soul not a temple, but a part or member of God" (*Con. Faust.* xx. 15); and thus, "identifying themselves with the nature and substance of God" (*ibid.* xii. 13), they did not refer their sin to themselves, but to the race of darkness, and so did not "prevail over their sin." That is, they denied original sin, and asserted that it necessarily resulted from the soul's contact with the body. To this Augustin steadily replied, that as the soul was not of the nature of God, but created by Him and endowed with free will, man was responsible for his transgressions. Again, referring to the *Confessions,* we find Augustin speaking consistently with his then belief, when he says that he had not then learned that the soul was not a "chief and unchangeable good" (sec. 24), or that "it was not that nature of truth" (sec. 25); and that when he transgressed "he accused flesh" rather than himself; and, as a result of his Manichæan errors (sec. 26), "contended that God's immutable substance erred of constraint, rather than admit that his mutable substance had gone astray of free will, and erred as a punishment."

---

of Bacon (*Essay on Adversity*), that while "prosperity is the blessing of the Old Testament, adversity is the blessing of the New." He would have been nearer the truth had he said that while temporal rewards were the special promise of the Old Testament, spiritual rewards were the special promise of the New. For though Christ's immediate followers had to suffer "adversity" in the planting of our faith, adversity cannot properly be said to be the result of following Christ. It has yet to be shown that, on the whole, the greatest amount of real happiness does not result, even in this life, from a Christian life, for virtue is, even here, its own reward. The fulness of the reward, however, will only be received in the life to come. Augustin's remark, therefore, still holds good that "life eternal is the supreme good, and death eternal the supreme evil, and that to obtain the one and escape the other we must live rightly" (*ibid.* sec. 4); and again, that even in the midst of the troubles of life, "as we are saved, so we are made happy, by hope. And as we do not as yet possess a present, but look for a future salvation, so it is with our happiness, . . . we ought patiently to endure till we come to the ineffable enjoyment of unmixed good." See Abbé Anselme, *Sur le Souverain Bien,* vol. v. serm. 1; and the last chapter of Professor Sidgwick's *Methods of Ethics,* for the conclusions at which a mind at once lucid and dispassionate has arrived on this question.

[1] Or 'an unintelligent soul;' very good MSS. reading '*sensu*,' the majority, it appears, '*sexu*.' If we read '*sexu*,' the absolute unity of the first principle, or Monad, may be insisted upon, and in the inferior principle, divided into 'violence' and 'lust,' 'violence,' as implying strength, may be looked on as the male, 'lust' was, in mythology, represented as female; if we take '*sensu*' it will express the living but unintelligent soul of the world in the Manichæan, as a pantheistic system."—E. B. P.

[2] Ps. xviii. 28. Augustin constantly urges our recognition of the truth that God is the "Father of lights." From Him as our central sun, all light, whether of wisdom or knowledge, proceedeth, and if, changing the figure, our candle which He hath lighted be blown out, He again must light it. Compare *Enar. in Ps.* xciii. 147; and *Sermons,* 67 and 341.

[3] John i. 16.

[4] John i. 9.

[5] Jas. i. 17.

[6] Jas. iv. 6, and 1 Pet. v. 5.

Truth, to Thy inward melody, pondering on the "fair and fit," and longing to stay and listen to Thee, and to rejoice greatly at the Bridegroom's voice,[1] and I could not; for by the voices of my own errors was I driven forth, and by the weight of my own pride was I sinking into the lowest pit. For Thou didst not "make me to hear joy and gladness;" nor did the bones which were not yet humbled rejoice.[2]

CHAP. XVI.—HE VERY EASILY UNDERSTOOD THE LIBERAL ARTS AND THE CATEGORIES OF ARISTOTLE, BUT WITHOUT TRUE FRUIT.

28. And what did it profit me that, when scarce twenty years old, a book of Aristotle's, entitled *The Ten Predicaments*, fell into my hands,—on whose very name I hung as on something great and divine, when my rhetoric master of Carthage, and others who were esteemed learned, referred to it with cheeks swelling with pride,—I read it alone and understood it? And on my conferring with others, who said that with the assistance of very able masters—who not only explained it orally, but drew many things in the dust[3]—they scarcely understood it, and could tell me no more about it than I had acquired in reading it by myself alone? And the book appeared to me to speak plainly enough of substances, such as man is, and of their qualities,—such as the figure of a man, of what kind it is; and his stature, how many feet high; and his relationship, whose brother he is; or where placed, or when born; or whether he stands or sits, or is shod or armed, or does or suffers anything; and whatever innumerable things might be classed under these nine categories,[4]—of which I have given some examples,—or under that chief category of substance.

29. What did all this profit me, seeing it even hindered me, when, imagining that whatsoever existed was comprehended in those ten categories, I tried so to understand, O my God, Thy wonderful and unchangeable unity as if Thou also hadst been subjected to Thine own greatness or beauty, so that they should exist in Thee as their subject, like as in bodies, whereas Thou Thyself art Thy greatness and beauty? But a body is not great or fair because it is a body, seeing that, though it were less great or fair, it should nevertheless be a body. But that which I had conceived of Thee was falsehood, not truth,—fictions of my misery, not the supports of Thy blessedness. For Thou hadst commanded, and it was done in me, that the earth should bring forth briars and thorns to me,[5] and that with labour I should get my bread.[6]

30. And what did it profit me that I, the base slave of vile affections, read unaided, and understood, all the books that I could get of the so-called liberal arts? And I took delight in them, but knew not whence came whatever in them was true and certain. For my back then was to the light, and my face towards the things enlightened; whence my face, with which I discerned the things enlightened, was not itself enlightened. Whatever was written either on rhetoric or logic, geometry, music, or arithmetic, did I, without any great difficulty, and without the teaching of any man, understand, as Thou knowest, O Lord my God, because both quickness of comprehension and acuteness of perception are Thy gifts. Yet did I not thereupon sacrifice to Thee. So, then, it served not to my use, but rather to my destruction, since I went about to get so good a portion of my substance[7] into my own power; and I kept not my strength for Thee,[8] but went away from Thee into a far country, to waste it upon harlotries.[9] For what did good abilities profit me, if I did not employ them to good uses? For I did not perceive that those arts were acquired with great difficulty, even by the studious and those gifted with genius, until I endeavoured to explain them to such; and he was the most proficient in them who followed my explanations not too slowly.

31. But what did this profit me, supposing that Thou, O Lord God, the Truth, wert a bright and vast body,[10] and I a piece of that body? Perverseness too great! But such was I. Nor do I blush, O my God, to confess to Thee Thy mercies towards me, and to call upon Thee—I, who blushed not then to avow before men my blasphemies, and to bark against Thee. What profited me then my nimble wit in those sciences and all those knotty volumes, disentangled by me without help from a human master, seeing that I erred so odiously, and with such sacrilegious baseness, in the doctrine of piety? Or what impediment was it to Thy

---

[1] John iii. 29.
[2] Ps. li. 8, *Vulg.*
[3] As the mathematicians did their figures, in dust or sand.
[4] "The categories enumerated by Aristotle are οὐσία, πόσον, ποῖον, πρόστι, ποῦ, πότε, κεῖσθαι, ἔχειν, ποιεῖν, πάσχειν; which are usually rendered, as adequately as perhaps they can be in our language, substance, quantity, quality, relation, place, time, situation, possession, action, suffering. The catalogue (which certainly is but a very crude one) has been by some writers enlarged, as it is evident may easily be done by subdividing some of the heads; and by others curtailed, as it is no less evident that all may ultimately be referred to the two heads of *substance* and *attribute*, or, in the language of some logicians, 'accident'" (Whately's *Logic*, iv. 2, sec. 1, note). "These are called in Latin the *prædicaments*, because they can be said or predicated in the same sense of all other terms, as well as of all the objects denoted by them, whereas no other term can be correctly said of them, because no other is employed to express the full extent of their meaning" (Gillies, *Analysis of Aristotle*, c. 2).

[5] Isa. xxxii. 13.
[6] Gen. iii. 19.
[7] Luke xv. 12.
[8] Ps. lix. 9, *Vulg.*
[9] Luke xv. 13.
[10] See iii. 12; iv. 3, 12; v. 19.

little ones to have a far slower wit, seeing that they departed not far from Thee, that in the nest of Thy Church they might safely become fledged, and nourish the wings of charity by the food of a sound faith? O Lord our God, under the shadow of Thy wings let us hope,[1] defend us, and carry us. Thou wilt carry us both when little, and even to grey hairs wilt Thou carry us;[2] for our firmness, when it is Thou, then is it firmness; but when it is our own, then it is infirmity. Our good lives always with Thee, from which when we are averted we are perverted. Let us now, O Lord, return, that we be not overturned, because with Thee our good lives without any eclipse,—which good Thou Thyself art.[3] And we need not fear lest we should find no place unto which to return because we fell away from it; for when we were absent, our home—Thy Eternity—fell not.

[1] Ps. xxxvi. 7.
[2] Isa. xlvi. 4.

[3] See xi. sec. 5, note, below.

BOOK V.

HE DESCRIBES THE TWENTY-NINTH YEAR OF HIS AGE, IN WHICH, HAVING DISCOVERED THE FALLACIES OF THE MANICHÆANS, HE PROFESSED RHETORIC AT ROME AND MILAN. HAVING HEARD AMBROSE, HE BEGINS TO COME TO HIMSELF.

CHAP. I.—THAT IT BECOMES THE SOUL TO PRAISE GOD, AND TO CONFESS UNTO HIM.

1. ACCEPT the sacrifice of my confessions by the agency of my tongue, which Thou hast formed and quickened, that it may confess to Thy name; and heal Thou all my bones, and let them say, "Lord, who is like unto Thee?"[1] For neither does he who confesses to Thee teach Thee what may be passing within him, because a closed heart doth not exclude Thine eye, nor does man's hardness of heart repulse Thine hand, but Thou dissolvest it when Thou willest, either in pity or in vengeance, "and there is no one who can hide himself from Thy heat."[2] But let my soul praise Thee, that it may love Thee; and let it confess Thine own mercies to Thee, that it may praise Thee. Thy whole creation ceaseth not, nor is it silent in Thy praises—neither the spirit of man, by the voice directed unto Thee, nor animal nor corporeal things, by the voice of those meditating thereon;[3] so that our souls may from their weariness arise towards Thee, leaning on those things which Thou hast made, and passing on to Thee, who hast made them wonderfully; and there is there refreshment and true strength.

CHAP. II.—ON THE VANITY OF THOSE WHO WISHED TO ESCAPE THE OMNIPOTENT GOD.

2. Let the restless and the unjust depart and flee from Thee. Thou both seest them and distinguishest the shadows. And lo! all things with them are fair, yet are they themselves foul.[4] And how have they injured Thee?[5] Or in what have they disgraced Thy government, which is just and perfect from heaven even to the lowest parts of the earth. For whither fled they when they fled from Thy presence?[6] Or where dost Thou not find them? But they fled that they might not see Thee seeing them, and blinded might stumble against Thee;[7] since Thou forsakest nothing that Thou hast made[8]—that the unjust might stumble against Thee, and justly be hurt,[9] withdrawing themselves from Thy gentleness, and stumbling against Thine uprightness, and falling upon their own roughness. Forsooth, they know not that Thou art everywhere whom no place encompasseth, and that Thou alone art near even to those that remove far from Thee.[10] Let them, then, be con-

---

[1] Ps. xxxv. 10.
[2] Ps. xix. 6.
[3] St. Paul speaks of a "minding of the flesh" and a "minding of the spirit" (Rom. viii. 6, margin), and we are prone to be attracted and held by the carnal surroundings of life; that is, "quæ per carnem sentiri querunt id est per oculos, per aures, ceterosque corporis sensus" (De Vera Relig. xxiv.). But God would have us, as we meditate on the things that enter by the gates of the senses, to arise towards Him, through these His creatures. Our Father in heaven might have ordered His creation simply in a utilitarian way, letting, for example, hunger be satisfied without any of the pleasures of taste, and so of the other senses. But He has not so done. To every sense He has given its appropriate pleasure as well as its proper use. And though this presents to us a source of temptation, still ought we for it to praise His goodness to the full, and that corde ore opere.—Bradward. ii. c. 23. See also i. sec. 1, note 3, and iv. sec. 18, above.

[4] Augustin frequently recurs to the idea, that in God's overruling Providence, the foulness and sin of man does not disturb the order and fairness of the universe. He illustrates the idea by reference to music, painting, and oratory. "For as the beauty of a picture is increased by well-managed shadows, so, to the eye that has skill to discern it, the universe is beautified even by sinners, though, considered by themselves, their deformity is a sad blemish" (De Civ. Dei, xi. 23). So again, he says, God would never have created angels or men whose future wickedness he foreknew, unless He could turn them to the use of the good, "thus embellishing the course of the ages as it were an exquisite poem set off with antitheses" (ibid. xi. 18); and further on, in the same section, "as the oppositions of contraries lend beauty to language, so the beauty of the course of this world is achieved by the opposition of contraries, arranged, as it were, by an eloquence not of words, but of things." These reflections affected Augustin's views as to the last things. They seemed to him to render the idea entertained by Origen (De Princ. i. 6) and other Fathers as to a general restoration [ἀποκατάστασις] unnecessary. See Hagenbach's Hist. of Doct. etc. i. 383 (Clark).
[5] "In Scripture they are called God's enemies who oppose His rule not by nature but by vice, having no power to hurt Him, but only themselves. For they are His enemies not through their power to hurt, but by their will to oppose Him. For God is unchangeable, and wholly proof against injury" (De Civ. Dei, xii. 3).
[6] Ps. cxxxix. 7.
[7] Gen. xvi. 13, 14.
[8] Wisd. ii. 26. Old ver.
[9] He also refers to the injury man does himself by sin in ii. sec. 13, above; and elsewhere he suggests the law which underlies it: "The vice which makes those who are called God's enemies resist Him, is an evil not to God but to themselves. And to them it is an evil solely because it corrupts the good of their nature." And when we suffer for our sins we should thank God that we are not unpunished (De Civ. Dei, xii. 3). But if, when God punishes us, we still continue in our sin, we shall be more confirmed in habits of sin, and then, as Augustin in another place (in Ps. vii. 15) warns us, "our facility in sinning will be the punishment of God for our former yieldings to sin." See also Butler's Analogy, Pt. i. ch. 5, "On a state of probation as intended for moral discipline and improvement."
[10] Ps. lxxiii. 27.

79

verted and seek Thee; because not as they have forsaken their Çreator hast Thou forsaken Thy creature. Let them be converted and seek Thee; and behold, Thou art there in their hearts, in the hearts of those who confess to Thee, and cast themselves upon Thee, and weep on Thy bosom after their obdurate ways, even Thou gently wiping away their tears. And they weep the more, and rejoice in weeping, since Thou, O Lord, not man, flesh and blood, but Thou, Lord, who didst make, remakest and comfortest them. And where was I when I was seeking Thee? And Thou wert before me, but I had gone away even from myself; nor did I find myself, much less Thee!

CHAP. III.—HAVING HEARD FAUSTUS, THE MOST LEARNED BISHOP OF THE MANICHÆANS, HE DISCERNS THAT GOD, THE AUTHOR BOTH OF THINGS ANIMATE AND INANIMATE, CHIEFLY HAS CARE FOR THE HUMBLE.

3. Let me lay bare before my God that twenty-ninth year of my age. There had at this time come to Carthage a certain bishop of the Manichæans, by name Faustus, a great snare of the devil, and many were entangled by him through the allurement of his smooth speech; the which, although I did commend, yet could I separate from the truth of those things which I was eager to learn. Nor did I esteem the small dish of oratory so much as the science, which this their so praised Faustus placed before me to feed upon. Fame, indeed, had before spoken of him to me, as most skilled in all becoming learning, and pre-eminently skilled in the liberal sciences. And as I had read and retained in memory many injunctions of the philosophers, I used to compare some teachings of theirs with those long fables of the Manichæans; and the former things which they declared, who could only prevail so far as to estimate this lower world, while its lord they could by no means find out,[1] seemed to me the more probable. For Thou art great, O Lord, and hast "respect unto the lowly, but the proud Thou knowest afar off."[2] Nor dost Thou draw near but to the contrite heart,[3] nor art Thou found by the proud,[4]—not even could they number by cunning skill the stars and the sand, and measure the starry regions, and trace the courses of the planets.

4. For with their understanding and the capacity which Thou hast bestowed upon them they search out these things; and much have they found out, and foretold many years before, —the eclipses of those luminaries, the sun and moon, on what day, at what hour, and from how many particular points they were likely to come. Nor did their calculation fail them; and it came to pass even as they foretold. And they wrote down the rules found out, which are read at this day; and from these others foretell in what year, and in what month of the year, and on what day of the month, and at what hour of the day, and at what quarter of its light, either moon or sun is to be eclipsed, and thus it shall be even as it is foretold. And men who are ignorant of these things marvel and are amazed, and they that know them exult and are exalted; and by an impious pride, departing from Thee, and forsaking Thy light, they foretell a failure of the sun's light which is likely to occur so long before, but see not their own, which is now present. For they seek not religiously whence they have the ability wherewith they seek out these things. And finding that Thou hast made them, they give not themselves up to Thee, that Thou mayest preserve what Thou hast made, nor sacrifice themselves to Thee, even such as they have made themselves to be; nor do they slay their own pride, as fowls of the air,[5] nor their own curiosities, by which (like the fishes of the sea) they wander over the unknown paths of the abyss, nor their own extravagance, as the "beasts of the field,"[6] that Thou, Lord, "a consuming fire,"[7] mayest burn up their lifeless cares and renew them immortally.

5. But the way—Thy Word,[8] by whom Thou didst make these things which they number, and themselves who number, and the sense by which they perceive what they number, and the judgment out of which they number—they knew not, and that of Thy wisdom there is no number.[9] But the Only-begotten has been "made unto us wisdom, and righteousness, and sanctification,"[10] and has been numbered amongst us, and paid tribute to Cæsar.[11] This way, by which they might descend to Him from themselves, they knew not; nor that through Him they might ascend unto Him.[12] This way they knew not, and they think themselves exalted with the stars[13] and shining, and lo! they fell upon the earth,[14] and "their foolish heart

---

[5] He makes use of the same illustrations on Psalms viii. and xi., where the birds of the air represent the proud, the fishes of the sea those who have too great a curiosity, while the beasts of the field are those given to carnal pleasures. It will be seen that there is a correspondence between them and the lust of the flesh, the lust of the eye, and the pride of life, in 1 John ii. 16. See also above, Book iii. sec. 16; and below, Book x. sec. 41, etc.
[6] Ps. viii. 7, 8.
[7] Deut. iv. 24.
[8] John i. 3.
[9] Ps. cxlvii. 5, *Vulg.*
[10] 1 Cor. i. 30.
[11] Matt. xvii. 27.
[12] In *Sermon* 123, sec. 3, we have: "Christ as God is the country to which we go—Christ as man is the way by which we go." See note on Book iv. sec. 19, above.
[13] Isa. xiv. 13.
[14] Rev. xii. 4.

---

[1] Wisd. xiii. 9.
[2] Ps. cxxxviii. 6.
[3] Ps. xxxiv. 18, and cxlv. 18.
[4] See Book iv. sec. 19, note, above.

was darkened."[1] They say many true things concerning the creature; but Truth, the Artificer of the creature, they seek not with devotion, and hence they find Him not. Or if they find Him, knowing that He is God, they glorify Him not as God, neither are they thankful,[2] but become vain in their imaginations, and say that they themselves are wise,[3] attributing to themselves what is Thine; and by this, with most perverse blindness, they desire to impute to Thee what is their own, forging lies against Thee who art the Truth, and changing the glory of the incorruptible God into an image made like corruptible man, and to birds, and four-footed beasts, and creeping things,[4]—changing Thy truth into a lie, and worshipping and serving the creature more than the Creator.[5]

6. Many truths, however, concerning the creature did I retain from these men, and the cause appeared to me from calculations, the succession of seasons, and the visible manifestations of the stars; and I compared them with the sayings of Manichæus, who in his frenzy has written most extensively on these subjects, but discovered not any account either of the solstices, or the equinoxes, the eclipses of the luminaries, or anything of the kind I had learned in the books of secular philosophy. But therein I was ordered to believe, and yet it corresponded not with those rules acknowledged by calculation and my own sight, but was far different.

CHAP. IV.—THAT THE KNOWLEDGE OF TERRESTRIAL AND CELESTIAL THINGS DOES NOT GIVE HAPPINESS, BUT THE KNOWLEDGE OF GOD ONLY.

7. Doth, then, O Lord God of truth, whosoever knoweth those things therefore please Thee? For unhappy is the man who knoweth all those things, but knoweth Thee not; but happy is he who knoweth Thee, though these he may not know.[6] But he who knoweth both Thee and them is not the happier on account of them, but is happy on account of Thee only, if knowing Thee he glorify Thee as

God, and gives thanks, and becomes not vain in his thoughts.[7] But as he is happier who knows how to possess a tree, and for the use thereof renders thanks to Thee, although he may not know how many cubits high it is, or how wide it spreads, than he that measures it and counts all its branches, and neither owns it nor knows or loves its Creator; so a just man, whose is the entire world of wealth,[8] and who, as having nothing, yet possesseth all things[9] by cleaving unto Thee, to whom all things are subservient, though he know not even the circles of the Great Bear, yet it is foolish to doubt but that he may verily be better than he who can measure the heavens, and number the stars, and weigh the elements, but is forgetful of Thee, "who hast set in order all things in number, weight, and measure."[10]

CHAP. V.—OF MANICHÆUS PERTINACIOUSLY TEACHING FALSE DOCTRINES, AND PROUDLY ARROGATING TO HIMSELF THE HOLY SPIRIT.

8. But yet who was it that ordered Manichæus to write on these things likewise, skill in which was not necessary to piety? For Thou hast told man to behold piety and wisdom,[11] of which he might be in ignorance although having a complete knowledge of these other things; but since, knowing not these things, he yet most impudently dared to teach them, it is clear that he had no acquaintance with piety. For even when we have a knowledge of these worldly matters, it is folly to make a profession of them; but confession to Thee is piety. It was therefore with this view that this straying one spake much of these matters, that, standing convicted by those who had in truth learned them, the understanding that he really had in those more difficult things might be made plain. For he wished not to be lightly esteemed, but went about trying to persuade men " that the Holy Ghost, the Comforter and Enricher of Thy faithful ones, was with full authority personally resident in him."[12] When, therefore, it was dis-

---

[1] Rom. i. 21.
[2] Ibid.
[3] Rom. i. 22.
[4] Rom. i. 23.
[5] Rom. 1. 25.
[6] What a contrast does his attitude here present to his supreme regard for secular learning before his conversion! We have constantly in his writings expressions of the same kind. On Psalm ciii. he dilates lovingly on the fount of happiness the word of God is, as compared with the writings of Cicero, Tully, and Plato; and again on Psalm xxxviii. he shows that the word is the source of all true joy. So likewise in De Trin. iv. 1 : " That mind is more praiseworthy which knows even its own weakness, than that which, without regard to this, searches out and even comes to know the ways of the stars, or which holds fast such knowledge already acquired, while ignorant of the way by which itself to enter into its own proper health and strength. . . . Such a one has preferred to know his own weakness, rather than to know the walls of the world, the foundations of the earth, and the pinnacles of heaven." See iii. sec. 9, note, above.

[7] Rom. i. 21.
[8] Prov. xvii. 6, in the LXX.
[9] 2 Cor. vi. 10.
[10] Wisd. xi. 20.
[11] Job xxviii. 28 in LXX. reads : 'Ιδοὺ ἡ θεοσέβειά ἐστι σοφία.
[12] This claim of Manichæus was supported by referring to the Lord's promise (John xvi. 12, 13) to send the Holy Ghost, the Comforter, to guide the apostles into that truth which they were as yet "not able to bear." The Manichæans used the words " Paraclete" and " Comforter," as indeed the names of the other two persons of the blessed Trinity, in a sense entirely different from that of the gospel. These terms were little more than the bodily frame, the soul of which was his own heretical belief. Whenever opposition appeared between his belief and the teaching of Scripture, their ready answer was that the Scriptures had been corrupted (De Mor. Ecc. Cath. xxviii. and xxix.) ; and in such a case, as we find Faustus contending (Con. Faust. xxxii. 6), the Paraclete taught them what part to receive and what to reject, according to the promise of Jesus that He should " guide them into all truth," and much more to the same effect. Augustin's whole argument in reply is well worthy of attention. Amongst other things, he points out that the Manichæan pretension to having received the promised Paraclete was precisely the same as that of the Montanists in the previous century. It should be observed that Beausobre (Histoire,

covered that his teaching concerning the heavens and stars, and the motions of sun and moon, was false, though these things do not relate to the doctrine of religion, yet his sacrilegious arrogance would become sufficiently evident, seeing that not only did he affirm things of which he knew nothing, but also perverted them, and with such egregious vanity of pride as to seek to attribute them to himself as to a divine being.

9. For when I hear a Christian brother ignorant of these things, or in error concerning them, I can bear with patience to see that man hold to his opinions; nor can I apprehend that any want of knowledge as to the situation or nature of this material creation can be injurious to him, so long as he does not entertain belief in anything unworthy of Thee, O Lord, the Creator of all. But if he conceives it to pertain to the form of the doctrine of piety, and presumes to affirm with great obstinacy that whereof he is ignorant, therein lies the injury. And yet even a weakness such as this in the dawn of faith is borne by our Mother Charity, till the new man may grow up "unto a perfect man," and not be "carried about with every wind of doctrine."[1] But in him who thus presumed to be at once the teacher, author, head, and leader of all whom he could induce to believe this, so that all who followed him believed that they were following not a simple man only, but Thy Holy Spirit, who would not judge that such great insanity, when once it stood convicted of false teaching, should be abhorred and utterly cast off? But I had not yet clearly ascertained whether the changes of longer and shorter days and nights, and day and night itself, with the eclipses of the greater lights, and whatever of the like kind I had read in other books, could be expounded consistently with his words. Should I have found myself able to do so, there would still have remained a doubt in my mind whether it were so or no, although I might, on the strength of his reputed godliness,[2] rest my faith on his authority.

CHAP. VI.—FAUSTUS WAS INDEED AN ELEGANT SPEAKER, BUT KNEW NOTHING OF THE LIBERAL SCIENCES.

10. And for nearly the whole of those nine years during which, with unstable mind, I had been their follower, I had been looking forward with but too great eagerness for the arrival of this same Faustus. For the other members of the sect whom I had chanced to light upon, when unable to answer the questions I raised, always bade me look forward to his coming, when, by discoursing with him, these, and greater difficulties if I had them, would be most easily and amply cleared away. When at last he did come, I found him to be a man of pleasant speech, who spoke of the very same things as they themselves did, although more fluently, and in better language. But of what profit to me was the elegance of my cup-bearer, since he offered me not the more precious draught for which I thirsted? My ears were already satiated with similar things; neither did they appear to me more conclusive, because better expressed; nor true, because oratorical; nor the spirit necessarily wise, because the face was comely and the language eloquent. But they who extolled him to me were not competent judges; and therefore, as he was possessed of suavity of speech, he appeared to them to be prudent and wise. Another sort of persons, however, was, I was aware, suspicious even of truth itself, if enunciated in smooth and flowing language. But me, O my God, Thou hadst already instructed by wonderful and mysterious ways, and therefore I believe that Thou instructedst me because it is truth; nor of truth is there any other teacher—where or whencesoever it may shine upon us[3]—but Thee. From Thee, therefore, I had now learned, that because a thing is eloquently expressed, it should not of necessity seem to be true; nor, because uttered with stammering lips, should it be false; nor, again, perforce true, because unskilfully delivered; nor consequently untrue, because the language is fine; but that wisdom and folly are as food both wholesome and unwholesome, and courtly or simple words as town-made or rustic vessels,—and both kinds of food may be served in either kind of dish.

11. That eagerness, therefore, with which I had so long waited for this man was in truth delighted with his action and feeling when disputing, and the fluent and apt words with which he clothed his ideas. I was therefore filled with joy, and joined with others (and even exceeded them) in exalting and praising him. It was, however, a source of annoyance to me that I was not allowed at those meetings of his auditors to introduce and impart[4] any of those questions that troubled me in familiar exchange of arguments with him. When I might speak, and began, in conjunction with my friends, to engage his attention at such times as it was not unseeming for him to enter into a discussion with me,

i. 254, 264, etc.) vigorously rebuts the charge brought against Manichæus of claiming to *be* the Holy Ghost. An interesting examination of the claims of Montanus will be found in Kaye's *Tertullian*, pp. 13 to 33.
[1] Eph. iv. 13, 14.
[2] See vi. sec. 12, note, below.

[3] Sec. vii. sec. 15, below.
[4] "This was the old fashion of the East, where the scholars had liberty to ask questions of their masters, and to move doubts as the professors were reading, or so soon as the lecture was done. Thus did our Saviour with the doctors (Luke ii. 46). So it is still in some European Universities."—W. W.

and had mooted such questions as perplexed me, I discovered him first to know nothing of the liberal sciences save grammar, and that only in an ordinary way. Having, however, read some of Tully's *Orations*, a very few books of Seneca, and some of the poets, and such few volumes of his own sect as were written coherently in Latin, and being day by day practised in speaking, he so acquired a sort of eloquence, which proved the more delightful and enticing in that it was under the control of ready tact, and a sort of native grace. Is it not even as I recall, O Lord my God, Thou judge of my conscience? My heart and my memory are laid before Thee, who didst at that time direct me by the inscrutable mystery of Thy Providence, and didst set before my face those vile errors of mine, in order that I might see and loathe them.

CHAP. VII.—CLEARLY SEEING THE FALLACIES OF THE MANICHÆANS, HE RETIRES FROM THEM, BEING REMARKABLY AIDED BY GOD.

12. For when it became plain to me that he was ignorant of those arts in which I had believed him to excel, I began to despair of his clearing up and explaining all the perplexities which harassed me: though ignorant of these, however, he might still have held the truth of piety, had he not been a Manichæan. For their books are full of lengthy fables[1] concerning the heaven and stars, the sun and moon, and I had ceased to think him able to decide in a satisfactory manner what I ardently desired,

—whether, on comparing these things with the calculations I had read elsewhere, the explanations contained in the works of Manichæus were preferable, or at any rate equally sound? But when I proposed that these subjects should be deliberated upon and reasoned out, he very modestly did not dare to endure the burden. For he was aware that he had no knowledge of these things, and was not ashamed to confess it. For he was not one of those loquacious persons, many of whom I had been troubled with, who covenanted to teach me these things, and said nothing; but this man possessed a heart, which, though not right towards Thee, yet was not altogether false towards himself. For he was not altogether ignorant of his own ignorance, nor would he without due consideration be inveigled in a controversy, from which he could neither draw back nor extricate himself fairly. And for that I was even more pleased with him, for more beautiful is the modesty of an ingenuous mind than the acquisition of the knowledge I desired,—and such I found him to be in all the more abstruse and subtle questions.

13. My eagerness after the writings of Manichæus having thus received a check, and despairing even more of their other teachers,— seeing that in sundry things which puzzled me, he, so famous amongst them, had thus turned out,—I began to occupy myself with him in the study of that literature which he also much affected, and which I, as Professor of Rhetoric, was then engaged in teaching the young Carthaginian students, and in reading with him either what he expressed a wish to hear, or I deemed suited to his bent of mind. But all my endeavours by which I had concluded to improve in that sect, by acquaintance with that man, came completely to an end: not that I separated myself altogether from them, but, as one who could find nothing better, I determined in the meantime upon contenting myself with what I had in any way lighted upon, unless, by chance, something more desirable should present itself. Thus that Faustus, who had entrapped so many to their death,—neither willing nor witting it,—now began to loosen the snare in which I had been taken. For Thy hands, O my God, in the hidden design of Thy Providence, did not desert my soul; and out of the blood of my mother's heart, through the tears that she poured out by day and by night, was a sacrifice offered unto Thee for me; and by marvellous ways didst Thou deal with me.[2] It was Thou, O my God, who didst it, for the steps of a man are ordered by the Lord, and He shall dispose his way.[3] Or how can we procure salvation but from Thy hand, remaking what it hath made?

---

[1] We have referred in the note on iii. sec. 10, above, to the way in which the Manichæans parodied Scripture names. In these "fables" this is remarkably evidenced. "To these filthy rags of yours," says Augustin (*Con. Faust.* xx. 6), "you would unite the mystery of the Trinity; for you say that the Father dwells in a secret light, the power of the Son in the sun, and His wisdom in the moon, and the Holy Spirit in the air." The Manichæan doctrine as to the mixture of the divine nature with the substance of evil, and the way in which that nature was released by the "elect," has already been pointed out (see note iii. sec. 18, above). The part of sun and moon, also, in accomplishing this release, is alluded to in his *De Mor. Manich.* "This part of God," he says (c. xxxvi.), "is daily being set free in all parts of the world, and restored to its own domain. But in its passage upwards as vapour from earth to heaven, it enters plants, because their roots are fixed in the earth, and so gives fertility and strength to all herbs and shrubs." These parts of God, arrested in their rise by the vegetable world, were released, as above stated, by the "elect." All that escaped from them in the act of eating, as well as what was set free by evaporation, passed into the sun and moon, as into a kind of purgatorial state—they being purer light than the only recently emancipated good nature. In his letter to Januarius (*Ep.* lv. 6), he tells us that the moon's waxing and waning were said by the Manichæans to be caused by its receiving souls from matter as it were into a ship, and transferring them "into the sun as into another ship." The sun was called Christ, and was worshipped; and accordingly we find Augustin, after alluding to these monstrous doctrines, saying (*Con. Faust.* v. 11): "If your affections were set upon spiritual and intellectual good instead of material forms, you would not pay homage to the material sun as a divine substance and as the light of wisdom." Many other interesting quotations might be added, but we must content ourselves with the following. In his *Reply to Faustus* (xx. 6), he says : "You call the sun a ship, so that you are not only astray worlds off, as the saying is, but adrift. Next, while every one sees that the sun is round, which is the form corresponding from its perfection to his position among the heavenly bodies, you maintain that he is triangular [perhaps in allusion to the early symbol of the Trinity]; that is, that his light shines on the earth through a triangular window in heaven. Hence it is that you bend and bow your heads to the sun, while you worship not this visible sun, but some imaginary ship, which you suppose to be shining through a triangular opening."

[2] Joel ii. 26.
[3] Ps. xxxvii. 23.

CHAP. VIII.—HE SETS OUT FOR ROME, HIS MOTHER IN VAIN LAMENTING IT.

14. Thou dealedst with me, therefore, that I should be persuaded to go to Rome, and teach there rather what I was then teaching at Carthage. And how I was persuaded to do this, I will not fail to confess unto Thee; for in this also the profoundest workings of Thy wisdom, and Thy ever present mercy to usward, must be pondered and avowed. It was not my desire to go to Rome because greater advantages and dignities were guaranteed me by the friends who persuaded me into this,—although even at this period I was influenced by these considerations,—but my principal and almost sole motive was, that I had been informed that the youths studied more quietly there, and were kept under by the control of more rigid discipline, so that they did not capriciously and impudently rush into the school of a master not their own, into whose presence they were forbidden to enter unless with his consent. At Carthage, on the contrary, there was amongst the scholars a shameful and intemperate license. They burst in rudely, and, with almost furious gesticulations, interrupt the system which any one may have instituted for the good of his pupils. Many outrages they perpetrate with astounding phlegm, which would be punishable by law were they not sustained by custom; that custom showing them to be the more worthless, in that they now do, as according to law, what by Thy unchangeable law will never be lawful. And they fancy they do it with impunity, whereas the very blindness whereby they do it is their punishment, and they suffer far greater things than they do. The manners, then, which as a student I would not adopt,[1] I was compelled as a teacher to submit to from others; and so I was too glad to go where all who knew anything about it assured me that similar things were not done. But Thou, "my refuge and my portion in the land of the living,"[2] didst while at Carthage goad me, so that I might thereby be withdrawn from it, and exchange my worldly habitation for the preservation of my soul; whilst at Rome Thou didst offer me enticements by which to attract me there, by men enchanted with this dying life,—the one doing insane actions, and the other making assurances of vain things; and, in order to correct my footsteps, didst secretly employ their and my perversity. For both they who disturbed my tranquillity were blinded by a shameful madness, and they who allured me elsewhere smacked of the earth. And I, who hated real misery here, sought fictitious happiness there.

15. But the cause of my going thence and going thither, Thou, O God, knewest, yet revealedst it not, either to me or to my mother, who grievously lamented my journey, and went with me as far as the sea. But I deceived her, when she violently restrained me either that she might retain me or accompany me, and I pretended that I had a friend whom I could not quit until he had a favourable wind to set sail. And I lied to my mother—and such a mother!—and got away. For this also Thou hast in mercy pardoned me, saving me, thus replete with abominable pollutions, from the waters of the sea, for the water of Thy grace, whereby, when I was purified, the fountains of my mother's eyes should be dried, from which for me she day by day watered the ground under her face. And yet, refusing to go back without me, it was with difficulty I persuaded her to remain that night in a place quite close to our ship, where there was an oratory[3] in memory of the blessed Cyprian. That night I secretly left, but she was not backward in prayers and weeping. And what was it, O Lord, that she, with such an abundance of tears, was asking of Thee, but that Thou wouldest not permit me to sail? But Thou, mysteriously counselling and hearing the real purpose of her desire, granted not what she then asked, in order to make me what she was ever asking. The wind blew and filled our sails, and withdrew the shore from our sight; and she, wild with grief, was there on the morrow, and filled Thine ears with complaints and groans, which Thou didst disregard; whilst, by the means of my longings, Thou wert hastening me on to the cessation of all longing, and the gross part of her love to me was whipped out by the just lash of sorrow. But, like all mothers,—though even more than others,—she loved to have me with her, and knew not what joy Thou wert preparing for her by my absence. Being ignorant of this, she did weep and mourn, and in her agony was seen the inheritance of Eve,—seeking in sorrow what in sorrow she had brought forth. And yet, after accusing my perfidy and cruelty, she again continued her intercessions for me with Thee, returned to her accustomed place, and I to Rome.

CHAP. IX.—BEING ATTACKED BY FEVER, HE IS IN GREAT DANGER.

16. And behold, there was I received by the scourge of bodily sickness, and I was descending into hell burdened with all the sins that I had committed, both against Thee, myself, and others, many and grievous, over and above that bond of original sin whereby we all die in Adam.[4] For none of these things hadst Thou

---

[1] See iiii. sec. 6, note, above.
[2] Ps. cxlii. 5.

[3] See vi. sec. 2, note, below.
[4] 1 Cor. xv. 22.

forgiven me in Christ, neither had He "abolished" by His cross "the enmity"[1] which, by my sins, I had incurred with Thee. For how could He, by the crucifixion of a phantasm,[2] which I supposed Him to be? As true, then, was the death of my soul, as that of His flesh appeared to me to be untrue; and as true the death of His flesh as the life of my soul, which believed it not, was false. The fever increasing, I was now passing away and perishing. For had I then gone hence, whither should I have gone but into the fiery torments meet for my misdeeds, in the truth of Thy ordinance? She was ignorant of this, yet, while absent, prayed for me. But Thou, everywhere present, hearkened to her where she was, and hadst pity upon me where I was, that I should regain my bodily health, although still frenzied in my sacrilegious heart. For all that peril did not make me wish to be baptized, and I was better when, as a lad, I entreated it of my mother's piety, as I have already related and confessed.[3] But I had grown up to my own dishonour, and all the purposes of Thy medicine I madly derided,[4] who wouldst not suffer me, though such a one, to die a double death. Had my mother's heart been smitten with this wound, it never could have been cured. For I cannot sufficiently express the love she had for me, nor how she now travailed for me in the spirit with a far keener anguish than when she bore me in the flesh.

17. I cannot conceive, therefore, how she could have been healed if such a death of mine had transfixed the bowels of her love. Where then would have been her so earnest, frequent, and unintermitted prayers to Thee alone? But couldst Thou, most merciful God, despise the "contrite and humble heart"[5] of that pure and prudent widow, so constant in alms-deeds, so gracious and attentive to Thy saints, not permitting one day to pass without oblation at Thy altar, twice a day, at morning and even-tide, coming to Thy church without intermission—not for vain gossiping, nor old wives' "fables,"[6]

but in order that she might listen to Thee in Thy sermons, and Thou to her in her prayers?[7] Couldst Thou—Thou by whose gift she was such—despise and disregard without succouring the tears of such a one, wherewith she entreated Thee not for gold or silver, nor for any changing or fleeting good, but for the salvation of the soul of her son? By no means, Lord. Assuredly Thou wert near, and wert hearing and doing in that method in which Thou hadst predetermined that it should be done. Far be it from Thee that Thou shouldst delude her in those visions and the answers she had from Thee,—some of which I have spoken of,[8] and others not,[9]—which she kept[10] in her faithful breast, and, always petitioning, pressed upon Thee as Thine autograph. For Thou, "because Thy mercy endureth for ever,"[11] condescendest to those whose debts Thou hast pardoned, to become likewise a debtor by Thy promises.

CHAP. X.—WHEN HE HAD LEFT THE MANICHÆANS, HE RETAINED HIS DEPRAVED OPINIONS CONCERNING SIN AND THE ORIGIN OF THE SAVIOUR.

18. Thou restoredst me then from that illness, and made sound the son of Thy handmaid meanwhile in body, that he might live for Thee, to endow him with a higher and

---

[1] Eph. ii. 15, and Col. i. 20, etc.
[2] The Manichæan belief in regard to the unreal nature of Christ's body may be gathered from Augustin's *Reply to Faustus*: "You ask," argues Faustus (xxvi. i.), "if Jesus was not born, how did He die? . . . In return I ask you, how did Elias not die, though he was a man? Could a mortal encroach upon the limits of immortality, and could not Christ add to His immortality whatever experience of death was required? . . . Accordingly, if it is a good argument that Jesus was a man because He died, it is an equally good argument that Elias was not a man because he did not die. . . . As, from the outset of His taking the likeness of man, He underwent in appearance all the experiences of humanity, it was quite consistent that He should complete the system by appearing to die." So that with him the whole life of Jesus was a "phantasm." His birth, circumcision, crucifixion, baptism, and temptation were (*ibid.* xxxii. 7) the mere result of the interpolation of crafty men, or sprung from the ignorance of the apostles, when as yet they had not reached perfection in knowledge. It is noticeable that Augustin, referring to Eph. ii. 15, substitutes His cross for His flesh, he, as a Manichæan, not believing in the real humanity of the Son of God. See iii. sec. 9, note, above.
[3] See i. sec. 10, above.
[4] See also iv. sec. 8, above, where he derides his friend's baptism.
[5] Ps. li. 19.
[6] 1 Tim. v. 10.

[7] Watts gives the following note here:—"Oblations were those offerings of bread, meal, or wine, for making of the Eucharist, or of alms besides for the poor, which the primitive Christians every time they communicated brought to the church, where it was received by the deacons, who presented them to the priest or bishop. Here note: (1) They communicated daily; (2) they had service morning and evening, and two sermons a day many times," etc. An interesting trace of an old use in this matter of oblations is found in the Queen's Coronation Service. After other oblations had been offered, the Queen knelt before the Archbishop and presented to him "oblations" of bread and wine *for* the Holy Communion. See also Palmer's *Origines Liturgicæ*, iv. 8, who demonstrates by reference to patristic writers that the custom was universal in the primitive Church:—"But though all the churches of the East and West agreed in this respect, they differed in appointing the time and place at which the oblations of the people were received." It would appear from the following account of early Christian worship, that in the time of Justin Martyr the oblations were collected after the reception of the Lord's Supper. In his *First Apology* we read (c. lxvii.): "On the day called Sunday [τοῦ ἡλίου λεγομένη ἡμέρᾳ] all who live in cities or in the country gather together to one place, and the memoirs of the apostles or the writings of the prophets are read, as long as time permits them. When the reader has ceased, the president [ὁ προεστὼς] verbally instructs, and exhorts to the imitation of these good things. Then we all rise together and pray [εὐχὰς πέμπομεν], and, as we before said, when our prayer is ended, bread and wine and water are brought, and the president in like manner offers prayers and thanksgivings according to his ability [Kaye renders (p. 89) εὐχὰς ὁμοίως καὶ εὐχαριστίας, ὅση δύναμις αὐτῷ, ἀναπέμπει, "with his utmost power"], and the people assent, saying Amen; and there is a distribution to each, and a participation of that over which thanks had been given, and to those who are absent a portion is sent by the deacons. And they who are well-to-do, and willing, give what each thinks fit; and what is collected [τὸ συλλεγόμενον] is deposited with the president, who succours the orphans and widows, and those who, through sickness or any other cause, are in want, and those who are in bonds, and the stranger sojourning among us, and, in a word, takes care of all who are in need." The whole passage is given, as portions of it will be found to have a bearing on other parts of the *Confessions*. Bishop Kaye's *Justin Martyr*, c. iv., may be referred to for his view of the controverted points in the passage. See also Bingham's *Antiquities*, ii. 2–9; and notes to vi. sec. 2, and ix. secs. 6 and 27, below.
[8] See above, iii. 11, 12.
[9] *Ibid.* iii. 12.
[10] Luke ii. 19.
[11] Ps. cxviii. 1.

more enduring health. And even then at Rome I joined those deluding and deluded "saints;" not their "hearers" only,—of the number of whom was he in whose house I had fallen ill, and had recovered,—but those also whom they designate "The Elect."[1] For it still seemed to me "that it was not we that sin, but that I know not what other nature sinned in us."[2] And it gratified my pride to be free from blame, and, after I had committed any fault, not to acknowledge that I had done any,—"that Thou mightest heal my soul because it had sinned against Thee;"[3] but I loved to excuse it, and to accuse something else (I wot not what) which was with me, but was not I. But assuredly it was wholly I, and my impiety had divided me against myself; and that sin was all the more incurable in that I did not deem myself a sinner. And execrable iniquity it was, O God omnipotent, that I would rather have Thee to be overcome in me to my destruction, than myself of Thee to salvation! Not yet, therefore, hadst Thou set a watch before my mouth, and kept the door of my lips, that my heart might not incline to wicked speeches, to make excuses of sins, with men that work iniquity[4] —and, therefore, was I still united with their "Elect."

19. But now, hopeless of making proficiency in that false doctrine, even those things with which I had decided upon contenting myself, providing that I could find nothing better, I now held more loosely and negligently. For I was half inclined to believe that those philosophers whom they call "Academics"[5] were more sagacious than the rest, in that they held that we ought to doubt everything, and ruled that man had not the power of comprehending any truth; for so, not yet realizing their meaning, I also was fully persuaded that they thought just as they are commonly held to do. And I did not fail frankly to restrain in my host that assurance which I observed him to have in those fictions of which the works of Manichæus are full. Notwithstanding, I was on terms of more intimate friendship with them than with others who were not of this heresy. Nor did I defend it with my former ardour; still my familiarity with that sect (many of them being concealed in Rome) made me slower[6] to seek any other way,—particularly since I was hopeless of finding the truth, from which in Thy Church, O Lord of heaven and earth, Creator of all things visible and invisible, they had turned me aside, —and it seemed to me most unbecoming to believe Thee to have the form of human flesh, and to be bounded by the bodily lineaments of our members. And because, when I desired to meditate on my God, I knew not what to think of but a mass of bodies[7] (for what was not such did not seem to me to be), this was the greatest and almost sole cause of my inevitable error.

20. For hence I also believed evil to be a similar sort of substance, and to be possessed of its own foul and misshapen mass—whether dense, which they denominated earth, or thin and subtle, as is the body of the air, which they fancy some malignant spirit crawling through that earth. And because a piety—such as it was—compelled me to believe that the good God never created any evil nature, I conceived two masses, the one opposed to the other, both infinite, but the evil the more contracted, the good the more expansive. And from this mischievous commencement the other profanities followed on me. For when my mind tried to revert to the Catholic faith, I was cast back, since what I had held to be the Catholic faith was not so. And it appeared to me more de-

---

[1] See iv. sec. 1, note, above.
[2] iv. sec. 26, note 2, above.
[3] Ps. xli. 4.
[4] Ps. cxli. 3, 4, Old Vers. See also Augustin's Commentary on the Psalms, where, using his Septuagint version, he applies this passage to the Manichæans.
[5] "Amongst these philosophers," i.e. those who have founded their systems on denial, "some are satisfied with denying certainty, admitting at the same time probability, and these are the New Academics; the others, who are the Pyrrhonists, have denied even this probability, and have maintained that all things are equally certain and uncertain" (Port. Roy. Log. iv. 1). There are, according to the usual divisions, three Academies, the old, the middle, and the new; and some subdivide the middle and the new each into two schools, making five schools of thought in all. These begin with Plato, the founder (387 B.C.), and continue to the fifth school, founded by Antiochus (83 B.C.), who, by combining his teachings with that of Aristotle and Zeno, prepared the way for Neo-Platonism and its development of the dogmatic side of Plato's teaching. In the second Academic school, founded by Arcesilas,—of whom Aristo, the Stoic, parodying the line in the Iliad (vi. 181), Πρόσθε λέων, ὄπιθεν δὲ δράκων, μέσση δὲ χίμαιρα, said sarcastically he was "Plato in front, Pyrrho behind, and Diodorus in the middle," —the "sceptical" tendency in Platonism began to develope itself, which, under Carneades, was expanded into the doctrine of the third Academic school. Arcesilas had been a pupil of Polemo when he was head of the old Academy. Zeno also, dissatisfied with the cynical philosophy of Crates, had learnt Platonic doctrine from Polemo, and was, as Cicero tells us (De Fin. iv. 16), greatly influenced by his teaching. Zeno, however, soon founded his own school of Stoical philosophy, which was violently opposed by Arcesilas (Cicero, Acad. Post. i. 12). Arcesilas, according to Cicero (ibid.), taught his pupils that we cannot know anything, not even that we are unable to know. It is exceedingly probable, however, that he taught esoterically the doctrines of Plato to those of his pupils he thought able to receive them, keeping them back from the multitude because of the prevalence of the new doctrine. This appears to have been Augustin's view when he had arrived at a fuller knowledge of their doctrines than that he possessed at the time referred to in his Confessions. In his treatises against the Academicians (iii. 17) he maintains the wisdom of Arcesilas in this matter. He says: "As the multitude are prone to rush into false opinions, and, from being accustomed to bodies, readily, but to their hurt, believe everything to be corporeal, this most acute and learned man determined rather to unteach those who had suffered from bad teaching, than to teach those whom he did not think teachable." Again, in the first of his Letters, alluding to these treatises, he says: "It seems to me to be suitable enough to the times in which they flourished, that whatever issued pure from the fountain-head of Platonic philosophy should be rather conducted into dark and thorny thickets for the refreshment of a very few men, than left to flow in open meadow-land, where it would be impossible to keep it clear and pure from the inroads of the vulgar herd. I use the word 'herd' advisedly, for what is more brutish than the opinion that the soul is material?" and more to the same purpose. In his De Civ. Dei, xix. 18, he contrasts the uncertainty ascribed to the doctrines of these teachers with the certainty of the Christian faith. See Burton's Bampton Lectures, note 33, and Archer Butler's Ancient Philosophy, ii. 313, 348, etc. See also vii. sec. 13, note, below.
[6] See iii. sec. 21, above.
[7] See iv. secs. 3, 12, and 31, above.

vout to look upon Thee, my God,—to whom I make confession of Thy mercies,—as infinite, at least, on other sides, although on that side where the mass of evil was in opposition to Thee[1] I was compelled to confess Thee finite, that if on every side I should conceive Thee to be confined by the form of a human body. And better did it seem to me to believe that no evil had been created by Thee—which to me in my ignorance appeared not only some substance, but a bodily one, because I had no conception of the mind excepting as a subtle body, and that diffused in local spaces—than to believe that anything could emanate from Thee of such a kind as I considered the nature of evil to be. And our very Saviour Himself, also, Thine only-begotten,[2] I believed to have been reached forth, as it were, for our salvation out of the lump of Thy most effulgent mass, so as to believe nothing of Him but what I was able to imagine in my vanity. Such a nature, then, I thought could not be born of the Virgin Mary without being mingled with the flesh; and how that which I had thus figured to myself could be mingled without being contaminated, I saw not. I was afraid, therefore, to believe Him to be born in the flesh, lest I should be compelled to believe Him contaminated by the flesh.[3] Now will Thy spiritual ones blandly and lovingly smile at me if they shall read these my confessions; yet such was I.

CHAP. XI.—HELPIDIUS DISPUTED WELL AGAINST THE MANICHÆANS AS TO THE AUTHENTICITY OF THE NEW TESTAMENT.

21. Furthermore, whatever they had censured[4] in Thy Scriptures I thought impossible to be defended; and yet sometimes, indeed, I desired to confer on these several points with some one well learned in those books, and to try what he thought of them. For at this time the words of one Helpidius, speaking and disputing face to face against the said Manichæans, had begun to move me even at Carthage, in that he brought forth things from the Scriptures not easily withstood, to which their answer appeared to me feeble. And this answer they did not give forth publicly, but only to us in private, —when they said that the writings of the New Testament had been tampered with by I know

not whom, who were desirous of ingrafting the Jewish law upon the Christian faith;[5] but they themselves did not bring forward any uncorrupted copies.[6] But I, thinking of corporeal things, very much ensnared and in a measure stifled, was oppressed by those masses;[7] panting under which for the breath of Thy Truth, I was not able to breathe it pure and undefiled.

CHAP. XII.—PROFESSING RHETORIC AT ROME, HE DISCOVERS THE FRAUD OF HIS SCHOLARS.

22. Then began I assiduously to practise that for which I came to Rome—the teaching of rhetoric; and first to bring together at my home some to whom, and through whom, I had begun to be known; when, behold, I learnt that other offences were committed in Rome which I had not to bear in Africa. For those subvertings by abandoned young men were not practised here, as I had been informed; yet, suddenly, said they, to evade paying their master's fees, many of the youths conspire together, and remove themselves to another,—breakers of faith, who, for the love of money, set a small value on justice. These also my heart "hated," though not with a "perfect hatred;"[8] for, perhaps, I hated them more in that I was to suffer by them, than for the illicit acts they committed. Such of a truth are base persons, and they are unfaithful to Thee, loving these transitory mockeries of temporal things, and vile gain, which begrimes the hand that lays hold on it; and embracing the fleeting world, and scorning Thee, who abidest, and invitest to return, and pardonest the prostituted human soul when it returneth to Thee. And now I hate such crooked and perverse men, although I love them if they are to be corrected so as to prefer the learning they obtain to money, and to learning Thee, O God, the truth and fulness of certain good and most chaste peace. But then was the wish stronger in me for my own sake not to suffer them evil, than was the wish that they should become good for Thine.

CHAP. XIII.—HE IS SENT TO MILAN, THAT HE, ABOUT TO TEACH RHETORIC, MAY BE KNOWN BY AMBROSE.

23. When, therefore, they of Milan had sent

---

[1] See iv. 26, note 2, above.
[2] See above, sec. 12, note.
[3] The dualistic belief of the Manichæan ever led him to contend that Christ only appeared in a resemblance of flesh, and did not touch its substance so as to be defiled. Hence Faustus characteristically speaks of the Incarnation (*Con. Faust.* xxxii. 7) as "the shameful birth of Jesus from a woman," and when pressed (*ibid.* xi. 1) with such passages as, Christ was "born of the seed of David according to the flesh" (Rom. i. 3), he would fall back upon what in these days we are familiar with as that "higher criticism," which rejects such parts of Scripture as it is inconvenient to receive. Paul, he said, then only "spoke as a child" (1 Cor. xiii. 11), but when he became a man in doctrine, he put away childish things, and then declared, "Though we have known Christ after the flesh, yet now henceforth know we Him no more." See above, sec. 16, note 3.
[4] See iii. sec. 14, above.

[5] On this matter reference may be made to *Con. Faust.* xviii. 1, 3; xix. 5, 6; xxxiii. 1, 3.
[6] They might well not like to give the answer in public, for, as Augustin remarks (*De Mor. Eccles. Cath.* sec. 14), every one could see "that this is all that is left for men to say when it is proved that they are wrong." The astonishment that he experienced now, that they did "not bring forward any uncorrupted copies," had fast hold of him, and after his conversion he confronted them on this very ground. "You ought to bring forward," he says (*ibid.* sec. 61), "another manuscript with the same contents, but incorrupt and more correct, with only the passage wanting which you charge with being spurious. . . . You say you will not, lest you be suspected of corrupting it. This is your usual reply, and a true one." See also *De Mor. Manich.* sec. 55; and *Con. Faust.* xi. 2, xiii. 5, xviii. 7, xxii. 15, xxxii. 16.
[7] See above, sec. 19, *Fin.*
[8] Ps. cxxxix. 22.

to Rome to the prefect of the city, to provide them with a teacher of rhetoric for their city, and to despatch him at the public expense, I made interest through those identical persons, drunk with Manichæan vanities, to be freed from whom I was going away,—neither of us, however, being aware of it,—that Symmachus, the then prefect, having proved me by proposing a subject, would send me. And to Milan I came, unto Ambrose the bishop, known to the whole world as among the best of men, Thy devout servant; whose eloquent discourse did at that time strenuously dispense unto Thy people the flour of Thy wheat, the "gladness" of Thy "oil," and the sober intoxication of Thy "wine."[1] To him was I unknowingly led by Thee, that by him I might knowingly be led to Thee. That man of God received me like a father, and looked with a benevolent and episcopal kindliness on my change of abode. And I began to love him, not at first, indeed, as a teacher of the truth,—which I entirely despaired of in Thy Church,—but as a man friendly to myself. And I studiously hearkened to him preaching to the people, not with the motive I should, but, as it were, trying to discover whether his eloquence came up to the fame thereof, or flowed fuller or lower than was asserted; and I hung on his words intently, but of the matter I was but as a careless and contemptuous spectator; and I was delighted with the pleasantness of his speech, more erudite, yet less cheerful and soothing in manner, than that of Faustus. Of the matter, however, there could be no comparison; for the latter was straying amid Manichæan deceptions, whilst the former was teaching salvation most soundly. But "salvation is far from the wicked,"[2] such as I then stood before him; and yet I was drawing nearer gradually and unconsciously.

CHAP. XIV.—HAVING HEARD THE BISHOP, HE PERCEIVES THE FORCE OF THE CATHOLIC FAITH, YET DOUBTS, AFTER THE MANNER OF THE MODERN ACADEMICS.

24. For although I took no trouble to learn what he spake, but only to hear how he spake (for that empty care alone remained to me, despairing of a way accessible for man to Thee), yet, together with the words which I prized, there came into my mind also the things about which I was careless; for I could not separate them. And whilst I opened my heart to admit "how skilfully he spake," there also entered

with it, but gradually, "and how truly he spake!" For first, these things also had begun to appear to me to be defensible; and the Catholic faith, for which I had fancied nothing could be said against the attacks of the Manichæans, I now conceived might be maintained without presumption; especially after I had heard one or two parts of the Old Testament explained, and often allegorically—which when I accepted literally, I was "killed" spiritually.[3] Many places, then, of those books having been expounded to me, I now blamed my despair in having believed that no reply could be made to those who hated and derided[4] the Law and the Prophets. Yet I did not then see that for that reason the Catholic way was to be held because it had its learned advocates, who could at length, and not irrationally, answer objections; nor that what I held ought therefore to be condemned because both sides were equally defensible. For that way did not appear to me to be vanquished; nor yet did it seem to me to be victorious.

25. Hereupon did I earnestly bend my mind to see if in any way I could possibly prove the Manichæans guilty of falsehood. Could I have realized a spiritual substance, all their strongholds would have been beaten down, and cast utterly out of my mind; but I could not. But yet, concerning the body of this world, and the whole of nature, which the senses of the flesh can attain unto, I, now more and more considering and comparing things, judged that the greater part of the philosophers held much the more probable opinions. So, then, after the manner of the Academics (as they are supposed),[5] doubting of everything and fluctuating between all, I decided that the Manichæans were to be abandoned; judging that, even while in that period of doubt, I could not remain in a sect to which I preferred some of the philosophers; to which philosophers, however, because they were without the saving name of Christ, I utterly refused to commit the cure of my fainting soul. I resolved, therefore, to be a catechumen[6] in the Catholic Church, which my parents had commended to me, until something settled should manifest itself to me whither I might steer my course.[7]

---

[3] 1 Cor. xiii. 12, and 2 Cor. iii. 6. See vi. sec. 6, note, below.
[4] He frequently alludes to this scoffing spirit, so characteristic of these heretics. As an example, he says (in Ps. cxlvi. 13) : " There has sprung up a certain accursed sect of the Manichæans which derides the Scriptures it takes and reads. It wishes to censure what it does not understand, and by disturbing and censuring what it understands not, has deceived many." See also sec. 16, and iv. sec. 8, above.
[5] See above, sec. 19, and note.
[6] See vi. sec. 2, note, below.
[7] In his Benefit of Believing, Augustin adverts to the above experiences with a view to the conviction of his friend Honoratus, who was then a Manichæan.

---

[1] Ps. iv. 7, and civ. 15.
[2] Ps. cxix 155.

BOOK VI.

ATTAINING HIS THIRTIETH YEAR, HE, UNDER THE ADMONITION OF THE DISCOURSES OF AMBROSE, DIS-
COVERED MORE AND MORE THE TRUTH OF THE CATHOLIC DOCTRINE, AND DELIBERATES AS TO THE
BETTER REGULATION OF HIS LIFE.

CHAP. I.—HIS MOTHER HAVING FOLLOWED HIM
TO MILAN, DECLARES THAT SHE WILL NOT
DIE BEFORE HER SON SHALL HAVE EMBRACED
THE CATHOLIC FAITH.

1. O THOU, my hope from my youth,[1] where
wert Thou to me, and whither hadst Thou gone?
For in truth, hadst Thou not created me, and
made a difference between me and the beasts of
the field and fowls of the air? Thou hadst made
me wiser than they, yet did I wander about in
dark and slippery places, and sought Thee
abroad out of myself, and found not the God
of my heart;[2] and had entered the depths of
the sea, and distrusted and despaired finding
out the truth. By this time my mother, made
strong by her piety, had come to me, following
me over sea and land, in all perils feeling secure
in Thee. For in the dangers of the sea she
comforted the very sailors (to whom the inexperienced passengers, when alarmed, were wont
rather to go for comfort), assuring them of a
safe arrival, because she had been so assured by
Thee in a vision. She found me in grievous
danger, through despair of ever finding truth.
But when I had disclosed to her that I was now
no longer a Manichæan, though not yet a Catholic Christian, she did not leap for joy as at what
was unexpected; although she was now reassured
as to that part of my misery for which she had
mourned me as one dead, but who would be
raised to Thee, carrying me forth upon the bier
of her thoughts, that Thou mightest say unto
the widow's son, "Young man, I say unto Thee,
arise," and he should revive, and begin to speak,
and Thou shouldest deliver him to his mother.[3]
Her heart, then, was not agitated with any violent exultation, when she had heard that to be
already in so great a part accomplished which
she daily, with tears, entreated of Thee might
be done,—that though I had not yet grasped the
truth, I was rescued from falsehood. Yea,
rather, for that she was fully confident that

Thou, who hadst promised the whole, wouldst
give the rest, most calmly, and with a breast
full of confidence, she replied to me, "She
believed in Christ, that before she departed
this life, she would see me a Catholic believer."[4] And thus much said she to me; but
to Thee, O Fountain of mercies, poured she
out more frequent prayers and tears, that Thou
wouldest hasten Thy aid, and enlighten my
darkness; and she hurried all the more assiduously to the church, and hung upon the words
of Ambrose, praying for the fountain of water
that springeth up into everlasting life.[5] For she
loved that man as an angel of God, because she
knew that it was by him that I had been
brought, for the present, to that perplexing
state of agitation[6] I was now in, through which
she was fully persuaded that I should pass from

---

[4] *Fidelem Catholicum*—those who are baptized being usually designated *Fideles*. The following extract from Kaye's *Tertullian*
(pp. 230, 231) is worthy of note :—"As the converts from heathenism, to use Tertullian's expression, were not born, but became Christians [*fiunt, non nascuntur, Christiani*], they went through a
course of instruction in the principles and doctrines of the gospel,
and were subjected to a strict probation before they were admitted
to the rite of baptism. In this stage of their progress they were
called catechumens, of whom, according to Suicer, there were two
classes,—one called 'Audientes,' who had only entered upon their
course, and begun to hear the word of God ; the other, συναιτοῦντες,
or 'Competentes,' who had made such advances in Christian knowledge and practice as to be qualified to appear at the font. Tertullian,
however, appears either not to have known or to have neglected
this distinction, since he applies the names of 'Audientes' and 'Au-
ditores' indifferently to all who had not partaken of the rite of baptism. When the catechumens had given full proof of the ripeness
of their knowledge, and of the stedfastness of their faith, they were
baptized, admitted to the table of the Lord, and styled *Fideles*. The
importance which Tertullian attached to this previous probation of
the candidates for baptism, appears from the fact that he founds
upon the neglect of it one of his charges against the heretics.
'Among them,' he says, 'no distinction is made between the catechumen and the faithful or confirmed Christian ; the catechumen is
pronounced fit for baptism before he is instructed ; all come in indis-
criminately ; all hear, all pray together.'" There were certain peculiar forms used in the admission of catechumens ; as, for example,
anointing with oil, imposition of hands, and the consecration and
giving of salt ; and when, from the progress of Christianity, Tertullian's above description as to converts from heathenism had
ceased to be correct, these forms were continued in many churches
as part of the baptismal service, whether of infants or adults. See
Palmer's *Origines Liturgicæ*, v. 1, and also i. sec. 17, above, where
Augustin says : "I was signed with the sign of the cross, and was
seasoned with His salt, even from the womb of my mother."
[5] John iv. 14.
[6] "Sermons," says Goodwin in his *Evangelical Communicant*,
"are, for the most part, as showers of rain that water for the instant ; such as may tickle the ear and warm the affections, and put
the soul into a posture of obedience. Hence it is that men are ofttimes sermon-sick, as some are sea-sick ; very ill, much troubled for
the present, but by and by all is well again as they were."

---

[1] Ps. lxxi. 5.
[2] See iv. sec. 18, note, above.
[3] Luke vii. 12-15.

89

sickness unto health, after an excess, as it were, of a sharper fit, which doctors term the "crisis."

CHAP. II.—SHE, ON THE PROHIBITION OF AMBROSE, ABSTAINS FROM HONOURING THE MEMORY OF THE MARTYRS.

2. When, therefore, my mother had at one time—as was her custom in Africa—brought to the oratories built in the memory of the saints[1] certain cakes, and bread, and wine, and was forbidden by the door-keeper, so soon as she learnt that it was the bishop who had forbidden it, she so piously and obediently acceded to it, that I myself marvelled how readily she could bring herself to accuse her own custom, rather than question his prohibition. For wine-bibbing did not take possession of her spirit, nor did the love of wine stimulate her to hatred of the truth, as it doth too many, both male and female, who nauseate at a song of sobriety, as men well drunk at a draught of water. But she, when she had brought her basket with the festive meats, of which she would taste herself first and give the rest away, would never allow herself more than one little cup of wine, diluted according to her own temperate palate, which, out of courtesy, she would taste. And if there were many oratories of departed saints that ought to be honoured in the same way, she still carried round

with her the selfsame cup, to be used everywhere; and this, which was not only very much watered, but was also very tepid with carrying about, she would distribute by small sips to those around; for she sought their devotion, not pleasure. As soon, therefore, as she found this custom to be forbidden by that famous preacher and most pious prelate, even to those who would use it with moderation, lest thereby an occasion of excess[2] might be given to such as were drunken, and because these, so to say, festivals in honour of the dead were very like unto the superstition of the Gentiles, she most willingly abstained from it. And in lieu of a basket filled with fruits of the earth, she had learned to bring to the oratories of the martyrs a heart full of more purified petitions, and to give all that she could to the poor;[3] that so the communion of the Lord's body might be rightly celebrated there, where, after the example of His passion, the martyrs had been sacrificed and crowned. But yet it seems to me, O Lord my God, and thus my heart thinks of it in thy sight, that my mother perhaps would not so easily have given way to the relinquishment of this custom had it been forbidden by another whom she loved not as Ambrose,[4] whom, out of regard for my salvation, she loved most dearly; and he loved her truly, on account of her most religious conversation, whereby, in good works so "fervent in spirit,"[5] she frequented the church; so that he would often, when he saw me, burst forth into her praises, congratulating me that I had such a mother—little knowing what a son she had in me, who was in doubt as to all these things,

---

[1] That is, as is explained further on in the section, the *Martyrs.* Tertullian gives us many indications of the veneration in which the martyrs were held towards the close of the second century. The anniversary of the martyr's death was called his *natalitium*, or natal day, as his martyrdom ushered him into eternal life, and *oblationes pro defunctis* were then offered. (*De Exhor. Cast.* c. 11; *De Coro.* c. 3). Many extravagant things were said about the glory of martyrdom, with the view, doubtless, of preventing apostasy in time of persecution. It was described (*De Bap.* c. 16; and *De Pat.* c. 13) as a second baptism, and said to secure for a man immediate entrance into heaven, and complete enjoyment of its happiness. These views developed in Augustin's time into all the wildness of Donatism. Augustin gives us an insight into the customs prevailing in his day, and their significance, which greatly illustrates the present section. In his *De Civ. Dei*, viii. 27, we read : "But, nevertheless, we do not build temples, and ordain priests, rites, and sacrifices for these same martyrs; for they are not our gods, but their God is our God. Certainly we honour their reliquaries, as the memorials of holy men of God, who strove for the truth even to the death of their bodies, that the true religion might be made known, and false and fictitious religions exposed. . . . But who ever heard a priest of the faithful, standing at an altar built for the honour and worship of God over the holy body of some martyr, say in the prayers, I offer to thee a sacrifice, O Peter, or O Paul, or O Cyprian? For it is to God that sacrifices are offered at their tombs,—the God who made them both men and martyrs, and associated them with holy angels in celestial honour; and the reason why we pay such honours to their memory is, that by so doing we may both give thanks to the true God for their victories, and, by recalling them afresh to remembrance, may stir ourselves up to imitate them by seeking to obtain like crowns and palms, calling to our help that same God on whom they called. Therefore, whatever honours the religious may pay in the places of the martyrs, they are but honours rendered to their memory [*ornamenta memoriarum*], not sacred rites or sacrifices offered to dead men as to gods. And even such as bring thither food—which, indeed, is not done by the better Christians, and in most places of the world is not done at all—do so in order that it may be sanctified to them through the merits of the martyrs, in the name of the Lord of the martyrs, first presenting the food and offering prayer, and thereafter taking it away to be eaten, or to be in part bestowed upon the needy. But he who knows the one sacrifice of Christians, which is the sacrifice offered in those places, also knows that these are not sacrifices offered to the martyrs." He speaks to the same effect in Book xxii. sec. 10; and in his *Reply to Faustus* (xx. 21), who had charged the Christians with imitating the Pagans, "and appeasing the 'shades' of the departed with wine and food." See v. sec. 17, note.

[2] Following the example of Ambrose, Augustin used all his influence and eloquence to correct such shocking abuses in the churches. In his letter to Alypius, Bishop of Thagaste (when as yet only a presbyter assisting the venerable Valerius), he gives an account of his efforts to overcome them in the church of Hippo. The following passage is instructive (*Ep.* xxix. 9) :—" I explained to them the circumstances out of which this custom seems to have necessarily risen in the Church, namely, that when, in the peace which came after such numerous and violent persecutions, crowds of heathen who wished to assume the Christian religion were kept back, because, having been accustomed to celebrate the feasts connected with their worship of idols in revelling and drunkenness, they could not easily refrain from pleasures so hurtful and so habitual, it had seemed good to our ancestors, making for the time a concession to this infirmity, to permit them to celebrate, instead of the festivals which they renounced, other feasts in honour of the holy martyrs, which were observed, not as before with a profane design, but with similar self-indulgence."

[3] See v. sec. 17, note 5, above.

[4] On another occasion, when Monica's mind was exercised as to non-essentials, Ambrose gave her advice which has perhaps given origin to the proverb, "When at Rome, do as Rome does." It will be found in the letter to Casulanus (*Ep.* xxxvi. 32), and is as follows :—" When my mother was with me in that city, I, as being only a catechumen, felt no concern about these questions; but it was to her a question causing anxiety, whether she ought, after the custom of our own town, to fast on the Saturday, or, after the custom of the church of Milan, not to fast. To deliver her from perplexity, I put the question to the man of God whom I have first named. He answered, ' What else can I recommend to others than what I do myself?' When I thought that by this he intended simply to prescribe to us that we should take food on Saturdays,— for I knew this to be his own practice,—he, following me, added these words: ' When I am here I do not fast on Saturday, but when I am at Rome I do; whatever church you may come to, conform to its custom, if you would avoid either receiving or giving offence.' " We find the same incident referred to in *Ep.* liv. 3.

[5] Rom. xii. 11.

and did not imagine the way of life could be found out.

CHAP. III.—AS AMBROSE WAS OCCUPIED WITH BUSINESS AND STUDY, AUGUSTIN COULD SELDOM CONSULT HIM CONCERNING THE HOLY SCRIPTURES.

3. Nor did I now groan in my prayers that Thou wouldest help me; but my mind was wholly intent on knowledge, and eager to dispute. And Ambrose himself I esteemed a happy man, as the world counted happiness, in that such great personages held him in honour; only his celibacy appeared to me a painful thing. But what hope he cherished, what struggles he had against the temptations that beset his very excellences, what solace in adversities, and what savoury joys Thy bread possessed for the hidden mouth of his heart when ruminating[1] on it, I could neither conjecture, nor had I experienced. Nor did he know my embarrassments, nor the pit of my danger. For I could not request of him what I wished as I wished, in that I was debarred from hearing and speaking to him by crowds of busy people, whose infirmities he devoted himself to. With whom when he was not engaged (which was but a little time), he either was refreshing his body with necessary sustenance, or his mind with reading. But while reading, his eyes glanced over the pages, and his heart searched out the sense, but his voice and tongue were silent. Ofttimes, when we had come (for no one was forbidden to enter, nor was it his custom that the arrival of those who came should be announced to him), we saw him thus reading to himself, and never otherwise; and, having long sat in silence (for who durst interrupt one so intent?), we were fain to depart, inferring that in the little time he secured for the recruiting of his mind, free from the clamour of other men's business, he was unwilling to be taken off. And perchance he was fearful lest, if the author he studied should express aught vaguely, some doubtful and attentive hearer should ask him to expound it, or to discuss some of the more abstruse questions, as

that, his time being thus occupied, he could not turn over as many volumes as he wished; although the preservation of his voice, which was very easily weakened, might be the truer reason for his reading to himself. But whatever was his motive in so doing, doubtless in such a man was a good one.

4. But verily no opportunity could I find of ascertaining what I desired from that Thy so holy oracle, his breast, unless the thing might be entered into briefly. But those surgings in me required to find him at full leisure, that I might pour them out to him, but never were they able to find him so; and I heard him, indeed, every Lord's day, "rightly dividing the word of truth"[2] among the people; and I was all the more convinced that all those knots of crafty calumnies, which those deceivers of ours had knit against the divine books, could be unravelled. But so soon as I understood, withal, that man made "after the image of Him that created him"[3] was not so understood by Thy spiritual sons (whom of the Catholic mother Thou hadst begotten again through grace), as though they believed and imagined Thee to be bounded by human form,—although what was the nature of a spiritual substance[4] I had not the faintest or dimmest suspicion,—yet rejoicing, I blushed that for so many years I had barked, not against the Catholic faith, but against the fables of carnal imaginations. For I had been both impious and rash in this, that what I ought inquiring to have learnt, I had pronounced on condemning. For Thou, O most high and most near, most secret, yet most present, who hast not limbs some larger some smaller, but art wholly everywhere, and nowhere in space, nor art Thou of such corporeal form, yet hast Thou created man after Thine own image, and, behold, from head to foot is he confined by space.

CHAP. IV.—HE RECOGNISES THE FALSITY OF HIS OWN OPINIONS, AND COMMITS TO MEMORY THE SAYING OF AMBROSE.

5. As, then, I knew not how this image of Thine should subsist, I should have knocked and propounded the doubt how it was to be believed, and not have insultingly opposed it, as if it were believed. Anxiety, therefore, as to what to retain as certain, did all the more sharply gnaw into my soul, the more shame I felt that, having been so long deluded and de-

---

[1] In his *Reply to Faustus* (vi. 7), he, conformably with this idea, explains the division into clean and unclean beasts under the Levitical law symbolically. "No doubt," he says, "the animal is pronounced unclean by the law because it does not chew the cud, which is not a fault, but its nature. But the men of whom this animal is a symbol are unclean, not by nature, but from their own fault; because, though they gladly hear the words of wisdom, they never reflect on them afterwards. For to recall, in quiet repose, some useful instruction from the stomach of memory to the mouth of reflection, is a kind of spiritual rumination. The animals above mentioned are a symbol of those people who do not do this. And the prohibition of the flesh of these animals is a warning against this fault. Another passage of Scripture (Prov. xxi. 20) speaks of the precious treasure of wisdom, and describes ruminating as clean, and not ruminating as unclean: 'A precious treasure resteth in the mouth of a wise man, but a foolish man swallows it up.' Symbols of this kind, either in words or in things, give useful and pleasant exercise to intelligent minds in the way of inquiry and comparison."

[2] 2 Tim. ii. 15.
[3] Col. iii. 10, and Gen. i. 26, 27. And because we are created in the image of God, Augustin argues (*Serm.* lxxxviii. 6), we have the ability to see and know Him, just as, having eyes to see, we can look upon the sun. And hereafter, too (*Ep.* xcii. 3), "We shall see Him according to the measure in which we shall be like Him; because now the measure in which we do not see Him is according to the measure of our unlikeness to Him."
[4] See iii. sec. 12, note, above.

ceived by the promise of certainties, I had, with puerile error and petulance, prated of so many uncertainties as if they were certainties. For that they were falsehoods became apparent to me afterwards. However, I was certain that they were uncertain, and that I had formerly held them as certain when with a blind contentiousness I accused Thy Catholic Church, which though I had not yet discovered to teach truly, yet not to teach that of which I had so vehemently accused her. In this manner was I confounded and converted, and I rejoiced, O my God, that the one Church, the body of Thine only Son (wherein the name of Christ had been set upon me when an infant), did not appreciate these infantile trifles, nor maintained, in her sound doctrine, any tenet that would confine Thee, the Creator of all, in space—though ever so great and wide, yet bounded on all sides by the restraints of a human form.

6. I rejoiced also that the old Scriptures of the law and the prophets were laid before me, to be perused, not now with that eye to which they seemed most absurd before, when I censured Thy holy ones for so thinking, whereas in truth they thought not so; and with delight I heard Ambrose, in his sermons to the people, oftentimes most diligently recommend this text as a rule,—"The letter killeth, but the Spirit giveth life;"[1] whilst, drawing aside the mystic veil, he spiritually laid open that which, accepted according to the "letter," seemed to teach perverse doctrines—teaching herein nothing that offended me, though he taught such things as I knew not as yet whether they were true. For all this time I restrained my heart from assenting to anything, fearing to fall headlong; but by hanging in suspense I was the worse killed. For my desire was to be as well assured of those things that I saw not, as I was that seven and three are ten. For I was not so insane as to believe that this could not be comprehended; but I desired to have other things as clear as this, whether corporeal things, which were not present to my senses, or spiritual, whereof I knew not how to conceive except corporeally. And by believing I might have been cured, that so the sight of my soul being cleared,[2] it might in some way be directed towards Thy truth, which abideth always, and faileth in naught. But as it happens that he who has tried a bad physician fears to trust himself with a good one, so was it with the health of my soul, which could not be healed but by believing, and, lest it should believe falsehoods, refused to be cured—resisting Thy hands, who hast prepared for us the medicaments of faith, and hast applied them to the maladies of the whole world, and hast bestowed upon them so great authority.

CHAP. V.—FAITH IS THE BASIS OF HUMAN LIFE; MAN CANNOT DISCOVER THAT TRUTH WHICH HOLY SCRIPTURE HAS DISCLOSED.

7. From this, however, being led to prefer the Catholic doctrine, I felt that it was with more moderation and honesty that it commanded things to be believed that were not demonstrated

---

[1] 2 Cor. iii. 6. The spiritual or allegorical meaning here referred to is one that Augustin constantly sought, as did many of the early Fathers, both Greek and Latin. He only employs this method of interpretation, however, in a qualified way—never going to the lengths of Origen or Clement of Alexandria. He does not depreciate the letter of Scripture, though, as we have shown above (iii. sec. 14, note), he went as far as he well could in interpreting the history spiritually. He does not seem, however, quite consistent in his statements as to the relative prominence to be given to the literal and spiritual meanings, as may be seen by a comparison of the latter portions of secs. 1 and 3 of book xvii. of the *City of God.* His general idea may be gathered from the following passage in the 21st sec. of book xiii. :—"Some allegorize all that concerns paradise itself, where the first men, the parents of the human race, are, according to the truth of Holy Scripture, recorded to have been; and they understand all its trees and fruit-bearing plants as virtues and habits of life, as if they had no existence in the external world, but were only so spoken of or related for the sake of spiritual meanings. As if there could not be a real terrestrial paradise! As if there never existed these two women, Sarah and Hagar, nor the two sons who were born to Abraham, the one of the bond-woman, the other of the free, because the apostle says that in them the two covenants were prefigured! or as if water never flowed from the rock when Moses struck it, because therein Christ can be seen in a figure, as the same apostle says : ' Now that rock was Christ' (1 Cor. x. 4). . . . . These and similar allegorical interpretations may be suitably put upon paradise without giving offence to any one, while *yet we believe the strict truth of the history,* confirmed by its circumstantial narrative of facts." The allusion in the above passage to Sarah and Hagar invites the remark, that in Galatians iv. 24, the words in our version rendered, " which things are an allegory," should be, "which things are such as may be allegorized." [Ἅτινά ἐστιν ἀλληγορούμενα. See Jelf, 398, sec. 2.] It is important to note this, as the passage has been quoted in support of the more extreme method of allegorizing, though it could clearly go no further than to sanction allegorizing by way of spiritual meditation upon Scripture, and not in the interpretation of it—which first, as Waterland thinks (*Works,* vol. v. p. 311), was the end contemplated by most of the Fathers. Thoughtful students of Scripture will feel that we have no right to make historical facts typical or allegorical, unless (as in the case of the manna, the brazen serpent, Jacob's ladder, etc.) we have divine authority for so doing; and few such will dissent from the opinion of Bishop Marsh (Lecture vi.) that the type must not only resemble the antitype, but must have been *designed* to resemble it, and further, that we must have the authority of Scripture for the existence of such design. The text, " The letter killeth, but the Spirit giveth life," as a perusal of the context will show, has nothing whatever to do with either " literal " or " spiritual " meanings. Augustin himself interprets it in one place (*De Spir. et Lit.* cc. 4, 5) as meaning the killing letter of the law, as compared with the quickening power of the gospel. "An opinion," to conclude with the thoughtful words of Alfred Morris on this chapter (*Words for the Heart and Life,* p. 203), " once common must therefore be rejected. Some still talk of ' letter' and ' spirit' in a way which has no sanction here. The ' letter' with them is the literal meaning of the text, the ' spirit' is its symbolic meaning. And, as the ' spirit' possesses an evident superiority to the ' letter,' they fly away into the region of secret senses and hidden doctrines, find types where there is nothing typical, and allegories where there is nothing allegorical ; make Genesis more evangelical than the Epistle to the Romans, and Leviticus than the Epistle to the Hebrews ; mistaking lawful criticism for legal Christianity, they look upon the exercise of a sober judgment as a proof of a depraved taste, and forget that diseased as well as very powerful eyes may see more than others. It is not the obvious meaning and the secret meaning that are intended by ' letter' and ' spirit,' nor any two meanings of Christianity, nor two meanings of any thing or things, but the two systems of Moses and of Christ." Reference may be made on this whole subject of allegorical interpretation in the writings of the Fathers to Blunt's *Right Use of the Early Fathers,* series i. lecture 9.

[2] Augustin frequently dilates on this idea. In sermon 88 (cc. 5, 6, etc.), he makes the whole of the ministries of religion subservient to the clearing of the inner eye of the soul ; and in his *De Trin.* i. 3, he says : "And it is necessary to purge our minds, in order to be able to see ineffably that which is ineffable [*i. e.* the Godhead], whereto not having yet attained, we are to be nourished by faith, and led by such ways as are more suited to our capacity, that we may be rendered apt and able to comprehend it."

(whether it was that they could be demonstrated, but not to any one, or could not be demonstrated at all), than was the method of the Manichæans, where our credulity was mocked by audacious promise of knowledge, and then so many most fabulous and absurd things were forced upon belief because they were not capable of demonstration.[1] After that, O Lord, Thou, by little and little, with most gentle and most merciful hand, drawing and calming my heart, didst persuade me,—taking into consideration what a multiplicity of things which I had never seen, nor was present when they were enacted, like so many of the things in secular history, and so many accounts of places and cities which I had not seen ; so many of friends, so many of physicians, so many now of these men, now of those, which unless we should believe, we should do nothing at all in this life ; lastly, with how unalterable an assurance I believed of what parents I was born, which it would have been impossible for me to know otherwise than by hearsay,—taking into consideration all this, Thou persuadest me that not they who believed Thy books (which, with so great authority, Thou hast established among nearly all nations), but those who believed them not were to be blamed ;[2] and that those men were not to be listened unto who should say to me, "How dost thou know that those Scriptures were imparted unto mankind by the Spirit of the one true and most true God ?" For it was the same thing that was most of all to be believed, since no wranglings of blasphemous questions, whereof I had read so many amongst the self-contradicting philosophers, could once

wring the belief from me that Thou art,—whatsoever Thou wert, though what I knew not,—or that the government of human affairs belongs to Thee.

8. Thus much I believed, at one time more strongly than another, yet did I ever believe both that Thou wert, and hadst a care of us, although I was ignorant both what was to be thought of Thy substance, and what way led, or led back to Thee. Seeing, then, that we were too weak by unaided reason to find out the truth, and for this cause needed the authority of the holy writings, I had now begun to believe that Thou wouldest by no means have given such excellency of authority to those Scriptures throughout all lands, had it not been Thy will thereby to be believed in, and thereby sought. For now those things which heretofore appeared incongruous to me in the Scripture, and used to offend me, having heard divers of them expounded reasonably, I referred to the depth of the mysteries, and its authority seemed to me all the more venerable and worthy of religious belief, in that, while it was visible for all to read it, it reserved the majesty of its secret[3] within its profound significance, stooping to all in the great plainness of its language and lowliness of its style, yet exercising the application of such as are not light of heart ; that it might receive all into its common bosom, and through narrow passages waft over some few towards Thee, yet many more than if it did not stand upon such a height of authority, nor allured multitudes within its bosom by its holy humility. These things I meditated upon, and Thou wert with me ; I sighed, and Thou heardest me ; I vacillated, and Thou didst guide me ; I roamed through the broad way[4] of the world, and Thou didst not desert me.

CHAP. VI.—ON THE SOURCE AND CAUSE OF TRUE JOY,—THE EXAMPLE OF THE JOYOUS BEGGAR BEING ADDUCED.

9. I longed for honours, gains, wedlock ; and Thou mockedst me. In these desires I underwent most bitter hardships, Thou being the more gracious the less Thou didst suffer anything which was not Thou to grow sweet to me. Behold my heart, O Lord, who wouldest that I should recall all this, and confess unto Thee. Now let my soul cleave to Thee, which Thou hast freed from that fast-holding bird-lime of death. How wretched was it ! And Thou didst irritate the feeling of its wound, that, forsaking all else, it might be converted unto Thee, —who art above all, and without whom all things would be naught,—be converted and be healed.

---

[1] He similarly exalts the claims of the Christian Church over Manichæanism in his *Reply to Faustus* (xxxii. 19) : " If you submit to receive a load of endless fictions at the bidding of an obscure and irrational authority, so that you believe all those things because they are written in the books which your misguided judgment pronounces trustworthy, though there is no evidence of their truth, why not rather submit to the evidence of the gospel, which is so well-founded, so confirmed, so generally acknowledged and admired, and which has an unbroken series of testimonies from the apostles down to our own day, that so you may have an intelligent belief, and may come to know that all your objections are the fruit of folly and perversity?" And again, in his *Reply to Manichæus' Fundamental Epistle* (sec. 18), alluding to the credulity required in those who accept Manichæan teaching on the mere authority of the teacher : " Whoever thoughtlessly yields this becomes a Manichæan, not by knowing undoubted truth, but by believing doubtful statements. Such were we when in our inexperienced youth we were deceived."

[2] He has a like train of thought in another place (*De Fide Rer. quæ non Vid.* sec. 4) : " If, then (harmony being destroyed), human society itself would not stand if we believe not that we see not, how much more should we have faith in things, though we see them not ; which if we have it not, we do not violate the friendship of a few men, but the profoundest religion—so as to have as its consequence the profoundest misery." Again, referring to belief in Scripture, he argues (*Con. Faust.* xxxiii. 6) that, if we doubt its evidence, we may equally doubt that of any book, and asks, " How do we know the authorship of the works of Plato, Aristotle, Cicero, Varro, and other similar writers, but by the unbroken chain of evidence?" And once more he contends (*De Mor. Cath. Eccles.* xxix. 60) that, " The utter overthrow of all literature will follow, and there will be an end to all books handed down from the past, if what is supported by such a strong popular belief, and established by the uniform testimony of so many men and so many times, is brought into such suspicion that it is not allowed to have the credit and the authority of common history."

[3] See i. sec. 10, note, above.
[4] Matt. vii. 13.

How wretched was I at that time, and how didst Thou deal with me, to make me sensible of my wretchedness on that day wherein I was preparing to recite a panegyric on the Emperor,[1] wherein I was to deliver many a lie, and lying was to be applauded by those who knew I lied; and my heart panted with these cares, and boiled over with the feverishness of consuming thoughts. For, while walking along one of the streets of Milan, I observed a poor mendicant,—then, I imagine, with a full belly,—joking and joyous; and I sighed, and spake to the friends around me of the many sorrows resulting from our madness, for that by all such exertions of ours,—as those wherein I then laboured, dragging along, under the spur of desires, the burden of my own unhappiness, and by dragging increasing it,—we yet aimed only to attain that very joyousness which that mendicant had reached before us, who, perchance, never would attain it! For what he had obtained through a few begged pence, the same was I scheming for by many a wretched and tortuous turning,—the joy of a temporary felicity. For he verily possessed not true joy, but yet I, with these my ambitions, was seeking one much more untrue. And in truth he was joyous, I anxious; he free from care, I full of alarms. But should any one inquire of me whether I would rather be merry or fearful, I would reply, Merry. Again, were I asked whether I would rather be such as he was, or as I myself then was, I should elect to be myself, though beset with cares and alarms, but out of perversity; for was it so in truth? For I ought not to prefer myself to him because I happened to be more learned than he, seeing that I took no delight therein, but sought rather to please men by it; and that not to instruct, but only to please. Wherefore also didst Thou break my bones with the rod of Thy correction.[2]

10. Away with those, then, from my soul, who say unto it, "It makes a difference from whence a man's joy is derived. That mendicant rejoiced in drunkenness; thou longedst to rejoice in glory." What glory, O Lord? That which is not in Thee. For even as his was no true joy, so was mine no true glory;[3] and it subverted my soul more. He would digest his drunkenness that same night, but many a night had I slept with mine, and risen again with it, and was to sleep again and again to rise with it, I know not how oft. It does indeed "make a difference whence a man's joy is derived." I

know it is so, and that the joy of a faithful hope is incomparably beyond such vanity. Yea, and at that time was he beyond me, for he truly was the happier man; not only for that he was thoroughly steeped in mirth, I torn to pieces with cares, but he, by giving good wishes, had gotten wine, I, by lying, was following after pride. Much to this effect said I then to my dear friends, and I often marked in them how it fared with me; and I found that it went ill with me, and fretted, and doubled that very ill. And if any prosperity smiled upon me, I loathed to seize it, for almost before I could grasp it it flew away.

CHAP. VII.—HE LEADS TO REFORMATION HIS FRIEND ALYPIUS, SEIZED WITH MADNESS FOR THE CIRCENSIAN GAMES.

11. These things we, who lived like friends together, jointly deplored, but chiefly and most familiarly did I discuss them with Alypius and Nebridius, of whom Alypius was born in the same town as myself, his parents being of the highest rank there, but he being younger than I. For he had studied under me, first, when I taught in our own town, and afterwards at Carthage, and esteemed me highly, because I appeared to him good and learned; and I esteemed him for his innate love of virtue, which, in one of no great age, was sufficiently eminent. But the vortex of Carthaginian customs (amongst whom these frivolous spectacles are hotly followed) had inveigled him into the madness of the Circensian games. But while he was miserably tossed about therein, I was professing rhetoric there, and had a public school. As yet he did not give ear to my teaching, on account of some ill-feeling that had arisen between me and his father. I had then found how fatally he doted upon the circus, and was deeply grieved that he seemed likely—if, indeed, he had not already done so—to cast away his so great promise. Yet had I no means of advising, or by a sort of restraint reclaiming him, either by the kindness of a friend or by the authority of a master. For I imagined that his sentiments towards me were the same as his father's; but he was not such. Disregarding, therefore, his father's will in that matter, he commenced to salute me, and, coming into my lecture-room, to listen for a little and depart.

12. But it slipped my memory to deal with him, so that he should not, through a blind and headstrong desire of empty pastimes, undo so great a wit. But Thou, O Lord, who governest the helm of all Thou hast created, hadst not forgotten him, who was one day to be amongst Thy sons, the President of Thy sacrament;[4]

[1] In the Benedictine edition it is suggested that this was probably Valentinian the younger, whose court was, according to Possidius (c. i.), at Milan when Augustin was professor of rhetoric there, who writes (Con. Litt. Petil. iii. 25) that he in that city recited a panegyric to Bauto, the consul, on the first of January, according to the requirements of his profession of rhetoric.
[2] Prov. xxii. 15.
[3] Here, as elsewhere, we have the feeling which finds its expression in i. sec. 1, above: "Thou hast formed us for Thyself, and our hearts are restless till they find rest in Thee."

[4] Compare v. sec. 17, note, above, and sec. 15, note, below.

and that his amendment might plainly be attributed to Thyself, Thou broughtest it about through me, but I knowing nothing of it. For one day, when I was sitting in my accustomed place, with my scholars before me, he came in, saluted me, sat himself down, and fixed his attention on the subject I was then handling. It so happened that I had a passage in hand, which while I was explaining, a simile borrowed from the Circensian games occurred to me, as likely to make what I wished to convey pleasanter and plainer, imbued with a biting jibe at those whom that madness had enthralled. Thou knowest, O our God, that I had no thought at that time of curing Alypius of that plague. But he took it to himself, and thought that I would not have said it but for his sake. And what any other man would have made a ground of offence against me, this worthy young man took as a reason for being offended at himself, and for loving me more fervently. For Thou hast said it long ago, and written in Thy book, " Rebuke a wise man, and he will love thee." [1] But I had not rebuked him, but Thou, who makest use of all consciously or unconsciously, in that order which Thyself knowest (and that order is right), wroughtest out of my heart and tongue burning coals, by which Thou mightest set on fire and cure the hopeful mind thus languishing. Let him be silent in Thy praises who meditates not on Thy mercies, which from my inmost parts confess unto Thee. For he upon that speech rushed out from that so deep pit, wherein he was wilfully plunged, and was blinded by its miserable pastimes ; and he roused his mind with a resolute moderation ; whereupon all the filth of the Circensian pastimes [2] flew off from him, and he did not approach them further. Upon this, he prevailed with his reluctant father to let him be my pupil. He gave in and consented. And Alypius, beginning again to hear me, was involved in the same superstition as I was, loving in the Manichæans that ostentation of continency [3] which he believed to be true and unfeigned. It was, however, a senseless and seducing continency, ensnaring precious souls, not able as yet to reach the height of virtue, and easily beguiled with the veneer of what was but a shadowy and feigned virtue.

CHAP. VIII.—THE SAME WHEN AT ROME, BEING LED BY OTHERS INTO THE AMPHITHEATRE, IS DELIGHTED WITH THE GLADIATORIAL GAMES.

13. He, not relinquishing that worldly way which his parents had bewitched him to pursue, had gone before me to Rome, to study law, and there he was carried away in an extraordinary manner with an incredible eagerness after the gladiatorial shows. For, being utterly opposed to and detesting such spectacles, he was one day met by chance by divers of his acquaintance and fellow-students returning from dinner, and they with a friendly violence drew him, vehemently objecting and resisting, into the amphitheatre, on a day of these cruel and deadly shows, he thus protesting : " Though you drag my body to that place, and there place me, can you force me to give my mind and lend my eyes to these shows ? Thus shall I be absent while present, and so shall overcome both you and them." They hearing this, dragged him on nevertheless, desirous, perchance, to see whether he could do as he said. When they had arrived thither, and had taken their places as they could, the whole place became excited with the inhuman sports. But he, shutting up the doors of his eyes, forbade his mind to roam abroad after such naughtiness ; and would that he had shut his ears also ! For, upon the fall of one in the fight, a mighty cry from the whole audience stirring him strongly, he, overcome by curiosity, and prepared as it were to despise and rise superior to it, no matter what it were, opened his eyes, and was struck with a deeper wound in his soul than the other, whom he desired to see, was in his body ; [4] and

---

[1] Prov. ix. 8.

[2] The games in the provinces of the empire were on the same model as those held in the Circus Maximus at Rome, though not so imposing. This circus is one of those vast works executed by Tarquinius Priscus. Hardly a vestige of it at the present time remains, though the Cloaca Maxima, another of his stupendous works, has not, after more than 2500 years, a stone displaced, and still performs its appointed service of draining the city of Rome into the Tiber. In the circus were exhibited chariot and foot races, fights on horseback, representations of battles (on which occasion camps were pitched in the circus), and the Grecian athletic sports introduced after the conquest of that country. See also sec. 13, note, below.

[3] Augustin, in book v. sec. 9, above, refers to the reputed sanctity of Manichæus, and it may well be questioned whether the sect deserved that unmitigated reprobation he pours out upon them in his De Moribus, and in parts of his controversy with Faustus. Certain it is that Faustus laid claim, on behalf of his sect, to a very different moral character to that Augustin would impute to them. He says (Con. Faust. v. 1) : " Do I believe the gospel ? You ask me if I believe it, though my obedience to its commands shows that I do. I should rather ask you if you believe it, since you give no proof of your belief. I have left my father, mother, wife, and children, and all else that the Gospel requires (Matt. xix. 29) ; and do you ask if I believe the gospel ? Perhaps you do not know what is called the gospel. The gospel is nothing else than the preaching and the precept of Christ. I have parted with all gold and silver, and have left off carrying money in my purse ; content with daily food ; without anxiety for to-morrow ; and without solicitude about how I shall be fed, or wherewithal I shall be clothed : and do you ask if I believe the gospel ? You see in me the blessings of the gospel (Matt. v. 3-11) ; and do you ask if I believe the gospel ? You see me poor, meek, a peacemaker, pure in heart, mourning, hungering, thirsting, bearing persecutions and enmity for righteousness' sake ; and do you doubt my belief in the gospel ? " It is difficult to understand that Manichæanism can have spread as largely as it did at that time, if the asceticism of many amongst them had not been real. It may be noted that in his controversy with Fortunatus, Augustin strangely declines to discuss the charges of immorality that had been brought against the Manichæans : and in the last chapter of his De Moribus, it appears to be indicated that one, if not more, of those whose evil deeds are there spoken of had a desire to follow the rule of life laid down by Manichæus.

[4] The scene of this episode was, doubtless, the great Flavian Amphitheatre, known by us at this day as the Colosseum. It stands in the valley between the Cælian and Esquiline hills, on the site of a lake formerly attached to the palace of Nero. Gibbon, in his graphic way, says of the building (Decline and Fall, i. 355) : " Posterity admires, and will long admire, the awful remains of the amphitheatre of Titus, which so well deserved the epithet of colossal. It was a building of an elliptic figure, five hundred and sixty-four feet in length, and four hundred and sixty-seven in breadth, founded on

he fell more miserably than he on whose fall that mighty clamour was raised, which entered through his ears, and unlocked his eyes, to make way for the striking and beating down of his soul, which was bold rather than valiant hitherto; and so much the weaker in that it presumed on itself, which ought to have depended on Thee. For, directly he saw that blood, he therewith imbibed a sort of savageness; nor did he turn away, but fixed his eye, drinking in madness unconsciously, and was delighted with the guilty contest, and drunken

with the bloody pastime. Nor was he now the same he came in, but was one of the throng he came unto, and a true companion of those who had brought him thither. Why need I say more? He looked, shouted, was excited, carried away with him the madness which would stimulate him to return, not only with those who first enticed him, but also before them, yea, and to draw in others. And from all this didst Thou, with a most powerful and most merciful hand, pluck him, and taughtest him not to repose confidence in himself, but in Thee—but not till long after.

CHAP. IX.—INNOCENT ALYPIUS, BEING APPREHENDED AS A THIEF, IS SET AT LIBERTY BY THE CLEVERNESS OF AN ARCHITECT.

14. But this was all being stored up in his memory for a medicine hereafter. As was that also, that when he was yet studying under me at Carthage, and was meditating at noonday in the market-place upon what he had to recite (as scholars are wont to be exercised), Thou sufferedst him to be apprehended as a thief by the officers of the market-place. For no other reason, I apprehend, didst Thou, O our God, suffer it, but that he who was in the future to prove so great a man should now begin to learn that, in judging of causes, man should not with a reckless credulity readily be condemned by man. For as he was walking up and down alone before the judgment-seat with his tablets and pen, lo, a young man, one of the scholars, the real thief, privily bringing a hatchet, got in without Alypius' seeing him as far as the leaden bars which protect the silversmiths' shops, and began to cut away the lead. But the noise of the hatchet being heard, the silversmiths below began to make a stir, and sent to take in custody whomsoever they should find. But the thief, hearing their voices, ran away, leaving his hatchet, fearing to be taken with it. Now Alypius, who had not seen him come in, caught sight of him as he went out, and noted with what speed he made off. And, being curious to know the reasons, he entered the place, where, finding the hatchet, he stood wondering and pondering, when behold, those that were sent caught him alone, hatchet in hand, the noise whereof had startled them and brought them thither. They lay hold of him and drag him away, and, gathering the tenants of the market-place about them, boast of having taken a notorious thief, and thereupon he was being led away to apppear before the judge.

15. But thus far was he to be instructed. For immediately, O Lord, Thou camest to the succour of his innocency, whereof Thou wert the sole witness. For, as he was being led either to prison or to punishment, they were met by a

---

fourscore arches, and rising, with four successive orders of architecture, to the height of one hundred and forty feet. The outside of the edifice was encrusted with marble, and decorated with statues. The slopes of the vast concave which formed the inside were filled and surrounded with sixty or eighty rows of seats of marble, likewise covered with cushions, and capable of receiving with ease above fourscore thousand spectators. Sixty-four vomitories (for by that name the doors were very aptly distinguished) poured forth the immense multitude; and the entrances, passages, and staircases were contrived with such exquisite skill, that each person, whether of the senatorial, the equestrian, or the plebeian order, arrived at his destined place without trouble or confusion. Nothing was omitted which in any respect could be subservient to the convenience or pleasure of the spectators. They were protected from the sun and rain by an ample canopy occasionally drawn over their heads. The air was continually refreshed by the playing of fountains, and profusely impregnated by the grateful scent of aromatics. In the centre of the edifice, the arena, or stage, was strewed with the finest sand, and successively assumed the most different forms; at one moment it seemed to rise out of the earth, like the garden of the Hesperides, and was afterwards broken into the rocks and caverns of Thrace. The subterraneous pipes conveyed an inexhaustible supply of water; and what had just before appeared a level plain might be suddenly converted into a wide lake, covered with armed vessels and replenished with the monsters of the deep. In the decoration of these scenes the Roman emperors displayed their wealth and liberality; and we read, on various occasions, that the whole furniture of the amphitheatre consisted either of silver, or of gold, or of amber." In this magnificent building were enacted *venatios* or hunting scenes, sea-fights, and gladiatorial shows, in all of which the greatest lavishness was exhibited. The men engaged were for the most part either criminals or captives taken in war. On the occasion of the triumph of Trajan for his victory over the Dacians, it is said that ten thousand gladiators were engaged in combat, and that in the *naumachia* or sea-fight shown by Domitian, ships and men in force equal to two real fleets were engaged, at an enormous expenditure of human life. "If," says James Martineau (*Endeavours after the Christian Life*, pp. 261, 262), "you would witness a scene characteristic of the popular life of old, you must go to the amphitheatre of Rome, mingle with its eighty thousand spectators, and watch the eager faces of senators and people; observe how the masters of the world spend the wealth of conquest, and indulge the pride of power. See every wild creature that God has made to dwell, from the jungles of India to the mountains of Wales, from the forests of Germany to the deserts of Nubia, brought hither to be hunted down in artificial groves by thousands in an hour, behold the captives of war, noble, perhaps, and wise in their own land, turned loose, amid yells of insult, more terrible for their foreign tongue, to contend with brutal gladiators, trained to make death the favourite amusement, and present the most solemn of individual realities as a wholesale public sport; mark the light look with which the multitude, by uplifted finger, demands that the wounded combatant be slain before their eyes; notice the troop of Christian martyrs awaiting hand in hand the leap from the tiger's den. And when the day's spectacle is over, and the blood of two thousand victims stains the ring, follow the giddy crowd as it streams from the vomitories into the street, trace its lazy course into the Forum, and hear it there scrambling for the bread of private indolence doled out by the purse of public corruption; and see how it suns itself to sleep in the open ways, or crawls into foul dens till morning brings the hope of games and merry blood again;—and you have an idea of the Imperial people, and their passionate living for the moment, which the gospel found in occupation of the world." The desire for these shows increased as the empire advanced. Constantine failed to put a stop to them at Rome, though they were not admitted into the Christian capital he established at Constantinople. We have already shown (iii. sec. 2, note, above) how strongly attendance at stage-plays and scenes like these was condemned by the Christian teachers. The passion, however, for these exhibitions was so great, that they were only brought to an end after the monk Telemachus—horrified that Christians should witness such scenes—had been battered to death by the people in their rage at his flinging himself between the swordsmen to stop the combat. This tragic episode occurred in the year 403, at a show held in commemoration of a temporary success over the troops of Alaric.

certain architect, who had the chief charge of the public buildings. They were specially glad to come across him, by whom they used to be suspected of stealing the goods lost out of the market-place, as though at last to convince him by whom these thefts were committed. He, however, had at divers times seen Alypius at the house of a certain senator, whom he was wont to visit to pay his respects; and, recognising him at once, he took him aside by the hand, and inquiring of him the cause of so great a misfortune, heard the whole affair, and commanded all the rabble then present (who were very uproarious and full of threatenings) to go with him. And they came to the house of the young man who had committed the deed. There, before the door, was a lad so young as not to refrain from disclosing the whole through the fear of injuring his master. For he had followed his master to the market-place. Whom, so soon as Alypius recognised, he intimated it to the architect; and he, showing the hatchet to the lad, asked him to whom it belonged. "To us," quoth he immediately; and on being further interrogated, he disclosed everything. Thus, the crime being transferred to that house, and the rabble shamed, which had begun to triumph over Alypius, he, the future dispenser of Thy word, and an examiner of numerous causes in Thy Church,[1] went away better experienced and instructed.

CHAP. X.—THE WONDERFUL INTEGRITY OF ALYPIUS IN JUDGMENT. THE LASTING FRIENDSHIP OF NEBRIDIUS WITH AUGUSTIN.

16. Him, therefore, had I lighted upon at Rome, and he clung to me by a most strong tie, and accompanied me to Milan, both that he might not leave me, and that he might practise something of the law he had studied, more with a view of pleasing his parents than himself. There had he thrice sat as assessor with an uncorruptness wondered at by others, he rather wondering at those who could prefer gold to integrity. His character was tested, also, not only by the bait of covetousness, but by the spur of fear. At Rome, he was assessor to the Count of the Italian Treasury.[2] There was at that time a most potent senator, to whose favours many were indebted, of whom also many stood in fear. He would fain, by his usual power, have a thing granted him which was forbidden by the

laws. This Alypius resisted; a bribe was promised, he scorned it with all his heart; threats were employed, he trampled them under foot, —all men being astonished at so rare a spirit, which neither coveted the friendship nor feared the enmity of a man at once so powerful and so greatly famed for his innumerable means of doing good or ill. Even the judge whose councillor Alypius was, although also unwilling that it should be done, yet did not openly refuse it, but put the matter off upon Alypius, alleging that it was he who would not permit him to do it; for verily, had the judge done it, Alypius would have decided otherwise. With this one thing in the way of learning was he very nearly led away,—that he might have books copied for him at prætorian prices.[3] But, consulting justice, he changed his mind for the better, esteeming equity, whereby he was hindered, more gainful than the power whereby he was permitted. These are little things, but "He that is faithful in that which is least, is faithful also in much."[4] Nor can that possibly be void which proceedeth out of the mouth of Thy Truth. "If, therefore, ye have not been faithful in the unrighteous mammon, who will commit to your trust the true riches? And if ye have not been faithful in that which is another man's, who shall give you that which is your own?"[5] He, being such, did at that time cling to me, and wavered in purpose, as I did, what course of life was to be taken.

17. Nebridius also, who had left his native country near Carthage, and Carthage itself, where he had usually lived, leaving behind his fine paternal estate, his house, and his mother, who intended not to follow him, had come to Milan, for no other reason than that he might live with me in a most ardent search after truth and wisdom. Like me he sighed, like me he wavered, an ardent seeker after true life, and a most acute examiner of the most abstruse questions.[6] So were there three begging mouths, sighing out their wants one to the other, and waiting upon Thee, that Thou mightest give them their meat in due season.[7] And in all the bitterness which by Thy mercy followed our worldly pursuits, as we contemplated the end, why this suffering should be ours, darkness came upon us; and we turned away groaning and exclaiming, "How long shall these things be?" And this we often said; and saying so, we did not relinquish them, for as yet we had discovered noth-

---

1 "Alypius became Bishop of Thagaste (Aug. *De Gestis c. Emerit.* secs. 1 and 5). On the necessity which bishops were under of hearing secular causes, and its use, see Bingham, ii. c. 7."—E. B. P.
2 "The Lord High Treasurer of the Western Empire was called *Comes Sacrarum largitionum.* He had six other treasurers in so many provinces under him, whereof he of Italy was one under whom this Alypius had some office of judicature, something like (though far inferior) to our Baron of the Exchequer. See Sir Henry Spelman's *Glossary,* in the word *Comes;* and Cassiodor, Var. v. c. 40."—W. W.

3 *Pretiis prætorianis.* Du Cange says that "*Pretium regium* is the right of a king or lord to purchase commodities at a certain and definite price." This may perhaps help us to understand the phrase as above employed.
4 Luke xvi. 10.
5 Luke xvi. 11, 12.
6 Augustin makes a similar allusion to Nebridius' ardour in examining difficult questions, especially those which refer *ad doctrinam pietatis,* in his 98th Epistle.
7 Ps. cxlv. 15.

ing certain to which, when relinquished, we might betake ourselves.

CHAP. XI.—BEING TROUBLED BY HIS GRIEVOUS ERRORS, HE MEDITATES ENTERING ON A NEW LIFE.

18. And I, puzzling over and reviewing these things, most marvelled at the length of time from that my nineteenth year, wherein I began to be inflamed with the desire of wisdom, resolving, when I had found her, to forsake all the empty hopes and lying insanities of vain desires. And behold, I was now getting on to my thirtieth year, sticking in the same mire, eager for the enjoyment of things present, which fly away and destroy me, whilst I say, "To-morrow I shall discover it; behold, it will appear plainly, and I shall seize it; behold, Faustus will come and explain everything! O ye great men, ye Academicians, it is then true that nothing certain for the ordering of life can be attained! Nay, let us search the more diligently, and let us not despair. Lo, the things in the ecclesiastical books, which appeared to us absurd aforetime, do not appear so now, and may be otherwise and honestly interpreted. I will set my feet upon that step, where, as a child, my parents placed me, until the clear truth be discovered. But where and when shall it be sought? Ambrose has no leisure,—we have no leisure to read. Where are we to find the books? Whence or when procure them? From whom borrow them? Let set times be appointed, and certain hours be set apart for the health of the soul. Great hope has risen upon us, the Catholic faith doth not teach what we conceived, and vainly accused it of. Her learned ones hold it as an abomination to believe that God is limited by the form of a human body. And do we doubt to 'knock,' in order that the rest may be 'opened'?[1] The mornings are taken up by our scholars; how do we employ the rest of the day? Why do we not set about this? But when, then, pay our respects to our great friends, of whose favours we stand in need? When prepare what our scholars buy from us? When recreate ourselves, relaxing our minds from the pressure of care?"

19. "Perish everything, and let us dismiss these empty vanities, and betake ourselves solely to the search after truth! Life is miserable, death uncertain. If it creeps upon us suddenly, in what state shall we depart hence, and where shall we learn what we have neglected here? Or rather shall we not suffer the punishment of this negligence? What if death itself should cut off and put an end to all care and feeling? This also, then, must be inquired into. But

God forbid that it should be so. It is not without reason, it is no empty thing, that the so eminent height of the authority of the Christian faith is diffused throughout the entire world. Never would such and so great things be wrought for us, if, by the death of the body, the life of the soul were destroyed. Why, therefore, do we delay to abandon our hopes of this world, and give ourselves wholly to seek after God and the blessed life? But stay! Even those things are enjoyable; and they possess some and no little sweetness. We must not abandon them lightly, for it would be a shame to return to them again. Behold, now is it a great matter to obtain some post of honour! And what more could we desire? We have crowds of influential friends, though we have nothing else, and if we make haste a presidentship may be offered us; and a wife with some money, that she increase not our expenses; and this shall be the height of desire. Many men, who are great and worthy of imitation, have applied themselves to the study of wisdom in the marriage state."

20. Whilst I talked of these things, and these winds veered about and tossed my heart hither and thither, the time passed on; but I was slow to turn to the Lord, and from day to day deferred to live in Thee, and deferred not daily to die in myself. Being enamoured of a happy life, I yet feared it in its own abode, and, fleeing from it, sought after it. I conceived that I should be too unhappy were I deprived of the embracements of a woman;[2] and of Thy merciful medicine to cure that infirmity I thought not, not having tried it. As regards continency, I imagined it to be under the control of our own strength (though in myself I found it not), being so foolish as not to know what is written, that none can be continent unless Thou give it;[3] and that Thou wouldst give it, if with heartfelt groaning I should knock at Thine ears, and should with firm faith cast my care upon Thee.

CHAP. XII.—DISCUSSION WITH ALYPIUS CONCERNING A LIFE OF CELIBACY.

21. It was in truth Alypius who prevented me from marrying, alleging that thus we could

---

[1] Matt. vii. 7.

[2] "I was entangled in the life of this world, clinging to dull hopes of a beauteous wife, the pomp of riches, the emptiness of honours, and the other hurtful and destructive pleasures" (Aug. *De Util. Credendi*, sec. 3). "After I had shaken off the Manichæans and escaped, especially when I had crossed the sea, the Academics long detained me tossing in the waves, winds from all quarters beating against my helm. And so I came to this shore, and there found a pole-star to whom to entrust myself. For I often observed in the discourses of our priest [Ambrose], and sometimes in yours [Theodorus], that you had no corporeal notions when you thought of God, or even of the soul, which of all things is next to God. But I was withheld, I own, from casting myself speedily into the bosom of true wisdom by the alluring hopes of marriage and honours; meaning, when I had obtained these, to press (as few singularly happy had before me) with oar and sail into that haven, and there rest" (Aug. *De Vita Beata*, sec. 4).—E. B. P.

[3] Wisd. viii. 2, *Vulg.*

by no means live together, having so much un-distracted leisure in the love of wisdom, as we had long desired. For he himself was so chaste in this matter that it was wonderful—all the more, too, that in his early youth he had entered upon that path, but had not clung to it; rather had he, feeling sorrow and disgust at it, lived from that time to the present most continently. But I opposed him with the examples of those who as married men had loved wisdom, found favour with God, and walked faithfully and lov-ingly with their friends. From the greatness of whose spirit I fell far short, and, enthralled with the disease of the flesh and its deadly sweetness, dragged my chain along, fearing to be loosed, and, as if it pressed my wound, re-jected his kind expostulations, as it were the hand of one who would unchain me. More-over, it was by me that the serpent spake unto Alypius himself, weaving and laying in his path, by my tongue, pleasant snares, wherein his hon-ourable and free feet[1] might be entangled.

22. For when he wondered that I, for whom he had no slight esteem, stuck so fast in the bird-lime of that pleasure as to affirm whenever we discussed the matter that it would be impos-sible for me to lead a single life, and urged in my defence when I saw him wonder that there was a vast difference between the life that he had tried by stealth and snatches (of which he had now but a faint recollection, and might therefore, without regret, easily despise), and my sustained acquaintance with it, whereto if but the honourable name of marriage were added, he would not then be astonished at my inability to contemn that course,—then began he also to wish to be married, not as if overpowered by the lust of such pleasure, but from curiosity. For, as he said, he was anxious to know what that could be without which my life, which was so pleasing to him, seemed to me not life but a penalty. For his mind, free from that chain, was astounded at my slavery, and through that astonishment was going on to a desire of trying it, and from it to the trial itself, and thence, perchance, to fall into that bondage whereat he

was so astonished, seeing he was ready to enter into "a covenant with death;"[2] and he that loves danger shall fall into it.[3] For whatever the conjugal honour be in the office of well-ordering a married life, and sustaining children, influenced us but slightly. But that which did for the most part afflict me, already made a slave to it, was the habit of satisfying an insatiable lust; him about to be enslaved did an admiring wonder draw on. In this state were we, until Thou, O most High, not forsaking our lowliness, commiserating our misery, didst come to our rescue by wonderful and secret ways.

CHAP. XIII.—BEING URGED BY HIS MOTHER TO TAKE A WIFE, HE SOUGHT A MAIDEN THAT WAS PLEASING UNTO HIM.

23. Active efforts were made to get me a wife. I wooed, I was engaged, my mother taking the greatest pains in the matter, that when I was once married, the health-giving bap-tism might cleanse me; for which she rejoiced that I was being daily fitted, remarking that her desires and Thy promises were being fulfilled in my faith. At which time, verily, both at my request and her own desire, with strong heartfelt cries did we daily beg of Thee that Thou would-est by a vision disclose unto her something con-cerning my future marriage; but Thou wouldest not. She saw indeed certain vain and fantastic things, such as the earnestness of a human spirit, bent thereon, conjured up; and these she told me of, not with her usual confidence when Thou hadst shown her anything, but slighting them. For she could, she declared, through some feel-ing which she could not express in words, dis-cern the difference betwixt Thy revelations and the dreams of her own spirit. Yet the affair was pressed on, and a maiden sued who wanted two years of the marriageable age; and, as she was pleasing, she was waited for.

CHAP. XIV.—THE DESIGN OF ESTABLISHING A COMMON HOUSEHOLD WITH HIS FRIENDS IS SPEEDILY HINDERED.

24. And many of us friends, consulting on and abhorring the turbulent vexations of human life, had considered and now almost determined upon living at ease and separate from the tur-moil of men. And this was to be obtained in this way; we were to bring whatever we could severally procure, and make a common house-hold, so that, through the sincerity of our friend-ship, nothing should belong more to one than the other; but the whole, being derived from all, should as a whole belong to each, and the whole unto all. It seemed to us that this

---

[1] " Paulinus says that though he lived among the people and sat over them, ruling the sheep of the Lord's fold, as a watchful shep-herd, with anxious sleeplessness, yet by renunciation of the world, and denial of flesh and blood, he had made himself a wilderness, severed from the many, called among the few " (Ap. Aug. *Ep.* 24, sec. 2). St. Jerome calls him " his holy and venerable brother, Father (Papa) Alypius " (*Ep.* 39, *ibid.*). Earlier, Augustin speaks of him as " abiding in union with him, to be an example to the brethren who wished to avoid the cares of this world " (*Ep.* 22); and to Paulinus (*Ep.* 27), [Romanianus] " is a relation of the ven-erable and truly blessed Bishop Alypius, whom you embrace with your whole heart deservedly ; for whosoever thinks favourably of that man, thinks of the great mercy of God. Soon, by the help of God, I shall transfuse Alypius wholly into your soul [Paulinus had asked Alypius to write him his life, and Augustin had, at Alypius' request, undertaken to relieve him, and to do it] ; for I feared chiefly lest he should shrink from laying open all which the Lord has bestowed upon him, lest, if read by any ordinary person (for it would not be read by you only), he should seem not so much to set forth the gifts of God committed to men, as to exalt himself."— E. B. P.

[2] Isa. xxviii. 15.
[3] Ecclus. iii. 27.

society might consist of ten persons, some of whom were very rich, especially Romanianus,[1] our townsman, an intimate friend of mine from his childhood, whom grave business matters had then brought up to Court; who was the most earnest of us all for this project, and whose voice was of great weight in commending it, because his estate was far more ample than that of the rest. We had arranged, too, that two officers should be chosen yearly, for the providing of all necessary things, whilst the rest were left undisturbed. But when we began to reflect whether the wives which some of us had already, and others hoped to have, would permit this, all that plan, which was being so well framed, broke to pieces in our hands, and was utterly wrecked and cast aside. Thence we fell again to sighs and groans, and our steps to follow the broad and beaten ways[2] of the world; for many thoughts were in our heart, but Thy counsel standeth for ever.[3] Out of which counsel Thou didst mock ours, and preparedst Thine own, purposing to give us meat in due season, and to open Thy hand, and to fill our souls with blessing.[4]

CHAP. XV.—HE DISMISSES ONE MISTRESS, AND CHOOSES ANOTHER.

25. Meanwhile my sins were being multiplied, and my mistress being torn from my side as an impediment to my marriage, my heart, which clave to her, was racked, and wounded, and bleeding. And she went back to Africa, making a vow unto Thee never to know another man, leaving with me my natural son by her. But I, unhappy one, who could not imitate a woman, impatient of delay, since it was not until two years' time I was to obtain her I sought,—being not so much a lover of marriage as a slave to lust,—procured another (not a wife, though), that so by the bondage of a lasting

habit the disease of my soul might be nursed up, and kept up in its vigour, or even increased, into the kingdom of marriage. Nor was that wound of mine as yet cured which had been caused by the separation from my former mistress, but after inflammation and most acute anguish it mortified,[5] and the pain became numbed, but more desperate.

CHAP. XVI.—THE FEAR OF DEATH AND JUDGMENT CALLED HIM, BELIEVING IN THE IMMORTALITY OF THE SOUL, BACK FROM HIS WICKEDNESS, HIM WHO AFORETIME BELIEVED IN THE OPINIONS OF EPICURUS.

26. Unto Thee be praise, unto Thee be glory, O Fountain of mercies! I became more wretched, and Thou nearer. Thy right hand was ever ready to pluck me out of the mire, and to cleanse me, but I was ignorant of it. Nor did anything recall me from a yet deeper abyss of carnal pleasures, but the fear of death and of Thy future judgment, which, amid all my fluctuations of opinion, never left my breast. And in disputing with my friends, Alypius and Nebridius, concerning the nature of good and evil, I held that Epicurus had, in my judgment, won the palm, had I not believed that after death there remained a life for the soul, and places of recompense, which Epicurus would not believe.[6] And I demanded, "Supposing us to be immortal, and to be living in the enjoyment of perpetual bodily pleasure, and that without any fear of losing it, why, then, should we not be happy, or why should we search for anything else?"—not knowing that even this very thing was a part of my great misery, that, being thus sunk and blinded, I could not discern that light

[5] In his *De Natura Con. Manich.* he has the same idea. He is speaking of the evil that has no pain, and remarks: "Likewise in the body, better is a wound with pain than putrefaction without pain, which is specially styled corruption;" and the same idea is embodied in the extract from Caird's *Sermons*, on p. 5, note 7.

[6] The ethics of Epicurus were a modified Hedonism (Diog. Laërt. *De Vitis*, etc., x. 123). With him the earth was a congeries of atoms (*ibid.* 38, 40), which atoms existed from eternity, and *formed themselves*, uninfluenced by the gods. The soul he held to be material. It was diffused through the body, and was in its nature somewhat like air. At death it was resolved into its original atoms, when the being ceased to exist (*ibid.* 63, 64). Hence death was a matter of indifference to man [ὁ θάνατος οὐδὲν πρὸς ἡμᾶς, *ibid.* 124, etc.]. In that great upheaval after the scholasticism of the Middle Ages, the various ancient philosophies were revived. This of Epicurus was disentombed and, as it were, vitalized by Gassendi, in the beginning of the seventeenth century; and it has a special importance from its bearing on the physical theories and investigations of modern times. Archer Butler, adverting to the inadequacy of the chief philosophical schools to satisfy the wants of the age in the early days of the planting of Christianity (*Lectures on Ancient Philosophy*, ii. 333), says of the Epicurean: "Its popularity was unquestioned; its adaptation to a luxurious age could not be doubted. But it was not formed to satisfy the wants of the time, however it might minister to its pleasures. It was, indeed, as it still continues to be, the tacit philosophy of the careless, and might thus number a larger army of disciples than any contemporary system. But its supremacy existed only when it estimated numbers; it ceased when tried by *weight*. The eminent men of Rome were often its avowed favourers; but they were for the most part men eminent in arms and statesmanship, rather than the influential directors of the world of speculation. Nor could the admirable poetic art of Lucretius, or the still more attractive ease of Horace, confer such strength or dignity upon the system as to enable it to compete with the new and mysterious elements now upon all sides gathering into conflict."

[1] Romanianus was a relation of Alypius (Aug. *Ep.* 27, *ad Paulin.*), of talent which astonished Augustin himself (*C. Acad.* i. 1, ii. 1), "surrounded by affluence from early youth, and snatched by what are thought adverse circumstances from the absorbing whirlpools of life" (*ibid.*). Augustin frequently mentions his great wealth, as also this vexatious suit, whereby he was harassed (*C. Acad.* i. 1, ii. 1, 2), and which so clouded his mind that his talents were almost unknown (*C. Acad.* ii. 2); as also his very great kindness to himself, when, "as a poor lad, setting out to foreign study, he had received him in his house, supported and (yet more) encouraged him; when deprived of his father, comforted, animated, aided him; when returning to Carthage, in pursuit of a higher employment, supplied him with all necessaries." "Lastly," says Augustin, "whatever ease I now enjoy, that I have escaped the bonds of useless desires, that, laying aside the weight of dead cares, I breathe, recover, return to myself, that with all earnestness I am seeking the truth [Augustin wrote this the year before his baptism], that I am attaining it, that I trust wholly to arrive at it, you encouraged, impelled, effected" (*C. Acad.* ii. 2). Augustin had "cast him headlong with himself" (as so many other of his friends) into the Manichæan heresy (*ibid.* i. sec. 3), and it is to be hoped that he extricated him with himself; but we only learn positively that he continued to be fond of the works of Augustin (*Ep.* 27), whereas in that which he dedicated to him (*C. Acad.*), Augustin writes very doubtingly to him, and afterwards recommends him to Paulinus, "to be cured wholly or in part by his conversation" (*Ep.* 27).—E. B. P.

[2] Matt. vii. 13.
[3] Ps. xxxiii. 11.
[4] Ps. cxlv. 15, 16.

of honour and beauty to be embraced for its own sake,[1] which cannot be seen by the eye of the flesh, it being visible only to the inner man. Nor did I, unhappy one, consider out of what vein it emanated, that even these things, loathsome as they were, I with pleasure discussed with my friends. Nor could I, even in accordance with my then notions of happiness, make myself happy without friends, amid no matter how great abundance of carnal pleasures. And these friends assuredly I loved for their own sakes, and I knew myself to be loved of them again for my own sake. O crooked ways! Woe to the audacious soul which hoped that, if it forsook Thee, it would find some better thing! It hath turned and re-turned, on back, sides, and belly, and all was hard,[2] and Thou alone rest. And behold, Thou art near, and deliverest us from our wretched wanderings, and stablishest us in Thy way, and dost comfort us, and say, "Run; I will carry you, yea, I will lead you, and there also will I carry you."

---

[1] See viii. sec. 17, note, below.

[2] See above, iv. cc. 1, 10, and 12.

BOOK VII.

HE RECALLS THE BEGINNING OF HIS YOUTH, *i. e.* THE THIRTY-FIRST YEAR OF HIS AGE, IN WHICH VERY GRAVE ERRORS AS TO THE NATURE OF GOD AND THE ORIGIN OF EVIL BEING DISTINGUISHED, AND THE SACRED BOOKS MORE ACCURATELY KNOWN, HE AT LENGTH ARRIVES AT A CLEAR KNOWLEDGE OF GOD, NOT YET RIGHTLY APPREHENDING JESUS CHRIST.

CHAP. I.—HE REGARDED NOT GOD INDEED UNDER THE FORM OF A HUMAN BODY, BUT AS A CORPOREAL SUBSTANCE DIFFUSED THROUGH SPACE.

1. DEAD now was that evil and abominable youth of mine, and I was passing into early manhood: as I increased in years, the fouler became I in vanity, who could not conceive of any substance but such as I saw with my own eyes. I thought not of Thee, O God, under the form of a human body. Since the time I began to hear something of wisdom, I always avoided this; and I rejoiced to have found the same in the faith of our spiritual mother, Thy Catholic Church. But what else to imagine Thee I knew not. And I, a man, and such a man, sought to conceive of Thee, the sovereign and only true God; and I did in my inmost heart believe that Thou wert incorruptible, and inviolable, and unchangeable; because, not knowing whence or how, yet most plainly did I see and feel sure that that which may be corrupted must be worse than that which cannot, and what cannot be violated did I without hesitation prefer before that which can, and deemed that which suffers no change to be better than that which is changeable. Violently did my heart cry out against all my phantasms, and with this one blow I endeavoured to beat away from the eye of my mind all that unclean crowd which fluttered around it.[1] And lo, being scarce put off, they, in the twinkling of an eye, pressed in multitudes around me, dashed against my face, and beclouded it; so that, though I thought not of Thee under the form of a human body, yet was I constrained to image Thee to be something corporeal in space, either infused into the world, or infinitely diffused beyond it, —even that incorruptible, inviolable, and unchangeable, which I preferred to the corruptible, and violable, and changeable; since whatsoever I conceived, deprived of this space, appeared as nothing to me, yea, altogether nothing, not even a void, as if a body were removed from its place and the place should remain empty of any body at all, whether earthy, terrestrial, watery, aerial, or celestial, but should remain a void place—a spacious nothing, as it were.

2. I therefore being thus gross-hearted, nor clear even to myself, whatsoever was not stretched over certain spaces, nor diffused, nor crowded together, nor swelled out, or which did not or could not receive some of these dimensions, I judged to be altogether nothing.[2] For over such forms as my eyes are wont to range did my heart then range; nor did I see that this same observation, by which I formed those same images, was not of this kind, and yet it could not have formed them had not itself been something great. In like manner did I conceive of Thee, Life of my life, as vast through infinite spaces, on every side penetrating the whole mass of the world, and beyond it, all ways, through immeasurable and boundless spaces; so that the earth should have Thee, the heaven have Thee, all things have Thee, and they bounded in Thee, but Thou nowhere. For as the body of this air which is above the earth preventeth not the light of the sun from passing through it, penetrating it, not by bursting or by cutting, but by filling it entirely, so I imagined the body, not of heaven, air, and sea only, but of the earth also, to be pervious

---

[1] See iii. sec. 12, iv. secs. 3 and 12, and v. sec. 19, above.

[2] "For with what understanding can man apprehend God, who does not yet apprehend that very understanding itself of his own by which he desires to apprehend Him? And if he does already apprehend this, let him carefully consider that there is nothing in his own nature better than it; and let him see whether he can there see any outlines of forms, or brightness of colours, or greatness of space, or distance of parts, or extension of size, or any movements through intervals of place, or any such thing at all. Certainly we find nothing of all this in that, than which we find nothing better in our own nature, that is, in our own intellect, by which we apprehend wisdom according to our capacity. What, therefore, we do not find in that, which is our own best, we ought not to seek in Him, who is far better than that best of ours; that so we may understand God, if we are able, and as much as we are able, as good without quality, great without quantity, a Creator though He lack nothing, ruling but from no position, sustaining all things without 'having' them, in His wholeness everywhere yet without place, eternal without time, making things that are changeable without change of Himself, and without passion. Whoso thus thinks of God, although he cannot yet find out in all ways what He is, yet piously takes heed, as much as he is able, to think nothing of Him that He is not."—*De Trin.* v. 2.

to Thee, and in all its greatest parts as well as smallest penetrable to receive Thy presence, by a secret inspiration, both inwardly and outwardly governing all things which Thou hast created. So I conjectured, because I was unable to think of anything else; for it was untrue. For in this way would a greater part of the earth contain a greater portion of Thee, and the less a lesser; and all things should so be full of Thee, as that the body of an elephant should contain more of Thee than that of a sparrow by how much larger it is, and occupies more room; and so shouldest Thou make the portions of Thyself present unto the several portions of the world, in pieces, great to the great, little to the little. But Thou art not such a one; nor hadst Thou as yet enlightened my darkness.

CHAP. II. — THE DISPUTATION OF NEBRIDIUS AGAINST THE MANICHÆANS, ON THE QUESTION "WHETHER GOD BE CORRUPTIBLE OR INCORRUPTIBLE."

3. It was sufficient for me, O Lord, to oppose to those deceived deceivers and dumb praters (dumb, since Thy word sounded not forth from them) that which a long while ago, while we were at Carthage, Nebridius used to propound, at which all we who heard it were disturbed: "What could that reputed nation of darkness, which the Manichæans are in the habit of setting up as a mass opposed to Thee, have done unto Thee hadst Thou objected to fight with it? For had it been answered, 'It would have done Thee some injury,' then shouldest Thou be subject to violence and corruption; but if the reply were: 'It could do Thee no injury,' then was no cause assigned for Thy fighting with it; and so fighting as that a certain portion and member of Thee, or offspring of Thy very substance, should be blended with adverse powers and natures not of Thy creation, and be by them corrupted and deteriorated to such an extent as to be turned from happiness into misery, and need help whereby it might be delivered and purged; and that this offspring of Thy substance was the soul, to which, being enslaved, contaminated, and corrupted, Thy word, free, pure, and entire, might bring succour; but yet also the word itself being corruptible, because it was from one and the same substance. So that should they affirm Thee, whatsoever Thou art, that is, Thy substance whereby Thou art, to be incorruptible, then were all these assertions false and execrable; but if corruptible, then that were false, and at the first utterance to be abhorred."[1] This argument, then, was

enough against those who wholly merited to be vomited forth from the surfeited stomach, since they had no means of escape without horrible sacrilege, both of heart and tongue, thinking and speaking such things of Thee.

CHAP. III.—THAT THE CAUSE OF EVIL IS THE FREE JUDGMENT OF THE WILL.

4. But I also, as yet, although I said and was firmly persuaded, that Thou our Lord, the true God, who madest not only our souls but our bodies, and not our souls and bodies alone, but all creatures and all things, wert uncontaminable and inconvertible, and in no part mutable; yet understood I not readily and clearly what was the cause of evil. And yet, whatever it was, I perceived that it must be sought out as not to constrain me by it to believe that the immutable God was mutable, lest I myself

him to the true faith. Again, in his *De Moribus* (sec. 25), where he examines the answers which had been given, he commences: "For this gives rise to the question, which used to throw us into great perplexity, even when we were your zealous disciples, nor could we find any answer,—what the race of darkness would have done to God, supposing He had refused to fight with it at the cost of such calamity to part of Himself. For if God would not have suffered any loss by remaining quiet, we thought it hard that we had been sent to endure so much. Again, if He would have suffered, His nature cannot have been incorruptible, as it behooves the nature of God to be." We have already, in the note to book iv. sec. 26, referred to some of the matters touched on in this section; but they call for further elucidation. The following passage, quoted by Augustin from Manichæus himself (*Con. Ep. Manich.* 19), discloses to us (1) their ideas as to the nature and position of the two kingdoms: "In one direction, on the border of this bright and holy region, there was a land of darkness, deep and vast in extent, where abode fiery bodies, destructive races. Here was boundless darkness flowing from the same source in immeasurable abundance, with the productions properly belonging to it. Beyond this were muddy, turbid waters, with their inhabitants; and inside of them winds terrible and violent, with their prince and their progenitors. Then, again, a fiery region of destruction, with its chiefs and peoples. And similarly inside of this, a race full of smoke and gloom, where abode the dreadful prince and chief of all, having around him innumerable princes, himself the mind and source of them all. Such are the five natures of the region of corruption." Augustin also designates them (*ibid.* sec. 20) "the five dens of the race of darkness." The nation of darkness desires to possess the kingdom of light, and prepares to make war upon it; and in the controversy with Faustus we have (2) the beginning and issue of the war (*Con. Faust.* ii. 3; see also *De Hæres*, 46). Augustin says: " You dress up for our benefit some wonderful First Man, who came down from the race of light, to war with the race of darkness, armed with his waters against the waters of the enemy, and with his fire against their fire, and with his winds against their winds." And again (*ibid.* sec. 5): "You say that he mingled with the principles of darkness in his conflict with the race of darkness, that by capturing these principles the world might be made out of the mixture. So that, by your profane fancies, Christ is not only mingled with heaven and all the stars, but conjoined and compounded with the earth and all its productions,—a Saviour no more, but needing to be saved by you, by your eating and disgorging Him. This foolish custom of making your disciples bring you food, that your teeth and stomach may be the means of relieving Christ, who is bound up in it, is a consequence of your profane fancies. You declare that Christ is liberated in this way,—not, however, entirely; for you hold that some tiny particles of no value still remain in the excrement, to be mixed up and compounded again and again in various material forms, and to be released and purified at any rate by the fire in which the world will be burned up, if not before. Nay, even then, you say, Christ is not entirely liberated, but some extreme particles of His good and divine nature, which have been so defiled that they cannot be cleansed, are condemned to stay for ever in the mass of darkness." The result of this commingling of the light with the darkness was, that a certain portion and member of God was turned "from happiness into misery," and placed in bondage in the world, and was in need of help "whereby it might be delivered and purged." (See also *Con. Fortunat.* i. 1.) Reference may be made (3), for information as to the method by which the divine substance was released in the eating of the elect, to the notes on book iii. sec. 18, above; and for the influence of the sun and moon in accomplishing that release, to the note on book v. sec. 12, above.

[1] Similar arguments are made use of in his controversy with Fortunatus (*Dis.* ii. 5), where he says, that as Fortunatus could find no answer, so neither could he when a Manichæan, and that this led

should become the thing that I was seeking out. I sought, therefore, for it free from care, certain of the untruthfulness of what these asserted, whom I shunned with my whole heart; for I perceived that through seeking after the origin of evil, they were filled with malice, in that they liked better to think that Thy Substance did suffer evil than that their own did commit it.[1]

5. And I directed my attention to discern what I now heard, that free will[2] was the cause of our doing evil, and Thy righteous judgment of our suffering it. But I was unable clearly to discern it. So, then, trying to draw the eye of my mind from that pit, I was plunged again therein, and trying often, was as often plunged back again. But this raised me towards Thy light, that I knew as well that I had a will as that I had life: when, therefore, I was willing or unwilling to do anything, I was most certain that it was none but myself that was willing and unwilling; and immediately I perceived that there was the cause of my sin. But what I did against my will I saw that I suffered rather than did, and that judged I not to be my fault, but my punishment; whereby, believing Thee to be most just, I quickly confessed myself to be not unjustly punished. But again I said: "Who made me? Was it not my God, who is not only good, but goodness itself? Whence came I then to will to do evil, and to be unwilling to do good, that there might be cause for my just punishment? Who was it that put this in me, and implanted in me the root of bitterness, seeing I was altogether made by my most sweet God? If the devil were the author, whence is that devil? And if he also, by his own perverse will, of a good angel became a devil, whence also was the evil will in him whereby he became a devil, seeing that the angel was made altogether good by that most good Creator?" By these reflections was I again cast down and stifled; yet not plunged into that hell of error (where no man confesseth unto Thee),[3] to think that Thou dost suffer evil, rather than that man doth it.

CHAP. IV.—THAT GOD IS NOT CORRUPTIBLE, WHO, IF HE WERE, WOULD NOT BE GOD AT ALL.

6. For I was so struggling to find out the rest, as having already found that what was incorruptible must be better than the corruptible; and Thee, therefore, whatsoever Thou wert, did I acknowledge to be incorruptible. For never yet was, nor will be, a soul able to conceive of anything better than Thou, who art the highest and best good. But whereas most truly and certainly that which is incorruptible

is to be preferred to the corruptible (like as I myself did now prefer it), then, if Thou were not incorruptible, I could in my thoughts have reached unto something better than my God. Where, then, I saw that the incorruptible was to be preferred to the corruptible, there ought I to seek Thee, and there observe "whence evil itself was," that is, whence comes the corruption by which Thy substance can by no means be profaned. For corruption, truly, in no way injures our God,—by no will, by no necessity, by no unforeseen chance,—because He is God, and what He wills is good, and Himself is that good; but to be corrupted is not good. Nor art Thou compelled to do anything against Thy will in that Thy will is not greater than Thy power. But greater should it be wert Thou Thyself greater than Thyself; for the will and power of God is God Himself. And what can be unforeseen by Thee, who knowest all things? Nor is there any sort of nature but Thou knowest it. And what more should we say "why that substance which God is should not be corruptible," seeing that if it were so it could not be God?

CHAP. V.—QUESTIONS CONCERNING THE ORIGIN OF EVIL IN REGARD TO GOD, WHO, SINCE HE IS THE CHIEF GOOD, CANNOT BE THE CAUSE OF EVIL.

7. And I sought "whence is evil?" And sought in an evil way; nor saw I the evil in my very search. And I set in order before the view of my spirit the whole creation, and whatever we can discern in it, such as earth, sea, air, stars, trees, living creatures; yea, and whatever in it we do not see, as the firmament of heaven, all the angels, too, and all the spiritual inhabitants thereof. But these very beings, as though they were bodies, did my fancy dispose in such and such places, and I made one huge mass of all Thy creatures, distinguished according to the kinds of bodies,—some of them being real bodies, some what I myself had feigned for spirits. And this mass I made huge,—not as it was, which I could not know, but as large as I thought well, yet every way finite. But Thee, O Lord, I imagined on every part environing and penetrating it, though every way infinite; as if there were a sea everywhere, and on every side through immensity nothing but an infinite sea; and it contained within itself some sponge, huge, though finite, so that the sponge would in all its parts be filled from the immeasurable sea. So conceived I Thy creation to be itself finite, and filled by Thee, the Infinite. And I said, Behold God, and behold what God hath created; and God is good, yea, most mightily and incomparably better than all these; but yet He, who is good, hath created them good, and

---

[1] See iv. sec. 26, note, above.
[2] See iii. sec. 12, note, and iv. sec. 26, note, above.
[3] Ps. vi. 5.

behold how He encircleth and filleth them. Where, then, is evil, and whence, and how crept it in hither? What is its root, and what its seed? Or hath it no being at all? Why, then, do we fear and shun that which hath no being? Or if we fear it needlessly, then surely is that fear evil whereby the heart is unnecessarily pricked and tormented,—and so much a greater evil, as we have naught to fear, and yet do fear. Therefore either that is evil which we fear, or the act of fearing is in itself evil. Whence, therefore, is it, seeing that God, who is good, hath made all these things good? He, indeed, the greatest and chiefest Good, hath created these lesser goods; but both Creator and created are all good. Whence is evil? Or was there some evil matter of which He made and formed and ordered it, but left something in it which He did not convert into good? But why was this? Was He powerless to change the whole lump, so that no evil should remain in it, seeing that He is omnipotent? Lastly, why would He make anything at all of it, and not rather by the same omnipotency cause it not to be at all? Or could it indeed exist contrary to His will? Or if it were from eternity, why did He permit it so to be for infinite spaces of times in the past, and was pleased so long after to make something out of it? Or if He wished now all of a sudden to do something, this rather should the Omnipotent have accomplished, that this evil matter should not be at all, and that He only should be the whole, true, chief, and infinite Good. Or if it were not good that He, who was good, should not also be the framer and creator of what was good, then that matter which was evil being removed, and brought to nothing, He might form good matter, whereof He might create all things. For He would not be omnipotent were He not able to create something good without being assisted by that matter which had not been created by Himself.[1] Such like things did I revolve in my miserable breast, overwhelmed with most gnawing cares lest I should die ere I discovered the truth; yet was the faith of Thy Christ, our Lord and Saviour, as held in the Catholic Church, fixed firmly in my heart, unformed, indeed, as yet upon many points, and diverging from doctrinal rules, but yet my mind did not utterly leave it, but every day rather drank in more and more of it.

CHAP. VI.—HE REFUTES THE DIVINATIONS OF THE ASTROLOGERS, DEDUCED FROM THE CONSTELLATIONS.

8. Now also had I repudiated the lying divinations and impious absurdities of the astrologers. Let Thy mercies, out of the depth of my soul, confess unto thee[2] for this also, O my God. For Thou, Thou altogether,—for who else is it that calls us back from the death of all errors, but that Life which knows not how to die, and the Wisdom which, requiring no light, enlightens the minds that do, whereby the universe is governed, even to the fluttering leaves of trees?—Thou providedst also for my obstinacy wherewith I struggled with Vindicianus,[3] an acute old man, and Nebridius, a young one of remarkable talent; the former vehemently declaring, and the latter frequently, though with a certain measure of doubt, saying, "That no art existed by which to foresee future things, but that men's surmises had oftentimes the help of luck, and that of many things which they foretold some came to pass unawares to the predicters, who lighted on it by their oft speaking." Thou, therefore, didst provide a friend for me, who was no negligent consulter of the astrologers, and yet not thoroughly skilled in those arts, but, as I said, a curious consulter with them; and yet knowing somewhat, which he said he had heard from his father, which, how far it would tend to overthrow the estimation of that art, he knew not. This man, then, by name Firminius, having received a liberal education, and being well versed in rhetoric, consulted me, as one very dear to him, as to what I thought on some affairs of his, wherein his worldly hopes had risen, viewed with regard to his so-called constellations; and I, who had now begun to lean in this particular towards Nebridius' opinion, did not indeed decline to speculate about the matter, and to tell him what came into my irresolute mind, but still added that I was now almost persuaded that these were but empty and ridiculous follies. Upon this he told me that his father had been very curious in such books, and that he had a friend who was as interested in them as he was himself, who, with combined study and consultation, fanned the flame of their affection for these toys, insomuch that they would observe the moment when the very dumb animals which bred in their houses brought forth, and then observed the position of the heavens with regard to them, so as to gather fresh proofs of this so-called art. He said, moreover, that his father had told him, that at the time his mother was about to give birth to him (Firminius), a female servant of that friend of his father's was also great with child, which could not be hidden from her master, who took care with most diligent exactness to know of the birth of his very dogs. And so it came to pass that (the one for his wife, and the other for his ser-

---

[1] See xi. sec. 7, note, below.

[2] Ps. cvii. 8, *Vulg.*
[3] See iv. sec. 5, note, above.

vant, with the most careful observation, calculating the days and hours, and the smaller divisions of the hours) both were delivered at the same moment, so that both were compelled to allow the very selfsame constellations, even to the minutest point, the one for his son, the other for his young slave. For so soon as the women began to be in travail, they each gave notice to the other of what was fallen out in their respective houses, and had messengers ready to despatch to one another so soon as they had information of the actual birth, of which they had easily provided, each in his own province, to give instant intelligence. Thus, then, he said, the messengers of the respective parties met one another in such equal distances from either house, that neither of them could discern any difference either in the position of the stars or other most minute points. And yet Firminius, born in a high estate in his parents' house, ran his course through the prosperous paths of this world, was increased in wealth, and elevated to honours; whereas that slave—the yoke of his condition being unrelaxed—continued to serve his masters, as Firminius, who knew him, informed me.

9. Upon hearing and believing these things, related by so reliable a person, all that resistance of mine melted away; and first I endeavoured to reclaim Firminius himself from that curiosity, by telling him, that upon inspecting his constellations, I ought, were I to foretell truly, to have seen in them parents eminent among their neighbours, a noble family in its own city, good birth, becoming education, and liberal learning. But if that servant had consulted me upon the same constellations, since they were his also, I ought again to tell him, likewise truly, to see in them the meanness of his origin, the abjectness of his condition, and everything else altogether removed from and at variance with the former. Whence, then, looking upon the same constellations, I should, if I spoke the truth, speak diverse things, or if I spoke the same, speak falsely; thence assuredly was it to be gathered, that whatever, upon consideration of the constellations, was foretold truly, was not by art, but by chance; and whatever falsely, was not from the unskilfulness of the art, but the error of chance.

10. An opening being thus made, I ruminated within myself on such things, that no one of those dotards (who followed such occupations, and whom I longed to assail, and with derision to confute) might urge against me that Firminius had informed me falsely, or his father him: I turned my thoughts to those that are born twins, who generally come out of the womb so near one to another, that the small distance of time between them—how much force soever

they may contend that it has in the nature of things—cannot be noted by human observation, or be expressed in those figures which the astrologer is to examine that he may pronounce the truth. Nor can they be true; for, looking into the same figures, he must have foretold the same of Esau and Jacob,[1] whereas the same did not happen to them. He must therefore speak falsely; or if truly, then, looking into the same figures, he must not speak the same things. Not then by art, but by chance, would he speak truly. For Thou, O Lord, most righteous Ruler of the universe, the inquirers and inquired of knowing it not, workest by a hidden inspiration that the consulter should hear what, according to the hidden deservings of souls, he ought to hear, out of the depth of Thy righteous judgment, to whom let not man say, "What is this?" or "Why that?" Let him not say so, for he is man.

CHAP. VII.—HE IS SEVERELY EXERCISED AS TO THE ORIGIN OF EVIL.

11. And now, O my Helper, hadst Thou freed me from those fetters; and I inquired, "Whence is evil?" and found no result. But Thou sufferedst me not to be carried away from the faith by any fluctuations of thought, whereby I believed Thee both to exist, and Thy substance to be unchangeable, and that Thou hadst a care of and wouldest judge men; and that in Christ, Thy Son, our Lord, and the Holy Scriptures, which the authority of Thy Catholic Church pressed upon me, Thou hadst planned the way of man's salvation to that life which is to come after this death. These things being safe and immoveably settled in my mind, I eagerly inquired, "Whence is evil?" What torments did my travailing heart then endure! What sighs, O my God! Yet even there were Thine ears open, and I knew it not; and when in stillness I sought earnestly, those silent contritions of my soul were strong cries unto Thy mercy. No man knoweth, but only Thou, what I endured. For what was that which was thence through my tongue poured into the ears of my most familiar friends? Did the whole tumult of my soul, for which neither time nor speech was sufficient, reach them? Yet went the whole into Thine ears, all of which I bellowed out from the sighings of my heart; and my desire was before Thee, and the light of mine eyes was not with me;[2] for that was within, I without. Nor was that in place, but my attention was directed to things contained in place; but there did I find no resting-place, nor did they receive me in such a way as that I could say, "It is

---

[1] He uses the same illustration when speaking of the *mathematici*, or astrologers, in his *De Doct. Christ.* ii. 33.
[2] Ps. xxxvii. 9-11, *Vulg.*

sufficient, it is well;" nor did they let me turn back, where it might be well enough with me. For to these things was I superior, but inferior to Thee; and Thou art my true joy when I am subjected to Thee, and Thou hadst subjected to me what Thou createdst beneath me.[1] And this was the true temperature and middle region of my safety, to continue in Thine image, and by serving Thee to have dominion over the body. But when I lifted myself proudly against Thee, and "ran against the Lord, even on His neck, with the thick bosses" of my buckler,[2] even these inferior things were placed above me, and pressed upon me, and nowhere was there alleviation or breathing space. They encountered my sight on every side in crowds and troops, and in thought the images of bodies obtruded themselves as I was returning to Thee, as if they would say unto me, "Whither goest thou, unworthy and base one?" And these things had sprung forth out of my wound; for thou humblest the proud like one that is wounded,[3] and through my own swelling was I separated from Thee; yea, my too much swollen face closed up mine eyes.

CHAP. VIII.—BY GOD'S ASSISTANCE HE BY DEGREES ARRIVES AT THE TRUTH.

12. "But Thou, O Lord, shalt endure for ever,"[4] yet not for ever art Thou angry with us, because Thou dost commiserate our dust and ashes; and it was pleasing in Thy sight to reform my deformity, and by inward stings didst Thou disturb me, that I should be dissatisfied until Thou wert made sure to my inward sight. And by the secret hand of Thy remedy was my swelling lessened, and the disordered and darkened eyesight of my mind, by the sharp anointings of healthful sorrows, was from day to day made whole.

CHAP. IX.—HE COMPARES THE DOCTRINE OF THE PLATONISTS CONCERNING THE Λόγος WITH THE MUCH MORE EXCELLENT DOCTRINE OF CHRISTIANITY.

13. And Thou, willing first to show me how Thou "resistest the proud, but givest grace unto the humble,"[5] and by how great an act of mercy Thou hadst pointed out to men the path of humility, in that Thy "Word was

made flesh" and dwelt among men,—Thou procuredst for me, by the instrumentality of one inflated with most monstrous pride, certain books of the Platonists,[6] translated from Greek into Latin.[7] And therein I read, not indeed in the same words, but to the selfsame effect,[8] enforced by many and divers reasons,

[6] "This," says Watts, "was likely to be the book of Amelius the Platonist, who hath indeed this beginning of St. John's Gospel, calling the apostle a barbarian." This Amelius was a disciple of Plotinus, who was the first to develope and formulate the Neo-Platonic doctrines, and of whom it is said that he would not have his likeness taken, nor be reminded of his birthday, because it would recall the existence of the body he so much despised. A popular account of the theories of Plotinus, and their connection with the doctrines of Plato and of Christianity respectively, will be found in Archer Butler's *Lectures on Ancient Philosophy*, vol. ii. pp. 348-358. For a more systematic view of his writings, see Ueberweg's *History of Philosophy*, sec. 68. Augustin alludes again in his *De Vita Beata* (sec. 4) to the influence the Platonic writings had on him at this time; and it is interesting to note how in God's providence they were drawing him to seek a fuller knowledge of Him, just as in his nineteenth year (book iii. sec. 7, above) the *Hortensius* of Cicero stimulated him to the pursuit of wisdom. Thus in his experience was exemplified the truth embodied in the saying of Clemens Alexandrinus,—" Philosophy led the Greeks to Christ, as the law did the Jews." Archbishop Trench, in his *Hulsean Lectures* (lecs. 1 and 3, 1846, "Christ the Desire of all Nations"), enters with interesting detail into this question, specially as it relates to the heathen world. "None," he says in lecture 3, "can thoughtfully read the early history of the Church without marking how hard the Jewish Christians found it to make their own true idea of a Son of God, as indeed is witnessed by the whole Epistle to the Hebrews—how comparatively easy the Gentile converts; how the Hebrew Christians were continually in danger of sinking down into Ebionite heresies, making Christ but a man as other men, refusing to go on unto perfection, or to realize the truth of His higher nature; while, on the other hand, the genial promptness is as remarkable with which the Gentile Church welcomed and embraced the offered truth, 'God manifest in the flesh.' We feel that there must have been effectual preparations in the latter, which wrought its greater readiness for receiving and heartily embracing this truth when it arrived." The passage from Amelius the Platonist, referred to at the beginning of this note, is examined in Burton's *Bampton Lectures*, note 90. It has been adverted to by Eusebius, Theodoret, and perhaps by Augustin in the *De Civ. Dei*, x. 29, quoted in note 2, sec. 25, below. See Kayes' *Clement*, pp. 116-124.

[7] See i. sec. 23, note, above, and also his *Life*, in the last vol. of the Benedictine edition of his works, for a very fair estimate of his knowledge of Greek.

[8] The Neo-Platonic ideas as to the "Word" or Λόγος, which Augustin (1) contrasts during the remainder of this book with the doctrine of the gospel, had its germ in the philosophy of Plato. The Greek term expresses both *reason* and the *expression of reason* in speech; and the Fathers frequently illustrate, by reference to this connection between ideas and uttered words, the fact that the "Word" that was *with God* had an incarnate existence in the world as the "Word" *made flesh*. By the Logos of the Alexandrian school something very different was meant from the Christian doctrine as to the incarnation, of which the above can only be taken as a dim illustration. It has been questioned, indeed, whether the philosophers, from Plotinus to the Gnostics of the time of St. John, believed the Logos and the supreme God to have in any sense separate "personalities." Dr. Burton, in his *Bampton Lectures*, concludes that they did not (lect. vii. p. 215, and note 93; compare Dorner, *Person of Christ*, i. 27, Clark); and quotes Origen when he points out to Celsus, that "while the heathen use the reason of God as another term for God Himself, the Christians use the term *Logos* for the Son of God." Another point of difference which appears in Augustin's review of Platonism above, is found in the Platonist's discarding the idea of the *Logos* becoming man. This the very genius of their philosophy forbade them to hold, since they looked on matter as impure. (2) It has been charged against Christianity by Gibbon and other sceptical writers, that it has borrowed largely from the doctrines of Plato; and it has been said that this doctrine of the *Logos* was taken from them by Justin Martyr. This charge, says Burton (*ibid.* p. 194), "has laid open in its supporters more inconsistencies and more misstatements than any other which ever has been advanced." We have alluded in the note to book iii. sec. 2, above, to Justin Martyr's search after truth. He endeavoured to find it successively in the Stoical, the Peripatetic, the Pythagorean, and the Platonic schools; and he appears to have thought as highly of Plato's philosophy as did Augustin. He does not, however, fail to criticise his doctrine when inconsistent with Christianity (see Burton, *ibid.* notes 18 and 86). Justin Martyr has apparently been chosen for attack as being the earliest of the post-apostolic Fathers. Burton, however, shows that Ignatius, who knew St. John, and was bishop of Antioch thirty years before his death, used precisely the same expression as applied to Christ (*ibid.* p. 204). This would appear to be a conclu-

[1] Man can only control the forces of nature by yielding obedience to nature's laws; and our true joy and safety is only to be found in being "subjected" to God. So Augustin says in another place (*De Trin.* x. 7), the soul is enjoined to know itself, "in order that it may consider itself, and live according to its own nature; that is, seek to be regulated according to its own nature, viz. under Him to whom it ought to be subject, and above those things to which it is to be preferred; under Him by whom it ought to be ruled, above those things which it ought to rule."

[2] Job xv. 26.
[3] Ps. lxxxix. 11, *Vulg.*
[4] Ps. cii. 12.
[5] Jas. iv. 6, and 1 Pet. v. 5.

that, " In the beginning was the Word, and the Word was with God, and the Word was God. The same was in the beginning with God. All things were made by Him; and without Him was not any thing made that was made." That which was made by Him is " life; and the life was the light of men. And the light shineth in darkness; and the darkness comprehendeth it not." [1] And that the soul of man, though it " bears witness of the light," [2] yet itself " is not that light; [3] but the Word of God, being God, is that true light that lighteth every man that cometh into the world." [4] And that " He was in the world, and the world was made by Him, and the world knew Him not." [5] But that " He came unto His own, and His own received Him not. [6] But as many as received Him, to them gave He power to become the sons of God, even to them that believe on His name." [7] This I did not read there.

14. In like manner, I read there that God the Word was born not of flesh, nor of blood, nor of the will of man, nor of the will of the flesh, but of God. But that " the Word was made flesh, and dwelt among us," [8] I read not there. For I discovered in those books that it was in many and divers ways said, that the Son was in the form of the Father, and " thought it not robbery to be equal with God," for that naturally He was the same substance. But that He emptied Himself, " and took upon Him the form of a servant, and was made in the likeness of men: and being found in fashion as a man, He humbled Himself, and became obedient unto death, even the death of the cross. Wherefore God also hath highly exalted Him "

from the dead, " and given Him a name above every name; that at the name of Jesus every knee should bow, of things in heaven, and things in earth, and things under the earth; and that every tongue should confess that Jesus Christ is Lord, to the glory of God the Father;" [9] those books have not. For that before all times, and above all times, Thy only-begotten Son remaineth unchangeably co-eternal with Thee; and that of " His fulness " souls receive, [10] that they may be blessed; and that by participation of the wisdom remaining in them they are renewed, that they may be wise, is there. But that " in due time Christ died for the ungodly," [11] and that Thou sparedst not Thine only Son, but deliveredst Him up for us all, [12] is not there. " Because Thou hast hid these things from the wise and prudent, and hast revealed them unto babes;" [13] that they " that labour and are heavy laden " might " come " unto Him and He might refresh them, [14] because He is " meek and lowly in heart." [15] " The meek will He guide in judgment; and the meek will He teach His way;" [16] looking upon our humility and our distress, and forgiving all our sins. [17] But such as are puffed up with the elation of would-be sublimer learning, do not hear Him saying, " Learn of Me; for I am meek and lowly in heart: and ye shall find rest unto your souls." [18] " Because that, when they knew God, they glorified Him not as God, neither were thankful; but became vain in their imaginations, and their foolish heart was darkened. Professing themselves to be wise, they became fools." [19]

15. And therefore also did I read there, that they had changed the glory of Thy incorruptible nature into idols and divers forms,—" into an image made like to corruptible man, and to birds, and four-footed beasts, and creeping things," [20] namely, into that Egyptian food [21] for which Esau lost his birthright; [22] for that Thy first-born people worshiped the head of a four-footed beast instead of Thee, turning back in heart towards Egypt, and prostrating Thy image—their own soul—before the image " of

sive answer to this objection. (3) It may be well to note here Burton's general conclusions as to the employment of this term *Logos* in St. John, since it occurs frequently in this part of the *Confessions*. Every one must have observed St. John's use of the term is peculiar as compared with the other apostles, but it is not always borne in mind that a generation probably elapsed between the date of his gospel and that of the other apostolic writings. In this interval the Gnostic heresy had made great advances; and it would appear that John, finding this term *Logos* prevalent when he wrote, infused into it a nobler meaning, and pointed out to those being led away by this heresy that there was indeed One who might be called " the Word"—One who was not, indeed, God's mind, or as the word that comes from the mouth and passes away, but One who, while He had been " made flesh " like unto us, was yet co-eternal with God. " You will perceive," says Archer Butler (*Ancient Philosophy*, vol. ii. p. 10), " how natural, or rather how necessary, is such a process, when you remember that this is exactly what every teacher must do who speaks of God to a heathen; he adopts the term, but he refines and exalts its meaning. Nor, indeed, is the procedure different in any use whatever of language in sacred senses and for sacred purposes. It has been justly remarked, by (I think) Isaac Casaubon, that the principle of all these adaptations is expressed in the sentence of St. Paul, Ὃν ἀγνοοῦντες εὐσεβεῖτε, τοῦτον ἐγὼ καταγγέλλω ὑμῖν." On the charge against Christianity of having borrowed from heathenism, reference may be made to Trench's *Hulsean Lectures*, lect. i. (1846); and for the sources of Gnosticism, and St. John's treatment of heresies as to the " Word," lects. ii. and v. in Mansel's *Gnostic Heresies* will be consulted with profit.

[1] John i. 1–5.
[2] *Ibid.* i. 7, 8.
[3] See note, sec. 23, below.
[4] John i. 9.
[5] *Ibid.* i. 10.
[6] *Ibid.* i. 11.
[7] *Ibid.* i. 12.
[8] *Ibid.* i. 14.

[9] Phil. ii. 6–11.
[10] John i. 16.
[11] Rom. v. 6.
[12] Rom. viii. 32.
[13] Matt. xi. 25.
[14] *Ibid.* ver. 28.
[15] *Ibid.* ver. 29.
[16] Ps. xxv. 9.
[17] *Ibid.* ver. 18.
[18] Matt. xi. 29.
[19] Rom. i. 21, 22.
[20] *Ibid.* i. 23.
[21] In the Benedictine edition we have reference to Augustin's *in Ps.* xlvi. 6, where he says: " We find the lentile is an Egyptian food, for it abounds in Egypt, whence the Alexandrian lentile is esteemed so as to be brought to our country, as if it grew not here. Esau, by desiring Egyptian food, lost his birthright; and so the Jewish people, of whom it is said they turned back in heart to Egypt, in a manner craved for lentiles, and lost their birthright." See Ex. xvi. 3; Num. xi. 5.
[22] Gen. xxv. 33, 34.

an ox that eateth grass."[1] These things found I there; but I fed not on them. For it pleased Thee, O Lord, to take away the reproach of diminution from Jacob, that the elder should serve the younger;[2] and Thou hast called the Gentiles into Thine inheritance. And I had come unto Thee from among the Gentiles, and I strained after that gold which Thou willedst Thy people to take from Egypt, seeing that wheresoever it was it was Thine.[3] And to the Athenians Thou saidst by Thy apostle, that in Thee "we live, and move, and have our being;" as one of their own poets has said.[4] And verily these books came from thence. But I set not my mind on the idols of Egypt, whom they ministered to with Thy gold,[5] "who changed the truth of God into a lie, and worshipped and served the creature more than the Creator."[6]

CHAP. X. — DIVINE THINGS ARE THE MORE CLEARLY MANIFESTED TO HIM WHO WITHDRAWS INTO THE RECESSES OF HIS HEART.

16. And being thence warned to return to myself, I entered into my inward self, Thou leading me on; and I was able to do it, for Thou wert become my helper. And I entered, and with the eye of my soul (such as it was) saw above the same eye of my soul, above my mind, the Unchangeable Light.[7] Not this common light, which all flesh may look upon, nor, as it were, a greater one of the same kind, as though the brightness of this should be much more resplendent, and with its greatness fill up all things. Not like this was that light, but different, yea, very different from all these. Nor was it above my mind as oil is above water, nor as heaven above earth; but above it was, because it made me, and I below it, because I was made by it. He who knows the Truth knows that Light; and he that knows it knoweth eternity. Love knoweth it. O Eternal Truth, and true Love, and loved Eternity![8] Thou art my God; to Thee do I sigh both night and day. When I first knew Thee, Thou liftedst me up, that I might see there was that which I might see, and that yet it was not I that did see. And Thou didst beat back the infirmity of my sight, pouring forth upon me most strongly Thy beams of light, and I trembled with love and fear; and I found myself to be far off from Thee, in the region of dissimilarity, as if I heard this voice of Thine from on high: "I am the food of strong men; grow, and thou shalt feed upon me; nor shalt thou convert me, like the food of thy flesh, into thee, but thou shalt be converted into me." And I learned that Thou for iniquity dost correct man, and Thou dost make my soul to consume away like a spider.[9] And I said, "Is Truth, therefore, nothing because it is neither diffused through space, finite, nor infinite?" And Thou criedst to me from afar, "Yea, verily, 'I AM THAT I AM.'"[10] And I heard this, as things

---

[1] Ps. cvi. 20; Ex. xxxii. 1-6.
[2] Rom. ix. 12.
[3] Similarly, as to all truth being God's, Justin Martyr says: "Whatever things were rightly said among all men are the property of us Christians" (Apol. ii. 13). In this he parallels what Augustin claims in another place (De Doctr. Christ. ii. 28): "Let every good and true Christian understand that wherever truth may be found, it belongs to his Master." Origen has a similar allusion to that of Augustin above (Ep. ad Gregor. vol. i. 30), but echoes the experience of our erring nature, when he says that the gold of Egypt more frequently becomes transformed into an idol, than into an ornament for the tabernacle of God. Augustin gives us at length his views on this matter in his De Doctr. Christ. ii. 60, 61: "If those who are called philosophers, and especially the Platonists, have said aught that is true and in harmony with our faith, we are not only not to shrink from it, but to claim it for our own use from those who have unlawful possession of it. For, as the Egyptians had not only the idols and heavy burdens which the people of Israel hated and fled from, but also vessels and ornaments of gold and silver, and garments, which the same people when going out of Egypt appropriated to themselves, designing them for a better use,—not doing this on their own authority, but by the command of God, the Egyptians themselves, in their ignorance, providing them with things which they themselves were not making a good use of (Ex. iii. 21, 22, xii. 35, 36); in the same way all branches of heathen learning have not only false and superstitious fancies and heavy burdens of unnecessary toil, which every one of us, when going out under the leadership of Christ from the fellowship of the heathen, ought to abhor and avoid, but they contain also liberal instruction, which is better adapted to the use of the truth, and some most excellent precepts of morality; and some truths in regard even to the worship of the One God are found among them. Now these are, so to speak, their gold and silver, which they did not create themselves, but dug out of the mines of God's providence which are everywhere scattered abroad, and are perversely and unlawfully prostituting to the worship of devils. These, therefore, the Christian, when he separates himself in spirit from the miserable fellowship of these men, ought to take away from them, and to devote to their proper use in preaching the gospel. Their garments, also,— that is, human institutions such as are adapted to that intercourse with men which is indispensable in this life,—we must take and turn to a Christian use. And what else have many good and faithful men among our brethren done? Do we not see with what a quantity of gold and silver, and garments, Cyprian, that most persuasive teacher and most blessed martyr, was loaded when he came out of Egypt? How much Lactantius brought with him! And Victorinus, and Optatus, and Hilary, not to speak of living men! How much Greeks out of number have borrowed! And, prior to all these, that most faithful servant of God, Moses, had done the same thing; for of him it is written that he was learned in all the wisdom of the Egyptians (Acts vii. 22). . . . For what was done at the time of the exodus was no doubt a type prefiguring what happens now."
[4] Acts xvii. 28.
[5] Hosea ii. 8.
[6] Rom. i. 25.

[7] Not the "corporeal brightness" which as a Manichee he had believed in, and to which reference has been made in iii. secs. 10, 12, iv. sec. 3, and sec. 2, above. The Christian belief he indicates in his De Trin. viii. 2: "God is Light (1 John i. 5), not in such way that these eyes see, but in such way as the heart sees when it is said, 'He is Truth.'" See also note 1, sec. 23, above.
[8] If we knew not God, he says, we could not love Him (De Trin. viii. 12); but in language very similar to that above, he tells us "we are men, created in the image of our Creator, whose eternity is true, and whose truth is eternal; whose love is eternal and true, and who Himself is the eternal, true, and adorable Trinity, without confusion, without separation" (De Civ. Dei, xi. 28); God, then, as even the Platonists hold, being the principle of all knowledge. "Let Him," he concludes, in his De Civ. Dei (viii. 4), "be sought in whom all things are secured to us, let Him be discovered in whom all truth becomes certain to us, let Him be loved in whom all becomes right to us."
[9] Ps. xxxix. 11, Vulg.
[10] Ex. iii. 14. Augustin, when in his De Civ. Dei (viii. 11, 12) he makes reference to this text, leans to the belief, from certain parallels between Plato's doctrines and those of the word of God, that he may have derived information concerning the Old Testament Scriptures from an interpreter when in Egypt. He says: "The most striking thing in this connection, and that which most of all inclines me almost to assent to the opinion that Plato was not ignorant of those writings, is the answer which was given to the question elicited from the holy Moses when the words of God were conveyed to him by the angel; for when he asked what was the name of that God who was commanding him to go and deliver the Hebrew people out of Egypt, this answer was given: 'I am who am; and thou shalt say to the children of Israel, He who is sent me unto you;' as though, compared with Him that truly is, because

are heard in the heart, nor was there room for doubt; and I should more readily doubt that I live than that Truth is not, which is "clearly seen, being understood by the things that are made."[1]

CHAP. XI.—THAT CREATURES ARE MUTABLE AND GOD ALONE IMMUTABLE.

17. And I viewed the other things below Thee, and perceived that they neither altogether are, nor altogether are not. They are, indeed, because they are from Thee; but are not, because they are not what Thou art. For that truly is which remains immutably.[2] It is good, then, for me to cleave unto God,[3] for if I remain not in Him, neither shall I in myself; but He, remaining in Himself, reneweth all things.[4] And Thou art the Lord my God, since Thou standest not in need of my goodness.[5]

CHAP. XII.—WHATEVER THINGS THE GOOD GOD HAS CREATED ARE VERY GOOD.

18. And it was made clear unto me that those things are good which yet are corrupted, which, neither were they supremely good, nor unless they were good, could be corrupted; because if supremely good, they were incorruptible, and if not good at all, there was nothing in them to be corrupted. For corruption harms, but, unless it could diminish goodness, it could not harm. Either, then, corruption harms not, which cannot be; or, what is most certain, all which is corrupted is deprived of good. But if they be deprived of all good, they will cease to be. For if they be, and cannot be at all corrupted, they will become better, because they shall remain incorruptibly. And what more monstrous than to assert that those things which have lost all their goodness are made better? Therefore, if they shall be deprived of all good, they shall no longer be. So long,

therefore, as they are, they are good; therefore whatsoever is, is good. That evil, then, which I sought whence it was, is not any substance; for were it a substance, it would be good. For either it would be an incorruptible substance, and so a chief good, or a corruptible substance, which unless it were good it could not be corrupted. I perceived, therefore, and it was made clear to me, that Thou didst make all things good, nor is there any substance at all that was not made by Thee; and because all that Thou hast made are not equal, therefore all things are; because individually they are good, and altogether very good, because our God made all things very good.[6]

CHAP. XIII.—IT IS MEET TO PRAISE THE CREATOR FOR THE GOOD THINGS WHICH ARE MADE IN HEAVEN AND EARTH.

19. And to Thee is there nothing at all evil, and not only to Thee, but to Thy whole creation; because there is nothing without which can break in, and mar that order which Thou hast appointed it. But in the parts thereof, some things, because they harmonize not with others, are considered evil;[7] whereas those very things harmonize with others, and are good, and in themselves are good. And all these things which do not harmonize together harmonize with the inferior part which we call earth, having its own cloudy and windy sky concordant to it. Far be it from me, then, to say, "These things should not be." For should I see nothing but these, I should indeed desire better; but yet, if only for these, ought I to praise Thee; for that Thou art to be praised is shown from the "earth, dragons, and all deeps; fire, and hail; snow, and vapours; stormy winds fulfilling Thy word; mountains, and all hills; fruitful trees, and all cedars; beasts, and all cattle; creeping things, and flying fowl; kings of the earth, and all people; princes, and all judges of the earth; both young men and maidens; old men and children," praise Thy name. But when, "from the heavens," these praise Thee, praise Thee, our God, "in the heights," all Thy "angels," all Thy "hosts," "sun and moon," all ye stars and light, "the heavens of heavens," and the "waters that be above the heavens," praise Thy name.[8] I did not now desire better things, because I was thinking of all; and with a better judgment I reflected that the things above were better than those below, but that all were better than those above alone.

He is unchangeable, those things which have been created mutable *are* not,—a truth which Plato vehemently held, and most diligently commended. And I know not whether this sentiment is anywhere to be found in the books of those who were before Plato, unless in that book where it is said, 'I am who am; and thou shalt say to the children of Israel, *Who is* sent me unto you.' But we need not determine from what source he learned these things,—whether it was from the books of the ancients who preceded him, or, as is more likely, from the words of the apostle (Rom. i. 20), 'Because that which is known of God has been manifested among them, for God hath manifested it to them. For His invisible things from the creation of the world are clearly seen, being understood by those things which have been made, also His eternal power and Godhead.' "—*De Civ. Dei*, viii. 11, 12.

[1] Rom. i. 20.

[2] Therefore, he argues, is God called the I AM (*De Nat. Boni*, 19); for *omnis mutatio facit non esse quod erat*. Similarly, we find him speaking in his *De Mor. Manich.* (c. i.): "For that exists in the highest sense of the word which continues always the same, which is throughout like itself, which cannot in any part be corrupted or changed, which is not subject to time, which admits of no variation in its present as compared with its former condition. This is existence in its true sense." See also note 3, p. 158.

[3] Ps. lxxiii. 28.

Wisd. vii. 27.

Ps. xvi. 2.

---

[6] Gen i. 31, and Ecclus. xxxix. 21. Evil, with Augustin, is a "privation of good." See iii. sec. 12, note, above.

[7] See v. sec. 2, note 1, above, where Augustin illustrates the existence of good and evil by the lights and shades in a painting, etc.

[8] Ps. cxlviii. 1-12.

CHAP. XIV.—BEING DISPLEASED WITH SOME PART OF GOD'S CREATION, HE CONCEIVES OF TWO ORIGINAL SUBSTANCES.

20. There is no wholeness in them whom aught of Thy creation displeaseth; no more than there was in me, when many things which Thou madest displeased me. And, because my soul dared not be displeased at my God, it would not suffer aught to be Thine which displeased it. Hence it had gone into the opinion of two substances, and resisted not, but talked foolishly. And, returning thence, it had made to itself a god, through infinite measures of all space; and imagined it to be Thee, and placed it in its heart, and again had become the temple of its own idol, which was to Thee an abomination. But after Thou hadst fomented the head of me unconscious of it, and closed mine eyes lest they should "behold vanity,"[1] I ceased from myself a little, and my madness was lulled to sleep; and I awoke in Thee, and saw Thee to be infinite, though in another way; and this sight was not derived from the flesh.

CHAP. XV.—WHATEVER IS, OWES ITS BEING TO GOD.

21. And I looked back on other things, and I perceived that it was to Thee they owed their being, and that they were all bounded in Thee; but in another way, not as being in space, but because Thou holdest all things in Thine hand in truth: and all things are true so far as they have a being; nor is there any falsehood, unless that which is not is thought to be. And I saw that all things harmonized, not with their places only, but with their seasons also. And that Thou, who only art eternal, didst not begin to work after innumerable spaces of times; for that all spaces of times, both those which have passed and which shall pass, neither go nor come, save through Thee, working and abiding.[2]

CHAP. XVI.—EVIL ARISES NOT FROM A SUBSTANCE, BUT FROM THE PERVERSION OF THE WILL.

22. And I discerned and found it no marvel, that bread which is distasteful to an unhealthy palate is pleasant to a healthy one; and that the light, which is painful to sore eyes, is delightful to sound ones. And Thy righteousness displeaseth the wicked; much more the viper and little worm, which Thou hast created good, fitting in with inferior parts of Thy creation; with which the wicked themselves also fit in, the more in proportion as they are unlike Thee, but with the superior creatures, in proportion as they become like to Thee.[3] And I inquired what iniquity was, and ascertained it not to be

a substance, but a perversion of the will, bent aside from Thee, O God, the Supreme Substance, towards these lower things, and casting out its bowels,[4] and swelling outwardly.

CHAP. XVII.—ABOVE HIS CHANGEABLE MIND, HE DISCOVERS THE UNCHANGEABLE AUTHOR OF TRUTH.

23. And I marvelled that I now loved Thee, and no phantasm instead of Thee. And yet I did not merit to enjoy my God, but was transported to Thee by Thy beauty, and presently torn away from Thee by mine own weight, sinking with grief into these inferior things. This weight was carnal custom. Yet was there a remembrance of Thee with me; nor did I any way doubt that there was one to whom I might cleave, but that I was not yet one who could cleave unto Thee; for that the body which is corrupted presseth down the soul, and the earthly dwelling weigheth down the mind which thinketh upon many things.[5] And most certain I was that Thy "invisible things from the creation of the world are clearly seen, being understood by the things that are made, even Thy eternal power and Godhead."[6] For, inquiring whence it was that I admired the beauty of bodies whether celestial or terrestrial, and what supported me in judging correctly on things mutable, and pronouncing, "This should be thus, this not,"—inquiring, then, whence I so judged, seeing I did so judge, I had found the unchangeable and true eternity of Truth, above my changeable mind. And thus, by degrees, I passed from bodies to the soul, which makes use of the senses of the body to perceive; and thence to its inward[7] faculty, to which the bodily senses represent outward things, and up to which reach the capabilities of beasts; and thence, again, I passed on to the reasoning faculty,[8] unto which whatever is received from

---

1 Ps. cxix. 37.
2 See xi. secs. 15, 16, 26, etc., below.
3 See v. sec. 2, note 1, above.

4 Ecclus. x. 9. Commenting on this passage of the Apocrypha (*De Mus.* vi. 40), he says, that while the soul's happiness and life is in God, "what is to go into outer things, but to cast out its *inward parts*, that is, to place itself far from God—not by distance of place, but by the affection of the mind?"
5 Wisd. ix. 15.
6 Rom. i. 20.
7 See above, sec. 10.
8 Here, and more explicitly in sec. 25, we have before us what has been called the "trichotomy" of man. This doctrine Augustin does not deny in theory, but appears to consider (*De Anima*, iv. 32) it prudent to overlook in practice. The biblical view of psychology may well be considered here not only on its own account, but as enabling us clearly to apprehend this passage and that which follows it. It is difficult to understand how any one can doubt that St. Paul, when speaking in 1 Thess. v. 23, of our "*spirit, soul, and body*" being preserved unto the coming of our Lord Jesus Christ," implies a belief in a kind of trinity in man. And it is very necessary to the understanding of other Scriptures that we should realize what special attributes pertain to the soul and the spirit respectively. It may be said, generally, that the soul ($\psi\nu\chi\dot{\eta}$) is that passionate and affectionate nature which is common to us and the inferior creatures, while the spirit ($\pi\nu\epsilon\hat{\nu}\mu\alpha$) is the higher intellectual nature which is peculiar to man. Hence our Lord in His agony in the garden says (Matt. xxvi. 38), "My SOUL is exceeding *sorrowful*"—the soul being liable to emotions of pleasure and pain. In the same passage (ver 41) he says to the apostles who had slept during His great agony, "The SPIRIT indeed is *willing*, but the flesh is weak," so that the spirit is the seat of the will. And that the spirit is also

the senses of the body is referred to be judged, which also, finding itself to be variable in me, raised itself up to its own intelligence, and from habit drew away my thoughts, withdrawing itself from the crowds of contradictory phantasms; that so it might find out that light[1] by which it was besprinkled, when, without all doubting, it cried out, " that the unchangeable was to be preferred before the changeable; " whence also it knew that unchangeable, which, unless it had in some way known, it could have had no sure ground for preferring it to the changeable. And thus, with the flash of a trembling glance, it arrived at that which is. And then I saw Thy invisible things understood by the things that are made.[2] But I was not able to fix my gaze thereon; and my infirmity being beaten back, I was thrown again on my accustomed habits, carrying along with me naught but a loving memory thereof, and an appetite for what I had, as it were, smelt the odour of, but was not yet able to eat.

CHAP. XVIII.—JESUS CHRIST, THE MEDIATOR, IS THE ONLY WAY OF SAFETY.

24. And I sought a way of acquiring strength sufficient to enjoy Thee; but I found it not until I embraced that " Mediator between God and man, the man Christ Jesus,"[3] " who is over all, God blessed for ever,"[4] calling unto me, and saying, " I am the way, the truth, and the life,"[5] and mingling that food which I was unable to receive with our flesh. For " the Word was made flesh,"[6] that Thy wisdom, by which Thou createdst all things, might provide milk for our infancy. For I did not grasp my Lord Jesus,—I, though humbled, grasped not the humble One;[7] nor did I know what lesson that infirmity of His would teach us. For Thy Word, the Eternal Truth, pre-eminent above the higher parts of Thy creation, raises up those that are subject unto Itself; but in this lower world built for Itself a humble habitation of our clay, whereby He intended to abase from themselves such as would be subjected and bring them over unto Himself, allaying their swelling, and fostering their love; to the end that they might go on no further in self-confidence, but rather should become weak, seeing before their feet the Divinity weak by taking our " coats of skins; "[8] and wearied, might cast themselves down upon It, and It rising, might lift them up.

CHAP. XIX.—HE DOES NOT YET FULLY UNDERSTAND THE SAYING OF JOHN, THAT " THE WORD WAS MADE FLESH."

25. But I thought differently, thinking only of my Lord Christ as of a man of excellent wisdom, to whom no man could be equalled; especially for that, being wonderfully born of a virgin, He seemed, through the divine care for us, to have attained so great authority of leadership,—for an example of contemning temporal things for the obtaining of immortality. But what mystery there was in, " The Word was

---

the seat of *consciousness* we gather from St. Paul's words (1 Cor. ii. 11), " What man knoweth the things of a man, save the spirit of man which is in him? even so the things of God knoweth no man, but the Spirit of God." And it is *on the spirit of man that the Spirit of God operates;* whence we read (Rom. viii. 16), " The Spirit beareth witness with our spirit, that we are the children of God." It is important to note that the word " flesh " ($\sigma\alpha\rho\xi$) has its special significance, as distinct from body. The word comes to us from the Hebrew through the Hellenistic Greek of the LXX., and in biblical language (see Bishop Pearson's *Præfatio Parænetica* to his edition of the LXX.) stands for our human nature with its worldly surroundings and liability to temptation; so that when it is said, " The Word was made flesh," we have what is equivalent to, " The Word put on human nature." It is, therefore, the flesh and the spirit that are ever represented in conflict one with the other when men are in the throes of temptation. So it must be while life lasts; for it is characteristic of our position in the world that we possess *soulish* bodies (to employ the barbarous but expressive word of Dr. Candlish in his *Life in a Risen Saviour*, p. 182), and only on the morning of the resurrection will the body be *spiritual* and suited to the new sphere of its existence: " It is sown a natural [$\psi\upsilon\chi\iota\kappa\grave{o}\nu$, " soulish "] body, it is raised a spiritual [$\pi\nu\epsilon\upsilon\mu\alpha\tau\iota\kappa\acute{o}\nu$] body" (1 Cor. xv. 44); " for," as Augustin says in his *Enchiridion* (c. xci.), " just as now the body is called *animate* (or, using the Greek term, as above, instead of the Latin, " soulish "), though it is a body and not a soul, so then the body shall be called *spiritual*, though it shall be a body, not a spirit. . . . No part of our nature shall be in discord with another; but as we shall be free from enemies without, so we shall not have ourselves for enemies within." For further information on this most interesting subject, see Delitzsch, *Biblical Psychology*, ii. 4 (" The True and False Trichotomy "); Olshausen, *Opuscula Theologica*, iv. (" De Trichotomia "); and cc. 2, 17, and 18 of R. W. Evans' *Ministry of the Body*, where the subject is discussed with thoughtfulness and spiritual insight. This matter is also treated of in the introductory chapters of Schlegel's *Philosophy of Life*.
[1] That light which illumines the soul, he tells us in his *De Gen. ad Lit.* (xii. 31), is God Himself, from whom all light cometh; and, though created in His image and likeness, when it tries to discover Him, *palpitat infirmitate, et minus valet*. In sec. 13, above, speaking of Platonism, he describes it as holding " that the soul of man, though it ' bears witness of the Light,' yet itself ' is not that Light.' " In his *De Civ. Dei*, x. 2, he quotes from Plotinus (mentioned in note 2, sec. 13, above) in regard to the Platonic doctrine as to enlightenment from on high. He says: " Plotinus, commenting on Plato, repeatedly and strongly asserts that not even the soul, which they believe to be the soul of the world, derives its blessedness from any other source than we do, viz. from that Light which is distinct from it and created it, and by whose intelligible illumination it enjoys light in things intelligible. He also compares those spiritual things to the vast and conspicuous heavenly bodies, as if God were the sun, and the soul the moon; for they suppose that the moon derives its light from the sun. That great Platonist, therefore, says that the rational soul, or rather the intellectual soul,— in which class he comprehends the souls of the blessed immortals who inhabit heaven,—has no nature superior to it save God, the Creator of the world and the soul itself, and that these heavenly spirits derive their blessed life, and the light of truth, from the same source as ourselves, agreeing with the gospel where we read, ' There was a man sent from God, whose name was John. The same came for a witness, to bear witness of that Light, that through Him all might believe. He was not that Light, but that he might bear witness of the Light. That was the true Light, which lighteth every man that cometh into the world ' (John i. 6-9);—a distinction which sufficiently proves that the rational or intellectual soul, such as John had, cannot be its own light, but needs to receive illumination from another, the true Light. This John himself avows when he delivers his witness (*ibid.* 16): ' We have all received of His fulness.' " Comp. Tertullian, *De Testim. Anim.*, and the note to iv. sec. 25, above, where other references to God's being the Father of Lights are given.

[2] Rom. i. 20.
[3] 1 Tim. ii. 5.
[4] Rom. ix. 5.
[5] John xiv. 6.
[6] John i. 14.
[7] Christ descended that we may ascend. See iv. sec. 19, notes 1 and 3, above.
[8] Gen. iii. 21. Augustin frequently makes these " coats of skin" symbolize the mortality to which our first parents became subject by being deprived of the tree of life (see iv. sec. 15, note 3, above; and in his *Enarr. in Ps.* (ciii. 1, 8), he says they are thus symbolical inasmuch as the skin is only taken from animals when dead.

made flesh,"[1] I could not even imagine. Only I had learnt out of what is delivered to us in writing of Him, that He did eat, drink, sleep, walk, rejoice in spirit, was sad, and discoursed; that flesh alone did not cleave unto Thy Word, but with the human soul and body. All know thus who know the unchangeableness of Thy Word, which I now knew as well as I could, nor did I at all have any doubt about it. For, now to move the limbs of the body at will, now not; now to be stirred by some affection, now not; now by signs to enunciate wise sayings, now to keep silence, are properties of a soul and mind subject to change. And should these things be falsely written of Him, all the rest would risk the imputation, nor would there remain in those books any saving faith for the human race. Since, then, they were written truthfully, I acknowledged a perfect man to be in Christ—not the body of a man only, nor with the body a sensitive soul without a rational, but a very man; whom, not only as being a form of truth, but for a certain great excellency of human nature and a more perfect participation of wisdom, I decided was to be preferred before others. But Alypius imagined the Catholics to believe that God was so clothed with flesh, that, besides God and flesh, there was no soul in Christ, and did not think that a human mind was ascribed to Him. And, because He was thoroughly persuaded that the actions which were recorded of Him could not be performed except by a vital and rational creature, he moved the more slowly towards the Christian faith. But, learning afterwards that this was the error of the Apollinarian heretics,[2] he rejoiced

in the Catholic faith, and was conformed to it. But somewhat later it was, I confess, that I learned how in the sentence, "The Word was made flesh," the Catholic truth can be distinguished from the falsehood of Photinus.[3] For the disapproval of heretics makes the tenets of Thy Church and sound doctrine to stand out boldly.[4] For there must be also heresies, that the approved may be made manifest among the weak.[5]

CHAP. XX.—HE REJOICES THAT HE PROCEEDED FROM PLATO TO THE HOLY SCRIPTURES, AND NOT THE REVERSE.

26. But having then read those books of the

---

[1] We have already seen, in note 1, sec. 13, above, how this text (1) runs counter to Platonic beliefs as to the *Logos*. The following passage from Augustin's *De Civ. Dei*, x. 29, is worth putting on record in this connection:—"Are ye ashamed to be corrected? This is the vice of the proud. It is, forsooth, a degradation for learned men to pass from the school of Plato to the discipleship of Christ, who by His Spirit taught a fisherman to think and to say, 'In the beginning was the Word, and the Word was with God, and the Word was God. The same was in the beginning with God. All things were made by Him, and without Him was not any thing made that was made. In Him was life; and the life was the light of men. And the light shineth in darkness; and the darkness comprehended it not' (John i. 1-5). The old saint Simplicianus, afterwards Bishop of Milan, used to tell me that a certain Platonist was in the habit of saying that this opening passage of the holy Gospel entitled, 'According to John,' should be written in letters of gold, and hung up in all churches in the most conspicuous place. But the proud scorn to take God for their Master, because 'the Word was made flesh and dwelt among us' (John i. 14). So that with these miserable creatures it is not enough that they are sick, but they boast of their sickness, and are ashamed of the medicine which could heal them. And doing so, they secure not elevation, but a more disastrous fall." This text, too, as Irenæus has remarked, (2) entirely opposes the false teaching of the *Docetæ*, who, as their name imports, believed, with the Manichæans, that Christ only *appeared* to have a body; as was the case, they said, with the angels entertained by Abraham (see Burton's *Bampton Lectures*, lect. 6). It is curious to note here that Augustin maintained that the Angel of the Covenant was not an anticipation, as it were, of the incarnation of the Word, but only a created angel (*De Civ. Dei*, xvi. 29, and *De Trin.* iii. 11), thus unconsciously playing into the hands of the Arians. See Bull's *Def. Fid. Nic.* i. 1, sec. 2, etc., and iv. 3, sec. 14.

[2] The founder of this heresy was Apollinaris the younger, Bishop of Laodicea, whose erroneous doctrine was condemned at the Council of Constantinople, A. D. 381. Note 4, sec. 23, above, on the "trichotomy," affords help in understanding it. Apollinaris seems to have desired to exalt the Saviour, not to detract from His

honour, like Arius. Before his time men had written much on the divine and much on the human side of our Lord's nature. He endeavoured to show (see Dorner's *Person of Christ*, A. ii. 252, etc., Clark) in what the two natures united differed from human nature. He concluded that our Lord had no need of the human πνεῦμα, and that its place was supplied by the divine nature, so that God "the Word," the body and the ψυχή, constituted the being of the Saviour. Dr. Pusey quotes the following passages hereon:—" The faithful who believes and confesses in the Mediator a real human, *i. e.* our nature, although God the Word, taking it in a singular manner, sublimated it into the only Son of God, so that He who took it, and what He took, was one person in the Trinity. For, after man was assumed, there became not a quaternity but remained the Trinity, that assumption making in an ineffable way the truth of one person in God and man. Since we do not say that Christ is only God, as do the Manichæan heretics, nor only man, as the Photinian heretics, nor in such wise man as not to have anything which certainly belongs to human nature, whether the soul, or in the soul itself the rational mind, or the flesh not taken of the woman, but made of the Word, converted and changed into flesh, which three false and vain statements made three several divisions of the Apollinarian heretics; but we say that Christ is true God, born of God the Father, without any beginning of time, and also true man, born of a human mother in the fulness of time; and that His humanity, whereby He is inferior to the Father, does not derogate from His divinity, whereby He is equal to the Father" (*De Dono Persev.* sec. *ult.*). "There was formerly a heresy—its remnants perhaps still exist—of some called Apollinarians. Some of them said that that man whom the Word took, when 'the Word was made flesh,' had not the human, *i. e.* rational (λογικόν) mind, but was only a soul without human intelligence, but that the very Word of God was in that man instead of a mind. They were cast out,—the Catholic faith rejected them, and they made a heresy. It was established in the Catholic faith that that man whom the wisdom of God took had nothing less than other men, with regard to the integrity of man's nature, but as to the excellency of His person, had more than other men. For other men may be said to be partakers of the Word of God, having the Word of God, but none of them can be called the Word of God, which He was called when it is said, 'The Word was made flesh'" (*in Ps.* xxix., *Enarr.* ii. sec. 2). "But when they reflected that, if their doctrine were true, they must confess that the only-begotten Son of God, the Wisdom and Word of the Father, *by whom all things were made*, is believed to have taken a sort of brute with the figure of a human body, they were dissatisfied with themselves; yet not so as to amend, and confess that the whole man was assumed by the wisdom of God, without any diminution of nature, but still more boldly denied to Him the soul itself, and everything of any worth in man, and said that He only took human flesh" (*De 83, Div. Quæst.* qu. 80). Reference on the questions touched on in this note may be made to Neander's *Church History*, ii. 401, etc. (Clark); and Hagenbach, *History of Doctrines*, i. 270 (Clark).

[3] See notes on p. 107.

[4] Archbishop Trench's words on this sentence in the *Confessions* (*Hulsean Lectures*, lect. v. 1845) have a special interest in the present attitude of the Roman Church :—" Doubtless there is a true idea of scriptural developments which has always been recognised, to which the great Fathers of the Church have set their seal; this, namely, that the Church, informed and quickened by the Spirit of God, more and more discovers what in Holy Scripture is given her; but not this, that she unfolds by an independent power anything further therefrom. She has always possessed what she now possesses of doctrine and truth, only not always with the same distinctness of consciousness. She has not added to her wealth, but she has become more and more aware of that wealth; her dowry has remained always the same, but that dowry was so rich and so rare, that only little by little she has counted over and taken stock and inventory of her jewels. She has consolidated her doctrine, compelled to this by the challenges and provocation of enemies, or induced to it by the growing sense of her own needs." Perhaps no one, to turn from the Church to individual men, has been more indebted than was Augustin to controversies with heretics for the evolvement of truth.

[5] 1 Cor. xi. 19.

Platonists, and being admonished by them to search for incorporeal truth, I saw Thy invisible things, understood by those things that are made;[1] and though repulsed, I perceived what that was, which through the darkness of my mind I was not allowed to contemplate,—assured that Thou wert, and wert infinite, and yet not diffused in space finite or infinite; and that Thou truly art, who art the same ever,[2] varying neither in part nor motion; and that all other things are from Thee, on this most sure ground alone, that they are. Of these things was I indeed assured, yet too weak to enjoy Thee. I chattered as one well skilled; but had I not sought Thy way in Christ our Saviour, I would have proved not skilful, but ready to perish. For now, filled with my punishment, I had begun to desire to seem wise; yet mourned I not, but rather was puffed up with knowledge.[3] For where was that charity building upon the "foundation" of humility, "which is Jesus Christ"?[4] Or, when would these books teach me it? Upon these, therefore, I believe, it was Thy pleasure that I should fall before I studied Thy Scriptures, that it might be impressed on my memory how I was affected by them; and that afterwards when I was subdued by Thy books, and when my wounds were touched by Thy healing fingers, I might discern and distinguish what a difference there is between presumption and confession,—between those who saw whither they were to go, yet saw not the way, and the way which leadeth not only to behold but to inhabit the blessed country.[5] For had I first been moulded in Thy Holy Scriptures, and hadst Thou, in the familiar use of them, grown sweet unto me, and had I afterwards fallen upon those volumes, they might perhaps have withdrawn me from the solid ground of piety; or, had I stood firm in that wholesome disposition which I had thence imbibed, I might have thought that it could have been attained by the study of those books alone.

CHAP. XXI.—WHAT HE FOUND IN THE SACRED BOOKS WHICH ARE NOT TO BE FOUND IN PLATO.

27. Most eagerly, then, did I seize that venerable writing of Thy Spirit, but more especially the Apostle Paul;[6] and those difficulties vanished away, in which he at one time appeared to me to contradict himself, and the text of his discourse not to agree with the testimonies of the Law and the Prophets. And the face of that pure speech appeared to me one and the same; and I learned to "rejoice with trembling."[7] So I commenced, and found that whatsoever truth I had there read was declared here with the recommendation of Thy grace; that he who sees may not so glory as if he had not received[8] not only that which he sees, but also that he can see (for what hath he which he hath not received?); and that he may not only be admonished to see Thee, who art ever the same, but also may be healed, to hold Thee; and that he who from afar off is not able to see, may still walk on the way by which he may reach, behold, and possess Thee. For though a man "delight in the law of God after the inward man,"[9] what shall he do with that other law in his members which warreth against the law of his mind, and bringeth him into captivity to the law of sin, which is in his members?[10] For Thou art righteous, O Lord, but we have sinned and committed iniquity, and have done wickedly,[11] and Thy hand is grown heavy upon us, and we are justly delivered over unto that ancient sinner, the governor of death; for he induced our will to be like his will, whereby he remained not in Thy truth. What shall "wretched man" do? "Who shall deliver him from the body of this death," but Thy grace only, "through Jesus Christ our Lord,"[12] whom Thou hast begotten co-eternal, and createdst[13] in the begin-

---

[1] Rom. i. 20.
[2] See sec. 17, note, above.
[3] 1 Cor. viii. 1.
[4] 1 Cor. iii. 11.
[5] We have already quoted a passage from Augustin's *Sermons* (v. sec. 5, note 7, above), where Christ as God is described as the country we seek, while as man He is the way to go to it. The Fathers frequently point out in their controversies with the philosophers that it little profited that they should know of a goal to be attained unless they could learn the *way* to reach it. And, in accordance with this sentiment, Augustin says: "For it is as man that He is the Mediator and the Way. Since, if the way lieth between him who goes and the place whither he goes, there is hope of his reaching it; but if there be no way, or if he know not where it is, what boots it to know whither he should go?" (*De Civ. Dei*, xi. 2.) And again, in his *De Trin.* iv. 15: "But of what use is it for the proud man,

[6] Literally, "The venerable *pen* of Thy Spirit (*venerabilem stilum Spiritus Tui*); words which would seem to imply a belief on Augustin's part in a verbal inspiration of Scripture. That he gave Scripture the highest honour as God's inspired word is clear not only from this, but other passages in his works. It is equally clear, however, that he gave full recognition to the human element in the word. See *De Cons. Evang.* ii. 12, where both these aspects are plainly discoverable. Compare also *ibid.* c. 24.
[7] Ps. ii. 11.
[8] 1 Cor. iv. 7.
[9] Rom. vii. 22.
[10] *Ibid.* ver. 23.
[11] Song of the Three Children, 4 *sq.*
[12] Rom. vii. 24, 25.
[13] Prov. viii. 22, as quoted from the old Italic version. It must not be understood to teach that the Lord is a creature. (1) Augustin, as indeed is implied in the *Confessions* above, understands the passage of the incarnation of Christ, and in his *De Doct. Christ.* i. 38, he distinctly so applies it : "For Christ . . . desiring to be Himself the Way to those who are just setting out, determined to take a fleshly body. Whence also that expression, 'The Lord created me in the beginning of his Way,'—that is, that those who wish to come might begin their journey in Him" Again, in a remarkable passage in his *De Trin.* i. 24, he makes a similar application of the words : "According to the form of a servant, it is said, 'The Lord created me in the beginning of His ways.' Because, according to the form of God, he said, 'I am the Truth;' and, according to the form of a servant, 'I am the Way.'" (2) Again, *creasti* is from the LXX. ἔκτισε, which is that version's rendering in this verse of the Hebrew קָנָנִי. The *Vulgate*, more correctly translating from the Hebrew, gives *possedit*, thus corresponding to our English version, "The Lord *possessed* me," etc. The LXX. would appear to have made an erroneous rendering here, for κτίζω is generally in that

---

who, on that account, is ashamed to embark upon the ship of wood, to behold from afar his country beyond the sea? Or how can it hurt the humble man not to behold it from so great a distance, when he is actually coming to it by that wood upon which the other disdains to be borne?"

ning of Thy ways, in whom the Prince of this world found nothing worthy of death,[1] yet killed he Him, and the handwriting which was contrary to us was blotted out?[2] This those writings contain not. Those pages contain not the expression of this piety,—the tears of confession, Thy sacrifice, a troubled spirit, "a broken and a contrite heart,"[3] the salvation of the people, the espoused city,[4] the earnest of the Holy Ghost,[5] the cup of our redemption.[6] No man sings there, Shall not my soul be subject unto God? For of Him cometh my salvation, for He is my God and my salvation, my defender, I shall not be further moved.[7] No one there hears Him calling, "Come unto me all ye that labour." They scorn to learn of Him, because He is meek and lowly of heart;[8] for "Thou hast hid those things from the wise and prudent, and hast revealed them unto babes."[9] For it is one thing, from the mountain's wooded

summit to see the land of peace,[10] and not to find the way thither,—in vain to attempt impassable ways, opposed and waylaid by fugitives and deserters, under their captain the "lion"[11] and the "dragon;"[12] and another to keep to the way that leads thither, guarded by the host of the heavenly general, where they rob not who have deserted the heavenly army, which they shun as torture. These things did in a wonderful manner sink into my bowels, when I read that "least of Thy apostles,"[13] and had reflected upon Thy works, and feared greatly.

---

[10] Deut. xxxii. 49.
[11] 1 Pet. v. 8.
[12] Rev. xii. 3.
[13] 1 Cor. xv. 9. In giving an account, remarks Pusey, of this period to his friend and patron Romanianus, St. Augustin seems to have blended together this and the history of his completed conversion, which was also wrought in connection with words in the same apostle, but the account of which he uniformly suppresses, for fear, probably, of injuring the individual to whom he was writing (see on book ix. sec. 4, note, below). "Since that vehement flame which was about to seize me as yet was not, I thought that by which I was slowly kindled was the very greatest. When lo! certain books, when they had distilled a very few drops of most precious unguent on that tiny flame, it is past belief, Romanianus, past belief, and perhaps past what even you believe of me (and what could I say more?), nay, to myself also is it past belief, what a conflagration of myself they lighted. What ambition, what human show, what empty love of fame, or, lastly, what incitement or band of this mortal life could hold me then? I turned speedily and wholly back into myself. I cast but a glance, I confess, as one passing on, upon that religion which was implanted into us as boys, and interwoven with our very inmost selves; but she drew me unknowing to herself. So then, stumbling, hurrying, hesitating, I seized the Apostle Paul; 'for never,' said I, 'could they have wrought such things, or lived as it is plain they did live, if their writings and arguments were opposed to this so high good.' I read the whole most intently and carefully. But then, never so little light having been shed thereon, such a countenance of wisdom gleamed upon me, that if I could exhibit it—I say not to you, who ever hungeredst after her, though unknown—but to your very adversary (see book vi. sec. 24, note, above), casting aside and abandoning whatever now stimulates him so keenly to whatsoever pleasures, he would, amazed, panting, enkindled, fly to her Beauty" (*Con. Acad.* ii. 5).

---

version the equivalent for בָּרָא, "to create," while קָנָה is usually rendered by κτάομαι, "to possess," "to acquire." It is true that Gesenius supposes that in a few passages, and Prov. viii. 22 among them, קָנָה should be rendered "to create;" but these very passages our authorized version renders "to get," or "to possess;" and, as Dr. Tregelles observes, referring to M'Call on the Divine Sonship, "in all passages cited for that sense, 'to possess' appears to be the true meaning."

[1] John xviii. 38.
[2] Col. ii. 14.
[3] Ps. li. 17.
[4] Rev. xxi. 2.
[5] 2 Cor. v. 5.
[6] Ps. cxvi. 13.
[7] Ps. lxii. 1, 2.
[8] Matt. xi. 28, 29.
[9] Matt. xi. 25.

BOOK VIII.

CHAP. I.—HE, NOW GIVEN TO DIVINE THINGS, AND YET ENTANGLED BY THE LUSTS OF LOVE, CONSULTS SIMPLICIANUS IN REFERENCE TO THE RENEWING OF HIS MIND.

1. O MY God, let me with gratitude remember and confess unto Thee Thy mercies bestowed upon me. Let my bones be steeped in Thy love, and let them say, Who is like unto Thee, O Lord?[1] "Thou hast loosed my bonds, I will offer unto Thee the sacrifice of thanksgiving."[2] And how Thou hast loosed them I will declare; and all who worship Thee when they hear these things shall say: "Blessed be the Lord in heaven and earth, great and wonderful is His name." Thy words had stuck fast into my breast, and I was hedged round about by Thee on every side.[3] Of Thy eternal life I was now certain, although I had seen it "through a glass darkly."[4] Yet I no longer doubted that there was an incorruptible substance, from which was derived all other substance; nor did I now desire to be more certain of Thee, but more stedfast in Thee. As for my temporal life, all things were uncertain, and my heart had to be purged from the old leaven.[5] The "Way,"[6] the Saviour Himself, was pleasant unto me, but as yet I disliked to pass through its straightness. And Thou didst put into my mind, and it seemed good in my eyes, to go unto Simplicianus,[7] who appeared to me a faithful servant of Thine, and Thy grace

shone in him. I had also heard that from his very youth he had lived most devoted to Thee. Now he had grown into years, and by reason of so great age, passed in such zealous following of Thy ways, he appeared to me likely to have gained much experience; and so in truth he had. Out of which experience I desired him to tell me (setting before him my griefs) which would be the most fitting way for one afflicted as I was to walk in Thy way.

2. For the Church I saw to be full, and one went this way, and another that. But it was displeasing to me that I led a secular life; yea, now that my passions had ceased to excite me as of old with hopes of honour and wealth, a very grievous burden it was to undergo so great a servitude. For, compared with Thy sweetness, and the beauty of Thy house, which I loved,[8] those things delighted me no longer. But still very tenaciously was I held by the love of women; nor did the apostle forbid me to marry, although he exhorted me to something better, especially wishing that all men were as he himself was.[9] But I, being weak, made choice of the more agreeable place, and because of this alone was tossed up and down in all beside, faint and languishing with withering cares, because in other matters I was compelled, though unwilling, to agree to a married life, to which I was given up and enthralled. I had heard from the mouth of truth that "there be eunuchs, which have made themselves eunuchs for the kingdom of heaven's sake;" but, saith He, "he that is able to receive it, let him receive it."[10] Vain, assuredly, are all men in whom the knowledge of God is not, and who could not, out of the good things which are seen, find out Him who is good.[11] But I was no longer in that vanity; I had surmounted it, and by the united testimony of Thy whole creation had found Thee, our Creator,[12] and Thy

---

[1] Ps. xxxv. 10.
[2] Ps. cxvi. 16, 17.
[3] Job. i. 10.
[4] 1 Cor. xiii. 12.
[5] 1 Cor. v. 7.
[6] John xiv. 6.
[7] "Simplicianus 'became a successor of the most blessed Ambrose, Bishop of the Church of Milan' (Aug. *Retract.* ii. 1). To him St. Augustin wrote two books, *De Diversis Quæstionibus* (*Op.* t. vi. p. 82 *sq.*), and calls him 'father' (*ibid.*), speaks of his 'fatherly affections from his most benevolent heart, not recent or sudden, but tried and known' (*Ep.* 37), requests his 'remarks and corrections of any books of his which might chance to fall into his holy hands' (*ibid.*). St. Ambrose mentions his 'having traversed the whole world, for the sake of the faith, and of acquiring divine knowledge, and having given the whole period of this life to holy reading, night and day; that he had an acute mind, whereby he took in intellectual studies, and was in the habit of proving how far the books of philosophy were gone astray from the truth,' *Ep.* 65, sec. 5, p. 1052, ed. Ben. See also Tillemont, H. E. t. 10, Art. 'S. Simplicien.'"—E. B. P.

[8] Ps. xxvi. 8.
[9] 1 Cor. vii. 7.
[10] Matt. xix. 12.
[11] Wisd. xiii. 1.
[12] See iv. sec. 18, and note, above.

Word, God with Thee, and together with Thee and the Holy Ghost[1] one God, by whom Thou createdst all things. There is yet another kind of impious men, who "when they knew God, they glorified Him not as God, neither were thankful."[2] Into this also had I fallen; but Thy right hand held me up,[3] and bore me away, and Thou placedst me where I might recover. For Thou hast said unto man, "Behold, the fear of the Lord, that is wisdom;"[4] and desire not to seem wise,[5] because, "Professing themselves to be wise, they became fools."[6] But I had now found the goodly pearl,[7] which, selling all that I had,[8] I ought to have bought; and I hesitated.

CHAP. II.—THE PIOUS OLD MAN REJOICES THAT HE READ PLATO AND THE SCRIPTURES, AND TELLS HIM OF THE RHETORICIAN VICTORINUS HAVING BEEN CONVERTED TO THE FAITH THROUGH THE READING OF THE SACRED BOOKS.

3. To Simplicianus then I went,—the father of Ambrose[9] (at that time a bishop) in receiving Thy grace, and whom he truly loved as a father. To him I narrated the windings of my error. But when I mentioned to him that I had read certain books of the Platonists, which Victorinus, sometime Professor of Rhetoric at Rome (who died a Christian, as I had been told), had translated into Latin, he congratulated me that I had not fallen upon the writings of other philosophers, which were full of fallacies and deceit, "after the rudiments of the world,"[10] whereas they,[11] in many ways, led to the belief in God and His word.[12] Then, to

exhort me to the humility of Christ,[13] hidden from the wise, and revealed to little ones,[14] he spoke of Victorinus himself,[15] whom, whilst he was at Rome, he had known very intimately; and of him he related that about which I will not be silent. For it contains great praise of Thy grace, which ought to be confessed unto Thee, how that most learned old man, highly skilled in all the liberal sciences, who had read, criticised, and explained so many works of the philosophers; the teacher of so many noble senators; who also, as a mark of his excellent discharge of his duties, had (which men of this world esteem a great honour) both merited and obtained a statue in the Roman Forum, he,—even to that age a worshipper of idols, and a participator in the sacrilegious rites to which almost all the nobility of Rome were wedded, and had inspired the people with the love of

> "The dog Anubis, and a medley crew
> Of monster gods [who] 'gainst Neptune stand in arms,
> 'Gainst Venus and Minerva, steel-clad Mars,"[16]

whom Rome once conquered, now worshipped, all which old Victorinus had with thundering eloquence defended so many years,—he now blushed not to be the child of Thy Christ, and an infant at Thy fountain, submitting his neck to the yoke of humility, and subduing his forehead to the reproach of the Cross.

4. O Lord, Lord, who hast bowed the heavens and come down, touched the mountains and they did smoke,[17] by what means didst Thou convey Thyself into that bosom? He used to read, as Simplicianus said, the Holy Scripture, most studiously sought after and searched into all the Christian writings, and said to Simplicianus,—not openly, but secretly, and as a friend,—"Know thou that I am a Christian." To which he replied, "I will not believe it, nor will I rank you among the Christians unless I see you in the Church of Christ." Whereupon he replied derisively, "Is it then the walls that make Christians?" And this he

---

1 "And the Holy Ghost." These words, though in the text of the Benedictine edition are not, as the editors point out, found in the majority of the best MSS.

2 Rom. i. 21.

3 Ps. xviii. 35.

4 Job xxviii. 28.

5 Prov. iii. 7.

6 Rom. i. 22.

7 In his *Quæst. ex Matt.* 13, likewise, Augustin compares Christ to the pearl of great price, who is in every way able to satisfy the cravings of man.

8 Matt. xiii. 46.

9 Simplicianus succeeded Ambrose, 397 A. D. He has already been referred to, in the extract from *De Civ. Dei*, in note 1, p. 113, above, as "the old saint Simplicianus, afterwards Bishop of Milan." In *Ep.* 37, Augustin addresses him as "his father, most worthy of being cherished with respect and sincere affection." When Simplicianus is spoken of above as "the father of Ambrose in receiving Thy grace," reference is doubtless made to his having been instrumental in his conversion—he having "begotten" him "through the gospel" (1 Cor. iv. 15). Ambrose, when writing to him (*Ep.* 65), concludes, "Vale, et nos parentis affectu dilige, ut facis."

10 Col. ii. 8.

11 *i. e.* the Platonists.

12 In like manner Augustin, in his *De Civ. Dei* (viii. 5), says: "No philosophers come nearer to us than the Platonists;" and elsewhere, in the same book, he speaks, in exalted terms, of their superiority to other philosophers. When he speaks of the Platonists, he means the Neo-Platonists, from whom he conceived that he could best derive a knowledge of Plato, who had, by pursuing the Socratic method in concealing his opinions, rendered it difficult "to discover clearly what he himself thought on various matters, any more than it is to discover what were the real opinions of Socrates" (*ibid.* sec. 4). Whether Plato himself had or not knowledge of the revelation contained in the Old Testament Scriptures, as Augustin supposed (*De Civ. Dei*, viii. 11, 12), it is clear that the later Platonists

were considerably affected by Judaic ideas, even as the philosophizing Jews were indebted to Platonism. This view has been embodied in the proverb frequently found in the Fathers, Latin as well as Greek, Ἡ Πλάτων φιλονίζει ἢ Φίλων πλατωνίζει. Archer Butler, in the fourth of his *Lectures on Ancient Philosophy*, treats of the vitality of Plato's teaching and the causes of its influence, and shows how in certain points there is a harmony between his ideas and the precepts of the gospel. On the difficulty of unravelling the subtleties of the Platonic philosophy, see Burton's *Bampton Lectures* (lect. 3).

13 See iv. sec. 19, above.

14 Matt. xi. 25.

15 "Victorinus, by birth an African, taught rhetoric at Rome under Constantius, and in extreme old age, giving himself up to the faith of Christ, wrote some books against Arius, dialectically [and so] very obscure, which are not understood but by the learned, and a commentary on the Apostle" [Paul] (Jerome, *De Viris Ill.* c. 101). It is of the same, probably, that Gennadius speaks (*De Viris Ill.* c. 60), "that he commented in a Christian and pious strain, but inasmuch as he was a man taken up with secular literature, and not trained in the Divine Scriptures by any teacher, he produced what was comparatively of little weight." Comp. Jerome, *Præf. in Comm. in Gal.*, and see Tillemont, l. c. p. 179, *sq.* Some of his works are extant.—E. B. P.

16 *Æneid.*, viii. 736–8. The Kennedys.

17 Ps. cxliv. 5.

often said, that he already was a Christian ; and Simplicianus making the same answer, the conceit of the "walls" was by the other as often renewed. For he was fearful of offending his friends, proud demon-worshippers, from the height of whose Babylonian dignity, as from cedars of Lebanon which had not yet been broken by the Lord,[1] he thought a storm of enmity would descend upon him. But after that, from reading and inquiry, he had derived strength, and feared lest he should be denied by Christ before the holy angels if he now was afraid to confess Him before men,[2] and appeared to himself guilty of a great fault in being ashamed of the sacraments[3] of the humility of Thy word, and not being ashamed of the sacrilegious rites of those proud demons, whose pride he had imitated and their rites adopted, he became bold-faced against vanity, and shame-faced toward the truth, and suddenly and unexpectedly said to Simplicianus,— as he himself informed me,—" Let us go to the church ; I wish to be made a Christian." But he, not containing himself for joy, accompanied him. And having been admitted to the first sacraments of instruction,[4] he not long

after gave in his name, that he might be regenerated by baptism,—Rome marvelling, and the Church rejoicing. The proud saw, and were enraged ; they gnashed with their teeth, and melted away![5] But the Lord God was the hope of Thy servant, and He regarded not vanities and lying madness.[6]

5. Finally, when the hour arrived for him to make profession of his faith (which at Rome they who are about to approach Thy grace are wont to deliver[7] from an elevated place, in view of the faithful people, in a set form of words learnt by heart),[8] the presbyters, he said, offered

---

[1] Ps. xxix. 5.

[2] Luke ix. 26.

[3] " The Fathers gave the name of *sacrament*, or *mystery*, to everything which conveyed one signification or property to unassisted reason, and another to faith. Hence Cyprian speaks of the ' sacraments' of the Lord's Prayer, meaning the hidden meaning conveyed therein, which could only be appreciated by a Christian. The Fathers sometimes speak of confirmation as a sacrament, because the chrism signified the grace of the Holy Ghost ; and the imposition of hands was not merely a bare sign, but the form by which it was conveyed. See Bingham, book xii. c. 1, sec. 4. Yet at the same time they continually speak of *two* great sacraments of the Christian Church " (Palmer's *Origines Liturgicæ*, vol. ii. c. 6, sec. 1, p. 201).

[4] That is, he became a *catechumen*. In addition to the information on this subject, already given in the note to book vi. sec. 2, above, the following references to it may prove instructive. (1) Justin Martyr, describing the manner of receiving converts into the Church in his day, says (*Apol.* i. 61) : "As many as are persuaded and believe that what we teach and say is true, and undertake to be able to live accordingly, are instructed to pray, and to entreat God with fasting for the remission of their sins that are past, we praying and fasting with them. Then they are brought by us where there is water, and are regenerated in the same manner in which we were ourselves regenerated. And this washing is called illumination, because they who learn these things are illuminated in their understandings." And again (*ibid.* 65) : "We, after we have thus washed him who has been convinced and has assented to our teaching, bring him to the place where those who are called brethren are assembled, in order that we may offer hearty prayers, in common for ourselves and for the baptized [illuminated] person, and for all others in every place. . . . Having ended the prayers, we salute one another with a kiss. There is then brought to the president of the brethren bread, and a cup of wine mixed with water ; and he, taking them, gives praise and glory to the Father of the universe, through the name of the Son and of the Holy Ghost. . . . And when the president has given thanks, and all the people have expressed their assent, those who are called by us deacons give to each of those present, to partake of, the bread and wine mixed with water over which the thanksgiving was pronounced, and to those who are absent they carry away a portion." And once more (*ibid.* 66) : " This food is called among us Εὐχαριστία [the Eucharist], of which no one is allowed to partake but the man who believes that the things which we teach are true, and who has been washed with the washing that is for the remission of sins, and unto regeneration, and who is so living as Christ has enjoined." (2) In Watts' translation, we have the following note on this episode in our text: " Here be divers particulars of the primitive fashion, in this story of Victorinus. First, being converted, he was to take some well-known Christian (who was to be his godfather) to go with him to the bishop, who, upon notice of it, admitted him a *catechumenus*, and gave him those six points of catechistical doctrine mentioned Heb. vi. 1, 2. When the time of baptism drew near, the young Christian

came to give in his heathen name, which was presently registered, submitting himself to examination. On the eve, was he, in a set form, first, to renounce the devil, and to pronounce, I confess to Thee, O Christ, repeating the Creed with it, in the form here recorded. The time for giving in their names must be within the two first weeks in Lent ; and the solemn day to renounce upon was Maundy Thursday. So bids the Council of Laodicea (Can. 45 and 46)." The *renunciation* adverted to by Watts in the above passage may be traced to an early period in the writings of the Fathers. It is mentioned by Tertullian, Ambrose, and Jerome ; and " in the fourth century," says Palmer (*Origines Liturgicæ*, c. 5, sec. 2, where the authorities will be found), " the renunciation was made with great solemnity. Cyril of Jerusalem, speaking to those who had been recently baptized, said, ' First, you have entered into the vestibule of the baptistry, and, standing towards the west, you have heard, and been commanded, and stretch forth your hands, and renounce Satan as if he were present.' This rite of turning to the west at the renunciation of Satan is also spoken of by Jerome, Gregory, Nazianzen, and Ambrose ; and it was sometimes performed by exsufflations and other external-signs of enmity to Satan, and rejection of him and his works. To the present day these customs remain in the patriarchate of Constantinople, where the candidates for baptism turn to the west to renounce Satan, stretching forth their hands, and using an exsufflation as a sign of enmity against him. And the Monophysites of Antioch and Jerusalem, Alexandria and Armenia, also retain the custom of renouncing Satan with faces turned to the west."

[5] Ps. cxii. 10.

[6] Ps. xxxi. 6, 14, 18.

[7] Literally, " give back," *reddere*.

[8] Anciently, as Palmer has noted in the introduction to his *Origines Liturgicæ*, the liturgies of the various churches were learnt by heart. They probably began to be committed to writing about Augustin's day. The reference, however, in this place, is to the Apostles' Creed, which, Dr. Pusey in a note remarks, was delivered orally to the catechumens to commit to memory, and by them *delivered back, i. e.* publicly repeated before they were baptized. " The symbol [creed] bearing hallowed testimony, which ye have together received, and are this day severally to give back [*reddidistis*], are the words in which the faith of our mother the Church is solidly constructed on a stable foundation, which is Christ the Lord. ' For other foundation can no man lay,' etc. Ye have received them, and given back [*reddidistis*] what ye ought to retain in heart and mind, what ye should repeat in your beds, think on in the streets, and forget not in your meals, and while sleeping in body, in heart watch therein For this is the faith, and the rule of salvation, that ' We believe in God, the Father Almighty,' " etc. (Aug. *Serm.* 215, *in Redditione Symboli*). " On the Sabbath day [Saturday], when we shall keep a vigil through the mercy of God, ye will give back [*reddituri*] not the [Lord's] Prayer, but the Creed " (*Serm.* 58, sec. *ult.*). " What ye have briefly heard, ye ought not only to believe, but to commit to memory in so many words, and utter with your mouth " (*Serm.* 214, *in Tradit. Symb.* 3, sec. 2). " Nor, in order to retain the very words of the Creed, ought ye any wise to write it, but *to learn it thoroughly by hearing*, nor, when ye have learnt it, ought ye to write it, but always to keep and refresh it in your memories. —' This is my covenant, which I will make with them after those days,' saith the Lord ; ' I will place my law in their minds, and in their hearts will I write it.' To convey this, *the Creed is learnt by hearing, and not written* on tables or any other substance, but on the heart " (*Serm.* 212, sec. 2). See the Roman Liturgy (*Assem. Cod. Liturg.* t. i. p. 11 *sq.*, 16), and the Gothic and Gallican (pp. 30 *sq.*, 38 *sq.*, 40 *sq.*, etc.). " The renunciation of Satan," to quote once more from Palmer's *Origines* (c. 5, sec. 3), " was always followed by a profession of faith in Christ, as it is now in the English ritual. . . . The promise of obedience and faith in Christ was made by the catechumens and sponsors, with their faces turned towards the east, as we learn from Cyril of Jerusalem and many other writers. Tertullian speaks of the profession of faith made at baptism, in the Father, Son, and Holy Spirit, and in the Church. Cyprian mentions the interrogation, ' Dost thou believe in eternal life, and remission of sins through the Holy Church ?' Eusebius and many other Fathers also speak of the profession of faith made at this time ; and it is especially noted in the Apostolical Constitutions,

Victorinus to make his profession more privately, as the custom was to do to those who were likely, through bashfulness, to be afraid; but he chose rather to profess his salvation in the presence of the holy assembly. For it was not salvation that he taught in rhetoric, and yet he had publicly professed that. How much less, therefore, ought he, when pronouncing Thy word, to dread Thy meek flock, who, in the delivery of his own words, had not feared the mad multitudes! So, then, when he ascended to make his profession, all, as they recognised him, whispered his name one to the other, with a voice of congratulation. And who was there amongst them that did not know him? And there ran a low murmur through the mouths of all the rejoicing multitude, "Victorinus! Victorinus!" Sudden was the burst of exultation at the sight of him; and suddenly were they hushed, that they might hear him. He pronounced the true faith with an excellent boldness, and all desired to take him to their very heart—yea, by their love and joy they took him thither; such were the hands with which they took him.

CHAP. III.—THAT GOD AND THE ANGELS REJOICE MORE ON THE RETURN OF ONE SINNER THAN OF MANY JUST PERSONS.

6. Good God, what passed in man to make him rejoice more at the salvation of a soul despaired of, and delivered from greater danger, than if there had always been hope of him, or the danger had been less? For so Thou also, O merciful Father, dost "joy over one sinner that repenteth, more than over ninety and nine just persons that need no repentance." And with much joyfulness do we hear, whenever we hear, how the lost sheep is brought home again on the Shepherd's shoulders, while the angels rejoice, and the drachma is restored to Thy treasury, the neighbours rejoicing with the woman who found it;[1] and the joy of the solemn service of Thy house constraineth to tears, when in Thy house it is read of Thy younger son that he "was dead, and is alive again, and was lost, and is found."[2] For Thou rejoicest both in us and in Thy angels, holy through holy charity. For Thou art ever the same; for all things which abide neither the same nor for ever, Thou ever knowest after the same manner.

7. What, then, passes in the soul when it more delights at finding or having restored to it

the thing it loves than if it had always possessed them? Yea, and other things bear witness hereunto; and all things are full of witnesses, crying out, "So it is." The victorious commander triumpheth; yet he would not have conquered had he not fought, and the greater the peril of the battle, the more the rejoicing of the triumph. The storm tosses the voyagers, threatens shipwreck, and every one waxes pale at the approach of death; but sky and sea grow calm, and they rejoice much, as they feared much. A loved one is sick, and his pulse indicates danger; all who desire his safety are at once sick at heart: he recovers, though not able as yet to walk with his former strength, and there is such joy as was not before when he walked sound and strong. Yea, the very pleasures of human life—not those only which rush upon us unexpectedly, and against our wills, but those that are voluntary and designed—do men obtain by difficulties. There is no pleasure at all in eating and drinking unless the pains of hunger and thirst go before. And drunkards eat certain salt meats with the view of creating a troublesome heat, which the drink allaying causes pleasure. It is also the custom that the affianced bride should not immediately be given up, that the husband may not less esteem her whom, as betrothed, he longed not for.[3]

8. This law obtains in base and accursed joy; in that joy also which is permitted and lawful; in the sincerity of honest friendship; and in Him who was dead, and lived again, had been lost, and was found.[4] The greater joy is everywhere preceded by the greater pain. What meaneth this, O Lord my God, when Thou art an everlasting joy unto Thine own self, and some things about Thee are ever rejoicing in Thee?[5] What meaneth this, that this portion of things thus ebbs and flows, alternately offended and reconciled? Is this the fashion of them, and is this all Thou hast allotted to them, whereas from the highest heaven to the lowest earth, from the beginning of the world to its end, from the angel to the worm, from the first movement unto the last, Thou settedst each in its right place, and appointedst each its proper seasons, everything good after its kind? Woe is me! How high art Thou in the highest, and how deep in the deepest! Thou withdrawest no whither, and scarcely do we *return* to Thee.

CHAP. IV.—HE SHOWS BY THE EXAMPLE OF VICTORINUS THAT THERE IS MORE JOY IN THE CONVERSION OF NOBLES.

9. Haste, Lord, and act; stir us up, and call us back; inflame us, and draw us to Thee; stir

---

which were written in the East at the end of the third or beginning of the fourth century. The profession of faith in the Eastern churches has generally been made by the sponsor, or the person to be baptized, not in the form of answers to questions, but by repeating the Creed after the priest. In the Western churches, the immemorial custom has been, for the priest to interrogate the candidate for baptism, or his sponsor, on the principal articles of the Christian faith."
[1] Luke xv. 4–10.
[2] Luke xv. 32.

[3] See ix. sec. 19, note.
[4] Luke xv. 32.
[5] See xii. sec. 12, and xiii. sec. 11, below.

us up, and grow sweet unto us; let us now love Thee, let us "run after Thee."[1] Do not many men, out of a deeper hell of blindness than that of Victorinus, return unto Thee, and approach, and are enlightened, receiving that light, which they that receive, receive power from Thee to become Thy sons?[2] But if they be less known among the people, even they that know them joy less for them. For when many rejoice together, the joy of each one is the fuller, in that they are incited and inflamed by one another. Again, because those that are known to many influence many towards salvation, and take the lead with many to follow them. And, therefore, do they also who preceded them much rejoice in regard to them, because they rejoice not in them alone. May it be averted that in Thy tabernacle the persons of the rich should be accepted before the poor, or the noble before the ignoble; since rather "Thou hast chosen the weak things of the world to confound the things which are mighty; and base things of the world, and things which are despised, hast Thou chosen, yea, and things which are not, to bring to naught things that are."[3] And yet, even that "least of the apostles,"[4] by whose tongue Thou soundest out these words, when Paulus the proconsul[5]—his pride overcome by the apostle's warfare—was made to pass under the easy yoke[6] of Thy Christ, and became a provincial of the great King,—he also, instead of Saul, his former name, desired to be called Paul,[7] in testimony of so great a victory. For the enemy is more overcome in one of whom he hath more hold, and by whom he hath hold of more. But the proud hath he more hold of by reason of their nobility; and by them of more, by reason of their authority.[8] By how

much the more welcome, then, was the heart of Victorinus esteemed, which the devil had held as an unassailable retreat, and the tongue of Victorinus, with which mighty and cutting weapon he had slain many; so much the more abundantly should Thy sons rejoice, seeing that our King hath bound the strong man,[9] and they saw his vessels taken from him and cleansed,[10] and made meet for Thy honour, and become serviceable for the Lord unto every good work.[11]

CHAP. V.—OF THE CAUSES WHICH ALIENATE US FROM GOD.

10. But when that man of Thine, Simplicianus, related this to me about Victorinus, I burned to imitate him; and it was for this end he had related it. But when he had added this also, that in the time of the Emperor Julian, there was a law made by which Christians were forbidden to teach grammar and oratory,[12] and he, in obedience to this law, chose rather to abandon the wordy school than Thy word, by which Thou makest eloquent the tongues of the dumb[13],—he appeared to me not more brave than happy, in having thus discovered an opportunity of waiting on Thee only, which thing I was sighing for, thus bound, not with the irons of another, but my own iron will. My will was the enemy master of, and thence had made a chain for me and bound me. Because of a perverse will was lust made; and lust indulged in became custom; and custom not resisted became necessity. By which links, as it were, joined together (whence I term it a "chain") did a hard bondage hold me enthralled.[14] But that

---

[1] Cant. i. 4.

[2] John i. 12.

[3] 1 Cor. i. 27, 28.

[4] 1 Cor. xv. 9.

[5] Acts. xiii. 12.

[6] Matt. xi. 30.

[7] " 'As Scipio, after the conquest of Africa, took the name of Africanus, so Saul also, being sent to preach to the Gentiles, brought back his trophy out of the first spoils won by the Church, the proconsul Sergius Paulus, and set up his banner, in that for Saul he was called Paul' (Jerome, *Comm. in Ep. ad Philem. init*). Origen mentions the same opinion (which is indeed suggested by the relation in the Acts), but thinks that the apostle had originally two names (*Præf. in Comm. in Ep. ad Rom.*), which, as a Roman, may very well have been, and yet that he made use of his Roman name Paul first in connection with the conversion of the proconsul; Chrysostom says that it was doubtless changed at the command of God, which is to be supposed, but still may have been at this time."—E. B P.

[8] "Satan makes choice of *persons of place and power*. These are either in the commonwealth or church. If he can, he will secure the throne and the pulpit, as the two forts that command the whole line. . . . A prince or a ruler may stand for a thousand; therefore saith Paul to Elymas, when he would have turned the deputy from the faith, 'O full of all subtilty, thou child of the devil!' (Acts. xiii. 10). As if he had said, 'You have learned this of your father the devil,—to haunt the courts of princes, wind into the favour of great ones. There is a double policy Satan hath in gaining such to his side :—(a) None have such advantage to draw others to their way. Corrupt the captain, and it is hard if he bring not off his troop with him. When the princes—men of renown in their tribes—stood up with Korah, presently a multitude are drawn into the conspiracy (Num. xvi. 2, 19). Let Jeroboam set up idolatry, and Israel is soon in a snare. It is said [that] the people willingly walked after

his commandment (Hos. v. 11). (b) Should the sin stay at court, and the infection go no further, yet the sin of such a one, though a good man, may cost a whole kingdom dear. 'Satan stood up against Israel, and provoked David to number Israel' (1 Chron. xxi. 1). He owed Israel a spite, and he pays them home in their king's sin, which dropped in a fearful plague upon their heads."—GURNALL, *The Christian in Complete Armour*, vol. i. part 2.

[9] Matt. xii. 29.

[10] Luke xi. 22, 25.

[11] 2 Tim. ii. 21.

[12] During the reign of Constantius, laws of a persecuting character were enacted against Paganism, which led multitudes *nominally* to adopt the Christian faith. When Julian the Apostate came to the throne, he took steps immediately to reinstate Paganism in all its ancient splendour. His court was filled with Platonic philosophers and diviners, and he sacrificed daily to the gods. But, instead of imitating the example of his predecessor, and enacting laws against the Christians, he endeavoured by *subtlety* to destroy their faith. In addition to the measures mentioned by Augustin above, he endeavoured to foment divisions in the Church by recalling the banished Donatists, and stimulating them to disseminate their doctrines, and he himself wrote treatises against it. In order, if possible, to counteract the influence of Christianity, he instructed his priests to imitate the Christians in their relief of the poor and care for the sick. But while in every way enacting measures of disability against the Christians, he showed great favour to the Jews, and with the view of confuting the predictions of Christ, went so far as to encourage them to rebuild the Temple.

[13] Wisd. x. 21.

[14] There would appear to be a law at work in the moral and spiritual worlds similar to that of gravitation in the natural, which "acts inversely as the square of the distance." As we are more affected, for example, by events that have taken place near us either in time or place, than by those which are more remote, so in spiritual things, the monitions of conscience would seem to become feeble with far greater rapidity than the continuance of our resistance would lead us to expect, while the power of sin, in like proportion, becomes strong. When tempted, men see not the end from

new will which had begun to develope in me, freely to worship Thee, and to wish to enjoy Thee, O God, the only sure enjoyment, was not able as yet to overcome my former wilfulness, made strong by long indulgence. Thus did my two wills, one old and the other new, one carnal, the other spiritual, contend within me; and by their discord they unstrung my soul.

11. Thus came I to understand, from my own experience, what I had read, how that "the flesh lusteth against the Spirit, and the Spirit against the flesh."[1] I verily lusted both ways;[2] yet more in that which I approved in myself, than in that which I disapproved in myself. For in this last it was now rather not "I,"[3] because in much I rather suffered against my will than did it willingly. And yet it was through me that custom became more combative against me, because I had come willingly whither I willed not. And who, then, can with any justice speak against it, when just punishment follows the sinner?[4] Nor had I now any longer my wonted excuse, that as yet I hesitated to be above the world and serve Thee, because my perception of the truth was uncertain; for now it was certain. But I, still bound to the earth, refused to be Thy soldier; and was as much afraid of being freed from all embarrassments, as we ought to fear to be embarrassed.

12. Thus with the baggage of the world was I sweetly burdened, as when in slumber; and the thoughts wherein I meditated upon Thee were like unto the efforts of those desiring to awake, who, still overpowered with a heavy drowsiness, are again steeped therein. And as no one desires to sleep always, and in the sober judgment of all waking is better, yet does a man generally defer to shake off drowsiness, when there is a heavy lethargy in all his limbs, and, though displeased, yet even after it is time to rise with pleasure yields to it, so was I assured that it were much better for me to give up myself to Thy charity, than to yield myself to my own cupidity; but the former course satisfied

and vanquished me, the latter pleased me and fettered me.[5] Nor had I aught to answer Thee calling to me, "Awake, thou that sleepest, and arise from the dead, and Christ shall give thee light."[6] And to Thee showing me on every side, that what Thou saidst was true, I, convicted by the truth, had nothing at all to reply, but the drawling and drowsy words: "Presently, lo, presently;" "Leave me a little while." But "presently, presently," had no present; and my "leave me a little while" went on for a long while.[7] In vain did I "delight in Thy law after the inner man," when "another law in my members warred against the law of my mind, and brought me into captivity to the law of sin which is in my members." For the law of sin is the violence of custom, whereby the mind is drawn and held, even against its will; deserving to be so held in that it so willingly falls into it. "O wretched man that I am! who shall deliver me from the body of this death" but Thy grace only, through Jesus Christ our Lord?[8]

CHAP. VI.—PONTITIANUS' ACCOUNT OF ANTONY, THE FOUNDER OF MONACHISM, AND OF SOME WHO IMITATED HIM.

13. And how, then, Thou didst deliver me out of the bonds of carnal desire, wherewith I was most firmly fettered, and out of the drudgery of worldly business, will I now declare and confess unto Thy name, "O Lord, my strength and my Redeemer."[9] Amid increasing anxiety, I was transacting my usual affairs, and daily

---

the beginning. The allurement, however, which at first is but as a gossamer thread, is soon felt to have the strength of a cable. "Evil men and seducers wax worse and worse" (2 Tim. iii. 13), and when it is too late they learn that the embrace of the siren is but the prelude to destruction. "Thus," as Gurnall has it (*The Christian in Complete Armour*, vol. i. part 2), "Satan leads poor creatures down into the depths of sin by winding stairs, that let them not see the bottom whither they are going. . . . Many who at this day lie in open profaneness, never thought they should have rolled so far from their modest beginnings. O Christians, give not place to Satan, no, not an inch, in his first motions. He that is a beggar and a modest one without doors, will command the house if let in. Yield at first, and thou givest away thy strength to resist him in the rest; when the hem is worn, the whole garment will ravel out, if it be not mended by timely repentance." See Müller, *Lehre von der Sünde*, book v., where the beginnings and alarming progress of evil in the soul are graphically described. See ix. sec. 18, note, below.
[1] Gal. v. 17.
[2] See iv. sec. 26, note, and v. sec. 18, above.
[3] Rom. vii. 20.
[4] See v. sec. 2, note 6, above.

[5] *Illud placebat et vincebat; hoc libebat et vinciebat.* Watts renders freely, "But notwithstanding that former course pleased and overcame my reason, yet did this latter tickle and enthrall my senses."
[6] Eph. v. 14.
[7] As Bishop Wilberforce, eloquently describing this condition of mind, says, in his sermon on *The Almost Christian,* "New, strange wishes were rising in his heart. The Mighty One was brooding over its currents, was stirring up its tides, was fain to over-rule their troubled flow—to arise in open splendour on his eyes; to glorify his life with His own blessed presence. And he himself was evidently conscious of the struggle; he was almost won; he was drawn towards that mysterious birth, and he well-nigh yielded. He even knew what was passing within his soul; he could appreciate something of its importance, of the living value of that moment. If that conflict was indeed visible to higher powers around him; if they who longed to keep him in the kingdom of darkness, and they who were ready to rejoice at his repentance—if they could see the inner waters of that troubled heart, as they surged and eddied underneath these mighty influences, how must they have waited for the doubtful choice! how would they strain their observation to see if that ALMOST should turn into an ALTOGETHER, or die away again, and leave his heart harder than it had been before!"
[8] Rom. vii. 22-24. This *difficilis et periculosus locus* (*Serm.* cliv. 1) he interprets differently at different periods of his life. In this place, as elsewhere in his writings, he makes the passage refer (according to the general interpretation in the Church up to that time) to man convinced of sin under the influence of the law, but not under grace. In his *Retractations,* however (i. 23, sec. 1), he points out that he had found reason to interpret the passage not of man convinced of sin, but of man renewed and regenerated in Christ Jesus. This is the view constantly taken in his anti-Pelagian writings, which were published subsequently to the date of his *Confessions;* and indeed this change in interpretation probably arose from the pressure of the Pelagian controversy (see *Con. Duas Ep. Pel.* i. 10, secs. 18 and 22), and the fear lest the old view should too much favour the heretics, and their exaltation of the powers of the natural man to the disparagement of the influence of the grace of God.
[9] Ps. xix. 14.

sighing unto Thee. I resorted as frequently to Thy church as the business, under the burden of which I groaned, left me free to do. Alypius was with me, being after the third sitting disengaged from his legal occupation, and awaiting further opportunity of selling his counsel, as I was wont to sell the power of speaking, if it can be supplied by teaching. But Nebridius had, on account of our friendship, consented to teach under Verecundus, a citizen and a grammarian of Milan, and a very intimate friend of us all; who vehemently desired, and by the right of friendship demanded from our company, the faithful aid he greatly stood in need of. Nebridius, then, was not drawn to this by any desire of gain (for he could have made much more of his learning had he been so inclined), but, as a most sweet and kindly friend, he would not be wanting in an office of friendliness, and slight our request. But in this he acted very discreetly, taking care not to become known to those personages whom the world esteems great; thus avoiding distraction of mind, which he desired to have free and at leisure as many hours as possible, to search, or read, or hear something concerning wisdom.

14. Upon a certain day, then, Nebridius being away (why, I do not remember), lo, there came to the house to see Alypius and me, Pontitianus, a countryman of ours, in so far as he was an African, who held high office in the emperor's court. What he wanted with us I know not, but we sat down to talk together, and it fell out that upon a table before us, used for games, he noticed a book; he took it up, opened it, and, contrary to his expectation, found it to be the Apostle Paul,—for he imagined it to be one of those books which I was wearing myself out in teaching. At this he looked up at me smilingly, and expressed his delight and wonder that he had so unexpectedly found this book, and this only, before my eyes. For he was both a Christian and baptized, and often prostrated himself before Thee our God in the church, in constant and daily prayers. When, then, I had told him that I bestowed much pains upon these writings, a conversation ensued on his speaking of Antony,[1] the Egyptian

monk, whose name was in high repute among Thy servants, though up to that time not familiar to us. When he came to know this, he lingered on that topic, imparting to us a knowledge of this man so eminent, and marvelling at our ignorance. But we were amazed, hearing Thy wonderful works most fully manifested in times so recent, and almost in our own, wrought in the true faith and the Catholic Church. We all wondered—we, that they were so great, and he, that we had never heard of them.

15. From this his conversation turned to the companies in the monasteries, and their manners so fragrant unto Thee, and of the fruitful deserts of the wilderness, of which we knew nothing. And there was a monastery at Milan[2] full of good brethren, without the walls of the city, under the fostering care of Ambrose, and we were ignorant of it. He went on with his relation, and we listened intently and in silence. He then related to us how on a certain afternoon, at Triers, when the emperor was taken up with seeing the Circensian games,[3] he and three others, his comrades, went out for a walk in the gardens close to the city walls, and there, as they chanced to walk two and two, one strolled away with him, while the other two went by themselves; and these, in their ram-

---

[1] It may be well here to say a few words in regard to Monachism and Antony's relation to it:—(1) There is much in the later Platonism, with its austerities and bodily mortifications (see vii. sec. 13, note 2, above), which is in common with the asceticism of the early Church. The Therapeutæ of Philo, indeed, of whom there were numbers in the neighbourhood of Alexandria in the first century, may be considered as the natural forerunners of the Egyptian monks. (2) Monachism, according to Sozomen (i. 12), had its origin in a desire to escape persecution by retirement into the wilderness. It is probable, however, that, as in the case of Paul the hermit of Thebais, the desire for freedom from the cares of life, so that by contemplation and mortification of the body, the λόγος or inner reason (which was held to be an emanation of God) might be purified, had as much to do with the hermit life as a fear of persecution. Mosheim, indeed (*Ecc. Hist.* i. part 2, c. 3), supposes Paul to have been influenced entirely by these Platonic notions. (3) Antony was born in the district of Thebes, A. D. 251, and visited Paul in the Egyptian desert a little before his death. To Antony is the world indebted

for establishing communities of monks, as distinguished from the solitary asceticism of Paul; he therefore is rightly viewed as the founder of Monachism. He appears to have known little more than how to speak his native Coptic, yet during his long life (said to have been 100 years) he by his fervent enthusiasm made for himself a name little inferior to that of the "king of men," Athanasius, whom in the time of the Arian troubles he stedfastly supported, and by whom his life has been handed down to us. Augustin, in his *De Doctr. Christ.* (Prol. sec. 4), speaks of him as "a just and holy man, who, not being able to read himself, is said to have committed the Scriptures to memory through hearing them read by others, and by dint of wise meditation to have arrived at a thorough understanding of them." (4) According to Sozomen (iii. 14), monasteries had not been established in Europe A. D. 340. They were, Baronius tells us, introduced into Rome about that date by Athanasius, during a visit to that city. Athanasius mentions "ascetics" as dwelling at Rome A. D. 355. Ambrose, Bishop of Milan, Martin, Bishop of Tours, and Jerome were enthusiastic supporters of the system. (5) Monachism in Europe presented more of its practical and less of its contemplative side, than in its cradle in the East. An example of how the monks of the East did work for the good of others is seen in the instance of the monks of Pachomius; still in this respect, as in matters of doctrine, the West has generally shown itself more practical than the East. Probably climate and the style of living consequent thereon have much to do with this. Sulpicius Severus (dial. i. 2, *De Vita Martini*) may be taken to give a quaint illustration of this, when he makes one of his characters say, as he hears of the mode of living of the Eastern monks, that their diet was only suited to angels. However mistaken we may think the monkish systems to be, it cannot be concealed that in the days of anarchy and semi-barbarism they were oftentimes centres of civilisation. Certainly in its originating idea of meditative seclusion, there is much that is worthy of commendation; for, as Farindon has it (*Works*, iv. 130), "This has been the practice not only of holy men, but of heathen men. Thus did Tully, and Antony, and Crassus make way to that honour and renown which they afterwards purchased in eloquence (Cicero, *De Officiis*, ii. 13, viii. 7); thus did they pass *a solitudine in scholas, a scholis in forum,—'* from their secret retirement into the schools, and from the schools into the pleading-place.'"

[2] Augustin, when comparing Christian with Manichæan asceticism, says in his *De Mor. Eccl. Cath.* (sec. 70), "I saw at Milan a lodging-house of saints, in number not a few, presided over by one presbyter, a man of great excellence and learning." In the previous note we have given the generally received opinion, that the first monastery in Europe was established at Rome. It may be mentioned here that Muratori maintains that the institution was transplanted from the East first to Milan; others contend that the first European society was at Aquileia.

[3] See vi. sec. 12, note 1, above.

bling, came upon a certain cottage inhabited by some of Thy servants, "poor in spirit," of whom "is the kingdom of heaven,"[1] where they found a book in which was written the life of Antony. This one of them began to read, marvel at, and be inflamed by it; and in the reading, to meditate on embracing such a life, and giving up his worldly employments to serve Thee. And these were of the body called "Agents for Public Affairs."[2] Then, suddenly being overwhelmed with a holy love and a sober sense of shame, in anger with himself, he cast his eyes upon his friend, exclaiming, "Tell me, I entreat thee, what end we are striving for by all these labours of ours. What is our aim? What is our motive in doing service? Can our hopes in court rise higher than to be ministers of the emperor? And in such a position, what is there not brittle, and fraught with danger, and by how many dangers arrive we at greater danger? And when arrive we thither? But if I desire to become a friend of God, behold, I am even now made it." Thus spake he, and in the pangs of the travail of the new life, he turned his eyes again upon the page and continued reading, and was inwardly changed where Thou sawest, and his mind was divested of the world, as soon became evident; for as he read, and the surging of his heart rolled along, he raged awhile, discerned and resolved on a better course, and now, having become Thine, he said to his friend, "Now have I broken loose from those hopes of ours, and am determined to serve God; and this, from this hour, in this place, I enter upon. If thou art reluctant to imitate me, hinder me not." The other replied that he would cleave to him, to share in so great a reward and so great a service. Thus both of them, being now Thine, were building a tower at the necessary cost,[3]—of forsaking all that they had and following

Thee. Then Pontitianus, and he that had walked with him through other parts of the garden, came in search of them to the same place, and having found them, reminded them to return as the day had declined. But they, making known to him their resolution and purpose, and how such a resolve had sprung up and become confirmed in them, entreated them not to molest them, if they refused to join themselves unto them. But the others, no whit changed from their former selves, did yet (as he said) bewail themselves, and piously congratulated them, recommending themselves to their prayers; and with their hearts inclining towards earthly things, returned to the palace. But the other two, setting their affections upon heavenly things, remained in the cottage. And both of them had affianced brides, who, when they heard of this, dedicated also their virginity unto God.

CHAP. VII.—HE DEPLORES HIS WRETCHEDNESS, THAT HAVING BEEN BORN THIRTY-TWO YEARS, HE HAD NOT YET FOUND OUT THE TRUTH.

16. Such was the story of Pontitianus. But Thou, O Lord, whilst he was speaking, didst turn me towards myself, taking me from behind my back, where I had placed myself while unwilling to exercise self-scrutiny; and Thou didst set me face to face with myself, that I might behold how foul I was, and how crooked and sordid, bespotted and ulcerous. And I beheld and loathed myself; and whither to fly from myself I discovered not. And if I sought to turn my gaze away from myself, he continued his narrative, and Thou again opposedst me unto myself, and thrustedst me before my own eyes, that I might discover my iniquity, and hate it.[4] I had known it, but acted as though I knew it not,—winked at it, and forgot it.

17. But now, the more ardently I loved those whose healthful affections I heard tell of, that they had given up themselves wholly to Thee to be cured, the more did I abhor myself when compared with them. For many of my years (perhaps twelve) had passed away since my nineteenth, when, on the reading of Cicero's *Hortensius*,[5] I was roused to a desire for wisdom; and still I was delaying to reject mere worldly happiness, and to devote myself to search out that whereof not the finding alone, but the bare search,[6] ought to have been pre-

---

[1] Matt. v. 3. Roman commentators are ever ready to use this text of Scripture as an argument in favour of monastic poverty, and some may feel disposed from its context to imagine such an interpretation to be implied in this place. This, however, can hardly be so. Augustin constantly points out in his sermons, etc. in what the poverty that is pleasing to God consists. "Pauper Dei," he says (*in Ps.* cxxxi. 15), "in animo est, non in sacculo;" and his interpretation of this passage in his *Exposition of the Sermon on the Mount* (i. 3) is entirely opposed to the Roman view. We there read: "The poor in spirit are rightly understood here as meaning the humble and God-fearing, *i. e.* those who have not a spirit which puffeth up. Nor ought blessedness to begin at any other point whatever, if indeed it is to reach the highest wisdom. 'The fear of the Lord is the beginning of wisdom' (Ps. cxi. 10); whereas, on the other hand also, 'pride' is entitled 'the beginning of all sin' (Ecclus. x. 13). Let the proud, therefore, seek after and love the kingdoms of the earth; but 'blessed are the poor in spirit, for theirs is the kingdom of heaven.'"

[2] "*Agentes in rebus.* There was a society of them still about the court. Their militia or employments were to gather in the emperor's tributes; to fetch in offenders; to do *Palatini obsequia*, offices of court; provide corn, etc., ride on errands like messengers of the chamber, lie abroad as spies and intelligencers. They were often preferred to places of magistracy in the provinces; such were called *Principes* or *Magistriani*. St. Hierome upon Abdias, c. 1, calls them messengers. They succeeded the *Frumentarii*, between which two and the *Curiosi* and the *Speculatores* there was not much difference."—W. W.

[3] Luke xiv. 26–35.

[4] Ps. xxxvi. 2.
[5] See iii. sec. 7, above.
[6] It is interesting to compare with this passage the views contained in Augustin's three books, *Con. Academicos*,—the earliest of his extant works, and written about this time. Licentius there maintains that the "bare search" for truth renders a man happy, while Trygetius contends that the "finding alone" can produce happiness. Augustin does not agree with the doctrine of the former, and points out that while the Academics held the probable to be attain-

ferred before the treasures and kingdoms of this world, though already found, and before the pleasures of the body, though encompassing me at my will. But I, miserable young man, supremely miserable even in the very outset of my youth, had entreated chastity of Thee, and said, "Grant me chastity and continency, but not yet." For I was afraid lest Thou shouldest hear me soon, and soon deliver me from the disease of concupiscence, which I desired to have satisfied rather than extinguished. And I had wandered through perverse ways in a sacrilegious superstition; not indeed assured thereof, but preferring that to the others, which I did not seek religiously, but opposed maliciously.

18. And I had thought that I delayed from day to day to reject worldly hopes and follow Thee only, because there did not appear anything certain whereunto to direct my course. And now had the day arrived in which I was to be laid bare to myself, and my conscience was to chide me. "Where art thou, O my tongue? Thou saidst, verily, that for an uncertain truth thou wert not willing to cast off the baggage of vanity. Behold, now it is certain, and yet doth that burden still oppress thee; whereas they who neither have so worn themselves out with searching after it, nor yet have spent ten years and more in thinking thereon, have had their shoulders unburdened, and gotten wings to fly away." Thus was I inwardly consumed and mightily confounded with an horrible shame, while Pontitianus was relating these things. And he, having finished his story, and the business he came for, went his way. And unto myself, what said I not within myself? With what scourges of rebuke lashed I not my soul to make

it follow me, struggling to go after Thee! Yet it drew back; it refused, and exercised not itself. All its arguments were exhausted and confuted. There remained a silent trembling; and it feared, as it would death, to be restrained from the flow of that custom whereby it was wasting away even to death.

CHAP. VIII.—THE CONVERSATION WITH ALYPIUS BEING ENDED, HE RETIRES TO THE GARDEN, WHITHER HIS FRIEND FOLLOWS HIM.

19. In the midst, then, of this great strife of my inner dwelling, which I had strongly raised up against my soul in the chamber of my heart,[1] troubled both in mind and countenance, I seized upon Alypius, and exclaimed: "What is wrong with us? What is this? What heardest thou? The unlearned start up and 'take' heaven,[2] and we, with our learning, but wanting heart, see where we wallow in flesh and blood! Because others have preceded us, are we ashamed to follow, and not rather ashamed at not following?" Some such words I gave utterance to, and in my excitement flung myself from him, while he gazed upon me in silent astonishment. For I spoke not in my wonted tone, and my brow, cheeks, eyes, colour, tone of voice, all expressed my emotion more than the words. There was a little garden belonging to our lodging, of which we had the use, as of the whole house; for the master, our landlord, did not live there. Thither had the tempest within my breast hurried me, where no one might impede the fiery struggle in which I was engaged with myself, until it came to the issue that Thou knewest, though I did not. But I was mad that I might be whole, and dying that I might have life, knowing what evil thing I was, but not knowing what good thing I was shortly to become. Into the garden, then, I retired, Alypius following my steps. For his presence was no bar to my solitude; or how could he desert me so troubled? We sat down at as great a distance from the house as we could. I was disquieted in spirit, being most impatient with myself that I entered not into Thy will and covenant, O my God, which all my bones cried out unto me to enter, extolling it to the skies. And we enter not therein by ships, or chariots, or feet, no, nor by going so far as I had come from the house to that place where we were sitting. For not to go only, but to enter there, was naught else but to will to go, but to will it resolutely and thoroughly; not to stagger and sway about this way and that, a changeable and half-wounded will, wrestling, with one part falling as another rose.

---

able, it could not be so without the true, by which the probable is measured and known. And, in his *De Vita Beata*, he contends that he who seeks truth and finds it not, has not attained happiness, and that though the grace of God be indeed guiding him, he must not expect complete happiness (*Retractations*, i. 2) till after death. Perhaps no sounder philosophy can be found than that evidenced in the life of Victor Hugo's good Bishop Myriel, who rested in the practice of love, and was content to look for perfect happiness, and a full unfolding of God's mysteries, to the future life:—" Aimezvous les uns les autres, il declarait cela complet, ne souhaitait rien de plus et c'était là toute sa doctrine. Un jour, cet homme qui se croyait 'philosophe,' ce senateur, déjà nommé, dit à l'évêque: 'Mais voyez donc le spectacle du monde; guerre de tous contre tous; le plus fort a la plus d'ésprit. Votre aimez-vous les uns les autres est une bêtise.'—' Eh bien,' répondit Monseigneur Bienvenu, sans disputer, 'si c'est une bêtise, l'âme doit s'y enfermer comme la perle dans l'huître.' Il s'y enfermait donc, il y vivait, il s'en satisfaisait absolument, laissant de côté les questions prodigieuses qui attirent et qui épouvantent, les perspectives insoudables de l'abstraction, les précipices de la métaphysique, toutes ces profondeurs convergentes, pour l'apôtre, à Dieu, pour l'athée, au néant: la destinée, le bien et le mal, la guerre de l'être contre l'être, la conscience de l'homme, le somnambulisme pensif de l'animal, la transformation par la mort, la récapitulation d'existences qui contient le tombeau, la greffe incompréhensible des amours successifs sur le moi persistant, l'essence, la substance, le Nil et l'Ens, l'âme, la nature, la liberté, la nécessité; problèmes à pic, épaisseurs sinistres, où se penchent les gigantesques archanges de l'ésprit humain; formidables abimes que Lucrèce, Manon, Saint Paul, et Dante contemplent avec cet œil fulgurant qui semble, en regardant fixement l'infini, y faire eclore les étoiles. Monseigneur Bienvenu était simplement un homme qui constatait du dehors les questions mystérieuses sans les scruter, sans les agiter, et sans en troubler son propre ésprit; et qui avait dans l'âme le grave respect de l'ombre." —*Les Misérables*, c. xiv.

---

[1] Isa. xxvi. 20, and Matt. vi. 6.
[2] Matt. xi. 12.

20. Finally, in the very fever of my irreso-
lution, I made many of those motions with my
body which men sometimes desire to do, but
cannot, if either they have not the limbs, or if
their limbs be bound with fetters, weakened by
disease, or hindered in any other way. Thus,
if I tore my hair, struck my forehead, or if, en-
twining my fingers, I clasped my knee, this I
did because I willed it. But I might have willed
and not done it, if the power of motion in my
limbs had not responded. So many things,
then, I did, when to have the will was not to
have the power, and I did not that which both
with an unequalled desire I longed more to do,
and which shortly when I should will I should
have the power to do; because shortly when I
should will, I should will thoroughly. For in
such things the power was one with the will,
and to will was to do, and yet was it not done;
and more readily did the body obey the slightest wish of the soul in the moving its limbs at
the order of the mind, than the soul obeyed
itself to accomplish in the will alone this its
great will.

CHAP. IX.—THAT THE MIND COMMANDETH THE MIND, BUT IT WILLETH NOT ENTIRELY.

21. Whence is this monstrous thing? And
why is it? Let Thy mercy shine on me, that I
may inquire, if so be the hiding-places of man's
punishment, and the darkest contritions of the
sons of Adam, may perhaps answer me. Whence
is this monstrous thing? and why is it? The
mind commands the body, and it obeys forthwith; the mind commands itself, and is resisted.
The mind commands the hand to be moved,
and such readiness is there that the command is
scarce to be distinguished from the obedience.
Yet the mind is mind, and the hand is body.
The mind commands the mind to will, and yet,
though it be itself, it obeyeth not. Whence this
monstrous thing? and why is it? I repeat, it
commands itself to will, and would not give the
command unless it willed; yet is not that done
which it commandeth. But it willeth not entirely; therefore it commandeth not entirely.
For so far forth it commandeth, as it willeth;
and so far forth is the thing commanded not
done, as it willeth not. For the will commandeth that there be a will;—not another, but itself.
But it doth not command entirely, therefore
that is not which it commandeth. For were
it entire, it would not even command it to be,
because it would already be. It is, therefore,
no monstrous thing partly to will, partly to be
unwilling, but an infirmity of the mind, that it
doth not wholly rise, sustained by truth, pressed
down by custom. And so there are two wills,
because one of them is not entire; and the one
is supplied with what the other needs.

CHAP. X.—HE REFUTES THE OPINION OF THE MANICHÆANS AS TO TWO KINDS OF MINDS,— ONE GOOD AND THE OTHER EVIL.

22. Let them perish from Thy presence,[1] O
God, as "vain talkers and deceivers"[2] of the
soul do perish, who, observing that there were two
wills in deliberating, affirm that there are two
kinds of minds in us,—one good, the other
evil.[3] They themselves verily are evil when
they hold these evil opinions; and they shall
become good when they hold the truth, and
shall consent unto the truth, that Thy apostle
may say unto them, "Ye were sometimes darkness, but now are ye light in the Lord."[4] But
they, desiring to be light, not "in the Lord,"
but in themselves, conceiving the nature of the
soul to be the same as that which God is,[5] are
made more gross darkness; for that through a
shocking arrogancy they went farther from
Thee, "the true Light, which lighteth every
man that cometh into the world."[6] Take
heed what you say, and blush for shame; draw
near unto Him and be "lightened," and your
faces shall not be "ashamed."[7] I, when I was
deliberating upon serving the Lord my God
now, as I had long purposed,—I it was who
willed, I who was unwilling. It was I, even I
myself. I neither willed entirely, nor was entirely unwilling. Therefore was I at war with
myself, and destroyed by myself. And this
destruction overtook me against my will, and
yet showed not the presence of another mind,
but the punishment of mine own.[8] "Now,
then, it is no more I that do it, but sin
that dwelleth in me,"[9]—the punishment of a
more unconfined sin, in that I was a son of
Adam.

23. For if there be as many contrary natures
as there are conflicting wills, there will not now
be two natures only, but many. If any one
deliberate whether he should go to their con-
venticle, or to the theatre, those men[10] at once
cry out, "Behold, here are two natures,—one
good, drawing this way, another bad, drawing
back that way; for whence else is this indecision
between conflicting wills?" But I reply that
both are bad—that which draws to them, and
that which draws back to the theatre. But they
believe not that will to be other than good which
draws to them. Supposing, then, one of us

1 Ps. lxviii. 2.
2 Titus i. 10.
3 And that therefore they were not responsible for their evil deeds,
it not being they that sinned, but the nature of evil in them. See
iv. sec. 26, and note, above, where the Manichæan doctrines in this
matter are fully treated.
4 Eph. v. 8.
5 See iv. sec. 26, note, above.
6 John i. 9.
7 Ps. xxxiv. 5.
8 See v. sec. 2, note 6, above, and x. sec. 5, note, below.
9 Rom. vii. 17.
10 The Manichæans.

should deliberate, and through the conflict of his two wills should waver whether he should go to the theatre or to our church, would not these also waver what to answer? For either they must confess, which they are not willing to do, that the will which leads to our church is good, as well as that of those who have received and are held by the mysteries of theirs, or they must imagine that there are two evil natures and two evil minds in one man, at war one with the other; and that will not be true which they say, that there is one good and another bad; or they must be converted to the truth, and no longer deny that where any one deliberates, there is one soul fluctuating between conflicting wills.

24. Let them no more say, then, when they perceive two wills to be antagonistic to each other in the same man, that the contest is between two opposing minds, of two opposing substances, from two opposing principles, the one good and the other bad. For Thou, O true God, dost disprove, check, and convince them; like as when both wills are bad, one deliberates whether he should kill a man by poison, or by the sword; whether he should take possession of this or that estate of another's, when he cannot both; whether he should purchase pleasure by prodigality, or retain his money by covetousness; whether he should go to the circus or the theatre, if both are open on the same day; or, thirdly, whether he should rob another man's house, if he have the opportunity; or, fourthly, whether he should commit adultery, if at the same time he have the means of doing so,—all these things concurring in the same point of time, and all being equally longed for, although impossible to be enacted at one time. For they rend the mind amid four, or even (among the vast variety of things men desire) more antagonistic wills, nor do they yet affirm that there are so many different substances. Thus also is it in wills which are good. For I ask them, is it a good thing to have delight in reading the apostle, or good to have delight in a sober psalm, or good to discourse on the gospel? To each of these they will answer, "It is good." What, then, if all equally delight us, and all at the same time? Do not different wills distract the mind, when a man is deliberating which he should rather choose? Yet are they all good, and are at variance until one be fixed upon, whither the whole united will may be borne, which before was divided into many. Thus, also, when above eternity delights us, and the pleasure of temporal good holds us down below, it is the same soul which willeth not that or this with an entire will, and is therefore torn asunder with grievous perplexities, while out of truth it prefers that, but out of custom forbears not this.

CHAP. XI.—IN WHAT MANNER THE SPIRIT STRUGGLED WITH THE FLESH, THAT IT MIGHT BE FREED FROM THE BONDAGE OF VANITY.

25. Thus was I sick and tormented, accusing myself far more severely than was my wont, tossing and turning me in my chain till that was utterly broken, whereby I now was but slightly, but still was held. And Thou, O Lord, pressedst upon me in my inward parts by a severe mercy, redoubling the lashes of fear and shame, lest I should again give way, and that same slender remaining tie not being broken off, it should recover strength, and enchain me the faster. For I said mentally, "Lo, let it be done now, let it be done now." And as I spoke, I all but came to a resolve. I all but did it, yet I did it not. Yet fell I not back to my old condition, but took up my position hard by, and drew breath. And I tried again, and wanted but very little of reaching it, and somewhat less, and then all but touched and grasped it; and yet came not at it, nor touched, nor grasped it, hesitating to die unto death, and to live unto life; and the worse, whereto I had been habituated, prevailed more with me than the better, which I had not tried. And the very moment in which I was to become another man, the nearer it approached me, the greater horror did it strike into me; but it did not strike me back, nor turn me aside, but kept me in suspense.

26. The very toys of toys, and vanities of vanities, my old mistresses, still enthralled me; they shook my fleshly garment, and whispered softly, "Dost thou part with us? And from that moment shall we no more be with thee for ever? And from that moment shall not this or that be lawful for thee for ever?" And what did they suggest to me in the words "this or that?" What is it that they suggested, O my God? Let Thy mercy avert it from the soul of Thy servant. What impurities did they suggest! What shame! And now I far less than half heard them, not openly showing themselves and contradicting me, but muttering, as it were, behind my back, and furtively plucking me as I was departing, to make me look back upon them. Yet they did delay me, so that I hesitated to burst and shake myself free from them, and to leap over whither I was called,—an unruly habit saying to me, "Dost thou think thou canst live without them?"

27. But now it said this very faintly; for on that side towards which I had set my face, and whither I trembled to go, did the chaste dignity of Continence appear unto me, cheerful, but not dissolutely gay, honestly alluring me to come and doubt nothing, and extending her holy hands, full of a multiplicity of good examples, to receive and embrace me. There

were there so many young men and maidens, a multitude of youth and every age, grave widows and ancient virgins, and Continence herself in all, not barren, but a fruitful mother of children of joys, by Thee, O Lord, her Husband. And she smiled on me with an encouraging mockery, as if to say, "Canst not thou do what these youths and maidens can? Or can one or other do it of themselves, and not rather in the Lord their God? The Lord their God gave me unto them. Why standest thou in thine own strength, and so standest not? Cast thyself upon Him; fear not, He will not withdraw that thou shouldest fall; cast thyself upon Him without fear, He will receive thee, and heal thee." And I blushed beyond measure, for I still heard the muttering of those toys, and hung in suspense. And she again seemed to say, "Shut up thine ears against those unclean members of thine upon the earth, that they may be mortified.[1] They tell thee of delights, but not as doth the law of the Lord thy God."[2] This controversy in my heart was naught but self against self. But Alypius, sitting close by my side, awaited in silence[3] the result of my unwonted emotion.

CHAP. XII.—HAVING PRAYED TO GOD, HE POURS FORTH A SHOWER OF TEARS, AND, ADMONISHED BY A VOICE, HE OPENS THE BOOK AND READS THE WORDS IN ROM. XIII. 13; BY WHICH, BEING CHANGED IN HIS WHOLE SOUL, HE DISCLOSES THE DIVINE FAVOUR TO HIS FRIEND AND HIS MOTHER.

28. But when a profound reflection had, from the secret depths of my soul, drawn together and heaped up all my misery before the sight of my heart, there arose a mighty storm, accompanied by as mighty a shower of tears. Which, that I might pour forth fully, with its natural expressions, I stole away from Alypius; for it suggested itself to me that solitude was fitter for the business of weeping.[4] So I retired to such a distance that even his presence could not be oppressive to me. Thus was it with me at that time, and he perceived it; for something, I believe, I had spoken, wherein the sound of my voice appeared choked with weeping, and in that state had I risen up. He then remained where we had been sitting, most completely astonished. I flung myself down, how, I know not, under a certain fig-tree, giving free course to my tears, and the streams of mine eyes gushed out, an acceptable sacrifice unto Thee.[5] And, not indeed in these words, yet to this effect, spake I much unto Thee,—"But Thou, O Lord, how long?"[6] "How long, Lord? Wilt Thou be angry for ever? Oh, remember not against us former iniquities;"[7] for I felt that I was enthralled by them. I sent up these sorrowful cries,—"How long, how long? To-morrow, and to-morrow? Why not now? Why is there not this hour an end to my uncleanness?"

29. I was saying these things and weeping in the most bitter contrition of my heart, when, lo, I heard the voice as of a boy or girl, I know not which, coming from a neighbouring house, chanting, and oft repeating, "Take up and read; take up and read." Immediately my countenance was changed, and I began most earnestly to consider whether it was usual for children in any kind of game to sing such words; nor could I remember ever to have heard the like. So, restraining the torrent of my tears, I rose up, interpreting it no other way than as a command to me from Heaven to open the book, and to read the first chapter I should light upon. For I had heard of Antony,[8] that, accidentally coming in whilst the gospel was being read, he received the admonition as if what was read were addressed to him, "Go and sell that thou hast, and give to the poor, and thou shalt have treasure in heaven; and come and follow me."[9] And by such oracle was he forthwith converted unto Thee. So quickly I returned to the place where Alypius was sitting; for there had I put down the volume of the apostles, when I rose thence. I grasped, opened, and in silence read that paragraph on which my eyes first fell,—"Not in rioting and drunkenness, not in chambering and wantonness, not in strife and envying; but put ye on the Lord Jesus Christ, and make not provision for the flesh, to fulfil the lusts thereof."[10] No further would I read, nor did I need; for instantly, as

---

[1] Col. iii. 5.
[2] Ps. cxix. 85, Old ver.
[3] As in nature, the men of science tell us, no two atoms touch, but that, while an inner magnetism draws them together, a secret repulsion keeps them apart, so it is with human souls. Into our deepest feelings our dearest friends cannot enter. In the throes of conversion, for example, God's ministering servants may assist, but He alone can bring the soul to the birth. So it was here in the case of Augustin. He felt that now even the presence of his dear friend would be a burden,—God alone could come near, so as to heal the sore wound of his spirit,—and Alypius was a friend who knew how to *keep silence*, and to await the issue of his friend's profound emotion. How comfortable a thing to find in those who would give consolation the spirit that animated the friends of Job, when "they sat down with him upon the ground seven days and seven nights, and *none spake a word unto him*; for they saw that his grief was very great" (Job ii. 13). Well has Rousseau said: "Les consolations indiscrètes ne font qu'aigrir les violentes afflictions. L'indifférence et la froideur trouvent aisément des paroles, mais la tristesse et *le silence* sont alors le vrai langage de l'amitié." A beautiful exemplification of this is found in Victor Hugo's portrait of Bishop Myriel, in *Les Misérables* (c. iv.), from which we have quoted a few pages back :—" Il savait s'asseoir et *se taire de longues heures* auprès de l'homme qui avait perdu la femme qu'il aimait, de la mère qui avait perdu son enfant. Comme il savait le moment de *se taire*, il savait aussi le moment de parler. O admirable consolateur! il ne cherchait pas à effacer la douleur par l'oubli, mais à l'agrandir et à la dignifier par l'espérance."

[4] See note 3, page 71.
[5] 1 Pet. ii. 5.
[6] Ps. vi. 3.
[7] Ps. lxxix. 5, 8.
[8] See his *Life* by St. Athanasius, secs. 2, 3.
[9] Matt. xix. 21.
[10] Rom. xiii. 13, 14.

the sentence ended,—by a light, as it were, of security infused into my heart,—all the gloom of doubt vanished away.

30. Closing the book, then, and putting either my finger between, or some other mark, I now with a tranquil countenance made it known to Alypius. And he thus disclosed to me what was wrought in him, which I knew not. He asked to look at what I had read. I showed him; and he looked even further than I had read, and I knew not what followed. This it was, verily, "Him that is weak in the faith, receive ye;"[1] which he applied to himself, and discovered to me. By this admonition was he strengthened; and by a good resolution and purpose, very much in accord with his character (wherein, for the better, he was always far different from me), without any restless delay he

joined me. Thence we go in to my mother. We make it known to her,—she rejoiceth. We relate how it came to pass,—she leapeth for joy, and triumpheth, and blesseth Thee, who art "able to do exceeding abundantly above all that we ask or think;[2] for she perceived Thee to have given her more for me than she used to ask by her pitiful and most doleful groanings. For Thou didst so convert me unto Thyself, that I sought neither a wife, nor any other of this world's hopes,—standing in that rule of faith[3] in which Thou, so many years before, had showed me unto her in a vision. And thou didst turn her grief into a gladness,[4] much more plentiful than she had desired, and much dearer and chaster than she used to crave, by having grandchildren of my body.

[1] Rom. xiv. 1.

[2] Eph. iii. 20.
[3] See book iii. sec. 19.
[4] Ps. xxx. 11.

BOOK IX.

HE SPEAKS OF HIS DESIGN OF FORSAKING THE PROFESSION OF RHETORIC; OF THE DEATH OF HIS FRIENDS, NEBRIDIUS AND VERECUNDUS; OF HAVING RECEIVED BAPTISM IN THE THIRTY-THIRD YEAR OF HIS AGE; AND OF THE VIRTUES AND DEATH OF HIS MOTHER, MONICA.

CHAP. I.—HE PRAISES GOD, THE AUTHOR OF SAFETY, AND JESUS CHRIST, THE REDEEMER, ACKNOWLEDGING HIS OWN WICKEDNESS.

1. "O LORD, truly I am Thy servant; I am Thy servant, and the son of Thine handmaid: Thou hast loosed my bonds. I will offer to Thee the sacrifice of thanksgiving."[1] Let my heart and my tongue praise Thee, and let all my bones say, "Lord, who is like unto Thee?"[2] Let them so say, and answer Thou me, and "say unto my soul, I am Thy salvation."[3] Who am I, and what is my nature? How evil have not my deeds been; or if not my deeds, my words; or if not my words, my will? But Thou, O Lord, art good and merciful, and Thy right hand had respect unto the profoundness of my death, and removed from the bottom of my heart that abyss of corruption. And this was the result, that I willed not to do what I willed, and willed to do what thou willedst.[4] But where, during all those years, and out of what deep and secret retreat was my free will summoned forth in a moment, whereby I gave my neck to Thy "easy yoke," and my shoulders to Thy "light burden,"[5] O Christ Jesus, "my strength and my Redeemer"?[6] How sweet did it suddenly become to me to be without the delights of trifles! And what at one time I feared to lose, it was now a joy to me to put away.[7] For Thou didst cast them away from me, Thou true and highest sweetness. Thou didst cast them away, and instead of them didst enter in Thyself,[8]—sweeter than all pleasure, though not to flesh and blood; brighter than all light, but more veiled than all mysteries; more exalted than all honour, but not to the exalted in their own conceits. Now was my soul free from the gnawing cares of seeking and getting, and of wallowing and exciting the itch of lust. And I babbled unto Thee my brightness, my riches, and my health, the Lord my God.

CHAP. II.—AS HIS LUNGS WERE AFFECTED, HE MEDITATES WITHDRAWING HIMSELF FROM PUBLIC FAVOUR.

2. And it seemed good to me, as before Thee, not tumultuously to snatch away, but gently to withdraw the service of my tongue from the talker's trade; that the young, who thought not on Thy law, nor on Thy peace, but on mendacious follies and forensic strifes, might no longer purchase at my mouth equipments for their vehemence. And opportunely there wanted but a few days unto the Vacation of the Vintage;[9] and I determined to endure them, in order to leave in the usual way, and, being redeemed by Thee, no more to return for sale. Our intention then was known to Thee; but to men—excepting our own friends—was it not known. For we had determined among ourselves not to let it get abroad to any; although Thou hadst given to us, ascending from the valley of tears,[10] and singing the song of degrees, "sharp arrows," and destroying coals, against the "deceitful tongue,"[11] which in giving coun-

[1] Ps. cxvi. 16, 17.
[2] Ibid. xxxv. 10.
[3] Ibid. xxxv. 3.
[4] Volebas, though a few MSS. have nolebas; and Watts accordingly renders "nilledst.'
[5] Matt. xi. 30.
[6] Ps. xix. 14.
[7] Archbishop Trench, in his exposition of the parable of the Hid Treasure, which the man who found sold all that he had to buy, remarks on this passage of the Confessions: "Augustin excellently illustrates from his own experience this part of the parable. Describing the crisis of his own conversion, and how easy he found it, through this joy, to give up all those pleasures of sin that he had long dreaded to be obliged to renounce, which had long held him fast bound in the chains of evil custom, and which if he renounced, it had seemed to him as though life itself would not be worth the living, he exclaims, 'How sweet did it suddenly become to me,'" etc.
[8] His love of earthly things was expelled by the indwelling love of God, "for," as he says in his De Musica, vi. 52, "the love of the things of time could only be expelled by some sweetness of things eternal." Compare also Dr. Chalmers' sermon on The Ex-

pulsive Power of a New Affection (the ninth of his "Commercial Discourses"), where this idea is expanded.
[9] "In harvest and vintage time had the lawyers their vacation. So Minutius Felix. Scholars, their Non Terminus, as here; yea, divinity lectures and catechizings then ceased. So Cyprian, Ep. 2. The law terms gave way also to the great festivals of the Church. Theodosius forbade any process to go out from fifteen days before Easter till the Sunday after. For the four Terms, see Caroli Calvi, Capitula, Act viii. p. 90."—W. W.
[10] Ps. lxxxiv. 6.
[11] Ps. cxx. 3, 4, according to the Old Ver. This passage has many difficulties we need not enter into. The Vulgate, however, we may say, renders verse 3: "Quid detur tibi aut quid apponatur tibi ad linguam dolosam,"—that is, shall be given as a defence against the tongues of evil speakers. In this way Augustin understands it, and in his commentary on this place interprets the fourth verse give the answer to the third. Thus, "sharp arrows" he interprets to be the word of God, and "destroying coals" those who, being converted to Him, have become examples to the ungodly.

sel opposes, and in showing love consumes, as it is wont to do with its food.

3. Thou hadst penetrated our hearts with Thy charity, and we carried Thy words fixed, as it were, in our bowels; and the examples of Thy servant, whom of black Thou hadst made bright, and of dead, alive, crowded in the bosom of our thoughts, burned and consumed our heavy torpor, that we might not topple into the abyss; and they enkindled us exceedingly, that every breath of the deceitful tongue of the gainsayer might inflame us the more, not extinguish us. Nevertheless, because for Thy name's sake which Thou hast sanctified throughout the earth, this, our vow and purpose, might also find commenders, it looked like a vaunting of oneself not to wait for the vacation, now so near, but to leave beforehand a public profession, and one, too, under general observation; so that all who looked on this act of mine, and saw how near was the vintage-time I desired to anticipate, would talk of me a great deal as if I were trying to appear to be a great person. And what purpose would it serve that people should consider and dispute about my intention, and that our good should be evil spoken of?[1]

4. Furthermore, this very summer, from too great literary labour, my lungs[2] began to be weak, and with difficulty to draw deep breaths; showing by the pains in my chest that they were affected, and refusing too loud or prolonged speaking. This had at first been a trial to me, for it compelled me almost of necessity to lay down that burden of teaching; or, if I could be cured and become strong again, at least to leave it off for a while. But when the full desire for leisure, that I might see that Thou art the Lord,[3] arose, and was confirmed in me, my God, Thou knowest I even began to rejoice that I had this excuse ready,—and that not a feigned one,—which might somewhat temper the offence taken by those who for their sons' good wished me never to have the freedom of sons. Full, therefore, with such joy, I bore it till that period of time had passed,—perhaps it was some twenty days,—yet they were bravely borne; for the cupidity which was wont to sustain part of this weighty business had departed, and I had remained overwhelmed had not its place been supplied by patience. Some of Thy servants, my brethren, may perchance say that I sinned in this, in that having once fully, and from my heart, entered on Thy warfare, I permitted myself to sit a single hour in the seat of falsehood. I will not contend. But hast not

Thou, O most merciful Lord, pardoned and remitted this sin also, with my others, so horrible and deadly, in the holy water?

CHAP. III.—HE RETIRES TO THE VILLA OF HIS FRIEND VERECUNDUS, WHO WAS NOT YET A CHRISTIAN, AND REFERS TO HIS CONVERSION AND DEATH, AS WELL AS THAT OF NEBRIDIUS.

5. Verecundus was wasted with anxiety at that our happiness, since he, being most firmly held by his bonds, saw that he would lose our fellowship. For he was not yet a Christian, though his wife was one of the faithful;[4] and yet hereby, being more firmly enchained than by anything else, was he held back from that journey which we had commenced. Nor, he declared, did he wish to be a Christian on any other terms than those that were impossible. However, he invited us most courteously to make use of his country house so long as we should stay there. Thou, O Lord, wilt "recompense" him for this "at the resurrection of the just,"[5] seeing that Thou hast already given him "the lot of the righteous."[6] For although, when we were absent at Rome, he, being overtaken with bodily sickness, and therein being made a Christian, and one of the faithful, departed this life, yet hadst Thou mercy on him, and not on him only, but on us also;[7] lest, thinking on the exceeding kindness of our friend to us, and unable to count him in Thy flock, we should be tortured with intolerable grief. Thanks be unto Thee, our God, we are Thine. Thy exhortations, consolations, and faithful promises assure us that Thou now repayest Verecundus for that country house at Cassiacum, where from the fever of the world we found rest in Thee, with the perpetual freshness of Thy Paradise, in that Thou hast forgiven him his earthly sins, in that mountain flowing with milk,[8] that fruitful mountain,— Thine own.

6. He then was at that time full of grief; but Nebridius was joyous. Although he also, not being yet a Christian, had fallen into the pit of that most pernicious error of believing Thy Son to be a phantasm,[9] yet, coming out thence, he

---

[1] Rom. xiv. 16.
[2] In his *De Vita Beata*, sec. 4, and *Con. Acad.* i. 3, he also alludes to this weakness of his chest. He was therefore led to give up his professorship, partly from this cause, and partly from a desire to devote himself more entirely to God's service. See also p. 115, note.
[3] Ps. xlvi. 10.

[4] See vi. sec. 1, note, above.
[5] Luke xiv. 14.
[6] Ps. cxxv. 2.
[7] Phil. ii. 27.
[8] Literally, *In monte incaseato*, "the mountain of curds," from the *Old Ver.* of Ps. lxviii. 16. The *Vulgate* renders *coagulatus*. But the Authorized Version is nearer the true meaning, when it renders גַּבְנֻנִּים, *hunched*, as "high." The LXX. renders τετυρωμένος, *condensed*, as if from גְּבִינָה, *cheese*. This divergence arises from the unused root גָּבַן, *to be curved*, having derivatives meaning (1) "hunch-backed," when applied to the body, and (2) "cheese" or "curds," when applied to milk. Augustin, in his exposition of this place, makes the "mountain" to be Christ, and parallels it with Isa. ii. 2; and the "milk" he interprets of the grace that comes from Him for Christ's little ones: *Ipse est mons incaseatus, propter parvulos gratia tanquam lacte nutriendos.*
[9] See v. 16, note, above.

held the same belief that we did; not as yet initiated in any of the sacraments of Thy Church, but a most earnest inquirer after truth.[1] Whom, not long after our conversion and regeneration by Thy baptism, he being also a faithful member of the Catholic Church, and serving Thee in perfect chastity and continency amongst his own people in Africa, when his whole household had been brought to Christianity through him, didst Thou release from the flesh; and now he lives in Abraham's bosom. Whatever that may be which is signified by that bosom,[2] there lives my Nebridius, my sweet friend, Thy son, O Lord, adopted of a freedman; there he liveth. For what other place could there be for such a soul? There liveth he, concerning which he used to ask me much, —me, an inexperienced, feeble one. Now he puts not his ear unto my mouth, but his spiritual mouth unto Thy fountain, and drinketh as much as he is able, wisdom according to his desire,—happy without end. Nor do I believe that he is so inebriated with it as to forget me,[3] seeing Thou, O Lord, whom he drinketh, art mindful of us. Thus, then, were we comforting the sorrowing Verecundus (our friendship being untouched, concerning our conversion, and exhorting him to a faith according to his condition, I mean, his married state. And tarrying for Nebridius to follow us, which, being so near, he was just about to do, when, behold, those days passed over at last; for long and many they seemed, on account of my love of easeful liberty, that I might sing unto Thee from my very marrow. My heart said unto Thee,—I have sought Thy face; "Thy face, Lord, will I seek."[4]

CHAP. IV.—IN THE COUNTRY HE GIVES HIS ATTENTION TO LITERATURE, AND EXPLAINS THE FOURTH PSALM IN CONNECTION WITH THE HAPPY CONVERSION OF ALYPIUS. HE IS TROUBLED WITH TOOTHACHE.

7. And the day arrived on which, in very deed, I was to be released from the Professorship of Rhetoric, from which in intention I had been already released. And done it was; and Thou didst deliver my tongue whence Thou hadst already delivered my heart; and full of joy I blessed Thee for it, and retired with all mine to the villa.[5] What I accomplished here in writing, which was now wholly devoted to Thy service, though still, in this pause as it were, panting from the school of pride, my books testify,[6]—those in which I disputed with my friends, and those with myself alone[7] before Thee; and what with the absent Nebridius, my letters[8] testify. And when can I find time to recount all Thy great benefits which Thou bestowedst upon us at that time, especially as I am hasting on to still greater mercies? For my memory calls upon me, and pleasant it is to me, O Lord, to confess unto Thee, by what inward goads Thou didst subdue me, and how Thou didst make me low, bringing down the mountains and hills of my imaginations, and didst straighten my crookedness, and smooth my rough ways;[9] and by what means Thou also didst subdue that brother of my heart, Alypius, unto the name of Thy only-begotten, our Lord and Saviour Jesus Christ, which he at first refused to have inserted in our writings. For he rather desired that they should savour of the "cedars" of the schools, which the Lord hath now broken down,[10] than of the wholesome herbs of the Church, hostile to serpents.

8. What utterances sent I up unto Thee, my God, when I read the Psalms of David,[11] those faithful songs and sounds of devotion which exclude all swelling of spirit, when new to Thy true love, at rest in the villa with Alypius, a catechumen like myself, my mother cleaving unto us,—in woman's garb truly, but with a man's faith, with the peacefulness of age, full of motherly love and Christian piety! What utterances used I to send up unto Thee in those Psalms, and how was I inflamed towards Thee by them, and burned to rehearse them, if it

---

[1] See vi. 17, note 6, above.

[2] Though Augustin, in his *Quæst. Evang.* ii. qu. 38, makes Abraham's bosom to represent the rest into which the Gentiles entered after the Jews had put it from them, yet he, for the most part, in common with the early Church (see *Serm.* xiv. 3; *Con. Faust.* xxxiii. 5; and *Eps.* clxiv. 7, and clxxxvii. Compare also Tertullian, *De Anima*, lviii.), takes it to mean the resting-place of the souls of the righteous after death. Abraham's bosom, indeed, is the same as the "Paradise" of Luke xxiii. 43. The souls of the faithful after they are delivered from the flesh are in "joy and felicity" (*De Civ. Dei*, i. 13, and xiii. 19); but they will not have "their perfect consummation and bliss both in *body and soul*" until the morning of the resurrection, when they shall be endowed with "spiritual *bodies*." See note p. 111; and for the difference between the ᾅδης of Luke xvi. 23, that is, the place of departed spirits,—into which it is said in the Apostles' Creed Christ descended,—and γέεννα, or Hell, see Campbell on *The Gospels*, i. 253. In the A. V. both Greek words are rendered "Hell."

[3] See sec. 37, note, below.

[4] Ps. xxvii. 8.

[5] As Christ went into the wilderness after His baptism (Matt. iv. 1), and Paul into Arabia after his conversion (Gal. i. 17), so did Augustin here find in his retirement a preparation for his future work. He tells us of this time of his life (*De Ordin.* i. 6) that his habit was to spend the beginning or end, and often almost half the night, in watching and searching for truth, and says further (*ibid.* 29), that "he almost daily asked God with tears that his wounds might be healed, and often proved to himself that he was unworthy to be healed as soon as he wished."

[6] These books are (*Con. Acad.* i. 4) his three disputations *Against the Academics*; his *De Vita Beata*, begun (*ibid.* 6) "Idibus Novembris die ejus natali;" and (*Retract.* i. 3) his two books *De Ordine*.

[7] That is, his two books of *Soliloquies*. In his *Retractations*, i. 4, sec. 1, he tells us that in these books he held an argument,— *me interrogans, mihique respondens, tanquam duo essemus, ratio et ego.*

[8] Several of these letters to Nebridius will be found in the two vols. of *Letters* in this series.

[9] Luke iii. 5.

[10] Ps. xxix. 5.

[11] Reference may with advantage be made to Archbishop Trench's *Hulsean Lectures* (1845), who in his third lect., on "The Manifoldness of Scripture," adverts to this very passage, and shows in an interesting way how the Psalms have ever been to the saints of God, as Luther said, "a Bible in little," affording satisfaction to their needs in every kind of trial, emergency, and experience.

were possible, throughout the whole world, against the pride of the human race! And yet they are sung throughout the whole world, and none can hide himself from Thy heat.[1] With what vehement and bitter sorrow was I indignant at the Manichæans; whom yet again I pitied, for that they were ignorant of those sacraments, those medicaments, and were mad against the antidote which might have made them sane! I wished that they had been somewhere near me then, and, without my being aware of their presence, could have beheld my face, and heard my words, when I read the fourth Psalm in that time of my leisure,—how that Psalm wrought upon me. When I called upon Thee, Thou didst hear me, O God of my righteousness; Thou hast enlarged me when I was in distress; have mercy upon me, and hear my prayer.[2] Oh that they might have heard what I uttered on these words, without my knowing whether they heard or no, lest they should think that I spake it because of them! For, of a truth, neither should I have said the same things, nor in the way I said them, if I had perceived that I was heard and seen by them; and had I spoken them, they would not so have received them as when I spake by and for myself before Thee, out of the private feelings of my soul.

9. I alternately quaked with fear, and warmed with hope, and with rejoicing in Thy mercy, O Father. And all these passed forth, both by mine eyes and voice, when Thy good Spirit, turning unto us, said, O ye sons of men, how long will ye be slow of heart? "How long will ye love vanity, and seek after leasing?"[3] For I had loved vanity, and sought after leasing. And Thou, O Lord, hadst already magnified Thy Holy One, raising Him from the dead, and setting Him at Thy right hand,[4] whence from on high He should send His promise,[5] the Paraclete, "the Spirit of Truth."[6] And He had already sent Him,[7] but I knew it not; He had sent Him, because He was now magnified, rising again from the dead, and ascending into heaven. For till then "the Holy Ghost was not yet given, because that Jesus was not yet glorified."[8] And the prophet cries out, How long will ye be slow of heart? How long will ye love vanity, and seek after leasing? Know this, that the Lord hath magnified His Holy One. He cries out, "How long?" He cries out, "Know this," and I, so long ignorant, "loved vanity, and sought after leasing." And

therefore I heard and trembled, because these words were spoken unto such as I remembered that I myself had been. For in those phantasms which I once held for truths was there "vanity" and "leasing." And I spake many things loudly and earnestly, in the sorrow of my remembrance, which, would that they who yet "love vanity and seek after leasing" had heard! They would perchance have been troubled, and have vomited it forth, and Thou wouldest hear them when they cried unto Thee;[9] for by a true[10] death in the flesh He died for us, who now maketh intercession for us[11] with Thee.

10. I read further, "Be ye angry, and sin not."[12] And how was I moved, O my God, who had now learned to "be angry" with myself for the things past, so that in the future I might not sin! Yea, to be justly angry; for that it was not another nature of the race of darkness[13] which sinned for me, as they affirm it to be who are not angry with themselves, and who treasure up to themselves wrath against the day of wrath, and of the revelation of Thy righteous judgment.[14] Nor were my good things[15] now without, nor were they sought after with eyes of flesh in that sun;[16] for they that would have joy from without easily sink into oblivion, and are wasted upon those things which are seen and temporal, and in their starving thoughts do lick their very shadows. Oh, if only they were wearied out with their fasting, and said, "Who will show us any good?"[17] And we would answer, and they hear, O Lord. The light of Thy countenance is lifted up upon us.[18] For we are not that Light, which lighteth every man,[19] but we are enlightened by Thee, that we, who were sometimes darkness, may be light in Thee.[20] Oh that they could behold the internal Eternal,[21] which having tasted I gnashed my teeth that I could not show It to them, while they brought me their heart in their eyes, roaming abroad from Thee, and said, "Who will show us any good?" But there, where I was angry with myself in my chamber, where I was inwardly pricked, where I had offered my "sacrifice," slaying my old man, and beginning the resolution of a new life, putting my trust in Thee,[22]—there hadst Thou begun to grow sweet unto me, and to "put gladness in

---

[1] Ps. xix. 6.
[2] Ps. iv. 1.
[3] *Ibid.* ver. 23.
[4] Eph. i. 20.
[5] Luke xxiv. 49.
[6] John xiv. 16, 17.
[7] Acts ii. 1–4.
[8] John vii. 39.

[9] Ps. iv. 1.
[10] See v. 16, note, above.
[11] Rom. viii. 34.
[12] Eph. iv. 26.
[13] See iv. 26, note, above.
[14] Rom. ii. 5.
[15] Ps. iv. 6.
[16] See v. 12, note, above.
[17] Ps. iv. 6.
[18] *Ibid.*
[19] John i. 9.
[20] Eph. v. 8.
[21] *Internum æternum,* but some MSS. read *internum lumen æternum.*
[22] Ps. iv. 5.

my heart."[1] And I cried out as I read this outwardly, and felt it inwardly. Nor would I be increased[2] with worldly goods, wasting time and being wasted by time; whereas I possessed in Thy eternal simplicity other corn, and wine, and oil.[3]

11. And with a loud cry from my heart, I called out in the following verse, "Oh, in peace!" and "the self-same!"[4] Oh, what said he, "I will lay me down and sleep!"[5] For who shall hinder us, when "shall be brought to pass the saying that is written, Death is swallowed up in victory?"[6] And Thou art in the highest degree "the self-same," who changest not; and in Thee is the rest which forgetteth all labour, for there is no other beside Thee, nor ought we to seek after those many other things which are not what Thou art; but Thou, Lord, only makest me to dwell in hope.[7] These things I read, and was inflamed; but discovered not what to do with those deaf and dead, of whom I had been a pestilent member, —a bitter and a blind declaimer against the writings be-honied with the honey of heaven and luminous with Thine own light; and I was consumed on account of the enemies of this Scripture.

12. When shall I call to mind all that took place in those holidays? Yet neither have I forgotten, nor will I be silent about the severity of Thy scourge, and the amazing quickness of Thy mercy.[8] Thou didst at that time torture me with toothache;[9] and when it had become so exceeding great that I was not able to speak, it came into my heart to urge all my friends who were present to pray for me to Thee, the God of all manner of health. And I wrote it down on wax,[10] and gave it to them to read.

Presently, as with submissive desire we bowed our knees, that pain departed. But what pain? Or how did it depart? I confess to being much afraid, my Lord my God, seeing that from my earliest years I had not experienced such pain. And Thy purposes were profoundly impressed upon me; and, rejoicing in faith, I praised Thy name. And that faith suffered me not to be at rest in regard to my past sins, which were not yet forgiven me by Thy baptism.

CHAP. V.—AT THE RECOMMENDATION OF AMBROSE, HE READS THE PROPHECIES OF ISAIAH, BUT DOES NOT UNDERSTAND THEM.

13. The vintage vacation being ended, I gave the citizens of Milan notice that they might provide their scholars with another seller of words; because both of my election to serve Thee, and my inability, by reason of the difficulty of breathing and the pain in my chest, to continue the Professorship. And by letters I notified to Thy bishop,[11] the holy man Ambrose, my former errors and present resolutions, with a view to his advising me which of Thy books it was best for me to read, so that I might be readier and fitter for the reception of such great grace. He recommended Isaiah the Prophet;[12] I believe, because he foreshows more clearly than others the gospel, and the calling of the Gentiles. But I, not understanding the first portion of the book, and imagining the whole to be like it, laid it aside, intending to take it up hereafter, when better practised in our Lord's words.

CHAP. VI.—HE IS BAPTIZED AT MILAN WITH ALYPIUS AND HIS SON ADEODATUS. THE BOOK "DE MAGISTRO."

14. Thence, when the time had arrived at which I was to give in my name,[13] having left the country, we returned to Milan. Alypius also was pleased to be born again with me in Thee, being now clothed with the humility appropriate to Thy sacraments, and being so brave a tamer of the body, as with unusual fortitude to tread the frozen soil of Italy with his naked feet. We took into our company the boy Adeodatus, born of me carnally, of my sin. Well hadst Thou made him. He was barely

---

[1] Ps. iv. 7.
[2] That is, lest they should distract him from the true riches. For, as he says in his exposition of the fourth Psalm, "Cum dedita temporalibus voluptatibus anima semper exardescit cupiditate, nec satiari potest." He knew that the prosperity of the soul (3 John 2) might be injuriously affected by the prosperity of the body; and disregarding the lower life (βίος) and its "worldly goods," he pressed on to increase the treasure he had within,—the true life (ζωή) which he had received from God. See also *Enarr. in Ps.* xxxviii. 6.
[3] Ps. iv. 7.
[4] *Ibid.* ver. 8, *Vulg.*
[5] Ps. iv. 8; in his comment whereon, Augustin applies this passage as above.
[6] 1 Cor. xv. 54.
[7] Ps. iv. 9, *Vulg.*
[8] Compare the beautiful Talmudical legend quoted by Jeremy Taylor (*Works*, viii. 397, Eden's ed.), that of the two archangels, Gabriel and Michael, Gabriel has two wings that he may "fly swiftly" (Dan. ix. 21) to bring the message of peace, while Michael has but one, that he may labour in his flight when he comes forth on his ministries of justice.
[9] In his *Soliloquies* (see note, sec. 7, above), he refers in i. 21 to this period. He there tells us that his pain was so great that it prevented his learning anything afresh, and only permitted him to revolve in his mind what he had already learnt. Compare De Quincey's description of the agonies he had to endure from toothache in his *Confessions of an Opium Eater.*
[10] That is, on the waxen tablet used by the ancients. The iron *stilus*, or pencil, used for writing, was pointed at one end and flattened at the other—the flattened circular end being used to erase the writing by smoothing down the wax. Hence *vertere stilum* signifies *to put out* or *correct.* See sec. 19, below.

[11] *Antistiti.*
[12] In his *De Civ. Dei*, xviii. 29, he likewise alludes to the evangelical character of the writings of Isaiah.
[13] "They were baptized at Easter, and gave up their names before the second Sunday in Lent, the rest of which they were to spend in fasting, humility, prayer, and being examined in the scrutinies (Tertull. *Lib. de Bapt.* c. 20). Therefore went they to Milan, that the bishop might see their preparation. Adjoining to the cathedrals were there certain lower houses for them to lodge and be exercised in, till the day of baptism" (Euseb. x. 4).—W. W. See also Bingham, x. 2, sec. 6; and above, note 4, p. 89; note 4, p. 118, and note 8, p. 118.

fifteen years, yet in wit excelled many grave and learned men.[1] I confess unto Thee Thy gifts, O Lord my God, Creator of all, and of exceeding power to reform our deformities; for of me was there naught in that boy but the sin. For that we fostered him in Thy discipline, Thou inspiredst us, none other,—Thy gifts I confess unto Thee. There is a book of ours, which is entitled *The Master*.[2] It is a dialogue between him and me. Thou knowest that all things there put into the mouth of the person in argument with me were his thoughts in his sixteenth year. Many others more wonderful did I find in him. That talent was a source of awe to me. And who but Thou could be the worker of such marvels? Quickly didst Thou remove his life from the earth; and now I recall him to mind with a sense of security, in that I fear nothing for his childhood or youth, or for his whole self. We took him coeval with us in Thy grace, to be educated in Thy discipline; and we were baptized,[3] and solicitude about our past life left us. Nor was I satiated in those days with the wondrous sweetness of considering the depth of Thy counsels concerning the salvation of the human race. How greatly did I weep in Thy hymns and canticles, deeply moved by the voices of Thy sweet-speaking Church! The voices flowed into mine ears, and the truth was poured forth into my heart, whence the agitation of my piety overflowed, and my tears ran over, and blessed was I therein.

CHAP. VII.—OF THE CHURCH HYMNS INSTITUTED AT MILAN; OF THE AMBROSIAN PERSECUTION RAISED BY JUSTINA; AND OF THE DISCOVERY OF THE BODIES OF TWO MARTYRS.

15. Not long had the Church of Milan begun to employ this kind of consolation and exhortation, the brethren singing together with great earnestness of voice and heart. For it was about a year, or not much more, since Justina, the mother of the boy-Emperor Valentinian, persecuted[4] Thy servant Ambrose in the interest of her heresy, to which she had been seduced by the Arians. The pious people kept guard in the church, prepared to die with their bishop, Thy servant. There my mother, Thy handmaid, bearing a chief part of those cares and watchings, lived in prayer. We, still unmelted by the heat of Thy Spirit, were yet moved by the astonished and disturbed city. At this time it was instituted that, after the manner of the Eastern Church, hymns and psalms should be sung, lest the people should pine away in the tediousness of sorrow; which custom, retained from then till now, is imitated by many, yea, by almost all of Thy congregations throughout the rest of the world.

16. Then didst Thou by a vision make known to Thy renowned bishop[5] the spot where lay the bodies of Gervasius and Protasius, the martyrs (whom Thou hadst in Thy secret storehouse preserved uncorrupted for so many years), whence Thou mightest at the fitting time produce them to repress the feminine but royal fury. For when they were revealed and dug up and with due honour transferred to the Ambrosian Basilica, not only they who were troubled with unclean spirits (the devils confessing themselves) were healed, but a certain man also, who had been blind[6] many years, a well-known citizen of that city, having asked and been told the reason of the people's tumultuous joy, rushed forth, asking his guide to lead him thither. Arrived there, he begged to be permitted to touch with his handkerchief the bier of Thy saints, whose death is precious in Thy sight.[7] When he had done this, and put it to his eyes, they were forthwith opened. Thence did the fame spread; thence did Thy praises burn,—shine; thence was the mind of that enemy, though not yet enlarged to the wholeness of believing, restrained from the fury of persecuting. Thanks be to Thee, O my God. Whence and whither hast Thou thus led my remembrance, that I should confess these

---

[1] In his *De Vita Beata*, sec. 6, he makes a similar illusion to the genius of Adeodatus.

[2] This book, in which he and his son are the interlocutors, will be found in vol. i. of the Benedictine edition, and is by the editors assumed to be written about A.D. 389. Augustin briefly gives its argument in his *Retractations*, i. 12. He says: "There it is disputed, sought, and discovered that there is no master who teaches man knowledge save God, as it is written in the gospel (Matt. xxiii. 10), 'One is your Master, even Christ.'"

[3] He was baptized by Ambrose, and tradition says, as he came out of the water, they sang alternate verses of the *Te Deum* (ascribed by some to Ambrose), which, in the old offices of the English Church is called "The Song of Ambrose and Augustin." In his *Con. Julian. Pelag.* i. 10, he speaks of Ambrose as being one whose devoted labours and perils were known throughout the whole Roman world, and says: "In Christo enim Jesu per evangelium ipse me genuit, et *eo Christi ministro lavacrum regenerationis accepi.*" See also the last sec. of his *De Nupt. et Concup.*, and *Ep.* cxlvii. 23. In notes 3, p. 50, and 4, p. 89, will be found references to the usages of the early Church as to baptism.

[4] The Bishop of Milan who preceded Ambrose was an Arian, and though Valentinian the First approved the choice of Ambrose as bishop, Justina, on his death, greatly troubled the Church. Ambrose subsequently had great influence over both Valentinian the Second and his brother Gratian. The persecution referred to above, says Pusey, was "to induce him to give up to the Arians a church,—the Portian Basilica without the walls; afterwards she asked for the new Basilica within the walls, which was larger." See Ambrose, *Epp.* 20–22; *Serm. c. Auxentium de Basilicis Tradendis*, pp. 852–880, ed. Bened.; cf. Tillemont, *Hist. Eccl. St. Ambroise*, art. 44–48, pp. 76–82. Valentinian was then at Milan. See next sec., the beginning of note.

[5] *Antistiti.*

[6] Augustin alludes to this, amongst other supposed miracles, in his *De Civ. Dei*, xxii. 8; and again in *Serm.* cclxxxvi. sec. 4, where he tells us that the man, after being cured, made a vow that he would for the remainder of his life serve in that Basilica where the bodies of the martyrs lay. St. Ambrose also examines the miracle at great length in one of his sermons. We have already referred in note 5, p. 69 to the origin of these false miracles in the early Church. Lecture vi. series 2, of Blunt's *Lectures on the Right Use of the Early Fathers*, is devoted to an examination of the various passages in the Ante-Nicene Fathers where the continuance of miracles in the Church is either expressed or implied. The reader should also refer to the note on p. 485 of vol. ii. of the *City of God*, in this series.

[7] Ps. cxvi. 15.

things also unto Thee,—great, though I, forgetful, had passed them over? And yet then, when the "savour" of Thy "ointments" was so fragrant, did we not "run after Thee."[1] And so I did the more abundantly weep at the singing of Thy hymns, formerly panting for Thee, and at last breathing in Thee, as far as the air can play in this house of grass.

CHAP. VIII.—OF THE CONVERSION OF EVODIUS, AND THE DEATH OF HIS MOTHER WHEN RETURNING WITH HIM TO AFRICA; AND WHOSE EDUCATION HE TENDERLY RELATES.

17. Thou, who makest men to dwell of one mind in a house,[2] didst associate with us Evodius also, a young man of our city, who, when serving as an agent for Public Affairs,[3] was converted unto Thee and baptized prior to us; and relinquishing his secular service, prepared himself for Thine. We were together,[4] and together were we about to dwell with a holy purpose. We sought for some place where we might be most useful in our service to Thee, and were going back together to Africa. And when we were at the Tiberine Ostia my mother died. Much I omit, having much to hasten. Receive my confessions and thanksgivings, O my God, for innumerable things concerning which I am silent. But I will not omit aught that my soul has brought forth as to that Thy handmaid who brought me forth,—in her flesh, that I might be born to this temporal light, and in her heart, that I might be born to life eternal.[5] I will speak not of her gifts, but Thine in her; for she neither made herself nor educated herself. Thou createdst her, nor did her father nor her mother know what a being was to proceed from them. And it was the rod of Thy Christ, the discipline of Thine only Son, that trained her in Thy fear, in the house of one of Thy faithful ones, who was a sound member of Thy Church. Yet this good discipline did she not so much attribute to the diligence of her mother, as that of a certain decrepid maid-servant, who had carried about her father when an infant, as little ones are wont to be carried on the backs of elder girls. For which reason, and on account of her extreme age and very good character, was she much respected by the heads of that Christian house. Whence also was committed to her the care of her master's daughters, which she with diligence performed,

and was earnest in restraining them when necessary, with a holy severity, and instructing them with a sober sagacity. For, excepting at the hours in which they were very temperately fed at their parents' table, she used not to permit them, though parched with thirst, to drink even water; thereby taking precautions against an evil custom, and adding the wholesome advice, "You drink water only because you have not control of wine; but when you have come to be married, and made mistresses of storeroom and cellar, you will despise water, but the habit of drinking will remain." By this method of instruction, and power of command, she restrained the longing of their tender age, and regulated the very thirst of the girls to such a becoming limit, as that what was not seemly they did not long for.

18. And yet—as Thine handmaid related to me, her son—there had stolen upon her a love of wine. For when she, as being a sober maiden, was as usual bidden by her parents to draw wine from the cask, the vessel being held under the opening, before she poured the wine into the bottle, she would wet the tips of her lips with a little, for more than that her inclination refused. For this she did not from any craving for drink, but out of the overflowing buoyancy of her time of life, which bubbles up with sportiveness, and is, in youthful spirits, wont to be repressed by the gravity of elders. And so unto that little, adding daily littles (for "he that contemneth small things shall fall by little and little"),[6] she contracted such a habit as to drink off eagerly her little cup nearly full of wine. Where, then, was the sagacious old woman with her earnest restraint? Could anything prevail against a secret disease if Thy medicine, O Lord, did not watch over us? Father, mother, and nurturers absent, Thou present, who hast created, who callest, who also by those who are set over us workest some good for the salvation of our souls, what didst Thou at that time, O my God? How didst Thou

---

[1] Cant. i. 3, 4.
[2] Ps. lxviii. 6.
[3] See viii. sec. 15, note, above.
[4] We find from his *Retractations* (i. 7, sec. 1), that at this time he wrote his *De Moribus Ecclesiæ Catholicæ* and his *De Moribus Manichæorum.* He also wrote (*ibid.* 8, sec. 1) his *De Animæ Quantitate,* and (*ibid.* 9, sec. 1) his three books *De Libero Arbitrio.*
[5] In his *De Vita Beata* and in his *De Dono Persev.* he attributes all that he was to his mother's tears and prayers.

[6] Ecclus. xix. 1. Augustin frequently alludes to the subtle power of little things. As when he says,—illustrating (*Serm.* cclxxviii.) by the plagues of Egypt,—tiny insects, if they be numerous enough, will be as harmful as the bite of great beasts; and (*Serm.* lvi.) a hill of sand, though composed of tiny grains, will crush a man as surely as the same weight of lead. Little drops (*Serm.* lviii.) make the river, and little leaks sink the ship; wherefore, he urges, little things must not be despised. "Men have usually," says Sedgwick in his *Anatomy of Secret Sins,* "been first wading in lesser sins who are now swimming in great transgressions." It is in the little things of evil that temptation has its greatest strength. The snow-flake is little and not to be accounted of, but from its multitudinous accumulation results the dread power of the avalanche. Satan often seems to act as it is said Pompey did, when he could not gain entrance to a city. He persuaded the citizens to admit a few of his weak and wounded soldiers, who, when they had become strong, opened the gates to his whole army. But if little things have such subtlety in temptation, they have likewise higher ministries. The Jews, in their Talmudical writings, have many parables illustrating how God by little things tries and proves men to see if they are fitted for greater things. They say, for example, that He tried David when keeping sheep in the wilderness, to see whether he would be worthy to rule over Israel, the sheep of his inheritance. See Ch. Schoettgen, *Hor. Heb. et Talmud,* i. 300.

heal her? How didst Thou make her whole? Didst Thou not out of another woman's soul evoke a hard and bitter insult, as a surgeon's knife from Thy secret store, and with one thrust remove all that putrefaction?[1] For the maid-servant who used to accompany her to the cellar, falling out, as it happens, with her little mistress, when she was alone with her, cast in her teeth this vice, with very bitter insult, calling her a "wine-bibber." Stung by this taunt, she perceived her foulness, and immediately condemned and renounced it. Even as friends by their flattery pervert, so do enemies by their taunts often correct us. Yet Thou renderest not unto them what Thou dost by them, but what was proposed by them. For she, being angry, desired to irritate her young mistress, not to cure her; and did it in secret, either because the time and place of the dispute found them thus, or perhaps lest she herself should be exposed to danger for disclosing it so late. But Thou, Lord, Governor of heavenly and earthly things, who convertest to Thy purposes the deepest torrents, and disposest the turbulent current of the ages,[2] healest one soul by the unsoundness of another; lest any man, when he remarks this, should attribute it unto his own power if another, whom he wishes to be reformed, is so through a word of his.

CHAP. IX.—HE DESCRIBES THE PRAISEWORTHY HABITS OF HIS MOTHER; HER KINDNESS TOWARDS HER HUSBAND AND HER SONS.

19. Being thus modestly and soberly trained, and rather made subject by Thee to her parents, than by her parents to Thee, when she had arrived at a marriageable age, she was given to a husband whom she served as her lord. And she busied herself to gain him to Thee, preaching Thee unto him by her behaviour; by which Thou madest her fair, and reverently amiable, and admirable unto her husband. For she so bore the wronging of her bed as never to have any dissension with her husband on account of it. For she waited for Thy mercy upon him, that by believing in Thee he might become chaste. And besides this, as he was earnest in friendship, so was he violent in anger; but she

had learned that an angry husband should not be resisted, neither in deed, nor even in word. But so soon as he was grown calm and tranquil, and she saw a fitting moment, she would give him a reason for her conduct, should he have been excited without cause. In short, while many matrons, whose husbands were more gentle, carried the marks of blows on their dishonoured faces, and would in private conversation blame the lives of their husbands, she would blame their tongues, monishing them gravely, as if in jest: "That from the hour they heard what are called the matrimonial tablets[3] read to them, they should think of them as instruments whereby they were made servants; so, being always mindful of their condition, they ought not to set themselves in opposition to their lords." And when they, knowing what a furious husband she endured, marvelled that it had never been reported, nor appeared by any indication, that Patricius had beaten his wife, or that there had been any domestic strife between them, even for a day, and asked her in confidence the reason of this, she taught them her rule, which I have mentioned above. They who observed it experienced the wisdom of it, and rejoiced; those who observed it not were kept in subjection, and suffered.

20. Her mother-in-law, also, being at first prejudiced against her by the whisperings of evil-disposed servants, she so conquered by submission, persevering in it with patience and meekness, that she voluntarily disclosed to her son the tongues of the meddling servants, whereby the domestic peace between herself and her daughter-in-law had been agitated, begging him to punish them for it. When, therefore, he had—in conformity with his mother's wish, and with a view to the discipline of his family, and to ensure the future harmony of its members—corrected with stripes those discovered, according to the will of her who had discovered them, she promised a similar reward to any who, to please her, should say anything evil to her of her daughter-in-law. And, none now daring to do so, they lived together with a wonderful sweetness of mutual good-will.

21. This great gift Thou bestowedst also, my God, my mercy, upon that good handmaid of Thine, out of whose womb Thou createdst me,

---

[1] "'Animam oportet assiduis saliri tentationibus,' says St. Ambrose. Some errors and offences do rub salt upon a good man's integrity, that it may not putrefy with presumption."—Bishop Hacket's *Sermons*, p. 210.

[2] Not only is this true in private, but in public concerns. Even in the crucifixion of our Lord, the wicked rulers did (Acts. iv. 26) what God's hand and God's counsel had before determined to be done. Perhaps by reason of His infinite knowledge it is that God, who knows our thoughts long before (Ps. cxxxix. 2, 4), weaves man's self-willed purposes into the pattern which His inscrutable Providence has before ordained. Or, to use Augustin's own words (*De Civ. Dei*, xxii. 2), "It is true that wicked men do many things contrary to God's will; but so great is His wisdom and power, that all things which seem adverse to His purpose do still tend towards those just and good ends and issues which He Himself has foreknown."

[3] That is, not only from the time of actual marriage, but from the time of betrothal, when the contract was written upon tablets (see note 10, p. 133), and signed by the contracting parties. The future wife was then called *sponsa sperata* or *pacta*. Augustin alludes to this above (viii. sec. 7), when he says, "It is also the custom that the affianced bride (*pactæ sponsæ*) should not immediately be given up, that the husband may not less esteem her whom, as betrothed, he longed not for" (*non suspiraverit sponsus*). It should be remembered, in reading this section, that women amongst the Romans were not confined after the Eastern fashion of the Greeks to separate apartments, but had charge of the domestic arrangements and the training of the children.

even that, whenever she could, she showed herself such a peacemaker between any differing and discordant spirits, that when she had heard on both sides most bitter things, such as swelling and undigested discord is wont to give vent to, when the crudities of enmities are breathed out in bitter speeches to a present friend against an absent enemy, she would disclose nothing about the one unto the other, save what might avail to their reconcilement. A small good this might seem to me, did I not know to my sorrow countless persons, who, through some horrible and far-spreading infection of sin, not only disclose to enemies mutually enraged the things said in passion against each other, but add some things that were never spoken at all; whereas, to a generous man, it ought to seem a small thing not to incite or increase the enmities of men by ill-speaking, unless he endeavour likewise by kind words to extinguish them. Such a one was she,—Thou, her most intimate Instructor, teaching her in the school of her heart.

22. Finally, her own husband, now towards the end of his earthly existence, did she gain over unto Thee; and she had not to complain of that in him, as one of the faithful, which, before he became so, she had endured. She was also the servant of Thy servants. Whosoever of them knew her, did in her much magnify, honour, and love Thee; for that through the testimony of the fruits of a holy conversation, they perceived Thee to be present in her heart. For she had "been the wife of one man," had requited her parents, had guided her house piously, was "well-reported of for good works," had "brought up children,"[1] as often travailing in birth of them[2] as she saw them swerving from Thee. Lastly, to all of us, O Lord (since of Thy favour Thou sufferest Thy servants to speak), who, before her sleeping in Thee,[3] lived associated together, having received the grace of Thy baptism, did she devote care such as she might if she had been mother of us all; served us as if she had been child of all.

CHAP. X.—A CONVERSATION HE HAD WITH HIS MOTHER CONCERNING THE KINGDOM OF HEAVEN.

23. As the day now approached on which she was to depart this life (which day Thou knewest, we did not), it fell out—Thou, as I believe, by Thy secret ways arranging it—that she and I stood alone, leaning in a certain window, from which the garden of the house we occupied at Ostia could be seen; at which place, removed

from the crowd, we were resting ourselves for the voyage, after the fatigues of a long journey. We then were conversing alone very pleasantly; and, "forgetting those things which are behind, and reaching forth unto those things which are before,"[4] we were seeking between ourselves in the presence of the Truth, which Thou art, of what nature the eternal life of the saints would be, which eye hath not seen, nor ear heard, neither hath entered into the heart of man.[5] But yet we opened wide the mouth of our heart, after those supernal streams of Thy fountain, "the fountain of life," which is "with Thee;"[6] that being sprinkled with it according to our capacity, we might in some measure weigh so high a mystery.

24. And when our conversation had arrived at that point, that the very highest pleasure of the carnal senses, and that in the very brightest material light, seemed by reason of the sweetness of that life not only not worthy of comparison, but not even of mention, we, lifting ourselves with a more ardent affection towards "the Selfsame,"[7] did gradually pass through all corporeal things, and even the heaven itself, whence sun, and moon, and stars shine upon the earth; yea, we soared higher yet by inward musing, and discoursing, and admiring Thy works; and we came to our own minds, and went beyond them, that we might advance as high as that region of unfailing plenty, where Thou feedest Israel[8] for ever with the food of truth, and where life is that Wisdom by whom all these things are made, both which have been, and which are to come; and she is not made, but is as she hath been, and so shall ever be; yea, rather, to "have been," and "to be hereafter," are not in her, but only "to be," seeing she is eternal, for to "have been" and "to be hereafter" are not eternal. And while we were thus speaking, and straining after her, we slightly touched her with the whole effort of our heart; and we sighed, and there left bound "the first-fruits of the Spirit;"[9] and returned to the noise of our own mouth, where the word uttered has both beginning and end. And what is like unto Thy Word, our Lord, who remaineth in Himself without becoming old, and "maketh all things new"?[10]

25. We were saying, then, If to any man the tumult of the flesh were silenced,—silenced the phantasies of earth, waters, and air,—silenced, too, the poles; yea, the very soul be silenced to herself, and go beyond herself by not think-

---

[1] 1 Tim. v. 4, 9, 10, 14.
[2] Gal. iv. 19.
[3] 1 Thess. iv. 14.
[4] Phil. iii. 13.
[5] 1 Cor. ii. 9; Isa. lxiv. 4.
[6] Ps. xxxvi. 9.
[7] Ps. iv. 8, *Vulg.*
[8] Ps. lxxx. 5.
[9] Rom. viii. 23.
[10] Wisd. vii. 27.

ing of herself,—silenced fancies and imaginary revelations, every tongue, and every sign, and whatsoever exists by passing away, since, if any could hearken, all these say, "We created not ourselves, but were created by Him who abideth for ever:" If, having uttered this, they now should be silenced, having only quickened our ears to Him who created them, and He alone speak not by them, but by Himself, that we may hear His word, not by fleshly tongue, nor angelic voice, nor sound of thunder, nor the obscurity of a similitude, but might hear Him— Him whom in these we love—without these, like as we two now strained ourselves, and with rapid thought touched on that Eternal Wisdom which remaineth over all. If this could be sustained, and other visions of a far different kind be withdrawn, and this one ravish, and absorb, and envelope its beholder amid these inward joys, so that his life might be eternally like that one moment of knowledge which we now sighed after, were not this "Enter thou into the joy of Thy Lord"?[1] And when shall that be? When we shall all rise again; but all shall not be changed.[2]

26. Such things was I saying; and if not after this manner, and in these words, yet, Lord, Thou knowest, that in that day when we were talking thus, this world with all its delights grew contemptible to us, even while we spake. Then said my mother, "Son, for myself, I have no longer any pleasure in aught in this life. What I want here further, and why I am here, I know not, now that my hopes in this world are satisfied. There was indeed one thing for which I wished to tarry a little in this life, and that was that I might see thee a Catholic Christian before I died.[3] My God has exceeded this abundantly, so that I see thee despising all earthly felicity, made His servant,—what do I here?"

CHAP. XI.—HIS MOTHER, ATTACKED BY FEVER, DIES AT OSTIA.

27. What reply I made unto her to these things I do not well remember. However, scarcely five days after, or not much more, she was prostrated by fever; and while she was sick, she one day sank into a swoon, and was

for a short time unconscious of visible things. We hurried up to her; but she soon regained her senses, and gazing on me and my brother as we stood by her, she said to us inquiringly, "Where was I?" Then looking intently at us stupefied with grief, "Here," saith she, "shall you bury your mother." I was silent, and refrained from weeping; but my brother said something, wishing her, as the happier lot, to die in her own country and not abroad. She, when she heard this, with anxious countenance arrested him with her eye, as savouring of such things, and then gazing at me, "Behold," saith she, "what he saith;" and soon after to us both she saith, "Lay this body anywhere, let not the care for it trouble you at all. This only I ask, that you will remember me at the Lord's altar, wherever you be." And when she had given forth this opinion in such words as she could, she was silent, being in pain with her increasing sickness.

28. But, as I reflected on Thy gifts, O thou invisible God, which Thou instillest into the hearts of Thy faithful ones, whence such marvellous fruits do spring, I did rejoice and give thanks unto Thee, calling to mind what I knew before, how she had ever burned with anxiety respecting her burial-place, which she had provided and prepared for herself by the body of her husband. For as they had lived very peacefully together, her desire had also been (so little is the human mind capable of grasping things divine) that this should be added to that happiness, and be talked of among men, that after her wandering beyond the sea, it had been granted her that they both, so united on earth, should lie in the same grave. But when this uselessness had, through the bounty of Thy goodness, begun to be no longer in her heart, I knew not, and I was full of joy admiring what she had thus disclosed to me; though indeed in that our conversation in the window also, when she said, "What do I here any longer?" she appeared not to desire to die in her own country. I heard afterwards, too, that at the time we were at Ostia, with a maternal confidence she one day, when I was absent, was speaking with certain of my friends on the contemning of this life, and the blessing of death; and when they—amazed at the courage which Thou hadst given to her, a woman—asked her whether she did not dread leaving her body at such a distance from her own city, she replied, "Nothing is far to God; nor need I fear lest He should be ignorant at the end of the world of the place whence He is to raise me up." On the ninth day, then, of her sickness, the fifty-sixth year of her age, and the thirty-third of mine, was that religious and devout soul set free from the body.

---

[1] Matt. xxv. 21.
[2] 1 Cor. xv. 51, however, is, "we *shall* all be changed."
[3] Dean Stanley (*Canterbury Sermons*, serm. 10) draws the following, amongst other lessons, from God's dealings with Augustin. "It is an example," he says, "like the conversion of St. Paul, of the fact that from time to time God calls His servants not by gradual, but by sudden changes. These conversions are, it is true, the exceptions and not the rule of Providence, but such examples as Augustin show us that we must acknowledge the truth of the exceptions when they do occur. It is also an instance how, even in such sudden conversions, previous good influences have their weight. The prayers of his mother, the silent influence of his friend, the high character of Ambrose, the preparation for Christian truth in the writings of heathen philosophers, were all laid up, as it were, waiting for the spark, and, when it came, the fire flashed at once through every corner of his soul."

CHAP. XII. — HOW HE MOURNED HIS DEAD
MOTHER.

29. I closed her eyes; and there flowed a
great sadness into my heart, and it was passing
into tears, when mine eyes at the same time, by
the violent control of my mind, sucked back
the fountain dry, and woe was me in such a
struggle! But, as soon as she breathed her last,
the boy Adeodatus burst out into wailing, but,
being checked by us all, he became quiet. In
like manner also my own childish feeling, which
was, through the youthful voice of my heart,
finding escape in tears, was restrained and
silenced. For we did not consider it fitting to
celebrate that funeral with tearful plaints and
groanings;[1] for on such wise are they who die
unhappy, or are altogether dead, wont to be
mourned. But she neither died unhappy, nor
did she altogether die. For of this were we
assured by the witness of her good conversation,
her "faith unfeigned,"[2] and other sufficient
grounds.

30. What, then, was that which did grievously pain me within, but the newly-made
wound, from having that most sweet and dear
habit of living together suddenly broken off?
I was full of joy indeed in her testimony, when,
in that her last illness, flattering my dutifulness,
she called me "kind," and recalled, with great
affection of love, that she had never heard any
harsh or reproachful sound come out of my
mouth against her. But yet, O my God, who
madest us, how can the honour which I paid to
her be compared with her slavery for me? As,
then, I was left destitute of so great comfort in
her, my soul was stricken, and that life torn
apart as it were, which, of hers and mine together, had been made but one.

31. The boy then being restrained from
weeping, Evodius took up the Psalter, and began to sing—the whole house responding—the
Psalm, "I will sing of mercy and judgment:
unto Thee, O Lord."[3] But when they heard

what we were doing, many brethren and religious women came together; and whilst they
whose office it was were, according to custom,
making ready for the funeral, I, in a part of the
house where I conveniently could, together
with those who thought that I ought not to be
left alone, discoursed on what was suited to the
occasion; and by this alleviation of truth mitigated the anguish known unto Thee—they being unconscious of it, listened intently, and
thought me to be devoid of any sense of sorrow.
But in Thine ears, where none of them heard,
did I blame the softness of my feelings, and restrained the flow of my grief, which yielded a
little unto me; but the paroxysm returned
again, though not so as to burst forth into tears,
nor to a change of countenance, though I knew
what I repressed in my heart. And as I was
exceedingly annoyed that these human things
had such power over me,[4] which in the due
order and destiny of our natural condition must
of necessity come to pass, with a new sorrow I
sorrowed for my sorrow, and was wasted by a
twofold sadness.

32. So, when the body was carried forth, we
both went and returned without tears. For
neither in those prayers which we poured forth
unto Thee when the sacrifice of our redemption[5]
was offered up unto Thee for her,—the dead
body being now placed by the side of the grave,
as the custom there is, prior to its being laid
therein,—neither in their prayers did I shed
tears; yet was I most grievously sad in secret
all the day, and with a troubled mind entreated
Thee, as I was able, to heal my sorrow, but
Thou didst not; fixing, I believe, in my memory by this one lesson the power of the bonds
of all habit, even upon a mind which now feeds
not upon a fallacious word. It appeared to me
also a good thing to go and bathe, I having
heard that the bath [balneum] took its name
from the Greek βαλανεῖον, because it drives
trouble from the mind. Lo, this also I confess
unto Thy mercy, "Father of the fatherless,"[6]
that I bathed, and felt the same as before I had
done so. For the bitterness of my grief exuded
not from my heart. Then I slept, and on
awaking found my grief not a little mitigated;
and as I lay alone upon my bed, there came

[1] For this would be to sorrow as those that have no hope.
Chrysostom accordingly frequently rebukes the Roman custom of
hiring persons to wail for the dead (see *e. g. Hom.* xxxii. *in Matt.*);
and Augustin in Serm. 2 of his *De Consol. Mor.* makes the same
objection, and also reproves those Christians who imitated the Romans in wearing black as the sign of mourning. But still (as in his
own case on the death of his mother) he admits that there is a grief
at the departure of friends that is both natural and seemly. In a
beautiful passage in his *De Civ. Dei* (xix. 8), he says: "That he
who will have none of this sadness must, if possible, have no
friendly intercourse. . . . Let him burst with ruthless insensibility the bonds of every human relationship;" and he continues:
"Though the cure is effected all the more easily and rapidly the
better condition the soul is in, we must not on this account suppose
that there is nothing at all to heal." See p. 140, note 2, below.
[2] 1 Tim. i. 5.
[3] Ps. ci. 1. "I suppose they continued to the end of Psalm cii.
This was the primitive fashion; Nazianzen says that his speechless
sister Gorgonia's lips muttered the fourth Psalm : 'I will lie down
in peace and sleep.' As St. Austen lay a dying, the company
prayed (Possid.). That they had prayers between the departure
and burial, see Tertull. *De Anima,* c. 51. They used to sing both
at the departure and burial. Nazianzen, *Orat.* 10, says, the dead
Cæsarius was carried from hymns to hymns. The priests were

called to sing (Chrysost. *Hom.* 70, *ad Antioch*). They sang the
116th Psalm usually (see Chrysost. *Hom.* 4, *in c. 2, ad Hebræos*)."
—W. W. See also note 13, p.141.
[4] In addition to the remarks quoted in note 1, see Augustin's
recognition of the naturalness and necessity of exercising human
affections, such as sorrow, in his *De Civ. Dei,* xiv. 9.
[5] "Here my Popish translator says, that the sacrifice of the mass
was offered for the dead. That the ancients had communion with
their burials, I confess. But for what? (1) To testify their dying
in the communion of the Church. (2) To give thanks for their departure. (3) To pray God to give them place in His Paradise, (4)
and a part in the first resurrection; but not as a propitiatory sacrifice to deliver them out of purgatory, which the mass is now only
meant for."—W. W. See also note 13, p. 141.
[6] Ps. lxviii. 5.

into my mind those true verses of Thy Ambrose, for Thou art—

> " Deus creator omnium,
> Polique rector, vestiens
> Diem decora lumine,
> Noctem sopora gratia;
> Artus solutos ut quies
> Reddat laboris usui,
> Mentesque fessas allevet,
> Luctusque solvat anxios."[1]

33. And then little by little did I bring back my former thoughts of Thine handmaid, her devout conversation towards Thee, her holy tenderness and attentiveness towards us, which was suddenly taken away from me; and it was pleasant to me to weep in Thy sight, for her and for me, concerning her and concerning myself. And I set free the tears which before I repressed, that they might flow at their will, spreading them beneath my heart; and it rested in them, for Thy ears were nigh me,—not those of man, who would have put a scornful interpretation on my weeping. But now in writing I confess it unto Thee, O Lord! Read it who will, and interpret how he will; and if he finds me to have sinned in weeping for my mother during so small a part of an hour,—that mother who was for a while dead to mine eyes, who had for many years wept for me, that I might live in Thine eyes,—let him not laugh at me, but rather, if he be a man of a noble charity, let him weep for my sins against Thee, the Father of all the brethren of Thy Christ.

CHAP. XIII.—HE ENTREATS GOD FOR HER SINS, AND ADMONISHES HIS READERS TO REMEMBER HER PIOUSLY.

34. But,—my heart being now healed of that wound, in so far as it could be convicted of a carnal[2] affection,—I pour out unto Thee, O our God, on behalf of that Thine handmaid, tears of a far different sort, even that which flows from a spirit broken by the thoughts of the dangers of every soul that dieth in Adam. And although she, having been " made alive " in Christ[3] even before she was freed from the flesh,

had so lived as to praise Thy name both by her faith and conversation, yet dare I not say[4] that from the time Thou didst regenerate her by baptism, no word went forth from her mouth against Thy precepts.[5] And it hath been declared by Thy Son, the Truth, that " Whosoever shall say to his brother, Thou fool, shall be in danger of hell fire."[6] And woe even unto the praiseworthy life of man, if, putting away mercy, Thou shouldest investigate it. But because Thou dost not narrowly inquire after sins, we hope with confidence to find some place of indulgence with Thee. But whosoever recounts his true merits[7] to Thee, what is it that he recounts to Thee but Thine own gifts? Oh, if men would know themselves to be men; and that " he that glorieth " would " glory in the Lord ! "[8]

35. I then, O my Praise and my Life, Thou God of my heart, putting aside for a little her good deeds, for which I joyfully give thanks to Thee, do now beseech Thee for the sins of my mother. Hearken unto me, through that Medicine of our wounds who hung upon the tree, and who, sitting at Thy right hand, " maketh intercession for us."[9] I know that she acted mercifully, and from the heart[10] forgave her debtors their debts; do Thou also forgive her debts,[11] whatever she contracted during so many

<hr>

[1] Rendered as follows in a translation of the first ten books of the Confessions, described on the title-page as " Printed by J. C., for John Crook, and are to be sold at the sign of the 'Ship,' in St. Paul's Churchyard. 1660 ":—

> " O God, the world's great Architect,
> Who dost heaven's rowling orbs direct;
> Cloathing the day with beauteous light,
> And with sweet slumbers silent night;
> When wearied limbs new vigour gain
> From rest, new labours to sustain,
> When hearts oppressed do meet relief,
> And anxious minds forget their grief."

See x. sec. 52, below, where this hymn is referred to.

[2] Rom. viii. 7.

[3] 1 Cor. xv. 22. The universalists of every age have interpreted the word " all " here so as to make salvation by Christ Jesus extend to every child of Adam. If their interpretation were true, Monica's spirit need not have been troubled at the thought of the danger of unregenerate souls. But Augustin in his De Civ. Dei, xiii. 23, gives the import of the word: " Not that all who die in Adam shall be members of Christ,—for the great majority shall be punished in eternal death,—but he uses the word 'all' in both

clauses because, as no one dies in an animal body except in Adam, *so no one is quickened a spiritual body save in Christ."* See x. sec. 68, note 1, below.

[4] For to have done so would have been to go perilously near to the heresy of the Pelagians, who laid claim to the possibility of attaining perfection in this life by the power of free-will, and without the assistance of divine grace; and went even so far, he tells us (Ep. clxxvi. 2), as to say that those who had so attained need not utter the petition for forgiveness in the Lord's Prayer,—*ut ei non sit jam necessarium dicere " Dimitte nobis debita nostra."* Those in our own day who enunciate perfectionist theories,— though, it is true, not denying the grace of God as did these,—may well ponder Augustin's forcible words in his De Pecc. Mer. et Rem. iii. 13: " Optandum est ut fiat, conandum est ut fiat, supplicandum est ut fiat; non tamen quasi factum fuerit, confitendum." We are indeed commanded to be perfect (Matt. v. 48); and the philosophy underlying the command is embalmed in the words of the proverb, " Aim high, and you will strike high." But he who lives nearest to God will have the humility of heart which will make him ready to confess that in His sight he is a " miserable sinner." Some interesting remarks on this subject will be found in Augustin's De Civ. Dei, xiv. 9, on the text, " If we say we have no sin," etc. (1 John i. 8.) On sins after baptism, see note on next section.

[5] Matt. xii. 36.

[6] Matt. v. 22.

[7] There is a passage parallel to this in his Ep. to Sextus (cxciv. 19). " Merits " therefore would appear to be used simply in the sense of good actions. Compare sec. 17, above, xiii. sec. 1, below, and Ep. cv. That righteousness is not by merit, appears from Ep. cxciv.; Ep. clxxvii., to Innocent; and Serm. ccxciii.

[8] 2 Cor. x. 17.

[9] Rom. viii. 34.

[10] Matt. xviii. 35.

[11] Matt. vi. 12. Augustin here as elsewhere applies this petition in the Lord's Prayer to the forgiveness of *sins after baptism.* He does so constantly. For example, in his Ep. cclxv. he says: " We do not ask for those to be forgiven which we doubt not were forgiven in baptism; but those which, though small, are frequent, and spring from the frailty of human nature." Again, in his Con. Ep. Parmen. ii. 10, after using almost the same words, he points out that it is a prayer against *daily* sins; and in his De Civ. Dei, xxi. 27, where he examines the passage in relation to various erroneous beliefs, he says it " was a *daily* prayer He [Christ] was teaching, and it was certainly to disciples already justified He was speaking. What, then, does He mean by ' your sins' (Matt. vi. 14), but those sins from which not even you *who are justified and sanctified can be free?* " See note on the previous section; and also for the feeling in the early Church as to sins after baptism, the note on i. sec. 17, above.

years since the water of salvation. Forgive her, O Lord, forgive her, I beseech Thee; "enter not into judgment" with her.[1] Let Thy mercy be exalted above Thy justice,[2] because Thy words are true, and Thou hast promised mercy unto "the merciful;"[3] which Thou gavest them to be who wilt "have mercy" on whom Thou wilt "have mercy," and wilt "have compassion" on whom Thou hast had compassion.[4]

36. And I believe Thou hast already done that which I ask Thee; but "accept the free-will offerings of my mouth, O Lord."[5] For she, when the day of her dissolution was near at hand, took no thought to have her body sumptuously covered, or embalmed with spices; nor did she covet a choice monument, or desire her paternal burial-place. These things she entrusted not to us, but only desired to have her name remembered at Thy altar, which she had served without the omission of a single day;[6] whence she knew that the holy sacrifice was dispensed, by which the handwriting that was against us is blotted out;[7] by which the enemy was triumphed over,[8] who, summing up our offences, and searching for something to bring against us, found nothing in Him[9] in whom we conquer. Who will restore to Him the innocent blood? Who will repay Him the price with which He bought us, so as to take us from Him? Unto the sacrament of which our ransom did Thy handmaid bind her soul by the bond of faith. Let none separate her from Thy protection. Let not the "lion" and the "dragon"[10] introduce himself by force or fraud. For she will not reply that she owes nothing, lest she be convicted and got the better of by the wily deceiver; but she will answer that her

"sins are forgiven"[11] by Him to whom no one is able to repay that price which He, owing nothing, laid down for us.

37. May she therefore rest in peace with her husband, before or after whom she married none; whom she obeyed, with patience bringing forth fruit[12] unto Thee, that she might gain him also for Thee. And inspire, O my Lord my God, inspire Thy servants my brethren, Thy sons my masters, who with voice and heart and writings I serve, that so many of them as shall read these confessions may at Thy altar remember Monica, Thy handmaid, together with Patricius, her sometime husband, by whose flesh Thou introducedst me into this life, in what manner I know not. May they with pious affection be mindful of my parents in this transitory light, of my brethren that are under Thee our Father in our Catholic mother, and of my fellow-citizens in the eternal Jerusalem, which the wandering of Thy people sigheth for from their departure until their return. That so my mother's last entreaty to me may, through my confessions more than through my prayers, be more abundantly fulfilled to her through the prayers of many.[13]

---

[1] Ps. cxliii. 2.
[2] Jas. ii. 13.
[3] Matt. v. 7.
[4] Rom. ix. 15.
[5] Ps. cxix. 108.
[6] See v. sec. 17, above.
[7] Col. ii. 14.
[8] See his *De Trin.* xiii. 18, the passage beginning, "What then is the righteousness by which the devil was conquered?"
[9] John xiv. 30.
[10] Ps. xci. 13.

[11] Matt. ix. 2.
[12] Luke viii. 15.
[13] The origin of prayers for the dead dates back probably to the close of the second century. In note 1, p. 90, we have quoted from Tertullian's *De Corona Militis*, where he says, "*Oblationes pro defunctis pro natalitiis annua die facimus.*" In his *De Monogamia*, he speaks of a widow praying for her departed husband, that "he might have rest, and be a partaker in the first resurrection." From this time a *catena* of quotations from the Fathers might be given, if space permitted, showing how, beginning with early expressions of *hope* for the dead, there, in process of time, arose *prayers* even for the unregenerate, until at last there was developed purgatory on the one side, and creature-worship on the other. That Augustin did not entertain the idea of creature-worship will be seen from his *Ep.* to Maximus, xvii. 5. In his *De Dulcit. Quæst.* 2 (where he discusses the whole question), he concludes that prayer must not be made for all, because all have not led the same life in the flesh. Still, in his *Enarr. in Ps.* cviii. 17, he argues from the case of the rich man in the parable, that the departed do certainly "have a care for us." Aërius, towards the close of the fourth century, objected to prayers for the dead, chiefly on the ground (see Usher's *Answer to a Jesuit,* iii. 258) of their uselessness. In the Church of England, as will be seen by reference to Keeling's *Liturgicæ Britannicæ,* pp. 210, 335, 339, and 341, prayers for the dead were eliminated from the second Prayer Book; and to the prudence of this step Palmer bears testimony in his *Origines Liturgicæ,* iv. 10, justifying it on the ground that the retaining of these prayers implied a belief in her holding the doctrine of purgatory. Reference may be made to Epiphanius, *Adv. Hær.* 75; Bishop Bull, *Sermon* 3; and Bingham, xv. 3, secs. 15, 16, and xxiii. 3, sec. 13.

BOOK X.

HAVING MANIFESTED WHAT HE WAS AND WHAT HE IS, HE SHOWS THE GREAT FRUIT OF HIS CON-
FESSION; AND BEING ABOUT TO EXAMINE BY WHAT METHOD GOD AND THE HAPPY LIFE MAY
BE FOUND, HE ENLARGES ON THE NATURE AND POWER OF MEMORY. THEN HE EXAMINES HIS
OWN ACTS, THOUGHTS AND AFFECTIONS, VIEWED UNDER THE THREEFOLD DIVISION OF TEMP-
TATION; AND COMMEMORATES THE LORD, THE ONE MEDIATOR OF GOD AND MEN.

CHAP. I.—IN GOD ALONE IS THE HOPE AND JOY OF MAN.

1. LET me know Thee, O Thou who knowest me; let me know Thee, as I am known.[1] O Thou strength of my soul, enter into it, and prepare it for Thyself, that Thou mayest have and hold it without "spot or wrinkle."[2] This is my hope, "therefore have I spoken;"[3] and in this hope do I rejoice, when I rejoice soberly. Other things of this life ought the less to be sorrowed for, the more they are sorrowed for; and ought the more to be sorrowed for, the less men do sorrow for them. For behold, "Thou desirest truth,"[4] seeing that he who does it "cometh to the light."[5] This wish I to do in confession in my heart before Thee, and in my writing before many witnesses.

CHAP. II.—THAT ALL THINGS ARE MANIFEST TO GOD. THAT CONFESSION UNTO HIM IS NOT MADE BY THE WORDS OF THE FLESH, BUT OF THE SOUL, AND THE CRY OF REFLECTION.

2. And from Thee, O Lord, unto whose eyes the depths of man's conscience are naked,[6] what in me could be hidden though I were unwilling to confess to Thee? For so should I hide Thee from myself, not myself from Thee. But now, because my groaning witnesseth that I am dis-satisfied with myself, Thou shinest forth, and satisfiest, and art beloved and desired; that I may blush for myself, and renounce myself, and choose Thee, and may neither please Thee nor myself, except in Thee. To Thee, then, O Lord, am I manifest, whatever I am, and with what fruit I may confess unto Thee I have spoken. Nor do I it with words and sounds of the flesh, but with the words of the soul, and that cry of reflection which Thine ear knoweth.

For when I am wicked, to confess to Thee is naught but to be dissatisfied with myself; but when I am truly devout, it is naught but not to attribute it to myself, because Thou, O Lord, dost "bless the righteous;"[7] but first Thou justifiest him "ungodly."[8] My confession, therefore, O my God, in Thy sight, is made unto Thee silently, and yet not silently. For in noise it is silent, in affection it cries aloud. For neither do I give utterance to anything that is right unto men which Thou hast not heard from me before, nor dost Thou hear any-thing of the kind from me which Thyself saidst not first unto me.

CHAP. III.—HE WHO CONFESSETH RIGHTLY UNTO GOD BEST KNOWETH HIMSELF.

3. What then have I to do with men, that they should hear my confessions, as if they were going to cure all my diseases?[9] A people curious to know the lives of others, but slow to correct their own. Why do they desire to hear from me what I am, who are unwilling to hear from Thee what they are? And how can they tell, when they hear from me of myself, whether I speak the truth, seeing that no man knoweth what is in man, "save the spirit of man which is in him"?[10] But if they hear from Thee aught concerning themselves, they will not be able to say, "The Lord lieth." For what is it to hear from Thee of themselves, but to know them-selves? And who is he that knoweth himself and saith, "It is false," unless he himself lieth? But because "charity believeth all things"[11] (amongst those at all events whom by union with itself it maketh one), I too, O Lord, also so confess unto Thee that men may hear, to whom I cannot prove whether I confess the truth, yet do they believe me whose ears charity openeth unto me.

---

[1] 1 Cor. xiii. 12.
[2] Eph. v. 27.
[3] Ps. cxvi. 10.
[4] Ps. li. 6.
[5] John iii. 20.
[6] Heb. iv. 13.

[7] Ps. v. 12.
[8] Rom. iv. 5.
[9] Ps. ciii. 3.
[10] 1 Cor. ii. 11.
[11] 1 Cor. xiii. 7.

4. But yet do Thou, my most secret Physician, make clear to me what fruit I may reap by doing it. For the confessions of my past sins,—which Thou hast "forgiven" and "covered,"[1] that Thou mightest make me happy in Thee, changing my soul by faith and Thy sacrament,—when they are read and heard, stir up the heart, that it sleep not in despair and say, "I cannot;" but that it may awake in the love of Thy mercy and the sweetness of Thy grace, by which he that is weak is strong,[2] if by it he is made conscious of his own weakness. As for the good, they take delight in hearing of the past errors of such as are now freed from them; and they delight, not because they are errors, but because they have been and are so no longer. For what fruit, then, O Lord my God, to whom my conscience maketh her daily confession, more confident in the hope of Thy mercy than in her own innocency,—for what fruit, I beseech Thee, do I confess even to men in Thy presence by this book what I am at this time, not what I have been? For that fruit I have both seen and spoken of, but what I am at this time, at the very moment of making my confessions, divers people desire to know, both who knew me and who knew me not,—who have heard of or from me,—but their ear is not at my heart, where I am whatsoever I am. They are desirous, then, of hearing me confess what I am within, where they can neither stretch eye, nor ear, nor mind; they desire it as those willing to believe,—but will they understand? For charity, by which they are good, says unto them that I do not lie in my confessions, and she in them believes me.

CHAP. IV.—THAT IN HIS CONFESSIONS HE MAY DO GOOD, HE CONSIDERS OTHERS.

5. But for what fruit do they desire this? Do they wish me happiness when they learn how near, by Thy gift, I come unto Thee; and to pray for me, when they learn how much I am kept back by my own weight? To such will I declare myself. For it is no small fruit, O Lord my God, that by many thanks should be given to Thee on our behalf,[3] and that by many Thou shouldest be entreated for us. Let the fraternal soul love that in me which Thou teachest should be loved, and lament that in me which Thou teachest should be lamented. Let a fraternal and not an alien soul do this, nor that "of strange children, whose mouth speaketh vanity, and their right hand is a right hand of falsehood,"[4] but that fraternal one which, when it approves me, rejoices for me, but when it disap-

proves me, is sorry for me; because whether it approves or disapproves it loves me. To such will I declare myself; let them breathe freely at my good deeds, and sigh over my evil ones. My good deeds are Thy institutions and Thy gifts, my evil ones are my delinquencies and Thy judgments.[5] Let them breathe freely at the one, and sigh over the other; and let hymns and tears ascend into Thy sight out of the fraternal hearts—Thy censers.[6] And do Thou, O Lord, who takest delight in the incense of Thy holy temple, have mercy upon me according to Thy great mercy,[7] "for Thy name's sake;"[8] and on no account leaving what Thou hast begun in me, do Thou complete what is imperfect in me.

6. This is the fruit of my confessions, not of what I was, but of what I am, that I may confess this not before Thee only, in a secret exultation with trembling,[9] and a secret sorrow with hope, but in the ears also of the believing sons of men,—partakers of my joy, and sharers of my mortality, my fellow-citizens and the companions of my pilgrimage, those who are gone before, and those that are to follow after, and the comrades of my way. These are Thy servants, my brethren, those whom Thou wishest to be Thy sons; my masters, whom Thou hast commanded me to serve, if I desire to live with and of Thee. But this Thy word were little to me did it command in speaking, without going before in acting. This then do I both in deed and word, this I do under Thy wings, in too great danger, were it not that my soul, under Thy wings, is subject unto Thee, and my weakness known unto Thee. I am a little one, but my Father liveth for ever, and my Defender is "sufficient"[10] for me. For He is the same who begat me and who defends me; and Thou Thyself art all my good; even Thou, the Omnipotent, who art with me, and that before I am with Thee. To such, therefore, whom Thou commandest me to serve will I declare, not what I was, but what I now am, and what I still am. But neither do I judge myself.[11] Thus then I would be heard.

CHAP. V.—THAT MAN KNOWETH NOT HIMSELF WHOLLY.

7. For it is Thou, Lord, that judgest me;[12] for although no "man knoweth the things of a

---

[1] Ps. xxxii. 1.
[2] 2 Cor. xii. 10.
[3] 2 Cor. i. 11.
[4] Ps. cxliv. 11.

[5] In note 9, p. 79, we have seen how God makes man's sin its own punishment. Reference may also be made to Augustin's *Con. Advers. Leg. et Proph.* i. 14, where he argues that "the punishment of a man's disobedience is found in himself, when he in his turn cannot get obedience even from himself." And again, in his *De Lib. Arb.* v. 18, he says, God punishes by taking from him that which he does not use well, "et qui recte facere cum possit noluit amittat posse cum velit." See also *Serm.* clxxi. 4, and *Ep.* cliii.
[6] Rev. viii. 3.
[7] Ps. li. 1.
[8] Ps. xxv. 11.
[9] Ps. ii. 11.
[10] 2 Cor. xii. 9.
[11] 1 Cor. iv. 3.
[12] 1 Cor. iv. 4.

man, save the spirit of man which is in him,"[1] yet is there something of man which "the spirit of man which is in him" itself knoweth not. But Thou, Lord, who hast made him, knowest him wholly. I indeed, though in Thy sight I despise myself, and reckon "myself but dust and ashes,"[2] yet know something concerning Thee, which I know not concerning myself. And assuredly "now we see through a glass darkly," not yet "face to face."[3] So long, therefore, as I be "absent" from Thee, I am more "present" with myself than with Thee;[4] and yet know I that Thou canst not suffer violence;[5] but for myself I know not what temptations I am able to resist, and what I am not able.[6] But there is hope, because Thou art faithful, who wilt not suffer us to be tempted above that we are able, but wilt with the temptation also make a way to escape, that we may be able to bear it.[7] I would therefore confess what I know concerning myself; I will confess also what I know not concerning myself. And because what I do know of myself, I know by Thee enlightening me; and what I know not of myself, so long I know not until the time when my "darkness be as the noonday"[8] in Thy sight.

CHAP. VI.—THE LOVE OF GOD, IN HIS NATURE SUPERIOR TO ALL CREATURES, IS ACQUIRED BY THE KNOWLEDGE OF THE SENSES AND THE EXERCISE OF REASON.

8. Not with uncertain, but with assured consciousness do I love Thee, O Lord. Thou hast stricken my heart with Thy word, and I loved Thee. And also the heaven, and earth, and all that is therein, behold, on every side they say that I should love Thee; nor do they cease to speak unto all, "so that they are without excuse."[9] But more profoundly wilt Thou have mercy on whom Thou wilt have mercy, and compassion on whom Thou wilt have compassion,[10] otherwise do both heaven and earth tell forth Thy praises to deaf ears. But what is it that I love in loving Thee? Not corporeal beauty, nor the splendour of time, nor the radiance of the light, so pleasant to our eyes, nor the sweet melodies of songs of all kinds, nor the fragrant smell of flowers, and ointments, and spices, not manna and honey, not limbs

pleasant to the embracements of flesh. I love not these things when I love my God; and yet I love a certain kind of light, and sound, and fragrance, and food, and embracement in loving my God, who is the light, sound, fragrance, food, and embracement of my inner man—where that light shineth unto my soul which no place can contain, where that soundeth which time snatcheth not away, where there is a fragrance which no breeze disperseth, where there is a food which no eating can diminish, and where that clingeth which no satiety can sunder. This is what I love, when I love my God.

9. And what is this? I asked the earth; and it answered, "I am not He;" and whatsoever are therein made the same confession. I asked the sea and the deeps, and the creeping things that lived, and they replied, "We are not thy God, seek higher than we." I asked the breezy air, and the universal air with its inhabitants answered, "Anaximenes[11] was deceived, I am not God." I asked the heavens, the sun, moon, and stars: "Neither," say they, "are we the God whom thou seekest." And I answered unto all these things which stand about the door of my flesh, "Ye have told me concerning my God, that ye are not He; tell me something about Him." And with a loud voice they exclaimed, "He made us." My questioning was my observing of them; and their beauty was their reply.[12] And I directed my thoughts to myself, and said, "Who art thou?" And I answered, "A man." And lo, in me there appear both body and soul, the one without, the other within. By which of these should I seek my God, whom I had sought through the body from earth to heaven, as far as I was able to send messengers—the beams of mine eyes? But the better part is that which is inner; for to it, as both president and judge, did all these my corporeal messengers render the answers of heaven and earth and all things therein, who said, "We are not God, but He made us." These things was my inner man cognizant of by the ministry of the outer; I, the inner man, knew all this—I, the soul, through the senses of my body. I asked the vast bulk of the earth of my God, and it answered me, "I am not He, but He made me."

10. Is not this beauty visible to all whose senses are unimpaired? Why then doth it not speak the same things unto all? Animals, the

---

[1] 1 Cor. ii. 11.
[2] Gen. xviii. 27.
[3] 1 Cor. xiii. 12.
[4] 2 Cor. v. 6.
[5] See Nebridius' argument against the Manichæans, as to God's not being violable, in vii. sec. 3, above, and the note thereon.
[6] See his *Enarr. in Ps.* lv. 8 and xciii. 19, where he beautifully describes how the winds and waves of temptation will be stilled if Christ be present in the ship. See also *Serm.* lxiii.; and *Eps.* cxxx. 22, and clxxvii. 4.
[7] 1 Cor. x. 13.
[8] Isa. lviii. 10.
[9] Rom. i. 20.
[10] Rom. ix. 15.

[11] Anaximenes of Miletus was born about 520 B. C. According to his philosophy the air was animate, and from it, as from a first principle, all things in heaven, earth, and sea sprung, first by condensation (πύκνωσις), and after that by a process of rarefaction (ἀραίωσις). See *Ep.* cxviii. 23; and Aristotle, *Phys.* iii. 4. Compare this theory and that of Epicurus (p. 100, above) with those of modern physicists; and see thereon *The Unseen Universe,* arts. 85, etc., and 117, etc.
[12] *In Ps.* cxliv. 13, the earth he describes as "dumb," but as speaking to us while we meditate upon its beauty—*Ipsa inquisitio interrogatio est.*

very small and the great, see it, but they are unable to question it, because their senses are not endowed with reason to enable them to judge on what they report. But men can question it, so that "the invisible things of Him . . . are clearly seen, being understood by the things that are made;"[1] but by loving them, they are brought into subjection to them; and subjects are not able to judge. Neither do the creatures reply to such as question them, unless they can judge; nor will they alter their voice (that is, their beauty),[2] if so be one man only sees, another both sees and questions, so as to appear one way to this man, and another to that; but appearing the same way to both, it is mute to this, it speaks to that—yea, verily, it speaks unto all; but they only understand it who compare that voice received from without with the truth within. For the truth declareth unto me, "Neither heaven, nor earth, nor any body is thy God." This, their nature declareth unto him that beholdeth them. "They are a mass; a mass is less in part than in the whole." Now, O my soul, thou art my better part, unto thee I speak; for thou animatest the mass of thy body, giving it life, which no body furnishes to a body; but thy God is even unto thee the Life of life.

CHAP. VII.—THAT GOD IS TO BE FOUND NEITHER FROM THE POWERS OF THE BODY NOR OF THE SOUL.

11. What then is it that I love when I love my God? Who is He that is above the head of my soul? By my soul itself will I mount up unto Him. I will soar beyond that power of mine whereby I cling to the body, and fill the whole structure of it with life. Not by that power do I find my God; for then the horse and the mule, "which have no understanding,"[3] might find Him, since it is the same power by which their bodies also live. But there is another power, not that only by which I quicken, but that also by which I endow with sense my flesh, which the Lord hath made for me; bidding the eye not to hear, and the ear not to see; but that, for me to see by, and this, for me to hear by; and to each of the other senses its own proper seat and office, which being different, I, the single mind, do through them govern. I will soar also beyond this power of mine; for this the horse and mule possess, for they too discern through the body.

CHAP. VIII.—OF THE NATURE AND THE AMAZING POWER OF MEMORY.

12. I will soar, then, beyond this power of my nature also, ascending by degrees unto Him who made me. And I enter the fields and roomy chambers of memory, where are the treasures of countless images, imported into it from all manner of things by the senses. There is treasured up whatsoever likewise we think, either by enlarging or diminishing, or by varying in any way whatever those things which the sense hath arrived at; yea, and whatever else hath been entrusted to it and stored up, which oblivion hath not yet engulfed and buried. When I am in this storehouse, I demand that what I wish should be brought forth, and some things immediately appear; others require to be longer sought after, and are dragged, as it were, out of some hidden receptacle; others, again, hurry forth in crowds, and while another thing is sought and inquired for, they leap into view, as if to say, " Is it not we, perchance?" These I drive away with the hand of my heart from before the face of my remembrance, until what I wish be discovered making its appearance out of its secret cell. Other things suggest themselves without effort, and in continuous order, just as they are called for,—those in front giving place to those that follow, and in giving place are treasured up again to be forthcoming when I wish it. All of which takes place when I repeat a thing from memory.

13. All these things, each of which entered by its own avenue, are distinctly and under general heads there laid up: as, for example, light, and all colours and forms of bodies, by the eyes; sounds of all kinds by the ears; all smells by the passage of the nostrils; all flavours by that of the mouth; and by the sensation of the whole body is brought in what is hard or soft, hot or cold, smooth or rough, heavy or light, whether external or internal to the body. All these doth that great receptacle of memory, with its many and indescribable departments, receive, to be recalled and brought forth when required; each, entering by its own door, is laid up in it. And yet the things themselves do not enter it, but only the images of the things perceived are ready at hand for thought to recall. And who can tell how these images are formed, notwithstanding that it is evident by which of the senses each has been fetched in and treasured up? For even while I live in darkness and silence, I can bring out colours in memory if I wish, and discern between black and white, and what others I wish; nor yet do sounds break in and disturb what is drawn in by mine eyes, and which I am considering, seeing that they also are there, and are concealed,— laid up, as it were, apart. For these too I can summon if I please, and immediately they appear. And though my tongue be at rest, and my throat silent, yet can I sing as much as I will; and those images of colours, which not-

[1] Rom. i. 20.
[2] See note 2 to previous section.
[3] Ps. xxxii. 9.

withstanding are there, do not interpose themselves and interrupt when another treasure is under consideration which flowed in through the ears. So the remaining things carried in and heaped up by the other senses, I recall at my pleasure. And I discern the scent of lilies from that of violets while smelling nothing; and I prefer honey to grape-syrup, a smooth thing to a rough, though then I neither taste nor handle, but only remember.

14. These things do I within, in that vast chamber of my memory. For there are nigh me heaven, earth, sea, and whatever I can think upon in them, besides those which I have forgotten. There also do I meet with myself, and recall myself,—what, when, or where I did a thing, and how I was affected when I did it. There are all which I remember, either by personal experience or on the faith of others. Out of the same supply do I myself with the past construct now this, now that likeness of things, which either I have experienced, or, from having experienced, have believed; and thence again future actions, events, and hopes, and upon all these again do I meditate as if they were present. "I will do this or that," say I to myself in that vast womb of my mind, filled with the images of things so many and so great, "and this or that shall follow upon it." "Oh that this or that might come to pass!" "God avert this or that!" Thus speak I to myself; and when I speak, the images of all I speak about are present, out of the same treasury of memory; nor could I say anything at all about them were the images absent.

15. Great is this power of memory, exceeding great, O my God,—an inner chamber large and boundless! Who has plumbed the depths thereof? Yet it is a power of mine, and appertains unto my nature; nor do I myself grasp all that I am. Therefore is the mind too narrow to contain itself. And where should that be which it doth not contain of itself? Is it outside and not in itself? How is it, then, that it doth not grasp itself? A great admiration rises upon me; astonishment seizes me. And men go forth to wonder at the heights of mountains, the huge waves of the sea, the broad flow of the rivers, the extent of the ocean, and the courses of the stars, and omit to wonder at themselves; nor do they marvel that when I spoke of all these things, I was not looking on them with my eyes, and yet could not speak of them unless those mountains, and waves, and rivers, and stars which I saw, and that ocean which I believe in, I saw inwardly in my memory, and with the same vast spaces between as when I saw them abroad. But I did not by seeing appropriate them when I looked on them with my eyes; nor are the things themselves with me, but their images. And I knew by what corporeal sense each made impression on me.

CHAP. IX.—NOT ONLY THINGS, BUT ALSO LITERATURE AND IMAGES, ARE TAKEN FROM THE MEMORY, AND ARE BROUGHT FORTH BY THE ACT OF REMEMBERING.

16. And yet are not these all that the illimitable capacity of my memory retains. Here also is all that is apprehended of the liberal sciences, and not yet forgotten—removed as it were into an inner place, which is not a place; nor are they the images which are retained, but the things themselves. For what is literature, what skill in disputation, whatsoever I know of all the many kinds of questions there are, is so in my memory, as that I have not taken in the image and left the thing without, or that it should have sounded and passed away like a voice imprinted on the ear by that trace, whereby it might be recorded, as though it sounded when it no longer did so; or as an odour while it passes away, and vanishes into wind, affects the sense of smell, whence it conveys the image of itself into the memory, which we realize in recollecting; or like food, which assuredly in the belly hath now no taste, and yet hath a kind of taste in the memory, or like anything that is by touching felt by the body, and which even when removed from us is imagined by the memory. For these things themselves are not put into it, but the images of them only are caught up, with a marvellous quickness, and laid up, as it were, in most wonderful garners, and wonderfully brought forth when we remember.

CHAP. X.—LITERATURE IS NOT INTRODUCED TO THE MEMORY THROUGH THE SENSES, BUT IS BROUGHT FORTH FROM ITS MORE SECRET PLACES.

17. But truly when I hear that there are three kinds of questions, "Whether a thing is?—what it is?—of what kind it is?" I do indeed hold fast the images of the sounds of which these words are composed, and I know that those sounds passed through the air with a noise, and now are not. But the things themselves which are signified by these sounds I never arrived at by any sense of the body, nor ever perceived them otherwise than by my mind; and in my memory have I laid up not their images, but themselves, which, how they entered into me, let them tell if they are able. For I examine all the gates of my flesh, but find not by which of them they entered. For the eyes say, "If they were coloured, we announced them." The ears say, "If they sounded, we gave notice of them." The nos-

trils say, " If they smell, they passed in by us."
The sense of taste says, " If they have no
flavour, ask not me." The touch says, " If it
have not body, I handled it not, and if I never
handled it, I gave no notice of it." Whence
and how did these things enter into my memory? I know not how. For when I learned
them, I gave not credit to the heart of another
man, but perceived them in my own; and I
approved them as true, and committed them to
it, laying them up, as it were, whence I might
fetch them when I willed. There, then, they
were, even before I learned them, but were
not in my memory. Where were they, then,
or wherefore, when they were spoken, did I
acknowledge them, and say, " So it is, it is
true," unless as being already in the memory,
though so put back and concealed, as it were,
in more secret caverns, that had they not been
drawn forth by the advice of another I would
not, perchance, have been able to conceive of
them?

CHAP. XI.—WHAT IT IS TO LEARN AND TO THINK.

18. Wherefore we find that to learn these
things, whose images we drink not in by our
senses, but perceive within as they are by themselves, without images, is nothing else but by
meditation as it were to concentrate, and by
observing to take care that those notions which
the memory did before contain scattered and
confused, be laid up at hand, as it were, in that
same memory, where before they lay concealed,
scattered and neglected, and so the more easily
present themselves to the mind well accustomed
to observe them. And how many things of this
sort does my memory retain which have been
found out already, and, as I said, are, as it
were, laid up ready to hand, which we are said
to have learned and to have known; which,
should we for small intervals of time cease to
recall, they are again so submerged and slide
back, as it were, into the more remote chambers, that they must be evolved thence again as
if new (for other sphere they have none), and
must be marshalled [*cogenda*] again that they
may become known; that is to say, they must
be collected [*colligenda*], as it were, from their
dispersion; whence we have the word *cogitare*.
For *cogo* [*I collect*] and *cogito* [*I re-collect*] have
the same relation to each other as *ago* and *agito*,
facio and *factito*. But the mind has appropriated to itself this word [cogitation], so that not
that which is collected anywhere, but what is
collected,[1] that is marshalled,[2] in the mind, is
properly said to be "cogitated."[3]

1 Colligitur.
2 Cogitur.
3 Cogitari.

CHAP. XII.—ON THE RECOLLECTION OF THINGS MATHEMATICAL.

19. The memory containeth also the reasons
and innumerable laws of numbers and dimensions, none of which hath any sense of the
body impressed, seeing they have neither colour,
nor sound, nor taste, nor smell, nor sense of
touch. I have heard the sound of the words
by which these things are signified when they
are discussed; but the sounds are one thing,
the things another. For the sounds are one
thing in Greek, another in Latin; but the
things themselves are neither Greek, nor Latin,
nor any other language. I have seen the lines
of the craftsmen, even the finest, like a spider's
web; but these are of another kind, they are
not the images of those which the eye of my
flesh showed me; he knoweth them who, without any idea whatsoever of a body, perceives
them within himself. I have also observed the
numbers of the things with which we number
all the senses of the body; but those by which
we number are of another kind, nor are they
the images of these, and therefore they certainly are. Let him who sees not these things
mock me for saying them; and I will pity him,
whilst he mocks me.

CHAP. XIII.—MEMORY RETAINS ALL THINGS.

20. All these things I retain in my memory,
and how I learnt them I retain. I retain also
many things which I have heard most falsely
objected against them, which though they be
false, yet is it not false that I have remembered
them; and I remember, too, that I have
distinguished between those truths and these
falsehoods uttered against them; and I now see
that it is one thing to distinguish these things,
another to remember that I often distinguished
them, when I often reflected upon them. I
both remember, then, that I have often understood these things, and what I now distinguish
and comprehend I store away in my memory,
that hereafter I may remember that I understood
it now. Therefore also I remember that I have
remembered; so that if afterwards I shall call
to mind that I have been able to remember these
things, it will be through the power of memory
that I shall call it to mind.

CHAP. XIV.—CONCERNING THE MANNER IN WHICH JOY AND SADNESS MAY BE BROUGHT BACK TO THE MIND AND MEMORY.

21. This same memory contains also the affections of my mind; not in the manner in which
the mind itself contains them when it suffers
them, but very differently according to a power
peculiar to memory. For without being joyous,
I remember myself to have had joy; and with-

out being sad, I call to mind my past sadness; and that of which I was once afraid, I remember without fear; and without desire recall a former desire. Again, on the contrary, I at times remember when joyous my past sadness, and when sad my joy. Which is not to be wondered at as regards the body; for the mind is one thing, the body another. If I, therefore, when happy, recall some past bodily pain, it is not so strange a thing. But now, as this very memory itself is mind (for when we give orders to have a thing kept in memory, we say, "See that you bear this in mind;" and when we forget a thing, we say, "It did not enter my mind," and, "It slipped from my mind," thus calling the memory itself mind), as this is so, how comes it to pass that when being joyful I remember my past sorrow, the mind has joy, the memory sorrow, —the mind, from the joy than is in it, is joyful, yet the memory, from the sadness that is in it, is not sad? Does not the memory perchance belong unto the mind? Who will say so? The memory doubtless is, so to say, the belly of the mind, and joy and sadness like sweet and bitter food, which, when entrusted to the memory, are, as it were, passed into the belly, where they can be reposited, but cannot taste. It is ridiculous to imagine these to be alike; and yet they are not utterly unlike.

22. But behold, out of my memory I educe it, when I affirm that there be four perturbations of the mind,—desire, joy, fear, sorrow; and whatsoever I shall be able to dispute on these, by dividing each into its peculiar species, and by defining it, there I find what I may say, and thence I educe it; yet am I not disturbed by any of these perturbations when by remembering them I call them to mind; and before I recollected and reviewed them, they were there; wherefore by remembrance could they be brought thence. Perchance, then, even as meat is in ruminating brought up out of the belly, so by calling to mind are these educed from the memory. Why, then, does not the disputant, thus recollecting, perceive in the mouth of his meditation the sweetness of joy or the bitterness of sorrow? Is the comparison unlike in this because not like in all points? For who would willingly discourse on these subjects, if, as often as we name sorrow or fear, we should be compelled to be sorrowful or fearful? And yet we could never speak of them, did we not find in our memory not merely the sounds of the names according to the images imprinted on it by the senses of the body, but the notions of the things themselves, which we never received by any door of the flesh, but which the mind itself, recognising by the experience of its own passions, entrusted to the memory, or else which the memory itself retained without their being entrusted to it.

CHAP. XV.—IN MEMORY THERE ARE ALSO IMAGES OF THINGS WHICH ARE ABSENT.

23. But whether by images or no, who can well affirm? For I name a stone, I name the sun, and the things themselves are not present to my senses, but their images are near to my memory. I name some pain of the body, yet it is not present when there is no pain; yet if its image were not in my memory, I should be ignorant what to say concerning it, nor in arguing be able to distinguish it from pleasure. I name bodily health when sound in body; the thing itself is indeed present with me, but unless its image also were in my memory, I could by no means call to mind what the sound of this name signified. Nor would sick people know, when health was named, what was said, unless the same image were retained by the power of memory, although the thing itself were absent from the body. I name numbers whereby we enumerate; and not their images, but they themselves are in my memory. I name the image of the sun, and this, too, is in my memory. For I do not recall the image of that image, but itself, for the image itself is present when I remember it. I name memory, and I know what I name. But where do I know it, except in the memory itself? Is it also present to itself by its image, and not by itself?

CHAP. XVI.—THE PRIVATION OF MEMORY IS FORGETFULNESS.

24. When I name forgetfulness, and know, too, what I name, whence should I know it if I did not remember it? I do not say the sound of the name, but the thing which it signifies; which, had I forgotten, I could not know what that sound signified. When, therefore, I remember memory, then is memory present with itself, through itself. But when I remember forgetfulness, there are present both memory and forgetfulness,—memory, whereby I remember, forgetfulness, which I remember. But what is forgetfulness but the privation of memory? How, then, is that present for me to remember, since, when it is so, I cannot remember? But if what we remember we retain in memory, yet, unless we remembered forgetfulness, we could never at the hearing of the name know the thing meant by it, then is forgetfulness retained by memory. Present, therefore, it is, lest we should forget it; and being so, we do forget. Is it to be inferred from this that forgetfulness, when we remember it, is not present to the memory through itself, but through its image; because, were forgetfulness present through itself, it would not lead us to remember, but to forget? Who will now investigate this? Who shall understand how it is?

25. Truly, O Lord, I labour therein, and labour in myself. I am become a troublesome soil that requires overmuch labour. For we are not now searching out the tracts of heaven, or measuring the distances of the stars, or inquiring about the weight of the earth. It is I myself—I, the mind—who remember. It is not much to be wondered at, if what I myself am not be far from me. But what is nearer to me than myself? And, behold, I am not able to comprehend the force of my own memory, though I cannot name myself without it. For what shall I say when it is plain to me that I remember forgetfulness? Shall I affirm that that which I remember is not in my memory? Or shall I say that forgetfulness is in my memory with the view of my not forgetting? Both of these are most absurd. What third view is there? How can I assert that the image of forgetfulness is retained by my memory, and not forgetfulness itself, when I remember it? And how can I assert this, seeing that when the image of anything is imprinted on the memory, the thing itself must of necessity be present first by which that image may be imprinted? For thus do I remember Carthage; thus, all the places to which I have been; thus, the faces of men whom I have seen, and things reported by the other senses; thus, the health or sickness of the body. For when these objects were present, my memory received images from them, which, when they were present, I might gaze on and reconsider in my mind, as I remembered them when they were absent. If, therefore, forgetfulness is retained in the memory through its image, and not through itself, then itself was once present, that its image might be taken. But when it was present, how did it write its image on the memory, seeing that forgetfulness by its presence blots out even what it finds already noted? And yet, in whatever way, though it be incomprehensible and inexplicable, yet most certain I am that I remember also forgetfulness itself, whereby what we do remember is blotted out.

CHAP. XVII.—GOD CANNOT BE ATTAINED UNTO BY THE POWER OF MEMORY, WHICH BEASTS AND BIRDS POSSESS.

26. Great is the power of memory; very wonderful is it, O my God, a profound and infinite manifoldness; and this thing is the mind, and this I myself am. What then am I, O my God? Of what nature am I? A life various and manifold, and exceeding vast. Behold, in the numberless fields, and caves, and caverns of my memory, full without number of numberless kinds of things, either through images, as all bodies are; or by the presence of the things themselves, as are the arts; or by some notion

or observation, as the affections of the mind are, which, even though the mind doth not suffer, the memory retains, while whatsoever is in the memory is also in the mind: through all these do I run to and fro, and fly; I penetrate on this side and that, as far as I am able, and nowhere is there an end. So great is the power of memory, so great the power of life in man, whose life is mortal. What then shall I do, O Thou my true life, my God? I will pass even beyond this power of mine which is called memory—I will pass beyond it, that I may proceed to Thee, O Thou sweet Light. What sayest Thou to me? Behold, I am soaring by my mind towards Thee who remainest above me. I will also pass beyond this power of mine which is called memory, wishful to reach Thee whence Thou canst be reached, and to cleave unto Thee whence it is possible to cleave unto Thee. For even beasts and birds possess memory, else could they never find their lairs and nests again, nor many other things to which they are used; neither indeed could they become used to anything, but by their memory. I will pass, then, beyond memory also, that I may reach Him who has separated me from the four-footed beasts and the fowls of the air, making me wiser than they. I will pass beyond memory also, but where shall I find Thee, O Thou truly good and assured sweetness? But where shall I find Thee? If I find Thee without memory, then am I unmindful of Thee. And how now shall I find Thee, if I do not remember Thee?

CHAP. XVIII.—A THING WHEN LOST COULD NOT BE FOUND UNLESS IT WERE RETAINED IN THE MEMORY.

27. For the woman who lost her drachma, and searched for it with a lamp,[1] unless she had remembered it, would never have found it. For when it was found, whence could she know whether it were the same, had she not remembered it? I remember to have lost and found many things; and this I know thereby, that when I was searching for any of them, and was asked, "Is this it?" "Is that it?" I answered "No," until such time as that which I sought were offered to me. Which had I not remembered, —whatever it were,—though it were offered me, yet would I not find it, because I could not recognise it. And thus it is always, when we search for and find anything that is lost. Notwithstanding, if anything be by accident lost from the sight, not from the memory,—as any visible body,—the image of it is retained within, and is searched for until it be restored to sight; and when it is found, it is recognised by

1 Luke xv. 8.

the image which is within. Nor do we say that we have found what we had lost unless we recognise it; nor can we recognise it unless we remember it. But this, though lost to the sight, was retained in the memory.

CHAP. XIX.—WHAT IT IS TO REMEMBER.

28. But how is it when the memory itself loses anything, as it happens when we forget anything and try to recall it? Where finally do we search, but in the memory itself? And there, if perchance one thing be offered for another, we refuse it, until we meet with what we seek; and when we do, we exclaim, "This is it!" which we should not do unless we knew it again, nor should we recognise it unless we remembered it. Assuredly, therefore, we had forgotten it. Or, had not the whole of it slipped our memory, but by the part by which we had hold was the other part sought for; since the memory perceived that it did not revolve together as much as it was accustomed to do, and halting, as if from the mutilation of its old habit, demanded the restoration of that which was wanting. For example, if we see or think of some man known to us, and, having forgotten his name, endeavour to recover it, whatsoever other thing presents itself is not connected with it; because it was not used to be thought of in connection with him, and is consequently rejected, until that is present whereon the knowledge reposes fittingly as its accustomed object. And whence, save from the memory itself, does that present itself? For even when we recognise it as put in mind of it by another, it is thence it comes. For we do not believe it as something new, but, as we recall it, admit what was said to be correct. But if it were entirely blotted out of the mind, we should not, even when put in mind of it, recollect it. For we have not as yet entirely forgotten what we remember that we have forgotten. A lost notion, then, which we have entirely forgotten, we cannot even search for.

CHAP. XX.—WE SHOULD NOT SEEK FOR GOD AND THE HAPPY LIFE UNLESS WE HAD KNOWN IT.

29. How, then, do I seek Thee, O Lord? For when I seek Thee, my God, I seek a happy life.[1] I will seek Thee, that my soul may live.[2] For my body liveth by my soul, and my soul liveth by Thee. How, then, do I seek a happy life, seeing that it is not mine till I can say, "It is enough!" in that place where I ought to say it? How do I seek it? Is it by remembrance, as though I had forgotten it, knowing too that I had forgotten it? or, longing to learn it as a

thing unknown, which either I had never known, or had so forgotten it as not even to remember that I had forgotten it? Is not a happy life the thing that all desire, and is there any one who altogether desires it not? But where did they acquire the knowledge of it, that they so desire it? Where have they seen it, that they so love it? Truly we have it, but how I know not. Yea, there is another way in which, when any one hath it, he is happy; and some there be that are happy in hope. These have it in an inferior kind to those that are happy in fact; and yet are they better off than they who are happy neither in fact nor in hope. And even these, had they it not in some way, would not so much desire to be happy, which that they do desire is most certain. How they come to know it, I cannot tell, but they have it by some kind of knowledge unknown to me, who am in much doubt as to whether it be in the memory; for if it be there, then have we been happy once; whether all individually, or as in that man who first sinned, in whom also we all died,[3] and from whom we are all born with misery, I do not now ask; but I ask whether the happy life be in the memory? For did we not know it, we should not love it. We hear the name, and we all acknowledge that we desire the thing; for we are not delighted with the sound only. For when a Greek hears it spoken in Latin, he does not feel delighted, for he knows not what is spoken; but we are delighted,[4] as he too would be if he heard it in Greek; because the thing itself is neither Greek nor Latin, which Greeks and Latins, and men of all other tongues, long so earnestly to obtain. It is then known unto all, and could they with one voice be asked whether they wished to be happy, without doubt they would all answer that they would. And this could not be unless the thing itself, of which it is the name, were retained in their memory.

CHAP. XXI.—HOW A HAPPY LIFE MAY BE RETAINED IN THE MEMORY.

30. But is it so as one who has seen Carthage remembers it? No. For a happy life is not visible to the eye, because it is not a body. Is it, then, as we remember numbers? No. For he that hath these in his knowledge strives not to attain further; but a happy life we have in our knowledge, and, therefore, do we love it, while yet we wish further to attain it that we may be happy. Is it, then, as we remember eloquence? No. For although some, when they hear this name, call the thing to mind, who, indeed, are not yet eloquent, and many

---

[1] See note, p. 75, above.
[2] Amos v. 4.

[3] 1 Cor. xv. 22; see p. 140, note 3, and note p. 73, above.
[4] That is, as knowing Latin.

who wish to be so, whence it appears to be in their knowledge; yet have these by their bodily perceptions noticed that others are eloquent, and been delighted with it, and long to be so, —although they would not be delighted save for some interior knowledge, nor desire to be so unless they were delighted,—but a happy life we can by no bodily perception make experience of in others. Is it, then, as we remember joy? It may be so; for my joy I remember, even when sad, like as I do a happy life when I am miserable. Nor did I ever with perception of the body either see, hear, smell, taste, or touch my joy; but I experienced it in my mind when I rejoiced; and the knowledge of it clung to my memory, so that I can call it to mind, sometimes with disdain and at others with desire, according to the difference of the things wherein I now remember that I rejoiced. For even from unclean things have I been bathed with a certain joy, which now calling to mind, I detest and execrate; at other times, from good and honest things, which, with longing, I call to mind, though perchance they be not nigh at hand, and then with sadness do I call to mind a former joy.

31. Where and when, then, did I experience my happy life, that I should call it to mind, and love and long for it? Nor is it I alone or a few others who wish to be happy, but truly all; which, unless by certain knowledge we knew, we should not wish with so certain a will. But how is this, that if two men be asked whether they would wish to serve as soldiers, one, it may be, would reply that he would, the other that he would not; but if they were asked whether they would wish to be happy, both of them would unhesitatingly say that they would; and this one would wish to serve, and the other not, from no other motive but to be happy? Is it, perchance, that as one joys in this, and another in that, so do all men agree in their wish for happiness, as they would agree, were they asked, in wishing to have joy,—and this joy they call a happy life? Although, then, one pursues joy in this way, and another in that, all have one goal, which they strive to attain, namely, to have joy. This life, being a thing which no one can say he has not experienced, it is on that account found in the memory, and recognised whenever the name of a happy life is heard.

CHAP. XXII.—A HAPPY LIFE IS TO REJOICE IN GOD, AND FOR GOD.

32. Let it be far, O Lord,—let it be far from the heart of Thy servant who confesseth unto Thee; let it be far from me to think myself happy, be the joy what it may. For there is a joy which is not granted to the "wicked,"[1] but to those who worship Thee thankfully, whose joy Thou Thyself art. And the happy life is this,—to rejoice unto Thee, in Thee, and for Thee; this it is, and there is no other.[2] But those who think there is another follow after another joy, and that not the true one. Their will, however, is not turned away from some shadow of joy.

CHAP. XXIII.—ALL WISH TO REJOICE IN THE TRUTH.

33. It is not, then, certain that all men wish to be happy, since those who wish not to rejoice in Thee, which is the only happy life, do not verily desire the happy life. Or do all desire this, but because "the flesh lusteth against the spirit, and the spirit against the flesh," so that they "cannot do the things that they would,"[3] they fall upon that which they are able to do, and with that are content; because that which they are not able to do, they do not so will as to make them able?[4] For I ask of every man, whether he would rather rejoice in truth or in falsehood. They will no more hesitate to say, "in truth," than to say, "that they wish to be happy." For a happy life is joy in the truth. For this is joy in Thee, who art "the truth,"[5] O God, "my light,"[6] "the health of my countenance, and my God."[7] All wish for this happy life; this life do all wish for, which is the only happy one; joy in the truth do all wish for.[8] I have had experience of many who wished to deceive, but not one who wished to be deceived. Where, then, did they know this happy life, save where they knew also the truth? For they love it, too, since they would not be deceived. And when they love a happy life, which is naught else but joy in the truth, assuredly they love also the truth; which yet they would not love were there not some knowledge of it in the memory. Wherefore, then, do they not rejoice in it? Why are they not happy? Because they are more entirely occupied with other things which rather make them miserable, than that which would make them happy, which they remember so little of. For there is yet a little light in men; let them walk —let them "walk," that the "darkness" seize them not.[9]

1 Isa. xlviii. 22.
2 Since "life eternal is the supreme good," as he remarks in his *De Civ. Dei*, xix. 4. Compare also *ibid*. viii. sec. 8, where he argues that the highest good is God, and that he who loves Him is in the enjoyment of that good. See also note on the chief good, p. 75, above.
3 Gal. v. 17.
4 See viii. sec. 20, above.
5 John xiv. 6.
6 Ps. xxvii. 1.
7 Ps. xlii. 11.
8 See sec. 29, above.
9 John xii. 35.

34. Why, then, doth truth beget hatred,[1] and that man of thine,[2] preaching the truth, become an enemy unto them, whereas a happy life is loved, which is naught else but joy in the truth; unless that truth is loved in such a sort as that those who love aught else wish that to be the truth which they love, and, as they are willing to be deceived, are unwilling to be convinced that they are so? Therefore do they hate the truth for the sake of that thing which they love instead of the truth. They love truth when she shines on them, and hate her when she rebukes them. For, because they are not willing to be deceived, and wish to deceive, they love her when she reveals herself, and hate her when she reveals them. On that account shall she so requite them, that those who were unwilling to be discovered by her she both discovers against their will, and discovers not herself unto them. Thus, thus, truly thus doth the human mind, so blind and sick, so base and unseemly, desire to lie concealed, but wishes not that anything should be concealed from it. But the opposite is rendered unto it,—that itself is not concealed from the truth, but the truth is concealed from it. Yet, even while thus wretched, it prefers to rejoice in truth rather than in falsehood. Happy then will it be, when, no trouble intervening, it shall rejoice in that only truth by whom all things else are true.

CHAP. XXIV.—HE WHO FINDS TRUTH, FINDS GOD.

35. Behold how I have enlarged in my memory seeking Thee, O Lord; and out of it have I not found Thee. Nor have I found aught concerning Thee, but what I have retained in memory from the time I learned Thee. For from the time I learned Thee have I never forgotten Thee. For where I found truth, there found I my God, who is the Truth itself,[3] which from the time I learned it have I not forgotten. And thus since the time I learned Thee, Thou abidest in my memory; and there do I find Thee whensoever I call Thee to remembrance, and delight in Thee. These are my holy delights, which Thou hast bestowed upon me in Thy mercy, having respect unto my poverty.

CHAP. XXV.—HE IS GLAD THAT GOD DWELLS IN HIS MEMORY.

36. But where in my memory abidest Thou, O Lord, where dost Thou there abide? What manner of chamber hast Thou there formed for Thyself? What sort of sanctuary hast Thou erected for Thyself? Thou hast granted this honour to my memory, to take up Thy abode in it; but in what quarter of it Thou abidest, I am considering. For in calling Thee to mind,[4] I soared beyond those parts of it which the beasts also possess, since I found Thee not there amongst the images of corporeal things; and I arrived at those parts where I had committed the affections of my mind, nor there did I find Thee. And I entered into the very seat of my mind, which it has in my memory, since the mind remembers itself also—nor wert Thou there. For as Thou art not a bodily image, nor the affection of a living creature, as when we rejoice, condole, desire, fear, remember, forget, or aught of the kind; so neither art Thou the mind itself, because Thou art the Lord God of the mind; and all these things are changed, but Thou remainest unchangeable over all, yet vouchsafest to dwell in my memory, from the time I learned Thee. But why do I now seek in what part of it Thou dwellest, as if truly there were places in it? Thou dost dwell in it assuredly, since I have remembered Thee from the time I learned Thee, and I find Thee in it when I call Thee to mind.

CHAP. XXVI.—GOD EVERYWHERE ANSWERS THOSE WHO TAKE COUNSEL OF HIM.

37. Where, then, did I find Thee, so as to be able to learn Thee? For Thou wert not in my memory before I learned Thee. Where, then, did I find Thee, so as to be able to learn Thee, but in Thee above me? Place there is none; we go both "backward" and "forward,"[5] and there is no place. Everywhere, O Truth, dost Thou direct all who consult Thee, and dost at once answer all, though they consult Thee on divers things. Clearly dost Thou answer, though all do not with clearness hear. All consult Thee upon whatever they wish, though they hear not always that which they wish. He is Thy best servant who does not so much look to hear that from Thee which he himself wisheth, as to wish that which he heareth from Thee.

CHAP. XXVII.—HE GRIEVES THAT HE WAS SO LONG WITHOUT GOD.

38. Too late did I love Thee, O Fairness, so ancient, and yet so new! Too late did I love Thee! For behold, Thou wert within, and I without, and there did I seek Thee; I, unlovely, rushed heedlessly among the things of beauty Thou madest.[6] Thou wert with me, but I was

---

[1] "Veritas parit odium." Compare Terence, *Andria*, i. 1, 41: "Obsequium amicos, veritas odium parit."
[2] John viii. 40.
[3] See iv. c. 12, and vii. c. 10, above.

[4] In connection with Augustin's views as to memory, Locke's *Essay on the Human Understanding*, ii. 10, and Stewart's *Philosophy of the Human Mind*, c. 6, may be profitably consulted.
[5] Job xxiii. 8.
[6] See p. 74, note 1, above.

not with Thee. Those things kept me far from Thee, which, unless they were in Thee, were not. Thou calledst, and criedst aloud, and forcedst open my deafness. Thou didst gleam and shine, and chase away my blindness. Thou didst exhale odours, and I drew in my breath and do pant after Thee. I tasted, and do hunger and thirst. Thou didst touch me, and I burned for Thy peace.

CHAP. XXVIII.—ON THE MISERY OF HUMAN LIFE.

39. When I shall cleave unto Thee with all my being, then shall I in nothing have pain and labour; and my life shall be a real life, being wholly full of Thee. But now since he whom Thou fillest is the one Thou liftest up, I am a burden to myself, as not being full of Thee. Joys of sorrow contend with sorrows of joy; and on which side the victory may be I know not. Woe is me! Lord, have pity on me. My evil sorrows contend with my good joys; and on which side the victory may be I know not. Woe is me! Lord, have pity on me. Woe is me! Lo, I hide not my wounds; Thou art the Physician, I the sick; Thou merciful, I miserable. Is not the life of man upon earth a temptation?[1] Who is he that wishes for vexations and difficulties? Thou commandest them to be endured, not to be loved. For no man loves what he endures, though he may love to endure. For notwithstanding he rejoices to endure, he would rather there were naught for him to endure.[2] In adversity, I desire prosperity; in prosperity, I fear adversity. What middle place, then, is there between these, where human life is not a temptation? Woe unto the prosperity of this world, once and again, from fear of misfortune and a corruption of joy! Woe unto the adversities of this world, once and again, and for the third time, from the desire of prosperity; and because adversity itself is a hard thing, and makes shipwreck of endurance! Is not the life of man upon earth a temptation, and that without intermission?[3]

CHAP. XXIX.—ALL HOPE IS IN THE MERCY OF GOD.

40. And my whole hope is only in Thy exceeding great mercy. Give what Thou commandest, and command what Thou wilt. Thou imposest continency upon us,[4] "nevertheless, when I perceived," saith one, "that I could not otherwise obtain her, except God gave her me; . . . that was a point of wisdom also to know whose gift she was."[5] For by continency are we bound up and brought into one, whence we were scattered abroad into many. For he loves Thee too little who loves aught with Thee, which he loves not for Thee,[6] O love, who ever burnest, and art never quenched! O charity, my God, kindle me! Thou commandest continency; give what Thou commandest, and command what Thou wilt.

CHAP. XXX.—OF THE PERVERSE IMAGES OF DREAMS, WHICH HE WISHES TO HAVE TAKEN AWAY.

41. Verily, Thou commandest that I should be continent from the "lust of the flesh, and the lust of the eyes, and the pride of life."[7] Thou hast commanded me to abstain from concubinage; and as to marriage itself, Thou hast advised something better than Thou hast allowed. And because Thou didst give it, it was done; and that before I became a dispenser of Thy sacrament. But there still exist in my memory—of which I have spoken much—the images of such things as my habits had fixed there; and these rush into my thoughts, though strengthless, when I am awake; but in sleep they do so not only so as to give pleasure, but even to obtain consent, and what very nearly resembles reality.[8] Yea, to such an extent prevails the illusion of the image, both in my soul and in my flesh, that the false persuade me,

---

[1] Job vii. 1. The *Old Ver.* rendering צבא by *tentatio*, after the LXX. πειρατήριον. The *Vulg.* has *militia*, which = "warfare" in margin of A. V.

[2] "It will not be safe," says Anthony Farindon (vol. iv. *Christ's Temptation*, serm. 107), "for us to challenge and provoke a temptation, but to arm and prepare ourselves against it; to stand upon our guard, and neither to offer battle nor yet refuse it. *Sapiens feret ista, non eliget:* 'It is the part of a wise man not to seek for evil, but to *endure* it.' And to this end it concerneth every man to exercise τὴν πνευματικὴν σύνεσιν, 'his spiritual wisdom,' that he may discover *Spiritûs ductiones et diaboli seductiones*, 'the Spirit's leadings and the devil's seducements.'" See also Augustin's *Serm.* lxxvi. 4, and p. 79, note 9, above.

[3] We have ever to endure temptation, either in the sense of a *testing*, as when it is said, "God did tempt Abraham" (Gen. xxii. 1); or with the additional idea of *yielding* to the temptation, and so committing sin, as in the use of the word in the Lord's Prayer (Matt. vi. 13); for, as Dyke says in his *Michael and the Dragon* (Works, i. 203, 204): "No sooner have we bathed and washed our souls in the waters of *Repentance*, but we must presently expect the fiery darts of Satan's temptations to be driving at us. What we get and gain from Satan by *Repentance*, he seeks to regain and re-

cover by his *Temptations*. We must not think to pass quietly out of Egypt without Pharaoh's pursuit, nor to travel the wilderness of this world without the opposition of the Amalekites." Compare Augustin, *In Ev. Joann.* Tract. xliii. 6, and *Serm.* lvii. 9. See also p. 79, note 3, above.

[4] In his 38th *Sermon*, he distinguishes between *continentia* and *sustinentia;* the first guarding us from the allurements of worldliness and sin, while the second enables us to endure the troubles of life.

[5] Wisd. viii. 21.

[6] In his *De Trin.* ix. 13 ("*In what desire and love differ*"), he says, that when the creature is loved for itself, and the love of it is not referred to its Creator, it is desire (*cupiditas*) and not true love. See also p. 129, note 8, above.

[7] 1 John ii. 16. Dilating on Ps. viii. he makes these three roots of sin to correspond to the threefold nature of our Lord's temptation in the wilderness. See also p. 80, note 5, above.

[8] In Augustin's view, then, dreams appear to result from our thoughts and feelings when awake. In this he has the support of Aristotle (*Ethics*, i. 13), as also that of Solomon, who says (Eccles. v. 3), "A dream cometh through the multitude of business." An apt illustration of this is found in the life of the great Danish sculptor, Thorwaldsen. It is said that he could not satisfy himself with his models for *The Christ*, in the Frauenkirche at Copenhagen,—as Da Vinci before him was *never* able to paint the face of the Christ in His noble fresco of the Last Supper,—and that it was only in consequence of a dream (that dream doubtless the result of his stedfast search for an ideal) that this great work was accomplished. But see *Ep.* clix.

when sleeping, unto that which the true are not able when waking. Am I not myself at that time, O Lord my God? And there is yet so much difference between myself and myself, in that instant wherein I pass back from waking to sleeping, or return from sleeping to waking! Where, then, is the reason which when waking resists such suggestions? And if the things themselves be forced on it, I remain unmoved. Is it shut up with the eyes? Or is it put to sleep with the bodily senses? But whence, then, comes it to pass, that even in slumber we often resist, and, bearing our purpose in mind, and continuing most chastely in it, yield no assent to such allurements? And there is yet so much difference that, when it happeneth otherwise, upon awaking we return to peace of conscience; and by this same diversity do we discover that it was not we that did it, while we still feel sorry that in some way it was done in us.

42. Is not Thy hand able, O Almighty God, to heal all the diseases of my soul,[1] and by Thy more abundant grace to quench even the lascivious motions of my sleep? Thou wilt increase in me, O Lord, Thy gifts more and more, that my soul may follow me to Thee, disengaged from the bird-lime of concupiscence; that it may not be in rebellion against itself, and even in dreams not simply not, through sensual images, commit those deformities of corruption, even to the pollution of the flesh, but that it may not even consent unto them. For it is no great thing for the Almighty, who is "able to do . . . above all that we ask or think,"[2] to bring it about that no such influence—not even so slight a one as a sign might restrain—should afford gratification to the chaste affection even of one sleeping; and that not only in this life, but at my present age. But what I still am in this species of my ill, have I confessed unto my good Lord; rejoicing with trembling[3] in that which Thou hast given me, and bewailing myself for that wherein I am still imperfect; trusting that Thou wilt perfect Thy mercies in me, even to the fulness of peace, which both that which is within and that which is without[4] shall have with Thee, when death is swallowed up in victory.[5]

CHAP. XXXI.—ABOUT TO SPEAK OF THE TEMPTA-TIONS OF THE LUST OF THE FLESH, HE FIRST COMPLAINS OF THE LUST OF EATING AND DRINKING.

43. There is another evil of the day that I would were "sufficient" unto it.[6] For by eat-ing and drinking we repair the daily decays of the body, until Thou destroyest both food and stomach, when Thou shalt destroy my want with an amazing satiety, and shalt clothe this corruptible with an eternal incorruption.[7] But now is necessity sweet unto me, and against this sweetness do I fight, lest I be enthralled; and I carry on a daily war by fastings,[8] oftentimes "bringing my body into subjection,"[9] and my pains are expelled by pleasure. For hunger and thirst are in some sort pains; they consume and destroy like unto a fever, unless the medicine of nourishment relieve us. The which, since it is at hand through the comfort we receive of Thy gifts, with which land and water and air serve our infirmity, our calamity is called pleasure.

44. This much hast Thou taught me, that I should bring myself to take food as medicine. But during the time that I am passing from the uneasiness of want to the calmness of satiety, even in the very passage doth that snare of concupiscence lie in wait for me. For the passage itself is pleasure, nor is there any other way of passing thither, whither necessity compels us to pass. And whereas health is the reason of eating and drinking, there joineth itself as an handmaid a perilous delight, which mostly tries to precede it, in order that I may do for her sake what I say I do, or desire to do, for health's sake. Nor have both the same limit; for what is sufficient for health is too little for pleasure. And oftentimes it is doubtful whether it be the necessary care of the body which still asks nourishment, or whether a sensual snare of desire offers its ministry. In this uncertainty does my unhappy soul rejoice, and therein prepares an excuse as a defence, glad that it doth not appear what may be sufficient for the moderation of health, that so under the pretence of health it may conceal the business of pleasure. These temptations do I daily endeavour to resist, and I summon Thy right hand·to my help, and refer my excitements to Thee, because as yet I have no resolve in this matter.

45. I hear the voice of my God commanding, let not "your hearts be overcharged with surfeiting and drunkenness."[10] "Drunkenness," it is far from me; Thou wilt have mercy, that it approach not near unto me. But "surfeiting" sometimes creepeth upon Thy servant; Thou wilt have mercy, that it may be far from me. For no man can be continent unless Thou give it.[11] Many things which we pray for dost

[1] Ps. ciii. 3.
[2] Eph. iii. 20.
[3] Ps. ii. 11.
[4] See note 4, p. 140, above.
[5] 1 Cor. xv. 54.
[6] Matt. vi. 34.

[7] 1 Cor. xv. 54.
[8] In Augustin's time, and indeed till the Council of Orleans, A. D. 538, fasting appears to have been left pretty much to the individual conscience. We find Tertullian in his *De Jejunio* lamenting the slight observance it received during his day. We learn, however, from the passage in Justin Martyr, quoted in note 4, on p. 118, above, that in his time it was enjoined as a preparation for Baptism.
[9] 1 Cor. ix. 27.
[10] Luke xxi. 34.
[11] Wisd. viii. 21.

Thou give us; and what good soever we receive before we prayed for it, do we receive from Thee, and that we might afterwards know this did we receive it from Thee. Drunkard was I never, but I have known drunkards to be made sober men by Thee. Thy doing, then, was it, that they who never were such might not be so, as from Thee it was that they who have been so heretofore might not remain so always; and from Thee, too, was it, that both might know from whom it was. I heard another voice of Thine, "Go not after thy lusts, but refrain thyself from thine appetites."[1] And by Thy favour have I heard this saying likewise, which I have much delighted in, "Neither if we eat, are we the better; neither if we eat not, are we the worse;"[2] which is to say, that neither shall the one make me to abound, nor the other to be wretched. I heard also another voice, "For I have learned, in whatsoever state I am, therewith to be content, I know both how to be abased, and I know how to abound. . . . I can do all things through Christ which strengtheneth me."[3] Lo! a soldier of the celestial camp—not dust as we are. But remember, O Lord, "that we are dust,"[4] and that of dust Thou hast created man;[5] and he "was lost, and is found."[6] Nor could he do this of his own power, seeing that he whom I so loved, saying these things through the afflatus of Thy inspiration, was of that same dust. "I can," saith he, "do all things through Him which strengtheneth me."[7] Strengthen me, that I may be able. Give what Thou commandest, and command what Thou wilt.[8] He confesses to have received, and when he glorieth, he glorieth in the Lord.[9] Another have I heard entreating that he might receive,—"Take from me," saith he, "the greediness of the belly;"[10] by which it appeareth, O my holy God, that Thou givest when what Thou commandest to be done is done.

46. Thou hast taught me, good Father, that "unto the pure all things are pure;"[11] but "it is evil for that man who eateth with offence;"[12] "and that every creature of Thine is good, and nothing to be refused, if it be received with thanksgiving;"[13] and that "meat commendeth us not to God;"[14] and that no man should

"judge us in meat or in drink;"[15] and that he that eateth, let him not despise him that eateth not; and let not him that eateth not judge him that eateth.[16] These things have I learned, thanks and praise be unto Thee, O my God and Master, who dost knock at my ears and enlighten my heart; deliver me out of all temptation. It is not the uncleanness of meat that I fear, but the uncleanness of lusting. I know that permission was granted unto Noah to eat every kind of flesh[17] that was good for food;[18] that Elias was fed with flesh;[19] that John, endued with a wonderful abstinence, was not polluted by the living creatures (that is, the locusts[20]) which he fed on. I know, too, that Esau was deceived by a longing for lentiles,[21] and that David took blame to himself for desiring water,[22] and that our King was tempted not by flesh but bread.[23] And the people in the wilderness, therefore, also deserved reproof, not because they desired flesh, but because, in their desire for food, they murmured against the Lord.[24]

47. Placed, then, in the midst of these temptations, I strive daily against longing for food and drink. For it is not of such a nature as that I am able to resolve to cut it off once for all, and not touch it afterwards, as I was able to do with concubinage. The bridle of the throat, therefore, is to be held in the mean of slackness and tightness.[25] And who, O Lord, is he who is not in some degree carried away beyond the bounds of necessity? Whoever he is, he is great; let him magnify Thy name. But I am not such a one, "for I am a sinful man."[26] Yet do I also magnify Thy name; and He who hath "overcome the world"[27] maketh intercession to Thee for my sins,[28] accounting me among the "feeble members" of His body,[29] because Thine eyes saw that of him which was imperfect; and in Thy book all shall be written.[30]

---

[1] Ecclus. xviii. 30.
[2] 1 Cor. viii. 8.
[3] Phil. iv. 11–14.
[4] Ps. ciii. 14.
[5] Gen. iii. 19.
[6] Luke xv. 32.
[7] Phil. iv. 13.
[8] In his *De Dono Persev.* sec. 53, he tells us that these words were quoted to Pelagius, when at Rome, by a certain bishop, and that they excited him to contradict them so warmly as nearly to result in a rupture between Pelagius and the bishop.
[9] 1 Cor. i. 31.
[10] Ecclus. xxiii. 6.
[11] Titus i. 15.
[12] Rom. xiv. 20.
[13] 1 Tim. iv. 4.
[14] 1 Cor. viii. 8.

[15] Col. ii. 16.
[16] Rom. xiii. 23.
[17] He here refers to the doctrine of the Manichæans in the matter of eating flesh. In his *De Mor. Manich.* secs. 36, 37, he discusses the prohibition of flesh to the "Elect." From *Ep.* ccxxxvi. we find that the "Hearers" had not to practise abstinence from marriage and from eating flesh. For other information on this subject, see notes, pp. 66 and 83.
[18] Gen. ix. 3.
[19] 1 Kings xvii. 6.
[20] Matt. iii. 4.
[21] Gen. xxv. 34.
[22] 2 Sam. xxiii. 15–17.
[23] Matt. iv. 3.
[24] Num. xi.
[25] So all God's gifts are to be used, but not abused; and those who deny the right use of any, do so by virtually accepting the principle of asceticism. As Augustin, in his *De Mor. Ecc. Cath.* sec. 39, says of all transient things, we "should use them as far as is required for the purposes and duties of life, with the moderation of an employer instead of the ardour of a lover."
[26] Luke v. 8.
[27] John xvi. 33.
[28] Rom. viii. 34.
[29] 1 Cor. xii. 22.
[30] Ps. cxxxix. 16; he similarly applies this passage when commenting on it *in Ps.* cxxxviii. 21, and also in *Serm.* cxxxv.

CHAP. XXXII.—OF THE CHARMS OF PERFUMES
    WHICH ARE MORE EASILY OVERCOME.

48. With the attractions of odours I am not
much troubled. When absent I do not seek
them; when present I do not refuse them; and
am prepared ever to be without them. At any
rate thus I appear to myself; perchance I am
deceived. For that also is a lamentable darkness wherein my capacity that is in me is concealed, so that my mind, making inquiry into
herself concerning her own powers, ventures
not readily to credit herself; because that which
is already in it is, for the most part, concealed,
unless experience reveal it. And no man ought
to feel secure[1] in this life, the whole of which is
called a temptation,[2] that he, who could be
made better from worse, may not also from
better be made worse. Our sole hope, our sole
confidence, our sole assured promise, is Thy
mercy.

CHAP. XXXIII.—HE OVERCAME THE PLEASURES
    OF THE EAR, ALTHOUGH IN THE CHURCH HE
    FREQUENTLY DELIGHTED IN THE SONG, NOT
    IN THE THING SUNG.

49. The delights of the ear had more powerfully inveigled and conquered me, but Thou
didst unbind and liberate me. Now, in those
airs which Thy words breathe soul into, when
sung with a sweet and trained voice, do I somewhat repose; yet not so as to cling to them,
but so as to free myself when I wish. But with
the words which are their life do they, that they
may gain admission into me, strive after a
place of some honour in my heart; and I can
hardly assign them a fitting one. Sometimes I
appear to myself to give them more respect than
is fitting, as I perceive that our minds are more
devoutly and earnestly elevated into a flame of
piety by the holy words themselves when they
are thus sung, than when they are not; and
that all affections of our spirit, by their own
diversity, have their appropriate measures in
the voice and singing, wherewith by I know not
what secret relationship they are stimulated.
But the gratification of my flesh, to which the
mind ought never to be given over to be ener-
vated, often beguiles me, while the sense does

not so attend on reason as to follow her
patiently; but having gained admission merely
for her sake, it strives even to run on before
her, and be her leader. Thus in these things
do I sin unknowing, but afterwards do I know it.

50. Sometimes, again, avoiding very earnestly this same deception, I err out of too great
preciseness; and sometimes so much as to desire that every air of the pleasant songs to which
David's Psalter is often used, be banished both
from my ears and those of the Church itself;
and that way seemed unto me safer which I remembered to have been often related to me of
Athanasius, Bishop of Alexandria, who obliged
the reader of the psalm to give utterance to it
with so slight an inflection of voice, that it was
more like speaking than singing. Notwithstanding, when I call to mind the tears I shed
at the songs of Thy Church, at the outset of my
recovered faith, and how even now I am moved
not by the singing but by what is sung, when
they are sung with a clear and skilfully modu-
lated voice, I then acknowledge the great utility of this custom. Thus vacillate I between
dangerous pleasure and tried soundness; being
inclined rather (though I pronounce no irrevo-
cable opinion upon the subject) to approve of
the use of singing in the church, that so by the
delights of the ear the weaker minds may be
stimulated to a devotional frame. Yet when it
happens to me to be more moved by the singing than by what is sung, I confess myself to
have sinned criminally, and then I would rather
not have heard the singing. See now the condition I am in! Weep with me, and weep for
me, you who so control your inward feelings as
that good results ensue. As for you who do
not thus act, these things concern you not.
But Thou, O Lord my God, give ear, behold
and see, and have mercy upon me, and heal
me,[3]—Thou, in whose sight I am become a
puzzle to myself; and "this is my infirmity."[4]

CHAP. XXXIV.—OF THE VERY DANGEROUS ALLURE-
    MENTS OF THE EYES; ON ACCOUNT OF BEAUTY
    OF FORM, GOD, THE CREATOR, IS TO BE
    PRAISED.

51. There remain the delights of these eyes
of my flesh, concerning which to make my confessions in the hearing of the ears of Thy temple, those fraternal and devout ears; and so to
conclude the temptations of "the lust of the
flesh"[5] which still assail me, groaning and desiring to be clothed upon with my house from
heaven.[6] The eyes delight in fair and varied
forms, and bright and pleasing colours. Suffer

---

[1] "For some," says Thomas Taylor (Works, vol. 1. "Christ's
Temptation," p. 11), "through vain presidence of God's protection, run in times of contagion into infected houses, which upon just
calling a man may: but for one to run out of his calling in the way
of an ordinary visitation, he shall find that God's angels have commission to protect him no longer than he is in his way (Ps. xci. 11),
and that being out of it, this arrow of the Lord shall sooner hit him
than another that is not half so confident." We should not, as
Fuller quaintly says, "hollo in the ears of a sleeping temptation;"
and when we are tempted, let us remember that if (Hibbert, Syn-
tagma Theologicum, p. 342) "a giant knock while the door is shut,
he may with ease be still kept out; but if once open, that he gets in
but a limb of himself, then there is no course left to keep out the
remaining bulk." See also Augustin on Peter's case, De Cor-
rept. et Grat. c. 9.
[2] Job vii. 1, Old Vers. See p. 153, note 1.

[3] Ps. vi. 2.
[4] Ps. lxxvii. 10.
[5] 1 John ii. 16.
[6] 2 Cor. v. 2.

not these to take possession of my soul; let God rather possess it, He who made these things "very good"[1] indeed; yet is He my good, not these. And these move me while awake, during the day; nor is rest from them granted me, as there is from the voices of melody, sometimes, in silence, from them all. For that queen of colours, the light, flooding all that we look upon, wherever I be during the day, gliding past me in manifold forms, doth soothe me when busied about other things, and not noticing it. And so strongly doth it insinuate itself, that if it be suddenly withdrawn it is looked for longingly, and if long absent doth sadden the mind.

52. O Thou Light, which Tobias saw,[2] when, his eyes being closed, he taught his son the way of life; himself going before with the feet of charity, never going astray. Or that which Isaac saw, when his fleshly "eyes were dim, so that he could not see"[3] by reason of old age; it was permitted him, not knowingly to bless his sons, but in blessing them to know them. Or that which Jacob saw, when he too, blind through great age, with an enlightened heart, in the persons of his own sons, threw light upon the races of the future people, presignified in them; and laid his hands, mystically crossed, upon his grandchildren by Joseph, not as their father, looking outwardly, corrected them, but as he himself distinguished them.[4] This is the light, the only one, and all those who see and love it are one. But that corporeal light of which I was speaking seasoneth the life of the world for her blind lovers, with a tempting and fatal sweetness. But they who know how to praise Thee for it, "O God, the world's great Architect,"[5] take it up in Thy hymn, and are not taken up with it[6] in their sleep. Such desire I to be. I resist seductions of the eyes, lest my feet with which I advance on Thy way be entangled; and I raise my invisible eyes to Thee, that Thou wouldst be pleased to "pluck my feet out of the net."[7] Thou dost continually pluck them out, for they are ensnared. Thou never ceasest to pluck them out, but I constantly remain fast in the snares set all around me; because Thou "that keepest Israel shall neither slumber nor sleep."[8]

53. What numberless things, made by divers arts and manufactures, both in our apparel, shoes, vessels, and every kind of work, in pictures, too, and sundry images, and these going far beyond necessary and moderate use and holy signification, have men added for the enthralment of the eyes; following outwardly what they make, forsaking inwardly Him by whom they were made, yea, and destroying that which they themselves were made! But I, O my God and my Joy, do hence also sing a hymn unto Thee, and offer a sacrifice of praise unto my Sanctifier,[9] because those beautiful patterns, which through the medium of men's souls are conveyed into their artistic hands,[10] emanate from that Beauty which is above our souls, which my soul sigheth after day and night. But as for the makers and followers of those outward beauties, they from thence derive the way of approving them, but not of using them.[11] And though they see Him not, yet is He there, that they might not go astray, but keep their strength for Thee,[12] and not dissipate it upon delicious lassitudes. And I, though I both say and perceive this, impede my course with such beauties, but Thou dost rescue me, O Lord, Thou dost rescue me; "for Thy loving-kindness is before mine eyes."[13] For I am taken miserably, and Thou rescuest me mercifully; sometimes not perceiving it, in that I had come upon them hesitatingly; at other times with pain, because I was held fast by them.

CHAP. XXXV.—ANOTHER KIND OF TEMPTATION IS CURIOSITY, WHICH IS STIMULATED BY THE LUST OF THE EYES.

54. In addition to this there is another form of temptation, more complex in its peril. For besides that concupiscence of the flesh which lieth in the gratification of all senses and pleasures, wherein its slaves who "are far from Thee perish,"[14] there pertaineth to the soul, through the same senses of the body, a certain vain and curious longing, cloaked under the name of knowledge and learning, not of having pleasure in the flesh, but of making experiments through the flesh. This longing, since it originates in an appetite for knowledge, and the sight being the chief amongst the senses in the acquisition of knowledge, is called in divine language, "the lust of the eyes."[15] For seeing belongeth properly to the eyes; yet we apply this word to the other senses also, when we exercise them in the search after knowledge. For we do not say, Listen how it glows, smell how it glistens, taste how it shines, or feel how it flashes, since all these are said to be seen. And yet we say

---

[1] Gen. i. 31.
[2] Tobit iv.
[3] Gen. xxvii. 1.
[4] Gen. xlviii. 13–19.
[5] From the beginning of the hymn of St. Ambrose, part of which is quoted, ix. sec. 32, above.
[6] *Assumunt eam, in hymno tuo, non absumuntur ab ea.*
[7] Ps. xxv. 15.
[8] Ps. cxxi. 4.

[9] *Sanctificatori meo*, but some MSS. have *sacrificatori*.
[10] See xi. sec. 7, and note, below.
[11] See note 6, sec. 40, above.
[12] Ps. lviii. 10, *Vulg.*
[13] Ps. xxvi. 3.
[14] Ps. lxiii. 27.
[15] 1 John ii. 16.

not only, See how it shineth, which the eyes alone can perceive; but also, See how it soundeth, see how it smelleth, see how it tasteth, see how hard it is. And thus the general experience of the senses, as was said before, is termed "the lust of the eyes," because the function of seeing, wherein the eyes hold the pre-eminence, the other senses by way of similitude take possession of, whensoever they seek out any knowledge.

55. But by this is it more clearly discerned, when pleasure and when curiosity is pursued by the senses; for pleasure follows after objects that are beautiful, melodious, fragrant, savoury, soft; but curiosity, for experiment's sake, seeks the contrary of these,—not with a view of undergoing uneasiness, but from the passion of experimenting upon and knowing them. For what pleasure is there to see, in a lacerated corpse, that which makes you shudder? And yet if it lie near, we flock thither, to be made sad, and to turn pale. Even in sleep they fear lest they should see it. Just as if when awake any one compelled them to go and see it, or any report of its beauty had attracted them! Thus also is it with the other senses, which it were tedious to pursue. From this malady of curiosity are all those strange sights exhibited in the theatre. Hence do we proceed to search out the secret powers of nature (which is beside our end), which to know profits not,[1] and wherein men desire nothing but to know. Hence, too, with that same end of perverted knowledge we consult magical arts. Hence, again, even in religion itself, is God tempted, when signs and wonders are eagerly asked of Him,—not desired for any saving end, but to make trial only.

56. In this so vast a wilderness, replete with snares and dangers, lo, many of them have I lopped off, and expelled from my heart, as Thou, O God of my salvation, hast enabled me to do. And yet when dare I say, since so many things of this kind buzz around our daily life,— when dare I say that no such thing makes me intent to see it, or creates in me vain solicitude? It is true that the theatres never now carry me away, nor do I now care to know the courses of the stars, nor hath my soul at any time consulted departed spirits; all sacrilegious oaths I abhor. O Lord my God, to whom I owe all humble and single-hearted service, with what subtlety of suggestion does the enemy influence me to require some sign from Thee! But by our King, and by our pure and chaste country Jerusalem, I beseech Thee, that as any consenting unto such thoughts is far from me, so may it always be farther and farther. But when I entreat Thee for the salvation of any, the end I aim at is far otherwise, and Thou who doest what Thou wilt, givest and wilt give me willingly to "follow" Thee.[2]

57. Nevertheless, in how many most minute and contemptible things is our curiosity daily tempted, and who can number how often we succumb? How often, when people are narrating idle tales, do we begin by tolerating them, lest we should give offence unto the weak; and then gradually we listen willingly! I do not now-a-days go to the circus to see a dog chasing a hare;[3] but if by chance I pass such a coursing in the fields, it possibly distracts me even from some serious thought, and draws me after it,—not that I turn the body of my beast aside, but the inclination of my mind. And except Thou, by demonstrating to me my weakness, dost speedily warn me, either through the sight itself, by some reflection to rise to Thee, or wholly to despise and pass it by, I, vain one, am absorbed by it. How is it, when sitting at home, a lizard catching flies, or a spider entangling them as they rush into her nets, oftentimes arrests me? Is the feeling of curiosity not the same because these are such tiny creatures? From them I proceed to praise Thee, the wonderful Creator and Disposer of all things; but it is not this that first attracts my attention. It is one thing to get up quickly, and another not to fall, and of such things is my life full; and my only hope is in Thy exceeding great mercy. For when this heart of ours is made the receptacle of such things, and bears crowds of this abounding vanity, then are our prayers often interrupted and disturbed thereby; and whilst in Thy presence we direct the voice of our heart to Thine ears, this so great a matter is broken off by the influx of I know not what idle thoughts.

CHAP. XXXVI.—A THIRD KIND IS "PRIDE," WHICH IS PLEASING TO MAN, NOT TO GOD.

58. Shall we, then, account this too amongst such things as are to be lightly esteemed, or shall anything restore us to hope, save Thy complete mercy, since Thou hast begun to change us? And Thou knowest to what extent Thou hast already changed me, Thou who

---

[1] Augustin's great end was to attain the knowledge of God. Hence, in his *Soliloquia*, i. 7, we read: "Deum et animam scire cupio. Nihilne plus? Nihil omnino." And he only esteemed the knowledge of physical laws so far as they would lead to Him. (See v. sec. 7, above, and the note there.) In his *De Ordine*, ii. 14, 15, etc., writing at the time of his conversion, he had contended that the knowledge of the liberal sciences would lead to a knowledge of the divine wisdom; but in his *Retractations* (i. 3, sec. 2) he regrets this, pointing out that while many holy men have not this knowledge, many who have it are not holy. Compare also *Enchir.* c. 16; *Serm.* lxviii. 1, 2; and *De Civ. Dei*, ix. 22.

[2] John xxi. 22.
[3] In allusion to those *venatios*, or hunting scenes, in which the less savage animals were slain. These were held in the circus, which was sometimes planted for the occasion, so as to resemble a forest. See Smith's *Greek and Roman Antiquities*, under "Venatio," and vi. sec. 13, note, above.

first healest me of the lust of vindicating myself, that so Thou mightest forgive all my remaining "iniquities," and heal all my "diseases," and redeem my life from corruption, and crown me with "loving-kindness and tender mercies," and satisfy my desire with "good things;"[1] who didst restrain my pride with Thy fear, and subdue my neck to Thy "yoke." And now I bear it, and it is "light"[2] unto me, because so hast Thou promised, and made it, and so in truth it was, though I knew it not, when I feared to take it up. But, O Lord,—Thou who alone reignest without pride, because Thou art the only true Lord, who hast no lord,—hath this third kind of temptation left me, or can it leave me during this life?

59. The desire to be feared and loved of men, with no other view than that I may experience a joy therein which is no joy, is a miserable life, and unseemly ostentation. Hence especially it arises that we do not love Thee, nor devoutly fear Thee. And therefore dost Thou resist the proud, but givest grace unto the humble;[3] and Thou thunderest upon the ambitious designs of the world, and "the foundations of the hills" tremble.[4] Because now certain offices of human society render it necessary to be loved and feared of men, the adversary of our true blessedness presseth hard upon us, everywhere scattering his snares of "well done, well done;" that while acquiring them eagerly, we may be caught unawares, and disunite our joy from Thy truth, and fix it on the deceits of men; and take pleasure in being loved and feared, not for Thy sake, but in Thy stead, by which means, being made like unto him, he may have them as his, not in harmony of love, but in the fellowship of punishment; who aspired to exalt his throne in the north,[5] that dark and cold they might serve him, imitating Thee in perverse and distorted ways. But we, O Lord, lo, we are Thy "little flock;"[6] do Thou possess us, stretch Thy wings over us, and let us take refuge under them. Be Thou our glory; let us be loved for Thy sake, and Thy word feared in us. They who desire to be commended of men when Thou blamest, will not be defended of men when Thou judgest; nor will they be delivered when Thou condemnest. But when not the sinner is praised in the desires of his soul, nor he blessed who doeth unjustly,[7] but a man is praised for some gift that Thou hast bestowed upon him, and he is more gratified at the praise for himself, than that he possesses the gift for which he is praised, such a one is praised while Thou blamest. And better truly is he who praised than the one who was praised. For the gift of God in man was pleasing to the one, while the other was better pleased with the gift of man than that of God.

CHAP. XXXVII.—HE IS FORCIBLY GOADED ON BY THE LOVE OF PRAISE.

60. By these temptations, O Lord, are we daily tried; yea, unceasingly are we tried. Our daily "furnace"[8] is the human tongue. And in this respect also dost Thou command us to be continent. Give what Thou commandest, and command what Thou wilt. Regarding this matter, Thou knowest the groans of my heart, and the rivers[9] of mine eyes. For I am not able to ascertain how far I am clean of this plague, and I stand in great fear of my "secret faults,"[10] which Thine eyes perceive, though mine do not. For in other kinds of temptations I have some sort of power of examining myself; but in this, hardly any. For, both as regards the pleasures of the flesh and an idle curiosity, I see how far I have been able to hold my mind in check when I do without them, either voluntarily or by reason of their not being at hand;[11] for then I inquire of myself how much more or less troublesome it is to me not to have them. Riches truly which are sought for in order that they may minister to some one of these three "lusts,"[12] or to two, or the whole of them, if the mind be not able to see clearly whether, when it hath them, it despiseth them, they may be cast on one side, that so it may prove itself. But if we desire to test our power of doing without praise, need we live ill, and that so flagitiously and immoderately as that every one who knows us shall detest us? What greater madness than this can be either said or conceived? But if praise both is wont and ought to be the companion of a good life and of good works, we should as little forego its companionship as a good life itself. But unless a thing be absent, I do not know whether I shall be contented or troubled at being without it.

61. What, then, do I confess unto Thee, O Lord, in this kind of temptation? What, save that I am delighted with praise, but more with the truth itself than with praise? For were I to have my choice, whether I had rather, being

---

[1] Ps. ciii. 3-5.
[2] Matt. xi. 30.
[3] Jas. iv. 6.
[4] Ps. xviii. 7.
[5] Isa. xiv. 13, 14.
[6] Luke xii. 32.
[7] Ps. x. 3, in *Vulg.* and LXX.

[8] Isa. xlviii. 10, and Prov. xxvii. 21.
[9] Lam. iii. 48.
[10] Ps. xix. 12. See note 5, page 47, above.
[11] In his *De Vera Relig.* sec. 92, he points out that adversity also, when it comes to a good man, will disclose to him how far his heart is set on worldly things : "Hoc enim sine amore nostro aderat, quod sine dolore discedit."
[12] 1 John ii. 16. See beginning of sec. 41, above.

mad, or astray on all things, be praised by all men, or, being firm and well-assured in the truth, be blamed by all, I see which I should choose. Yet would I be unwilling that the approval of another should even add to my joy for any good I have. Yet I admit that it doth increase it, and, more than that, that dispraise doth diminish it. And when I am disquieted at this misery of mine, an excuse presents itself to me, the value of which Thou, God, knowest, for it renders me uncertain. For since it is not continency alone that Thou hast enjoined upon us, that is, from what things to hold back our love, but righteousness also, that is, upon what to bestow it, and hast wished us to love not Thee only, but also our neighbour,[1]—often, when gratified by intelligent praise, I appear to myself to be gratified by the proficiency or towardliness of my neighbour, and again to be sorry for evil in him when I hear him dispraise either that which he understands not, or is good. For I am sometimes grieved at mine own praise, either when those things which I am displeased at in myself be praised in me, or even lesser and trifling goods are more valued than they should be. But, again, how do I know whether I am thus affected, because I am unwilling that he who praiseth me should differ from me concerning myself—not as being moved with consideration for him, but because the same good things which please me in myself are more pleasing to me when they also please another? For, in a sort, I am not praised when my judgment of myself is not praised; since either those things which are displeasing to me are praised, or those more so which are less pleasing to me. Am I then uncertain of myself in this matter?

62. Behold, O Truth, in Thee do I see that I ought not to be moved at my own praises for my own sake, but for my neighbour's good. And whether it be so, in truth I know not. For concerning this I know less of myself than dost Thou. I beseech Thee now, O my God, to reveal to me myself also, that I may confess unto my brethren, who are to pray for me, what I find in myself weak. Once again let me more diligently examine myself.[2] If, in mine own praise, I am moved with consideration for my neighbour, why am I less moved if some other man be unjustly dispraised than if it be myself? Why am I more irritated at that reproach which is cast upon myself, than at that which is with equal injustice cast upon another in my presence? Am I ignorant of this also? or does it remain that I deceive myself,[3] and do not the "truth"[4] before Thee in my heart and tongue? Put such madness far from me, O Lord, lest my mouth be to me the oil of sinners, to anoint my head.[5]

CHAP. XXXVIII.—VAIN-GLORY IS THE HIGHEST DANGER.

63. "I am poor and needy,"[6] yet better am I while in secret groanings I displease myself, and seek for Thy mercy, until what is lacking in me be renewed and made complete, even up to that peace of which the eye of the proud is ignorant. Yet the word which proceedeth out of the mouth, and actions known to men, have a most dangerous temptation from the love of praise, which, for the establishing of a certain excellency of our own, gathers together solicited suffrages. It tempts, even when within I reprove myself for it, on the very ground that it is reproved; and often man glories more vainly of the very scorn of vain-glory; wherefore it is not any longer scorn of vain-glory whereof it glories, for he does not truly contemn it when he inwardly glories.

CHAP. XXXIX.—OF THE VICE OF THOSE WHO, WHILE PLEASING THEMSELVES, DISPLEASE GOD.

64. Within also, within is another evil, arising out of the same kind of temptation; whereby they become empty who please themselves in themselves, although they please not, or displease, or aim at pleasing others. But in pleasing themselves, they much displease Thee, not merely taking pleasure in things not good as if they were good, but in Thy good things as though they were their own; or even as if in Thine, yet as though of their own merits; or even as if though of Thy grace, yet not with friendly rejoicings, but as envying that grace to others.[7] In all these and similar perils and labours Thou perceivest the trembling of my heart, and I rather feel my wounds to be cured by Thee than not inflicted by me.

---

[1] Lev. xix. 18. See book xii. secs. 35, 41, below.

[2] It may be well, in connection with the striking piece of soul-anatomy in this and the last two sections, to advert to other passages in which Augustin speaks of the temptation arising from the praise of men. In *Serm.* cccxxxix. 1, he says that he does not altogether dislike praise when it comes from the good, though feeling it to be a snare, and does not reject it: " Ne *ingrati* sint quibus prædico." That is, as he says above, he accepted it for his " neighbour's good," since, had his neighbour not been ready to give praise, it would have indicated a wrong condition of heart in him. We are, therefore, as he argues in his *De Serm. Dom. in Mon.* ii. 1, 2, 6, to see that the *design* of our acts be not that men should see and praise us (compare also *Enarr. in Ps.* lxv. 2). If they praise us it is well, since it shows that their heart is right; but if we " act rightly only *because* of the praise of men" (Matt. vi. 2, 5), we seek our own glory and not that of God. See also *Serms.* xciii. 9, clix. 10, etc.; and *De Civ. Dei*, v. 13, 14.

[3] Gal. vi. 3.
[4] 1 John i. 8.
[5] Ps. cxli. 5, according to the *Vulg.* and LXX. The Authorized Version (with which the *Targum* is in accord) gives the more probable sense, when it makes the oil to be that of the righteous and not that of the sinner: " Let the righteous smite me, it shall be a kindness; and let him reprove me, it shall be an excellent oil, which shall not break my head."
[6] Ps. cix. 22.
[7] See his *De Civ. Dei*, v. 20, where he compares the truly pious man, who attributes all his good to God's mercy, " giving thanks for what in him is healed, and pouring out prayers for the healing of that which is yet unhealed," with the philosophers who make their chief end pleasure or human glory.

CHAP. XL.—THE ONLY SAFE RESTING-PLACE FOR THE SOUL IS TO BE FOUND IN GOD.

65. Where hast Thou not accompanied me, O Truth,[2] teaching me both what to avoid and what to desire, when I submitted to Thee what I could perceive of sublunary things, and asked Thy counsel? With my external senses, as I could, I viewed the world, and noted the life which my body derives from me, and these my senses. Thence I advanced inwardly into the recesses of my memory,—the manifold rooms, wondrously full of multitudinous wealth; and I considered and was afraid, and could discern none of these things without Thee, and found none of them to be Thee. Nor was I myself the discoverer of these things,—I, who went over them all, and laboured to distinguish and to value everything according to its dignity, accepting some things upon the report of my senses, and questioning about others which I felt to be mixed up with myself, distinguishing and numbering the reporters themselves, and in the vast storehouse of my memory investigating some things, laying up others, taking out others. Neither was I myself when I did this (that is, that ability of mine whereby I did it), nor was it Thou, for Thou art that never-failing light which I took counsel of as to them all, whether they were what they were, and what was their worth; and I heard Thee teaching and commanding me. And this I do often; this is a delight to me, and, as far as I can get relief from necessary duties, to this gratification do I resort. Nor in all these which I review when consulting Thee, find I a secure place for my soul, save in Thee, into whom my scattered members may be gathered together, and nothing of me depart from Thee.[2] And sometimes Thou dost introduce me to a most rare affection, inwardly, to an inexplicable sweetness, which, if it should be perfected in me, I know not to what point that life might not arrive. But by these wretched weights[3] of mine do I relapse into these things, and am sucked in by my old customs, and am held, and sorrow much, yet am much held. To such an extent does the burden of habit press us down. In this way I can be, but will not; in that I will, but cannot,—on both ways miserable.

CHAP. XLI.—HAVING CONQUERED HIS TRIPLE DESIRE, HE ARRIVES AT SALVATION.

66. And thus have I reflected upon the weariness of my sins, in that threefold "lust,"[4] and have invoked Thy right hand to my aid. For with a wounded heart have I seen Thy

brightness, and being beaten back I exclaimed, "Who can attain unto it?" "I am cut off from before Thine eyes."[5] Thou art the Truth, who presidest over all things, but I, through my covetousness, wished not to lose Thee, but with Thee wished to possess a lie; as no one wishes so to speak falsely as himself to be ignorant of the truth. So then I lost Thee, because Thou deignest not to be enjoyed with a lie.

CHAP. XLII.—IN WHAT MANNER MANY SOUGHT THE MEDIATOR.

67. Whom could I find to reconcile me to Thee? Was I to solicit the angels? By what prayer? By what sacraments? Many striving to return unto Thee, and not able of themselves, have, as I am told, tried this, and have fallen into a longing for curious visions,[6] and were held worthy to be deceived. For they, being exalted, sought Thee by the pride of learning, thrusting themselves forward rather than beating their breasts, and so by correspondence of heart drew unto themselves the princes of the air,[7] the conspirators and companions in pride, by whom, through the power of magic,[8] they were deceived, seeking a mediator by whom they might be cleansed; but none was there. For the devil it was, transforming himself into an angel of light.[9] And he much allured proud flesh, in that he had no fleshly body. For they were mortal, and sinful; but Thou, O Lord, to whom they arrogantly sought to be reconciled, art immortal, and sinless. But a mediator between God and man ought to have something like unto God, and something like unto man; lest being in both like unto man, he should be far from God; or if in both like unto God, he should be far from man, and so should not be a mediator. That deceitful mediator, then, by whom in Thy secret judgments pride deserved to be deceived, hath one thing in common with man, that is, sin; another he would appear to have with God, and, not being clothed with mortality of flesh, would boast that he was immortal.[10] But since "the wages of sin is death,"[11] this hath he in common with men, that together with them he should be condemned to death.

1 See xii. sec. 35, below.
2 See ix. sec. 10, note, above, and xi. sec. 39, below.
3 Heb. xii. 1.
4 See p. 153, note 7, above.

5 Ps. xxxi. 22.
6 It would be easy so to do, since even amongst believers, as we find from Evodius' letter to Augustin (*Ep.* clvi.), there was a prevalent belief that the blessed dead visited the earth, and that visions had an important bearing on human affairs. See also Augustin's answer to Evodius, in *Ep.* clix.; Chrysostom, *De Sacer.* vi. 4; and on Visions, see sec. 41, note, above.
7 Eph. ii. 2.
8 See note 5, p. 69, above.
9 2 Cor. xi. 14.
10 In his *De Civ. Dei*, x. 24, in speaking of the Incarnation of Christ as a mystery unintelligible to Porphyry's pride, he has a similar passage, in which he speaks of the "true and benignant Mediator," and the "malignant and deceitful mediators." See vii. sec. 24, above.
11 Rom. vi. 23.

CHAP. XLIII.—THAT JESUS CHRIST, AT THE SAME TIME GOD AND MAN, IS THE TRUE AND MOST EFFICACIOUS MEDIATOR.

68. But the true Mediator, whom in Thy secret mercy Thou hast pointed out to the humble, and didst send, that by His example[1] also they might learn the same humility—that "Mediator between God and men, the man Christ Jesus,"[2] appeared between mortal sinners and the immortal Just One—mortal with men, just with God; that because the reward of righteousness is life and peace, He might, by righteousness conjoined with God, cancel the death of justified sinners, which He willed to have in common with them.[3] Hence He was pointed out to holy men of old; to the intent that they, through faith in His Passion to come,[4] even as we through faith in that which is past, might be saved. For as man He was Mediator; but as the Word He was not between,[5] because equal to God, and God with God, and together with the Holy Spirit[6] one God.

69. How hast Thou loved us,[7] O good Father, who sparedst not Thine only Son, but deliveredst Him up for us wicked ones![8] How hast Thou loved us, for whom He, who thought it no robbery to be equal with Thee, "became obedient unto death, even the death of the cross;"[9] He alone "free among the dead,"[10] that had power to lay down His life, and power to take it again;[11] for us was He unto Thee both Victor and Victim, and the Victor as being the Victim; for us was He unto Thee both Priest and Sacrifice, and Priest as being the Sacrifice; of slaves making us Thy sons, by being born of Thee, and serving us. Rightly, then, is my hope strongly fixed on Him, that Thou wilt heal all my diseases[12] by Him who sitteth at Thy right hand and maketh intercession for us;[13] else should I utterly despair.[14] For numerous and great are my infirmities, yea, numerous and great are they; but Thy medicine is greater. We might think that Thy Word was removed from union with man, and despair of ourselves had He not been "made flesh and dwelt among us."[15]

70. Terrified by my sins and the load of my misery, I had resolved in my heart, and meditated flight into the wilderness;[16] but Thou didst forbid me, and didst strengthen me, saying, therefore, Christ "died for all, that they which live should not henceforth live unto themselves, but unto Him which died for them."[17] Behold, O Lord, I cast my care upon Thee,[18] that I may live, and "behold wondrous things out of Thy law."[19] Thou knowest my unskilfulness and my infirmities; teach me, and heal me. Thine only Son—He "in whom are hid all the treasures of wisdom and knowledge"[20]—hath redeemed me with His blood. Let not the proud speak evil of me,[21] because I consider my ransom, and eat and drink, and distribute; and poor, desire to be satisfied from Him, together with those who eat and are satisfied, and they praise the Lord that seek him.[22]

---

[1] See notes 3, p. 71, and 9 and 11, p. 74, above.

[2] 1 Tim. ii. 5.

[3] Not that our Lord is to be supposed, as some have held, to have been under the law of death in Adam, because "in Adam all die" (1 Cor. xv. 22; see the whole of c. 23, in *De Civ. Dei,* xiii., and compare sec. 34, note 3, above); for he says in *Serm.* ccxxxii. 5: "As there was nothing in us from which life could spring, so there was nothing in Him from which death could come." He *laid down* His life (John x. 18), and as being partaker of the divine nature, could *see no corruption* (Acts ii. 27). This is the explanation Augustin gives in his comment on Ps. lxxxv. 5 (quoted in the next section) of Christ's being "free among the dead." So also in his *De Trin.* xiii. 18, he says he was thus free because "solus enim a debito mortis liber est mortuus." The true analogy between the first and second Adam is surely then to be found in our Lord's being free from the law of death by reason of His divine nature, and Adam before his transgression being able to avert death by partaking of the Tree of Life. Christ was, it is true, a child of Adam, but a child of Adam miraculously born. See note 3, p. 73, above.

[4] See *De Trin.* iv. 2; and Trench, *Hulsean Lectures* (1845), latter part of lect. iv.

[5] *Medius,* alluding to *mediator* immediately before. See his *De Civ. Dei,* ix. 15, and xi. 2, for an enlargement of this distinction between Christ as man and Christ as the Word. Compare also *De Trin.* i. 20 and xiii. 13; and Mansel, *Bampton Lectures,* lect. v. note 20.

[6] Some MSS. omit *Cum spiritu sancto.*

[7] Christ did not, as in the words of a well-known hymn, "change the wrath to love." For, as Augustin remarks in a very beautiful passage in *Ev. Joh. Tract.* cx. 6, God loved us before the foundation of the world, and the reconcilement wrought by Christ must not be "so understood as if the Son reconciled us unto Him in this respect, that He now began to love those *whom He formerly hated,* in the same way as enemy is reconciled to enemy, so that thereafter they become friends, and mutual love takes the place of their mutual hatred; but we were reconciled unto Him who *already loved us,* but with whom we were at enmity because of our sin. Whether I say the truth on this let the apostle testify, when he says: 'God commendeth His love towards us, in that, while we were yet sinners, Christ died for us'" (Rom. v. 8, 9). He similarly applies the text last quoted in his *De Trin.* xiii. 15. See also *ibid.* sec. 21, where he speaks of the wrath of God, and *ibid.* iv. 2. Compare Archbishop Thomson, *Bampton Lectures,* lect. vii., and note 95.

[8] Rom. viii. 34, which is not "for us wicked ones," but "for us all," as the Authorized Version has it; and we must not narrow the words. Augustin, in *Ev. Joh. Tract.* cx. 2, it will be remembered, when commenting on John xvii. 21, "that they all may be one . . . that the world may believe Thou hast sent me," limits "the world" to the *believing world,* and continues (*ibid.* sec. 4), "Ipsi sunt enim mundus, non permanens inimicus, qualis est mundis damnationi prædestinatus." On Christ being a ransom for *all,* see Archbishop Thomson, *Bampton Lectures,* lect. vii. part 5, and note 101.

[9] Phil. ii. 6, 8.

[10] Ps. lxxxviii. 5; see sec. 68, note, above.

[11] John x. 18.

[12] Ps. ciii. 3.

[13] Rom. viii. 34.

[14] See note 11, p. 140, above.

[15] John i. 14.

[16] Ps. lv. 7.

[17] 2 Cor. v. 15.

[18] Ps. lv. 22.

[19] Ps. cxix. 18.

[20] Col. ii. 3. Compare Dean Mansel, *Bampton Lectures,* lect. v. and note 22.

[21] Ps. cxix. 122, *Old Ver.* He may perhaps here allude to the spiritual pride of the Donatists, who, holding rigid views as to purity of discipline, disparaged both his life and doctrine, pointing to his Manichæanism and the sinfulness of life before baptism. In his *Answer to Petilian,* iii. 11, 20, etc., and *Serm.* 3, sec. 19, on Ps. xxxvi., he alludes at length to the charges brought against him, referring then finally to his own confessions in book iii. above.

[22] Ps. xxii. 26. Augustin probably alludes here to the Lord's Supper, in accordance with the general Patristic interpretation.

BOOK XI.

THE DESIGN OF HIS CONFESSIONS BEING DECLARED, HE SEEKS FROM GOD THE KNOWLEDGE OF THE HOLY SCRIPTURES, AND BEGINS TO EXPOUND THE WORDS OF GENESIS I. I, CONCERNING THE CREATION OF THE WORLD. THE QUESTIONS OF RASH DISPUTERS BEING REFUTED, "WHAT DID GOD BEFORE HE CREATED THE WORLD?" THAT HE MIGHT THE BETTER OVERCOME HIS OPPONENTS, HE ADDS A COPIOUS DISQUISITION CONCERNING TIME.

CHAP. I.—BY CONFESSION HE DESIRES TO STIMULATE TOWARDS GOD HIS OWN LOVE AND THAT OF HIS READERS.

1. O LORD, since eternity is Thine, art Thou ignorant of the things which I say unto Thee? Or seest Thou at the time that which cometh to pass in time? Why, therefore, do I place before Thee so many relations of things? Not surely that Thou mightest know them through me, but that I may awaken my own love and that of my readers towards Thee, that we may all say, "Great is the Lord, and greatly to be praised."[1] I have already said, and shall say, for the love of Thy love do I this. For we also pray, and yet Truth says, "Your Father knoweth what things ye have need of before ye ask Him."[2] Therefore do we make known unto Thee our love, in confessing unto Thee our own miseries and Thy mercies upon us, that Thou mayest free us altogether, since Thou hast begun, that we may cease to be wretched in ourselves, and that we may be blessed in Thee; since Thou hast called us, that we may be poor in spirit, and meek, and mourners, and hungering and athirst after righteousness, and merciful, and pure in heart, and peacemakers.[3] Behold, I have told unto Thee many things, which I could and which I would, for Thou first wouldest that I should confess unto Thee, the Lord my God, for Thou art good, since Thy "mercy endureth for ever."[4]

CHAP. II—HE BEGS OF GOD THAT THROUGH THE HOLY SCRIPTURES HE MAY BE LED TO TRUTH.

2. But when shall I suffice with the tongue of my pen to express all Thy exhortations, and all Thy terrors, and comforts, and guidances, whereby Thou hast led me to preach Thy Word and to dispense Thy Sacrament[5] unto Thy people? And if I suffice to utter these things in order, the drops[6] of time are dear to me. Long time have I burned to meditate in Thy law, and in it to confess to Thee my knowledge and ignorance, the beginning of Thine enlightening, and the remains of my darkness, until infirmity be swallowed up by strength. And I would not that to aught else those hours should flow away, which I find free from the necessities of refreshing my body, and the care of my mind, and of the service which we owe to men, and which, though we owe not, even yet we pay.[7]

3. O Lord my God, hear my prayer, and let Thy mercy regard my longing, since it burns not for myself alone, but because it desires to benefit brotherly charity; and Thou seest into my heart, that so it is. I would sacrifice to Thee the service of my thought and tongue; and do Thou give what I may offer unto Thee. For "I am poor and needy,"[8] Thou rich unto all that call upon Thee,[9] who free from care carest for us. Circumcise from all rashness and

---

[5] He very touchingly alludes in *Serm.* ccclv. 2 to the way in which he was forced against his will (as was frequently the custom in those days), first, to become a presbyter (A.D. 391), and, four years later, coadjutor to Valerius, Bishop of Hippo (*Ep.* xxxi. 4, and *Ep.* ccxiii. 4), whom on his death he succeeded. His own wish was to establish a monastery, and to this end he sold his patrimony, "which consisted of only a few small fields" (*Ep.* cxxvi. 7). He absolutely dreaded to become a bishop, and as he knew his name was highly esteemed in the Church, he avoided cities in which the see was vacant. His former backsliding had made him humble; and he tells us in the sermon above referred to, "Cavebam hoc, et agebam quantam poteram, ut in loco humili salvarer *ne in alto periclitarer.*" Augustin also alludes to his ordination in *Ep.* xxi., addressed to Bishop Valerius.

[6] "He alludes to the hour-glasses of his time, which went by water, as ours do now by sand."—W. W.

[7] Augustin, in common with other bishops, had his time much invaded by those who sought his arbitration or judicial decision in secular matters, and in his *De Op. Monach.* sec. 37, he says, what many who have much mental toil will readily appreciate, that he would rather have spent the time not occupied in prayer and the study of the Scriptures in working with his hands, as did the monks, than have to bear these *tumultuosissimas perplexitates.* In the year 426 we find him (*Ep.* ccxiii.) designating Eraclius, in public assembly, as his successor in the see, and to relieve him (though, meanwhile, remaining a presbyter) of these anxious duties. See vi. sec. 15, and note 1, above; and also *ibid.* sec. 3.

[8] Ps. lxxxvi. 1.

[9] Rom. x. 12.

---

[1] Ps. xcvi. 4. See note 3, page 45, above.
[2] Matt. vi. 8.
[3] Matt. v. 3-9.
[4] Ps. cxviii. 1.

from all lying my inward and outward lips.[1] Let Thy Scriptures be my chaste delights. Neither let me be deceived in them, nor deceive out of them.[2] Lord, hear and pity, O Lord my God, light of the blind, and strength of the weak; even also light of those that see, and strength of the strong, hearken unto my soul, and hear it crying "out of the depths."[3] For unless Thine ears be present in the depths also, whither shall we go? whither shall we cry? "The day is Thine, and the night also is Thine."[4] At Thy nod the moments flee by. Grant thereof space for our meditations amongst the hidden things of Thy law, nor close it against us who knock. For not in vain hast Thou willed that the obscure secret of so many pages should be written. Nor is it that those forests have not their harts,[5] betaking themselves therein, and ranging, and walking, and feeding, lying down, and ruminating. Perfect me, O Lord, and reveal them unto me. Behold, Thy voice is my joy, Thy voice surpasseth the abundance of pleasures. Give that which I love, for I do love; and this hast Thou given. Abandon not Thine own gifts, nor despise Thy grass that thirsteth. Let me confess unto Thee whatsoever I shall have found in Thy books, and let me hear the voice of praise, and let me imbibe Thee, and reflect on the wonderful things of Thy law;[6] even from the beginning, wherein Thou madest the heaven and the earth, unto the everlasting kingdom of Thy holy city that is with Thee.

4. Lord, have mercy on me and hear my desire. For I think that it is not of the earth, nor of gold and silver, and precious stones, nor gorgeous apparel, nor honours and powers, nor the pleasures of the flesh, nor necessaries for the body, and this life of our pilgrimage; all which are added to those that seek Thy kingdom and Thy righteousness.[7] Behold, O Lord my God, whence is my desire. The unrighteous have told me of delights, but not such as Thy law, O Lord.[8] Behold whence is my desire. Behold, Father, look and see, and approve; and let it be pleasing in the sight of Thy mercy, that I may find grace before Thee, that the secret things of Thy Word may be opened unto me when I knock.[9] I beseech, by our Lord Jesus Christ, Thy Son, "the Man of Thy right hand, the Son of man, whom Thou madest strong for Thyself,"[10] as Thy Mediator and ours, through whom Thou hast sought us, although not seeking Thee, but didst seek us that we might seek Thee,[11]—Thy Word through whom Thou hast made all things,[12] and amongst them me also,— Thy Only-begotten, through whom Thou hast called to adoption the believing people, and therein me also. I beseech Thee through Him, who sitteth at Thy right hand, and "maketh intercession for us,"[13] "in whom are hid all treasures of wisdom and knowledge."[14] Him[15] do I seek in Thy books. Of Him did Moses write;[16] this saith Himself; this saith the Truth.

CHAP. III.—HE BEGINS FROM THE CREATION OF THE WORLD—NOT UNDERSTANDING THE HEBREW TEXT.

5. Let me hear and understand how in the beginning Thou didst make the heaven and the earth.[17] Moses wrote this; he wrote and departed,—passed hence from Thee to Thee. Nor now is he before me; for if he were I would hold him, and ask him, and would adjure him by Thee that he would open unto me these things, and I would lend the ears of my body to the sounds bursting forth from his mouth. And should he speak in the Hebrew tongue, in vain would it beat on my senses, nor would aught touch my mind; but if in Latin, I should know what he said. But whence should I know whether he said what was true? But if I knew this even, should I know it from him? Verily within me, within in the chamber of my thought,

---

[1] Ex. vi. 12.
[2] Augustin is always careful to distinguish between the certain truths of faith and doctrine which all may know, and the mysteries of Scripture which all have not the ability equally to apprehend. "Among the things," he says (De Doctr. Christ. ii. 14), "that are plainly laid down in Scripture, are to be found all matters that concern faith, and the manner of life." As to the Scriptures that are obscure, he is slow to come to conclusions, lest he should "be deceived in them or deceive out of them." In his De Gen. ad Lit. i. 37, he gives a useful warning against forcing our own meaning on Scripture in doubtful questions, and, ibid. viii. 5, we have the memorable words: "Melius est dubitare de rebus occultis, quam litigare de incertis." For examples of how careful he is in such matters not to go beyond what is written, see his answer to the question raised by Evodius,—a question which reminds us of certain modern speculations (see The Unseen Universe, arts. 61, 201, etc.), —whether the soul on departing from the body has not still a body of some kind, and at least some of the senses proper to a body; and also (Ep. clxiv.) his endeavours to unravel Evodius' difficulties as to Christ's preaching to the spirits in prison (1 Pet. iii. 18-21). Similarly, he says, as to the Antichrist of 2 Thess. ii. 1-7 (De Civ. Dei, xx. 19): "I frankly confess I know not what he means. I will, nevertheless, mention such conjectures as I have heard or read." See notes, pp. 64 and 92, above.
[3] Ps. cxxx. 1.
[4] Ps. lxxiv. 16.
[5] Ps. xxix. 9. In his comment on this place as given in the Old Version, "vox Domini perficientis cervos," he makes the forest with its thick darkness to symbolize the mysteries of Scripture, while the harts ruminating thereon represent the pious Christian meditating on those mysteries (see vi. sec. 3, above). In this same passage he speaks of those who are thus being perfected as overcoming the poisoned tongues. This is an allusion to the fabled power the stags had of enticing serpents from their holes by their breath, and then destroying them. Augustin is very fond of this kind of fable from natural history. In his Enarr. in Ps. cxxix. and cxli., we have similar allusions to the supposed habits of stags; and, ibid. ci., we have the well-known fable of the pelican in its charity reviving its young, and feeding them with its own blood. This use of fables was very common with the mediæval writers, and those familiar with the writings of the sixteenth and seventeenth centuries will recall many illustrations of it amongst the preachers of those days.
[6] Ps. xxvi. 7.

[7] Matt. vi. 33.
[8] Ps. cxix. 85.
[9] See p. 48, note 5, above.
[10] Ps. lxxx. 17.
[11] See note 9, p. 74, above.
[12] John i. 3.
[13] Rom. viii. 34.
[14] Col. ii. 3.
[15] Many MSS., however, read ipsos, and not ipsum.
[16] John v. 4-6.
[17] Gen. i. 1.

Truth, neither Hebrew,[1] nor Greek, nor Latin, nor barbarian, without the organs of voice and tongue, without the sound of syllables, would say, "He speaks the truth," and I, forthwith assured of it, confidently would say unto that man of Thine, "Thou speakest the truth." As, then, I cannot inquire of him, I beseech Thee,—Thee, O Truth, full of whom he spake truth,—Thee, my God, I beseech, forgive my sins; and do Thou, who didst give to that Thy servant to speak these things, grant to me also to understand them.

CHAP. IV.—HEAVEN AND EARTH CRY OUT THAT THEY HAVE BEEN CREATED BY GOD.

6. Behold, the heaven and earth are; they proclaim that they were made, for they are changed and varied. Whereas whatsoever hath not been made, and yet hath being, hath nothing in it which there was not before; this is what it is to be changed and varied. They also proclaim that they made not themselves; "therefore we are, because we have been made; we were not therefore before we were, so that we could have made ourselves." And the voice of those that speak is in itself an evidence. Thou, therefore, Lord, didst make these things; Thou who art beautiful, for they are beautiful; Thou who art good, for they are good; Thou who art, for they are. Nor even so are they beautiful, nor good, nor are they, as Thou their Creator art; compared with whom they are neither beautiful, nor good, nor are at all.[2] These things we know, thanks be to Thee. And our knowledge, compared with Thy knowledge, is ignorance.

CHAP. V.—GOD CREATED THE WORLD NOT FROM ANY CERTAIN MATTER, BUT IN HIS OWN WORD.

7. But how didst Thou make the heaven and the earth, and what was the instrument of Thy so mighty work? For it was not as a human worker fashioning body from body, according to the fancy of his mind, in somewise able to assign a form which it perceives in itself by its inner eye.[3] And whence should he be able to do this, hadst not Thou made that mind? And he assigns to it already existing, and as it were having a being, a form, as clay, or stone, or wood, or gold, or such like. And whence should these things be, hadst not Thou appointed them? Thou didst make for the workman his body,—Thou the mind commanding the limbs,—Thou the matter whereof he makes anything,[4]—Thou the capacity whereby he may apprehend his art, and see within what he may do without,—Thou the sense of his body, by which, as by an interpreter, he may from mind unto matter convey that which he doeth, and report to his mind what may have been done, that it within may consult the truth, presiding over itself, whether it be well done. All these things praise Thee, the Creator of all. But how dost Thou make them? How, O God, didst Thou make heaven and earth? Truly, neither in the heaven nor in the earth didst Thou make heaven and earth; nor in the air, nor in the waters, since these also belong to the heaven and the earth; nor in the whole world didst Thou make the whole world; because there was no place wherein it could be made before it was made, that it might be; nor didst Thou hold anything in Thy hand wherewith to make heaven and earth. For whence couldest Thou have what Thou hadst not made, whereof to make anything? For what is, save because Thou art? Therefore Thou didst speak and they were made,[5] and in Thy Word Thou madest these things.[6]

CHAP. VI.—HE DID NOT, HOWEVER, CREATE IT BY A SOUNDING AND PASSING WORD.

8. But how didst Thou speak? Was it in that manner in which the voice came from the cloud, saying, "This is my beloved Son"?[7] For that voice was uttered and passed away, began and ended. The syllables sounded and passed by, the second after the first, the third after the second, and thence in order, until the last after the rest, and silence after the last. Hence it is clear and plain that the motion of a creature expressed it, itself temporal, obeying Thy Eternal will. And these thy words formed at the time, the outer ear conveyed to the intel-

---

[1] Augustin was not singular amongst the early Fathers in not knowing Hebrew, for of the Greeks only Origen, and of the Latins Jerome, knew anything of it. We find him confessing his ignorance both here and elsewhere (*Enarr. in Ps.* cxxxvi. 7, and *De Doctr. Christ.* ii. 22); and though he recommends a knowledge of Hebrew as well as Greek, to correct "the endless diversity of the Latin translators" (*De Doctr. Christ.* ii. 16); he speaks as strongly as does Grinfield, in his *Apology for the Septuagint*, in favour of the claims of that version to "biblical and canonical authority" (*Eps.* xxviii., lxxi., and lxxv.; *De Civ. Dei*, xviii. 42, 43; *De Doctr. Christ.* ii. 22). He discountenanced Jerome's new translation, probably from fear of giving offence, and, as we gather from *Ep.* lxxi. 5, not without cause. From the tumult he there describes as ensuing upon Jerome's version being read, the outcry would appear to have been as great as when, on the change of the old style of reckoning to the new, the ignorant mob clamoured to have their eleven days! [2] It was the doctrine of Aristotle that excellence of character is the proper object of love, and in proportion as we recognise such excellence in others are we attracted to become like them (see Sidgwick's *Methods of Ethics*, book iv. c. 5, sec. 4). If this be true of the creature, how much more should it be so of the Creator, who is the perfection of all that we can conceive of goodness and truth. Compare *De Trin.* viii. 3–6, *De Vera Relig.* 57, and an extract from Athanase Coquerel in Archbishop Thomson's *Bampton Lectures*, note 73.

[3] See x. sec. 40, note 6, and sec. 53, above. [4] That is, the artificer makes, God creates. **The creation of matter** is distinctively a doctrine of revelation. The ancient philosophers believed in the eternity of matter. As Lucretius puts it (i. 51): "Nullam rem e nihilo gigni divinitus unquam." See Burton, *Bampton Lectures*, lect. iii. and notes 18–21, and Mansel, *Bampton Lectures*, lect. iii. note 12. See also p. 76, note 8, above, for the Manichæan doctrine as to the ὕλη; and *The Unseen Universe*, arts. 85, 86, 151, and 160, for the modern doctrine of " continuity." See also Kalisch, *Commentary* on Gen. i. 1. [5] Ps. xxxiii. 9. [6] *Ibid.* ver. 6. [7] Matt. xvii. 5.

ligent mind, whose inner ear lay attentive to Thy eternal word. But it compared these words sounding in time with Thy eternal word in silence, and said, "It is different, very different. These words are far beneath me, nor are they, since they flee and pass away; but the Word of my Lord remaineth above me for ever." If, then, in sounding and fleeting words Thou didst say that heaven and earth should be made, and didst thus make heaven and earth, there was already a corporeal creature before heaven and earth by whose temporal motions that voice might take its course in time. But there was nothing corporeal before heaven and earth; or if there were, certainly Thou without a transitory voice hadst created that whence Thou wouldest make the passing voice, by which to say that the heaven and the earth should be made. For whatsoever that were of which such a voice was made, unless it were made by Thee, it could not be at all. By what word of Thine was it decreed that a body might be made, whereby these words might be made?

CHAP. VII.—BY HIS CO-ETERNAL WORD HE SPEAKS, AND ALL THINGS ARE DONE.

9. Thou callest us, therefore, to understand the Word, God with Thee, God,[1] which is spoken eternally, and by it are all things spoken eternally. For what was spoken was not finished, and another spoken until all were spoken; but all things at once and for ever. For otherwise have we time and change, and not a true eternity, nor a true immortality. This I know, O my God, and give thanks. I know, I confess to Thee, O Lord, and whosoever is not unthankful to certain truth, knows and blesses Thee with me. We know, O Lord, we know; since in proportion as anything is not what it was, and is what it was not, in that proportion does it die and arise. Not anything, therefore, of Thy Word giveth place and cometh into place again, because it is truly immortal and eternal. And, therefore, unto the Word co-eternal with Thee, Thou dost at once and for ever say all that Thou dost say; and whatever Thou sayest shall be made, is made; nor dost Thou make otherwise than by speaking; yet all things are not made both together and ever-lasting which Thou makest by speaking

CHAP. VIII.—THAT WORD ITSELF IS THE BEGIN-NING OF ALL THINGS, IN THE WHICH WE ARE INSTRUCTED AS TO EVANGELICAL TRUTH.

10. Why is this, I beseech Thee, O Lord my God? I see it, however; but how I shall express it, I know not, unless that everything which begins to be and ceases to be, then begins and

ceases when in Thy eternal Reason it is known that it ought to begin or cease where nothing beginneth or ceaseth. The same is Thy Word, which is also "the Beginning," because also It speaketh unto us.[2] Thus, in the gospel He speaketh through the flesh; and this sounded outwardly in the ears of men, that it might be believed and sought inwardly, and that it might be found in the eternal Truth, where the good and only Master teacheth all His disciples. There, O Lord, I hear Thy voice, the voice of one speaking unto me, since He speaketh unto us who teacheth us. But He that teachth us not, although He speaketh, speaketh not to us. Moreover, who teacheth us, unless it be the immutable Truth? For even when we are admonished through a changeable creature, we are led to the Truth immutable. There we learn truly while we stand and hear Him, and rejoice greatly "because of the Bridegroom's voice,"[3] restoring us to that whence we are. And, therefore, the Beginning, because unless It remained, there would not, where we strayed, be whither to return. But when we return from error, it is by knowing that we return. But that we may know, He teacheth us, because He is the Beginning and speaketh unto us.

CHAP. IX.—WISDOM AND THE BEGINNING.

11. In this Beginning, O God, hast Thou made heaven and earth,—in Thy Word, in Thy Son, in Thy Power, in Thy Wisdom, in Thy Truth, wondrously speaking and wondrously making. Who shall comprehend? who shall relate it? What is that which shines through me, and strikes my heart without injury, and I both shudder and burn? I shudder inasmuch as I am unlike it; and I burn inasmuch as I am like it. It is Wisdom itself that shines through me, clearing my cloudiness, which again over-whelms me, fainting from it, in the darkness and amount of my punishment. For my strength is brought down in need,[4] so that I cannot endure my blessings, until Thou, O Lord, who hast

---

[1] John i. 1.

[2] John viii. 25, *Old Ver.* Though some would read, *Qui et loquitur*, making it correspond to the Vulgate, instead of *Quia et loquitur*, as above, the latter is doubtless the correct reading, since we find the text similarly quoted *In Ev. Joh. Tract.* xxxviii. 11, where he enlarges on "The Beginning," comparing *principium* with ἀρχή. It will assist to the understanding of this section to refer to the early part of the note on p. 107, above, where the Platonic view of the *Logos*, as ἐνδιάθετος and προφορικός, or in the "bosom of the Father" and "made flesh," is given; which terminology, as Dr. Newman tells us (*Arians*, pt. i. c. 2, sec. 4), was accepted by the Church. Augustin, consistently with this idea, says (on John viii. 25, as above): "For if the Beginning, as it is in itself, had remained so with the Father as not to receive the form of a servant and speak as man with men, how could they have believed in Him, since their weak hearts could not have heard the word intelligently without some voice that would appeal to their senses? Therefore, said He, believe me to be the Beginning; for that you may believe, I not only am, but also speak to you." Newman, as quoted above, may be referred to for the significance of ἀρχή as applied to the Son, and *ibid.* sec. 3, also, on the "Word." For the difference between a mere "voice" and the "Word," compare Aug. *Serm.* ccxciii. sec. 3, and Origen, *In Joann.* ii. 36.

[3] John iii. 29.

[4] Ps. xxxi. 10.

been gracious to all mine iniquities, heal also all mine infirmities; because Thou shalt also redeem my life from corruption, and crown me with Thy loving-kindness and mercy, and shalt satisfy my desire with good things, because my youth shall be renewed like the eagle's.[1] For by hope we are saved; and through patience we await Thy promises.[2] Let him that is able hear Thee discoursing within. I will with confidence cry out from Thy oracle, How wonderful are Thy works, O Lord, in Wisdom hast Thou made them all.[3] And this Wisdom is the Beginning, and in that Beginning hast Thou made heaven and earth.

CHAP. X.—THE RASHNESS OF THOSE WHO INQUIRE WHAT GOD DID BEFORE HE CREATED HEAVEN AND EARTH.

12. Lo, are they not full of their ancient way, who say to us, "What was God doing before He made heaven and earth? For if," say they, "He were unoccupied, and did nothing, why does He not for ever also, and from henceforth, cease from working, as in times past He did? For if any new motion has arisen in God, and a new will, to form a creature which He had never before formed, however can that be a true eternity where there ariseth a will which was not before? For the will of God is not a creature, but before the creature; because nothing could be created unless the will of the Creator were before it. The will of God, therefore, pertaineth to His very Substance. But if anything hath arisen in the Substance of God which was not before, that Substance is not truly called eternal. But if it was the eternal will of God that the creature should be, why was not the creature also from eternity?"

CHAP. XI.—THEY WHO ASK THIS HAVE NOT AS YET KNOWN THE ETERNITY OF GOD, WHICH IS EXEMPT FROM THE RELATION OF TIME.

13. Those who say these things do not as yet understand Thee, O Thou Wisdom of God, Thou light of souls; not as yet do they understand how these things be made which are made by and in Thee. They even endeavour to comprehend things eternal; but as yet their heart flieth about in the past and future motions of things, and is still wavering. Who shall hold it and fix it, that it may rest a little, and by degrees catch the glory of that ever-standing eternity, and compare it with the times which never stand, and see that it is incomparable; and that a long time cannot become long, save from the many motions that pass by, which cannot at the same

instant be prolonged; but that in the Eternal nothing passeth away, but that the whole is present; but no time is wholly present; and let him see that all time past is forced on by the future, and that all the future followeth from the past, and that all, both past and future, is created and issues from that which is always present? Who will hold the heart of man, that it may stand still, and see how the still-standing eternity, itself neither future nor past, uttereth the times future and past? Can my hand accomplish this, or the hand of my mouth by persuasion bring about a thing so great?[4]

CHAP. XII.—WHAT GOD DID BEFORE THE CREATION OF THE WORLD.

14. Behold, I answer to him who asks, "What was God doing before He made heaven and earth?" I answer not, as a certain person is reported to have done facetiously (avoiding the pressure of the question), "He was preparing hell," saith he, "for those who pry into mysteries." It is one thing to perceive, another to laugh,—these things I answer not. For more willingly would I have answered, "I know not what I know not," than that I should make him a laughing-stock who asketh deep things, and gain praise as one who answereth false things. But I say that Thou, our God, art the Creator of every creature; and if by the term "heaven and earth" every creature is understood, I boldly say, "That before God made heaven and earth, He made not anything. For if He did, what did He make unless the creature?" And would that I knew whatever I desire to know to my advantage, as I know that no creature was made before any creature was made.

CHAP. XIII.—BEFORE THE TIMES CREATED BY GOD, TIMES WERE NOT.

15. But if the roving thought of any one should wander through the images of bygone time, and wonder that Thou, the God Almighty, and All-creating, and All-sustaining, the Architect of heaven and earth, didst for innumerable ages refrain from so great a work before Thou wouldst make it, let him awake and consider that he wonders at false things. For whence could innumerable ages pass by which Thou didst not make, since Thou art the Author and Creator of all ages? Or what times should those be which were not made by Thee? Or how should they pass by if they had not been? Since, therefore, Thou art the Creator of all times, if any time was before Thou madest heaven and earth, why is it said that Thou didst refrain from working? For that very time Thou madest, nor could times pass by before Thou madest times.

---

[1] Ps. ciii. 3–5.
[2] Rom viii. 24, 25.
[3] Ps. civ. 24.

[4] See note 12, p. 174, below.

But if before heaven and earth there was no time, why is it asked, What didst Thou then? For there was no "then" when time was not.

16. Nor dost Thou by time precede time; else wouldest not Thou precede all times. But in the excellency of an ever-present eternity, Thou precedest all times past, and survivest all future times, because they are future, and when they have come they will be past; but "Thou art the same, and Thy years shall have no end." [1] Thy years neither go nor come; but ours both go and come, that all may come. All Thy years stand at once since they do stand; nor were they when departing excluded by coming years, because they pass not away; but all these of ours shall be when all shall cease to be. Thy years are one day, and Thy day is not daily, but to-day; because Thy to-day yields not with to-morrow, for neither doth it follow yesterday. Thy to-day is eternity; therefore didst Thou beget the Co-eternal, to whom Thou saidst, "This day have I begotten Thee." [2] Thou hast made all time; and before all times Thou art, nor in any time was there not time.

CHAP. XIV.—NEITHER TIME PAST NOR FUTURE, BUT THE PRESENT ONLY, REALLY IS.

17. At no time, therefore, hadst Thou not made anything, because Thou hadst made time itself. And no times are co-eternal with Thee, because Thou remainest for ever; but should these continue, they would not be times. For what is time? Who can easily and briefly explain it? Who even in thought can comprehend it, even to the pronouncing of a word concerning it? But what in speaking do we refer to more familiarly and knowingly than time? And certainly we understand when we speak of it; we understand also when we hear it spoken of by another. What, then, is time? If no one ask of me, I know; if I wish to explain to him who asks, I know not. Yet I say with confidence, that I know that if nothing passed away, there would not be past time; and if nothing were coming, there would not be future time; and if nothing were, there would not be present time. Those two times, therefore, past and future, how are they, when even the past now is not, and the future is not as yet? But should the present be always present, and should it not pass into time past, time truly it could not be, but eternity. If, then, time present—if it be time —only comes into existence because it passes into time past, how do we say that even this is, whose cause of being is that it shall not be— namely, so that we cannot truly say that time is, unless because it tends not to be?

[1] Ps. cii. 27.
[2] Ps. ii. 7, and Heb. v. 5.

CHAP. XV.—THERE IS ONLY A MOMENT OF PRESENT TIME.

18. And yet we say that "time is long and time is short;" nor do we speak of this save of time past and future. A long time past, for example, we call a hundred years ago; in like manner a long time to come, a hundred years hence. But a short time past we call, say, ten days ago: and a short time to come, ten days hence. But in what sense is that long or short which is not? For the past is not now, and the future is not yet. Therefore let us not say, "It is long;" but let us say of the past, "It hath been long," and of the future, "It will be long." O my Lord, my light, shall not even here Thy truth deride man? For that past time which was long, was it long when it was already past, or when it was as yet present? For then it might be long when there was that which could be long, but when past it no longer was; wherefore that could not be long which was not at all. Let us not, therefore, say, "Time past hath been long;" for we shall not find what may have been long, seeing that since it was past it is not; but let us say "that present time was long, because when it was present it was long." For it had not as yet passed away so as not to be, and therefore there was that which could be long. But after it passed, that ceased also to be long which ceased to be.

19. Let us therefore see, O human soul, whether present time can be long; for to thee is it given to perceive and to measure periods of time. What wilt thou reply to me? Is a hundred years when present a long time? See, first, whether a hundred years can be present. For if the first year of these is current, that is present, but the other ninety and nine are future, and therefore they are not as yet. But if the second year is current, one is already past, the other present, the rest future. And thus, if we fix on any middle year of this hundred as present, those before it are past, those after it are future; wherefore a hundred years cannot be present. See at least whether that year itself which is current can be present. For if its first month be current, the rest are future; if the second, the first hath already passed, and the remainder are not yet. Therefore neither is the year which is current as a whole present; and if it is not present as a whole, then the year is not present. For twelve months make the year, of which each individual month which is current is itself present, but the rest are either past or future. Although neither is that month which is current present, but one day only: if the first, the rest being to come, if the last, the rest being past; if any of the middle, then between past and future.

20. Behold, the present time, which alone we

found could be called long, is abridged to the space scarcely of one day. But let us discuss even that, for there is not one day present as a whole. For it is made up of four-and-twenty hours of night and day, whereof the first hath the rest future, the last hath them past, but any one of the intervening hath those before it past, those after it future. And that one hour passeth away in fleeting particles. Whatever of it hath flown away is past, whatever remaineth is future. If any portion of time be conceived which cannot now be divided into even the minutest particles of moments, this only is that which may be called present; which, however, flies so rapidly from future to past, that it cannot be extended by any delay. For if it be extended, it is divided into the past and future; but the present hath no space. Where, therefore, is the time which we may call long? Is it future? Indeed we do not say, "It is long," because it is not yet, so as to be long; but we say, "It will be long." When, then, will it be? For if even then, since as yet it is future, it will not be long, because what may be long is not as yet; but it shall be long, when from the future, which as yet is not, it shall already have begun to be, and will have become present, so that there could be that which may be long; then doth the present time cry out in the words above that it cannot be long.

CHAP. XVI.—TIME CAN ONLY BE PERCEIVED OR MEASURED WHILE IT IS PASSING.

21. And yet, O Lord, we perceive intervals of times, and we compare them with themselves, and we say some are longer, others shorter. We even measure by how much shorter or longer this time may be than that; and we answer, "That this is double or treble, while that is but once, or only as much as that." But we measure times passing when we measure them by perceiving them; but past times, which now are not, or future times, which as yet are not, who can measure them? Unless, perchance, any one will dare to say, that that can be measured which is not. When, therefore, time is passing, it can be perceived and measured; but when it has passed, it cannot, since it is not.

CHAP. XVII.—NEVERTHELESS THERE IS TIME PAST AND FUTURE.

22. I ask, Father, I do not affirm. O my God, rule and guide me. "Who is there who can say to me that there are not three times (as we learned when boys, and as we have taught boys), the past, present, and future, but only present, because these two are not? Or are they also; but when from future it becometh present, cometh it forth from some secret place, and when from the present it becometh past, doth it retire into anything secret? For where have they, who have foretold future things, seen these things, if as yet they are not? For that which is not cannot be seen. And they who relate things past could not relate them as true, did they not perceive them in their mind. Which things, if they were not, they could in no wise be discerned. There are therefore things both future and past.

CHAP. XVIII.—PAST AND FUTURE TIMES CANNOT BE THOUGHT OF BUT AS PRESENT.

23. Suffer me, O Lord, to seek further; O my Hope, let not my purpose be confounded. For if there are times past and future, I desire to know where they are. But if as yet I do not succeed, I still know, wherever they are, that they are not there as future or past, but as present. For if there also they be future, they are not as yet there; if even there they be past, they are no longer there. Wheresoever, therefore, they are, whatsoever they are, they are only so as present. Although past things are related as true, they are drawn out from the memory,—not the things themselves, which have passed, but the words conceived from the images of the things which they have formed in the mind as footprints in their passage through the senses. My childhood, indeed, which no longer is, is in time past, which now is not; but when I call to mind its image, and speak of it, I behold it in the present, because it is as yet in my memory. Whether there be a like cause of foretelling future things, that of things which as yet are not the images may be perceived as already existing, I confess, my God, I know not. This certainly I know, that we generally think before on our future actions, and that this premeditation is present; but that the action whereon we premeditate is not yet, because it is future; which when we shall have entered upon, and have begun to do that which we were premeditating, then shall that action be, because then it is not future, but present.

24. In whatever manner, therefore, this secret preconception of future things may be, nothing can be seen, save what is. But what now is is not future, but present. When, therefore, they say that things future are seen, it is not themselves, which as yet are not (that is, which are future); but their causes or their signs perhaps are seen, the which already are. Therefore, to those already beholding them, they are not future, but present, from which future things conceived in the mind are foretold. Which conceptions again now are, and they who foretell those things behold these conceptions present before them. Let now so multitudinous a variety of things afford me some example. I

behold daybreak; I foretell that the sun is about to rise. That which I behold is present; what I foretell is future,—not that the sun is future, which already is; but his rising, which is not yet. Yet even its rising I could not predict unless I had an image of it in my mind, as now I have while I speak. But that dawn which I see in the sky is not the rising of the sun, although it may go before it, nor that imagination in my mind; which two are seen as present, that the other which is future may be foretold. Future things, therefore, are not as yet; and if they are not as yet, they are not. And if they are not, they cannot be seen at all; but they can be foretold from things present which now are, and are seen.

CHAP. XIX.—WE ARE IGNORANT IN WHAT MANNER GOD TEACHES FUTURE THINGS.

25. Thou, therefore, Ruler of Thy creatures, what is the method by which Thou teachest souls those things which are future? For Thou hast taught Thy prophets. What is that way by which Thou, to whom nothing is future, dost teach future things; or rather of future things dost teach present? For what is not, of a certainty cannot be taught. Too far is this way from my view; it is too mighty for me, I cannot attain unto it;[1] but by Thee I shall be enabled, when Thou shalt have granted it, sweet light of my hidden eyes.

CHAP. XX.—IN WHAT MANNER TIME MAY PROPERLY BE DESIGNATED.

26. But what now is manifest and clear is, that neither are there future nor past things. Nor is it fitly said, "There are three times, past, present and future;" but perchance it might be fitly said, "There are three times; a present of things past, a present of things present, and a present of things future." For these three do somehow exist in the soul, and otherwise I see them not: present of things past, memory; present of things present, sight; present of things future, expectation. If of these things we are permitted to speak, I see three times, and I grant there are three. It may also be said, "There are three times, past, present and future," as usage falsely has it. See, I trouble not, nor gainsay, nor reprove; provided always that which is said may be understood, that neither the future, nor that which is past, now is. For there are but few things which we speak properly, many things improperly; but what we may wish to say is understood.

CHAP. XXI.—HOW TIME MAY BE MEASURED.

27. I have just now said, then, that we measure times as they pass, that we may be able

to say that this time is twice as much as that one, or that this is only as much as that, and so of any other of the parts of time which we are able to tell by measuring. Wherefore, as I said, we measure times as they pass. And if any one should ask me, "Whence dost thou know?" I can answer, "I know, because we measure; nor can we measure things that are not; and things past and future are not." But how do we measure present time, since it hath not space? It is measured while it passeth; but when it shall have passed, it is not measured; for there will not be aught that can be measured. But whence, in what way, and whither doth it pass while it is being measured? Whence, but from the future? Which way, save through the present? Whither, but into the past? From that, therefore, which as yet is not, through that which hath no space, into that which now is not. But what do we measure, unless time in some space? For we say not single, and double, and triple, and equal, or in any other way in which we speak of time, unless with respect to the spaces of times. In what space, then, do we measure passing time? Is it in the future, whence it passeth over? But what yet we measure not, is not. Or is it in the present, by which it passeth? But no space, we do not measure. Or in the past, whither it passeth? But that which is not now, we measure not.

CHAP. XXII.—HE PRAYS GOD THAT HE WOULD EXPLAIN THIS MOST ENTANGLED ENIGMA.

28. My soul yearns to know this most entangled enigma. Forbear to shut up, O Lord my God, good Father,—through Christ I beseech Thee,—forbear to shut up these things, both usual and hidden, from my desire, that it may be hindered from penetrating them; but let them dawn through Thy enlightening mercy, O Lord. Of whom shall I inquire concerning these things? And to whom shall I with more advantage confess my ignorance than to Thee, to whom these my studies, so vehemently kindled towards Thy Scriptures, are not troublesome? Give that which I love; for I do love, and this hast Thou given me. Give, Father, who truly knowest to give good gifts unto Thy children.[2] Give, since I have undertaken to know, and trouble is before me until Thou dost open it.[3] Through Christ, I beseech Thee, in His name, Holy of Holies, let no man interrupt me. For I believed, and therefore do I speak.[4] This is my hope; for this do I live, that I may contemplate the delights of the Lord.[5] Behold, Thou hast made my days old,[6] and they pass away, and

---

[1] Ps. cxxxix. 6.

[2] Matt. vii. 11.
[3] Ps. lxxiii. 16.
[4] Ps. cxvi. 10.
[5] Ps. xxvii. 4.
[6] Ps. xxxix. 5.

in what manner I know not. And we speak as to time and time, times and times,—"How long is the time since he said this?" "How long the time since he did this?" and, "How long the time since I saw that?" and, "This syllable hath double the time of that single short syllable." These words we speak, and these we hear; and we are understood, and we understand. They are most manifest and most usual, and the same things again lie hid too deeply, and the discovery of them is new.

CHAP. XXIII.—THAT TIME IS A CERTAIN EXTENSION.

29. I have heard from a learned man that the motions of the sun, moon, and stars constituted time, and I assented not.[1] For why should not rather the motions of all bodies be time? What if the lights of heaven should cease, and a potter's wheel run round, would there be no time by which we might measure those revolutions, and say either that it turned with equal pauses, or, if it were moved at one time more slowly, at another more quickly, that some revolutions were longer, others less so? Or while we were saying this, should we not also be speaking in time? Or should there in our words be some syllables long, others short, but because those sounded in a longer time, these in a shorter? God grant to men to see in a small thing ideas common to things great and small. Both the stars and luminaries of heaven are "for signs and for seasons, and for days and years."[2] No doubt they are; but neither should I say that the circuit of that wooden wheel was a day, nor yet should he say that therefore there was no time.

30. I desire to know the power and nature of time, by which we measure the motions of bodies, and say (for example) that this motion is twice as long as that. For, I ask, since "day" declares not the stay only of the sun upon the earth, according to which day is one thing, night another, but also its entire circuit from east even to east,—according to which we say, "So many days have passed" (the nights being included when we say "so many days," and their spaces not counted apart),—since, then, the day is finished by the motion of the

sun, and by his circuit from east to east, I ask, whether the motion itself is the day, or the period in which that motion is completed, or both? For if the first be the day, then would there be a day although the sun should finish that course in so small a space of time as an hour. If the second, then that would not be a day if from one sunrise to another there were but so short a period as an hour, but the sun must go round four-and-twenty times to complete a day. If both, neither could that be called a day if the sun should run his entire round in the space of an hour; nor that, if, while the sun stood still, so much time should pass as the sun is accustomed to accomplish his whole course in from morning to morning. I shall not therefore now ask, what that is which is called day, but what time is, by which we, measuring the circuit of the sun, should say that it was accomplished in half the space of time it was wont, if it had been completed in so small a space as twelve hours; and comparing both times, we should call that single, this double time, although the sun should run his course from east to east sometimes in that single, sometimes in that double time. Let no man then tell me that the motions of the heavenly bodies are times, because, when at the prayer of one the sun stood still in order that he might achieve his victorious battle, the sun stood still, but time went on. For in such space of time as was sufficient was that battle fought and ended.[3] I see that time, then, is a certain extension. But do I see it, or do I seem to see it? Thou, O Light and Truth, wilt show me.

CHAP. XXIV.—THAT TIME IS NOT A MOTION OF A BODY WHICH WE MEASURE BY TIME.

31. Dost Thou command that I should assent, if any one should say that time is "the motion of a body?" Thou dost not command me. For I hear that no body is moved but in time. This Thou sayest; but that the very motion of a body is time, I hear not; Thou sayest it not. For when a body is moved, I by time measure how long it may be moving from the time in which it began to be moved till it left off. And if I saw not whence it began, and it continued to be moved, so that I see not when it leaves off, I cannot measure unless, perchance, from the time I began until I cease to see. But if I look long, I only proclaim that the time is long, but not how long it may be; because when we say, "How long," we speak by comparison, as, "This is as long as that," or, "This is double as long as that," or any other thing of the kind. But if we were able to note down the distances of places whence and whither cometh the body

---

1 Compare Gillies (*Analysis of Aristotle*, c. 2, p. 138): "As our conception of space originates in that of body, and our conception of motion in that of space, so our conception of time originates in that of motion; and particularly in those regular and equable motions carried on in the heavens, the parts of which, from their perfect similarity to each other, are correct measures of the continuous and successive quantity called Time, with which they are conceived to co-exist. Time, therefore, may be defined the perceived number of successive movements; for, as number ascertains the greater or lesser quantity of things numbered, so time ascertains the greater or lesser quantity of motion performed." And with this accords Monboddo's definition of time (*Ancient Metaphysics*, vol. i. book 4, chap. i.), as "the measure of the duration of things that exist in succession by the motion of the heavenly bodies." See xii. sec. 40, and note, below.
2 Gen. i. 14.

3 Josh. x. 12-14.

which is moved, or its parts, if it moved as in a wheel, we can say in how much time the motion of the body or its part, from this place unto that, was performed. Since, then, the motion of a body is one thing, that by which we measure how long it is another, who cannot see which of these is rather to be called time? For, although a body be sometimes moved, sometimes stand still, we measure not its motion only, but also its standing still, by time; and we say, "It stood still as much as it moved;" or, "It stood still twice or thrice as long as it moved;" and if any other space which our measuring hath either determined or imagined, more or less, as we are accustomed to say. Time, therefore, is not the motion of a body.

CHAP. XXV.—HE CALLS ON GOD TO ENLIGHTEN HIS MIND.

32. And I confess unto Thee, O Lord, that I am as yet ignorant as to what time is, and again I confess unto Thee, O Lord, that I know that I speak these things in time, and that I have already long spoken of time, and that very "long" is not long save by the stay of time. How, then, know I this, when I know not what time is? Or is it, perchance, that I know not in what wise I may express what I know? Alas for me, that I do not at least know the extent of my own ignorance! Behold, O my God, before Thee I lie not. As I speak, so is my heart. Thou shalt light my candle; Thou, O Lord my God, wilt enlighten my darkness.[1]

CHAP. XXVI.—WE MEASURE LONGER EVENTS BY SHORTER IN TIME.

33. Doth not my soul pour out unto Thee truly in confession that I do measure times? But do I thus measure, O my God, and know not what I measure? I measure the motion of a body by time; and the time itself do I not measure? But, in truth, could I measure the motion of a body, how long it is, and how long it is in coming from this place to that, unless I should measure the time in which it is moved? How, therefore, do I measure this very time itself? Or do we by a shorter time measure a longer, as by the space of a cubit the space of a crossbeam? For thus, indeed, we seem by the space of a short syllable to measure the space of a long syllable, and to say that this is double. Thus we measure the spaces of stanzas by the spaces of the verses, and the spaces of the verses by the spaces of the feet, and the spaces of the feet by the spaces of the syllables, and the spaces of long by the spaces of short syllables; not measuring by pages (for in that manner we measure spaces, not times), but when in uttering the words they pass by, and we say, "It is a long stanza because it is made up of so many verses; long verses, because they consist of so many feet; long feet, because they are prolonged by so many syllables; a long syllable, because double a short one." But neither thus is any certain measure of time obtained; since it is possible that a shorter verse, if it be pronounced more fully, may take up more time than a longer one, if pronounced more hurriedly. Thus for a stanzas, thus for a foot, thus for a syllable. Whence it appeared to me that time is nothing else than protraction; but of what I know not. It is wonderful to me, if it be not of the mind itself. For what do I measure, I beseech Thee, O my God, even when I say either indefinitely, "This time is longer than that;" or even definitely, "This is double that?" That I measure time, I know. But I measure not the future, for it is not yet; nor do I measure the present, because it is extended by no space; nor do I measure the past, because it no longer is. What, therefore, do I measure? Is it times passing, not past? For thus had I said.

CHAP. XXVII.—TIMES ARE MEASURED IN PROPORTION AS THEY PASS BY.

34. Persevere, O my mind, and give earnest heed. God is our helper; He made us, and not ourselves.[2] Give heed, where truth dawns. Lo, suppose the voice of a body begins to sound, and does sound, and sounds on, and lo! it ceases,—it is now silence, and that voice is past and is no longer a voice. It was future before it sounded, and could not be measured, because as yet it was not; and now it cannot, because it longer is. Then, therefore, while it was sounding, it might, because there was then that which might be measured. But even then it did not stand still, for it was going and passing away. Could it, then, on that account be measured the more? For, while passing, it was being extended into some space of time, in which it might be measured, since the present hath no space. If, therefore, then it might be measured, lo! suppose another voice hath begun to sound, and still soundeth, in a continued tenor without any interruption, we can measure it while it is sounding; for when it shall have ceased to sound, it will be already past, and there will not be that which can be measured. Let us measure it truly, and let us say how much it is. But as yet it sounds, nor can it be measured, save from that instant in which it began to sound, even to the end in which it left off. For the interval itself we measure from

---

[1] Ps. xviii. 28.   [2] Ps. c. 3.

some beginning unto some end. On which account, a voice which is not yet ended cannot be measured, so that it may be said how long or how short it may be; nor can it be said to be equal to another, or single or double in respect of it, or the like. But when it is ended, it no longer is. In what manner, therefore, may it be measured? And yet we measure times; still not those which as yet are not, nor those which no longer are, nor those which are protracted by some delay, nor those which have no limits. We, therefore, measure neither future times, nor past, nor present, nor those passing by; and yet we do measure times.

35. *Deus Creator omnium;* this verse of eight syllables alternates between short and long syllables. The four short, then, the first, third, fifth and seventh, are single in respect of the four long, the second, fourth, sixth, and eighth. Each of these hath a double time to every one of those. I pronounce them, report on them, and thus it is, as is perceived by common sense. By common sense, then, I measure a long by a short syllable, and I find that it has twice as much. But when one sounds after another, if the former be short the latter long, how shall I hold the short one, and how measuring shall I apply it to the long, so that I may find out that this has twice as much, when indeed the long does not begin to sound unless the short leaves off sounding? That very long one I measure not as present, since I measure it not save when ended. But its ending is its passing away. What, then, is it that I can measure? Where is the short syllable by which I measure? Where is the long one which I measure? Both have sounded, have flown, have passed away, and are no longer; and still I measure, and I confidently answer (so far as is trusted to a practised sense), that as to space of time this syllable is single, that double. Nor could I do this, unless because they have past, and are ended. Therefore do I not measure themselves, which now are not, but something in my memory, which remains fixed.

36. In thee, O my mind, I measure times.[1] Do not overwhelm me with thy clamour. That is, do not overwhelm thyself with the multitude of thy impressions. In thee, I say, I measure times; the impression which things as they pass by make on Thee, and which, when they have passed by, remains, that I measure as time present, not those things which have passed by, that the impression should be made. This I measure when I measure times. Either, then, these are times, or I do not measure times. What when we measure silence, and say that this silence hath lasted as long as that voice lasts? Do we not extend our thought to the measure of a voice, as if it sounded, so that we may be able to declare something concerning the intervals of silence in a given space of time? For when both the voice and tongue are still, we go over in thought poems and verses, and any discourse, or dimensions of motions; and declare concerning the spaces of times, how much this may be in respect of that, not otherwise than if uttering them we should pronounce them. Should any one wish to utter a lengthened sound, and had with forethought determined how long it should be, that man hath in silence verily gone through a space of time, and, committing it to memory, he begins to utter that speech, which sounds until it be extended to the end proposed; truly it hath sounded, and will sound. For what of it is already finished hath verily sounded, but what remains will sound; and thus does it pass on, until the present intention carry over the future into the past; the past increasing by the diminution of the future, until, by the consumption of the future, all be past.

CHAP. XXVIII.—TIME IN THE HUMAN MIND, WHICH EXPECTS, CONSIDERS, AND REMEMBERS.

37. But how is that future diminished or consumed which as yet is not? Or how doth the past, which is no longer, increase, unless in the mind which enacteth this there are three things done? For it both expects, and considers, and remembers, that that which it expecteth, through that which it considereth, may pass into that which it remembereth. Who, therefore, denieth that future things as yet are not? But yet there is already in the mind the expectation of things future. And who denies that past things are now no longer? But, however, there is still in the mind the memory of things past. And who denies that time present wants space, because it passeth away in a moment? But yet our consideration endureth, through which that which may be present may proceed to become absent. Future time, which is not, is not therefore long; but a "long future" is "a long expectation of the future." Nor is time past, which is now no longer, long; but a long past is "a long memory of the past."

---

1 With the argument in this and the previous sections, compare Dr. Reid's remarks in his *Intellectual Powers,* iii. 5: "We may measure duration by the succession of thoughts in the mind, as we measure length by inches or feet, but the notion or idea of duration must be antecedent to the mensuration of it, as the notion of length is antecedent to its being measured. . . . Reason, from the contemplation of finite extended things, leads us necessarily to the belief of an *immensity* that contains them. In like manner, memory gives us the conception and belief of finite intervals of duration. From the contemplation of these, reason leads us necessarily to the belief of an *eternity,* which comprehends all things that have a beginning and an end." The student will with advantage examine a monograph on this subject by C. Fortlage, entitled, *Aurelii Augustini doctrina de tempore ex libro* xi. *Confessionum deprompta, Aristotelicæ, Kantianæ, aliarumque theoriarium recensione aucta, et congruis hodiernæ philosophiæ ideis amplificata* (Heidelbergæ, 1836). He says that amongst all the philosophers none have so nearly approached truth as Augustin.

38. I am about to repeat a psalm that I know. Before I begin, my attention is extended to the whole; but when I have begun, as much of it as becomes past by my saying it is extended in my memory; and the life of this action of mine is divided between my memory, on account of what I have repeated, and my expectation, on account of what I am about to repeat; yet my consideration is present with me, through which that which was future may be carried over so that it may become past. Which the more it is done and repeated, by so much (expectation being shortened) the memory is enlarged, until the whole expectation be exhausted, when that whole action being ended shall have passed into memory. And what takes place in the entire psalm, takes place also in each individual part of it, and in each individual syllable: this holds in the longer action, of which that psalm is perchance a portion; the same holds in the whole life of man, of which all the actions of man are parts; the same holds in the whole age of the sons of men, of which all the lives of men are parts.

CHAP. XXIX.—THAT HUMAN LIFE IS A DISTRACTION, BUT THAT THROUGH THE MERCY OF GOD HE WAS INTENT ON THE PRIZE OF HIS HEAVENLY CALLING.

39. But "because Thy loving-kindness is better than life,"[1] behold, my life is but a distraction,[2] and Thy right hand upheld me[3] in my Lord, the Son of man, the Mediator between Thee,[4] The One, and us the many,—in many distractions amid many things,—that through Him I may apprehend in whom I have been apprehended, and may be re-collected from my old days, following The One, forgetting the things that are past; and not distracted, but drawn on,[5] not to those things which shall be and shall pass away, but to those things which are before,[6] not distractedly, but intently, I follow on for the prize of my heavenly calling,[7] where I may hear the voice of

Thy praise, and contemplate Thy delights,[8] neither coming nor passing away. But now are my years spent in mourning.[9] And Thou, O Lord, art my comfort, my Father everlasting. But I have been divided amid times, the order of which I know not; and my thoughts, even the inmost bowels of my soul, are mangled with tumultuous varieties, until I flow together unto Thee, purged and molten in the fire of Thy love.[10]

CHAP. XXX.—AGAIN HE REFUTES THE EMPTY QUESTION, "WHAT DID GOD BEFORE THE CREATION OF THE WORLD?"

40. And I will be immoveable, and fixed in Thee, in my mould, Thy truth; nor will I endure the questions of men, who by a penal disease thirst for more than they can hold, and say, "What did God make before He made heaven and earth?" Or, "How came it into His mind to make anything, when He never before made anything?" Grant to them, O Lord, to think well what they say, and to see that where there is no time, they cannot say "never." What, therefore, He is said "never to have made," what else is it but to say, that in no time was it made? Let them therefore see that there could be no time without a created being,[11] and let them cease to speak that vanity. Let them also be extended unto those things which are before,[12] and understand that thou, the eternal Creator of all times, art before all times, and that no times are co-eternal with Thee, nor any creature, even if there be any creature beyond all times.

CHAP. XXXI.—HOW THE KNOWLEDGE OF GOD DIFFERS FROM THAT OF MAN.

41. O Lord my God, what is that secret place of Thy mystery, and how far thence have the consequences of my transgressions cast me? Heal my eyes, that I may enjoy Thy light. Surely, if there be a mind, so greatly abounding in knowledge and foreknowledge, to which all things past and future are so known as one psalm is well known to me, that mind is exceedingly wonderful, and very astonishing; because whatever is so past, and whatever is to come of after ages, is no more concealed from Him than was it hidden from me when singing that psalm, what and how much of it had been sung from the beginning, what and how much remained unto the end. But far be it that Thou, the Creator of the universe, the Creator of souls and

---

[1] Ps. lxiii. 3.
[2] *Distentio.* It will be observed that there is a play on the word throughout the section.
[3] Ps. lxiii. 8.
[4] 1 Tim. ii. 5.
[5] *Non distentus sed extentus.* So in *Serm.* cclv. 6, we have: "Unum nos *extendat*, ne multa *distendant*, et abrumpant ab uno."
[6] Phil iii. 13.
[7] Phil. iii. 14. Many wish to attain the prize who never earnestly pursue it. And it may be said here in view of the subject of this book, that there is no stranger delusion than that which possesses the idle and the worldly as to the influence of time in ameliorating their condition. They have "good intentions," and hope that time in the future may do for them what it has not in the past. But in truth, time merely affords an opportunity for energy and life to work. To quote that lucid and nervous thinker, Bishop Copleston (*Remains*, p. 123): "One of the commonest errors is to regard *time* as an *agent*. But in reality time *does* nothing, and *is* nothing. We use it as a compendious expression for all those causes which operate slowly and imperceptibly; but, unless some positive cause is in action, no change takes place in the lapse of one thousand years; *e. g.*, a drop of water encased in a cavity of silex."

[8] Ps. xxvi. 7.
[9] Ps. xxvii. 4.
[10] Ps. xxxi. 10.
[11] He argues similarly in his *De Civ. Dei*, xi. 6: "That the world and time had both one beginning."
[12] Phil. iii. 13.

bodies,—far be it that Thou shouldest know all things future and past. Far, far more wonderfully, and far more mysteriously, Thou knowest them.[1] For it is not as the feelings of one singing known things, or hearing a known song, are —through expectation of future words, and in remembrance of those that are past—varied, and

his senses divided, that anything happeneth unto Thee, unchangeably eternal, that is, the truly eternal[2] Creator of minds. As, then, Thou in the Beginning knewest the heaven and the earth without any change of Thy knowledge, so in the Beginning didst Thou make heaven and earth without any distraction of Thy action.[3] Let him who understandeth confess unto Thee; and let him who understandeth not, confess unto Thee. Oh, how exalted art Thou, and yet the humble in heart are Thy dwelling-place; for Thou raisest up those that are bowed down,[4] and they whose exaltation Thou art fall not.

---

[1] Dean Mansel's argument, in his *Bampton Lectures*, as to our knowledge of the Infinite, is well worthy of consideration. He refers to Augustin's views on the subject of this book in note 13 to his third lecture, and in the text itself says : " The limited character of all existence which can be conceived as having a continuous duration, or as made up of successive moments, is so far manifest, that it has been assumed almost as an axiom, by philosophical theologians, that in the existence of God there is no distinction between past, present, and future. ' In the changes of things,' says Augustin, ' there is a past and a future ; in God there is a present, in which neither past nor future can be.' ' Eternity,' says Beethius, ' is the perfect possession of interminable life, and of all that life at once ; ' and Aquinas, accepting the definition, adds, ' Eternity has no succession, but exists all together.' But whether this assertion be literally true or not (and this we have no means of ascertaining), it is clear that such a mode of existence is altogether inconceivable by us, and that the words in which it is described represent not thought, but the refusal to think at all. " See notes to xiii. 12, below.

[2] " With God, indeed, all things are arranged and fixed ; and when He seemeth to act upon sudden motive, He doth nothing but what He foreknew that He should do from eternity " (Aug. *in Ps.* cvi. 35). With this passage may well be compared Dean Mansel's remarks (*Bampton Lectures*, lect. vi., and notes 23–25) on the doctrine, that the world is but a machine and is not under the continual government and direction of God. See also note 4, on p. 80 and note 2 on p. 136, above.
[3] See p. 166, note 2.
[4] Ps. cxlvi. 8.

BOOK XII.

HE CONTINUES HIS EXPLANATION OF THE FIRST CHAPTER OF GENESIS ACCORDING TO THE SEPTUAGINT, AND BY ITS ASSISTANCE HE ARGUES, ESPECIALLY, CONCERNING THE DOUBLE HEAVEN, AND THE FORMLESS MATTER OUT OF WHICH THE WHOLE WORLD MAY HAVE BEEN CREATED; AFTERWARDS OF THE INTERPRETATIONS OF OTHERS NOT DISALLOWED, AND SETS FORTH AT GREAT LENGTH THE SENSE OF THE HOLY SCRIPTURE.

CHAP. I.—THE DISCOVERY OF TRUTH IS DIFFICULT, BUT GOD HAS PROMISED THAT HE WHO SEEKS SHALL FIND.

1. My heart, O Lord, affected by the words of Thy Holy Scripture, is much busied in this poverty of my life; and therefore, for the most part, is the want of human intelligence copious in language, because inquiry speaks more than discovery, and because demanding is longer than obtaining, and the hand that knocks is more active than the hand that receives. We hold the promise; who shall break it? "If God be for us, who can be against us?"[1] "Ask, and ye shall have; seek, and ye shall find; knock, and it shall be opened unto you: for every one that asketh receiveth; and he that seeketh findeth; and to him that knocketh it shall be opened."[2] These are Thine own promises; and who need fear to be deceived where the Truth promiseth?

CHAP. II.—OF THE DOUBLE HEAVEN,—THE VISIBLE, AND THE HEAVEN OF HEAVENS.

2. The weakness of my tongue confesseth unto Thy Highness, seeing that Thou madest heaven and earth. This heaven which I see, and this earth upon which I tread (from which is this earth that I carry about me), Thou hast made. But where is that heaven of heavens,[3] O Lord, of which we hear in the words of the Psalm, The heaven of heavens are the Lord's, but the earth hath He given to the children of men?[4] Where is the heaven, which we behold not, in comparison of which all this, which we behold, is earth? For this corporeal whole, not as a whole everywhere, hath thus received its beautiful figure in these lower parts, of which the bottom is our earth; but compared with that heaven of heavens, even the heaven of our earth is but earth; yea, each of these great bodies is not absurdly called earth, as compared with that, I know not what manner of heaven, which is the Lord's, not the sons' of men.

CHAP. III.—OF THE DARKNESS UPON THE DEEP, AND OF THE INVISIBLE AND FORMLESS EARTH.

3. And truly this earth was invisible and formless,[5] and there was I know not what profundity of the deep upon which there was no light,[6] because it had no form. Therefore didst Thou command that it should be written, that darkness was upon the face of the deep; what else was it than the absence of light?[7] For had there been light, where should it have been save by being above all, showing itself aloft, and enlightening? Where, therefore, light was as yet not, why was it that darkness was present, unless because light was absent? Darkness therefore was upon it, because the light above was absent; as silence is there present where sound is not. And what is it to have silence there, but not to have sound there? Hast not Thou, O Lord, taught this soul which confesseth unto Thee? Hast not Thou taught me, O Lord, that before Thou didst form and separate this formless matter, there was nothing, neither colour, nor figure, nor body, nor spirit? Yet not altogether nothing; there was a certain formlessness without any shape.

CHAP. IV.—FROM THE FORMLESSNESS OF MATTER, THE BEAUTIFUL WORLD HAS ARISEN.

4. What, then, should it be called, that even in some ways it might be conveyed to those of

---

[1] Rom. viii. 31.
[2] Matt. vii. 7, 8.
[3] That is, not the atmosphere which surrounds the earth, as when we say, "the birds of heaven" (Jer. iv. 25), "the dew of heaven" (Gen. xxvii. 28); nor that "firmament of heaven" (Gen. i. 17) in which the stars have their courses; nor both these together; but that "third heaven" to which Paul was "caught up" (2 Cor. xii. 1) in his rapture, and where God most manifests His glory, and the angels do Him homage.
[4] Ps. cxv. 16, after the LXX., Vulgate, and Syriac.

[5] Gen. i. 2, as rendered by the *Old Ver.* from the LXX. : ἀόρατος καὶ ἀκατασκεύαστος. Kalisch in his *Commentary* translates תֹהוּ וָבֹהוּ: "dreariness and emptiness."
[6] The reader should keep in mind in reading what follows the Manichæan doctrine as to the kingdom of light and darkness. See notes, pp. 68 and 103, above.
[7] Compare *De Civ. Dei*, xi. 9, 10.

duller mind, save by some conventional word? But what, in all parts of the world, can be found nearer to a total formlessness than the earth and the deep? For, from their being of the lowest position, they are less beautiful than are the other higher parts, all transparent and shining. Why, therefore, may I not consider the formlessness of matter—which Thou hadst created without shape, whereof to make this shapely world—to be fittingly intimated unto men by the name of earth invisible and formless?

CHAP. V.—WHAT MAY HAVE BEEN THE FORM OF MATTER.

5. So that when herein thought seeketh what the sense may arrive at, and saith to itself, "It is no intelligible form, such as life or justice, because it is the matter of bodies; nor perceptible by the senses, because in the invisible and formless there is nothing which can be seen and felt;—while human thought saith these things to itself, it may endeavour either to know it by being ignorant, or by knowing it to be ignorant.

CHAP. VI.—HE CONFESSES THAT AT ONE TIME HE HIMSELF THOUGHT ERRONEOUSLY OF MATTER.

6. But were I, O Lord, by my mouth and by my pen to confess unto Thee the whole, whatever Thou hast taught me concerning that matter, the name of which hearing beforehand, and not understanding (they who could not understand it telling me of it), I conceived[1] it as having innumerable and varied forms. And therefore did I not conceive it; my mind revolved in disturbed order foul and horrible "forms," but yet "forms;" and I called it formless, not that it lacked form, but because it had such as, did it appear, my mind would turn from, as unwonted and incongruous, and at which human weakness would be disturbed. But even that which I did conceive was formless, not by the privation of all form, but in comparison of more beautiful forms; and true reason persuaded me that I ought altogether to remove from it all remnants of any form whatever, if I wished to conceive matter wholly without form; and I could not. For sooner could I imagine that that which should be deprived of all form was not at all, than conceive anything between form and nothing,—neither formed, nor nothing, formless, nearly nothing. And my mind hence ceased to question my spirit, filled (as it was) with the images of formed bodies, and changing and varying them according to its will; and I applied myself to the bodies themselves, and looked more deeply into their mutability, by which they cease to be what they had been, and begin to be what they were not; and

this same transit from form unto form I have looked upon to be through some formless condition, not through a very nothing; but I desired to know, not to guess. And if my voice and my pen should confess the whole unto Thee, whatsoever knots Thou hast untied for me concerning this question, who of my readers would endure to take in the whole? Nor yet, therefore, shall my heart cease to give Thee honour, and a song of praise, for those things which it is not able to express. For the mutability of mutable things is itself capable of all those forms into which mutable things are changed. And this mutability, what is it? Is it soul? Is it body? Is it the outer appearance of soul or body? Could it be said, "Nothing were something," and "That which is, is not," I would say that this were it; and yet in some manner was it already, since it could receive these visible and compound shapes.

CHAP. VII.—OUT OF NOTHING GOD MADE HEAVEN AND EARTH.

7. And whence and in what manner was this, unless from Thee, from whom are all things, in so far as they are? But by how much the farther from Thee, so much the more unlike unto Thee; for it is not distance of place. Thou, therefore, O Lord, who art not one thing in one place, and otherwise in another, but the Self-same, and the Self-same, and the Self-same,[2] Holy, Holy, Holy, Lord God Almighty, didst in the beginning,[3] which is of Thee, in Thy Wisdom, which was born of Thy Substance, create something, and that out of nothing.[4] For Thou didst create heaven and earth, not out of Thyself, for then they would be equal to Thine Only-begotten, and thereby even to Thee;[5] and in no wise would it be right that anything should be equal to Thee which was not of Thee. And aught else except Thee there was not whence Thou mightest create these things, O God, One Trinity, and Trine Unity; and, therefore, out of nothing didst Thou create heaven and earth,—a great thing and a small,—because Thou art Almighty and Good, to make all things good, even the great heaven and the small earth. Thou wast, and there was nought else from which Thou didst create heaven and earth; two such things, one near unto Thee, the other near to nothing,[6]—one to which Thou shouldest be superior, the other to which nothing should be inferior.

---

[1] See iii. sec. 11, and p. 103, note, above.

[2] See ix. sec. 11, above.
[3] See p. 166, note, above.
[4] See p. 165, note 2, above.
[5] In the beginning of sec. 10, book xi. of his *De Civ. Dei*, he similarly argues that the world was, not like the Son, "begotten of the simple good," but "created." See also note 8, p. 76, above.
[6] "Because at the first creation, it had no form nor thing in it."—W. W.

CHAP. VIII.—HEAVEN AND EARTH WERE MADE "IN THE BEGINNING;" AFTERWARDS THE WORLD, DURING SIX DAYS, FROM SHAPELESS MATTER.

8. But that heaven of heavens was for Thee, O Lord; but the earth, which Thou hast given to the sons of men,[1] to be seen and touched, was not such as now we see and touch. For it was invisible and "without form,"[2] and there was a deep over which there was not light; or, darkness was over the deep, that is, more than in the deep. For this deep of waters, now visible, has, even in its depths, a light suitable to its nature, perceptible in some manner unto fishes and creeping things in the bottom of it. But the entire deep was almost nothing, since hitherto it was altogether formless; yet there was then that which could be formed. For Thou, O Lord, hast made the world of a formless matter, which matter, out of nothing, Thou hast made almost nothing, out of which to make those great things which we, sons of men, wonder at. For very wonderful is this corporeal heaven, of which firmament, between water and water, the second day after the creation of light, Thou saidst, Let it be made, and it was made.[3] Which firmament Thou calledst heaven, that is, the heaven of this earth and sea, which Thou madest on the third day, by giving a visible shape to the formless matter which Thou madest before all days. For even already hadst Thou made a heaven before all days, but that was the heaven of this heaven; because in the beginning Thou hadst made heaven and earth. But the earth itself which Thou hadst made was formless matter, because it was invisible and without form, and darkness was upon the deep. Of which invisible and formless earth, of which formlessness, of which almost nothing, Thou mightest make all these things of which this changeable world consists, and yet consisteth not; whose very changeableness appears in this, that times can be observed and numbered in it. Because times are made by the changes of things, while the shapes, whose matter is the invisible earth aforesaid, are varied and turned.

CHAP. IX.—THAT THE HEAVEN OF HEAVENS WAS AN INTELLECTUAL CREATURE, BUT THAT THE EARTH WAS INVISIBLE AND FORMLESS BEFORE THE DAYS THAT IT WAS MADE.

9. And therefore the Spirit, the Teacher of Thy servant,[4] when He relates that Thou didst in the Beginning create heaven and earth, is silent as to times, silent as to days. For, doubtless, that heaven of heavens, which Thou in the Beginning didst create, is some intellectual creature, which, although in no wise co-eternal unto Thee, the Trinity, is yet a partaker of Thy eternity, and by reason of the sweetness of that most happy contemplation of Thyself, doth greatly restrain its own mutability, and without any failure, from the time in which it was created, in clinging unto Thee, surpasses all the rolling change of times. But this shapelessness—this earth invisible and without form—has not itself been numbered among the days. For where there is no shape nor order, nothing either cometh or goeth; and where this is not, there certainly are no days, nor any vicissitude of spaces of times.

CHAP. X.—HE BEGS OF GOD THAT HE MAY LIVE IN THE TRUE LIGHT, AND MAY BE INSTRUCTED AS TO THE MYSTERIES OF THE SACRED BOOKS.

10. Oh, let Truth, the light of my heart,[5] not my own darkness, speak unto me! I have descended to that, and am darkened. But thence, even thence, did I love Thee. I went astray, and remembered Thee. I heard Thy voice behind me bidding me return, and scarcely did I hear it for the tumults of the unquiet ones. And now, behold, I return burning and panting after Thy fountain. Let no one prohibit me; of this will I drink, and so have life. Let me not be my own life; from myself have I badly lived,—death was I unto myself; in Thee do I revive. Do Thou speak unto me; do Thou discourse unto me. In Thy books have I believed, and their words are very deep.[6]

CHAP. XI.—WHAT MAY BE DISCOVERED TO HIM BY GOD.

11. Already hast Thou told me, O Lord, with a strong voice, in my inner ear, that Thou art eternal, having alone immortality.[7] Since Thou art not changed by any shape or motion, nor is Thy will altered by times, because no will which changes is immortal. This in Thy sight is clear to me, and let it become more and more clear, I beseech Thee; and in that manifestation let me abide more soberly under Thy wings. Likewise hast Thou said to me, O Lord, with a strong voice, in my inner ear, that Thou hast made all natures and substances, which are not what Thou Thyself art, and yet they are; and that only is not from Thee which is not, and the motion of

---

[1] Ps. cxv. 16.
[2] Gen. i. 2.
[3] Gen. i. 6-8.
[4] Of Moses.

[5] See note 2, p. 76, above.
[6] As Gregory the Great has it, Revelation is a river broad and deep, "In quo et agnus ambulet, et elephas natet." And these deep things of God are to be learned only by patient searching. We must, says St. Chrysostom (De Prec. serm. ii.), dive down into the sea as those who would fetch up pearls from its depths. The very mysteriousness of Scripture is, doubtless, intended by God to stimulate us to search the Scriptures, and to strengthen our spiritual insight (Enar. in Ps cxlvi. 6). See also, p. 48, note 5; p. 164, note 2, above; and the notes on pp. 370, 371, below.
[7] 1 Tim. vi. 16.

the will from Thee who art, to that which in a less degree is, because such motion is guilt and sin;[1] and that no one's sin doth either hurt Thee, or disturb the order of Thy rule,[2] either first or last. This, in Thy sight, is clear to me, and let it become more and more clear, I beseech Thee; and in that manifestation let me abide more soberly under Thy wings.

12. Likewise hast Thou said to me, with a strong voice, in my inner ear, that that creature, whose will Thou alone art, is not co-eternal unto Thee, and which, with a most persevering purity[3] drawing its support from Thee, doth, in place and at no time, put forth its own mutability;[4] and Thyself being ever present with it, unto whom with its entire affection it holds itself, having no future to expect nor conveying into the past what it remembereth, is varied by no change, nor extended into any times.[5] O blessed one,—if any such there be,—in clinging unto Thy Blessedness; blest in Thee, its everlasting Inhabitant and its Enlightener! Nor do I find what the heaven of heavens, which is the Lord's, can be better called than Thine house, which contemplateth Thy delight without any defection of going forth to another; a pure mind, most peacefully one, by that stability of peace of holy spirits,[6] the citizens of Thy city " in the heavenly places," above these heavenly places which are seen.[7]

13. Whence the soul, whose wandering has been made far away, may understand, if now she thirsts for Thee, if now her tears have become bread to her, while it is daily said unto her "Where is thy God?"[8] if she now seeketh of Thee one thing, and desireth that she may dwell in Thy house all the days of her life.[9] And what is her life but Thee? And what are Thy days but Thy eternity, as Thy years which fail not, because Thou art the same? Hence, therefore, can the soul, which is able, understand how far beyond all times Thou art eternal; when Thy house, which has not wandered from Thee, although it be not co-eternal with Thee, yet by continually and unfailingly clinging unto Thee, suffers no vicissitude of times. This in Thy sight is clear unto me, and may it become more and more clear unto me, I beseech Thee; and in this manifestation may I abide more soberly under Thy wings.

14. Behold, I know not what shapelessness there is in those changes of these last and lowest creatures. And who shall tell me, unless it be some one who, through the emptiness of his own heart, wanders and is staggered by his own fancies? Who, unless such a one, would tell me that (all figure being diminished and consumed), if the formlessness only remain, through which the thing was changed and was turned from one figure into another, that that can exhibit the changes of times? For surely it could not be, because without the change of motions times are not, and there is no change where there is no figure.

CHAP. XII.—FROM THE FORMLESS EARTH GOD CREATED ANOTHER HEAVEN AND A VISIBLE AND FORMED EARTH.

15. Which things considered as much as Thou givest, O my God, as much as Thou excitest me to "knock," and as much as Thou openest unto me when I knock,[10] two things I find which Thou hast made, not within the compass of time, since neither is co-eternal with Thee. One, which is so formed that, without any failing of contemplation, without any interval of change, although changeable, yet not changed, it may fully enjoy Thy eternity and unchangeableness; the other, which was so formless, that it had not that by which it could be changed from one form into another, either of motion or of repose, whereby it might be subject unto time. But this Thou didst not leave to be formless, since before all days, in the beginning Thou createdst heaven and earth,—these two things of which I spoke. But the earth was invisible and without form, and darkness was upon the deep.[11] By which words its shapelessness is conveyed unto us,— that by degrees those minds may be drawn on which cannot wholly conceive the privation of all form without coming to nothing,—whence another heaven might be created, and another earth visible and well-formed, and water beautifully ordered, and whatever besides is, in the formation of this world, recorded to have been, not without days, created; because such things are so that in them the vicissitudes of times may take place, on account of the appointed changes of motions and of forms.[12]

CHAP. XIII.—OF THE INTELLECTUAL HEAVEN AND FORMLESS EARTH, OUT OF WHICH, ON ANOTHER DAY, THE FIRMAMENT WAS FORMED.

16. Meanwhile I conceive this, O my God, when I hear Thy Scripture speak, saying, In the beginning God made heaven and earth;

---

[1] For Augustin's view of evil as a " privation of good," see p. 64, note 1, above, and with it compare vii. sec. 22, above; Con. Secundin. c. 12; and De Lib. Arb. ii. 53. Parker, in his Theism, Atheism, etc. p. 119, contends that God Himself must in some way be the author of evil, and a similar view is maintained by Schleiermacher, Christliche Glaube, sec. 80.
[2] See ii. sec. 13, and v. sec. 2, notes 4, 9, above.
[3] See iv. sec. 3, and note 1, above.
[4] See sec. 19, below.
[5] See xi. sec. 38, above, and sec. 18, below.
[6] See xiii. sec. 50, below.
[7] Eph. i. 20, etc.
[8] Ps. xlii. 2, 3, 10.
[9] Ps. xxvii. 4.
[10] Matt. vii. 7.
[11] Gen. i. 2.
[12] See end of sec. 40, below.

but the earth was invisible and without form, and darkness was upon the deep, and not stating on what day Thou didst create these things. Thus, meanwhile, do I conceive, that it is on account of that heaven of heavens, that intellectual heaven, where to understand is to know all at once,—not "in part," not "darkly," not "through a glass,"[1] but as a whole, in manifestation, "face to face;" not this thing now, that anon, but (as has been said) to know at once without any change of times; and on account of the invisible and formless earth, without any change of times; which change is wont to have "this thing now, that anon," because, where there is no form there can be no distinction between "this" or "that;"—it is, then, on account of these two,—a primitively formed, and a wholly formless; the one heaven, but the heaven of heavens, the other earth, but the earth invisible and formless;—on account of these two do I meanwhile conceive that Thy Scripture said without mention of days, "In the beginning God created the heaven and the earth." For immediately it added of what earth it spake. And when on the second day the firmament is recorded to have been created, and called heaven, it suggests to us of which heaven He spake before without mention of days.

CHAP. XIV.—OF THE DEPTH OF THE SACRED SCRIPTURE, AND ITS ENEMIES.

17. Wonderful is the depth of Thy oracles, whose surface is before us, inviting the little ones; and yet wonderful is the depth, O my God, wonderful is the depth.[2] It is awe to look into it; and awe of honour, and a tremor of love. The enemies thereof I hate vehemently.[3] Oh, if Thou wouldest slay them with Thy two-edged sword,[4] that they be not its enemies! For thus do I love, that they should be slain unto themselves that they may live unto Thee. But behold others not reprovers, but praisers of the book of Genesis,—"The Spirit of God," say they, "Who by His servant Moses wrote these things, willed not that these words should be thus understood. He willed not that it should be understood as Thou sayest, but as we say." Unto whom, O God of us all, Thyself being Judge, do I thus answer.

CHAP. XV.—HE ARGUES AGAINST ADVERSARIES CONCERNING THE HEAVEN OF HEAVENS.

18. "Will you say that these things are false, which, with a strong voice, Truth tells me in my inner ear, concerning the very eternity of the Creator, that His substance is in no wise changed by time, nor that His will is separate from His substance? Wherefore, He willeth not one thing now, another anon, but once and for ever He willeth all things that He willeth; not again and again, nor now this, now that; nor willeth afterwards what He willeth not before, nor willeth not what before He willed. Because such a will is mutable, and no mutable thing is eternal; but our God is eternal.[5] Likewise He tells me, tells me in my inner ear, that the expectation of future things is turned to sight when they have come; and this same sight is turned to memory when they have passed. Moreover, all thought which is thus varied is mutable, and nothing mutable is eternal; but our God is eternal." These things I sum up and put together, and I find that my God, the eternal God, hath not made any creature by any new will, nor that His knowledge suffereth anything transitory.

19. What, therefore, will ye say, ye objectors? Are these things false? "No," they say. "What is this? Is it false, then, that every nature already formed, or matter formable, is only from Him who is supremely good, because He is supreme?" "Neither do we deny this," say they. "What then? Do you deny this, that there is a certain sublime creature, clinging with so chaste a love with the true and truly eternal God, that although it be not co-eternal with Him, yet it separateth itself not from Him, nor floweth into any variety and vicissitude of times, but resteth in the truest contemplation of Him only?" Since Thou, O God, showest Thyself unto him, and sufficest him, who loveth Thee as muce as Thou commandest, and, therefore, he declineth not from Thee, nor toward himself.[6] This is the house of God,[7] not earthly, nor of any celestial bulk corporeal, but a spiritual house and a partaker of Thy eternity, because without blemish for ever. For Thou hast made it fast for ever and ever; Thou hast given it a law, which it shall not pass.[8] Nor yet is it co-eternal with Thee, O God, because not without beginning, for it was made.

20. For although we find no time before it, for wisdom was created before all things,[9]— not certainly that Wisdom manifestly co-eternal and equal unto Thee, our God, His Father,

---

[1] 1 Cor. xiii. 12.

[2] See p. 112, note 2, and p. 178, note 2, above, See also Trench, *Hulsean Lectures* (1845), lect. 6, "The Inexhaustibility of Scripture."

[3] Ps. cxxxix. 21.

[4] Ps. cxlix. 6. He refers to the Manichæans (see p. 71, note 1). In his comment on this place, he interprets the "two-edged sword" to mean the Old and New Testament, called two-edged, he says, because it speaks of things temporal and eternal.

[5] See xi. sec. 41, above.

[6] In his *De Vera Relig.* c. 13, he says : "We must confess that the angels are in their nature mutable as God is Immutable. Yet by that will with which they love God more than themselves, they remain firm and staple in Him, and enjoy His majesty, being most willingly subject to Him alone."

[7] In his *Con. Adv. Leg. et Proph.* i. 2, he speaks of all who are holy, whether angels or men, as being God's dwelling-place.

[8] Ps. cxlviii. 6.

[9] Ecclus. i. 4.

and by Whom all things were created, and in Whom, as the Beginning, Thou createdst heaven and earth; but truly that wisdom which has been created, namely, the intellectual nature,[1] which, in the contemplation of light, is light. For this, although created, is also called wisdom. But as great as is the difference between the Light which enlighteneth and that which is enlightened,[2] so great is the difference between the Wisdom that createth and that which hath been created; as between the Righteousness which justifieth, and the righteousness which has been made by justification. For we also are called Thy righteousness; for thus saith a certain servant of Thine: "That we might be made the righteousness of God in Him."[3] Therefore, since a certain created wisdom was created before all things, the rational and intellectual mind of that chaste city of Thine, our mother which is above, and is free,[4] and "eternal in the heavens"[5] (in what heavens, unless in those that praise Thee, the "heaven of heavens," because this also is the "heaven of heavens,"[6] which is the Lord's) —although we find not time before it, because that which hath been created before all things also precedeth the creature of time, yet is the Eternity of the Creator Himself before it, from Whom, having been created, it took the beginning, although not of time,—for time as yet was not,—yet of its own very nature.

21. Hence comes it so to be of Thee, our God, as to be manifestly another than Thou, and not the Self-same.[7] Since, although we find time not only not before it, but not in it (it being proper ever to behold Thy face, nor is ever turned aside from it, wherefore it happens that it is varied by no change), yet is there in it that mutability itself whence it would become dark and cold, but that, clinging unto Thee with sublime love, it shineth and gloweth from Thee like a perpetual noon. O house, full of light and splendour! I have loved thy beauty, and the place of the habitation of the glory of my Lord,[8] thy builder and owner. Let my wandering sigh after thee; and I speak unto Him that made thee, that He may possess me also in thee, seeing He hath made me likewise. "I have gone astray, like a lost sheep;"[9] yet upon the shoulders of my Sheperd,[10] thy builder, I hope that I may be brought back to thee.

22. "What say ye to me, O ye objectors whom I was addressing, and who yet believe that Moses was the holy servant of God, and that his books were the oracles of the Holy Ghost? Is not this house of God, not indeed co-eternal with God, yet, according to its measure, eternal in the heavens,[11] where in vain you seek for changes of times, because you will not find them? For that surpasseth all extension, and every revolving space of time, to which it is ever good to cleave fast to God."[12] "It is," say they. "What, therefore, of those things which my heart cried out unto my God, when within it heard the voice of His praise, what then do you contend is false? Or is it because the matter was formless, wherein, as there was no form, there was no order? But where there was no order there could not be any change of times; and yet this 'almost nothing,' inasmuch as it was not altogether nothing, was verily from Him, from Whom is whatever is, in what state soever anything is." "This also," say they, "we do not deny."

CHAP. XVI.—HE WISHES TO HAVE NO INTERCOURSE WITH THOSE WHO DENY DIVINE TRUTH.

23. With such as grant that all these things which Thy truth indicates to my mind are true, I desire to confer a little before Thee, O my God. For let those who deny these things bark and drown their own voices with their clamour as much as they please; I will endeavour to persuade them to be quiet, and to suffer Thy word to reach them. But should they be unwilling, and should they repel me, I beseech, O my God, that Thou "be not silent to me."[13] Do Thou speak truly in my heart, for Thou only so speakest, and I will send them away blowing upon the dust from without, and raising it up into their own eyes; and I will myself enter into my chamber,[14] and sing there unto Thee songs of love,—groaning with groaning unutterable[15] in my pilgrimage, and remembering Jerusalem, with heart raised up towards it,[16]

---

[1] "Pet. Lombard. lib. sent. 2, dist. 2, affirms that by Wisdom, Ecclus. i. 4, the angels be understood, the whole spiritual intellectual nature; namely, this highest heaven, in which the angels were created, and it by them instantly filled."—W. W.
[2] On God as the Father of Lights, see p. 76, note 2. In addition to the references there given, compare in Ev. Joh. Tract. ii. sec. 7; xiv. secs. 1, 2; and xxxv. sec. 3. See also p. 373, note, below.
[3] 2 Cor. v. 21.
[4] Gal. iv. 26.
[5] 2 Cor. v. 1.
[6] Ps. cxlviii. 4.
[7] Against the Manichæans. See iv. sec. 26, and part 2 of note on p. 76, above.
[8] Ps. xxvi. 8.
[9] Ps. cxix. 176.
[10] Luke xv. 5.
[11] 2 Cor. v. 1.
[12] Ps. lxxiii. 28.
[13] Ps. xxviii. 1.
[14] Isa. xxvi. 20.
[15] Rom. viii. 26.
[16] Baxter has a noteworthy passage on our heavenly citizenship in his Saints' Rest : " As Moses, before he died, went up into Mount Nebo, to take a survey of the land of Canaan, so the Christian ascends the Mount of Contemplation, and by faith surveys his rest. . . . As Daniel in his captivity daily opened his window towards Jerusalem, though far out of sight, when he went to God in his devotions, so may the believing soul, in this captivity of the flesh, look towards 'Jerusalem which is above' (Gal. iv. 26). And as Paul was to the Colossians (ii. 5), so may the believer be with the glorified spirits, 'though absent in the flesh,' yet with them 'in the spirit,' joying and beholding their heavenly 'order.' And as the lark sweetly sings while she soars on high, but is suddenly silenced when she falls to the earth, so is the frame of the soul most delightful and divine while it keeps in the views of God by contemplation. Alas, we make there too short a stay, fall down again, and lay by our music!" (Fawcett's Ed. p. 327).

Jerusalem my country, Jerusalem my mother, and Thyself, the Ruler over it, the Enlightener, the Father, the Guardian, the Husband, the chaste and strong delight, the solid joy, and all good things ineffable, even all at the same time, because the one supreme and true Good. And I will not be turned away until Thou collect all that I am, from this dispersion [1] and deformity, into the peace of that very dear mother, where are the first-fruits of my spirit, [2] whence these things are assured to me, and Thou conform and confirm it for ever, my God, my Mercy. But with reference to those who say not that all these things which are true and false, who honour Thy Holy Scripture set forth by holy Moses, placing it, as with us, on the summit of an authority [3] to be followed, and yet who contradict us in some particulars, I thus speak: Be Thou, O our God, judge between my confessions and their contradictions.

CHAP. XVII.—HE MENTIONS FIVE EXPLANATIONS OF THE WORDS OF GENESIS i. I.

24. For they say, "Although these things be true, yet Moses regarded not those two things, when by divine revelation he said, 'In the beginning God created the heaven and the earth.' [4] Under the name of heaven he did not indicate that spiritual or intellectual creature which always beholds the face of God; nor under the name of earth, that shapeless matter." "What then?" "That man," say they, "meant as we say; this it is that he declared by those words." "What is that?" "By the name of heaven and earth," say they, "did he first wish to set forth, universally and briefly, all this visible world, that afterwards by the enumeration of the days he might distribute, as if in detail, all those things which it pleased the Holy Spirit thus to reveal. For such men were that rude and carnal people to which he spoke, that he judged it prudent that only those works of God as were visible should be entrusted to them." They agree, however, that the earth invisible and formless, and the darksome deep (out of which it is subsequently pointed out that all these visible things, which are known to all, were made and set in order during those "days"), may not unsuitably be understood of this formless matter.

25. What, now, if another should say "That this same formlessness and confusion of matter was first introduced under the name of heaven and earth, because out of it this visible world, with all those natures which most manifestly appear in it, and which is wont to be called by the name of heaven and earth, was created and perfected"? But what if another should say, that "That invisible and visible nature is not inaptly called heaven and earth; and that consequently the universal creation, which God in His wisdom hath made,—that is, 'in the beginning,'—was comprehended under these two words. Yet, since all things have been made, not of the substance of God, but out of nothing [5] (because they are not that same thing that God is, and there is in them all a certain mutability, whether they remain, as doth the eternal house of God, or be changed, as are the soul and body of man), therefore, that the common matter of all things invisible and visible,—as yet shapeless, but still capable of form,—out of which was to be created heaven and earth (that is, the invisible and visible creature already formed), was spoken of by the same names by which the earth invisible and formless and the darkness upon the deep would be called; with this difference, however, that the earth invisible and formless is understood as corporeal matter, before it had any manner of form, but the darkness upon the deep as spiritual matter, before it was restrained at all of its unlimited fluidity, and before the enlightening of wisdom."

26. should any man wish, he may still say, "That the already perfected and formed natures, invisible and visible, are not signified under the name of heaven and earth when it is read, 'In the beginning God created the heaven and the earth;' but that the yet same formless beginning of things, the matter capable of being formed and made, was called by these names, because contained in it there were these confused things not as yet distinguished by their qualities and forms, the which now being digested in their own orders, are called heaven and earth, the former being the spiritual, the latter the corporeal creature."

CHAP. XVIII.—WHAT ERROR IS HARMLESS IN SACRED SCRIPTURE.

27. All which things having been heard and considered, I am unwilling to contend about words, [6] for that is profitable to nothing but to the subverting of the hearers. [7] But the law is good to edify, if a man use it lawfully; [8] for the end of it "is charity out of a pure heart, and of a good conscience, and of faith unfeigned." [9] And well did our Master know, upon which two commandments He hung all the Law and

---

[1] See ii. sec. 1; ix. sec. 10; x. sec. 40, note; *ibid.* sec. 65; and xi. sec. 39, above.
[2] See ix. sec. 24, above; and xiii. sec. 13, below.
[3] See p. 118, note 12, above.
[4] Gen. i. 1.

[5] See p. 165, note 4, above.
[6] See p. 164, note 2, above
[7] 2 Tim. ii. 14.
[8] 1 Tim. i. 8.
[9] *Ibid.* ver. 5.

the Prophets.[1] And what doth it hinder me, O my God, Thou light of my eyes in secret, while ardently confessing these things,—since by these words many things may be understood, all of which are yet true,—what, I say, doth it hinder me, should I think otherwise of what the writer thought than some other man thinketh? Indeed, all of us who read endeavour to trace out and to understand that which he whom we read wished to convey; and as we believe him to speak truly, we dare not suppose that he has spoken anything which we either know or suppose to be false. Since, therefore, each person endeavours to understand in the Holy Scriptures that which the writer understood, what hurt is it if a man understand what Thou, the light of all true-speaking minds, dost show him to be true although he whom he reads understood not this, seeing that he also understood a Truth, not, however, this Truth?

CHAP. XIX.—HE ENUMERATES THE THINGS CONCERNING WHICH ALL AGREE.

28. For it is true, O Lord, that Thou hast made heaven and earth; it is also true, that the Beginning is Thy Wisdom, in Which Thou hast made all things.[2] It is likewise true, that this visible world hath its own great parts, the heaven and the earth, which in a short compass comprehends all made and created natures. It is also true, that everything mutable sets before our minds a certain want of form, whereof it taketh a form, or is changed and turned. It is true, that that is subject to no times which so cleaveth to the changeless form as that, though it be mutable, it is not changed. It is true, that the formlessness, which is almost nothing, cannot have changes, of times. It is true, that that of which anything is made may by a certain mode of speech be called by the name of that thing which is made of it; whence that formlessness of which heaven and earth were made might it be called "heaven and earth." It is true, that of all things having form, nothing is nearer to the formless than the earth and the deep. It is true, that not only every created and formed thing, but also whatever is capable of creation and of form, Thou hast made, "by whom are all things."[3] It is true, that every-

thing that is formed from that which is formless was formless before it was formed.

CHAP. XX.—OF THE WORDS, "IN THE BEGINNING," VARIOUSLY UNDERSTOOD.

29. From all these truths, of which they doubt not whose inner eye Thou hast granted to see such things, and who immoveably believe Moses, Thy servant, to have spoken in the spirit of truth; from all these, then, he taketh one who saith, "In the beginning God created the heaven and the earth,"—that is, "In His Word, co-eternal with Himself, God made the intelligible and the sensible, or the spiritual and corporeal creature." He taketh another, who saith, "In the beginning God created the heaven and the earth,"—that is, "In His Word, co-eternal with Himself, God made the universal mass of this corporeal world, with all those manifest and known natures which it containeth." He, another, who saith, "In the beginning God created the heaven and the earth,"—that is, "In His Word, co-eternal with Himself, God made the formless matter of the spiritual[4] and corporeal creature." He, another, who saith, "In the beginning God created the heaven and the earth,"—that is, "In His Word, co-eternal with Himself, God made the formless matter of the corporeal creature, wherein heaven and earth lay as yet confused, which being now distinguished and formed, we, at this day, see in the mass of this world." He, another, who saith, "In the beginning God created heaven and earth,"—that is, "In the very beginning of creating and working, God made that formless matter confusedly containing heaven and earth, out of which, being formed, they now stand out, and are manifest, with all the things that are in them."

CHAP. XXI.—OF THE EXPLANATION OF THE WORDS, "THE EARTH WAS INVISIBLE."

30. And as concerns the understanding of

---

[1] Matt. xxii. 40. For he says in his *Con. Faust.* xvii. 6, remarking on John i. 17, a text which he often quotes in this connection : "The law itself by being fulfilled becomes grace and truth. Grace is the fulfilment of love." And so in *ibid.* xix. 27 we read : "From the words, 'I came not to destroy the law but to fulfil it,' we are not to understand that Christ by His precepts filled up what was wanting in the law; but what the literal command failed in doing from the pride and disobedience of men is accomplished by grace. . . . So, the apostle says, 'faith worketh by love.'" So, again, we read in *Serm.* cxxv. : "Quia venit dare caritatem, et caritas perficit legem ; merito dixit non veni legem solvere sed implere." And hence in his letter to Jerome (*Ep.* clxvii. 19), he speaks of the "royal law" as being "the law of liberty, which is the law of love." See p. 348, note 4, above.
[2] Ps civ. 24. See p. 297 note 1, above,
[3] 1 Cor. viii. 6.

[4] Augustin, in his letter to Jerome (*Ep.* clxvi. 4) on "The origin of the human soul," says : "The soul, whether it be termed material or immaterial, has a certain nature of its own, created from a substance superior to the elements of this world." And in his *De Gen. ad Lit.* vii. 10, he speaks of the soul being formed from a certain "spiritual matter," even as flesh was formed from the earth. It should be observed that at one time Augustin held to the theory that the souls of infants were created by God out of nothing at each fresh birth, and only rejected this view for that of its being generated by the parents under the pressure of the Pelagian controversy. The first doctrine was generally held by the Schoolmen ; and William of Conches maintained this belief on the authority of Augustin,—apparently being unaware of any modification in his opinion : "Cum Augustino," he says (Victor Cousin, *Ouvrages ined. d'Abelard*, p. 673), "credo et sentio quotidie novas animas *non ex traduce*, non ex aliqua substantia, sed *ex nihilo, solo jussu creatoris* creari." Those who held the first-named belief were called *Creatiani* ; those who held the second, *Truduciani*. It may be noted as to the word "Traduciani," that Tertullian, in his *De Anima*, chaps. 24-27, etc., frequently uses the word *tradux* in this connection. Augustin, in his *Retractations*, ii. 45, refers to his letter to Jerome, and urges that if so obscure a matter is to be discussed at all, that solution only should be received : "Quæ contraria non sit apertissimis rebus quas de originati peccato fides catholica novit in parvulis, nisi regenerentur in Christo, sine dubitatione damnandis." On Tertullian's views, see Bishop Kays, p. 178, etc.

the following words, out of all those truths he selected one to himself, who saith, "But the earth was invisible and without form, and darkness was upon the deep,"—that is, "That corporeal thing, which God made, was as yet the formless matter of corporeal things, without order, without light." He taketh another, who saith, "But the earth was invisible and without form, and darkness was upon the deep,"—that is, "This whole, which is called heaven and earth, was as yet formless and darksome matter, out of which the corporeal heaven and the corporeal earth were to be made, with all things therein which are known to our corporeal senses." He, another, who saith, "But the earth was invisible and without form, and darkness was upon the deep,"—that is, "This whole, which is called heaven and earth, was as yet a formless and darksome matter, out of which were to be made that intelligible heaven, which is otherwise called the heaven of heavens, and the earth, namely, the whole corporeal nature, under which name may also be comprised this corporeal heaven,—that is, from which every invisible and visible creature would be created." He, another, who saith, "But the earth was invisible and without form, and darkness was upon the deep,"—"The Scripture called not that formlessness by the name of heaven and earth, but that formlessness itself," saith he, "already was, which he named the earth invisible and formless and the darksome deep, of which he had said before, that God had made the heaven and the earth, namely, the spiritual and corporeal creature." He, another, who saith, "But the earth was invisible and formless, and darkness was upon the deep,"—that is, "There was already a formless matter, whereof the Scripture before said, that God had made heaven and earth, namely, the entire corporeal mass of the world, divided into two very great parts, the superior and the inferior, with all those familiar and known creatures which are in them."

CHAP. XXII.—HE DISCUSSES WHETHER MATTER WAS FROM ETERNITY, OR WAS MADE BY GOD.[1]

31. For, should any one endeavour to contend against these last two opinions, thus,—"If you will not admit that this formlessness of matter appears to be called by the name of heaven and earth, then there was something which God had not made out of which He could make heaven and earth; for Scripture hath not told us that God made this matter, unless we understand it to be implied in the term of hea-

ven and earth, or of earth only, when it is said, 'In the beginning God created heaven and earth,' as that which follows, but the earth was invisible and formless, although it was pleasing to him so to call the formless matter, we may not yet understand any but that which God made in that text which hath been already written, 'God made heaven and earth.'" The maintainers of either one or the other of these two opinions which we have put last will, when they have heard these things, answer and say, "We deny not indeed that this formless matter was created by God, the God of whom are all things, very good; for, as we say that that is a greater good which is created and formed, so we acknowledge that that is a minor good which is capable of creation and form, but yet good. But yet the Scripture hath not declared that God made this formlessness, any more than it hath declared many other things; as the 'Cherubim,' and 'Seraphim,'[2] and those of which the apostle distinctly speaks, 'Thrones,' 'Dominions,' 'Principalities,' 'Powers,'[3] all of which it is manifest God made. Or if in that which is said, 'He made heaven and earth,' all things are comprehended, what do we say of the waters upon which the Spirit of God moved? For if they are understood as incorporated in the word earth, how then can formless matter be meant in the term earth when we see the waters so beautiful? Or if it be so meant, why then is it written that out of the same formlessness the firmament was made and called heaven, and yet it is not written that the waters were made? For those waters, which we perceive flowing in so beautiful a manner, remain not formless and invisiblee. But if, then, they received that beauty when God said, Let the water which is under the firmament be gathered together,[4] so that the gathering be the very formation, what will be answered concerning the waters which are above the firmament, because if formless they would not have deserved to receive a seat so honourable, nor is it written by what word they were formed? If, then, Genesis is silent as to anything that God has made, which, however, neither sound faith nor unerring understanding doubteth that God hath made,[5] let not any sober teaching dare to say that these waters were co-eternal with God because we find them mentioned in the book of Genesis; but when they were created, we find not. Why—truth instructing us—may we not understand that that formless matter, which the Scripture calls the earth invisible and without form, and the darksome deep,[6] have been made

1 See xi. sec. 7, and note, above; and xii. sec. 33, and note, below. See also the subtle reasoning of Dean Mansel (*Bampton Lectures*, lect. ii.), on the inconsequence of receiving the idea of the creation out of nothing on other than Christian principles. And compare Coleridge, *The Friend*, iii. 213.

2 Isa. vi. 2, and xxxvii. 16.
3 Col. i. 16.
4 Gen. i. 9.
5 See p. 165, note 4, above.
6 See p. 176, note 5, above.

by God out of nothing, and therefore that they are not co-eternal with Him, although that narrative hath failed to tell when they were made?"

CHAP. XXIII. — TWO KINDS OF DISAGREEMENTS IN THE BOOKS TO BE EXPLAINED.

32. These things, therefore, being heard and perceived according to my weakness of apprehension, which I confess unto Thee, O Lord, who knowest it, I see that two sorts of differences may arise when by signs anything is related, even by true reporters, — one concerning the truth of the things, the other concerning the meaning of him who reports them. For in one way we inquire, concerning the forming of the creature, what is true; but in another, what Moses, that excellent servant of Thy faith, would have wished that the reader and hearer should understand by these words. As for the first kind, let all those depart from me who imagine themselves to know as true what is false. And as for the other also, let all depart from me who imagine Moses to have spoken things that are false. But let me be united in Thee, O Lord, with them, and in Thee delight myself with them that feed on Thy truth, in the breadth of charity; and let us approach together unto the words of Thy book, and in them make search for Thy will, through the will of Thy servant by whose pen Thou hast dispensed them.

CHAP. XXIV. — OUT OF THE MANY TRUE THINGS, IT IS NOT ASSERTED CONFIDENTLY THAT MOSES UNDERSTOOD THIS OR THAT.

33. But which of us, amid so many truths which occur to inquirers in these words, understood as they are in different ways, shall so discover that one interpretation as to confidently say "that Moses thought this," and "that in that narrative he wished this to be understood," as confidently as he says "that this is true," whether he thought this thing or the other? For behold, O my God, I Thy servant, who in this book have vowed unto Thee a sacrifice of confession, and beseech Thee that of Thy mercy I may pay my vows unto Thee,[1] behold, can I, as I confidently assert that Thou in Thy immutable word hast created all things, invisible and visible, with equal confidence assert that Moses meant nothing else than this when he wrote, "In the beginning God created the heaven and the earth."[2] No. Because it is not as clear to me that this was in his mind when he wrote these things, as I see it to be certain in Thy truth. For his thoughts might be set upon the very beginning of the creation when he said, "In the beginning;" and he might wish it to be understood that, in this place, "the heaven and the earth" were no formed and perfected nature, whether spiritual or corporeal, but each of them newly begun, and as yet formless. Because I see, that whichsoever of these had been said, it might have been said truly; but which of them he may have thought in these words, I do not so perceive. Although, whether it were one of these, or some other meaning which has not been mentioned by me, that this great man saw in his mind when he used these words, I make no doubt but that he saw it truly, and expressed it suitably.

CHAP. XXV. — IT BEHOVES INTERPRETERS, WHEN DISAGREEING CONCERNING OBSCURE PLACES, TO REGARD GOD THE AUTHOR OF TRUTH, AND THE RULE OF CHARITY.

34. Let no one now trouble me by saying, "Moses thought not as you say, but as I say." For should he ask me, "Whence knowest thou that Moses thought this which you deduce from his words?" I ought to take it contentedly,[3] and reply perhaps as I have before, or somewhat more fully should he be obstinate. But when he says, "Moses meant not what you say, but what I say," and yet denies not what each of us says, and that both are true, O my God, life of the poor, in whose bosom there is no contradiction, pour down into my heart Thy soothings, that I may patiently bear with such as say this to me; not because they are divine, and because they have seen in the heart of Thy servant what they say, but because they are proud, and have not known the opinion of Moses, but love their own, — not because it is true, but because it is their own. Otherwise they would equally love another true opinion, as I love what they say when they speak what is true; not because it is theirs, but because it is true, and therefore now not theirs because true. But if they therefore love that because it is true, it is now both theirs and mine, since it is common to all the lovers of truth. But because they contend that Moses meant not what I say, but what they themselves say, this I neither like nor love; because, though it were so, yet that rashness is not of knowledge, but of audacity; and not vision, but vanity brought it forth. And therefore, O Lord, are Thy judgments to be dreaded, since Thy truth is neither mine, nor his, nor another's, but of all of us, whom Thou publicly callest to have it in common, warning

---

[1] Ps. xxii. 25.
[2] It is curious to note here Fichte's strange idea (*Anweisung zum seligen Leben*, Werke, v. 479), that St. John, at the commencement of his Gospel, in his teaching as to the "Word," intended to confute the Mosaic statement, which Fichte — since it ran counter to that idea of "the absolute" which he made the point of departure in his philosophy — antagonizes as a heathen and Jewish error. On "In the Beginning," see p. 166, note 2, above.

[3] See p. 48, note, and p. 164, note 2, above.

us terribly not to hold it as specially for ourselves, lest we be deprived of it. For whosoever claims to himself as his own that which Thou appointed to all to enjoy, and desires that to be his own which belongs to all, is forced away from what is common to all to that which is his own — that is, from truth to falsehood. For he that "speaketh a lie, speaketh of his own." [1]

35. Hearken, O God, Thou best Judge! Truth itself, hearken to what I shall say to this gainsayer; hearken, for before Thee I say it, and before my brethren who use Thy law lawfully, to the end of charity; [2] hearken and behold what I shall say to him, if it be pleasing unto Thee. For this brotherly and peaceful word do I return unto him: "If we both see that that which thou sayest is true, and if we both see that what I say is true, where, I ask, do we see it? Certainly not I in thee, nor thou in me, but both in the unchangeable truth itself, [3] which is above our minds." When, therefore, we may not contend about the very light of the Lord our God, why do we contend about the thoughts of our neighbour, which we cannot so see as incommutable truth is seen; when, if Moses himself had appeared to us and said, "This I meant," not so should we see it, but believe it? Let us not, then, "be puffed up for one against the other," [4] above that which is written; let us love the Lord our God with all our heart, with all our soul, and with all our mind, and our neighbour as ourself. [5] As to which two precepts of charity, unless we believe that Moses meant whatever in these books he did mean, we shall make God a liar when we think otherwise concerning our fellow-servants' mind than He hath taught us. Behold, now, how foolish it is, in so great an abundance of the truest opinions which can be extracted from these words, rashly to affirm which of them Moses particularly meant; and with pernicious contentions to offend charity itself, on account of which he hath spoken all the things whose words we endeavour to explain!

CHAP. XXVI. — WHAT HE MIGHT HAVE ASKED OF GOD HAD HE BEEN ENJOINED TO WRITE THE BOOK OF GENESIS.

36. And yet, O my God, Thou exaltation of my humility, and rest of my labour, who hearest my confessions, and forgivest my sins, since Thou commandest me that I should love my neighbour as myself, I cannot believe that Thou gavest to Moses, Thy most faithful servant, a less gift than I should wish and desire for myself from Thee, had I been born in his time, and hadst Thou placed me in that position that through the service of my heart and of my tongue those books might be distributed, which so long after were to profit all nations, and through the whole world, from so great a pinnacle of authority, were to surmount the words of all false and proud teachings. I should have wished truly had I then been Moses (for we all come from the same mass; and what is man, saving that Thou art mindful of him? [6]). I should then, had I been at that time what he was, and enjoined by Thee to write the book of Genesis, have wished that such a power of expression and such a method of arrangement should be given me, that they who cannot as yet understand how God creates might not reject the words as surpassing their powers; and they who are already able to do this, would find, in what true opinion soever they had by thought arrived at, that it was not passed over in the few words of Thy servant; and should another man by the light of truth have discovered another, neither should that fail to be found in those same words.

CHAP. XXVII. — THE STYLE OF SPEAKING IN THE BOOK OF GENESIS IS SIMPLE AND CLEAR.

37. For as a fountain in a limited space is more plentiful, and affords supply for more streams over larger spaces than any one of those streams which, after a wide interval, is derived from the same fountain; so the narrative of Thy dispenser, destined to benefit many who were likely to discourse thereon, does, from a limited measure of language, overflow into streams of clear truth, whence each one may draw out for himself that truth which he can concerning these subjects, — this one that truth, that one another, by larger circumlocutions of discourse. For some, when they read or hear these words, think that God as a man or some mass gifted with immense power, by some new and sudden resolve, had, outside itself, as if at distant places, created heaven and earth, two great bodies above and below, wherein all things were to be contained. And when they hear, God said, Let it be made, and it was made, they think of words begun and ended, sounding in times and passing away, after the departure of which that came into being which was commanded to be; and whatever else of the kind their familiarity with the world [7] would suggest. In whom, being as yet little ones, [8] while their weakness by this humble kind of speech is carried on as if in a mother's bosom, their faith is healthfully built

---

[1] John viii. 44.
[2] 1 Tim. i. 8.
[3] As to all truth being God's, see vii. sec. 16, and note 3, above; and compare x. sec. 65, above.
[4] 1 Cor. iv. 6.
[5] Mark xii. 30, 31.

[6] Ps. viii. 8.
[7] "Ex familiaritate carnis," literally, "from familiarity with the flesh."
[8] "Parvulis animalibus."

up, by which they have and hold as certain that God made all natures, which in wondrous variety their senses perceive on every side. Which words, if any one despising them, as if trivial, with proud weakness shall have stretched himself beyond his fostering cradle, he will, alas, fall miserably. Have pity, O Lord God, lest they who pass by trample on the unfledged bird; and send Thine angel, who may restore it to its nest, that it may live until it can fly.[1]

CHAP. XXVIII. — THE WORDS, "IN THE BEGINNING," AND, "THE HEAVEN AND THE EARTH," ARE DIFFERENTLY UNDERSTOOD.

38. But others, to whom these words are no longer a nest, but shady fruit-bowers, see the fruits concealed in them, fly around rejoicing, and chirpingly search and pluck them. For they see when they read or hear these words, O God, that all times past and future are surmounted by Thy eternal and stable abiding, and still that there is no temporal creature which Thou hast not made. And by Thy will, because it is that which Thou art, Thou hast made all things, not by any changed will, nor by a will which before was not, — not out of Thyself, in Thine own likeness, the form of all things, but out of nothing, a formless unlikeness which should be formed by Thy likeness (having recourse to Thee the One, after their settled capacity, according as it has been given to each thing in his kind), and might all be made very good; whether they remain around Thee, or, being by degrees removed in time and place, make or undergo beautiful variations. These things they see, and rejoice in the light of Thy truth, in the little degree they here may.

39. Again, another of these directs his attention to that which is said, "In the beginning God made the heaven and the earth," and beholdeth Wisdom, — the Beginning,[2] because It also speaketh unto us.[3] Another likewise directs his attention to the same words, and by "beginning" understands the commencement of things created; and receives it thus, — In the beginning He made, as if it were said, He at first made. And among those who understand "In the beginning" to mean, that "in Thy Wisdom Thou hast created heaven and earth," one believes the matter out of which the heaven and earth were to be created to be there called "heaven and earth;" another, that they are natures already formed and distinct; another, one formed nature, and that a spiritual, under the name of heaven, the other formless, of corporeal matter, under the name of earth.

But they who under the name of "heaven and earth" understand matter as yet formless, out of which were to be formed heaven and earth, do not themselves understand it in one manner; but one, that matter out of which the intelligible and the sensible creature were to be completed; another, that only out of which this sensible corporeal mass was to come, holding in its vast bosom these visible and prepared natures. Nor are they who believe that the creatures already set in order and arranged are in this place called heaven and earth of one accord; but the one, both the invisible and visible; the other, the visible only, in which we admire the luminous heaven and darksome earth, and the things that are therein.

CHAP. XXIX. — CONCERNING THE OPINION OF THOSE WHO EXPLAIN IT "AT FIRST HE MADE."

40. But he who does not otherwise understand, "In the beginning He made," than if it were said, "At first He made," can only truly understand heaven and earth of the matter of heaven and earth, namely, of the universal, that is, intelligible and corporeal creation. For if he would have it of the universe, as already formed, it might rightly be asked of him: "If at first God made this, what made He afterwards?" And after the universe he will find nothing; thereupon must he, though unwilling, hear, "How is this first, if there is nothing afterwards?" But when he says that God made matter first formless, then formed, he is not absurd if he be but able to discern what precedes by eternity, what by time, what by choice, what by origin. By eternity, as God is before all things; by time, as the flower is before the fruit; by choice, as the fruit is before the flower; by origin, as sound is before the tune. Of these four, the first and last which I have referred to are with much difficulty understood; the two middle very easily. For an uncommon and too lofty vision it is to behold, O Lord, Thy Eternity, immutably making things mutable, and thereby before them. Who is so acute of mind as to be able without great labour to discover how the sound is prior to the tune, because a tune is a formed sound; and a thing not formed may exist, but that which existeth not cannot be formed?[4] So is the matter prior to that which is made from it; not prior because it maketh it, since itself is rather made, nor is it prior by an interval of time. For we do not as to time first utter formless sounds without singing, and then adapt or fashion them into the form of a song, just as wood or silver from which a chest or vessel is made. Because such materials do by

---

[1] In allusion, perhaps, to Prov. xxvii. 8: "As a bird that wandereth from her nest, so is a man that wandereth from his place."
[2] See p. 166, note 2.
[3] John viii. 23.

[4] See a similar argument in his *Con. adv. Leg. et Proph.* i. 9; and sec. 29, and note, above.

time also precede the forms of the things which are made from them; but in singing this is not so. For when it is sung, its sound is heard at the same time; seeing there is not first a formless sound, which is afterwards formed into a song. For as soon as it shall have first sounded it passeth away; nor canst thou find anything of it, which being recalled thou canst by art compose. And, therefore, the song is absorbed in its own sound, which sound of it is its matter. Because this same is formed that it may be a tune; and therefore, as I was saying, the matter of the sound is prior to the form of the tune, not before through any power of making it a tune; for neither is a sound the composer of the tune, but is sent forth from the body and is subjected to the soul of the singer, that from it he may form a tune. Nor is it first in time, for it is given forth together with the tune; nor first in choice, for a sound is not better than a tune, since a tune is not merely a sound, but a beautiful sound. But it is first in origin, because the tune is not formed that it may become a sound, but the sound is formed that it may become a tune. By this example, let him who is able understand that the matter of things was first made, and called heaven and earth, because out of it heaven and earth were made. Not that it was made first in time, because the forms of things give rise to time,[1] but that was formless; but now, in time, it is perceived together with its form. Nor yet can anything be related concerning that matter, unless as if it were prior in time, while it is considered last (because things formed are assuredly superior to things formless), and is preceded by the Eternity of the Creator, so that there might be out of nothing that from which something might be made.

CHAP. XXX. — IN THE GREAT DIVERSITY OF OPINIONS, IT BECOMES ALL TO UNITE CHARITY AND DIVINE TRUTH.

41. In this diversity of true opinions let Truth itself beget concord;[2] and may our God have mercy upon us, that we may use the law lawfully,[3] the end of the commandment, pure charity.[4] And by this if any one asks of me, "Which of

---

[1] See xi. sec. 29, above, and Gillies' note thereon; and compare with it Augustin's *De. Gen. ad Lit.* v. 5: "In vain we inquire after time before the creation as though we could find time before time, for if there were no motion of the spiritual or corporeal creatures whereby through the present the future might succeed the past, there would be no time at all. But the creature could not have motion unless it were. Time, therefore, begins rather from the creation, than creation from time, but both are from God."
[2] See p. 164, note 2, above.
[3] 1 Tim. i. 8.
[4] See p. 183, note, above; and on the supremacy of this law of love, may be compared Jeremy Taylor's curious story (Works, iv. 477, Eden's ed.): "St. Lewis, the king, having sent Ivo, Bishop of Chartres, on an embassy, the bishop met a woman on the way, grave, sad, fantastic, and melancholy, with fire in one hand, and water in the other. He asked what those symbols meant. She answered, 'My purpose is with fire to burn Paradise, and with my water to quench the flames of hell, that men may serve God without the incentives of hope and fear, and purely for the love of God.'"

these was the meaning of Thy servant Moses?" these were not the utterances of my confessions, should I not confess unto Thee, "I know not;" and yet I know that those opinions are true, with the exception of those carnal ones concerning which I have spoken what I thought well. However, these words of Thy Book affright not those little ones of good hope, treating few of high things in a humble fashion, and few things in varied ways.[5] But let all, whom I acknowledge to see and speak the truth in these words, love one another, and equally love Thee, our God, fountain of truth, — if we thirst not for vain things, but for it; yea, let us so honour this servant of Thine, the dispenser of this Scripture, full of Thy Spirit, as to believe that when Thou revealedst Thyself to him, and he wrote these things, he intended that which in them chiefly excels both for light of truth and fruitfulness of profit.

CHAP. XXXI. — MOSES IS SUPPOSED TO HAVE PERCEIVED WHATEVER OF TRUTH CAN BE DISCOVERED IN HIS WORDS.

42. Thus, when one shall say, "He [Moses] meant as I do," and another, "Nay, but as I do," I suppose that I am speaking more religiously when I say, "Why not rather as both, if both be true?" And if there be a third truth, or a fourth, and if any one seek any truth altogether different in those words, why may not he be believed to have seen all these, through whom one God hath tempered the Holy Scriptures to the senses of many, about to see therein things true but different? I certainly, — and I fearlessly declare it from my heart, — were I to write anything to have the highest authority, should prefer so to write, that whatever of truth any one might apprehend concerning these matters, my words should re-echo, rather than that I should set down one true opinion so clearly on this as that I should exclude the rest, that which was false in which could not offend me. Therefore am I unwilling, O my God, to be so headstrong as not to believe that from Thee this man [Moses] hath received so much. He, surely, when he wrote those words, perceived and thought whatever of truth we have been able to discover, yea, and whatever we have not been able, nor yet are able, though still it may be found in them.

CHAP. XXXII. — FIRST, THE SENSE OF THE WRITER IS TO BE DISCOVERED, THEN THAT IS TO BE BROUGHT OUT WHICH DIVINE TRUTH INTENDED.

43. Finally, O Lord, who art God, and not flesh and blood, if man doth see anything less,

---

[5] See end of note 17, p. 197, below.

can anything lie hid from "Thy good Spirit," who shall "lead me into the land of uprightness,"[1] which Thou Thyself, by those words, wert about to reveal to future readers, although he through whom they were spoken, amid the many interpretations that might have been found, fixed on but one? Which, if it be so, let that which he thought on be more exalted than the rest. But to us, O Lord, either point out the same, or any other true one which may be pleasing unto Thee; so that whether Thou makest known to us that which Thou didst to that man of Thine, or some other by occasion of the same words, yet Thou mayest feed us, not error deceive us.[2] Behold, O Lord my God, how many things we have written concerning a few words, — how many, I beseech Thee! What strength of ours, what ages would suffice for all Thy books after this manner? Permit me, therefore, in these more briefly to confess unto Thee, and to select some one true, certain, and good sense, that Thou shalt inspire, although many senses offer themselves, where many, indeed, may; this being the faith of my confession, that if I should say that which Thy minister felt, rightly and profitably, this I should strive for; the which if I shall not attain, yet I may say that which Thy Truth willed through Its words to say unto me, which said also unto him what It willed.

---

[1] Ps. cxliii. 10.

[2] Augustin, as we have seen (see notes, pp. 65 and 92), was frequently addicted to allegorical interpretation, but he, none the less, laid stress on the necessity of avoiding obscure and allegorical passages when it was necessary to convince the opponent of Christianity (*De Unit. Eccl.* ch. 5). It should also be noted that, however varied the meaning deduced from a doubtful Scripture, he ever maintained that such meaning must be *sacræ fidei congruam*. Compare *De Gen. ad Lit.* end of book i.; and *ibid.* viii. 4 and 7. See also notes, pp. 164 and 178, above.

BOOK XIII.

OF THE GOODNESS OF GOD EXPLAINED IN THE CREATION OF THINGS, AND OF THE TRINITY AS FOUND IN THE FIRST WORDS OF GENESIS. THE STORY CONCERNING THE ORIGIN OF THE WORLD (GEN. I.) IS ALLEGORICALLY EXPLAINED, AND HE APPLIES IT TO THOSE THINGS WHICH GOD WORKS FOR SANCTIFIED AND BLESSED MAN. FINALLY, HE MAKES AN END OF THIS WORK, HAVING IMPLORED ETERNAL REST FROM GOD.

CHAP. I. — HE CALLS UPON GOD, AND PROPOSES TO HIMSELF TO WORSHIP HIM.

1. I CALL upon Thee, my God, my mercy, who madest me, and who didst not forget me, though forgetful of Thee. I call Thee into [1] my soul, which by the desire which Thou inspirest in it Thou preparest for Thy reception. Do not Thou forsake me calling upon Thee, who didst anticipate me before I called, and didst importunately urge with manifold calls that I should hear Thee from afar, and be converted, and call upon Thee who calledst me. For Thou, O Lord, hast blotted out all my evil deserts, that Thou mightest not repay into my hands wherewith I have fallen from Thee, and Thou hast anticipated all my good deserts, that Thou mightest repay into Thy hands wherewith Thou madest me ; because before I was, Thou wast, nor was I [anything] to which Thou mightest grant being. And yet behold, I am, out of Thy goodness, anticipating all this which Thou hast made me, and of which Thou hast made me. For neither hadst Thou stood in need of me, nor am I such a good as to be helpful unto Thee,[2] my Lord and God ; not that I may so serve Thee as though Thou wert fatigued in working, or lest Thy power may be less if lacking my assistance ; nor that, like the land, I may so cultivate Thee that Thou wouldest be uncultivated did I cultivate Thee not ; but that I may serve and worship Thee, to the end that I may have well-being from Thee, from whom it is that I am one susceptible of well-being.

CHAP. II. — ALL CREATURES SUBSIST FROM THE PLENITUDE OF DIVINE GOODNESS.

2. For of the plenitude of Thy goodness Thy creature subsists, that a good, which could profit Thee nothing, nor though of Thee was equal to Thee, might yet be, since it could be made of Thee. For what did heaven and earth, which Thou madest in the beginning, deserve of Thee? Let those spiritual and corporeal natures, which Thou in Thy wisdom madest, declare what they deserve of Thee to depend thereon, — even the inchoate and formless, each in its own kind, either spiritual or corporeal, going into excess, and into remote unlikeness unto Thee (the spiritual, though formless, more excellent than if it were a formed body ; and the corporeal, though formless, more excellent than if it were altogether nothing), and thus they as formless would depend upon Thy Word, unless by the same Word they were recalled to Thy Unity, and endued with form, and from Thee, the one sovereign Good, were all made very good. How have they deserved of Thee, that they should be even formless, since they would not be even this except from Thee?

3. How has corporeal matter deserved of Thee, to be even invisible and formless,[3] since it were not even this hadst Thou not made it ; and therefore since it was not, it could not deserve of Thee that it should be made? Or how could the inchoate spiritual creature [4] deserve of Thee, that even it should flow darksomely like the deep, — unlike Thee, had it not been by the same Word turned to that by Whom it was created, and by Him so enlightened become light, although not equally, yet conformably to that Form which is equal unto Thee? For as to a body, to be is not all one with being beautiful, for then it could not be deformed ; so also to a created spirit, to live is not all one with living wisely, for then it would be wise unchangeably. But it is good [5] for it always to hold fast unto Thee,[6] lest, in turning from Thee, it lose that light which it hath obtained in turning to Thee,

---

[1] See i. sec. 2, above.
[2] Similar views as to God's not having need of us, though He created us, and as to our service being for our and not His advantage, will be found in his *De Gen. ad Lit.* viii. 11 ; and *Con. Adv. Leg. et Proph.* i. 4.

[3] Gen. i. 2.
[4] In his *De Gen. ad Lit.* i. 5, he maintains that the spiritual creature may have a formless life, since it has its form — its wisdom and happiness — by being turned to the Word of God, the Immutable Light of Wisdom.
[5] Ps. lxxiii. 28.
[6] Similarly, in his *De Civ. Dei*, xii. 1, he argues that true blessedness is to be attained "by adhering to the Immutable Good, the Supreme God." This, indeed, imparts the only true life (see note, p. 133, above) ; for, as Origen says (*in S. Joh*. ii. 7), "the good man is he who truly exists," and "to be evil and to be wicked are the same as not to be." See notes, pp. 75 and 151, above.

and relapse into a light resembling the darksome deep. For even we ourselves, who in respect of the soul are a spiritual creature, having turned away from Thee, our light, were in that life "sometimes darkness;"[1] and do labour amidst the remains of our darkness, until in Thy Only One we become Thy righteousness, like the mountains of God. For we have been Thy judgments, which are like the great deep.[2]

CHAP. III. — GENESIS I. 3, — OF "LIGHT," — HE UNDERSTANDS AS IT IS SEEN IN THE SPIRITUAL CREATURE.

4. But what Thou saidst in the beginning of the creation, "Let there be light, and there was light,"[3] I do not unfitly understand of the spiritual creature; because there was even then a kind of life, which Thou mightest illuminate. But as it had not deserved of Thee that it should be such a life as could be enlightened, so neither, when it already was, hath it deserved of Thee that it should be enlightened. For neither could its formlessness be pleasing unto Thee, unless it became light, — not by merely existing, but by beholding the illuminating light, and cleaving unto it; so also, that it lives, and lives happily,[4] it owes to nothing whatsoever but to Thy grace; being converted by means of a better change unto that which can be changed neither into better nor into worse; the which Thou only art because Thou only simply art, to whom it is not one thing to live, another to live blessedly, since Thou art Thyself Thine own Blessedness.

CHAP. IV. — ALL THINGS HAVE BEEN CREATED BY THE GRACE OF GOD, AND ARE NOT OF HIM AS STANDING IN NEED OF CREATED THINGS.

5. What, therefore, could there be wanting unto Thy good, which Thou Thyself art, although these things had either never been, or had remained formless, — the which Thou madest not out of any want, but out of the plenitude of Thy goodness, restraining them and converting them to form not as though Thy joy were perfected by them? For to Thee, being perfect, their imperfection is displeasing, and therefore were they perfected by Thee, and were pleasing unto Thee; but not as if Thou wert imperfect, and wert to be perfected in their perfection. For Thy good Spirit was borne over the waters,[5] not borne up by them as if He rested upon them.

For those in whom Thy good Spirit is said to rest,[6] He causes to rest in Himself. But Thy incorruptible and unchangeable will, which in itself is all-sufficient for itself, was borne over that life which Thou hadst made, to which to live is not all one with living happily, since, flowing in its own darkness, it liveth also; for which it remaineth to be converted unto Him by whom it was made, and to live more and more by "the fountain of life," and in His light to "see light,"[7] and to be perfected, and enlightened, and made happy.

CHAP. V. — HE RECOGNISES THE TRINITY IN THE FIRST TWO VERSES OF GENESIS.

6. Behold now, the Trinity appears unto me in an enigma, which Thou, O my God, art, since Thou, O Father, in the Beginning of our wisdom, — Which is Thy Wisdom, born of Thyself, equal and co-eternal unto Thee, — that is, in Thy Son, hast created heaven and earth. Many things have we said of the heaven of heavens, and of the earth invisible and formless, and of the darksome deep, in reference to the wandering defects of its spiritual deformity, were it not converted unto Him from whom was its life, such as it was, and by His enlightening became a beauteous life, and the heaven of that heaven which was afterwards set between water and water. And under the name of God, I now held the Father, who made these things; and under the name of the Beginning,[8] the Son, in whom He made these things; and believing, as I did, that my God was the Trinity, I sought further in His holy words, and behold, Thy Spirit was borne over the waters. Behold the Trinity, O my God, Father, Son, and Holy Ghost, — the Creator of all creation.

CHAP. VI. — WHY THE HOLY GHOST SHOULD HAVE BEEN MENTIONED AFTER THE MENTION OF HEAVEN AND EARTH.

7. But what was the cause, O Thou true-speaking Light? Unto Thee do I lift up my heart, let it not teach me vain things; disperse its darkness, and tell me, I beseech Thee, by our mother charity, tell me, I beseech Thee, the reason why, after the mention of heaven, and of the earth invisible and formless, and darkness upon the deep, Thy Scripture should then at length mention Thy Spirit? Was it because it was meet that it should be spoken of Him that He was "borne over," and this could not be said, unless that were first mentioned "over" which Thy Spirit may be understood to have been "borne?" For neither was He "borne over"

---

[1] Eph. v. 8.
[2] Ps. xxxvi. 6, as in the Vulgate, which renders the Hebrew more correctly than the Authorized Version. This passage has been variously interpreted. Augustin makes "the mountains of God" to mean the saints, prophets, and apostles, while "the great deep" he interprets of the wicked and sinful. Compare *In Ev. Joh. Tract.* i. 2; and *in Ps.* xxxv. 7, sec. 10.
[3] Gen. i. 3.
[4] Compare the end of chap. 24 of book xi of the *De Civ Dei*, where he says that the life and light and joy of the holy city which is above is in God.
[5] Gen. i. 2.

[6] Num. xi. 25.
[7] Ps. xxxvi. 9.
[8] See also xi. sec. 10, and note, above.

the Father, nor the Son, nor could it rightly be said that He was "borne over" if He were "borne over" nothing. That, therefore, was first to be spoken of "over" which He might be "borne;" and then He, whom it was not meet to mention otherwise than as having been "borne." Why, then, was it not meet that it should otherwise be mentioned of Him, than as having been "borne over?"

CHAP. VII. — THAT THE HOLY SPIRIT BRINGS US TO GOD.

8. Hence let him that is able now follow Thy apostle with his understanding where he thus speaks, because Thy love "is shed abroad in our hearts by the Holy Ghost, which is given unto us;" [1] and where, "concerning spiritual gifts," he teacheth and showeth unto us a more excellent way of charity; [2] and where he bows his knees unto Thee for us, that we may know the super-eminent knowledge of the love of Christ. [3] And, therefore, from the beginning was He supereminently "borne above the waters." To whom shall I tell this? How speak of the weight of lustful desires, pressing downwards to the steep abyss? and how charity raises us up again, through Thy Spirit which was "borne over the waters?" To whom shall I tell it? How tell it? For neither are there places in which we are merged and emerge. [4] What can be more like, and yet more unlike? They be affections, they be loves; the filthiness of our spirit flowing away downwards with the love of cares, and the sanctity of Thine raising us upwards by the love of freedom from care; that we may lift our hearts [5] unto Thee where Thy Spirit is "borne over the waters;" and that we may come to that pre-eminent rest, when our soul shall have passed through the waters which have no substance. [6]

CHAP. VIII. — THAT NOTHING WHATEVER, SHORT OF GOD, CAN YIELD TO THE RATIONAL CREATURE A HAPPY REST.

9. The angels fell, the soul of man fell, [7] and they have thus indicated the abyss in that dark deep, ready for the whole spiritual creation, unless Thou hadst said from the beginning, "Let there be light," and there had been light, and every obedient intelligence of Thy celestial City had cleaved to Thee, and rested in Thy Spirit, which unchangeably is "borne over" everything changeable. Otherwise, even the heaven of heavens itself would have been a darksome deep, whereas now it is light in the Lord. For even in that wretched restlessness of the spirits who fell away, and, when unclothed of the garments of Thy light, discovered their own darkness, dost Thou sufficiently disclose how noble Thou hast made the rational creature; to which nought which is inferior to Thee will suffice to yield a happy rest, [8] and so not even herself. For Thou, O our God, shalt enlighten our darkness; [9] from Thee are derived our garments of light, [10] and then shall our darkness be as the noonday. [11] Give Thyself unto me, O my God, restore Thyself unto me; behold, I love Thee, and if it be too little, let me love Thee more strongly. I cannot measure my love, so that I may come to know how much there is yet wanting in me, ere my life run into Thy embracements, and not be turned away until it be hidden in the secret place of Thy Presence. [12] This only I know, that woe is me except in Thee, — not only without, but even also within myself; and all plenty which is not my God is poverty to me. [13]

CHAP. IX. — WHY THE HOLY SPIRIT WAS ONLY "BORNE OVER" THE WATERS.

10. But was not either the Father or the Son "borne over the waters?" If we understand this to mean in space, as a body, then neither was the Holy Spirit; but if the incommutable super-eminence of Divinity above everything mutable, then both Father, and Son, and Holy

---

c. xxix., that "the restored part of humanity will fill up the gap which the rebellion and fall of the devils had left in the company of the angels. For this is the promise to the saints, that at the resurrection they shall be equal to the angels of God (Luke xx. 36). And thus the Jerusalem which is above, which is the mother of us all, the City of God, shall not be spoiled of any of the number of her citizens, shall perhaps reign over even a more abundant population." He speaks to the same effect at the close of ch. 1 of his *De Civ. Dei*, xxii. This doctrine was enlarged upon by some of the writers of the seventeenth century.

[8] See his *De Civ. Dei*, xxii. 1, where he beautifully compares sin to blindness, in that it makes us miserable in depriving us of the sight of God. Also his *De Cat. Rud.* sec. 24, where he shows that the restlessness and changefulness of the world cannot give rest. Comp. p. 46, note 7, above.

[9] Ps. xviii. 28.

[10] Ps. civ. 2.

[11] Ps. cxxxix. 12.

[12] Ps. xxxi. 20. "In abscondito vultus tui," *Old Ver.* Augustin in his comment on this passage (*Enarr.* 4, sec. 8) gives us his interpretation. He points out that the refuge of a particular place (*e.g.* the bosom of Abraham) is not enough. We must have God with us here as our refuge, and then we will be hidden in His countenance hereafter; or in other words, if we receive Him into our heart now, He will hereafter receive us into His countenance — *Ille post hoc sæculum excipiet te vultu suo.* For heaven is a prepared place for a prepared people, and we must be fitted to live with Him there by going to Him now, and this, to quote from his *De Serm. Dom. in Mon.* i. 27, "not with a slow movement of the body, but with the swift impulse of love."

[13] See p. 133, note 2, above.

---

[1] Rom. v. 5.
[2] 1 Cor. xii. 1, 31.
[3] Eph. iii. 14-19.
[4] "Neque enim loca sunt quibus mergimur et emergimus."
[5] Watts remarks here: "This sentence was generally in the Church service and communion. Nor is there scarce any one old liturgy but hath it, *Sursum corda, Habemus ad Dominum.*" Palmer, speaking of the Lord's Supper, says, in his *Origines Liturgicæ*, iv. 14, that "Cyprian, in the third century, attested the use of the form, 'Lift up your hearts,' and its response, in the liturgy of Africa (Cyprian, *De Orat. Dom.* p. 152, *Opera*, ed. Fell). Augustin, at the beginning of the fifth century, speaks of these words as being used in *all* churches" (Aug. *De Vera Relig.* iii.). We find from the same writer, *ibid.* v. 5, that in several churches this sentence was used in the office of baptism.
[6] "Sine substantia," the *Old Ver.* rendering of Ps. cxxiv. 5. The Vulgate gives "aquam intolerabilem." The Authorized Version, however, correctly renders the Hebrew by "proud waters," that is, *swollen*, as the water of sins: "for," he says, "sins have not substance; they have weakness, not substance; want, not substance." Augustin, *in Ps.* cxxiii. 5, sec. 9, explains the "aqua sine substantia," as the water of sins: "for," he says, "sins have not substance; they have weakness, not substance; want, not substance."
[7] We may note here that Augustin maintains the existence of the relationship between these two events. He says in his *Enchiridion*,

Ghost were borne "over the waters." Why, then, is this said of Thy Spirit only? Why is it said of Him alone? As if He had been in place who is not in place, of whom only it is written, that He is Thy gift?[1] In Thy gift we rest; there we enjoy Thee. Our rest is our place. Love lifts us up thither, and Thy good Spirit lifteth our lowliness from the gates of death.[2] In Thy good pleasure lies our peace.[3] The body by its own weight gravitates towards its own place. Weight goes not downward only, but to its own place. Fire tends upwards, a stone downwards. They are propelled by their own weights, they seek their own places. Oil poured under the water is raised above the water; water poured upon oil sinks under the oil. They are propelled by their own weights, they seek their own places. Out of order, they are restless; restored to order, they are at rest. My weight is my love;[4] by it am I borne whithersoever I am borne. By Thy Gift we are inflamed, and are borne upwards; we wax hot inwardly, and go forwards. We ascend Thy ways that be in our heart,[5] and sing a song of degrees; we glow inwardly with Thy fire, with Thy good fire, and we go, because we go upwards to the peace of Jerusalem; for glad was I when they said unto me, "Let us go into the house of the Lord."[6] There hath Thy good pleasure placed us, that we may desire no other thing than to dwell there for ever.

CHAP. X. — THAT NOTHING AROSE SAVE BY THE GIFT OF GOD.

11. Happy creature, which, though in itself it was other than Thou, hath known no other state than that as soon as it was made, it was, without any interval of time, by Thy Gift, which is borne over everything mutable, raised up by that calling whereby Thou saidst, "Let there be light, and there was light." Whereas in us there is a difference of times, in that we were darkness, and are made light;[7] but of that it is only said what it would have been had it not been enlightened. And this is so spoken as if it had been fleeting and darksome before; that so the cause whereby it was made to be otherwise might appear, — that is to say, being turned to the unfailing Light it might become light. Let him who is able understand this; and let him who is not,[8] ask of Thee. Why should he

trouble me, as if I could enlighten any "man that cometh into the world?"[9]

CHAP. XI. — THAT THE SYMBOLS OF THE TRINITY IN MAN, TO BE, TO KNOW, AND TO WILL, ARE NEVER THOROUGHLY EXAMINED.

12. Which of us understandeth the Almighty Trinity?[10] And yet which speaketh not of It, if indeed it be It? Rare is that soul which, while it speaketh of It, knows what it speaketh of. And they contend and strive, but no one without peace seeth that vision. I could wish that men would consider these three things that are in themselves. These three are far other than the Trinity; but I speak of things in which they may exercise and prove themselves, and feel how far other they be.[11] But the three things I speak of are, To Be, to Know, and to Will. For I Am, and I Know, and I Will; I Am Knowing and Willing; and I Know myself to Be and to Will; and I Will to Be and to Know. In these three, therefore, let him who can see how inseparable a life there is, — even one life, one mind, and one essence; finally, how inseparable is the distinction, and yet a distinction. Surely a man hath it before him; let him look into himself, and see, and tell me. But

---

[1] See *De Trin.* xv. 17-19.
[2] Ps. ix. 13.
[3] Luke ii. 14, *Vulg.*
[4] Compare *De Civ. Dei*, xi. 28: "For the specific gravity of bodies is, as it were, their love, whether they are carried downwards by their weight, or upwards by their levity."
[5] Ps. lxxxiv. 5.
[6] Ps. cxxii. 1.
[7] Eph. v. 8.
[8] *Et qui non potest*, which words, however, some MSS. omit, reading, *Qui potest intelligat ; a te petat.*

[9] John i. 9; see p. 76, note 2, and p. 181, note 2, above.
[10] As Augustin constantly urges of God, "Cujus nulla scientia est in anima, nisi scire quomodo eum nesciat" (*De Ord.* ii. 18), so we may say of the Trinity. The objectors to the doctrine sometimes speak as if it were irrational (Mansel's *Bampton Lectures*, lect. vi., notes 9, 10). But while the doctrine is *above* reason, it is not *contrary* thereto; and, as Dr. Newman observes in his *Grammar of Assent*, v. 2 (a book which the student should remember has been written since his union with the Roman Church), though the doctrine be mysterious, and, when taken as a whole, transcends all our experience, there is that on which the spiritual life of the Christian can repose in its "propositions taken one by one, and that not in the case of intellectual and thoughtful minds only, but of all religious minds whatever, in the case of a child or a peasant as well as of a philosopher." With the above compare the words of Leibnitz in his "Discours de la Conformité de la Foi avec la Raison," sec. 56: "Il en est de même des autres mystères, où les esprits modérés trouveront toujours une explication suffisante pour croire, et jamais autant qu'il en faut pour comprendre. Il nous suffit d'un certain *ce que c'est* (τί ἐστι); mais le *comment* (πῶς) nous passe, et ne nous est point nécessaire" (*Œuvres de Locke et Leibnitz*). See also p. 175, note 1, above, on the "incomprehensibility" of eternity.
[11] While giving illustrations of the Trinity like the above, he would not have a man think "that he has discovered that which is above these, Unchangeable." (See also *De Trin.* xv. 5, end.) He is very fond of such illustrations. In his *De Civ. Dei*, xi. 26, 27, for example, we have a parallel to this in our text, in the union of existence, knowledge, and love in man; in his *De Trin.* ix. 4, 17, 18, we have mind, knowledge, and love; *ibid.* x. 19, memory, understanding, and will; and *ibid.* xi. 16, memory, thought, and will. In his *De Lib. Arb.* ii. 7, again, we have the doctrine illustrated by the union of being, life, and knowledge in man. He also finds illustrations of the doctrine in other created things, as in their measure, weight, and number (*De Trin.* xi. 18), and their existence, figure, and order (*De Vera Relig.* xiii.). The nature of these illustrations would at first sight seem to involve him in the Sabellian heresy, which denied the fulness of the Godhead to each of the three Persons of the Trinity; but this is only in appearance. He does not use these illustrations as presenting anything *analogous* to the union of the three Persons in the Godhead, but as dimly illustrative of it. He declares his belief in the Athanasian doctrine, which, as Dr. Newman observes (*Grammar of Assent*, v. 2), "may be said to be summed up in this very formula on which St. Augustin lays so much stress, — 'Tres et Unus,' not merely 'Unum.'" Nothing can be clearer than his words in his *De Civ. Dei*, xi. 24: "When we inquire regarding each singly, it is said that each is God and Almighty; and when we speak of all together, it is said that there are not three Gods, nor three Almighties, but one God Almighty." Compare with this his *De Trin.* vii., end of ch. 11, where the language is equally emphatic. See also Mansel, as above, lect. vi. and notes 11 and 12.

when he discovers and can say anything of these, let him not then think that he has discovered that which is above these Unchangeable, which Is unchangeably, and Knows unchangeably, and Wills unchangeably. And whether on account of these three there is also, where they are, a Trinity; or whether these three be in Each, so that the three belong to Each; or whether both ways at once, wondrously, simply, and yet diversely, in Itself a limit unto Itself, yet illimitable; whereby It is, and is known unto Itself, and sufficeth to Itself, unchangeably the Self-same, by the abundant magnitude of its Unity, — who can readily conceive? Who in any wise express it? Who in any way rashly pronounce thereon?

CHAP. XII. — ALLEGORICAL EXPLANATION OF GENE- SIS, CHAP. I., CONCERNING THE ORIGIN OF THE CHURCH AND ITS WORSHIP.

13. Proceed in thy confession, say to the Lord thy God, O my faith, Holy, Holy, Holy, O Lord my God, in Thy name have we been baptized, Father, Son, and Holy Ghost, in Thy name do we baptize, Father, Son, and Holy Ghost,[1] because among us also in His Christ did God make heaven and earth, namely, the spiritual and carnal people of His Church.[2] Yea, and our earth, before it received the "form of doctrine,"[3] was invisible and formless, and we were covered with the darkness of ignorance. For Thou correctest man for iniquity,[4] and "Thy judgments are a great deep."[5] But because Thy Spirit was "borne over the waters,"[6] Thy mercy forsook not our misery,[7] and Thou saidst, "Let there be light," "Repent ye, for the kingdom of heaven is at hand."[8] Repent ye, let there be light.[9] And because our soul was troubled within us,[10] we remembered Thee, O Lord, from the land of Jordan, and that mountain[11] equal unto Thyself, but little for our sakes; and upon our being displeased with our darkness, we turned unto Thee, "and there was light." And, behold, we were sometimes darkness, but now light in the Lord.[12]

CHAP. XIII. — THAT THE RENEWAL OF MAN IS NOT COMPLETED IN THIS WORLD.

14. But as yet "by faith, not by sight,"[13] for "we are saved by hope; but hope that is seen is not hope."[14] As yet deep calleth unto deep[15] but in "the noise of Thy waterspouts."[16] And as yet doth he that saith, I "could not speak unto you as unto spiritual, but as unto carnal,"[17] even he, as yet, doth not count himself to have apprehended, and forgetteth those things which are behind, and reacheth forth to those things which are before,[18] and groaneth being burdened;[19] and his soul thirsteth after the living God, as the hart after the water-brooks, and saith, "When shall I come?"[20] "desiring to be clothed upon with his house which is from heaven;"[21] and calleth upon this lower deep, saying, "Be not conformed to this world, but be ye transformed by the renewing of your mind."[22] And, "Be not children in understanding, howbeit in malice be ye children," that in "understanding ye may be perfect;"[23] and "O foolish Galatians, who hath bewitched you?"[24] But now not in his own voice, but in Thine who sentest Thy Spirit from above;[25] through Him who "ascended up on high,"[26] and set open the flood-gates of His gifts,[27] that the force of His streams might make glad the city of God.[28] For, for Him doth "the friend of the bridegroom"[29] sigh, having now the first-fruits of the Spirit laid up with Him, yet still groaning within himself, waiting for the adoption, to wit, the redemption of his body;[30] to Him he sighs, for he is a member of the Bride; for Him is he jealous, for he is the friend of the Bridegroom;[29] for Him is he jealous, not for himself; because in the voice of Thy "waterspouts,"[16] not in his own voice, doth he call on that other deep, for whom being jealous he feareth, lest that, as the serpent beguiled Eve through his subtilty, so their minds should be corrupted from the simplicity that is in our Bridegroom, Thine only Son.[31] What a light of beauty will that be when "we shall see Him as He is,"[32] and those tears be passed away

---

[1] Matt. xxviii. 19.
[2] He similarly interprets "heaven and earth" in his De Gen. ad Lit. ii. 4. With this compare Chrysostom's illustration in his De Pœnit. hom. 8. The Church is like the ark of Noah, yet different from it. Into that ark the animals entered, so they came forth. The fox remained a fox, the hawk a hawk, and the serpent a serpent. But with the spiritual ark it is not so, for in it evil dispositions are changed. This illustration of Chrysostom is used with an effective but rough eloquence by the Italian preacher Segneri, in his Quaresimale, serm. iv. sec.
[3] Rom. vi. 17.
[4] Ps. xxxix. 11.
[5] Ps. xxxvi. 6.
[6] Gen. i. 3.
[7] See p. 47, note 10, above.
[8] Matt. iii. 2.
[9] "His putting repentance and light together is, for that baptism was anciently called illumination, as Heb. vi. 4, Ps. xlii. 2." — W. W. See also p. 118, note 4, part 1, above, for the meaning of "illumination."
[10] Ps. xlii. 6.
[11] That is, Christ. See p. 130, note 8, part 2, above; and compare the De Div. Quæst. lxxxiii. 6.
[12] Eph. v. 8.

[13] 2 Cor. v. 7.
[14] Rom. viii. 24.
[15] The "deep" Augustin interprets (as do the majority of Patristic commentators), in Ps. xli. 8, sec. 13, to be the heart of man; and the "deep" that calls unto it, is the preacher who has his own "deep" of infirmity, even as Peter had.
[16] Ps. xlii. 7.
[17] 1 Cor. iii. 1.
[18] Phil. iii. 13.
[19] 2 Cor. v. 2, 4.
[20] Ps. xlii. 1, 2.
[21] 2 Cor. v. 2.
[22] Rom. xii. 2.
[23] 1 Cor. xiv. 20 (margin).
[24] Gal. iii. 1.
[25] Acts ii. 19.
[26] Eph. iv. 8.
[27] Mal. iii. 10.
[28] Ps. xlvi. 4.
[29] John iii. 29.
[30] Rom. viii. 23.
[31] 2 Cor. xi. 3, and 1 John iii. 3.
[32] Ibid. ver. 2.

which "have been my meat day and night, while they continually say unto me, Where is thy God?"[1]

CHAP. XIV. — THAT OUT OF THE CHILDREN OF THE NIGHT AND OF THE DARKNESS, CHILDREN OF THE LIGHT AND OF THE DAY ARE MADE.

15. And so say I too, O my God, where art Thou? Behold where Thou art! In Thee I breathe a little, when I pour out my soul by myself in the voice of joy and praise, the sound of him that keeps holy-day.[2] And yet it is "cast down," because it relapses and becomes a deep, or rather it feels that it is still a deep. Unto it doth my faith speak which Thou hast kindled to enlighten my feet in the night, "Why art thou cast down, O my soul? and why art thou disquieted in me? hope thou in God;"[3] His "word is a lamp unto my feet."[4] Hope and endure until the night, — the mother of the wicked, — until the anger of the Lord be overpast,[5] whereof we also were once children who were sometimes darkness,[6] the remains whereof we carry about us in our body, dead on account of sin,[7] "until the day break and the shadows flee away."[8] "Hope thou in the Lord." In the morning I shall stand in Thy presence, and contemplate Thee;[9] I shall for ever confess unto Thee.[10] In the morning I shall stand in Thy presence, and shall see "the health of my countenance,"[11] my God, who also shall quicken our mortal bodies by the Spirit that dwelleth in us,[12] because in mercy He was borne over our inner darksome and floating deep. Whence we have in this pilgrimage received "an earnest"[13] that we should now be light, whilst as yet we "are saved by hope,"[14] and are the children of light, and the children of the day, — not the children of the night nor of the darkness,[15] which yet we have been.[16] Betwixt whom and us, in this as yet uncertain state of human knowledge, Thou only dividest, who provest our hearts[17] and callest the light day, and the darkness night.[18] For who discerneth us but Thou? But what have we that we have not received of Thee?[19] Out of the same lump vessels unto honour, of which others also are made to dishonour.[20]

CHAP. XV. — ALLEGORICAL EXPLANATION OF THE FIRMAMENT AND UPPER WORKS, VER. 6.

16. Or who but Thou, our God, made for us that firmament[21] of authority over us in Thy divine Scripture?[22] As it is said, For heaven shall be folded up like a scroll;[23] and now it is extended over us like a skin.[24] For Thy divine Scripture is of more sublime authority, since those mortals through whom Thou didst dispense it unto us underwent mortality. And Thou knowest, O Lord, Thou knowest, how Thou with skins didst clothe men[25] when by sin they became mortal. Whence as a skin hast Thou stretched out the firmament of Thy Book;[26] that is to say, Thy harmonious words, which by the ministry of mortals Thou hast spread over us. For by their very death is that solid firmament of authority in Thy discourses set forth by them more sublimely extended above all things that are under it, the which, while they were living here, was not so eminently extended.[27] Thou hadst not as yet spread abroad the heaven like a skin; Thou hadst not as yet noised everywhere the report of their deaths.

17. Let us look, O Lord, "upon the heavens, the work of Thy fingers;"[28] clear from our eyes that mist with which Thou hast covered them. There is that testimony of Thine which giveth wisdom unto the little ones.[29] Perfect, O my God, Thy praise out of the mouth of babes and sucklings.[30] Nor have we known any other books so destructive to pride, so destructive to the enemy and the defender,[31] who resisteth Thy reconciliation in defence of his own sins.[32] I know not, O Lord, I know not other such "pure"[33] words which so persuade me to confession, and make my neck submissive to Thy yoke, and invite me to serve Thee for nought. Let me understand these things, good Father. Grant this to me, placed under them; because Thou hast established these things for those placed under them.

---

[1] Ps. xlii. 3.
[2] *Ibid.* ver. 4.
[3] *Ibid.* ver. 5.
[4] Ps. cxix. 105.
[5] Job xiv. 13.
[6] Eph. ii. 3, and v. 8.
[7] Rom. viii. 10.
[8] Cant. ii. 17.
[9] Ps. v. 3.
[10] Ps. xxx. 12.
[11] Ps. xliii. 5.
[12] Rom. viii. 11.
[13] 2 Cor. i. 22.
[14] Rom. viii. 24.
[15] Though *of* the light, we are not yet *in* the light; and though, in this grey dawn of the coming day, we have a foretaste of the vision that shall be, we cannot hope, as he says *in Ps.* v. 4, to " see Him as He is" until the darkness of sin be overpast.
[16] Eph. v. 8, and 1 Thess. v. 5.
[17] Ps. vii. 9.
[18] Gen. i. 5.
[19] 1 Cor. iv. 7.

[20] Rom. ix. 21.
[21] Gen. i. 6.
[22] See sec. 33, below, and references there given.
[23] Isa. xxxiv. 4, and Rev. vi. 14.
[24] Ps. civ. 2; in the *Vulg.* being, "extendens cœlum *sicut pellem.*" The LXX. agrees with the *Vulg.* in translating בִּירִיעָה, "as a curtain," by "as a skin."
[25] Gen. iii. 21. Skins he makes the emblems of mortality, as being taken from dead animals. See p. 112, note 8, above.
[26] That is, the firmament of Scripture was after man's sin stretched over him as a parchment scroll, — stretched over him for his enlightenment by the ministry of mortal men. This idea is enlarged on *in Ps.* viii. 4, sec. 7, etc., xviii. sec. 2, xxxii. 6, 7, and cxlvi. 8, sec. 15.
[27] We have the same idea *in Ps.* ciii. sec. 8: "Cum enim viverent nondum erat extenta pellis, nondum erat extentum cœlum, ut tegeret orbem terrarum."
[28] Ps. viii. 3.
[29] Ps. xix. 7. See p. 62, note 6, above.
[30] Ps. viii. 2.
[31] He alludes to the Manichæans. See notes, pp. 67, 81, and 87.
[32] See part 2 of note 8 on p. 76, above.
[33] Ps. xix. 8.

18. Other "waters" there be "above" this "firmament," I believe immortal, and removed from earthly corruption. Let them praise Thy Name, — those super-celestial people, Thine angels, who have no need to look up at this firmament, or by reading to attain the knowledge of Thy Word, — let them praise Thee. For they always behold Thy face,[1] and therein read without any syllables in time what Thy eternal will willeth. They read, they choose, they love.[2] They are always reading; and that which they read never passeth away. For, by choosing and by loving, they read the very unchangeableness of Thy counsel. Their book is not closed, nor is the scroll folded up,[3] because Thou Thyself art this to them, yea, and art so eternally; because Thou hast appointed them above this firmament, which Thou hast made firm over the weakness of the lower people, where they might look up and learn Thy mercy, announcing in time Thee who hast made times. "For Thy mercy, O Lord, is in the heavens, and Thy faithfulness reacheth unto the clouds."[4] The clouds pass away, but the heaven remaineth. The preachers of Thy Word pass away from this life into another; but Thy Scripture is spread abroad over the people, even to the end of the world. Yea, both heaven and earth shall pass away, but Thy Words shall not pass away.[5] Because the scroll shall be rolled together,[3] and the grass over which it was spread shall with its goodliness pass away; but Thy Word remaineth for ever,[6] which now appeareth unto us in the dark image of the clouds, and through the glass of the heavens, not as it is;[7] because we also, although we be the well-beloved of Thy Son, yet it hath not yet appeared what we shall be.[8] He looketh through the lattice[9] of our flesh, and He is fair-speaking, and hath inflamed us, and we run after His odours.[10] But "when He shall appear, then shall we be like Him, for we shall see Him as He is."[8] As He is, O Lord, shall we see Him, although the time be not yet.

CHAP. XVI. — THAT NO ONE BUT THE UNCHANGE-
ABLE LIGHT KNOWS HIMSELF.

19. For altogether as Thou art, Thou only knowest, Who art unchangeably, and knowest unchangeably, and willest unchangeably. And

Thy Essence Knoweth and Willeth unchangeably; and Thy Knowledge Is, and Willeth unchangeably; and Thy Will Is, and Knoweth unchangeably. Nor doth it appear just to Thee, that as the Unchangeable Light knoweth Itself, so should It be known by that which is enlightened and changeable.[11] Therefore unto Thee is my soul as "land where no water is,"[12] because as it cannot of itself enlighten itself, so it cannot of itself satisfy itself. For so is the fountain of life with Thee, like as in Thy light we shall see light.[13]

CHAP. XVII. — ALLEGORICAL EXPLANATION OF THE
SEA AND THE FRUIT-BEARING EARTH — VERSES
9 AND 11.

20. Who hath gathered the embittered together into one society? For they have all the same end, that of temporal and earthly happiness, on account of which they do all things, although they may fluctuate with an innumerable variety of cares. Who, O Lord, unless Thou, saidst, Let the waters be gathered together into one place, and let the dry land appear,[14] which "thirsteth after Thee"?[15] For the sea also is Thine, and Thou hast made it, and Thy hands prepared the dry land.[16] For neither is the bitterness of men's wills, but the gathering together of waters called sea; for Thou even curbest the wicked desires of men's souls, and fixest their bounds, how far they may be permitted to advance,[17] and that their waves may be broken against each other; and thus dost Thou make it a sea, by the order of Thy dominion over all things.

21. But as for the souls that thirst after Thee, and that appear before Thee (being by other bounds divided from the society of the sea), them Thou waterest by a secret and sweet spring, that the earth may bring forth her fruit,[18] and,

---

[1] Matt. xviii. 10.
[2] "Legunt, eligunt, et diligunt."
[3] Isa. xxxiv. 4.
[4] Ps. xxxvi. 5.
[5] Matt. xxiv. 35.
[6] Isa. xl. 6-8. The law of storms, and that which regulates the motions of the stars or the ebbing and flowing of the tides, may change at the "end of the world." But the moral law can know no change, for while the first is arbitrary, the second is absolute. On the difference between moral and natural law, see Candlish, *Reason and Revelation*, "Conscience and the Bible."
[7] 1 Cor. xiii. 12.
[8] 1 John iii. 2.
[9] Cant. ii. 9.
[10] Cant. i. 3.

[11] See Dean Mansel on this place (*Bampton Lectures*, lect. v. note 18), who argues that revelation is clear and devoid of mystery when viewed as intended "for our practical guidance," and not as a matter of speculation. He says: " The utmost deficiency that can be charged against human faculties amounts only to this, that we cannot say that we know God as God knows Himself, — that the truth of which our finite minds are susceptible may, for aught we know, be but the passing shadow of some higher reality, which exists only in the Infinite Intelligence." He shows also that this deficiency pertains to the human faculties as such, and that, whether they set themselves to consider the things of nature or revelation. See also p 193, note 8, above, and notes, pp. 197, 198, below.
[12] Ps. lxiii. 1.
[13] Ps. xxxvi. 9.
[14] Gen. i. 9. In his comment on Psalm lxiv. 6 (sec. 9), he interprets "the sea," allegorically, of the wicked world. Hence were the disciples called "fishers of men." If the fishers have taken us in the nets of faith, we are to rejoice, because the net will be dragged to the shore. On the providence of God, regulating the wickedness of men, see p. 79, note 4, above.
[15] Ps. cxliii. 6, and lxiii. 1.
[16] Ps. xcv. 5.
[17] Ps. civ. 9, and Job xxxviii. 11, 12.
[18] Gen. i. 11. As he interprets (see sec. 20, note, above) the *sea* as the world, so he tells us *in Ps.* lxvi. 6, sec. 8, that when the *earth*, full of thorns, thirsted for the waters of heaven, God in His mercy sent His apostles to preach the gospel, whereon the earth brought forth that fruit which fills the world; that is, the earth bringing forth fruit represents the Church.

Thou, O Lord God, so commanding, our soul may bud forth works of mercy according to their kind,[1] — loving our neighbour in the relief of his bodily necessities, having seed in itself according to its likeness, when from our infirmity we compassionate even to the relieving of the needy; helping them in a like manner as we would that help should be brought unto us if we were in a like need; not only in the things that are easy, as in "herb yielding seed," but also in the protection of our assistance, in our very strength, like the tree yielding fruit; that is, a good turn in delivering him who suffers an injury from the hand of the powerful, and in furnishing him with the shelter of protection by the mighty strength of just judgment.

CHAP. XVIII. — OF THE LIGHTS AND STARS OF HEAVEN — OF DAY AND NIGHT, VER. 14.

22. Thus, O Lord, thus, I beseech Thee, let there arise, as Thou makest, as Thou givest joy and ability, — let "truth spring out of the earth, and righteousness look down from heaven,"[1] and let there be "lights in the firmament."[2] Let us break our bread to the hungry, and let us bring the houseless poor to our house.[3] Let us clothe the naked, and despise not those of our own flesh.[3] The which fruits having sprung forth from the earth, behold, because it is good;[4] and let our temporary light burst forth;[5] and let us, from this inferior fruit of action, possessing the delights of contemplation and of the Word of Life above, let us appear as lights in the world,[6] clinging to the firmament of Thy Scripture. For therein Thou makest it plain unto us, that we may distinguish between things intelligible and things of sense, as if between the day and the night; or between souls, given, some to things intellectual, others to things of sense; so that now not Thou only in the secret of Thy judgment, as before the firmament was made, dividest between the light and the darkness, but Thy spiritual children also, placed and ranked in the same firmament (Thy grace being manifest throughout the world), may give light upon the earth, and divide between the day and night, and be for signs of times; because "old things have passed away," and "behold all things are become new;"[7] and "because our salvation is nearer than when we believed;"[8] and because "the night is far spent, the day is at hand;"[8] and because Thou wilt crown Thy year with blessing,[9] sending the labourers of Thy goodness

into Thy harvest,[10] in the sowing of which others have laboured, sending also into another field, whose harvest shall be in the end.[11] Thus Thou grantest the prayers of him that asketh, and blessest the years of the just;[12] but Thou art the same, and in Thy years which fail not[13] Thou preparest a garner for our passing years. For by an eternal counsel Thou dost in their proper seasons bestow upon the earth heavenly blessings.

23. For, indeed, to one is given by the Spirit the word of wisdom, as if the greater light, on account of those who are delighted with the light of manifest truth, as in the beginning of the day; but to another the word of knowledge by the same Spirit, as if the lesser light;[14] to another faith; to another the gift of healing; to another the working of miracles; to another prophecy; to another the discerning of spirits; to another divers kinds of tongues. And all these as stars. For all these worketh the one and self-same Spirit, dividing to every man his own as He willeth;[15] and making stars appear manifestly, to profit withal.[16] But the word of knowledge, wherein are contained all sacraments,[17] which are varied in their periods like the moon, and the other conceptions of gifts, which are successively reckoned up as stars, inasmuch as they come short of that splendour of wisdom in which the fore-mentioned day rejoices, are only for the beginning of the night. For they are necessary to such as he Thy most prudent servant could not speak unto as unto spiritual, but as unto carnal[18] — even he who speaketh wisdom among those that are perfect.[19] But the natural man, as a babe in Christ, — and a drinker of milk, — until he be strengthened for solid meat,[20] and his eye be enabled to look upon

---

[10] Matt. ix. 38.
[11] Matt. xiii. 39.
[12] Prov. x. 6.
[13] Ps. cii. 27.
[14] Compare his *De Trin.* xii. 22–55, where, referring to 1 Cor. xii. 8, he explains that "knowledge" has to do with *action*, or that by which we use rightly things temporal; while wisdom has to do with the *contemplation* of things eternal. See also *in Ps.* cxxxv. sec. 8.
[15] 1 Cor. xii. 8–11.
[16] 1 Cor. xii. 7.
[17] 1 Cor. xiii. 2.   The Authorized Version and the Vulgate render more correctly, "mysteries." From Palmer (see p. 118, note 3, above), we learn that "the Fathers gave the name of *sacrament* or *mystery* to everything which conveyed one signification or property to unassisted reason, and another to faith;" while, at the same time, they included Baptism and the Lord's Supper as the two great sacraments. The sacraments, then, used in this sense are "varied in their periods," and Augustin, *in Ps.* lxxiii. 2, speaks of distinguishing between the sacraments of the Old Testament and the sacraments of the New. "Sacramenta novi Testamenti" he says, "dant salutem, sacramenta veteris Testamenti promiserunt salvatorem." So also *in Ps.* xlvi. he says: "Our Lord God varying, indeed, the sacraments of the words, but commending unto us one faith, hath diffused through the sacred Scriptures manifoldly and variously the faith in which we live, and by which we live. For one and the same thing is said in many ways, that it may be varied in the manner of speaking in order to prevent aversion, but may be preserved as one with a view to concord."
[18] 1 Cor. iii. 1.
[19] 1 Cor. ii. 6.
[20] 1 Cor. iii. 2, and Heb. v. 12. The allusion in our text is to what is called the *Disciplina Arcani* of the early Church. Clement of Alexandria, in his *Stromata*, enters at large into the matter of esoteric teaching, and traces its use amongst the Hebrews, Greeks,

---

[1] Ps. lxxxv. 11.
[2] Gen. i 14.
[3] Isa. lviii. 7.
[4] Gen. i. 12.
[5] Isa. lviii. 8.
[6] Phil. ii. 15.
[7] 2 Cor. v. 17.
[8] Rom. xiii. 11, 12.
[9] Ps. lxv. 11.

the Sun,[1] let him not dwell in his own deserted night, but let him be contented with the light of the moon and the stars. Thou reasonest these things with us, our All-wise God, in Thy Book, Thy firmament, that we may discern all things in an admirable contemplation, although as yet in signs, and in times, and in days, and in years.

CHAP. XIX. — ALL MEN SHOULD BECOME LIGHTS IN THE FIRMAMENT OF HEAVEN.

24. But first, "Wash you, make you clean;"[2] put away iniquity from your souls, and from before mine eyes, that the dry land may appear. "Learn to do well; judge the fatherless; plead for the widow,"[3] that the earth may bring forth the green herb for meat, and the tree bearing fruit;[4] and come let us reason together, saith the Lord,[5] that there may be lights in the firmament of heaven, and that they may shine upon the earth.[6] That rich man asked of the good Master what he should do to attain eternal life.[7] Let the good Master, whom he thought a man, and nothing more, tell him (but He is "good" because He is God) — let Him tell him, that if he would "enter into life" he must "keep the commandments;"[8] let him banish from himself the bitterness of malice and wickedness;[9] let him not kill, nor commit adultery,

nor steal, nor bear false witness; that the dry land may appear, and bud forth the honouring of father and mother, and the love of our neighbour.[10] All these, saith he, have I kept.[11] Whence, then, are there so many thorns, if the earth be fruitful? Go, root up the woody thicket of avarice; sell that thou hast, and be filled with fruit by giving to the poor, and thou shalt have treasure in heaven; and follow the Lord "if thou wilt be perfect,"[12] coupled with those amongst whom He speaketh wisdom, Who knoweth what to distribute to the day and to the night, that thou also mayest know it, that for thee also there may be lights in the firmament of heaven, which will not be unless thy heart be there;[13] which likewise also will not be unless thy treasure be there, as thou hast heard from the good Master. But the barren earth was grieved,[14] and the thorns choked the word.[15]

25. But you, "chosen generation,"[16] you weak things of the world," who have forsaken all things that you might "follow the Lord," go after Him, and "confound the things which are mighty;"[17] go after Him, ye beautiful feet,[18] and shine in the firmament,[19] that the heavens may declare His glory, dividing between the light of the perfect, though not as of the angels, and the darkness of the little, though not despised ones. Shine over all the earth, and let the day, lightened by the sun, utter unto day the word of wisdom; and let night, shining by the moon, announce unto night the word of knowledge.[20] The moon and the stars shine for the night, but the night obscureth them not, since they illumine it in its degree. For behold God (as it were) saying, "Let there be lights in the firmament of the heaven." There came suddenly a sound from heaven, as it had been the rushing of a mighty wind, and there appeared cloven tongues like as of fire, and it sat upon each of them.[21] And there were made lights in the firmament of heaven, having the word of life.[22] Run ye to and fro everywhere, ye holy fires, ye beautiful fires; for ye are the light of the world,[23] nor are ye put under a bushel.[24] He to whom ye cleave is exalted, and hath exalted you. Run ye to and fro, and be known unto all nations.

---

and Egyptians. Clement, like Chrysostom and other Fathers, supports this principle of interpretation on the authority of St. Paul in Heb. v. and vi., referred to by Augustin above. He says (as quoted by Bishop Kaye, *Clement of Alexandria*, ch. iv. p. 183): "Babes must be fed with milk, the perfect man with solid food; milk is catechetical instruction, the first nourishment of the soul; solid food, contemplation penetrating into all mysteries (ἡ ἐποπτικὴ θεωρία), the blood and flesh of the Word, the comprehension of the Divine power and essence." Augustin, therefore, when he speaks of being "contented with the light of the moon and stars," alludes to the partial knowledge imparted to the catechumen during his probationary period before baptism. It was only as *competentes*, and ready for baptism, that the catechumens were taught the Lord's Prayer and the Creed. We have already adverted to this matter in note 4 on p. 89, and need not now do more than refer the reader to Dr. Newman's *Arians*. In ch. i. sec. 3 of that work, there are some most interesting pages on this subject, in its connection with the Catechetical School of Alexandria. See also p. 118, note 8, above; Palmer, *Origines Liturgicæ*, iv. sec. 7; and note 1, below.

[1] Those ready for strong meat were called "illuminated" (see p. 118, note 4, above), as their eyes were "enabled to look upon the Sun." We have frequent traces in Augustin's writings of the Neo-Platonic doctrine that the soul has a capacity to see God, even as the eye the sun. In *Serm.* lxxxviii. 6 he says: "Daretne tibi unde videres solem quem fecit, et non tibi daret unde videres eum qui te fecit, cum te ad imaginem suam fecerit?" And, referring to 1 John iii. 2, he tells us in *Ep.* xcii. 3, that not with the bodily eye shall we see God, but with the inner, which is to be renewed day by day: "We shall, therefore, see Him according to the measure in which we shall be like Him; because now the measure in which we do not see Him is according to the measure of our unlikeness to Him." Compare also Justin Martyr, *Dialogue with Trypho*, c. 4: "Plato, indeed, says, that the mind's eye is of such a nature, and has been given for this end, that we may see that very Being who is the cause of all when the mind is pure itself." Some interesting remarks on this subject, and on the three degrees of divine knowledge as held by the Neo-Platonists, will be found in John Smith's *Select Discourses*, pp. 2 and 165 (Cambridge 1860). On growth in grace, see note 4, p. 140, above.
[2] "He alludes to the sacrament of Baptism." — W. W.
[3] Isa. i. 16, 19.
[4] Gen. i. 11, 30.
[5] Isa. i. 18.
[6] Gen. i. 15.
[7] Matt. xix. 16.
[8] *Ibid.* ver. 17.
[9] 1 Cor. v. 8.

[10] Matt. xix. 16–19.
[11] *Ibid.* ver. 20.
[12] *Ibid.* ver. 21.
[13] Matt. vi. 21.
[14] Matt. xix. 22.
[15] Matt. xiii. 7, 22.
[16] 1 Pet. ii. 9.
[17] 1 Cor. i. 27.
[18] Isa. lii. 7.
[19] Dan. xii. 3.
[20] Ps. xix.
[21] Acts ii. 3.
[22] 1 John i. 1.
[23] That is, as having their light from Him who is their central Sun (see p. 76, note 2, above). For it is true of all Christians in relation to their Lord, as he says of John the Baptist (*Serm.* ccclxxxii. 7): "Johannes lumen illuminatum: Christus lumen illuminans." See also note 1, above.
[24] Matt. v. 14.

CHAP. XX. — CONCERNING REPTILES AND FLYING CREATURES (VER. 20), — THE SACRAMENT OF BAPTISM BEING REGARDED.

26. Let the sea also conceive and bring forth your works, and let the waters bring forth the moving creatures that have life.[1] For ye, who "take forth the precious from the vile,"[2] have been made the mouth of God, through which He saith, "Let the waters bring forth," not the living creature which the earth bringeth forth, but the moving creature having life, and the fowls that fly above the earth. For Thy sacraments, O God, by the ministry of Thy holy ones, have made their way amid the billows of the temptations of the world, to instruct the Gentiles in Thy Name, in Thy Baptism. And amongst these things, many great works of wonder have been wrought, like as great whales; and the voices of Thy messengers flying above the earth, near to the firmament of Thy Book; that being set over them as an authority, under which they were to fly whithersoever they were to go. For "there is no speech, nor language, where their voice is not heard;" seeing their sound[3] "hath gone through all the earth, and their words to the end of the world," because Thou, O Lord, hast multiplied these things by blessing.[4]

27. Whether do I lie, or do I mingle and confound, and not distinguish between the clear knowledge of these things that are in the firmament of heaven, and the corporeal works in the undulating sea and under the firmament of heaven? For of those things whereof the knowledge is solid and defined, without increase by generation, as it were lights of wisdom and knowledge, yet of these self-same things the material operations are many and varied; and one thing in growing from another is multiplied by Thy blessing, O God, who hast refreshed the fastidiousness of mortal senses; so that in the knowledge of our mind, one thing may, through the motions of the body, be in many ways[5] set out and expressed. These sacraments have the waters brought forth;[6] but in Thy Word. The wants of the people estranged from the eternity of Thy truth have produced them, but in Thy Gospel; because the waters themselves have cast them forth, the bitter weakness of which was the cause of these things being sent forth in Thy Word.

28. Now all things are fair that Thou hast made, but behold, Thou art inexpressibly fairer who hast made all things; from whom had not Adam fallen, the saltness of the sea would never have flowed from him, — the human race so profoundly curious, and boisterously swelling, and restlessly moving; and thus there would be no need that Thy dispensers should work in many waters,[7] in a corporeal and sensible manner, mysterious doings and sayings. For so these creeping and flying creatures now present themselves to my mind, whereby men, instructed, initiated, and subjected by corporeal sacraments, should not further profit, unless their soul had a higher spiritual life, and unless, after the word of admission, it looked forwards to perfection.[8]

CHAP. XXI. — CONCERNING THE LIVING SOUL, BIRDS, AND FISHES (VER. 24), — THE SACRAMENT OF THE EUCHARIST BEING REGARDED.

29. And hereby, in Thy Word, not the depth of the sea, but the earth parted from the bitterness of the waters,[9] bringeth forth not the creeping and flying creature that hath life,[1] but the living soul itself.[10] For now hath it no longer need of baptism, as the heathen have, and as itself had when it was covered with the waters, — for no other entrance is there into the kingdom of heaven,[11] since Thou hast appointed that this should be the entrance, — nor does it seek great works of miracles by which to cause faith; for it is not such that, unless it shall have seen signs and wonders, it will not believe,[12] when now the faithful earth is separated from the waters of the sea, rendered bitter by infidelity; and "tongues are for a sign, not to those that believe, but to those that believe not."[13] Nor then doth the earth, which Thou hast founded above the waters,[14] stand in need of that flying kind which at Thy word the waters brought forth. Send Thy word forth into it by Thy messengers. For we relate their works, but it is Thou who workest in them, that in it they may work out a living soul. The earth bringeth it forth, because the

---

[1] Gen. i. 20.
[2] Jer. xv. 19.
[3] Ps. xix. 3, 4. The word "sound" in this verse (as given in the LXX. and _Vulg._), is in the Hebrew קַו, which is rightly rendered in the Authorized Version a "line" or "rule." It may be noted, in connection with Augustin's interpretation, that the word "firmament" in the first verse of this psalm is the רְקִיעַ of Gen. i. 7; translated in both places by the LXX. στερέωμα. The "heavens" and the "firmament" are constantly interpreted by the Fathers as referring to the apostles and their firmness in teaching the word; and this is supported by reference to St. Paul's quotation of the text in Rom. x. 18: "But I say, Have they not heard? Yes, verily, their sound went into all the earth, and their words unto the ends of the world."
[4] Gen. i. 4.
[5] See end of note 17, p. 197, above.
[6] "He alludes to Baptism in water, accompanied with the word of the gospel; of the institution whereof man's misery was the occasion." — W. W.

[7] See sec. 20, note, above.
[8] "He means that Baptism, which is the sacrament of initiation, was not so profitable without the Lord's Supper, which ancients called the sacrament of perfection or consummation." — W. W. Compare also sec. 24, note, and p. 140, note 3, above.
[9] See sec. 20, note, and sec. 21, note, above.
[10] Gen. ii. 7.
[11] John iii. 5.
[12] John iv. 48.
[13] 1 Cor. xiv. 22.
[14] "Fundasti super aquas," which is the _Old Ver._ of Ps. cxxxvi. 6. Augustin sometimes uses a version with "firmavit terram," which corresponds to the LXX., but the Authorized Version renders the Hebrew more accurately by "stretched out." In his comment on this place he applies this text to baptism as being the entrance into the Church, and in this he is followed by many mediæval writers.

earth is the cause that they work these things in the soul; as the sea has been the cause that they wrought upon the moving creatures that have life, and the fowls that fly under the firmament of heaven, of which the earth hath now no need; although it feeds on the fish which was taken out of the deep, upon that table which Thou hast prepared in the presence of those that believe.[1] For therefore He was raised from the deep, that He might feed the dry land; and the fowl, though bred in the sea, is yet multiplied upon the earth. For of the first preachings of the Evangelists, the infidelity of men was the prominent cause; but the faithful also are exhorted, and are manifoldly blessed by them day by day. But the living soul takes its origin from the earth, for it is not profitable, unless to those already among the faithful, to restrain themselves from the love of this world, that so their soul may live unto Thee, which was dead while living in pleasures,[2] — in death-bearing pleasures, O Lord, for Thou art the vital delight of the pure heart.

30. Now, therefore, let Thy ministers work upon the earth, — not as in the waters of infidelity, by announcing and speaking by miracles, and sacraments, and mystic words; in which ignorance, the mother of admiration, may be intent upon them, in fear of those hidden signs. For such is the entrance unto the faith for the sons of Adam forgetful of Thee, while they hide themselves from Thy face,[3] and become a darksome deep. But let Thy ministers work even as on the dry land, separated from the whirlpools of the great deep; and let them be an example unto the faithful, by living before them, and by stimulating them to imitation. For thus do men hear not with an intent to hear merely, but to act also. Seek the Lord, and your soul shall live,[4] that the earth may bring forth the living soul. "Be not conformed to this world."[5] Restrain yourselves from it; the soul lives by avoiding those things which it dies by affecting. Restrain yourselves from the unbridled wildness of pride, from the indolent voluptuousness of luxury, and from the false name of knowledge;[6] so that wild beasts may be tamed, the cattle subdued, and serpents harmless. For these are the motions of the mind in allegory; that is to say, the haughtiness of pride, the delight of lust, and the poison of curiosity are the motions of the dead soul; for the soul dies not so as to lose all motion, because it dies by forsaking the fountain of life,[7] and so is received by this transitory world, and is conformed unto it.

31. But Thy Word, O God, is the fountain of eternal life, and passeth not away; therefore this departure is kept in check by Thy word when it is said unto us, "Be not conformed unto this world,"[8] so that the earth may bring forth a living soul in the fountain of life, — a soul restrained in Thy Word, by Thy Evangelists, by imitating the followers of Thy Christ.[9] For this is after his kind; because a man is stimulated to emulation by his friend.[10] "Be ye," saith he, "as I am, for I am as you are."[11] Thus in the living soul shall there be good beasts, in gentleness of action. For Thou hast commanded, saying, Go on with thy business in meekness, and thou shalt be beloved by all men;[12] and good cattle, which neither if they eat, shall they over-abound, nor if they do not eat, have they any want;[13] and good serpents, not destructive to do hurt, but "wise"[14] to take heed; and exploring only so much of this temporal nature as is sufficient that eternity may be "clearly seen, being understood by the things that are."[15] For these animals are subservient to reason,[16] when, being kept in check from a deadly advance, they live, and are good.

CHAP. XXII. — HE EXPLAINS THE DIVINE IMAGE (VER. 26) OF THE RENEWAL OF THE MIND.

32. For behold, O Lord our God, our Creator, when our affections have been restrained from the love of the world, by which we died by living ill, and began to be a "living soul" by living well;[17] and Thy word which Thou spakest by Thy apostle is made good in us, "Be not conformed to this world;" next also follows that which Thou presently subjoinedst, saying, "But be ye transformed by the renewing of your mind,"[8] — not now after your kind, as if following your neighbour who went before you, nor as if living after the example of a better man (for Thou hast not said, "Let man be made after his kind," but, "Let us make man in our image,

---

[1] Ps. xxiii. 5. Many of the Fathers interpret this text of the Lord's Supper, as Augustin does above. The fish taken out of the deep, which is fed upon, means Christ, in accordance with the well-known acrostic of ΙΧΘΥΣ. "If," he says in his *De Civ. Dei*, xviii. 23, "you join the initial letters of these five Greek words, Ἰησοῦς Χριστὸς Θεοῦ Υἱὸς Σωτήρ, which mean, 'Jesus Christ the Son of God, the Saviour,' they will make the word ἰχθύς, — that is, 'fish,' in which word Christ is mystically understood, because He was able to live, that is, to exist without sin in the abyss of this mortality as in the depth of waters." So likewise we find Tertullian saying in his *De Bapt*. chap. i.: "Nos pisciculi, secundum ΙΧΘΥΝ nostrum Jesum Christum in aqua nascimur; nec aliter quam in aqua permanendo salvi sumus." See Bishop Kaye's *Tertullian*, pp. 43, 44; and sec. 34, below.
[2] 1 Tim. v. 6.
[3] Gen. iii. 8.
[4] Ps. lxix. 32.
[5] Rom. xii. 2.
[6] 1 Tim. vi. 20. See p. 153, note 7, above.

[7] Jer. ii. 13. See p. 133, note 2, and p. 129, note 8, above.
[8] Rom. xii. 2.
[9] 1 Cor. xi. 1.
[10] See p. 71, note 3, above.
[11] Gal. iv. 12.
[12] Ecclus. iii. 17, etc.
[13] 1 Cor. viii. 8.
[14] Matt. x. 16.
[15] Rom. i. 20.
[16] In his *De Gen. con. Manich*. i. 20, he interprets the dominion given to man over the beasts of his keeping in subjection the passions of the soul, so as to attain true happiness.
[17] As Origen has it: "The good man is he who truly exists." See p. 190, note 6, above; and compare the use made of the idea in Archbishop Thomson's *Bampton Lectures*, lect. i.

after our likeness"),[1] that we may prove what Thy will is. For to this purpose said that dispenser of Thine, — begetting children by the gospel,[2] — that he might not always have them "babes," whom he would feed on milk, and cherish as a nurse;[3] "be ye transformed," saith He, "by the renewing of your mind, that he may prove what is that good, and acceptable, and perfect will of God."[4] Therefore Thou sayest not, "Let man be made," but, "Let us make man." Nor sayest Thou, "after his kind," but, after "our image" and "likeness." Because, being renewed in his mind, and beholding and apprehending Thy truth, man needeth not man as his director[5] that he may imitate his kind; but by Thy direction proveth what is that good, and acceptable, and perfect will of Thine. And Thou teachest him, now made capable, to perceive the Trinity of the Unity, and the Unity of the Trinity. And therefore this being said in the plural, "Let us make man," it is yet subjoined in the singular, "and God made man;" and this being said in the plural, "after our likeness," is subjoined in the singular, "after the image of God."[6] Thus is man renewed in the knowledge of God, after the image of Him that created him;[7] and being made spiritual, he judgeth all things, — all things that are to be judged, — "yet he himself is judged of no man."[8]

CHAP. XXIII. — THAT TO HAVE POWER OVER ALL THINGS (VER. 26) IS TO JUDGE SPIRITUALLY OF ALL.

33. But that he judgeth all things answers to his having dominion over the fish of the sea, and over the fowls of the air, and over all cattle and wild beasts, and over all the earth, and over every creeping thing that creepeth upon the earth. For this he doth by the discernment of his mind, whereby he perceiveth the things "of the Spirit of God;"[9] whereas, otherwise, man being placed in honour, had no understanding, and is compared unto the brute beasts, and is become like unto them.[10] In Thy Church, therefore, O our God, according to Thy grace which Thou hast accorded unto it, since we are Thy workmanship created in good works,[11] there are not only those who are spiritually set over, but those also who are spiritually subjected to those placed over them; for in this manner hast Thou made man, male and female,[6] in Thy grace spiritual, where, according to the sex of body,

there is not male and female, because neither Jew nor Greek, nor bond nor free.[12] Spiritual persons, therefore, whether those that are set over, or those who obey, judge spiritually; not of that spiritual knowledge which shines in the firmament, for they ought not to judge as to an authority so sublime, nor doth it behove them to judge of Thy Book itself, although there be something that is not clear therein; because we submit our understanding unto it, and esteem as certain that even that which is shut up from our sight is rightly and truly spoken.[13] For thus man, although now spiritual and renewed in the knowledge of God after His image that created him, ought yet to be the "doer of the law, not the judge."[14] Neither doth he judge of that distinction of spiritual and carnal men, who are known to Thine eyes, O our God, and have not as yet made themselves manifest unto us by works, that by their fruits we may know them;[15] but Thou, O Lord, dost already know them, and Thou hast divided and hast called them in secret, before the firmament was made. Nor doth that man, though spiritual, judge the restless people of this world; for what hath he to do to judge them that are without,[16] knowing not which of them may afterwards come into the sweetness of Thy grace, and which continue in the perpetual bitterness of impiety?

34. Man, therefore, whom Thou hast made after Thine own image, received not dominion over the lights of heaven, nor over the hidden heaven itself, nor over the day and the night, which Thou didst call before the foundation of the heaven, nor over the gathering together of the waters, which is the sea; but he received dominion over the fishes of the sea, and the fowls of the air, and over all cattle, and over all the earth, and over all creeping things which creep upon the earth. For He judgeth and approveth what He findeth right, but disapproveth what He findeth amiss, whether in the celebration of those sacraments by which are

[1] Gen. i. 26.
[2] 1 Cor. iv. 15.
[3] 1 Thess. ii. 7.
[4] Rom. xii. 2.
[5] Jer. xxxi. 34.
[6] Gen. i. 27.
[7] Col. iii. 10.
[8] 1 Cor. ii. 15.
[9] 1 Cor. ii. 14.
[10] Ps. xlix. 20.
[11] Eph. ii. 10.

[12] Gal. iii. 28.
[13] In his De Civ. Dei, xi. 3, he defines very distinctly (as he does in other of his writings) the knowledge received 'by sight" — that is, by experience, as distinguished from that which is received "by faith" — that is, by revelation (2 Cor. v. 7). He, in common with all the Fathers who had knowledge of the Pagan philosophy, would feel how utterly that philosophy had failed to "find out" (Job xi. 7) with certitude anything as to God and His character, — the Creation of the world, — the Atonement wrought by Christ, — the doctrine of the Resurrection, as distinguished from the Immortality of the Soul, — our Immortal Destiny after death, or "the Restitution of all things." As to the knowledge of God, see Justin Martyr's experience in the schools of philosophy, Dialogue with Trypho, ch. ii.; and on the doctrine of Creation, see p. 165, note 4. On the "Restitution of all things," etc., reference may be made to Mansel's Gnostics, who points out (Introd. p. 3) that "in the Greek philosophical systems the idea of evil holds a very subordinate and insignificant place, and that the idea of redemption seems not to be recognised at all." He shows further (ibid. p. 4), that "there is no idea of the delivery of the creature from the bondage of corruption. The great year of the Stoics, the commencement of the new cycle which takes its place after the destruction of the old world, is but a repetition of the old evil." See also p. 164, note 2, above.
[14] Jas. iv. 11.
[15] Matt. viii. 20.
[16] 1 Cor. v. 12.

initiated those whom Thy mercy searches out in many waters; or in that in which the Fish[1] Itself is exhibited, which, being raised from the deep, the devout earth feedeth upon; or in the signs and expressions of words, subject to the authority of Thy Book, — such signs as burst forth and sound from the mouth, as it were flying under the firmament, by interpreting, expounding, discoursing, disputing, blessing, calling upon Thee, so that the people may answer, *Amen*. The vocal pronunciation of all which words is caused by the deep of this world, and the blindness of the flesh, by which thoughts cannot be seen, so that it is necessary to speak aloud in the ears; thus, although flying fowls be multiplied upon the earth, yet they derive their beginning from the waters. The spiritual man judgeth also by approving what is right and reproving what he finds amiss in the works and morals of the faithful, in their alms, as if in "the earth bringing forth fruit;" and he judgeth of the "living soul," rendered living by softened affections, in chastity, in fastings, in pious thoughts; and of those things which are perceived through the senses of the body. For it is now said, that he should judge concerning those things in which he has also the power of correction.

CHAP. XXIV. — WHY GOD HAS BLESSED MEN, FISHES, FLYING CREATURES, AND NOT HERBS AND THE OTHER ANIMALS (VER. 28).

35. But what is this, and what kind of mystery is it? Behold, Thou blessest men, O Lord, that they may "be fruitful and multiply, and replenish the earth;"[2] in this dost Thou not make a sign unto us that we may understand something? Why hast Thou not also blessed the light, which Thou calledst day, nor the firmament of heaven, nor the lights, nor the stars, nor the earth, nor the sea? I might say, O our God, that Thou, who hast created us after Thine Image, — I might say, that Thou hast willed to bestow this gift of blessing especially upon man, hadst Thou not in like manner blessed the fishes and the whales, that they should be fruitful and multiply, and replenish the waters of the sea, and that the fowls should be multiplied upon the earth. Likewise might I say, that this blessing belonged properly unto such creatures as are propagated from their own kind, if I had found it in the shrubs, and the fruit trees, and beasts of the earth. But now is it not said either unto the herbs, or trees, or beasts, or serpents, "Be fruitful and multiply;" since all these also, as well as fishes, and fowls, and men, do by propagation increase and preserve their kind.

36. What, then, shall I say, O Thou Truth, my Light, — "that it was idly and vainly said?"

Not so, O Father of piety; far be it from a minister of Thy word to say this. But if I understand not what Thou meanest by that phrase, let my betters — that is, those more intelligent than I — use it better, in proportion as Thou, O my God, hast given to each to understand. But let my confession be also pleasing before Thine eyes, in which I confess to Thee that I believe, O Lord, that Thou hast not thus spoken in vain; nor will I be silent as to what this lesson suggests to me. For it is true, nor do I see what should prevent me from thus understanding the figurative sayings[3] of Thy books. For I know a thing may be manifoldly signified by bodily expression which is understood in one manner by the mind; and that that may be manifoldly understood in the mind which is in one manner signified by bodily expression. Behold, the single love of God and of our neighbour, by what manifold sacraments and innumerable languages, and in each several language in how innumerable modes of speaking, it is bodily expressed. Thus do the young of the waters increase and multiply. Observe again, whosoever thou art who readest; behold what Scripture delivers, and the voice pronounces in one only way, "In the beginning God created heaven and earth;" is it not manifoldly understood, not by any deceit of error, but by divers kinds of true senses?[4] Thus are the offspring of men "fruitful" and do "multiply."

37. If, therefore, we conceive of the natures of things, not allegorically, but properly, then does the phrase, "be fruitful and multiply," correspond to all things which are begotten of seed. But if we treat those words as taken figuratively (the which I rather suppose the Scripture intended, which doth not, verily, superfluously attribute this benediction to the offspring of marine animals and man only), then do we find that "multitude" belongs also to creatures both spiritual and corporeal, as in heaven and in earth; and to souls both righteous and unrighteous, as in light and darkness; and to holy authors, through whom the law has been furnished unto us, as in the firmament[5] which has been firmly placed betwixt waters and waters; and to the society of people yet endued with bitterness, as in the sea; and to the desire of holy souls, as in the dry land; and to works of mercy pertaining to this present life, as in the seed-bearing herbs and fruit-bearing trees; and to spiritual gifts shining forth for edification, as in the lights of heaven; and to affections formed unto temperance, as in the living soul. In all these cases we meet with multitudes, abundance, and increase; but what shall thus "be fruitful and multiply,"

1 See sec. 29, note.
2 Gen. i. 28.
3 See p. 92, note 1, above.
4 See p. 189, note 2, above.
5 See p. 199, note 3, above.

that one thing may be expressed in many ways, and one expression understood in many ways, we discover not, unless in signs corporeally expressed, and in things mentally conceived. We understand the signs corporeally pronounced as the generations of the waters, necessarily occasioned by carnal depth; but things mentally conceived we understand as human generations, on account of the fruitfulness of reason. And therefore do we believe that to each kind of these it has been said by Thee, O Lord, " Be fruitful and multiply." For in this blessing I acknowledge that a power and faculty has been granted unto us, by Thee, both to express in many ways what we understand but in one, and to understand in many ways what we read as obscurely delivered but in one. Thus are the waters of the sea replenished, which are not moved but by various significations; thus even with the human offspring is the earth also replenished, the dryness[1] whereof appeareth in its desire, and reason ruleth over it.

CHAP. XXV. — HE EXPLAINS THE FRUITS OF THE EARTH (VER. 29) OF WORKS OF MERCY.

38. I would also say, O Lord my God, what the following Scripture reminds me of; yea, I will say it without fear. For I will speak the truth, Thou inspiring me as to what Thou willest that I should say out of these words. For by none other than Thy inspiration do I believe that I can speak the truth, since Thou art the Truth, but every man a liar.[2] And therefore he that " speaketh a lie, he speaketh of his own ; "[3] therefore that I may speak the truth, I will speak of Thine. Behold, Thou hast given unto us for food " every herb bearing seed," which is upon the face of all the earth, " and every tree in the which is the fruit of a tree yielding seed."[4] Nor to us only, but to all the fowls of the air, and to the beasts of the earth, and to all creeping things ;[5] but unto the fishes, and great whales, Thou hast not given these things. Now we were saying, that by these fruits of the earth works of mercy were signified and figured in an allegory, the which are provided for the necessities of this life out of the fruitful earth. Such an earth was the godly Onesiphorus, unto whose house Thou didst give mercy, because he frequently refreshed Thy Paul, and was not ashamed of his chain.[6] This did also the brethren, and such fruit did they bear, who out of Macedonia supplied what was wanting unto him.[7] But how doth he grieve for certain trees, which did not

afford him the fruit due unto him, when he saith, " At my first answer no man stood with me, but all men forsook me : I pray God that it may not be laid to their charge."[8] For these fruits are due to those who minister spiritual[9] doctrine, through their understanding of the divine mysteries; and they are due to them as men. They are due to them, too, as to the living soul, supplying itself as an example in all continency; and due unto them likewise as flying creatures, for their blessings which are multiplied upon the earth, since their sound went out into all lands.[10]

CHAP. XXVI. — IN THE CONFESSING OF BENEFITS, COMPUTATION IS MADE NOT AS TO THE " GIFT," BUT AS TO THE " FRUIT," — THAT IS, THE GOOD AND RIGHT WILL OF THE GIVER.

39. But they who are delighted with them are fed by those fruits ; nor are they delighted with them " whose god is their belly."[11] For neither in those that yield them are the things given the fruit, but in what spirit they give them. Therefore he who serves God and not his own belly,[12] I plainly see why he may rejoice ; I see it, and I rejoice with him exceedingly. For he hath received from the Philippians those things which they had sent from Epaphroditus ;[13] but yet I see why he rejoiced. For whereat he rejoices, upon that he feeds ; for speaking in truth, " I rejoiced," saith he, " in the Lord greatly, that now at the last your care of me hath flourished again, wherein ye were also careful,"[14] but it had become wearisome unto you. These Philippians, then, by protracted wearisomeness, had become enfeebled, and as it were dried up, as to bringing forth this fruit of a good work ; and he rejoiceth for them, because they flourished again, not for himself, because they ministered to his wants. Therefore, adds he, " not that I speak in respect of want, for I have learned in whatsoever state I am therewith to be content. I know both how to be abased, and I know how to abound ; everywhere and in all things I am instructed both to be full and to be hungry, both to abound and to suffer need. I can do all things through Christ which strengtheneth me."[15]

40. Whereat, then, dost thou rejoice in all things, O great Paul? Whereat dost thou rejoice? Whereon dost thou feed, O man, re-

---

[1] See sec. 21, and note, above.
[2] Rom. iii. 4, and Ps. cxvi. 11.
[3] John viii. 44.
[4] Gen. i. 29.
[5] Ibid ver. 30.
[6] 2 Tim. i. 16.
[7] 2 Cor. xi. 9.

[8] 2 Tim. iv. 16.
[9] " Rationalem. An old epithet to most of the holy things. So, reasonable service, Rom. xii. 1, λογικὸν γάλα; 1 Pet. ii. 2, sincere milk. Clem. Alex. calls Baptism so, Pedag. i. 6. And in Constitut. Apost. vi. 23, the Eucharist is styled, a reasonable Sacrifice. The word was used to distinguish Christian mysteries from Jewish. Rationale est spirituale." — W. W.
[10] Ps. xix. 4.
[11] Phil. iii. 19.
[12] Rom. xvi. 18.
[13] Phil. iv. 18.
[14] Ibid. ver. 10.
[15] Ibid. vers. 11-13.

newed in the knowledge of God, after the image of Him that created thee, thou living soul of so great continency, and thou tongue like flying fowls, speaking mysteries, — for to such creatures is this food due, — what is that which feeds thee? Joy. Let us hear what follows.' "Notwithstanding," saith he, "ye have well done that ye did communicate with my affliction."[1] Hereat doth he rejoice, hereon doth he feed; because they have well done,[2] not because his strait was relieved, who saith unto thee, "Thou hast enlarged me when I was in distress;"[3] because he knew both "to abound and to suffer need,"[4] in Thee Who strengthenest him. For, saith he, "ye Philippians know also that in the beginning of the gospel, when I departed from Macedonia, no Church communicated with me as concerning giving and receiving, but ye only. For even in Thessalonica ye sent once and again unto my necessity."[5] Unto these good works he now rejoiceth that they have returned; and is made glad that they flourished again, as when a fruitful field recovers its greenness.

41. Was it on account of his own necessities that he said, "Ye have sent unto my necessity"? Rejoiceth he for that? Verily not for that. But whence know we this? Because he himself continues, "Not because I desire a gift, but I desire fruit."[6] From Thee, O my God, have I learned to distinguish between a "gift" and "fruit." A gift is the thing itself which he gives who bestows these necessaries, as money, food, drink, clothing, shelter, aid; but the fruit is the good and right will of the giver. For the good Master saith not only, "He that receiveth a prophet," but addeth, "in the name of a prophet." Nor saith He only, "He that receiveth a righteous man," but addeth, "in the name of a righteous man." So, verily, the former shall receive the reward of a prophet, the latter that of a righteous man. Nor saith He only, "Whosoever shall give to drink unto one of these little ones a cup of cold water," but addeth, "in the name of a disciple;" and so concludeth, "Verily I say unto you, he shall in no wise lose his reward."[7] The gift is to receive a prophet, to receive a righteous man, to hand a cup of cold water to a disciple; but the fruit is to do this in the name of a prophet, in the name of a righteous man, in the name of a disciple. With fruit was Elijah fed by the widow, who knew that she fed a man of God, and on this account fed him; but by the raven

was he fed with a gift. Nor was the inner man[8] of Elijah fed, but the outer only, which might also from want of such food have perished.

CHAP. XXVII. — MANY ARE IGNORANT AS TO THIS, AND ASK FOR MIRACLES, WHICH ARE SIGNIFIED UNDER THE NAMES OF "FISHES" AND "WHALES."

42. Therefore will I speak before Thee, O Lord, what is true, when ignorant men and infidels (for the initiating and gaining of whom the sacraments of initiation and great works of miracles are necessary,[9] which we believe to be signified under the name of "fishes" and "whales") undertake that Thy servants should be bodily refreshed, or should be otherwise succoured for this present life, although they may be ignorant wherefore this is to be done, and to what end; neither do the former feed the latter, nor the latter the former; for neither do the one perform these things through a holy and right intent, nor do the other rejoice in the gifts of those who behold not as yet the fruit. For on that is the mind fed wherein it is gladdened. And, therefore, fishes and whales are not fed on such food as the earth bringeth not forth until it had been separated and divided from the bitterness of the waters of the sea.

CHAP. XXVIII. — HE PROCEEDS TO THE LAST VERSE, "ALL THINGS ARE VERY GOOD," — THAT IS, THE WORK BEING ALTOGETHER GOOD.

43. And Thou, O God, sawest everything that Thou hadst made, and behold it was very good.[10] So we also see the same, and behold all are very good. In each particular kind of Thy works, when Thou hadst said, "Let them be made," and they were made, Thou sawest that it was good. Seven times have I counted it written that Thou sawest that that which Thou madest was "good;" and this is the eighth, that Thou sawest all things that Thou hadst made, and behold they are not only good, but also "very good," as being now taken together. For individually they were only good, but all taken together they were both good and very good. All beautiful bodies also express this; for a body which consists of members, all of which are beautiful, is by far more beautiful than the several members individually are by whose well-ordered union the whole is completed, though these members also be severally beautiful.[11]

---

[1] Phil. iv. 14.
[2] Compare p. 160, note 2, above.
[3] Ps. iv. 1.
[4] Compare his *De Bono Conjug* ch. xxi., where he points out that while any may suffer need and abound, to *know* how to suffer belongs only to great souls, and to *know* how to abound to those whom abundance does not corrupt.
[5] Phil. iv. 15, 16.
[6] *Ibid.* ver. 17.
[7] Matt. x. 41, 42.

[8] 1 Kings xvii. See p. 133, note 2, above.
[9] We have already referred (p. 69, note 5, above) to the cessation of miracles. Augustin has a beautiful passage in *Serm.* ccxliv. 8, on the evidence which we have in the spread of Christianity — it doing for us what miracles did for the early Church. Compare also *De Civ. Dei*, xxii. 8. And he frequently alludes, as, for example, *in Ps.* cxxx., to "charity" being more desirable than the power of working miracles.
[10] Gen. i. 31.
[11] In his *De Gen. con. Manich.* i. 21, he enlarges to the same effect on Gen. i. 31.

CHAP. XXIX. — ALTHOUGH IT IS SAID EIGHT TIMES THAT "GOD SAW THAT IT WAS GOOD," YET TIME HAS NO RELATION TO GOD AND HIS WORD.

44. And I looked attentively to find whether seven or eight times Thou sawest that Thy works were good, when they were pleasing unto Thee; but in Thy seeing I found no times, by which I might understand that thou sawest so often what Thou madest. And I said, "O Lord, is not this Thy Scripture true, since Thou art true, and being Truth hast set it forth? Why, then, dost Thou say unto me that in Thy seeing there are no times, while this Thy Scripture tell-eth me that what Thou madest each day, Thou sawest to be good; and when I counted them I found how often?" Unto these things Thou repliest unto me, for Thou art my God, and with strong voice tellest unto Thy servant in his inner ear, bursting through my deafness, and crying, "O man, that which My Scripture saith, I say; and yet doth that speak in time; but time has no reference to My Word, because My Word existeth in equal eternity with Myself. Thus those things which ye see through My Spirit, I see, just as those things which ye speak through My Spirit, I speak. And so when ye see those things in time, I see them not in time; as when ye speak them in time, I speak them not in time."

CHAP. XXX. — HE REFUTES THE OPINIONS OF THE MANICHÆANS AND THE GNOSTICS CONCERNING THE ORIGIN OF THE WORLD.

45. And I heard, O Lord my God, and drank up a drop of sweetness from Thy truth, and understood that there are certain men to whom Thy works are displeasing, who say that many of them Thou madest being compelled by neces-sity; — such as the fabric of the heavens and the courses of the stars, and that Thou madest them not of what was Thine, but, that they were elsewhere and from other sources created; that Thou mightest bring together and compact and interweave, when from Thy conquered enemies Thou raisedst up the walls of the universe, that they, bound down by this structure, might not be able a second time to rebel against Thee. But, as to other things, they say Thou neither madest them nor compactedst them, — such as all flesh and all very minute creatures, and what-soever holdeth the earth by its roots; but that a mind hostile unto Thee, and another nature not created by Thee, and in everywise contrary unto Thee, did, in these lower places of the world, beget and frame these things.[1] Infatu-ated are they who speak thus, since they see

not Thy works through Thy Spirit, nor recog-nise Thee in them.

CHAP. XXXI. — WE DO NOT SEE "THAT IT WAS GOOD" BUT THROUGH THE SPIRIT OF GOD, WHICH IS IN US.

46. But as for those who through Thy Spirit see these things, Thou seest in them. When, therefore, they see that these things are good, Thou seest that they are good; and whatsoever things for Thy sake are pleasing, Thou art pleased in them; and those things which through Thy Spirit are pleasing unto us, are pleasing unto Thee in us. "For what man knoweth the things of a man, save the spirit of a man which is in him? Even so the things of God knoweth no man, but the Spirit of God. Now we," saith he, "have received not the spirit of the world, but the Spirit which is of God, that we might know the things that are freely given to us of God."[2] And I am reminded to say, "Truly, 'the things of God knoweth no man, but the Spirit of God;' how, then, do we also know 'what things are given us by God'?" It is answered unto me, "Because the things which we know by His Spirit, even these 'knoweth no man, but the Spirit of God.' For, as it is rightly said unto those who were to speak by the Spirit of God, 'It is not ye that speak,'[3] so is it rightly said to them who know by the Spirit of God, 'It is not ye that know.' None the less, then, is it rightly said to those that see by the Spirit of God, 'It is not ye that see;' so whatever they see by the Spirit of God that it is good, it is not they, but God who 'sees that it is good.'" It is one thing, then, for a man to suppose that to be bad which is good, as the fore-named do; another, that what is good a man should see to be good (as Thy creatures are pleasing unto many, be-cause they are good, whom, however, Thou pleasest not in them when they wish to enjoy them rather than enjoy Thee); and another, that when a man sees a thing to be good, God should in him see that it is good, — that in truth He may be loved in that which He made,[4] who cannot be loved unless by the Holy Ghost, which He hath given. "Because the love of God is shed abroad in our hearts by the Holy Ghost which is given unto us;"[5] by whom we see that whatsoever in any degree is, is good. Because it is from Him who Is not in any de-gree, but He Is that He Is.

CHAP. XXXII. — OF THE PARTICULAR WORKS OF GOD, MORE ESPECIALLY OF MAN.

47. Thanks to Thee, O Lord. We behold the heaven and the earth, whether the corporeal

---

[1] He alludes in the above statements to the heretical notions of the Manichæans. Their speculations on these matters are enlarged on in note 8 on p. 76.

[2] 1 Cor. ii. 12.
[3] Matt. x. 20.
[4] See the end of note 1, p. 74.
[5] Rom. v. 5.

part, superior and inferior, or the spiritual and corporeal creature ; and in the embellishment of these parts, whereof the universal mass of the world or the universal creation consisteth, we see light made, and divided from the darkness. We see the firmament of heaven,[1] whether the primary body of the world between the spiritual upper waters and the corporeal lower waters, or — because this also is called heaven — this expanse of air, through which wander the fowls of heaven, between the waters which are in vapours borne above them, and which in clear nights drop down in dew, and those which being heavy flow along the earth. We behold the waters gathered together through the plains of the sea ; and the dry land both void and formed, so as to be visible and compact, and the matter of herbs and trees. We behold the lights shining from above, — the sun to serve the day, the moon and the stars to cheer the night ; and that by all these, times should be marked and noted. We behold on every side a humid element, fruitful with fishes, beasts, and birds ; because the density of the air, which bears up the flights of birds, is increased by the exhalation of the waters.[2] We behold the face of the earth furnished with terrestrial creatures, and man, created after Thy image and likeness, in that very image and likeness of Thee (that is, the power of reason and understanding) on account of which he was set over all irrational creatures. And as in his soul there is one power which rules by directing, another made subject that it might obey, so also for the man was corporeally made a woman,[3] who, in the mind of her rational understanding should also have a like nature, in the sex, however, of her body should be in like manner subject to the sex of her husband, as the appetite of action is subjected by reason of the mind, to conceive the skill of acting rightly. These things we behold, and they are severally good, and all very good.

CHAP. XXXIII. — THE WORLD WAS CREATED BY GOD OUT OF NOTHING.

48. Let Thy works praise Thee, that we may love Thee ; and let us love Thee, that Thy works may praise Thee, the which have beginning and end from time, — rising and setting, growth and decay, form and privation. They have therefore their successions of morning and

evening, partly hidden, partly apparent ; for they were made from nothing by Thee, not of Thee, nor of any matter not Thine, or which was created before, but of concreated matter (that is, matter at the same time created by Thee), because without any interval of time Thou didst form its formlessness.[4] For since the matter of heaven and earth is one thing, and the form of heaven and earth another, Thou hast made the matter indeed of almost nothing, but the form of the world Thou hast formed of formless matter ; both, however, at the same time, so that the form should follow the matter with no interval of delay.

CHAP. XXXIV. — HE BRIEFLY REPEATS THE ALLEGORICAL INTERPRETATION OF GENESIS (CH. I.), AND CONFESSES THAT WE SEE IT BY THE DIVINE SPIRIT.

49. We have also examined what Thou willedst to be shadowed forth, whether by the creation, or the description of things in such an order. And we have seen that things severally are good, and all things very good,[5] in Thy Word, in Thine Only-Begotten, both heaven and earth, the Head and the body of the Church, in Thy predestination before all times, without morning and evening. But when Thou didst begin to execute in time the things predestinated, that Thou mightest make manifest things hidden, and adjust our disorders (for our sins were over us, and we had sunk into profound darkness away from Thee, and Thy good Spirit was borne over us to help us in due season), Thou didst both justify the ungodly,[6] and didst divide them from the wicked ; and madest firm the authority of Thy Book between those above, who would be docile unto Thee, and those under, who would be subject unto them ; and Thou didst collect the society of unbelievers into one conspiracy, in order that the zeal of the faithful might appear, and that they might bring forth works of mercy unto Thee, even distributing unto the poor earthly riches, to obtain heavenly. And after this didst Thou kindle certain lights in the firmament, Thy holy ones, having the word of life, and shining with an eminent authority preferred by spiritual gifts ; and then again, for the instruction of the unbelieving Gentiles, didst Thou out of corporeal matter produce the sacraments and visible miracles, and sounds of words according to the firmament be Thy Book, by which the faithful should of blessed. Next didst Thou form the living soul of the faithful, through affections ordered by the vigour of continency ; and afterwards, the mind

---

[1] In his *Retractations*, ii. 6, he says: "Non satis considerate dictum est ; res enim in abdito est valde."
[2] Compare *De Gen. con. Manich.* ii. 15.
[3] "'Concipiendam,' or the reading may be 'concupiscendam,' according to St. Augustin's interpretation of Gen. iii. 16, in the *De Gen. con. Manich.* ii. 15. 'As an instance hereof was woman made, who is in the order of things made subject to the man ; that what appears more evidently in two human beings, the man and the woman, may be contemplated in the one, man ; viz. that the inward man, as it were manly reason, should have in subjection the appetite of the soul, whereby we act through the bodily members.'" — E. B. P.

[4] See p. 165, note 4, above.
[5] Gen. i. 31.
[6] Rom. iv. 5.

subjected to Thee alone, and needing to imitate no human authority,[1] Thou didst renew after Thine image and likeness ; and didst subject its rational action to the excellency of the under-standing, as the woman to the man ; and to all Thy ministries, necessary for the perfecting of the faithful in this life, Thou didst will that, for their temporal uses, good things, fruitful in the future time, should be given by the same faith-ful.[2] We behold all these things, and they are very good, because Thou dost see them in us, — Thou who hast given unto us Thy Spirit, whereby we might see them, and in them love Thee.

CHAP. XXXV. — HE PRAYS GOD FOR THAT PEACE OF REST WHICH HATH NO EVENING.

50. O Lord God, grant Thy peace unto us, — for Thou hast supplied us with all things, — the peace of rest, the peace of the Sabbath, which hath no evening. For all this most beautiful order of things, " very good " (all their courses being finished), is to pass away, for in them there was morning and evening.

CHAP. XXXVI. — THE SEVENTH DAY, WITHOUT EVENING AND SETTING, THE IMAGE OF ETERNAL LIFE AND REST IN GOD.

51. But the seventh day is without any even-ing, nor hath it any setting, because Thou hast sanctified it to an everlasting continuance ; that that which Thou didst after Thy works, which were very good, resting on the seventh day, although in unbroken rest Thou madest them, that the voice of Thy Book may speak before-hand unto us, that we also after our works (therefore very good, because Thou hast given

them unto us) may repose in Thee also in the Sabbath of eternal life.

CHAP. XXXVII. — OF REST IN GOD, WHO EVER WORKETH, AND YET IS EVER AT REST.

52. For even then shalt Thou so rest in us, as now Thou dost work in us ; and thus shall that be Thy rest through us, as these are Thy works through us.[3] But Thou, O Lord, ever workest, and art ever at rest. Nor seest Thou in time, nor movest Thou in time, nor restest Thou in time ; and yet Thou makest the scenes of time, and the times themselves, and the rest which results from time.

CHAP. XXXVIII. — OF THE DIFFERENCE BETWEEN THE KNOWLEDGE OF GOD AND OF MEN, AND OF THE REPOSE WHICH IS TO BE SOUGHT FROM GOD ONLY.

53. We therefore see those things which Thou madest, because they are ; but they are because Thou seest them. And we see without that they are, and within that they are good, but Thou didst see them there, when made, where Thou didst see them to be made. And we were at another time moved to do well, after our hearts had conceived of Thy Spirit ; but in the former time, forsaking Thee, we were moved to do evil ; but Thou, the One, the Good God, hast never ceased to do good. And we also have certain good works, of Thy gift, but not eternal ; after these we hope to rest in Thy great hal-lowing. But Thou, being the Good, needing no good, art ever at rest, because Thou Thyself art Thy rest. And what man will teach man to understand this ? Or what angel, an angel ? Or what angel, a man ? Let it be asked of Thee, sought in Thee, knocked for at Thee ; so, even so shall it be received, so shall it be found, so shall it be opened.[4]   *Amen.*

---

[1] See p. 165, note 2, above.

[2] " The peace of heaven," says Augustin in his *De Civ. Dei,* xix. 17, " alone can be truly called and esteemed the peace of the reason-able creatures, consisting as it does in the perfectly ordered and har-monious enjoyment of God, and of one another in God. When we shall have reached that peace, this mortal life shall give place to one that is eternal, and our body shall be no more this animal body which by its corruption weighs down the soul, but a spiritual body feeling no want, and in all its members subjected to the will." See p. 111, note 8 (end), above.

[3] Compare his *De Gen. ad Lit.* iv. 9: " For as God is properly said to do what we do when He works in us, so is God properly said to rest when by His gift we rest."

[4] Matt. vii. 7.

LETTERS

OF

ST. AUGUSTIN

TRANSLATED BY

THE REV. J. G. CUNNINGHAM, M.A.

PREFACE.

THE importance of the letters of eminent men, as illustrations of their life, character, and times, is too well understood to need remark. The Letters of Cicero and Pliny have given us a more vivid conception of Roman life than the most careful history could have given; the Letters of Erasmus, Luther, and Calvin furnish us with the most trustworthy material for understanding the rapid movement and fierce conflict of their age; when we read the voluminous correspondence of Pope and his compeers, or the unstudied beauties of Cowper's letters of friendship, we seem to be in the company of living men; and modern history has in nothing more distinctly proved its sagacity, than by its diligence in publishing the Letters of Cromwell, of Washington, of Chatham, and of other historical personages.

For biography, familiar letters are the most important material. In a man's published writings we see the general character of his mind, and we ascertain his opinions in so far as he deemed it safe or advisable to lay these before a perhaps unsympathizing public; in his letters he reveals his whole character, his feelings as well as his judgments, his motives, his personal history, and the various ramifications of his interest. In his familiar correspondence we see the man as he is known to his intimate friends, in his times of relaxation and unstudied utterance.[1] Few men, in writing for the public, can resist the tendency towards a constrained attitudinizing, or throw off the fixed expression of one sitting for his portrait; and it is only in conversation, spoken or written, that we get the whole man revealed in a series of constantly varying and unconstrained expressions. And even where, as in Augustin's case, we have an autobiography, we derive from the letters many additional traits of character, much valuable illustration of opinions and progress.[2]

In their function of appendices to history they are equally valuable. It was a characteristic remark of Horace Walpole's, that "nothing gives so just an idea of an age as genuine letters; nay, history waits for its last seal from them." A still greater authority, Bacon, in his marvellous distribution of all knowledge, gives to letters the highest place among the "Appendices to History." "Letters," he says, "are, according to all the variety of occasions, advertisements, advices, directions, propositions, petitions commendatory, expostulatory, satisfactory; of compliment, of pleasure, of discourse, and all other passages of action. And such as are written from wise men are, of all the words of man, in my judgment, the best; for they are more natural than orations and public speeches, and more advised than conferences or present speeches. So, again, letters of affairs from such as manage them, or are privy to them, are of all others the best instructions for history, and to a diligent reader the best histories in themselves."[3] This is especially true of the Letters of Augustin. A large number of them are ecclesiastical and theological, and would in our day have appeared as pamphlets, or would have been delivered as lectures. There are none of his writings which do not receive some supplementary light from his letters. The subjects of his more elaborate writings are here handled in an easier manner, and their sources,

---

[1] "Ut oculi aliis corporis sensibus praestant, ita illustrium virorum Epistolae caeteris eorum scriptis passim antecellunt." — Benedictine Preface to the *Ep. Aug.*

[2] "Si, dans le vaste naufrage des temps, par un malheur que la Providence n'a pas permis, les ouvrages proprement dits de Saint Augustin eussent péri et qu'il ne fût resté que ses lettres, nous aurions encore toute sa doctrine, tout son génie: les *Lettres de Saint Augustin, c'est tout Saint Augustin.*" — Poujoulat, *Lettres de. S. Aug.* vii.

[3] *Advancement of Learning*, p. 125.

motives, and origin are disclosed.   Difficulties which his published works had occasioned are here removed, new illustrations are noted, further developments and fresh complications of heresy are alluded to, and the whole theological movement of the time is here reflected in a vivid and interesting shape.   No controversy of his age was settled without his voice, and it is in his letters we chiefly see the vastness of his empire, the variety of subjects on which appeal was made to him, and the deference with which his judgment was received.   Inquiring philosophers, puzzled statesmen, angry heretics, pious ladies, all found their way to the Bishop of Hippo.   And while he continually complains of want of leisure, of the multifarious business of his episcopate, of the unwarranted demands made upon him, he yet carefully answers all.   Sometimes he writes with the courier who is to carry his letter impatiently chafing outside the door; sometimes a promptly written reply is carried round the whole known world by some faithless messenger before it reaches his anxious correspondent; but, amidst difficulties unthought of under a postal system, his indefatigable diligence succeeds in diffusing intelligence and counsel to the most distant inquirers.

In the present volume we have, as usual, followed the Benedictine edition.   Among the many labours which the Benedictine Fathers encountered in editing the works of Augustin, they under-took the onerous task of rearranging the Epistles in chronological order.   The manner in which this task has been executed is eminently characteristic of their unostentatious patience and skill. Their order has been universally adopted; it is to this order that reference is made when any writer cites a letter of Augustin's; and therefore it matters less whether in each case the date assigned by the Benedictine editors can be accepted as accurate.   It will be seen that we have not considered it desirable to translate all the letters.   Of those addressed to Augustin we have omitted a few which were neither important in themselves nor indispensable for the understanding of his replies; and, when any of his own letters is a mere repetition of what he has previously written to another correspondent, we have contented ourselves, and, we hope, shall satisfy our readers, with a reference to the former letter in which the arguments and illustrations now repeated may be found.

No English translation of these Letters has previously appeared.   The French have in this, as in other patristic studies, been before us.   Two hundred years ago a translation into the French tongue was published, and this has lately been superseded by M. Poujoulat's four readable and fairly accurate volumes.

THE EDITOR.

1872.

In the second volume of Letters in Clark's series the editor adds the following

PREFATORY NOTE.

OF the two hundred and seventy-two letters given in the Benedictine edition of Augustin's works, one hundred and sixty are translated in this selection.   In the former volume few were omitted, and the reason for each omission was given in its own place.   As the proportion of untranslated letters is in this volume much larger, it may be more convenient to indicate briefly here the general reasons which have guided us in the selection.

We have omitted —

I. Almost all the letters referring to the Donatist schism, as there is enough on this subject in the works on the Donatist controversy (vol. iii. of this series) and in numerous earlier letters. This excludes — 105, 106, 107, 108, 128, 129, 134, 141, 142, and 204.

II. Almost all the letters relating to Pelagianism, as the series contains three volumes of Augustin's anti-Pelagian writings (vols. iv. xii. xv.).   This excludes — 156, 157, 175, 176, 177, 178, 179, 181, 182, 183, 184, 184 *bis*, 186, 193, 194, 214, 215, 216, 217.

III. Almost all the letters referring to the doctrine of the Trinity, as this has been already given, partly in earlier letters, and more fully in the volume on the Trinity (vol. vii. of this series). This excludes — 119, 120, 170, 174, 238, 239, 240, 241, 242.

IV. Almost all those which in design, style, and prolixity, are exegetical or doctrinal treatises rather than letters. This excludes — 140, 147, 149, 152, 153, 154, 155, 162, 187, 190, 196, 197, 198, 199, 202 *bis*, 205.

V. Some of the letters written by others to Augustin. This excludes — 94, 109, 121, 160, 168, 225, 226, 230, 270.

VI. A large number of miscellaneous smaller letters, as, in order to avoid going beyond the limits of one volume, it was necessary to select only the more interesting and important of these. This excludes — 110, 112, 113, 114, 127, 161, 162, 171, 200, 206, 207, 221, 222, 223, 224, 233, 234, 235, 236, 243, 244, 247, 248, 249, 251, 252, 253, 255, 256, 257, 258, 259, 260, 261, 262, 264, 265, 266, 267, 268.

CONTENTS OF THE LETTERS.

LETTERS OF ST. AUGUSTIN.

LETTER I.

(A.D. 386.)

TO HERMOGENIANUS [1] AUGUSTIN SENDS GREETING.

1. I WOULD not presume, even in playful discussion, to attack the philosophers of the Academy; [2] for when could the authority of such eminent men fail to move me, did I not believe their views to be widely different from those commonly ascribed to them? Instead of confuting them, which is beyond my power, I have rather imitated them to the best of my ability. For it seems to me to have been suitable enough to the times in which they flourished, that whatever issued pure from the fountainhead of Platonic philosophy should be rather conducted into dark and thorny thickets for the refreshment of a very few *men*, than left to flow in open meadow-land, where it would be impossible to keep it clear and pure from the inroads of the vulgar herd. I use the word herd advisedly; for what is more brutish than the opinion that the soul is material? For defence against the men who held this, it appears to me that such an art and method of concealing the truth [3] was wisely contrived by the new Academy. But in this age of ours, when we see none who are philosophers, — for I do not consider those who merely wear the cloak of a philosopher to be worthy of that venerable name, — it seems to me that men (those, at least, whom the teaching of the Academicians has, through the subtlety of the terms in which it was expressed, deterred from attempting to understand its actual meaning) should be brought back to the hope of discovering the truth, lest that which was then for the time useful in eradicating obstinate error, should begin now to hinder the casting in of the seeds of true knowledge.

2. In that age the studies of contending schools of philosophers were pursued with such ardour, that the one thing to be feared was the possibility of error being approved. For every one who had been driven by the arguments of the sceptical philosophers from a position which he had supposed to be impregnable, set himself to seek some other in its stead, with a perseverance and caution corresponding to the greater industry which was characteristic of the men of that time, and the strength of the persuasion then prevailing, that truth, though deep and hard to be deciphered, does lie hidden in the nature of things and of the human mind. Now, however, such is the indisposition to strenuous exertion, and the indifference to the liberal arts, that so soon as it is noised abroad that, in the opinion of the most acute philosophers, truth is unattainable, men send their minds to sleep, and cover them up for ever. For they presume not, forsooth, to imagine themselves to be so superior in discernment to those great men, that they shall find out what, during his singularly long life, Carneades, [4] with all his diligence, talents, and leisure, besides his extensive and varied learning, failed to discover. And if, contending somewhat against indolence, they rouse themselves so far as to read those books in which it is, as it were, proved that the perception of truth is denied to man, they relapse into lethargy so profound, that not even by the heavenly trumpet can they be aroused.

3. Wherefore, although I accept with the greatest pleasure your candid estimate of my brief treatise, and esteem you so much as to rely not less on the sagacity of your judgment than on the sincerity of your friendship, I beg you to give more particular attention to one point, and to write me again concerning it, — namely, whether you approve of that which, in the end of the third book, [5] I have given as my opinion, in a tone perhaps of hesitation rather than of certainty, but in statements, as I think, more likely to be found useful than to be rejected as incredible. But whatever be the value of those treatises

---

[1] Hermogenianus was one of the earliest and most intimate friends of Augustin, and his associate in literary and philosophical studies.

[2] [Academy was a grove dedicated to the Attic hero Academos, on the banks of the Kephissos near Athens, where Plato taught. Hence it became the name of the Platonic school of philosophy. It had three branches, — the Older, the Middle, and the Younger Academy. The study of Platonism was a preparatory step to the conversion of Augustin in 386. — P. S.]

[3] We follow the reading " *tegendi veri.*"

[4] [Carneades of Cyrene (B.C. 214-129), the founder of the third Academic school, who came to Rome B.C. 155, went further in the direction of scepticism than Arcesilas, and taught that certain knowledge was impossible. See Ueberweg, *History of Philosophy,* i. 133, 136 (transl. of Morris). — P. S.]

[5] Augustin's work, *De Academicis,* b. iii. c. 20.

[the books against the Academicians], what I most rejoice in is, not that I have vanquished the Academicians, as you express it (using the language rather of friendly partiality than of truth), but that I have broken and cast away from me the odious bonds by which I was kept back from the nourishing breasts of philosophy, through despair of attaining that truth which is the food of the soul.

LETTER II.

(A.D. 386.)

TO ZENOBIUS AUGUSTIN SENDS GREETING.[1]

1. We are, I suppose, both agreed in maintaining that all things with which our bodily senses acquaint us are incapable of abiding unchanged for a single moment, but, on the contrary, are moving and in perpetual transition, and have no present reality, that is, to use the language of Latin philosophy, do not exist.[2] Accordingly, the true and divine philosophy admonishes us to check and subdue the love of these things as most dangerous and disastrous, in order that the mind, even while using this body, may be wholly occupied and warmly interested in those things which are ever the same, and which owe their attractive power to no transient charm. Although this is all true, and although my mind, without the aid of the senses, sees you as you really are, and as an object which may be loved without disquietude, nevertheless I must own that when you are absent in body, and separated by distance, the pleasure of meeting and seeing you is one which I miss, and which, therefore, while it is attainable, I earnestly covet. This my infirmity (for such it must be) is one which, if I know you aright, you are well pleased to find in me; and though you wish every good thing for your best and most loved friends, you rather fear than desire that they should be cured of this infirmity. If, however, your soul has attained to such strength that you are able both to discern this snare, and to smile at those who are caught therein, truly you are great, and different from what I am. For my part, as long as I regret the absence of any one from me, so long do I wish him to regret my absence. At the same time, I watch and strive to set my love as little as possible on anything which can be separated from me against my will. Regarding this as my duty, I remind you, in the meantime, whatever be your frame of mind, that the discussion which I have begun with you must be finished, if we care for each other. For I can by no means consent to its

being finished with Alypius, even if he wished it. But he does not wish this; for he is not the man to join with me now in endeavouring, by as many letters as we could send, to detain you with us, when you decline this, under the pressure of some necessity to us unknown.

LETTER III.

(A.D. 387.)

TO NEBRIDIUS AUGUSTIN SENDS GREETING.[3]

1. Whether I am to regard it as the effect of what I may call your flattering language, or whether the thing be really so, is a point which I am unable to decide. For the impression was sudden, and I am not yet resolved how far it deserves to be believed. You wonder what this can be. What do you think? You have almost made me believe, not indeed that I am happy — for that is the heritage of the wise alone — but that I am at least in a sense happy: as we apply the designation *man* to beings who deserve the name only in a sense if compared with Plato's ideal man, or speak of things which we see as *round* or *square*, although they differ widely from the perfect figure which is discerned by the mind of a few. I read your letter beside my lamp after supper: immediately after which I lay down, but not at once to sleep; for on my bed I meditated long, and talked thus with myself — Augustin addressing and answering Augustin: "Is it not true, as Nebridius affirms, that I am happy?" "Absolutely true it cannot be, for that I am still far from wise he himself would not deny." "But may not a happy life be the lot even of those who are not wise?" "That is scarcely possible; because, in that case, lack of wisdom would be a small misfortune, and not, as it actually is, the one and only source of unhappiness." "How, then, did Nebridius come to esteem me happy? Was it that, after reading these little books of mine, he ventured to pronounce me wise? Surely the vehemence of joy could not make him so rash, especially seeing that he is a man to whose judgment I well know so much weight is to be attached. I have it now: he wrote what he thought would be most gratifying to me, because he had been gratified by what I had written in those treatises; and he wrote in a joyful mood, without accurately weighing the sentiments entrusted to his joyous pen. What, then, would he have said if he had read my *Soliloquies?* He would have rejoiced with much more exultation, and yet could find no loftier name to bestow on me than this which he has already given in calling me happy. All at once, then, he has lavished on me the highest

---

[1] Zenobius was the friend to whom Augustin dedicated his books *De Ordine.* In book i. ch. 1 and 2, we have a delightful description of the character of Zenobius.
[2] *Ut latiné loquar, non esse.*

[3] The character of Nebridius, and the intimacy of friendship between him and Augustin, may be seen in the *Confessions,* b. ix. c. 3.

possible name, and has not reserved a single word to add to my praises, if at any time he were made by me more joyful than he is now. See what joy does."

2. But where is that truly happy life? where? ay, where? Oh! if it were attained, one would spurn the atomic theory of Epicurus. Oh! if it were attained, one would know that there is nothing here below but the visible world. Oh! if it were attained, one would know that in the rotation of a globe on its axis, the motion of points near the poles is less rapid than of those which lie half way between them, — and other such like things which we likewise know. But now, how or in what sense can I be called happy, who know not why the world is such in size as it is, when the proportions of the figures according to which it is framed do in no way hinder its being enlarged to any extent desired? Or how might it not be said to me — nay, might we not be compelled to admit that matter is infinitely divisible; so that, starting from any given base (so to speak), a definite number of corpuscles must rise to a definite and ascertainable quantity? Wherefore, seeing that we do not admit that any particle is so small as to be insusceptible of further diminution, what compels us to admit that any assemblage of parts is so great that it cannot possibly be increased? Is there perchance some important truth in what I once suggested confidentially to Alypius, that since number, as cognisable by the understanding, is susceptible of infinite augmentation, but not of infinite diminution,[1] because we cannot reduce it lower than to the units, number, as cognisable by the senses (and this, of course, just means quantity of material parts or bodies), is on the contrary susceptible of infinite diminution, but has a limit to its augmentation? This may perhaps be the reason why philosophers justly pronounce riches to be found in the things about which the understanding is exercised, and poverty in those things with which the senses have to do. For what is poorer than to be susceptible of endless diminution? and what more truly rich than to increase as much as you will, to go whither you will, to return when you will and as far as you will, and to have as the object of your love that which is large and cannot be made less? For whoever understands these numbers loves nothing so much as the unit; and no wonder, seeing that it is through it that all the other numbers can be loved by him. But to return: Why is the world the size that it is,

seeing that it might have been greater or less? I do not know: its dimensions are what they are, and I can go no further. Again: Why is the world in the place it now occupies rather than in another? Here, too, it is better not to put the question; for whatever the answer might be, other questions would still remain. This one thing greatly perplexed me, that bodies could be infinitely subdivided. To this perhaps an answer has been given, by setting over against it the converse property of abstract number [viz. its susceptibility of infinite multiplication].

3. But stay: let us see what is that indefinable object[2] which is suggested to the mind. This world with which our senses acquaint us is surely the image of some world which the understanding apprehends. Now it is a strange phenomenon which we observe in the images which mirrors reflect to us, — that however great the mirrors be, they do not make the images larger than the objects placed before them, be they ever so small; but in small mirrors, such as the pupil of the eye, although a large surface be placed over against them, a very small image is formed, proportioned to the size of the mirror.[3] Therefore if the mirrors be reduced in size, the images reflected in them are also reduced; but it is not possible for the images to be enlarged by enlarging the mirrors. Surely there is in this something which might reward further investigation; but meanwhile, I must sleep.[4] Moreover, if I seem to Nebridius to be happy, it is not because I seek, but because perchance I have found something. What, then, is that something? Is it that chain of reasoning which I am wont so to caress as if it were my sole treasure, and in which perhaps I take too much delight?

4. "Of what parts do we consist?" "Of soul and body." "Which of these is the nobler?" "Doubtless the soul." "What do men praise in the body?" "Nothing that I see but comeliness." "And what is comeliness of body?" "Harmony of parts in the form, together with a certain agreeableness of colour." "Is this comeliness better where it is true or where it is illusive?" "Unquestionably it is better where it is true." "And where is it found true?" "In the soul." "The soul, therefore, is to be loved more than the body; but in what part of the soul does this truth reside?" "In the mind and understanding." "With what has the understanding to contend?" "With the senses." "Must we then resist the senses with all our might?" "Certainly." "What, then, if the things with which the senses acquaint us give us pleasure?" "We must prevent them from doing so." "How?"

---

[1] Had Augustin been acquainted with the decimal notation, he would not have made this remark to Alypius; for in the decimal scale, when the point is inserted, fractional parts go on diminishing according to the number of cyphers between them and the point (e.g. .001), precisely as the integers increase according to the number of cyphers between them and the decimal point (e.g. 100.), — there being no limit to the descending series on the right hand of the decimal point, any more than to the ascending series on the left hand of the same point.

[2] Nescio quid.
[3] Augustin's acquaintance with the first principles of optics, and with the properties of reflection possessed by convex, plane, and concave mirrors, was very limited.
[4] Wisely resolved.

"By acquiring the habit of doing without them, and desiring better things." "But if the soul die, what then?" "Why, then truth dies, or intelligence is not truth, or intelligence is not a part of the soul, or that which has some part immortal is liable to die : conclusions all of which I demonstrated long ago in my *Soliloquies* to be absurd because impossible ; and I am firmly persuaded that this is the case, but somehow through the influence of custom in the experience of evils we are terrified, and hesitate. But even granting, finally, that the soul dies, which I do not see to be in any way possible, it remains nevertheless true that a happy life does not consist in the evanescent joy which sensible objects can yield : this I have pondered deliberately, and proved."

Perhaps it is on account of reasonings such as these that I have been judged by my own Nebridius to be, if not absolutely happy, at least in a sense happy. Let me also judge myself to be happy : for what do I lose thereby, or why should I grudge to think well of my own estate? Thus I talked with myself, then prayed according to my custom, and fell asleep.

5. These things I have thought good to write to you. For it gratifies me that you should thank me when I write freely to you whatever crosses my mind ; and to whom can I more willingly write nonsense[1] than to one whom I cannot displease? But if it depends upon fortune whether one man love another or not, look to it, I pray you, how can I be justly called happy when I am so elated with joy by fortune's favours, and avowedly desire that my store of such good things may be largely increased? For those who are most truly wise, and whom alone it is right to pronounce happy, have maintained that fortune's favours ought not to be the objects of either fear or desire.

Now here I used the word "*cupi* :"[2] will you tell me whether it should be "*cupi*" or "*cupiri?*" And I am glad this has come in the way, for I wish you to instruct me in the inflexion of this verb "*cupio*," since, when I compare similar verbs with it, my uncertainty as to the proper inflexion increases. For "*cupio*" is like "*fugio*," "*sapio*," "*jacio*," "*capio*;" but whether the infinitive mood is "*fugiri*" or "*fugi*," "*sapiri*" or "*sapi*," I do not know. I might regard "*jaci*" and "*capi*"[3] as parallel instances answering my question as to the others, were I not afraid lest some grammarian should "catch" and "throw" me like a ball in sport wherever he pleased, by reminding me that the form of the supines "*jactum*" and "*captum*" is different from that

found in the other verbs "*fugitum*," "*cupitum*," and "*sapitum*." As to these three words, moreover, I am likewise ignorant whether the penultimate is to be pronounced long and with circumflex accent, or without accent and short. I would like to provoke you to write a reasonably long letter. I beg you to let me have what it will take some time to read. For it is far beyond my power to express the pleasure which I find in reading what you write.

LETTER IV.

(A.D. 387.)

TO NEBRIDIUS AUGUSTIN SENDS GREETING.

1. It is very wonderful how completely I was taken by surprise, when, on searching to discover which of your letters still remained unanswered, I found only one which held me as your debtor, — that, namely, in which you request me to tell you how far in this my leisure, which you suppose to be great, and which you desire to share with me, I am making progress in learning to discriminate those things in nature with which the senses are conversant, from those about which the understanding is employed. But I suppose it is not unknown to you, that if one becomes more and more fully imbued with false opinions, the more fully and intimately one exercises himself in them, the corresponding effect is still more easily produced in the mind by contact with truth. Nevertheless my progress, like our physical development, is so gradual, that it is difficult to define its steps distinctly, just as though there is a very great difference between a boy and a young man, no one, if daily questioned from his boyhood onward, could at any one date say that now he was no more a boy, but a young man.

2. I would not have you, however, so to apply this illustration as to suppose that, in the vigour of a more powerful understanding, I have arrived as it were at the beginning of the soul's manhood. For I am yet but a boy, though perhaps, as we say, a promising boy, rather than a good-for-nothing. For although the eyes of my mind are for the most part perturbed and oppressed by the distractions produced by blows inflicted through things sensible, they are revived and raised up again by that brief process of reasoning : "The mind and intelligence are superior to the eyes and the common faculty of sight ; which could not be the case unless the things which we perceive by intelligence were more real than the things which we perceive by the faculty of sight." I pray you to help me in examining whether any valid objection can be brought against this reasoning. By it, meanwhile, I find myself restored and refreshed ; and when, after calling upon God for help, I begin to rise

---

[1] *Ineptiam.*
[2] Present infinitive passive of *cupere*, to desire.
[3] Infinitive passive of verbs signifying respectively to "throw" and to "catch."

to Him, and to those things which are in the highest sense real, I am at times satisfied with such a grasp and enjoyment of the things which eternally abide, that I sometimes wonder at my requiring any such reasoning as I have above given to persuade me of the reality of those things which in my soul are as truly present to me as I am to myself.

Please look over your letters yourself, for I own that you will be in this matter at greater pains than I, in order to make sure that I am not perchance unwittingly still owing an answer to any of them : for I can hardly believe that I have so soon got from under the burden of debts which I used to reckon as so numerous ; albeit, at the same time, I cannot doubt that you have had some letters from me to which I have as yet received no reply.

LETTER V.

(A.D. 388.)

TO AUGUSTIN NEBRIDIUS SENDS GREETING.

Is it true, my beloved Augustin, that you are spending your strength and patience on the affairs of your fellow-citizens (in Thagaste), and that the leisure from distractions which you so earnestly desired is still withheld from you? Who, I would like to know, are the men who thus take advantage of your good nature, and trespass on your time? I believe that they do not know what you love most and long for. Have you no friend at hand to tell them what your heart is set upon? Will neither Romanianus nor Lucinianus do this? Let them hear me at all events. I will proclaim aloud ; I will protest that God is the supreme object of your love, and that your heart's desire is to be His servant, and to cleave to Him. Fain would I persuade you to come to my home in the country, and rest here ; I shall not be afraid of being denounced as a robber by those countrymen of yours, whom you love only too well, and by whom you are too warmly loved in return.

LETTER VI.

(A.D. 389.)

TO AUGUSTIN NEBRIDIUS SENDS GREETING.

1. Your letters I have great pleasure in keeping as carefully as my own eyes. For they are great, not indeed in length, but in the greatness of the subjects discussed in them, and in the great ability with which the truth in regard to these subjects is demonstrated. They shall bring to my ear the voice of Christ, and the teaching of Plato and of Plotinus. To me, therefore, they shall ever be pleasant to hear, because of their eloquent style ; easy to read, because of their brevity ; and profitable to understand, because of the wisdom which they contain. Be at pains, therefore, to teach me everything which, to your judgment, commends itself as holy or good. As to this letter in particular, answer it when you are ready to discuss a subtle problem in regard to memory, and the images presented by the imagination.[1] My opinion is, that although there can be such images independently of memory, there is no exercise of memory independently of such images.[2] You will say, What, then, takes place when memory is exercised in recalling an act of understanding or of thought? I answer this objection by saying, that such acts can be recalled by memory for this reason, that in the supposed act of understanding or of thought we gave birth to something conditioned by space or by time, which is of such a nature that it can be reproduced by the imagination : for either we connected the use of words with the exercise of the understanding and with the thoughts, and words are conditioned by time, and thus fall within the domain of the senses or of the imaginative faculty ; or if we did not join words with the mental act, our intellect at all events experienced in the act of thinking something which was of such a nature as could produce in the mind that which, by the aid of the imaginative faculty, memory could recall. These things I have stated, as usual, without much consideration, and in a somewhat confused manner : do you examine them, and, rejecting what is false, acquaint me by letter with what you hold as the truth on this subject.

2. Listen also to this question : Why, I should like to know, do we not affirm that the phantasy [imaginative faculty] derives all its images from itself, rather than say that it receives these from the senses? For it is possible that, as the intellectual faculty of the soul is indebted to the senses, not for the objects upon which the intellect is exercised, but rather for the admonition arousing it to see these objects, in the same manner the imaginative faculty may be indebted to the senses, not for the images which are the objects upon which it is exercised, but rather for the admonition arousing it to contemplate these images. And perhaps it is in this way that we are to explain the fact that the imagination perceives some objects which the senses never perceived, whereby it is shown that it has all its images within itself, and from itself. You will answer me what you think of this question also.

---

[1] *Phantasia.*
[2] *Quamvis non omnis phantasia cum memoria sit, omnis tamen memoria, sine phantasia esse non possit.*

LETTER VII.

(A.D. 389.)

TO NEBRIDIUS AUGUSTIN SENDS GREETING.

CHAP. I. — *Memory may be exercised independently of such images as are presented by the imagination.*

1. I shall dispense with a formal preface, and to the subject on which you have for some time wished to hear my opinion I shall address myself at once; and this I do the more willingly, because the statement must take some time.

It seems to you that there can be no exercise of memory without images, or the apprehension of some objects presented by the imagination, which you have been pleased to call "phantasiæ." For my part, I entertain a different opinion. In the first place, we must observe that the things which we remember are not always things which are passing away, but are for the most part things which are permanent. Wherefore, seeing that the function of memory is to retain hold of what belongs to time past, it is certain that it embraces on the one hand things which leave us, and on the other hand things from which we go away. When, for example, I remember my father, the object which memory recalls is one which has left me, and is now no more; but when I remember Carthage, the object is in this case one which still exists, and which I have left. In both cases, however, memory retains what belongs to past time. For I remember that man and this city, not by seeing them now, but by having seen them in the past.

2. You perhaps ask me at this point, Why bring forward these facts? And you may do this the more readily, because you observe that in both the examples quoted the object remembered can come to my memory in no other way than by the apprehension of such an image as you affirm to be always necessary. For my purpose it suffices meanwhile to have proved in this way that memory can be spoken of as embracing also those things which have not yet passed away: and now mark attentively how this supports my opinion. Some men raise a groundless objection to that most famous theory invented by Socrates, according to which the things that we learn are not introduced to our minds as new, but brought back to memory by a process of recollection; supporting their objection by affirming that memory has to do only with things which have passed away, whereas, as Plato himself has taught, those things which we learn by the exercise of the understanding are permanent, and being imperishable, cannot be numbered among things which have passed away: the mistake into which they have fallen arising obviously from this, that they do not consider that it is only the mental act of apprehension by which we have discerned these things which belongs to the past; and that it is because we have, in the stream of mental activity, left these behind, and begun in a variety of ways to attend to other things, that we require to return to them by an effort of recollection, that is, by memory. If, therefore, passing over other examples, we fix our thoughts upon eternity itself as something which is for ever permanent, and consider, on the one hand, that it does not require any image fashioned by the imagination as the vehicle by which it may be introduced into the mind; and, on the other hand, that it could never enter the mind otherwise than by our remembering it, — we shall see that, in regard to some things at least, there can be an exercise of memory without any image of the thing remembered being presented by the imagination.

CHAP. II. — *The mind is destitute of images presented by the imagination, so long as it has not been informed by the senses of external things.*

3. In the second place, as to your opinion that it is possible for the mind to form to itself images of material things independently of the services of the bodily senses, this is refuted by the following argument: — If the mind is able, before it uses the body as its instrument in perceiving material objects, to form to itself the images of these; and if, as no sane man can doubt, the mind received more reliable and correct impressions before it was involved in the illusions which the senses produce, it follows that we must attribute greater value to the impressions of men asleep than of men awake, and of men insane than of those who are free from such mental disorder: for they are, in these states of mind, impressed by the same kind of images as impressed them before they were indebted for information to these most deceptive messengers, the senses; and thus, either the sun which they see must be more real than the sun which is seen by men in their sound judgment and in their waking hours, or that which is an illusion must be better than what is real. But if these conclusions, my dear Nebridius, are, as they obviously are, wholly absurd, it is demonstrated that the image of which you speak is nothing else than a blow inflicted by the senses, the function of which in connection with these images is not, as you write, the mere suggestion or admonition occasioning their formation by the mind within itself, but the actual bringing in to the mind, or, to speak more definitely, impressing upon it of the illusions to which through the senses we are subject. The difficulty which you feel as to the question how

it comes to pass that we can conceive in thought, faces and forms which we have never seen, is one which proves the acuteness of your mind. I shall therefore do what may extend this letter beyond the usual length; not, however, beyond the length which you will approve, for I believe that the greater the fulness with which I write to you, the more welcome shall my letter be.

4. I perceive that all those images which you as well as many others call *phantasiæ*, may be most conveniently and accurately divided into three classes, according as they originate with the senses, or the imagination, or the faculty of reason. Examples of the first class are when the mind forms within itself and presents to me the image of your face, or of Carthage, or of our departed friend Verecundus, or of any other thing at present or formerly existing, which I have myself seen and perceived. Under the second class come all things which we imagine to have been, or to be so and so: *e.g.* when, for the sake of illustration in discourse, we ourselves suppose things which have no existence, but which are not prejudicial to truth; or when we call up to our own minds a lively conception of the things described while we read history, or hear, or compose, or refuse to believe fabulous narrations. Thus, according to my own fancy, and as it may occur to my own mind, I picture to myself the appearance of Æneas, or of Medea with her team of winged dragons, or of Chremes, or Parmeno.[1] To this class belong also those things which have been brought forward as true, either by wise men wrapping up some truth in the folds of such inventions, or by foolish men building up various kinds of superstition; *e.g.* the Phlegethon of Tartarus, and the five caves of the nation of darkness,[2] and the North Pole supporting the heavens, and a thousand other prodigies of poets and of heretics. Moreover, we often say, when carrying on a discussion, "Suppose that three worlds, such as the one which we inhabit, were placed one above another;" or, "Suppose the earth to be enclosed within a four-sided figure," and so on: for all such things we picture to ourselves, and imagine according to the mood and direction of our thoughts. As for the third class of images, it has to do chiefly with numbers and measure; which are found partly in the nature of things, as when the figure of the entire world is discovered, and an image consequent upon this discovery is formed in the mind of one thinking upon it; and partly in sciences, as in geometrical figures and musical harmonies, and in the infinite variety of numerals: which, although

they are, as I think, true in themselves as objects of the understanding, are nevertheless the causes of illusive exercises of the imagination, the misleading tendency of which reason itself can only with difficulty withstand; although it is not easy to preserve even the science of reasoning free from this evil, since in our logical divisions and conclusions we form to ourselves, so to speak, calculi or counters to facilitate the process of reasoning.

5. In this whole forest of images, I believe that you do not think that those of the first class belong to the mind previous to the time when they find access through the senses. On this we need not argue any further. As to the other two classes a question might reasonably be raised, were it not manifest that the mind is less liable to illusions when it has not yet been subjected to the deceptive influence of the senses, and of things sensible; and yet who can doubt that these images are much more unreal than those with which the senses acquaint us? For the things which we suppose, or believe, or picture to ourselves, are in every point wholly unreal; and the things which we perceive by sight and the other senses, are, as you see, far more near to the truth than these products of imagination. As to the third class, whatever extension of body in space I figure to myself in my mind by means of an image of this class, although it seems as if a process of thought had produced this image by scientific reasonings which did not admit of error, nevertheless I prove it to be deceptive, these same reasonings serving in turn to detect its falsity. Thus it is wholly impossible for me to believe [as, accepting your opinion, I must believe] that the soul, while not yet using the bodily senses, and not yet rudely assaulted through these fallacious instruments by that which is mortal and fleeting, lay under such ignominious subjection to illusions.

CHAP. III. — *Objection answered.*

6. "Whence then comes our capacity of conceiving in thought things which we have never seen?" What, think you, can be the cause of this, but a certain faculty of diminution and addition which is innate in the mind, and which it cannot but carry with it whithersoever it turns (a faculty which may be observed especially in relation to numbers)? By the exercise of this faculty, if the image of a crow, for example, which is very familiar to the eye, be set before the eye of the mind, as it were, it may be brought, by the taking away of some features and the addition of others, to almost any image such as never was seen by the eye. By this faculty also it comes to pass, that when men's minds habitually ponder such things, figures of

---

[1] *Dramatis personæ* in Terence.
[2] Referring to Manichæan notions.

this kind force their way as it were unbidden into their thoughts. Therefore it is possible for the mind, by taking away, as has been said, some things from objects which the senses have brought within its knowledge, and by adding some things, to produce in the exercise of imagination that which, as a whole, was never within the observation of any of the senses; but the parts of it had all been within such observation, though found in a variety of different things : e.g., when we were boys, born and brought up in an inland district, we could already form some idea of the sea, after we had seen water even in a small cup; but the flavour of strawberries and of cherries could in no wise enter our conceptions before we tasted these fruits in Italy. Hence it is also, that those who have been born blind know not what to answer when they are asked about light and colours. For those who have never perceived coloured objects by the senses are not capable of having the images of such objects in the mind.

7. And let it not appear to you strange, that though the mind is present in and intermingled with all those images which in the nature of things are figured or can be pictured by us, these are not evolved by the mind from within itself before it has received them through the senses from without. For we also find that, along with anger, joy, and other such emotions, we produce changes in our bodily aspect and complexion, before our thinking faculty even conceives that we have the power of producing such images [or indications of our feeling]. These follow upon the experience of the emotion in those wonderful ways (especially deserving your attentive consideration), which consist in the repeated action and reaction of hidden numbers [1] in the soul, without the intervention of any image of illusive material things. Whence I would have you understand — perceiving as you do that so many movements of the mind go on wholly independently of the images in question — that of all the movements of the mind by which it may conceivably attain to the knowledge of bodies, every other is more likely than the process of creating forms of sensible things by unaided thought, because I do not think that it is capable of any such conceptions before it uses the body and the senses.

Wherefore, my well beloved and most amiable brother, by the friendship which unites us, and by our faith in the divine law itself,[2] I would warn you never to link yourself in friendship with those shadows of the realm of darkness, and to break off without delay whatever friendship may have been begun between you and them. That resistance to the sway of the bodily senses which it is our most sacred duty to practise, is wholly abandoned if we treat with fondness and flattery the blows and wounds which the senses inflict upon us.

LETTER VIII.

(A.D. 389.)

TO AUGUSTIN NEBRIDIUS SENDS GREETING.

1. As I am in haste to come to the subject of my letter, I dispense with any preface or introduction. When at any time it pleases higher (by which I mean heavenly) powers to reveal anything to us by dreams in our sleep, how is this done, my dear Augustin, or what is the method which they use? What, I say, is their method, i.e. by what art or magic, by what agency or enchantments, do they accomplish this? Do they by their thoughts influence our minds, so that we also have the same images presented in our thoughts? Do they bring before us, and exhibit as actually done in their own body or in their own imagination, the things which we dream? But if they actually do these things in their own body, it follows that, in order to our seeing what they thus do, we must be endowed with other bodily eyes beholding what passes within while we sleep. If, however, they are not assisted by their bodies in producing the effects in question, but frame such things in their own imaginative faculty, and thus impress our imaginations, thereby giving visible form to what we dream; why is it, I ask, that I cannot compel your imagination to reproduce those dreams which I have myself first formed by my imagination? I have undoubtedly the faculty of imagination, and it is capable of presenting to my own mind the picture of whatever I please; and yet I do not thereby cause any dream in you, although I see that even our bodies have the power of originating dreams in us. For by means of the bond of sympathy uniting it to the soul, the body compels us in strange ways to repeat or reproduce by imagination anything which it has once experienced. Thus often in sleep, if we are thirsty, we dream that we drink; and if we are hungry, we seem to ourselves to be eating; and many other instances there are in which, by some mode of exchange, so to speak, things are transferred through the imagination from the body to the soul.

Be not surprised at the want of elegance and subtlety with which these questions are here stated to you; consider the obscurity in which the subject is involved, and the inexperience of the writer; be it yours to do your utmost to supply his deficiencies.

---

[1] Numeri actitantur occulti.
[2] Pro ipsius divini juris fide.

LETTER IX.

(A.D. 389.)

TO NEBRIDIUS AUGUSTIN SENDS GREETING.

1. Although you know my mind well, you are perhaps not aware how much I long to enjoy your society. This great blessing, however, God will some day bestow on me. I have read your letter, so genuine in its utterances, in which you complain of your being in solitude, and, as it were, forsaken by your friends, in whose society you found the sweetest charm of life. But what else can I suggest to you than that which I am persuaded is already your exercise? Commune with your own soul, and raise it up, as far as you are able, unto God. For in Him you hold us also by a firmer bond, not by means of bodily images, which we must meanwhile be content to use in remembering each other, but by means of that faculty of thought through which we realize the fact of our separation from each other.

2. In considering your letters, in answering all of which I have certainly had to answer questions of no small difficulty and importance, I was not a little stunned by the one in which you ask me by what means certain thoughts and dreams are put into our minds by higher powers or by superhuman agents.[1] The question is a great one, and, as your own prudence must convince you, would require, in order to its being satisfactorily answered, not a mere letter, but a full oral discussion or a whole treatise. I shall try, however, knowing as I do your talents, to throw out a few germs of thought which may shed light on this question, in order that you may either complete the exhaustive treatment of the subject by your own efforts, or at least not despair of the possibility of this important matter being investigated with satisfactory results.

3. It is my opinion that every movement of the mind affects in some degree the body. We know that this is patent even to our senses, dull and sluggish though they are, when the movements of the mind are somewhat vehement, as when we are angry, or sad, or joyful. Whence we may conjecture that, in like manner, when thought is busy, although no bodily effect of the mental act is discernible by us, there may be some such effect discernible by beings of aërial or etherial essence whose perceptive faculty is in the highest degree acute, — so much so, that, in comparison with it, our faculties are scarcely worthy to be called perceptive. Therefore these footprints of its motion, so to speak, which the mind impresses on the body, may perchance not only remain, but remain as it were with the force of a habit; and it may be that, when these are secretly stirred and played upon, they bear thoughts and dreams into our minds, according to the pleasure of the person moving or touching them: and this is done with marvellous facility. For if, as is manifest, the attainments of our earth-born and sluggish bodies in the department of exercise, e.g. in the playing of musical instruments, dancing on the tight-rope, etc., are almost incredible, it is by no means unreasonable to suppose that beings which act with the powers of an aërial or etherial body upon our bodies, and are by the constitution of their natures able to pass unhindered through these bodies, should be capable of much greater quickness in moving whatever they wish, while we, though not perceiving what they do, are nevertheless affected by the results of their activity. We have a somewhat parallel instance in the fact that we do not perceive how it is that superfluity of bile impels us to more frequent outbursts of passionate feeling; and yet it does produce this effect, while this superfluity of bile is itself an effect of our yielding to such passionate feelings.

4. If, however, you hesitate to accept this example as a parallel one, when it is thus cursorily stated by me, turn it over in your thoughts as fully as you can. The mind, if it be continually obstructed by some difficulty in the way of doing and accomplishing what it desires, is thereby made continually angry. For anger, so far as I can judge of its nature, seems to me to be a tumultuous eagerness to take out of the way those things which restrict our freedom of action. Hence it is that usually we vent our anger not only on men, but on such a thing, for example, as the pen with which we write, bruising or breaking it in our passion; and so does the gambler with his dice, the artist with his pencil, and every man with the instrument which he may be using, if he thinks that he is in some way thwarted by it. Now medical men themselves tell us that by these frequent fits of anger bile is increased. But, on the other hand, when the bile is increased, we are easily, and almost without any provocation whatever, made angry. Thus the effect which the mind has by its movement produced upon the body, is capable in its turn of moving the mind again.

5. These things might be treated at very great length, and our knowledge of the subject might be brought to greater certainty and fulness by a large induction from relevant facts. But take along with this letter the one which I sent you lately concerning images and memory,[2] and study it somewhat more carefully; for it was manifest to me, from your reply, that it had not been fully

---

[1] Dæmonibus.

[2] See Letter VII.

understood. When, to the statements now before you, you add the portion of that letter in which I spoke of a certain natural faculty whereby the mind does in thought add to or take from any object as it pleases, you will see that it is possible for us both in dreams and in waking thoughts to conceive the images of bodily forms which we have never seen.

LETTER X.

(A.D. 389.)

TO NEBRIDIUS AUGUSTIN SENDS GREETING.

1. No question of yours ever kept me so disturbed while reflecting upon it, as the remark which I read in your last letter, in which you chide me for being indifferent as to making arrangements by which it may be possible for us to live together. A grave charge, and one which, were it not unfounded, would be most perilous. But since satisfactory reasons seem to prove that we can live as we would wish to do better here than at Carthage, or even in the country, I am wholly at a loss, my dear Nebridius, what to do with you. Shall such a conveyance as may best suit your state of health be sent from us to you? Our friend Lucinianus informs me that you can be carried without injury in a palanquin. But I consider, on the other hand, how your mother, who could not bear your absence from her when you were in health, will be much less able to bear it when you are ill. Shall I myself then come to you? This I cannot do, for there are some here who cannot accompany me, and whom I would think it a crime for me to leave. For you already can pass your time agreeably when left to the resources of our own mind; but in their case the object of present efforts is that they may attain to this. Shall I go and come frequently, and so be now with you, now with them? But this is neither to live together, nor to live as we would wish to do. For the journey is not a short one, but so great at least that the attempt to perform it frequently would prevent our gaining the wished-for leisure. To this is added the bodily weakness through which, as you know, I cannot accomplish what I wish, unless I cease wholly to wish what is beyond my strength.

2. To occupy one's thoughts throughout life with journeyings which you cannot perform tranquilly and easily, is not the part of a man whose thoughts are engaged with that last journey which is called death, and which alone, as you understand, really deserves serious consideration. God has indeed granted to some few men whom He has ordained to bear rule over churches, the capacity of not only awaiting calmly, but even desiring eagerly, that last journey, while at the same time they can meet without disquietude the toils of those other journeyings; but I do not believe

that either to those who are urged to accept such duties through desire for worldly honour, or to those who, although occupying a private station, covet a busy life, so great a boon is given as that amid bustle and agitating meetings, and journeyings hither and thither, they should acquire that familiarity with death which we seek: for both of these classes had it in their power to seek edification[1] in retirement. Or if this be not true, I am, I shall not say the most foolish of all men, but at least the most indolent, since I find it impossible, without the aid of such an interval of relief from care and toil, to taste and relish that only real good. Believe me, there is need of much withdrawal of oneself from the tumult of the things which are passing away, in order that there may be formed in man, not through insensibility, not through presumption, not through vainglory, not through superstitious blindness, the ability to say, "I fear nought." By this means also is attained that enduring joy with which no pleasurable excitement found elsewhere is in any degree to be compared.

3. But if such a life does not fall to the lot of man, how is it that calmness of spirit is our occasional experience? Wherefore is this experience more frequent, in proportion to the devotion with which any one in his inmost soul worships God? Why does this tranquillity for the most part abide with one in the business of life, when he goes forth to its duties from that sanctuary? Why are there times in which, speaking, we do not fear death, and, silent, even desire it? I say to you — for I would not say it to every one — to you whose visits to the upper world I know well, Will you, who have often felt how sweetly the soul lives when it dies to all mere bodily affections, deny that it is possible for the whole life of man to become at length so exempt from fear, that he may be justly called wise? Or will you venture to affirm that this state of mind on which reason leans has ever been your lot, except when you were shut up to commune with your own heart? Since these things are so, you see that it remains only for you to share with me the labour of devising how we may arrange to live together. You know much better than I do what is to be done in regard to your mother, whom your brother Victor, of course, does not leave alone. I will write no more, lest I turn your mind away from considering this proposal.

LETTER XI.

(A.D. 389.)

TO NEBRIDIUS AUGUSTIN SENDS GREETING.

1. When the question, which has long been brought before me by you with something even

---

[1] Text, "*deificari*" for "*ædificari*" (?).

of friendly chiding, as to the way in which we might live together, was seriously disturbing my mind, and I had resolved to write to you, and to beg an answer from you bearing exclusively on this subject, and to employ my pen on no other theme pertaining to our studies, in order that the discussion of this matter between us might be brought to an end, the very short and indisputable conclusion stated in your letter lately received at once delivered me from all further solicitude; your statement being to the effect that on this matter there ought to be no further deliberation, because as soon as it is in my power to come to you, or in your power to come to me, we shall feel alike constrained to improve the opportunity. My mind being thus, as I have said, at rest, I looked over all your letters, that I might see what yet remained unanswered. In these I have found so many questions, that even if they were easily solved, they would by their mere number more than exhaust the time and talents of any man. But they are so difficult, that if the answering of even one of them were laid upon me, I would not hesitate to confess myself heavily burdened. The design of this introductory statement is to make you desist for a little from asking new questions until I am free from debt, and that you confine yourself in your answer to the statement of your opinion of my replies. At the same time, I know that it is to my own loss that I postpone for even a little while the participation of your divine thoughts.

2. Hear, therefore, the view which I hold concerning the mystery of the Incarnation which the religion wherein we have been instructed commends to our faith and knowledge as having been accomplished in order to our salvation; which question I have chosen to discuss in preference to all the rest, although it is not the most easily answered. For those questions which are proposed by you concerning this world do not appear to me to have a sufficiently direct reference to the obtaining of a happy life; and whatever pleasure they yield when investigated, there is reason to fear lest they take up time which ought to be devoted to better things. With regard, then, to the subject which I have at this time undertaken, first of all I am surprised that you were perplexed by the question why not the Father, but the Son, is said to have become incarnate, and yet were not also perplexed by the same question in regard to the Holy Spirit. For the union of Persons in the Trinity is in the Catholic faith set forth and believed, and by a few holy and blessed ones understood, to be so inseparable, that whatever is done by the Trinity must be regarded as being done by the Father, and by the Son, and by the Holy Spirit together; and that nothing is done by the Father which is not also done by the Son and by the Holy Spirit;

and nothing done by the Holy Spirit which is not also done by the Father and by the Son; and nothing done by the Son which is not also done by the Father and by the Holy Spirit. From which it seems to follow as a consequence, that the whole Trinity assumed human nature; for if the Son did so, but the Father and the Spirit did not, there is something in which they act separately.[1] Why, then, in our mysteries and sacred symbols, is the Incarnation ascribed only to the Son? This is a very great question, so difficult, and on a subject so vast, that it is impossible either to give a sufficiently clear statement, or to support it by satisfactory proofs. I venture, however, since I am writing to you, to indicate rather than explain what my sentiments are, in order that you, from your talents and our intimacy, through which you thoroughly know me, may for yourself fill up the outline.

3. There is no nature, Nebridius—and, indeed, there is no substance—which does not contain in itself and exhibit these three things: first, that it *is;* next, that it is *this* or *that;* and third, that as far as possible it *remains* as it is. The first of these three presents the original cause of nature from which all things exist; the second presents the form[2] according to which all things are fashioned and formed in a particular way; the third presents a certain permanence, so to speak, in which all things are. Now, if it be possible that a thing can *be,* and yet not be *this* or *that,* and not *remain* in its own generic form; or that a thing can be *this* or *that,* and yet not *be,* and not *remain* in its own generic form, so far as it is possible for it to do so; or that a thing can *remain* in its own generic form according to the force belonging to it, and yet not *be,* and not be *this* or *that,*—then it is also possible that in that Trinity one Person can do something in which the others have no part. But if you see that whatever *is* must forthwith be *this* or *that,* and must *remain* so far as possible in its own generic form, you see also that these Three do nothing in which all have not a part. I see that as yet I have only treated a portion of this question, which makes its solution difficult. But I wished to open up briefly to you—if, indeed, I have succeeded in this—how great in the system of Catholic truth is the doctrine of the inseparability of the Persons of the Trinity, and how difficult to be understood.

4. Hear now how that which disquiets your mind may disquiet it no more. The mode of existence (Species—the second of the three above named) which is properly ascribed to the Son, has to do with training, and with a certain art, if I may use that word in regard to such things, and with the exercise of intellect, by

---

[1] *Aliquid præter invicem faciunt.*
[2] Species.

which the mind itself is moulded in its thoughts upon things. Therefore, since by that assumption of human nature the work accomplished was the effective presentation to us of a certain training in the right way of living, and exemplification of that which is commanded, under the majesty and perspicuousness of certain sentences, it is not without reason that all this is ascribed to the Son. For in many things which I leave your own reflection and prudence to suggest, although the constituent elements be many, some one nevertheless stands out above the rest, and therefore not unreasonably claims a right of possession, as it were, of the whole for itself: as, *e.g.*, in the three kinds of questions above mentioned,[1] although the question raised be whether a thing *is* or not, this involves necessarily also both *what* it is (this or that), for of course it cannot *be* at all unless it be something, and whether it ought to be approved of or disapproved of, for whatever *is* is a fit subject for some opinion as to its *quality;* in like manner, when the question raised is *what* a thing is, this necessarily involves both that it *is*, and that its quality may be tried by some standard; and in the same way, when the question raised is what is the *quality* of a thing, this necessarily involves that that thing *is*, and is *something*, since all things are inseparably joined to themselves; — nevertheless, the question in each of the above cases takes its name not from all the three, but from the special point towards which the inquirer directed his attention. Now there is a certain training necessary for men, by which they might be instructed and formed after some model. We cannot say, however, regarding that which is accomplished in men by this training, either that it does not exist, or that it is not a thing to be desired [*i.e.* we cannot say *what* it is, without involving an affirmation both of its *existence* and of its *quality*]; but we seek first to know *what* it is, for in knowing this we know that by which we may infer that it is something, and in which we may remain. Therefore the first thing necessary was, that a certain rule and pattern of training be plainly exhibited; and this was done by the divinely appointed method of the Incarnation, which is properly to be ascribed to the Son, in order that from it should follow both our knowledge, through the Son, of the Father Himself, *i.e.* of the one first principle whence all things have their being, and a certain inward and ineffable charm and sweetness of remaining in that knowledge, and of despising all mortal things, — a gift and work which is properly ascribed to the Holy Spirit. Wherefore, although in all things the Divine Persons act perfectly in common, and without possibility of separation,

nevertheless their operations behoved to be exhibited in such a way as to be distinguished from each other, on account of the weakness which is in us, who have fallen from unity into variety. For no one ever succeeds in raising another to the height on which he himself stands, unless he stoop somewhat towards the level which that other occupies.

You have here a letter which may not indeed put an end to your disquietude in regard to this doctrine, but which may set your own thoughts to work upon a kind of solid foundation; so that, with the talents which I well know you to possess, you may follow, and, by the piety in which especially we must be stedfast, may apprehend that which still remains to be discovered.

LETTER XII.

(A.D. 389.)

Omitted, as only a fragment of the text of the letter is preserved.

LETTER XIII.

(A.D. 389.)

TO NEBRIDIUS AUGUSTIN SENDS GREETING.

1. I do not feel pleasure in writing of the subjects which I was wont to discuss; I am not at liberty to write of new themes. I see that the one would not suit you, and that for the other I have no leisure. For, since I left you, neither opportunity nor leisure has been given me for taking up and revolving the things which we are accustomed to investigate together. The winter nights are indeed too long, and they are not entirely spent in sleep by me; but when I have leisure, other subjects [than those which we used to discuss] present themselves as having a prior claim on my consideration.[2] What, then, am I to do? Am I to be to you as one dumb, who cannot speak, or as one silent, who will not speak? Neither of these things is desired, either by you or by me. Come, then, and hear what the end of the night succeeded in eliciting from me during the time in which it was devoted to following out the subject of this letter.

2. You cannot but remember that a question often agitated between us, and which kept us agitated, breathless, and excited, was one concerning a body or kind of body, which belongs perpetually to the soul, and which, as you recollect, is called by some its vehicle. It is manifest that this thing, if it moves from place to place, is not cognisable by the understanding. But whatever is not cognisable by the understanding cannot be understood. It is not, however, utterly

---

[1] *An sit, quid sit, quale sit.*

[2] We leave untranslated the words "quæ *diffirmando* sunt otio necessaria," the text here being evidently corrupt.

impossible to form an opinion approximating to the truth concerning a thing which is outside the province of the intellect, if it lies within the province of the senses. But when a thing is beyond the province of the intellect and of the senses, the speculations to which it gives rise are too baseless and trifling; and the thing of which we treat now is of this nature, if indeed it exists. Why, then, I ask, do we not finally dismiss this unimportant question, and with prayer to God raise ourselves to the supreme serenity of the Highest existing nature?

3. Perhaps you may here reply: "Although bodies cannot be perceived by the understanding, we can perceive with the understanding many things concerning material objects; *e.g.* we know that matter exists. For who will deny this, or affirm that in this we have to do with the probable rather than the true? Thus, though matter itself lies among things probable, it is a most indisputable truth that something like it exists in nature. Matter itself is therefore pronounced to be an object cognisable by the senses; but the assertion of its existence is pronounced to be a truth cognisable by the intellect, for it cannot be perceived otherwise. And so this unknown body, about which we inquire, upon which the soul depends for its power to move from place to place, may possibly be cognisable by senses more powerful than we possess, though not by ours; and at all events, the question whether it exists is one which may be solved by our understandings."

4. If you intend to say this, let me remind you that the mental act we call understanding is done by us in two ways: either by the mind and reason within itself, as when we understand that the intellect itself exists; or by occasion of suggestion from the senses, as in the case above mentioned, when we understand that matter exists. In the first of these two kinds of acts we understand through ourselves, *i.e.* by asking instruction of God concerning that which is within us; but in the second we understand by asking instruction of God regarding that of which intimation is given to us by the body and the senses. If these things be found true, no one can by his understanding discover whether that body of which you speak exists or not, but the person to whom his senses have given some intimation concerning it. If there be any living creature to which the senses give such intimation, since we at least see plainly that we are not among the number, I regard the conclusion established which I began to state a little ago, that the question [about the vehicle of the soul] is one which does not concern us. I wish you would consider this over and over again, and take care to let me know the product of your consideration.

LETTER XIV.

(A.D. 389.)

TO NEBRIDIUS AUGUSTIN SENDS GREETING.

1. I have preferred to reply to your last letter, not because I undervalued your earlier questions, or enjoyed them less, but because in answering you I undertake a greater task than you think. For although you enjoined me to send you a superlatively long[1] letter, I have not so much leisure as you imagine, and as you know I have always wished to have, and do still wish. Ask not why it is so: for I could more easily enumerate the things by which I am hindered, than explain why I am hindered by them.

2. You ask why it is that you and I, though separate individuals, do many things which are the same, but the sun does not the same as the other heavenly bodies. Of this thing I must attempt to explain the cause. Now, if you and I do the same things, the sun also does many things which the other heavenly bodies do: if in some things it does not the same as the others, this is equally true of you and me. I walk, and you walk; it is moved, and they are moved: I keep awake, and you keep awake; it shines, and they shine: I discuss, and you discuss; it goes its round, and they go their rounds. And yet there is no fitness of comparison between mental acts and things visible. If, however, as is reasonable, you compare mind with mind, the heavenly bodies, if they have any mind, must be regarded as even more uniform than men in their thoughts or contemplations, or whatever term may more conveniently express such activity in them. Moreover, as to the movements of the body, you will find, if you reflect on this with your wonted attention, that it is impossible for precisely the same thing to be done by two persons. When we walk together, do you think that we both necessarily do the same thing? Far be such thought from one of your wisdom! For the one of us who walks on the side towards the north, must either, in taking the same step as the other, get in advance of him, or walk more slowly than he does. Neither of these things is perceptible by the senses; but you, if I am not mistaken, look to what we know by the understanding rather than to what we learn by the senses. If, however, we move from the pole towards the south, joined and clinging to each other as closely as possible, and treading on a sheet of marble or even ivory smooth and level, a perfect identity is as unattainable in our motions as in the throbbings of our pulses, or in our figures and faces. Put us aside, and place in our stead the sons of Glaucus, and you gain

---

[1] The phrase used by Nebridius had been "*longior quam longissima*," which Augustin here quotes, and afterwards playfully alludes to in sec. 3.

nothing by this substitution: for even in these twins so perfectly resembling each other, the necessity for the motions of each being peculiarly his own, is as great as the necessity for their birth as separate individuals.

3. You will perhaps say: "The difference in this case is one which only reason can discover; but the difference between the sun and the other heavenly bodies is to the senses also patent." If you insist upon my looking to their difference in magnitude, you know how many things may be said as to the distances by which they are removed from us, and into how great uncertainty that which you speak of as obvious may thus be brought back. I may, however, concede that the actual size corresponds with the apparent size of the heavenly bodies, for I myself believe this; and I ask you to show me any one whose senses were incapable of remarking the prodigious stature of Nævius, exceeding by a foot that of the tallest man.[1] By the way, I think you have been just too eager to discover some man to match him; and when you did not succeed in the search, have resolved to make me stretch out my letter so as to rival his dimensions.[2] If therefore even on earth such variety in size may be seen, I think that it need not surprise us to find the like in the heavens. If, however, the thing which moves your surprise is that the light of no other heavenly body than the sun fills the day, who, I ask you, has ever been manifested to men so great as that Man whom God took into union with Himself, in another way entirely than He has taken all other holy and wise men who ever lived? for if you compare Him with other men who were wise, He is separated from them by superiority greater far than that which the sun has above the other heavenly bodies. This comparison let me charge you by all means attentively to study; for it is not impossible that to your singularly gifted mind I may have suggested, by this cursory remark, the solution of a question which you once proposed to me concerning the humanity of Christ.

4. You also ask me whether that highest Truth and highest Wisdom and Form (or Archetype) of things, by whom all things were made, and whom our creeds confess to be the only-begotten Son of God, contains the idea[3] of mankind in general, or also of each individual of our race. A great question. My opinion is, that in the creation of man there was in Him the idea only of man generally, and not of you or me as individuals; but that in the cycle of time the idea of each individual, with all the varieties distinguishing men from each other, lives in that pure

Truth. This I grant is very obscure; yet I know not by what kind of illustration light may be shed upon it, unless perhaps we betake ourselves to those sciences which lie wholly within our minds. In geometry, the idea of an angle is one thing, the idea of a square is another. As often, therefore, as I please to describe an angle, the idea of the angle, and that alone, is present to my mind; but I can never describe a square unless I fix my attention upon the idea of four angles at the same time. In like manner, every man, considered as an individual man, has been made according to one idea proper to himself; but in the making of a nation, although the idea according to which it is made be also one, it is the idea not of one, but of many men collectively. If, therefore, Nebridius is a part of this universe, as he is, and the whole universe is made up of parts, the God who made the universe could not but have in His plan the idea of all the parts. Wherefore, since there is in this idea of a very great number of men, it does not belong to man himself as such; although, on the other hand, all the individuals are in wonderful ways reduced to one. But you will consider this at your convenience. I beg you meanwhile to be content with what I have written, although I have already outdone Nævius himself.

LETTER XV.

(A.D. 390.)

TO ROMANIANUS AUGUSTIN SENDS GREETING.

1. This letter indicates a scarcity of paper,[4] but not so as to testify that parchment is plentiful here. My ivory tablets I used in the letter which I sent to your uncle. You will more readily excuse this scrap of parchment, because what I wrote to him could not be delayed, and I thought that not to write to you for want of better material would be most absurd. But if any tablets of mine are with you, I request you to send them to meet a case of this kind. I have written something, as the Lord has deigned to enable me, concerning the Catholic religion, which before my coming I wish to send to you, if my paper does not fail me in the meantime. For you will receive with indulgence any kind of writing from the office of the brethren who are with me. As to the manuscripts of which you speak, I have entirely forgotten them, except the books *de Oratore;* but I could not have written anything better than that you should take such of them as you please, and I am still of the same mind; for at this distance I know not what else I can do in the matter.

2. It gave me very great pleasure that in your

[1] The text contains the word "sex" here, which is omitted in the translation. The reading is uncertain.
[2] See note on sec. 1.
[3] *Ratio.*
[4] *Charta.*

last letter you desired to make me a sharer of your joy at home ; but

> " Wouldst thou have me forget how soon the deep,
> So tranquil now, may wear another face,
> And rouse these slumbering waves ? " [1]

Yet I know you would not have me forget this, nor are you yourself unmindful of it. Wherefore, if some leisure is granted you for more profound meditation, improve this divine blessing. For when these things fall to our lot, we should not only congratulate ourselves, but show our gratitude to those to whom we owe them ; for if in the stewardship of temporal blessings we act in a manner that is just and kind, and with the moderation and sobriety of spirit which befits the transient nature of these possessions, — if they are held by us without laying hold on us, are multiplied without entangling us, and serve us without bringing us into bondage, — such conduct entitles us to the recompense of eternal blessings. For by Him who is the Truth it was said : " If ye have not been faithful in that which is another man's, who will give you that which is your own ? " Let us therefore disengage ourselves from care about the passing things of time ; let us seek the blessings that are imperishable and sure : let us soar above our worldly possessions. The bee does not the less need its wings when it has gathered an abundant store ; for if it sink in the honey it dies.

LETTER XVI.

(A.D. 390.)

FROM MAXIMUS OF MADAURA TO AUGUSTIN.

1. Desiring to be frequently made glad by communications from you, and by the stimulus of your reasoning with which in a most pleasant way, and without violation of good feeling, you recently attacked me, I have not forborne from replying to you in the same spirit, lest you should call my silence an acknowledgment of being in the wrong. But I beg you to give these sentences an indulgent kindly hearing, if you judge them to give evidence of the feebleness of old age. Grecian mythology tells us, but without sufficient warrant for our believing the statement, that Mount Olympus is the dwelling-place of the gods. But we actually see the market-place of our town occupied by a crowd of beneficent deïties ; and we approve of this. Who could ever be so frantic and infatuated as to deny that there is one supreme God, without beginning, without natural offspring, who. is, as it were, the great and mighty Father of all? The powers of this Deity, diffused throughout the universe which

He has made, we worship under many names, as we are all ignorant of His true name, the name God [2] being common to all kinds of religious belief. Thus it comes, that while in diverse supplications we approach separately, as it were, certain parts of the Divine Being, we are seen in reality to be the worshippers of Him in whom all these parts are one.

2. Such is the greatness of your delusion in another matter, that I cannot conceal the impatience with which I regard it. For who can bear to find Mygdo honoured above that Jupiter who hurls the thunderbolt ; or Sanæ above Juno, Minerva, Venus, and Vesta ; or the arch-martyr Namphanio (oh horror !) above all the immortal gods together? Among the immortals, Lucitas also is looked up to with no less religious reverence, and others in an endless list (having names abhorred both by gods and by men), who, when they met the ignominious end which their character and conduct had deserved, put the crowning act upon their criminal career by affecting to die nobly in a good cause, though conscious of the infamous deeds for which they were condemned. The tombs of these men (it is a folly almost beneath our notice) are visited by crowds of simpletons, who forsake our temples and despise the memory of their ancestors, so that the prediction of the indignant bard is notably fulfilled : " Rome shall, in the temples of the gods, swear by the shades of men." [3] To me it almost seems at this time as if a second campaign of Actium had begun, in which Egyptian monsters, doomed soon to perish, dare to brandish their weapons against the gods of the Romans.

3. But, O man of great wisdom, I beseech you, lay aside and reject for a little while the vigour of your eloquence, which has made you everywhere renowned ; lay down also the arguments of Chrysippus, which you are accustomed to use in debate ; leave for a brief season your logic, which aims in the forthputting of its energies to leave nothing certain to any one ; and show me plainly and actually who is that God whom you Christians claim as belonging specially to you, and pretend to see present among you in secret places. For it is in open day, before the eyes and ears of all men, that we worship our gods with pious supplications, and propitiate them by acceptable sacrifices ; and we take pains that these things be seen and approved by all.

4. Being, however, infirm and old, I withdraw myself from further prosecution of this contest, and willingly consent to the opinion of the rhetorician of Mantua, " Each one is drawn by that which pleases himself best." [4]

---

[1] " Mene salis placidı vultum fluctusque quietos
Ignorare jubes ? " — Æn. v. 848, 849.

[2] *Deus.*

[3] " Inque Deûm templis jurabit Roma per umbras."
Lucan, *Pharsalia,* vii. 459.

[4] Virg. *Eclog.* ii. 65: " Trahit sua quemque voluptas."

After this, O excellent man, who hast turned aside from my faith, I have no doubt that this letter will be stolen by some thief, and destroyed by fire or otherwise. Should this happen, the paper will be lost, but not my letter, of which I will always retain a copy, accessible to all religious persons. May you be preserved by the gods, through whom we all, who are mortals on the surface of this earth, with apparent discord but real harmony, revere and worship Him who is the common Father of the gods and of all mortals.

LETTER XVII.

(A.D. 390.)

TO MAXIMUS OF MADAURA.

1. Are we engaged in serious debate with each other, or is it your desire that we merely amuse ourselves? For, from the language of your letter, I am at a loss to know whether it is due to the weakness of your cause, or through the courteousness of your manners, that you have preferred to show yourself more witty than weighty in argument. For, in the first place, a comparison was drawn by you between Mount Olympus and your market-place, the reason for which I cannot divine, unless it was in order to remind me that on the said mountain Jupiter pitched his camp when he was at war with his father, as we are taught by history, which your religionists call sacred; and that in the said market-place Mars is represented in two images, the one unarmed, the other armed, and that a statue of a man placed over against these restrains with three extended fingers the fury of their demonship from the injuries which he would willingly inflict on the citizens. Could I then ever believe that by mentioning that market-place you intended to revive my recollection of such divinities, unless you wished that we should pursue the discussion in a jocular spirit rather than in earnest? But in regard to the sentence in which you said that such gods as these are members, so to speak, of the one great God, I admonish you by all means, since you vouchsafe such an opinion, to abstain very carefully from profane jestings of this kind. For if you speak of the One God, concerning whom learned and unlearned are, as the ancients have said, agreed, do you affirm that those whose savage fury — or, if you prefer it, whose power — the image of a dead man keeps in check are members of Him? I might say more on this point, and your own judgment may show you how wide a door for the refutation of your views is here thrown open. But I restrain myself, lest I should be thought by you to act more as a rhetorician than as one earnestly defending truth.

2. As to your collecting of certain Carthaginian names of deceased persons, by which you think reproach may be cast, in what seems to you a witty manner, against our religion, I do not know whether I ought to answer this taunt, or to pass it by in silence. For if to your good sense these things appear as trifling as they really are, I have not time to spare for such pleasantry. If, however, they seem to you important, I am surprised that it did not occur to you, who are apt to be disturbed by absurdly-sounding names, that your religionists have among their priests Eucaddires, and among their deities, Abaddires. I do not suppose that these were absent from your mind when you were writing, but that, with your courtesy and genial humour, you wished for the unbending of our minds, to recall to our recollection what ludicrous things are in your superstition. For surely, considering that you are an African, and that we are both settled in Africa, you could not have so forgotten yourself when writing to Africans as to think that Punic names were a fit theme for censure. For if we interpret the signification of these words, what else does Namphanio mean than "man of the good foot," i.e. whose coming brings with it some good fortune, as we are wont to say of one whose coming to us has been followed by some prosperous event, that he came with a lucky foot? And if the Punic language is rejected by you, you virtually deny what has been admitted by most learned men, that many things have been wisely preserved from oblivion in books written in the Punic tongue. Nay, you ought even to be ashamed of having been born in the country in which the cradle of this language is still warm, i.e. in which this language was originally, and until very recently, the language of the people. If, however, it is not reasonable to take offence at the mere sound of names, and you admit that I have given correctly the meaning of the one in question, you have reason for being dissatisfied with your friend Virgil, who gives to your god Hercules an invitation to the sacred rites celebrated by Evander in his honour, in these terms, "Come to us, and to these rites in thine honour, with auspicious foot." [1] He wishes him to come "with auspicious foot;" that is to say, he wishes Hercules to come as a Namphanio, the name about which you are pleased to make much mirth at our expense. But if you have a penchant for ridicule, you have among yourselves ample material for witticisms — the god Stercutius, the goddess Cloacina, the Bald Venus, the gods Fear and Pallor, and the goddess Fever, and others of the same kind without number, to whom the ancient Roman idolaters erected temples, and judged it right to offer worship; which if you neglect, you are neg-

---

[1] Virg. Æneid, viii. 302: "Et nos et tua dexter adi pede sacra secundo."

lecting Roman gods, thereby making it manifest that you are not thoroughly versed in the sacred rites of Rome ; and yet you despise and pour contempt on Punic names, as if you were a devotee at the altars of Roman deities.

3. In truth, however, I believe that perhaps you do not value these sacred rites any more than we do, but only take from them some unaccountable pleasure in your time of passing through this world : for you have no hesitation about taking refuge under Virgil's wing, and defending yourself with a line of his :

" Each one is drawn by that which pleases himself best."[1]

If, then, the authority of Maro pleases you, as you indicate that it does, you will be pleased with such lines as these : " First Saturn came from lofty Olympus, fleeing before the arms of Jupiter, an exile bereft of his realms,"[2] — and other such statements, by which he aims at making it understood that Saturn and your other gods like him were men. For he had read much history, confirmed by ancient authority, which Cicero also had read, who makes the same statement in his dialogues, in terms more explicit than we would venture to insist upon, and labours to bring it to the knowledge of men so far as the times in which he lived permitted.

4. As to your statement, that your religious services are to be preferred to ours because you worship the gods in public, but we use more retired places of meeting, let me first ask you how you could have forgotten your Bacchus, whom you consider it right to exhibit only to the eyes of the few who are initiated. You, however, think that, in making mention of the public celebration of your sacred rites, you intended only to make sure that we would place before our eyes the spectacle presented by your magistrates and the chief men of the city when intoxicated and raging along your streets ; in which solemnity, if you are possessed by a god, you surely see of what nature he must be who deprives men of their reason. If, however, this madness is only feigned, what say you to this keeping of things hidden in a service which you boast of as public, or what good purpose is served by so base an imposition? Moreover, why do you not foretell future events in your songs, if you are endowed with the prophetic gift? or why do you rob the bystanders, if you are in your sound mind ?

5. Since, then, you have recalled to our remembrance by your letter these and other things which I think it better to pass over meanwhile, why may not we make sport of your gods, which, as every one who knows your mind, and has read your letters, is well aware, are made sport of abundantly by yourself? Therefore, if you wish us to discuss these subjects in a way becoming your years and wisdom, and, in fact, as may be justly required of us, in connection with our purpose, by our dearest friends, seek some topic worthy of being debated between us ; and be careful to say on behalf of your gods such things as may prevent us from supposing that you are intentionally betraying your own cause, when we find you rather bringing to our remembrance things which may be said against them than alleging anything in their defence. In conclusion, however, lest this should be unknown to you, and you might thus be brought unwittingly into jestings which are profane, let me assure you that by the Christian Catholics (by whom a church has been set up in your own town also) no deceased person is worshipped, and that nothing, in short, which has been made and fashioned by God is worshipped as a divine power. This worship is rendered by them only to God Himself, who framed and fashioned all things.[3]

These things shall be more fully treated of, with the help of the one true God, whenever I learn that you are disposed to discuss them seriously.

LETTER XVIII.

(A.D. 390.)

TO CŒLESTINUS AUGUSTIN SENDS GREETING.

1. Oh how I wish that I could continually say one thing to you ! It is this : Let us shake off the burden of unprofitable cares, and bear only those which are useful. For I do not know whether anything like complete exemption from care is to be hoped for in this world. I wrote to you, but have received no reply. I sent you as many of my books against the Manichæans as I could send in a finished and revised condition, and as yet nothing has been communicated to me as to the impression they have made on your[4] judgment and feelings. It is now a fitting opportunity for me to ask them back, and for you to return them. I beg you therefore not to lose time in sending them, along with a letter from yourself, by which I eagerly long to know what you are doing with them, or with what further help you think that you require still to be furnished in order to assail that error with success.

---

1 " Trahit sua quemque voluptas."
2 " Primus ab æthereo venit Saturnis Olympo
  Arma Jovis fugiens et regnis exsul ademptis."
                                    Æn. viii. 319, 320.

3 We give the original of this important sentence: " Scias a Christianis catholicis (quorum in vestro oppido etiam ecclesia constituta est) nullum coli mortuorum, nihil denique ut numen adorari quod sit factum et conditum a Deo, sed unum ipsum Deum qui fecit et condidit omnia."
4 The sense here obviously requires " *vestri*" instead of " *nostri*," which is in the text.

2. As I know you well, I ask you to accept and ponder the following brief sentences on a great theme. There is a nature which is susceptible of change with respect to both place and time, namely, the corporeal. There is another nature which is in no way susceptible of change with respect to place, but only with respect to time, namely, the spiritual. And there is a third Nature which can be changed neither in respect to place nor in respect to time: that is, God. Those natures of which I have said that they are mutable in some respect are called creatures; the Nature which is immutable is called Creator. Seeing, however, that we affirm the existence of anything only in so far as it continues and is one (in consequence of which, unity is the condition essential to beauty in every form), you cannot fail to distinguish, in this classification of natures, which exists in the highest possible manner; and which occupies the lowest place, yet is within the range of existence; and which occupies the middle place, greater than the lowest, but coming short of the highest. That highest is essential blessedness; the lowest, that which cannot be either blessed or wretched; and the intermediate nature lives in wretchedness when it stoops towards that which is lowest, and in blessedness when it turns towards that which is highest. He who believes in Christ does not sink his affections in that which is lowest, is not proudly self-sufficient in that which is intermediate, and thus he is qualified for union and fellowship with that which is highest; and this is the sum of the active life to which we are commanded, admonished, and by holy zeal impelled to aspire.

LETTER XIX.

(A.D. 390.)

TO GAIUS AUGUSTIN SENDS GREETING.

1. Words cannot express the pleasure with which the recollection of you filled my heart after I parted with you, and has often filled my heart since then. For I remember that, notwithstanding the amazing ardour which pervaded your inquiries after truth, the bounds of proper moderation in debate were never transgressed by you. I shall not easily find any one who is more eager in putting questions, and at the same time more patient in hearing answers, than you approved yourself. Gladly therefore would I spend much time in converse with you; for the time thus spent, however much it might be, would not seem long. But what avails it to discuss the hindrances on account of which it is difficult for us to enjoy such converse? Enough that it is exceedingly difficult. Perhaps at some future period it may be made very easy; may

God grant this! Meanwhile it is otherwise. I have given to the brother by whom I have sent this letter the charge of submitting all my writings to your eminent wisdom and charity, that they may be read by you. For nothing written by me will find in you a reluctant reader; for I know the goodwill which you cherish towards me. Let me say, however, that if, on reading these things, you approve of them, and perceive them to be true, you must not consider them to be mine otherwise than as given to me; and you are at liberty to turn to that same source whence proceeds also the power given you to appreciate their truth. For no one discerns the truth of that which he reads from anything which is in the mere manuscript, or in the writer, but rather by something within himself, if the light of truth, shining with a clearness beyond what is men's common lot, and very far removed from the darkening influence of the body, has penetrated his own mind. If, however, you discover some things which are false and deserve to be rejected, I would have you know that these things have fallen as dew from the mists of human frailty, and these you are to reckon as truly mine. I would exhort you to persevere in seeking the truth, were it not that I seem to see the mouth of your heart already opened wide to drink it in. I would also exhort you to cling with manly tenacity to the truth which you have learned, were it not that you already manifest in the clearest manner that you possess strength of mind and fixedness of purpose. For all that lives within you has, in the short time of our fellowship, revealed itself to me, almost as if the bodily veil had been rent asunder. And surely the merciful providence of our God can in no wise permit a man so good and so remarkably gifted as you are to be an alien from the flock of Christ.

LETTER XX.

(A.D. 390.)

TO ANTONINUS AUGUSTIN SENDS GREETING.

1. As letters are due to you by two of us, a part of our debt is repaid with very abundant usury when you see one of the two in person; and since by his voice you, as it were, hear my own, I might have refrained from writing, had I not been called to do it by the urgent request of the very person whose journey to you seemed to me to make this unnecessary. Accordingly I now hold converse with you even more satisfactorily than if I were personally with you, because you both read my letter, and you listen to the words of one in whose heart you know that I dwell. I have with great joy studied and pondered the letter sent by your Holiness, because

it exhibits both your Christian spirit unsullied by the guile of an evil age, and your heart full of kindly feeling towards myself.

2. I congratulate you, and I give thanks to our God and Lord, because of the hope and faith and love which are in you; and I thank you, in Him, for thinking so well of me as to believe me to be a faithful servant of God, and for the love which with guileless heart you cherish towards that which you commend in me; although, indeed, there is occasion rather for congratulation than for thanks in acknowledging your goodwill in this thing. For it is profitable for yourself that you should love for its own sake that goodness which he of course loves who loves another because he believes him to be good, whether that other be or be not what he is supposed to be. One error only is to be carefully avoided in this matter, that we do not think otherwise than truth demands, not of the individual, but of that which is true goodness in man. But, my brother well-beloved, seeing that you are not in any degree mistaken either in believing or in knowing that the great good for men is to serve God cheerfully and purely, when you love any man because you believe him to share this good, you reap the reward, even though the man be not what you suppose him to be. Wherefore it is fitting that you should on this account be congratulated; but the person whom you love is to be congratulated, not because of his being for that reason loved, but because of his being truly (if it is the case) such an one as the person who for this reason loves him esteems him to be. As to our real character, therefore, and as to the progress we may have made in the divine life, this is seen by Him whose judgment, both as to that which is good in man, and as to each man's personal character, cannot err. For your obtaining the reward of blessedness so far as this matter is concerned, it is sufficient that you embrace me with your whole heart because you believe me to be such a servant of God as I ought to be. To you, however, I also render many thanks for this, that you encourage me wonderfully to aspire after such excellence, by your praising me as if I had already attained it. Many more thanks still shall be yours, if you not only claim an interest in my prayers, but also cease not to pray for me. For intercession on behalf of a brother is more acceptable to God when it is offered as a sacrifice of love.

3. I greet very kindly your little son, and I pray that he may grow up in the way of obedience to the salutary requirements of God's law. I desire and pray, moreover, that the one true faith and worship, which alone is catholic, may prosper and increase in your house; and if you think any labour on my part necessary for the

promotion of this end, do not scruple to claim my service, relying upon Him who is our common Lord, and upon the law of love which we must obey. This especially would I recommend to your pious discretion, that by reading the word of God, and by serious conversation with your partner,[1] you should either plant the seed or foster the growth in her heart of an intelligent fear of God. For it is scarcely possible that any one who is concerned for the soul's welfare, and is therefore without prejudice resolved to know the will of the Lord, should fail, when enjoying the guidance of a good instructor, to discern the difference which exists between every form of schism and the one Catholic Church.

LETTER XXI.

(A.D. 391.)

TO MY LORD BISHOP VALERIUS, MOST BLESSED AND VENERABLE, MY FATHER MOST WARMLY CHERISHED WITH TRUE LOVE IN THE SIGHT OF THE LORD, AUGUSTIN, PRESBYTER, SENDS GREETING IN THE LORD.

1. Before all things I ask your pious wisdom to take into consideration that, on the one hand, if the duties of the office of a bishop, or presbyter, or deacon, be discharged in a perfunctory and time-serving manner, no work can be in this life more easy, agreeable, and likely to secure the favour of men, especially in our day, but none at the same time more miserable, deplorable, and worthy of condemnation in the sight of God; and, on the other hand, that if in the office of bishop, or presbyter, or deacon, the orders of the Captain of our salvation be observed, there is no work in this life more difficult, toilsome, and hazardous, especially in our day, but none at the same time more blessed in the sight of God.[2] But what the proper mode of discharging these duties is, I did not learn either in boyhood or in the earlier years of manhood; and at the time when I was beginning to learn it, I was constrained as a just correction for my sins (for I know not what else to think) to accept the second place at the helm, when as yet I knew not how to handle an oar.

2. But I think that it was the purpose of my Lord hereby to rebuke me, because I presumed, as if entitled by superior knowledge and excellence, to reprove the faults of many sailors before I had learned by experience the nature of their work. Therefore, after I had been sent in among them to share their labours, then I began to feel the rashness of my censures; although even before that time I judged this office to be beset

---

[1] *Infirmiori vasi tuo.*
[2] [A most noble sentence, which contains, as in a nutshell, a whole system of pastoral theology. — P. S.]

with many dangers. And hence the tears which some of my brethren perceived me shedding in the city at the time of my ordination, and because of which they did their utmost with the best intentions to console me, but with words which, through their not knowing the causes of my sorrow, did not reach my case at all.[1] But my experience has made me realize these things much more both in degree and in measure than I had done in merely thinking of them : not that I have now seen any new waves or storms of which I had not previous knowledge by observation, or report, or reading, or meditation ; but because I had not known my own skill or strength for avoiding or encountering them, and had estimated it to be of some value instead of none. The Lord, however, laughed at me, and was pleased to show me by actual experience what I am.

3. But if He has done this not in judgment, but in mercy, as I confidently hope even now, when I have learned my infirmity, my duty is to study with diligence all the remedies which the Scriptures contain for such a case as mine, and to make it my business by prayer and reading to secure that my soul be endued with the health and vigour necessary for labours so responsible. This I have not yet done, because I have not had time ; for I was ordained at the very time when I was thinking of having, along with others, a season of freedom from all other occupation, that we might acquaint ourselves with the divine Scriptures, and was intending to make such arrangements as would secure unbroken leisure for this great work. Moreover, it is true that I did not at any earlier period know how great was my unfitness for the arduous work which now disquiets and crushes my spirit. But if I have by experience learned what is necessary for a man who ministers to a people in the divine sacraments and word, only to find myself prevented from now obtaining what I have learned that I do not possess, do you bid me perish, father Valerius ? Where is your charity ? Do you indeed love me ? Do you indeed love the Church to which you have appointed me, thus unqualified, to minister ? I am well assured that you love both ; but you think me qualified, whilst I know myself better ; and yet I would not have come to know myself if I had not learned by experience.

4. Perhaps your Holiness replies : I wish to know what is lacking to fit you for your office. The things which I lack are so many, that I could more easily enumerate the things which I have than those which I desire to have. I may venture to say that I know and unreserved-

ly believe the doctrines pertaining to our salvation. But my difficulty is in the question how I am to use this truth in ministering to the salvation of others, seeking what is profitable not for myself alone, but for many, that they may be saved. And perhaps there may be, nay, beyond all question there are, written in the sacred books, counsels by the knowledge and acceptance of which the man of God may so discharge his duties to the Church in the things of God, or at least so keep a conscience void of offence in the midst of ungodly men, whether living or dying, as to secure that that life for which alone humble and meek Christian hearts sigh is not lost. But how can this be done, except, as the Lord Himself tells us, by asking, seeking, knocking, that is, by praying, reading, and weeping ? For this I have by the brethren made the request, which in this petition I now renew, that a short time, say till Easter, be granted me by your unfeigned and venerable charity.

5. For what shall I answer to the Lord my Judge ? Shall I say, " I was not able to acquire the things of which I stood in need, because I was engrossed wholly with the affairs of the Church " ? What if He thus reply : " Thou wicked servant, if property belonging to the Church (in the collection of the fruits of which great labour is expended) were suffering loss under some oppressor, and it was in thy power to do something in defence of her rights at the bar of an earthly judge, wouldst thou not, leaving the field which I have watered with my blood, go to plead the cause with the consent of all, and even with the urgent commands of some ? And if the decision given were against the Church, wouldst thou not, in prosecuting an appeal, go across the sea ; and would no complaint be heard summoning thee home from an absence of a year or more, because thy object was to prevent another from taking possession of land required not for the souls, but for the bodies of the poor, whose hunger might nevertheless be satisfied in a way much easier and more acceptable to me by my living trees, if these were cultivated with care ? Wherefore, then, dost thou allege that thou hadst not time to learn how to cultivate my field ? " Tell me, I beseech you, what could I reply ? Are you perchance willing that I should say, " The aged Valerius is to blame ; for, believing me to be instructed in all things necessary, he declined, with a determination proportioned to his love for me, to give me permission to learn what I had not acquired " ?

6. Consider all these things, aged Valerius ; consider them, I beseech you, by the goodness and severity of Christ, by His mercy and judgment, by Him who has inspired you with such love for me that I dare not displease you, even when the advantage of my soul is at stake.

---

[1] They thought Augustin was disappointed at being made only presbyter and not colleague of Valerius as bishop. See Possidius, *Aug. Vita*, c. 4.

You, moreover, appeal to God and to Christ to bear witness to me concerning your innocence and charity, and the sincere love which you bear to me, just as if all these were not things about which I may myself willingly take my oath. I therefore appeal to the love and affection which you have thus avouched. Have pity on me, and grant me, for the purpose for which I have asked it, the time which I have asked; and help me with your prayers, that my desire may not be in vain, and that my absence may not be without fruit to the Church of Christ, and to the profit of my brethren and fellow-servants. I know that the Lord will not despise your love interceding for me, especially in such a cause as this; and accepting it as a sacrifice of sweet savour, He will restore me to you, perhaps, within a period shorter than I have craved, thoroughly furnished for His service by the profitable counsels of His written word.

LETTER XXII.

(A.D. 392.)

TO BISHOP AURELIUS, AUGUSTIN, PRESBYTER, SENDS GREETING.

CHAP. I. — 1. When, after long hesitation, I knew not how to frame a suitable reply to the letter of your Holiness (for all attempts to express my feelings were baffled by the strength of affectionate emotions which, rising spontaneously, were by the reading of your letter much more vehemently inflamed), I cast myself at last upon God, that He might, according to my strength, so work in me that I might address to you such an answer as should be suitable to the zeal for the Lord and the care of His Church which we have in common, and in accordance with your dignity and the respect which is due to you from me. And, first of all, as to your belief that you are aided by my prayers, I not only do not decline this assurance, but I do even willingly accept it. For thus, though not through my prayers, assuredly in yours, our Lord will hear me. As to your most benignant approval of the conduct of brother Alypius in remaining in connection with us, to be an example to the brethren who desire to withdraw themselves from this world's cares, I thank you more warmly than words can declare. May the Lord recompense this to your own soul! The whole company, therefore, of brethren which has begun to grow up together beside me, is bound to you by gratitude for this great favour; in bestowing which, you, being far separated from us only by distance on the surface of the earth, have consulted our interest as one in spirit very near to us. Wherefore, to the utmost of our power we give ourselves to prayer that the Lord may be pleased to uphold along with you the flock which has been committed to you, and may never anywhere forsake you, but be present as your help in all times of need, showing in His dealings with His Church, through your discharge of priestly functions, such mercy as spiritual men with tears and groanings implore Him to manifest.

2. Know, therefore, most blessed lord, venerable for the superlative fulness of your charity, that I do not despair, but rather cherish lively hope that, by means of that authority which you wield, and which, as we trust, has been committed to your spirit, not to your flesh alone, our Lord and God may be able, through the respect due to councils [1] and to yourself, to bring healing to the many carnal blemishes and disorders which the African Church is suffering in the conduct of many, and is bewailing in the sorrow of a few of her members. For whereas the apostle had in one passage briefly set forth as fit to be hated and avoided three classes of vices, from which there springs an innumerable crop of vicious courses, only one of these — that, namely, which he has placed second — is very strictly punished by the Church; but the other two, viz. the first and third, appear to be tolerable in the estimation of men, and so it may gradually come to pass that they shall even cease to be regarded as vices. The words of the chosen vessel are these: "Not in rioting and drunkenness, not in chambering and wantonness, not in strife and envying: but put ye on the Lord Jesus Christ, and make not provision for the flesh, to fulfil the lusts thereof." [2]

3. Of these three, then, chambering and wantonness are regarded as crimes so great, that any one stained with these sins is deemed unworthy not merely of holding office in the Church, but also of participation in the sacraments; and rightly so. But why restrict such censure to this form of sin alone? For rioting and drunkenness are so tolerated and allowed by public opinion, that even in services designed to honour the memory of the blessed martyrs, and this not only on the annual festivals (which itself must be regarded as deplorable by every one who looks with a spiritual eye upon these things), but every day, they are openly practised. Were this corrupt practice objectionable only because of its being disgraceful, and not on the ground of impiety, we might consider it as a scandal to be tolerated with such amount of forbearance as is within our power. And yet, even in that case, what are we to make of the fact that, when the same apostle had given a long list of vices, among which he mentioned drunkenness, he concluded with the warning that we should not even eat bread

---

[1] We adopt the conjectural reading "*conciliorum.*" Compare sec. 4, p. 240.
[2] Rom. xiii. 13, 14.

with those who are guilty of such things?[1] But let us, if it must be so, bear with these things in the luxury and disorder of families, and of those convivial meetings which are held within the walls of private houses; and let us take the body of Christ in communion with those with whom we are forbidden to eat even the bread which sustains our bodies; but at least let this outrageous insult be kept far away from the tombs of the sainted dead, from the scenes of sacramental privilege, and from the houses of prayer. For who may venture to forbid in private life excesses which, when they are practised by crowds in holy places, are called an honouring of the martyrs?

4. If Africa were the first country in which an attempt were made to put down these things, her example would deserve to be esteemed worthy of imitation by all other countries;[2] but when, both throughout the greater part of Italy and in all or almost all the churches beyond the sea, these practices either, as in some places, never existed, or, as in other places where they did exist, have been, whether they were recent or of long standing, rooted out and put down by the diligence and the censures of bishops who were holy men, entertaining true views concerning the life to come;—when this, I say, is the case, do we hesitate as to the possibility of removing this monstrous defect in our morals, after an example has been set before us in so many lands? Moreover, we have as our bishop a man belonging to those parts, for which we give thanks earnestly to God; although he is a man of such moderation and gentleness, in fine, of such prudence and zeal in the Lord, that even had he been a native of Africa, the persuasion would have been wrought in him by the Scriptures, that a remedy must be applied to the wound which this loose and disorderly custom has inflicted. But so wide and deep is the plague caused by this wickedness, that, in my opinion, it cannot be completely cured without interposition of a council's authority. If, however, a beginning is to be made by one church, it seems to me, that as it would be presumptuous for any other church to attempt to change what the Church of Carthage still maintained, so would it also be the height of effrontery for any other to wish to persevere in a course which the Church of Carthage had condemned. And for such a reform in Carthage, what better bishop could be desired than the prelate who, while he was a deacon, solemnly denounced these practices?

5. But that over which you then sorrowed you ought now to suppress, not harshly, but as it is

written, "in the spirit of meekness."[3] Pardon my boldness, for your letter revealing to me your true brotherly love gives me such confidence, that I am encouraged to speak as freely to you as I would to myself. These offences are taken out of the way, at least in my judgment, by other methods than harshness, severity, and an imperious mode of dealing,—namely, rather by teaching than by commanding, rather by advice than by denunciation.[4] Thus at least we must deal with the multitude; in regard to the sins of a few, exemplary severity must be used. And if we do employ threats, let this be done sorrowfully, supporting our threatenings of coming judgment by the texts of Scripture, so that the fear which men feel through our words may be not of us in our own authority, but of God Himself. Thus an impression shall be made in the first place upon those who are spiritual, or who are nearest to that state of mind; and then by means of the most gentle, but at the same time most importunate exhortations, the opposition of the rest of the multitude shall be broken down.[5]

6. Since, however, these drunken revels and luxurious feasts in the cemeteries are wont to be regarded by the ignorant and carnal multitude as not only an honour to the martyrs, but also a solace to the dead, it appears to me that they might be more easily dissuaded from such scandalous and unworthy practices in these places, if, besides showing that they are forbidden by Scripture, we take care, in regard to the offerings for the spirits of those who sleep, which indeed we are bound to believe to be of some use, that they be not sumptuous beyond what is becoming respect for the memory of the departed, and that they be distributed without ostentation, and cheerfully to all who ask a share of them; also that they be not sold, but that if any one desires to offer any money as a religious act, it be given on the spot to the poor. Thus the appearance of neglecting the memory of their deceased friends, which might cause them no small sorrow of heart, shall be avoided, and that which is a pious and honourable act of religious service shall be celebrated as it should be in the Church. This may suffice meanwhile in regard to rioting and drunkenness.

CHAP. II.—7. As to "strife and deceit,"[6] what right have I to speak, seeing that these vices prevail more seriously among our own order than among our congregations? Let me, however, say that the source of these evils is pride, and a desire for the praises of men, which also frequently produces hypocrisy. This is successfully re-

---

[1] 1 Cor. v. 11.
[2] Manifestly the correct punctuation here is: *Hæc si prima Africa tentaret auferre, a cæteris terris imitatione digna esse deberet.*
[3] Gal. vi. 1.
[4] *Magis monendo quam minando.*
[5] One may see in Letter XXIX. how admirably Augustin illustrated in his own practice the directions here given.
[6] "*De contentione et dolo*" is Augustin's translation of the words in Rom. xiii. 13.

sisted only by him who is penetrated with love and fear of God, through the multiplied declarations of the divine books; provided, however, that such a man exhibit in himself a pattern both of patience and of humility, by assuming as his due less praise and honour than is offered to him: at the same time neither accepting all nor refusing all that is rendered to him by those who honour him; and as to the portion which he does accept, receiving it not for his own sake, seeing that he ought to live wholly in the sight of God and to despise human applause, but for the sake of those whose welfare he cannot promote if by too great self-abasement he lose his place in their esteem. For to this pertains that word, " Let no man despise thy youth;"[1] while he who said this says also in another place, " If I yet pleased men, I should not be the servant of Christ."[2]

8. It is a great matter not to exult in the honours and praises which come from men, but to reject all vain pomp; and, if some of this be necessary, to make whatever is thus retained contribute to the benefit and salvation of those who confer the honour. For it has not been said in vain, " God will break the bones of those who seek to please men."[3] For what could be feebler, what more destitute of the firmness and strength which the bones here spoken of figuratively represent, than the man who is prostrated by the tongue of slanderers, although he knows that the things spoken against him are false? The pain arising from this thing would in no wise rend the bowels of his soul, if its bones had not been broken by the love of praise. I take for granted your strength of mind: therefore it is to myself that I say those things which I am now stating to you. Nevertheless you are willing, I believe, to consider along with me how important and how difficult these things are. For the man who has not declared war against this enemy has no idea of its power; for if it be comparatively easy to dispense with praise so long as it is denied to him, it is difficult to forbear from being captivated with praise when it is offered. And yet the hanging of our minds upon God ought to be so great, that we would at once correct those with whom we may take that liberty, when we are by them undeservedly praised, so as to prevent them from either thinking us to possess what is not in us, or regarding that as ours which belongs to God, or commending us for things which, though we have them, and perhaps have them in abundance, are nevertheless in their nature not worthy of commendation, such as are all those good things which we have in common with the lower animals or with wicked men. If,

however, we are deservedly praised on account of what God has given us, let us congratulate those to whom what is really good yields pleasure; but let us not congratulate ourselves on the fact of our pleasing men, but on the fact of our being (if it is the case) such in the sight of God as we are in their esteem, and because praise is given not to us, but to God, who is the giver of all things which are truly and justly praised. These things are daily repeated to me by myself, or rather by Him from whom proceed all profitable instructions, whether they are found in the reading of the divine word or are suggested from within to the mind; and yet, although strenuously contending with my adversary, I often receive wounds from him when I am unable to put away from myself the fascinating power of the praise which is offered to me.

9. These things I have written, in order that, if they are not now necessary for your Holiness (your own thoughts suggesting to you other and more useful considerations of this kind, or your Holiness being above the need of such remedies), my disorders at least may be known to you, and you may know that which may move you to deign to plead with God for me as my infirmity demands: and I beseech you, by the humanity of Him who hath commanded us to bear each other's burdens, that you offer such intercession most importunately on my behalf. There are many things in regard to my life and conversation, of which I will not write, which I would confess with tears if we were so situated that nothing was required but my mouth and your ears as the means of communication between my heart and your heart. If, however, the aged Saturninus, venerated by us and beloved by all here with unreserved and unfeigned affection, whose brotherly love and devotion to you I observed when I was with you, — if he, I say, is pleased to visit us so soon as he finds it convenient, whatever converse we may be able to enjoy with that holy and spiritually-minded man shall be esteemed by us very little, if at all, different from personal conference with your Excellency. With entreaties too earnest for words to express their urgency, I beg you to condescend to join us in asking and obtaining from him this favour. For the people of Hippo fear much, and far more than they ought, to let me go so great a distance from them, and will on no account trust me by myself so far as to permit me to see the field given by your care and generosity to the brethren, of which, before your letter came, we had heard through our brother and fellow-servant Parthenius, from whom we have also learned many other things which we longed to know. The Lord will accomplish the fulfilment of all the other things which we still desiderate.

---

[1] 1 Tim. iv. 12.
[2] Gal. i. 10.
[3] Ps. lii. 6, Sept.

LETTER XXIII.

(A.D. 392.)

TO MAXIMIN, MY WELL-BELOVED LORD AND BROTHER, WORTHY OF HONOUR, AUGUSTIN, PRESBYTER OF THE CATHOLIC CHURCH, SENDS GREETING IN THE LORD.

1. Before entering on the subject on which I have resolved to write to your Grace, I shall briefly state my reasons for the terms used in the title of this letter, lest these should surprise either yourself or any other person. I have written "to my lord," because it is written: "Brethren, ye have been called unto liberty; only use not liberty for an occasion to the flesh, but by love serve one another."[1] Seeing, therefore, that in this duty of writing to you I am actually by love serving you, I do only what is reasonable in calling you "my lord," for the sake of that one true Lord who gave us this command. Again, as to my having written "well-beloved," God knoweth that I not only love you, but love you as I love myself; for I am well aware that I desire for you the very blessings which I am fain to make my own. As to my adding the words "worthy of honour," I did not mean, by adding this, to say that I honour your episcopal office, for to me you are not a bishop; and this I trust you will take as spoken with no intention to give offence, but from the conviction that in our mouth Yea should be Yea, and Nay, Nay: for neither you nor any one who knows us can fail to know that you are not my bishop, and I am not your presbyter. "Worthy of honour" I therefore willingly call you on this ground, that I know you to be a man; and I know that man was made in the image and likeness of God, and is placed in honour by the very order and law of nature, if by understanding the things which he ought to understand he retain his honour. For it is written, "Man being placed in honour did not understand: he is compared to the brutes devoid of reason, and is made like unto them."[2] Why then may I not address you as worthy of honour, inasmuch as you are a man, especially since I dare not despair of your repentance and salvation so long as you are in this life? Moreover, as to my calling you "brother," you are well acquainted with the precept divinely given to us, according to which we are to say, "Ye are our brethren," even to those who deny that they are our brethren; and this has much to do with the reason which has made me resolve to write to you, my brother. Now that the reason for my making such an introduction to my letter has been given, I bespeak your calm attention to what follows.

2. When I was in your district, and was with all my power expressing my abhorrence of the sad and deplorable custom followed by men who, though they boast of the name of Christians, do not hesitate to rebaptize Christians, there were not wanting some who said in praise of you, that you do not conform to this custom. I confess that at first I did not believe them; but afterwards, considering that it was possible for the fear of God to take possession of a human soul exercised in meditation upon the life to come, in such a way as to restrain a man from most manifest wickedness, I believed their statement, rejoicing that by holding such a resolution you showed yourself averse to complete alienation from the Catholic Church. I was even on the outlook for an opportunity of conversing with you, in order that, if it were possible, the small difference which still remained between us might be taken away, when, behold, a few days ago it was reported to me that you had rebaptized a deacon of ours belonging to Mutugenna! I was deeply grieved both for his melancholy fall and for your sin, my brother, which surprised and disappointed me. For I know what the Catholic Church is. The nations are Christ's inheritance, and the ends of the earth are His possession. You also know what the Catholic Church is; or if you do not know it, apply your attention to discern it, for it may be very easily known by those who are willing to be taught. Therefore, to rebaptize even a heretic who has received in baptism the seal of holiness which the practice[3] of the Christian Church has transmitted to us, is unquestionably a sin; but to rebaptize a Catholic is one of the worst of crimes. As I did not, however, believe the report, because I still retained my favourable impression of you, I went in person to Mutugenna. The miserable man himself I did not succeed in finding, but I learned from his parents that he had been made one of your deacons. Nevertheless I still think so favourably of you, that I will not believe that he has been rebaptized.

3. Wherefore, my beloved brother, I beseech you, by the divine and human natures of our Lord Jesus Christ, have the kindness to reply to this letter, telling me what has been done, and so to write as knowing that I intend to read your letter aloud to our brethren in the church. This I have written, lest, by afterwards doing that which you did not expect me to do, I should give offence to your Charity, and give you occasion for making a just complaint against me to our common friends. What can reasonably prevent you from answering this letter I do not see. For if you do rebaptize, you have nothing to apprehend from your colleagues when you write

---

[1] Gal. v. 13.
[2] Ps. xlix. 12, version of the LXX.
[3] *Disciplina.*

that you are doing that which they would command you to do even if you were unwilling ; and if you, moreover, defend this by the best arguments known to you, as a thing which ought to be done, your colleagues, so far from being displeased on this account, will praise you. But if you do not rebaptize, hold fast your Christian liberty, my brother Maximin ; hold it fast, I implore you : fixing your eye on Christ, fear not the censure, tremble not before the power of any man. Fleeting is the honour of this world, and fleeting are all the objects to which earthly ambition aspires. Neither thrones ascended by flights of steps,[1] nor canopied pulpits,[2] nor processions and chantings of crowds of consecrated virgins, shall be admitted as available for the defence of those who have now these honours, when at the judgment-seat of Christ conscience shall begin to lift its accusing voice, and He who is the Judge of the consciences of men shall pronounce the final sentence. What is here esteemed an honour shall then be a burden : what uplifts men here, shall weigh heavily on them in that day. Those things which meanwhile are done for the Church's welfare as tokens of respect to us, shall then be vindicated, it may be, by a conscience void of offence ; but they will avail nothing as a screen for a guilty conscience.

4. If, then, it be indeed the case that, under the promptings of a devout and pious mind, you abstain from dispensing a second baptism, and rather accept the baptism of the Catholic Church as the act of the one true Mother, who to all nations both offers a welcome to her bosom, that they may be regenerated, and gives a mother's nourishment to them when they are regenerated, and as the token of admission into Christ's one possession, which reaches to the ends of the earth ; if, I say, you indeed do this, why do you not break forth into a joyful and independent confession of your sentiments? Why do you hide under a bushel the lamp which might so profitably shine? Why do you not rend and cast from you the old sordid livery of your craven-hearted bondage, and go forth clad in the panoply of Christian boldness, saying, " I know but one baptism consecrated and sealed with the name of the Father, and the Son, and the Holy Ghost : this sacrament, wherever I find it, I am bound to acknowledge and approve ; I do not destroy what I discern to be my Lord's ; I do not treat with dishonour the banner of my King"? Even the men who parted the raiment of Christ among them did not rudely rend in pieces the seamless robe ;[3] and they were men who had not then any faith in Christ's resurrection ; nay, they were witnessing His death. If,

then, persecutors forbore from rending the vesture of Christ when He was hanging upon the cross, why should Christians destroy the sacrament of His institution now when He is sitting in heaven upon His throne? Had I been a Jew in the time of that ancient people, when there was nothing better that I could be, I would undoubtedly have received circumcision. That " seal of the righteousness which is by faith " was of so great importance in that dispensation before it was abrogated[4] by the Lord's coming, that the angel would have strangled the infant-child of Moses, had not the child's mother, seizing a stone, circumcised the child, and by this sacrament averted impending death.[5] This sacrament also arrested the waters of the Jordan, and made them flow back towards their source. This sacrament the Lord Himself received in infancy, although He abrogated it when He was crucified. For these signs of spiritual blessings were not condemned, but gave place to others which were more suitable to the later dispensation. For as circumcision was abolished by the first coming of the Lord, so baptism shall be abolished by His second coming. For as now, since the liberty of faith has come, and the yoke of bondage has been removed, no Christian receives circumcision in the flesh ; so then, when the just are reigning with the Lord, and the wicked have been condemned, no one shall be baptized, but the reality which both ordinances prefigure — namely, circumcision of the heart and cleansing of the conscience — shall be eternally abiding. If, therefore, I had been a Jew in the time of the former dispensation, and there had come to me a Samaritan who was willing to become a Jew, abandoning the error which the Lord Himself condemned when He said, " Ye worship ye know not what ; we know what we worship, for salvation is of the Jews ; "[6] — if, I say, a Samaritan whom Samaritans had circumcised had expressed his willingness to become a Jew, there would have been no scope for the boldness which would have insisted on the repetition of the rite ; and instead of this, we would have been compelled to approve of that which God had commanded, although it had been done by heretics. But if, in the flesh of a circumcised man, I could not find place for the repetition of the circumcision, because there is but one member which is circumcised, much less is place found in the one heart of man for the repetition of the baptism of Christ. Ye, therefore, who wish to baptize twice, must seek as subjects of such double baptism men who have double hearts.

---

[1] *Absidæ gradatæ.*
[2] *Cathedræ velatæ.*
[3] John xix. 24.

[4] *Evacuaretur.*
[5] Ex iv. 24, 25. Augustin believes that the angel sought to slay, not Moses, but the child, for which he gives reasons in his *Quæstiones in Exodum.* See Rosenmüller, *Scholia.*
[6] John iv. 22.

5. Publish frankly, therefore, that you are doing what is right, if it be the case that you do not rebaptize; and write me to that effect, not only without fear, but with joy. Let no Councils of your party deter you, my brother, from this step: for if this displease them, they are not worthy to have you among them; but if it please them, we trust that there shall soon be peace between you and us, through the mercy of our Lord, who never forsakes those who fear to displease Him, and who labour to do what is acceptable in His sight; and let not our honours — a dangerous burden, of which an account must yet be given — be a hindrance, making it unhappily impossible for our people who believe in Christ, and who share with one another in daily bread at home, to sit down at the same table of Christ. Do we not grievously lament that husband and wife do in most cases, when marriage makes them one flesh, vow mutual fidelity in the name of Christ, and yet rend asunder Christ's own body by belonging to separate communions? If, by your moderate measures and wisdom, and by your exercise of that love which we all owe to Him who shed His blood for us, this schism, which is such a grievous scandal, causing Satan to triumph and many souls to perish, be taken out of the way in these parts, who can adequately express how illustrious is the reward which the Lord prepares for you, in that from you should proceed an example which, if imitated, as it may so easily be, would bring health to all His other members, which throughout the whole of Africa are lying now miserably exhausted? How much I fear lest, since you cannot see my heart, I appear to you to speak rather in irony than in the sincerity of love! But what more can I do than present my words before your eye, and my heart before God?

6. Let us put away from between us those vain objections which are wont to be thrown at each other by the ignorant on either side. Do not on your part cast up to me the persecutions of Macarius. I, on mine, will not reproach you with the excesses of the Circumcelliones. If you are not to blame for the latter, neither am I for the former; they pertain not to us. The Lord's floor is not yet purged — it cannot be without chaff; be it ours to pray, and to do what in us lies that we may be good grain. I could not pass over in silence the rebaptizing of our deacon; for I know how much harm my silence might do to myself. For I do not propose to spend my time in the empty enjoyment of ecclesiastical dignity; but I propose to act as mindful of this, that to the one Chief Shepherd I must give account of the sheep committed unto me. If you would rather that I should not thus write to you, you must, my brother, excuse me on the ground of my fears; for I do fear greatly, lest, if I were silent and concealed my sentiments, others might be rebaptized by you. I have resolved, therefore, with such strength and opportunity as the Lord may grant, so to manage this discussion, that by our peaceful conferences, all who belong to our communion may know how far apart from heresy and schism is the position of the Catholic Church, and with what care they should guard against the destruction which awaits the tares and the branches cut off from the Lord's vine. If you willingly accede to such conference with me, by consenting to the public reading of the letters of both, I shall unspeakably rejoice. If this proposal is displeasing to you, what can I do, my brother, but read our letters, even without your consent, to the Catholic congregation, with a view to its instruction? But if you do not condescend to write me a reply, I am resolved at least to read my own letter, that, when your misgivings as to your procedure are known, others may be ashamed to be rebaptized.

7. I shall not, however, do this in the presence of the soldiery, lest any of you should think that I wish to act in a violent way, rather than as the interests of peace demand; but only after their departure, that all who hear me may understand, that I do not propose to compel men to embrace the communion of any party, but desire the truth to be made known to persons who, in their search for it, are free from disquieting apprehensions. On our side there shall be no appeal to men's fear of the civil power; on your side, let there be no intimidation by a mob of Circumcelliones. Let us attend to the real matter in debate, and let our arguments appeal to reason and to the authoritative teaching of the Divine Scriptures, dispassionately and calmly, so far as we are able; let us ask, seek, and knock, that we may receive and find, and that to us the door may be opened, and thereby may be achieved, by God's blessing on our united efforts and prayers, the first step towards the entire removal from our district of that impiety which is such a disgrace to Africa. If you do not believe that I am willing to postpone the discussion until after the soldiery have left, you may delay your answer until they have gone; and if, while they are still here, I should wish to read my own letter to the people, the production of the letter will of itself convict me of breaking my word. May the Lord in His mercy prevent me from acting in a way so contrary to morality, and to the good resolutions with which, by laying His yoke on me, He has been pleased to inspire me!

8. My bishop would perhaps have preferred to send a letter himself to your Grace, if he had been here; or my letter would have been written, if not by his order, at least with his sanction.

But in his absence, seeing that the rebaptizing of this deacon is said to have occurred recently, I have not by delay allowed the feelings caused by the action to cool down, being moved by the promptings of the keenest anguish on account of what I regard as really the death of a brother. This my grief the compensating joy of reconciliation between us and you may perhaps be appointed to heal, through the help of the mercy and providence of our Lord. May the Lord our God grant thee a calm and conciliatory spirit, my dearly beloved lord and brother !

LETTER XXIV.

This letter, written in 394 to Alypius by Paulinus, owes its place in the collection of Augustin's letters to the notice of the treatises written by Augustin against the Manichæans, and its connection with the following letter addressed by Paulinus to Augustin himself. It is obviously one of those which, in making a selection of letters, may be safely omitted.

LETTER XXV.

(A.D. 394.)

TO AUGUSTIN, OUR LORD AND BROTHER BELOVED AND VENERABLE, FROM PAULINUS AND THERASIA, SINNERS.

1. The love of Christ which constrains us, and which unites us, though separated by distance, in the bond of a common faith, has itself emboldened me to dismiss my fear and address a letter to you ; and it has given you a place in my inmost heart by means of your writings — so full of the stores of learning, so sweet with celestial honey, the medicine and the nourishment of my soul. These I at present have in five books, which, through the kindness of our blessed and venerable Bishop Alypius, I received, not only as a means of my own instruction, but for the use of the Church in many towns. These books I am now reading : in them I take great delight : in them I find food, not that which perisheth, but that which imparts the substance of eternal life through our faith, whereby we are in our Lord Jesus Christ made members of His body ; for the writings and examples of the faithful do greatly strengthen that faith which, not looking at things seen, longs after things not seen with that love which accepts implicitly all things which are according to the truth of the omnipotent God. O true salt of the earth, by which our hearts are preserved from being corrupted by the errors of the world ! O light worthy of your place on the candlestick of the Church, diffusing widely in the Catholic towns the brightness of a flame fed by the oil of the seven-branched lamp of the upper sanctuary, you also disperse even the thick mists of heresy,

and rescue the light of truth from the confusion of darkness by the beams of your luminous demonstrations.

2. You see, my brother beloved, esteemed, and welcomed in Christ our Lord, with what intimacy I claim to know you, with what amazement I admire and with what love I embrace you, seeing that I enjoy daily converse with you by the medium of your writings, and am fed by the breath of your mouth. For your mouth I may justly call a pipe conveying living water, and a channel from the eternal fountain ; for Christ has become in you a fountain of " living water springing up into eternal life." [1] Through desire for this my soul thirsted within me, and my parched ground longed to be flooded with the fulness of your river. Since, therefore, you have armed me completely by this your Pentateuch against the Manichæans, if you have prepared any treatises in defence of the Catholic faith against other enemies (for our enemy, with his thousand pernicious stratagems, must be defeated by weapons as various as the artifices by which he assails us), I beg you to bring these forth from your armoury for me, and not refuse to furnish me with the " armour of righteousness." For I am oppressed even now in my work with a heavy burden, being, as a sinner, a veteran in the ranks of sinners, but an untrained recruit in the service of the King eternal. The wisdom of this world I have unhappily hitherto regarded with admiration, and, devoting myself to literature which I now see to be unprofitable, and wisdom which I now reject, I was in the sight of God foolish and dumb. When I had become old in the fellowship of my enemies, and had laboured in vain in my thoughts, I lifted mine eyes to the mountains, looking up to the precepts of the law and to the gifts of grace, whence my help came from the Lord, who, not requiting me according to mine iniquity, enlightened my blindness, loosed my bonds, humbled me who had been sinfully exalted, in order that He might exalt me when graciously humbled.

3. Therefore I follow, with halting pace indeed as yet, the great examples of the just, if I may through your prayers apprehend that for which I have been apprehended by the compassion of God. Guide, therefore, this infant creeping on the ground, and by your steps teach him to walk. For I would not have you judge of me by the age which began with my natural birth, but by that which began with my spiritual new birth. For as to the natural life, my age is that which the cripple, healed by the apostles by the power of their word at the gate Beautiful, had attained.[2] But with respect to the birth of my soul, mine is as yet the age of those infants

[1] John iv. 14.
[2] Acts iii. 7 and iv. 22.

who, being sacrificed by the death-blows which were aimed at Christ, preceded with blood worthy of such honour the offering of the Lamb, and were the harbingers of the passion of the Lord.[1] Therefore, as I am but a babe in the word of God, and as to spiritual age a sucking child, satisfy my vehement desire by nourishing me with your words, the breasts of faith, and wisdom, and love. If you consider only the office which we both hold, you are my brother; but if you consider the ripeness of your understanding and other powers, you are, though my junior in years, a father to me; because the possession of a venerable wisdom has promoted you, though young, to a maturity of worth, and to the honour which belongs to those who are old. Foster and strengthen me, then, for I am, as I have said, but a child in the sacred Scriptures and in spiritual studies; and seeing that, after long contendings and frequent shipwreck, I have but little skill, and am even now with difficulty rising above the waves of this world, do you, who have already found firm footing on the shore, receive me into the safe refuge of your bosom, that, if it please you, we may together sail towards the harbour of salvation. Meanwhile, in my efforts to escape from the dangers of this life and the abyss of sin, support me by your prayers, as by a plank, that from this world I may escape as one does from a shipwreck, leaving all behind.

4. I have therefore been at pains to rid myself of all baggage and garments which might impede my progress, in order that, obedient to the command and sustained by the help of Christ, I may swim, unhindered by any clothing for the flesh or care for the morrow, across the sea of this present life, which, swelling with waves and echoing with the barking of our sins, like the dogs of Scylla, separates between us and God. I do not boast that I have accomplished this: even if I might so boast, I would glory only in the Lord, whose it is to accomplish what it is our part to desire; but my soul is in earnest that the judgments of the Lord be her chief desire. You can judge how far he is on the way to efficiently performing the will of God, who is desirous that he may desire to perform it. Nevertheless, so far as in me lies, I have loved the beauty of His sanctuary, and, if left to myself, would have chosen to occupy the lowest place in the Lord's house. But to Him who was pleased to separate me from my mother's womb, and to draw me away from the friendship of flesh and blood to His grace, it has seemed good to raise me from the earth and from the gulf of misery, though destitute of all merit, and to take me from the mire and from the dunghill, to set me among the princes of His

people, and appoint my place in the same rank with yourself; so that, although you excel me in worth, I should be associated with you as your equal in office.

5. It is not therefore by my own presumption, but in accordance with the pleasure and appointment of the Lord, that I appropriate the honour of which I own myself unworthy, claiming for myself the bond of brotherhood with you; for I am persuaded, from the holiness of your character, that you are taught by the truth "not to mind high things, but to condescend to men of low estate." Therefore I hope that you will readily and kindly accept the assurance of the love which in humility we bear to you, and which, I trust, you have already received through the most blessed priest Alypius, whom (with his permission) we call our father. For he doubtless has himself given you an example of loving us both while we are yet strangers, and above our desert; for he has found it possible, in the spirit of far-reaching and self-diffusing genuine love, to behold us by affection, and to come in contact with us by writing, even when we were unknown to him, and severed by a wide interval both of land and sea. He has presented us with the first proofs of his affection to us, and evidences of your love, in the above-mentioned gift of books. And as he was greatly concerned that we should be constrained to ardent love for you, when known to us, not by his testimony alone, but more fully by the eloquence and the faith seen in your own writings; so do we believe that he has taken care, with equal zeal, to bring you to imitate his example in cherishing a very warm love towards us in return. O brother in Christ, beloved, venerable, and ardently longed for, we desire that the grace of God, as it is with you, may abide for ever. We salute, with the utmost affection of cordial brotherhood, your whole household, and every one who is in the Lord a companion and imitator of your holiness. We beg you to bless, in accepting it, one loaf which we have sent to your Charity, in token of our oneness of heart with you.

LETTER XXVI.

(A.D. 395.)

TO LICENTIUS [2] FROM AUGUSTIN.

1. I have with difficulty found an opportunity for writing to you: who would believe it? Yet Licentius must take my word for it. I do not wish you to search curiously for the causes and reasons of this; for though they could be given,

---

[1] Matt. ii. 16.

[2] Licentius, son of Romanianus, had been a pupil of Augustin when he was in retirement at Cassiacum. In this letter and in the next we see proofs of Augustin's pious solicitude for his welfare.

your confidence in me acquits me of obligation to furnish them. Moreover, I received your letters by messengers who were not available for the carrying back of my reply. And as to the thing which you asked me to ask, I attended to it by letter as far as it seemed to me right to bring it forward; but with what result you may have seen. If I have not yet succeeded, I will press the matter more earnestly, either when the result comes to my knowledge, or when you yourself remind me of it. Thus far I have spoken to you of the things in which we hear the sound of the chains of this life. I pass from them. Receive now in a few words the utterance of my heart's anxieties concerning your hope for eternity, and the question how a way may be opened for you to God.

2. I fear, my dear Licentius, that you, while repeatedly rejecting and dreading the restraints of wisdom, as if these were bonds, are becoming firmly and fatally in bondage to mortal things. For wisdom, though at first it restrains men, and subdues them by some labours in the way of discipline, gives them presently true freedom, and enriches them, when free, with the possession and enjoyment of itself; and though at first it educates them by the help of temporary restraints, it folds them afterwards in its eternal embrace, the sweetest and strongest of all conceivable bonds. I admit, indeed, that these initial restraints are somewhat hard to bear; but the ultimate restraints of wisdom I cannot call grievous, because they are most sweet; nor can I call them easy, because they are most firm: in short, they possess a quality which cannot be described, but which can be the object of faith, and hope, and love. The bonds of this world, on the other hand, have a real harshness and a delusive charm, certain pain and uncertain pleasure, hard toil and troubled rest, an experience full of misery, and a hope devoid of happiness. And are you submitting neck and hands and feet to these chains, desiring to be burdened with honours of this kind, reckoning your labours to be in vain if they are not thus rewarded, and spontaneously aspiring to become fixed in that to which neither persuasion nor force ought to have induced you to go? Perhaps you answer, in the words of the slave in Terence,

"So ho, you are pouring out wise words here."

Receive my words, then, that I may pour them out without wasting them. But if I sing, while you prefer to dance to another tune, even thus I do not regret my effort to give advice; for the exercise of singing yields pleasure even when the song fails to stir to responsive motion the person for whom it is sung with loving care. There were in your letters some verbal mistakes

which attracted my attention, but I judge it trifling to discuss these when solicitude about your actions and your whole life disturbs me.

3. If your verses were marred by defective arrangement, or violated the laws of prosody, or grated on the ears of the hearer by imperfect rhythm, you would doubtless be ashamed, and you would lose no time, you would take no rest, until you arranged, corrected, remodelled, and balanced your composition, devoting any amount of earnest study and toil to the acquisition and practice of the art of versification: but when you yourself are marred by disorderly living, when you violate the laws of God, when your life accords neither with the honourable desires of friends on your behalf, nor with the light given by your own learning, do you think this is a trifle to be cast out of sight and out of mind? As if, forsooth, you thought yourself of less value than the sound of your own voice, and esteemed it a smaller matter to displease God by ill-ordered life, than to provoke the censure of grammarians by ill-ordered syllables.

4. You write thus: "Oh that the morning light of other days could with its gladdening chariot bring back to me bright hours that are gone, which we spent together in the heart of Italy and among the high mountains, when proving the generous leisure and pure privileges which belong to the good! Neither stern winter with its frozen snow, nor the rude blasts of Zephyrs and raging of Boreas, could deter me from following your footsteps with eager tread. You have only to express your wish." [1]

Woe be to me if I do not express this wish, nay, if I do not compel and command, or beseech and implore you to follow me. If, however, your ear is shut against my voice, let it be open to your own voice, and give heed to your own poem: listen to yourself, O friend, most unyielding, unreasonable, and unimpressible. What care I for your tongue of gold, while your heart is of iron? How shall I, not in verses, but in lamentations, sufficiently bewail these verses of yours, in which I discover what a soul, what a mind that is which I am not permitted to seize and present as an offering to our God? You are waiting for me to express the wish that you should become good, and enjoy rest and happiness: as if any day could shine more pleasantly on me than that in which I shall enjoy in God your gifted mind, or as if you did not know how I hunger and thirst for you, or as if you did not in this poem itself confess this. Return to the mind in which you wrote these things; say to me now again, "You have only to express your wish." Here then is my wish, if my expression of it be enough to move you

---

[1] Extract from a long poem, by Licentius, forming § 3 of the text.

to comply: Give yourself to me — give your-self to my Lord, who is the Lord of us both, and who has endowed you with your faculties: for what am I but through Him your servant, and under Him your fellow-servant?

5. Nay, has not He given expression to His will? Hear the gospel: it declares, "Jesus stood and cried."[1] "Come unto me, all ye that labour and are heavy laden, and I will give you rest. Take my yoke upon you, and learn of me; for I am meek and lowly in heart: so shall ye find rest to your souls. For my yoke is easy, and my burden is light."[2] If these words are not heard, or are heard only with the ear, do you, Licentius, expect Augustin to issue his command to his fellow-servant, and not rather complain that the will of his Lord is despised, when He orders, nay invites, and as it were en-treats all who labour to seek rest in Him? But to your strong and proud neck, forsooth, the yoke of the world seems easier than the yoke of Christ; yet consider, in regard to the yoke which He imposes, by whom and with what recompense it is imposed. Go to Campania, learn in the case of Paulinus, that eminent and holy servant of God, how great worldly honours he shook off, without hesitation, from neck truly noble because humble, in order that he might place it, as he has done, beneath the yoke of Christ; and now, with his mind at rest, he meekly rejoices in Him as the guide of his way. Go, learn with what wealth of mind he offers to Him the sacrifice of praise, rendering unto Him all the good which he has received from Him, lest, by failing to store all that he has in Him from whom he received it, he should lose it all.

6. Why are you so excited? why so wavering? why do you turn your ear away from us, and lend it to the imaginations of fatal pleasures? They are false, they perish, and they lead to perdition. They are false, Licentius. "May the truth," as you desire, "be made plain to us by demonstra-tion, may it flow more clear than Eridanus." The truth alone declares what is true: Christ is the truth; let us come to Him that we may be released from labour. That He may heal us, let us take His yoke upon us, and learn of Him who is meek and lowly in heart, and we shall find rest unto our souls: for His yoke is easy, and His burden is light. The devil desires to wear you as an ornament. Now, if you found in the earth a golden chalice, you would give it to the Church of God. But you have received from God talents that are spiritually valuable as gold; and do you devote these to the service of your lusts, and surrender yourself to Satan? Do it not, I entreat you. May you at some time perceive with what a sad and sorrowful heart I have written these things; and I pray you, have pity on me if you have ceased to be precious in your own eyes.

LETTER XXVII.

(A.D. 395.)

TO MY LORD, HOLY AND VENERABLE, AND WORTHY OF HIGHEST PRAISE IN CHRIST, MY BROTHER PAULINUS, AUGUSTIN SENDS GREETING IN THE LORD.

1. O excellent man and excellent brother, there was a time when you were unknown to my mind; and I charge my mind to bear pa-tiently your being still unknown to my eyes, but it almost — nay, altogether — refuses to obey. Does it indeed bear this patiently? If so, why then does a longing for your presence rack my inmost soul? For if I were suffering bodily in-firmities, and these did not interrupt the serenity of my mind, I might be justly said to bear them patiently; but when I cannot bear with equa-nimity the privation of not seeing you, it would be intolerable were I to call my state of mind patience. Nevertheless, it would perhaps be still more intolerable if I were to be found patient while absent from you, seeing that you are such an one as you are. It is well, therefore, that I am unsatisfied under a privation which is such that, if I were satisfied under it, every one would justly be dissatisfied with me. What has befallen me is strange, yet true: I grieve because I do not see you, and my grief itself comforts me; for I neither admire nor covet a fortitude easily consoled under the absence of good men such as you are. For do we not long for the heav-enly Jerusalem? and the more impatiently we long for it, do we not the more patiently sub-mit to all things for its sake? Who can so withhold himself from joy in seeing you, as to feel no pain when you are no longer seen? I at least can do neither; and seeing that if I could, it could only be by trampling on right and natu-ral feeling, I rejoice that I cannot, and in this rejoicing I find some consolation. It is there-fore not the removal, but the contemplation, of this sorrow that consoles me. Blame me not, I beseech you, with that devout seriousness of spirit which so eminently distinguishes you; say not that I do wrong to grieve because of my not yet knowing you, when you have disclosed to my sight your mind, which is the inner man. For if, when sojourning in any place, or in the city to which you belong, I had come to know you as my brother and friend, and as one so eminent as a Christian, so noble as a man, how could you think that it would be no disappoint-

---

[1] John vii 37.
[2] Matt. xi. 28-30.

ment to me if I were not permitted to know your dwelling? How, then, can I but mourn because I have not yet seen your face and form, the dwelling-place of that mind which I have come to know as if it were my own?

2. For I have read your letter, which flows with milk and honey, which exhibits the simplicity of heart wherewith, under the guidance of piety, you seek the Lord, and which brings glory and honour to Him. The brethren have read it also, and find unwearied and ineffable satisfaction in those abundant and excellent gifts with which God has endowed you. As many as have read it carry it away with them, because, while they read, it carries them away. Words cannot express how sweet is the savour of Christ which your letter breathes. How strong is the wish to be more fully acquainted with you which that letter awakens by presenting you to our sight! for it at once permits us to discern and prompts us to desire you. For the more effectually that it makes us in a certain sense realize your presence, the more does it render us impatient under your absence. All love you as seen therein, and wish to be loved by you. Praise and thanksgiving are offered to God, by whose grace you are what you are. In your letter, Christ is awakened that He may be pleased to calm the winds and the waves for you, directing your steps towards His perfect stedfastness.[1] In it the reader beholds a wife[2] who does not bring her husband to effeminacy, but by union to him is brought herself to share the strength of his nature; and unto her in you, as completely one with you, and bound to you by spiritual ties which owe their strength to their purity, we desire to return our salutations with the respect due to your Holiness. In it, the cedars of Lebanon, levelled to the ground, and fashioned by the skilful craft of love into the form of the Ark, cleave the waves of this world, fearless of decay. In it, glory is scorned that it may be secured, and the world given up that it may be gained. In it, the little ones, yea, the mightier sons of Babylon, the sins of turbulence and pride, are dashed against the rock.

3. These and other such most delightful and hallowed spectacles are presented to the readers of your letter, — that letter which exhibits a true faith, a good hope, a pure love. How it breathes to us your thirst, your longing and fainting for the courts of the Lord! With what holy love it is inspired! How it overflows with the abundant treasure of a true heart! What thanksgivings it renders to God! What blessings it procures from Him! Is it elegance or fervour, light or life-giving power, which shines most in your letter? For how can it at once soothe us and animate us? how can it combine fertilizing rains with the brightness of a cloudless sky? How is this? I ask; or how shall I repay you, except by giving myself to be wholly yours in Him whose you wholly are? If this be little, it is at least all I have to give. But you have made me think it not little, by your deigning to honour me in that letter with such praises, that when I requite you by giving myself to you, I would be chargeable if I counted the gift a small one, with refusing to believe your testimony. I am ashamed, indeed, to believe so much good spoken of myself, but I am yet more unwilling to refuse to believe you. I have one way of escape from the dilemma: I shall not credit your estimate of my character, because I do not recognise myself in the portrait you have drawn; but I shall believe myself to be beloved by you, because I perceive and feel this beyond all doubt. Thus I shall be found neither rash in judging of myself, nor ungrateful for your esteem. Moreover, when I offer myself to you, it is not a small offering; for I offer one whom you very warmly love, and one who, though he is not what you suppose him to be, is nevertheless one for whom you are praying that he may become such. And your prayers I now beg the more earnestly, lest, thinking me to be already what I am not, you should be less solicitous for the supply of that which I lack.

4. The bearer of this letter[3] to your Excellency and most eminent Charity is one of my dearest friends, and most intimately known to me from early years. His name is mentioned in the treatise *De Religione*, which your Holiness, as you indicate in your letter, has read with very great pleasure, doubtless because it was made more acceptable to you by the recommendation of so good a man as he who sent it to you.[4] I would not wish you, however, to give credence to the statements which, perchance, one who is so intimately my friend may have made in praise of me. For I have often observed, that, without intending to say what was untrue, he was, by the bias of friendship, mistaken in his opinion concerning me, and that he thought me to be already possessed of many things, for the gift of which my heart earnestly waited on the Lord. And if he did such things in my presence, who may not conjecture that out of the fulness of his heart he may utter many things more excellent than true concerning me when absent? He will submit to your esteemed attention, and review all my treatises; for I am not aware of having written anything, either addressed to those who are beyond the pale of the Church, or to the brethren, which is not in his possession. But when you are reading these,

---

[1] Compare end of sec. 3 in Letter XXV. p. 246.
[2] Therasia.

[3] Romanianus. See *De Religione*, ch. vii. n. 12.
[4] Alypius.

my holy Paulinus, let not those things which Truth has spoken by my weak instrumentality, so carry you away as to prevent your carefully observing what I myself have spoken, lest, while you drink in with eagerness the things good and true which have been given to me as a servant, you should forget to pray for the pardon of my errors and mistakes. For in all that shall, if observed, justly displease you, I myself am seen; but in all which in my books is justly approved by you, through the gift of the Holy Spirit bestowed on you, He is to be loved, He is to be praised, with whom is the fountain of life, and in whose light we shall see light,[1] not darkly as we do here, but face to face.[2] When, in reading over my writings, I discover in them anything which is due to the working of the old leaven in me, I blame myself for it with true sorrow; but if anything which I have spoken is, by God's gift, from the unleavened bread of sincerity and truth, I rejoice therein with trembling. For what have we that we have not received? Yet it may be said, his portion is better whom God has endowed with larger and more numerous gifts, than his on whom smaller and fewer have been conferred. True; but, on the other hand, it is better to have a small gift, and to render to Him due thanks for it, than, having a large gift, to wish to claim the merit of it as our own. Pray for me, my brother, that I may make such acknowledgments sincerely, and that my heart may not be at variance with my tongue. Pray, I beseech you, that, not coveting praise to myself, but rendering praise to the Lord, I may worship Him; and I shall be safe from mine enemies.

5. There is yet another thing which may move you to love more warmly the brother who bears my letter; for he is a kinsman of the venerable and truly blessed bishop Alypius, whom you love with your whole heart, and justly: for whoever thinks highly of that man, thinks highly of the great mercy and wonderful gifts which God has bestowed on him. Accordingly, when he had read your request, desiring him to write for you a sketch of his history, and, while willing to do it because of your kindness, was yet unwilling to do it because of his humility, I, seeing him unable to decide between the respective claims of love and humility, transferred the burden from his shoulders to my own, for he enjoined me by letter to do so. I shall therefore, with God's help, soon place in your heart Alypius just as he is: for this I chiefly feared, that he would be afraid to declare all that God has conferred on him, lest (since what he writes would be read by others besides you) he should seem to any who

are less competent to discriminate to be commending not God's goodness bestowed on men, but his own merits; and that thus you, who know what construction to put on such statements, would, through his regard for the infirmity of others, be deprived of that which to you as a brother ought to be imparted. This I would have done already, and you would already be reading my description of him, had not my brother suddenly resolved to set out earlier than we expected. For him I bespeak a welcome from your heart and from your lips as kindly as if your acquaintance with him was not beginning now, but of as long standing as my own. For if he does not shrink from laying himself open to your heart, he will be in great measure, if not completely, healed by your lips; for I desire him to be often made to hear the words of those who cherish for their friends a higher love than that which is of this world.

6. Even if Romanianus had not been going to visit your Charity, I had resolved to recommend to you by letter his son [Licentius], dear to me as my own (whose name you will find also in some of my books), in order that he may be encouraged, exhorted, and instructed, not so much by the sound of your voice, as by the example of your spiritual strength. I desire earnestly, that while his life is yet in the green blade, the tares may be turned into wheat, and he may believe those who know by experience the dangers to which he is eager to expose himself. From the poem of my young friend, and my letter to him, your most benevolent and considerate wisdom may perceive my grief, fear, and care on his account. I am not without hope that, by the Lord's favour, I may through your means be set free from such disquietude regarding him.

As you are now about to read much that I have written, your love will be much more gratefully esteemed by me, if, moved by compassion, and judging impartially, you correct and reprove whatever displeases you. For you are not one whose oil anointing my head would make me afraid.[3]

The brethren, not those only who dwell with us, and those who, dwelling elsewhere, serve God in the same way as we do, but almost all who are in Christ our warm friends, send you salutations, along with the expression of their veneration and affectionate longing for you as a brother, as a saint, and as a man.[4] I dare not ask; but if you have any leisure from ecclesiastical duties, you may see for what favour all Africa, with myself, is thirsting.

[1] Ps. xxxvi. 10.
[2] 1 Cor. xiii. 12.

[3] The reference is to Ps. cxli. 5, the words of which, translated from the LXX. version, are given in full in the succeeding letter.
[4] This may approximate to a translation of the three titles in the original, " Germanitas, Beatitudo, Humanitas tua."

LETTER XXVIII.

(A.D. 394 OR 395.)

TO JEROME, HIS MOST BELOVED LORD, AND BROTHER AND FELLOW-PRESBYTER, WORTHY OF BEING HONOURED AND EMBRACED WITH THE SINCEREST AFFECTIONATE DEVOTION, AUGUSTIN SENDS GREETING.[1]

CHAP. I. — 1. Never was the face of any one more familiar to another, than the peaceful, happy, and truly noble diligence of your studies in the Lord has become to me. For although I long greatly to be acquainted with you, I feel that already my knowledge of you is deficient in respect of nothing but a very small part of you, —namely, your personal appearance; and even as to this, I cannot deny that since my most blessed brother Alypius (now invested with the office of bishop, of which he was then truly worthy) has seen you, and has on his return been seen by me, it has been almost completely imprinted on my mind by his report of you; nay, I may say that before his return, when he saw you there, I was seeing you myself with his eyes. For any one who knows us may say of him and me, that in body only, and not in mind, we are two, so great is the union of heart, so firm the intimate friendship subsisting between us; though in merit we are not alike, for his is far above mine. Seeing, therefore, that you love me, both of old through the communion of spirit by which we are knit to each other, and more recently through what you know of me from the mouth of my friend, I feel that it is not presumptuous in me (as it would be in one wholly unknown to you) to recommend to your brotherly esteem the brother Profuturus, in whom we trust that the happy omen of his name (Good-speed) may be fulfilled through our efforts furthered after this by your aid; although, perhaps, it may be presumptuous on this ground, that he is so great a man, that it would be much more fitting that I should be commended to you by him, than he by me. I ought perhaps to write no more, if I were willing to content myself with the style of a formal letter of introduction; but my mind overflows into conference with you, concerning the studies with which we are occupied in Christ Jesus our Lord, who is pleased to furnish us largely through your love with many benefits, and

some helps by the way, in the path which He has pointed out to His followers.

CHAP. II. — 2. We therefore, and with us all that are devoted to study in the African churches, beseech you not to refuse to devote care and labour to the translation of the books of those who have written in the Greek language most able commentaries on our Scriptures. You may thus put us also in possession of these men, and especially of that one whose name you seem to have singular pleasure in sounding forth in your writings [Origen]. But I beseech you not to devote your labour to the work of translating into Latin the sacred canonical books, unless you follow the method in which you have translated Job, viz. with the addition of notes, to let it be seen plainly what differences there are between this version of yours and that of the LXX., whose authority is worthy of highest esteem. For my own part, I cannot sufficiently express my wonder that anything should at this date be found in the Hebrew MSS. which escaped so many translators perfectly acquainted with the language. I say nothing of the LXX., regarding whose harmony in mind and spirit, surpassing that which is found in even one man, I dare not in any way pronounce a decided opinion, except that in my judgment, beyond question, very high authority must in this work of translation be conceded to them. I am more perplexed by those translators who, though enjoying the advantage of labouring after the LXX. had completed their work, and although well acquainted, as it is reported, with the force of Hebrew words and phrases, and with Hebrew syntax, have not only failed to agree among themselves, but have left many things which, even after so long a time, still remain to be discovered and brought to light. Now these things were either obscure or plain: if they were obscure, it is believed that you are as likely to have been mistaken as the others; if they were plain, it is not believed that they [the LXX.] could possibly have been mistaken. Having stated the grounds of my perplexity, I appeal to your kindness to give me an answer regarding this matter.

CHAP. III. — 3. I have been reading also some writings, ascribed to you, on the Epistles of the Apostle Paul. In reading your exposition of the Epistle to the Galatians, that passage came to my hand in which the Apostle Peter is called back from a course of dangerous dissimulation. To find there the defence of falsehood undertaken, whether by you, a man of such weight, or by any author (if it is the writing of another), causes me, I must confess, great sorrow, until at least those things which decide my opinion in the matter are refuted, if indeed they admit of refutation. For it seems to me that most disastrous consequences must follow upon our be-

---

[1] [The letters to Jerome, and Jerome's replies, are among the most interesting and important in this correspondence, especially those parts which relate to Jerome's revision of the Latin version of the Bible, and his interpretation of Gal. ii. 11–14. See Letters 40, 71, 72, 73, 75, 81, 82, 172, 195, 202. Augustin was inferior to Jerome in learning, especially as a linguist, but superior in Christian temper and humility. Jerome's false interpretation of the dispute between Paul and Peter at Antioch, which involved both apostles in hypocrisy, offended Augustin's keener sense of veracity. He here protests against it in this letter (ch. iii.), and again in Letter 40, and thereby provokes Jerome's irritable temper. His last letters to Augustin, however, show sincere esteem and affection.—P. S.]

lieving that anything false is found in the sacred books : that is to say, that the men by whom the Scripture has been given to us, and committed to writing, did put down in these books anything false. It is one question whether it may be at any time the duty of a good man to deceive ; but it is another question whether it can have been the duty of a writer of Holy Scripture to deceive : nay, it is not another question — it is no question at all. For if you once admit into such a high sanctuary of authority one false statement as made in the way of duty,[1] there will not be left a single sentence of those books which, if appearing to any one difficult in practice or hard to believe, may not by the same fatal rule be explained away, as a statement in which, intentionally, and under a sense of duty, the author declared what was not true.

4. For if the Apostle Paul did not speak the truth when, finding fault with the Apostle Peter, he said : " If thou, being a Jew, livest after the manner of Gentiles, and not as do the Jews, why compellest thou the Gentiles to live as do the Jews ? " — if, indeed, Peter seemed to him to be doing what was right, and if, notwithstanding, he, in order to soothe troublesome opponents, both said and wrote that Peter did what was wrong ;[2] — if we say thus, what then shall be our answer when perverse men such as he himself prophetically described arise, forbidding marriage,[3] if they defend themselves by saying that, in all which the same apostle wrote in confirmation of the lawfulness of marriage,[4] he was, on account of men who, through love for their wives, might become troublesome opponents, declaring what was false, — saying these things, forsooth, not because he believed them, but because their opposition might thus be averted ? It is unnecessary to quote many parallel examples. For even things which pertain to the praises of God might be represented as piously intended falsehoods, written in order that love for Him might be enkindled in men who were slow of heart ; and thus nowhere in the sacred books shall the authority of pure truth stand sure. Do we not observe the great care with which the same apostle commends the truth to us, when he says : "And if Christ be not risen, then is our preaching vain, and your faith is also vain : yea, and we are found false witnesses of God ; because we have testified of God that He raised up Christ ; whom He raised not up, if so be that the dead rise not."[5] If any one said to him, " Why are you so shocked by this falsehood, when the thing which you have said, even if it were false, tends very greatly to the glory of God ? " would he not, abhorring the madness of such a man, with every word and sign which could express his feelings, open clearly the secret depths of his own heart, protesting that to speak well of a falsehood uttered on behalf of God, was a crime not less, perhaps even greater, than to speak ill of the truth concerning Him ? We must therefore be careful to secure, in order to our knowledge of the divine Scriptures, the guidance only of such a man as is imbued with a high reverence for the sacred books, and a profound persuasion of their truth, preventing him from flattering himself in any part of them with the hypothesis of a statement being made not because it was true, but because it was expedient, and making him rather pass by what he does not understand, than set up his own feelings above that truth. For, truly, when he pronounces anything to be untrue, he demands that he be believed in preference, and endeavours to shake our confidence in the authority of the divine Scriptures.

5. For my part, I would devote all the strength which the Lord grants me, to show that every one of those texts which are wont to be quoted in defence of the expediency of falsehood ought to be otherwise understood, in order that everywhere the sure truth of these passages themselves may be consistently maintained. For as statements adduced in evidence must not be false, neither ought they to favour falsehood. This, however, I leave to your own judgment. For if you apply more thorough attention to the passage, perhaps you will see it much more readily than I have done. To this more careful study that piety will move you, by which you discern that the authority of the divine Scriptures becomes unsettled (so that every one may believe what he wishes, and reject what he does not wish) if this be once admitted, that the men by whom these things have been delivered unto us, could in their writings state some things which were not true, from considerations of duty ;[6] unless, perchance, you propose to furnish us with certain rules by which we may know when a falsehood might or might not become a duty. If this can be done, I beg you to set forth these rules with reasonings which may be neither equivocal nor precarious ; and I beseech you by our Lord, in whom Truth was incarnate, not to consider me burdensome or presumptuous in making this request. For a mistake of mine which is in the interest of truth cannot deserve great blame, if indeed it deserves blame at all, when it is possible for you to use truth in the interest of falsehood without doing wrong.

CHAP. IV. — 6. Of many other things I would wish to discourse with your most ingenuous heart,

---

[1] *Officiosum mendacium.*
[2] Gal. ii. 11-14.
[3] 1 Tim. iv. 3.
[4] 1 Cor. vii. 10-16.
[5] 1 Cor. xv. 14, 15.
[6] *Aliqua officiose mentiri.*

and to take counsel with you concerning Christian studies; but this desire could not be satisfied within the limits of any letter. I may do this more fully by means of the brother bearing this letter, whom I rejoice in sending to share and profit by your sweet and useful conversation. Nevertheless, although I do not reckon myself superior in any respect to him, even he may take less from you than I would desire; and he will excuse my saying so, for I confess myself to have more room for receiving from you than he has. I see his mind to be already more fully stored, in which unquestionably he excels me. Therefore, when he returns, as I trust he may happily do by God's blessing, and when I become a sharer in all with which his heart has been richly furnished by you, there will still be a consciousness of void unsatisfied in me, and a longing for personal fellowship with you. Hence of the two I shall be the poorer, and he the richer, then as now. This brother carries with him some of my writings, which if you condescend to read, I implore you to review them with candid and brotherly strictness. For the words of Scripture, "The righteous shall correct me in compassion, and reprove me; but the oil of the sinner shall not anoint my head,"[1] I understand to mean that he is the truer friend who by his censure heals me, than the one who by flattery anoints my head. I find the greatest difficulty in exercising a right judgment when I read over what I have written, being either too cautious or too rash. For I sometimes see my own faults, but I prefer to hear them reproved by those who are better able to judge than I am; lest after I have, perhaps justly, charged myself with error, I begin again to flatter myself, and think that my censure has arisen from an undue mistrust of my own judgment.

LETTER XXIX.

(A.D. 395.)

A LETTER FROM THE PRESBYTER OF THE DISTRICT OF HIPPO TO ALYPIUS THE BISHOP OF THAGASTE, CONCERNING THE ANNIVERSARY OF THE BIRTH OF LEONTIUS,[2] FORMERLY BISHOP OF HIPPO.

1. In the absence of brother Macharius, I have not been able to write anything definite concerning a matter about which I could not feel otherwise than anxious: it is said, however, that he will soon return, and whatever can be with God's help done in the matter shall be done. Although also our brethren, citizens of your town, who were with us, might sufficiently assure you of our solicitude on their behalf when they returned, never-

theless the thing which the Lord has granted to me is one worthy to be the subject of that epistolary intercourse which ministers so much to the comfort of us both; it is, moreover, a thing in the obtaining of which I believe that I have been greatly assisted by your own solicitude regarding it, seeing that it could not but constrain you to intercession on our behalf.

2. Therefore let me not fail to relate to your Charity what has taken place; so that, as you joined us in pouring out prayers for this mercy before it was obtained, you may now join us in rendering thanks for it after it has been received. When I was informed after your departure that some were becoming openly violent, and declaring that they could not submit to the prohibition (intimated while you were here) of that feast which they call Lætitia, vainly attempting to disguise their revels under a fair name, it happened most opportunely for me, by the hidden fore-ordination of the Almighty God, that on the fourth holy day that chapter of the Gospel fell to be expounded in ordinary course, in which the words occur: "Give not that which is holy unto the dogs, neither cast ye your pearls before swine."[3] I discoursed therefore concerning dogs and swine in such a way as to compel those who clamour with obstinate barking against the divine precepts, and who are given up to the abominations of carnal pleasures, to blush for shame; and followed it up by saying, that they might plainly see how criminal it was to do, under the name of religion, within the walls of the church, that which, if it were practised by them in their own houses, would make it necessary for them to be debarred from that which is holy, and from the privileges which are the pearls of the Church.

3. Although these words were well received, nevertheless, as few had attended the meeting, all had not been done which so great an emergency required. When, however, this discourse was, according to the ability and zeal of each, made known abroad by those who had heard it, it found many opponents. But when the morning of Quadragesima came round, and a great multitude had assembled at the hour of exposition of Scripture, that passage in the Gospel was read in which our Lord said, concerning those sellers who were driven out of the temple, and the tables of the money-changers which He had overthrown, that the house of His Father had been made a den of thieves instead of a house of prayer.[4] After awakening their attention by bringing forward the subject of immoderate indulgence in wine, I myself also read this chapter, and added to it an argument to prove with how much greater anger and vehemence our Lord would cast forth drunken revels, which are every-

---

[1] Ps. cxli. 5, translated from the Septuagint.
[2] Leontius was Bishop of Hippo in the latter part of the second century. He built a church which was called after him, and in which some of the sermons of Augustin were delivered.

[3] Matt. vii. 6.
[4] Matt. xxi. 12.

where disgraceful, from that temple from which He thus drove out merchandise lawful elsewhere, especially when the things sold were those required for the sacrifices appointed in that dispensation; and I asked them whether they regarded a place occupied by men selling what was necessary, or one used by men drinking to excess, as bearing the greater resemblance to a den of thieves.

4. Moreover, as passages of Scripture which I had prepared were held ready to be put into my hands, I went on to say that the Jewish nation, with all its lack of spirituality in religion, never held feasts, even temperate feasts, much less feasts disgraced by intemperance, in their temple, in which at that time the body and blood of the Lord were not yet offered, and that in history they are not found to have been excited by wine on any public occasion bearing the name of worship, except when they held a feast before the idol which they had made.[1] While I said these things I took the manuscript from the attendant, and read that whole passage. Reminding them of the words of the apostle, who says, in order to distinguish Christians from the obdurate Jews, that they are his epistle written, not on tables of stone, but on the fleshly tables of the heart,[2] I asked further, with the deepest sorrow, how it was that, although Moses the servant of God broke both the tables of stone because of these rulers of Israel, I could not break the hearts of those who, though men of the New Testament dispensation, were desiring in their celebration of saints' days to repeat often the public perpetration of excesses of which the people of the Old Testament economy were guilty only once, and that in an act of idolatry.

5. Having then given back the manuscript of Exodus, I proceeded to enlarge, so far as my time permitted, on the crime of drunkenness, and took up the writings of the Apostle Paul, and showed among what sins it is classed by him, reading the text, "If any man that is called a brother be a fornicator, or covetous, or an idolater, or a railer, or a drunkard, or an extortioner; with such an one (ye ought) not even to eat;"[3] pathetically reminding them how great is our danger in eating with those who are guilty of intemperance even in their own houses. I read also what is added, a little further on, in the same epistle: "Be not deceived: neither fornicators, nor idolaters, nor adulterers, nor effeminate, nor abusers of themselves with mankind, nor thieves, nor covetous, nor drunkards, nor revilers, nor extortioners, shall inherit the kingdom of God. And such were some of you: but ye are washed, but ye are sanctified, but ye

are justified in the name of the Lord Jesus, and by the Spirit of our God."[4] After reading these, I charged them to consider how believers could hear these words, "but ye are washed," if they still tolerated in their own hearts — that is, in God's inner temple — the abominations of such lusts as these against which the kingdom of heaven is shut. Then I went on to that passage: "When ye come together into one place, this is not to eat the Lord's supper: for in eating, every one taketh before other his own supper; and one is hungry, and another is drunken. What! have ye not houses to eat and to drink in, or despise ye the church of God?"[5] After reading which, I more especially begged them to remark that not even innocent and temperate feasts were permitted in the church: for the apostle said not, "Have ye not houses of your own in which to be drunken?" — as if it was drunkenness alone which was unlawful in the church; but, "Have ye not houses to eat and to drink in?" — things lawful in themselves, but not lawful in the church, inasmuch as men have their own houses in which they may be recruited by necessary food: whereas now, by the corruption of the times and the relaxation of morals, we have been brought so low, that, no longer insisting upon sobriety in the houses of men, all that we venture to demand is, that the realm of tolerated excess be restricted to their own homes.

6. I reminded them also of a passage in the Gospel which I had expounded the day before, in which it is said of the false prophets: "Ye shall know them by their fruits."[6] I also bade them remember that in that place our works are signified by the word fruits. Then I asked among what kind of fruits drunkenness was named, and read that passage in the Epistle to the Galatians: "Now the works of the flesh are manifest, which are these: adultery, fornication, uncleanness, lasciviousness, idolatry, witchcraft, hatred, variance, emulations, wrath, strife, seditions, heresies, envyings, murder, drunkenness, revellings, and such like; of the which I tell you before, as I have told you in time past, that they which do such things shall not inherit the kingdom of God."[7] After these words, I asked how, when God has commanded that Christians be known by their fruits, we could be known as Christians by this fruit of drunkenness? I added also, that we must read what follows there: "But the fruit of the Spirit is love, joy, peace, longsuffering, gentleness, goodness, faith, meekness, temperance."[8] And I pled with them to consider how shameful and lamentable it would be,

---

[1] Ex. xxxii. 6.
[2] 2 Cor. iii. 3.
[3] 1 Cor. v. 11.
[4] 1 Cor. vi. 9-11.
[5] 1 Cor. xi. 20-22.
[6] Matt. vii. 16.
[7] Gal. v. 19-21.
[8] Gal. v. 22, 23.

if, not content with living at home in the practice of these works of the flesh, they even wished by them, forsooth, to honour the church, and to fill the whole area of so large a place of worship, if they were permitted, with crowds of revellers and drunkards : and yet would not present to God those fruits of the Spirit which, by the authority of Scripture, and by my groans, they were called to yield, and by the offering of which they would most suitably celebrate the saints' days.

7. This being finished, I returned the manuscript ; and being asked to speak,[1] I set before their eyes with all my might, as the danger itself constrained me, and as the Lord was pleased to give strength, the danger shared by them who were committed to my care, and by me, who must give account to the Chief Shepherd, and implored them by His humiliation, by the unparalleled insults, the buffetings and spitting on the face which He endured, by His pierced hands and crown of thorns, and by His cross and blood, to have pity on me at least, if they were displeased with themselves, and to consider the inexpressible love cherished towards me by the aged and venerable Valerius, who had not scrupled to assign to me for their sakes the perilous burden of expounding to them the word of truth, and had often told them that in my coming here his prayers were answered ; not rejoicing, surely, that I had come to share or to behold the death of our hearers, but rejoicing that I had come to share his labours for their eternal life. In conclusion, I told them that I was resolved to trust in Him who cannot lie, and who has given us a promise by the mouth of the prophet, saying of our Lord Jesus Christ, "If His children forsake my law, and walk not in my judgments ; if they break my statutes, and keep not my commandments ; then will I visit their transgression with the rod, and their iniquity with stripes : nevertheless my loving-kindness will I not utterly take from Him."[2] I declared, therefore, that I put my trust in Him, that if they despised the weighty words which had now been read and spoken to them, He would visit them with the rod and with stripes, and not leave them to be condemned with the world. In this appeal I put forth all the power in thought and utterance which, in an emergency so great and hazardous, our Saviour and Ruler was pleased to supply. I did not move them to weep by first weeping myself ; but while these things were being spoken, I own that, moved by the tears which they began to shed, I myself could not refrain from following their example. And when we had thus wept together, I concluded my sermon with full persuasion that they

would be restrained by it from the abuses denounced.

8. Next morning, however, when the day dawned, which so many were accustomed to devote to excess in eating and drinking, I received notice that some, even of those who were present when I preached, had not yet desisted from complaint, and that so great was the power of detestable custom with them, that, using no other argument, they asked, "Wherefore is this now prohibited? Were they not Christians who in former times did not interfere with this practice?" On hearing this, I knew not what more powerful means for influencing them I could devise ; but resolved, in the event of their judging it proper to persevere, that after reading in Ezekiel's prophecy that the watchman has delivered his own soul if he has given warning, even though the persons warned refuse to give heed to him, I would shake my garments and depart. But then the Lord showed me that He leaves us not alone, and taught me how He encourages us to trust Him ; for before the time at which I had to ascend the pulpit,[3] the very persons of whose complaint against interference with long-established custom I had heard came to me. Receiving them kindly, I by a few words brought them round to a right opinion ; and when it came to the time for my discourse, having laid aside the lecture which I had prepared as now unnecessary, I said a few things concerning the question mentioned above, "Wherefore *now* prohibit this custom?" saying that to those who might propose it the briefest and best answer would be this : "Let us now at last put down what ought to have been earlier prohibited."

9. Lest, however, any slight should seem to be put by us on those who, before our time, either tolerated or did not dare to put down such manifest excesses of an undisciplined multitude, I explained to them the circumstances out of which this custom seems to have necessarily risen in the Church, — namely, that when, in the peace which came after such numerous and violent persecutions, crowds of heathen who wished to assume the Christian religion were kept back, because, having been accustomed to celebrate the feasts connected with their worship of idols in revelling and drunkenness, they could not easily refrain from pleasures so hurtful and so habitual, it had seemed good to our ancestors, making for the time a concession to this infirmity, to permit them to celebrate, instead of the festivals which they renounced, other feasts in honour of the holy martyrs, which were observed, not as before with a profane design, but with similar self-indulgence. I

---

[1] *Imperatâ oratione.*
[2] Ps. lxxxix. 30–33.

[3] *Exhedra.*

added that now upon them, as persons bound together in the name of Christ, and submissive to the yoke of His august authority, the wholesome restraints of sobriety were laid — restraints with which the honour and fear due to Him who appointed them should move them to comply — and that therefore the time had now come in which all who did not dare to cast off the Christian profession should begin to walk according to Christ's will; and being now confirmed Christians, should reject those concessions to infirmity which were made only for a time in order to their becoming such.

10. I then exhorted them to imitate the example of the churches beyond the sea, in some of which these practices had never been tolerated, while in others they had been already put down by the people complying with the counsel of good ecclesiastical rulers; and as the examples of daily excess in the use of wine in the church of the blessed Apostle Peter were brought forward in defence of the practice, I said in the first place, that I had heard that these excesses had been often forbidden, but because the place was at a distance from the bishop's control, and because in such a city the multitude of carnally-minded persons was great, the foreigners especially, of whom there is a constant influx, clinging to that practice with an obstinacy proportioned to their ignorance, the suppression of so great an evil had not yet been possible. If, however, I continued, we would honour the Apostle Peter, we ought to hear his words, and look much more to the epistles by which his mind is made known to us, than to the place of worship, by which it is not made known; and immediately taking the manuscript, I read his own words: "Forasmuch then as Christ hath suffered for us in the flesh, arm yourselves likewise with the same mind: for he that hath suffered in the flesh hath ceased from sin; that he no longer should live the rest of his time in the flesh to the lusts of men, but to the will of God. For the time past of our life may suffice us to have wrought the will of the Gentiles, when we walked in lasciviousness, lusts, excess of wine, revellings, banquetings, and abominable idolatries." [1] After this, when I saw that all were with one consent turning to a right mind, and renouncing the custom against which I had protested, I exhorted them to assemble for the reading of God's word and singing of psalms; stating that we had resolved thus to celebrate the festival in a way much more accordant with purity and piety; and that, by the number of worshippers who should assemble for this purpose, it would plainly appear who were guided by reason, and who were the slaves of appetite. With these words the discourse concluded.

11. In the afternoon a greater number assembled than in the forenoon, and there was reading and praise alternately up to the hour at which I went out in company with the bishop; and after our coming two psalms were read. Then the old man [Valerius] constrained me by his express command to say something to the people; from which I would rather have been excused, as I was longing for the close of the anxieties of the day. I delivered a short discourse in order to express our gratitude to God. And as we heard the noise of the feasting, which was going on as usual in the church of the heretics, who still prolonged their revelry while we were so differently engaged, I remarked that the beauty of day is enhanced by contrast with the night, and that when anything black is near, the purity of white is the more pleasing; and that, in like manner, our meeting for a spiritual feast might perhaps have been somewhat less sweet to us, but for the contrast of the carnal excesses in which the others indulged; and I exhorted them to desire eagerly such feasts as we then enjoyed, if they had tasted the goodness of the Lord. At the same time, I said that those may well be afraid who seek anything which shall one day be destroyed as the chief object of their desire, seeing that every one shares the portion of that which he worships; a warning expressly given by the apostle to such, when he says of them their "god is their belly," [2] inasmuch as he has elsewhere said, "Meats for the belly, and the belly for meats; but God shall destroy both it and them." [3] I added that it is our duty to seek that which is imperishable, which, far removed from carnal affections, is obtained through sanctification of the spirit; and when those things which the Lord was pleased to suggest to me had been spoken on this subject as the occasion required, the daily evening exercises of worship were performed; and when with the bishop I retired from the church, the brethren said a hymn there, a considerable multitude remaining in the church, and engaging in praise [4] even till daylight failed.

12. I have thus related as concisely as I could that which I am sure you longed to hear. Pray that God may be pleased to protect our efforts from giving offence or provoking odium in any way. In the tranquil prosperity which you enjoy we do with lively warmth of affection participate in no small measure, when tidings so frequently reach us of the gifts possessed by the highly spiritual church of Thagaste. The ship bringing our brethren has not yet arrived. At Hasna, where our brother Argentius is presbyter, the Circumcelliones, entering our church,

---

[1] 1 Pet. iv. 1–3.

[2] Phil. iii. 19.
[3] 1 Cor. vi. 13.
[4] *Psallente.*

demolished the altar. The case is now in process of trial; and we earnestly ask your prayers that it may be decided in a peaceful way, and as becomes the Catholic Church, so as to silence the tongues of turbulent heretics. I have sent a letter to the Asiarch.[1]

Brethren most blessed, may ye persevere in the Lord, and remember us. Amen.

LETTER XXX.

(A.D. 396.)

This letter of Paulinus was written before receiving a reply to his former letter, No. 27, p. 248.

TO AUGUSTIN, OUR LORD AND HOLY AND BELOVED BROTHER, PAULINUS AND THERASIA, SINNERS, SEND GREETING.

1. My beloved brother in Christ the Lord, having through your holy and pious works come to know you without your knowledge, and to see you though absent long ago, my mind embraced you with unreserved affection, and I hastened to secure the gratification of hearing you through familiar brotherly exchange of letters. I believe also that by the Lord's hand and favour my letter has reached you; but as the youth whom, before winter, we had sent to salute you and others equally loved in God's name, has not returned, we could no longer either put off what we feel to be our duty, or restrain the vehemence of our desire to hear from you. If, then, my former letter has been found worthy to reach you, this is the second; if, however, it was not so fortunate as to come to your hand, accept this as the first.

2. But, my brother, judging all things as a spiritual man, do not estimate our love to you by the duty which we render, or the frequency of our letters. For the Lord, who everywhere, as one and the same, worketh His love in His own, is witness that, from the time when, by the kindness of the venerable bishops Aurelius and Alypius, we came to know you through your writings against the Manichæans, love for you has taken such a place in us, that we seemed not so much to be acquiring a new friendship as reviving an old affection. Now at length we address you in writing; and though we are novices in expressing, we are not novices in feeling love to you; and by communion of the spirit, which is the inner man, we are as it were acquainted with you. Nor is it strange that though distant we are near, though unknown we are well known to each other; for we are members of one body, having one Head, enjoying the effusion of the same grace, living by the same bread, walking in the same way, and dwelling in the same home. In short, in all that makes up our being, — in the whole faith and hope by which we stand in the present life, or labour for that which is to come, — we are both in the spirit and in the body of Christ so united, that if we fell from this union we would cease to be.

3. How small a thing, therefore, is that which our bodily separation denies to us! — for it is nothing more than one of those fruits that gratify the eyes, which are occupied only with the things of time. And yet, perhaps, we should not number this pleasure which in the body we enjoy among the blessings which are only in time the portion of spiritual men, to whose bodies the resurrection will impart immortality; as we, though in ourselves unworthy, are bold to expect, through the merit of Christ and the mercy of God the Father. Wherefore I pray that the grace of God by our Lord Jesus Christ may grant unto us this favour too, that we may yet see your face. Not only would this bring great gratification to our desires; but by it illumination would be brought to our minds, and our poverty would be enriched by your abundance. This indeed you may grant to us even while we are absent from you, especially on the present occasion, through our sons Romanus and Agilis, beloved and most dear to us in the Lord (whom as our second selves we commend to you), when they return to us in the Lord's name, after fulfilling the labour of love in which they are engaged; in which work we beg that they may especially enjoy the goodwill of your Charity. For you know what high rewards the Most High promises to the brother who gives his brother help. If you are pleased to impart to me any gift of the grace that has been bestowed on you, you may safely do it through them; for, believe me, they are of one heart and of one mind with us in the Lord. May the grace of God always abide as it is with you, O brother beloved, venerable, most dear, and longed for in Christ the Lord! Salute on our behalf all the saints in Christ who are with you, for doubtless such attach themselves to your fellowship; commend us to them all, that they may, along with yourself, remember us in prayer.

[1] A magistrate who was also charged with the affairs pertaining to the protection of religion. The title belonged primarily to those who in the province of Asia had charge of the games. — *Codex Theodosianus,* xv. 9.

SECOND DIVISION.

LETTERS WHICH WERE WRITTEN BY AUGUSTIN AFTER HIS BECOMING BISHOP OF HIPPO, AND BEFORE THE CONFERENCE HELD WITH THE DONATISTS AT CARTHAGE, AND THE DISCOVERY OF THE HERESY OF PELAGIUS IN AFRICA (A.D. 396–410).

LETTER XXXI.

(A.D. 396.)

TO BROTHER PAULINUS AND TO SISTER THERASIA, MOST BELOVED AND SINCERE, TRULY MOST BLESSED AND MOST EMINENT FOR THE VERY ABUNDANT GRACE OF GOD BESTOWED ON THEM, AUGUSTIN SENDS GREETING IN THE LORD.

1. ALTHOUGH in my longing to be without delay near you in one sense, while still remote in another, I wished much that what I wrote in answer to your former letter (if, indeed, any letter of mine deserves to be called an answer to yours) should go with all possible expedition to your Grace,[1] my delay has brought me the advantage of a second letter from you. The Lord is good, who often withholds what we desire, that He may add to it what we would prefer. For it is one pleasure to me that you will write me on receiving my letter, and it is another that, through not receiving it at once, you have written now. The joy which I have felt in reading this letter would have been lost to me if my letter to your Holiness had been quickly conveyed to you, as I intended and earnestly desired. But now, to have this letter, and to expect a reply to my own, multiplies my satisfaction. The blame of the delay cannot be laid to my charge; and the Lord, in His more abundant kindness, has done that which He judged to be more conducive to my happiness.

2. We welcomed with great gladness in the Lord the holy brothers Romanus and Agilis, who were, so to speak, an additional letter from you, capable of hearing and answering our voices, whereby most agreeably your presence was in part enjoyed by us, although only to make us long the more eagerly to see you. It would be at all times and in every way impossible for you to give, and unreasonable for us to ask, as much information from you concerning yourself by letter as we received from them by word of mouth. There was manifest also in them (what no paper could convey) such delight in telling us of you, that by their very countenance and eyes while they spoke, we could with unspeakable joy read you written on their hearts. Moreover, a sheet of paper, of whatever kind it be, and however excellent the things written upon

it may be, enjoys no benefit itself from what it contains, though it may be unfolded with great benefit to others; but, in reading this letter of yours — namely, the minds of these brethren — when conversing with them, we found that the blessedness of those upon whom you had written was manifestly proportioned to the fulness with which they had been written upon by you. In order, therefore, to attain to the same blessedness, we transcribed in our own hearts what was written in theirs, by most eager questioning as to everything concerning you.

3. Notwithstanding all this, it is with deep regret that we consent to their so soon leaving us, even to return to you. For observe, I beseech you, the conflicting emotions by which we are agitated. Our obligation to let them go without delay was increased according to the vehemence of their desire to obey you; but the greater the vehemence of this desire in them, the more completely did they set you forth as almost present with us, because they let us see how tender your affections are. Therefore our reluctance to let them go increased with our sense of the reasonableness of their urgency to be permitted to go. Oh insupportable trial, were it not that by such partings we are not, after all, separated from each other, — were it not that we are "members of one body, having one Head, enjoying the effusion of the same grace, living by the same bread, walking in the same way, and dwelling in the same home!"[2] You recognise these words, I suppose, as quoted from your own letter; and why should not I also use them? Why should they be yours any more than mine, seeing that, inasmuch as they are true, they proceed from communion with the same head? And in so far as they contain something that has been specially given to you, I have so loved them the more on that account, that they have taken possession of the way leading through my breast, and would suffer no words to pass from my heart to my tongue until they went first, with the priority which is due to them as yours. My brother and sister, holy and beloved in God, members of the same body with us, who could doubt that we are animated by one spirit, except those who are strangers to that affection by which we are bound to each other?

4. Yet I am curious to know whether you

bear with more patience and ease than I do this bodily separation. If it be so, I do not, I confess, take any pleasure in your fortitude in this respect, unless perhaps because of its reasonableness, seeing that I confess myself much less worthy of your affectionate longing than you are of mine. At all events, if I found in myself a power of bearing your absence patiently, this would displease me, because it would make me relax my efforts to see you; and what could be more absurd than to be made indolent by power of endurance? But I beg to acquaint your Charity with the ecclesiastical duties by which I am kept at home, inasmuch as the blessed father Valerius (who with me salutes you, and thirsts for you with a vehemence of which you will hear from our brethren), not content with having me as his presbyter, has insisted upon adding the greater burden of sharing the episcopate with him. This office I was afraid to decline, being persuaded, through the love of Valerius and the importunity of the people, that it was the Lord's will, and being precluded from excusing myself on other grounds by some precedents of similar appointments. The yoke of Christ, it is true, is in itself easy, and His burden light;[1] yet, through my perversity and infirmity, I may find the yoke vexatious and the burden heavy in some degree; and I cannot tell how much more easy and light my yoke and burden would become if I were comforted by a visit from you, who live, as I am informed, more disengaged and free from such cares.[2] I therefore feel warranted in asking, nay, demanding and imploring you to condescend to come over into Africa, which is more oppressed with thirst for men such as you are than even by the well-known aridity of her soil.[3]

5. God knoweth that I long for your visiting this country, not merely to gratify my own desire, nor merely on account of those who through me, or by public report, have heard of your pious resolution;[4] I long for it for the sake of others also who either have not heard, or, hearing, have not believed the fame of your piety, but who might be constrained to love excellence of which they could then be no longer in ignorance or doubt. For although the perseverance and purity of your compassionate benevolence is good, more is required of you; namely, "Let your light so shine before men, that they may behold your good works, and may glorify your Father which is in heaven."[5] The fishermen of Galilee found pleasure not only in leaving

their ships and their nets at the Lord's command, but also in declaring that they had left all and followed Him.[6] And truly he despises all who despises not only all that he was able, but also all that he was desirous to possess. What may have been desired is seen only by the eyes of God; what was actually possessed is seen also by the eyes of men. Moreover, when things trivial and earthly are loved by us, we are somehow more firmly wedded to what we have than to what we desire to have. For whence was it that he who sought from the Lord counsel as to the way of eternal life, went away sorrowful upon hearing that, if he would be perfect, he must sell all, and distribute to the poor, and have treasure in heaven, unless because, as the Gospel tells us, he had great possessions?[7] For it is one thing to forbear from appropriating what is wanting to us; it is another thing to rend away that which has become a part of ourselves: the former action is like declining food, the latter is like cutting off a limb. How great and how full of wonder is the joy with which Christian charity beholds in our day a sacrifice cheerfully made in obedience to the Gospel of Christ, which that rich man grieved and refused to make at the bidding of Christ Himself!

6. Although language fails to express that which my heart has conceived and labours to utter, nevertheless, since you perceive with your discernment and piety that the glory of this is not yours, that is to say, not of man, but the glory of the Lord in you (for you yourselves are most carefully on your guard against your Adversary, and most devoutly strive to be found as learners of Christ, meek and lowly in heart; and, indeed, it were better with humility to retain than with pride to renounce this world's wealth); — since, I say, you are aware that the glory here is not yours, but the Lord's, you see how weak and inadequate are the things which I have spoken. For I have been speaking of the praises of Christ, a theme transcending the tongue of angels. We long to see this glory of Christ brought near to the eyes of our people; that in you, united in the bonds of wedlock, there may be given to both sexes an example of the way in which pride must be trodden under foot, and perfection hopefully pursued. I know not any way in which you could give greater proof of your benevolence, than in resolving to be not less willing to permit your worth to be seen, than you are zealous to acquire and retain it.

7. I recommend to your kindness and charity this boy Vetustinus, whose case might draw forth the sympathy even of those who are not religious: the causes of his affliction and of his leav-

---

[1] Matt. xi. 30.
[2] Paulinus was then at Nola, having gone thither from Barcelona in A.D. 393 or 394. He became Bishop of Nola in 409.
[3] *Nobilitate siccitatis.*
[4] This refers to the voluntary poverty which Paulinus and Therasia, though of high rank and great wealth, embraced, selling all that they had in order to give to the poor.
[5] Matt. v. 16.

[6] Matt. xix. 27.
[7] Luke xviii. 22, 23.

ing his country you will hear from his own lips. As to his pious resolution—his promise, namely, to devote himself to the service of God—it will be more decisively known after some time has elapsed, when his strength has been confirmed, and his present fear is removed. Perceiving the warmth of your love for me, and encouraged thereby to believe that you will not grudge the labour of reading what I have written, I send to your Holiness and Charity three books: would that the size of the volumes were an index of the completeness of the discussion of so great a subject; for the question of free-will is handled in them! I know that these books, or at least some of them, are not in the possession of our brother Romanianus; but almost everything which I have been able for the benefit of any readers to write is, as I have intimated, accessible to your perusal through him, because of your love to me, although I did not charge him to carry them to you. For he already had them all, and was carrying them with him: moreover, it was by him that my answer to your first letter was sent. I suppose that your Holiness has already discovered, by that spiritual sagacity which the Lord has given you, how much that man bears in his soul of what is good, and how far he still comes short through infirmity. In the letter sent through him you have, as I trust, read with what anxiety I commended himself and his son to your sympathy and love, as well as how close is the bond by which they are united to me. May the Lord build them up by your means! This must be asked from Him rather than from you, for I know how much it is already your desire.

8. I have heard from the brethren that you are writing a treatise against the Pagans: if we have any claim on your heart, send it at once to us to read. For your heart is such an oracle of divine truth, that we expect from it answers which shall satisfactorily and clearly decide the most prolix debates. I understand that your Holiness has the books of the most blessed father [1] Ambrose, of which I long greatly to see those which, with much care and at great length, he has written against some most ignorant and pretentious men, who affirm that our Lord was instructed by the writings of Plato.[2]

9. Our most blessed brother Severus, formerly of our community, now president [3] of the church in Milevis, and well known by the brethren in that city, joins me in respectful salutation to your Holiness. The brethren also who are with me serving the Lord salute you as warmly as they long to see you: they long for you as much as they love you; and they love you as your eminent goodness merits. The loaf which we send

you will become more rich as a blessing through the love with which your kindness receives it. May the Lord keep you for ever from this generation,[4] my brother and sister most beloved and sincere, truly benevolent, and most eminently endowed with abundant grace from the Lord.

LETTER XXXII.

This letter from Paulinus to Romanianus and Licentius expresses the satisfaction with which he heard of the promotion of Augustin to the episcopate, and conveys both in prose and in verse excellent counsels to Licentius: it is one which in this selection may without loss be omitted.

LETTER XXXIII.

(A.D. 396.)

TO PROCULEIANUS, MY LORD, HONOURABLE AND MOST BELOVED, AUGUSTIN SENDS GREETING.

1. The titles prefixed to this letter I need not defend or explain at any length to you, though they may give offence to the vain prejudices of ignorant men. For I rightly address you as *lord*, seeing that we are both seeking to deliver each other from error, although to some it may seem uncertain which of us is in error before the matter has been fully debated; and therefore we are mutually *serving* one another, if we sincerely labour that we may both be delivered from the perversity of discord. That I labour to do this with a sincere heart, and with the fear and trembling of Christian humility, is not perhaps to most men manifest, but is seen by Him to whom all hearts are open. What I without hesitation esteem *honourable* in you, you readily perceive. For I do not esteem worthy of any honour the error of schism, from which I desire to have all men delivered, so far as is within my power; but yourself I do not for a moment hesitate to regard as worthy of honour, chiefly because you are knit to me in the bonds of a common humanity, and because there are conspicuous in you some indications of a more gentle disposition, by which I am encouraged to hope that you may readily embrace the truth when it has been demonstrated to you. As for my *love* to you, I owe not less than He commanded who so loved us as to bear the shame of the cross for our sakes.

2. Be not, however, surprised that I have so long forborne from addressing your Benevolence; for I did not think that your views were such as were with great joy declared to me by brother Evodius, whose testimony I cannot but believe. For he tells me that, when you met accidentally at the same house, and conversation began between you concerning our hope, that is to say, the inheritance of Christ, you were kindly pleased

---

[1] *Beatissimi papæ.*
[2] These books of Ambrose are lost.
[3] *Antistes.*

[4] See Ps. xii. 7.

to say that you were willing to have a conference with me in the presence of good men. I am truly glad that you have condescended to make this proposal: and I can in no wise forego so important an opportunity, given by your kindness, of using whatever strength the Lord may be pleased to give me in considering and debating with you what has been the cause, or source, or reason of a division so lamentable and deplorable in that Church of Christ to which He said: "Peace I give you, my peace I leave unto you."[1]

3. I heard from the brother aforesaid that you had complained of his having said something in answer to you in an insulting manner; but, I pray you, do not regard it as an insult, for I am sure it did not proceed from an overbearing spirit, as I know my brother well. But if, in disputing in defence of his own faith and the Church's love, he spoke perchance with a degree of warmth something which you regarded as wounding your dignity, that deserves to be called, not contumacy, but boldness. For he desired to debate and discuss the question, not to be merely submitting to you and flattering you. For such flattery is the oil of the sinner, with which the prophet does not desire to have his head anointed; for he saith: "The righteous shall correct me in compassion, and rebuke me; but the oil of the sinner shall not anoint my head."[2] For he prefers to be corrected by the stern compassion of the righteous, rather than to be commended with the soothing oil of flattery. Hence also the saying of the prophet: "They who pronounce you happy cause you to err."[3] Therefore also it is commonly and justly said of a man whom false compliments have made proud, "his head has grown;"[4] for it has been increased by the oil of the sinner, that is, not of one correcting with stern truth, but of one commending with smooth flattery. Do not, however, suppose me to mean by this, that I wish it to be understood that you have been corrected by brother Evodius, as by a righteous man; for I fear lest you should think that anything is spoken by me also in an insulting manner, against which I desire to the utmost of my power to be on guard. But He is righteous who hath said, "I am the truth."[5] When, therefore, any true word has been uttered, though it may be somewhat rudely, by the mouth of any man, we are corrected not by the speaker, who may perhaps be not less a sinner than ourselves, but by the truth itself, that is to say, by Christ who is righteous, lest the unction of smooth but pernicious flattery, which is the oil of the sinner, should anoint our head. Although, therefore, brother Evodius, through undue ex-

citement in defending the communion to which he belongs, may have said something too vehemently through strong feeling, you ought to excuse him on the ground of his age, and of the importance of the matter in his estimation.

4. I beseech you, however, to remember what you have been pleased to promise; namely, to investigate amicably with me a matter of so great importance, and so closely pertaining to the common salvation, in the presence of such spectators as you may choose (provided only that our words are not uttered so as to be lost, but are taken down with the pen; so that we may conduct the discussion in a more calm and orderly manner, and anything spoken by us which escapes the memory may be recalled by reading the notes taken). Or, if you prefer it, we may discuss the matter without the interference of any third party, by means of letters or conference and reading, wherever you please, lest perchance some hearers, unwisely zealous, should be more concerned with the expectation of a conflict between us, than the thought of our mutual profit by the discussion. Let the people, however, be afterwards informed through us of the debate, when it is concluded; or, if you prefer to have the matter discussed by letters exchanged, let these letters be read to the two congregations, in order that they may yet come to be no longer divided, but one. In fact, I willingly accede to whatever terms you wish, or prescribe, or prefer. And as to the sentiments of my most blessed and venerable father Valerius, who is at present from home, I undertake with fullest confidence that he will hear of this with great joy; for I know how much he loves peace, and how free he is from being influenced by any paltry regard for vain parade of dignity.

5. I ask you, what have we to do with the dissensions of a past generation? Let it suffice that the wounds which the bitterness of proud men inflicted on our members have remained until now; for we have, through the lapse of time, ceased to feel the pain to remove which the physician's help is usually sought. You see how great and miserable is the calamity by which the peace of Christian homes and families is broken. Husbands and wives, agreeing together at the family hearth, are divided at the altar of Christ. By Him they pledge themselves to be at peace between themselves, yet in Him they cannot be at peace. Children have the same home, but not the same house of God, with their own parents. They desire to be secure of the earthly inheritance of those with whom they wrangle concerning the inheritance of Christ. Servants and masters divide their common Lord, who took on Him the form of a servant that He might deliver all from bondage. Your party honours us, and our party honours you. Your

---

[1] John xiv. 27.
[2] Ps. cxli. 5.
[3] Isa. iii. 12, according to the LXX. version.
[4] *Crevit caput.*
[5] John xiv. 6.

members appeal to us by our episcopal insignia,[1] and our members show the same respect to you. We receive the words of all, we desire to give offence to none. Why then, finding cause of offence in none besides, do we find it in Christ, whose members we rend asunder? When we may be serviceable to men that are desirous of terminating through our help disputes concerning secular affairs, they address us as saints and servants of God, in order that they may have their questions as to property disposed of by us: let us at length, unsolicited, take up a matter which concerns both our own salvation and theirs. It is not about gold or silver, or land, or cattle, — matters concerning which we are daily saluted with lowly respect, in order that we may bring disputes to a peaceful termination, — but it is concerning our Head Himself that this dissension, so unworthy and pernicious, exists between us. However low they bow their heads who salute us in the hope that we may make them agree together in regard to the things of this world, our Head stooped from heaven even to the cross, and yet we do not agree together in Him.

6. I beg and beseech you, if there be in you that brotherly feeling for which some give you credit, let your goodness be approved sincere, and not feigned with a view to passing honours, by this, that your bowels of compassion be moved, so that you consent to have this matter discussed; joining with me in persevering prayer, and in peaceful discussion of every point. Let not the respect paid by the unhappy people to our dignities be found, in the judgment of God, aggravating our condemnation; rather let them be recalled along with us, through our unfeigned love, from errors and dissensions, and guided into the ways of truth and peace.

My lord, honourable and most beloved, I pray that you may be blessed in the sight of God.

LETTER XXXIV.

(A.D. 396.)

TO EUSEBIUS, MY EXCELLENT LORD AND BROTHER, WORTHY OF AFFECTION AND ESTEEM, AUGUSTIN SENDS GREETING.

1. God, to whom the secrets of the heart of man are open, knoweth that it is because of my love for Christian peace that I am so deeply moved by the profane deeds of those who basely and impiously persevere in dissenting from it. He knoweth also that this feeling of mine is one tending towards peace, and that my desire is, not that any one should against his will be co-erced into the Catholic communion, but that to all who are in error the truth may be openly declared, and being by God's help clearly exhibited through my ministry, may so commend itself as to make them embrace and follow it.

2. Passing many other things unnoticed, what could be more worthy of detestation than what has just happened? A young man is reproved by his bishop for frequently beating his mother like a madman, and not restraining his impious hands from wounding her who bore him, even on those days on which the sternness of law shows mercy to the most guilty criminals.[2] He then threatens his mother that he would pass to the party of the Donatists, and that he would kill her whom he is accustomed to beat with incredible ferocity. He utters these threats, then passes over to the Donatists, and is rebaptized while filled with wicked rage, and is arrayed in white vestments while he is burning to shed his mother's blood. He is placed in a prominent and conspicuous position within the railing in the church; and to the eyes of sorrowful and indignant beholders, he who is purposing matricide is exhibited as a regenerate man.

3. I appeal to you, as a man of most mature judgment, can these things find favour in your eyes? I do not believe this of you: I know your wisdom. A mother is wounded by her son in the members of that body which bore and nursed the ungrateful wretch; and when the Church, his spiritual mother, interferes, she too is wounded in those sacraments by which, to the same ungrateful son, she ministered life and nourishment. Do you not seem to hear the young man gnashing his teeth in rage for a parent's blood, and saying, "What shall I do to the Church which forbids my wounding my mother? I have found out what to do: let the Church herself be wounded by such blows as she can suffer; let that be done in me which may cause her members pain. Let me go to those who know how to despise the grace with which she gave me spiritual birth, and to mar the form which in her womb I received. Let me vex both my natural and my spiritual mother with cruel tortures: let the one who was the second to give me birth be the first to give me burial; for her sorrow let me seek spiritual death, and for the other's death let me prolong my natural life." Oh, Eusebius! I appeal to you as an honourable man, what else may we expect than that now he shall feel himself, as a Donatist, so armed as to have no fear in assailing that unhappy woman, decrepit with age and helpless in her widowhood, from wounding whom he was restrained while he remained a Catholic? For what else had he purposed in his passionate

---

[1] *Corona.*

[2] During Lent and the Easter holidays.

heart when he said to his mother, "I will pass over to the party of Donatus, and I will drink your blood?" Behold, arrayed in white vestments, but with conscience crimson with blood, he has fulfilled his threat in part; the other part remains, viz. that he drink his mother's blood. If, therefore, these things find favour in your eyes, let him be urged by those who are now his clergy and his sanctifiers to fulfil within eight days the remaining portion of his vow.

4. The Lord's right hand indeed is strong, so that He may keep back this man's rage from that unhappy and desolate widow, and, by means known unto His own wisdom, may deter him from his impious design; but could I do otherwise than utter my feelings when my heart was pierced with such grief? Shall they do such things, and am I to be commanded to hold my peace? When He commands me by the mouth of the apostle, saying that those who teach what they ought not must be rebuked by the bishop,[1] shall I be silent through dread of their displeasure? The Lord deliver me from such folly! As to my desire for having such an impious crime recorded in our public registers, it was desired by me chiefly for this end, that no one who may hear me bewailing these proceedings, especially in other towns where it may be expedient for me to do so, may think that I am inventing a falsehood, and the rather, because in Hippo itself it is already affirmed that Proculeianus did not issue the order which was in the official report ascribed to him.

5. In what more temperate way could we dispose of this important matter than through the mediation of such a man as you, invested with most illustrious rank, and possessing calmness as well as great prudence and goodwill? I beg, therefore, as I have already done by our brethren, good and honourable men, whom I sent to your Excellency, that you will condescend to inquire whether it is the case that the presbyter Victor did not receive from his bishop the order which the public official records reported; or whether, since Victor himself has said otherwise, they have in their records laid a thing falsely to his charge, though they belong to the same communion with him. Or, if he consents to our calmly discussing the whole question of our differences, in order that the error which is already manifest may become yet more so, I willingly embrace the opportunity. For I have heard that he proposed that without popular tumult, in the presence only of ten esteemed and honourable men from each party, we should investigate what is the truth in this matter according to the Scriptures. As to another proposal which some have reported to me as made by him, that

I should rather go to Constantina,[2] because in that town his party was more numerous; or that I should go to Milevis, because there, as they say, they are soon to hold a council;—these things are absurd, for my special charge does not extend beyond the Church of Hippo. The whole importance of this question to me, in the first place, is as it affects Proculeianus and myself; and if, perchance, he thinks himself not a match for me, let him implore the aid of any one whom he pleases as his colleague in the debate. For in other towns we interfere with the affairs of the Church only so far as is permitted or enjoined by our brethren bearing the same priestly office with us, the bishops of these towns.

6. And yet I cannot comprehend what there is in me, a novice, that should make him, who calls himself a bishop of so many years' standing, unwilling and afraid to enter into discussion with me. If it be my acquaintance with liberal studies, which perhaps he did not pursue at all, or at least not so much as I have done, what has this to do with the question in debate, which is to be decided by the Holy Scriptures or by ecclesiastical or public documents, with which he has for so many years been conversant, that he ought to be more skilled in them than I am? Once more, I have here my brother and colleague Samsucius, bishop of the Church of Turris,[3] who has not learned any of those branches of culture of which he is said to be afraid: let him attend in my place, and let the debate be between them. I will ask him, and, as I trust in the name of Christ, he will readily consent to take my place in this matter; and the Lord will, I trust, give aid to him when contending for the truth: for although unpolished in language, he is well instructed in the true faith. There is therefore no reason for his referring me to others whom I do not know, instead of letting us settle between ourselves that which concerns ourselves. However, as I have said, I will not decline meeting them if he himself asks their assistance.

LETTER XXXV.

(A.D. 396.)

(Another letter to Eusebius on the same subject.)

TO EUSEBIUS, MY EXCELLENT LORD AND BROTHER, WORTHY OF AFFECTION AND ESTEEM, AUGUSTIN SENDS GREETING.

1. I did not impose upon you, by importunate exhortation or entreaty in spite of your reluctance, the duty, as you call it, of arbitrating between bishops. Even if I had desired to move

---

[1] Tit. i. 9–13.

[2] Constantina, a chief city of Numidia.
[3] Turris, a town in Numidia.

you to this, I might perhaps have easily shown how competent you are to judge between us in a cause so clear and simple ; nay, I might show how you are already doing this, inasmuch as you, who are afraid of the office of judge, do not hesitate to pronounce sentence in favour of one of the parties before you have heard both. But of this, as I have said, I do not meanwhile say anything. For I had asked nothing else from your honourable good-nature, — and I beseech you to be pleased to remark it in this letter, if you did not in the former, — than that you should ask Proculeianus whether he himself said to his presbyter Victor that which the public registers have by official report ascribed to him, or whether those who were sent have written in the public registers not what they heard from Victor, but a falsehood ; and further, what his opinion is as to our discussing the whole question between us. I think that he is not constituted judge between parties, who is only requested by the one to put a question to the other, and condescend to write what reply he has received. This also I now again ask you not to refuse to do, because, as I know by experiment, he does not wish to receive a letter from me, otherwise I would not employ your Excellency's mediation. Since, therefore, he does not wish this, what could I do less likely to give offence, than to apply through you, so good a man and such a friend of his, for an answer concerning a matter about which the burden of my responsibility forbids me to hold my peace? Moreover, you say (because the son's beating of his mother is disapproved by your sound judgment), "If Proculeianus had known this, he would have debarred that man from communion with his party." I answer in a sentence, "He knows it now, let him now debar him."

2. Let me mention another thing. A man who was formerly a subdeacon of the church at Spana, Primus by name, when, having been forbidden such intercourse with nuns as contravened the laws of the Church,[1] he treated with contempt the established and wise regulations, was deprived of his clerical office, — this man also, being provoked by the divinely warranted discipline, went over to the other party, and was by them rebaptized. Two nuns also, who were settled in the same lands of the Catholic Church with him, either taken by him to the other party, or following him, were likewise rebaptized : and now, among bands of Circumcelliones and troops of homeless women, who have declined matrimony that they may avoid restraint, he proudly boasts himself in excesses of detestable revelry, rejoicing that he now has without hindrance the utmost freedom in that misconduct from which in the Catholic Church he was restrained. Perhaps Proculeianus knows nothing about this case either. Let it therefore through you, as a man of grave and dispassionate spirit, be made known to him ; and let him order that man to be dismissed from his communion, who has chosen it for no other reason than that he had, on account of insubordination and dissolute habits, forfeited his clerical office in the Catholic Church.

3. For my own part, if it please the Lord, I purpose to adhere to this rule, that whoever, after being deposed among them by a sentence of discipline, shall express a desire to pass over into the Catholic Church, must be received on condition of submitting to give the same proofs of penitence as those which, perhaps, they would have constrained him to give if he had remained among them. But consider, I beseech you, how worthy of abhorrence is their procedure in regard to those whom we check by ecclesiastical censures for unholy living, persuading them first to come to a second baptism, in order to their being qualified for which they declare themselves to be pagans (and how much blood of martyrs has been poured out rather than that such a declaration should proceed from the mouth of a Christian !) ; and thereafter, as if renewed and sanctified, but in truth more hardened in sin, to defy with the impiety of new madness, under the guise of new grace, that discipline to which they could not submit. If, however, I am wrong in attempting to obtain the correction of these abuses through your benevolent interposition, let no one find fault with my causing them to be made known to Proculeianus by the public registers, — a means of notification which in this Roman city cannot, I believe, be refused to me. For, since the Lord commands us to speak and proclaim the truth, and in teaching to rebuke what is wrong, and to labour in season and out of season, as I can prove by the words of the Lord and of the apostles,[2] let no man think that I am to be persuaded to be silent concerning these things. If they meditate any bold measures of violence or outrage, the Lord, who has subdued under His yoke all earthly kingdoms in the bosom of His Church spread abroad through the whole world, will not fail to defend her from wrong.

4. The daughter of one of the cultivators of the property of the Church here, who had been one of our catechumens, had been, against the will of her parents, drawn away by the other party, and after being baptized among them, had assumed the profession of a nun. Now her father wished to compel her by severe treatment to return to the Catholic Church ; but I was unwilling

---

[1] Accessus indisciplinatus sanctimonialium.

[2] 2 Tim. iv. 2 and Tit. i. 9-11.

that this woman, whose mind was so perverted, should be received by us unless with her own will, and choosing, in the free exercise of judgment, that which is better: and when the countryman began to attempt to compel his daughter by blows to submit to his authority, I immediately forbade his using any such means. Notwithstanding, after all, when I was passing through the Spanian district, a presbyter of Proculeianus, standing in a field belonging to an excellent Catholic woman, shouted after me with a most insolent voice that I was a Traditor and a persecutor; and he hurled the same reproach against that woman, belonging to our communion, on whose property he was standing. But when I heard his words, I not only refrained from pursuing the quarrel, but also held back the numerous company which surrounded me. Yet if I say, Let us inquire and ascertain who are or have been indeed Traditors and persecutors, they reply, "We will not debate, but we will rebaptize. Leave us to prey upon your flocks with crafty cruelty, like wolves; and if you are good shepherds, bear it in silence." For what else has Proculeianus commanded but this, if indeed the order is justly ascribed to him: "If thou art a Christian," said he, "leave this to the judgment of God; whatever we do, hold thou thy peace." The same presbyter, moreover, dared to utter a threat against a countryman who is overseer of one of the farms belonging to the Church.

5. I pray you to inform Proculeianus of all these things. Let him repress the madness of his clergy, which, honoured Eusebius, I have felt constrained to report to you. Be pleased to write to me, not your own opinion concerning them all, lest you should think that the responsibility of a judge is laid upon you by me, but the answer which they give to my questions. May the mercy of God preserve you from harm, my excellent lord and brother, most worthy of affection and esteem.

LETTER XXXVI.

(A.D. 396.)

TO MY BROTHER AND FELLOW-PRESBYTER CASULANUS, MOST BELOVED AND LONGED FOR, AUGUSTIN SENDS GREETING IN THE LORD.

CHAP. I. — 1. I know not how it was that I did not reply to your first letter; but I know that my neglect was not owing to want of esteem for you. For I take pleasure in your studies, and even in the words in which you express your thoughts; and it is my desire as well as advice that you make great attainments in your early years in the word of God, for the edification of the Church. Having now received a second

letter from you, in which you plead for an answer on the most just and amiable ground of that brotherly love in which we are one, I have resolved no longer to postpone the gratification of the desire expressed by your love; and although in the midst of most engrossing business, I address myself to discharge the debt due to you.

2. As to the question on which you wish my opinion, "whether it is lawful to fast on the seventh day of the week," [1] I answer, that if it were wholly unlawful, neither Moses nor Elijah, nor our Lord Himself, would have fasted for forty successive days. But by the same argument it is proved that even on the Lord's day fasting is not unlawful. And yet, if any one were to think that the Lord's day should be appointed a day of fasting, in the same way as the seventh day is observed by some, such a man would be regarded, and not unjustly, as bringing a great cause of offence into the Church. For in those things concerning which the divine Scriptures have laid down no definite rule, the custom of the people of God, or the practices instituted by their fathers, are to be held as the law of the Church.[2] If we choose to fall into a debate about these things, and to denounce one party merely because their custom differs from that of others, the consequence must be an endless contention, in which the utmost care is necessary lest the storm of conflict overcast with clouds the calmness of brotherly love, while strength is spent in mere controversy which cannot adduce on either side any decisive testimonies of truth. This danger the author has not been careful to avoid, whose prolix dissertation you deemed worth sending to me with your former letter, that I might answer his arguments.

CHAP. II. — 3. I have not at my disposal sufficient leisure to enter on the refutation of his opinions one by one: my time is demanded by other and more important work. But if you devote a little more carefully to this treatise of an anonymous Roman author,[3] the talents which by your letters you prove yourself to possess, and which I greatly love in you as God's gift, you will see that he has not hesitated to wound by his most injurious language almost the whole Church of Christ, from the rising of the sun to its going down. Nay, I may say not almost, but absolutely, the whole Church. For he is found to have not even spared the Roman Christians, whose custom he seems to himself to defend; but he is not aware how the force of his invectives recoils upon them, for it has escaped his observation. For when arguments to prove the

---

[1] Sabbato.
[2] We give the *ipsissima verba* of this canon: "In his enim rebus de quibus nihil certi statuit Scriptura divina mos populi Dei vel instituta majorum pro lege tenenda sunt."
[3] In the text the name is Urbicus, from Urbs Roma.

obligation to fast on the seventh day of the week fail him, he enters on a vehement blustering protest against the excesses of banquets and drunken revelries, and the worst licence of intoxication, as if there were no medium between fasting and rioting. Now if this be admitted, what good can fasting on Saturday do to the Romans? since on the other days on which they do not fast they must be presumed, according to his reasoning, to be gluttonous, and given to excess in wine. If, therefore, there is any difference between loading the heart with surfeiting and drunkenness, which is always sinful, and relaxing the strictness of fasting, with due regard to self-restraint and temperance on the other, which is done on the Lord's day without censure from any Christian, — if, I say, there is a difference between these two things, let him first mark the distinction between the repasts of saints and the excessive eating and drinking of those whose god is their belly, lest he charge the Romans themselves with belonging to the latter class on the days on which they do not fast; and then let him inquire, not whether it is lawful to indulge in drunkenness on the seventh day of the week, which is not lawful on the Lord's day, but whether it is incumbent on us to fast on the seventh day of the week, which we are not wont to do on the Lord's day.

4. This question I would wish to see him investigate, and resolve in such a manner as would not involve him in the guilt of openly speaking against the whole Church diffused throughout the world, with the exception of the Roman Christians, and hitherto a few of the Western communities. Is it, I ask, to be endured among the entire Eastern Christian communities, and many of those in the West, that this man should say of so many and so eminent servants of Christ, who on the seventh day of the week refresh themselves soberly and moderately with food, that they "are in the flesh, and cannot please God;" and that of them it is written, "Let the wicked depart from me, I will not know their way;" and that they make their belly their god, that they prefer Jewish rites to those of the Church, and are sons of the bondwoman; that they are governed not by the righteous law of God, but by their own good pleasure, consulting their own appetites instead of submitting to salutary restraint; also that they are carnal, and savour of death, and other such charges, which if he had uttered against even one servant of God, who would listen to him, who would not be bound to turn away from him? But now, when he assails with such reproachful and abusive language the Church bearing fruit and increasing throughout the whole world, and in almost all places observing no fast on the seventh day of the week, I warn him,

whoever he is, to beware. For in wishing to conceal from me his name, you plainly showed your unwillingness that I should judge him.

CHAP. III. — 5. "The Son of man," he says, "is Lord of the Sabbath, and in that day it is by all means lawful to do good rather than do evil."[1] If, therefore, we do evil when we break our fast, there is no Lord's day upon which we live as we should. As to his admission that the apostles did eat upon the seventh day of the week, and his remark upon this, that the time for their fasting had not then come, because of the Lord's own words, "The days will come when the Bridegroom shall be taken away from them, and then shall the children of the Bridegroom fast;"[2] since there is "a time to rejoice, and a time to mourn,"[3] he ought first to have observed, that our Lord was speaking there of fasting in general, but not of fasting upon the seventh day. Again, when he says that by fasting grief is signified, and that by food joy is represented, why does he not reflect what it was which God designed to signify by that which is written, "that He rested on the seventh day from all His works," — namely, that joy, and not sorrow, was set forth in that rest? Unless, perchance, he intends to affirm that in God's resting and hallowing of the Sabbath, joy was signified to the Jews, but grief to the Christians. But God did not lay down a rule concerning fasting or eating on the seventh day of the week, either at the time of His hallowing that day because in it He rested from His works, or afterwards, when He gave precepts to the Hebrew nation concerning the observance of that day. The only thing enjoined on man there is, that he abstain from doing work himself, or requiring it from his servants. And the people of the former dispensation, accepting this rest as a shadow of things to come, obeyed the command by such abstinence from work as we now see practised by the Jews; not, as some suppose, through their being carnal, and misunderstanding what the Christians rightly understand. Nor do we understand this law better than the prophets, who, at the time when this was still binding, observed such rest on the Sabbath as the Jews believe ought to be observed to this day. Hence also it was that God commanded them to stone to death a man who had gathered sticks on the Sabbath;[4] but we nowhere read of any one being stoned, or deemed worthy of any punishment whatever, for either fasting or eating on the Sabbath. Which of the two is more in keeping with rest, and which with toil, let our author himself decide, who has regarded joy as the portion of

[1] Matt. xii. 8-12.
[2] Matt. ix. 15.
[3] Eccles. iii. 4.
[4] Num. xv. 35.

those who eat, and sorrow as the portion of those who fast, or at least has understood that these things were so regarded by the Lord, when, giving answer concerning fasting, He said: "Can the children of the bride-chamber mourn as long as the Bridegroom is with them?"[1]

6. Moreover, as to his assertion, that the reason of the apostles eating on the seventh day (a thing forbidden by the tradition of the elders) was, that the time for their fasting on that day had not come; I ask, if the time had not then come for the abolition of the Jewish rest from work on that day? Did not the tradition of the elders prohibit fasting on the one hand, and enjoin rest on the other? and yet the disciples of Christ, of whom we read that they did eat on the Sabbath, did on the same day pluck the ears of corn, which was not then lawful, because forbidden by the tradition of the elders. Let him therefore consider whether it might not with more reason be said in reply to him, that the Lord desired to have these two things, the plucking of the ears of corn and the taking of food, done in the same day by His disciples, for this reason, that the former action might confute those who would prohibit all work on the seventh day, and the latter action confute those who would enjoin fasting on the seventh day; since by the former action He taught that the rest from labour was now, through the change in the dispensation, an act of superstition; and by the latter He intimated His will, that under both dispensations the matter of fasting or not was left to every man's choice. I do not say this by way of argument in support of my view, but only to show how, in answer to him, things much more forcible than what he has spoken might be advanced.

CHAP. IV. — 7. "How shall we," says our author, "escape sharing the condemnation of the Pharisee, if we fast twice in the week?"[2] As if the Pharisee had been condemned for fasting twice in the week, and not for proudly vaunting himself above the publican. He might as well say that those also are condemned with that Pharisee, who give a tenth of all their possessions to the poor, for he boasted of this among his other works; whereas I would that it were done by many Christians, instead of a very small number, as we find. Or let him say, that whosoever is not an unjust man, or adulterer, or extortioner, must be condemned with that Pharisee, because he boasted that he was none of these; but the man who could think thus is, beyond question, beside himself. Moreover, if these things which the Pharisee mentioned as found in him, being admitted by all to be good in themselves, are not to be retained with the haughty boastfulness

which was manifest in him, but are to be retained with the lowly piety which was not in him; by the same rule, to fast twice in the week is in a man such as the Pharisee unprofitable, but is in one who has humility and faith a religious service. Moreover, after all, the Scripture does not say that the Pharisee was condemned, but only that the publican was "justified rather than the other."

8. Again, when our author insists upon interpreting, in connection with this matter, the words of the Lord, "Except your righteousness shall exceed the righteousness of the scribes and Pharisees, ye shall not enter into the kingdom of heaven,"[3] and thinks that we cannot fulfil this precept unless we fast oftener than twice in the week, let him mark well that there are seven days in the week. If, then, from these any one subtract two, not fasting on the seventh day nor on the Lord's day, there remain five days in which he may surpass the Pharisee, who fasts but twice in the week. For I think that if any man fast three times in the week, he already surpasses the Pharisee who fasted but twice. And if a fast is observed four times, or even so often as five times, passing over only the seventh day and the Lord's day without fasting, — a practice observed by many through their whole lifetime, especially by those who are settled in monasteries, — by this not the Pharisee alone is surpassed in the labour of fasting, but that Christian also whose custom is to fast on the fourth, and sixth, and seventh days, as the Roman community does to a large extent. And yet your nameless metropolitan disputant calls such an one carnal, even though for five successive days of the week, excepting the seventh and the Lord's day, he so fast as to withhold all refection from the body; as if, forsooth, food and drink on other days had nothing to do with the flesh, and condemns him as making a god of his belly, as if it was only the seventh day's repast which entered into the belly.

•   •   •   •   •   •   •   •   •

We have no compunction in passing over about eight columns here of this letter, in which Augustin exposes, with a tedious minuteness and with a waste of rhetoric, other feeble and irrelevant puerilities of the Roman author whose work Casulanus had submitted to his review. Instead of accompanying him into the shallow places into which he was drawn while pursuing such an insignificant foe, let us resume the translation at the point at which Augustin gives his own opinion regarding the question whether it is binding on Christians to fast on Saturday.

•   •   •   •   •   •   •   •   •

CHAP. XI. — 25. As to the succeeding paragraphs with which he concludes his treatise, they are, like some other things in it which I have not thought worthy of notice, even more irrelevant

---

[1] Matt. ix. 15.
[2] Luke xviii. 11, 12.

[3] Matt. v. 21.

to a discussion of the question whether we should fast or eat on the seventh day of the week. But I leave it to yourself, especially if you have found any help from what I have already said, to observe and dispose of these. Having now to the best of my ability, and as I think sufficiently, replied to the reasonings of this author, if I be asked what is my own opinion in this matter, I answer, after carefully pondering the question, that in the Gospels and Epistles, and the entire collection of books for our instruction called the New Testament, I see that fasting is enjoined. But I do not discover any rule definitely laid down by the Lord or by the apostles as to days on which we ought or ought not to fast. And by this I am persuaded that exemption from fasting on the seventh day is more suitable, not indeed to obtain, but to foreshadow, that eternal rest in which the true Sabbath is realized, and which is obtained only by faith, and by that righteousness whereby the daughter of the King is all glorious within.

26. In this question, however, of fasting or not fasting on the seventh day, nothing appears to me more safe and conducive to peace than the apostle's rule: "Let not him that eateth despise him that eateth not, and let not him which eateth not judge him that eateth:"[1] "for neither if we eat are we the better, neither if we eat not are we the worse;"[2] our fellowship with those among whom we live, and along with whom we live in God, being preserved undisturbed by these things. For as it is true that, in the words of the apostles, "it is evil for that man who eateth with offence,"[3] it is equally true that it is evil for that man who fasteth with offence. Let us not therefore be like those who, seeing John the Baptist neither eating nor drinking, said, "He hath a devil;" but let us equally avoid imitating those who said, when they saw Christ eating and drinking, "Behold a man gluttonous, and a winebibber, a friend of publicans and sinners."[4] After mentioning these sayings, the Lord subjoined a most important truth in the words, "But Wisdom is justified of her children;" and if you ask who these are, read what is written, "The sons of Wisdom are the congregation of the righteous:"[5] they are they who, when they eat, do not despise others who do not eat; and when they eat not, do not judge those who eat, but who do despise and judge those who, with offence, either eat or abstain from eating.

CHAP. XII. — 27. As to the seventh day of the week there is less difficulty in acting on the rule above quoted, because both the Roman Church and some other churches, though few, near to it

or remote from it, observe a fast on that day; but to fast on the Lord's day is a great offence, especially since the rise of that detestable heresy of the Manichæans, so manifestly and grievously contradicting the Catholic faith and the divine Scriptures: for the Manichæans have prescribed to their followers the obligation of fasting upon that day; whence it has resulted that the fast upon the Lord's day is regarded with the greater abhorrence. Unless, perchance, some one be able to continue an unbroken fast for more than a week, so as to approach as nearly as may be to the fast of forty days, as we have known some do; and we have even been assured by brethren most worthy of credit, that one person did attain to the full period of forty days. For as, in the time of the Old Testament fathers, Moses and Elijah did not do anything against liberty of eating on the seventh day of the week, when they fasted forty days; so the man who has been able to go beyond seven days in fasting has not chosen the Lord's day as a day of fasting, but has only come upon it in course among the days for which, so far as he might be able, he had vowed to prolong his fast. If, however, a continuous fast is to be concluded within a week, there is no day upon which it may more suitably be concluded than the Lord's day; but if the body is not refreshed until more than a week has elapsed, the Lord's day is not in that case selected as a day of fasting, but is found occurring within the number of days for which it had seemed good to the person to make a vow.

28. Be not moved by that which the Priscillianists[6] (a sect very like the Manichæans) are wont to quote as an argument from the Acts of the Apostles, concerning what was done by the Apostle Paul in Troas. The passage is as follows: "Upon the first day of the week, when the disciples came together to break bread, Paul preached unto them, ready to depart on the morrow; and continued his speech until midnight."[7] Afterwards, when he had come down from the supper chamber where they had been gathered together, that he might restore the young man who, overpowered with sleep, had fallen from the window and was taken up dead, the Scripture states further concerning the apostle: "When he therefore was come up again, and had broken bread, and eaten and talked a long while, even till break of day, so he departed."[8] Far be it from us to accept this as affirming that the apostles were accustomed to fast habitually on the Lord's day. For the day now known as the Lord's day was then called

---

[1] Rom. xiv. 3.
[2] 1 Cor. viii. 8.
[3] Rom. xiv. 20.
[4] Matt. xi. 19.
[5] Ecclus. iii. 1.

[6] Priscillian, Bishop of Avila in Spain, adopted Gnostic and Manichæan errors and practices. He was condemned by the Synod of Saragossa in 381 A.D., and beheaded, along with his principal followers, by order of Maximus in 385 A.D.
[7] Acts xx. 7.
[8] Acts xx. 11.

the first day of the week, as is more plainly seen in the Gospels; for the day of the Lord's resurrection is called by Matthew μία σαββάτων, and by the other three evangelists ἡ μία (τῶν) σαββάτων,[1] and it is well ascertained that the same is the day which is now called the Lord's day. Either, therefore, it was after the close of the seventh day that they had assembled, — namely, in the beginning of the night which followed, and which belonged to the Lord's day, or the first day of the week, — and in this case the apostle, before proceeding to break bread with them, as is done in the sacrament of the body of Christ, continued his discourse until midnight, and also, after celebrating the sacrament, continued still speaking again to those who were assembled, being much pressed for time in order that he might set out at dawn upon the Lord's day; or if it was on the first day of the week, at an hour before sunset on the Lord's day, that they had assembled, the words of the text, " Paul preached unto them, ready to depart on the morrow," themselves expressly state the reason for his prolonging his discourse, — namely, that he was about to leave them, and wished to give them ample instruction. The passage does not therefore prove that they habitually fasted on the Lord's day, but only that it did not seem meet to the apostle to interrupt, for the sake of taking refreshment, an important discourse, which was listened to with the ardour of most lively interest by persons whom he was about to leave, and whom, on account of his many other journeyings, he visited but seldom, and perhaps on no other occasion than this, especially because, as subsequent events prove, he was then leaving them without expectation of seeing them again in this life. Nay, by this instance, it is rather proved that such fasting on the Lord's day was not customary, because the writer of the history, in order to prevent this being thought, has taken care to state the reason why the discourse was so prolonged, that we might know that in an emergency dinner is not to stand in the way of more important work. But indeed the example of these most eager listeners goes further; for by them all bodily refreshment, not dinner only, but supper also, was disregarded when thirsting vehemently, not for water, but for the word of truth; and considering that the fountain was about to be removed from them, they drank in with unabated desire whatever flowed from the apostle's lips.

29. In that age, however, although fasting upon the Lord's day was not usually practised, it was not so great an offence to the Church when, in any similar emergency to that in which Paul was at Troas, men did not attend to the refreshment of the body throughout the whole of the Lord's day until midnight, or even until the dawn of the following morning. But now, since heretics, and especially these most impious Manichæans, have begun not to observe an occasional fast upon the Lord's day, when constrained by circumstances, but to prescribe such fasting as a duty binding by sacred and solemn institution, and this practice of theirs has become well known to Christian communities; even were such an emergency arising as that which the apostle experienced, I verily think that what he then did should not now be done, lest the harm done by the offence given should be greater than the good received from the words spoken. Whatever necessity may arise, or good reason, compelling a Christian to fast on the Lord's day, — as we find, e.g., in the Acts of the Apostles, that in peril of shipwreck they fasted on board of the ship in which the apostle was for fourteen days successively, within which the Lord's day came round twice,[2] — we ought to have no hesitation in believing that the Lord's day is not to be placed among the days of voluntary fasting, except in the case of one vowing to fast continuously for a period longer than a week.

CHAP. XIII. — 30. The reason why the Church prefers to appoint the fourth and sixth days of the week for fasting, is found by considering the gospel narrative. There we find that on the fourth day of the week[3] the Jews took counsel to put the Lord to death. One day having intervened, — on the evening of which, at the close, namely, of the day which we call the fifth day of the week, the Lord ate the passover with His disciples, — He was thereafter betrayed on the night which belonged to the sixth day of the week, the day (as is everywhere known) of His passion. This day, beginning with the evening, was the first day of unleavened bread. The evangelist Matthew, however, says that the fifth day of the week was the first of unleavened bread, because in the evening following it the paschal supper was to be observed, at which they began to eat the unleavened bread, and the lamb offered in sacrifice. From which it is inferred that it was upon the fourth day of the week that the Lord said, " You know that after two days is the feast of the passover, and the Son of man is betrayed to be crucified;"[4] and for this reason that day has been regarded as one suitable for fasting, because, as the evangelist immediately adds: " Then assembled together the chief priests and the scribes and the elders of the people unto the palace of the high priest, who is called Caiaphas, and consulted that they might take Jesus by subtilty and kill Him."[5] After

---

1 " Prima Sabbati a Matthæo, a cæteris autem tribus una Sabbati dicitur." Matt. xxviii. 1; Mark xvi. 2; Luke xxiv. 1; John xx. 1.

2 Acts xxvii. 33.
3 Commonly called *quarta feria*.
4 Matt. xxvi. 2.
5 Matt. xxvi. 3, 4.

the intermission of one day, — the day, namely, of which the evangelist writes : [1] "Now, on the first day of the feast of unleavened bread, the disciples came to Jesus, saying unto Him, Where wilt Thou that we prepare for Thee to eat the passover ? " — the Lord suffered on the sixth day of the week, as is admitted by all : wherefore the sixth day also is rightly reckoned a day for fasting, as fasting is symbolical of humiliation ; whence it is said, " I humbled my soul with fasting." [2]

31. The next day is the Jewish Sabbath, on which day Christ's body rested in the grave, as in the original fashioning of the world God rested on that day from all His works. Hence originated that variety in the robe of His bride [3] which we are now considering : some, especially the Eastern communities, preferring to take food on that day, that their action might be emblematic of the divine rest ; others, namely the Church of Rome, and some churches in the West, preferring to fast on that day because of the humiliation of the Lord in death. Once in the year, namely at Easter, all Christians observe the seventh day of the week by fasting, in memory of the mourning with which the disciples, as men bereaved, lamented the death of the Lord (and this is done with the utmost devoutness by those who take food on the seventh day throughout the rest of the year) ; thus providing a symbolical representation of both events, — of the disciples' sorrow on one seventh day in the year, and of the blessing of repose on all the others. There are two things which make the happiness of the just and the end of all their misery to be confidently expected, viz. death and the resurrection of the dead. In death is that rest of which the prophet speaks : " Come, my people, enter thou into thy chambers, and shut thy doors about thee : hide thyself as it were for a little moment, until the indignation be overpast." [4] In resurrection blessedness is consummated in the whole man, both body and soul. Hence it came to be thought that both of these things [death and resurrection] should be symbolized, not by the hardship of fasting, but rather by the cheerfulness of refreshment with food, excepting only the Easter Saturday, on which, as I have said, it had been resolved to commemorate by a more protracted fast the mourning of the disciples, as one of the events to be had in remembrance.

CHAP. XIV. — 32. Since, therefore (as I have said above), we do not find in the Gospels or in the apostolical writings, belonging properly to the revelation of the New Testament, that any

law was laid down as to fasts to be observed on particular days ; and since this is consequently one of many things, difficult to enumerate, which make up a variety in the robe of the King's daughter,[5] that is to say, of the Church, — I will tell you the answer given to my questions on this subject by the venerable Ambrose Bishop of Milan, by whom I was baptized. When my mother was with me in that city, I, as being only a catechumen, felt no concern about these questions ; but it was to her a question causing anxiety, whether she ought, after the custom of our own town, to fast on the Saturday, or, after the custom of the Church of Milan, not to fast. To deliver her from perplexity, I put the question to the man of God whom I have just named. He answered, " What else can I recommend to others than what I do myself ? " When I thought that by this he intended simply to prescribe to us that we should take food on Saturdays — for I knew this to be his own practice — he, following me, added these words : " When I am here I do not fast on Saturday ; but when I am at Rome I do : whatever church you may come to, conform to its custom, if you would avoid either receiving or giving offence." This reply I reported to my mother, and it satisfied her, so that she scrupled not to comply with it ; and I have myself followed the same rule. Since, however, it happens, especially in Africa, that one church, or the churches within the same district, may have some members who fast and others who do not fast on the seventh day, it seems to me best to adopt in each congregation the custom of those to whom authority in its government has been committed. Wherefore, if you are quite willing to follow my advice, especially because in regard to this matter I have spoken at greater length than was necessary, do not in this resist your own bishop, but follow his practice without scruple or debate.

LETTER XXXVII.

(A.D. 397.)

TO SIMPLICIANUS,[6] MY LORD MOST BLESSED, AND MY FATHER MOST WORTHY OF BEING CHERISHED WITH RESPECT AND SINCERE AFFECTION, AUGUSTIN SENDS GREETING IN THE LORD.

1. I received the letter which your Holiness kindly sent, — a letter full of occasions of much joy to me, because assuring me that you remember me, that you love me as you used to do, and that you take great pleasure in every one of the gifts which the Lord has in His compassion

---

[1] Matt. xxvi. 17.
[2] Ps. xxxv. 13.
[3] Ps. xlv. 13, 14.
[4] Isa. xxvi. 20.

[5] Ps. xlv. 13.
[6] Simplicianus succeeded Ambrose in the see of Milan in 397 A.D. This letter is the preface to the two books addressed to Simplicianus, and contained in vol. vi. of the Benedictine edition of Augustin.

been pleased to bestow on me. In reading that letter, I have eagerly welcomed the fatherly affection which flows from your benignant heart towards me : and this I have not found for the first time, as something short-lived and new, but long ago proved and well known, my lord, most blessed, and most worthy of being cherished with respect and sincere love.

2. Whence comes so great a recompense for the literary labour given by me to the writing of a few books as this, that your Excellency should condescend to read them? Is it not that the Lord, to whom my soul is devoted, has purposed thus to comfort me under my anxieties, and to lighten the fear with which in such labour I cannot but be exercised, lest, notwithstanding the evenness of the plain of truth, I stumble through want either of knowledge or of caution? For when what I write meets your approval, I know by whom it is approved, for I know who dwells in you ; and the Giver and Dispenser of all spiritual gifts designs by your approbation to confirm my obedience to Him. For whatever in these writings of mine merits your approbation is from God, who has by me as His instrument said, "Let it be done," and it was done ; and in your approval God has pronounced that what was done is "good."[1]

3. As for the questions which you have condescended to command me to resolve, even if through the dulness of my mind I did not understand them, I might through the assistance of your merits find an answer to them. This only I ask, that on account of my weakness you intercede with God for me, and that whatever writings of mine come into your sacred hands, whether on the topics to which you have in a manner so kind and fatherly directed my attention, or on any others, you will not only take pains to read them, but also accept the charge of reviewing and correcting them ; for I acknowledge the mistakes which I myself have made, as readily as the gifts which God has bestowed on me.

LETTER XXXVIII.

(A.D. 397.)

TO HIS BROTHER PROFUTURUS AUGUSTIN SENDS GREETING.

1. As for my spirit, I am well, through the Lord's good pleasure, and the strength which He condescends to impart ; but as for my body, I am confined to bed. I can neither walk, nor stand, nor sit, because of the pain and swelling of a boil or tumour.[2] But even in such a case, since this is the will of the Lord, what else can I say than that I am well? For if we do not

wish that which He is pleased to do, we ought rather to take blame to ourselves than to think that He could err in anything which He either does or suffers to be done. All this you know well ; but what shall I more willingly say to you than the things which I say to myself, seeing that you are to me a second self? I commend therefore both my days and my nights to your pious intercessions. Pray for me, that I may not waste my days through want of self-control, and that I may bear my nights with patience : pray that, though I walk in the midst of the shadow of death, the Lord may so be with me that I shall fear no evil.

2. You have heard, doubtless, of the death of the aged Megalius,[3] for it is now twenty-four days since he put off this mortal body. I wish to know, if possible, whether you have seen, as you proposed, his successor in the primacy. We are not delivered from offences, but it is equally true that we are not deprived of our refuge ; our griefs do not cease, but our consolations are equally abiding. And well do you know, my excellent brother, how, in the midst of such offences, we must watch lest hatred of any one gain a hold upon the heart, and so not only hinder us from praying to God with the door of our chamber closed,[4] but also shut the door against God Himself ; for hatred of another insidiously creeps upon us, while no one who is angry considers his anger to be unjust. For anger habitually cherished against any one becomes hatred, since the sweetness which is mingled with what appears to be righteous anger makes us detain it longer than we ought in the vessel, until the whole is soured, and the vessel itself is spoiled. Wherefore it is much better for us to forbear from anger, even when one has given us just occasion for it, than, beginning with what seems just anger against any one, to fall, through this occult tendency of passion, into hating him. We are wont to say that, in entertaining strangers, it is much better to bear the inconvenience of receiving a bad man than to run the risk of having a good man shut out, through our caution lest any bad man be admitted ; but in the passions of the soul the opposite rule holds true. For it is incomparably more for our soul's welfare to shut the recesses of the heart against anger, even when it knocks with a just claim for admission, than to admit that which it will be most difficult to expel, and which will rapidly grow from a mere sapling to a strong tree. Anger dares to increase with

---

[1] Gen. i. 3, 4.
[2] *Rhagas vel exochas.*

[3] Megalius, Bishop of Calama and Primate of Numidia, by whom two years before Augustin had been ordained Bishop of Hippo. The reflections upon anger which follow the allusion here to the death of Megalius were probably suggested by the remembrance of an incident in the life of that bishop. While Augustin was a presbyter, Megalius had written in anger a letter to him for which he afterwards apologized, formally retracting calumny which it contained.
[4] Matt. vi. 6.

boldness more suddenly than men suppose, for it does not blush in the dark, when the sun has gone down upon it.[1] You will understand with how great care and anxiety I write these things, if you consider the things which lately on a certain journey you said to me.

3. I salute my brother Severus, and those who are with him. I would perhaps write to them also, if the limited time before the departure of the bearer permitted me. I beseech you also to assist me in persuading our brother Victor (to whom I desire through your Holiness to express my thanks for his informing me of his setting out to Constantina) not to refuse to return by way of Calama, on account of a business known to him, in which I have to bear a very heavy burden in the importunate urgency of the elder Nectarius concerning it; he gave me his promise to this effect. Farewell!

LETTER XXXIX.

(A.D. 397.)

TO MY LORD AUGUSTIN, A FATHER[2] TRULY HOLY AND MOST BLESSED, JEROME SENDS GREETING IN CHRIST.

CHAP. I. — 1. Last year I sent by the hand of our brother, the sub-deacon Asterius, a letter conveying to your Excellency a salutation due to you, and readily rendered by me; and I think that my letter was delivered to you. I now write again, by my holy brother the deacon Præsidius, begging you in the first place not to forget me, and in the second place to receive the bearer of this letter, whom I commend to you with the request that you recognise him as one very near and dear to me, and that you encourage and help him in whatever way his circumstances may demand; not that he is in need of anything (for Christ has amply endowed him), but that he is most eagerly desiring the friendship of good men, and thinks that in securing this he obtains the most valuable blessing. His design in travelling to the West you may learn from his own lips.

CHAP. II. — 2. As for us, established here in our monastery, we feel the shock of waves on every side, and are burdened with the cares of our lot as pilgrims. But we believe in Him who hath said, " Be of good cheer, I have overcome the world,"[3] and are confident that by His grace and guidance we shall prevail against our adversary the devil.

I beseech you to give my respectful salutation to the holy and venerable brother, our father Alypius. The brethren who, with me, devote themselves to serve the Lord in this monastery, salute you warmly. May Christ our Almighty God guard you from harm, and keep you mindful of me, my lord and father truly holy and venerable.

LETTER XL.

(A.D. 397.)

TO MY LORD MUCH BELOVED, AND BROTHER WORTHY OF BEING HONOURED AND EMBRACED WITH THE MOST SINCERE DEVOTION OF CHARITY, MY FELLOW-PRESBYTER JEROME, AUGUSTIN SENDS GREETING.

CHAP. I. — 1. I thank you that, instead of a mere formal salutation, you wrote me a letter, though it was much shorter than I would desire to have from you; since nothing that comes from you is tedious, however much time it may demand. Wherefore, although I am beset with great anxieties about the affairs of others, and that, too, in regard to secular matters, I would find it difficult to pardon the brevity of your letter, were it not that I consider that it was written in reply to a yet shorter letter of my own. Address yourself, therefore, I entreat you, to that exchange of letters by which we may have fellowship, and may not permit the distance which separates us to keep us wholly apart from each other; though we are in the Lord bound together by the unity of the Spirit, even when our pens rest and we are silent. The books in which you have laboured to bring treasures from the Lord's storehouse give me almost a complete knowledge of you. For if I may not say, " I know you," because I have not seen your face, it may with equal truth be said that you do not know yourself, for you cannot see your own face. If, however, it is this alone which constitutes your acquaintance with yourself, that you know your own mind, we also have no small knowledge of it through your writings, in studying which we bless God that to yourself, to us, to all who read your works, He has given you as you are.

CHAP. II. — 2. It is not long since, among other things, a certain book of yours came into my hands, the name of which I do not yet know, for the manuscript itself had not the title written, as is customary, on the first page. The brother with whom it was found said that its title is *Epitaphium*, — a name which we might believe you to have approved, if we found in the work a notice of the lives or writings of those only who are deceased. Inasmuch, however, as mention is there made of the works of some who were, at the time when it was written, or are even now, alive, we wonder why you either gave this title to it, or permitted others to believe that you had done so. The book itself has our complete approval as a useful work.

---

[1] Eph. iv. 26.
[2] [*Papa.*]
[3] John xvi. 33.

CHAP. III. — 3. In your exposition of the Epistle of Paul to the Galatians I have found one thing which causes me much concern. For if it be the case that statements untrue in themselves, but made, as it were, out of a sense of duty in the interest of religion,[1] have been admitted into the Holy Scriptures, what authority will be left to them? If this be conceded, what sentence can be produced from these Scriptures, by the weight of which the wicked obstinacy of error can be broken down? For as soon as you have produced it, if it be disliked by him who contends with you, he will reply that, in the passage alleged, the writer was uttering a falsehood under the pressure of some honourable sense of duty. And where will any one find this way of escape impossible, if it be possible for men to say and believe that, after introducing his narrative with these words, " The things which I write unto you, behold, before God, I lie not,"[2] the apostle lied when he said of Peter and Barnabas, " I saw that they walked not uprightly, according to the truth of the gospel "?[3] For if they did walk uprightly, Paul wrote what was false ; and if he wrote what was false *here*, when did he say what was true ? Shall he be supposed to say what is true when his teaching corresponds with the predilection of his reader, and shall everything which runs counter to the impressions of the reader be reckoned a falsehood uttered by him under a sense of duty? It will be impossible to prevent men from finding reasons for thinking that he not only might have uttered a falsehood, but was bound to do so, if we admit this canon of interpretation. There is no need for many words in pursuing this argument, especially in writing to you, for whose wisdom and prudence enough has already been said. I would by no means be so arrogant as to attempt to enrich by my small coppers[4] your mind, which by the divine gift is golden ; and none is more able than yourself to revise and correct that work to which I have referred.

CHAP. IV. — 4. You do not require me to teach you in what sense the apostle says, " To the Jews I became as a Jew, that I might gain the Jews,"[5] and other such things in the same passage, which are to be ascribed to the compassion of pitying love, not the artifices of intentional deceit. For he that ministers to the sick becomes as if he were sick himself ; not, indeed, falsely pretending to be under the fever, but considering, with the mind of one truly sympathizing, what he would wish done for himself if he were in the sick man's place. Paul was indeed a Jew ; and when he had become a Christian, he had not aban-doned those Jewish sacraments which that people had received in the right way, and for a certain appointed time. Therefore, even although he was an apostle of Christ, he took part in observing these ; but with this view, that he might show that they were in no wise hurtful to those who, even after they had believed in Christ, desired to retain the ceremonies which by the law they had learned from their fathers ; provided only that they did not build on these their hope of salvation, since the salvation which was foreshadowed in these has now been brought in by the Lord Jesus. For the same reason, he judged that these ceremonies should by no means be made binding on the Gentile converts, because, by imposing a heavy and superfluous burden, they might turn aside from the faith those who were unaccustomed to them.

5. The thing, therefore, which he rebuked in Peter was not his observing the customs handed down from his fathers — which Peter, if he wished, might do without being chargeable with deceit or inconsistency, for, though now superfluous, these customs were not hurtful to one who had been accustomed to them — but his compelling the Gentiles to observe Jewish ceremonies,[3] which he could not do otherwise than by so acting in regard to them as if their observance was, even after the Lord's coming, still necessary to salvation, against which truth protested through the apostolic office of Paul. Nor was the Apostle Peter ignorant of this, but he did it through fear of those who were of the circumcision. Manifestly, therefore, Peter was truly corrected, and Paul has given a true narrative of the event, unless, by the admission of a falsehood here, the authority of the Holy Scriptures given for the faith of all coming generations is to be made wholly uncertain and wavering. For it is neither possible nor suitable to state within the compass of a letter how great and how unutterably evil must be the consequences of such a concession. It might, however, be shown seasonably, and with less hazard, if we were conversing together.

6. Paul had forsaken everything peculiar to the Jews that was evil, especially this : " That, being ignorant of God's righteousness, and going about to establish their own righteousness, they had not submitted themselves unto the righteousness of God."[6] In this, moreover, he differed from them : that after the passion and resurrection of Christ, in whom had been given and made manifest the mystery of grace, according to the order of Melchizedek, they still considered it binding on them to celebrate, not out of mere reverence for old customs, but as necessary to salvation, the sacraments of the old econ-

---

[1] [*Velut officiosa mendacia.*]
[2] Gal. i. 20.
[3] Gal. ii. 14.
[4] [*Obolis meis.*]
[5] 1 Cor. ix. 20.

[6] Rom. x. 3.

omy, which were indeed at one time necessary, else had it been unprofitable and vain for the Maccabees to suffer martyrdom, as they did, for their adherence to them.[1] Lastly, in this also Paul differed from the Jews : that they persecuted the Christian preachers of grace as enemies of the law. These and all similar errors and sins he declares that he " counted but loss and dung that he might win Christ ; "[2] but he does not, in so saying, disparage the ceremonies of the Jewish law, if only they were observed after the custom of their fathers, in the way in which he himself observed them, without regarding them as necessary to salvation, and not in the way in which the Jews affirmed that they must be observed, nor in the exercise of deceptive dissimulation such as he had rebuked in Peter. For if Paul observed these sacraments in order, by pretending to be a Jew, to gain the Jews, why did he not also take part with the Gentiles in heathen sacrifices, when to them that were without law he became as without law, that he might gain them also? The explanation is found in this, that he took part in the Jewish sacrifices, as being himself by birth a Jew ; and that when he said all this which I have quoted, he meant, not that he pretended to be what he was not, but that he felt with true compassion that he must bring such help to them as would be needful for himself if he were involved in their error. Herein he exercised not the subtlety of a deceiver, but the sympathy of a compassionate deliverer. In the same passage the apostle has stated the principle more generally : " To the weak became I as weak, that I might gain the weak ; I am made all things to all men, that I might by all means save some," [3] — the latter clause of which guides us to understand the former as meaning that he showed himself one who pitied the weakness of another as much as if it had been his own. For when he said, " Who is weak, and I am not weak ? " [4] he did not wish it to be supposed that he pretended to suffer the infirmity of another, but rather that he showed it by sympathy.

7. Wherefore I beseech you, apply to the correction and emendation of that book a frank and truly Christian severity, and chant what the Greeks call παλινῳδια. For incomparably more lovely than the Grecian Helen is Christian truth : In her defence, our martyrs have fought against Sodom with more courage than the heroes of Greece displayed against Troy for Helen's sake. I do not say this in order that you may recover the faculty of spiritual sight,[5] — far be it from

me to say that you have lost it ! — but that, having eyes both clear and quick in discernment, you may turn them towards that from which, in unaccountable dissimulation, you have turned them away, refusing to see the calamitous consequences which would follow on our once admitting that a writer of the divine books could in any part of his work honourably and piously utter a falsehood.

CHAP. V. — 8. I had written some time ago a letter to you on this subject,[6] which was not delivered to you, because the bearer to whom it was entrusted did not finish his journey to you. From it I may quote a thought which occurred to me while I was dictating it, and which I ought not to omit in this letter, in order that, if your opinion is still different from mine, and is better, you may readily forgive the anxiety which has moved me to write. It is this : If your opinion is different, and is according to truth (for only in that case can it be better than mine), you will grant that " a mistake of mine, which is in the interest of truth, cannot deserve great blame, if indeed it deserves blame at all, when it is possible for you to use truth in the interest of falsehood without doing wrong." [7]

9. As to the reply which you were pleased to give me concerning Origen, I did not need to be told that we should, not only in ecclesiastical writers, but in all others, approve and commend what we find right and true, but reject and condemn what we find false and mischievous. What I craved from your wisdom and learning (and I still crave it), was that you should acquaint us definitely with the points in which that remarkable man is proved to have departed from the belief of the truth. Moreover, in that book in which you have mentioned all the ecclesiastical writers whom you could remember, and their works, it would, I think, be a more convenient arrangement if, after naming those whom you know to be heretics (since you have chosen not to pass them without notice), you would add in what respect their doctrine is to be avoided. Some of these heretics also you have omitted, and I would fain know on what grounds. If, however, perchance it has been from a desire not to enlarge that volume unduly that you refrained from adding to a notice of heretics, the statement of the things in which the Catholic Church has authoritatively condemned them, I beg you not to grudge bestowing on this subject, to which with humility and brotherly love I direct your attention, a portion of that literary labour by which already, by the grace of the Lord our God, you have in no small measure stimulated and assisted the saints in the study of the Latin tongue, and publish in one small book (if your

---

[1] 2 Macc. vii. 1.
[2] Phil. iii. 8.
[3] 1 Cor. ix. 22.
[4] 2 Cor. xi. 29.
[5] The reference here is to the story of the poet Stesichorus, who, having lost his sight as a judgment for writing an attack on Helen, was miraculously healed when he wrote a poem in retractation.

[6] [Epist. XXVIII.]
[7] See Letter XXVIII. sec. 5.

other occupations permit you) a digest of the perverse dogmas of all the heretics who up to this time have, through arrogance, or ignorance, or self-will, attempted to subvert the simplicity of the Christian faith; a work most necessary for the information of those who are prevented, either by lack of leisure or by their not knowing the Greek language, from reading and understanding so many things. I would urge my request at greater length, were it not that this is commonly a sign of misgivings as to the benevolence of the party from whom a favour is sought. Meanwhile I cordially recommend to your goodwill in Christ our brother Paulus, to whose high standing in these regions I bear before God willing testimony.

LETTER XLI.

(A.D. 397.)

TO FATHER AURELIUS, OUR LORD MOST BLESSED AND WORTHY OF VENERATION, OUR BROTHER MOST SINCERELY BELOVED, AND OUR PARTNER IN THE SACERDOTAL OFFICE, ALYPIUS AND AUGUSTIN SEND GREETING IN THE LORD.

1. " Our mouth is filled with laughter, and our tongue with singing," [1] by your letter informing us that, by the help of that God whose inspiration guided you, you have carried into effect your pious purpose concerning all our brethren in orders, and especially concerning the regular delivering of a sermon to the people in your presence by the presbyters, through whose tongues thus engaged your love sounds louder in the hearts than their voice does in the ears of men. Thanks be unto God! Is there anything better for us to have in our heart, or utter with our lips, or record with our pen, than this? Thanks be unto God! No other phrase is more easily spoken, and nothing more pleasant in sound, profound in significance, and profitable in practice, than this. Thanks be unto God, who has endowed you with a heart so true to the interests of your sons, and who has brought to light what you had latent in the inner soul, beyond the reach of human eye, giving you not only the will to do good, but the means of realizing your desires. So be it, certainly so be it! let these works shine before men, that they may see them, and rejoice and glorify your Father in heaven.[2] In such things delight yourself in the Lord; and may your prayers for these presbyters be graciously heard on their behalf by Him whose voice you do not consider it beneath you to hear when He speaks by them! May they go on, and walk, yea, run in the way 'of the Lord! May the small and the great be

blessed together, being made glad by those who say unto them, " Let us go into the house of the Lord!" [3] Let the stronger lead; let the weaker imitate their example, being followers of them, as they are of Christ. May we all be as ants pursuing eagerly the path of holy industry, as bees labouring amidst the fragrance of holy duty; and may fruit be brought forth in patience by the saving grace of stedfastness unto the end! May the Lord "not suffer us to be tempted above that we are able, but with the temptation may He make a way to escape, that we may be able to bear it"![4]

2. Pray for us: we value your prayers as worthy to be heard, since you go to God with so great an offering of unfeigned love, and of praise brought to Him by your works. Pray that in us also these works may shine, for He to whom you pray knows with what fulness of joy we behold them shining in you. Such are our desires; such are the abounding comforts which in the multitude of our thoughts within us delight our souls.[5] It is so now because such is the promise of God; and as He hath promised, so shall it be in the time to come. We beseech you, by Him who hath blessed you, and has by you bestowed this blessing on the people whom you serve, to order any of the presbyters' sermons which you please to be transcribed, and after revisal sent to us. For I on my part am not neglecting what you required of me; and as I have written often before, I am still longing to know what you think of Tychonius' seven Rules or Keys.[6]

We warmly commend to you our brother Hilarinus, leading physician and magistrate of Hippo. As to our brother Romanus, we know how actively you are exerting yourself on his behalf, and that we need ask nothing but that God may prosper your endeavours.

LETTER XLII.

(A.D. 397.)

TO PAULINUS AND THERASIA, MY BROTHER AND SISTER IN CHRIST, WORTHY OF RESPECT AND PRAISE, MOST EMINENT FOR PIETY, AUGUSTIN SENDS GREETING IN THE LORD.

Could this have been hoped or expected by us, that now by our brother Severus we should have to claim the answer which your love has not yet written to us, so long and so impatiently desiring your reply? Why have we been doomed through two summers (and these in the

---

[1] Ps. cxxvi. 1.
[2] Matt. v. 16.

[3] Ps. cxxii. 1.
[4] 1 Cor. ix. 13.
[5] Ps. xciv. 19.
[6] On this work of Tychonius, see Augustin, *De Doctrina Christiana*, b. iii., in which these seven keys for the opening of Scripture are stated and examined.

parched land of Africa) to bear this thirst? What more can I say? O generous man, who art daily giving away what is your own, be just, and pay what is a debt to us. Perhaps the reason of your long delay is your desire to finish and transmit to me that book against heathen worship, in writing which I had heard that you were engaged, and for which I had expressed a very earnest desire. O that you might by so rich a feast satisfy the hunger which has been sharpened by fasting (so far as your pen was concerned) for more than a year! but if this be not yet prepared, our complaints will not cease unless meanwhile you prevent us from being famished before that is finished. Salute our brethren, especially Romanus and Agilis.[1] From this place all who are with me salute you, and they would be less provoked by your delay in writing if they loved you less than they do.

LETTER XLIII.

(A.D. 397.)

TO GLORIUS, ELEUSIUS, THE TWO FELIXES, GRAMMATICUS, AND ALL OTHERS TO WHOM THIS MAY BE ACCEPTABLE, MY LORDS MOST BELOVED AND WORTHY OF PRAISE, AUGUSTIN SENDS GREETING.

CHAP. I. — 1. The Apostle Paul hath said: "A man that is an heretic after the first and second admonition reject, knowing that he that is such is subverted and sinneth, being condemned of himself."[2] But though the doctrine which men hold be false and perverse, if they do not maintain it with passionate obstinacy, especially when they have not devised it by the rashness of their own presumption, but have accepted it from parents who had been misguided and had fallen into error, and if they are with anxiety seeking the truth, and are prepared to be set right when they have found it, such men are not to be counted heretics. Were it not that I believe you to be such, perhaps I would not write to you. And yet even in the case of a heretic, however puffed up with odious conceit, and insane through the obstinacy of his wicked resistance to truth, although we warn others to avoid him, so that he may not deceive the weak and inexperienced, we do not refuse to strive by every means in our power for his correction. On this ground I wrote even to some of the chief of the Donatists, not indeed letters of communion, which on account of their perversity they have long ceased to receive from the undivided Catholic Church which is spread throughout the world, but letters of a private kind, such as we may send even to pagans. These letters,

however, though they have sometimes read them, they have not been willing, or perhaps it is more probable, have not been able, to answer. In these cases, it seems to me that I have discharged the obligation laid on me by that love which the Holy Spirit teaches us to render, not only to our own, but to all, saying by the apostle: "The Lord make you to increase and abound in love one toward another, and toward all men."[3] In another place we are warned that those who are of a different opinion from us must be corrected with meekness, "if God peradventure will give them repentance to the acknowledging of the truth, and that they may recover themselves out of the snare of the devil, who are taken captive by him at his will."[4]

2. I have said these things by way of preface, lest any one should think, because you are not of our communion, that I have been influenced by forwardness rather than consideration in sending this letter, and in desiring thus to confer with you regarding the welfare of the soul; though I believe that, if I were writing to you about an affair of property, or the settlement of some dispute about money, no one would find fault with me. So precious is this world in the esteem of men, and so small is the value which they set upon themselves! This letter, therefore, shall be a witness in my vindication at the bar of God, who knows the spirit in which I write, and who has said: "Blessed are the peacemakers: for they shall be called the sons of God."[5]

CHAP. II. — 3. I beg you, therefore, to call to mind that, when I was in your town,[6] and was discussing with you a little concerning the communion of Christian unity, certain Acts were brought forward by you, from which a statement was read aloud that about seventy bishops condemned Cæcilianus, formerly our Bishop of Carthage, along with his colleagues, and those by whom he was ordained. In the same Acts was given a full account of the case of Felix of Aptunga, as one singularly odious and criminal. When all these had been read, I answered that it was not to be wondered at if the men who then caused that schism, and who did not scruple to tamper with Acts, thought that it was right to condemn those against whom they had been instigated by envious and wicked men, although the sentence was passed without deliberation, in the absence of the parties condemned, and without acquainting them with the matter laid to their charge. I added that we have other ecclesiastical Acts, according to which Secundus of Tigisis, who was for the time

---

[1] See Epistle XXXI. p. 258.
[2] Tit. iii. 10, 11.

[3] 1 Thess. iii. 12.
[4] 2 Tim. ii. 25, 26.
[5] Matt. v. 9.
[6] Tubursi, a town recently identified, half-way between Calama and Madaura.

Primate of Numidia, left those who, being there present, confessed themselves traditors to the judgment of God, and permitted them to remain in the episcopal sees which they then occupied; and I stated that the names of these men are in the list of those who condemned Cæcilianus, and that this Secundus himself was president of the Council in which he secured the condemnation of those who, being absent, were accused as traditors, by the votes of those whom he pardoned when, being present, they confessed the same crime.

4. I then said that some time after the ordination of Majorinus, whom they with impious wickedness set up against Cæcilianus, raising one altar against another, and rending with infatuated contentiousness the unity of Christ, they applied to Constantine, who was then emperor, to appoint bishops to act as judges and arbiters concerning the questions which, having arisen in Africa, disturbed the peace of the Church.[1] This having been done, Cæcilianus and those who had sailed from Africa to accuse him being present, and the case tried by Melchiades, who was then Bishop of Rome, along with the assessors whom at the request of the Donatists the Emperor had sent, nothing could be proved against Cæcilianus; and thus, while he was confirmed in his episcopal see, Donatus, who was present as his opponent, was condemned. After all this, when they all still persevered in the obstinacy of their most sinful schism, the Emperor being appealed to, took pains to have the matter again more carefully examined and settled at Arles. They, however, declining an ecclesiastical decision, appealed to Constantine himself to hear their cause. When this trial came on, both parties being present, Cæcilianus was pronounced innocent, and they retired vanquished; but they still persisted in the same perversity. At the same time the case of Felix of Aptunga was not forgotten, and he too was acquitted of the crimes laid to his charge, after an investigation by the proconsul at the order of the same prince.

5. Since, however, I was only saying these things, not reading from the record, I seemed to you to be doing less than my earnestness had led you to expect. Perceiving this, I sent at once for that which I had promised to read. While I went on to visit the Church at Gelizi, intending to return thence to you, all these Acts were brought to you before two days had passed, and were read to you, as you know, so far as time permitted, in one day. We read first how Se-

cundus of Tigisis did not dare to depose his colleagues in office who confessed themselves to be traditors; but afterwards, by the help of these very men, dared to condemn, without their confessing the crime, and in their absence, Cæcilianus and others who were his colleagues. And we next read the proconsular Acts in which Felix was, after a most thorough investigation, proved innocent. These, as you will remember, were read in the forenoon. In the afternoon I read to you their petition to Constantine, and the ecclesiastical record of the proceedings in Rome of the judges whom he appointed, by which the Donatists were condemned, and Cæcilianus confirmed in his episcopal dignity. In conclusion, I read the letters of the Emperor Constantine, in which the evidence of all these things was established beyond all possibility of dispute.

CHAP. III. — 6. What more do you ask, sirs? what more do you ask? The matter in question here is not your gold and silver; it is not your land, nor property, nor bodily health that is at stake. I appeal to your souls concerning their obtaining eternal life, and escaping eternal death. At length awake! I am not handling an obscure question, nor searching into some hidden mystery, for the investigation of which capacity is found in no human intellect, or at least in only a few: the thing is clear as day. Is anything more obvious? could anything be more quickly seen? I affirm that parties innocent and absent were condemned by a Council, very numerous indeed, but hasty in their decisions. I prove this by the proconsular Acts, in which that man was wholly cleared from the charge of being a traditor, whom the Acts of the Council which your party brought forward proclaimed as most specially guilty. I affirm further, that the sentence against those who were said to be traditors was passed by men who had confessed themselves guilty of that very crime. I prove this by the ecclesiastical Acts in which the names of those men are set forth, to whom Secundus of Tigisis, professing a desire to preserve peace, granted pardon of a crime which he knew them to have committed, and by whose help he afterwards, notwithstanding the destruction of peace, passed sentence upon others of whose crime he had no evidence; whereby he made it manifest that in the former decision he had been moved, not by a regard for peace, but by fear for himself. For Purpurius, Bishop of Limata, had alleged against him that he himself, when he had been put in custody by a curator and his soldiers, in order to compel him to give up the Scriptures, was let go, doubtless not without paying a price, in either giving up something, or ordering others to do so for him. He, fearing that this suspicion might be easily enough confirmed, having

---

[1] They asked judges from Gaul, as a country in which none had been guilty of surrendering the sacred books under pressure of persecution. The bishops appointed were Maternus of Agrippina, Rheticius of Augustodunum, and Marinus of Arles. They were sent to Rome with fifteen Italian bishops; Melchiades, Bishop of Rome, presided in their meeting in A.D. 313, and acquitted Cæcilianus.

obtained the advice of Secundus the younger, his own kinsman, and having consulted all his colleagues in the episcopal office, remitted crimes which required no proof to be judged by God, and in so doing appeared to be protecting the peace of the Church: which was false, for he was only protecting himself.

7. For if, in truth, regard for peace had any place in his heart, he would not afterwards at Carthage have joined those traditors whom he had left to the judgment of God when they were present, and confessed their fault, in passing sentence for the same crime upon others who were absent, and against whom no one had proved the charge. He was bound, moreover, to be the more afraid on that occasion of disturbing the peace, inasmuch as Carthage was a great and famous city, from which any evil originating there might extend, as from the head of the body, throughout all Africa. Carthage was also near to the countries beyond the sea, and distinguished by illustrious renown, so that it had a bishop of more than ordinary influence, who could afford to disregard even a number of enemies conspiring against him, because he saw himself united by letters of communion both to the Roman Church, in which the supremacy of an apostolic chair has always flourished,[1] and to all other lands from which Africa itself received the gospel, and was prepared to defend himself before these Churches if his adversaries attempted to cause an alienation of them from him. Seeing, therefore, that Cæcilianus declined to come before his colleagues, whom he perceived or suspected (or, as they affirm, pretended to suspect) to be biassed by his enemies against the real merits of his case, it was all the more the duty of Secundus, if he wished to be the guardian of true peace, to prevent the condemnation in their absence of those who had wholly declined to compear at their bar. For it was not a matter concerning presbyters or deacons or clergy of inferior order, but concerning colleagues who might refer their case wholly to the judgment of other bishops, especially of apostolical churches, in which the sentence passed against them in their absence would have no weight, since they had not deserted their tribunal after having compeared before it, but had always declined compearance because of the suspicions which they entertained.

8. This consideration ought to have weighed much with Secundus, who was at that time Primate, if his desire, as president of the Council, was to promote peace; for he might perhaps have quieted or restrained the mouths of those who were raging against men who were absent, if he had spoken thus: "Ye see, brethren, how after so great havoc of persecution peace has been given to us, through God's mercy, by the princes of this world; surely we, being Christians and bishops, ought not to break up the Christian unity which even pagan enemies have ceased to assail. Either, therefore, let us leave to God, as Judge, all those cases which the calamity of a most troublous time has brought upon the Church; or if there be some among you who have such certain knowledge of the guilt of other parties, that they are able to bring against them a definite indictment, and prove it if they plead not guilty, and who also shrink from having communion with such persons, let them hasten to our brethren and peers, the bishops of the churches beyond the sea, and present to them in the first place a complaint concerning the conduct and contumacy of the accused, as having through consciousness of guilt declined the jurisdiction of their peers in Africa, so that by these foreign bishops they may be summoned to compear and answer before them regarding the things laid to their charge. If they disobey this summons, their criminality and obduracy will become known to those other bishops; and by a synodical letter sent in their name to all parts of the world throughout which the Church of Christ is now extended, the parties accused will be excluded from communion with all churches, in order to prevent the springing up of error in the see of the Church at Carthage. When that has been done, and these men have been separated from the whole Church, we shall without fear ordain another bishop over the community in Carthage; whereas, if now another bishop be ordained by us, communion will most probably be withheld from him by the Church beyond the sea, because they will not recognise the validity of the deposition of the bishop, whose ordination was everywhere acknowledged, and with whom letters of communion had been exchanged; and thus, through our undue eagerness to pronounce without deliberation a final sentence, the great scandal of schism within the Church, when it has rest from without, may arise, and we may be found presuming to set up another altar, not against Cæcilianus, but against the universal Church, which, uninformed of our procedure, would still hold communion with him."

9. If any one had been disposed to reject sound and equitable counsels such as these, what could he have done? or how could he have procured the condemnation of any one of his absent peers, when he could not have any decisions with the authority of the Council, seeing that the Primate was opposed to him? And if such a serious revolt against the authority of

---

[1] "In qua semper apostolicæ cathedræ viguit principatus." The use in the translation of the indefinite article, "*an* apostolic chair," is vindicated by the language of Augustin in sec. 26 of this letter regarding Carthage, and by the words in Letter CCXXXII. sec. 3: "Christianæ societatis quæ per sedes apostolorum et successiones episcoporum certa per orbem propagatione diffunditur."

the Primate himself arose, that some were resolved to condemn at once those whose case he desired to postpone, how much better would it have been for him to separate himself by dissent from such quarrelsome and factious men, than from the communion of the whole world ! But because there were no charges which could be proved at the bar of foreign bishops against Cæcilianus and those who took part in his ordination, those who condemned them were not willing to delay passing sentence ; and when they had pronounced it, were not at any pains to intimate to the Church beyond the sea the names of those in Africa with whom, as condemned traditors, she should avoid communion. For if they had attempted this, Cæcilianus and the others would have defended themselves, and would have vindicated their innocence against their false accusers by a most thorough trial before the ecclesiastical tribunal of bishops beyond the sea.

10. Our belief concerning that perverse and unjust Council is, that it was composed chiefly of traditors whom Secundus of Tigisis had pardoned on their confession of guilt; and who, when a rumour had gone abroad that some had been guilty of delivering up the sacred books, sought to turn aside suspicion from themselves by bringing a calumny upon others, and to escape the detection of their crime, through surrounding themselves with a cloud of lying rumours, when men throughout all Africa, believing their bishops, said what was false concerning innocent men, that they had been condemned at Carthage as traditors. Whence you perceive, my beloved friends, how that which some of your party affirmed to be improbable could indeed happen, viz. that the very men who had confessed their own guilt as traditors, and had obtained the remission of their case to the divine tribunal, afterwards took part in judging and condemning others who, not being present to defend themselves, were accused of the same crime. For their own guilt made them more eagerly embrace an opportunity by which they might overwhelm others with a groundless accusation, and by thus finding occupation for the tongues of men, which screen their own misdeeds from investigation. Moreover, if it were inconceivable that a man should condemn in another the wrong which he had himself done, the Apostle Paul would not have had occasion to say : " Therefore thou art inexcusable, O man, whosoever thou art that judgest : for wherein thou judgest another, thou condemnest thyself; for thou that judgest doest the same things." [1] This is exactly what these men did, so that the words of the apostle may be fully and appropriately applied to them.

11. Secundus, therefore, was not acting in the interests of peace and unity when he remitted to the divine tribunal the crimes which these men confessed : for, if so, he would have been much more careful to prevent a schism at Carthage, when there were none present to whom he might be constrained to grant pardon of a crime which they confessed ; when, on the contrary, all that the preservation of peace demanded was a refusal to condemn those who were absent. They would have acted unjustly to these innocent men, had they even resolved to *pardon* them, when they were not proved guilty, and had not confessed the guilt, but were actually not present at all. For the guilt of a man is established beyond question when he accepts a pardon. How much more outrageous and blind were they who thought that they had power to condemn for crimes which, as unknown, they could not even have forgiven ! In the former case, crimes that were known were remitted to the divine arbitration, lest others should be inquired into ; in the latter case, crimes that were not known were made ground of condemnation, that those which were known might be concealed. But it will be said, the crime of Cæcilianus and the others was known. Even if I were to admit this, the fact of their absence ought to have protected them from such a sentence. For they were not chargeable with deserting a tribunal before which they had never stood ; nor was the Church so exclusively represented in these African bishops, that in refusing to appear before them they could be supposed to decline all ecclesiastical jurisdiction. For there remained thousands of bishops in countries beyond the sea, before whom it was manifest that those who seemed to distrust their peers in Africa and Numidia could be tried. Have you forgotten what Scripture commands : "Blame no one before you have examined him ; and when you have examined him, let your correction be just"? [2] If, then, the Holy Spirit has forbidden us to blame or correct any one before we have questioned him, how much greater is the crime of not merely blaming or correcting, but actually condemning men who, being absent, could not be examined as to the charges brought against them !

12. Moreover, as to the assertion of these judges, that though the parties accused were absent, having not fled from trial, but always avowed their distrust of that faction, and declined to appear before them, the crimes for which they condemned them were well known ; I ask, my brethren, how did they know them? You reply, We cannot tell, since the evidence is not stated in the public Acts. But I will tell you how they knew them. Observe carefully the

---

[1] Rom. ii. 1.

[2] Ecclus. xi. 7.

case of Felix of Aptunga, and first read how much more vehement they were against him; for they had just the same grounds for their knowledge in the case of the others as in his, who was afterwards proved most completely innocent by a thorough and severe investigation. How much greater the justice and safety and readiness with which we are warranted in believing the innocence of the others whose indictment was less serious, and their condemnation less severe, seeing that the man against whom they raged much more furiously has been proved innocent!

CHAP. IV.—13. Some one may perhaps make an objection which, though it was disapproved by you when it was brought forward, I must not pass over, for it has been made by others, viz.: It was not meet that a bishop should be acquitted by trial before a proconsul: as if the bishop had himself procured this trial, and it had not been done by order of the Emperor, to whose care this matter, as one concerning which he was responsible to God, especially belonged. For they themselves had constituted the Emperor the arbiter and judge in this question regarding the surrender of the sacred books, and regarding the schism, by their sending petitions to him, and afterwards appealing to him; and nevertheless they refuse to acquiesce in his decision. If, therefore, he is to be blamed whom the magistrate absolved, though he had not himself applied to that tribunal, how much more worthy of blame are those who desired an earthly king to be the judge of their cause! For if it be not wrong to appeal to the Emperor, it is not wrong to be tried by the Emperor, and consequently not wrong to be tried by him to whom the Emperor refers the case. One of your friends was anxious to make out a ground of complaint on the fact that, in the case of the bishop Felix, one witness was suspended on the rack, and another tortured with pincers.[1] But was it in the power of Felix to prevent the prosecution of the inquiry with diligence, and even severity, when the case regarding which the advocate was labouring to discover the truth was his own? For what else would such a resistance to investigation have been construed to signify, than a confession of his crime? And yet this proconsul, surrounded with the awe-inspiring voices of heralds, and the blood-stained hands of executioners at his service, would not have condemned one of his peers in absence, who declined to come before his tribunal, if there was any other place where his cause could be disposed of. Or if he had in such circumstances pronounced sentence, he would himself assuredly have suffered the due and just award prescribed by civil law.

CHAP. V.—14. If, however, you repudiate the Acts of a proconsul, submit yourselves to the Acts of the Church. These have all been read over to you in their order. Perhaps you will say that Melchiades, bishop of the Roman Church, along with the other bishops beyond the sea who acted as his colleagues, had no right to usurp the place of judge in a matter which had been already settled by seventy African bishops, over whom the bishop of Tigisis as Primate presided. But what will you say if he in fact did not usurp this place? For the Emperor, being appealed to, sent bishops to sit with him as judges, with authority to decide the whole matter in the way which seemed to them just. This we prove, both by the petitions of the Donatists and the words of the Emperor himself, both of which were, as you remember, read to you, and are now accessible to be studied or transcribed by you. Read and ponder all these. See with what scrupulous care for the preservation or restoration of peace and unity everything was discussed; how the legal standing of the accusers was inquired into, and what defects were proved in this matter against some of them; and how it was clearly proved by the testimony of those present that they had nothing to say against Cæcilianus, but wished to transfer the whole matter to the people belonging to the party of Majorinus,[2] that is, to the seditious multitude who were opposed to the peace of the Church, in order, forsooth, that Cæcilianus might be accused by that crowd which they believed to be powerful enough to bend aside to their views the minds of the judges by mere turbulent clamour, without any documentary evidence or examination as to the truth; unless it was likely that true accusations should be brought against Cæcilianus by a multitude infuriated and infatuated by the cup of error and wickedness, in a place where seventy bishops had with insane precipitancy condemned, in their absence, men who were their peers, and who were innocent, as was proved in the case of Felix of Aptunga. They wished to have Cæcilianus accused by a mob such as that to which they had given way themselves, when they pronounced sentence upon parties who were absent, and who had not been examined. But assuredly they had not come to judges who could be persuaded to such madness.

15. Your own prudence may enable you to remark here both the obstinacy of these men, and the wisdom of the judges, who to the last persisted in refusing to admit accusations against Cæcilianus from the populace who were of the faction of Majorinus, who had no legal standing in the case. You will also remark how they

---

[1] *Ungulæ,* mentioned in Codex Justinianus, ix. 18. 7.

[2] Ordained by the Donatists bishop of Carthage in room of Cæcilianus.

were required to bring forward the men who had come with them from Africa as accusers or witnesses, or in some other connection with the case, and how it was said that they had been present, but had been withdrawn by Donatus. The said Donatus promised that he would produce them, and this promise he made repeatedly; yet, after all, declined to appear again in presence of that tribunal before which he had already confessed so much, that it seemed as if by his refusal to return he desired only to avoid being present to hear himself condemned; but the things for which he was to be condemned had been proved against him in his own presence, and after examination. Besides this, a libel bringing charges against Cæcilianus was handed in by some parties. How the inquiry was thereupon opened anew, what persons brought up the libel, and how nothing after all could be proved against Cæcilianus, I need not state, seeing that you have heard it all, and can read it as often as you please.

16. As to the fact that there were seventy bishops in the Council [which condemned Cæcilianus], you remember what was said in the way of pleading against him the venerable authority of so great a number. Nevertheless these most venerable men resolved to keep their judgment unembarrassed by endless questions of hopeless intricacy, and did not care to inquire either what was the number of those bishops, or whence they had been collected, when they saw them to be blinded with such reckless presumption as to pronounce rash sentence upon their peers in their absence, and without having examined them. And yet what a decision was finally pronounced by the blessed Melchiades himself; how equitable, how complete, how prudent, and how fitted to make peace! For he did not presume to depose from his own rank those peers against whom nothing had been proved; and, laying blame chiefly upon Donatus, whom he had found the cause of the whole disturbance, he gave to all the others restoration if they chose to accept it, and was prepared to send letters of communion even to those who were known to have been ordained by Majorinus; so that wherever there were two bishops, through this dissension doubling their number, he decided that the one who was prior in the date of ordination should be confirmed in his see, and a new congregation found for the other. O excellent man! O son of Christian peace, father of the Christian people! Compare now this handful with that multitude of bishops, not counting, but weighing them: on the one side you have moderation and circumspection; on the other, precipitancy and blindness. On the one side, clemency has not wronged justice, nor has justice been at variance with clemency; on the other

side, fear was hiding itself under passion, and passion was goaded to excess by fear. In the one case, they assembled to clear the innocent from false accusations by discovering where the guilt really lay; in the other, they had met to screen the guilty from true accusations by bringing false charges against the innocent.

CHAP. VI.—17. Could Cæcilianus leave himself to be tried and judged by these men, when he had such others before whom, if his case were argued, he could most easily prove his innocence? He could not have left himself in their hands even had he been a stranger recently ordained over the Church at Carthage, and consequently not aware of the power in perverting the minds of men, either worthless or unwise, which was then possessed by a certain Lucilla, a very wealthy woman, whom he had offended when he was a deacon, by rebuking her in the exercise of church discipline; for this evil influence was also at work to bring about that iniquitous transaction. For in that Council, in which men absent and innocent were condemned by persons who had confessed themselves to be traditors, there were a few who wished, by defaming others, to hide their own crimes, that men, led astray by unfounded rumours, might be turned aside from inquiring into the truth. The number of those who were especially interested in this was not great, although the preponderating authority was on their side; because they had with them Secundus himself, who, yielding to fear, had pardoned them. But the rest are said to have been bribed and instigated specially against Cæcilianus by the money of Lucilla. There are Acts in the possession of Zenophilus, a man of consular rank, according to which one Nundinarius, a deacon who had been (as we learn from the same Acts) deposed by Sylvanus, bishop of Cirta, having failed in an attempt to recommend himself to that party by the letters of other bishops, in the heat of passion revealed many secrets, and brought them forward in open court; amongst which we read this on the record, that the rearing of rival altars in the Church of Carthage, the chief city of Africa, was due to the bishops being bribed by the money of Lucilla. I am aware that I did not read these Acts to you, but you remember that there was not time. Besides these influences, there was also some bitterness arising from mortified pride, because they had not themselves ordained Cæcilianus bishop of Carthage.

18. When Cæcilianus knew that these men had assembled, not as impartial judges, but hostile and perverted through all these things, was it possible that either he should consent, or the people over whom he presided should allow him, to leave the church and go into a private dwelling, where he was not to be tried fairly by his

peers, but to be slain by a small faction, urged on by a woman's spite, especially when he saw that his case might have an unbiassed and equitable hearing before the Church beyond the sea, which was uninfluenced by private enmities on either side in the dispute? If his adversaries declined pleading before that tribunal, they would thereby cut themselves off from that communion with the whole world which innocence enjoys. And if they attempted there to bring a charge against him, then he would compear for himself, and defend his innocence against all their plots, as you have learned that he afterwards did, when they, already guilty of schism, and stained with the atrocious crime of having actually reared their rival altar, applied — but too late — for the decision of the Church beyond the sea. For this they would have done at first, if their cause had been supported by truth; but their policy was to come to the trial after false rumours had gained strength by lapse of time, and public report of old standing, so to speak, had prejudged the case; or, which seems more likely, having first condemned Cæcilianus as they pleased, they relied for safety upon their number, and did not dare to open the discussion of so bad a case before other judges, by whom, as they were not influenced by bribery, the truth might be discovered.

CHAP. VII. — 19. But when they actually found that the communion of the whole world with Cæcilianus continued as before, and that letters of communion from churches beyond the sea were sent to him, and not to the man whom they had flagitiously ordained, they became ashamed of being always silent; for it might be objected to them: Why did they suffer the Church in so many countries to go on in ignorance, communicating with men that were condemned; and especially why did they cut themselves off from communion with the whole world, against which they had no charge to make, by their bearing in silence the exclusion from that communion of the bishop whom they had ordained in Carthage? They chose, therefore, as it is reported, to bring their dispute with Cæcilianus before the foreign churches, in order to secure one of two things, either of which they were prepared to accept: if, on the one hand, by any amount of craft, they succeeded in making good the false accusation, they would abundantly satisfy their lust of revenge; if, however, they failed, they might remain as stubborn as before, but would now have, as it were, some excuse for it, in alleging that they had suffered at the hands of an unjust tribunal, — the common outcry of all worthless litigants, though they have been defeated by the clearest light of truth, — as if it might not have been said, and most justly said, to them: "Well, let us suppose that those bishops who decided the case at Rome were not good judges; there still remained a plenary Council of the universal Church, in which these judges themselves might be put on their defence; so that, if they were convicted of mistake, their decisions might be reversed." Whether they have done this or not, let them prove: for we easily prove that it was not done, by the fact that the whole world does not communicate with them; or if it was done, they were defeated there also, of which their state of separation from the Church is a proof.

20. What they actually did afterwards, however, is sufficiently shown in the letter of the Emperor. For it was not before other bishops, but at the bar of the Emperor, that they dared to bring the charge of wrong judgment against ecclesiastical judges of so high authority as the bishops by whose sentence the innocence of Cæcilianus and their own guilt had been declared. He granted them the second trial at Arles, before other bishops; not because this was due to them, but only as a concession to their stubbornness, and from a desire by all means to restrain so great effrontery. For this Christian Emperor did not presume so to grant their unruly and groundless complaints as to make himself the judge of the decision pronounced by the bishops who had sat at Rome; but he appointed, as I have said, other bishops, from whom, however, they preferred again to appeal to the Emperor himself; and you have heard the terms in which he disapproved of this. Would that even then they had desisted from their most insane contentions, and had yielded at last to the truth, as he yielded to them when (intending afterwards to apologize for this course to the reverend prelates) he consented to try their case after the bishops, on condition that, if they did not submit to his decision, for which they had themselves appealed, they should thenceforward be silent! For he ordered that both parties should meet him at Rome to argue the case. When Cæcilianus, for some reason, failed to compear there, he, at their request, ordered all to follow him to Milan. Then some of their party began to withdraw, perhaps offended that Constantine did not follow their example, and condemn Cæcilianus in his absence at once and summarily. When the prudent Emperor was aware of this, he compelled the rest to come to Milan in charge of his guards. Cæcilianus having come thither, he brought him forward in person, as he has written; and having examined the matter with the diligence, caution, and prudence which his letters on the subject indicate, he pronounced Cæcilianus perfectly innocent, and them most criminal.

CHAP. VIII. — 21. And to this day they administer baptism outside of the communion of the Church, and, if they can, they rebaptize the members of the Church: they offer sacrifice in discord and schism, and salute in the name of peace communities which they pronounce beyond the bounds of the peace of salvation. The unity of Christ is rent asunder, the heritage of Christ is reproached, the baptism of Christ is treated with contempt; and they refuse to have these errors corrected by constituted human authorities, applying penalties of a temporal kind in order to prevent them from being doomed to eternal punishment for such sacrilege. We blame them for the rage which has driven them to schism, the madness which makes them rebaptize, and for the sin of separation from the heritage of Christ, which has been spread abroad through all lands. In using manuscripts which are in their hands as well as in ours, we mention churches, the names of which are now read by them also, but with which they have now no communion; and when these are pronounced in their conventicles, they say to the reader, " Peace be with thee; " and yet they have no peace with those to whom these letters were written. They, on the other hand, blame us for crimes of men now dead, making charges which either are false, or, if true, do not concern us; not perceiving that in the things which we lay to their charge they are all involved, but in the things which they lay to our charge the blame is due to the chaff or the tares in the Lord's harvest, and the crime does not belong to the good grain; not considering, moreover, that within our unity those only have fellowship with the wicked who take pleasure in their being such, whereas those who are displeased with their wickedness yet cannot correct them, — as they do not presume to root out the tares before the harvest, lest they root out the wheat also,[1] — have fellowship with them, not in their deeds, but in the altar of Christ; so that not only do they avoid being defiled by them, but they deserve commendation and praise according to the word of God, because, in order to prevent the name of Christ from being reproached by odious schisms, they tolerate in the interest of unity that which in the interest of righteousness they hate.

22. If they have ears, let them hear what the Spirit saith to the churches. For in the Apocalypse of John we read: " Unto the angel of the Church of Ephesus write: These things saith He that holdeth the seven stars in His right hand, who walketh in the midst of the seven golden candlesticks; I know thy works, and thy labour, and thy patience, and how thou canst not bear them which are evil: and thou hast tried them which say they are apostles, and are not, and hast found them liars: and hast borne, and hast patience, and for My name's sake hast tolerated them,[2] and hast not fainted."[3] Now, if He wished this to be understood as addressed to a celestial angel, and not to those invested with authority in the Church, He would not go on to say: " Nevertheless I have somewhat against thee, because thou hast left thy first love. Remember therefore from whence thou art fallen, and repent, and do the first works; or else I will come unto thee quickly, and will remove thy candlestick out of his place, except thou repent."[4] This could not be said to the heavenly angels, who retain their love unchanged, as the only beings of their order that have departed and fallen from their love are the devil and his angels. The first love here alluded to is that which was proved in their tolerating for Christ's name's sake the false apostles. To this He commands them to return, and to do " their first works." Now we are reproached with the crimes of bad men, not done by us, but by others; and some of them, moreover, not known to us. Nevertheless, even if they were actually committed, and that under our own eyes, and we bore with them for the sake of unity, letting the tares alone on account of the wheat, whosoever with open heart receives the Holy Scriptures would pronounce us not only free from blame, but worthy of no small praise.

23. Aaron bears with the multitude demanding, fashioning, and worshipping an idol. Moses bears with thousands murmuring against God, and so often offending His holy name. David bears with Saul his persecutor, even when forsaking the things that are above by his wicked life, and following after the things that are beneath by magical arts, avenges his death, and calls him the Lord's anointed,[5] because of the venerable right by which he had been consecrated. Samuel bears with the reprobate sons of Eli, and his own perverse sons, whom the people refused to tolerate, and were therefore rebuked by the warning and punished by the severity of God. Lastly, he bears with the nation itself, though proud and despising God. Isaiah bears with those against whom he hurls so many merited denunciations. Jeremiah bears with those at whose hands he suffers so many things. Zechariah bears with the scribes and Pharisees, as to whose character in those days Scripture informs us. I know that I have omitted many examples: let those who are willing and able read the divine records for themselves: they will find that all the holy servants and friends of God have always had to bear with some among their

---

[1] Matt. xiii. 29.

[2] Augustin translates ἐβάστασας (E. V. " hast laboured ") by "sustinuisti eos" — " hast tolerated *them;*" and upon this his argument turns.
[3] Rev. ii. 1-3.
[4] Rev. ii. 4, 5.
[5] *Christum Domini.*

own people, with whom, nevertheless, they partook in the sacraments of that dispensation, and in so doing not only were not defiled by them, but were to be commended for their tolerant spirit, "endeavouring to keep," as the apostle says, "the unity of the Spirit in the bond of peace."[1] Let them also observe what has occurred since the Lord's coming, in which time we would find many more examples of this toleration in all parts of the world, if they could all be written down and authenticated: but attend to those which are on record. The Lord Himself bears with Judas, a devil, a thief, His own betrayer; He permits him, along with the innocent disciples, to receive that which believers know as our ransom.[2] The apostles bear with false apostles; and in the midst of men who sought their own things, and not the things of Jesus Christ, Paul, not seeking his own, but the things of Christ, lives in the practice of a most noble toleration. In fine, as I mentioned a little while ago, the person presiding under the title of Angel over a Church, is commended, because, though he hated those that were evil, he yet bore with them for the Lord's name's sake, even when they were tried and discovered.

24. In conclusion, let them ask themselves: Do they not bear with the murders and devastations by fire which are perpetrated by the Circumcelliones, who treat with honour the dead bodies of those who cast themselves down from dangerous heights? Do they not bear with the misery which has made all Africa groan for years beneath the incredible outrages of one man, Optatus [bishop of Thamugada]? I forbear from specifying the tyrannical acts of violence and public depredations in districts, towns, and properties throughout Africa; for it is better to leave you to speak of these to each other, whether in whispers or openly, as you please. For wherever you turn your eyes, you will find the things of which I speak, or, more correctly, refrain from speaking. Nor do we on this ground accuse those whom, when they do such things, you love. What we dislike in that party is not their bearing with those who are wicked, but their intolerable wickedness in the matter of schism, of raising altar against altar, and of separation from the heritage of Christ now spread, as was so long ago promised, throughout the world. We behold with grief and lamentation peace broken, unity rent asunder, baptism administered a second time, and contempt poured on the sacraments, which are holy even when ministered and received by the wicked. If they regard these things as trifles, let them observe those examples by which it has been proved how

they are esteemed by God. The men who made an idol perished by a common death, being slain with the sword:[3] but when the men endeavoured to make a schism in Israel, the leaders were swallowed up by the opening earth, and the crowd of their accomplices was consumed by fire.[4] In the difference between the punishments, the different degrees of demerit may be discerned.

Chap. ix.—25. These, then, are the facts: In time of persecution, the sacred books are surrendered to the persecutors. Those who were guilty of this surrender confess it, and are remitted to the divine tribunal; those who were innocent are not examined, but condemned at once by rash men. The integrity of that one who, of all the men thus condemned in their absence, was the most vehemently accused, is afterwards vindicated before unimpeachable judges. From the decision of bishops an appeal is made to the Emperor; the Emperor is chosen judge; and the sentence of the Emperor, when pronounced, is set at naught. What was then done you have read; what is now being done you have before your eyes. If, after all that you have read, you are still in doubt, be convinced by what you see. By all means let us give up arguing from ancient manuscripts, public archives, or the acts of courts, civil or ecclesiastical. We have a greater book — the world itself. In it I read the accomplishment of that of which I read the promise in the Book of God: "The Lord hath said unto me, Thou art my Son, this day have I begotten Thee: ask of Me, and I shall give Thee the heathen for Thine inheritance, and the uttermost parts of the earth for Thy possession."[5] He that has not communion with this inheritance may know himself to be disinherited, whatever books he may plead to the contrary. He that assails this inheritance is plainly enough declared to be an outcast from the family of God. The question is raised as to the parties guilty of surrendering the divine books in which that inheritance is promised. Let him be believed to have delivered the testament to the flames, who is resisting the intentions of the testator. O faction of Donatus, what has the Corinthian Church done against you? In speaking of this one Church, I wish to be understood as asking the same question in regard to all similar churches remote from you. What have these churches done against you, which could not know even what you had done, or the names of the men whom you branded with condemnation? Or is it so, that because Cæcilianus gave offence to Lucilla in Africa, the light of Christ is lost to the whole world?[6]

---

[1] Eph. iv. 3.
[2] Augustin holds that Judas was present at the institution of the Lord's Supper. See Letter XLIV. sec. 10, p. 288.
[3] Ex. xxxii. 27, 28.
[4] Num. xvi. 31, 35.
[5] Ps. ii. 7, 8.
[6] The original has a play on the words Lucillam and Lucem.

26. Let them at last become sensible of what they have done; for in the lapse of years, by a just retribution, their work has recoiled upon themselves. Ask by what woman's instigation Maximianus [1] (said to be a kinsman of Donatus) withdrew himself from the communion of Primianus, and how, having gathered a faction of bishops, he pronounced sentence against Primianus in his absence, and had himself ordained as a rival bishop in his place, — precisely as Majorinus, under the influence of Lucilla, assembled a faction of bishops, and, having condemned Cæcilianus in his absence, was ordained bishop in opposition to him. Do you admit, as I suppose you do, that when Primianus was delivered by the other bishops of his communion in Africa from the sentence pronounced by the faction of Maximianus, this decision was valid and sufficient? And will you refuse to admit the same in the case of Cæcilianus, when he was released by the bishops of the same one Church beyond the sea from the sentence pronounced by the faction of Majorinus? Pray, my brethren, what great thing do I ask of you? What difficulty is there in comprehending what I bring before you? The African Church, if it be compared with the churches in other parts of the world, is very different from them, and is left far behind both in numbers and in influence; and even if it had retained its unity, is far smaller when compared with the universal Church in other nations, than was the faction of Maximianus when compared with that of Primianus. I ask, however, only this — and I believe it to be just — that you give no more weight to the Council of Secundus of Tigisis, which Lucilla stirred up against Cæcilianus when absent, and against an apostolic see and the whole world in communion with Cæcilianus, than you give to the Council of Maximianus, which in like manner some other woman stirred up against Primianus when absent, and against the rest of the multitude throughout Africa which was in communion with him. What case could be more transparent? what demand more just?

27. You see and know all these things, and you groan over them; and yet God at the same time sees that nothing compels you to remain in such fatal and impious schism, if you would but subdue the lust of the flesh in order to win the spiritual kingdom; and in order to escape from eternal punishment, have courage to forfeit the friendship of men, whose favour will not avail at the bar of God. Go now, and take counsel together: find what you can say in reply to that which I have written. If you bring forward manuscripts on your side, we do the same; if your party say that our documents are not to be trusted, let them not take it amiss if we retort

the charge. No one can erase from heaven the divine decree, no one can efface from earth the Church of God. His decree has promised the whole world, and the Church has filled it; and it includes both bad and good. On earth it loses none but the bad, and into heaven it admits none but the good.

In writing this discourse, God is my witness with what sincere love to peace and to you I have taken and used that which He has given. It shall be to you a means of correction if you be willing, and a testimony against you whether you will or not.

LETTER XLIV.

(A.D. 398.)

TO MY LORDS MOST BELOVED, AND BRETHREN WORTHY OF ALL PRAISE, ELEUSIUS, GLORIUS, AND THE TWO FELIXES, AUGUSTIN SENDS GREETING.

CHAP. I. — 1. In passing through Tubursi on my way to the church at Cirta, though pressed for time, I visited Fortunius, your bishop there, and found him to be, in truth, just such a man as you were wont most kindly to lead me to expect. When I sent him notice of your conversation with me concerning him, and expressed a desire to see him, he did not decline the visit. I therefore went to him, because I thought it due to his age that I should go to him, instead of insisting upon his first coming to me. I went, therefore, accompanied by a considerable number of persons, who, as it happened, were at that time beside me. When, however, we had taken our seats in his house, the thing becoming known, a considerable addition was made to the crowd assembled; but in that whole multitude there appeared to me to be very few who desired the matter to be discussed in a sound and profitable manner, or with the deliberation and solemnity which so great a question demands. All the others had come rather in the mood of playgoers, expecting a scene in our debates, than in Christian seriousness of spirit, seeking instruction in regard to salvation. Accordingly they could neither favour us with silence when we spoke, nor speak with care, or even with due regard to decorum and order, — excepting, as I have said, those few persons about whose pious and sincere interest in the matter there was no doubt. Everything was therefore thrown into confusion by the noise of men speaking loudly, and each according to the unchecked impulse of his own feelings; and though both Fortunius and I used entreaty and remonstrance, we utterly failed in persuading them to listen silently to what was spoken.

2. The discussion of the question was opened notwithstanding, and for some hours we persevered, speeches being delivered by each

---

[1] A deacon in the Donatist communion at Carthage. This matter is more fully gone into by Augustin in his second sermon on Ps. xxxvi.

side in turn, so far as was permitted by an occasional respite from the voices of the noisy onlookers. In the beginning of the debate, perceiving that things which had been spoken were liable to be forgotten by myself, or by those about whose salvation I was deeply concerned; being desirous also that our debate should be managed with caution and self-restraint, and that both you and other brethren who were absent might be able to learn from a record what passed in the discussion, I demanded that our words should be taken down by reporters. This was for a long time resisted, either by Fortunius or by those on his side. At length, however, he agreed to it; but the reporters who were present, and were able to do the work thoroughly, declined, for some reason unknown to me, to take notes. I urged them, that at least the brethren who accompanied me, though not so expert in the work, should take notes, and promised that I would leave the tablets on which the notes were taken in the hands of the other party. This was agreed to. Some words of mine were first taken down, and some statements on the other side were dictated and recorded. After that, the reporters, not being able to endure the disorderly interruptions vociferated by the opposing party, and the increased vehemence with which under this pressure our side maintained the debate, gave up their task. This, however, did not close the discussion, many things being still said by each as he obtained an opportunity. This discussion of the whole question, or at least so much of all that was said as I can remember, I have resolved, my beloved friends, that you shall not lose; and you may read this letter to Fortunius, that he may either confirm my statements as true, or himself inform you, without hesitation, of anything which his more accurate recollection suggests.

CHAP. II.—3. He was pleased to begin with commending my manner of life, which he said he had come to know through your statements (in which I am sure there was more kindness than truth), adding that he had remarked to you that I might have done well all the things which you had told him of me, if I had done them within the Church. I thereupon asked him what was the Church within which it was the duty of a man so to live; whether it was that one which, as Sacred Scripture had long foretold, was spread over the whole world, or that one which a small section of Africans, or a small part of Africa, contained. To this he at first attempted to reply, that his communion was in all parts of the earth. I asked him whether he was able to issue letters of communion, which we call regular,[1] to places which I might select; and I affirmed, what was obvious to all, that in

this way the question might be most simply settled. In the event of his agreeing to this, my intention was that we should send such letters to those churches which we both knew, on the authority of the apostles, to have been already founded in their time.

4. As the falsity of his statement, however, was apparent, a hasty retreat from it was made in a cloud of confused words, in the midst of which he quoted the Lord's words: "Beware of false prophets, which come to you in sheep's clothing, but inwardly they are ravening wolves. Ye shall know them by their fruits."[2] When I said that these words of the Lord might also be applied by us to them, he went on to magnify the persecution which he affirmed that his party had often suffered; intending thereby to prove that his party were Christians because they endured persecution. When I was preparing, as he went on with this, to answer him from the Gospel, he himself anticipated me in bringing forward the passage in which the Lord says: "Blessed are they which are persecuted for righteousness' sake: for theirs is the kingdom of heaven."[3] Thanking him for the apt quotation, I immediately added that this behoved therefore to be inquired into, whether they had indeed suffered persecution for righteousness' sake. In following up this inquiry I wished this to be ascertained, though indeed it was patent to all, whether the persecutions under Macarius[4] fell upon them while they were within the unity of the Church, or after they had been severed from it by schism; so that those who wished to see whether they had suffered persecution for righteousness' sake might turn rather to the prior question, whether they had done rightly in cutting themselves off from the unity of the whole world. For if they were found in this to have done wrong, it was manifest that they suffered persecution for unrighteousness' sake rather than for righteousness' sake, and could not therefore be numbered among those of whom it is said, "Blessed are they which are persecuted for righteousness' sake." Thereupon mention was made of the surrender of the sacred books, a matter about which much more has been spoken than has ever been proved true. On our side it was said in reply, that their leaders rather than ours had been traditors; but that if they would not believe the documents with which we supported this charge, we could not be compelled to accept those which they brought forward.

---

[1] *Formatæ.*

[2] Matt. vii. 15, 16.
[3] Matt. v. 10.
[4] Macarius was sent in A.D. 348 by the Emperor Constans to Africa, to exhort all to cherish the unity of the Catholic Church, and at the same time to collect for the relief of the poor. The vehement opposition with which the Donatists met him led to conflicts and bloodshed, the Donatists claiming the honour of martyrdom for all of their party who fell in fighting with the imperial soldiers.

CHAP. III. — 5. Having therefore laid aside that question as one on which there was a doubt, I asked how they could justify their separation of themselves from all other Christians who had done them no wrong, who throughout the world preserved the order of succession, and were established in the most ancient churches, but had no knowledge whatever as to who were traditors in Africa; and who assuredly could not hold communion with others than those whom they had heard of as occupying the episcopal sees. He answered that the foreign churches had done them no wrong, up to the time when they had consented to the death of those who, as he had said, had suffered in the Macarian persecution. Here I might have said that it was impossible for the innocence of the foreign churches to be affected by the offence given in the time of Macarius, seeing that it could not be proved that he had done with their sanction what he did. I preferred, however, to save time by asking whether, supposing that the foreign churches had, through the cruelties of Macarius, lost their innocence from the time in which they were said to have approved of these, it could even be proved that up to that time the Donatists had remained in unity with the Eastern churches and other parts of the world.

6. Thereupon he produced a certain volume, by which he wished to show that a Council at Sardica had sent a letter to African bishops who belonged to the party of Donatus. When this was read aloud, I heard the name Donatus among the bishops to whom the writing had been sent. I therefore insisted upon being told whether this was the Donatus from whom their faction takes its name; as it was possible that they had written to some bishop named Donatus belonging to another section [heresy], especially since in these names no mention had been made of Africa. How then, I asked, could it be proved that we must believe the Donatus here named to be the Donatist bishop, when it could not even be proved that this letter had been specially directed to bishops in Africa? For although Donatus is a common African name, there is nothing improbable in the supposition, that either some one in other countries should be found bearing an African name, or that a native of Africa should be made a bishop there. We found, moreover, no day or name of consul given in the letter, from which any certain light might have been furnished by comparison of dates. I had indeed once heard that the Arians, when they had separated from the Catholic communion, had endeavoured to ally the Donatists in Africa with themselves; and my brother Alypius recalled this to me at the time in a whisper. Having then taken up the volume itself, and glancing over the decrees of the said Council, I read that Athanasius,

Catholic bishop of Alexandria, who was so conspicuous as a debater in the keen controversies with the Arians, and Julius, bishop of the Roman Church, also a Catholic, had been condemned by that Council of Sardica; from which we were sure that it was a Council of Arians, against which heretics these Catholic bishops had contended with singular fervour. I therefore wished to take up and carry with me the volume, in order to give more pains to find out the date of the Council. He refused it, however, saying that I could get it there if I wished to study anything in it. I asked also that he would allow me to mark the volume; for I feared, I confess, lest, if perchance necessity arose for my asking to consult it, another should be substituted in its room. This also he refused.

CHAP. IV. — 7. Thereafter he began to insist upon my answering categorically this question: Whether I thought the persecutor or the persecuted to be in the right? To which I answered, that the question was not fairly stated: it might be that both were in the wrong, or that the persecution might be made by the one who was the more righteous of the two parties; and therefore it was not always right to infer that one is on the better side because he suffers persecution, although that is almost always the case. When I perceived that he still laid great stress upon this, wishing to have the justice of the cause of his party acknowledged as beyond dispute because they had suffered persecution, I asked him whether he believed Ambrose, bishop of the Church of Milan, to be a righteous man and a Christian? He was compelled to deny expressly that that man was a Christian and a righteous man; for if he had admitted this, I would at once have objected to him that he esteemed it necessary for him to be rebaptized. When, therefore, he was compelled to pronounce concerning Ambrose that he was not a Christian nor a righteous man, I related the persecution which he endured when his church was surrounded with soldiers. I also asked whether Maximianus, who had made a schism from their party at Carthage, was in his view a righteous man and a Christian. He could not but deny this. I therefore reminded him that he had endured such persecution that his church had been razed to the foundations. By these instances I laboured to persuade him, if possible, to give up affirming that the suffering of persecution is the most infallible mark of Christian righteousness.

8. He also related that, in the infancy of their schism, his predecessors, being anxious to devise some way of hushing up the fault of Cæcilianus, lest a schism should take place, had appointed over the people belonging to his communion in Carthage an interim bishop before Majorinus was ordained in opposition to Cæcilianus. He

alleged that this interim bishop was murdered in his own meeting house by our party. This, I confess, I had never heard before, though so many charges brought by them against us have been refuted and disproved, while by us greater and more numerous crimes have been alleged against them. After having narrated this story, he began again to insist on my answering whether in this case I thought the murderer or the victim the more righteous man; as if he had already proved that the event had taken place as he had stated. I therefore said that we must first ascertain the truth of the story, for we ought not to believe without examination all that is said: and that even were it true, it was possible either that both were equally bad, or that one who was bad had caused the death of another yet worse than himself. For, in truth, it is possible that his guilt is more heinous who rebaptizes the whole man than his who kills the body only.

9. After this there was no occasion for the question which he afterwards put to me. He affirmed that even a bad man should not be killed by Christians and righteous men; as if we called those who in the Catholic Church do such things righteous men: a statement, moreover, which it is more easy for them to affirm than to prove to us, so long as they themselves, with few exceptions, bishops, presbyters, and clergy of all kinds, go on gathering mobs of most infatuated men, and causing, wherever they are able, so many violent massacres, and devastations to the injury not of Catholics only, but sometimes even of their own partisans. In spite of these facts, Fortunius, affecting ignorance of the most villanous doings, which were better known by him than by me, insisted upon my giving an example of a righteous man putting even a bad man to death. This was, of course, not relevant to the matter in hand; for I conceded that wherever such crimes were committed by men having the name of Christians, they were not the actions of good men. Nevertheless, in order to show him what was the true question before us, I answered by inquiring whether Elijah seemed to him to be a righteous man; to which he could not but assent. Thereupon I reminded him how many false prophets Elijah slew with his own hand.[1] He saw plainly herein, as indeed he could not but see, that such things were then lawful to righteous men. For they did these things as prophets guided by the Spirit and sanctioned by the authority of God, who knows infallibly to whom it may be even a benefit to be put to death.[2] He therefore required me to show him one who, being a righteous man, had in the New Testament times put any one, even a criminal and impious man, to death.

CHAP. V. — 10. I then returned to the argument used in my former letter,[3] in which I laboured to show that it was not right either for us to reproach them with atrocities of which some of their party had been guilty, or for them to reproach us if any such deeds were found by them to have been done on our side. For I granted that no example could be produced from the New Testament of a righteous man putting any one to death; but I insisted that by the example of our Lord Himself, it could be proved that the wicked had been tolerated by the innocent. For His own betrayer, who had already received the price of His blood, He suffered to remain undistinguished from the innocent who were with Him, even up to that last kiss of peace. He did not conceal from the disciples the fact that in the midst of them was one capable of such a crime; and, nevertheless, He administered to them all alike, without excluding the traitor, the first sacrament of His body and blood.[4] When almost all felt the force of this argument, Fortunius attempted to meet it by saying, that before the Lord's Passion that communion with a wicked man did no harm to the apostles, because they had not as yet the baptism of Christ, but the baptism of John only. When he said this, I asked him to explain how it was written that Jesus baptized more disciples than John, though Jesus Himself baptized not, but His disciples, that is to say, baptized by means of His disciples?[5] How could they give what they had not received (a question often used by the Donatists themselves)? Did Christ baptize with the baptism of John? I was prepared to ask many other questions in connection with this opinion of Fortunius; such as — how John himself was interrogated as to the Lord's baptizing, and replied that He had the bride, and was the Bridegroom?[6] Was it, then, lawful for the Bridegroom to baptize with the baptism of him who was but a friend or servant? Again, how could they receive the Eucharist if not previously baptized? or how could the Lord in that case have said in reply to Peter, who was willing to be wholly washed by Him, "He that is washed needeth not save to wash his feet, but is clean every whit"?[7] For perfect cleansing is by the baptism, not of John, but of the Lord, if the person receiving it be worthy; if, however, he be unworthy, the sacraments abide in him, not to his salvation, but to his perdition. When I was about to put these questions, Fortunius himself saw that he ought not to have mooted the subject of the baptism of the disciples of the Lord.

11. From this we passed to something else,

---

[1] 1 Kings xviii. 40.
[2] *Qui novit cui etiam prosit occidi.*

[3] Let. XLIII. pp. 283, 284.
[4] Matt. xxvi. 20–28.
[5] John iv. 1, 2.
[6] John iii. 29.
[7] John xiii. 10.

many on both sides discoursing to the best of their ability. Among other things it was alleged that our party was still intending to persecute them; and he [Fortunius] said that he would like to see how I would act in the event of such persecution, whether I would consent to such cruelty, or withhold from it all countenance. I said that God saw my heart, which was unseen by them; also that they had hitherto had no ground for apprehending such persecution, which if it did take place would be the work of bad men, who were, however, not so bad as some of their own party; but that it was not incumbent on us to withdraw ourselves from communion with the Catholic Church on the ground of anything done against our will, and even in spite of our opposition (if we had an opportunity of testifying against it), seeing that we had learned that toleration for the sake of peace which the apostle prescribes in the words: "Forbearing one another in love, endeavouring to keep the unity of the Spirit in the bond of peace."[1] I affirmed that they had not preserved this peace and forbearance, when they had caused a schism, within which, moreover, the more moderate among them now tolerated more serious evils, lest that which was already a fragment should be broken again, although they did not, in order to preserve unity, consent to exercise forbearance in smaller things. I also said that in the ancient economy the peace of unity and forbearance had not been so fully declared and commended as it is now by the example of the Lord and the charity of the New Testament; and yet prophets and holy men were wont to protest against the sins of the people, without endeavouring to separate themselves from the unity of the Jewish people, and from communion in partaking along with them of the sacraments then appointed.

12. After that, mention was made, I know not in what connection, of Genethlius of blessed memory, the predecessor of Aurelius in the see of Carthage, because he had suppressed some edict granted against the Donatists, and had not suffered it to be carried into effect. They were all praising and commending him with the utmost kindness. I interrupted their commendatory speeches with the remark that, for all this, if Genethlius himself had fallen into their hands, it would have been declared necessary to baptize him a second time. (We were by this time all standing, as the time of our going away was at hand.) On this the old man said plainly, that a rule had now been made, according to which every believer who went over from us to them must be baptized; but he said this with the most manifest reluctance and sincere regret.

When he himself most frankly bewailed many of the evil deeds of his party, making evident, as was further proved by the testimony of the whole community, how far he was from sharing in such transactions, and told us what he was wont to say in mild expostulation to those of his own party; when also I had quoted the words of Ezekiel — "As the soul of the father, so also the soul of the son is mine: the soul that sinneth it shall die"[2] — it which it is written that the son's fault is not to be reckoned to his father, nor the father's fault reckoned to his son, it was agreed by all that in such discussions the excesses of bad men ought not to be brought forward by either party against the other. There remained, therefore, only the question as to schism. I therefore exhorted him again and again that he should with tranquil and undisturbed mind join me in an effort to bring to a satisfactory end, by diligent research, the examination of so important a matter. When he kindly replied that I myself sought this with a single eye, but that others who were on my side were averse to such examination of the truth, I left him with this promise, that I would bring to him more of my colleagues, ten at least, who desire this question to be sifted with the same good-will and calmness and pious care which I saw that he had discovered and now commended in myself. He gave me a similar promise regarding a like number of his colleagues.

CHAP. VI. — 13. Wherefore I exhort you, and by the blood of the Lord implore you, to put him in mind of his promise, and to insist urgently that what has been begun, and is now, as you see, nearly finished, may be concluded. For, in my opinion, you will have difficulty in finding among your bishops another whose judgment and feelings are so sound as we have seen that old man's to be. The next day he came to me himself, and we began to discuss the matter again. I could not, however, remain long with him, as the ordination of a bishop required my departing from the place. I had already sent a messenger to the chief man of the Cœlicolæ,[3] of whom I had heard that he had introduced a new baptism among them, and had by this impiety led many astray, intending, so far as my limited time permitted, to confer with him. Fortunius, when he learned that he was coming, perceiving that I was to be otherwise engaged, and having himself some other duty calling him from home, bade me a kind and friendly farewell.

14. It seems to me that if we would avoid the attendance of a noisy crowd, rather hindering than helping the debate, and if we wish to com-

---

[1] Eph. iv. 2, 3.

[2] Ezek. xviii. 4.
[3] The Cœlicolæ are mentioned in some laws of Honorius as heretics whose heresy, if they refused to abandon it, involved them in civil penalties.

plete by the Lord's help so great a work begun in a spirit of unfeigned good-will and peace, we ought to meet in some small village in which neither party has a church, and which is inhabited by persons belonging to both churches, such as Titia. Let this or any other such place be agreed upon in the region of Tubursi or of Thagaste, and let us take care to have the canonical books at hand for reference. Let any other documents be brought thither which either party may judge useful; and laying all other things aside, uninterrupted, if it please God, by other cares, devoting our time for as many days as we can to this one work, and each imploring in private the Lord's guidance, we may, by the help of Him to whom Christian peace is most sweet, bring to a happy termination the inquiry which has been in such a good spirit opened. Do not fail to write in reply what you or Fortunius think of this.

LETTER XLV.

A short letter to Paulinus and Therasia repeating the request made in Letter XLII., and again complaining of the long silence of his friend.

LETTER XLVI.

(A.D. 398.)

A letter propounding several cases of conscience.

TO MY BELOVED AND VENERABLE FATHER THE BISHOP AUGUSTIN, PUBLICOLA SENDS GREETING.

It is written: "Ask thy father, and he will show thee; thy elders, and they will tell thee." [1] I have therefore judged it right to "seek the law at the mouth of the priest" in regard to a certain case which I shall state in this letter, desiring at the same time to be instructed in regard to several other matters. I have distinguished the several questions by stating each in a separate paragraph, and I beg you kindly to give an answer to each in order.

I. In the country of the Arzuges it is customary, as I have heard, for the barbarians to take an oath, swearing by their false gods, in the presence of the decurion stationed on the frontier or of the tribune, when they have come under engagement to carry baggage to any part, or to protect the crops from depredation; and when the decurion certifies in writing that this oath has been taken, the owners or farmers of land employ them as watchmen of their crops; or travellers who have occasion to pass through their country hire them, as if assured of their now being trustworthy. Now a doubt has arisen

in my mind whether the landowner who thus employs a barbarian, of whose fidelity he is persuaded in consequence of such an oath, does not make himself and the crops committed to that man's charge to share the defilement of that sinful oath; and so also with the traveller who may employ his services. I should mention, however, that in both cases the barbarian is rewarded for his services with money. Nevertheless in both transactions there comes in, besides the pecuniary remuneration, this oath before the decurion or tribune involving mortal sin. I am concerned as to whether this sin does not defile either him who accepts the oath of the barbarian, or at least the things which are committed to the barbarian's keeping. For whatever other terms be in the arrangement, even such as the payment of gold, and giving of hostages in security, nevertheless this sinful oath has been a real part of the transaction. Be pleased to resolve my doubts definitely and positively. For if your answer indicate that you are in doubt yourself, I may fall into greater perplexity than before.

II. I have also heard that my own land-stewards receive from the barbarians hired to protect the crops an oath in which they appeal to their false gods. Does not this oath so defile these crops, that if a Christian uses them or takes the money realized by their sale, he is himself defiled? Do answer this.

III. Again, I have heard from one person that no oath was taken by the barbarian in making agreement with my steward, but another has said to me that such an oath was taken. Suppose now that the latter statement were false, tell me if I am bound to forbear from using these crops, or the money obtained for them, merely because I have heard the statement made, according to the scriptural rule: "If any man say unto you, This is offered in sacrifice unto idols, eat not, for his sake that showed it." [2] Is this case parallel to the case of meat offered to idols; and if it is, what am I to do with the crops, or with the price of them?

IV. In this case ought I to examine both him who said that no oath was taken before my steward, and the other who said that the oath was taken, and bring witnesses to prove which of the two spoke truly, leaving the crops or their price untouched so long as there is uncertainty in the matter?

V. If the barbarian who swears this sinful oath were to require of the steward or of the tribune stationed on the frontier, that he, being a Christian, should give him assurance of his faithfulness to his part of the engagement about watching the crops, by the same oath which he

---

[1] Deut. xxxii. 7.

[2] 1 Cor. x. 28.

himself has taken, involving mortal sin, does the oath pollute only that Christian man? Does it not also pollute the things regarding which he took the oath? Or if a pagan who has authority on the frontier thus give to a barbarian this oath in token of acting faithfully to him, does he not involve in the defilement of his own sin those in whose interest he swears? If I send a man to the Arzuges, is it lawful for him to take from a barbarian that sinful oath? Is not the Christian who takes such an oath from him also defiled by his sin?

VI. Is it lawful for a Christian to use wheat or beans from the threshing-floor, wine or oil from the press, if, with his knowledge, some part of what has been taken thence was offered in sacrifice to a false god?

VII. May a Christian use for any purpose wood which he knows to have been taken from one of their idols' groves?

VIII. If a Christian buy in the market meat which has not been offered to idols, and have in his mind conflicting doubts as to whether it has been offered to idols or not, but eventually adopt the opinion that it was not, does he sin if he partake of this meat?

IX. If a man does an action good in itself, about which he has some misgivings as to whether it is good or bad, can it be reckoned as a sin to him if he does it believing it to be good, although formerly he may have thought it bad?

X. If any one has falsely said that some meat has been offered to idols, and afterwards confess that it was a falsehood, and this confession is believed, may a Christian use the meat regarding which he heard that statement, or sell it, and use the price obtained?

XI. If a Christian on a journey, overpowered by want, having fasted for one, two, or several days, so that he can no longer endure the privation, should by chance, when in the last extremity of hunger, and when he sees death close at hand, find food placed in an idol's temple, where there is no man near him, and no other food to be found; whether should he die or partake of that food?

XII. If a Christian is on the point of being killed by a barbarian or a Roman, ought he to kill the aggressor to save his own life? or ought he even, without killing the assailant, to drive him back and fight with him, seeing it has been said, "Resist not evil"?[1]

XIII. May a Christian put a wall for defence against an enemy round his property? and if some use that wall as a place from which to fight and kill the enemy, is the Christian the cause of the homicide?

XIV. May a Christian drink at a fountain or well into which anything from a sacrifice has been cast? May he drink from a well found in a deserted temple? If there be in a temple where an idol is worshipped a well or fountain which nothing has defiled, may he draw water thence, and drink of it?

XV. May a Christian use baths[2] in places in which sacrifice is offered to images? May he use baths which are used by pagans on a feast-day, either while they are there or after they have left?

XVI. May a Christian use the same sedan-chair[3] as has been used by pagans coming down from their idols on a feast-day, if in that chair they have performed any part of their idolatrous service, and the Christian is aware of this?

XVII. If a Christian, being the guest of another, has forborne from using meat set before him, concerning which it was said to him that it had been offered in sacrifice, but afterwards by some accident finds the same meat for sale and buys it, or has it presented to him at another man's table, and then eat of it, without knowing that it is the same, is he guilty of sin?

XVIII. May a Christian buy and use vegetables or fruit which he knows to have been brought from the garden of a temple or of the priests of an idol?

That you may not be put to trouble in searching the Scriptures concerning the oath of which I have spoken and the idols, I resolved to set before you those texts which, by the Lord's help, I have found; but if you have found anything better or more to the purpose in Scripture, be so good as let me know. For example, when Laban said to Jacob, "The God of Abraham and the God of Nahor judge betwixt us,"[4] Scripture does not declare which god is meant. Again, when Abimelech came to Isaac, and he and those who were with him sware to Isaac, we are not told what kind of oath it was.[5] As to the idols, Gideon was commanded by the Lord to make a whole burnt-offering of the bullock which he killed.[6] And in the book of Joshua the son of Nun, it is said of Jericho that all the silver, and gold, and brass should be brought into the treasures of the Lord, and the things found in the accursed city were called sacred.[7] Also we read in Deuteronomy:[8] "Neither shalt thou bring an abomination into thine house, lest thou be a cursed thing like it."

May the Lord preserve thee. I salute thee. Pray for me.

---

[1] Matt. v. 39.

[2] *Balneis vel thermis.*
[3] The Benedictine Fathers translate this, in their note, sitz-bath.
[4] Gen. xxxi. 53.
[5] Gen. xxvi. 31.
[6] Judg. vi. 26.
[7] Josh. vi. 19.
[8] Deut. vii. 26.

LETTER XLVII.

(A.D. 398.)

TO THE HONOURABLE PUBLICOLA, MY MUCH BELOVED SON, AUGUSTIN SENDS GREETING IN THE LORD.

1. Your perplexities have, since I learned them by your letter, become mine also, not because all those things by which you tell me that you are disturbed, disturb my mind: but I have been much perplexed, I confess, by the question how your perplexities were to be removed; especially since you require me to give a conclusive answer, lest you should fall into greater doubts than you had before you applied to me to have them resolved. For I see that I cannot give this, since, though I may write things which appear to me most certain, if I do not convince you, you must be beyond question more at a loss than before; and though it is in my power to use arguments which weigh with myself, I may fail of convincing another by these. However, lest I should refuse the small service which your love claims, I have resolved after some consideration to write in reply.

2. One of your doubts is as to using the services of a man who has guaranteed his fidelity by swearing by his false gods. In this matter I beg you to consider whether, in the event of a man failing to keep his word after having pledged himself by such an oath, you would not regard him as guilty of a twofold sin. For if he kept the engagement which he had confirmed by this oath, he would be pronounced guilty in this only, that he swore by such deities; but no one would justly blame him for keeping his engagement. But in the case supposed, seeing that he both swore by those whom he should not worship, and did, notwithstanding his promise, what he should not have done, he was guilty of two sins: whence it is obvious that in using, not for an evil work, but for some good and lawful end, the service of a man whose fidelity is known to have been confirmed by an oath in the name of false gods, one participates, not in the sin of swearing by the false gods, but in the good faith with which he keeps his promise. The faith which I here speak of as kept is not that on account of which those who are baptized in Christ are called faithful: that is entirely different and far removed from the faith desiderated in regard to the arrangements and compacts of men. Nevertheless it is, beyond all doubt, worse to swear falsely by the true God than to swear truly by the false gods; for the greater the holiness of that by which we swear, the greater is the sin of perjury. It is therefore a different question whether he is not guilty who requires another to pledge himself by taking an oath in the name of his gods, seeing that he worships false gods. In answering this question, we may accept as decisive those examples which you yourself quoted of Laban and of Abimelech (if Abimelech did swear by his gods, as Laban swore by the god of Nahor). This is, as I have said, another question, and one which would perchance perplex me, were it not for those examples of Isaac and Jacob, to which, for aught I know, others might be added. It may be that some scruple might yet be suggested by the precept in the New Testament, "Swear not at all;"[1] words which were in my opinion spoken, not because it is a sin to swear a true oath, but because it is a heinous sin to forswear oneself: from which crime our Lord would have us keep at a great distance, when He charged us not to swear at all. I know, however, that your opinion is different: wherefore it should not be discussed at present; let us rather treat of that about which you have thought of asking my advice. On the same ground on which you forbear from swearing yourself, you may, if such be your opinion, regard it as forbidden to exact an oath from another, although it is expressly said, Swear not; but I do not remember reading anywhere in Holy Scripture that we are not to take another's oath. The question whether we ought to take advantage of the concord which is established between other parties by their exchange of oaths is entirely different. If we answer this in the negative, I know not whether we could find any place on earth in which we could live. For not only on the frontier, but throughout all the provinces, the security of peace rests on the oaths of barbarians. And from this it would follow, that not only the crops which are guarded by men who have sworn fidelity in the name of their false gods, but all things which enjoy the protection secured by the peace which a similar oath has ratified, are defiled. If this be admitted by you to be a complete absurdity, dismiss with it your doubts on the cases which you named.

3. Again, if from the threshing-floor or wine-press of a Christian anything be taken, with his knowledge, to be offered to false gods, he is guilty in permitting this to be done, if it be in his power to prevent it. If he finds that it has been done, or has not the power to prevent it, he uses without scruple the rest of the grain or wine, as uncontaminated, just as we use fountains from which we know that water has been taken to be used in idol-worship. The same principle decides the question about baths. For we have no scruple about inhaling the air into which we know that the smoke from all the altars and incense of idolaters ascends. From which it is manifest, that the thing forbidden is

[1] Matt. v. 34, 36.

our devoting anything to the honour of the false gods, or appearing to do this by so acting as to encourage in such worship those who do not know our mind, although in our heart we despise their idols. And when temples, idols, groves, etc., are thrown down by permission from the authorities, although our taking part in this work is a clear proof of our not honouring, but rather abhorring, these things, we must nevertheless forbear from appropriating any of them to our own personal and private use; so that it may be manifest that in overthrowing these we are influenced, not by greed, but by piety. When, however, the spoils of these places are applied to the benefit of the community or devoted to the service of God, they are dealt with in the same manner as the men themselves when they are turned from impiety and sacrilege to the true religion. We understand this to be the will of God from the examples quoted by yourself: the grove of the false gods from which He commanded wood to be taken [by Gideon] for the burnt-offering; and Jericho, of which all the gold, silver, and brass was to be brought into the Lord's treasury. Hence also the precept in Deuteronomy: "Thou shalt not desire the silver or gold that is on them, nor take it unto thee, lest thou be snared therein; for it is an abomination to the Lord thy God. Neither shalt thou bring an abomination into thine house, lest thou become a cursed thing like it: but thou shalt utterly detest it, and thou shalt utterly abhor it; for it is a cursed thing."[1] From which it appears plainly, that either the appropriation of such spoils to their own private use was absolutely forbidden, or they were forbidden to carry anything of that kind into their own houses with the intention of giving to it honour; for then this would be an abomination and accursed in the sight of God; whereas the honour impiously given to such idols is, by their public destruction, utterly abolished.

4. As to meats offered to idols, I assure you we have no duty beyond observing what the apostle taught concerning them. Study, therefore, his words on the subject, which, if they were obscure to you, I would explain as well as I could. He does not sin who, unwittingly, afterwards partakes of food which he formerly refused because it had been offered to an idol. A kitchen-herb, or any other fruit of the ground, belongs to Him who created it; for "the earth is the Lord's, and the fulness thereof," and "every creature of God is good."[2] But if that which the earth has borne is consecrated or offered to an idol, then we must reckon it among the things offered to idols. We must beware lest, in pronouncing that we ought not

to eat the fruits of a garden belonging to an idol-temple, we be involved in the inference that it was wrong for the apostle to take food in Athens, since that city belonged to Minerva, and was consecrated to her as the guardian deity. The same answer I would give as to the well or fountain enclosed in a temple, though my scruples would be somewhat more awakened if some part of the sacrifices be thrown into the said well or fountain. But the case is, as I have said before, exactly parallel to our using of the air which receives the smoke of these sacrifices; or, if this be thought to make a difference, that the sacrifice, the smoke whereof mingles with the air, is not offered to the air itself, but to some idol or false god, whereas sometimes offerings are cast into the water with the intention of sacrificing to the waters themselves, it is enough to say that the same principle would preclude us from using the light of the sun, because wicked men continually worship that luminary wherever they are tolerated in doing so. Sacrifices are offered to the winds, which we nevertheless use for our convenience, although they seem, as it were, to inhale and swallow greedily the smoke of these sacrifices. If any one be in doubt regarding meat, whether it has been offered to an idol or not, and the fact be that it has not, when he eats that meat under the impression that it has not been offered to an idol, he by no means does wrong; because neither in fact, nor now in his judgment, is it food offered to an idol, although he formerly thought it was. For surely it is lawful to correct false impressions by others that are true. But if any one believes that to be good which is evil, and acts accordingly, he sins in entertaining that belief; and these are all sins of ignorance, in which one thinks that to be right which it is wrong for him to do.

5. As to killing others in order to defend one's own life, I do not approve of this, unless one happen to be a soldier or public functionary acting, not for himself, but in defence of others or of the city in which he resides, if he act according to the commission lawfully given him, and in the manner becoming his office.[3] When, however, men are prevented, by being alarmed, from doing wrong, it may be said that a real service is done to themselves. The precept, "Resist not evil,"[4] was given to prevent us from taking pleasure in revenge, in which the mind is gratified by the sufferings of others, but not to make us neglect the duty of restraining men from sin. From this it follows that one is not guilty of homicide, because he has put up a wall

---

[1] Deut. vii. 25, 26.
[2] Ps. xxiv. 1; 1 Cor. x. 25, 26; and 1 Tim. iv. 4.
[3] For Augustin's mature view on this subject, see his work, *De Libero Arbitrio*, i. 5. 13: "That it is wrong to shed the blood of our fellow-men in defence of those things which ought to be despised by us."
[4] Matt. v. 39.

round his estate, if any one is killed by the wall falling upon him when he is throwing it down. For a Christian is not guilty of homicide though his ox may gore or his horse kick a man, so that he dies. On such a principle, the oxen of a Christian should have no horns, and his horses no hoofs, and his dogs no teeth. On such a principle, when the Apostle Paul took care to inform the chief captain that an ambush was laid for him by certain desperadoes, and received in consequence an armed escort,[1] if the villains who plotted his death had thrown themselves on the weapons of the soldiers, Paul would have had to acknowledge the shedding of their blood as a crime with which he was chargeable. God forbid that we should be blamed for accidents which, without our desire, happen to others through things done by us or found in our possession, which are in themselves good and lawful. In that event, we ought to have no iron implements for the house or the field, lest some one should by them lose his own life or take another's; no tree or rope on our premises, lest some one hang himself; no window in our house, lest some one throw himself down from it. But why mention more in a list which must be interminable? For what good and lawful thing is there in use among men which may not become chargeable with being an instrument of destruction?

6. I have now only to notice (unless I am mistaken) the case which you mentioned of a Christian on a journey overcome by the extremity of hunger; whether, if he could find nothing to eat but meat placed in an idol's temple, and there was no man near to relieve him, it would be better for him to die of starvation than to take that food for his nourishment? Since in this question it is not assumed that the food thus found was offered to the idol (for it might have been left by mistake or designedly by persons who, on a journey, had turned aside there to take refreshment; or it might have been put there for some other purpose), I answer briefly thus: Either it is certain that this food was offered to the idol, or it is certain that it was not, or neither of these things is known. If it is certain, it is better to reject it with Christian fortitude. In either of the other alternatives, it may be used for his necessity without any conscientious scruple.

LETTER XLVIII.

(A.D. 398.)

TO MY LORD EUDOXIUS, MY BROTHER AND FELLOW-PRESBYTER, BELOVED AND LONGED FOR, AND TO THE BRETHREN WHO ARE WITH HIM,[2] AUGUSTIN AND THE BRETHREN WHO ARE HERE SEND GREETING.

1. When we reflect upon the undisturbed rest which you enjoy in Christ, we also, although engaged in labours manifold and arduous, find rest with you, beloved. We are one body under one Head, so that you share our toils, and we share your repose: for "if one member suffer, all the members suffer with it; or if one member be honoured, all the members rejoice with it."[3] Therefore we earnestly exhort and beseech you, by the deep humility and most compassionate majesty of Christ, to be mindful of us in your holy intercessions; for we believe you to be more lively and undistracted in prayer than we can be, whose prayers are often marred and weakened by the darkness and confusion arising from secular occupations: not that we have these on our own account, but we can scarcely breathe for the pressure of such duties imposed upon us by men compelling us, so to speak, to go with them one mile, with whom we are commanded by our Lord to go farther than they ask.[4] We believe, nevertheless, that He before whom the sighing of the prisoner comes[5] will look on us persevering in the ministry in which He was pleased to put us, with promise of reward, and, by the assistance of your prayers, will set us free from all distress.

2. We exhort you in the Lord, brethren, to be stedfast in your purpose, and persevere to the end; and if the Church, your Mother, calls you to active service, guard against accepting it, on the one hand, with too eager elation of spirit, or declining it, on the other, under the solicitations of indolence; and obey God with a lowly heart, submitting yourselves in meekness to Him who governs you, who will guide the meek in judgment, and will teach them His way.[6] Do not prefer your own ease to the claims of the Church; for if no good men were willing to minister to her in her bringing forth of her spiritual children, the beginning of your own spiritual life would have been impossible. As men must keep the way carefully in walking between fire and water, so as to be neither burned nor drowned, so must we order our steps between the pinnacle of pride and the whirlpool of indolence; as it is written, "declining neither to the right hand nor to the left."[7] For some, while guarding too anxiously against being lifted up and raised, as it were, to the dangerous heights on the right hand, have

---

[1] Acts xxiii. 17–24.

[2] The monastery of these brethren was in the island of Capraria — the same, I suppose, with Caprera — now so widely famous as Garibaldi's home.
[3] 1 Cor. xii. 26.
[4] Matt. v. 41.
[5] Ps. lxxix. 11.
[6] Ps. xxv. 9.
[7] Deut. xvii. 11.

fallen and been engulphed in the depths on the left. Again, others, while turning too eagerly from the danger on the left hand of being immersed in the torpid effeminacy of inaction, are, on the other hand, so destroyed and consumed by the extravagance of self-conceit, that they vanish into ashes and smoke. See then, beloved, that in your love of ease you restrain yourselves from all mere earthly delight, and remember that there is no place where the fowler who fears lest we fly back to God may not lay snares for us ; let us account him whose captives we once were to be the sworn enemy of all good men ; let us never consider ourselves in possession of perfect peace until iniquity shall have ceased, and "judgment shall have returned unto righteousness." [1]

3. Moreover, when you are exerting yourselves with energy and fervour, whatever you do, whether labouring diligently in prayer, fasting, or almsgiving, or distributing to the poor, or forgiving injuries, " as God also for Christ's sake hath forgiven us," [2] or subduing evil habits, and chastening the body and bringing it into subjection,[3] or bearing tribulation, and especially bearing with one another in love (for what can he bear who is not patient with his brother?), or guarding against the craft and wiles of the tempter, and by the shield of faith averting and extinguishing his fiery darts,[4] or " singing and making melody to the Lord in your hearts," or with voices in harmony with your hearts ; [5]—whatever you do, I say, " do all to the glory of God," [6] who " worketh all in all," [7] and be so " fervent in spirit " [8] that your " soul may make her boast in the Lord." [9] Such is the course of those who walk in the "straight way," whose "eyes are ever upon the Lord, for He shall pluck their feet out of the net." [10] Such a course is neither interrupted by business, nor benumbed by leisure, neither boisterous nor languid, neither presumptuous nor desponding, neither reckless nor supine. " These things do, and the God of peace shall be with you." [11]

4. Let your charity prevent you from accounting me forward in wishing to address you by letter. I remind you of these things, not because I think you come short in them, but because I thought that I would be much commended unto God by you, if, in doing your duty to Him, you do it with a remembrance of my exhortation. For good report, even before the coming of the

brethren Eustasius and Andreas from you, had brought to us, as they did, the good savour of Christ, which is yielded by your holy conversation. Of these, Eustasius has gone before us to that land of rest, on the shore of which beat no rude waves such as those which encompass your island home, and in which he does not regret Caprera, for the homely raiment [12] with which it furnished him he wears no more.

LETTER XLIX.

This letter, written to Honoratus, a Donatist bishop, contains nothing on the Donatist schism which is not already found in Letters XLIII. and XLIV., or supplied in Letter LIII.

LETTER L.[13]

(A.D. 399.)

TO THE MAGISTRATES AND LEADING MEN, OR ELDERS, OF THE COLONY OF SUFFECTUM, BISHOP AUGUSTIN SENDS GREETING.

Earth reels and heaven trembles at the report of the enormous crime and unprecedented cruelty which has made your streets and temples run red with blood, and ring with the shouts of murderers. You have buried the laws of Rome in a dishonoured grave, and trampled in scorn the reverence due to equitable enactments. The authority of emperors you neither respect nor fear. In your city there has been shed the innocent blood of sixty of our brethren ; and whoever approved himself most active in the massacre, was rewarded with your applause, and with a high place in your Council. Come now, let us arrive at the chief pretext for this outrage. If you say that Hercules belonged to you, by all means we will make good your loss : we have metals at hand, and there is no lack of stone ; nay, we have several varieties of marble, and a host of artisans. Fear not, your god is in the hands of his makers, and shall be with all diligence hewn out and polished and ornamented. We will give in addition some red ochre, to make him blush in such a way as may well harmonize with your devotions. Or if you say that the Hercules must be of your own making, we will raise a subscription in pennies,[14] and buy a god from a workman of your own for you. Only do you at the same time make restitution to us ; and as your god Hercules is given back to you, let the lives of the many men whom your violence has destroyed be given back to us.

---

1 Ps. lvii. 1 and xciv. 15.
2 Eph. iv. 32.
3 1 Cor. ix. 27.
4 Eph. vi. 16.
5 Eph. v. 19.
6 1 Cor. x. 31.
7 1 Cor. xii. 6.
8 Rom. xii. 11.
9 Ps. xxxiv. 2.
10 Ps. xxv. 15.
11 Phil. iv. 9.

12 Cilicium, the garment of goats' hair worn by the brethren. These were the staple article of manufacture in Caprera, " the goat island."
13 This letter is found only in the Vatican MS. On this ground, and because of its tone and style, its composition has been ascribed to another hand than Augustin's. The reader may judge for himself. The sixty Christians of Suffectum (a town in the territory of Tunis), whose death is here mentioned, are commemorated in the martyrology of the Roman Catholic Church. Their day in the Calendar is Aug. 30.
14 Singulis nummis.

LETTER LI.

(A.D. 399 OR 400.)

An invitation to Crispinus, Donatist bishop at Calama, to discuss the whole question of the Donatist schism.

(No salutation at the beginning of the letter.)

1. I have adopted this plan in regard to the heading of this letter, because your party are offended by the humility which I have shown in the salutations prefixed to others. I might be supposed to have done it as an insult to you, were it not that I trust that you will do the same in your reply to me. Why should I say much regarding your promise at Carthage, and my urgency to have it fulfilled? Let the manner in which we then acted to each other be forgotten with the past, lest it should obstruct future conference. Now, unless I am mistaken, there is, by the Lord's help, no obstacle in the way: we are both in Numidia, and located at no great distance from each other. I have heard it said that you are still willing to examine, in debate with me, the question which separates us from communion with each other. See how promptly all ambiguities may be cleared away: send me an answer to this letter if you please, and perhaps that may be enough, not only for us, but for those also who desire to hear us; or if it is not, let us exchange letters again and again until the discussion is exhausted. For what greater benefit could be secured to us by the comparative nearness of the towns which we inhabit? I have resolved to debate with you in no other way than by letters, in order both to prevent anything that is said from escaping from our memory, and to secure that others interested in the question, but unable to be present at a debate, may not forfeit the instruction. You are accustomed, not with any intention of falsehood, but by mistake, to reproach us with charges such as may suit your purpose, concerning past transactions, which we repudiate as untrue. Therefore, if you please, let us weigh the question in the light of the present, and let the past alone. You are doubtless aware that in the Jewish dispensation the sin of idolatry was committed by the people, and once the book of the prophet of God was burned by a defiant king;[1] the punishment of the sin of schism would not have been more severe than that with which these two were visited, had not the guilt of it been greater. You remember, of course, how the earth opening swallowed up alive the leaders of a schism, and fire from heaven breaking forth destroyed their accomplices.[2] Neither the making and worshipping of an idol, nor the burning of the Holy Book, was deemed worthy of such punishment.

2. You are wont to reproach us with a crime, not proved against us, indeed, though proved beyond question against some of your own party, — the crime, namely, of yielding up, through fear of persecution, the Scriptures[3] to be burned. Let me ask, therefore, why you have received back men whom you condemned for the crime of schism by the "unerring voice of your plenary Council" (I quote from the record), and replaced them in the same episcopal sees as they were in at the time when you passed sentence against them? I refer to Felicianus of Musti and Prætextatus of Assuri.[4] These were not, as you would have the ignorant believe, included among those to whom your Council appointed and intimated a certain time, after the lapse of which, if they had not returned to your communion, the sentence would become final; but they were included among the others whom you condemned, without delay, on the day on which you gave to some, as I have said, a respite. I can prove this, if you deny it. Your own Council is witness. We have also the proconsular Acts, in which you have not once, but often, affirmed this. Provide, therefore, some other line of defence if you can, lest, denying what I can prove, you cause loss of time. If, then, Felicianus and Prætextatus were innocent, why were they thus condemned? If they were guilty, why were they thus restored? If you prove them to have been innocent, can you object to our believing that it was possible for innocent men, falsely charged with being traditors, to be condemned by a much smaller number of your predecessors, if it is found possible for innocent men, falsely charged with being schismatics, to be condemned by three hundred and ten of their successors, whose decision is magniloquently described as proceeding from "the unerring voice of a plenary Council"? If, however, you prove them to have been justly condemned, what can you plead in defence of their being restored to office in the same episcopal sees, unless, magnifying the importance and benefit of peace, you maintain that even such things as these should be tolerated in order to preserve unbroken the bond of unity? Would to God that you would urge this plea, not with the lips only, but with the whole heart! You could not fail then to perceive that no calumnies whatever could justify the breaking up of the peace of Christ throughout the world, if it is lawful in Africa for men, once condemned for impious schism, to be restored to the same office which they held, rather than break up the peace of Donatus and his party.

---

[1] Jer. xxxvi. 23.
[2] Num. xvi. 31-35.

[3] *Dominici libri.*
[4] Felicianus and Prætextatus were two of the twelve bishops by whom Maximianus was ordained. They were condemned by the Donatist Council of Bagæ; but finding it impossible to eject them from their sees, the Donatists yielded after a time, and restored them to their office. See Letter LIII. p. 299.

3. Again, you are wont to reproach us with persecuting you by the help of the civil power. In regard to this, I do not draw an argument either from the demerit involved in the enormity of so great an impiety, nor from the Christian meekness moderating the severity of our measures. I take up this position : if this be a crime, why have you harshly persecuted the Maximianists by the help of judges appointed by those emperors whose spiritual birth by the gospel was due to our Church? Why have you driven them, by the din of controversy, the authority of edicts, and the violence of soldiery, from those buildings for worship which they possessed, and in which they were when they seceded from you? The wrongs endured by them in that struggle in every place are attested by the existing traces of events so recent. Documents declare the orders given. The deeds done are notorious throughout regions in which also the sacred memory of your leader Optatus is mentioned with honour.

4. Again, you are wont to say that we have not the baptism of Christ, and that beyond your communion it is not to be found. On this I would enter into a more lengthened argument; but in dealing with you this is not necessary, seeing that, along with Felicianus and Prætextatus, you admitted also the baptism of the Maximianists as valid. For all whom these bishops baptized so long as they were in communion with Maximianus, while you were doing your utmost in a protracted contest in the civil courts to expel these very men [Felicianus and Prætextatus] from their churches, as the Acts testify, —all those, I say, whom they baptized during that time, they now have in fellowship with them and with you ; and though these were baptized by them when excommunicated and in the guilt of schism, not only in cases of extremity through dangerous sickness, but also at the Easter services, in the large number of churches belonging to their cities, and in these important cities themselves, — in the case of none of them has the rite of baptism been repeated. And I wish you could prove that those whom Felicianus and Prætextatus had baptized, as it were, in vain, when they were excommunicated and in the guilt of schism, were satisfactorily baptized again by them when they were restored. For if the renewal of baptism was necessary for the people, the renewal of ordination was not less necessary for the bishops. For they had forfeited their episcopal office by leaving you, if they could not baptize beyond your communion ; because, if they had not forfeited their episcopal office by leaving you, they could still baptize. But if they had forfeited their episcopal office, they should have received ordination when they returned, so that what they had lost might be restored. Let not this, however, alarm you. As it is certain that they returned with the same standing as bishops with which they had gone forth from you, so is it also certain that they brought back with themselves to your communion, without any repetition of their baptism, all those whom they had baptized in the schism of Maximianus.

5. How can we weep enough when we see the baptism of the Maximianists acknowledged by you, and the baptism of the Church universal despised? Whether it was with or without hearing their defence, whether it was justly or unjustly, that you condemned Felicianus and Prætextatus, I do not ask ; but tell me what bishop of the Corinthian Church ever defended himself at your bar, or received sentence from you? or what bishop of the Galatians has done so, or of the Ephesians, Colossians, Philippians, Thessalonians, or of any of the other cities included in the promise : " All the kindreds of the nations shall worship before Thee "? [1] Yet you accept the baptism of the former, while that of the latter is despised ; whereas baptism belongs neither to the one nor to the other, but to Him of whom it was said : " This same is He that baptizeth with the Holy Ghost." [2] I do not, however, dwell on this in the meantime : take notice of the things which are beside us — behold what might make an impression even on the blind ! Where do we find the baptism which you acknowledge? With those, forsooth, whom you have condemned, but not with those who were never even tried at your bar ! — with those who were denounced by name, and cast forth from you for the crime of schism, but not with those who, unknown to you, and dwelling in remote lands, never were accused or condemned by you ! — with those who are but a fraction of the inhabitants of a fragment of Africa, but not with those from whose country the gospel first came to Africa ! Why should I add to your burden? Let me have an answer to these things. Look to the charge made by your Council against the Maximianists as guilty of impious schism : look to the persecutions by the civil courts to which you appealed against them : look to the fact that you restored some of them without re-ordination, and accepted their baptism as valid : and answer, if you can, whether it is in your power to hide, even from the ignorant, the question why you have separated yourselves from the whole world, in a schism much more heinous than that which you boast of having condemned in the Maximianists? May the peace of Christ triumph in your heart ! Then all shall be well. [3]

---

[1] Ps. xxii. 27.
[2] John i. 33.
[3] We conjecture this to be the meaning of the elliptical expression ΕΥΤΥΧΩΣ with which the letter ends.

LETTER LII.

This letter to his kinsman Severinus, exhorting him to withdraw from the Donatists, contains no new argument.

LETTER LIII.

(A.D. 400.)

TO GENEROSUS, OUR MOST LOVED AND HONOURABLE BROTHER, FORTUNATUS, ALYPIUS, AND AUGUSTIN SEND GREETING IN THE LORD.

CHAP. I. — 1. Since you were pleased to acquaint us with the letter sent to you by a Donatist presbyter, although, with the spirit of a true Catholic, you regarded it with contempt, nevertheless, to aid you in seeking his welfare if his folly be not incurable, we beg you to forward to him the following reply. He wrote that an angel had enjoined him to declare to you the episcopal succession[1] of the Christianity of your town; to you, forsooth, who hold the Christianity not of your own town only, nor of Africa only, but of the whole world, the Christianity which has been published, and is now published to all nations. This proves that they think it a small matter that they themselves are not ashamed of being cut off, and are taking no measures, while they may, to be engrafted anew; they are not content unless they do their utmost to cut others off, and bring them to share their own fate, as withered branches fit for the flames. Wherefore, even if you had yourself been visited by that angel whom he affirms to have appeared to him, — a statement which we regard as a cunning fiction; and if the angel had said to you the very words which he, on the warrant of the alleged command, repeated to you, — even in that case it would have been your duty to remember the words of the apostle: "Though we, or an angel from heaven, preach any other gospel unto you than that we have preached unto you, let him be accursed."[2] For to you it was proclaimed by the voice of the Lord Jesus Christ Himself, that His "gospel shall be preached unto all nations, and then shall the end come."[3] To you it has moreover been proclaimed by the writings of the prophets and of the apostles, that the promises were given to Abraham and to his seed, which is Christ,[4] when God said unto him: "In thy seed shall all nations of the earth be blessed." Having then such promises, if an angel from heaven were to say to thee, "Let go the Christianity of the whole earth, and cling to the faction of Donatus, the episcopal succession of which is set forth

in a letter of their bishop in your town," he ought to be accursed in your estimation; because he would be endeavouring to cut you off from the whole Church, and thrust you into a small party, and make you forfeit your interest in the promises of God.

2. For if the lineal succession of bishops is to be taken into account, with how much more certainty and benefit to the Church do we reckon back till we reach Peter himself, to whom, as bearing in a figure the whole Church,[5] the Lord said: "Upon this rock will I build my Church, and the gates of hell shall not prevail against it!"[6] The successor of Peter was Linus, and his successors in unbroken continuity were these: — Clement, Anacletus, Evaristus, Alexander, Sixtus, Telesphorus, Iginus, Anicetus, Pius, Soter, Eleutherius, Victor, Zephirinus, Calixtus, Urbanus, Pontianus, Antherus, Fabianus, Cornelius, Lucius, Stephanus, Xystus, Dionysius, Felix, Eutychianus, Gaius, Marcellinus, Marcellus, Eusebius, Miltiades, Sylvester, Marcus, Julius, Liberius, Damasus, and Siricius, whose successor is the present Bishop Anastasius. In this order of succession no Donatist bishop is found. But, reversing the natural course of things, the Donatists sent to Rome from Africa an ordained bishop, who, putting himself at the head of a few Africans in the great metropolis, gave some notoriety to the name of "mountain men," or Cutzupits, by which they were known.

3. Now, even although some traditor had in the course of these centuries, through inadvertence, obtained a place in that order of bishops, reaching from Peter himself to Anastasius, who now occupies that see, — this fact would do no harm to the Church and to Christians having no share in the guilt of another; for the Lord, providing against such a case, says, concerning officers in the Church who are wicked: "All whatsoever they bid you observe, that observe and do; but do not ye after their works: for they say, and do not."[7] Thus the stability of the hope of the faithful is secured, inasmuch as being fixed, not in man, but in the Lord, it never can be swept away by the raging of impious schism; whereas they themselves are swept away who read in the Holy Scriptures the names of churches to which the apostles wrote, and in which they have no bishop. For what could more clearly prove their perversity and their folly, than their saying to their clergy, when they read these letters, "Peace be with thee,"[8] at the very time that they are themselves disjoined from the peace of those churches to which the letters were originally written?

---

[1] "Ordo." The phrase is afterwards given (sec. 2) more fully, "ordo episcoporum sibi succedentium."
[2] Gal. i. 8.
[3] Matt. xxiv. 14.
[4] Gal. iii. 16

[5] *Totius Ecclesiæ figuram gerenti.*
[6] Matt. xvi. 18.
[7] Matt. xxiii. 3.
[8] Compare the allusion to the same custom in Letter XLIII. sec. 21, p. 155.

CHAP. II. — 4. Lest, however, he should congratulate himself too much on the succession of bishops in Constantina, your own city, read to him the records of proceedings before Munatius Felix, the resident Flamen [heathen priest], who was governor of your city in the consulship of Diocletian for the eighth time, and Maximian for the seventh, on the eleventh day before the calends of June. By these records it is proved that the bishop Paulus was a traditor; the fact being that Sylvanus was then one of his subdeacons, and, along with him, produced and surrendered certain things belonging to the Lord's house, which had been most carefully concealed, namely a box [1] and a lamp of silver, upon seeing which a certain Victor is reported to have said, "You would have been put to death if you had not found these." Your Donatist priest makes great account of this Sylvanus, this clearly convicted traditor, in the letter which he writes you, mentioning him as then ordained to the office of bishop by the Primate Secundus of Tigisis. Let them keep their proud tongues silent, let them admit the charges which may truly be brought against themselves, and not utter foolish calumnies against others. Read to him also, if he permits it, the ecclesiastical records of the proceedings of this same Secundus of Tigisis in the house of Urbanus Donatus, in which he remitted to God, as judge, men who confessed themselves to have been traditors — Donatus of Masculi, Marinus of Aquæ Tibilitanæ, Donatus of Calama, with whom as his colleagues, though they were confessed traditors, he ordained their bishop Sylvanus, of whose guilt in the same matter I have given the history above. Read to him also the proceedings before Zenophilus, a man of consular rank, in the course of which a certain deacon of theirs, Nundinarius, being angry with Sylvanus for having excommunicated him, brought all these facts into court, proving them incontestably by authentic documents, and the questioning of witnesses, and the reading of public records and many letters.

5. There are many other things which you might read in his hearing, if he is disposed not to dispute angrily, but to listen prudently, such as: the petition of the Donatists to Constantine, begging him to send from Gaul bishops who should settle this controversy which divided the African bishops; the Acts recording what took place in Rome, when the case was taken up and decided by the bishops whom he sent thither: also you might read in other letters how the Emperor aforesaid states that they had made a complaint to him against the decision of their peers — the bishops, namely, whom he had sent to Rome; how he appointed other bishops to try the case over again at Arles; how they appealed from that tribunal also to the Emperor again; how at last he himself investigated the matter; and how he most emphatically declares that they were vanquished by the innocence of Cæcilianus. Let him listen to these things if he be willing, and he will be silent and desist from plotting against the truth.

CHAP. III. — 6. We rely, however, not so much on these documents as on the Holy Scriptures, wherein a dominion extending to the ends of the earth among all nations is promised as the heritage of Christ, separated from which by their sinful schism they reproach us with the crimes which belong to the chaff in the Lord's threshing-floor, which must be permitted to remain mixed with the good grain until the end come, until the whole be winnowed in the final judgment. From which it is manifest that, whether these charges be true or false, they do not belong to the Lord's wheat,[2] which must grow until the end of the world throughout the whole field, i.e. the whole earth; as we know, not by the testimony of a false angel such as confirmed your correspondent in his error, but from the words of the Lord in the Gospel. And because these unhappy Donatists have brought the reproach of many false and empty accusations against Christians who were blameless, but who are throughout the world mingled with the chaff or tares, i.e. with Christians unworthy of the name, therefore God has, in righteous retribution, appointed that they should, by their universal Council, condemn as schismatics the Maximianists, because they had condemned Primianus, and baptized while not in communion with Primianus, and rebaptized those whom he had baptized, and then after a short interval should, under the coercion of Optatus the minion of Gildo, reinstate in the honours of their office two of these, the bishops Felicianus of Musti and Prætextatus of Assuri, and acknowledge the baptism of all whom they, while under sentence and excommunicated, had baptized. If, therefore, they are not defiled by communion with the men thus restored again to their office, — men whom with their own mouth they had condemned as wicked and impious, and whom they compared to those first heretics whom the earth swallowed up alive,[3] — let them at last awake and consider how great is their blindness and folly in pronouncing the whole world defiled by unknown crimes of Africans, and the heritage of Christ (which according to the promise has been shown unto all nations) destroyed through the sins of these Africans by the maintenance of communion with them; while they refuse to acknowledge themselves to be destroyed and defiled

---

[1] *Capitulata.*

[2] Matt. xiii. 30.
[3] Num. xvi. 31–33.

by communicating with men whose crimes they had both known and condemned.

7. Wherefore, since the Apostle Paul says in another place, that even Satan transforms himself into an angel of light, and that therefore it is not strange that his servants should assume the guise of ministers of righteousness: [1] if your correspondent did indeed see an angel teaching him error, and desiring to separate Christians from the Catholic unity, he has met with an angel of Satan transforming himself into an angel of light. If, however, he has lied to you, and has seen no such vision, he is himself a servant of Satan, assuming the guise of a minister of righteousness. And yet, if he be not incorrigibly obstinate and perverse, he may, by considering all the things now stated, be delivered both from misleading others, and from being himself misled. For, embracing the opportunity which you have given, we have met him without any rancour, remembering in regard to him the words of the apostle: "The servant of the Lord must not strive; but be gentle unto all men, apt to teach, patient; in meekness instructing those that oppose themselves; if God peradventure will give them repentance to the acknowledging of the truth; and that they may recover themselves out of the snare of the devil, who are taken captive by him at his will." [2] If, therefore, we have said anything severe, let him know that it arises not from the bitterness of controversy, but from love vehemently desiring his return to the right path. May you live safe in Christ, most beloved and honourable brother!

LETTER LIV.

Styled also Book I. of Replies to Questions of Januarius.

(A.D. 400.)

TO HIS BELOVED SON JANUARIUS, AUGUSTIN SENDS GREETING IN THE LORD.

CHAP. I. — 1. In regard to the questions which you have asked me, I would like to have known what your own answers would have been; for thus I might have made my reply in fewer words, and might most easily confirm or correct your opinions, by approving or amending the answers which you had given. This I would have greatly preferred. But desiring to answer you at once, I think it better to write a long letter than incur loss of time. I desire you therefore, in the first place, to hold fast this as the fundamental principle in the present discussion, that our Lord Jesus Christ has appointed to us a "light yoke" and an "easy burden," as He declares in the Gospel: [3] in accordance with which He has

bound His people under the new dispensation together in fellowship by sacraments, which are in number very few, in observance most easy, and in significance most excellent, as baptism solemnized in the name of the Trinity, the communion of His body and blood, and such other things as are prescribed in the canonical Scriptures, with the exception of those enactments which were a yoke of bondage to God's ancient people, suited to their state of heart and to the times of the prophets, and which are found in the five books of Moses. As to those other things which we hold on the authority, not of Scripture, but of tradition, and which are observed throughout the whole world, it may be understood that they are held as approved and instituted either by the apostles themselves, or by plenary Councils, whose authority in the Church is most useful, e.g. the annual commemoration, by special solemnities, of the Lord's passion, resurrection, and ascension, and of the descent of the Holy Spirit from heaven, and whatever else is in like manner observed by the whole Church wherever it has been established.

CHAP. II. — 2. There are other things, however, which are different in different places and countries: e.g., some fast on Saturday, others do not; some partake daily of the body and blood of Christ, others receive it on stated days: in some places no day passes without the sacrifice being offered; in others it is only on Saturday and the Lord's day, or it may be only on the Lord's day. In regard to these and all other variable observances which may be met anywhere, one is at liberty to comply with them or not as he chooses; and there is no better rule for the wise and serious Christian in this matter, than to conform to the practice which he finds prevailing in the Church to which it may be his lot to come. For such a custom, if it is clearly not contrary to the faith nor to sound morality, is to be held as a thing indifferent, and ought to be observed for the sake of fellowship with those among whom we live.

3. I think you may have heard me relate before, [4] what I will nevertheless now mention. When my mother followed me to Milan, she found the Church there not fasting on Saturday. She began to be troubled, and to hesitate as to what she should do; upon which I, though not taking a personal interest then in such things, applied on her behalf to Ambrose, of most blessed memory, for his advice. He answered that he could not teach me anything but what he himself practised, because if he knew any better rule, he would observe it himself. When I supposed that he intended, on the ground of his authority alone, and without supporting it by

---

[1] 2 Cor. xi. 13-15.
[2] 2 Tim. ii. 24-26.
[3] Matt. xi. 30.

[4] Compare Letter XXXVI. sec. 32, p. 270.

any argument, to recommend us to give up fasting on Saturday, he followed me, and said: "When I visit Rome, I fast on Saturday; when I am here, I do not fast. On the same principle, do you observe the custom prevailing in whatever Church you come to, if you desire neither to give offence by your conduct, nor to find cause of offence in another's." When I reported this to my mother, she accepted it gladly; and for myself, after frequently reconsidering his decision, I have always esteemed it as if I had received it by an oracle from heaven. For often have I perceived, with extreme sorrow, many disquietudes caused to weak brethren by the contentious pertinacity or superstitious vacillation of some who, in matters of this kind, which do not admit of final decision by the authority of Holy Scripture, or by the tradition of the universal Church, or by their manifest good influence on manners, raise questions, it may be, from some crotchet of their own, or from attachment to the custom followed in one's own country, or from preference for that which one has seen abroad, supposing that wisdom is increased in proportion to the distance to which men travel from home, and agitate these questions with such keenness, that they think all is wrong except what they do themselves.

CHAP. III. — 4. Some one may say, "The Eucharist ought not to be taken every day." You ask, "On what grounds?" He answers, "Because, in order that a man may approach worthily to so great a sacrament, he ought to choose those days upon which he lives in more special purity and self-restraint; for 'whosoever eateth and drinketh unworthily, eateth and drinketh judgment to himself.'"[1] Another answers, "Certainly; if the wound inflicted by sin and the violence of the soul's distemper be such that the use of these remedies must be put off for a time, every man in this case should be, by the authority of the bishop, forbidden to approach the altar, and appointed to do penance,[2] and should be afterwards restored to privileges by the same authority; for this would be partaking unworthily, if one should partake of it at a time when he ought to be doing penance; and it is not a matter to be left to one's own judgment to withdraw himself from the communion of the Church, or restore himself, as he pleases. If, however, his sins are not so great as to bring him justly under sentence of excommunication, he ought not to withdraw himself from the daily use of the Lord's body for the healing of his soul." Perhaps a third party interposes with a more just decision of the question, reminding them that the principal thing is to remain united in the peace of Christ, and that each should be free to do what,

according to his belief, he conscientiously regards as his duty. For neither of them lightly esteems the body and blood of the Lord; on the contrary, both are contending who shall most highly honour the sacrament fraught with blessing. There was no controversy between those two mentioned in the Gospel, Zacchæus and the Centurion; nor did either of them think himself better than the other, though, whereas the former received the Lord joyfully into his house,[3] the latter said, "I am not worthy that Thou shouldest come under my roof,"[4]—both honouring the Saviour, though in ways diverse and, as it were, mutually opposed; both miserable through sin, and both obtaining the mercy they required. We may further borrow an illustration here, from the fact that the manna given to the ancient people of God tasted in each man's mouth as he desired that it might.[5] It is the same with this world-subduing sacrament in the heart of each Christian. For he that dares not take it every day, and he who dares not omit it any day, are both alike moved by a desire to do it honour. That sacred food will not submit to be despised, as the manna could not be loathed with impunity. Hence the apostle says that it was unworthily partaken of by those who did not distinguish between this and all other meats, by yielding to it the special veneration which was due; for to the words quoted already, "eateth and drinketh judgment to himself," he has added these, "not discerning the Lord's body;" and this is apparent from the whole of that passage in the first Epistle to the Corinthians, if it be carefully studied.

CHAP. IV. — 5. Suppose some foreigner visit a place in which during Lent it is customary to abstain from the use of the bath, and to continue fasting on Thursday. "I will not fast to-day," he says. The reason being asked, he says, "Such is not the custom in my own country." Is not he, by such conduct, attempting to assert the superiority of his custom over theirs? For he cannot quote a decisive passage on the subject from the Book of God; nor can he prove his opinion to be right by the unanimous voice of the universal Church, wherever spread abroad; nor can he demonstrate that they act contrary to the faith, and he according to it, or that they are doing what is prejudicial to sound morality, and he is defending its interests. Those men injure their own tranquillity and peace by quarrelling on an unnecessary question. I would rather recommend that, in matters of this kind, each

---

[1] 1 Cor. xi. 29.
[2] Agere pænitentiam.

[3] Luke xix. 6.
[4] Matt. viii. 8.
[5] In his Retractations, b. ii. ch. xx., Augustin remarks on this statement: "I do not recollect any passage by which it could be substantiated, except from the book of Wisdom (ch. xvi. 21), which the Jews do not admit to be of canonical authority." He says, in the same place, that this peculiarity of the manna must have been enjoyed only by the pious in Israel, not by the murmurers who said, "Our soul loatheth this light bread" (Num. xxi. 5).

man should, when sojourning in a country in which he finds a custom different from his own, consent to do as others do. If, on the other hand, a Christian, when travelling abroad in some region where the people of God are more numerous, and more easily assembled together, and more zealous in religion, has seen, *e.g.*, the sacrifice twice offered, both morning and evening, on the Thursday of the last week in Lent, and therefore, on his coming back to his own country, where it is offered only at the close of the day, protests against this as wrong and unlawful, because he has himself seen another custom in another land, this would show a childish weakness of judgment against which we should guard ourselves, and which we must bear with in others, but correct in all who are under our influence.

CHAP. V. — 6. Observe now to which of these three classes the first question in your letter is to be referred. You ask, "What ought to be done on the Thursday of the last week of Lent? Ought we to offer the sacrifice in the morning, and again after supper, on account of the words in the Gospel, 'Likewise also . . . after supper'?[1] Or ought we to fast and offer the sacrifice only after supper? Or ought we to fast until the offering has been made, and then take supper as we are accustomed to do?" I answer, therefore, that if the authority of Scripture has decided which of these methods is right, there is no room for doubting that we should do according to that which is written; and our discussion must be occupied with a question, not of duty, but of interpretation as to the meaning of the divine institution. In like manner, if the universal Church follows any one of these methods, there is no room for doubt as to our duty; for it would be the height of arrogant madness to discuss whether or not we should comply with it. But the question which you propose is not decided either by Scripture or by universal practice. It must therefore be referred to the third class — as pertaining, namely, to things which are different in different places and countries. Let every man, therefore, conform himself to the usage prevailing in the Church to which he may come. For none of these methods is contrary to the Christian faith or the interests of morality, as favoured by the adoption of one custom more than the other. If this were the case, that either the faith or sound morality were at stake, it would be necessary either to change what was done amiss, or to appoint the doing of what had been neglected. But mere change of custom, even though it may be of advantage in some respects, unsettles men by reason of the novelty: therefore, if it brings no

advantage, it does much harm by unprofitably disturbing the Church.

7. Let me add, that it would be a mistake to suppose that the custom prevalent in many places, of offering the sacrifice on that day after partaking of food, is to be traced to the words, "Likewise after supper," etc. For the Lord might give the name of supper to what they had received, in already partaking of His body, so that it was after this that they partook of the cup: as the apostle says in another place, "When ye come together into one place, this is not to *eat*[2] the Lord's Supper,"[3] giving to the receiving of the Eucharist to that extent (*i.e.* the eating of the bread) the name of the Lord's Supper.

CHAP. VI. — As to the question whether upon that day it is right to partake of food before either offering or partaking of the Eucharist, these words in the Gospel might go far to decide our minds, "As they were eating, Jesus took bread and blessed it;" taken in connection with the words in the preceding context, "When the even was come, He sat down with the twelve: and as they did eat, He said, Verily I say unto you, that one of you shall betray Me." For it was after that that He instituted the sacrament; and it is clear that when the disciples first received the body and blood of the Lord, they had not been fasting.

8. Must we therefore censure the universal Church because the sacrament is everywhere partaken of by persons fasting? Nay, verily, for from that time it pleased the Holy Spirit to appoint, for the honour of so great a sacrament, that the body of the Lord should take the precedence of all other food entering the mouth of a Christian; and it is for this reason that the custom referred to is universally observed. For the fact that the Lord instituted the sacrament after other food had been partaken of, does not prove that brethren should come together to partake of that sacrament after having dined or supped, or imitate those whom the apostle reproved and corrected for not distinguishing between the Lord's Supper and an ordinary meal. The Saviour, indeed, in order to commend the depth of that mystery more affectingly to His disciples, was pleased to impress it on their hearts and memories by making its institution His last act before going from them to His Passion. And therefore He did not prescribe the order in which it was to be observed, reserving this to be done by the apostles, through whom He intended to arrange all things pertaining to the Churches. Had He appointed that the sacrament should be always partaken of after other food, I believe that no one would have departed from that practice. But when

---

[1] Luke xxii. 20.

[2] *Manducare.*
[3] 1 Cor. xi. 20.

the apostle, speaking of this sacrament, says, "Wherefore, my brethren, when ye come together to eat, tarry one for another: and if any man hunger, let him eat at home; that ye come not together unto condemnation," he immediately adds, "and the rest will I set in order when I come." [1] Whence we are given to understand that, since it was too much for him to prescribe completely in an epistle the method observed by the universal Church throughout the world, it was one of the things set in order by him in person, for we find its observance uniform amid all the variety of other customs.

CHAP. VII. — 9. There are, indeed, some to whom it has seemed right (and their view is not unreasonable), that it is lawful for the body and blood of the Lord to be offered and received after other food has been partaken of, on one fixed day of the year, the day on which the Lord instituted the Supper, in order to give special solemnity to the service on that anniversary. I think that, in this case, it would be more seemly to have it celebrated at such an hour as would leave it in the power of any who have fasted to attend the service before [2] the repast which is customary at the ninth hour. Wherefore we neither compel nor do we dare to forbid any one to break his fast before the Lord's Supper on that day. I believe, however, that the real ground upon which this custom rests is, that many, nay, almost all, are accustomed in most places to use the bath on that day. And because some continue to fast, it is offered in the morning, for those who take food, because they cannot bear fasting and the use of the bath at the same time; and in the evening, for those who have fasted all day.

10. If you ask me whence originated the custom of using the bath on that day, nothing occurs to me, when I think of it, as more likely than that it was to avoid the offence to decency which must have been given at the baptismal font, if the bodies of those to whom that rite was to be administered were not washed on some preceding day from the uncleanness consequent upon their strict abstinence from ablutions during Lent; and that this particular day was chosen for the purpose because of its being the anniversary of the institution of the Supper. And this being granted to those who were about to receive baptism, many others desired to join them in the luxury of a bath, and in relaxation of their fast.

Having discussed these questions to the best of my ability, I exhort you to observe, in so far as you may be able, what I have laid down, as becomes a wise and peace-loving son of the Church. The remainder of your questions I purpose, if the Lord will, to answer at another time.

LETTER LV.

Or Book II. of Replies to Questions of Januarius.

(A.D. 400.)

CHAP. I. — 1. Having read the letter in which you have put me in mind of my obligation to give answers to the remainder of those questions which you submitted to me a long time ago, I cannot bear to defer any longer the gratification of that desire for instruction which it gives me so much pleasure and comfort to see in you; and although encompassed by an accumulation of engagements, I have given the first place to the work of supplying you with the answers desired. I will make no further comment on the contents of your letter, lest my doing so should prevent me from paying at length what I owe.

2. You ask, "Wherefore does the anniversary on which we celebrate the Passion of the Lord not fall, like the day which tradition has handed down as the day of His birth, on the same day every year?" and you add, "If the reason of this is connected with the week and the month, what have we to do with the day of the week or the state of the moon in this solemnity?" The first thing which you must know and remember here is, that the observance of the Lord's natal day is not sacramental, but only commemorative of His birth, and that therefore no more was in this case necessary, than that the return of the day on which the event took place should be marked by an annual religious festival. The celebration of an event becomes sacramental in its nature, only when the commemoration of the event is so ordered that it is understood to be significant of something which is to be received with reverence as sacred. [3] Therefore we observe Easter [4] in such a manner as not only to recall the facts of the death and resurrection of Christ to remembrance, but also to find a place for all the other things which, in connection with these events, give evidence as to the import of the sacrament. For since, as the apostle wrote, "He was delivered for our offences, and was raised again for our justification," [5] a certain transition from death to life has been consecrated in that Passion and Resurrection of the Lord. For the word Pascha itself is not, as is commonly thought, a Greek word: those who are acquainted with both languages affirm it to be a Hebrew word. It is not derived, therefore, from the Passion, because of the Greek word πάσχειν, signifying to suffer, but it takes its name from the transition, of which I have spoken, from death to life; the meaning of the Hebrew word Pascha being, as those who are acquainted with

---

[1] 1 Cor. xi. 33, 34.
[2] "Ante" is the reading of seven MSS. The Benedictine edition gives "post" in the text. We think the former gives better sense.
[3] *Sancte accipiendum*
[4] *Pascha.*
[5] Rom. iv. 25.

it assure us,[1] a passing over or transition. To this the Lord Himself designed to allude, when He said, " He that believeth in Me is passed from death to life."[2] And the same evangelist who records that saying is to be understood as desiring to give emphatic testimony to this, when, speaking of the Lord as about to celebrate with His disciples the passover, at which He instituted the sacramental supper, he says, " When Jesus knew that His hour was come, that He should depart[3] from this world unto the Father."[4] This passing over from this mortal life to the other, the immortal life, that is, from death to life, is set forth in the Passion and Resurrection of the Lord.

Chap. II. — 3. This passing from death to life is meanwhile wrought in us by faith, which we have for the pardon of our sins and the hope of eternal life, when we love God and our neighbour ; " for faith worketh by love,"[5] and " the just shall live by his faith ; "[6] " and hope that is seen is not hope : for what a man seeth, why doth he yet hope for? But if we hope for that we see not, then do we with patience wait for it."[7] According to this faith and hope and love, by which we have begun to be " under grace," we are already dead together with Christ, and buried together with Him by baptism into death ;[8] as the apostle hath said, " Our old man is crucified with Him ; "[9] and we have risen with Him, for " He hath raised us up together, and made us sit with Him in heavenly places."[10] Whence also he gives this exhortation : " If ye then be risen with Christ, seek those things which are above, where Christ sitteth on the right hand of God. Set your affection on things above, not on things on the earth."[11] In the next words, " For ye are dead, and your life is hid with Christ in God ; when Christ, who is our life, shall appear, then shall ye also appear with Him in glory,"[12] he plainly gives us to understand that our passing in this present time from death to life by faith is accomplished in the hope of that future final resurrection and glory, when " this corruptible," that is, this flesh in which we now groan, " shall put on incorruption, and this mortal shall put on immortality."[13] For now, indeed, we have by faith " the first-fruits of the Spirit ; " but still we " groan within ourselves, waiting for the adoption,

to wit, the redemption of the body : for we are saved by hope." While we are in this hope, " the body indeed is dead because of sin, but the spirit is life because of righteousness." Now mark what follows : " But if the Spirit of Him that raised up Jesus from the dead dwell in you, He that raised up Christ from the dead shall also quicken your mortal bodies by His Spirit that dwelleth in you."[14] The whole Church, therefore, while here in the conditions of pilgrimage and mortality, expects that to be accomplished in her at the end of the world which has been shown first in the body of our Lord Jesus Christ, who is " the first-begotten from the dead," seeing that the body of which He is the Head is none other than the Church.[15]

Chap. III. — 4. Some, indeed, studying the words so frequently used by the apostle, about our being dead with Christ and raised together with Him, and misunderstanding the sense in which they are used, have thought that the resurrection is already past, and that no other is to be hoped for at the end of time : " Of whom," he says, " are Hymenæus and Philetus ; who concerning the truth have erred, saying that the resurrection is past already ; and overthrow the faith of some."[16] The same apostle who thus reproves and testifies against them, teaches nevertheless that we are risen with Christ. How is the apparent contradiction to be removed, unless he means that this is accomplished in us by faith and hope and love, according to the first-fruits of the Spirit? But because " hope which is seen is not hope," and therefore " if we hope for that we see not, we do with patience wait for it," it is beyond question that there remains, as still future, the redemption of the body, in longing for which we " groan within ourselves." Hence also that saying, " Rejoicing in hope, patient in tribulation."[17]

5. This renewal, therefore, of our life is a kind of transition from death to life' which is made first by faith, so that we rejoice in hope and are patient in tribulation, while still " our outward man perisheth, but the inward man is renewed day by day."[18] It is because of this beginning of a new life, because of the new man which we are commanded to put on, putting off the old man,[19] " purging out the old leaven, that we may be a new lump, because Christ our passover is sacrificed for us ; "[20] it is, I say, because of this newness of life in us, that the first of the months of the year has been appointed as the season of this solemnity. This very name is given to

---

[1] Had Augustin not been obliged to take his Hebrew at second hand, he might have seen that the word פֶּסַח does not bear out his interpretation. Ex. xii. 13, 27.
[2] John v. 24.
[3] *Transiret.*
[4] John xiii. 1.
[5] Gal. v. 6.
[6] Hab. ii. 4.
[7] Rom. viii. 24, 25.
[8] Col. ii. 12 and Rom. vi. 4
[9] Rom. vi. 6.
[10] Eph. ii. 6.
[11] Col. iii. 1, 2.
[12] Col. iii. 3, 4.
[13] 1 Cor. xv. 53.

[14] Rom. viii. 23, 24, 10, 11.
[15] Col. i. 18.
[16] 2 Tim. ii. 17.
[17] Rom. xii. 12.
[18] 2 Cor. iv. 16.
[19] Col. iii. 9, 10.
[20] 1 Cor. v. 7.

it, the month Abib, or beginning of months.[1] Again, the resurrection of the Lord was upon the third day, because with it the third epoch of the world began. The first Epoch was before the Law, the second under the Law, the third under Grace, in which there is now the manifestation of the mystery,[2] which was formerly hidden under dark prophetic sayings. This is accordingly signified also in the part of the month appointed for the celebration; for, since the number seven is usually employed in Scripture as a mystical number, indicating perfection of some kind, the day of the celebration of Easter is within the third week of the month, namely, between the fourteenth and the twenty-first day.

CHAP. IV. — 6. There is in this another mystery,[2] and you are not to be distressed if perhaps it be not so readily perceived by you, because of your being less versed in such studies; nor are you to think me any better than you, because I learned these things in early years: for the Lord saith, "Let him that glorieth glory in this, that he understandeth and knoweth Me, that I am the Lord."[3] Some men who give attention to such studies, have investigated many things concerning the numbers and motions of the heavenly bodies. And those who have done this most ably have found that the waxing and waning of the moon are due to the turning of its globe, and not to any such actual addition to or diminution of its substance as is supposed by the foolish Manichæans, who say that as a ship is filled, so the moon is filled with a fugitive portion of the Divine Being, which they, with impious heart and lips, do not hesitate to believe and to declare to have become mingled with the rulers of darkness, and contaminated with their pollution. And they account for the waxing of the moon by saying that it takes place when that lost portion of the Deity, being purified from contamination by great labours, escaping from the whole world,[4] and from all foul abominations,[5] is restored to the Deity, who mourns till it returns; that by this the moon is filled up till the middle of the month, and that in the latter half of the month this is poured back into the sun as into another ship. Amid these execrable blasphemies, they have never succeeded in devising any way of explaining why the moon in the beginning or end of its brightness shines with its light in the shape of a horn, or why it begins at the middle of the month to wane, and does not go on full until it pour back its increase into the sun.

7. Those, however, to whom I refer have inquired into these things with trustworthy calculations, so that they can not only state the reason of eclipses, both solar and lunar, but also predict their occurrence long before they take place, and are able to determine by mathematical computation the precise intervals at which these must happen, and to state the results in treatises, by reading and understanding which any others may foretell as well as they the coming of these eclipses, and find their prediction verified by the event. Such men, — and they deserve censure, as Holy Scripture teaches, because "though they had wisdom enough to measure the periods of this world, they did not much more easily come," as by humble piety they might have done, "to the knowledge of its Lord,"[6] — such men, I say, have inferred from the horns of the moon, which both in waxing and in waning are turned from the sun, either that the moon is illuminated by the sun, and that the farther it recedes from the sun the more fully does it lie exposed to its rays on the side which is visible from the earth; but that the more it approaches the sun, after the middle of the month, on the other half of its orbit, it becomes more fully illuminated on the upper part, and less and less open to receive the sun's rays on the side which is turned to the earth, and seems to us accordingly to decrease: or, that if the moon has light in itself, it has this light in the hemisphere on one side only, which side it gradually turns more to the earth as it recedes from the sun, until it is fully displayed, thereby exhibiting an apparent increase, not by the addition of what was deficient, but by disclosing what was already there; and that, in like manner, going towards the sun, the moon again gradually turns from our view that which had been disclosed, and so appears to decrease. Whichever of these two theories be correct, this at least is plain, and is easily discovered by any careful observer, that the moon does not to our eyes increase except when it is receding from the sun, nor decrease except when returning towards the sun.

CHAP. V. — 8. Now mark what is said in Proverbs: "The wise man is fixed like the sun; but the fool changes like the moon."[7] And who is the wise that has no changes, but that Sun of Righteousness of whom it is said, "The Sun of righteousness has risen upon me," and of which the wicked shall say, when mourning in the day of judgment that it has not risen upon them, "The light of righteousness hath not shone upon us, and the sun hath not risen upon us"?[8] For that sun which is visible to the eye of sense, God makes to rise upon the evil and the good alike, as He sendeth rain upon the just and the unjust;[9] but apt similitudes are often

[1] Ex. xxiii. 15.
[2] Sacramentum.
[3] Jer. ix. 24.
[4] Mundus.
[5] Cloacis.
[6] Wisd. xiii. 9.
[7] Ecclus. xxvii. 12.
[8] Wisd. v. 6.
[9] Matt. v. 45.

borrowed from things visible to explain things invisible. Again, who is the "fool" who "changes like the moon," if not Adam, in whom all have sinned? For the soul of man, receding from the Sun of righteousness, that is to say, from the internal contemplation of unchangeable truth, turns all its strength towards external things, and becomes more and more darkened in its deeper and nobler powers; but when the soul begins to return to that unchangeable wisdom, the more it draws near to it with pious desire, the more does the outward man perish, but the inward man is renewed day by day, and all that light of the soul which was inclining to things that are beneath is turned to the things that are above, and is thus withdrawn from the things of earth; so that it dies more and more to this world, and its life is hid with Christ in God.

9. It is therefore for the worse that the soul is changed when it moves in the direction of external things, and throws aside that which pertains to the inner life; and to the earth, i.e. to those who mind earthly things, the soul looks better in such a case, for by them the wicked is commended for his heart's desire, and the unrighteous is blessed.[1] But it is for the better that the soul is changed, when it gradually turns away its aims and ambition from earthly things, which appear important in this world, and directs them to things nobler and unseen; and to the earth, i.e. to men who mind earthly things, the soul in such a case seems worse. Hence those wicked men who at last shall in vain repent of their sins, will say this among other things: "These are the men whom once we derided and reproached; we in our folly esteemed their way of life to be madness."[2] Now the Holy Spirit, drawing a comparison from things visible to things invisible, from things corporeal to spiritual mysteries, has been pleased to appoint that the feast symbolical of the passing from the old life to the new, which is signified by the name Pascha, should be observed between the 14th and 21st days of the month,—after the 14th, in order that a twofold illustration of spiritual realities might be gained, both with respect to the third epoch of the world, which is the reason of its occurrence in the third week, as I have already said, and with respect to the turning of the soul from external to internal things,—a change corresponding to the change in the moon when on the wane; not later than the 21st, because of the number 7 itself, which is often used to represent the notion of the universe, and is also applied to the Church on the ground of her likeness to the universe.

CHAP. VI.—10. For this reason the Apostle John writes in the Apocalypse to *seven* churches.

The Church, moreover, while it remains under the conditions of our mortal life in the flesh, is, on account of her liability to change, spoken of in Scripture by the name of the moon; e.g., "They have made ready their arrows in the quiver, that they may, while the moon is obscured, wound those who are upright in heart."[3] For before that comes to pass of which the apostle says, "When Christ, who is our life, shall appear, then shall ye also appear with Him in glory,"[4] the Church seems in the time of her pilgrimage obscured, groaning under many iniquities; and at such a time, the snares of those who deceive and lead astray are to be feared, and these are intended by the word "arrows" in this passage. Again, we have another instance in Psalm lxxxix.,[5] where, because of the faithful witnesses which she everywhere brings forth on the side of truth, the Church is called "the moon, a faithful witness in heaven." And when the Psalmist sang of the Lord's kingdom, he said, "In His days shall be righteousness and abundance of peace, until the moon be destroyed;"[6] i.e. abundance of peace shall increase so greatly, until He shall at length take away all the changeableness incidental to this mortal condition. Then shall death, the last enemy, be destroyed; and whatever obstacle to the perfection of our peace is due to the infirmity of our flesh shall be utterly consumed when this corruptible shall have put on incorruption, and this mortal shall have put on immortality.[7] We have another instance in this, that the walls of the town named Jericho — which in the Hebrew tongue is said to signify "moon" — fell when they had been compassed for the seventh time by the ark of the covenant borne round the city. For what else is conveyed by the promise of the coming of the heavenly kingdom, which was symbolized in the carrying of the ark round Jericho, than that all the strongholds of this mortal life, i.e. every hope pertaining to this world which resists the hope of the world to come, must be destroyed, with the soul's free consent, by the sevenfold gift of the Holy Spirit. Therefore it was, that when the ark was going round, those walls fell, not by violent assault, but of themselves. There are, besides these, other passages in Scripture which, speaking of the moon, impress upon us under that figure the condition of the Church while here, amid cares and labours, she is a pilgrim under the lot of mortality, and far from that Jerusalem of which the holy angels are the citizens.

11. These foolish men who refuse to be changed for the better have no reason, however, to imagine

---

[1] Ps. x. 3, as rendered by Aug.
[2] Wisd. v. 3, 4.

[3] Ps. xi. 3: in the LXX. version, τοῦ κατατοξεῦσαι ἐν σκοτομήνῃ τοὺς εὐθεῖς τῇ καρδίᾳ.
[4] Col. iii. 4.
[5] Ver. 39.
[6] Ps. lxxii. 7, Septuagint version.
[7] 1 Cor. xv. 26, 53, 54.

that worship is due to those heavenly luminaries because a similitude is occasionally borrowed from them for the representation of divine mysteries ; for such are borrowed from every created thing. Nor is there any reason for our incurring the sentence of condemnation which is pronounced by the apostle on some who worshipped and served the creature more than the Creator, who is blessed for ever.[1] We do not adore sheep or cattle, although Christ is called both a Lamb,[2] and by the prophet a young bullock ;[3] nor any beast of prey, though He is called the Lion of the tribe of Judah ;[4] nor a stone, although Christ is called a Rock ;[5] nor Mount Zion, though in it there was a type of the Church.[6] And, in like manner, we do not adore the sun or the moon, although, in order to convey instruction in holy mysteries, figures of sacred things are borrowed from these celestial works of the Creator, as they are also from many of the things which He hath made on earth.

CHAP. VII. — 12. We are therefore bound to denounce with abhorrence and contempt the ravings of the astrologers, who, when we find fault with the empty inventions by which they cast other men down into the delusions whereinto they themselves have fallen, imagine that they answer well when they say, " Why, then, do you regulate the time of the observance of Easter by calculation of the positions of the sun and moon ? " — as if that with which we find fault was the arrangements of the heavenly bodies, or the succession of the seasons, which are appointed by God in His infinite power and goodness, and not their perversity in abusing, for the support of the most absurd opinions, those things which God has ordered in perfect wisdom. If the astrologer may on this ground forbid us from drawing comparisons from the heavenly bodies for the mystical representation of sacramental realities, then the augurs may with equal reason prevent the use of these words of Scripture, " Be harmless as doves ; " and the snake-charmers may forbid that other exhortation, " Be wise as serpents ; "[7] while the play-actors may interfere with our mentioning the harp in the book of Psalms. Let them therefore say, if they please, that, because similitudes for the exhibition of the mysteries of God's word are taken from the things which I have named, we are chargeable either with consulting the omens given by the flight of birds, or with concocting the poisons of the charmer, or with taking pleasure in the excesses of the theatre, — a statement which would be the climax of absurdity.

13. We do not forecast the issues of our enterprises by studying the sun and moon, and the times of the year or of the month, lest in the most trying emergencies of life, we, being dashed against the rocks of a wretched bondage, shall make shipwreck of our freedom of will ; but with the most pious devoutness of spirit, we accept similitudes adapted to the illustration of holy things, which these heavenly bodies furnish, just as from all other works of creation, the winds, the sea, the land, birds, fishes, cattle, trees, men, etc., we borrow in our discourses manifold figures ; and in the celebration of sacraments, the very few things which the comparative liberty of the Christian dispensation has prescribed, such as water, bread, wine, and oil. Under the bondage, however, of the ancient dispensation many rites were prescribed, which are made known to us only for our instruction as to their meaning. We do not now observe years, and months, and seasons, lest the words of the apostle apply to us, " I am afraid of you, lest I have bestowed upon you labour in vain." [8] For he blames those who say, " ₁ will not set out to-day, because it is an unlucky day, or because the moon is so and so ; " or, " I will go to-day, that things may prosper with me, because the position of the stars is this or that ; I will do no business this month, because a particular star rules it ; " or, " I will do business, because another star has succeeded in its place ; I will not plant a vineyard this year, because it is leap year." No man of ordinary sense would, however, suppose that those men deserve reproof for studying the seasons, who say, e.g., " I will not set out to-day, because a storm has begun ; " or, " I will not put to sea, because the winter is not yet past ; " or, " It is time to sow my seed, for the earth has been saturated with the showers of autumn ; " and so on, in regard to any other natural effects of the motion and moisture of the atmosphere which have been observed in connection with that consummately ordered revolution of the heavenly bodies concerning which it was said when they were made, " Let them be for signs, and for seasons, and for days, and for years." [9] And in like manner, whensoever illustrative symbols are borrowed, for the declaration of spiritual mysteries, from created things, not only from the heaven and its orbs, but also from meaner creatures, this is done to give to the doctrine of salvation an eloquence adapted to raise the affections of those who receive it from things seen, corporeal and temporal, to things unseen, spiritual and eternal.

CHAP. VIII. — 14. None of us gives any consideration to the circumstance that, at the time at which we observe Easter, the sun is in the Ram,

---

[1] Rom. i. 25.
[2] John i. 29.
[3] Ezek. xliii. 19.
[4] Rev. v. 5.
[5] 1 Cor. x. 4.
[6] 1 Pet. ii. 4.
[7] Matt x. 16.

[8] Gal. iv. 11.
[9] Gen. i 14.

as they call a certain region of the heavenly bodies, in which the sun is, in fact, found at the beginning of the months; but whether they choose to call that part of the heavens the Ram or anything else, we have learned this from the Sacred Scriptures, that God made all the heavenly bodies, and appointed their places as it pleased Him; and whatever the parts may be into which astronomers divide the regions set apart and ordained for the different constellations, and whatever the names by which they distinguish them, the place occupied by the sun in the first month is that in which the celebration of this sacrament behoved to find that luminary, because of the illustration of a holy mystery in the renovation of life, of which I have already spoken sufficiently. If, however, the name of Ram could be given to that portion of the heavenly bodies because of some correspondence between their form and the name, the word of God would not hesitate to borrow from anything of this kind an illustration of a holy mystery, as it has done not only from other celestial bodies, but also from terrestrial things, *e.g.* from Orion and the Pleiades, Mount Zion, Mount Sinai, and the rivers of which the names are given, Gihon, Pison, Tigris, Euphrates, and particularly from the river Jordan, which is so often named in the sacred mysteries.

15. But who can fail to perceive how great is the difference between useful observations of the heavenly bodies in connection with the weather, such as farmers or sailors make; or in order to mark the part of the world in which they are, and the course which they should follow, such as are made by pilots of ships or men going through the trackless sandy deserts of southern Africa; or in order to present some useful doctrine under a figure borrowed from some facts concerning heavenly bodies;—and the vain hallucinations of men who observe the heavens not to know the weather, or their course, or to make scientific calculations, or to find illustrations of spiritual things, but merely to pry into the future and learn now what fate has decreed?

Chap. IX. — 16. Let us now direct our minds to observe the reason why, in the celebration of Easter, care is taken to appoint the day so that Saturday precedes it: for this is peculiar to the Christian religion. The Jews keep the Passover from the 14th to the 21st of the first month, on whatever day that week begins. But since at the Passover at which the Lord suffered, it was the case that the Jewish Sabbath came in between His death and His resurrection, our fathers have judged it right to add this specialty to their celebration of Easter, both that our feast might be distinguished from the Jewish Passover, and that succeeding generations might retain in their annual commemoration of His Passion that

which we must believe to have been done for some good reason, by Him who is before the times, by whom also the times have been made, and who came in the fulness of the times, and who, when He said, Mine hour is not yet come, had the power of laying down His life and taking it again, and was therefore waiting for an hour not fixed by blind fate, but suitable to the holy mystery which He had resolved to commend to our observation.

17. That which we here hold in faith and hope, and to which by love we labour to come, is, as I have said above, a certain holy and perpetual rest from the whole burden of every kind of care; and from this life unto that rest we make a transition which our Lord Jesus Christ condescended to exemplify and consecrate in His Passion. This rest, however, is not a slothful inaction, but a certain ineffable tranquillity caused by work in which there is no painful effort. For the repose on which one enters at the end of the toils of this life is of such a nature as consists with lively joy in the active exercises of the better life. Forasmuch, however, as this activity is exercised in praising God without bodily toil or mental anxiety, the transition to that activity is not made through a repose which is to be followed by labour, *i.e.* a repose which, at the point where activity begins, ceases to be repose: for in these exercises there is no return to toil and care; but that which constitutes rest —namely, exemption from weariness in work and from uncertainty in thought—is always found in them. Now, since through rest we get back to that original life which the soul lost by sin, the emblem of this rest is the seventh day of the week. But that original life itself which is restored to those who return from their wanderings, and receive in token of welcome the robe which they had at first,[1] is represented by the first day of the week, which we call the Lord's day. If, in reading Genesis, you search the record of the seven days, you will find that there was no evening of the seventh day, which signified that the rest of which it was a type was eternal. The life originally bestowed was not eternal, because man sinned; but the final rest, of which the seventh day was an emblem, is eternal, and hence the eighth day also will have eternal blessedness, because that rest, being eternal, is taken up by the eighth day, not destoyed by it; for if it were thus destroyed, it would not be eternal. Accordingly the eighth day, which is the first day of the week, represents to us that original life, not taken away, but made eternal.

Chap. X. — 18. Nevertheless the seventh day was appointed to the Jewish nation as a day to be observed by rest of the body, that it might

---

[1] *Primam stolam.*

be a type of sanctification to which men attain through rest in the Holy Spirit. We do not read of sanctification in the history given in Genesis of all the earlier days : of the Sabbath alone it is said that "God blessed the seventh day, and sanctified it."[1] Now the souls of men, whether good or bad, love rest, but how to attain to that which they love is to the greater part unknown : and that which bodies seek for their weight, is precisely what souls seek for their love, namely, a resting-place. For as, according to its specific gravity, a body descends or rises until it reaches a place where it can rest, — oil, for example, falling if poured into the air, but rising if poured into water, — so the soul of man struggles towards the things which it loves, in order that, by reaching them, it may rest. There are indeed many things which please the soul through the body, but its rest in these is not eternal, nor even long continued ; and therefore they rather debase the soul and weigh it down, so as to be a drag upon that pure imponderability by which it tends towards higher things. When the soul finds pleasure from itself, it is not yet seeking delight in that which is unchangeable ; and therefore it is still proud, because it is giving to itself the highest place, whereas God is higher. In such sin the soul is not left unpunished, for "God resisteth the proud, but giveth grace to the humble."[2] When, however, the soul delights in God, there it finds the true, sure, and eternal rest, which in all other objects was sought in vain. Therefore the admonition is given in the book of Psalms, "Delight thyself in the Lord, and He shall give thee the desires of thine heart."[3]

19. Because, therefore, "the love of God[4] is shed abroad in our hearts by the Holy Spirit which is given to us,"[5] sanctification was associated with the seventh day, the day in which rest was enjoined. But inasmuch as we neither are able to do any good work, except as helped by the gift of God, as the apostle says, "For it is God that worketh in you both to will and to do His good pleasure,"[6] nor will be able to rest, after all the good works which engage us in this life, except as sanctified and perfected by the same gift to eternity ; for this reason it is said of God Himself, that when He had made all things "very good," He rested "on the seventh day from all His works which He had made."[7] For He, in so doing, presented a type of that future rest which He purposed to bestow on us men after our good works are done. For

as in our good works He is said to work in us, by whose gift we are enabled to work what is good, so in our rest He is said to rest by whose gift we rest.

CHAP. XI. — 20. This, moreover, is the reason why the law of the Sabbath is placed third among the three commandments of the Decalogue which declare our duty to God (for the other seven relate to our neighbour, that is, to man ; the whole law hanging on these two commandments).[8] The first commandment, in which we are forbidden to worship any likeness of God made by human contrivance, we are to understand as referring to the Father : this prohibition being made, not because God has no image, but because no image of Him but that One which is the same with Himself, ought to be worshipped ; and this One not in His stead, but along with Him. Then, because a creature is mutable, and therefore it is said, "The whole creation is subject to vanity,"[9] since the nature of the whole is manifested also in any part of it, lest any one should think that the Son of God, the Word by whom all things were made, is a creature, the second commandment is, "Thou shalt not take the name of the Lord thy God in vain."[10] And because God sanctified the seventh day, on which He rested, the Holy Spirit — in whom is given to us that rest which we love everywhere, but find only in loving God, when "His love is shed abroad in us, by the Holy Ghost given unto us"[11] — is presented to our minds in the third commandment, which was written concerning the observance of the Sabbath, not to make us suppose that we attain to rest in this present life, but that all our labours in what is good may point towards nothing else than that eternal rest. For I would specially charge you to remember the passage quoted above : "We are saved by hope ; but hope that is seen is not hope."[12]

21. For the feeding and fanning of that ardent love by which, under a law like that of gravitation, we are borne upwards or inwards to rest, the presentation of truth by emblems has a great power : for, thus presented, things move and kindle our affection much more than if they were set forth in bald statements, not clothed with sacramental symbols. Why this should be, it is hard to say ; but it is the fact that anything which we are taught by allegory or emblem affects and pleases us more, and is more highly esteemed by us, than it would be if most clearly stated in plain terms. I believe that the emotions are less easily kindled while the soul is wholly involved in earthly things ; but if it be

---

1 Gen. ii. 3.
2 Jas. iv. 6.
3 Ps. xxxvii. 4.
4 Augustin interprets the "love of God" here as meaning our love to Him, and equivalent to delighting in Him.
5 Rom. v. 5.
6 Phil. ii. 13.
7 Gen. i. 31, ii. 2.

8 Matt. xxii. 10.
9 Rom. viii. 20.
10 Ex. xx. 7; Deut. v. 11.
11 Rom. v. 5.
12 Rom. viii. 24.

brought to those corporeal things which are emblems of spiritual things, and then taken from these to the spiritual realities which they represent, it gathers strength by the mere act of passing from the one to the other, and, like the flame of a lighted torch, is made by the motion to burn more brightly, and is carried away to rest by a more intensely glowing love.

CHAP. XII. — 22. It is also for this reason, that of all the ten commandments, that which related to the Sabbath was the only one in which the thing commanded was typical;[1] the bodily rest enjoined being a type which we have received as a means of our instruction, but not as a duty binding also upon us. For while in the Sabbath a figure is presented of the spiritual rest, of which it is said in the Psalm, "Be still, and know that I am God,"[2] and unto which men are invited by the Lord Himself in the words, "Come unto Me, all ye that labour and are heavy laden, and I will give you rest. Take My yoke upon you, and learn of Me; for I am meek and lowly in heart: so shall ye find rest unto your souls;"[3] as to all the things enjoined in the other commandments, we are to yield to them an obedience in which there is nothing typical. For we have been taught literally not to worship idols; and the precepts enjoining us not to take God's name in vain, to honour our father and mother, not to commit adultery, or kill, or steal, or bear false witness, or covet our neighbour's wife, or covet anything that is our neighbour's,[4] are all devoid of typical or mystical meaning, and are to be literally observed. But we are not commanded to observe the day of the Sabbath literally, in resting from bodily labour, as it is observed by the Jews; and even their observance of the rest as prescribed is to be deemed worthy of contempt, except as signifying another, namely, spiritual rest. From this we may reasonably conclude, that all those things which are figuratively set forth in Scripture, are powerful in stimulating that love by which we tend towards rest; since the only figurative or typical precept in the Decalogue is the one in which that rest is commended to us, which is desired everywhere, but is found sure and sacred in God alone.

CHAP. XIII. — 23. The Lord's day, however, has been made known not to the Jews, but to Christians, by the resurrection of the Lord, and from Him it began to have the festive character which is proper to it.[5] For the souls of the pious dead are, indeed, in a state of repose before the resurrection of the body, but they are not engaged in the same active exercises as shall engage the strength of their bodies when restored. Now, of this condition of active exercise the eighth day (which is also the first of the week) is a type, because it does not put an end to that repose, but glorifies it. For with the reunion of the body no hindrance of the soul's rest returns, because in the restored body there is no corruption: for "this corruptible must put on incorruption, and this mortal must put on immortality."[6] Wherefore, although the sacramental import of the 8th number, as signifying the resurrection, was by no means concealed from the holy men of old who were filled with the spirit of prophecy (for in the title of Psalms [vi. and xii.] we find the words "for the eighth," and infants were circumcised on the eighth day; and in Ecclesiastes it is said, with allusion to the two covenants, "Give a portion to seven, and also to eight"[7]); nevertheless, before the resurrection of the Lord, it was reserved and hidden, and the Sabbath alone was appointed to be observed, because before that event there was indeed the repose of the dead (of which the Sabbath rest was a type), but there was not any instance of the resurrection of one who, rising from the dead, was no more to die, and over whom death should no longer have dominion; this being done in order that, from the time when such a resurrection did take place in the Lord's own body (the Head of the Church being the first to experience that which His body, the Church, expects at the end of time), the day upon which He rose, the eighth day namely (which is the same with the first of the week), should begin to be observed as the Lord's day. The same reason enables us to understand why, in regard to the day of keeping the passover, on which the Jews were commanded to kill and eat a lamb, which was most clearly a foreshadowing of the Lord's Passion, there was no injunction given to them that they should take the day of the week into account, waiting until the Sabbath was past, and making the beginning of the third week of the moon coincide with the beginning of the third week of the first month; the reason being, that the Lord might rather in His own Passion declare the significance of that day, as He had come also to declare the mystery of the day now known as the Lord's day, the eighth namely, which is also the first of the week.

CHAP. XIV. — 24. Consider now with attention these three most sacred days, the days signalized by the Lord's crucifixion, rest in the grave, and resurrection. Of these three, that of which the cross is the symbol is the business of our present life: those things which are symbolized by His rest in the grave and His resurrection we hold

---

1 *Figurate observandum præcipitur.*
2 Ps. xlvi. 11.
3 Matt. xi. 28, 29.
4 Ex. xx. 1-17; Deut. v. 6-21.
5 *Ex illo habere cœpit festivitatem suam.*
6 1 Cor. xv. 53.
7 Eccles. xi. 2, which Aug. translates, " Da illis septem, et illis octo."

by faith and hope. For *now* the command is given to each man, "Take up thy cross, and follow me." [1] But the flesh is crucified, when our members which are upon the earth are mortified, such as fornication, uncleanness, luxury, avarice, etc., of which the apostle says in another passage: "If ye live after the flesh, ye shall die; but if ye through the Spirit do mortify the deeds of the body, ye shall live." [2] Hence also he says of himself: "The world is crucified unto me, and I unto the world." [3] And again: "Knowing this, that our old man is crucified with Him, that the body of sin might be destroyed, that henceforth we should not serve sin." [4] The period during which our labours tend to the weakening and destruction of the body of sin, during which the outward man is perishing, that the inward man may be renewed day by day, — that is the period of the cross.

25. These are, it is true, good works, having rest for their recompense, but they are meanwhile laborious and painful: therefore we are told to be "rejoicing in hope," that while we contemplate the future rest, we may labour with cheerfulness in present toil. Of this cheerfulness the breadth of the cross in the transverse beam to which the hands were nailed is an emblem: for the hands we understand to be symbolical of working, and the breadth to be symbolical of cheerfulness in him who works, for sadness straitens the spirit. In the height of the cross, against which the head is placed, we have an emblem of the expectation of recompense from the sublime justice of God, "who will render to every man according to his deeds; to them who, by patient continuance in well-doing, seek for glory, and honour, and immortality, eternal life." [5] Therefore the length of the cross, along which the whole body is extended, is an emblem of that patient continuance in the will of God, on account of which those who are patient are said to be long-suffering. The depth also, *i.e.* the part which is fixed in the ground, represents the occult nature of the holy mystery. For you remember, I suppose, the words of the apostle, which in this description of the cross I aim at expounding: "That ye, being rooted and grounded in love, may be able to comprehend with all saints what is the breadth, and length, and depth, and height." [6]

Those things which we do not yet see or possess, but hold in faith and hope, are the things represented in the events by which the second and third of the three memorable days above mentioned were signalized [viz. the Lord's rest in the grave, and His resurrection]. But the things which keep us occupied in this present life, while we are held fast in the fear of God by the commandments, as by nails driven through the flesh (as it is written, "Make my flesh fast with nails by fear of Thee" [7]), are to be reckoned among things necessary, not among those which are for their own sakes to be desired and coveted. Hence Paul says that he desired, as something far better, to depart and to be with Christ: "nevertheless," he adds, "to remain in the flesh is expedient for you" [8] — necessary for your welfare. This departing and being with Christ is the beginning of the rest which is not interrupted, but glorified by the resurrection; and this rest is now enjoyed by faith, "for the just shall live by faith." [9] "Know ye not," saith the same apostle, "that so many of us as were baptized into Jesus Christ, were baptized into His death? Therefore we are buried with Him by baptism unto death." [10] How? By faith. For this is not actually completed in us so long as we are still "groaning within ourselves, and waiting for the adoption, to wit, the redemption of our body: for we are saved by hope; but hope that is seen is not hope: for what a man seeth why doth he yet hope for? But if we hope for that we see not, then do we with patience wait for it." [11]

26. Remember how often I repeat this to you, that we are not to think that we ought to be made happy and free from all difficulties in this present life, and are therefore at liberty to murmur profanely against God when we are straitened in the things of this world, as if He were not performing what He promised. He hath indeed promised the things which are necessary for this life, but the consolations which mitigate the misery of our present lot are very different from the joys of those who are perfect in blessedness. "In the multitude of my thoughts within me," saith the believer, "Thy comforts, O Lord, delight my soul." [12] Let us not therefore murmur because of difficulties; let us not lose that breadth of cheerfulness, of which it is written, "Rejoicing in hope," because this follows, — "patient in tribulation." [13] The new life, therefore, is meanwhile begun in faith, and maintained by hope: for it shall only then be perfect when this mortal shall be swallowed up in life, and death swallowed up in victory; when the last enemy, death, shall be destroyed; when we shall be changed, and made like the angels: for "we shall all rise again, but we shall not all be

---

[1] Matt. xvi. 24.
[2] Rom. viii. 13.
[3] Gal. vi. 14.
[4] Rom. vi. 6.
[5] Rom. ii. 6, 7.
[6] Eph. iii. 17, 18.

[7] Ps. cxix. 120; Septuagint version, καθήλωσον ἐκ τοῦ φόβου σου τὰς σάρκας μου.
[8] Phil. i. 23, 24.
[9] Hab. ii. 4.
[10] Rom. vi. 3, 4.
[11] Rom. viii. 23, 25.
[12] Ps. xciv. 19.
[13] Rom. xii. 12.

changed." [1]   Again, the Lord saith, "They shall be equal unto the angels." [2]   We now are apprehended by Him in fear by faith : then we shall apprehend Him in love by sight.   For "whilst we are at home in the body, we are absent from the Lord : for we walk by faith, not by sight." [3]   Hence the apostle himself, who says, "I follow after, if that I may apprehend that for which also I am apprehended of Christ Jesus," confesses frankly that he has not attained to it.   "Brethren," he says, "I count not myself to have apprehended." [4]   Since, however, our hope is sure, because of the truth of the promise, when he said elsewhere, "Therefore we are buried with Him by baptism into death," he adds these words, "that like as Christ was raised up from the dead by the glory of the Father, even so we also should walk in newness of life." [5]   We walk, therefore, in actual labour, but in hope of rest, in the flesh of the old life, but in faith of the new.   For he says again : "The body is dead because of sin ; but the spirit is life because of righteousness.   But if the Spirit of Him that raised up Jesus from the dead dwell in you, He that raised up Christ from the dead shall also quicken your mortal bodies by His Spirit that dwelleth in you."

27. Both the authority of the Divine Scriptures and the consent of the whole Church spread throughout the world have combined to ordain the annual commemoration of these things at Easter, by observances which are, as you now see, full of spiritual significance.   From the Old Testament Scriptures we are not taught as to the precise day of holding Easter, beyond the limitation to the period between the 14th and 21st days of the first month ; but because we know from the Gospel beyond doubt which days of the week were signalized in succession by the Lord's crucifixion, His resting in the grave, and His resurrection, the observance of these days has been enjoined in addition by Councils of the Fathers, and the whole Christian world has arrived unanimously at the persuasion that this is the proper mode of observing Easter.

CHAP. XV. — 28.[6] The Fast of Forty Days has its warrant both in the Old Testament, from the fasting of Moses [7] and of Elijah,[8] and in the Gospel from the fact that our Lord fasted the same number of days ; [9] proving thereby that the Gospel is not at variance with the Law and the Prophets.   For the Law and the Prophets are represented in the persons of Moses and Elijah respectively ; between whom also He appeared in glory on the Mount, that what the apostle says of Him, that He is "witnessed unto both by the Law and the Prophets," [10] might be made more clearly manifest.   Now, in what part of the year could the observance of the Fast of Forty Days be more appropriately placed, than in that which immediately precedes and borders on the time of the Lord's Passion?   For by it is signified this life of toil, the chief work in which is to exercise self-control, in abstaining from the world's friendship, which never ceases deceitfully caressing us, and scattering profusely around us its bewitching allurements.   As to the reason why this life of toil and self-control is symbolized by the number 40, it seems to me that the number ten (in which is the perfection of our blessedness, as in the number eight, because it returns to the unit) has a like place in this number [as the unit has in giving its significance to eight] ; [11] and therefore I regard the number forty as a fit symbol for this life, because in it the creature (of which the symbolical number is seven) cleaves to the Creator, in whom is revealed that unity of the Trinity which is to be published while time lasts throughout this whole world, — a world swept by four winds, constituted of four elements, and experiencing the changes of four seasons in the year.   Now four times ten [seven added to three] are forty ; but the number forty reckoned in along with [one of] its parts adds the number ten, [as seven reckoned in along with one of its parts adds the unit,] and the total is fifty, — the symbol, as it were, of the reward of the toil and self-control. [12]   For it is not without reason that the Lord Himself continued for forty days on this earth and in this life in fellowship with His disciples after His resurrection, and, when He ascended into heaven, sent the promised Holy Spirit, after an interval of ten days more, when the day of Pentecost was fully come.   This fiftieth day, moreover, has wrapped up in it another holy mystery : [13] for 7 times 7 days are 49.   And when we return to the beginning of another seven, and add the eighth, which is also the first day of the week, we have the 50 days complete ; which period of fifty days we celebrate after the Lord's resurrection, as

---

[1] 1 Cor. xv. 54, 26, 51 — the last of these verses being rendered by Augustin here, not as in the English version, but as given above.
[2] Luke xx. 36.
[3] 2 Cor. v. 6, 7.
[4] Phil. iii. 12, 13.
[5] Rom. vi 4.
[6] In translating, we have ventured to take this title of Chap. xv. out of the place which the Benedictines have given to it, in the middle of a sentence of the preceding paragraph.   There it almost hopelessly bewildered the reader.   Here it prepares him for a new topic.
[7] Ex. xxxiv. 28.
[8] 1 Kings xix. 8
[9] Matt. iv. 2.

[10] Rom. iii. 21.
[11] Compare "octavus qui et primus," and the remarks on the meaning of the number 8 in § 23.
[12] We give the original of this very obscure paragraph : — " Numero autem quadragenario vitam istam propter ea figurari arbitror, quia denarius in quo est perfectio beatitudinis nostræ, sicut in octonario, quia redit ad primum, ita in hoc mihi videtur exprimi : quia creatura, quæ septenario figuratur adhæret Creatori in quo declaratur unitas Trinitatis per universum mundum temporaliter annuntianda ; qui mundus et a quatuor ventis delimatur et quatuor elementis erigitur, et quatuor anni temporum vicibus variatur.   Decem autem quater in quadraginta consummantur, quadragenarius autem partibus suis computatus, addit ipsum denarium et fiunt quinquaginta tanquam merces laboris et continentiæ."
[13] Sacramentum.

representing not toil, but rest and gladness. For this reason we do not fast in them ; and in praying we stand upright, which is an emblem of resurrection. Hence, also, every Lord's day during the fifty days, this usage is observed at the altar, and the Alleluia is sung, which signifies that our future exercise shall consist wholly in praising God, as it is written : " Blessed are they who dwell in Thy house, O Lord : they will be still (*i.e.* eternally) praising Thee." [1]

CHAP. XVI. — 29. The fiftieth day is also commended to us in Scripture ; and not only in the Gospel, by the fact that on that day the Holy Spirit descended, but also in the books of the Old Testament. For in them we learn, that after the Jews observed the first passover with the slaying of the lamb as appointed, 50 days intervened between that day and the day on which upon Mount Sinai there was given to Moses the Law written with the finger of God ; [2] and this " finger of God " is in the Gospels most plainly declared to signify the Holy Spirit : for where one evangelist quotes our Lord's words thus, " I with the finger of God cast out devils," [3] another quotes them thus, " I cast out devils by the Spirit of God." [4] Who would not prefer the joy which these divine mysteries impart, when the light of healing truth beams from them on the soul to all the kingdoms of this world, even though these were held in perfect prosperity and peace ? May we not say, that as the two seraphim answer each other in singing the praise of the Most High, " Holy, holy, holy is the Lord God of Hosts," [5] so the Old Testament and the New, in perfect harmony, give forth their testimony to sacred truth? The lamb is slain, the passover is celebrated, and after 50 days the Law is given, which inspires fear, written by the finger of God. Christ is slain, being led as a lamb to the slaughter, as Isaiah testifies ; [6] the true Passover is celebrated ; and after 50 days is given the Holy Spirit, who is the finger of God, and whose fruit is love, and who is therefore opposed to men who seek their own, and consequently bear a grievous yoke and heavy burden, and find no rest for their souls ; for love " seeketh not her own." [7] Therefore there is no rest in the unloving spirit of heretics, whom the apostle declares guilty of conduct like that of the magicians of Pharaoh, saying, " Now as Jannes and Jambres withstood Moses, so do these also resist the truth : men of corrupt minds, reprobate concerning the faith. But they shall proceed no further : for their folly shall be manifest to all

men, as theirs also was." [8] For because through this corruptness of mind they were utterly disquieted, they failed at the third miracle, confessing that the Spirit of God which was in Moses was opposed to them : for in owning their failure, they said, " This is the finger of God." [9] The Holy Spirit, who shows Himself reconciled and gracious to the meek and lowly in heart, and gives them rest, shows Himself an inexorable adversary to the proud and haughty, and vexes them with disquiet. Of this disquiet those despicable insects were a figure, under which Pharaoh's magicians owned themselves foiled, saying, " This is the finger of God."

30. Read the book of Exodus, and observe the number of days between the first passover and the giving of the Law. God speaks to Moses in the desert of Sinai on the first day of the third month. Mark, then, this as one day of the month, and then observe what (among other things) the Lord said on that day : " Go unto the people, and sanctify them to-day and to-morrow, and let them wash their clothes, and be ready against the third day ; for the third day the Lord will come down in the sight of all the people upon Mount Sinai." [10] The Law was accordingly given on the third day of the month. Now reckon the days between the 14th day of the first month, the day of the passover, and the 3d day of the third month, and you have 17 days of the first month, 30 of the second, and 3 of the third — 50 in all. The Law in the Ark of the Testimony represents holiness in the Lord's body, by whose resurrection is promised to us the future rest ; for our receiving of which, love is breathed into us by the Holy Spirit. But the Spirit had not then been given, for Jesus had not yet been glorified. [11] Hence that prophetic song, " Arise, O Lord, into Thy rest, Thou and the ark of Thy strength " [holiness, LXX.]. [12] Where there is rest, there is holiness. Wherefore we have now received a pledge of it, that we may love and desire it. For to the rest belonging to the other life, whereunto we are brought by that transition from this life of which the passover is a symbol, all are now invited in the name of the Father, the Son, and the Holy Spirit.

CHAP. XVII. — 31. Hence also, in the number of the large fishes which our Lord after His resurrection, showing this new life, commanded to be taken on the right side of the ship, there is found the number 50 three times multiplied, with the addition of three more [the symbol of the Trinity] to make the holy mystery more apparent ; and the disciples' nets were not

1 Ps. lxxxiv. 5.
2 Ex. xii. xix. xx. xxxi.
3 Luke xi. 20.
4 Matt. xii 28.
5 Isa. vi. 3.
6 Isa. liii. 7.
7 1 Cor. xiii. 5.

8 2 Tim. iii. 8.
9 Ex. viii. 19.
10 Ex. xix. 10, 11.
11 John vii. 39.
12 Ps. cxxxii. 8.

broken,[1] because in that new life there shall be no schism caused by the disquiet of heretics. Then [in this new life] man, made perfect and at rest, purified in body and in soul by the pure words of God, which are like silver purged from its dross, seven times refined,[2] shall receive his reward, the denarius;[3] so that with that reward the numbers 10 and 7 meet in him. For in this number [17] there is found, as in other numbers representing a combination of symbols, a wonderful mystery. Nor is it without good reason that the seventeenth Psalm[4] is the only one which is given complete in the book of Kings,[5] because it signifies that kingdom in which we shall have no enemy. For its title is, "A Psalm of David, in the day that the Lord delivered him from the hand of all his enemies, and from the hand of Saul." For of whom is David the type, but of Him who, according to the flesh, was born of the seed of David?[6] He in His Church, that is, in His body, still endures the malice of enemies. Therefore the words which from heaven fell upon the ear of that persecutor whom Jesus slew by His voice, and whom He transformed into a part of His body (as the food which we use becomes a part of ourselves), were these, "Saul, Saul, why persecutest thou Me?"[7] And when shall this His body be finally delivered from enemies? Is it not when the last enemy, Death, shall be destroyed? It is to that time that the number of the 153 fishes pertains. For if the number 17 itself be the side of an arithmetical triangle,[8] formed by placing above each other rows of units, increasing in number from 1 to 17, the whole sum of these units is 153: since 1 and 2 make 3; 3 and 3, 6; 6 and 4, 10; 10 and 5, 15; 15 and 6, 21; and so on: continue this up to 17, the total is 153.

32. The celebration of Easter and Pentecost is therefore most firmly based on Scripture. As to the observance of the forty days before Easter, this has been confirmed by the practice of the Church; as also the separation of the eight days of the neophytes, in such order that the eighth of these coincides with the first. The custom of singing the Alleluia on those 50 days only in the Church is not universal; for in other places it is sung also at various other times, but on these days it is sung everywhere. Whether the custom of standing at prayer on these days, and on all the Lord's days, is everywhere observed or not, I do not know; nevertheless, I have told you what guides the Church in this usage, and it is in my opinion sufficiently obvious.[9]

CHAP. XVIII. — 33. As to the feet-washing, since the Lord recommended this because of its being an example of that humility which He came to teach, as He Himself afterwards explained, the question has arisen at what time it is best, by literal performance of this work, to give public instruction in the important duty which it illustrates, and this time [of Lent] was suggested in order that the lesson taught by it might make a deeper and more serious impression. Many, however, have not accepted this as a custom, lest it should be thought to belong to the ordinance of baptism; and some have not hesitated to deny it any place among our ceremonies. Some, however, in order to connect its observance with the more sacred associations of this solemn season, and at the same time to prevent its being confounded with baptism in any way, have selected for this ceremony either the eighth day itself, or that on which the third eighth day occurs, because of the great significance of the number three in many holy mysteries.

34. I am surprised at your expressing a desire that I should write anything in regard to those ceremonies which are found different in different countries, because there is no necessity for my doing this; and, moreover, one most excellent rule must be observed in regard to these customs, when they do not in any way oppose either true doctrine or sound morality, but contain some incentives to the better life, viz., that wherever we see them observed, or know them to be established, we should not only refrain from finding fault with them, but even recommend them by our approval and imitation, unless restrained by fear of doing greater harm than good by this course, through the infirmity of others. We are not, however, to be restrained by this, if more good is to be expected from our consenting with those who are zealous for the ceremony, than loss to be feared from our displeasing those who protest against it. In such a case we ought by all means to adopt it, especially if it be something in defence of which Scripture can be alleged: as in the singing of hymns and psalms, for which we have on record both the example and the precepts of the Lord and of His apostles. In this religious exercise,

---

[1] John xxi. 6, 11.
[2] Ps. xii. 6.
[3] Matt. xx. 9, 10.
[4] The eighteenth in the English Bible.
[5] 2 Sam. xxii. 2–51. The title of that book is in the LXX. the 2d book of Kings.
[6] Rom. i. 3.
[7] Acts ix. 4.
[8] Such a triangle as this:

[9] He refers to the significance of the standing upright as an emblem of resurrection.

so useful for inducing a devotional frame of mind and inflaming the strength of love to God, there is diversity of usage, and in Africa the members of the Church are rather too indifferent in regard to it; on which account the Donatists reproach us with our grave chanting of the divine songs of the prophets in our churches, while they inflame their passions in their revels by the singing of psalms of human composition, which rouse them like the stirring notes of the trumpet on the battle-field. But when brethren are assembled in the church, why should not the time be devoted to singing of sacred songs, excepting of course while reading or preaching[1] is going on, or while the presiding minister prays aloud, or the united prayer of the congregation is led by the deacon's voice? At the other intervals not thus occupied, I do not see what could be a more excellent, useful, and holy exercise for a Christian congregation.

CHAP. XIX.[2] — 35. I cannot, however, sanction with my approbation those ceremonies which are departures from the custom of the Church, and are instituted on the pretext of being symbolical of some holy mystery; although, for the sake of avoiding offence to the piety of some and the pugnacity of others, I do not venture to condemn severely many things of this kind. But this I deplore, and have too much occasion to do so, that comparatively little attention is paid to many of the most wholesome rites which Scripture has enjoined; and that so many false notions everywhere prevail, that more severe rebuke would be administered to a man who should touch the ground with his feet bare during the octaves (before his baptism), than to one who drowned his intellect in drunkenness. My opinion therefore is, that wherever it is possible, all those things should be abolished without hesitation, which neither have warrant in Holy Scripture, nor are found to have been appointed by councils of bishops, nor are confirmed by the practice of the universal Church, but are so infinitely various, according to the different customs of different places, that it is with difficulty, if at all, that the reasons which guided men in appointing them can be discovered. For even although nothing be found, perhaps, in which they are against the true faith; yet the Christian religion, which God in His mercy made free, appointing to her sacraments very few in number, and very easily observed, is by these burdensome ceremonies so oppressed, that the condition of the Jewish Church itself is preferable: for although they have not known the time of their freedom, they are subjected to burdens imposed by the law of God, not by the vain conceits of men. The Church of God, however, being meanwhile so constituted as to enclose much chaff and many tares, bears with many things; yet if anything be contrary to faith or to holy life, she does not approve of it either by silence or by practice.

CHAP. XX. — 36. Accordingly, that which you wrote as to certain brethren abstaining from the use of animal food, on the ground of its being ceremonially unclean, is most clearly contrary to the faith and to sound doctrine. If I were to enter on anything like a full discussion of this matter, it might be thought by some that there was some obscurity in the precepts of the apostle in this matter; whereas he, among many other things which he said on this subject, expressed his abhorrence of this opinion of the heretics in these words: " Now the Spirit speaketh expressly, that in the latter times some shall depart from the faith, giving heed to seducing spirits and doctrines of devils; speaking lies in hypocrisy; having their conscience seared with a hot iron; forbidding to marry, and commanding to abstain from meats, which God hath created to be received with thanksgiving of them which believe and know the truth. For every creature of God is good, and nothing to be refused, if it be received with thanksgiving: for it is sanctified by the word of God and prayer." [3] Again, in another place, he says, concerning these things: " Unto the pure all things are pure: but unto them that are defiled and unbelieving is nothing pure; but even their mind and conscience is defiled." [4] Read the rest for yourself, and read these passages to others — to as many as you can — in order that, seeing that they have been called to liberty, they may not make void the grace of God toward them; only let them not use their liberty for an occasion to serve the flesh: let them not refuse to practise the purpose of curbing carnal appetite, abstinence from some kinds of food, on the pretext that it is unlawful to do so under the promptings of superstition or unbelief.

37. As to those who read futurity by taking at random a text from the pages of the Gospels, although it is better that they should do this than go to consult spirits of divination, nevertheless it is, in my opinion, a censurable practice to try to turn to secular affairs and the vanity of this life those divine oracles which were intended to teach us concerning the higher life.

CHAP. XXI. — 38. If you do not consider that I have now written enough in answer to your questions, you must have little knowledge of my capacities or of my engagements. For so far am I from being, as you have thought, ac-

---

[1] Preaching. The word in the original is " disputatur," — something much more lively and entertaining.
[2] I have taken the liberty here of putting the beginning of the chapter and paragraph a sentence further on than in the Benedictine edition, so as to finish in sec. 34 the remarks on psalm-singing.

[3] 1 Tim. iv. 1–5.
[4] Tit. i. 15.

quainted with everything, that I read nothing in your letter with more sadness than this statement, both because it is most manifestly untrue, and because I am surprised that you should not be aware, that not only are many things unknown to me in countless other departments, but that even in the Scriptures themselves the things which I do not know are many more than the things which I know. But I cherish a hope in the name of Christ, which is not without its reward, because I have not only believed the testimony of my God that "on these two commandments hang all the Law and the Prophets;"[1] but I have myself proved it, and daily prove it, by experience. For there is no holy mystery, and no difficult passage of the word of God, in which, when it is opened up to me, I do not find these same commandments: for "the end of the commandment is charity, out of a pure heart, and of a good conscience, and of faith unfeigned;"[2] and "love is the fulfilling of the law."[3]

39. I beseech you therefore also, my dearly beloved, whether studying these or other writings, so to read and so to learn as to bear in mind what hath been most truly said, "Knowledge puffeth up, but charity edifieth;"[4] but charity vaunteth not itself, is not puffed up. Let knowledge therefore be used as a kind of scaffolding by which may be erected the building of charity, which shall endure for ever when knowledge faileth.[5] Knowledge, if applied as a means to charity, is most useful; but apart from this high end, it has been proved not only superfluous, but even pernicious. I know, however, how holy meditation keeps you safe under the shadow of the wings of our God. These things I have stated, though briefly, because I know that this same charity of yours, which "vaunteth not itself," will prompt you to lend and read this letter to many.

LETTERS LVI. AND LVII.

are addressed (A.D. 400) to Celer, exhorting him to forsake the Donatist schismatics. They may be omitted, being brief, and containing no new argument.

LETTER LVIII.

(A.D. 401.)

TO MY NOBLE AND WORTHY LORD PAMMACHIUS, MY SON, DEARLY BELOVED IN THE BOWELS OF CHRIST, AUGUSTIN SENDS GREETING IN THE LORD.

1. The good works which spring from the grace of Christ in you have given you a claim to be esteemed by us His members, and have made you as truly known and as much beloved by us as you could be. For even were I daily seeing your face, this could add nothing to the completeness of the acquaintance with you which I now have, when in the shining light of one of your actions I have seen your inner being, fair with the loveliness of peace, and beaming with the brightness of truth. Seeing this has made me know you, and knowing you has made me love you; and therefore, in addressing you, I write to one who, notwithstanding our distance from each other, has become known to me, and is my beloved friend. The bond which binds us together is indeed of earlier date, and we were living united under One Head: for had you not been rooted in His love, the Catholic unity would not have been so dear to you, and you would not have dealt as you have done with your African tenants[6] settled in the midst of the consular province of Numidia, the very country in which the folly of the Donatists began, addressing them in such terms, and encouraging them with such enthusiasm, as to persuade them with unhesitating devotion to choose that course which they believed that a man of your character and position would not adopt on other grounds than truth ascertained and acknowledged, and to submit themselves, though so remote from you, to the same Head; so that along with yourself they are reckoned for ever as members of Him by whose command they are for the time dependent upon you.

2. Embracing you, therefore, as known to me by this transaction, I am moved by joyful feelings to congratulate you in Christ Jesus our Lord, and to send you this letter as a proof of my heart's love towards you; for I cannot do more. I beseech you, however, not to measure the amount of my love by this letter; but by means of this letter, when you have read it, pass on by the unseen inner passage which thought opens up into my heart, and see what is there felt towards you. For to the eye of love that sanctuary of love shall be unveiled which we shut against the disquieting trifles of this world when there we worship God; and there you will see the ecstasy of my joy in your good work, — an ecstasy which I cannot describe with tongue or pen, glowing and burning in the offering of praise to Him by whose inspiration you were made willing, and by whose help you were made able to serve Him in this way. "Thanks be unto God for His unspeakable gift!"[7]

3. Oh how we desire in Africa to see such work as this by which you have gladdened us done by many, who are, like yourself, senators in the State, and sons of the holy Church! It

---

[1] Matt. xxii. 40.
[2] 1 Tim. i. 5.
[3] Rom. xiii. 10.
[4] 1 Cor. viii. 1.
[5] 1 Cor. xiii. 4, 8.

[6] *Coloni.*
[7] 1 Cor. ix. 15.

is, however, hazardous to give them this exhortation: they may refuse to follow it, and the enemies of the Church will take advantage of this to deceive the weak, as if they had gained a victory over us in the minds of those who disregarded our counsel. But it is safe for me to express gratitude to you; for you have already done that by which, in the emancipation of those who were weak, the enemies of the Church are confounded. I have therefore thought it sufficient to ask you to read this letter with friendly boldness to any to whom you can do so on the ground of their Christian profession. For thus learning what you have achieved, they will believe that that, about which as an impossibility they are now indifferent, can be done in Africa. As to the snares which these heretics contrive in the perversity of their hearts, I have resolved not to speak of them in this letter, because I have been only amused at their imagining that they could gain any advantage over your mind, which Christ holds as His possession. You will hear them, however, from my brethren, whom I earnestly commend to your Excellency: they fear lest you should disdain some things which to you might seem unnecessary in connection with the great and unlooked for salvation of those men over whom, in consequence of your work, their Catholic Mother rejoices.

LETTER LIX.

(A.D. 401.)

TO MY MOST BLESSED LORD AND VENERABLE FATHER VICTORINUS, MY BROTHER IN THE PRIESTHOOD, AUGUSTIN SENDS GREETING IN THE LORD.

1. Your summons to the Council reached me on the fifth day before the Ides of November, in the evening, and found me very much indisposed, so that I could not possibly attend. However, I submit to your pious and wise judgment whether certain perplexities which the summons occasioned were due to my own ignorance or to sufficient grounds. I read in that summons that it was written also to the districts of Mauritania, which, as we know, have their own primates. Now, if these provinces were to be represented in a Council held in Numidia, it was by all means proper that the names of some of the more eminent bishops who are in Mauritania should be attached to the circular letter; and not finding this, I have been greatly surprised. Moreover, to the bishops of Numidia it has been addressed in such a confused and careless manner, that my own name I find in the third place, although I know my proper order to be much further down in the roll of bishops. This wrongs others, and grieves me. Moreover, our venerable father and colleague,

Xantippus of Tagosa, says that the primacy belongs to him, and by very many he is regarded as the primate, and he issues such letters as you have sent. Even supposing that this be a mistake, which your Holiness can easily discover and correct, certainly his name should not have been omitted in the summons which you have issued. If his name had been placed in the middle of the list, and not in the first line, I would have wondered much; how much greater, then, is my surprise, when I find in it no mention whatever made of him who, above all others, behoved to be present in the Council, that by the bishops of all the Numidian churches this question of the order of the primacy might be debated before any other!

2. For these reasons, I might even hesitate to come to the Council, lest the summons in which so many flagrant mistakes are found should be a forgery; even were I not hindered both by the shortness of the notice, and manifold other important engagements standing in the way. I therefore beg you, most blessed prelate, to excuse me, and to be pleased to give attention, in the first instance, to bring about between your Holiness and the aged Xantippus a cordial mutual understanding as to the question which of you ought to summon the Council; or at least, as I think would be still better, let both of you, without prejudging the claim of either, conjointly call together our colleagues, especially those who have been nearly as long in the episcopate as yourselves, who may easily discover and decide which of you has truth on his side,[1] that this question may be settled first among a few of you; and then, when the mistake has been rectified, let the younger bishops be gathered together, who, having no others whom it would be either possible or right for them to accept as witnesses in this matter but yourselves, are meanwhile at a loss to know to which of you the preference is to be given.

I have sent this letter sealed with a ring which represents a man's profile.

LETTER LX.

(A.D. 401.)

TO FATHER AURELIUS, MY LORD MOST BLESSED, AND REVERED WITH MOST JUSTLY MERITED RESPECT, MY BROTHER IN THE PRIESTHOOD, MOST SINCERELY BELOVED, AUGUSTIN SENDS GREETING IN THE LORD.

1. I have received no letter from your Holiness since we parted; but I have now read a letter of your Grace concerning Donatus and his brother, and I have long hesitated as to the

---

[1] The primacy in Numidia belonged not to the bishop of the most important town, but to the oldest bishop.

reply which I ought to give. After frequently reconsidering what is in such a case conducive to the welfare of those whom we serve in Christ, and seek to nourish in Him, nothing has occurred to me which would alter my opinion that it is not right to give occasion for God's servants to think that promotion to a better position is more readily given to those who have become worse. Such a rule would make monks less careful of falling, and a most grievous wrong would be done to the order of clergy, if those who have deserted their duty as monks be chosen to serve as clergy, seeing that our custom is to select for that office only the more tried and superior men of those who continue faithful to their calling as monks; unless, perchance, the common people are to be taught to joke at our expense, saying "a bad monk makes a good clerk," as they are wont to say that "a poor flute-player makes a good singer." It would be an intolerable calamity if we were to encourage the monks to such fatal pride, and were to consent to brand with so grievous disgrace the clerical order to which we ourselves belong: seeing that sometimes even a good monk is scarcely qualified to be a good clerk; for though he be proficient in self-denial, he may lack the necessary instruction, or be disqualified by some personal defect.

2. I believe, however, that your Holiness understood these monks to have left the monastery with my consent, in order that they might rather be useful to the people of their own district; but this was not the case: of their own accord they departed, of their own accord they deserted us, notwithstanding my resisting, from a regard to their welfare, to the utmost of my power. As to Donatus, seeing that he has obtained ordination before we could arrive at any decision in the Council[1] as to his case, do as your wisdom may guide you; it may be that his proud obstinacy has been subdued. But as to his brother, who was the chief cause of Donatus leaving the monastery, I know not what to write, since you know what I think of him. I do not presume to oppose what may seem best to one of your wisdom, rank, and piety; and I hope with all my heart that you will do whatever you judge most profitable for the members of the Church.

LETTER LXI.

(A.D. 401.)

TO HIS WELL-BELOVED AND HONOURABLE BROTHER
THEODORUS, BISHOP AUGUSTIN SENDS GREETING
IN THE LORD.

1. I have resolved to commit to writing in this letter what I said when you and I were conversing together as to the terms on which we would welcome clergy of the party of Donatus desiring to become Catholics, in order that, if any one asked you what are our sentiments and practice in regard to this, you might exhibit these by producing what I have written with my own hand. Be assured, therefore, that we detest nothing in the Donatist clergy but that which renders them schismatics and heretics, namely, their dissent from the unity and truth of the Catholic Church, in their not remaining in peace with the people of God, which is spread abroad throughout the world, and in their refusing to recognise the baptism of Christ in those who have received it. This their grievous error, therefore, we reject; but the good name of God which they bear, and His sacrament which they have received, we acknowledge in them, and embrace it with reverence and love. But for this very reason we grieve over their wandering, and long to gain them for God by the love of Christ, that they may have within the peace of the Church that holy sacrament for their salvation, which they meanwhile have beyond the pale of the Church for their destruction. If, therefore, there be taken away from between us the evil things which proceed from men, and if the good which comes from God and belongs to both parties in common be duly honoured, there will ensue such brotherly concord, such amiable peace, that the love of Christ shall gain the victory in men's hearts over the temptation of the devil.

2. When, therefore, any come to us from the party of Donatus, we do not welcome the evil which belongs to them, viz. their error and schism: these, the only obstacles to our concord, are removed from between us, and we embrace our brethren, standing with them, as the apostle says, in "the unity of the Spirit, in the bond of peace,"[2] and acknowledging in them the good things which are divine, as their holy baptism, the blessing conferred by ordination, their profession of self-denial, their vow of celibacy, their faith in the Trinity, and such like; all which things were indeed theirs before, but "profited them nothing, because they had not charity." For what truth is there in the profession of Christian charity by him who does not embrace Christian unity? When, therefore, they come to the Catholic Church, they gain thereby not what they already possessed, but something which they had not before,—namely, that those things which they possessed begin then to be profitable to them. For in the Catholic Church they obtain the root of charity in the bond of peace and in the fellowship of unity: so that all the sacraments of truth which they hold serve not to condemn, but to deliver them. The branches

---

[1] The Council held at Carthage in September 401.

[2] Eph. iv. 3.

ought not to boast that their wood is the wood of the vine, not of the thorn; for if they do not live by union to the root, they shall, notwithstanding their outward appearance, be cast into the fire. But of some branches which were broken off the apostle says that "God is able to graff them in again." [1] Wherefore, beloved brother, if you see any one of the Donatist party in doubt as to the place into which they shall be welcomed by us, show them this writing in my own hand, which is familiar to you, and let them have it to read if they desire it; for "I call God for a record upon my soul," that I will welcome them on such terms as that they shall retain not only the baptism of Christ which they have received, but also the honour due to their vow of holiness and to their self-denying virtue.

LETTER LXII.

(A.D. 401.)

ALYPIUS, AUGUSTIN, AND SAMSUCIUS, AND THE BRETHREN WHO ARE WITH THEM, SEND GREETING IN THE LORD TO SEVERUS,[2] THEIR LORD MOST BLESSED, AND WITH ALL REVERENCE MOST BELOVED, THEIR BROTHER IN TRUTH, AND PARTNER IN THE PRIESTLY OFFICE, AND TO ALL THE BRETHREN WHO ARE WITH HIM.

1. When we came to Subsana, and inquired into the things which had been done there in our absence and against our will, we found some things exactly as we had heard reported, and some things otherwise, but all things calling for lamentation and forbearance; and we endeavoured, in so far as the Lord gave His help, to put them right by reproof, admonition, and prayer. What distressed us most, since your departure from the place, was that the brethren who went thence to you were allowed to go without a guide, which we beg you to excuse, as having taken place not from malice, but from an excessive caution. For, believing as they did that these men were sent by our son Timotheus in order to move you to be displeased with us, and being anxious to reserve the whole matter untouched until we should come (when they hoped to see you along with us), they thought that the departure of these men would be prevented if they were not furnished with a guide. That they did wrong in thus attempting to detain the brethren we admit, — nay, who could doubt it? Hence also arose the story which was told to Fossor,[3] that Timotheus had already gone to you with these same brethren. This was wholly false, but the statement was not made by the presbyter; and that Carcedonius our brother was wholly unaware of all these things, was most clearly proved to us by all the ways in which such things are susceptible of proof.

2. But why spend more time on these circumstances! Our son Timotheus, being greatly disturbed because he found himself, altogether in spite of his own wish, in such unlooked for perplexity, informed us that, when you were urging him to serve God at Subsana, he broke forth vehemently, and swore that he would never on any account leave you. And when we questioned him as to his present wish, he replied that by this oath he was precluded from going to the place which we had previously wished him to occupy, even though his mind were set at rest by the evidence given as to his freedom from restraint. When we showed him that he would not be guilty of violating his oath if a bar was put in the way of his being with you, not by him, but by you, in order to avoid a scandal; seeing that he could by his oath bind only his own will, not yours, and he admitted that you had not bound yourself reciprocally by your oath; at last he said, as it became a servant of God and a son of the Church to say, that he would without hesitation agree to whatever should seem good to us, along with your Holiness, to appoint concerning him. We therefore ask, and by the love of Christ implore you, in the exercise of your sagacity, to remember all that we spoke to each other in this matter, and to make us glad by your reply to this letter. For "we that are strong" (if, indeed, amid so great and perilous temptations, we may presume to claim this title) are bound, as the apostle says, to "bear the infirmities of the weak."[4] Our brother Timotheus has not written to your Holiness, because your venerable brother has reported all to you. May you be joyful in the Lord, and remember us, our lord most blessed, and with all reverence most beloved, our brother in sincerity.

LETTER LXIII.

(A.D. 401.)

TO SEVERUS, MY LORD MOST BLESSED AND VENERABLE, A BROTHER WORTHY OF BEING EMBRACED WITH UNFEIGNED LOVE, AND PARTNER IN THE PRIESTLY OFFICE, AND TO THE BRETHREN THAT ARE WITH HIM, AUGUSTIN AND THE BRETHREN WITH HIM SEND GREETING IN THE LORD.

1. If I frankly say all that this case compels me to say, you may perhaps ask me where is my concern for the preservation of charity; but if

---

[1] Rom. xi. 23.
[2] Severus, bishop of Milevi in Numidia, had at one time been an inmate of the monastery of Augustin, and was held by him in the highest esteem.
[3] Tillemont suggests that this may be "the sexton," and not a proper name.

[4] Rom. xv. 1.

I may not thus say all that the case demands, may I not ask you where is the liberty conceded to friendship? Hesitating between these two alternatives, I have chosen to write so much as may justify me without accusing you. You wrote that you were surprised that we, notwithstanding our great grief at what was done, acquiesced in it, when it might have been remedied by our correction; as if when things wrongly done have been afterwards, so far as possible, corrected, they are no longer to be deplored; and more particularly, as if it were absurd for us to acquiesce in that which, though wrongly done, it is impossible for us to undo. Wherefore, my brother, sincerely esteemed as such, your surprise may cease. For Timotheus was ordained a subdeacon at Subsana against my advice and desire, at the time when the decision of his case was still pending as the subject of deliberation and conference between us. Behold me still grieving over this, although he has now returned to you; and we do not regret that in our consenting to his return we obeyed your will.

2. May it please you to hear how, by rebuke, admonition, and prayer, we had, even before he went away from this place, corrected the wrong which had been done, lest it should appear to you that up to that time nothing had been corrected by us because he had not returned to you. By *rebuke*, addressing ourselves first to Timotheus himself, because he did not obey you, but went away to your Holiness without consulting our brother Carcedonius, to which act of his the origin of this affliction is to be traced; and afterwards censuring the presbyter (Carcedonius) and Verinus, through whom we found that the ordination of Timotheus had been managed. When all of these admitted, under our rebuke, that in all the things alleged they had done wrong and begged forgiveness, we would have acted with undue haughtiness if we had refused to believe that they were sufficiently corrected. For they could not make that to be not done which had been done; and we by our rebuke were not expecting or desiring to do more than bring them to acknowledge their faults, and grieve over them. By *admonition*: first, in warning all never to dare again to do such things, lest they should incur God's wrath; and then especially charging Timotheus, who said that he was bound only by his oath to go to your Grace, that if your Holiness, considering all that we had spoken together on the matter, should, as we hoped might be the case, decide not to have him with you, out of regard for the weak for whom Christ died, who might be offended, and for the discipline of the Church, which it is perilous to disregard, seeing that he had begun to be a reader in this diocese, — he should then, being free from the bond of his oath, devote himself with undis-

turbed mind to the service of God, to whom we are to give an account of all our actions. By such admonitions as we were able to give, we had also persuaded our brother Carcedonius to submit with perfect resignation to whatever might be seen to be necessary in regard to him for the preservation of the discipline of the Church. By *prayer*, moreover, we had laboured to correct ourselves, commending both the guidance and the issues of our counsels to the mercy of God, and seeking that if any sinful anger had wounded us, we might be cured by taking refuge under His healing right hand. Behold how much we had corrected by rebuke, admonition, and prayer!

3. And now, considering the bond of charity, that we may not be possessed by Satan, — for we are not ignorant of his devices, — what else ought we to have done than obey your wish, seeing that you thought that what had been done could be remedied in no other way than by our giving back to your authority him in whose person you complained that wrong had been done to you. Even our brother Carcedonius himself consented to this, not indeed without much distress of spirit, on account of which I entreat you to pray for him, but eventually without opposition, believing that he submitted to Christ in submitting to you. Nay, even when I still thought it might be our duty to consider whether I should not write a second letter to you, my brother, while Timotheus still remained here, he himself, with filial reverence, feared to displease you, and cut my deliberations short by not only consenting, but even urging, that Timotheus should be restored to you.

4. I therefore, brother Severus, leave my case to be decided by you. For I am sure that Christ dwells in your heart, and by Him I beseech you to ask counsel from Him, submitting your mind to His direction regarding the question whether, when a man had begun to be a Reader in the Church confided to my care, having read, not once only, but a second and a third time, at Subsana, and in company with the presbyter of the Church of Subsana had done the same also at Turres and Ciza and Verbalis, it is either possible or right that he be pronounced to have never been a Reader. And as we have, in obedience to God, corrected that which was afterwards done contrary to our will, do you also, in obedience to Him, correct in like manner that which was formerly, through your not knowing the facts of the case, wrongly done. For I have no fear of your failing to perceive what a door is opened for breaking down the discipline of the Church, if, when a clergyman of any church has sworn to one of another church that he will not leave him, that other encourage him to remain with him, alleging that he does so that he

may not be the occasion of the breaking of an oath; seeing that he who forbids this, and declines to allow the other to remain with him (because that other could by his vow bind only his own conscience), unquestionably preserves the order which is necessary to peace in a way which none can justly censure.

LETTER LXIV.

(A.D. 401.)

TO MY LORD QUINTIANUS, MY MOST BELOVED BROTHER AND FELLOW-PRESBYTER, AUGUSTIN SENDS GREETING IN THE LORD.

1. We do not disdain to look upon bodies which are defective in beauty, especially seeing that our souls themselves are not yet so beautiful as we hope that they shall be when He who is of ineffable beauty shall have appeared, in whom, though now we see Him not, we believe; for then "we shall be like Him," when "we shall see Him as He is."[1] If you receive my counsel in a kindly and brotherly spirit, I exhort you to think thus of your soul, as we do of our own, and not presumptuously imagine that it is already perfect in beauty; but, as the apostle enjoins, "rejoice in hope," and obey the precept which he annexes to this, when he says, "Rejoicing in hope, patient in tribulation:"[2] "for we are saved by hope," as he says again; "but hope that is seen is not hope: for what a man seeth, why doth he yet hope for? But if we hope for that we see not, then do we with patience wait for it."[3] Let not this patience be wanting in thee, but with a good conscience "wait on the Lord; be of good courage, and He shall strengthen thine heart: wait, I say, on the Lord."[4]

2. It is, of course, obvious that if you come to us while debarred from communion with the venerable bishop Aurelius, you cannot be admitted to communion with us; but we would act towards you with that same charity which we are assured shall guide his conduct. Your coming to us, however, should not on this account be embarrassing to us, because the duty of submission to this, out of regard to the discipline of the Church, ought to be felt by yourself, especially if you have the approval of your own conscience, which is known to yourself and to God. For if Aurelius has deferred the examination of your case, he has done this not from dislike to you, but from the pressure of other engagements; and if you knew his circumstances as well as you know your own, the delay would cause you neither surprise nor sorrow. That it is the same

with myself, I entreat you to believe on my word, as you are equally unable to know how I am occupied. But there are other bishops older than I am, and both in authority more worthy and in place more convenient, by whose help you may more easily expedite the affairs now pending in the Church committed to your charge. I have not, however, failed to make mention of your distress, and of the complaint in your letter to my venerable brother and colleague the aged Aurelius, whom I esteem with the respect due to his worth; I took care to acquaint him with your innocence of the things laid to your charge, by sending him a copy of your letter. It was not until a day, or at the most two, before Christmas,[5] that I received the letter in which you informed me of his intention to visit the Church at Badesile, by which you fear lest the people be disturbed and influenced against you. I do not therefore presume to address by letter your people; for I could write a reply to any who had written to me, but how could I put myself forward unasked to write to a people not committed to my care?

3. Nevertheless, what I now say to you, who alone have written to me, may, through you, reach others who should hear it. I charge you then, in the first place, not to bring the Church into reproach by reading in the public assemblies those writings which the Canon of the Church has not acknowledged; for by these, heretics, and especially the Manichæans (of whom I hear that some are lurking, not without encouragement, in your district), are accustomed to subvert the minds of the inexperienced. I am amazed that a man of your wisdom should admonish me to forbid the reception into the monastery of those who have come from you to us, in order that a decree of the Council may be obeyed, and at the same time should forget another decree[6] of the same Council, declaring what are the canonical Scriptures which ought to be read to the people. Read again the proceedings of the Council, and commit them to memory: you will there find that the Canon which you refer to[7] as prohibiting the indiscriminate reception of applicants for admission to a monastery, was not framed in regard to laymen, but applies to the clergy alone. It is true there is no mention of monasteries in the canon; but it is laid down in general, that no one may receive a clergyman belonging to another diocese [except in such a way as upholds the discipline of the Church]. Moreover, it has been enacted in a recent Council,[8] that any who desert a monastery, or are expelled from one, shall not be else-

---

[1] 1 John iii. 2.
[2] Rom. xii 12.
[3] Rom. viii. 24, 25.
[4] Ps. xxvii. 14.

[5] *Pridie Natalis Domini.*
[6] See Council of Hippo, A D. 393, Can. 38, and the third Council of Carthage, A.D. 397, Can. 47.
[7] *Ibid.* Can. 21.
[8] Council of Carthage, 13th Sept. 401.

where admitted either to clerical office or to the charge of a monastery. If, therefore, you are in any measure disturbed regarding Privatio, let me inform you that he has not yet been received by us into the monastery; but that I have submitted his case to the aged Aurelius, and will act according to his decision. For it seems strange to me, if a man can be reckoned a Reader who has read only once in public, and on that occasion read writings which are not canonical. If for this reason he is regarded as an ecclesiastical reader, it follows that the writing which he read must be esteemed as sanctioned by the Church. But if the writing be not sanctioned by the Church as canonical, it follows that, although a man may have read it to a congregation, he is not thereby made an ecclesiastical reader, [but is, as before, a layman]. Nevertheless I must, in regard to the young man in question, abide by the decision of the arbiter whom I have named.

4. As to the people of Vigesile, who are to us as well as to you beloved in the bowels of Christ, if they have refused to accept a bishop who has been deposed by a plenary Council in Africa,[1] they act wisely, and cannot be compelled to yield, nor ought to be. And whoever shall attempt to compel them by violence to receive him, will show plainly what is his character, and will make men well understand what his real character was at an earlier time, when he would have had them believe no evil of him. For no one more effectually discovers the worthlessness of his cause, than the man who, employing the secular power, or any other kind of violent means, endeavours by agitating and complaining to recover the ecclesiastical rank which he has forfeited. For his desire is not to yield to Christ service which He claims, but to usurp over Christians an authority which they disown. Brethren, be cautious; great is the craft of the devil, but Christ is the wisdom of God.

LETTER LXV.

(A.D. 402.)

TO THE AGED [2] XANTIPPUS, MY LORD MOST BLESSED AND WORTHY OF VENERATION, AND MY FATHER AND COLLEAGUE IN THE PRIESTLY OFFICE, AUGUSTIN SENDS GREETING IN THE LORD.

1. Saluting your Excellency with the respect due to your worth, and earnestly seeking an interest in your prayers, I beg to submit to the consideration of your wisdom the case of a certain Abundantius, ordained a presbyter in the domain of Strabonia, belonging to my diocese. He had begun to be unfavourably reported of, through his not walking in the way which becomes the servants of God; and I being on this account alarmed, though not believing the rumours without examination, was made more watchful of his conduct, and devoted some pains to obtain, if possible, indisputable evidences of the evil courses with which he was charged. The first thing which I ascertained was, that he had embezzled the money of a countryman, entrusted to him for religious purposes, and could give no satisfactory account of his stewardship. The next thing proved against him, and admitted by his own confession, was, that on Christmas day, on which the fast was observed by the Church of Gippe as by all the other Churches, after taking leave of his colleague the presbyter of Gippe, as if going to his own church about 11 A.M., he remained, without having any ecclesiastic in his company, in the same parish, and dined, supped, and spent the night in the house of a woman of ill fame. It happened that lodging in the same place was one of our clergy of Hippo, who had gone thither; and as the facts were known beyond dispute to this witness, Abundantius could not deny the charge. As to the things which he did deny, I left them to the divine tribunal, passing sentence upon him only in regard to those things which he had not been permitted to conceal. I was afraid to leave him in charge of a Church, especially of one placed as his was, in the very midst of rabid and barking heretics. And when he begged me to give him a letter with a statement of his case to the presbyter of the parish of Armema, in the district of Bulla, from which he had come to us, so as to prevent any exaggerated suspicion there of his character, and in order that he might there live, if possible, a more consistent life, having no duties as a presbyter, I was moved by compassion to do as he desired. At the same time, it was very specially incumbent on me to submit to your wisdom these facts, lest any deception should be practised upon you.

2. I pronounced sentence in his case one hundred days before Easter Sunday, which falls this year on the 7th of April. I have taken care to acquaint you with the date, because of the decree of Council,[3] which I also did not conceal from him, but explained to him the law of the Church, that if he thought anything could be done to reverse my decision, unless he began proceedings with this view within a year, no one would, after the lapse of that time, listen to his pleading. For my own part, my lord most blessed, and father worthy of all veneration, I assure you that if I did not think that these instances of vicious conversation in an ecclesiastic, especially when accompanied with an evil reputation, deserved

---

[1] Council of Carthage, 13th Sept. 401.
[2] This title in the African Church seems equivalent to Primate when applied to a bishop. See Letter LIX.

[3] Held at Carthage, 13th Sept. 401.

to be visited with the punishment appointed by the Council, I would be compelled now to attempt to sift things which cannot be known, and either to condemn the accused upon doubtful evidence, or acquit him for want of proof. When a presbyter, upon a day of fasting which was observed as such also in the place in which he was, having taken leave of his colleague in the ministry in that place, and being unattended by any ecclesiastic, ventured to tarry in the house of a woman of ill fame, and to dine and sup and spend the night there, it seemed to me, whatever others might think, that he behoved to be deposed from his office, as I durst not commit to his charge a Church of God. If it should so happen that a different opinion be held by the ecclesiastical judges to whom he may appeal, seeing that it has been decreed by the Council[1] that the decision of six bishops be final in the case of a presbyter, let who will commit to him a Church within his jurisdiction, I confess, for my own part, that I fear to entrust any congregation whatever to persons like him, especially when nothing in the way of general good character can be alleged as a reason for excusing these delinquencies; lest, if he were to break forth into some more ruinous wickedness, I should be compelled with sorrow to blame myself for the harm done by his crime.

LETTER LXVI.

(A.D. 402.)

ADDRESSED, WITHOUT SALUTATION, TO CRISPINUS, THE DONATIST BISHOP OF CALAMA.

1. You ought to have been influenced by the fear of God; but since, in your work of rebaptizing the Mappalians,[2] you have chosen to take advantage of the fear with which as man you could inspire them, let me ask you what hinders the order of the sovereign from being carried out in the province, when the order of the governor of the province has been so fully enforced in a village? If you compare the persons concerned, you are but a vassal in possession; he is the Emperor. If you compare the positions of both, you are in a property, he is on a throne; if you compare the causes maintained by both, his aim is to heal division, and yours is to rend unity in twain. But we do not bid you stand in awe of man: though we might take steps to compel you to pay, according to the imperial decree, ten pounds of gold as the penalty of your outrage. Perhaps you might be unable to pay the fine imposed upon those who rebaptize members of the Church, having been involved in so much expense in buying people whom you might compel to submit to the rite. But, as I have said, we do not bid you be afraid of man : rather let Christ fill you with fear. I should like to know what answer you could give Him, if He said to you : "Crispinus, was it a great price which you paid in order to buy the fear of the Mappalian peasantry; and does My death, the price paid by Me to purchase the love of all nations, seem little in your eyes? Was the money which was counted out from your purse in acquiring these serfs in order to their being rebaptized, a more costly sacrifice than the blood which flowed from My side in redeeming the nations in order to their being baptized?" I know that, if you would listen to Christ, you might hear many more such appeals, and might, even by the possession which you have obtained, be warned how impious are the things which you have spoken against Christ. For if you think that your title to hold what you have bought with money is sure by human law, how much more sure, by divine law, is Christ's title to that which He hath bought with His own blood ! And it is true that He of whom it is written, "He shall have dominion from sea to sea, and from the river unto the ends of the earth," shall hold with invincible might all which He has purchased; but how can you expect with any assurance to retain that which you think you have made your own by purchase in Africa, when you affirm that Christ has lost the whole world, and been left with Africa alone as His portion?

2. But why multiply words? If these Mappalians have passed of their own free will into your communion, let them hear both you and me on the question which divides us, — the words of each of us being written down, and translated into the Punic tongue after having been attested by our signatures; and then, all pressure through fear of their superior being removed, let these vassals choose what they please. For by the things which we shall say it will be made manifest whether they remain in error under coercion, or hold what they believe to be truth with their own consent. They either understand these matters, or they do not: if they do not, how could you dare to transfer them in their ignorance to your communion? and if they do, let them, as I have said, hear both sides, and act freely for themselves. If there be any communities that have passed over from you to us, which you believe to have yielded to the pressure of their superiors, let the same be done in their case; let them hear both sides, and choose for themselves. Now, if you reject this proposal, who can fail to be convinced that your reliance is not upon the force of truth? But you ought to beware of the

---

[1] Held at Carthage, A.D. 318 or 319, Can. 11.

[2] About eighty persons, on a property which he had acquired, were compelled by Crispinus to undergo submersion, notwithstanding their groaning and protesting against this tyrannical act of their new landlord.

wrath of God both here and hereafter. I adjure you by Christ to give a reply to what I have written.

LETTER LXVII.

(A.D. 402.)

TO MY LORD MOST BELOVED AND LONGED FOR, MY HONOURED BROTHER IN CHRIST, AND FELLOW-PRESBYTER, JEROME, AUGUSTIN SENDS GREETING IN THE LORD.

CHAP. I. — 1. I have heard that my letter has come to your hand. I have not yet received a reply, but I do not on this account question your affection; doubtless something has hitherto prevented you. Wherefore I know and avow that my prayer should be, that God would put it in your power to forward your reply, for He has already given you power to prepare it, seeing that you can do so with the utmost ease if you feel disposed.

CHAP. II. — 2. I have hesitated whether to give credence or not to a certain report which has reached me; but I felt that I ought not to hesitate as to writing a few lines to you regarding the matter. To be brief, I have heard that some brethren have told your Charity that I have written a book against you and have sent it to Rome. Be assured that this is false: I call God to witness that I have not done this. But if perchance there be some things in some of my writings in which I am found to have been of a different opinion from you, I think you ought to know, or if it cannot be certainly known, at least to believe, that such things have been written not with a view of contradicting you, but only of stating my own views. In saying this, however, let me assure you that not only am I most ready to hear in a brotherly spirit the objections which you may entertain to anything in my writings which has displeased you, but I entreat, nay implore you, to acquaint me with them; and thus I shall be made glad either by the correction of my mistake, or at least by the expression of your goodwill.

3. Oh that it were in my power, by our living near each other, if not under the same roof, to enjoy frequent and sweet conference with you in the Lord! Since, however, this is not granted, I beg you to take pains that this one way in which we can be together in the Lord be kept up; nay more, improved and perfected. Do not refuse to write me in return, however seldom.

Greet with my respects our holy brother Paulinianus, and all the brethren who with you, and because of you, rejoice in the Lord. May you, remembering us, be heard by the Lord in regard to all your holy desires, my lord most beloved and longed for, my honoured brother in Christ.

LETTER LXVIII.

(A.D. 402.)

TO AUGUSTIN, MY LORD, TRULY HOLY AND MOST BLESSED FATHER,[1] JEROME SENDS GREETING IN CHRIST.

1. When my kinsman, our holy son Asterius, subdeacon, was just on the point of beginning his journey, the letter of your Grace arrived, in which you clear yourself of the charge of having sent to Rome a book written against your humble servant.[2] I had not heard that charge; but by our brother Sysinnius, deacon, copies of a letter addressed by some one apparently to me have come hither. In the said letter I am exhorted to sing the παλινωδία, confessing mistake in regard to a paragraph of the apostle's writing, and to imitate Stesichorus, who, vacillating between disparagement and praises of Helen, recovered, by praising her, the eyesight which he had forfeited by speaking against her.[3] Although the style and the method of argument appeared to be yours, I must frankly confess to your Excellency that I did not think it right to assume without examination the authenticity of a letter of which I had only seen copies, lest perchance, if offended by my reply, you should with justice complain that it was my duty first to have made sure that you were the author, and only after that was ascertained, to address you in reply. Another reason for my delay was the protracted illness of the pious and venerable Paula. For, while occupied long in attending upon her in severe illness, I had almost forgotten your letter, or more correctly, the letter written in your name, remembering the verse, "Like music in the day of mourning is an unseasonable discourse."[4] Therefore, if it is your letter, write me frankly that it is so, or send me a more accurate copy, in order that without any passionate rancour we may devote ourselves to discuss scriptural truth; and I may either correct my own mistake, or show that another has without good reason found fault with me.

2. Far be it from me to presume to attack anything which your Grace has written. For it is enough for me to prove my own views without controverting what others hold. But it is well known to one of your wisdom, that every one is satisfied with his own opinion, and that it is puerile self-sufficiency to seek, as young men have of old been wont to do, to gain glory to one's own name by assailing men who have become renowned. I am not so foolish as to think myself insulted by the fact that you give an explanation different from mine; since you, on the

---

[1] *Papæ.*
[2] *Parvitas mea.*
[3] See Letter XL. sec. 7, p. 274
[4] Ecclus. xxii. 6.

other hand, are not wronged by my views being contrary to those which you maintain. But that is the kind of reproof by which friends may truly benefit each other, when each, not seeing his own bag of faults, observes, as Persius has it, the wallet borne by the other.[1] Let me say further, love one who loves you, and do not because you are young challenge a veteran in the field of Scripture. I have had my time, and have run my course to the utmost of my strength. It is but fair that I should rest, while you in your turn run and accomplish great distances ; at the same time (with your leave, and without intending any disrespect), lest it should seem that to quote from the poets is a thing which you alone can do, let me remind you of the encounter between Dares and Entellus,[2] and of the proverb, " The tired ox treads with a firmer step." With sorrow I have dictated these words. Would that I could receive your embrace, and that by converse we might aid each other in learning !

3. With his usual effrontery, Calphurnius, surnamed Lanarius,[3] has sent me his execrable writings, which I understand that he has been at pains to disseminate in Africa also. To these I have replied in part, and shortly ; and I have sent you a copy of my treatise, intending by the first opportunity to send you a larger work, when I have leisure to prepare it. In this treatise I have been careful not to offend Christian feeling in any, but only to confute the lies and hallucinations arising from his ignorance and madness.

Remember me, holy and venerable father. See how sincerely I love thee, in that I am unwilling, even when challenged, to reply, and refuse to believe you to be the author of that which in another I would sharply rebuke. Our brother Communis sends his respectful salutation.

LETTER LXIX.

(A.D. 402.)

TO THEIR JUSTLY BELOVED LORD CASTORIUS, THEIR TRULY WELCOMED AND WORTHILY HONOURED SON, ALYPIUS AND AUGUSTIN SEND GREETING IN THE LORD.

1. An attempt was made by the enemy of Christians to cause, by occasion of our very dear and sweet son your brother, the agitation of a most dangerous scandal within the Catholic Church, which as a mother welcomed you to her affectionate embrace when you fled from a disinherited and separated fragment into the heritage of Christ ; the desire of that enemy being evidently to becloud with unseemly melancholy the calm beauty of joy which was imparted to us by the blessing of your conversion. But the Lord our God, who is compassionate and merciful, who comforteth them that are cast down, nourishing the infants, and cherishing the infirm, permitted him to gain in some measure success in this design, only to make us rejoice more over the prevention of the calamity than we grieved over the danger. For it is a far more magnanimous thing to have resigned the onerous responsibilities of the bishop's dignity in order to save the Church from danger, than to have accepted these in order to have a share in her government. He truly proves that he was worthy of holding that office, had the interests of peace permitted him to do so, who does not insist upon retaining it when he cannot do so without endangering the peace of the Church. It has accordingly pleased God to show, by means of your brother, our beloved son Maximianus, unto the enemies of His Church, that there are within her those who seek not their own things, but the things of Jesus Christ. For in laying down that ministry of stewardship of the mysteries of God, he was not deserting his duty under the pressure of some worldly desire, but acting under the impulse of a pious love of peace, lest, on account of the honour conferred upon him, there should arise among the members of Christ an unseemly and dangerous, perhaps even fatal, dissension. For could anything have been more infatuated and worthy of utter reprobation, than to forsake schismatics because of the peace of the Catholic Church, and then to trouble that same Catholic peace by the question of one's own rank and preferment? On the other hand, could anything be more praiseworthy, and more in accordance with Christian charity, than that, after having forsaken the frenzied pride of the Donatists, he should, in the manner of his cleaving to the heritage of Christ, give such a signal proof of humility under the power of love for the unity of the Church? As for him, therefore, we rejoice indeed that he has been proved of such stability that the storm of this temptation has not cast down what divine truth had built in his heart ; and therefore we desire and pray the Lord to grant that, by his life and conversation in the future, he may make it more and more manifest how well he would have discharged the responsibilities of that office which he would have accepted if that had been his duty. May that eternal peace which is promised to the Church be given in recompense to him, who discerned that the things which were not compatible with the peace of the Church were not expedient for him !

2. As for you, our dear son, in whom we have great joy, since you are not restrained from ac-

---

[1] " Ut nemo in sese tentat descendere, nemo;
Sed præcedenti spectatur mantica tergo." — *Sat.* iv. 29. See also *Phædrus,* iv. 10.
[2] Virgil, *Æneid,* v. 369 seq.
[3] Rufinus.

cepting the office of bishop by any such considerations as have guided your brother in declining it, it becomes one of your disposition to devote to Christ that which is in you by His own gift. Your talents, prudence, eloquence, gravity, self-control, and everything else which adorns your conversation, are the gifts of God. To what service can they be more fittingly devoted than to His by whom they were bestowed, in order that they may be preserved, increased, perfected, and rewarded by Him? Let them not be devoted to the service of this world, lest with it they pass away and perish. We know that, in dealing with you, it is not necessary to insist much on your reflecting, as you may so easily do, upon the hopes of vain men, their insatiable desires, and the uncertainty of life. Away, therefore, with every expectation of deceptive and earthly felicity which your mind had grasped: labour in the vineyard of God, where the fruit is sure, where so many promises have already received so large measure of fulfilment, that it would be the height of madness to despair as to those which remain. We beseech you by the divinity and humanity of Christ, and by the peace of that heavenly city where we receive eternal rest after labouring for the time of our pilgrimage, to take the place as the bishop of the Church of Vagina which your brother has resigned, not under ignominious deposition, but by magnanimous concession. Let that people for whom we expect the richest increase of blessings through your mind and tongue, endowed and adorned by the gifts of God, — let that people, we say, perceive through you, that in what your brother has done, he was consulting not his own indolence, but their peace.

We have given orders that this letter be not read to you until those to whom you are necessary hold you in actual possession.[1] For we hold you in the bond of spiritual love, because to us also you are very necessary as a colleague. Our reason for not coming in person to you, you shall afterwards learn.

LETTER LXX.

(A.D. 402.)

This letter is addressed by Alypius and Augustin to Naucelio, a person through whom they had discussed the question of the Donatist schism with Clarentius, an aged Donatist bishop (probably the same with the Numidian bishop of Tabraca, who took part in the Conference at Carthage in 411 A.D.). The ground traversed in the letter is the same as in pages 296 and 297, in Letter LI., regarding the inconsistencies of the Donatists in the case of Felicianus of Musti. We therefore leave it untranslated.

---

[1] It would seem that there was some reason to fear lest Castorius should elsewhere devote his talents to some other calling, and that a deputation from Vagina had been sent to seek him and bring him to that place. Alypius and Augustin for some reason did not accompany the deputation, but sent this letter with them.

LETTER LXXI.

(A.D. 403.)

TO MY VENERABLE LORD JEROME, MY ESTEEMED AND HOLY BROTHER AND FELLOW-PRESBYTER, AUGUSTIN SENDS GREETING IN THE LORD.

CHAP. I. — 1. Never since I began to write to you, and to long for your writing in return, have I met with a better opportunity for our exchanging communications than now, when my letter is to be carried to you by a most faithful servant and minister of God, who is also a very dear friend of mine, namely, our son Cyprian, deacon. Through him I expect to receive a letter from you with all the certainty which is in a matter of this kind possible. For the son whom I have named will not be found wanting in respect of zeal in asking, or persuasive influence in obtaining a reply from you; nor will he fail in diligently keeping, promptly bearing, and faithfully delivering the same. I only pray that if I be in any way worthy of this, the Lord may give His help and favour to your heart and to my desire, so that no higher will may hinder that which your brotherly goodwill inclines you to do.

2. As I have sent you two letters already to which I have received no reply, I have resolved to send you at this time copies of both of them, for I suppose that they never reached you. If they did reach you, and your replies have failed, as may be the case, to reach me, send me a second time the same as you sent before, if you have copies of them preserved: if you have not, dictate again what I may read, and do not refuse to send to these former letters the answer for which I have been waiting so long. My first letter to you, which I had prepared while I was a presbyter, was to be delivered to you by a brother of ours, Profuturus, who afterwards became my colleague in the episcopate, and has since then departed from this life; but he could not then bear it to you in person, because at the very time when he intended to begin his journey, he was prevented by his ordination to the weighty office of bishop, and shortly afterwards he died. This letter I have resolved also to send at this time, that you may know how long I have cherished a burning desire for conversation with you, and with what reluctance I submit to the remote separation which prevents my mind from having access to yours through our bodily senses, my brother, most amiable and honoured among the members of the Lord.

CHAP. II. — 3. In this letter I have further to say, that I have since heard that you have translated Job out of the original Hebrew, although in your own translation of the same prophet from the Greek tongue we had already a version of that book. In that earlier version you marked with asterisks the words found in the Hebrew but wanting in the Greek, and with obelisks the words found in the Greek but wanting in the Hebrew ; and this was done with such astonishing exactness, that in some places we have every word distinguished by a separate asterisk, as a sign that these words are in the Hebrew, but not in the Greek. Now, however, in this more recent version from the Hebrew, there is not the same scrupulous fidelity as to the words ; and it perplexes any thoughtful reader to understand either what was the reason for marking the asterisks in the former version with so much care that they indicate the absence from the Greek version of even the smallest grammatical particles which have not been rendered from the Hebrew, or what is the reason for so much less care having been taken in this recent version from the Hebrew to secure that these same particles be found in their own places. I would have put down here an extract or two in illustration of this criticism ; but at present I have not access to the MS. of the translation from the Hebrew. Since, however, your quick discernment anticipates and goes beyond not only what I have said, but also what I meant to say, you already understand, I think, enough to be able, by giving the reason for the plan which you have adopted, to explain what perplexes me.

4. For my part, I would much rather that you would furnish us with a translation of the Greek version of the canonical Scriptures known as the work of the Seventy translators. For if your translation begins to be more generally read in many churches, it will be a grievous thing that, in the reading of Scripture, differences must arise between the Latin Churches and the Greek Churches, especially seeing that the discrepancy is easily condemned in a Latin version by the production of the original in Greek, which is a language very widely known ; whereas, if any one has been disturbed by the occurrence of something to which he was not accustomed in the translation taken from the Hebrew, and alleges that the new translation is wrong, it will be found difficult, if not impossible, to get at the Hebrew documents by which the version to which exception is taken may be defended. And when they are obtained, who will submit to have so many Latin and Greek authorities pronounced to be in the wrong? Besides all this, Jews, if consulted as to the meaning of the Hebrew text, may give a different opinion from yours : in which case it will seem as if your presence were indispensable, as being the only one who could refute their view ; and it would be a miracle if one could be found capable of acting as arbiter between you and them.

CHAP. III. — 5. A certain bishop, one of our brethren, having introduced in the church over which he presides the reading of your version, came upon a word in the book of the prophet Jonah, of which you have given a very different rendering from that which had been of old familiar to the senses and memory of all the worshippers, and had been chanted for so many generations in the church.[1] Thereupon arose such a tumult in the congregation, especially among the Greeks, correcting what had been read, and denouncing the translation as false, that the bishop was compelled to ask the testimony of the Jewish residents (it was in the town of Oea). These, whether from ignorance or from spite, answered that the words in the Hebrew MSS. were correctly rendered in the Greek version, and in the Latin one taken from it. What further need I say? The man was compelled to correct your version in that passage as if it had been falsely translated, as he desired not to be left without a congregation, — a calamity which he narrowly escaped. From this case we also are led to think that you may be occasionally mistaken. You will also observe how great must have been the difficulty if this had occurred in those writings which cannot be explained by comparing the testimony of languages now in use.

CHAP. IV. — 6. At the same time, we are in no small measure thankful to God for the work in which you have translated the Gospels from the original Greek, because in almost every passage we have found nothing to object to, when we compared it with the Greek Scriptures. By this work, any disputant who supports an old false translation is either convinced or confuted with the utmost ease by the production and collation of MSS. And if, as indeed very rarely happens, something be found to which exception may be taken, who would be so unreasonable as not to excuse it readily in a work so useful that it cannot be too highly praised? I wish you would have the kindness to open up to me what you think to be the reason of the frequent discrepancies between the text supported by the Hebrew codices and the Greek Septuagint version. For the latter has no mean authority, seeing that it has obtained so wide circulation, and was the one which the apostles used, as is not only proved by looking to the text itself, but has also been, as I remember, affirmed by yourself. You would therefore confer upon us a much greater boon if you gave an exact Latin translation of the Greek Septuagint version : for the variations found in the different codices of the Latin text are intolerably numerous ; and it is so justly open to suspicion as possibly different from what is to be found in the Greek, that one has no confidence in either quoting it or proving anything by its help.

----

[1] Jonah iv. 6.

I thought that this letter was to be a short one, but it has somehow been as pleasant to me to go on with it as if I were talking with you. I conclude with entreating you by the Lord kindly to send me a full reply, and thus give me, so far as is in your power, the pleasure of your presence.

LETTER LXXII.

(A.D. 404.)

TO AUGUSTIN, MY LORD TRULY HOLY, AND MOST BLESSED FATHER, JEROME SENDS GREETING IN THE LORD.

CHAP. I. — 1. You are sending me letter upon letter, and often urging me to answer a certain letter of yours, a copy of which, without your signature, had reached me through our brother Sysinnius, deacon, as I have already written, which letter you tell me that you entrusted first to our brother Profuturus, and afterwards to some one else; but that Profuturus was prevented from finishing his intended journey, and having been ordained a bishop, was removed by sudden death; and the second messenger, whose name you do not give, was afraid of the perils of the sea, and gave up the voyage which he had intended. These things being so, I am at a loss to express my surprise that the same letter is reported to be in the possession of most of the Christians in Rome, and throughout Italy, and has come to every one but myself, to whom alone it was ostensibly sent. I wonder at this all the more, because the brother Sysinnius aforesaid tells me that he found it among the rest of your published works, not in Africa, not in your possession, but in an island of the Adriatic some five years ago.

2. True friendship can harbour no suspicion; a friend must speak to his friend as freely as to his second self. Some of my acquaintances, vessels of Christ, of whom there is a very large number in Jerusalem and in the holy places, suggested to me that this had not been done by you in a guileless spirit, but through desire for praise and celebrity, and *éclat* in the eyes of the people, intending to become famous at my expense; that many might know that you challenged me, and I feared to meet you; that you had written as a man of learning, and I had by silence confessed my ignorance, and had at last found one who knew how to stop my garrulous tongue. I, however, let me say it frankly, refused at first to answer your Excellency, because I did not believe that the letter, or as I may call it (using a proverbial expression), the honeyed sword, was sent from you. Moreover, I was cautious lest I should seem to answer uncourteously a bishop of my own communion, and to censure anything in the letter of one who censured me, especially as I judged some of its statements to be tainted with heresy.[1] Lastly, I was afraid lest you should have reason to remonstrate with me, saying, "What! had you seen the letter to be mine, — had you discovered in the signature attached to it the autograph of a hand well known to you, when you so carelessly wounded the feelings of your friend, and reproached me with that which the malice of another had conceived?"

CHAP. II. — 3. Wherefore, as I have already written, either send me the identical letter in question subscribed with your own hand, or desist from annoying an old man, who seeks retirement in his monastic cell. If you wish to exercise or display your learning, choose as your antagonists, young, eloquent, and illustrious men, of whom it is said that many are found in Rome, who may be neither unable nor afraid to meet you, and to enter the lists with a bishop in debates concerning the Sacred Scriptures. As for me, a soldier once, but a retired veteran now, it becomes me rather to applaud the victories won by you and others, than with my worn-out body to take part in the conflict; beware lest, if you persist in demanding a reply, I call to mind the history of the way in which Quintus Maximus by his patience defeated Hannibal, who was, in the pride of youth, confident of success.[2]

"Omnia fert ætas, animum quoque. Sæpe ego longos
Cantando puerum memini me condere soles:
Nunc oblita mihi tot carmina : vox quoque Mœrin
Jam fugit ipsa."[3]

Or rather, to quote an instance from Scripture: Barzillai of Gilead, when he declined in favour of his youthful son the kindnesses of King David and all the charms of his court, taught us that old age ought neither to desire these things, nor to accept them when offered.

4. As to your calling God to witness that you had not written a book against me, and of course had not sent to Rome what you had never written, adding that, if perchance some things were found in your works in which a different opinion from mine was advanced, no wrong had thereby been done to me, because you had, without any intention of offending me, written only what you believed to be right; I beg you to hear me with patience. You never wrote a book against me: how then has there been brought to me a copy, written by another hand, of a treatise containing a rebuke administered to me by you? How comes Italy to possess a treatise of yours which you did not write? Nay, how can you reasonably ask me to reply to that which you solemnly assure me was never written by you? Nor am I so foolish as to think that I am insulted by you, if

---

[1] I have taken the liberty of making chap. ii. begin at the end instead of the beginning of this sentence, where its interruption of the paragraph bewilders the reader.
[2] Livy, book xxii.
[3] Virgil, *Eclogue* ix.

in anything your opinion differs from mine. But if, challenging me as it were to single combat, you take exception to my views, and demand a reason for what I have written, and insist upon my correcting what you judge to be an error, and call upon me to recant it in a humble παλινῳδία, and speak of your curing me of blindness; in this I maintain that friendship is wounded, and the laws of brotherly union are set at nought. Let not the world see us quarrelling like children, and giving material for angry contention between those who may become our respective supporters or adversaries. I write what I have now written, because I desire to cherish towards you pure and Christian love, and not to hide in my heart anything which does not agree with the utterance of my lips. For it does not become me, who have spent my life from youth until now, sharing the arduous labours of pious brethren in an obscure monastery, to presume to write anything against a bishop of my own communion, especially against one whom I had begun to love before I knew him, who also sought my friendship before I sought his, and whom I rejoiced to see rising as a successor to myself in the careful study of the Scriptures. Wherefore either disown that book, if you are not its author, and give over urging me to reply to that which you never wrote; or if the book is yours, admit it frankly; so that if I write anything in self-defence, the responsibility may lie on you who gave, not on me who am forced to accept, the challenge.

CHAP. III. — 5. You say also, that if there be anything in your writings which has displeased me, and which I would wish to correct, you are ready to receive my criticism as a brother; and you not only assure me that you would rejoice in such proof of my goodwill toward you, but you earnestly ask me to do this. I tell you again, without reserve, what I feel: you are challenging an old man, disturbing the peace of one who asks only to be allowed to be silent, and you seem to desire to display your learning. It is not for one of my years to give the impression of enviously disparaging one whom I ought rather to encourage by approbation. And if the ingenuity of perverse men finds something which they may plausibly censure in the writings even of evangelists and prophets, are you amazed if, in your books, especially in your exposition of passages in Scripture which are exceedingly difficult of interpretation, some things be found which are not perfectly correct? This I say, however, not because I can at this time pronounce anything in your works to merit censure. For, in the first place, I have never read them with attention; and in the second place, we have not beside us a supply of copies of what you have written, excepting the books of Soliloquies and Commentaries on some of the Psalms; which,

if I were disposed to criticise them, I could prove to be at variance, I shall not say with my own opinion, for I am nobody, but with the interpretations of the older Greek commentators.

Farewell, my very dear friend, my son in years, my father in ecclesiastical dignity; and to this I most particularly request your attention, that henceforth you make sure that I be the first to receive whatever you may write to me.

LETTER LXXIII.

(A.D. 404.)

TO JEROME, MY VENERABLE AND MOST ESTEEMED BROTHER AND FELLOW-PRESBYTER, AUGUSTIN SENDS GREETING IN THE LORD.

CHAP. I. — 1. Although I suppose that, before this reaches you, you have received through our son the deacon Cyprian, a servant of God, the letter which I sent by him, from which you would be apprised with certainty that I wrote the letter of which you mentioned that a copy had been brought to you; in consequence of which I suppose that I have begun already, like the rash Dares, to be beaten and belaboured by the missiles and the merciless fists of a second Entellus[1] in the reply which you have written; nevertheless I answer in the meantime the letter which you have deigned to send me by our holy son Asterius, in which I have found many proofs of your most kind goodwill to me, and at the same time some signs of your having in some measure felt agrieved by me. In reading it, therefore, I was no sooner soothed by one sentence than I was buffeted in another; my wonder being especially called forth by this, that after alleging, as your reason for not rashly accepting as authentic the letter from me of which you had a copy, the fact that, offended by your reply, I might justly remonstrate with you, because you ought first to have ascertained that it was mine before answering it, you go on to command me to acknowledge the letter frankly if it is mine, or send a more reliable copy of it, in order that we may, without any bitterness of feeling, address ourselves to the discussion of scriptural doctrine. For how can we engage in such discussion without bitterness of feeling, if you have made up your mind to offend me? or, if your mind is not made up to this, what reason could I have had, when you did not offend me, for justly complaining as having been offended by you, that you ought first to have made sure that the letter was mine, and only then to have replied, that is to say, only then to have offended me? For if there had been nothing to offend me in your reply, I could have had no just ground of com-

---

[1] See Jerome's Letter, LXVIII., sec. 2, p. 325.

plaint. Accordingly, when you write such a reply to that letter as must offend me, what hope is left of our engaging without any bitterness in the discussion of scriptural doctrine? Far be it from me to take offence if you are willing and able to prove, by incontrovertible argument, that you have apprehended more correctly than I have the meaning of that passage in Paul's Epistle [to the Galatians], or of any other text in Holy Scripture : nay, more, far be it from me to count it aught else than gain to myself, and cause of thankfulness to you, if in anything I am either informed by your teaching or set right by your correction.

2. But, my very dear brother, you could not think that I could be offended by your reply, had you not thought that you were offended by what I had written. For I could never have entertained concerning you the idea that you had not felt yourself offended by me if you so framed your reply as to offend me in return. If, on the other hand, I have been supposed by you to be capable of such preposterous folly as to take offence when you had not written in such a way as to give me occasion, you have in this already wronged me, that you have entertained such an opinion of me. But surely you who are so cautious, that although you recognised my style in the letter of which you had a copy, you refused to believe its authenticity, would not without consideration believe me to be so different from what your experience has proved me to be. For if you had good reason for seeing that I might justly complain had you hastily concluded that a letter not written by me was mine, how much more reasonably may I complain if you form, without consideration, such an estimate of myself as is contradicted by your own experience ! You would not therefore go so far astray in your judgment as to believe, when you had written nothing by which I could be offended, that I would nevertheless be so foolish as to be capable of being offended by such a reply.

CHAP. II. — 3. There can therefore be no doubt that you were prepared to reply in such a way as would offend me, if you had only indisputable evidence that the letter was mine. Accordingly, since I do not believe that you would think it right to offend me unless you had just cause, it remains for me to confess, as I now do, my fault as having been the first to offend by writing that letter which I cannot deny to be mine. Why should I strive to swim against the current, and not rather ask pardon? I therefore entreat you by the mercy of Christ to forgive me wherein I have injured you, and not to render evil for evil by injuring me in return. For it will be an injury to me if you pass over in silence anything which you find wrong in either

word or action of mine. If, indeed, you rebuke in me that which merits no rebuke, you do wrong to yourself, not to me ; for far be it from one of your life and holy vows to rebuke merely from a desire to give offence, using the tongue of malice to condemn in me that which by the truth-revealing light of reason you know to deserve no blame. Therefore either rebuke kindly him whom, though he is free from fault, you think to merit rebuke ; or with a father's kindness soothe him whom you cannot bring to agree with you. For it is possible that your opinion may be at variance with the truth, while notwithstanding your actions are in harmony with Christian charity: for I also shall most thankfully receive your rebuke as a most friendly action, even though the thing censured be capable of defence, and therefore ought not to have been censured ; or else I shall acknowledge both your kindness and my fault, and shall be found, so far as the Lord enables me, grateful for the one, and corrected in regard to the other.

4. Why, then, shall I fear your words, hard, perhaps, like the boxing-gloves of Entellus, but certainly fitted to do me good? The blows of Entellus were intended not to heal, but to harm, and therefore his antagonist was conquered, not cured. But I, if I receive your correction calmly as a necessary medicine, shall not be pained by it. If, however, through weakness, either common to human nature or peculiar to myself, I cannot help feeling some pain from rebuke, even when I am justly reproved, it is far better to have a tumour in one's head cured, though the lance cause pain, than to escape the pain by letting the disease go on. This was clearly seen by him who said that, for the most part, our enemies who expose our faults are more useful than friends who are afraid to reprove us. For the former, in their angry recriminations, sometimes charge us with what we indeed require to correct ; but the latter, through fear of destroying the sweetness of friendship, show less boldness on behalf of right than they ought. Since, therefore, you are, to quote your own comparison, an ox [1] worn out, perhaps, as to your bodily strength by reason of years, but unimpaired in mental vigour, and toiling still assiduously and with profit in the Lord's threshing-floor ; here am I, and in whatever I have spoken amiss, tread firmly on me: the weight of your venerable age should not be grievous to me, if the chaff of my fault be so bruised under foot as to be separated from me.

5. Let me further say, that it is with the utmost affectionate yearning that I read or recollect the words at the end of your letter, "Would that I could receive your embrace, and that by

[1] See p. 325.

converse we might aid each other in learning."
For my part, I say, — Would that we were even
dwelling in parts of the earth less widely separated ; so that if we could not meet for converse, we might at least have a more frequent
exchange of letters. For as it is, so great is the
distance by which we are prevented from any
kind of access to each other through the eye and
ear, that I remember writing to your Holiness
regarding these words in the Epistle to the Galatians when I was young ; and behold I am now
advanced in age, and have not yet received a
reply, and a copy of my letter has reached you
by some strange accident earlier than the letter
itself, about the transmission of which I took no
small pains. For the man to whom I entrusted
it neither delivered it to you nor returned it to
me. So great in my esteem is the value of those
of your writings which we have been able to procure, that I should prefer to all other studies the
privilege, if it were attainable by me, of sitting
by your side and learning from you. Since I
cannot do this myself, I propose to send to you
one of my sons in the Lord, that he may for my
benefit be instructed by you, in the event of
my receiving from you a favourable reply in regard
to the matter. For I have not now, and I can
never hope to have, such knowledge of the Divine Scriptures as I see you possess. Whatever
abilities I may have for such study, I devote entirely to the instruction of the people whom God
has entrusted to me ; and I am wholly precluded
by my ecclesiastical occupations from having
leisure for any further prosecution of my studies
than is necessary for my duty in public teaching.

CHAP. III. — 6. I am not acquainted with the
writings speaking injuriously of you, which you
tell me have come into Africa. I have, however,
received the reply to these which you have been
pleased to send. After reading it, let me say
frankly, I have been exceedingly grieved that
the mischief of such painful discord has arisen
between persons once so loving and intimate, and
formerly united by the bond of a friendship which
was well known in almost all the Churches. In
that treatise of yours, any one may see how you
are keeping yourself under restraint, and holding
back the stinging keenness of your indignation,
lest you should render railing for railing. If,
however, even in reading this reply of yours, I
fainted with grief and shuddered with fear, what
would be the effect produced in me by the things
which he has written against you, if they should
come into my possession ! "Woe unto the
world because of offences !"[1] Behold the complete fulfilment of which He who is Truth foretold : "Because iniquity shall abound, the love
of many shall wax cold."[2] For what trusting

hearts can now pour themselves forth with any
assurance of their confidence being reciprocated?
Into whose breast may confiding love now throw
itself without reserve? In short, where is the
friend who may not be feared as possibly a future
enemy, if the breach that we deplore could arise
between Jerome and Rufinus? Oh, sad and pit-
iable is our portion ! Who can rely upon the
affection of his friends because of what he knows
them to be now, when he has no foreknowledge
of what they shall afterwards become? But why
should I reckon it cause for sorrow, that one man
is thus ignorant of what another may become,
when no man knows even what he himself is
afterwards to be? The utmost that he knows,
and that he knows but imperfectly, is his present
condition ; of what he shall hereafter become
he has no knowledge.

7. Do the holy and blessed angels possess not
only this knowledge of their actual character,
but also a foreknowledge of what they shall af-
terward become? If they do, I cannot see how
it was possible for Satan ever to have been happy,
even while he was still a good angel, knowing,
as in this case he must have known, his future
transgression and eternal punishment. I would
wish to hear what you think as to this question,
if indeed it be one which it would be profitable
for us to be able to answer. But mark here what
I suffer from the lands and seas which keep us,
so far as the body is concerned, distant from each
other. If I were myself the letter which you
are now reading, you might have told me already
what I have just asked ; but now, when will you
write me a reply? when will you get it sent away?
when will it come here? when shall I receive it?
And yet, would that I were sure that it would
come at last, though meanwhile I must summon
all the patience which I can command to endure
the unwelcome but unavoidable delay ! Wherefore I come back to those most delightful words
of your letter, filled with your holy longing, and
I in turn appropriate them as my own : "Would
that I might receive your embrace, and that by
converse we might aid each other in learning,"
— if indeed there be any sense in which I could
possibly impart instruction to you.

8. When by these words, now mine not less
than yours, I am gladdened and refreshed, and
when I am comforted not a little by the fact
that in both of us a desire for mutual fellowship
exists, though meanwhile unsatisfied, it is not
long before I am pierced through by darts of
keenest sorrow when I consider Rufinus and
you, to whom God had granted in fullest measure and for a length of time that which both of
us have longed for, so that in most close and
endearing fellowship you feasted together on the
honey of the Holy Scriptures, and think how
between you the blight of such exceeding bitter-

---

[1] Matt. xviii. 7.
[2] Matt. xxiv. 12.

ness has found its way, constraining us to ask when, where, and in whom the same calamity may not be reasonably feared; seeing that it has befallen you at the very time when, unencumbered, having cast away secular burdens, you were following the Lord and were living together in that very land which was trodden by the feet of our Lord, when He said, "Peace I leave with you, My peace I give unto you;"[1] being, moreover, men of mature age, whose life was devoted to the study of the word of God. Truly "man's life on earth is a period of trial."[2] If I could anywhere meet you both together — which, alas, I cannot hope to do — so strong are my agitation, grief, and fear, that I think I would cast myself at your feet, and there weeping till I could weep no more, would, with all the eloquence of love, appeal first to each of you for his own sake, then to both for each other's sake, and for the sake of those, especially the weak, "for whom Christ died,"[3] whose salvation is in peril, as they look on you who occupy a place so conspicuous on the stage of time; imploring you not to write and scatter abroad these hard words against each other, which, if at any time you who are now at variance were reconciled, you could not destroy, and which you could not then venture to read lest strife should be kindled anew.

9. But I say to your Charity, that nothing has made me tremble more than your estrangement from Rufinus, when I read in your letter some of the indications of your being displeased with me. I refer not so much to what you say of Entellus and of the wearied ox, in which you appear to me to use genial pleasantry rather than angry threat, but to that which you have evidently written in earnest, of which I have already spoken perhaps more than was fitting, but not more than my fears compelled me to do, — namely, the words, "lest perchance, being offended, you should have reason to remonstrate with me." If it be possible for us to examine and discuss anything by which our hearts may be nourished, without any bitterness of discord, I entreat you let us address ourselves to this. But if it is not possible for either of us to point out what he may judge to demand correction in the other's writings, without being suspected of envy and regarded as wounding friendship, let us, having regard to our spiritual life and health, leave such conference alone. Let us content ourselves with smaller attainments in that [knowledge] which puffeth up, if we can thereby preserve unharmed that [charity] which edifieth.[4] I feel that I come far short of that perfection of

which it is written, "If any man offend not in word, the same is a perfect man;"[5] but through God's mercy I truly believe myself able to ask your forgiveness for that in which I have offended you: and this you ought to make plain to me, that through my hearing you, you may gain your brother.[6] Nor should you make it a reason for leaving me in error, that the distance between us on the earth's surface makes it impossible for us to meet face to face. As concerns the subjects into which we inquire, if I know, or believe, or think that I have got hold of the truth in a matter in which your opinion is different from mine, I shall by all means endeavour, as the Lord may enable me, to maintain my view without injuring you. And as to any offence which I may give to you, so soon as I perceive your displeasure, I shall unreservedly beg your forgiveness.

10. I think, moreover, that your reason for being displeased with me can only be, that I have either said what I ought not, or have not expressed myself in the manner in which I ought: for I do not wonder that we are less thoroughly known to each other than we are to our most close and intimate friends. Upon the love of such friends I readily cast myself without reservation, especially when chafed and wearied by the scandals of this world; and in their love I rest without any disturbing care: for I perceive that God is there, on whom I confidingly cast myself, and in whom I confidingly rest. Nor in this confidence am I disturbed by any fear of that uncertainty as to the morrow which must be present when we lean upon human weakness, and which I have in a former paragraph bewailed. For when I perceive that a man is burning with Christian love, and feel that thereby he has been made a faithful friend to me, whatever plans or thoughts of mine I entrust to him I regard as entrusted not to the man, but to Him in whom his character makes it evident that he dwells: for "God is love, and he that dwelleth in love dwelleth in God, and God in him;"[7] and if he cease to dwell in love, his forsaking it cannot but cause as much pain as his abiding in it caused joy. Nevertheless, in such a case, when one who was an intimate friend has become an enemy, it is better that he should search out what ingenuity may help him to fabricate to our prejudice, than that he should find what anger may provoke him to reveal. This every one most easily secures, not by concealing what he does, but by doing nothing which he would wish to conceal. And this the mercy of God grants to good and pious men: they go out and in among their friends in liberty and without fear, whatever these friends may afterwards become: the sins which may

1 John xiv. 27.
2 Job vii. 1, according to the LXX., and more correctly than in E. V.
3 1 Cor. viii. 11.
4 1 Cor. viii. 1.
5 Jas iii. 2.
6 Matt. xviii. 18.
7 1 John iv. 16.

have been committed by others within their knowledge they do not reveal, and they themselves avoid doing what they would fear to see revealed. For when any false charge is fabricated by a slanderer, either it is disbelieved, or, if it is believed, our reputation alone is injured, our spiritual wellbeing is not affected. But when any sinful action is committed, that action becomes a secret enemy, even though it be not revealed by the thoughtless or malicious talk of one acquainted with our secrets. Wherefore any person of discernment may see in your own example how, by the comfort of a good conscience, you bear what would otherwise be insupportable — the incredible enmity of one who was formerly your most intimate and beloved friend; and how even what he utters against you, even what may to your disadvantage be believed by some, you turn to good account as the armour of righteousness on the left hand, which is not less useful than armour on the right hand[1] in our warfare with the devil. But truly I would rather see him less bitter in his accusations, than see you thus more fully armed by them. This is a great and a lamentable wonder, that you should have passed from such amity to such enmity: it would be a joyful and a much greater event, should you come back from such enmity to the friendship of former days.

LETTER LXXIV.

(A.D. 404.)

TO MY LORD PRÆSIDIUS, MOST BLESSED, MY BROTHER AND PARTNER IN THE PRIESTLY OFFICE, TRULY ESTEEMED, AUGUSTIN SENDS GREETING IN THE LORD.

1. I write to remind you of the request which I made to you as a sincere friend when you were here, that you would not refuse to send a letter of mine to our holy brother and fellow-presbyter Jerome; in order, moreover, to let your Charity know in what terms you ought to write to him on my behalf. I have sent a copy of my letter to him, and of his to me, by reading which your pious wisdom may easily see both the moderation of tone which I have been careful to preserve, and the vehemence on his part by which I have been not unreasonably filled with fear. If, however, I have written anything which I ought not to have written, or have expressed myself in an unbecoming way, let it not be to him, but to myself, in brotherly love, that you send your opinion of what I have done, in order that, if I am convinced of my fault by your rebuke, I may ask his forgiveness.

LETTER LXXV.

(A.D. 404.)

Jerome's answer to Letters XXVIII., XL., and LXXI.

TO AUGUSTIN, MY LORD TRULY HOLY, AND MOST BLESSED FATHER, JEROME SENDS GREETING IN CHRIST.

CHAP. I. — I. I have received by Cyprian, deacon, three letters, or rather three little books, at the same time, from your Excellency, containing what you call sundry questions, but what I feel to be animadversions on opinions which I have published, to answer which, if I were disposed to do it, would require a pretty large volume. Nevertheless I shall attempt to reply without exceeding the limits of a moderately long letter, and without causing delay to our brother, now in haste to depart, who only three days before the time fixed for his journey asked earnestly for a letter to take with him, in consequence of which I am compelled to pour out these sentences, such as they are, almost without premeditation, answering you in a rambling effusion, prepared not in the leisure of deliberate composition, but in the hurry of extemporaneous dictation, which usually produces a discourse that is more the offspring of chance than the parent of instruction; just as unexpected attacks throw into confusion even the bravest soldiers, and they are compelled to take to flight before they can gird on their armour.

2. But our armour is Christ; it is that which the Apostle Paul prescribes when, writing to the Ephesians, he says, "Take unto you the whole armour of God, that ye may be able to withstand in the evil day;" and again, "Stand, therefore, having your loins girt about with truth, and having on the breastplate of righteousness; and your feet shod with the preparation of the gospel of peace; above all, taking the shield of faith, wherewith ye shall be able to quench all the fiery darts of the wicked: and take the helmet of salvation, and the sword of the Spirit, which is the word of God."[2] Armed with these weapons, King David went forth in his day to battle; and taking from the torrent's bed five smooth rounded stones, he proved that, even amidst all the eddying currents of the world, his feelings were free both from roughness and from defilement; drinking of the brook by the way, and therefore lifted up in spirit, he cut off the head of Goliath, using the proud enemy's own sword as the fittest instrument of death,[3] smiting the profane boaster on the forehead and wounding him in the same place in which Uzziah was smitten with leprosy when he presumed to usurp the priestly office;[4]

---

[1] 2 Cor. vi. 7.

[2] Eph. vi. 13-17.
[3] 1 Sam. xvii. 40-51.
[4] 2 Chron. xvi. 19.

the same also in which shines the glory that makes the saints rejoice in the Lord, saying, "The light of Thy countenance is sealed upon us, O Lord." [1] Let us therefore also say, "My heart is fixed, O God, my heart is fixed: I will sing and give praise: awake up, my glory; awake, psaltery and harp; I myself will awake early;" [2] that in us may be fulfilled that word, "Open thy mouth wide, and I will fill it;" [3] and, "The Lord shall give the word with great power to them that publish it." [4] I am well assured that your prayer as well as mine, is that in our contendings the victory may remain with the truth. For you seek Christ's glory, not your own: if you are victorious, I also gain a victory if I discover my error. On the other hand, if I win the day, the gain is yours; for "the children ought not to lay up for the parents, but the parents for the children." [5] We read, moreover, in Chronicles, that the children of Israel went to battle with their minds set upon peace, [6] seeking even amid swords and bloodshed and the prostrate slain a victory not for themselves, but for peace. Let me therefore, if it be the will of Christ, give an answer to all that you have written, and attempt in a short dissertation to solve your numerous questions. I pass by the conciliatory phrases in your courteous salutation: I say nothing of the compliments by which you attempt to take the edge off your censure: let me come at once to the matters in debate.

CHAP. II. — 3. You say that you received from some brother a book of mine, in which I have given a list of ecclesiastical writers, both Greek and Latin, but which had no title; and that when you asked the brother aforesaid (I quote your own statement) why the title-page had no inscription, or what was the name by which the book was known, he answered that it was called "Epitaphium," i.e. "Obituary Notices:" upon which you display your reasoning powers, by remarking that the name Epitaphium would have been properly given to the book if the reader had found in it an account of the lives and writings of deceased authors, but that inasmuch as mention is made of the works of many who were living when the book was written, and are at this day still living, you wonder why I should have given the book a title so inappropriate. I think that it must be obvious to your own common sense, that you might have discovered the title of that book from its contents, without any other help. For you have read both Greek and Latin biographies of eminent men, and you know that they do not give to works of this kind the title Epitaphium, but simply "Illustrious Men," e.g. "Illustrious Generals," or "philosophers, orators, historians, poets," etc., as the case may be. An Epitaphium is a work written concerning the dead; such as I remember having composed long ago after the decease of the presbyter Nepotianus, of blessed memory. The book, therefore, of which you speak ought to be entitled, "Concerning Illustrious Men," or properly, "Concerning Ecclesiastical Writers," although it is said that by many who were not qualified to make any correction of the title, it has been called "Concerning Authors."

CHAP. III. — 4. You ask, in the second place, my reason for saying, in my commentary on the Epistle to the Galatians, that Paul could not have rebuked Peter for that which he himself had done, [7] and could not have censured in another the dissimulation of which he was himself confessedly guilty; and you affirm that that rebuke of the apostle was not a manœuvre of pious policy, [8] but real; and you say that I ought not to teach falsehood, but that all things in Scripture are to be received literally as they stand.

To this I answer, in the first place, that your wisdom ought to have suggested the remembrance of the short preface to my commentaries, saying of my own person, "What then? Am I so foolish and bold as to promise that which he could not accomplish? By no means; but I have rather, as it seems to me, with more reserve and hesitation, because feeling the deficiency of my strength, followed the commentaries of Origen in this matter. For that illustrious man wrote five volumes on the Epistle of Paul to the Galatians, and has occupied the tenth volume of his *Stromata* with a short treatise upon his explanation of the epistle. He also composed several treatises and fragmentary pieces upon it, which, if they even had stood alone, would have sufficed. I pass over my revered instructor Didymus [9] (blind, it is true, but quick-sighted in the discernment of spiritual things), and the bishop of Laodicea, [10] who has recently left the Church, and the early heretic Alexander, as well as Eusebius of Emesa and Theodorus of Heraclea, who have also left some brief disquisitions upon this subject. From these works if I were to extract even a few passages, a work which could not be altogether despised would be produced. Let me therefore frankly say that I have

---

[1] Ps. iv. 7, according to the LXX.
[2] Ps. lvii 7, 8.
[3] Ps lxxxi. 10
[4] Ps. lxviii 11, in LXX. version.
[5] 2 Cor. xii. 14
[6] 1 Chron. xii. 17, 18.

[7] Gal. ii. 14.
[8] *Dispensatoria.*
[9] "Videntem meum Didymum," — Didymus of Alexandria, who, at the time when Jerome wrote his book on ecclesiastical writers (A.D. 392), was above ninety-three years of age. He became blind when he was five years old, but by perseverance attained extraordinary learning, and was much esteemed.
[10] The younger Apollinarius, who in 380 was excommunicated for error regarding the Incarnation. His works were valuable, but have been almost all lost, being not transcribed because of his lapsing into heresy.

read all these; and storing up in my mind very many things which they contain, I have dictated to my amanuensis sometimes what was borrowed from other writers, sometimes what was my own, without distinctly remembering the method, or the words, or the opinions which belonged to each. I look now to the Lord in His mercy to grant that my want of skill and experience may not cause the things which others have well spoken to be lost, or to fail of finding among foreign readers the acceptance with which they have met in the language in which they were first written. If, therefore, anything in my explanation has seemed to you to demand correction, it would have been seemly for one of your learning to inquire first whether what I had written was found in the Greek writers to whom I have referred; and if they had not advanced the opinion which you censured, you could then with propriety condemn me for what I gave as my own view, especially seeing that I have in the preface openly acknowledged that I had followed the commentaries of Origen, and had dictated sometimes the view of others, sometimes my own, and have written at the end of the chapter with which you find fault: "If any one be dissatisfied with the interpretation here given, by which it is shown that neither did Peter sin, nor did Paul rebuke presumptuously a greater than himself, he is bound to show how Paul could consistently blame in another what he himself did." By which I have made it manifest that I did not adopt finally and irrevocably that which I had read in these Greek authors, but had propounded what I had read, leaving to the reader's own judgment whether it should be rejected or approved.

5. You, however, in order to avoid doing what I had asked, have devised a new argument against the view proposed; maintaining that the Gentiles who had believed in Christ were free from the burden of the ceremonial law, but that the Jewish converts were under the law, and that Paul, as the teacher of the Gentiles, rightly rebuked those who kept the law; whereas Peter, who was the chief of the "circumcision," [1] was justly rebuked for commanding the Gentile converts to do that which the converts from among the Jews were alone under obligation to observe. If this is your opinion, or rather since it is your opinion, that all from among the Jews who believe are debtors to do the whole law, you ought, as being a bishop of great fame in the whole world, to publish your doctrine, and labour to persuade all other bishops to agree with you. As for me in my humble cell,[2] along with the monks my fellow-sinners, I do not presume to dogmatize in regard to things

of great moment; I only confess frankly that I read the writings of the Fathers,[3] and, complying with universal usage, put down in my commentaries a variety of explanations, that each may adopt from the number given the one which pleases him. This method, I think, you have found in your reading, and have approved in connection with both secular literature and the Divine Scriptures.

6. Moreover, as to this explanation which Origen first advanced,[4] and which all the other commentators after him have adopted, they bring forward, chiefly for the purpose of answering the blasphemies of Porphyry, who accuses Paul of presumption because he dared to reprove Peter and rebuke him to his face, and by reasoning convict him of having done wrong; that is to say, of being in the very fault which he himself, who blamed another for transgressing, had committed. What shall I say also of John, who has long governed the Church of Constantinople, and holding pontifical rank,[5] who has composed a very large book upon this paragraph, and has followed the opinion of Origen and of the old expositors? If, therefore, you censure me as in the wrong, suffer me, I pray you, to be mistaken in company with such men; and when you perceive that I have so many companions in my error, you will require to produce at least one partisan in defence of your truth. So much on the interpretation of one paragraph of the Epistle to the Galatians.

7. Lest, however, I should seem to rest my answer to your reasoning wholly on the number of witnesses who are on my side, and to use the names of illustrious men as a means of escaping from the truth, not daring to meet you in argument, I shall briefly bring forward some examples from the Scriptures.

In the Acts of the Apostles, a voice was heard by Peter, saying unto him, "Rise, Peter, slay and eat," when all manner of four-footed beasts, and creeping things, and birds of the air, were presented before him; by which saying it is proved that no man is by nature [ceremonially] unclean, but that all men are equally welcome to the gospel of Christ. To which Peter answered, "Not so, Lord; for I have never eaten anything that is common or unclean." And the voice spake unto him again the second time, "What God hath cleansed, that call not thou common." Therefore he went to Cæsarea, and having entered the house of Cornelius, "he opened his mouth and said, Of a truth I perceive that God is no respecter of persons, but in every nation he that feareth Him and worketh righteousness is

---

[1] Gal ii. 8.
[2] *Parvo tuguriunculo.*

[3] *Majorum.*
[4] In the tenth book of his *Stromata*, where he expounds the Epistle to the Galatians.
[5] This year (404) was the year of John Chrysostom's banishment from Constantinople, after being pontiff there for ten years.

accepted with Him." Thereafter "the Holy Ghost fell on all them which heard the word; and they of the circumcision which believed were astonished, as many as came with Peter, because that on the Gentiles also was poured out the gift of the Holy Ghost. Then answered Peter, Can any man forbid water, that these should not be baptized, which have received the Holy Ghost as well as we? And he commanded them to be baptized in the name of the Lord."[1] "And the apostles and brethren that were in Judea heard that the Gentiles had also received the word of God. And when Peter was come up to Jerusalem, they that were of the circumcision contended with him, saying, Thou wentest in to men uncircumcised, and didst eat with them." To whom he gave a full explanation of the reasons of his conduct, and concluded with these words: "Forasmuch then as God gave them the like gift as He did unto us who believed on the Lord Jesus Christ, what was I, that I could withstand God? When they heard these things, they held their peace, and glorified God, saying, Then hath God also to the Gentiles granted repentance unto life."[2] Again, when, long after this, Paul and Barnabas had come to Antioch, and "having gathered the Church together, rehearsed all that God had done with them, and how He had opened the door of faith unto the Gentiles, certain men which came down from Judea taught the brethren, and said, Except ye be circumcised after the manner of Moses, ye cannot be saved. When therefore Paul and Barnabas had no small dissension and disputation with them, they determined that Paul and Barnabas, and certain other of them, should go up to Jerusalem unto the apostles and elders about this question. And when they were come to Jerusalem, there rose up certain of the sect of the Pharisees which believed, saying that it was needful to circumcise them, and to command them to keep the law of Moses." And when there had been much disputing, Peter rose up, with his wonted readiness, "and said, Men and brethren, ye know how that a good while ago God made choice among us, that the Gentiles by my mouth should hear the word of the gospel, and believe. And God, which knoweth the hearts, bare them witness, giving them the Holy Ghost, even as He did unto us; and put no difference between us and them, purifying their hearts by faith. Now therefore why tempt ye God, to put a yoke upon the neck of the disciples, which neither our fathers nor we were able to bear? But we believe that, through the grace of the Lord Jesus Christ, we shall be saved, even as they. Then all the multitude kept silence;" and to his opinion the Apostle James, and all the elders together, gave consent.[3]

8. These quotations should not be tedious to the reader, but useful both to him and to me, as proving that, even before the Apostle Paul, Peter had come to know that the law was not to be in force after the gospel was given; nay more, that Peter was the prime mover in issuing the decree by which this was affirmed. Moreover, Peter was of so great authority, that Paul has recorded in his epistle: "Then, after three years, I went up to Jerusalem to see Peter, and abode with him fifteen days."[4] In the following context, again, he adds: "Then, fourteen years after, I went up again to Jerusalem with Barnabas, and took Titus with me also. And I went up by revelation, and communicated unto them that gospel which I preach among the Gentiles;" proving that he had not had confidence in his preaching of the gospel if he had not been confirmed by the consent of Peter and those who were with him. The next words are, "but privately to them that were of reputation, lest by any means I should run, or had run, in vain." Why did he this privately rather than in public? Lest offence should be given to the faith of those who from among the Jews had believed, since they thought that the law was still in force, and that they ought to join observance of the law with faith in the Lord as their Saviour. Therefore also, when at that time Peter had come to Antioch (although the Acts of the Apostles do not mention this, but we must believe Paul's statement), Paul affirms that he "withstood him to the face, because he was to be blamed. For, before that certain came from James, he did eat with the Gentiles: but when they were come, he withdrew, and separated himself, fearing them which were of the circumcision. And the other Jews dissembled likewise with him; insomuch that Barnabas also was carried away with their dissimulation. But when I saw," he says, "that they walked not uprightly, according to the truth of the gospel, I said unto Peter before them all, If thou, being a Jew, livest after the manner of Gentiles, and not as do the Jews, why compellest thou the Gentiles to live as do the Jews?"[5] etc. No one can doubt, therefore, that the Apostle Peter was himself the author of that rule with deviation from which he is charged. The cause of that deviation, moreover, is seen to be fear of the Jews. For the Scripture says, that "at first he did eat with the Gentiles, but that when certain had come from James he withdrew, and separated himself, fearing them which were of the circumcision." Now he feared the Jews, to whom he had been appointed apostle, lest by occasion of

---

[1] Acts x. 13-48.
[2] Acts xi. 1-18.

[3] Acts xiv. 27, and xv. 1-12.
[4] Gal. i. 18.
[5] Gal. ii. 1, 2, 14.

the Gentiles they should go back from the faith in Christ; imitating the Good Shepherd in his concern lest he should lose the flock committed to him.

9. As I have shown, therefore, that Peter was thoroughly aware of the abrogation of the law of Moses, but was compelled by fear to pretend to observe it, let us now see whether Paul, who accuses another, ever did anything of the same kind himself. We read in the same book: "Paul passed through Syria and Cilicia, confirming the churches. Then came he to Derbe and Lystra: and, behold, a certain disciple was there, named Timotheus, the son of a certain woman which was a Jewess, and believed; but his father was a Greek: which was well reported of by the brethren that were at Lystra and Iconium. Him would Paul have to go forth with him; and he took and circumcised him, because of the Jews which were in those quarters: for they knew all that his father was a Greek."[1] O blessed Apostle Paul, who hadst rebuked Peter for dissimulation, because he withdrew himself from the Gentiles through fear of the Jews who came from James, why art thou, notwithstanding thine own doctrine, compelled to circumcise Timothy, the son of a Gentile, nay more, a Gentile himself (for he was not a Jew, having not been circumcised)? Thou wilt answer, "Because of the Jews which are in these quarters?" If, then, thou forgiveth thyself the circumcision of a disciple coming from the Gentiles, forgive Peter also, who has precedence above thee, his doing some things of the same kind through fear of the believing Jews. Again, it is written: "Paul after this tarried there yet a good while, and then took his leave of the brethren, and sailed thence into Syria, and with him Priscilla and Aquila; having shorn his head in Cenchrea, for he had a vow."[2] Be it granted that he was compelled through fear of the Jews in the other case to do what he was unwilling to do; wherefore did he let his hair grow in accordance with a vow of his own making, and afterwards, when in Cenchrea, shave his head according to the law, as the Nazarites, who had given themselves by vow to God, were wont to do, according to the law of Moses?

10. But these things are small when compared with what follows. The sacred historian Luke further relates: "And when we were come to Jerusalem, the brethren received us gladly;" and the day following, James, and all the elders who were with him, having expressed their approbation of his gospel, said to Paul: "Thou seest, brother, how many thousands of Jews there are which believe; and they are all zealous of the law: and they are informed of thee, that thou teachest all the Jews which are among the Gentiles to forsake Moses, saying that they ought not to circumcise their children, neither to walk after the customs. What is it therefore? The multitude must needs come together: for they will hear that thou art come. Do therefore this that we say to thee: We have four men which have a vow on them; them take, and purify thyself with them, and be at charges with them, that they may shave their heads: and all may know that those things, whereof they were informed concerning thee, are nothing; but that thou thyself also walkest orderly, and keepest the law. Then Paul took the men, and the next day purifying himself with them, entered into the temple, to signify the accomplishment of the days of purification, until an offering should be offered for every one of them."[3] O Paul, here again let me question thee: Why didst thou shave thy head, why didst thou walk barefoot according to Jewish ceremonial law, why didst thou offer sacrifices, why were victims slain for thee according to the law? Thou wilt answer, doubtless, "To avoid giving offence to those of the Jews who had believed." To gain the Jews, thou didst pretend to be a Jew; and James and all the other elders taught thee this dissimulation. But thou didst not succeed in escaping, after all. For when thou wast on the point of being killed in a tumult which had arisen, thou wast rescued by the chief captain of the band, and was sent by him to Cæsarea, guarded by a careful escort of soldiers, lest the Jews should kill thee as a dissembler, and a destroyer of the law; and from Cæsarea coming to Rome, thou didst, in thine own hired house, preach Christ to both Jews and Gentiles, and thy testimony was sealed under Nero's sword.[4]

11. We have learned, therefore, that through fear of the Jews both Peter and Paul alike pretended that they observed the precepts of the law. How could Paul have the assurance and effrontery to reprove in another what he had done himself? I at least, or, I should rather say, others before me, have given such explanation of the matter as they deemed best, not defending the use of falsehood in the interest of religion,[5] as you charge them with doing, but teaching the honourable exercise of a wise discretion;[6] seeking both to show the wisdom of the apostles, and to restrain the shameless blasphemies of Porphyry, who says that Peter and Paul quarrelled with each other in childish rivalry, and affirms that Paul had been inflamed with envy on account of the excellences of Peter,

[1] Acts xv. 41, xvi. 1-3.
[2] Acts xviii. 18.
[3] Acts xxi. 17-26.
[4] Acts xxiii. 23, xxviii. 14, 30.
[5] Officiosum mendacium.
[6] Honestam dispensationem.

and had written boastfully of things which he either had not done, or, if he did them, had done with inexcusable presumption, reproving in another that which he himself had done. They, in answering him, gave the best interpretation of the passage which they could find; what interpretation have you to propound? Surely you must intend to say something better than they have said, since you have rejected the opinion of the ancient commentators.

CHAP. IV.—12. You say in your letter:[1] "You do not require me to teach you in what sense the apostle says, 'To the Jews I became as a Jew, that I might gain the Jews;'[2] and other such things in the same passage, which are to be ascribed to the compassion of pitying love, not to the artifices of intentional deceit. For he that ministers to the sick becomes as if he were sick himself, not indeed falsely pretending to be under the fever, but considering with the mind of one truly sympathizing what he would wish done for himself if he were in the sick man's place. Paul was indeed a Jew; and when he had become a Christian, he had not abandoned those Jewish sacraments which that people had received in the right way, and for a certain appointed time. Therefore, even when he was an apostle of Christ, he took part in observing these, but with this view, that he might show that they were in no wise hurtful to those who, even after they had believed in Christ, desired to retain the ceremonies which by the law they had learned from their fathers; provided only that they did not build on these their hope of salvation, since the salvation which was foreshadowed in these has now been brought in by the Lord Jesus." The sum of your whole argument, which you have expanded into a most prolix dissertation, is this, that Peter did not err in supposing that the law was binding on those who from among the Jews had believed, but departed from the right course in this, that he compelled the Gentile converts to conform to Jewish observances. Now, if he compelled them, it was not by use of authority as a teacher, but by the example of his own practice. And Paul, according to your view, did not protest against what Peter had done personally, but asked wherefore Peter would compel those who were from among the Gentiles to conform to Jewish observances.

13. The matter in debate, therefore, or I should rather say your opinion regarding it, is summed up in this: that since the preaching of the gospel of Christ, the believing Jews do well in observing the precepts of the law, i.e. in offering sacrifices as Paul did, in circumcising their children, as Paul did in the case of Timothy, and

keeping the Jewish Sabbath, as all the Jews have been accustomed to do. If this be true, we fall into the heresy of Cerinthus and Ebion, who, though believing in Christ, were anathematized by the fathers for this one error, that they mixed up the ceremonies of the law with the gospel of Christ, and professed their faith in that which was new, without letting go what was old. Why do I speak of the Ebionites, who make pretensions to the name of Christian? In our own day there exists a sect among the Jews throughout all the synagogues of the East, which is called the sect of the Minei, and is even now condemned by the Pharisees. The adherents to this sect are known commonly as Nazarenes; they believe in Christ the Son of God, born of the Virgin Mary; and they say that He who suffered under Pontius Pilate and rose again, is the same as the one in whom we believe. But while they desire to be both Jews and Christians, they are neither the one nor the other. I therefore beseech you, who think that you are called upon to heal my slight wound, which is no more, so to speak, than a prick or scratch from a needle, to devote your skill in the healing art to this grievous wound, which has been opened by a spear driven home with the impetus of a javelin. For there is surely no proportion between the culpability of him who exhibits the various opinions held by the fathers in a commentary on Scripture, and the guilt of him who reintroduces within the Church a most pestilential heresy. If, however, there is for us no alternative but to receive the Jews into the Church, along with the usages prescribed by their law; if, in short, it shall be declared lawful for them to continue in the Churches of Christ what they have been accustomed to practise in the synagogues of Satan, I will tell you my opinion of the matter: they will not become Christians, but they will make us Jews.

14. For what Christian will submit to hear what is said in your letter? "Paul was indeed a Jew; and when he had become a Christian, he had not abandoned those Jewish sacraments which that people had received in the right way, and for a certain appointed time. Therefore, even when he was an apostle of Christ, he took part in observing these; but with this view, that he might show that they were in no wise hurtful to those who, even after they had believed in Christ, desired to retain the ceremonies which by the law they had learned from their fathers." Now I implore you to hear patiently my complaint. Paul, even when he was an apostle of Christ, observed Jewish ceremonies; and you affirm that they are in no wise hurtful to those who wish to retain them as they had received them from their fathers by the law. I, on the contrary, shall maintain, and, though the world

---

[1] Letter XL. 4, p. 273.
[2] 1 Cor. ix. 20.

were to protest against my view, I may boldly declare that the Jewish ceremonies are to Christians both hurtful and fatal; and that whoever observes them, whether he be Jew or Gentile originally, is cast into the pit of perdition. " For Christ is the end of the law for righteousness to every one that believeth," [1] that is, to both Jew and Gentile; for if the Jew be excepted, He is not the end of the law for righteousness to every one that believeth. Moreover, we read in the Gospel, "The law and the prophets were until John the Baptist." [2] Also, in another place: "Therefore the Jews sought the more to kill Him, because He had not only broken the Sabbath, but said also that God was His Father, making Himself equal with God." [3] Again: "Of His fulness have all we received, and grace for grace; for the law was given by Moses, but grace and truth came by Jesus Christ." [4] Instead of the grace of the law which has passed away, we have received the grace of the gospel which is abiding; and instead of the shadows and types of the old dispensation, the truth has come by Jesus Christ. Jeremiah also prophesied thus in God's name: "Behold, the days come, saith the Lord, that I will make a new covenant with the house of Israel, and with the house of Judah; not according to the covenant which I made with their fathers, in the day that I took them by the hand, to bring them out of the land of Egypt." [5] Observe what the prophet says, not to Gentiles, who had not been partakers in any former covenant, but to the Jewish nation. He who has given them the law by Moses, promises in place of it the new covenant of the gospel, that they might no longer live in the oldness of the letter, but in the newness of the spirit. Paul himself, moreover, in connection with whom the discussion of this question has arisen, delivers such sentiments as these frequently, of which I subjoin only a few, as I desire to be brief: "Behold, I Paul say unto you, that if ye be circumcised, Christ shall profit you nothing." Again: "Christ is become of no effect unto you, whosoever of you are justified by the law; ye are fallen from grace." Again: "If ye be led of the Spirit, ye are not under the law." [6] From which it is evident that he has not the Holy Spirit who submits to the law, not, as our fathers affirmed the apostles to have done, feignedly, under the promptings of a wise discretion, [7] but, as you suppose to have been the case, sincerely. As to the quality of these legal precepts, let us learn from God's own teaching: "I gave them," He says, "statutes that were not good, and judgments whereby they should not live." [8] I say these things, not that I may, like Manichæus and Marcion, destroy the law, which I know on the testimony of the apostle to be both holy and spiritual; but because when "faith came," and the fulness of times, "God sent forth His Son, made of a woman, made under the law, to redeem them that were under the law, that we might receive the adoption of sons," [9] and might live no longer under the law as our schoolmaster, but under the Heir, who has now attained to full age, and is Lord.

15. It is further said in your letter: "The thing, therefore, which he rebuked in Peter was not his observing the customs handed down from his fathers, which Peter, if he wished, might do without being chargeable with deceit or inconsistency." [10] Again I say: Since you are a bishop, a teacher in the Churches of Christ, if you would prove what you assert, receive any Jew who, after having become a Christian, circumcises any son that may be born to him, observes the Jewish Sabbath, abstains from meats which God has created to be used with thanksgiving, and on the evening of the fourteenth day of the first month slays a paschal lamb; and when you have done this, or rather, have refused to do it (for I know that you are a Christian, and will not be guilty of a profane action), you will be constrained, whether willingly or unwillingly, to renounce your opinion; and then you will know that it is a more difficult work to reject the opinion of others than to establish your own. Moreover, lest perhaps we should not believe your statement, or, I should rather say, understand it (for it is often the case that a discourse unduly extended is not intelligible, and is less censured by the unskilled in discussion because its weakness is not so easily perceived), you inculcate your opinion by reiterating the statement in these words: "Paul had forsaken everything peculiar to the Jews that was evil, especially this, that 'being ignorant of God's righteousness, and going about to establish their own righteousness, they had not submitted themselves to the righteousness of God.' [11] In this, moreover, he differed from them, that after the passion and resurrection of Christ, in whom had been given and made manifest the mystery of grace, according to the order of Melchizedek, they still considered it binding on them to celebrate, not out of mere reverence for old customs, but as necessary to salvation, the sacraments of the old dispensation; which were indeed at one time necessary, else had it been unprofitable and vain for the Maccabees to suffer martyrdom as

---

[1] Rom. x. 4.
[2] Matt. xi. 13 and Luke xvi. 16.
[3] John v. 18.
[4] John i. 16, 17.
[5] Jer. xxxi. 31, 32.
[6] Gal. v. 2, 4, 18.
[7] *Dispensativé.*

[8] Ezek. xx. 25.
[9] Gal. iv. 4.
[10] Letter XL. sec. 5, p. 273.
[11] Rom. x. 3.

they did for their adherence to them.[1] Lastly, in this also Paul differed from the Jews, that they persecuted the Christian preachers of grace as enemies of the law. These, and all similar errors and sins, he declares that he counted but loss and dung, that he might win Christ."[2]

16. We have learned from you what evil things peculiar to the Jews Paul had abandoned; let us now learn from your teaching what good things which were Jewish he retained. You will reply: "The ceremonial observances in which they continued to follow the practice of their fathers, in the way in which these were complied with by Paul himself, without believing them to be at all necessary to salvation." I do not fully understand what you mean by the words, "without believing them to be at all necessary to salvation." For if they do not contribute to salvation, why are they observed? And if they must be observed, they by all means contribute to salvation; especially seeing that, because of observing them, some have been made martyrs: for they would not be observed unless they contributed to salvation. For they are not things indifferent — neither good nor bad, as philosophers say. Self-control is good, self-indulgence is bad: between these, and indifferent, as having no moral quality, are such things as walking, blowing one's nose, expectorating phlegm, etc. Such an action is neither good nor bad; for whether you do it or leave it undone, it does not affect your standing as righteous or unrighteous. But the observance of legal ceremonies is not a thing indifferent; it is either good or bad. You say it is good. I affirm it to be bad, and bad not only when done by Gentile converts, but also when done by Jews who have believed. In this passage you fall, if I am not mistaken, into one error while avoiding another. For while you guard yourself against the blasphemies of Porphyry, you become entangled in the snares of Ebion; pronouncing that the law is binding on those who from among the Jews have believed. Perceiving, again, that what you have said is a dangerous doctrine, you attempt to qualify it by words which are only superfluous: viz., "The law must be observed not from any belief, such as prompted the Jews to keep it, that this is necessary to salvation, and not in any misleading dissimulation such as Paul reproved in Peter."

17. Peter therefore pretended to keep the law; but this censor of Peter boldly observed the things prescribed by the law. The next words of your letter are these: "For if Paul observed these sacraments in order, by pretending to be a Jew, to gain the Jews, why did he not also take part with the Gentiles in heathen sacrifices, when to them that were without law

he became as without law, that he might gain them also? The explanation is found in this, that he took part in the Jewish rites as being himself a Jew; and that when he said all this which I have quoted, he meant not that he pretended to be what he was not, but that he felt with true compassion that he must bring such help to them as would be needful for himself if he were involved in their error.[3] Herein he exercised not the subtlety of a deceiver, but the sympathy of a compassionate deliverer." A triumphant vindication of Paul! You prove that he did not pretend to share the error of the Jews, but was actually involved in it; and that he refused to imitate Peter in a course of deception, dissembling through fear of the Jews what he really was, but without reserve freely avowed himself to be a Jew. Oh, unheard-of compassion of the apostle! In seeking to make the Jews Christians, he himself became a Jew! For he could not have persuaded the luxurious to become temperate if he had not himself become luxurious like them; and could not have brought help, in his compassion, as you say, to the wretched, otherwise than by experiencing in his own person their wretchedness! Truly wretched, and worthy of most compassionate lamentation, are those who, carried away by vehemence of disputation, and by love for the law which has been abolished, have made Christ's apostle to be a Jew. Nor is there, after all, a great difference between my opinion and yours: for I say that both Peter and Paul, through fear of the believing Jews, practised, or rather pretended to practise, the precepts of the Jewish law; whereas you maintain that they did this out of pity, "not with the subtlety of a deceiver, but with the sympathy of a compassionate deliverer." But by both this is equally admitted, that (whether from fear or from pity) they pretended to be what they were not. As to your argument against our view, that he ought to have become to the Gentiles a Gentile, if to the Jews he became a Jew, this favours our opinion rather than yours: for as he did not actually become a Jew, so he did not actually become a heathen; and as he did not actually become a heathen, so he did not actually become a Jew. His conformity to the Gentiles consisted in this, that he received as Christians the uncircumcised who believed in Christ, and left them free to use without scruple meats which the Jewish law prohibited; but not, as you suppose, in taking part in their worship of idols. For "in Christ Jesus, neither circumcision availeth anything, nor uncircumcision, but the keeping of the commandments of God."[4]

18. I ask you, therefore, and with all urgency

[1] 2 Macc. vii. 1.
[2] Phil. iii. 8. Letter XL. sec. 6, p. 274.
[3] Letter XL. 6, p. 274.
[4] Gal. v. 6 and vi. 15.

press the request, that you forgive me this humble attempt at a discussion of the matter; and wherein I have transgressed, lay the blame upon yourself who compelled me to write in reply, and who made me out to be as blind as Stesichorus. And do not bring the reproach of teaching the practice of lying upon me who am a follower of Christ, who said, "I am the Way, the Truth, and the Life." [1] It is impossible for me, who am a worshipper of the Truth, to bow under the yoke of falsehood. Moreover, refrain from stirring up against me the unlearned crowd who esteem you as their bishop, and regard with the respect due the priestly office the orations which you deliver in the church, but who esteem lightly an old decrepit man like me, courting the retirement of a monastery far from the busy haunts of men; and seek others who may be more fitly instructed or corrected by you. For the sound of your voice can scarcely reach me, who am so far separated from you by sea and land. And if you happen to write me a letter, Italy and Rome are sure to be acquainted with its contents long before it is brought to me, to whom alone it ought to be sent.

CHAP. V. — 19. In another letter you ask why a former translation which I made of some of the canonical books was carefully marked with asterisks and obelisks, whereas I afterwards published a translation without these. You must pardon my saying that you seem to me not to understand the matter: for the former translation is from the Septuagint; and wherever obelisks are placed, they are designed to indicate that the Seventy have said more than is found in the Hebrew. But the asterisks indicate what has been added by Origen from the version of Theodotion. In that version I was translating from the Greek: but in the later version, translating from the Hebrew itself, I have expressed what I understood it to mean, being careful to preserve rather the exact sense than the order of the words. I am surprised that you do not read the books of the Seventy translators in the genuine form in which they were originally given to the world, but as they have been corrected, or rather corrupted, by Origen, with his obelisks and asterisks; and that you refuse to follow the translation, however feeble, which has been given by a Christian man, especially seeing that Origen borrowed the things which he has added from the edition of a man who, after the passion of Christ, was a Jew and a blasphemer. Do you wish to be a true admirer and partisan of the Seventy translators? Then do not read what you find under the asterisks; rather erase them from the volumes, that you may approve yourself indeed a follower of the ancients. If, however,

you do this, you will be compelled to find fault with all the libraries of the Churches; for you will scarcely find more than one MS. here and there which has not these interpolations.

CHAP. VI. — 20. A few words now as to your remark that I ought not to have given a translation, after this had been already done by the ancients; and the novel syllogism which you use: "The passages of which the Seventy have given an interpretation were either obscure or plain. If they were obscure, it is believed that you are as likely to have been mistaken as the others; if they were plain, it is not believed that the Seventy could have been mistaken." [2]

All the commentators who have been our predecessors in the Lord in the work of expounding the Scriptures, have expounded either what was obscure or what was plain. If some passages were obscure, how could you, after them, presume to discuss that which they were not able to explain? If the passages were plain, it was a waste of time for you to have undertaken to treat of that which could not possibly have escaped them. This syllogism applies with peculiar force to the book of Psalms, in the interpretation of which Greek commentators have written many volumes: viz. 1st, Origen: 2d, Eusebius of Cæsarea; 3d, Theodorus of Heraclea; 4th, Asterius of Scythopolis; 5th, Apollinaris of Laodicea; and, 6th, Didymus of Alexandria. There are said to be minor works on selections from the Psalms, but I speak at present of the whole book. Moreover, among Latin writers the bishops Hilary of Poitiers, and Eusebius of Verceil, have translated Origen and Eusebius of Cæsarea, the former of whom has in some things been followed by our own Ambrose. Now, I put it to your wisdom to answer why you, after all the labours of so many and so competent interpreters, differ from them in your exposition of some passages? If the Psalms are obscure, it must be believed that you are as likely to be mistaken as others; if they are plain, it is incredible that these others could have fallen into mistake. In either case, your exposition has been, by your own showing, an unnecessary labour; and on the same principle, no one would ever venture to speak on any subject after others have pronounced their opinion, and no one would be at liberty to write anything regarding that which another has once handled, however important the matter might be.

It is, however, more in keeping with your enlightened judgment, to grant to all others the liberty which you tolerate in yourself; for in my attempt to translate into Latin, for the benefit of those who speak the same language with myself, the corrected Greek version of the Scriptures, I

---

[1] John xiv. 6.

[2] Letter XXVIII. ch. ii. p. 251.

have laboured not to supersede what has been long esteemed, but only to bring prominently forward those things which have been either omitted or tampered with by the Jews, in order that Latin readers might know what is found in the original Hebrew. If any one is averse to reading it, none compels him against his will. Let him drink with satisfaction the old wine, and despise my new wine, *i.e.* the sentences which I have published in explanation of former writers, with the design of making more obvious by my remarks what in them seemed to me to be obscure.

As to the principles which ought to be followed in the interpretation of the Sacred Scriptures, they are stated in the book which I have written,[1] and in all the introductions to the divine books which I have in my edition prefixed to each; and to these I think it sufficient to refer the prudent reader. And since you approve of my labours in revising the translation of the New Testament, as you say, — giving me at the same time this as your reason, that very many are acquainted with the Greek language, and are therefore competent judges of my work, — it would have been but fair to have given me credit for the same fidelity in the Old Testament; for I have not followed my own imagination, but have rendered the divine words as I found them understood by those who speak the Hebrew language. If you have any doubt of this in any passage, ask the Jews what is the meaning of the original.

21. Perhaps you will say, "What if the Jews decline to answer, or choose to impose upon us?" Is it conceivable that the whole multitude of Jews will agree together to be silent if asked about my translation, and that none shall be found that has any knowledge of the Hebrew language? Or will they all imitate those Jews whom you mention as having, in some little town, conspired to injure my reputation? For in your letter you put together the following story : — "A certain bishop, one of our brethren, having introduced in the Church over which he presides the reading of your version, came upon a word in the book of the prophet Jonah, of which you have given a very different rendering from that which had been of old familiar to the senses and memory of all the worshippers, and had been chanted for so many generations in the Church. Thereupon arose such a tumult in the congregation, especially among the Greeks, correcting what had been read, and denouncing the translation as false, that the bishop was compelled to ask the testimony of the Jewish residents (it was in the town of Oea). These, whether from ignorance or from spite, answered

that the words in the Hebrew MSS. were correctly rendered in the Greek version, and in the Latin one taken from it. What further need I say? The man was compelled to correct your version in that passage as if it had been falsely translated, as he desired not to be left without a congregation, — a calamity which he narrowly escaped. From this case we also are led to think that you may be occasionally mistaken."[2]

CHAP. VII. — 22. You tell me that I have given a wrong translation of some word in Jonah, and that a worthy bishop narrowly escaped losing his charge through the clamorous tumult of his people, which was caused by the different rendering of this one word. At the same time, you withhold from me what the word was which I have mistranslated ; thus taking away the possibility of my saying anything in my own vindication, lest my reply should be fatal to your objection. Perhaps it is the old dispute about the gourd which has been revived, after slumbering for many long years since the illustrious man, who in that day combined in his own person the ancestral honours of the Cornelii and of Asinius Pollio,[3] brought against me the charge of giving in my translation the word "ivy" instead of "gourd." I have already given a sufficient answer to this in my commentary on Jonah. At present, I deem it enough to say that in that passage, where the Septuagint has "gourd," and Aquila and the others have rendered the word "ivy" ($\kappa\iota\sigma\sigma\circ\varsigma$), the Hebrew MS. has "ciceion," which is in the Syriac tongue, as now spoken, "ciceia." It is a kind of shrub having large leaves like a vine, and when planted it quickly springs up to the size of a small tree, standing upright by its own stem, without requiring any support of canes or poles, as both gourds and ivy do. If, therefore, in translating word for word, I had put the word "ciceia," no one would know what it meant ; if I had used the word "gourd," I would have said what is not found in the Hebrew. I therefore put down "ivy," that I might not differ from all other translators. But if your Jews said, either through malice or ignorance, as you yourself suggest, that the word is in the Hebrew text which is found in the Greek and Latin versions, it is evident that they were either unacquainted with Hebrew, or have been pleased to say what was not true, in order to make sport of the gourd-planters.

In closing this letter, I beseech you to have some consideration for a soldier who is now old and has long retired from active service, and not to force him to take the field and again expose

---

[1] *De optimo genere interpretandi.*

[2] Letter LXXI., sec. 5, p. 327.
[3] The critic here referred to was Canthelius, whom Jerome abuses in his commentary on the passage, insinuating that the reason why the gourds found in this scion of a noble house a champion so devoted, was that they had often rendered him a service which ivy could not have done, screening his secret potations from public notice.

his life to the chances of war. Do you, who are young, and who have been appointed to the conspicuous seat of pontifical dignity, give yourself to teaching the people, and enrich Rome with new stores from fertile Africa.[1] I am contented to make but little noise in an obscure corner of a monastery, with one to hear me or read to me.

LETTER LXXVI.

(A.D. 402.)

1. Hear, O Donatists, what the Catholic Church says to you: "O ye sons of men, how long will ye be slow of heart? why will ye love vanity, and follow after lies?"[2] Why have you severed yourselves, by the heinous impiety of schism, from the unity of the whole world? You give heed to the falsehoods concerning the surrendering of the divine books to persecutors, which men who are either deceiving you, or are themselves deceived, utter in order that you may die in a state of heretical separation: and you do not give heed to what these divine books themselves proclaim, in order that you may live in the peace of the Catholic Church. Wherefore do you lend an open ear to the words of men who tell you things which they have never been able to prove, and are deaf to the voice of God speaking thus: "The Lord hath said unto me, Thou art My Son; this day have I begotten Thee. Ask of Me, and I shall give Thee the heathen for Thine inheritance, and the uttermost parts of the earth for Thy possession"?[3] "To Abraham and his seed were the promises made. He saith not, 'And to seeds,' as of many, but as of one, 'And to thy seed,' which is Christ."[4] And the promise to which the apostle refers is this: "In thy seed shall all the nations of the earth be blessed."[5] Therefore lift up the eyes of your souls, and see how in the whole world all nations are blessed in Abraham's seed. Abraham, in his day, believed what was not yet seen; but you who see it refuse to believe what has been fulfilled.[6] The Lord's death was the ransom of the world; He paid the price for the whole world; and you do not dwell in concord with the whole world, as would be for your advantage, but stand apart and strive contentiously to destroy the whole world, to your own loss. Hear now what is said in the Psalm concerning this ransom: "They pierced my hands and my feet. I may tell all my bones; they look and stare upon me. They part my garments among them, and cast lots upon my vesture."[7] Wherefore will you be guilty of dividing the garments of the Lord, and not hold in common with the whole world that coat of charity, woven from above throughout, which even His executioners did not rend? In the same Psalm we read that the whole world holds this, for he says: "All the ends of the world shall remember and turn unto the Lord, and all the kindreds of the nations shall worship before Thee; for the kingdom is the Lord's, and He is the Governor among the nations."[8] Open the ears of your soul, and hear: "The mighty God, even the LORD, hath spoken, and called the earth, from the rising of the sun unto the going down thereof; out of Zion, the perfection of beauty."[9] If you do not wish to understand this, hear the gospel from the Lord's own lips, how He said: "All things must be fulfilled which were written in the Law of Moses, and in the Prophets, and in the Psalms, concerning Him; and that repentance and remission of sins should be preached in His name among all nations, beginning at Jerusalem."[10] The words in the Psalm, "the earth from the rising of the sun unto the going down thereof," correspond to these in the Gospel, "among all nations;" and as He said in the Psalm, "from Zion, the perfection of beauty," He has said in the Gospel, "beginning at Jerusalem."

2. Your imagination that you are separating yourselves, before the time of the harvest, from the tares which are mixed with the wheat, proves that you are only tares. For if you were wheat, you would bear with the tares, and not separate yourselves from that which is growing in Christ's field. Of the tares, indeed, it has been said, "Because iniquity shall abound, the love of many shall wax cold;" but of the wheat it is said, "He that shall endure unto the end, the same shall be saved."[11] What grounds have you for believing that the tares have increased and filled the world, and that the wheat has decreased, and is found now in Africa alone? You claim to be Christians, and you disclaim the authority of Christ. He said, "Let both grow together till the harvest;" He said not, "Let the wheat decrease, and let the tares multiply." He said, "The field is the world;" He said not, "The field is Africa." He said, "The harvest is the end of the world;" He said not, "The harvest is the time of Donatus." He said, "The reapers are the angels;" He said not, "The reapers are the captains of the Circumcelliones."[12] But you, by charging the good wheat with being tares, have proved yourselves to be tares; and

---

[1] Alluding to the extent to which Rome was indebted to Africa for corn.
[2] Ps. iv. 2.
[3] Ps. ii. 7, 8.
[4] Gal. iii. 16
[5] Gen. xxii. 18.
[6] The original here is antithetical: "jam vos videtis, et adhuc invidetis."
[7] Ps. xxii. 16, 17, 18.
[8] Ps. xxii. 27, 28.
[9] Ps. l. 1, 2.
[10] Luke xxiv. 44, 47.
[11] Matt. xxiv 12, 13.
[12] Matt. xiii. 30-39.

what is worse, you have prematurely separated yourselves from the wheat. For some of your predecessors, in whose impious schism you obstinately remain, delivered up to persecutors the sacred MSS. and the vessels of the Church (as may be seen in municipal records [1]) ; others of them passed over the fault which these men confessed, and remained in communion with them ; and both parties having come together to Carthage as an infatuated faction, condemned others without a hearing, on the charge of that fault which they had agreed, so far as they themselves were concerned, to forgive, and then set up a bishop against the ordained bishop, and erected an altar against the altar already recognised. Afterwards they sent to the Emperor Constantine a letter begging that bishops of churches beyond the sea should be appointed to arbitrate between the bishops of Africa. When the judges whom they sought were granted, and at Rome had given their decision, they refused to submit to it, and complained to the Emperor or against the bishops as having judged unrighteously. From the sentence of another bench of bishops sent to Arles to try the case, they appealed to the Emperor himself. When he had heard them, and they had been proved guilty of calumny, they still persisted in their wickedness. Awake to the interest of your salvation! love peace, and return to unity! Whensoever you desire it, we are ready to recite in detail the events to which we have referred.

3. He is the associate of wicked men who consents to the deeds of wicked men ; not he who suffers the tares to grow in the Lord's field unto the harvest, or the chaff to remain until the final winnowing time. If you hate those who do evil, shake yourselves free from the crime of schism. If you really feared to associate with the wicked, you would not for so many years have permitted Optatus [2] to remain among you when he was living in the most flagrant sin. And as you now give him the name of martyr, you must, if you are consistent, give him for whom he died the name of Christ. Finally, wherein has the Christian world offended you, from which you have insanely and wickedly cut yourselves off? and what claim upon your esteem have those followers of Maximianus, whom you have received back with honour after they had been condemned by you, and violently cast forth by warrant of the civil authorities from their churches? Wherein has the peace of Christ offended you, that you resist it by separating yourselves from those whom you calumniate? and wherein has the peace of Donatus earned

your favour, that to promote it you receive back those whom you condemned? Felicianus of Musti is now one of you. We have read concerning him, that he was formerly condemned by your council, and afterwards accused by you at the bar of the proconsul, and in the town of Musti was attacked as is stated in the municipal records.

4. If the surrendering of the sacred books to destruction is a crime which, in the case of the king who burned the book of Jeremiah,[3] God punished with death as a prisoner of war, how much greater is the guilt of schism! For those authors of schism to whom you have compared the followers of Maximianus, the earth opening, swallowed up alive.[4] Why, then, do you object against us the charge of surrendering the sacred books which you do not prove, and at the same time both condemn and welcome back those among yourselves who are schismatics? If you are proved to be in the right by the fact that you have suffered persecution from the Emperor, a still stronger claim than yours must be that of the followers of Maximianus, whom you have yourselves persecuted by the help of judges sent to you by Catholic emperors. If you alone have baptism, what weight do you attach to the baptism administered by followers of Maximianus in the case of those whom Felicianus baptized while he was under your sentence of condemnation, who came along with him when he was afterwards restored by you? Let your bishops answer these questions to your laity at least, if they will not debate with us ; and do you, as you value your salvation, consider what kind of doctrine that must be about which they refuse to enter into discussion with us. If the wolves have prudence enough to keep out of the way of the shepherds, why have the flock so lost their prudence, that they go into the dens of the wolves?

LETTER LXXVII.

(A.D. 404.)

TO FELIX AND HILARINUS, MY LORDS MOST BELOVED, AND BRETHREN WORTHY OF ALL HONOUR, AUGUSTIN SENDS GREETING IN THE LORD.

1. I do not wonder to see the minds of believers disturbed by Satan, whom resist, continuing in the hope which rests on the promises of God, who cannot lie, who has not only condescended to promise in eternity rewards to us who believe and hope in Him, and who persevere in love unto the end, but has also foretold that in time offences by which our faith must be tried and proved shall not be wanting ; for He said, "Because iniquity shall abound, the love

---

[1] Proceedings before Munatius Felix, Letter LIII. sec. 4, p. 299.
[2] Optatus, Donatist bishop of Thamugada, was cast into prison A.D. 397, and died there. He was a partisan of Gildo in his rebellion against Honorius, and shared the misfortunes, as he had participated in the crimes, of his chief.

[3] Jer. xxxvi. 23, 30.
[4] Num. xvi. 31-33.

of many shall wax cold;" but He added immediately, "and he that shall endure to the end, the same shall be saved."[1] Why, therefore, should it seem strange that men bring calumnies against the servants of God, and being unable to turn them aside from an upright life, endeavour to blacken their reputation, seeing that they do not cease uttering blasphemies daily against God, the Lord of these servants, if they are displeased by anything in which the execution of His righteous and secret counsel is contrary to their desire? Wherefore I appeal to your wisdom, my lords most beloved, and brethren worthy of all honour, and exhort you to exercise your minds in the way which best becomes Christians, setting over against the empty calumnies and groundless suspicions of men the written word of God, which has foretold that these things should come, and has warned us to meet them with fortitude.

2. Let me therefore say in a few words to your Charity, that the presbyter Boniface has not been discovered by me to be guilty of any crime, and that I have never believed, and do not yet believe, any charge brought against him. How, then, could I order his name to be deleted from the roll of presbyters, when filled with alarm by that word of our Lord in the gospel: "With what judgment ye judge ye shall be judged"?[2] For, seeing that the dispute which has arisen between him and Spes has by their consent been submitted to divine arbitration in a way which, if you desire it, can be made known to you,[3] who am I, that I should presume to anticipate the divine award by deleting or passing over his name? As a bishop, I ought not rashly to suspect him; and as being only a man, I cannot decide infallibly concerning things which are hidden from me. Even in secular matters, when an appeal has been made to a higher authority, all procedure is sisted while the case awaits the decision from which there is no appeal; because if anything were changed while the matter is depending on his arbitration, this would be an insult to the higher tribunal. And how great the distance between even the highest human authority and the divine!

May the mercy of the Lord our God never forsake you, my lords most beloved, and brethren worthy of all honour.

LETTER LXXVIII.

(A.D. 404.)

TO MY MOST BELOVED BRETHREN, THE CLERGY, ELDERS, AND PEOPLE OF THE CHURCH OF HIP-PO, WHOM I SERVE IN THE LOVE OF CHRIST, I, AUGUSTIN, SEND GREETING IN THE LORD.

1. Would that you, giving earnest heed to the word of God, did not require counsel of mine to support you under whatsoever offences may arise! Would that your comfort rather came from Him by whom we also are comforted; who has foretold not only the good things which He designs to give to those who are holy and faithful, but also the evil things in which this world is to abound; and has caused these to be written, in order that we may expect the blessings which are to follow the end of this world with a certainty not less complete than that which attends our present experience of the evils which had been predicted as coming before the end of the world! Wherefore also the apostle says, "Whatsoever things were written aforetime, were written for our learning, that we through patience and comfort of the Scriptures might have hope."[4] And wherefore did our Lord Himself judge it necessary not only to say, "Then shall the righteous shine forth as the sun in the kingdom of their Father"[5] which shall come to pass after the end of the world, but also to exclaim, "Woe unto the world because of offences!"[6] if not to prevent us from flattering ourselves with the idea that we can reach the mansions of eternal felicity, unless we have overcome the temptation to yield when exercised by the afflictions of time? Why was it necessary for Him to say, "Because iniquity shall abound, the love of many shall wax cold," if not in order that those of whom He spoke in the next sentence, "but he that shall endure to the end shall be saved,"[1] might, when they saw love waxing cold through abounding iniquity, be saved from being put to confusion, or filled with fear, or crushed with grief about such things, as if they were strange and unlooked for, and might rather, through witnessing the events which had been predicted as appointed to occur before the end, be assisted in patiently enduring unto the end, so as to obtain after the end the reward of reigning in peace in that life which has no end?

2. Wherefore, beloved, in regard to that scandal by which some are troubled concerning the presbyter Boniface, I do not say to you that you are not to be grieved for it; for in men who do not grieve for such things the love of Christ is not, whereas those who take pleasure in such things are filled with the malice of the devil. Not, however, that anything has come to our knowledge which deserves censure in the presbyter aforesaid, but that two in our house are so situated that one of them must be regarded as

---

[1] Matt. xxiv. 12, 13.
[2] Matt. vii. 2.
[3] He refers to their visiting the tomb of Felix of Nola, in the hope that by some miracle there the innocent and the guilty would be distinguished. See Letter LXXVIII. sec. 3, p. 346.

[4] Rom. xv. 4.
[5] Matt. xiii. 43.
[6] Matt. xviii. 7.

beyond all doubt wicked; and though the conscience of the other be not defiled, his good name is forfeited in the eyes of some, and suspected by others. Grieve for these things, for they are to be lamented; but do not so grieve as to let your love grow cold, and yourselves be indifferent to holy living. Let it rather burn the more vehemently in the exercise of prayer to God, that if your presbyter is guiltless (which I am the more inclined to believe, because, when he had discovered the immoral and vile proposal of the other, he would neither consent to it nor conceal it), a divine decision may speedily restore him to the exercise of his official duties with his innocence vindicated; and that if, on the other hand, knowing himself to be guilty, which I dare not suspect, he has deliberately tried to destroy the good name of another when he could not corrupt his morals, as he charges his accuser with having done, God may not permit him to hide his wickedness, so that the thing which men cannot discover may be revealed by the judgment of God, to the conviction of the one or of the other.

3. For when this case had long disquieted me, and I could find no way of convicting either of the two as guilty, although I rather inclined to believe the presbyter innocent, I had at first resolved to leave both in the hand of God, without deciding the case, until something should be done by the one of whom I had suspicion, giving just and unquestionable reasons for his expulsion from our house. But when he was labouring most earnestly to obtain promotion to the rank of the clergy, either on the spot from myself, or elsewhere through letter of recommendation from me, and I could on no account be induced either to lay hands in the act of ordination upon one of whom I thought so ill, or to consent to introduce him through commendation of mine to any brother for the same purpose, he began to act more violently, demanding that if he was not to be promoted to clerical orders, Boniface should not be permitted to retain his status as a presbyter. This demand having been made, when I perceived that Boniface was unwilling that, through doubts as to his holiness of life, offence should be given to any who were weak and inclined to suspect him, and that he was ready to suffer the loss of his honour among men rather than vainly persist even to the disquieting of the Church in a contention the very nature of which made it impossible for him to prove his innocence (of which he was conscious) to the satisfaction of those who did not know him, or were in doubt or prone to suspicion in regard to him, I fixed upon the following as a means of discovering the truth. Both pledged themselves in a solemn compact to go to a holy place, where the more awe-inspiring works of God

might much more readily make manifest the evil of which either of them was conscious, and compel the guilty to confess, either by judgment or through fear of judgment. God is everywhere, it is true, and He that made all things is not contained or confined to dwell in any place; and He is to be worshipped in spirit and in truth by His true worshippers,[1] in order that, as He heareth in secret, He may also in secret justify and reward. But in regard to the answers to prayer which are visible to men, who can search out His reasons for appointing some places rather than others to be the scene of miraculous interpositions? To many the holiness of the place in which the body of the blessed Felix is buried is well known, and to this place I desired them to repair; because from it we may receive more easily and more reliably a written account of whatever may be discovered in either of them by divine interposition. For I myself knew how, at Milan, at the tomb of the saints, where demons are brought in a most marvellous and awful manner to confess their deeds, a thief who had come thither intending to deceive by perjuring himself, was compelled to own his theft, and to restore what he had taken away; and is not Africa also full of the bodies of holy martyrs? Yet we do not know of such things being done in any place here. Even as the gift of healing and the gift of discerning of spirits are not given to all saints,[2] as the apostle declares; so it is not at all the tombs of the saints that it has pleased Him who divideth to each severally as He will, to cause such miracles to be wrought.

4. Wherefore, although I had purposed not to let this most heavy burden on my heart come to your knowledge, lest I should disquiet you by a painful but useless vexation, it has pleased God to make it known to you, perhaps for this reason, that you may along with me devote yourselves to prayer, beseeching Him to condescend to reveal that which He knoweth, but which we cannot know in this matter. For I did not presume to suppress or erase from the roll of his colleagues the name of this presbyter, lest I should seem to insult the Divine Majesty, upon whose arbitration the case now depends, if I were to forestall His decision by any premature decision of mine: for even in secular affairs, when a perplexing case is referred to a higher authority, the inferior judges do not presume to make any change while the reference is pending. Moreover, it was decreed in a Council of bishops[3] that no clergyman who has not yet been proved guilty be suspended from communion, unless he fail to present himself for the examination of the charges against him. Boniface, however, humbly agreed to fore-

---

[1] John iv. 24.
[2] 1 Cor. xii. 9, 10, 30.
[3] Third Council of Carthage, A.D. 397, Can. 7, 8.

go his claim to a letter of commendation, by the use of which on his journey he might have secured the recognition of his rank, preferring that both should stand on a footing of equality in a place where both were alike unknown. And now, if you prefer that his name should not be read, that we "may cut off occasion," as the apostle says, from those that desire occasion [1] to justify their unwillingness to come to the Church, this omission of his name shall be not our deed, but theirs on whose account it may be done. For what does it harm any man, that men through ignorance refuse to have his name read from that tablet, so long as a guilty conscience does not blot his name out of the Book of Life?

5. Wherefore, my brethren who fear God, remember what the Apostle Peter says: Your adversary, the devil, as a roaring lion, walketh about, seeking whom he may devour." [2] When he cannot devour a man through seducing him into iniquity, he attempts to injure his good name, that if it be possible, he may give way under the reproaches of men and the calumnies of slandering tongues, and may thus fall into his jaws. If, however, he be unable even to sully the good name of one who is innocent, he tries to persuade him to cherish unkindly suspicions of his brother, and judge him harshly, and so become entangled, and be an easy prey. And who is able to know or to tell all his snares and wiles? Nevertheless, in reference to those three, which belong more especially to the case before us; in the first place, lest you should be turned aside to wickedness through following bad examples, God gives you by the apostle these warnings: "Be ye not unequally yoked together with unbelievers; for what fellowship hath righteousness with unrighteousness, and what communion hath light with darkness?" [3] and in another place: "Be not deceived; evil communications corrupt good manners: awake to righteousness,[4] and sin not." [5] Secondly, that ye may not give way under the tongues of slanderers, He saith by the prophet, "Hearken unto Me, ye that know righteousness, the people in whose heart is My law: fear ye not the reproach of men, neither be ye afraid of their revilings.[6] For the moth shall eat them up like a garment, and the worm shall eat them like wool; but My righteousness shall be for ever." [7] And thirdly, lest you should be undone through groundless and malevolent suspicions concerning any servants of God, remember that word of the apostle, "Judge nothing before the time, until the Lord come,

who both will bring to light the hidden things of darkness, and will make manifest the counsels of the hearts, and then shall every man have praise of God;" [8] and this also, "The things which are revealed belong to you, but the secret things belong unto the Lord your God." [9]

6. It is indeed manifest that such things do not take place in the Church without great sorrow on the part of saints and believers; but let Him be our Comforter who hath foretold all these events, and has warned us not to become cold in love through abounding iniquity, to endure to the end that we may be saved. For, as far as I am concerned, if there be in me a spark of the love of Christ, who among you is weak, and I am not weak? who among you is offended, and I burn not? [10] Do not therefore add to my distresses, by your yielding either by groundless suspicions or by occasion of other men's sins. Do not, I beseech you, lest I say of you, "They have added to the pain of my wounds." [11] For it is much more easy to bear the reproach of those who take open pleasure in these our pains, of whom it was foretold in regard to Christ Himself, "They that sit in the gate speak against Me, and I was the song of the drunkards," [12] for whom also we have been taught to pray, and to seek their welfare. For why do they sit at the gate, and what do they watch for, if it be not for this, that so soon as any bishop or clergyman or monk or nun has fallen, they may have ground for believing, and boasting, and maintaining that all are the same as the one that has fallen, but that all cannot be convicted and unmasked? Yet these very men do not straightway cast forth their wives, or bring accusation against their mothers, if some married woman has been discovered to be an adulteress. But the moment that any crime is either falsely alleged or actually proved against any one who makes a profession of piety, these men are incessant and unwearied in their efforts to make this charge be believed against all religious men. Those men, therefore, who eagerly find what is sweet to their malicious tongues in the things which grieve us, we may compare to those dogs (if, indeed, they are to be understood as increasing his misery) which licked the sores of the beggar who lay before the rich man's gate, and endured with patience every hardship and indignity until he should come to rest in Abraham's bosom.[13]

7. Do not add to my sorrows, O ye who have some hope toward God. Let not the wounds which these lick be multiplied by you, for whom

[1] 2 Cor. xi. 12.
[2] 1 Pet. v. 8.
[3] 2 Cor. vi. 14.
[4] Aug. translates, "be sober and righteous."
[5] 1 Cor. xv. 33, 34.
[6] "Nor count it a great thing that they despise you." — AUG.
[7] Isa. li. 7, 8.
[8] 1 Cor. iv. 5.
[9] Deut. xxix. 29. This verse is the nearest I can find to the words here quoted by the apostle. The reference in the Bened. edition to 1 Cor. v. 12 must be a mistake.
[10] 2 Cor. xi. 29.
[11] Ps. lxix. 26, as translated by Aug.
[12] Ps. lxix. 12.
[13] Luke xvi. 21–23.

we are in jeopardy every hour, having fightings without and fears within, and perils in the city, perils in the wilderness, perils by the heathen, and perils by false brethren.[1] I know that you are grieved, but is your grief more poignant than mine? I know that you are disquieted, and I fear lest by the tongues of slanderers some weak one for whom Christ died should perish. Let not my grief be increased by you, for it is not through my fault that this grief was made yours. For I used the utmost precautions to secure, if it were possible, both that the steps necessary for the prevention of this evil should not be neglected, and that it should not be brought to your knowledge, since this could only cause unavailing vexation to the strong, and dangerous disquietude to the weak, among you. But may He who hath permitted you to be tempted by knowing this, give you strength to bear the trial, and "teach you out of His law, and give you rest from the days of adversity, until the pit be digged for the wicked."[2]

8. I hear that some of you are more cast down with sorrow by this event, than by the fall of the two deacons who had joined us from the Donatist party, as if they had brought reproach upon the discipline of Proculeianus;[3] whereas this checks your boasting about me, that under my discipline no such inconsistency among the clergy had taken place. Let me frankly say to you, whoever you are that have done this, you have not done well. Behold, God hath taught you, "He that glorieth, let him glory in the Lord;"[4] and ye ought to bring no reproach against heretics but this, that they are not Catholics. Be not like these heretics, who, because they have nothing to plead in \defence of their schism, attempt nothing beyond heaping up charges against the men from whom they are separated, and most falsely boast that in these we have an unenviable pre-eminence, in order that since they can neither impugn nor darken the truth of the Divine Scripture, from which the Church of Christ spread abroad everywhere receives its testimony, they may bring into disfavour the men by whom it is preached, against whom they are capable of affirming anything — whatever comes into their mind. "But ye have not so learned Christ, if so be that ye have heard Him, and have been taught by Him."[5] For He Himself has guarded His believing people from undue disquietude concerning wickedness, even in stewards of the divine mysteries, as doing evil which was their own, but speaking good which was His. "All therefore whatsoever they bid you observe, that observe and do; but do not

ye after their works: for they say, and do not."[6] Pray by all means for me, lest perchance "when I have preached to others, I myself should be a castaway;"[7] but when you glory, glory not in me, but in the Lord. For however watchful the discipline of my house may be, I am but a man, and I live among men; and I do not presume to pretend that my house is better than the ark of Noah, in which among eight persons one was found a castaway;[8] or better than the house of Abraham, regarding which it was said, "Cast out the bondwoman and her son;"[9] or better than the house of Isaac, regarding whose twin sons it was said, "I loved Jacob, and I hated Esau;"[10] or better than the house of Jacob himself, in which Reuben defiled his father's bed;[11] or better than the house of David, in which one son wrought folly with his sister,[12] and another rebelled against a father of such holy clemency; or better than the band of companions of Paul the apostle, who nevertheless would not have said, as above quoted, "Without are fightings, and within are fears," if he had dwelt with none but good men; nor would have said, in speaking of the holiness and fidelity of Timothy, "I have no man like-minded who will naturally care for your state; for all seek their own, not the things which are Jesus Christ's;"[13] or better than the band of the disciples of the Lord Christ Himself, in which eleven good men bore with Judas, who was a thief and a traitor; or, finally, better than heaven itself, from which the angels fell.

9. I frankly avow to your Charity, before the Lord our God, whom I have taken, since the time when I began to serve Him, as a witness upon my soul, that as I have hardly found any men better than those who have done well in monasteries, so I have not found any men worse than monks who have fallen; whence I suppose that to them applies the word written in the Apocalypse, "He that is righteous, let him be still more righteous; and he that is filthy, let him be still more filthy."[14] Wherefore, if we be grieved by some foul blemishes, we are comforted by a much larger proportion of examples of an opposite kind. Let not, therefore, the dregs which offend your eyes cause you to hate the oil-presses whence the Lord's storehouses are supplied to their profit with a more brightly illuminating oil.

May the mercy of our Lord keep you in His peace, safe from all the snares of the enemy, my dearly beloved brethren.

---

[1] 2 Cor. vii. 5 and xi. 26.
[2] Ps. xciv. 12, 13.
[3] Donatist bishop of Hippo.
[4] 1 Cor. i. 31.
[5] Eph. iv. 20, 21.

[6] Matt. xxiii. 3.
[7] 1 Cor. ix. 27.
[8] Gen. ix. 27.
[9] Gen. xxi. 10.
[10] Mal. i. 2.
[11] Gen. xlix. 4.
[12] 2 Sam. xiii. 14.
[13] Phil. ii. 20, 21.
[14] Rev. xxii. 11.

LETTER LXXIX.

(A.D. 404.)

A short and stern challenge to some Manichæan teacher who had succeeded Fortunatus (supposed to be Felix).

Your attempts at evasion are to no purpose : your real character is patent even a long way off. My brethren have reported to me their conversation with you. You say that you do not fear death ; it is well : but you ought to fear that death which you are bringing upon yourself by your blasphemous assertions concerning God. As to your understanding that the visible death which all men know is a separation between soul and body, this is a truth which demands no great grasp of intellect. But as to the statement which you annex to this, that death is a separation between good and evil, do you not see that, if the soul be good and the body be evil, he who joined them together [1] is not good ? But you affirm that the good God has joined them together ; from which it follows that He is either evil, or swayed by fear of one who is evil. Yet you boast of your having no fear of man, when at the same time you conceive God to be such that, through fear of Darkness, He would join together good and evil. Be not uplifted, as your writing shows you to be, by supposing that I magnify you, by my resolving to check the outflowing of your poison, lest its insidious and pestilential power should do harm : for the apostle does not magnify those whom he calls "dogs," saying to the Philippians, " Beware of dogs ; " [2] nor does he magnify those of whom he says that their word doth eat as a canker.[3] Therefore, in the name of Christ, I demand of you to answer, if you are able, the question which baffled your predecessor Fortunatus.[4] For he went from the scene of our discussion declaring that he would not return, unless, after conferring with his party, he found something by which he could answer the arguments used by our brethren. And if you are not prepared to do this, begone from this place, and do not pervert the right ways of the Lord, ensnaring and infecting with your poison the minds of the weak, lest, by the Lord's right hand helping me, you be put to confusion in a way which you did not expect.

LETTER LXXX.

(A.D. 404.)

A letter to Paulinus, asking him to explain more fully how we may know what is the will of God and rule of our duty in the ordinary course of providence. This letter may be omitted as merely propounding a question, and containing nothing specially noticeable.

LETTER LXXXI.

(A.D. 405.)

TO AUGUSTIN, MY LORD TRULY HOLY, AND MOST BLESSED FATHER, JEROME SENDS GREETING IN THE LORD.

Having anxiously inquired of our holy brother Firmus regarding your state, I was glad to hear that you are well. I expected him to bring, or, I should rather say, I insisted upon his giving me, a letter from you ; upon which he told me that he had set out from Africa without communicating to you his intention. I therefore send to you my respectful salutations through this brother, who clings to you with a singular warmth of affection ; and at the same time, in regard to my last letter, I beg you to forgive the modesty which made it impossible for me to refuse you, when you had so long required me to write you in reply. That letter, moreover, was not an answer from me to you, but a confronting of my arguments with yours. And if it was a fault in me to send a reply (I beseech you hear me patiently), the fault of him who insisted upon it was still greater. But let us be done with such quarrelling ; let there be sincere brotherliness between us ; and henceforth let us exchange letters, not of controversy, but of mutual charity. The holy brethren who with me serve the Lord send you cordial salutations. Salute from us the holy brethren who with you bear Christ's easy yoke ; especially I beseech you to convey my respectful salutation to the holy father Alypius, worthy of all esteem. May Christ, our almighty God, preserve you safe, and not unmindful of me, my lord truly holy, and most blessed father. If you have read my commentary on Jonah, I think you will not recur to the ridiculous gourd-debate. If, moreover, the friend who first assaulted me with his sword has been driven back by my pen, I rely upon your good feeling and equity to lay blame on the one who brought, and not on the one who repelled, the accusation. Let us, if you please, exercise ourselves [5] in the field of Scripture without wounding each other.

LETTER LXXXII.

(A.D. 405.)

A Reply to Letters LXXII., LXXV., and LXXXI.

TO JEROME, MY LORD BELOVED AND HONOURED IN THE BOWELS OF CHRIST, MY HOLY BROTHER AND FELLOW-PRESBYTER, AUGUSTIN SENDS GREETING IN THE LORD.

1. Long ago I sent to your Charity a long letter in reply to the one which you remember sending to me by your holy son Asterius, who is now not only my brother, but also my colleague. Whether

---

[1] *Commiscuit.*
[2] Phil. iii. 2.
[3] 2 Tim. ii. 17.
[4] In his *Retractations*, i. 16, Augustin mentions his having defeated Fortunatus in discussion before he was made bishop of Hippo.

[5] *Ludamus.*

that reply reached you or not I do not know, unless I am to infer this from the words in your letter brought to me by our most sincere friend Firmus, that if the one who first assaulted you with his sword has been driven back by your pen, you rely upon my good feeling and equity to lay blame on the one who brought, not on the one who repelled, the accusation. From this one indication, though very slight, I infer that you have read my letter. In that letter I expressed indeed my sorrow that so great discord had arisen between you and Rufinus, over the strength of whose former friendship brotherly love was wont to rejoice in all parts to which the fame of it had come ; but I did not in this intend to re- buke you, my brother, whom I dare not say that I have found blameable in that matter. I only lamented the sad lot of men in this world, in whose friendships, depending as they do on the continuance of mutual regard, there is no stability, however great that regard may sometimes be. I would rather, however, have been informed by your letter whether you have granted me the pardon which I begged, of which I now desire you to give me more explicit assurance ; although the more genial and cheerful tone of your letter seems to signify that I have obtained what I asked in mine, if indeed it was despatched after mine had been read by you, which is, as I have said, not clearly indicated.

2. You ask, or rather you give a command with the confiding boldness of charity, that we should amuse ourselves [1] in the field of Scripture without wounding each other. For my part, I am by all means disposed to exercise myself in earnest much rather than in mere amusement on such themes. If, however, you have chosen this word because of its suggesting easy exercise, let me frankly say that I desire something more from one who has, as you have, great talents under the control of a benignant disposition, together with wisdom enlightened by erudition, and whose application to study, hindered by no other distractions, is year after year impelled by enthusiasm and guided by genius : the Holy Spirit not only giving you all these advantages, but expressly charging you to come with help to those who are engaged in great and difficult investigations ; not as if, in studying Scripture, they were amusing themselves on a level plain, but as men panting and toiling up a steep ascent. If, however, perchance, you selected the expres- sion "ludamus" [let us amuse ourselves] because of the genial kindliness which befits discussion between loving friends, whether the matter de- bated be obvious and easy, or intricate and diffi- cult, I beseech you to teach me how I may succeed in securing this ; so that when I am

dissatisfied with anything which, not through want of careful attention, but perhaps through my slowness of apprehension, has not been demonstrated to me, if I should, in attempting to make good an opposite opinion, express my- self with a measure of unguarded frankness, I may not fall under the suspicion of childish con- ceit and forwardness, as if I sought to bring my own name into renown by assailing illustrious men ; [2] and that if, when something harsh has been demanded by the exigencies of argument, I attempt to make it less hard to bear by stating it in mild and courteous phrases, I may not be pronounced guilty of wielding a "honeyed sword." The only way which I can see for avoiding both these faults, or the suspicion of either of them, is to consent that when I am thus arguing with a friend more learned than myself, I must approve of everything which he says, and may not, even for the sake of more accurate information, hesitate before accepting his decisions.

3. On such terms we might amuse ourselves without fear of offending each other in the field of Scripture, but I might well wonder if the amusement was not at my expense. For I con- fess to your Charity that I have learned to yield this respect and honour only to the canonical books of Scripture : of these alone do I most firmly believe that the authors were completely free from error. And if in these writings I am perplexed by anything which appears to me op- posed to truth, I do not hesitate to suppose that either the MS. is faulty, or the translator has not caught the meaning of what was said, or I my- self have failed to understand it. As to all other writings, in reading them, however great the su- periority of the authors to myself in sanctity and learning, I do not accept their teaching as true on the mere ground of the opinion being held by them ; but only because they have suc- ceeded in convincing my judgment of its truth either by means of these canonical writings themselves, or by arguments addressed to my reason. I believe, my brother, that this is your own opinion as well as mine. I do not need to say that I do not suppose you to wish your books to be read like those of prophets or of apostles, concerning which it would be wrong to doubt that they are free from error. Far be such arrogance from that humble piety and just estimate of yourself which I know you to have, and without which assuredly you would not have said, " Would that I could receive your embrace, and that by converse we might aid each other in learning ! " [3]

CHAP. II. — 4. Now if, knowing as I do your life and conversation, I do not believe in regard

---

[1] *Ludamus.* Letter LXXXI. On this unfortunate word of Jerome's Augustin lingers with most provoking ingenuity.

[2] See Letter LXXII., sec. 2.
[3] Letter LXVIII. sec. 2.

to you that you have spoken anything with an intention of dissimulation and deceit, how much more reasonable is it for me to believe, in regard to the Apostle Paul, that he did not think one thing and affirm another when he wrote of Peter and Barnabas: "When I saw that they walked not uprightly, according to the truth of the gospel, I said unto Peter before them all, 'If thou, being a Jew, livest after the manner of the Gentiles, and not as do the Jews, why compellest thou the Gentiles to live as do the Jews?'"[1] For whom can I confide in, as assuredly not deceiving me by spoken or written statements, if the apostle deceived his own "children," for whom he "travailed in birth again until Christ (who is the Truth) were formed in them"?[2] After having previously said to them, "The things which I write unto you, behold, before God, I lie not,"[3] could he in writing to these same persons state what was not true, and deceive them by a fraud which was in some way sanctioned by expediency, when he said that he had seen Peter and Barnabas not walking uprightly, according to the truth of the gospel, and that he had withstood Peter to the face because of this, that he was compelling the Gentiles to live after the manner of the Jews?

5. But you will say it is better to believe that the Apostle Paul wrote what was not true, than to believe that the Apostle Peter did what was not right. On this principle, we must say (which far be it from us to say), that it is better to believe that the gospel history is false, than to believe that Christ was denied by Peter;[4] and better to charge the book of Kings [second book of Samuel] with false statements, than believe that so great a prophet, and one so signally chosen by the Lord God as David was, committed adultery in lusting after and taking away the wife of another, and committed such detestable homicide in procuring the death of her husband.[5] Better far that I should read with certainty and persuasion of its truth the Holy Scripture, placed on the highest (even the heavenly) pinnacle of authority, and should, without questioning the trustworthiness of its statements, learn from it that men have been either commended, or corrected, or condemned, than that, through fear of believing that by men, who, though of most praiseworthy excellence, were no more than men, actions deserving rebuke might sometimes be done, I should admit suspicions affecting the trustworthiness of the whole "oracles of God."

6. The Manichæans maintain that the greater part of the Divine Scripture, by which their wicked error is in the most explicit terms confuted, is not worthy of credit, because they cannot pervert its language so as to support their opinions; yet they lay the blame of the alleged mistake not upon the apostles who originally wrote the words, but upon some unknown corrupters of the manuscripts. Forasmuch, however, as they have never succeeded in proving this by more numerous and by earlier manuscripts, or by appealing to the original language from which the Latin translations have been drawn, they retire from the arena of debate, vanquished and confounded by truth which is well known to all. Does not your holy prudence discern how great scope is given to their malice against the truth, if we say not (as they do) that the apostolic writings have been tampered with by others, but that the apostles themselves wrote what they knew to be untrue?

7. You say that it is incredible that Paul should have rebuked in Peter that which Paul himself had done. I am not at present inquiring about what Paul did, but about what he wrote. This is most pertinent to the matter which I have in hand,—namely, the confirmation of the universal and unquestionable truth of the Divine Scriptures, which have been delivered to us for our edification in the faith, not by unknown men, but by the apostles, and have on this account been received as the authoritative canonical standard. For if Peter did on that occasion what he ought to have done, Paul falsely affirmed that he saw him walking not uprightly, according to the truth of the gospel. For whoever does what he ought to do, walks uprightly. He therefore is guilty of falsehood, who, knowing that another has done what he ought to have done, says that he has not done uprightly. If, then, Paul wrote what was true, it is true that Peter was not then walking uprightly, according to the truth of the gospel. He was therefore doing what he ought not to have done; and if Paul had himself already done something of the same kind, I would prefer to believe that, having been himself corrected, he could not omit the correction of his brother apostle, than to believe that he put down any false statement in his epistle; and if in any epistle of Paul this would be strange, how much more in the one in the preface of which he says, "The things which I write unto you, behold, before God, I lie not"!

8. For my part, I believe that Peter so acted on this occasion as to compel the Gentiles to live as Jews: because I read that Paul wrote this, and I do not believe that he lied. And therefore Peter was not acting uprightly. For it was contrary to the truth of the gospel, that those who believed in Christ should think that without those ancient ceremonies they could not

[1] Gal. ii. 14.
[2] Gal. iv. 19.
[3] Ch. i. 21.
[4] Matt. xxvi 75.
[5] 2 Sam. xi. 4, 17.

be saved. This was the position maintained at Antioch by those of the circumcision who had believed; against whom Paul protested constantly and vehemently. As to Paul's circumcising of Timothy,[1] performing a vow at Cenchrea,[2] and undertaking on the suggestion of James at Jerusalem to share the performance of the appointed rites with some who had made a vow,[3] it is manifest that Paul's design in these things was not to give to others the impression that he thought that by these observances salvation is given under the Christian dispensation, but to prevent men from believing that he condemned as no better than heathen idolatrous worship, those rites which God had appointed in the former dispensation as suitable to it, and as shadows of things to come. For this is what James said to him, that the report had gone abroad concerning him that he taught men "to forsake Moses."[4] This would be by all means wrong for those who believe in Christ, to forsake him who prophesied of Christ, as if they detested and condemned the teaching of him of whom Christ said, " Had ye believed Moses, ye would have believed Me; for he wrote of Me."

9. For mark, I beseech you, the words of James: "Thou seest, brother, how many thousands of Jews there are which believe; and they are all zealous of the law: and they are informed of thee, that thou teachest all the Jews which are among the Gentiles to forsake Moses, saying that they ought not to circumcise their children, neither to walk after the customs. What is it therefore? the multitude must needs come together: for they will hear that thou art come. Do therefore this that we say to thee: We have four men which have a vow on them; them take, and purify thyself with them, and be at charges with them, that they may shave their heads: and all may know that those things, whereof they were informed concerning thee, are nothing; but that thou thyself also walkest orderly, and keepest the law. As touching the Gentiles which have believed, we have written and concluded that they observe no such thing, save only that they keep themselves from things offered to idols, and from blood, and from things strangled, and from fornication."[5] It is, in my opinion, very clear that the reason why James gave this advice was, that the falsity of what they had heard concerning him might be known to those Jews, who, though they had believed in Christ, were jealous for the honour of the law, and would not have it thought that the institutions which had been given by Moses to their fathers were condemned by the doctrine of Christ as if

they were profane, and had not been originally given by divine authority. For the men who had brought this reproach against Paul were not those who understood the right spirit in which observance of these ceremonies should be practised under the Christian dispensation by believing Jews, — namely, as a way of declaring the divine authority of these rites, and their holy use in the prophetic dispensation, and not as a means of obtaining salvation, which was to them already revealed in Christ and ministered by baptism. On the contrary, the men who had spread abroad this report against the apostle were those who would have these rites observed, as if without their observance there could be no salvation to those who believed the gospel. For these false teachers had found him to be a most zealous preacher of free grace, and a most decided opponent of their views, teaching as he did that men are not justified by these things, but by the grace of Jesus Christ, which these ceremonies of the law were appointed to foreshadow. This party, therefore, endeavouring to raise odium and persecution against him, charged him with being an enemy of the law and of the divine institutions; and there was no more fitting way in which he could turn aside the odium caused by this false accusation, than by himself celebrating those rites which he was supposed to condemn as profane, and thus showing that, on the one hand, the Jews were not to be debarred from them as if they were unlawful, and on the other hand, that the Gentiles were not to be compelled to observe them as if they were necessary.

10. For if he did in truth condemn these things in the way in which he was reported to have done, and undertook to perform these rites in order that he might, by dissembling, disguise his real sentiments, James would not have said to him, "and all shall know," but, "all shall *think* that those things whereof they were informed concerning thee are nothing;"[6] especially seeing that in Jerusalem itself the apostles had already decreed that no one should compel the Gentiles to adopt Jewish ceremonies, but had not decreed that no one should then prevent the Jews from living according to their customs, although upon them also Christian doctrine imposed no such obligation. Wherefore, if it was after the apostle's decree that Peter's dissimulation at Antioch took place, whereby he was compelling the Gentiles to live after the manner of the Jews, which he himself was not compelled to do, although he was not forbidden to use Jewish rites in order to declare the honour of the oracles of God which were committed to the Jews; — if this, I say, were

[1] Acts xvi. 3.
[2] Acts xviii. 18.
[3] Acts xxi. 26.
[4] Acts xxi. 21.
[5] Acts xxi. 20–25.

[6] Acts xxi. 24.

the case, was it strange that Paul should exhort him to declare freely that decree which he remembered to have framed in conjunction with the other apostles at Jerusalem?

11. If, however, as I am more inclined to think, Peter did this before the meeting of that council at Jerusalem, in that case also it is not strange that Paul wished him not to conceal timidly, but to declare boldly, a rule of practice in regard to which he already knew that they were both of the same mind; whether he was aware of this from having conferred with him as to the gospel which both preached, or from having heard that, at the calling of the centurion Cornelius, Peter had been divinely instructed in regard to this matter, or from having seen him eating with Gentile converts before those whom he feared to offend had come to Antioch. For we do not deny that Peter was already of the same opinion in regard to this question as Paul himself was. Paul, therefore, was not teaching Peter what was the truth concerning that matter, but was reproving his dissimulation as a thing by which the Gentiles were compelled to act as Jews did; for no other reason than this, that the tendency of all such dissembling was to convey or confirm the impression that they taught the truth who held that believers could not be saved without circumcision and other ceremonies, which were shadows of things to come.

12. For this reason also he circumcised Timothy, lest to the Jews, and especially to his relations by the mother's side, it should seem that the Gentiles who had believed in Christ abhorred circumcision as they abhorred the worship of idols; whereas the former was appointed by God, and the latter invented by Satan. Again, he did not circumcise Titus, lest he should give occasion to those who said that believers could not be saved without circumcision, and who, in order to deceive the Gentiles, openly declared that this was the view held by Paul. This is plainly enough intimated by himself, when he says: "But neither Titus, who was with me, being a Greek, was compelled to be circumcised: and that because of false brethren unawares brought in, who came in privily to spy out our liberty which we have in Christ Jesus, that they might bring us into bondage: to whom we gave place by subjection, no, not for an hour, that the truth of the gospel might continue with you." [1] Here we see plainly what he perceived them to be eagerly watching for, and why it was that he did not do in the case of Titus as he had done in the case of Timothy, and as he might otherwise have done in the exercise of that liberty, by which he had shown that these observances were neither to be demanded as necessary to salvation, nor denounced as unlawful.

[1] Gal. ii. 3–5.

13. You say, however, that in this discussion we must beware of affirming, with the philosophers, that some of the actions of men lie in a region between right and wrong, and are to be reckoned, accordingly, neither among good actions nor among the opposite; [2] and it is urged in your argument that the observance of legal ceremonies cannot be a thing indifferent, but either good or bad; so that if I affirm it to be good, I acknowledge that we also are bound to observe these ceremonies; but if I affirm it to be bad, I am bound to believe that the apostles observed them not sincerely, but in a way of dissimulation. I, for my part, would not be so much afraid of defending the apostles by the authority of philosophers, since these teach some measure of truth in their dissertations, as of pleading on their behalf the practice of advocates at the bar, in sometimes serving their clients' interests at the expense of truth. If, as is stated in your exposition of the Epistle to the Galatians, this practice of barristers may be in your opinion with propriety quoted as resembling and justifying dissimulation on the part of Peter and Paul, why should I fear to allege to you the authority of philosophers whose teaching we account worthless, not because everything which they say is false, but because they are in most things mistaken, and wherein they are found affirming truth, are notwithstanding strangers to the grace of Christ, who is the Truth?

14. But why may I not say regarding these institutions of the old economy, that they are neither good nor bad: not good, since men are not by them justified, they having been only shadows predicting the grace by which we are justified; and not bad, since they were divinely appointed as suitable both to the time and to the people? Why may I not say this, when I am supported by that saying of the prophet, that God gave unto His people "statutes that were not good"? [3] For we have in this perhaps the reason of his not calling them "bad," but calling them "not good," i.e. not such that either by them men could be made good, or that without them men could not possibly become good. I would esteem it a favour to be informed by your Sincerity, whether any saint, coming from the East to Rome, would be guilty of dissimulation if he fasted on the seventh day of each week, excepting the Saturday before Easter. For if we say that it is wrong to fast on the seventh day, we shall condemn not only the Church of Rome, but also many other churches, both neighbouring and more remote, in which the same custom continues to be observed. If, on the other hand, we pronounce it wrong not to fast on the seventh day, how great is our presumption in

[2] See Jerome's Letter, LXXV. sec. 16, p. 340.
[3] Ezek. xx. 25.

censuring so many churches in the East, and by far the greater part of the Christian world! Or do you prefer to say of this practice, that it is a thing indifferent in itself, but commendable in him who conforms with it, not as a dissembler, but from a seemly desire for the fellowship and deference for the feelings of others? No precept, however, concerning this practice is given to Christians in the canonical books. How much more, then, may I shrink from pronouncing that to be bad which I cannot deny to be of divine institution!—this fact being admitted by me in the exercise of the same faith by which I know that not through these observances, but by the grace of God through our Lord Jesus Christ, I am justified.

15. I maintain, therefore, that circumcision, and other things of this kind, were, by means of what is called the Old Testament, given to the Jews with divine authority, as signs of future things which were to be fulfilled in Christ; and that now, when these things have been fulfilled, the laws concerning these rights remained only to be read by Christians in order to their understanding the prophecies which had been given before, but not to be of necessity practised by them, as if the coming of that revelation of faith which they prefigured was still future. Although, however, these rites were not to be imposed upon the Gentiles, the compliance with them, to which the Jews had been accustomed, was not to be prohibited in such a way as to give the impression that it was worthy of abhorrence and condemnation. Therefore slowly, and by degrees, all this observance of these types was to vanish away through the power of the sound preaching of the truth of the grace of Christ, to which alone believers would be taught to ascribe their justification and salvation, and not to those types and shadows of things which till then had been future, but which were now newly come and present, as at the time of the calling of those Jews whom the personal coming of our Lord and the apostolic times had found accustomed to the observance of these ceremonial institutions. The toleration, for the time, of their continuing to observe these was enough to declare their excellence as things which, though they were to be given up, were not, like the worship of idols, worthy of abhorrence; but they were not to be imposed upon others, lest they should be thought necessary, either as means or as conditions of salvation. This was the opinion of those heretics who, while anxious to be both Jews and Christians, could not be either the one or the other. Against this opinion you have most benevolently condescended to warn me, although I never entertained it. This also was the opinion with which, through fear, Peter fell into the fault of pretending to

yield concurrence, though in reality he did not agree with it; for which reason Paul wrote most truly of him, that he saw him not walking uprightly, according to the truth of the gospel, and most truly said of him that he was compelling the Gentiles to live as did the Jews. Paul did not impose this burden on the Gentiles through his sincerely complying, when it was needful, with these ceremonies, with the design of proving that they were not to be utterly condemned (as idol-worship ought to be); for he nevertheless constantly preached that not by these things, but by the grace revealed to faith, believers obtain salvation, lest he should lead any one to take up these Jewish observances as necessary to salvation. Thus, therefore, I believe that the Apostle Paul did all these things honestly, and without dissimulation; and yet if any one now leave Judaism and become a Christian, I neither compel nor permit him to imitate Paul's example, and go on with the sincere observance of Jewish rites, any more than you, who think that Paul dissembled when he practised these rites, would compel or permit such an one to follow the apostle in that dissimulation.

16. Shall I also sum up "the matter in debate, or rather your opinion concerning it"[1] (to quote your own expression)? It seems to me to be this: that after the gospel of Christ has been published, the Jews who believe do rightly if they offer sacrifices as Paul did, if they circumcise their children as Paul circumcised Timothy, and if they observe the "seventh day of the week, as the Jews have always done, provided only that they do all this as dissemblers and deceivers." If this is your doctrine, we are now precipitated, not into the heresy of Ebion, or of those who are commonly called Nazarenes, or any other known heresy, but into some new error, which is all the more pernicious because it originates not in mistake, but in deliberate and designed endeavour to deceive. If, in order to clear yourself from the charge of entertaining such sentiments, you answer that the apostles were to be commended for dissimulation in these instances, their purpose being to avoid giving offence to the many weak Jewish believers who did not yet understand that these things were to be rejected, but that now, when the doctrine of Christ's grace has been firmly established throughout so many nations, and when, by the reading of the Law and the Prophets throughout all the churches of Christ, it is well known that these are not read for our observance, but for our instruction, any man who should propose to feign compliance with these rites would be regarded as a madman. What objection can there be to my affirming that the Apostle Paul, and

---

[1] See Letter LXXV. sec. 13, p. 338.

other sound and faithful Christians, were bound sincerely to declare the worth of these old observances by occasionally honouring them, lest it should be thought that these institutions, originally full of prophetic significance, and cherished sacredly by their most pious forefathers, were to be abhorred by their posterity as profane inventions of the devil? For now, when the faith had come, which, previously foreshadowed by these ceremonies, was revealed after the death and resurrection of the Lord, they became, so far as their office was concerned, defunct. But just as it is seemly that the bodies of the deceased be carried honourably to the grave by their kindred, so was it fitting that these rites should be removed in a manner worthy of their origin and history, and this not with pretence of respect, but as a religious duty, instead of being forsaken at once, or cast forth to be torn in pieces by the reproaches of their enemies, as by the teeth of dogs. To carry the illustration further, if now any Christian (though he may have been converted from Judaism) were proposing to imitate the apostles in the observance of these ceremonies, like one who disturbs the ashes of those who rest, he would be not piously performing his part in the obsequies, but impiously violating the sepulchre.

17. I acknowledge that in the statement contained in my letter, to the effect that the reason why Paul undertook (although he was an apostle of Christ) to perform certain rites, was that he might show that these ceremonies were not pernicious to those who desired to continue that which they had received by the Law from their fathers, I have not explicitly enough qualified the statement, by adding that this was the case *only in that time in which the grace of faith was at first revealed;* for at that time this was not pernicious. These observances were to be given up by all Christians step by step, as time advanced; not all at once, lest, if this were done, men should not perceive the difference between what God by Moses appointed to His ancient people, and the rites which the unclean spirit taught men to practise in the temples of heathen deities. I grant, therefore, that in this your censure is justifiable, and my omission deserved rebuke. Nevertheless, long before the time of my receiving your letter, when I wrote a treatise against Faustus the Manichæan, I did not omit to insert the qualifying clause which I have just stated, in a short exposition which I gave of the same passage, as you may see for yourself if you kindly condescend to read that treatise; or you may be satisfied in any other way that you please by the bearer of this letter, that I had long ago published this restriction of the general affirmation. And I now, as speaking in the sight of God, beseech you by the law of charity to believe

me when I say with my whole heart, that it never was my opinion that in our time, Jews who become Christians were either required or at liberty to observe in any manner, or from any motive whatever, the ceremonies of the ancient dispensation; although I have always held, in regard to the Apostle Paul, the opinion which you call in question, from the time that I became acquainted with his writings. Nor can these two things appear incompatible to you; for you do not think it is the duty of any one in our day to feign compliance with these Jewish observances, although you believe that the apostles did this.

18. Accordingly, as you in opposing me affirm, and, to quote your own words, "though the world were to protest against it, boldly declare that the Jewish ceremonies are to Christians both hurtful and fatal, and that whoever observes them, whether he was originally Jew or Gentile, is on his way to the pit of perdition," [1] I entirely indorse that statement, and add to it, "Whoever observes these ceremonies, whether he was originally Jew or Gentile, is on his way to the pit of perdition, not only if he is sincerely observing them, but also if he is observing them with dissimulation." What more do you ask? But as you draw a distinction between the dissimulation which you hold to have been practised by the apostles, and the rule of conduct befitting the present time, I do the same between the course which Paul, as I think, sincerely followed in all these examples then, and the matter of observing in our day these Jewish ceremonies, although it were done, as by him, without any dissimulation, since it was then to be approved, but is now to be abhorred. Thus, although we read that "the law and the prophets were until John," [2] and that "therefore the Jews sought the more to kill Him, because He not only had broken the Sabbath, but said also that God was His Father, making Himself equal with God," [3] and that "we have received grace for grace; for the law was given by Moses, but grace and truth came by Jesus Christ;" [4] and although it was promised by Jeremiah that God would make a new covenant with the house of Judah, not according to the covenant which He made with their fathers; [5] nevertheless I do not think that the circumcision of our Lord by His parents was an act of dissimulation. If any one object that He did not forbid this because He was but an infant, I go on to say that I do not think that it was with intention to deceive that He said to the leper, "Offer for thy cleansing those things which Moses commanded for a testimony unto

---

[1] See Letter LXXV. sec. 14, pp. 338, 339.
[2] Luke xvi. 16.
[3] John v. 18.
[4] John i. 16, 17.
[5] Jer. xxxi. 31.

them,"[1]—thereby adding His own precept to the authority of the law of Moses regarding that ceremonial usage. Nor was there dissimulation in His going up to the feast,[2] as there was also no desire to be seen of men; for He went up, not openly, but secretly.

19. But the words of the apostle himself may be quoted against me: "Behold, I Paul say unto you, that if ye be circumcised, Christ shall profit you nothing."[3] It follows from this that he deceived Timothy, and made Christ profit him nothing, for he circumcised Timothy. Do you answer that this circumcision did Timothy no harm, because it was done with an intention to deceive? I reply that the apostle has not made any such exception. He does not say, If ye be circumcised without dissimulation, any more than, If ye be circumcised with dissimulation. He says unreservedly, "If ye be circumcised, Christ shall profit you nothing." As, therefore, you insist upon finding room for your interpretation, by proposing to supply the words, "unless it be done as an act of dissimulation," I make no unreasonable demand in asking you to permit me to understand the words, "if ye be circumcised," to be in that passage addressed to those who demanded circumcision, for this reason, that they thought it impossible for them to be otherwise saved by Christ. Whoever was then circumcised because of such persuasion and desire, and with this design, Christ assuredly profited him nothing, as the apostle elsewhere expressly affirms, "If righteousness come by the law, Christ is dead in vain."[4] The same is affirmed in words which you have quoted: "Christ is become of no effect to you, whosoever of you is justified by the law; ye are fallen from grace."[5] His rebuke, therefore, was addressed to those who believed that they were to be justified by the law,—not to those who, knowing well the design with which the legal ceremonies were instituted as foreshadowing truth, and the time for which they were destined to be in force, observed them in order to honour Him who appointed them at first. Wherefore also he says elsewhere, "If ye be led of the Spirit, ye are not under the law,"[6]—a passage from which you infer, that evidently "he has not the Holy Spirit who submits to the Law, not, as our fathers affirmed the apostles to have done, feignedly under the promptings of a wise discretion, but"—as I suppose to have been the case—"sincerely."[7]

20. It seems to me important to ascertain precisely what is that submission to the law which the apostle here condemns; for I do not think that he speaks here of circumcision merely, or of the sacrifices then offered by our fathers, but now not offered by Christians, and other observances of the same nature. I rather hold that he includes also that precept of the law, "Thou shalt not covet,"[8] which we confess that Christians are unquestionably bound to obey, and which we find most fully proclaimed by the light which the Gospel has shed upon it.[9] "The law," he says, "is holy, and the commandment holy, and just, and good;" and then adds, "Was, then, that which is good made death unto me? God forbid." "But sin, that it might appear sin, wrought death in me by that which is good; that sin, by the commandment, might become exceeding sinful."[10] As he says here, "that sin by the commandment might become exceeding sinful," so elsewhere, "The law entered that the offence might abound; but where sin abounded, grace did much more abound."[11] Again, in another place, after affirming, when speaking of the dispensation of grace, that grace alone justifies, he asks, "Wherefore then serveth the law?" and answers immediately, "It was added because of transgressions, until the Seed should come to whom the promises were made."[12] The persons, therefore, whose submission to the law the apostle here pronounces to be the cause of their own condemnation, are those whom the law brings in guilty, as not fulfilling its requirements, and who, not understanding the efficacy of free grace, rely with self-satisfied presumption on their own strength to enable them to keep the law of God; for "love is the fulfilling of the law."[13] Now "the love of God is shed abroad in our hearts," not by our own power, but "by the Holy Ghost, which is given unto us."[14] The satisfactory discussion of this, however, would require too long a digression, if not a separate volume. If, then, that precept of the law, "Thou shalt not covet," holds under it as guilty the man whose human weakness is not assisted by the grace of God, and instead of acquitting the sinner, condemns him as a transgressor, how much more was it impossible for those ordinances which were merely typical, circumcision and the rest, which were destined to be abolished when the revelation of grace became more widely known, to be the means of justifying any man! Nevertheless they were not on this ground to be immediately shunned with abhorrence, like the diabolical impieties of heathenism, from the first beginning of the revelation of the grace which

---

[1] Mark i. 44.
[2] John vii. 10.
[3] Gal. v. 2.
[4] Gal. ii. 21.
[5] Gal. v. 4.
[6] Gal. v. 18.
[7] Jerome, Letter LXXV. sec. 14, p. 339.
[8] Ex. xx. 17 and Deut. v. 21.
[9] *Evangelica maxime illustratione prædicari.*
[10] Rom. vii. 13.
[11] Rom. v. 20.
[12] Gal. iii. 19.
[13] Rom. xiii. 10.
[14] Rom. v. 5.

had been by these shadows prefigured; but to be for a little while tolerated, especially among those who joined the Christian Church from that nation to whom these ordinances had been given. When, however, they had been, as it were, honourably buried, they were thenceforward to be finally abandoned by all Christians.

21. Now, as to the words which you use, "non dispensative, ut nostri voluere majores,"[1] — "not in a way justifiable by expediency, the ground on which our fathers were disposed to explain the conduct of the apostles," — pray what do these words mean? Surely nothing else than that which I call "officiosum mendacium," the liberty granted by expediency being equivalent to a call of duty to utter a falsehood with pious intention. I at least can see no other explanation, unless, of course, the mere addition of the words "permitted by expediency" be enough to make a lie cease to be a lie; and if this be absurd, why do you not openly say that a lie spoken in the way of duty[2] is to be defended? Perhaps the name offends you, because the word "officium" is not common in ecclesiastical books; but this did not deter our Ambrose from its use, for he has chosen the title "De Officiis" for some of his books that are full of useful rules. Do you mean to say, that whoever utters a lie from a sense of duty is to be blamed, and whoever does the same on the ground of expediency is to be approved? I beseech you, consider that the man who thinks this may lie whenever he thinks fit, because this involves the whole important question whether to say what is false be at any time the duty of a good man, especially of a Christian man, to whom it has been said, "Let your yea be yea, and your nay, nay, lest ye fall into condemnation,"[3] and who believes the Psalmist's word, "Thou wilt destroy all them that speak lies."[4]

22. This, however, is, as I have said, another and a weighty question; I leave him who is of this opinion to judge for himself the circumstances in which he is at liberty to utter a lie: provided, however, that it be most assuredly believed and maintained that this way of lying is far removed from the authors who were employed to write holy writings, especially the canonical Scriptures; lest those who are the stewards of Christ, of whom it is said, "It is required in stewards, that a man be found faithful,"[5] should seem to have proved their fidelity by learning as an important lesson to speak what is false when this is expedient for the truth's sake, although the word fidelity itself, in the Latin tongue, is said to signify originally a real

correspondence between what is said and what is done.[6] Now, where that which is spoken is actually done, there is assuredly no room for falsehood. Paul therefore, as a "faithful steward," doubtless is to be regarded as approving his fidelity in his writings; for he was a steward of truth, not of falsehood. Therefore he wrote the truth when he wrote that he had seen Peter walking not uprightly, according to the truth of the gospel, and that he had withstood him to the face because he was compelling the Gentiles to live as the Jews did. And Peter himself received, with the holy and loving humility which became him, the rebuke which Paul, in the interests of truth, and with the boldness of love, administered. Therein Peter left to those that came after him an example, that, if at any time they deviated from the right path, they should not think it beneath them to accept correction from those who were their juniors, — an example more rare, and requiring greater piety, than that which Paul's conduct on the same occasion left us, that those who are younger should have courage even to withstand their seniors if the defence of evangelical truth required it, yet in such a way as to preserve unbroken brotherly love. For while it is better for one to succeed in perfectly keeping the right path, it is a thing much more worthy of admiration and praise to receive admonition meekly, than to admonish a transgressor boldly. On that occasion, therefore, Paul was to be praised for upright courage, Peter was to be praised for holy humility; and so far as my judgment enables me to form an opinion, this ought rather to have been asserted in answer to the calumnies of Porphyry, than further occasion given to him for finding fault, by putting it in his power to bring against Christians this much more damaging accusation, that either in writing their letters or in complying with the ordinances of God they practised deceit.

CHAP. III. — 23. You call upon me to bring forward the name of even one whose opinion I have followed in this matter, and at the same time you have quoted the names of many who have held before you the opinion which you defend.[7] You also say that if I censure you for an error in this, you beg to be allowed to remain in error in company with such great men. I have not read their writings; but although they are only six or seven in all, you have yourself impugned the authority of four of them. For as to the Laodicean author,[8] whose name you do not give, you say that he has lately forsaken the Church; Alexander you describe as a heretic of old standing; and as to Origen and Didymus, I read in some of your more recent works,

[1] Letter LXXV. sec. 14, p. 339.
[2] Mendacium officiosum.
[3] Jas. v. 12; Matt. v. 37.
[4] Ps. v. 6.
[5] 1 Cor. iv. 2.

[6] Cum ipsa fides in latino sermone ab eo dicatur appellata quia fit quod dicitur.
[7] Jerome's Letter, LXXV. sec. 6, p. 335.
[8] Ibid. sec. 4, p. 334.

censure passed on their opinions, and that in no measured terms, nor in regard to insignificant questions, although formerly you gave Origen marvellous praise. I suppose, therefore, that you would not even yourself be contented to be in error with these men; although the language which I refer to is equivalent to an assertion that in this matter they have not erred. For who is there that would consent to be knowingly mistaken, with whatever company he might share his errors? Three of the seven therefore alone remain, Eusebius of Emesa, Theodorus of Heraclea, and John, whom you afterwards mention, who formerly presided as pontiff over the Church of Constantinople.

24. However, if you inquire or recall to memory the opinion of our Ambrose,[1] and also of our Cyprian,[2] on the point in question, you will perhaps find that I also have not been without some whose footsteps I follow in that which I have maintained. At the same time, as I have said already, it is to the canonical Scriptures alone that I am bound to yield such implicit subjection as to follow their teaching, without admitting the slightest suspicion that in them any mistake or any statement intended to mislead could find a place. Wherefore, when I look round for a third name that I may oppose three on my side to your three, I might indeed easily find one, I believe, if my reading had been extensive; but one occurs to me whose name is as good as all these others, nay, of greater authority — I mean the Apostle Paul himself. To him I betake myself; to himself I appeal from the verdict of all those commentators on his writings who advance an opinion different from mine. I interrogate him, and demand from himself to know whether he wrote what was true, or under some plea of expediency wrote what he knew to be false, when he wrote that he saw Peter not walking uprightly, according to the truth of the gospel, and withstood him to his face because by that dissimulation he was compelling the Gentiles to live after the manner of the Jews. And I hear him in reply proclaiming with a solemn oath in an earlier part of the epistle, where he began this narration, "The things that I write unto you, behold, before God, I lie not."[3]

25. Let those who think otherwise, however great their names, excuse my differing from them. The testimony of so great an apostle using, in his own writings, an oath as a confirmation of their truth, is of more weight with me than the opinion of any man, however learned, who is discussing the writings of another. Nor am I afraid lest men should say that, in vindi-

cating Paul from the charge of pretending to conform to the errors of Jewish prejudice, I affirm him to have actually so conformed. For as, on the one hand, he was not guilty of pretending conformity to error when, with the liberty of an apostle, such as was suitable to that period of transition, he did, by practising those ancient holy ordinances, when it was necessary to declare their original excellence as appointed not by the wiles of Satan to deceive men, but by the wisdom of God for the purpose of typically foretelling things to come; so, on the other hand, he was not guilty of real conformity to the errors of Judaism, seeing that he not only knew, but also preached constantly and vehemently, that those were in error who thought that these ceremonies were to be imposed upon the Gentile converts, or were necessary to the justification of any who believed.

26. Moreover, as to my saying that to the Jews he became as a Jew, and to the Gentiles as a Gentile, not with the subtlety of intentional deceit, but with the compassion of pitying love,[4] it seems to me that you have not sufficiently considered my meaning in the words; or rather, perhaps, I have not succeeded in making it plain. For I did not mean by this that I supposed him to have practised in either case a feigned conformity; but I said it because his conformity was sincere, not less in the things in which he became to the Jews as a Jew, than in those in which he became to the Gentiles as a Gentile, — a parallel which you yourself suggested, and by which I thankfully acknowledge that you have materially assisted my argument. For when I had in my letter asked you to explain how it could be supposed that Paul's becoming to the Jews as a Jew involved the supposition that he must have acted deceitfully in conforming to the Jewish observances, seeing that no such deceptive conformity to heathen customs was involved in his becoming as a Gentile to the Gentiles; your answer was, that his becoming to the Gentiles as a Gentile meant no more than his receiving the uncircumcised, and permitting the free use of those meats which were pronounced unclean by Jewish law. If, then, when I ask whether in this also he practised dissimulation, such an idea is repudiated as palpably most absurd and false: it is an obvious inference, that in his performing those things in which he became as a Jew to the Jews, he was using a wise liberty, not yielding to a degrading compulsion, nor doing what would be still more unworthy of him, viz. stooping from integrity to fraud out of a regard to expediency.

27. For to believers, and to those who know the truth, as the apostle testifies (unless here

[1] In his Commentary on Galatians.
[2] In his letter, LXX., to Quintus; *Ante-Nicene Fathers*, Am. ed. vol. v. p. 377.
[3] Gal. i. 20.

[4] Letter XL. sec. 4, p. 273, quoted also by Jerome, LXXV. sec. 12, p. 338.

too, perhaps, he is deceiving his readers), "every creature of God is good, and nothing to be refused, if it be received with thanksgiving."[1] Therefore to Paul himself, not only as a man, but as a steward eminently faithful, not only as knowing, but also as a teacher of the truth, every creature of God which is used for food was not feignedly but truly good. If, then, to the Gentiles he became as a Gentile, by holding and teaching the truth concerning meats and circumcision, although he feigned no conformity to the rites and ceremonies of the Gentiles, why say that it was impossible for him to become as a Jew to the Jews, unless he practised dissimulation in performing the rites of their religion? Why did he maintain the true faithfulness of a steward towards the wild olive branch that was engrafted, and yet hold up a strange veil of dissimulation, on the plea of expediency, before those who were the natural and original branches of the olive tree? Why was it that, in becoming as a Gentile to the Gentiles, his teaching and his conduct[2] are in harmony with his real sentiments; but that, in becoming as a Jew to the Jews, he shuts up one thing in his heart, and declares something wholly different in his words, deeds, and writings? But far be it from us to entertain such thoughts of him. To both Jews and Gentiles he owed "charity out of a pure heart, and of a good conscience, and of faith unfeigned;"[3] and therefore he became all things to all men, that he might gain all,[4] not with the subtlety of a deceiver, but with the love of one filled with compassion; that is to say, not by pretending himself to do all the evil things which other men did, but by using the utmost pains to minister with all compassion the remedies required by the evils under which other men laboured, as if their case had been his own.

28. When, therefore, he did not refuse to practise some of these Old Testament observances, he was not led by his compassion for Jews to feign this conformity, but unquestionably was acting sincerely; and by this course of action declaring his respect for those things which in the former dispensation had been for a time enjoined by God, he distinguished between them and the impious rites of heathenism. At that time, moreover, not with the subtlety of a deceiver, but with the love of one moved by compassion, he became to the Jews as a Jew, when, seeing them to be in error, which either made them unwilling to believe in Christ, or made them think that by these old sacrifices and ceremonial observances they could be cleansed from sin and made partakers of salvation, he desired so

to deliver them from that error as if he saw not them, but himself, entangled in it; thus truly loving his neighbour as himself, and doing to others as he would have others do to him if he required their help, — a duty to the statement of which our Lord added these words, "This is the law and the prophets."[5]

29. This compassionate affection Paul recommends in the same Epistle to the Galatians, saying: "If a man be overtaken in a fault, ye which are spiritual restore such an one in the spirit of meekness; considering thyself, lest thou also be tempted."[6] See whether he has not said, "Make thyself as he is, that thou mayest gain him." Not, indeed, that one should commit or pretend to have committed the same fault as the one who has been overtaken, but that in the fault of that other he should consider what might happen to himself, and so compassionately render assistance to that other, as he would wish that other to do to him if the case were his; that is, not with the subtlety of a deceiver, but with the love of one filled with compassion. Thus, whatever the error or fault in which Jew or Gentile or any man was found by Paul, to all men he became all things, — not by feigning what was not true, but by feeling, because the case might have been his own, the compassion of one who put himself in the other's place, — that he might gain all.

CHAP. IV. — 30. I beseech you to look, if you please, for a little into your own heart, — I mean, into your own heart as it stands affected towards myself, — and recall, or if you have it in writing beside you, read again, your own words in that letter (only too brief) which you sent to me by Cyprian our brother, now my colleague. Read with what sincere brotherly and loving earnestness you have added to a serious complaint of what I had done to you these words: "In this friendship is wounded, and the laws of brotherly union are set at nought. Let not the world see us quarrelling like children, and giving material for angry contention between those who may become our respective supporters or adversaries."[7] These words I perceive to be spoken by you from the heart, and from a heart kindly seeking to give me good advice. Then you add, what would have been obvious to me even without your stating it: "I write what I have now written, because I desire to cherish towards you pure and Christian love, and not to hide in my heart anything which does not agree with the utterance of my lips." O pious man, beloved by me, as God who seeth my soul is witness, with a true heart I believe your statement; and just as I do not question the sincerity of the profession which you have thus made in a letter to me, so do I by all

---

[1] 1 Tim. iv. 4.
[2] We follow here the reading of fourteen mss., "agit" instead of "ait."
[3] 1 Tim. i. 5.
[4] 1 Cor. ix. 19-22.

[5] Matt. vii. 12.
[6] Gal. vii. 2.
[7] Letter LXXII. sec. 4.

means believe the Apostle Paul when he makes the very same profession in his letter, addressed not to any one individual, but to Jews and Greeks, and all those Gentiles who were his children in the gospel, for whose spiritual birth he travailed, and after them to so many thousands of believers in Christ, for whose sake that letter has been preserved. I believe, I say, that he did not "hide in his heart anything which did not agree with the utterance of his lips."

31. You have indeed done yourself done towards me this very thing, — becoming to me as I am, — "not with the subtlety of deception, but with the love of compassion," when you thought that it behoved you to take as much pains to prevent me from being left in a mistake, in which you believed me to be, as you would have wished another to take for your deliverance if the case had been your own. Wherefore, gratefully acknowledging this evidence of your goodwill towards me, I also claim that you also be not displeased with me, if, when anything in your treatises disquieted me, I acquainted you with my distress, desiring the same course to be followed by all towards me as I have followed towards you, that whatever they think worthy of censure in my writings, they would neither flatter me with deceitful commendation nor blame me before others for that of which they are silent towards myself; thereby, as it seems to me, more seriously "wounding friendship and setting at nought the laws of brotherly union." For I would hesitate to give the name of Christian to those friendships in which the common proverb, "Flattery makes friends, and truth makes enemies,"[1] is of more authority than the scriptural proverb, "Faithful are the wounds of a friend, but the kisses of an enemy are deceitful."[2]

32. Wherefore let us rather do our utmost to set before our beloved friends, who most cordially wish us well in our labours, such an example that they may know that it is possible for the most intimate friends to differ so much in opinion, that the views of the one may be contradicted by the other without any diminution of their mutual affection, and without hatred being kindled by that truth which is due to genuine friendship, whether the contradiction be in itself in accordance with truth, or at least, whatever its intrinsic value is, be spoken from a sincere heart by one who is resolved not "to hide in his heart anything which does not agree with the utterance of his lips." Let therefore our brethren, your friends, of whom you bear testimony that they are vessels of Christ, believe me when I say that it was wholly against my will that my letter came into the hands of many others before it reached your own, and that my heart is filled with no small

sorrow for this mistake. How it happened would take long to tell, and this is now, if I am not mistaken, unnecessary; since, if my word is to be taken at all in regard to this, it suffices for me to say that it was not done by me with the sinister intention which is supposed by some, and that it was not by my wish, or arrangement, or consent, or design that this has taken place. If they do not believe this, which I affirm in the sight of God, I can do no more to satisfy them. Far be it, however, from me to believe that they made this suggestion to your Holiness with the malicious desire to kindle enmity between you and me, from which may God in His mercy defend us! Doubtless, without any intention of doing me wrong, they readily suspected me, as a man, to be capable of failings common to human nature. For it is right for me to believe this concerning them, if they be vessels of Christ appointed not to dishonour, but to honour, and made meet by God for every good work in His great house.[3] If, however, this my solemn protestation come to their knowledge, and they still persist in the same opinion of my conduct, you will yourself see that in this they will do wrong.

33. As to my having written that I had never sent to Rome a book against you, I wrote this because, in the first place, I did not regard the name "book" as applicable to my letter, and therefore was under the impression that you had heard of something else entirely different from it; in the second place, I had not sent the letter in question to Rome, but to you; and in the third place, I did not consider it to be against you, because I knew that I had been prompted by the sincerity of friendship, which should give liberty for the exchange of suggestions and corrections between us. Leaving out of sight for a little while your friends of whom I have spoken, I implore yourself, by the grace whereby we have been redeemed, not to suppose that I have been guilty of artful flattery in anything which I have said in my letters concerning the good gifts which have been by the Lord's goodness bestowed on you. If, however, I have in anything wronged you, forgive me. As to that incident in the life of some forgotten bard, which, with perhaps more pedantry than good taste, I quoted from classic literature, I beg you not to carry the application of it to yourself further than my words warranted; for I immediately added: "I do not say this in order that you may recover the faculty of spiritual sight — far be it from me to say that you have lost it! — but that, having eyes both clear and quick in discernment, you may turn them to this matter."[4] I thought a reference to that incident suitable exclusively in connection with the παλινῳδία, in which we ought all to imi-

tate Stesichorus if we have written anything which it becomes our duty to correct in a writing of later date, and not at all in connection with the blindness of Stesichorus, which I neither ascribed to your mind, nor feared as likely to befall you. And again, I beseech you to correct boldly whatever you see needful to censure in my writings. For although, so far as the titles of honour which prevail in the Church are concerned, a bishop's rank is above that of a presbyter, nevertheless in many things Augustin is inferior to Jerome; albeit correction is not to be refused nor despised, even when it comes from one who in all respects may be an inferior.

CHAP. V. — 34. As to your translation, you have now convinced me of the benefits to be secured by your proposal to translate the Scriptures from the original Hebrew, in order that you may bring to light those things which have been either omitted or perverted by the Jews. But I beg you to be so good as state by what Jews this has been done, whether by those who before the Lord's advent translated the Old Testament — and if so, by what one or more of them — or by the Jews of later times, who may be supposed to have mutilated or corrupted the Greek MSS., in order to prevent themselves from being unable to answer the evidence given by these concerning the Christian faith. I cannot find any reason which should have prompted the earlier Jewish translators to such unfaithfulness. I beg of you, moreover, to send us your translation of the Septuagint, which I did not know that you had published. I am also longing to read that book of yours which you named *De optimo genere interpretandi*, and to know from it how to adjust the balance between the product of the translator's acquaintance with the original language, and the conjectures of those who are able commentators on the Scripture, who, notwithstanding their common loyalty to the one true faith, must often bring forward various opinions on account of the obscurity of many passages;[1] although this difference of interpretation by no means involves departure from the unity of the faith; just as óne commentator may himself give, in harmony with the faith which he holds, two different interpretations of the same passage, because the obscurity of the passage makes both equally admissible.

35. I desire, moreover, your translation of the Septuagint, in order that we may be delivered, so far as is possible, from the consequences of the notable incompetency of those who, whether qualified or not, have attempted a Latin translation; and in order that those who think that I look with jealousy on your useful labours, may at

length, if it be possible, perceive that my only reason for objecting to the public reading of your translation from the Hebrew in our churches was, lest, bringing forward anything which was, as it were, new and opposed to the authority of the Septuagint version, we should trouble by serious cause of offence the flocks of Christ, whose ears and hearts have become accustomed to listen to that version to which the seal of approbation was given by the apostles themselves. Wherefore, as to that shrub in the book of Jonah,[2] if in the Hebrew it is neither "gourd" nor "ivy," but something else which stands erect, supported by its own stem without other props, I would prefer to call it "gourd" in all our Latin versions; for I do not think that the Seventy would have rendered it thus at random, had they not known that the plant was something like a gourd.

36. I think I have now given a sufficient answer (perhaps more than sufficient) to your three letters; of which I received two by Cyprian, and one by Firmus. In replying, send whatever you think likely to be of use in instructing me and others. And I shall take more care, as the Lord may help me, that any letter which I may write to you shall reach yourself before it falls into the hand of any other, by whom its contents may be published abroad; for I confess that I would not like any letter of yours to me to meet with the fate of which you justly complain as having befallen my letter to you. Let us, however, resolve to maintain between ourselves the liberty as well as the love of friends; so that in the letters which we exchange, neither of us shall be restrained from frankly stating to the other whatever seems to him open to correction, provided always that this be done in the spirit which does not, as inconsistent with brotherly love, displease God. If, however, you do not think that this can be done between us without endangering that brotherly love, let us not do it: for the love which I should like to see maintained between us is assuredly the greater love which would make this mutual freedom possible; but the smaller measure of it is better than none at all.[3]

LETTER LXXXIII.

(A.D. 405.)

TO MY LORD ALYPIUS MOST BLESSED, MY BROTHER AND COLLEAGUE, BELOVED AND LONGED FOR

---

[1] An important sentence, as indicating the estimation in which Augustin held the "consensus patrum" as an authority in the interpretation of Scripture.

[2] Ch. iv. 6.

[3] It is interesting to know that Jerome afterwards admitted the soundness of the view so ably and reasonably defended by Augustin in this letter concerning the rebuke of Peter at Antioch. In Letter CLXXX., addressed to Oceanus, we have these words: "This question the venerable Father Jerome and I have discussed fully in letters which we exchanged; and in the last work which he has published against Pelagius, under the name of *Critobulus*, he has maintained the same opinion concerning that event, and the sayings of the apostles, as I myself had adopted, following the blessed Cyprian." See Jerome, book i., against the Pelagians, and Cyprian, Letter LXX., to Quintus.

WITH SINCERE VENERATION, AND TO THE BRETH-
REN THAT ARE WITH HIM, AUGUSTIN AND THE
BRETHREN WITH HIM SEND GREETING IN THE
LORD.

1. The sorrow of the members of the Church at Thiave prevents my heart from having any rest until I hear that they have been brought again to be of the same mind towards you as they formerly were ; which must be accomplished without delay. For if the apostle was concerned about one individual, " lest perhaps such an one should be swallowed up with overmuch sorrow," adding in the same context the words, " lest Satan should get an advantage of us, for we are not ignorant of his devices," [1] how much more does it become us to act with caution, lest we cause similar grief to a whole flock, and especially one composed of persons who have lately been reconciled to the Catholic Church, and whom I can upon no account forsake ! As, however, the short time at our disposal did not permit us so to take counsel together as to arrive at a mature and satisfactory decision, may it please your Holiness to accept in this letter the finding which commended itself most to me when I had long reflected upon the matter since we parted ; and if you approve of it, let the enclosed letter,[2] which I have written to them in the name of both of us, be sent to them without delay.

2. You proposed that they should have the one half [of the property left by Honoratus], and that the other half should be made up to them by me from such resources as might be at my disposal. I think, however, that if the whole property had been taken from them, men might reasonably have said that we had taken the great pains in this matter which we have done, for the sake of justice, not for pecuniary advantage. But when we concede to them one half, and in that way settle with them by a com-promise, it will be manifest that our anxiety has been only about the money ; and you see what harm must follow from this. For, on the one hand, we shall be regarded by them as having taken away one half of a property to which we had no claim ; and, on the other hand, they will be regarded by us as dishonourably and unjustly consenting to accept aid from one half of a property of which the whole belonged to the poor. For your remark, " We must beware lest, in our efforts to obtain a right adjustment of a diffi-cult question, we cause more serious wounds," applies with no less force if the half be conceded to them. For those whose turning from the world to monastic life we desire to secure, will, for the sake of this half of their private estates, be disposed to find some excuse for putting off

the sale of these, in order that their case may be dealt with according to this precedent. More-over, would it not be strange, if, in a question like this, where much may be said on both sides, a whole community should, through our not avoiding the appearance of evil, be offended by the impression that their bishops, whom they hold in high esteem, are smitten with sordid avarice ?

3. For when any one is turned to adopt the life of a monk, if he is adopting it with a true heart, he does not think of that which I have just mentioned, especially if he be admonished of the sinfulness of such conduct. But if he be a deceiver, and is seeking " his own things, not the things which are Jesus Christ's," [3] he has not charity ; and without this, what does it profit him, " though he bestow all his goods to feed the poor, and though he give his body to be burned " ? [4] Moreover, as we agreed when con-versing together, this may be henceforth avoided, and an arrangement made with each individual who is disposed to enter a monastery, if he can-not be admitted to the society of the brethren before he has relieved himself of all these en-cumbrances, and comes as one at leisure from all business, because the property which belonged to him has ceased to be his. But there is no other way in which this spiritual death of weak brethren, and grievous obstacle to the salvation of those for whose reconciliation with the Catho-lic Church we so earnestly labour, can be avoided, than by our giving them most clearly to under-stand that we are by no means anxious about money in such cases as this. And this they cannot be made to understand, unless we leave to their use the estate which they always sup-posed to belong to their late presbyter ; because, even if it was not his, they ought to have known this from the beginning.

4. It seems to me, therefore, that in matters of this kind, the rule which ought to hold is, that whatever belonged, according to the ordinary civil laws regarding property, to him who is an ordained clergyman in any place, belongs after his death to the Church over which he was or-dained. Now, by civil law, the property in question belonged to the presbyter Honoratus ; so that not only on account of his being or-dained elsewhere, but even had he remained in the monastery of Thagaste, if he had died with-out having either sold his estate or handed it over by express deed of gift to any one, the right of succession to it would belong only to his heirs : as brother Æmilianus inherited those thirty shil-lings [5] left by the brother Privatus. This, there-fore, behoved to be considered and provided for

---

[1] 2 Cor. ii. 7, 11.
[2] This letter has not been preserved.

[3] Phil. ii. 21.
[4] 1 Cor. xiii. 3.
[5] *Solidi.*

in time ; but if no provision was made for it, we must, in the disposal of the estate, comply with the laws which have been appointed to regulate in civil society the holding or not holding of property ; that we may, so far as is in our power, abstain not only from the reality, but also from all appearance of evil, and preserve that good name which is so necessary to our office as stewards. How truly this procedure has the appearance of evil, I beseech your wisdom to observe. For having heard of their sorrow, which we ourselves witnessed at Thiave, fearing lest, as frequently happens, I should myself be mistaken through partiality for my own opinion, I stated the facts of the case to our brother and colleague Samsucius, without telling him at the time my present view of the matter, but rather stating the view taken up by both of us when we were resisting their demands. He was exceedingly shocked, and wondered that we had entertained such a view ; being moved by nothing else but the ugly appearance of the transaction, as one wholly unworthy not only of us, but of any man.

5. Wherefore I implore you to subscribe and transmit without delay the letter which I have written to them in name of both of us. And even if, perchance, you discern the other course to be a just one in the matter, let not these brethren who are weak be compelled to learn now what I myself cannot understand ; rather let this word of the Lord be remembered in dealing with them : "I have yet many things to say unto you, but ye cannot bear them now."[1] For He Himself, out of condescension to such weakness, said on another occasion (it was in reference to the payment of tribute), "Then are the children free ; notwithstanding lest we offend them," etc. ; and sent Peter to pay the didrachmæ which were then exacted.[2] For He knew another law according to which he was not bound to make any such payment ; but He made the payment which was imposed upon Him by that law according to which, as I have said, succession to the estate of Honoratus behoved to be regulated, if he died before either giving away or selling his property. Nay, even in regard to the law of the Church, Paul showed forbearance towards the weak, and did not insist upon his receiving the money due to him, although fully persuaded in his conscience that he might with perfect justice insist upon it ; waiving his claim, however, only because he thereby avoided a suspicion of his motives which would mar the sweet savour of Christ among them, and abstained from the appearance of evil in a region in which he knew that this was his duty, and probably even before he had known by experience the sorrow which it would occasion. Let us now, though we are somewhat behindhand, and have been admonished by experience, correct that which we ought to have foreseen.

6. I remember that you proposed when we parted that the brethren at Thagaste should hold me responsible to make up the half of the sum claimed ; let me say in conclusion, that as I fear everything which may make my attempt unsuccessful, if you clearly perceive that proposal to be a just one, I do not refuse to comply with it, on this condition, however, that I am to pay the amount only when I have it in my power, *i.e.* when something so considerable falls to our monastery at Hippo that this can be done without unduly straitening us, — the amount remaining after the subtraction of so large a sum being still such as to provide for our monastery here an equal share in proportion to the number of resident brethren.

LETTER LXXXIV.

(A.D. 405.)

TO MY LORD NOVATUS, MOST BLESSED, MY BROTHER AND PARTNER IN THE PRIESTLY OFFICE, ESTEEMED AND LONGED FOR, AND TO THE BRETHREN WHO ARE WITH HIM, AUGUSTIN AND THE BRETHREN WITH HIM SEND GREETING IN THE LORD.

1. I myself feel how hard-hearted I must appear to you, and I can scarcely excuse to myself my conduct in not consenting to send to your Holiness my son the deacon Lucillus, your own brother. But when your own time comes to surrender to the claims of Churches in remote places some of those whom you have educated, and who are most dear and sweet to you, then, and not till then, will you know the pangs of longing which pierce me through and through for some who, once united to me in the strongest and most pleasing intimacy, are no more beside me. Let me submit to your thoughts the case of one who is far away. However strong be the bond of kindred between brothers, it does not surpass the bond by which my brother Severus and I are united to each other, and yet you know how rarely I have the happiness of seeing him. And this has been caused neither by his wish nor by mine, but because of our giving to the claims of our mother the Church precedency above the claims of this present world, out of regard to that coming eternity in which we shall dwell together and part no more. How much more reasonable, therefore, is it for you to submit for the sake of the Church's welfare to the absence of that brother, with whom you have not shared the food which the Lord our Shepherd provides for nearly so long a period as I

---

[1] John xvi. 12.
[2] Matt. xvii. 26, 27.

did with my most amiable fellow-townsman Severus, who now only with an effort and at long intervals converses with me by means of brief letters, — letters, moreover, which are for the most part burdened with the cares and affairs of other men, instead of bearing to me any reminiscence of those green pastures in which we were wont to lie down under Christ's loving care !

2. You will perhaps reply, "What then? May not my brother be of service to the Church here also? Is it for any other end than usefulness to the Church that I desire to have him with me?" Truly, if his being beside you seemed to me to be as important for the gathering in or ruling of the Lord's flock as his presence here is for these ends, every one might justly blame me for being not merely hard-hearted, but unjust. But since he is conversant with the Punic[1] language, through want of which the preaching of the gospel is greatly hindered in these parts, whereas the use of that language is general with you, do you think that we would be doing our duty in consulting for the welfare of the Lord's flocks, if we were to send this talent to a place where it is not specially needful, and remove it from this region, where we thirst for it with such parched spirits? Forgive me, therefore, when I do, not only against your will, but also against my own feeling, what the care of the burden imposed upon me compels me to do. The Lord, to whom you have given your heart, will grant you such aid in your labours that you shall be recompensed for this kindness; for we acknowledge that you have with a good grace rather than of necessity conceded the deacon Lucillus to the burning thirst of the regions in which our lot is cast. For you will do me no small favour if you do not burden me with any further request upon this subject, lest I should have occasion to appear anything more than somewhat hard-hearted to you, whom I revere for your holy benignity of disposition.

LETTER LXXXV.

(A.D. 405.)

TO MY LORD PAULUS, MOST BELOVED, MY BROTHER AND COLLEAGUE IN THE PRIESTHOOD, WHOSE HIGHEST WELFARE IS SOUGHT BY ALL MY PRAYERS, AUGUSTIN SENDS GREETING IN THE LORD.

1. You would not call me so inexorable if you did not think me also a dissembler. For what else do you believe concerning my spirit, if I am to judge by what you have written, than that I cherish towards you dislike and antipathy which merit blame and detestation; as if in a matter about which there could be but one opinion I

was not careful lest, while warning others, I myself should deserve reproof,[2] or were wishing to cast the mote out of your eye while retaining and fostering the beam in my own?[3] It is by no means as you suppose. Behold! I repeat this, and call God to witness, that if you were only to desire for yourself what I desire on your behalf, you would now be living in Christ free from all disquietude, and would make the whole Church rejoice in glory brought by you to His name. Observe, I pray you, that I have addressed you not only as my brother, but also as my colleague. For it cannot be that any bishop whatsoever of the Catholic Church should cease to be my colleague, so long as he has not been condemned by any ecclesiastical tribunal. As to my refusing to hold communion with you, the only reason for this is that I cannot flatter you. For inasmuch as I have begotten you in Christ, I am under very special obligation to render to you the salutary severity of love in faithful admonition and reproof. It is true that I rejoice in the numbers who have been, by God's blessing on your work, gathered into the Catholic Church; but this does not make me less bound to weep that a greater number are being by you scattered from the Church. For you have so wounded the Church of Hippo,[4] that unless the Lord make you disengage yourself from all secular cares and burdens, and recall you to the manner of living and deportment which become the true bishop, the wound may soon be beyond remedy.

2. Seeing, however, that you continue to involve yourself more and more deeply in these affairs, and have, notwithstanding your vow of renunciation, entangled yourself again with the things which you had solemnly laid aside, — a step which could not be justified even by the laws of ordinary human affairs; seeing also that you are reported to be living in a style of extravagance which cannot be maintained by the slender income of your church, — why do you insist upon communion with me, while you refuse to hear my rebuke of your faults? Is it that men whose complaints I cannot bear, may justly blame me for whatever you do? You are, moreover, mistaken in suspecting that those who find fault with you are persons who have always been against you even in your earlier life. It is not so: and you have no reason to be surprised that many things escape your observation. But even were this the case, it is your duty to secure that they find nothing in your conduct which they might reasonably blame, and for which they might bring reproach against the Church. Perhaps you think that my reason for saying these

---

[1] The text here gives *latinâ*. All that we know of the languages then spoken in Hippo would lead us to suppose that *punicâ* must have been written here by Augustin.

[2] 1 Cor. ix. 27.
[3] Matt. vii. 4.
[4] Cataqua (?).

things is, that I have not accepted what you urged in your defence. Nay, rather my reason is, that if I were to say nothing regarding these things, I would be guilty of that for which I could urge nothing in my defence before God. I know your abilities; but even a man of dull mind is kept from disquietude if he sets his affections on heavenly things, whereas a man of acute mind has this gift in vain if he set his affections on earthly things. The office of a bishop is not designed to enable one to spend a life of vanity. The Lord God, who has closed against you all the ways by which you were disposed to make Him minister to your gain, in order that He may guide you, if you but understand Him, into that way, with a view to the pursuit of which that holy responsibility was laid upon you, will Himself teach you what I now say.

LETTER LXXXVI.

(A.D. 405.)

TO MY NOBLE LORD CÆCILIANUS, MY SON TRULY AND JUSTLY HONOURABLE AND ESTEEMED IN THE LOVE OF CHRIST, AUGUSTIN, BISHOP, SENDS GREETING IN THE LORD.

The renown of your administration and the fame of your virtues, as well as the praiseworthy zeal and faithful sincerity of your Christian piety, — gifts of God which make you rejoice in Him from whom they came, and from whom you hope to receive yet greater things, — have moved me to acquaint your Excellency by this letter with the cares which agitate my mind. As our joy is great that throughout the rest of Africa you have taken measures with remarkable success on behalf of Catholic unity, our sorrow is proportionately great because the district of Hippo[1] and the neighbouring regions on the borders of Numidia have not enjoyed the benefit of the vigour with which as a magistrate you have enforced your proclamation, my noble lord, and my son truly and justly honourable and esteemed in the love of Christ. Lest this should be regarded rather as due to the neglect of duty by me who bear the burden of the episcopal office at Hippo, I have considered myself bound to mention it to your Excellency. If you condescend to acquaint yourself with the extremities to which the effrontery of the heretics has proceeded in the region of Hippo, as you may do by questioning my brethren and colleagues, who are able to furnish your Excellency with information, or the presbyter whom I have sent with this letter, I am sure you will so deal with this tumour of impious presumption, that it shall be healed by warning rather than painfully removed afterwards by punishment.

LETTER LXXXVII.

(A.D. 405.)

TO HIS BROTHER EMERITUS, BELOVED AND LONGED FOR, AUGUSTIN SENDS GREETING.

1. I know that it is not on the possession of good talents and a liberal education that the salvation of the soul depends; but when I hear of any one who is thus endowed holding a different view from that which truth imperatively insists upon on a point which admits of very easy examination, the more I wonder at such a man, the more I burn with desire to make his acquaintance, and to converse with him; or if that be impossible, I long to bring his mind and mine into contact by exchanging letters, which wing their flight even between places far apart. As I have heard that you are such a man as I have spoken of, I grieve that you should be severed and shut out from the Catholic Church, which is spread abroad throughout the whole world, as was foretold by the Holy Spirit. What your reason for this separation is I do not know. For it is not disputed that the party of Donatus is wholly unknown to a great part of the Roman world, not to speak of the barbarian nations (to whom also the apostle said that he was a debtor[2]) whose communion in the Christian faith is joined with ours, and that in fact they do not even know at all when or upon what account the dissension began. Now, unless you admit these Christians to be innocent of those crimes with which you charge the Christians of Africa, you must confess that all of you are defiled by participation in the wicked actions of all worthless characters, so long as they succeed (to put the matter mildly) in escaping detection among you. For you do occasionally expel a member from your communion, in which case his expulsion takes place only after he has committed the crime for which he merited expulsion. Is there not some intervening time during which he escapes detection before he is discovered, convicted, and condemned by you? I ask, therefore, whether he involved you in his defilement so long as he was not discovered by you? You answer, "By no means." If, then, he were not to be discovered at all, he would in that case never involve you in his defilement; for it sometimes happens that the crimes committed by men come to light only after their death, yet this does not bring guilt upon those Christians who communicated with them while they were alive. Why, then, have you severed yourselves by so rash and profane schism from the communion of innumerable Eastern Churches, in which all that you truly or falsely affirm to have been done in Africa has been and still is utterly unknown?

---

[1] *Regionem Hipponensium Regiorum.*

[2] Rom. i. 14.

2. For it is quite another question whether or not there be truth in the assertions made by you. These assertions we disprove by documents much more worthy of credit than those which you bring forward, and we further find in your own documents more abundant proof of those positions which you assail. But this is, as I have said, another question altogether, to be taken up and discussed when necessary. Meanwhile, let your mind give special attention to this : that no one can be involved in the guilt of unknown crimes committed by persons unknown to him. Whence it is manifest that you have been guilty of impious schism in separating yourselves from the communion of the whole world, to which the things charged, whether truly or falsely, by you against some men in Africa, have been and still are wholly unknown ; although this also should not be forgotten, that even when known and discovered, bad men do not harm the good who are in a Church, if either the power of restraining them from communion be wanting, or the interests of the Church's peace forbid this to be done. For who were those who, according to the prophet Ezekiel,[1] obtained the reward of being marked before the destruction of the wicked, and of escaping unhurt when they were destroyed, but those who sighed and cried for the sins and iniquities of the people of God which were done in the midst of them? Now who sighs and cries for that which is unknown to him? On the same principle, the Apostle Paul bears with false brethren. For it is not of persons unknown to him that he says, "All seek their own, not the things which are Jesus Christ's ; " yet these persons he shows plainly to have been beside him. And to what class do the men belong who have chosen rather to burn incense to idols or surrender the divine books than to suffer death, if not to those who "seek their own, not the things of Jesus Christ"?

3. I omit many proofs which I might give from Scripture, that I may not make this letter longer than is needful ; and I leave many more things to be considered by yourself in the light of your own learning. But I beseech you mark this, which is quite enough to decide the whole question : If so many transgressors in the one nation, which was then the Church of God, did not make those who were associated with them to be guilty like themselves ; if that multitude of false brethren did not make the Apostle Paul, who was a member of the same Church with them, a seeker not of the things of Jesus Christ, but of his own, — it is manifest that a man is not made wicked by the wickedness of any one with whom he goes to the altar of Christ, even though he be not unknown to him, provided

only that he do not encourage him in his wickedness, but by a good conscience disallowing his conduct keep himself apart from him. It is therefore obvious that, to be art and part with a thief, one must either help him in the theft, or receive with approbation what he has stolen. This I say in order to remove out of the way endless and unnecessary questions concerning the conduct of men, which are wholly irrelevant when advanced against our position.

4. If, however, you do not agree with what I have said, you involve the whole of your party in the reproach of being such men as Optatus was, while, notwithstanding your knowledge of his crimes, he was tolerated in communion with you ; and far be it from me to say this of such a man as Emeritus, and of others of like integrity among you, who are, I am sure, wholly averse to such deeds as disgraced him. For we do not lay any charge against you but the one of schism, which by your obstinate persistence in it you have now made heresy. How great this crime is in the judgment of God Himself, you may see by reading what without doubt you have read ere now. You will find that Dathan and Abiram were swallowed up by an opening of the earth beneath them,[2] and that all the others who had conspired with them were devoured by fire breaking forth in the midst of them. As a warning to men to shun this crime, the Lord God signalized its commission with this immediate punishment, that He might show what He reserves for the final recompense of persons guilty of a similar transgression, whom His great forbearance spares for a time. We do not, indeed, find fault with the reasons by which you excuse your tolerating Optatus among you. We do not blame you, because at the time when he was denounced for his furious conduct in the mad abuse of power, when he was impeached by the groans of all Africa, — groans in which you also shared, if you are what good report declares you to be, — a report which, God knows, I most willingly believe, — you forbore from excommunicating him, lest he should under such sentence draw away many with him, and rend your communion asunder with the frenzy of schism. But this is the thing which is itself an indictment against you at the bar of God, O brother Emeritus, that although you saw that the division of the party of Donatus was so great an evil, that it was thought better that Optatus should be tolerated in your communion than that division should be introduced among you, you nevertheless perpetuate the evil which was wrought in the division of the Church of Christ by your forefathers.

5. Here perhaps you will be disposed, under

[1] Ch. ix. 4-6.　　　　[2] Num. xvi. 31-35.

the exigencies of debate, to attempt to defend Optatus. Do not so, I beseech you; do not so, my brother: it would not become you; and if it would perchance be seemly for any one to do it (though, in fact, nothing is seemly which is wrong), it assuredly would be unseemly for Emeritus to defend Optatus. Perhaps you reply that it would as little become you to accuse him. Granted, by all means. Take, then, the course which lies between defending and accusing him. Say, "Every man shall bear his own burden;"[1] "Who art thou that judgest another man's servant?"[2] If, then, notwithstanding the testimony of all Africa, — nay more, of all regions to which the name of Gildo was carried, for Optatus was not less notorious than he, — you have not dared to pronounce judgment concerning Optatus, lest you should rashly decide in regard to one unknown to you, is it, I ask, either possible or right for us, proceeding solely on your testimony, to pronounce sentence rashly upon persons whom we do not know? Is it not enough that you should charge them with things of which you have no certain knowledge, without our pronouncing them guilty of things of which we know as little as yourselves? For even though Optatus were in peril through the falsehood of detractors, you defend not him, but yourself, when you say, "I do not know what his character was." How much more obvious, then, is it that the Eastern world knows nothing of the character of those Africans with whom, though much less known to you than Optatus, you find fault! Yet you are disjoined by scandalous schism from Churches in the East, the names of which you have and you read in the sacred books. If your most famous and most scandalously notorious Bishop of Thamugada[3] was at that very time not known to his colleague, I shall not say in Cæsarea, but in Sitifa, so close at hand, how was it possible for the Churches of Corinth, Ephesus, Colosse, Philippi, Thessalonica, Antioch, Pontus, Galatia, Cappadocia, and others which were founded in Christ by the apostles, to know the case of these African traditors, whoever they were; or how was it consistent with justice that they should be condemned by you for not knowing it? Yet with these Churches you hold no communion. You say they are not Christian, and you labour to rebaptize their members. What need I say? What complaint, what protest is necessary here? If I am addressing a right-hearted man, I know that with you I share the keenness of the indignation which I feel. For you doubtless see at once what I might say if I would.

6. Perhaps, however, your forefathers formed of themselves a council, and placed the whole Christian world except themselves under sentence of excommunication. Have you come so to judge of things, as to affirm that the council of the followers of Maximianus who were cut off from you, as you were cut off from the Church, was of no authority against you, because their number was small compared with yours; and yet claim for your council an authority against the nations, which are the inheritance of Christ, and the ends of the earth, which are His possession?[4] I wonder if the man who does not blush at such pretensions has any blood in his body. Write me, I beseech you, in reply to this letter; for I have heard from some, on whom I could not but rely, that you would write me an answer if I were to address a letter to you. Some time ago, moreover, I sent you a letter; but I do not know whether you received it or answered it, and perhaps your reply did not reach me. Now, however, I beg you not to refuse to answer this letter, and state what you think. But do not occupy yourself with other questions than the one which I have stated, for this is the leading point of a well-ordered discussion of the origin of the schism.

7. The civil powers defend their conduct in persecuting schismatics by the rule which the apostle laid down: "Whoso resisteth the power, resisteth the ordinance of God; and they that resist shall receive to themselves judgment. For rulers are not a terror to good works, but to the evil. Wilt thou then not be afraid of the power? Do that which is good, and thou shalt have praise of the same: for he is the minister of God to thee for good. But if thou do that which is evil, be afraid; for he beareth not the sword in vain: for he is the minister of God, a revenger to execute wrath upon him that doeth evil."[5] The whole question therefore is, whether schism be not an evil work, or whether you have not caused schism, so that your resistance of the powers that be is in a good cause and not in an evil work, whereby you would bring judgment on yourselves. Wherefore with infinite wisdom the Lord not merely said, "Blessed are they who are persecuted," but added, "for righteousness' sake."[6] I desire therefore to know from you, in the light of what I have said above, whether it be a work of righteousness to originate and perpetuate your state of separation from the Church. I desire also to know whether it be not rather a work of unrighteousness to condemn unheard the whole Christian world, either because it has not heard what you have heard, or because no proof has been furnished to it of charges which were rashly believed, or without

[1] Gal. vi. 5.
[2] Rom. xiv. 4.
[3] Optatus.

[4] Ps. ii. 8.
[5] Rom. xiii. 2-4.
[6] Matt. v. 10.

sufficient evidence advanced by you, and to propose on this ground to baptize a second time the members of so many churches founded by the preaching and labours either of the Lord Himself while He was on earth, or of His apostles; and all this on the assumption that it is excusable for you either not to know the wickedness of your African colleagues who are living beside you, and are using the same sacraments with you, or even to tolerate their misdeeds when known, lest the party of Donatus should be divided, but that it is inexcusable for them, though they reside in most remote régions, to be ignorant of what you either know, or believe, or have heard, or imagine, concerning men in Africa. How great is the perversity of those who cling to their own unrighteousness, and yet find fault with the severity of the civil powers!

8. You answer, perhaps, that Christians ought not to persecute even the wicked. Be it so; let us admit that they ought not: but is it lawful to lay this objection in the way of the powers which are ordained for this very purpose? Shall we erase the apostle's words? Or do your MSS. not contain the words which I mentioned a little while ago? But you will say that we ought not to communicate with such persons. What then? Did you withdraw, some time ago, from communion with the deputy Flavianus, on the ground of his putting to death, in his administration of the laws, those whom he found guilty? Again, you will say that the Roman emperors are incited against you by us. Nay, rather blame yourselves for this, seeing that, as was long ago foretold in the promise concerning Christ, "Yea, all kings shall fall down before him,"[1] they are now members of the Church; and you have dared to wound the Church by schism, and still presume to insist upon rebaptizing her members. Our brethren indeed demand help from the powers which are ordained, not to persecute you, but to protect themselves against the lawless acts of violence perpetrated by individuals of your party, which you yourselves, who refrain from such things, bewail and deplore; just as, before the Roman Empire became Christian, the Apostle Paul took measures to secure that the protection of armed Roman soldiers should be granted him against the Jews who had conspired to kill him. But these emperors, whatever the occasion of their becoming acquainted with the crime of your schism might be, frame against you such decrees as their zeal and their office demand. For they bear not the sword in vain; they are the ministers of God to execute wrath upon those that do evil. Finally, if some of our party transgress the bounds of Christian moderation in this matter, it displeases us; nevertheless, we do not

on their account forsake the Catholic Church because we are unable to separate the wheat from the chaff before the final winnowing, especially since you yourselves have not forsaken the Donatist party on account of Optatus, when you had not courage to excommunicate him for his crimes.

9. You say, however, "Why seek to have us joined to you, if we be thus stained with guilt?" I reply: Because you still live, and may, if you are willing, be restored. For when you join yourselves to us, i.e. to the Church of God, the heritage of Christ, who has the ends of the earth as his possession, you are restored so that you live in vital union with the Root. For the apostle says of the branches which were broken off: "God is able to graff them in again."[2] We exhort you to change, in so far as concerns your dissent from the Church; although, as to the sacraments which you had, we admit that they are holy, since they are the same in all. Wherefore we desire to see you changed from your obstinacy, that is, in order that you who have been cut off may be vitally united to the Root again. For the sacraments which you have not changed are approved by us as you have them; else, in our attempting to correct your sin, we should do impious wrong to those mysteries of Christ which have not been deprived of their worth by your unworthiness. For even Saul did not, with all his sins, destroy the efficacy of the anointing which he received; to which anointing David, that pious servant of God, showed so great respect. We therefore do not insist upon rebaptizing you, because we only wish to restore to you connection with the Root: the form of the branch which has been cut off we accept with approval, if it has not been changed; but the branch, however perfect in its form, cannot bear fruit, except it be united to the root. As to the persecution, so gentle and tempered with clemency, which you say you suffer at the hands of our party, while unquestionably your own party inflict greater harm in a lawless and irregular way upon us,—this is one question: the question concerning baptism is wholly distinct from it; in regard to it, we inquire not where it is, but where it profits. For wherever it is, it is the same; but it cannot be said of him who receives it, that wherever he is, he is the same. We therefore detest the impiety of which men as individuals are guilty in a state of schism; but we venerate everywhere the baptism of Christ. If deserters carry with them the imperial standards, these standards are welcomed back again as they were, if they have remained unharmed, when the deserters are either punished with a severe sentence, or, in the exercise of clemency,

---

[1] Ps. lxxii. 11.

[2] Rom. xi. 23.

restored. If, in regard to this, any more partic- ular inquiry is to be made, that is, as I have said, another question ; for in these things, the prac- tice of the Church of God is the rule of our practice.

10. The question between us, however, is, whether your Church or ours is the Church of God. To resolve this, we must begin with the original inquiry, why you became schismatics. If you do not write me an answer, I believe that before the bar of God I shall be easily vindicated as having done my duty in this matter ; because I have sent a letter in the interests of peace to a man of whom I have heard that, excepting only his adherence to schismatics, he is a good and well-educated man. Be it yours to consider how you shall answer Him whose forbearance now demands your praise, and His judgment shall in the end demand your fears. If, however, you write a reply to me with as much care as you see me to have bestowed upon this, I believe that, by the mercy of God, the error which now keeps us apart shall perish before the love of peace and the logic of truth. Observe that I have said nothing about the followers of Rogatus,[1] who call you Firmiani, as you call us Macariani. Nor have I spoken of your bishop of Rucata (or Rusicada), who is said to have made an agree- ment with Firmus, promising, on condition of the safety of all his adherents, that the gates should be opened to him, and the Catholics given up to slaughter and pillage. Many other such things I pass unnoticed. Do you therefore in like manner desist from the commonplaces of rhetorical exaggeration concerning actions of men which you have either heard of or known ; for you see how I am silent concerning deeds of your party, in order to confine the debate to the question upon which the whole matter hinges, — namely, the origin of the schism.

My brother, beloved and longed for, may the Lord our God breathe into you thoughts tending towards reconciliation.

LETTER LXXXVIII.

(A.D. 406.)

TO JANUARIUS,[2] THE CATHOLIC CLERGY OF THE DISTRICT OF HIPPO[3] SEND THE FOLLOWING.

1. Your clergy and your Circumcelliones are venting against us their rage in a persecution of a new kind, and of unparalleled atrocity. Were we to render evil for evil, we should be trans- gressing the law of Christ. But now, when all

that has been done, both on your side and on ours, is impartially considered, it is found that we are suffering what is written, " They rewarded me evil for good ; "[4] and (in another Psalm), " My soul hath long dwelt with him that hateth peace. I am for peace : but when I speak, they are for war."[5] For, seeing that you have arrived at so great age, we suppose you to know per- fectly well that the party of Donatus, which at first was called at Carthage the party of Majori- nus, did of their own accord accuse Cæcilianus, then bishop of Carthage, before the famous Em- peror Constantine. Lest, however, you should have forgotten this, venerable sir, or should pre- tend not to know, or perhaps (which we scarcely think possible) may never have known it, we insert here a copy of the narrative of Anulinus, then proconsul, to whom the party of Majorinus appealed, requesting that by him as proconsul a statement of the charges which they brought against Cæcilianus should be sent to the Em- peror aforesaid : —

2. *To Constantine Augustus, from Anulinus, a man of consular rank, proconsul of Africa, these :*[6]

The welcome and adored celestial writing sent by your Majesty to Cæcilianus, and those over whom he presides, who are called clergy, have been, by the care of your Majesty's most hum- ble servant, engrossed in his Records ; and he has exhorted these parties that, heartily agreeing among themselves, since they are seen to be ex- empted from all other burdens by your Majesty's clemency, they should, preserving Catholic unity, devote themselves to their duties with the rev- erence due to the sanctity of law and to divine things. After a few days, however, there arose some persons to whom a crowd of people joined themselves, who thought that proceedings should be taken against Cæcilianus, and presented to me[7] a sealed packet wrapped in leather, and a small document without seal, and earnestly be- sought me to transmit them to your Majesty's sacred and venerable court, which your Ma- jesty's most humble servant[8] has taken care to do, Cæcilianus continuing meanwhile as he was. The Acts pertaining to the case are subjoined, in order that your Majesty may be able to arrive at a decision concerning the whole matter. The documents sent are two : the one in a leathern envelope, with this title, " A document of the Catholic Church containing charges against Cæ- cilianus, and furnished by the party of Majori-

---

[1] Rogatus, bishop of Cartenna in Mauritania, who left the Dona- tists and suffered much persecution at the hands of Firmus, a brother of Gildo; hence the Donatists were named by the Rogatists Firmiani. See Augustin, *Contra Literas Petiliani*, book ii ch. 83.
[2] Bishop of Casæ Nigræ in Numidia, and at that time the Dona- tist primate, as the oldest of their bishops.
[3] *Hipponensium Regiorum.*

[4] Ps. xxxv. 12.
[5] Ps. cxx. 6, 7.
[6] The actual heading of the Report stands thus: " A. GGG. NNN. Anulinus VC. proconsul Africæ." For the interpretation we are in- debted to the marginal note on the Codex Gervasianus.
[7] *Dicationi meæ.*
[8] *Parvitas mea.*

nus ; " the other attached without a seal to the same leathern envelope.

Given on the 17th day before the Calends of May, in the third consulship of our lord Constantine Augustus [*i.e.* April 15, A.D. 313].

3. After this report had been sent to him, the Emperor summoned the parties before a tribunal of bishops to be constituted at Rome. The ecclesiastical records show how the case was there argued and decided, and Cæcilianus pronounced innocent. Surely now, after the peacemaking decision of the tribunal of bishops, all the pertinacity of strife and bitterness should have given way. Your forefathers, however, appealed again to the Emperor, and complained that the decision was not just, and that their case had not been fully heard. Accordingly, he appointed a second tribunal of bishops to meet in Arles, a town of Gaul, where, after sentence had been pronounced against your worthless and diabolical schism, many of your party returned to a good understanding with Cæcilianus ; some, however, who were most obstinate and contentious, appealed to the Emperor again. Afterwards, when, yielding to their importunity, he personally interposed in this dispute, which belonged properly to the bishops to decide, having heard the case, he gave sentence against your party, and was the first to pass a law that the properties of your congregations should be confiscated ; of all which things we could insert the documentary evidence here, if it were not for making the letter too long. We must, however, by no means omit the investigation and decision in open court of the case of Felix of Aptunga, whom, in the Council of Carthage, under Secundus of Tigisis, primate, your fathers affirmed to be the original cause of all these evils. For the Emperor aforesaid, in a letter of which we annex a copy, bears witness that in this trial your party were before him as accusers and most strenuous prosecutors : —

4. *The Emperors Flavius Constantinus, Maximus Cæsar, and Valerius Licinius Cæsar, to Probianus, proconsul of Africa :*

Your predecessor Ælianus, who acted as substitute for Verus, the superintendent of the prefects, when that most excellent magistrate was by severe illness laid aside in that part of Africa which is under our sway, considered it, and most justly, to be his duty, amongst other things, to bring again under his investigation and decision the matter of Cæcilianus, or rather the odium which seems to have been stirred up against that bishop of the Catholic Church. Wherefore, having ordered the compearance of Superius, centurion, Cæcilianus, magistrate of Aptunga, and

Saturninus, the ex-president of police, and his successor in the office, Calibius the younger, and Solon, an official belonging to Aptunga, he heard the testimony of these witnesses ;[1] the result of which was, that whereas objection had been taken to Cæcilianus on the ground of his ordination to the office of bishop by Felix, against whom it seemed that the charge of surrendering and burning the sacred books had been made, the innocence of Felix in this matter was clearly established. Moreover, when Maximus affirmed that Ingentius, a decurion of the town of Ziqua, had forged a letter of the ex-magistrate Cæcilianus, we found, on examining the Acts which were before us, that this same Ingentius had been put on the rack[2] for that offence, and that the infliction of torture on him was not, as alleged, on the ground of his affirming that he was a decurion of Ziqua. Wherefore we desire you to send under a suitable guard to the court of Augustus Constantine the said Ingentius, that in the presence and hearing of those who are now pleading in this case, and who day after day persist in their complaints, it may be made manifest and fully known that they labour in vain to excite odium against the bishop Cæcilianus, and to clamour violently against him. This, we hope, will bring the people to desist, as they should do, from such contentions, and to devote themselves with becoming reverence to their religious duties, undistracted by dissension among themselves.

5. Since you see, therefore, that these things are so, why do you provoke odium against us on the ground of the imperial decrees which are in force against you, when you have yourselves done all this before we followed your example? If emperors ought not to use their authority in such cases, if care of these matters lies beyond the province of Christian emperors, who urged your forefathers to remit the case of Cæcilianus, by the proconsul, to the Emperor, and a second time to bring before the Emperor accusations against a bishop whom you had somehow condemned in absence, and on his acquittal to invent and bring before the same Emperor other calumnies against Felix, by whom the bishop aforesaid had been ordained? And now, what other law is in force against your party than that decision of the elder Constantine, to which your forefathers of their own choice appealed, which they extorted from him by their importunate

[1] The value of the evidence of these witnesses is apparent when we remember that they were all in a position to speak from personal knowledge of the persecution in A.D. 303 (under Diocletian and Maximian), and had in their public capacity some share in enforcing the demand made in that persecution for the surrender of the sacred books. These could tell whether Felix the Bishop of Aptunga was guilty or not of the unfaithfulness to his religion with which the faction of Majorinus reproached him.
[2] *Suspensum.*

complaints, and which they preferred to the decision of an episcopal tribunal? If you are dissatisfied with the decrees of emperors, who were the first to compel the emperors to set these in array against you? For you have no more reason for crying out against the Catholic Church because of the decrees of emperors against you, than those men would have had for crying out against Daniel, who, after his deliverance, were thrown in to be devoured by the same lions by which they first sought to have him destroyed; as it is written: "The king's wrath is as the roaring of a lion."[1] These slanderous enemies insisted that Daniel should be thrown into the den of lions: his innocence prevailed over their malice; he was taken from the den unharmed, and they, being cast into it, perished. In like manner, your forefathers cast Cæcilianus and his companions to be destroyed by the king's wrath; and when, by their innocence, they were delivered from this, you yourselves now suffer from these kings what your party wished them to suffer; as it is written: "Whoso diggeth a pit for his neighbour, shall himself fall therein."[2]

6. You have therefore no ground for complaint against us: nay more, the clemency of the Catholic Church would have led us to desist from even enforcing these decrees of the emperors, had not your clergy and Circumcelliones, disturbing our peace, and destroying us by their most monstrous crimes and furious deeds of violence, compelled us to have these decrees revived and put in force again. For before these more recent edicts of which you complain had come into Africa, these desperadoes laid ambush for our bishops on their journeys, abused our clergy with savage blows, and assaulted our laity in the same most cruel manner, and set fire to their habitations. A certain presbyter who had of his own free choice preferred the unity of our Church, was for so doing dragged out of his own house, cruelly beaten without form of law, rolled over and over in a miry pond, covered with a matting of rushes, and exhibited as an object of pity to some and of ridicule to others, while his persecutors gloried in their crime; after which they carried him away where they pleased, and reluctantly set him at liberty after twelve days. When Proculeianus[3] was challenged by our bishop concerning this outrage, at a meeting of the municipal courts, he at first endeavoured to evade inquiry into the matter by pretending that he knew nothing of it; and when the demand was immediately repeated, he publicly declared that he would say nothing more on the subject. And the perpetrators of that outrage are at this day among your presbyters, continuing moreover

to keep us in terror, and to persecute us to the utmost of their power.

7. Our bishop, however, did not complain to the emperors of the wrongs and persecution which the Catholic Church in our district suffered in those days. But when a Council had been convened,[4] it was agreed that you should be invited to meet our party peaceably, in order that, if it were possible, you [i.e. the bishops on both sides, for the letter is written by the clergy of Hippo] might have a conference, and the error being taken out of the way, brotherly love might rejoice in the bond of peace between us. You may learn from your own records the answer which Proculeianus made at first on that occasion, that you would call a Council together, and would there see what you ought to answer; and how afterwards, when he was again publicly reminded of his promise, he stated, as the Acts bear witness, that he refused to have any conference with a view to peace. After this, when the notorious atrocities of your clergy and Circumcelliones continued, a case was brought to trial;[5] and Crispinus being condemned as a heretic, although he was through the forbearance of the Catholics exempted from the fine which the imperial edict imposed on heretics of ten pounds of gold, nevertheless thought himself warranted in appealing to the emperors. As to the answer which was made to that appeal, was it not extorted by the preceding wickedness of your party and by his own appeal? And yet, even after that answer was given, he was permitted to escape the infliction of that fine, through the intercession of our bishops with the Emperor on his behalf. From that Council, however, our bishops sent deputies to the court, who obtained a decree that not all your bishops and clergy should be held liable to this fine of ten pounds of gold, which the decree had imposed on all heretics, but only those in whose districts the Catholic Church suffered violence at the hands of your party. But by the time that the deputation came to Rome, the wounds of the Catholic bishop of Bagæ, who had just then been dreadfully injured, had moved the Emperor to send such edicts as were actually sent. When these edicts came to Africa, seeing especially that strong pressure had begun to be brought upon you, not to any evil thing, but for your good, what should you have done but invited our bishops to meet you, as they had invited yours to meet them, that by a conference the truth might be brought to light?

8. Not only, however, have you failed to do this, but your party go on inflicting yet greater

---

[1] Prov. xix. 12.
[2] Ecclus. xxvii. 29, and Prov. xxvi. 27.
[3] Donatist bishop of Hippo. See Letter XXXIII. p. 260.

[4] At Carthage, A.D. 403.
[5] For a more detailed reference to this case, see Letter CV. sec. 4. Crispinus was charged with an attempt to kill Possidius the bishop of Calama. See also Aug. *Cont. Crescon.* b. iii. c. 46, n. 50, and c. 47, n. 51.

injuries upon us. Not contented with beating us with bludgeons and killing some with the sword, they even, with incredible ingenuity in crime, throw lime mixed with acid [? vitriol] into our people's eyes to blind them. For pillaging our houses, moreover, they have fashioned huge and formidable implements, armed with which they wander here and there, breathing out threats of slaughter, rapine, burning of houses, and blinding of our eyes; by which things we have been constrained in the first instance to complain to you, venerable sir, begging you to consider how, under these so-called terrible laws of Catholic emperors, many, nay all of you, who say that you are the victims of persecution, are settled in peace in the possessions which were your own, or which you have taken from others, while we suffer such unheard-of wrongs at the hands of your party. You say that you are persecuted, while we are killed with clubs and swords by your armed men. You say that you are persecuted, while our houses are pillaged by your armed robbers. You say that you are persecuted, while many of us have our eyesight destroyed by the lime and acid with which your men are armed for the purpose. Moreover, if their course of crime brings some of them to death, they make out that these deaths are justly the occasion of odium against us, and of glory to them. They take no blame to themselves for the harm which they do to us, and they lay upon us the blame of the harm which they bring upon themselves. They live as robbers, they die as Circumcelliones, they are honoured as martyrs! Nay, I do injustice to robbers in this comparison, for we have never heard of robbers destroying the eyesight of those whom they have plundered: they indeed take away those whom they kill from the light, but they do not take away the light from those whom they leave in life.

9. On the other hand, if at any time we get men of your party into our power, we keep them unharmed, showing great love towards them; and we tell them everything by which the error which has severed brother from brother is refuted. We do as the Lord Himself commanded us, in the words of the prophet Isaiah: "Hear the word of the Lord, ye that tremble at His word; say, Ye are our brethren, to those who hate you, and who cast you out, that the name of the Lord may be glorified, and that He may appear to them with joy; but let them be put to shame." [1] And thus some of them we persuade, through their considering the evidences of the truth and the beauty of peace, not to be baptized anew for this sign of allegiance to our king they have already received (though they were as deserters), but to accept that faith, and love of the Holy Spirit, and union to the body of Christ, which formerly they had not. For it is written, "Purifying their hearts by faith;" [2] and again, "Charity covereth a multitude of sins." [3] If, however, either through too great obduracy, or through shame making them unable to bear the taunts of those with whom they were accustomed to join so frequently in falsely reproaching us and contriving evil against us, or perhaps more through fear lest they should come to share along with us such injuries as they were formerly wont to inflict on us, — if, I say, from any of these causes, they refuse to be reconciled to the unity of Christ, they are allowed to depart, as they were detained, without suffering any harm. We also exhort our laity as far as we can to detain them without doing them any harm, and bring them to us for admonition and instruction. Some of them obey us and do this, if it is in their power: others deal with them as they would with robbers, because they actually suffer from them such things as robbers are wont to do. Some of them strike their assailants in protecting their own bodies from their blows: while others apprehend them and bring them to the magistrates; and though we intercede on their behalf, they do not let them off, because they are very much afraid of their savage outrages. Yet all the while, these men, though persisting in the practices of robbers, claim to be honoured as martyrs when they receive the due reward of their deeds!

10. Accordingly our desire, which we lay before you, venerable sir, by this letter and by the brethren whom we have sent, is as follows. In the first place, if it be possible, let a peaceable conference be held with our bishops, so that an end may be put to the error itself, not to the men who embrace it, and men corrected rather than punished; and as you formerly despised their proposals for agreement, let them now proceed from your side. How much better for you to have such a conference between your bishops and ours, the proceedings of which may be written down and sent with signature of the parties to the Emperor, than to confer with the civil magistrates, who cannot do otherwise than administer the laws which have been passed against you! For your colleagues who sailed from this country said that they had come to have their case heard by the prefects. They also named our holy father the Catholic bishop Valentinus, who was then at court, saying that they wished to be heard along with him. This the judge could not concede, as he was guided in his judicial functions by the laws which were passed against you: the bishop, moreover, had not

---

[1] Isa. lxvi. 5, as given by Augustin.

[2] Acts xv. 9.
[3] 1 Pet. iv. 8.

come on this footing, or with any such instructions from his colleagues. How much better qualified therefore will the Emperor himself be to decide regarding your case, when the report of that conference has been read before him, seeing that he is not bound by these laws, and has power to enact other laws instead of them; although it may be said to be a case upon which final decision was pronounced long ago! Yet, in wishing this conference with you, we seek not to have a second final decision, but to have it made known as already settled to those who meanwhile are not aware that it is so. If your bishops be willing to do this, what do you thereby lose? Do you not rather gain, inasmuch as your willingness for such conference will become known, and the reproach, hitherto deserved, that you distrust your own cause will be taken away? Do you, perchance, suppose that such conference would be unlawful? Surely you are aware that Christ our Lord spoke even to the devil concerning the law,[1] and that by the Apostle Paul debates were held not only with Jews, but even with heathen philosophers of the sect of the Stoics and of the Epicureans.[2] Is it, perchance, that the laws of the Emperor do not permit you to meet our bishops? If so, assemble together in the meantime your bishops in the region of Hippo, in which we are suffering such wrongs from men of your party. For how much more legitimate and open is the way of access to us for the writings which you might send to us, than for the arms with which they assail us!

11. Finally, we beg you to send back such writings by our brethren whom we have sent to you. If, however, you will not do this, at least hear us as well as those of your own party, at whose hands we suffer such wrongs Show us the truth for which you allege that you suffer persecution, at the time when we are suffering so great cruelties from your side. For if you convict us of being in error, perhaps you will concede to us an exemption from being rebaptized by you, because we were baptized by persons whom you have not condemned; and you granted this exemption to those whom Felicianus of Musti, and Prætextatus of Assuri, had baptized during the long period in which you were attempting to cast them out of their churches by legal interdicts, because they were in communion with Maximianus, along with whom they were condemned explicitly and by name in the Council of Bagæ. All which things we can prove by the judicial and municipal transactions, in which you brought forward the decisions of this same Council of yours, when you wished to show the judges that the persons whom you were expelling from your ecclesiastical buildings were persons by schism separated from you. Nevertheless, you who have by schism severed yourselves from the seed of Abraham, in whom all the nations of the earth are blessed,[3] refuse to be expelled from our ecclesiastical buildings, when the decree to this effect proceeds not from judges such as you employed in dealing with schismatics from your sect, but from the kings of the earth themselves, who worship Christ as the prophecy had foretold, and from whose bar you retired vanquished when you brought accusation against Cæcilianus.

12. If, however, you will neither instruct us nor listen to us, come yourselves, or send into the district of Hippo some of your party, with some of us as their guides, that they may see your army equipped with their weapons; nay, more fully equipped than ever army was before, for no soldier when fighting against barbarians was ever known to add to his other weapons lime and acid to destroy the eyes of his enemies. If you refuse this also, we beg you at least to write to them to desist now from these things, and refrain from murdering, plundering, and blinding our people. We will not say, condemn them; for it is for yourselves to see how no contamination is brought to you by the toleration within your communion of those whom we prove to be robbers, while contamination is brought to us by our having members against whom you have never been able to prove that they were traditors. If, however, you treat all our remonstrances with contempt, we shall never regret that we desired to act in a peaceful and orderly way. The Lord will so plead for His Church, that you, on the other hand, shall regret that you despised our humble attempt at conciliation.

LETTER LXXXIX.

(A.D. 406.)

TO FESTUS, MY LORD WELL BELOVED, MY SON HONOURABLE AND WORTHY OF ESTEEM, AUGUSTIN SENDS GREETING IN THE LORD.

1. If, on behalf of error and inexcusable dissension, and falsehoods which have been in every way possible disproved, men are so presumptuous as to persevere in boldly assailing and threatening the Catholic Church, which seeks their salvation, how much more is it reasonable and right for those who maintain the truth of Christian peace and unity, — truth which commends itself even to those who profess to deny it or attempt to resist it, — to labour constantly and with energy, not only in the defence of those who are already Catholics, but also for the correction of those who are not yet within the

---

[1] Matt. iv. 4.
[2] Acts xvii. 18.

[3] Gen. xxii. 18.

Church! For if obstinacy aims at the possession and exercise of indomitable strength, how great should be the strength of constancy which devotes persevering and unwearied labours to a cause which it knows to be both pleasing to God, and beyond all question necessarily approved by the judgment of wise men!

2. Could there, moreover, be anything more lamentable as an instance of perversity, than for men not only to refuse to be humbled by the correction of their wickedness, but even to claim commendation for their conduct, as is done by the Donatists, when they boast that they are the victims of persecution; either through incredible blindness not knowing, or through inexcusable passion pretending not to know, that men are made martyrs not by the amount of their suffering, but by the cause in which they suffer? This I would say even were I opposing men who were only involved in the darkness of error, and suffering penalties on that account most truly merited, and who had not dared to assault any one with insane violence. But what shall I say against those whose fatal obstinacy is such that it is checked only by fear of losses, and is taught only by exile how universal (as had been foretold) is the diffusion of the Church, which they prefer to attack rather then to acknowledge? And if the things which they suffer under this most gentle discipline be compared with those things which they in reckless fury perpetrate, who does not see to which party the name of persecutors more truly belongs? Nay, even though wicked sons abstain from violence, they do, by their abandoned way of life, inflict upon their affectionate parents a much more serious wrong than their father and mother inflict upon them, when, with a sternness proportioned to the strength of their love, they endeavour without dissimulation to compel them to live uprightly.

3. There exist the strongest evidences in public documents, which you can read if you please, or rather, which I beseech and exhort you to read, by which it is proved that their predecessors, who originally separated themselves from the peace of the Church, did of their own accord dare to bring accusation against Cæcilianus before the Emperor by means of Anulinus, who was proconsul at that time. Had they gained the day in that trial, what else would Cæcilianus have suffered at the hands of the Emperor than that which, when they were defeated, he awarded to them? But truly, if they having accused him had prevailed, and Cæcilianus and his colleagues had been expelled from their sees, or, through persisting in their conspiracy, had exposed themselves to severer punishments (for the imperial censure could not pass unpunished the resistance of persons who had been defeated in the civil courts), they would then have published as worthy of all praise the Emperor's wise measures and anxious care for the good of the Church. But now, because they have themselves lost their case, being wholly unable to prove the charges which they advanced, if they suffer anything for their iniquity, they call it persecution; and not only set no bounds to their wicked violence, but also claim to be honoured as martyrs: as if the Catholic Christian emperors were following in their measures against their most obstinate wickedness any other precedent than the decision of Constantine, to whom they of their own accord appealed as the accusers of Cæcilianus, and whose authority they so esteemed above that of all the bishops beyond the sea, that to him rather than to them they referred this ecclesiastical dispute. To him, again, they protested against the first judgment given against them by the bishops whom he had appointed to examine the case in Rome, and to him also they appealed against the second judgment given by the bishops at Arles: yet when at last they were defeated by his own decision, they remained unchanged in their perversity. I think that even the devil himself would not have had the assurance to persist in such a cause, if he had been so often overthrown by the authority of the judge to whom he had of his own will chosen to appeal.

4. It may be said, however, that these are human tribunals, and that they might have been cajoled, misguided, or bribed. Why, then, is the Christian world libelled and branded with the crime laid to the charge of some who are said to have surrendered to persecutors the sacred books? For surely it was neither possible for the Christian world, nor incumbent upon it, to do otherwise than believe the judges whom the plaintiffs had chosen, rather than the plaintiffs against whom these judges pronounced judgments. These judges are responsible to God for their opinion, whether just or unjust; but what has the Church, diffused throughout the world, done that it should be deemed necessary for her to be rebaptized by the Donatists upon no other ground than because, in a case in which she was not able to decide as to the truth, she has thought herself called upon to believe those who were in a position to judge it rightly, rather than those who, though defeated in the civil courts, refused to yield? O weighty indictment against all the nations to which God promised that they should be blessed in the seed of Abraham, and has now made His promise good! When they with one voice demand, Why do you wish to rebaptize us? the answer given is, Because you do not know what men in Africa were guilty of surrendering the sacred books; and being thus ignorant, accepted the testimony of the judges who decided

the case as more worthy of credit than that of those by whom the accusation was brought. No man deserves to be blamed for the crime of another; what, then, has the whole world to do with the sin which some one in Africa may have committed? No man deserves to be blamed for a crime about which he knows nothing; and how could the whole world possibly know the crime in this case, whether the judges or the party condemned were guilty? Ye who have understanding, judge what I say. Here is the justice of heretics: the party of Donatus condemns the whole world unheard, because the whole world does not condemn a crime unknown. But for the world, truly, it suffices to have the promises of God, and to see fulfilled in itself what prophets predicted so long ago, and to recognise the Church by means of the same Scriptures by which Christ her King is recognised. For as in them are foretold concerning Christ the things which we read in gospel history to have been fulfilled in Him, so also in them have been foretold concerning the Church the things which we now behold fulfilled in the world.

5. Possibly some thinking people might be disturbed by what they are accustomed to say regarding baptism, viz. that it is the true baptism of Christ only when it is administered by a righteous man, were it not that on this subject the Christian world holds what is most manifestly evangelical truth as taught in the words of John: "He that sent me to baptize with water, the same said unto me, Upon whom thou shalt see the Spirit descending, and remaining on him, the same is he which baptizeth with the Holy Ghost." [1] Wherefore the Church calmly declines to place her hope in man, lest she fall under the curse pronounced in Scripture, "Cursed be the man that trusteth in man," [2] but places her hope in Christ, who so took upon Him the form of a servant as not to lose the form of God, of whom it is said, "The same is He which baptizeth." Therefore, whoever the man be, and whatever office he bear who administers the ordinance, it is not he who baptizes, — that is the work of Him upon whom the dove descended. So great is the absurdity in which the Donatists are involved in consequence of these foolish opinions, that they can find no escape from it. For when they admit the validity and reality of baptism when one of their sect baptizes who is a guilty man, but whose guilt is concealed, we ask them, Who baptizes in this case? and they can only answer, God; for they cannot affirm that a man guilty of sin (say of adultery) can sanctify any one. If, then, when baptism is administered by a man known to be righteous, he sanctifies the person baptized; but when it is administered by a wicked man, whose wickedness is hidden, it is not he, but God, who sanctifies. Those who are baptized ought to wish to be baptized rather by men who are secretly bad than by men manifestly good, for God sanctifies much more effectually than any righteous man can do. If it be palpably absurd that one about to be baptized ought to wish to be baptized by a hypocritical adulterer rather than by a man of known chastity, it follows plainly, that whoever be the minister that dispenses the rite, the baptism is valid, because He Himself baptizes upon whom the dove descended.

6. Notwithstanding the impression which truth so obvious should produce on the ears and hearts of men, such is the whirlpool of evil custom by which some have been engulfed, that rather than yield, they will resist both authority and argument of every kind. Their resistance is of two kinds — either with active rage or with passive immobility. What remedies, then, must the Church apply when seeking with a mother's anxiety the salvation of them all, and distracted by the frenzy of some and the lethargy of others? Is it right, is it possible, for her to despise or give up any means which may promote their recovery? She must necessarily be esteemed burdensome by both, just because she is the enemy of neither. For men in frenzy do not like to be bound, and men in lethargy do not like to be stirred up; nevertheless the diligence of charity perseveres in restraining the one and stimulating the other, out of love to both. Both are provoked, but both are loved; both, while they continue under their infirmity, resent the treatment as vexatious; both express their thankfulness for it when they are cured.

7. Moreover, whereas they think and boast that we receive them into the Church just as they were, it is not so. We receive them completely changed, because they do not begin to be Catholics until they have ceased to be heretics. For their sacraments, which we have in common with them, are not the objects of dislike to us, because they are not human, but Divine. That which must be taken from them is the error, which is their own, and which they have wickedly imbibed; not the sacraments, which they have received like ourselves, and which they bear and have, — to their own condemnation, indeed, because they use them so unworthily; nevertheless, they truly have them. Wherefore, when their error is forsaken, and the perversity of schism corrected in them, they pass over from heresy into the peace of the Church, which they formerly did not possess, and without which all that they did possess was only doing them harm. If, however, in thus passing over they are not sincere, this is a matter not for us, but for God, to judge. And yet, some who were suspected of insincerity because they had passed over to us

[1] John i. 33.
[2] Jer. xvii. 5.

through fear, have been found in some subsequent temptations so faithful as to surpass others who had been originally Catholics. Therefore let it not be said that nothing is accomplished when strong measures are employed. For when the entrenchments of stubborn custom are stormed by fear of human authority, this is not all that is done, because at the same time faith is strengthened, and the understanding convinced, by authority and arguments which are Divine.

8. These things being so, be it known to your Grace that your men in the region of Hippo are still Donatists, and that your letter has had no influence upon them. The reason why it failed to move them I need not write ; but send some one, either a servant or a friend of your own, whose fidelity you can entrust with the commission, and let him come not to them in the first place, but to us without their knowledge ; and when he has carefully consulted with us as to what is best to be done, let him do it with the Lord's help. For in these measures we are acting not only for their welfare, but also on behalf of our own men who have become Catholics, to whom the vicinity of these Donatists is so dangerous, that it cannot be looked upon by us as a small matter.

I could have written much more briefly ; but I wished you to have a letter from me, by which you might not only be yourself informed of the reason of my solicitude, but also be provided with an answer to any one who might dissuade you from earnestly devoting your energies to the correction of the people who belong to you, and might speak against us for wishing you to do this. If in this I have done what was unnecessary, because you had yourself either learned or thought out these principles, or if I have been burdensome to you by inflicting so long a letter upon one so engrossed with public affairs, I beg you to forgive me. I only entreat you not to despise what I have brought before you and requested at your hands. May the mercy of God be your safeguard !

LETTER XC.

(A.D. 408.)

TO MY NOBLE LORD AND BROTHER, WORTHY OF ALL ESTEEM, BISHOP AUGUSTIN, NECTARIUS SENDS GREETING.

I do not dwell upon the strength of the love men bear to their native land, for you know it. It is the only emotion which has a stronger claim than love of kindred. If there were any limit or time beyond which it would be lawful for right-hearted men to withdraw themselves from its control, I have by this time well earned exemption from the burdens which it imposes.

But since love and gratitude towards our country gain strength every day, and the nearer one comes to the end of life, the more ardent is his desire to leave his country in a safe and prosperous condition, I rejoice, in beginning this letter, that I am addressing myself to a man who is versed in all kinds of learning, and therefore able to enter into my feelings.

There are many things in the colony of Calama which justly bind my love to it. I was born here, and I have (in the opinion of others) rendered great services to this community. Now, my lord most excellent and worthy of all esteem, this town has fallen disastrously by a grievous misdemeanour on the part of her citizens,[1] which must be punished with very great severity, if we are dealt with according to the rigour of the civil law. But a bishop is guided by another law. His duty is to promote the welfare of men, to interest himself in any case only with a view to the benefit of the parties, and to obtain for other men the pardon of their sins at the hand of the Almighty God. Wherefore I beseech you with all possible urgency to secure that, if the matter is to be made the subject of a prosecution, the guiltless be protected, and a distinction drawn between the innocent and those who did the wrong. This, which, as you see, is a demand in accordance with your own natural sentiments, I pray you to grant. An assessment to compensate for the losses caused by the tumult can be easily levied. We only deprecate the severity of revenge. May you live in the more full enjoyment of the Divine favour, my noble lord, and brother worthy of all esteem.

LETTER XCI.

(A.D. 408.)

TO MY NOBLE LORD AND JUSTLY HONOURED BROTHER NECTARIUS, AUGUSTIN SENDS GREETING.

1. I do not wonder that, though your limbs are chilled by age, your heart still glows with patriotic fire. I admire this, and, instead of grieving, I rejoice to learn that you not only remember, but by your life and practice illustrate, the maxim that there is no limit either in measure or in time to the claims which their country has upon the care and service of right-hearted men. Wherefore we long to have you enrolled in the service of a higher and nobler country, through holy love, to which (up to the measure of our capacity) we are sustained amid the perils and toils which we meet with among those whose welfare we seek in urging them to make that country their own. Oh that we had you such a

---

[1] He refers to a riot in which the Pagans, after celebrating a heathen festival, attacked the Christians on June 1, 408 A.D.

citizen of that country, that you would think that there ought to be no limit either in measure or in time to your efforts for the good of that small portion of her citizens who are on this earth pilgrims ! This would be a better loyalty, because you would be responding to the claims of a better country ; and if you resolved that in your time on earth your labours for her welfare should have no end, you would in her eternal peace be recompensed with joy that shall have no end.

2. But till this be done, — and it is not beyond hope that you should be able to gain, or should even now be most wisely considering that you ought to gain, that country to which your father has gone before you, — till this be done, I say, you must excuse us if, for the sake of that country which we desire never to leave, we cause some distress to that country which you desire to leave in the full bloom of honour and prosperity. As to the flowers which thus bloom in your country, if we were discussing this subject with one of your wisdom, we have no doubt that you would be easily convinced, or rather, would yourself readily perceive, in what way a commonwealth should flourish. The foremost of your poets has sung of certain flowers of Italy ; but in your own country we have been taught by experience, not how it has blossomed with heroes, so much as how it has gleamed with weapons of war : nay, I ought to write how it has burned rather than how it has gleamed ; and instead of the weapons of war, I should write the fires of incendiaries. If so great a crime were to remain unpunished, without any rebuke such as the miscreants have deserved, do you think that you would leave your country in the full bloom of honour and prosperity ? O blooming flowers, yielding not fruit, but thorns ! Consider now whether you would prefer to see your country flourish by the piety of its inhabitants, or by their escaping the punishment of their crimes ; by the correction of their manners, or by outrages to which impunity emboldens them. Compare these things, I say, and judge whether or not you love your country more than we do ; whether its prosperity and honour are more truly and earnestly sought by you or by us.

3. Consider for a little those books, *De Republica*, from which you imbibed that sentiment of a most loyal citizen, that there is no limit either in measure or in time to the claims which their country has upon the care and service of right-hearted men. Consider them, I beseech you, and observe how great are the praises there bestowed upon frugality, self-control, conjugal fidelity, and those chaste, honourable, and upright manners, the prevalence of which in any city entitles it to be spoken of as flourishing. Now the Churches which are multiplying throughout the world are,

as it were, sacred seminaries of public instruction, in which this sound morality is inculcated and learned, and in which, above all, men are taught the worship due to the true and faithful God, who not only commands men to attempt, but also gives grace to perform, all those things by which the soul of man is furnished and fitted for fellowship with God, and for dwelling in the eternal heavenly kingdom. For this reason He hath both foretold and commanded the casting down of the images of the many false gods which are in the world. For nothing so effectually renders men depraved in practice, and unfit to be good members of society, as the imitation of such deities as are described and extolled in pagan writings.

4. In fact, those most learned men (whose *beau idéal* of a republic or commonwealth in this world was, by the way, rather investigated or described by them in private discussions, than established and realized by them in public measures) were accustomed to set forth as models for the education of youth the examples of men whom they esteemed eminent and praiseworthy, rather than the example given by their gods. And there is no question that the young man in Terence,[1] who, beholding a picture upon the wall in which was portrayed the licentious conduct of the king of the gods, fanned the flame of the passion which mastered him, by the encouragement which such high authority gave to wickedness, would not have fallen into the desire, nor have plunged into the commission, of such a shameful deed if he had chosen to imitate Cato instead of Jupiter ; but how could he make such a choice, when he was compelled in the temples to worship Jupiter rather than Cato? Perhaps it may be said that we should not bring forward from a comedy arguments to put to shame the wantonness and the impious superstition of profane men. But read or recall to mind how wisely it is argued in the books above referred to, that the style and the plots of comedies would never be approved by the public voice if they did not harmonize with the manners of those who approved them ; wherefore, by the authority of men most illustrious and eminent in the commonwealth to which they belonged, and engaged in debating as to the conditions of a perfect commonwealth, our position is established, that the most degraded of men may be made yet worse if they imitate their gods, — gods, of course, which are not true, but false and invented.

5. You will perhaps reply, that all those things which were written long ago concerning the life and manners of the gods are to be far otherwise than literally understood and interpreted by the wise. Nay, we have heard within the last few

---

[1] *Eunuchus*, Act iii. Sc. 5.

days that such wholesome interpretations are now read to the people when assembled in the temples. Tell me, is the human race so blind to truth as not to perceive things so plain and palpable as these? When, by the art of painters, founders, hammermen, sculptors, authors, players, singers, and dancers, Jupiter is in so many places exhibited in flagrant acts of lewdness, how important it was that in his own Capitol at least his worshippers might have read a decree from himself prohibiting such crimes! If, through the absence of such prohibition, these monsters, in which shame and profanity culminate, are regarded with enthusiasm by the people, worshipped in their temples, and laughed at in their theatres; if, in order to provide sacrifices for them, even the poor must be despoiled of their flocks; if, in order to provide actors who shall by gesture and dance represent their infamous achievements, the rich squander their estates, can it be said of the communities in which these things are done, that they flourish? The flowers with which they bloom owe their birth not to a fertile soil, nor to a wealthy and bounteous virtue; for them a worthy parent is found in that goddess Flora,[1] whose dramatic games are celebrated with a profligacy so utterly dissolute and shameless, that any one may infer from them what kind of demon that must be which cannot be appeased unless — not birds, nor quadrupeds, nor even human life — but (oh, greater villany!) human modesty and virtue, perish as sacrifices on her altars.

6. These things I have said, because of your having written that the nearer you come to the end of life, the greater is your desire to leave your country in a safe and flourishing condition. Away with all these vanities and follies, and let men be converted to the true worship of God, and to chaste and pious manners: then will you see your country flourishing, not in the vain opinion of fools, but in the sound judgment of the wise; when your fatherland here on earth shall have become a portion of that Fatherland into which we are born not by the flesh, but by faith, and in which all the holy and faithful servants of God shall bloom in the eternal summer, when their labours in the winter of time are done. We are therefore resolved, neither on the one hand to lay aside Christian gentleness, nor on the other to leave in your city that which would be a most pernicious example for all others to follow. For success in this dealing we trust to the help of God, if His indignation against the evil-doers be not so great as to make Him with-

hold His blessing. For certainly both the gentleness which we desire to maintain, and the discipline which we shall endeavour without passion to administer, may be hindered, if God in His hidden counsels order it otherwise, and either appoint that this so great wickedness be punished with a more severe chastisement, or in yet greater displeasure leave the sin without punishment in this world, its guilty authors being neither reproved nor reformed.

7. You have, in the exercise of your judgment, laid down the principles by which a bishop should be influenced; and after saying that your town has fallen disastrously by a grievous misdemeanour on the part of your citizens, which must be punished with great severity if they are dealt with according to the rigour of the civil law, you add: "But a bishop is guided by another law; his duty is to promote the welfare of men, to interest himself in any case only with a view to the benefit of the parties, and to obtain for other men the pardon of their sins at the hand of the Almighty God."[2] This we by all means labour to secure, that no one be visited with undue severity of punishment, either by us or by any other who is influenced by our interposition; and we seek to promote the true welfare of men, which consists in the blessedness of well-doing, not in the assurance of impunity in evil-doing. We do also seek earnestly, not for ourselves alone, but on behalf of others, the pardon of sin: but this we cannot obtain, except for those who have been turned by correction from the practice of sin. You add, moreover: "I beseech you with all possible urgency to secure that if the matter is to be made the subject of a prosecution, the guiltless be protected, and a distinction drawn between the innocent and those who did the wrong."

8. Listen to a brief account of what was done, and let the distinction between innocent and guilty be drawn by yourself. In defiance of the most recent laws,[3] certain impious rites were celebrated on the Pagan feast-day, the calends of June, no one interfering to forbid them, and with such unbounded effrontery that a most insolent multitude passed along the street in which the church is situated, and went on dancing in front of the building, — an outrage which was never committed even in the time of Julian. When the clergy endeavoured to stop this most illegal and insulting procedure, the church was assailed with stones. About eight days after that, when the bishop had called the attention of the authorities to the well-known laws on the subject, and they were preparing to carry out that which the law prescribed, the church was a

---

[1] Here culminates in the original a play upon words, towards which Augustin has been working with the ingenuity of a rhetorician from the beginning of the second paragraph; but the zest of his wit is necessarily lost in translation, because in our language the words "flower" and "flourish" are not so immediately suggestive of each other as the corresponding noun and verb in Latin (*flos* and *florere*).

[2] Letter XC. p. 376.
[3] The law of Honorius, passed on Nov. 24, 407, forbidding the celebration of public heathen solemnities and festivals (*quidquam solemnitatis agitare*).

second time assailed with stones. When, on the following day, our people wished to make such complaint as they deemed necessary in open court, in order to make these villains afraid, their rights as citizens were denied them. On the same day there was a storm of hailstones, that they might be made afraid, if not by men, at least by the divine power, thus requiting them for their showers of stones against the church; but as soon as this was over they renewed the attack for the third time with stones, and at last endeavoured to destroy both the buildings and the men in them by fire: one servant of God who lost his way and met them they killed on the spot, all the rest escaping or concealing themselves as they best could; while the bishop hid himself in some crevice into which he forced himself with difficulty, and in which he lay folded double while he heard the voices of the ruffians seeking him to kill him, and expressing their mortification that through his escaping them their principal design in this grievous outrage had been frustrated. These things went on from about the tenth hour until the night was far advanced. No attempt at resistance or rescue was made by those whose authority might have had influence on the mob. The only one who interfered was a stranger, through whose exertions a number of the servants of God were delivered from the hands of those who were trying to kill them, and a great deal of property was recovered from the plunderers by force: whereby it was shown how easily these riotous proceedings might have been either prevented wholly or arrested, if the citizens, and especially the leading men, had forbidden them, either from the first or after they had begun.

9. Accordingly you cannot in that community draw a distinction between innocent and guilty persons, for all are guilty; but perhaps you may distinguish degrees of guilt. Those are in a comparatively small fault, who, being kept back by fear, especially by fear of offending those whom they knew to have leading influence in the community and to be hostile to the Church, did not dare to render assistance to the Christians; but all are guilty who consented to these outrages, though they neither perpetrated them nor instigated others to the crime: more guilty are those who perpetrated the wrong, and most guilty are those who instigated them to it. Let us, however, suppose that the instigation of others to these crimes is a matter of suspicion rather than of certain knowledge, and let us not investigate those things which can be found out in no other way than by subjecting witnesses to torture. Let us also forgive those who through fear thought it better for them to plead secretly with God for the bishop and His other servants, than openly to displease the powerful enemies

of the Church. What reason can you give for holding that those who remain should be subjected to no correction and restraint? Do you really think that a case of such cruel rage should be held up to the world as passing unpunished? We do not desire to gratify our anger by vindictive retribution for the past, but we are concerned to make provision in a truly merciful spirit for the future. Now, wicked men have something in respect to which they may be punished, and that by Christians, in a merciful way, and so as to promote their own profit and well-being. For they have these three things: the life and health of the body, the means of supporting that life, and the means and opportunities of living a wicked life. Let the two former remain untouched in the possession of those who repent of their crime: this we desire, and this we spare no pains to secure. But as to the third, upon it God will, if it please Him, inflict punishment in His great compassion, dealing with it as a decaying or diseased part, which must be removed with the pruning-knife. If, however, He be pleased either to go beyond this, or not to permit the punishment to go so far, the reason for this higher and doubtless more righteous counsel remains with Him: our duty is to devote pains and use our influence according to the light which is granted to us, beseeching His approval of our endeavours to do that which shall be most for the good of all, and praying Him not to permit us to do anything which He who knoweth all things much better than we do sees to be inexpedient both for ourselves and for His Church.

10. When I went recently to Calama, that under so grievous sorrow I might either comfort the downcast or soothe the indignant among our people, I used all my influence with the Christians to persuade them to do what I judged to be their duty at that time. I then at their own request admitted to an audience the Pagans also, the source and cause of all this mischief, in order that I might admonish them what they should do if they were wise, not only for the removal of present anxiety, but also for the obtaining of everlasting salvation. They listened to many things which I said, and they preferred many requests to me; but far be it from me to be such a servant as to find pleasure in being petitioned by those who do not humble themselves before my Lord to ask from Him. With your quick intelligence, you will readily perceive that our aim must be, while preserving Christian gentleness and moderation, to act so that we may either make others afraid of imitating their perversity, or have cause to desire others to imitate their profiting by correction. As for the loss sustained, this is either borne by the Christians or remedied by the help of their brethren.

What concerns us is the gaining of souls, which even at the risk of life we are impatient to secure ; and our desire is, that in your district we may have larger success, and that in other districts we may not be hindered by the influence of your example. May God in His mercy grant to us to rejoice in your salvation !

LETTER XCII.

(A.D. 408.)

TO THE NOBLE AND JUSTLY DISTINGUISHED LADY ITALICA, A DAUGHTER WORTHY OF HONOUR IN THE LOVE OF CHRIST, BISHOP AUGUSTIN SENDS GREETING IN THE LORD.

1. I have learned, not only by your letter, but also by the statements of the person who brought it to me, that you earnestly solicit a letter from me, believing that you may derive from it very great consolation. What you may gain from my letter it is for yourself to judge ; I at least felt that I should neither refuse nor delay compliance with your request. May your own faith and hope comfort you, and that love which is shed abroad in the hearts of the pious by the Holy Ghost,[1] whereof we have now a portion as an earnest of the whole, in order that we may learn to desire its consummate fulness. For you ought not to consider yourself desolate while you have Christ dwelling in your heart by faith ; nor ought you to sorrow as those heathens who have no hope, seeing that in regard to those friends, who are not lost, but only called earlier than ourselves to the country whither we shall follow them, we have hope, resting on a most sure promise, that from this life we shall pass into that other life, in which they shall be to us more beloved as they shall be better known, and in which our pleasure in loving them shall not be alloyed by any fear of separation.

2. Your late husband, by whose decease you are now a widow, was truly well known to you, but better known to himself than to you. And how could this be, when you saw his face, which he himself did not see, if it were not that the inner knowledge which we have of ourselves is more certain, since no man " knoweth the things of a man, save the spirit of man which is in man " ?[2] but when the Lord cometh, " who both will bring to light the hidden things of darkness, and will make manifest the counsels of the hearts," [3] then shall nothing in any one be concealed from his neighbour ; nor shall there be anything which any one might reveal to his friends, but keep hidden from strangers, for no stranger shall be there. What tongue can de-

scribe the nature and the greatness of that light by which all those things which are now in the hearts of men concealed shall be made manifest? who can with our weak faculties even approach it? Truly that Light is God Himself, for " God is Light, and in Him is no darkness at all ; " [4] but He is the Light of purified minds, not of these bodily eyes. And the mind shall then be, what meanwhile it is not, able to see that light.

3. But this the bodily eye neither now is, nor shall then be, able to see. For everything which can be seen by the bodily eye must be in some place, nor can be everywhere in its totality, but with a smaller part of itself occupies a smaller space, and with a larger part a larger space. It is not so with God, who is invisible and incorruptible, " who only hath immortality, dwelling in the light which no man can approach unto ; whom no man hath seen nor can see." [5] For He cannot be seen by men through the bodily organ by which men see corporeal things. For if He were inaccessible to the minds also of the saints, it would not be said, " They looked unto Him, and were lightened " [translated by Aug., " Draw near unto Him, and be enlightened "] ; [6] and if He was invisible to the minds of the saints, it would not be said, " We shall see Him as He is : " for consider the whole context there in that Epistle of John : " Beloved," he says, " now are we the sons of God ; and it doth not yet appear what we shall be : but we know that, when He shall appear, we shall be like Him ; for we shall see Him as He is." [7] We shall therefore see Him according to the measure in which we shall be like Him ; because now the measure in which we do not see Him is according to the measure of our unlikeness to Him. We shall therefore see Him by means of that in which we shall be like Him. But who would be so infatuated as to assert that we either are or shall be in our bodies like unto God? The likeness spoken of is therefore in the inner man, " which is renewed in knowledge after the image of Him that created him." [8] And we shall become the more like unto Him, the more we advance in knowledge of Him and in love ; because " though our outward man perish, our inward man is renewed day by day," [9] yet so as that, however far one may have become advanced in this life, he is far short of that perfection of likeness which is fitted for seeing God, as the apostle says, " face to face." [10] If by these words we were to understand the bodily face, it would follow that God has a face such as ours, and

---

[1] Rom. v. 5.
[2] 1 Cor. ii. 11.
[3] 1 Cor. iv. 5.

[4] 1 John i. 5.
[5] 1 Tim. vi. 16.
[6] Ps. xxxiv. 5.
[7] 1 John iii. 2.
[8] Col. iii. 10.
[9] 2 Cor. iv. 6.
[10] 1 Cor. xiii. 12.

that between our face and His there must be a space intervening when we shall see Him face to face. And if a space intervene, this presupposes a limitation and a definite conformation of members and other things, absurd to utter, and impious even to think of, by which most empty delusions the natural man, which "receiveth not the things of the Spirit of God,"[1] is deceived.

4. For some of those who talk thus foolishly affirm, as I am informed, that we see God now by our minds, but shall then see Him by our bodies; yea, they even say that the wicked shall in the same manner see Him. Observe how far they have gone from bad to worse, when, unpunished for their foolish speaking, they talk at random, unrestrained by either fear or shame. They used to say at first, that Christ endowed only His own flesh with this faculty of seeing God with the bodily eye; then they added to this, that all the saints shall see God in the same way when they have received their bodies again in the resurrection; and now they have granted that the same thing is possible to the wicked also. Well, let them grant what gifts they please, and to whom they please: for who may say anything against men giving away that which is their own? for he that speaketh a lie, speaketh of his own.[2] Be it yours, however, in common with all who hold sound doctrine, not to presume to take in this way from your own any of these errors; but when you read, "Blessed are the pure in heart, for they shall see God,"[3] learn from it that the impious shall not see Him: for the impious are neither blessed nor pure in heart. Moreover, when you read, "Now we see through a glass darkly,[4] but then face to face,"[5] learn from this that we shall then see Him face to face by the same means by which we now see Him through a glass darkly. In both cases alike, the vision of God belongs to the inner man, whether when we walk in this pilgrimage still by faith, in which it uses the glass and the αἴνιγμα, or when, in the country which is our home, we shall perceive by sight, which vision the words "face to face" denote.

5. Let the flesh raving with carnal imaginations hear these words: "God is a Spirit, and they that worship Him must worship Him in spirit and in truth."[6] If this be the manner of worshipping Him, how much more of seeing Him! For who durst affirm that the Divine essence is seen in a corporal manner, when He has not permitted it to be worshipped in a corporal manner? They think, however, that they

are very acute in saying and in pressing as a question for us to answer: Was Christ able to endow His flesh so as that He could with His eyes see the Father, or was He not? If we reply that He was not, they publish abroad that we have denied the omnipotence of God; if, on the other hand, we grant that He was able, they affirm that their argument is established by our reply. How much more excusable is the folly of those who maintain that the flesh shall be changed into the Divine substance, and shall be what God Himself is, in order that thus they may endow with fitness for seeing God that which is meanwhile removed by so great diversity of nature from likeness to Him! Yet I believe they reject from their creed, perhaps also refuse to hear, this error. Nevertheless, if they were in like manner pressed with the question above quoted, as to whether God can or cannot do this [viz. change our flesh into the Divine substance], which alternative will they choose? Will they limit His power by answering that He cannot; or if they concede that He can, will they by this concession grant that it shall be done? Let them get out of the dilemma which they have proposed to others as above, in the same way by which they get out of this dilemma proposed to others by them. Moreover, why do they contend that this gift is to be attributed only to the eyes, and not to all the other senses of Christ? Shall God then be a sound, that He may be perceived by the ear? and an exhalation, that He may be discerned by the sense of smell? and a liquid of some kind, that He may be also imbibed? and a solid body, that He may be also touched? No, they say. What then? we reply; can God be this, or can He not? If they say He cannot, why do they derogate from the omnipotence of God? If they say He can, but is not willing, why do they show favour to the eyes alone, and grudge the same honour to the other senses of Christ? Do they carry their folly just as far as they please? How much better is our course, who do not prescribe limits to their folly, but would fain prevent them from entering into it at all!

6. Many things may be brought forward for the confutation of that madness. Meanwhile, however, if at any time they assail your ears, read this letter to the supporters of such error, and do not count it too great a labour to write back to me as well as you can what they say in reply. Let me add that our hearts are purified by faith, because the vision of God is promised to us as the reward of faith. Now, if this vision of God were to be through the bodily eyes, in vain are the souls of saints exercised for receiving it; nay, rather, a soul which cherishes such sentiments is not exercised in itself, but is wholly in the flesh. For where will it dwell more reso-

---

[1] 1 Cor. ii. 14.
[2] John viii. 44.
[3] Matt. v. 8.
[4] ἐν αἰνίγματι.
[5] 1 Cor. xiii. 12.
[6] John iv. 24.

lutely and fixedly than in that by means of which it expects that it shall see God? How great an evil this would be I rather leave to your own intelligence to observe, than labour to prove by a long argument.

May your heart dwell always under the Lord's keeping, noble and justly distinguished lady, and daughter worthy of honour in the love of Christ! Salute from me, with the respect due to your worth, your sons, who are along with yourself honourable, and to me dearly beloved in the Lord.

LETTER XCIII.

(A.D. 408.)

TO VINCENTIUS, MY BROTHER DEARLY BELOVED, AUGUSTIN SENDS GREETING.

CHAP. I. — I. I have received a letter which I believe to be from you to me: at least I have not thought this incredible, for the person who brought it is one whom I know to be a Catholic Christian, and who, I think, would not dare to impose upon me. But even though the letter may perchance not be from you, I have considered it necessary to write a reply to the author, whoever he may be. You know me now to be more desirous of rest, and earnest in seeking it, than when you knew me in my earlier years at Carthage, in the lifetime of your immediate predecessor Rogatus. But we are precluded from this rest by the Donatists, the repression and correction of whom, by the powers which are ordained of God, appears to me to be labour not in vain. For we already rejoice in the correction of many who hold and defend the Catholic unity with such sincerity, and are so glad to have been delivered from their former error, that we admire them with great thankfulness and pleasure. Yet these same persons, under some indescribable bondage of custom, would in no way have thought of being changed to a better condition, had they not, under the shock of this alarm, directed their minds earnestly to the study of the truth; fearing lest, if without profit, and in vain, they suffered hard things at the hands of men, for the sake not of righteousness, but of their own obstinacy and presumption, they should afterwards receive nothing else at the hand of God than the punishment due to wicked men who despised the admonition which He so gently gave and His paternal correction; and being by such reflection made teachable, they found not in mischievous or frivolous human fables, but in the promises of the divine books, that universal Church which they saw extending according to the promise throughout all nations: just as, on the testimony of prophecy in the same Scriptures, they believed without hesitation that Christ is exalted above the heavens, though

He is not seen by them in His glory. Was it my duty to be displeased at the salvation of these men, and to call back my colleagues from a fatherly diligence of this kind, the result of which has been, that we see many blaming their former blindness? For they see that they were blind who believed Christ to have been exalted above the heavens although they saw Him not, and yet denied that His glory is spread over all the earth although they saw it; whereas the prophet has with so great plainness included both in one sentence, "Be Thou exalted, O God, above the heavens, and Thy glory above all the earth."[1]

2. Wherefore, if we were so to overlook and forbear with those cruel enemies who seriously disturb our peace and quietness by manifold and grievous forms of violence and treachery, as that nothing at all should be contrived and done by us with a view to alarm and correct them, truly we would be rendering evil for evil. For if any one saw his enemy running headlong to destroy himself when he had become delirious through a dangerous fever, would he not in that case be much more truly rendering evil for evil if he permitted him to run on thus, than if he took measures to have him seized and bound? And yet he would at that moment appear to the other to be most vexatious, and most like an enemy, when, in truth, he had proved himself most useful and most compassionate; although, doubtless, when health was recovered, would he express to him his gratitude with a warmth proportioned to the measure in which he had felt his refusal to indulge him in his time of phrenzy. Oh, if I could but show you how many we have even from the Circumcelliones, who are now approved Catholics, and condemn their former life, and the wretched delusion under which they believed that they were doing in behalf of the Church of God whatever they did under the promptings of a restless temerity, who nevertheless would not have been brought to this soundness of judgment had they not been, as persons beside themselves, bound with the cords of those laws which are distasteful to you! As to another form of most serious distemper, — that, namely, of those who had not, indeed, a boldness leading to acts of violence, but were pressed down by a kind of inveterate sluggishness of mind, and would say to us: "What you affirm is true, nothing can be said against it; but it is hard for us to leave off what we have received by tradition from our fathers," — why should not such persons be shaken up in a beneficial way by a law bringing upon them inconvenience in worldly things, in order that they might rise from their lethargic sleep, and

---

[1] Ps. cviii. 5.

awake to the salvation which is to be found in the unity of the Church? How many of them, now rejoicing with us, speak bitterly of the weight with which their ruinous course formerly oppressed them, and confess that it was our duty to inflict annoyance upon them, in order to prevent them from perishing under the disease of lethargic habit, as under a fatal sleep!

3. You will say that to some these remedies are of no service. Is the art of healing, therefore, to be abandoned, because the malady of some is incurable? You look only to the case of those who are so obdurate that they refuse even such correction. Of such it is written, "In vain have I smitten your children: they received no correction:"[1] and yet I suppose that those of whom the prophet speaks were smitten in love, not from hatred. But you ought to consider also the very large number over whose salvation we rejoice. For if they were only made afraid, and not instructed, this might appear to be a kind of inexcusable tyranny. Again, if they were instructed only, and not made afraid, they would be with more difficulty persuaded to embrace the way of salvation, having become hardened through the inveteracy of custom: whereas many whom we know well, when arguments had been brought before them, and the truth made apparent by testimonies from the word of God, answered us that they desired to pass into the communion of the Catholic Church, but were in fear of the violence of worthless men, whose enmity they would incur; which violence they ought indeed by all means to despise when it was to be borne for righteousness' sake, and for the sake of eternal life. Nevertheless the weakness of such men ought not to be regarded as hopeless, but to be supported until they gain more strength. Nor may we forget what the Lord Himself said to Peter when he was yet weak: "Thou canst not follow Me now, but thou shalt follow Me afterwards."[2] When, however, wholesome instruction is added to means of inspiring salutary fear, so that not only the light of truth may dispel the darkness of error, but the force of fear may at the same time break the bonds of evil custom, we are made glad, as I have said, by the salvation of many, who with us bless God, and render thanks to Him, because by the fulfilment of His covenant, in which He promised that the kings of the earth should serve Christ, He has thus cured the diseased and restored health to the weak.

CHAP. II. — 4. Not every one who is indulgent is a friend; nor is every one an enemy who smites. Better are the wounds of a friend than the proffered kisses of an enemy.[3] It is better with severity to love, than with gentleness to deceive. More good is done by taking away food from one who is hungry, if, through freedom from care as to his food, he is forgetful of righteousness, than by providing bread for one who is hungry, in order that, being thereby bribed, he may consent to unrighteousness. He who binds the man who is in a phrenzy, and he who stirs up the man who is in a lethargy, are alike vexatious to both, and are in both cases alike prompted by love for the patient. Who can love us more than God does? And yet He not only give us sweet instruction, but also quickens us by salutary fear, and this unceasingly. Often adding to the soothing remedies by which He comforts men the sharp medicine of tribulation, He afflicts with famine even the pious and devout patriarchs,[4] disquiets a rebellious people by more severe chastisements, and refuses, though thrice besought, to take away the thorn in the flesh of the apostle, that He may make His strength perfect in weakness.[5] Let us by all means love even our enemies, for this is right, and God commands us so to do, in order that we may be the children of our Father who is in heaven, "who maketh His sun to rise on the evil and on the good, and sendeth rain on the just and on the unjust."[6] But as we praise these His gifts, lets us in like manner ponder His correction of those whom He loves.

5. You are of opinion that no one should be compelled to follow righteousness; and yet you read that the householder said to his servants, "Whomsoever ye shall find, compel them to come in."[7] You also read how he who was at first Saul, and afterwards Paul, was compelled, by the great violence with which Christ coerced him, to know and to embrace the truth; for you cannot but think that the light which your eyes enjoy is more precious to men than money or any other possession. This light, lost suddenly by him when he was cast to the ground by the heavenly voice, he did not recover until he became a member of the Holy Church. You are also of opinion that no coercion is to be used with any man in order to his deliverance from the fatal consequences of error; and yet you see that, in examples which cannot be disputed, this is done by God, who loves us with more real regard for our profit than any other can; and you hear Christ saying, "No man can come to me except the Father draw him,"[8] which is done in the hearts of all those who, through fear of the wrath of God, betake themselves to Him. You know also that sometimes the thief scatters food before the flock that he may lead them

---

[1] Jer. ii. 30.
[2] John xiii. 36.
[3] Prov. xxvii. 6.

[4] Gen. xii., xxvi., xlii., and xliii.
[5] 2 Cor. xii. 7-9.
[6] Matt. v. 45.
[7] Luke xiv. 23.
[8] John vi. 44.

astray, and sometimes the shepherd brings wandering sheep back to the flock with his rod.

6. Did not Sarah, when she had the power, choose rather to afflict the insolent bondwoman? And truly she did not cruelly hate her whom she had formerly by an act of her own kindness made a mother; but she put a wholesome restraint upon her pride.[1] Moreover, as you well know, these two women, Sarah and Hagar, and their two sons Isaac and Ishmael, are figures representing spiritual and carnal persons. And although we read that the bondwoman and her son suffered great hardships from Sarah, nevertheless the Apostle Paul says that Isaac suffered persecution from Ishmael: "But as then he that was born after the flesh persecuted him that was born after the Spirit, even so it is now;"[2] whence those who have understanding may perceive that it is rather the Catholic Church which suffers persecution through the pride and impiety of those carnal men whom it endeavours to correct by afflictions and terrors of a temporal kind. Whatever therefore the true and rightful Mother does, even when something severe and bitter is felt by her children at her hands, she is not rendering evil for evil, but is applying the benefit of discipline to counteract the evil of sin, not with the hatred which seeks to harm, but with the love which seeks to heal. When good and bad do the same actions and suffer the same afflictions, they are to be distinguished not by what they do or suffer, but by the causes of each: e.g. Pharaoh oppressed the people of God by hard bondage; Moses afflicted the same people by severe correction when they were guilty of impiety:[3] their actions were alike; but they were not alike in the motive of regard to the people's welfare, — the one being inflated by the lust of power, the other inflamed by love. Jezebel slew prophets, Elijah slew false prophets;[4] I suppose that the desert of the actors and of the sufferers respectively in the two cases was wholly diverse.

7. Look also to the New Testament times, in which the essential gentleness of love was to be not only kept in the heart, but also manifested openly: in these the sword of Peter is called back into its sheath by Christ, and we are taught that it ought not to be taken from its sheath even in Christ's defence.[5] We read, however, not only that the Jews beat the Apostle Paul, but also that the Greeks beat Sosthenes, a Jew, on account of the Apostle Paul.[6] Does not the similarity of the events apparently join both; and, at the same time, does not the dissimilarity

of the causes make a real difference? Again, God spared not His own Son, but delivered Him up[7] for us all.[8] Of the Son also it is said, "who loved me, and gave Himself[9] for me;"[10] and it is also said of Judas that Satan entered into him that he might betray[11] Christ.[12] Seeing, therefore, that the Father delivered up His Son, and Christ delivered up His own body, and Judas delivered up his Master, wherefore is God holy and man guilty in this delivering up of Christ, unless that in the one action which both did, the reason for which they did it was not the same? Three crosses stood in one place: on one was the thief who was to be saved; on the second, the thief who was to be condemned; on the third, between them, was Christ, who was about to save the one thief and condemn the other. What could be more similar than these crosses? what more unlike than the persons who were suspended on them? Paul was given up to be imprisoned and bound,[13] but Satan is unquestionably worse than any gaoler: yet to him Paul himself gave up one man for the destruction of the flesh, that the spirit might be saved in the day of the Lord Jesus.[14] And what say we to this? Behold, both deliver a man to bondage; but he that is cruel consigns his prisoner to one less severe, while he that is compassionate consigns his to one who is more cruel. Let us learn, my brother, in actions which are similar to distinguish the intentions of the agents; and let us not, shutting our eyes, deal in groundless reproaches, and accuse those who seek men's welfare as if they did them wrong. In like manner, when the same apostle says that he had delivered certain persons unto Satan, that they might learn not to blaspheme,[15] did he render to these men evil for evil, or did he not rather esteem it a good work to correct evil men by means of the evil one?

8. If to suffer persecution were in all cases a praiseworthy thing, it would have sufficed for the Lord to say, "Blessed are they which are persecuted," without adding "for righteousness' sake."[16] Moreover, if to inflict persecution were in all cases blameworthy, it would not have been written in the sacred books, "Whoso privily slandereth his neighbour, him will I persecute [cut off, E.V.]."[17] In some cases, therefore, both he that suffers persecution is in the wrong, and he that inflicts it is in the right. But the truth is, that always both the bad have per-

[1] Gen. xvi. 5.
[2] Gal. iv. 29.
[3] Ex. v. 9 and xxxii. 27.
[4] 1 Kings xviii. 4, 40.
[5] Matt. xxvi. 52.
[6] Acts xvi. 22, 23, and xviii. 17.

[7] παρέδωκεν.
[8] Rom. viii. 32.
[9] παράδοντος.
[10] Gal. ii. 20.
[11] παραδῷ.
[12] John xiii. 2.
[13] Acts xxi. 23, 24.
[14] 1 Cor. v. 5.
[15] 1 Tim. i. 20.
[16] Matt. v. 10.
[17] Ps. ci. 5.

secuted the good, and the good have persecuted the bad : the former doing harm by their unrighteousness, the latter seeking to do good by the administration of discipline ; the former with cruelty, the latter with moderation ; the former impelled by lust, the latter under the constraint of love. For he whose aim is to kill is not careful how he wounds, but he whose aim is to cure is cautious with his lancet ; for the one seeks to destroy what is sound, the other that which is decaying. The wicked put prophets to death ; prophets also put the wicked to death. The Jews scourged Christ ; Christ also scourged the Jews. The apostles were given up by men to the civil powers ; the apostles themselves gave men up to the power of Satan. In all these cases, what is important to attend to but this : who were on the side of truth, and who on the side of iniquity ; who acted from a desire to injure, and who from a desire to correct what was amiss?

CHAP. III. — 9. You say that no example is found in the writings of evangelists and apostles, of any petition presented on behalf of the Church to the kings of the earth against her enemies. Who denies this? None such is found. But at that time the prophecy, "Be wise now, therefore, O ye kings ; be instructed, ye judges of the earth : serve the Lord with fear," was not yet fulfilled. Up to that time the words which we find at the beginning of the same Psalm were receiving their fulfilment, "Why do the heathen rage, and the people imagine a vain thing? The kings of the earth set themselves, and the rulers take counsel together against the Lord, and against His Anointed." [1] Truly, if past events recorded in the prophetic books were figures of the future, there was given under King Nebuchadnezzar a figure both of the time which the Church had under the apostles, and of that which she has now. In the age of the apostles and martyrs, that was fulfilled which was prefigured when the aforesaid king compelled pious and just men to bow down to his image, and cast into the flames all who refused. Now, however, is fulfilled that which was prefigured soon after in the same king, when, being converted to the worship of the true God, he made a decree throughout his empire, that whosoever should speak against the God of Shadrach, Meshach, and Abednego, should suffer the penalty which their crime deserved. The earlier time of that king represented the former age of emperors who did not believe in Christ, at whose hands the Christians suffered because of the wicked ; but the later time of that king represented the age of the successors to the imperial throne, now believing in Christ, at whose hands the wicked suffer because of the Christians.

10. It is manifest, however, that moderate severity, or rather clemency, is carefully observed towards those who, under the Christian name, have been led astray by perverse men, in the measures used to prevent them who are Christ's sheep from wandering, and to bring them back to the flock, when by punishments, such as exile and fines, they are admonished to consider what they suffer, and wherefore, and are taught to prefer the Scriptures which they read to human legends and calumnies. For which of us, yea, which of you, does not speak well of the laws issued by the emperors against heathen sacrifices? In these, assuredly, a penalty much more severe has been appointed, for the punishment of that impiety is death. But in repressing and restraining you, the thing aimed at has been rather that you should be admonished to depart from evil, than that you should be punished for a crime. For perhaps what the apostle said of the Jews may be said of you : "I bear them record that they have a zeal of God, but not according to knowledge : for, being ignorant of the righteousness of God, and going about to establish their own righteousness, they have not submitted themselves to the righteousness of God." [2] For what else than your own righteousness are you desiring to establish, when you say that none are justified but those who may have had the opportunity of being baptized by you? In regard to this statement made by the apostle concerning the Jews, you differ from those to whom it originally applied in this, that you have the Christian sacraments, of which they are still destitute. But in regard to the words, "being ignorant of God's righteousness, and going about to establish their own righteousness," and "they have a zeal of God, but not according to knowledge," you are exactly like them, excepting only those among you who know what is the truth, and who in the wilfulness of their perversity continue to fight against truth which is perfectly well known to them. The impiety of these men is perhaps even a greater sin than idolatry. Since, however, they cannot be easily convicted of this (for it is a sin which lies concealed in the mind), you are all alike restrained with a comparatively gentle severity, as being not so far alienated from us. And this I may say, both concerning all heretics without distinction, who, while retaining the Christian sacraments, are dissenters from the truth and unity of Christ, and concerning all Donatists without exception.

11. But as for you, who are not only, in common with these last, styled Donatists, from Donatus, but also specially named Rogatists, from Rogatus, you indeed seem to be more gentle in

---

[1] Ps. ii. 10, 11, 1, 2. [2] Rom. x. 2, 3.

disposition, because you do not rage up and down with bands of these savage Circumcelliones : but no wild beast is said to be gentle if, because of its not having teeth and claws, it wounds no one. You say that you have no wish to be cruel: I think that power, not will, is wanting to you. For you are in number so few, that even if you desire it, you dare not move against the multitudes which are opposed to you. Let us suppose, however, that you do not wish to do that which you have not strength to do ; let us suppose that the gospel rule, " If any man will sue thee at the law and take away thy coat, let him have thy cloak also," [1] is so understood and obeyed by you that resistance to those who persecute you is unlawful, whether they have right or wrong on their side. Rogatus, the founder of your sect, either did not hold this view, or was guilty of inconsistency ; for he fought with the keenest determination in a lawsuit about certain things which, according to your statement, belonged to you. If to him it had been said, Which of the apostles ever defended his property in a matter concerning faith by appeal to the civil courts? as you have put the question in your letter, " Which of the apostles ever invaded the property of other men in a matter concerning faith?" he could not find any example of this in the Divine writings ; but he might perhaps have found some true defence if he had not separated himself from the true Church, and then audaciously claimed to hold in the name of the true Church the disputed possession.

CHAP. IV.— 12. As to the obtaining or putting in force of edicts of the powers of this world against schismatics and heretics, those from whom you separated yourselves were very active in this matter, both against you, so far as we have heard, and against the followers of Maximianus, as we prove by the indisputable evidence of their own Records ; but you had not yet separated yourselves from them at the time when in their petition they said to the Emperor Julian that "nothing but righteousness found a place with him," — a man whom all the while they knew to be an apostate, and whom they saw to be so given over to idolatry, that they must either admit idolatry to be righteousness, or be unable to deny that they had wickedly lied when they said that nothing but righteousness had a place with him with whom they saw that idolatry had so large a place. Grant, however, that that was a mistake in the use of words, what say you as to the deed itself? If not even that which is just is to be sought by appeal to an emperor, why was that which was by you supposed to be just sought from Julian?

13. Do you reply that it is lawful to petition the Emperor in order to recover what is one's own, but not lawful to accuse another in order that he may be coerced by the Emperor? I may remark, in passing, that in even petitioning for the recovery of what is one's own, the ground covered by apostolic example is abandoned, because no apostle is found to have ever done this. But apart from this, when your predecessors brought before the Emperor Constantine, by means of the proconsul Anulinus, their accusations against Cæcilianus, who was then bishop of Carthage, with whom as a guilty person they refused to have communion, they were not endeavouring to recover something of their own which they had lost, but were by calumnies assailing one who was, as we think, and as the issue of the judicial proceedings showed, an innocent man ; and what more heinous crime could have been perpetrated by them than this? If, however, as you erroneously suppose, they did in his case deliver up to the judgment of the civil powers a man who was indeed guilty, why do you object to our doing that which your own party first presumed to do, and for doing which we would not find fault with them, if they had done it not with an envious desire to do harm, but with the intention of reproving and correcting what was wrong. But we have no hesitation in finding fault with you, who think that we are criminal in bringing any complaint before a Christian emperor against the enemies of our communion, seeing that a document given by your predecessors to Anulinus the proconsul, to be forwarded by him to the Emperor Constantine, bore this superscription : " Libellus Ecclesiæ Catholicæ, criminum Cæciliani, traditus a parte Majorini." [2] We find fault, moreover, with them more particularly, because when they had of their own accord gone to the Emperor with accusations against Cæcilianus, which they ought by all means to have in the first place proved before those who were his colleagues beyond the sea, and when the Emperor, acting in a much more orderly way than they had done, referred to bishops the decision of this case pertaining to bishops which had been brought before him, they, even when defeated by a decision against them, would not come to peace with their brethren. Instead of this, they next accused at the bar of the temporal sovereign, not Cæcilianus only, but also the bishops who had been appointed judges ; and finally, from a second episcopal tribunal they appealed to the Emperor again. Nor did they consider it their duty to yield either to truth or to peace when he himself inquired into the case and gave his decision.

---

[1] Matt. v. 40.

[2] See Letter LXXXVIII. § 2.

14. Now what else could Constantine have decreed against Cæcilianus and his friends, if they had been defeated when your predecessors accused them, than the things decreed against the very men who, having of their own accord brought the accusations, and having failed to prove what they alleged, refused even when defeated to acquiesce in the truth? The Emperor, as you know, in that case decreed for the first time that the property of those who were convicted of schism and obstinately resisted the unity of the Church should be confiscated. If, however, the issue had been that your predecessors who brought the accusations had gained their case, and the Emperor had made some such decree against the communion to which Cæcilianus belonged, you would have wished the emperors to be called the friends of the Church's interests, and the guardians of her peace and unity. But when such things are decreed by emperors against the parties who, having of their own accord brought forward accusations, were unable to substantiate them, and who, when a welcome back to the bosom of peace was offered to them on condition of their amendment, refused the terms, an outcry is raised that this is an unworthy wrong, and it is maintained that no one ought to be coerced to unity, and that evil should not be requited for evil to any one. What else is this than what one of yourselves wrote: "What we wish is holy"?[1] And in view of these things, it was not a great or difficult thing for you to reflect and discover how the decree and sentence of Constantine, which was published against you on the occasion of your predecessors so frequently bringing before the Emperor charges which they could not make good, should be in force against you; and how all succeeding emperors, especially those who are Catholic Christians, necessarily act according to it as often as the exigencies of your obstinacy make it necessary for them to take any measures in regard to you.

15. It was an easy thing for you to have reflected on these things, and perhaps some time to have said to yourselves: Seeing that Cæcilianus either was innocent, or at least could not be proved guilty, what sin has the Christian Church spread so far and wide through the world committed in this matter? On what ground could it be unlawful for the Christian world to remain ignorant of that which even those who made it matter of accusation against others could not prove? Why should those whom Christ has sown in His field, that is, in this world, and has commanded to grow alongside of the tares until the harvest,[2] — those many thousands of believers in all nations, whose multitude the Lord compared to the stars of heaven and the sand of the sea, to whom He promised of old, and has now given, the blessing in the seed of Abraham, — why, I ask, should the name of Christians be denied to all these, because, forsooth, in regard to this case, in the discussion of which they took no part, they preferred to believe the judges, who under grave responsibility gave their decision, rather than the plaintiffs, against whom the decision was given? Surely no man's crime can stain with guilt another who does not know of its commission. How could the faithful, scattered throughout the world, be cognisant of the crime of surrendering the sacred books as committed by men, whose guilt their accusers, even if they knew it, were at least unable to prove? Unquestionably this one fact of ignorance on their part most easily demonstrates that they had no share in the guilt of this crime. Why then should the innocent be charged with crimes which they never committed, because of their being ignorant of crimes which, justly or unjustly, are laid to the charge of others? What room is left for innocence, if it is criminal for one to be ignorant of the crimes of others? Moreover, if the mere fact of their ignorance proves, as has been said, the innocence of the people in so many nations, how great is the crime of separation from the communion of these innocent people! For the deeds of guilty parties which either cannot be proved to those who are innocent, or cannot be believed by them, bring no stain upon any one, since, even when known, they are borne with in order to preserve fellowship with those who are innocent. For the good are not to be deserted for the sake of the wicked, but the wicked are to be borne with for the sake of the good; as the prophets bore with those against whom they delivered such testimonies, and did not cease to take part in the sacraments of the Jewish people; as also our Lord bore with guilty Judas, even until he met the end which he deserved, and permitted him to take part in the sacred supper along with the innocent disciples; as the apostles bore with those who preached Christ through envy, — a sin peculiarly satanic;[3] as Cyprian bore with colleagues guilty of avarice, which, after the example of the apostle,[4] he calls idolatry. In fine, whatever was done at that time among these bishops, although perhaps it was known by some of them, is, unless there be respect of persons in judgment, unknown to all: why, then, is not peace loved by all? These thoughts might easily occur to you; perhaps you already entertain them. But it would be better for you to be devoted to earthly possessions, through fear of losing which you might be proved to consent to

---

[1] "Quod volumus sanctum est."— TYCHONIUS.
[2] Matt. xiii. 24–30.

[3] Phil. i. 15, 18.
[4] Col. iii. 5.

known truth, than to be devoted to that worthless vainglory which you think you will by such consent forfeit in the estimation of men.

CHAP. V. — 16. You now see therefore, I suppose, that the thing to be considered when any one is coerced, is not the mere fact of the coercion, but the nature of that to which he is coerced, whether it be good or bad: not that any one can be good in spite of his own will, but that, through fear of suffering what he does not desire, he either renounces his hostile prejudices, or is compelled to examine truth of which he had been contentedly ignorant; and under the influence of this fear repudiates the error which he was wont to defend, or seeks the truth of which he formerly knew nothing, and now willingly holds what he formerly rejected. Perhaps it would be utterly useless to assert this in words, if it were not demonstrated by so many examples. We see not a few men here and there, but many cities, once Donatist, now Catholic, vehemently detesting the diabolical schism, and ardently loving the unity of the Church; and these became Catholic under the influence of that fear which is to you so offensive by the laws of emperors, from Constantine, before whom your party of their own accord impeached Cæcilianus, down to the emperors of our own time, who most justly decree that the decision of the judge whom your own party chose, and whom they preferred to a tribunal of bishops, should be maintained in force against you.

17. I have therefore yielded to the evidence afforded by these instances which my colleagues have laid before me. For originally my opinion was, that no one should be coerced into the unity of Christ, that we must act only by words, fight only by arguments, and prevail by force of reason, lest we should have those whom we knew as avowed heretics feigning themselves to be Catholics. But this opinion of mine was overcome not by the words of those who controverted it, but by the conclusive instances to which they could point. For, in the first place, there was set over against my opinion my own town, which, although it was once wholly on the side of Donatus, was brought over to the Catholic unity by fear of the imperial edicts, but which we now see filled with such detestation of your ruinous perversity, that it would scarcely be believed that it had ever been involved in your error. There were so many others which were mentioned to me by name, that, from facts themselves, I was made to own that to this matter the word of Scripture might be understood as applying: "Give opportunity to a wise man, and he will be yet wiser." [1] For how many were already, as we assuredly know, willing to be Catholics, being

moved by the indisputable plainness of truth, but daily putting off their avowal of this through fear of offending their own party! How many were bound, not by truth — for you never pretended to that as yours — but by the heavy chains of inveterate custom, so that in them was fulfilled the divine saying: "A servant (who is hardened) will not be corrected by words; for though he understand, he will not answer"! [2] How many supposed the sect of Donatus to be the true Church, merely because ease had made them too listless, or conceited, or sluggish, to take pains to examine Catholic truth! How many would have entered earlier had not the calumnies of slanderers, who declared that we offered something else than we do upon the altar of God, shut them out! How many, believing that it mattered not to which party a Christian might belong, remained in the schism of Donatus only because they had been born in it, and no one was compelling them to forsake it and pass over into the Catholic Church!

18. To all these classes of persons the dread of those laws in the promulgation of which kings serve the Lord in fear has been so useful, that now some say we were willing for this some time ago; but thanks be to God, who has given us occasion for doing it at once, and has cut off the hesitancy of procrastination! Others say: We already knew this to be true, but we were held prisoners by the force of old custom: thanks be to the Lord, who has broken these bonds asunder, and has brought us into the bond of peace! Others say: We knew not that the truth was here, and we had no wish to learn it; but fear made us become earnest to examine it when we became alarmed, lest, without any gain in things eternal, we should be smitten with loss in temporal things: thanks be to the Lord, who has by the stimulus of fear startled us from our negligence, that now being disquieted we might inquire into those things which, when at ease, we did not care to know! Others say: We were prevented from entering the Church by false reports, which we could not know to be false unless we entered it; and we would not enter unless we were compelled: thanks be to the Lord, who by His scourge took away our timid hesitation, and taught us to find out for ourselves how vain and absurd were the lies which rumour had spread abroad against His Church: by this we are persuaded that there is no truth in the accusations made by the authors of this heresy, since the more serious charges which their followers have invented are without foundation. Others say: We thought, indeed, that it mattered not in what communion we held the faith of Christ; but thanks to the Lord, who has gath-

---

[1] Prov. ix. 9.

[2] Prov. xxix. 19.

ered us in from a state of schism, and has taught us that it is fitting that the one God be worshipped in unity.

19. Could I therefore maintain opposition to my colleagues, and by resisting them stand in the way of such conquests of the Lord, and prevent the sheep of Christ which were wandering on your mountains and hills — that is, on the swellings of your pride — from being gathered into the fold of peace, in which there is one flock and one Shepherd?[1] Was it my duty to obstruct these measures, in order, forsooth, that you might not lose what you call your own, and might without fear rob Christ of what is His: that you might frame your testaments according to Roman law, and might by calumnious accusations break the Testament made with the sanction of Divine law to the fathers, in which it was written, " In thy seed shall all the nations of the earth be blessed " :[2] that you might have freedom in your transactions in the way of buying and selling, and might be emboldened to divide and claim as your own that which Christ bought by giving Himself as its price: that any gift made over by one of you to another might remain unchallenged, and that the gift which the God of gods has bestowed upon His children, called from the rising of the sun to the going down thereof,[3] might become invalid: that you might not be sent into exile from the land of your natural birth, and that you might labour to banish Christ from the kingdom bought with His blood, which extends from sea to sea, and from the river to the ends of the earth?[4] Nay verily; let the kings of the earth serve Christ by making laws for Him and for His cause. Your predecessors exposed Cæcilianus and his companions to be punished by the kings of the earth for crimes with which they were falsely charged: let the lions now be turned to break in pieces the bones of the calumniators, and let no intercession for them be made by Daniel when he has been proved innocent, and set free from the den in which they meet their doom;[5] for he that prepareth a pit for his neighbour shall himself most justly fall into it.[6]

CHAP. VI. — 20. Save yourself therefore, my brother, while you have this present life, from the wrath which is to come on the obstinate and the proud. The formidable power of the authorities of this world, when it assails the truth, gives glorious opportunity of probation to the strong, but puts dangerous temptation before the weak who are righteous; but when it assists the proclamation of the truth, it is the means of profitable admonition to the wise, and of unprofitable vexation to the foolish among those who have gone astray. " For there is no power but of God: whosoever therefore resisteth the power, resisteth the ordinance of God; for rulers are not a terror to good works, but to the evil. Wilt thou then not be afraid of the power? Do that which is good, and thou shalt have praise of the same."[7] For if the power be on the side of the truth, and correct any one who was in error, he that is put right by the correction has praise from the power. If, on the other hand, the power be unfriendly to the truth, and cruelly persecute any one, he who is crowned victor in this contest receives praise from the power which he resists. But you do not that which is good, so as to avoid being afraid of the power; unless perchance this is good, to sit and speak against not one brother,[8] but against all your brethren that are found among all nations, to whom the prophets, and Christ, and the apostles bear witness in the words of Scripture, " In thy seed shall all the nations of the earth be blessed ; "[2] and again, " From the rising of the sun even unto the going down of the same, a pure offering shall be offered unto My name; for My name shall be great among the heathen, saith the Lord."[9] Mark this: " saith the Lord ; " not saith Donatus, or Rogatus, or Vincentius, or Ambrose, or Augustin, but " saith the Lord ; " and again, " All tribes of the earth shall be blessed in Him, and all nations shall call Him blessed. Blessed be the Lord God, the God of Israel, who only doeth wondrous things; and blessed be His glorious name for ever, and the whole earth shall be filled with His glory: so let it be, so let it be."[10] And you sit at Cartennæ, and with a remnant of half a score of Rogatists you say, " Let it not be! Let it not be!"

21. You hear Christ speaking thus in the Gospel: "All things must be fulfilled which were written in the law of Moses, and in the Prophets, and in the Psalms, concerning Me. Then opened He their understanding, that they might understand the Scriptures, and said unto them, Thus it is written, and thus it behoved Christ to suffer, and to rise from the dead the third day; and that repentance and remission of sins should be preached in His name among all nations, beginning at Jerusalem."[11] You read also in the Acts of the Apostles how this gospel began at Jerusalem, where the Holy Spirit first filled those hundred and twenty persons, and went forth thence into Judæa and Samaria, and to all nations, as He had said unto them when He was about to ascend into heaven, "Ye shall

---

[1] John x. 16.
[2] Gen. xxvi. 4.
[3] Ps l. 1.
[4] Ps. lxxii. 8.
[5] Dan. vi. 23, 24.
[6] Prov. xxvi. 27.

[7] Rom. xiii. 1-3.
[8] Ps. l. 20.
[9] Mal. i. 11.
[10] Ps. lxxii. 17-19.
[11] Luke xxiv. 44-47.

be witnesses unto Me both in Jerusalem, and in all Judæa, and in Samaria, and unto the uttermost parts of the earth;"[1] for "their sound went into all the earth, and their words unto the ends of the world."[2] And you contradict the Divine testimonies so firmly established and so clearly revealed, and attempt to bring about such an absolute confiscation of Christ's heritage, that although repentance is preached, as He said, in His name to all nations, whosoever may be in any part of the earth moved by that preaching, there is for him no possibility of remission of sins, unless he seek and discover Vincentius of Cartennæ, or some one of his nine or ten associates, in their obscurity in the imperial colony of Mauritania. What will the arrogance of insignificant mortals[3] not dare to do? To what extremities will the presumption of flesh and blood not hurry men? Is this your well-doing, on account of which you are not afraid of the power? You place this grievous stumbling-block in the way of your own mother's son,[4] for whom Christ died,[5] and who is yet in feeble infancy, not ready to use strong meat, but requiring to be nursed on a mother's milk;[6] and you quote against me the works of Hilary, in order that you may deny the fact of the Church's increase among all nations, even unto the end of the world, according to the promise which God, in order to subdue your unbelief, confirmed with an oath! And although you would by all means be most miserable if you stood against this when it was promised, you even now contradict it when the promise is fulfilled.

CHAP. VII. — 22. You, however, through your profound erudition, have discovered something which you think worthy to be alleged as a great objection against the Divine testimonies. For you say, "If we consider the parts comprehended in the whole world, it is a comparatively small portion in which the Christian faith is known:" either refusing to see, or pretending not to know, to how many barbarous nations the gospel has already penetrated, within a space of time so short, that not even Christ's enemies can doubt that in a little while that shall be accomplished which our Lord foretold, when, answering the question of His disciples concerning the end of the world, He said, "This gospel of the kingdom shall be preached in all the world for a witness unto all nations, and then shall the end come."[7] Meanwhile do all you can to proclaim and to maintain, that even though the gospel be published in Persia and India, as indeed it has been for a long time, no one who hears it can be in any degree cleansed from his sins, unless he come to Cartennæ, or to the neighbourhood of Cartennæ! If you have not expressly said this, it is evidently through fear lest men should laugh at you; and yet when you do say this, do you refuse that men should weep for you?

23. You think that you make a very acute remark when you affirm the name Catholic to mean universal, not in respect to the communion as embracing the whole world, but in respect to the observance of all Divine precepts and of all the sacraments, as if we (even accepting the position that the Church is called Catholic because it honestly holds the whole truth, of which fragments here and there are found in some heresies) rested upon the testimony of this word's signification, and not upon the promises of God, and so many indisputable testimonies of the truth itself, our demonstration of the existence of the Church of God in all nations. In fact, however, this is the whole which you attempt to make us believe, that the Rogatists alone remain worthy of the name Catholics, on the ground of their observing all the Divine precepts and all the sacraments; and that you are the only persons in whom the Son of man when He cometh shall find faith.[8] You must excuse me for saying we do not believe a word of this. For although, in order to make it possible for that faith to be found in you which the Lord said that He would not find on the earth, you may perhaps presume even to say that you are to be regarded as in heaven, not on earth, we at least have profited by the apostle's warning, wherein he has taught us that even an angel from heaven must be regarded as accursed if he were to preach to us any other gospel than that which we have received.[9] But how can we be sure that we have indisputable testimony to Christ in the Divine Word, if we do not accept as indisputable the testimony of the same Word to the Church? For as, however ingenious the complex subtleties which one may contrive against the simple truth, and however great the mist of artful fallacies with which he may obscure it, any one who shall proclaim that Christ has not suffered, and has not risen from the dead on the third day, must be accursed — because we have learned in the truth of the gospel, "that it behoved Christ to suffer, and to rise from the dead on the third day;"[10] — on the very same grounds must that man be accursed who shall proclaim that the Church is outside of[11] the communion which embraces all nations: for in the

---

[1] Acts i. 15, 8, and ii.
[2] Ps. xix. 4; Rom. x. 18.
[3] *Typhus morticinæ pelliculæ.*
[4] Ps. l. 20.
[5] 1 Cor. viii. 11.
[6] 1 Cor. iii. 2.
[7] Matt. xxiv. 14.

[8] Luke xviii. 8.
[9] Gal i. 8.
[10] Luke xxiv. 46.
[11] *Præter.*

next words of the same passage we learn also that repentance and remission of sins should be preached in His name among all nations, beginning at Jerusalem; [1] and we are bound to hold firmly this rule, "If any preach any other gospel unto you than that ye have received, let him be accursed." [2]

CHAP. VIII.— 24. If, moreover, we do not listen to the claims of the entire sect of Donatists when they pretend to be the Church of Christ, seeing that they do not allege in proof of this anything from the Divine Books, how much less, I ask, are we called upon to listen to the Rogatists, who will not attempt to interpret in the interest of their party the words of Scripture: "Where Thou feedest, where Thou dost rest in the south"! [3] For if by this the southern part of Africa is to be understood,— the district, namely, which is occupied by Donatists, because it is under a more burning portion of the heavens,— the Maximianists must excel all the rest of your party, as the flame of their schism broke forth in Byzantium [4] and in Tripoli. Let the Arzuges, if they please, dispute this point with them, and contest that to them more properly this text applies; but how shall the imperial province of Mauritania, lying rather to the west than to the south, since it refuses to be called Africa,— how shall it, I say, find in the word "the south" [5] a ground for boasting, I do not say against the world, but against even that sect of Donatus from which the sect of Rogatus, a very small fragment of that other and larger fragment, has been broken off? For what else is it than superlative impudence for one to interpret in his own favour any allegorical statements, unless he has also plain testimonies, by the light of which the obscure meaning of the former may be made manifest.

25. With how much greater force, moreover, may we say to you what we are accustomed to say to all the Donatists: If any can have good grounds (which indeed none can have) for separating themselves from the communion of the whole world, and calling their communion the Church of Christ, because of their having withdrawn warrantably from the communion of all nations,— how do you know that in the Christian society, which is spread so far and wide, there may not have been some in a very remote place, from which the fame of their righteousness could not reach you, who had already, before the date of your separation, separated themselves for some just cause from the communion of the whole world? How could the Church in that case be found in your sect, rather than in those who were separated before you? Thus it comes to pass, that so long as you are ignorant of this, you cannot make with certainty any claim: which is necessarily the portion of all who, in defending the cause of their party, appeal to their own testimony instead of the testimony of God. For you cannot say, If this had happened, it could not have escaped our knowledge; for, not going beyond Africa itself, you cannot tell, when the question is put to you, how many subdivisions of the party of Donatus have occurred: in connection with which we must especially bear in mind that in your view the smaller the number of those who separate themselves, the greater is the justice of their cause, and this paucity of numbers makes them undoubtedly more likely to remain unnoticed. Hence, also, you are by no means sure that there may not be some righteous persons, few in number, and therefore unknown, dwelling in some place far remote from the south of Africa, who, long before the party of Donatus had withdrawn their righteousness from fellowship with the unrighteousness of all other men, had, in their remote northern region, separated themselves in the same way for some most satisfactory reason, and now are, by a claim superior to yours, the Church of God, as the spiritual Zion which preceded all your sects in the matter of warrantable secession, and who interpret in their favour the words of the Psalm, "Mount Zion, on the sides of the north, the city of the Great King," [6] with much more reason than the party of Donatus interpret in their favour the words, "Where Thou feedest, where Thou dost rest in the south." [7]

26. You profess, nevertheless, to be afraid lest, when you are compelled by imperial edicts to consent to unity, the name of God be for a longer time blasphemed by the Jews and the heathen: as if the Jews were not aware how their own nation Israel, in the beginning of its history, wished to exterminate by war the two tribes and a half which had received possessions beyond Jordan, when they thought that these had separated themselves from the unity of their nation. [8] As to the Pagans, they may indeed with greater reason reproach us for the laws which Christian emperors have enacted against idolaters; and yet many of these have thereby been, and are now daily, turned from idols to the living and true God. In fact, however, both Jews and Pagans, if they thought the Christians to be as insignificant in number as you are,— who maintain, forsooth, that you alone are Christians,— would not condescend to say anything against us, but would never cease to treat us with ridicule and contempt. Are you not afraid

1 Luke xxiv. 47.
2 Gal. i. 9.
3 *Meridie;* at noon, E. V. Cant. i. 7.
4 Now Tunis.
5 *Meridie.*

6 Ps. xlviii. 2.
7 Cant. i. 7.
8 Josh. xxii. 9-12.

lest the Jews should say to you, " If your hand-ful of men be the Church of Christ, what be-comes of the statement of your Apostle Paul, that your Church is described in the words, 'Rejoice, thou barren that bearest not; break forth and cry, thou that travailest not: for the desolate hath many more children than she which hath an husband;'[1] in which he plainly declares the multitude of Christians to surpass that of the Jewish Church?" Will you say to them, "We are the more righteous because our number is not large;" and do you expect them not to reply, "Whoever[2] you claim to be, you are not those of whom it is said, 'She that was desolate hath *many* children,' if you are reduced to so small a number"?

27. Perhaps you will quote against this the example of that righteous man, who along with his family was alone found worthy of deliverance when the flood came. Do you see then how far you still are from being righteous? Most assur-edly we do not affirm you to be righteous on the ground of this instance until your associates be reduced to seven, yourself being the eighth per-son: provided always, however, that no other has, as I was saying, anticipated the party of Donatus in snatching up that righteousness, by having, in some far distant spot, withdrawn him-self along with seven more, under pressure of some good reason, from communion with the whole world, and so saved himself from the flood by which it is overwhelmed. Seeing, therefore, that you do not know whether this may not have been done, and been as entirely unheard of by you as the name of Donatus is unheard of by many nations of Christians in remote countries, you are unable to say with certainty where the Church is to be found. For it must be in that place in which what you have now done may happen to have been at an earlier date done by others, if there could possibly be any just reason for your separating yourselves from the com-munion of the whole world.

Chap. IX. — 28. We, however, are certain that no one could ever have been warranted in sepa-rating himself from the communion of all na-tions, because every one of us looks for the marks of the Church not in his own righteous-ness, but in the Divine Scriptures, and beholds it actually in existence, according to the prom-ises. For it is of the Church that it is said, "As the lily among thorns, so is my love among the daughters;"[3] which could be called on the one hand "thorns" only by reason of the wick-edness of their manners, and on the other hand "daughters" by reason of their participation in the same sacraments. Again, it is the Church

which saith, "From the end of the earth have I cried unto Thee when my heart was over-whelmed;"[4] and in another Psalm, "Horror hath kept me back from[5] the wicked that for-sake Thy law;" and, "I beheld the transgress-ors, and was grieved."[6] It is the same which says to her Spouse: "Tell me where Thou feed-est, where Thou dost rest at noon: for why should I be as one veiled beside the flocks of Thy companions?"[7] This is the same as is said in another place: "Make known to me Thy right hand, and those who are in heart taught in wisdom;"[8] in whom, as they shine with light and glow with love, Thou dost rest as in noon-tide; lest perchance, like one veiled, that is, hidden and unknown, I should run, not to Thy flock, but to the flocks of Thy companions, *i.e.* of heretics, whom the bride here calls compan-ions, just as He called the thorns[3] "daughters," because of common participation in the sacra-ments: of which persons it is elsewhere said: "Thou wast a man, mine equal, my guide, my acquaintance, who didst take sweet food to-gether with me; we walked unto the house of God in company. Let death seize upon them, and let them go down quick into hell,"[9] like Dathan and Abiram, the authors of an impious schism.

29. It is to the Church also that the answer is given immediately after in the passage quoted above: " If thou know not thyself,[10] O thou fair-est among women, go thy way forth by the foot-steps of the flocks,[11] and feed thy kids beside the shepherds' tents."[12] Oh, matchless sweet-ness of the Bridegroom, who thus replied to her question: "If thou knowest not thyself," He says; as if He said, "Surely the city which is set upon a mountain cannot be hid;[13] and there-fore, 'Thou art not as one veiled, that thou shouldst run to the flocks of my companions.' For I am the mountain established upon the top of the mountains, unto which all nations shall come.[14] 'If thou knowest not thyself,' by the knowledge which thou mayest gain, not in the words of false witnesses, but in the testimonies of My book; 'if thou knowest not thyself,' from such testimony as this concerning thee: 'Lengthen thy cords, and strengthen thy stakes: for thou shalt break forth on the right hand and on the left; and thy seed shall inherit the Gen-tiles, and make the desolate cities to be inhabited.

---

[1] Gal. iv. 27.
[2] *Quoslibet* is obviously the true reading.
[3] Cant. ii. 2.

[4] Ps. lxi. 2.
[5] In this and the other passages quoted, Augustin translates from the LXX.
[6] Ps. cxix. 53 and 158.
[7] Cant. i. 7.
[8] Ps. xc. 12.
[9] Ps. lv. 14, 15.
[10] *Nisi cognoveris temetipsam.*
[11] *Gregum.*
[12] Cant. i. 8.
[13] Matt. v. 14.
[14] Isa. ii. 2.

Fear not, for thou shalt not be ashamed ; neither be thou confounded, for thou shalt not be put to shame : for thou shalt forget the shame of thy youth, and shalt not remember the reproach of thy widowhood any more : for thy Maker is thine husband, the Lord of hosts is His name, and thy Redeemer the Holy One of Israel ; the God of the whole earth shall He be called.' ' If thou knowest not thyself,' O thou fairest among women, from this which hath been said of thee, ' The King hath greatly desired thy beauty,' and ' instead of thy fathers shall be thy children, whom thou mayest make princes upon the earth : ' [1] if, therefore, ' thou know not thyself,' go thy way forth : I do not cast thee forth, but ' go thy way forth,' that of thee it may be said, ' They went out from us, but they were not of us.' [2] ' Go thy way forth' by the footsteps of the flocks, not in My footsteps, but in the footsteps of the flocks ; and not of the one flock, but of flocks divided and going astray. ' And feed thy kids,' not as Peter, to whom it is said, ' Feed My sheep ; ' [3] but. ' Feed thy kids beside the shepherds' tents,' not beside the tent of the Shepherd, where there is ' one fold and one Shepherd.' " [4] But the Church knows herself, and thereby escapes from that lot which has befallen those who did not know themselves to be in her.

30. The same [Church] is spoken of, when, in regard to the fewness of her numbers as compared with the multitude of the wicked, it is said : " Strait is the gate and narrow is the way which leadeth unto life, and few there be that find it." [5] And again, it is of the same Church that it is said with respect to the multitude of her members : " I will multiply thy seed as the stars of heaven, and as the sand which is upon the sea-shore." [6] For the same Church of holy and good believers is both small if compared with the number of the wicked, which is greater, and large if considered by itself ; " for the desolate hath more sons than she which hath an husband," and " many shall come from the east and from the west, and shall sit down with Abraham, and Isaac, and Jacob, in the kingdom of God." [7] God, moreover, presents unto Himself a " numerous people, zealous of good works." [8] And in the Apocalypse, many thousands " which no man can number," from every tribe and tongue, are seen clothed in white robes, and with palms of victory.[9] It is the same Church which is occasionally obscured, and, as it were, beclouded by the multitude of offences, when sin-

ners bend the bow that they may shoot under the darkened moon [10] at the upright in heart.[11] But even at such a time the Church shines in those who are most firm in their attachment to her. And if, in the Divine promise above quoted, any distinct application of its two clauses should be made, it is perhaps not without reason that the seed of Abraham was compared both to the " stars of heaven," and to " the sand which is by the sea-shore : " that by " the stars " may be understood those who, in number fewer, are more fixed and more brilliant ; and that by " the sand on the sea-shore " may be understood that great multitude of weak and carnal persons within the Church, who at one time are seen at rest and free while the weather is calm, but are at another time covered and troubled under the waves of tribulation and temptation.

31. Now, such a troublous time was the time at which Hilary wrote in the passage which you have thought fit artfully to adduce against so many Divine testimonies, as if by it you could prove that the Church has perished from the earth.[12] You may just as well say that the numerous churches of Galatia had no existence at the time when the apostle wrote to them : " O foolish Galatians, who hath bewitched you," that, " having begun in the Spirit, ye are now made perfect in the flesh ? " [13] For thus you would misrepresent that learned man, who (like the apostle) was sternly rebuking the slow of heart and the timid, for whom he was travailing in birth a second time, until Christ should be formed in them.[14] For who does not know that many persons of weak judgment were at that time deluded by ambiguous phrases, so that they thought that the Arians believed the same doctrines as they themselves held ; and that others, through fear, had yielded and feigned consent, not walking uprightly according to the truth of the gospel, to whom you would have denied that forgiveness which, when they had been turned from their error, was extended to them ? But in refusing such pardon, you prove yourselves wholly ignorant of the word of God. For read what Paul has recorded concerning Peter,[15] and what Cyprian has expressed as his view on the ground of that statement, and do not blame the compassion of the Church, which does not scatter the members of Christ when they are gathered together, but labours to gather His scattered members into one. It is true that those who then stood most resolute, and were able to understand the treacherous phrases used by the

---

[1] Ps. xlv. 11-16.
[2] 1 John ii. 19.
[3] John xxi. 17.
[4] John x. 16.
[5] Matt. vii. 14.
[6] Gen. xxii. 14.
[7] Matt. viii. 11.
[8] Tit. ii. 14; περιούσιος being translated by Augustin " *abundans*," where our version has " peculiar."
[9] Rev. vii. 9.

[10] ἐν σκοτομήνῃ, LXX.
[11] Ps. xi. 2.
[12] Vincentius had quoted from Hilary's work, *De Synodis adversum Arianos*, a sentence to the effect that, with the exception of a very small remnant, the ten provinces of Asia in which he was settled were truly ignorant of God.
[13] Gal. iii. 1, 3.
[14] Gal. iv. 19.
[15] Gal. ii. 11-21.

heretics, were few in number when compared with the rest; but some of them it is to be remembered were then bravely enduring sentence of banishment, and others were hiding themselves for safety in all parts of the world. And thus the Church, which is increasing throughout all nations, has been preserved as the Lord's wheat, and shall be preserved unto the end, yea, until all nations, even the barbarous tribes, are within its embrace. For it is the Church which the Son of man has sown as good seed, and of which He has foretold that it should grow among the tares until the harvest. For the field is the world, and the harvest is the end of time.[1]

32. Hilary, therefore, either was rebuking not the wheat, but the tares, in those ten provinces of Asia, or was addressing himself to the wheat, because it was endangered through some unfaithfulness, and spoke as one who thought that the rebuke would be useful in proportion to the vehemence with which it was given. For the canonical Scriptures contain examples of the same manner of rebuke in which what is intended for some is spoken as if it applied to all. Thus the apostle, when he says to the Corinthians, "How say some among you, that there is no resurrection of the dead?"[2] proves clearly that all of them were not such; but he bears witness that those who were such were not outside of their communion, but among them. And shortly after, lest those who were of a different opinion should be led astray by them, he gave this warning: "Be not deceived: evil communications corrupt good manners. Awake to righteousness, and sin not; for some have not the knowledge of God: I speak this to your shame."[3] But when he says, "Whereas there is among you envying and strife, and divisions, are ye not carnal, and walk as men?"[4] he speaks as if it applied to all, and you see how grave a charge he makes. Wherefore, if it were not that we read in the same epistle, "I thank my God always on your behalf, for the grace of God which is given you by Jesus Christ; that in everything ye are enriched by Him, in all utterance, and in all knowledge; even as the testimony of Christ was confirmed in you: so that ye come behind in no gift,"[5] we would think that all the Corinthians had been carnal and natural, not perceiving the things of the spirit of God,[6] fond of strife, and full of envy, and "walking as men." In like manner it is said, on the one hand, "the whole world lieth in wickedness,"[7] because of the tares which are throughout the whole world; and, on the other hand, Christ "is the propitiation for our sins, and not for ours only, but also for the sins of the whole world,"[8] because of the wheat which is throughout the whole world.

33. The love of many, however, waxes cold because of offences, which abound increasingly the more that, within the communion of the sacraments of Christ, there are gathered to the glory of His name even those who are wicked, and who persist in the obstinacy of error; whose separation, however, as chaff from the wheat, is to be effected only in the final purging of the Lord's threshing-floor.[9] These do not destroy those who are the Lord's wheat — few, indeed, when compared with the others, but in themselves a great multitude; they do not destroy the elect of God, who are to be gathered at the end of the world from the four winds, from the one end of heaven to the other.[10] For it is from the elect that the cry comes, "Help, Lord! for the godly man ceaseth, for the faithful fail from among the children of men;"[11] and it is of them that the Lord saith, "He that shall endure to the end (when iniquity shall abound), the same shall be saved."[12] Moreover, that the psalm quoted is the language not of one man, but of many, is shown by the following context: "Thou shalt keep us, O Lord; Thou shalt preserve us from this generation for ever."[13] On account of this abounding iniquity which the Lord foretold, it is said in another place: "When the Son of man cometh, shall He find faith on the earth?" This doubt expressed by Him who knoweth all things prefigured the doubts which in Him we entertain, when the Church, being often disappointed in many from whom much was expected, but who have proved very different from what they were supposed to be, is so alarmed in regard to her own members, that she is slow to believe good of any one. Nevertheless it would be wrong to cherish doubt that those whose faith He shall find on the earth are growing along with the tares throughout the whole field.

34. Therefore it is the same Church also which within the Lord's net is swimming along with the bad fishes, but is in heart and in life separated from them, and departs from them, that she may be presented to her Lord a "glorious Church, not having spot or wrinkle."[14] But the actual visible separation she looks for only on the sea-shore, i.e. at the end of the world, — meanwhile correcting as many as she can, and bearing with those whom she cannot correct; but she does not abandon the unity of the good because of the wickedness of those whom she finds incorrigible.

[1] Matt. xiii. 24–39.
[2] 1 Cor. xv. 12.
[3] 1 Cor. xv. 33, 34.
[4] 1 Cor. iii. 3.
[5] 1 Cor. i. 4–7.
[6] 1 Cor. ii. 14.
[7] 1 John v. 19.

[8] 1 John ii. 2.
[9] Matt. iii. 12.
[10] Matt. xxiv. 31.
[11] Ps. xii. 1.
[12] Matt. xxiv. 12, 13.
[13] Ps. xii. 7.
[14] Eph. v. 27.

Chap. x. — 35. Wherefore, my brother, refrain from gathering together against divine testimonies so many, so perspicuous, and so unchallenged, the calumnies which may be found in the writings of bishops either of our communion, as Hilary, or of the undivided Church itself in the age preceding the schism of Donatus, as Cyprian or Agrippinus ;[1] because, in the first place, this class of writings must be, so far as authority is concerned, distinguished from the canon of Scripture. For they are not read by us as if a testimony brought forward from them was such that it would be unlawful to hold any different opinion, for it may be that the opinions which they held were different from those to which truth demands our assent. For we are amongst those who do not reject what has been taught us even by an apostle : " If in anything ye be otherwise minded, God shall reveal even this unto you ; nevertheless, whereto we have already attained, let us walk by the same rule,"[2] — in that way, namely, which Christ is ; of which way the Psalmist thus speaks : " God be merciful unto us, and bless us, and cause His face to shine upon us : that Thy way may be known upon earth, Thy saving health among all nations."[3]

36. In the next place, if you are charmed by the authority of that bishop and illustrious martyr St. Cyprian, which we indeed regard, as I have said, as quite distinct from the authority of canonical Scripture, why are you not charmed by such things in him as these : that he maintained with loyalty, and defended in debate, the unity of the Church in the world and in all nations ; that he censured, as full of self-sufficiency and pride, those who wished to separate themselves as righteous from the Church, holding them up to ridicule for assuming to themselves that which the Lord did not concede even to apostles, — namely, the gathering of the tares before the harvest, — and for attempting to separate the chaff from the wheat, as if to them had been assigned the charge of removing the chaff and cleansing the threshing-floor ; that he proved that no man can be stained with guilt by the sins of others, thus sweeping away the only ground alleged by the authors of schism for their separation ; that in the very matter in regard to which he was of a different opinion from his colleagues, he did not decree that those who thought otherwise than he did should be condemned or excommunicated ; that even in his letter to Jubaianus[4] (which was read for the first time in the Council,[5] the authority of which you are wont to plead in defence of the practice of rebaptizing), although he admits that in time

past persons who had been baptized in other communions had been received into the Church without being a second time baptized, on which ground they were regarded by him as having had no baptism, nevertheless he considers the use and benefit of peace within the Church to be so great, that for its sake he holds that these persons (though in his judgment unbaptized) should not be excluded from office in the Church ?

37. And by this you will very readily perceive (for I know the acuteness of your mind) that your cause is completely subverted and annihilated. For if, as you suppose, the Church which had been spread abroad throughout the world perished through her admitting sinners to partake in her sacraments (and this is the ground alleged for your separation), it had wholly perished long before, — at the time, namely, when, as Cyprian says, men were admitted into it without baptism, — and thus Cyprian himself had no Church within which to be born ; and if so, how much more must this have been the case with one who, like Donatus, the author of your schism, and the father of your sect, belonged to a later age ! But if at that time, although persons were being admitted into the Church without baptism, the Church nevertheless remained in being, so as to give birth to Cyprian and afterwards to Donatus, it is manifest that the righteous are not defiled by the sins of other men when they participate with them in the sacraments. And thus you have no excuse by which you can wash away the guilt of the schism whereby you have gone forth from the unity of the Church ; and in you is fulfilled that saying of Holy Writ : " There is a generation that esteem themselves right, and have not cleansed themselves from the guilt of their going forth."[6]

38. The man who, out of regard to the sameness of the sacraments, does not presume to insist on the second administration of baptism even to heretics, is not, by thus avoiding Cyprian's error, placed on a level with Cyprian in merit, any more than the man who does not insist upon the Gentiles conforming to Jewish ceremonies is thereby placed on a level in merit with the Apostle Peter. In Peter's case, however, the record not only of his halting, but also of his correction, is contained in the canonical Scriptures ; whereas the statement that Cyprian entertained opinions at variance with those approved by the constitution and practice of the Church is found, not in canonical Scripture, but in his own writings, and in those of a Council ; and although it is not found in the same records that he corrected that opinion, it is nevertheless by no means an unreasonable supposition that he did correct it, and that this fact may perhaps

---

1 Agrippinus, successor of Cyprian in the see of Carthage.
2 Phil. iii. 15, 16.
3 Ps. lxvii. 1, 2.
4 See *Ante-Nicene Fathers*, Am. ed. vol. v. p. 379.
5 Held at Carthage, A.D. 256.

6 Prov. xxx. 12, ἔκγονον κακὸν δίκαιον ἑαυτὸν κρίνει, τὴν δ' ἔξοδον αὐτοῦ οὐκ ἀπένιψεν.

have been suppressed by those who were too much pleased with the error into which he fell, and were unwilling to lose the patronage of so great a name. At the same time, there are not wanting some who maintain that Cyprian never held the view ascribed to him, but that this was an unwarrantable forgery passed off by liars under his name. For it was impossible for the integrity and authenticity of the writings of any one bishop, however illustrious, to be secured and preserved as the canonical Scriptures are through translation into so many languages, and through the regular and continuous manner in which the Church has used them in public worship. Even in the face of this, some have been found forging many things under the names of the apostles. It is true, indeed, that they made such attempts in vain, because the text of canonical Scripture was so well attested, and so generally used and known; but this effort of an unholy boldness, which has not forborne to assail writings which are defended by the strength of such notoriety, has proved what it is capable of essaying against writings which are not established upon canonical authority.

39. We, however, do not deny that Cyprian held the views ascribed to him: first, because his style has a certain peculiarity of expression by which it may be recognised; and secondly, because in this case our cause rather than yours is proved victorious, and the pretext alleged for your schism — namely, that you might not be defiled by the sins of other men — is in the most simple manner exploded; since it is manifest from the letters of Cyprian that participation in the sacraments was allowed to sinful men, when those who, in your judgment (and as you will have it, in his judgment also), were unbaptized were as such admitted to the Church, and that nevertheless the Church did not perish, but remained in the dignity belonging to her nature as the Lord's wheat scattered throughout the world. And, therefore, if in your consternation you thus betake yourselves to Cyprian's authority as to a harbour of refuge, you see the rock against which your error dashes itself in this course; if, on the other hand, you do not venture to flee thither, you are wrecked without any struggle for escape.

40. Moreover, Cyprian either did not hold at all the opinions which you ascribe to him, or did subsequently correct his mistake by the rule of truth, or covered this blemish, as we may call it, upon his otherwise spotless mind by the abundance of his love, in his most amply defending the unity of the Church growing throughout the whole world, and in his most stedfastly holding the bond of peace; for it is written, "Charity [love] covereth a multitude of sins."[1] To this

was also added, that in him, as a most fruitful branch, the Father removed by the pruning-knife of suffering whatever may have remained in him requiring correction: "For every branch in me," saith the Lord, "that beareth fruit He purgeth, that it may bring forth more fruit."[2] And whence this care of him, if not because, continuing as a branch in the far-spreading vine, he did not forsake the root of unity? "For though he gave his body to be burned, if he had not charity, it would profit him nothing."[3]

41. Attend now a little while to the letters of Cyprian, that you may see how he proves the man to be inexcusable who desires ostensibly on the ground of his own righteousness to withdraw himself from the unity of the Church (which God promised and has fulfilled in all nations), and that you may more clearly apprehend the truth of the text quoted by me shortly before: "There is a generation that esteem themselves righteous, and have not cleansed themselves from the guilt of their going forth." In a letter which he wrote to Antonianus[4] he discusses a matter very closely akin to that which we are now debating; but it is better for us to give his very words: "Some of our predecessors," he says, "in the episcopal office in this province were of opinion that the peace of the Church should not be given to fornicators, and finally closed the door of repentance against those who had been guilty of adultery. They did not, however, withdraw themselves from fellowship with their colleagues in the episcopate; nor did they rend asunder the unity of the Catholic Church, by such harshness and obstinate perseverance in their censure as to separate themselves from the Church because others granted while they themselves refused to adulterers the peace of the Church. The bond of concord remaining unbroken, and the sacrament of the Church continuing undivided, each bishop arranges and orders his own conduct as one who shall give account of his procedure to his Lord." What say you to that, brother Vincentius? Surely you must see that this great man, this peace-loving bishop and dauntless martyr, made nothing more earnestly his care than to prevent the sundering of the bond of unity. You see him travailing in birth for the souls of men, not only that they might, when conceived, be born in Christ, but also that, when born, they might not perish through their being shaken out of their mother's bosom.

42. Now give attention, I pray you, further to this thing which he has mentioned in protesting against impious schismatics. If those who granted peace to adulterers, who repented of

---

[1] 1 Pet. iv. 8.
[2] John xv. 2.
[3] 1 Cor. xiii. 3.
[4] Letter LI. 21. *Ante-Nicene Fathers*, Am. ed. vol. v. p. 332.

their sin, shared the guilt of adulterers, were those who did not so act defiled by fellowship with them as colleagues in office? If, again, it was a right thing, as truth asserts and the Church maintains, that peace should be given to adulterers who repented of their sin, those who utterly closed against adulterers the door of reconciliation through repentance were unquestionably guilty of impiety in refusing healing to the members of Christ, in taking away the keys of the Church from those who knocked for admission, and in opposing with heartless cruelty God's most compassionate forbearance, which permitted them to live in order that, repenting, they might be healed by the sacrifice of a contrite spirit and broken heart. Nevertheless this their heartless error and impiety did not defile the others, compassionate and peace-loving men, when these shared with them in the Christian sacraments, and tolerated them within the net of unity, until the time when, brought to the shore, they should be separated from each other; or if this error and impiety of others did defile them, then the Church was already at that time destroyed, and there was no Church to give Cyprian birth. But if, as is beyond question, the Church continued in existence, it is also beyond question that no man in the unity of Christ can be stained by the guilt of the sins of other men if he be not consenting to the deeds of the wicked, and thus defiled by actual participation in their crimes, but only, for the sake of the fellowship of the good, tolerating the wicked, as the chaff which lies until the final purging of the Lord's threshing-floor. These things being so, where is the pretext for your schism? Are ye not an "evil generation, esteeming yourselves righteous, yet not washed from the guilt of your going forth" [from the Church]?

43. If, now, I were disposed to quote anything against you from the writings of Tychonius, a man of your communion, who has written rather in defence of the Church and against you than the reverse, in vain disowning the communion of African Christians as traditors (by which one thing Parmenianus silences him), what else can you say in reply than what Tychonius himself said of you as I have shortly before reminded you: "That which is according to our will is holy"?[1] For this Tychonius — a man, as I have said, of your communion — writes that a Council was held at Carthage[2] by two hundred and seventy of your bishops; in which Council, after seventy-five days of deliberation, all past decisions on the matter being set aside, a carefully revised resolution was published, to the effect that to those who were guilty of a heinous crime

as traditors, the privilege of communion should be granted as to blameless persons, if they refused to be baptized. He says further, that Deuterius of Macriana, a bishop of your party, added to the Church a whole crowd of traditors, without making any distinction between them and others, making the unity of the Church open to these traditors, in accordance with the decree of the Council held by these two hundred and seventy of your bishops, and that after that transaction Donatus continued unbroken his communion with the said Deuterius, and not only with him, but also with all the Mauritanian bishops for forty years, who, according to the statement of Tychonius, admitted the traditors to communion without insisting on their being rebaptized, up to the time of the persecution made by Macarius.

44. You will say, "What has that Tychonius to do with me?" It is true that Tychonius is the man whom Parmenianus checked by his reply, and effectually warned not to write such things; but he did not refute the statements themselves, but, as I have said above, silenced him by this one thing, that while saying such things concerning the Church which is diffused throughout the world, and while admitting that the faults of other men within its unity cannot defile one who is innocent, he nevertheless withdrew himself from the contagion of communion with African Christians because of their being traditors, and was an adherent of the party of Donatus. Parmenianus, indeed, might have said that Tychonius had in all these things spoken falsely; but, as Tychonius himself observes, many were still living at that time by whom these things might be proved to be most unquestionably true and generally known.

45. Of these things, however, I say no more: maintain, if you choose, that Tychonius spoke falsely; I bring you back to Cyprian, the authority which you yourself have quoted. If, according to his writings, every one in the unity of the Church is defiled by the sins of other members, then the Church had utterly perished before Cyprian's time, and all possibility of Cyprian's own existence (as a member of the Church) is taken away. If, however, the very thought of this is impiety, and it be beyond question that the Church continued in being, it follows that no one is defiled by the guilt of the sins of other men within the Catholic unity; and in vain do you, "an evil generation," maintain that you are righteous, when you are "not washed from the guilt of your going forth."

CHAP. XI. — 46. You will say, "Why then do you seek us? Why do you receive those whom you call heretics?" Mark how simple and short is my reply. We seek you because you are lost, that we may rejoice over you when found, as

---

[1] P. 387.
[2] This Council at Carthage is not elsewhere mentioned.

over you while lost we grieved. Again we call you heretics; but the name applies to you only up to the time of your being turned to the peace of the Catholic Church, and extricated from the errors by which you have been ensnared. For when you pass over to us, you entirely abandon the position you formerly occupied, so that, as heretics no longer, you pass over to us. You will say, "Then baptize me." I would, if you were not already baptized, or if you had received the baptism of Donatus, or of Rogatus only, and not of Christ. It is not the Christian sacraments, but the crime of schism, which makes you a heretic. The evil which has proceeded from yourself is not a reason for our denying the good that is permanent in you, but which you possess to your own harm if you have it not in that Church from which proceeds its power to do good. For from the Catholic Church are all the sacraments of the Lord, which you hold and administer in the same way as they were held and administered even before you went forth from her. The fact, however, that you are no longer in that Church from which proceeded the sacraments which you have, does not make it the less true that you still have them. We therefore do not change in you that wherein you are at one with ourselves, for in many things you are at one with us; and of such it is said, "For in many things they were with me:"[1] but we correct those things in which you are not with us, and we wish you to receive those things which you have not where you now are. You are at one with us in baptism, in creed, and in the other sacraments of the Lord. But in the spirit of unity and bond of peace, in a word, in the Catholic Church itself, you are not with us. If you receive these things, the others which you already have will then not begin to be yours, but begin to be of use to you. We do not therefore, as you think, receive your men of your party as still belonging to you, but in the act of receiving them we incorporate with ourselves those who forsake you that they may be received by us; and in order that they may belong to us, their first step is to renounce their connection with you. Nor do we compel into union with us those who industriously serve an error which we abhor; but our reason for wishing those men to be united to us is, that they may no longer be worthy of our abhorrence.

47. But you will say, "The Apostle Paul baptized after John."[2] Did he then baptize after a heretic? If you do presume to call that friend of the Bridegroom a heretic, and to say that he was not in the unity of the Church, I beg that you will put this in writing. But if you believe that it would be the height of folly to think or

to say so, it remains for your own wisdom to resolve the question why the Apostle Paul baptized after John. For if he baptized after one who was his equal, you ought all to baptize after one another. If after one who was greater than himself, you ought to baptize after Rogatus; if after one who was less than himself, Rogatus ought to have baptized after you those whom you, as a presbyter, had baptized. If, however, the baptism which is now administered is in all cases of equal value to those who receive it, however unequal in merit the persons may be by whom it is administered, because it is the baptism of Christ, not of those who administer the right, I think you must already perceive that Paul administered the baptism of Christ to certain persons because they had received the baptism of John only, and not of Christ; for it is expressly called the baptism of John, as the Divine Scripture bears witness in many passages, and as the Lord Himself calls it, saying: "The baptism of John, whence was it? from heaven, or of men?"[3] But the baptism which Peter administered was the baptism, not of Peter, but of Christ; that which Paul administered was the baptism, not of Paul, but of Christ; that which was administered by those who, in the apostle's time, preached Christ not sincerely, but of contention,[4] was not their own, but the baptism of Christ; and that which was administered by those who, in Cyprian's time, either by artful dishonesty obtained their possessions, or by usury, at exorbitant interest, increased them, was not their own baptism, but the baptism of Christ. And because it was of Christ, therefore, although there was very great disparity in the persons by whom it was administered, it was equally useful to those by whom it was received. For if the excellency of baptism in each case is according to the excellency of the person by whom one is baptized, it was wrong in the apostle to give thanks that he had baptized none of the Corinthians, but Crispus, and Gaius, and the house of Stephanas;[5] for the baptism of the converts in Corinth, if administered by himself, would have been so much more excellent as Paul himself was more excellent than other men. Lastly, when he says, "I have planted, and Apollos watered,"[6] he seems to intimate that he had preached the gospel, and that Apollos had baptized. Is Apollos better than John? Why then did he, who baptized after John, not baptize after Apollos? Surely because, in the one case, the baptism, by whomsoever administered, was the baptism of Christ; and in the other case, by whomsoever admin-

[1] Ps. lv. 18, Septuagint.
[2] Acts xix. 5.
[3] Matt. xxi. 25.
[4] Phil. i. 15, 17.
[5] 1 Cor. i. 14.
[6] 1 Cor. iii. 6.

istered, it was, although preparing the way for Christ, only the baptism of John.

48. It seems to you an odious thing to say that baptism was given to some after John had baptized them, and yet that baptism is not to be given to men after heretics have baptized them; but it may be said with equal justice to be an odious thing that baptism was given to some after John had baptized them, and yet that baptism is not to be given to men after intemperate persons have baptized them. I name this sin of intemperance rather than others, because those in whom it reigns are not able to hide it: and yet what man, even though he be blind, does not know how many addicted to this vice are to be found everywhere? And yet among the works of the flesh, of which it is said that they who do them shall not inherit the kingdom of God, the apostle places this in an enumeration in which heresies also are specified: " Now the works of the flesh," he says, " are manifest, which are these: adultery, fornication, unclean-ness, lasciviousness, idolatry, witchcraft, hatred, variance, emulations, wrath, strife, seditions, heresies, envyings, murders, drunkenness, revel-lings, and such like; of the which I tell you before, as I have also told you in time past, that they who do such things shall not inherit the kingdom of God." ¹ Baptism, therefore, although it was administered after John, is not administered after a heretic, on the very same principle according to which, though adminis-tered after John, it is not administered after an intemperate man: for both heresies and drunken-ness are among the works which exclude those who do them from inheriting the kingdom of God. Does it not seem to you as if it were a thing intolerably unseemly, that although bap-tism was repeated after it had been administered by him who, not even moderately drinking wine, but wholly refraining from its use, prepared the way for the kingdom of God, and yet that it should not be repeated after being administered by an intemperate man, who shall not inherit the kingdom of God? What can be said in answer to this, but that the one was the baptism of John, after which the apostle administered the baptism of Christ; and that the other, adminis-tered by an intemperate man, was the baptism of Christ? Between John Baptist and an in-temperate man there is a great difference, as of opposites; between the baptism of Christ and the baptism of John there is no contrariety, but a great difference. Between the apostle and an intemperate man there is a great difference; but there is none between the baptism of Christ administered by an apostle, and the baptism of Christ administered by an intemperate man. In like manner, between John and a heretic there is a great difference, as of opposites; and between the baptism of John and the baptism of Christ which a heretic administers there is no contrari-ety, but there is a great difference. But between the baptism of Christ which an apostle adminis-ters, and the baptism of Christ which a heretic administers, there is no difference. For the form of the sacrament is acknowledged to be the same even when there is a great difference in point of worth between the men by whom it is administered.

49. But pardon me, for I have made a mis-take in wishing to convince you by arguing from the case of an intemperate man administering baptism; for I had forgotten that I am dealing with a Rogatist, not with one bearing the wider name of Donatist. For among your colleagues who are so few, and in the whole number of your clergy, perhaps you cannot find one addicted to this vice. For you are persons who hold that the name Catholic is given to the faith not be-cause communion of those who hold it embraces the whole world, but because they observe the whole of the Divine precepts and the whole of the sacraments; you are the persons in whom alone the Son of man when He cometh shall find faith, when on the earth He shall find no faith, forasmuch as you are not earth and on the earth, but heavenly and dwelling in heaven! Do you not fear, or do you not observe that " God resisteth the proud, but giveth grace to the hum-ble "? ² Does not that very passage in the Gos-pel startle you, in which the Lord saith, " When the Son of man cometh, shall He find faith in the earth?" ³ Immediately thereafter, as if foreseeing that some would proudly arrogate to themselves the possession of this faith, He spake to some who trusted in themselves that they were righteous, and despised others, the parable of the two men who went up to the temple to pray, the one a Pharisee, and the other a publi-can. The words which follow I leave for your-self to consider and to answer. Nevertheless examine more minutely your small sect, to see whether not so much as one who administers baptism is an intemperate man. For so wide-spread is the havoc wrought among souls by this plague, that I am greatly surprised if it has not reached even your infinitesimal flock, although it is your boast that already, before the coming of Christ, the one good Shepherd, you have separated between the sheep and the goats.

CHAP. XII. — 50. Listen to the testimony which through me is addressed to you by those who are the Lord's wheat, suffering meanwhile until the final winnowing,⁴ among the chaff in

---

¹ Gal. v. 19-21.

² Jas. iv. 6.
³ Luke xviii. 8.
⁴ Matt. iii. 12.

the Lord's threshing-floor, *i.e.* throughout the whole world, because "God hath called the earth from the rising of the sun unto the going down thereof," [1] and throughout the same wide field the "children praise Him." [2] We disapprove of every one who, taking advantage of this imperial edict, persecutes you, not with loving concern for your correction, but with the malice of an enemy. Moreover, although, since every earthly possession can be rightly retained only on the ground either of divine right, according to which all things belong to the righteous, or of human right, which is in the jurisdiction of the kings of the earth, you are mistaken in calling those things yours which you do not possess as righteous persons, and which you have forfeited by the laws of earthly sovereigns, and plead in vain, "We have laboured to gather them," seeing that you may read what is written, "The wealth of the sinner is laid up for the just;" [3] nevertheless we disapprove of any one who, availing himself of this law which the kings of the earth, doing homage to Christ, have published in order to correct your impiety, covetously seeks to possess himself of your property. Also we disapprove of any one who, on the ground not of justice, but of avarice, seizes and retains the provision pertaining to the poor, or the chapels [4] in which you meet for worship, which you once occupied in the name of the Church, and which are by all means the rightful property only of that Church which is the true Church of Christ. We disapprove of any one who receives a person that has been expelled by you for some disgraceful action or crime, on the same terms on which those are received who have lived among you chargeable with no other crime beyond the error through which you are separated from us. But these are things which you cannot easily prove; and although you can prove them, we bear with some whom we are unable to correct or even to punish; and we do not quit the Lord's threshing-floor because of the chaff which is there, nor break the Lord's net because of bad fishes enclosed therein, nor desert the Lord's flock because of goats which are to be in the end separated from it, nor go forth from the Lord's house because in it there are vessels destined to dishonour.

CHAP. XIII. — 51. But, my brother, if you forbear seeking the empty honour which comes from men, and despise the reproach of fools, who will be ready to say, "Why do you now destroy what you once laboured to build up?" it seems to me to be beyond doubt that you will now pass over to the Church which I perceive that you acknowledge to be the true Church: the proofs of which sentiment on your part I find at hand. For in the beginning of your letter which I am now answering you have these words: "I knew you, my excellent friend, as a man devoted to peace and uprightness, when you were still far removed from the Christian faith, and were in these earlier days occupied with literary pursuits; but since your conversion at a more recent time to the Christian faith, you give your time and labour, as I am informed by the statements of many persons, to theological controversies." [5] These words are undoubtedly your own, if you were the person who sent me that letter. Seeing, therefore, that you confess that I have been converted to the Christian faith, although I have not been converted to the sect of the Donatists or of the Rogatists, you unquestionably uphold the truth that beyond the pale of Rogatists and Donatists the Christian faith exists. This faith therefore is, as we say, spread abroad throughout all nations, which are according to God's testimony blessed in the seed of Abraham. [6] Why therefore do you still hesitate to adopt what you perceive to be true, unless it be that you are humbled because at some former time you did not perceive what you now see, or maintained some different view, and so, while ashamed to correct an error, are not ashamed (where shame would be much more reasonable) of remaining wilfully in error?

52. Such conduct the Scripture has not passed over in silence; for we read, "There is a shame which bringeth sin, and there is a shame which is graceful and glorious." [7] Shame brings sin, when through its influence any one forbears from changing a wicked opinion, lest he be supposed to be fickle, or be held as by his own judgment convicted of having been long in error: such persons descend into the pit alive, that is, conscious of their perdition; whose future doom the death of Dathan and Abiram and Korah, swallowed up by the opening earth, long ago prefigured. [8] But shame is graceful and glorious when one blushes for his own sin, and by repentance is changed to something better, which you are reluctant to do because overpowered by that false and fatal shame, fearing lest by men who know not whereof they affirm, that sentence of the apostle may be quoted against you: "If I build again the things which I destroyed, I make myself a transgressor." [9] If, however, this sentence admitted of application to those who, after being corrected, preach the truth which in their perversity they opposed, it might have been said at first against Paul himself, in regard to whom

---

[1] Ps. l. 1.
[2] Ps cxiii. 1–3.
[3] Prov. xiii. 22.
[4] *Basilicæ.*

[5] *Disputationibus legalibus.*
[6] Gen. xxii. 18.
[7] Ecclus. iv. 21.
[8] Num. xvi. 31–33.
[9] Gal. ii. 18.

the churches of Christ glorified God when they heard that he now "preached the faith which once he destroyed." [1]

53. Do not, however, imagine that one can pass from error to truth, or from any sin, be it great or small, to the correction of his sin, without giving some proof of his repentance. It is, however, an error of intolerable impertinence for men to blame the Church, which is proved by so many Divine testimonies to be the Church of Christ, for dealing in one way with those who forsake her, receiving them back on condition of correcting this fault by some acknowledgment of their repentance, and in another way with those who never were within her pale, and are receiving welcome to her peace for the first time; her method being to humble the former more fully, and to receive the latter upon easier terms, cherishing affection for both, and ministering with a mother's love to the health of both.

You have here perhaps a longer letter than you desired. It would have been much shorter if in my reply I had been thinking of you alone; but as it is, even though it should be of no use to yourself, I do not think that it can fail to be of use to those who shall take pains to read it in the fear of God, and without respect of persons. Amen.

LETTER XCIV.

(A.D. 408.)

A letter to Augustin from Paulinus and Therasia, the substance of which is sufficiently stated in the next letter, which contains the reply of Augustin to his friend's questions concerning the present life, the nature of the bodies of the blessed in the life to come, and the functions of the members of the body after the resurrection.

LETTER XCV.

(A.D. 408.)

TO BROTHER PAULINUS AND SISTER THERASIA, MOST BELOVED AND SINCERE, SAINTS WORTHY OF AFFECTION AND VENERATION, FELLOW-DISCIPLES WITH HIMSELF UNDER THE LORD JESUS AS MASTER, AUGUSTIN SENDS GREETING IN THE LORD.

1. When brethren most closely united to us, towards whom along with us you are accustomed both to cherish and to express sentiments of regard which we all cordially reciprocate, have frequent occasions of visiting you, this benefit is one by which we are comforted under evil rather than made to rejoice in increase of good. For we strive to the utmost of our power to avoid the causes and emergencies which necessitate their journeys, and yet, — I know not how, un-

less it be as just retribution, — they cannot be dispensed with : but when they return to us and see us, that word of Scripture is fulfilled in our experience : "In the multitude of my thoughts within me, Thy comforts delight my soul." [2] Accordingly, when you learn from our brother Possidius himself how sad is the occasion which has compelled him to go to Italy,[3] you will know how true the remarks I have made are in regard to the joy which he has in meeting you; and yet, if any of us should cross the sea for the one purpose of enjoying a meeting with you, what more cogent or worthy reason could be found? This, however, would not be compatible with those obligations by which we are bound to minister to those who are languid through infirmity, and not to withdraw our bodily presence from them, unless their malady, assuming a dangerous form, makes such departure imperative. Whether in these things we are receiving chastening or judgment I know not; but this I know, that He is not dealing with us according to our sins, nor requiting us according to our iniquities,[4] who mingles so great comfort with our tribulation, and who, by remedies which fill us with wonder, secures that we shall not love the world, and shall not by it be made to fall away.

2. I asked in a former letter your opinion as to the nature of the future life of the saints; but you have said in your reply that we have still much to study concerning our condition in this present life, and you do well, except in this, that you have expressed your desire to learn from me that of which you are either equally ignorant or equally well-informed with myself, or rather, of which you know much more perhaps than I do; for you have said with perfect truth, that before we meet the dissolution of this mortal body, we must die, in a gospel sense, by a voluntary departure, withdrawing ourselves, not by death, but by deliberate resolution, from the life of this world. This course is a simple one, and is beset with no waves of uncertainty, because we are of opinion that we ought so to live in this mortal life that we may be in some measure fitted for immortality. The whole question, however, which, when discussed and investigated, perplexes men like myself, is this — how we ought to live among or for the welfare of those who have not yet learned to live by dying, not in the dissolution of the body, but by turning themselves with a certain mental resolution away from the attractions of mere natural things. For in most cases, it seems to us that unless we in some small degree conform to them in regard to those very things from which we desire to see

---

[1] Gal. i. 23, 24.

[2] Ps. xciv. 19.
[3] Possidius, bishop of Calama, was going to Rome to complain of the outrage of the Pagans of Calama, described in Letter XCI. sec. 8, p. 378.
[4] Ps. ciii. 10.

them delivered, we shall not succeed in doing them any good. And when we do thus conform, a pleasure in such things steals upon ourselves, so that often we are pleased to speak and to listen to frivolous things, and not only to smile at them, but even to be completely overcome with laughter: thus burdening our souls with feelings which cleave to the dust, or even to the mire of this world, we experience greater difficulty and reluctance in raising ourselves to God that by dying a gospel-death we may live a gospel-life. And whensoever this state of mind is reached, immediately thereupon will follow the commendation, "Well done! well done!" not from men, for no man perceives in another the mental act by which divine things are apprehended, but in a certain inward silence there sounds I know not whence, "Well done! well done!" Because of this kind of temptation, the great apostle confesses that he was buffeted by the angel.[1] Behold whence it comes that our whole life on earth is a temptation; for man is tempted even in that thing in which he is being conformed so far as he can be to the likeness of the heavenly life.

3. What shall I say as to the infliction or remission of punishment, in cases in which we have no other desire than to forward the spiritual welfare of those in regard to whom we judge that they ought or ought not to be punished? Also, if we consider not only the nature and magnitude of faults, but also what each may be able or unable to bear according to his strength of mind, how deep and dark a question it is to adjust the amount of punishment so as to prevent the person who receives it not only from getting no good, but also from suffering loss thereby! Besides, I know not whether a greater number have been improved or made worse when alarmed under threats of such punishment at the hands of men as is an object of fear. What, then, is the path of duty, seeing that it often happens that if you inflict punishment on one he goes to destruction; whereas, if you leave him unpunished, another is destroyed? I confess that I make mistakes daily in regard to this, and that I know not when and how to observe the rule of Scripture: "Them that sin rebuke before all, that others may fear;"[2] and that other rule, "Tell him his fault between thee and him alone;"[3] and the rule, "Judge nothing before the time;"[4] "Judge not, that ye be not judged"[5] (in which command the Lord has not added the words, "before the time"); and this saying of Scripture, "Who art thou that judgest another man's servant? to his own master he

standeth or falleth: yea, he shall be holden up, for God is able to make him stand;"[6] by which words he makes it plain that he is speaking of those who are within the Church; yet, on the other hand, he commands them to be judged when he says, "What have I to do to judge them also that are without? do not ye judge them that are within? therefore put away from among yourselves that wicked person."[7] But when this is necessary, how much care and fear is occasioned by the question to what extent it should be done, lest that happen which, in his second epistle to them, the apostle is found admonishing these persons to beware of in that very example, saying, "lest, perhaps, such an one should be swallowed up with overmuch sorrow;" adding, in order to prevent men from thinking this a thing not calling for anxious care, "lest Satan should get an advantage of us; for we are not ignorant of his devices."[8] What trembling we feel in all these things, my brother Paulinus, O holy man of God! what trembling, what darkness! May we not think that with reference to these things it was said, "Fearfulness and trembling are come upon me, and horror hath overwhelmed me. And I said, Oh that I had wings like a dove! for then would I fly away, and be at rest. Lo, then would I wander far off, and remain in the wilderness." And yet even in the wilderness perchance he still experienced it; for he adds, "I waited for Him who should deliver me from weakness and from tempest."[9] Truly, therefore, is the life of man upon the earth a life of temptation.[10]

4. Moreover, as to the oracles of God, is it not true that they are lightly touched rather than grasped and handled by us, seeing that in by far the greater part of them we do not already possess opinions definite and ascertained, but are rather inquiring what our opinion ought to be? And this caution, though attended with abundant disquietude, is much better than the rashness of dogmatic assertion. Also, if a man is not carnally minded (which the apostle says is death), will he not be a great cause of offence to those who are still carnally minded, in many parts of Scripture in the exposition of which to say what you believe is most perilous, and to refrain from saying it is most grievous, and to say something else than what you believe is most pernicious? Nay more, when in the discourses or writings of those who are within the Church we find some things censurable, and do not conceal our disapprobation (supposing such correction to be according to the freedom of brotherly love), how great a sin is committed against us

---

[1] 2 Cor. xii. 7.
[2] 1 Tim. v. 20.
[3] Matt. xviii. 15.
[4] 1 Cor. iv. 5.
[5] Matt. vii. 1.

[6] Rom. xiv. 4.
[7] 1 Cor. v. 12, 13.
[8] 2 Cor. ii. 7, 11.
[9] Ps. lv. 5-8, as given in the LXX.
[10] Job vii. 1.

when we are suspected of being actuated in this by envy and not by goodwill! and how much do we sin against others, when we in like manner impute to those who find fault with our opinions a desire rather to wound than to correct us! Verily, there arise usually from this cause bitter enmities even between persons bound to each other by the greatest affection and intimacy, when, "thinking of men above that which is written, any one is puffed up for one against another;"[1] and while they bite and devour one another, "there is reason to fear lest they be consumed one of another."[2] Therefore, "Oh that I had wings like a dove! for then would I fly away, and be at rest."[3] For whether it be that the dangers by which one is beset seem to him greater than those of which he has no experience, or that my impressions are correct, I cannot help thinking that any amount of weakness and of tempest in the wilderness would be more easily borne than the things which we feel or fear in the busy world.

5. I therefore greatly approve of your saying that we should make the state in which men stand, or rather the course which they run, in this present life, the theme of our discussion. I add as another reason for our giving this subject the preference, that the finding and following of the course itself must come before our finding and possessing that towards which it leads. When, therefore, I asked your views on this, I acted as if, through holding and observing carefully the right rule of this life, we were already free from disquietude concerning its course, although I feel in so many things, and especially in those which I have mentioned, that I toil in the midst of very great dangers. Nevertheless, forasmuch as the cause of all this ignorance and embarrassment appears to me to be that, in the midst of a great variety of manners and of minds having inclinations and infirmities hidden altogether from our sight, we seek the interest of those who are citizens and subjects, not of Rome which is on earth, but of Jerusalem which is in heaven, it seemed to me more agreeable to converse with you about what we shall be, than about what we now are. For although we do not know the blessings which are to be enjoyed yonder, of one thing at least we are assured, and it is not a small thing, that yonder the evils which we experience here shall have no place.

6. Wherefore, as to the ordering of this present life in the way which we must follow in order to the attainment of eternal life, I know that our carnal appetites must be held in check, only so much concession being made to the gratification of the bodily senses as suffices for the support

of this life and the active discharge of its duties, and that all the vexations of this life which come upon us in connection with the truth of God, and the eternal welfare of ourselves or of our neighbours, must be borne with patience and fortitude. I know also that with all the zeal of love we should seek the good of our neighbour, that he may rightly spend the present life so as to obtain life eternal. I know also that we ought to prefer spiritual to carnal, immutable to mutable things, and that all this a man is so much more or less enabled to do, according as he is more or less helped by the grace of God through Jesus Christ our Lord. But I do not know the reason why one or another is more or less helped or not helped by that grace; this only I know, that God does this with perfect justice, and for reasons which to Himself are known as sufficient. In regard, however, to the things which I have mentioned above, as to the way in which we ought to live amongst men, if anything has become known to you through experience or meditation, I beseech you to give me instruction. And if these things perplex you not less than myself, make them the subject of conference with some judicious spiritual physician, whom you may find either where you reside, or in Rome, when you make your annual visit to the city, and thereafter write to me whatever the Lord may reveal to you through his instructions, or to you and him together when engaged in conversation on the subject.

7. As to the resurrection of the body, and the future offices of its members in the incorruptible and immortal state, since you have, in return for the questions which I put to you, inquired my views on these matters, listen to a brief statement which, if it be not sufficient, may afterwards, with the Lord's help, be amplified by fuller discussion. It is to be held most firmly, as a doctrine in regard to which the testimony of Holy Scripture is true and unmistakable, that these visible and earthly bodies which are now called natural,[4] shall, in the resurrection of the faithful and just, be spiritual bodies. At the same time, I do not know how the quality of a spiritual body can be comprehended or stated by us, seeing that it lies beyond the range of our experience. There shall be, assuredly, in such bodies no corruption, and therefore they shall not require the perishable nourishment which is now necessary; yet though unnecessary, it will not be impossible for them at their pleasure to take and actually consume food; otherwise it would not have been taken after His resurrection by the Lord, who has given us such an example of the resurrection of the body, that the apostle argues from it: "If the dead rise not, then is

---

[1] 1 Cor. iv. 6.
[2] Gal. v. 15.
[3] Ps. lv. 6.

[4] *Animalia*, 1 Cor. xv. 34.

not Christ raised." [1] But He, when He appeared to His disciples, having all His members, and using them according to their functions, also pointed out to them the places where His wounds had been, regarding which I have always supposed that they were the scars, not the wounds themselves, and that they were there, not of necessity, but according to His free exercise of power. He gave at that time the clearest evidence of the ease with which He exercised this power, both by showing Himself in another form to the two disciples, and by His appearing, not as a spirit, but in His true body, to the disciples in the upper chamber, although the doors were shut. [2]

8. From this arises the question as to angels, whether they have bodies adapted to their duties and their swift motions from place to place, or are only spirits? For if we say that they have bodies, we are met by the passage : " He maketh His angels spirits ; " [3] and if we say that they have not bodies, a still greater difficulty meets us in explaining how, if they are without bodily form, it is written that they appeared to the bodily senses of men, accepted offers of hospitality, permitted their feet to be washed, and used the meat and drink which was provided for them. [4] For it seems to involve us in less difficulty, if we suppose that the angels are there called spirits in the same manner as men are called souls, e.g. in the statement that so many souls (not signifying that they had not bodies also) went down with Jacob into Egypt, [5] than if we suppose that, without bodily form, all these things were done by angels. Again, a certain definite height is named in the Apocalypse as the stature of an angel, in dimensions which could apply only to bodies, proving that that which appeared to the eyes of men is to be explained, not as an illusion, but as resulting from the power which we have spoken of as easily put forth by spiritual bodies. But whether angels have bodies or not, and whether or not any one be able to show how without bodies they could do all these things, it is nevertheless certain, that in that city of the holy in which those of our race who have been redeemed by Christ shall be united for ever to thousands of angels, voices proceeding from organs of speech shall furnish expression to the thoughts of minds in which nothing is hidden ; for in that divine fellowship it will not be possible for any thought in one to remain concealed from another, but there shall be complete harmony and oneness of heart in the praise of God, and this shall find utterance not only from the spirit, but through the spiritual

body as its instrument ; this, at least, is what I believe.

9. Meanwhile, if you have already found or can learn from other teachers anything more fully agreeing with the truth than this, I am most eagerly longing to be instructed therein by you. Study carefully, if you please, my letter, in regard to which, as you pled in excuse for your very hurried reply the haste of the deacon who brought it to me, I do not make any complaint, but rather remind you of it, in order that what was then omitted in your answer may now be supplied. Look over it again, and observe what I wished to learn from you, both regarding your opinion concerning Christian retirement as a means to the acquisition and discussion of the truths of Christian wisdom, and regarding that retirement in which I supposed that you had found leisure, but in which it is reported to me that you are engrossed with occupation to an incredible extent.

May you, in whom the holy God has given us great joy and consolation, live mindful of us, and in true felicity. (*This sentence is added by another hand.*)

LETTER XCVI.

(A.D. 408.)

TO OLYMPIUS, MY LORD GREATLY BELOVED, AND MY SON WORTHY OF HONOUR AND REGARD AS A MEMBER OF CHRIST, AUGUSTIN SENDS GREETING.

1. Whatever your rank may be in connection with the course of this world, I have the greatest confidence in addressing you as my much-loved, true-hearted Christian fellow-servant Olympius. For I know that this name, in your esteem, excels all other glorious and lofty titles. Reports have indeed reached me that you have obtained some promotion in worldly honour, but no information confirming the truth of the rumour had come to me up to the time when this opportunity of writing to you occurred. Since, however, I know that you have learned from the Lord not to mind high things, but to condescend to those who are lightly esteemed by men, whatever the pinnacle to which you may have been raised, we take for granted, my lord greatly beloved, and son worthy of honour and regard as a member of Christ, that you will still make a letter from me welcome, just as you were wont to do. And as to your worldly prosperity, I do not doubt that you will wisely use it for your eternal gain ; so that the greater the influence which you acquire in the commonwealth on this earth, the more will you devote yourself to the interests of the heavenly city to which you owe your birth in Christ, forasmuch as this shall be more abundantly repaid to you in the land of the living,

---

[1] 1 Cor. xv. 16.
[2] Luke xxiv. 15–43; John xx. 14–29; Mark xvi. 12, 14.
[3] Ps. civ. 4 and Heb. i. 7.
[4] Gen. xviii. 2–9 and xix. 1–3.
[5] Gen. xlvi. 27.

and in the true peace which yields sure and endless joys.[1]

2. I again commend to your kind consideration the petition of my brother and colleague Boniface, in the hope that what could not be done before may be in your power now. He might perhaps, indeed, legally retain, without any further difficulty, that which his predecessor had acquired, though under another name than his own, and which he had begun to possess in name of the church; but we do not wish, since his predecessor was in debt to the public exchequer, to have this burden upon our conscience. For that act of fraud was none the less truly fraud because perpetrated at the expense of the public revenue. The same Paul (the predecessor of Boniface), when he was made bishop, being about to surrender all his effects because of the accumulated burden of arrears due to the public exchequer, having secured payment of a bond by which a certain sum of money was due to him, bought with it, as if for the church, in the name of a family then very powerful, these few fields by the produce of which he might support himself, in order that, in respect to these also, after his old practice, he might escape annoyance at the hands of the collectors of the revenue, although he was paying no tax. Boniface, however, when ordained over the same church, on his death, hesitated to take the fields which he had thus held; and although he might have contented himself with asking from the emperor no more than a remission of the fiscal arrears which his predecessor had incurred on this small property, he preferred to confess without reserve that Paul had bought the property at an auction with money of his own, at a time when he was bankrupt as a debtor to the public revenue, so that now the Church may, if possible, obtain possession of this, not through the secret fraud of her bishop, but by an open act of the Christian emperor's liberality. And if this be impossible, the servants of God prefer to bear the hardship of want, rather than obtain the supply of that which they require under reproaches of conscience for dishonourable dealing.

3. I beg you to condescend to give your support to this petition, because he has resolved not to bring forward the decision in his favour which was formerly obtained, lest it should preclude him from the liberty of making a second application; for the answer then given fell short of what he desired. And now, since you are of the same kindly disposition that you formerly were, but possessed of greater influence, I do not despair of this being easily granted by the

Lord's help, in consideration of your claims on the emperor; and if even you were to ask the gift of the property in your own name, and present it to the church of which I have spoken, who would find fault with your request; nay, rather, who would not commend it, as dictated not by personal covetousness, but by Christian piety? May the mercy of the Lord our God shield you, and make you more and more happy in Christ, my lord and son.

LETTER XCVII.

(A.D. 408.)

TO OLYMPIUS, MY EXCELLENT AND JUSTLY DISTINGUISHED LORD, AND MY SON WORTHY OF MUCH HONOUR IN CHRIST, AUGUSTIN SENDS GREETING IN THE LORD.

1. Although, when we heard recently of your having obtained merited promotion to the highest rank, we felt persuaded, however uncertain we still were in some degree as to the truth of the report, that towards the Church of which we rejoice to know that you are truly a son, there was no other feeling in your mind than that which you have now made patent to us in your letter, nevertheless, having now read that letter in which you have been pleased of your own accord to send to us, when we were full of backwardness and diffidence, a most gracious exhortation to use our humble efforts in pointing out to you how the Lord, by whose gift you are thus powerful, may from time to time, by means of your pious obedience, bring assistance to His Church, we write to you with the more abundant confidence, my excellent and justly distinguished lord, and my son worthy of much honour in Christ.

2. Many brethren, indeed, holy men who are my colleagues, have, by reason of the troubles of the church here, gone — I might almost say as fugitives — to the emperor's most illustrious court; and these brethren you may have already seen, or may have received from Rome their letters, in connection with their respective occasions of appeal. I have not had it in my power to consult them before writing; nevertheless, I was unwilling to miss the opportunity of sending a letter by the bearer, my brother and fellow-presbyter, who has been compelled, though in mid-winter, to make the best of his way into those parts, under pressing necessity, in order to save the life of a fellow-citizen. I write, therefore, to salute you, and to charge you by the love which you have in Christ Jesus our Lord, to see that your good work be hastened on with the utmost diligence, in order that the enemies of the Church may know that those laws concerning the demolition of idols and the correction of heretics which were sent into Africa

---

[1] This Olympius was appointed in 408 (A.D.) to the office of highest authority in the court of Honorius (magister officiorum), in room of Stilicho, who was put to death at Ravenna on account of suspected complicity with the authors of the sedition which threatened the life of the emperor at Pavia.

while Stilicho yet lived, were framed by the desire of our most pious and faithful emperor; for they either cunningly boast, or unwillingly imagine, that this was done without his knowledge, or against his will, and thus they render the minds of the ignorant full of seditious violence, and excite them to dangerous and vehement enmity against us.

3. I do not doubt that, in submitting this in the way of petition or respectful suggestion to the consideration of your Excellency, I act agreeably to the wishes of all my colleagues throughout Africa; and I think that it is your duty to take measures, as could be easily done, on whatever opportunity may first arise, to make it understood by these vain men (whose salvation we seek, although they resist us), that it was to the care, not of Stilicho, but of the son of Theodosius, that those laws which have been sent into Africa for the defence of the Church of Christ owed their promulgation. On account of these things, then, the presbyter whom I have mentioned already, the bearer of this letter, who is from the district of Milevi, was ordered by his bishop, the venerable Severus, who joins me in cordial salutations to you, whose love we esteem most genuine, to pass through Hippo-regius, where I am; because, when we happened to meet together in time of serious tribulation and distress to the Church, we sought an opportunity of writing to your Highness, but found none. I had indeed already sent one letter in regard to the business of our holy brother and colleague Boniface, bishop of Cataqua; but the heavier calamities destined to cause us greater agitation had not then befallen us, regarding which, and the means whereby something may be done with the best counsel for their prevention or punishment, according to the method of Christ, the bishops who have sailed hence on that errand will be able more conveniently to confer with you, in whose cordial goodwill towards us we rejoice, inasmuch as they are able to report to you something which has been, so far as limited time permitted, the result of careful and united consultation. But as to this other matter, namely, that the province be made to know how the mind of our most gracious and religious emperor stands towards the Church, I recommend, nay, I beg, beseech, and implore you, to take care that no time be lost, but that its accomplishment be hastened, even before you see the bishops who have gone from us, so soon as shall be possible for you, in the exercise of your most eminent vigilance on behalf of the members of Christ who are now in circumstances of the utmost danger; for the Lord has provided no small consolation for us under these trials, seeing that it has pleased Him to put much more now than formerly in your power, although we were already

filled with joy by the number and the magnitude of your good offices.

4. We rejoice much in the firm and stedfast faith of some, and these not few in number, who by means of these laws have been converted to the Christian religion, or from schism to Catholic peace, for whose eternal welfare we are glad to run the risk of forfeiting temporal welfare. For on this account especially we now have to endure at the hands of men, exceedingly and obdurately perverse, more grievous assaults of enmity, which some of them, along with us, bear most patiently; but we are in very great fear because of their weakness, until they learn, and are enabled by the help of the Lord's most compassionate grace, to despise with more abundant strength of spirit the present world and man's short day. May it please your Highness to deliver the letter of instructions which I have sent to my brethren the bishops when they come, if, as I suppose, they have not yet reached you. For we have such confidence in the unfeigned devotion of your heart, that with the Lord's help we desire to have you not only giving us your assistance, but also participating in our consultations.

LETTER XCVIII.

(A.D. 408.)

TO BONIFACE, HIS COLLEAGUE IN THE EPISCOPAL OFFICE, AUGUSTIN SENDS GREETING IN THE LORD.

1. You ask me to state "whether parents do harm to their baptized infant children, when they attempt to heal them in time of sickness by sacrifices to the false gods of the heathen." Also, "if they do thereby no harm to their children, how can any advantage come to these children at their baptism, through the faith of parents whose departure from the faith does them no harm?" To which I reply, that in the holy union of the parts of the body of Christ, so great is the virtue of that sacrament, namely, of baptism, which brings salvation, that so soon as he who owed his first birth to others, acting under the impulse of natural instincts, has been made partaker of the second birth by others, acting under the impulse of spiritual desires, he cannot be thenceforward held under the bond of that sin in another to which he does not with his own will consent. "Both the soul of the father is mine," saith the Lord, "and the soul of the son is mine: the soul that sinneth, it shall die;"[1] but he does not sin on whose behalf his parents or any other one resort, without his knowledge, to the impiety of worshipping heathen deities. That bond of guilt which was to be

---

[1] Ezek. xviii. 4.

cancelled by the grace of this sacrament he derived from Adam, for this reason, that at the time of Adam's sin he was not yet a soul having a separate life, *i.e.* another soul regarding which it could be said, "both the soul of the father is mine, and the soul of the son is mine." Therefore now, when the man has a personal, separate existence, being thereby made distinct from his parents, he is not held responsible for that sin in another which is performed without his consent. In the former case, he derived guilt from another, because, at the time when the guilt which he has derived was incurred, he was one with the person from whom he dervived it, and was in him. But one man does not derive guilt from another, when, through the fact that each has a separate life belonging to himself, the word may apply equally to both — "The soul that sinneth, it shall die."

2. But the possibility of regeneration through the office rendered by the will of another, when the child is presented to receive the sacred rite, is the work exclusively of the Spirit by whom the child thus presented is regenerated. For it is not written, "Except a man be born again by the will of his parents, or by the faith of those presenting the child, or of those administering the ordinance," but, "Except a man be born again of water and of the Spirit."[1] By the water, therefore, which holds forth the sacrament of grace in its outward form, and by the Spirit who bestows the benefit of grace in its inward power, cancelling the bond of guilt, and restoring natural goodness [reconcilians bonum naturæ], the man deriving his first birth originally from Adam alone, is regenerated in Christ alone. Now the regenerating Spirit is possessed in common both by the parents who present the child, and by the infant that is presented and is born again; wherefore, in virtue of this participation in the same Spirit, the will of those who present the infant is useful to the child. But when the parents sin against the child by presenting him to the false gods of the heathen, and attempting to bring him under impious bonds unto these false gods, there is not such community of souls subsisting between the parents and the child, that the guilt of one party can be common to both alike. For we are not made partakers of guilt along with others through their will, in the same way as we are made partakers of grace along with others through the unity of the Holy Spirit; because the one Holy Spirit can be in two different persons without their knowing in respect to each other that by Him grace is the common possession of both, but the human spirit cannot so belong to two individuals as to make the blame common to both

in a case in which one of the two sins, and the other does not sin. Therefore a child, having once received natural birth through his parents, can be made partaker of the second (or spiritual) birth by the Spirit of God, so that the bond of guilt which he inherited from his parents is cancelled; but he that has once received this second birth by the Spirit of God cannot be made again partaker of natural birth through his parents, so that the bond once cancelled should again bind him. And thus, when the grace of Christ has been once received, the child does not lose it otherwise than by his own impiety, if, when he becomes older, he turn out so ill. For by that time he will begin to have sins of his own, which cannot be removed by regeneration, but must be healed by other remedial measures.

3. Nevertheless, persons of more advanced years, whether they be parents bringing their children, or others bringing any little ones, who attempt to place those who have been baptized under obligation to profane worship of heathen gods, are guilty of spiritual homicide. True, they do not actually kill the children's souls, but they go as far towards killing them as is in their power. The warning, "Do not kill your little ones," may be with all propriety addressed to them; for the apostle says, "Quench not the Spirit;"[2] not that He can be quenched, but that those who so act as if they wished to have Him quenched are deservedly spoken of as quenchers of the Spirit. In this sense also may be rightly understood the words which most blessed Cyprian wrote in his letter concerning the lapsed, when, rebuking those who in the time of persecution had sacrificed to idols, he says, "And that nothing might be wanting to fill up the measure of their crime, their infant children, carried in arms, or led thither by the hands of their parents, lost, while yet in their infancy, that which they had received as soon as life began."[3] They lost it, he meant, so far at least as pertained to the guilt of the crime of those by whom they were compelled to incur the loss: they lost it, that is to say, in the purpose and wish of those who perpetrated on them such a wrong. For had they actually in their own persons lost it, they must have remained under the divine sentence of condemnation without any plea; but if holy Cyprian had been of this opinion, he would not have added in the immediate context a plea in their defence, saying, "Shall not these say, when the judgment-day has come: 'We have done nothing; we have not of our own accord hastened to participate in profane rites, forsaking the bread and

[1] John iii. 5.

[2] 1 Thess. v. 19.
[3] Cyprian, *de Lapsis*. See *Ante-Nicene Fathers*, Am. ed. vol. v. p. 439.

the cup of the Lord; the apostasy of others caused our destruction; we found our parents murderers, for they deprived us of our Mother the Church and of our Father the Lord, so that, through the wrong done by others, we were ensnared, because, while yet young and unable to think for ourselves, we were by the deed of others, and while wholly ignorant of such a crime, made partners in their sin'?" This plea in their defence he would not have subjoined had he not believed it to be perfectly just, and one which would be of service to these infants at the bar of divine judgment. For if it is said by them with truth, "We have done nothing," then "the soul that sinneth, it shall die;" and in the just dispensation of judgment by God, those shall not be doomed to perish whose souls their parents did, so far at least as concerns their own guilt in the transaction, bring to ruin.

4. As to the incident mentioned in the same letter, that a girl who was left as an infant in charge of her nurse, when her parents had escaped by sudden flight, and was made by that nurse to take part in the profane rites of idolatrous worship, had afterwards in the Church expelled from her mouth, by wonderful motions, the Eucharist when it was given to her, this seems to me to have been caused by divine interposition, in order that persons of riper years might not imagine that in this sin they do no wrong to the children, but rather might understand, by means of a bodily action of obvious significance on the part of those who were unable to speak, that a miraculous warning was given to themselves as to the course which would have been becoming in persons who, after so great a crime, rushed heedlessly to those sacraments from which they ought by all means, in proof of penitence, to have abstained. When Divine Providence does anything of this kind by means of infant children, we must not believe that they are acting under the guidance of knowledge and reason; just as we are not called upon to admire the wisdom of asses, because once God was pleased to rebuke the madness of a prophet by the voice of an ass.[1] If, therefore, a sound exactly like the human voice was uttered by an irrational animal, and this was to be ascribed to a divine miracle, not to faculties belonging to the ass, the Almighty could, in like manner, through the spirit of an infant (in which reason was not absent, but only slumbering undeveloped), make manifest by a motion of its body something to which those who had sinned against both their own souls and their children behoved to give heed. But since a child cannot return to become again a part of the author of his natural life, so as to be one with him and in him, but is

a wholly distinct individual, having a body and a soul of his own, "the soul that sinneth, it shall die."

5. Some, indeed, bring their little ones for baptism, not in the believing expectation that they shall be regenerated unto life eternal by spiritual grace, but because they think that by this as a remedy the children may recover or retain bodily health; but let not this disquiet your mind, because their regeneration is not prevented by the fact that this blessing has no place in the intention of those by whom they are presented for baptism. For by these persons the ministerial actions which are necessary are performed, and the sacramental words are pronounced, without which the infant cannot be consecrated to God. But the Holy Spirit who dwells in the saints, in those, namely, whom the glowing flame of love has fused together into the one Dove whose wings are covered with silver,[2] accomplishes His work even by the ministry of bond-servants, of persons who are sometimes not only ignorant through simplicity, but even culpably unworthy to be employed by Him. The presentation of the little ones to receive the spiritual grace is the act not so much of those by whose hands they are borne up (although it is theirs also in part, if they themselves are good believers) as of the whole society of saints and believers. For it is proper to regard the infants as presented by all who take pleasure in their baptism, and through whose holy and perfectly-united love they are assisted in receiving the communion of the Holy Spirit. Therefore this is done by the whole mother Church, which is in the saints, because the whole Church is the parent of all the saints, and the whole Church is the parent of each one of them. For if the sacrament of Christian baptism, being always one and the same, is of value even when administered by heretics, and though not in that case sufficing to secure to the baptized person participation in eternal life, does suffice to seal his consecration to God; and if this consecration makes him who, having the mark of the Lord, remains outside of the Lord's flock, guilty as a heretic, but reminds us at the same time that he is to be corrected by sound doctrine, but not to be a second time consecrated by repetition of the ordinance; — if this be the case even in the baptism of heretics, how much more credible is it that within the Catholic Church that which is only straw should be of service in bearing the grain to the floor in which it is to be winnowed, and by means of which it is to be prepared for being added to the heap of good grain!

6. I would, moreover, wish you not to remain under the mistake of supposing that the bond

---

[1] Num. xxii. 28.

[2] Ps. lxviii. 13.

of guilt which is inherited from Adam cannot be cancelled in any other way than by the parents themselves presenting their little ones to receive the grace of Christ; for you write: "As the parents have been the authors of the life which makes them liable to condemnation, the children should receive justification through the same channel, through the faith of the same parents;" whereas you see that many are not presented by parents, but also by any strangers whatever, as sometimes the infant children of slaves are presented by their masters. Sometimes also, when their parents are deceased, little orphans are baptized, being presented by those who had it in their power to manifest their compassion in this way. Again, sometimes foundlings which heartless parents have exposed in order to their being cared for by any passer-by, are picked up by holy virgins, and are presented for baptism by these persons, who neither have nor desire to have children of their own: and in this you behold precisely what was done in the case mentioned in the Gospel of the man wounded by thieves, and left half dead on the way, regarding whom the Lord asked who was neighbour to him, and received for answer: "He that showed mercy on him." [1]

7. That which you have placed at the end of your series of questions you have judged to be the most difficult, because of the jealous care with which you are wont to avoid whatever is false. You state it thus: "If I place before you an infant, and ask, 'Will this child when he grows up be chaste?' or 'Will he not be a thief?' you will reply, 'I know not.' If I ask, 'Is he in his present infantile condition thinking what is good or thinking what is evil?' you will reply, 'I know not.' If, therefore, you do not venture to take the responsibility of making any positive statement concerning either his conduct in after life or his thoughts at the time, what is that which parents do, when, in presenting their children for baptism, they as sureties (or sponsors) answer for the children, and say that they do that which at that age they are incapable even of understanding, or, at least, in regard to which their thoughts (if they can think) are hidden from us? For we ask those by whom the child is presented, 'Does he believe in God?' and though at that age the child does not so much as know that there is a God, the sponsors reply, 'He believes;' and in like manner answer is returned by them to each of the other questions. Now I am surprised that parents can in these things answer so confidently on the child's behalf as to say, at the time when they are answering the questions of the persons administering baptism, that the infant is doing what is so re-

markable and so excellent; and yet if at the same hour I were to add such questions as, 'Will the child who is now being baptized be chaste when he grows up? Will he not be a thief?' probably no one would presume to answer, 'He will' or 'He will not,' although there is no hesitation in giving the answer that the child believes in God, and turns himself to God." Thereafter you add this sentence in conclusion: "To these questions I pray you to condescend to give me a short reply, not silencing me by the traditional authority of custom, but satisfying me by arguments addressed to my reason."

8. While reading this letter of yours over and over again, and pondering its contents so far as my limited time permitted, memory recalled to me my friend Nebridius, who, while he was a most diligent and eager student of difficult problems, especially in the department of Christian doctrine, had an extreme aversion to the giving of a short answer to a great question. If any one insisted upon this, he was exceedingly displeased; and if he was not prevented by respect for the age or rank of the person, he indignantly rebuked such a questioner by stern looks and words; for he considered him unworthy to be investigating matters such as these, who did not know how much both might be said and behoved to be said on a subject of great importance. But I do not lose patience with you, as he was wont to do when one asked a brief reply; for you are, as I am, a bishop engrossed with many cares, and therefore have not leisure for reading any more than I have leisure for writing any prolix communication. He was then a young man, who was not satisfied with short statements on subjects of this kind, and being then himself at leisure, addressed his questions concerning the many topics discussed in our conversations to one who was also at leisure; whereas you, having regard to the circumstances both of yourself the questioner, and of me from whom you demand the reply, insist upon my giving you a short answer to the weighty question which you propound. Well, I shall do my best to satisfy you; the Lord help me to accomplish what you require.

9. You know that in ordinary parlance we often say, when Easter is approaching, "Tomorrow or the day after is the Lord's Passion," although He suffered so many years ago, and His passion was endured once for all time. In like manner, on Easter Sunday, we say, "This day the Lord rose from the dead," although so many years have passed since His resurrection. But no one is so foolish as to accuse us of falsehood when we use these phrases, for this reason, that we give such names to these days on the ground of a likeness between them and the days on which the events referred to actually tran-

spired, the day being called the day of that event, although it is not the very day on which the event took place, but one corresponding to it by the revolution of the same time of the year, and the event itself being said to take place on that day, because, although it really took place long before. it is on that day sacramentally celebrated. Was not Christ once for all offered up in His own person as a sacrifice? and yet, is He not likewise offered up in the sacrament as a sacrifice, not only in the special solemnities of Easter, but also daily among our congregations; so that the man who, being questioned, answers that He is offered as a sacrifice in that ordinance, declares what is strictly true? For if sacraments had not some points of real resemblance to the things of which they are the sacraments, they would not be sacraments at all. In most cases, moreover, they do in virtue of this likeness bear the names of the realities which they resemble. As, therefore, in a certain manner the sacrament of Christ's body is Christ's body, and the sacrament of Christ's blood is Christ's blood,[1] in the same manner the sacrament of faith is faith. Now believing is nothing else than having faith; and accordingly, when, on behalf of an infant as yet incapable of exercising faith, the answer is given that he believes, this answer means that he has faith because of the sacrament of faith, and in like manner the answer is made that he turns himself to God because of the sacrament of conversion, since the answer itself belongs to the celebration of the sacrament. Thus the apostle says, in regard to this sacrament of Baptism : "We are buried with Christ by baptism into death."[2] He does not say, "We have signified our being buried with Him," but "We have been buried with Him." He has therefore given to the sacrament pertaining to so great a transaction no other name than the word describing the transaction itself.

10. Therefore an infant, although he is not yet a believer in the sense of having that faith which includes the consenting will of those who exercise it, nevertheless becomes a believer through the sacrament of that faith. For as it is answered that he believes, so also he is called a believer, not because he assents to the truth by an act of his own judgment, but because he receives the sacrament of that truth. When, however, he begins to have the discretion of manhood, he will not repeat the sacrament, but understand its meaning, and become conformed to the truth which it contains, with his will also consenting. During the time in which he is by reason of youth unable to do this, the sacrament will avail for his protection against adverse powers, and will avail so much on his behalf, that if before he arrives at the use of reason he depart from this life, he is delivered by Christian help, namely, by the love of the Church commending him through this sacrament unto God, from that condemnation which by one man entered into the world.[3] He who does not believe this, and thinks that it is impossible, is assuredly an unbeliever, although he may have received the sacrament of faith ; and far before him in merit is the infant which, though not yet possessing a faith helped by the understanding, is not obstructing faith by any antagonism of the understanding, and therefore receives with profit the sacrament of faith.

I have answered your questions, as it seems to me, in a manner which, if I were dealing with persons of weaker capacity and disposed to gainsaying, would be inadequate, but which is perhaps more than sufficient to satisfy peaceable and sensible persons. Moreover, I have not urged in my defence the mere fact that the custom is thoroughly established, but have to the best of my ability advanced reasons in support of it as fraught with very abundant blessing.

LETTER XCIX.

(A.D. 408 OR BEGINNING OF 409.)

TO THE VERY DEVOUT ITALICA, AN HANDMAID OF GOD, PRAISED JUSTLY AND PIOUSLY BY THE MEMBERS OF CHRIST, AUGUSTIN SENDS GREETING IN THE LORD.

1. Up to the time of my writing this reply, I had received three letters from your Grace, of which the first asked urgently a letter from me, the second intimated that what I wrote in answer had reached you, and the third, which conveyed the assurance of your most benevolent solicitude for our interest in the matter of the house belonging to that most illustrious and distinguished young man Julian, which is in immediate contact with the walls of our Church. To this last letter, just now received, I lose no time in promptly replying, because your Excellency's agent has written to me that he can send my letter without delay to Rome. By his letter we have been greatly distressed, because he has taken pains to acquaint us[4] with the things which are taking place in the city (Rome) or around its walls, so as to give us reliable information concerning that which we were reluctant to believe on the authority of vague rumours. In the letters which

---

[1] As this is an important sentence, we give the original words: *Sicut ergo secundum quemdam modum sacramentum corporis Christi corpus Christi est, sacramentum sanguinis Christi sanguis Christi est, ita sacramentum fidei fides est.*
[2] Rom. vi. 4.

[3] Rom. v. 12.
[4] Tillemont (vol. xiii. note 44) conjectures that the word "*non*" before "*nobis insinuare curavit*" should not be in the text, — a conjecture which commends itself to our judgment, though it is unsupported by mss.
The calamities referred to are the events connected with the siege of Rome by Alaric in the end of 408.

were sent to us previously by our brethren, tidings were given to us of events, vexatious and grievous, it is true, but much less calamitous than those of which we now hear. I am surprised beyond expression that my brethren the holy bishops did not write to me when so favourable an opportunity of sending a letter by your messengers occurred, and that your own letter conveyed to us no information concerning such painful tribulation as has befallen you, — tribulation which, by reason of the tender sympathies of Christian charity, is ours as well as yours. I suppose, however, that you deemed it better not to mention these sorrows, because you considered that this could do no good, or because you did not wish to make us sad by your letter. But in my opinion, it does some good to acquaint us even with such events as these : in the first place, because it is not right to be ready to "rejoice with them that rejoice," but refuse to "weep with them that weep ; " and in the second place, because "tribulation worketh patience, and patience experience, and experience hope ; and hope maketh not ashamed, because the love of God is shed abroad in our hearts by the Holy Ghost which is given unto us."[1]

2. Far be it, therefore, from us to refuse to hear even of the bitter and sorrowful things which befall those who are very dear to us ! For in some way which I cannot explain, the pain suffered by one member is mitigated when all the other members suffer with it.[2] And this mitigation is effected not by actual participation in the calamity, but by the solacing power of love ; for although only some suffer the actual burden of the affliction, and the others share their suffering through knowing what these have to bear, nevertheless the tribulation is borne in common by them all, seeing that they have in common the same experience, hope, and love, and the same Divine Spirit. Moreover, the Lord provides consolation for us all, inasmuch as He hath both forewarned us of these temporal afflictions, and promised to us after them eternal blessings ; and the soldier who desires to receive a crown when the conflict is over, ought not to lose courage while the conflict lasts, since He who is preparing rewards ineffable for those who overcome, does Himself minister strength to them while they are on the field to battle.

3. Let not what I have now written take away your confidence in writing to me, especially since the reason which may be pled for your endeavouring to lessen our fears is one which cannot be condemned. We salute in return your little children, and we desire that they may be spared to you, and may grow up in Christ, since they discern even in their present tender age how

dangerous and baneful is the love of this world. God grant that the plants which are small and still flexible may be bent in the right direction in a time in which the great and hardy are being shaken. As to the house of which you speak, what can I say beyond expressing my gratitude for your very kind solicitude? For the house which we can give they do not wish ; and the house which they wish we cannot give, for it was not left to the church by my predecessor, as they have been falsely informed, but is one of the ancient properties of the church, and it is attached to the one ancient church in the same way as the house about which this question has been raised is attached to the other.[3]

LETTER C.

(A.D. 409.)

TO DONATUS, HIS NOBLE AND DESERVEDLY HONOURABLE LORD, AND EMINENTLY PRAISEWORTHY SON, AUGUSTIN SENDS GREETING IN THE LORD.

1. I would indeed that the African Church were not placed in such trying circumstances as to need the aid of any earthly power. But since, as the apostle says, "there is no power but of God,"[4] it is unquestionable that, when by you the sincere sons of your Catholic Mother help is given to her, our help is in the name of the Lord, "who made heaven and earth."[5] For oh, noble and deservedly honourable lord, and eminently praiseworthy son, who does not perceive that in the midst of so great calamities no small consolation has been bestowed upon us by God, in that you, such a man, and so devoted to the name of Christ, have been raised to the dignity of proconsul, so that power allied with your goodwill may restrain the enemies of the Church from their wicked and sacrilegious attempts? In fact, there is only one thing of which we are much afraid in your administration of justice, viz., lest perchance, seeing that every injury done by impious and ungrateful men against the Christian society is a more serious and heinous crime than if it had been done against others, you should on this ground consider that it ought to be punished with a severity corresponding to the enormity of the crime, and not with the moderation which is suitable to Christian forbearance. We beseech you, in the name of Jesus Christ, not to act in this manner. For we do not seek to revenge ourselves in this world ; nor ought the things which we suffer to reduce us to such distress of mind as to leave no room in our memory for the precepts in regard to this which we have

---

[1] Rom. xii. 15 and v. 3–5.
[2] 1 Cor. xii. 26.

[3] We have no further information regarding this affair. The prospect of an amicable settlement seems remote.
[4] Rom. xiii. 1.
[5] Ps. cxxiv. 8.

received from Him for whose truth and in whose name we suffer; we "love our enemies," and we "pray for them."[1] It is not their death, but their deliverance from error, that we seek to accomplish by the help of the terror of judges and of laws, whereby they may be preserved from falling under the penalty of eternal judgment; we do not wish either to see the exercise of discipline towards them neglected, or, on the other hand, to see them subjected to the severer punishments which they deserve. Do you, therefore, check their sins in such a way, that the sinners may be spared to repent of their sins.

2. We beg you, therefore, when you are pronouncing judgment in cases affecting the Church, how wicked soever the injuries may be which you shall ascertain to have been attempted or inflicted on the Church, to forget that you have the power of capital punishment, and not to forget our request. Nor let it appear to you an unimportant matter and beneath your notice, my most beloved and honoured son, that we ask you to spare the lives of the men on whose behalf we ask God to grant them repentance. For even granting that we ought never to deviate from a fixed purpose of overcoming evil with good, let your own wisdom take this also into consideration, that no person beyond those who belong to the Church is at pains to bring before you cases pertaining to her interests. If, therefore, your opinion be, that death must be the punishment of men convicted of these crimes, you will deter us from endeavouring to bring anything of this kind before your tribunal; and this being discovered, they will proceed with more unrestrained boldness to accomplish speedily our destruction, when upon us is imposed and enjoined the necessity of choosing rather to suffer death at their hands, than to bring them to death by accusing them at your bar. Disdain not, I beseech you, to accept this suggestion, petition, and entreaty from me. For I do not think that you are unmindful that I might have great boldness in addressing you, even were I not a bishop, and even though your rank were much above what you now hold. Meanwhile, let the Donatist heretics learn at once through the edict of your Excellency that the laws passed against their error, which they suppose and boastfully declare to be repealed, are still in force, although even when they know this they may not be able to refrain in the least degree from injuring us. You will, however, most effectively help us to secure the fruit of our labours and dangers, if you take care that the imperial laws for the restraining of their sect, which is full of conceit and of impious pride, be so used that they may not appear either to themselves or to others to be suffering hardship

in any form for the sake of truth and righteousness; but suffer them, when this is requested at your hands, to be convinced and instructed by incontrovertible proofs of things which are most certain, in public proceedings in the presence of your Excellency or of inferior judges, in order that those who are arrested by your command may themselves incline their stubborn will to the better part, and may read these things profitably to others of their party. For the pains bestowed are burdensome rather than really useful, when men are only compelled, not persuaded by instruction, to forsake a great evil and lay hold upon a great benefit.

LETTER CI.

(A.D. 409.)

TO MEMOR,[2] MY LORD MOST BLESSED, AND WITH ALL VENERATION MOST BELOVED, MY BROTHER AND COLLEAGUE SINCERELY LONGED FOR, AUGUSTIN SENDS GREETING IN THE LORD.

1. I ought not to write any letter to your holy Charity, without sending at the same time those books which by the irresistible plea of holy love you have demanded from me, that at least by this act of obedience I might reply to those letters by which you have put on me a high honour indeed, but also a heavy load. Albeit, while I bend because of the load, I am raised up because of your love. For it is not by an ordinary man that I am loved and raised up and made to stand erect, but by a man who is a priest of the Lord, and whom I know to be so accepted before Him, that when you raise to the Lord your good heart, having me in your heart, you raise me with yourself to Him. I ought, therefore, to have sent at this time those books which I had promised to revise. The reason why I have not sent them is that I have not revised them, and this not because I was unwilling, but because I was unable, having been occupied with many very urgent cares. But it would have shown inexcusable ingratitude and hardness of heart to have permitted the bearer, my holy colleague and brother Possidius, in whom you will find one who is very much the same as myself, either to miss becoming acquainted with you, who love me so much, or to come to know you without any letter from me. For he is one who has been by my labours nourished, not in those studies which men who are the slaves of every kind of passion call liberal, but with the Lord's bread, in so far as this could be supplied to him from my scanty store.

2. For to men who, though they are unjust and impious, imagine that they are well educated

---

[1] Matt. v. 44.

[2] We regard Memori, not Memorio, as the true reading.

in the liberal arts, what else ought we to say than what we read in those writings which truly merit the name of liberal, — "if the Son shall make you free, ye shall be free indeed." [1] For it is through Him that men come to know, even in those studies which are termed liberal by those who have not been called to this true liberty, anything in them which deserves the name. For they have nothing which is consonant with liberty, except that which in them is consonant with truth ; for which reason the Son Himself hath said : "The truth shall make you free." [2] The freedom which is our privilege has therefore nothing in common with the innumerable and impious fables with which the verses of silly poets are full, nor with the fulsome and highly-polished falsehoods of their orators, nor, in fine, with the rambling subtleties of philosophers themselves, who either did not know anything of God, or when they knew God, did not glorify Him as God, neither were thankful, but became vain in their imaginations, and their foolish heart was darkened ; so that, professing themselves to be wise, they became fools, and changed the glory of the incorruptible God into an image made like to corruptible man, and to birds and four-footed beasts, and to creeping things, or who, though not wholly or at all devoted to the worship of images, nevertheless worshipped and served the creature more than the Creator.[3] Far be it, therefore, from us to admit that the epithet liberal is justly bestowed on the lying vanities and hallucinations, or empty trifles and conceited errors of those men — unhappy men, who knew not the grace of God in Christ Jesus our Lord, by which alone we are " delivered from the body of this death," [4] and who did not even perceive the measure of truth which was in the things which they knew. Their historical works, the writers of which profess to be chiefly concerned to be accurate in narrating events, may perhaps, I grant, contain some things worthy of being known by "free" men, since the narration is true, whether the subject described in it be the good or the evil in human experience. At the same time, I can by no means see how men who were not aided in their knowledge by the Holy Spirit, and who were obliged to gather floating rumours under the limitations of human infirmity, could avoid being misled in regard to very many things ; nevertheless, if they have no intention of deceiving, and do not mislead other men otherwise than so far as they have themselves, through human infirmity, fallen into a mistake, there is in such writings an approach to liberty.

3. Forasmuch, however, as the powers belonging to numbers [5] in all kinds of movements are most easily studied as they are presented in sounds, and this study furnishes a way of rising to the higher secrets of truth, by paths gradually ascending, so to speak, in which Wisdom pleasantly reveals herself, and in every step of providence meets those who love her,[6] I desired, when I began to have leisure for study, and my mind was not engaged by greater and more important cares, to exercise myself by writing those books which you have requested me to send. I then wrote six books on rhythm alone, and proposed, I may add, to write other six on music,[7] as I at that time expected to have leisure. But from the time that the burden of ecclesiastical cares was laid upon me, all these recreations have passed from my hand so completely, that now, when I cannot but respect your wish and command, — for it is more than a request, — I have difficulty in even finding what I had written. If, however, I had it in my power to send you that treatise, it would occasion regret, not to me that I had obeyed your command, but to you that you had so urgently insisted upon its being sent. For five books of it are all but unintelligible, unless one be at hand who can in reading not only distinguish the part belonging to each of those between whom the discussion is maintained, but also mark by enunciation the time which the syllables should occupy, so that their distinctive measures may be expressed and strike the ear, especially because in some places there occur pauses of measured length, which of course must escape notice, unless the reader inform the hearer of them by intervals of silence where they occur.

The sixth book, however, which I have found already revised, and in which the product of the other five is contained, I have not delayed to send to your Charity ; it may, perhaps, be not wholly unsuited to one of your venerable age.[8] As to the other five books, they seem to me scarcely worthy of being known and read by Julian,[9] our son, and now our colleague, for, as a deacon, he is engaged in the same warfare with ourselves. Of him I dare not say, for it would not be true, that I love him more than I love you ; yet this I may say, that I long for him more than for you. It may seem strange, that when I love both equally, I long more ardently for the one than the other ; but the cause of the difference is, that I have greater hope of seeing him ; for I think that if ordered or sent by you he come to us, he will both be doing what is

---

[1] John viii. 36.
[2] John viii. 38.
[3] Rom. i. 21-25.
[4] Rom. vii. 24, 25.

[5] *Quid numeri valeant.*
[6] Wisd. vi. 17.
[7] *De melo.*
[8] *Gravitatem tuam.*
[9] Julian, son of Memor, afterwards a leading supporter of the Pelagian heresy.

suitable to one of his years, especially as he is not yet hindered by weightier responsibilities, and he will more speedily bring yourself to me.

I have not stated in this treatise the kinds of metre in which the lines of David's Psalms are composed, because I do not know them. For it was not possible for any one, in translating these from the Hebrew (of which language I know nothing), to preserve the metre at the same time, lest by the exigencies of the measure he should be compelled to depart from accurate translation further than was consistent with the meaning of the sentences. Nevertheless, I believe, on the testimony of those who are acquainted with that language, that they are composed in certain varieties of metre ; for that holy man loved sacred music, and has more than any other kindled in me a passion for its study.

May the shadow of the wings of the Most High be for ever the dwelling-place [1] of you all, who with oneness of heart occupy one home,[2] father and mother, bound in the same brotherhood with your sons, being all the children of the one Father. Remember us.

LETTER CII.

(A.D. 409.)

TO DEOGRATIAS, MY BROTHER IN ALL SINCERITY, AND MY FELLOW-PRESBYTER, AUGUSTIN SENDS GREETING IN THE LORD.

1. In choosing to refer to me questions which were submitted to yourself for solution, you have not done so, I suppose, from indolence, but because, loving me more than I deserve, you prefer to hear through me even those things which you already know quite well. I would rather, however, that the answers were given by yourself, because the friend who proposed the questions seems to be shy of following advice from me, if I may judge from the fact that he has written no reply to a letter of mine, for what reason he knows best. I suspect this, however, and there is neither ill-will nor absurdity in the suspicion ; for you also know very well how much I love him, and how great is my grief that he is not yet a Christian ; and it is not unreasonable to think that one whom I see unwilling to answer my letters is not willing to have anything written by me to him. I therefore implore you to comply with a request of mine, seeing that I have been obedient to you, and, notwithstanding most engrossing duties, have feared to disappoint the wish of one so dear to me by declining to comply with your request. What I ask is this, that you do not refuse yourself to give an answer to all his questions, see-

ing that, as you have told me, he begged this from you ; and it is a task to which, even before receiving this letter, you were competent ; for when you have read this letter, you will see that scarcely anything has been said by me which you did not already know, or which you could not have come to know though I had been silent. This work of mine, therefore, I beg you to keep for the use of yourself and of all other persons whose desire for instruction you deem it suited to satisfy. But as for the treatise of your own composition which I demand from you, give it to him to whom this treatise is most specially adapted, and not to him only, but also all others who find exceedingly acceptable such statements concerning these things as you are able to make, among whom I number myself. May you live always in Christ, and remember me.

2. QUESTION I. Concerning the resurrection. This question perplexes some, and they ask, Which of two kinds of resurrection corresponds to that which is promised to us? is it that of Christ, or that of Lazarus? They say, "If the former, how can this correspond with the resurrection of those who have been born by ordinary generations, seeing that He was not thus born?[3] If, on the other hand, the resurrection of Lazarus is said to correspond to ours, here also there seems to be a discrepancy, since the resurrection of Lazarus was accomplished in the case of a body not yet dissolved, but the same body in which he was known by the name of Lazarus ; whereas ours is to be rescued after many centuries from the mass in which it has ceased to be distinguishable from other things. Again, if our state after the resurrection is one of blessedness, in which the body shall be exempt from every kind of wound, and from the pain of hunger, what is meant by the statement that Christ took food, and showed his wounds after His resurrection? For if He did it to convince the doubting, when the wounds were not real, He practised on them a deception ; whereas, if He showed them what was real, it follows that wounds received by the body shall remain in the state which is to ensue after resurrection."

3. To this I answer, that the resurrection of Christ and not of Lazarus corresponds to that which is promised, because Lazarus was so raised that he died a second time, whereas of Christ it is written : "Christ, being raised from the dead, dieth no more ; death hath no more dominion over Him."[4] The same is promised to those who shall rise at the end of the world, and shall reign for ever with Christ. As to the difference in the manner of Christ's generation and that of other men, this has no bearing upon the nature

---

[1] Ps. xci. 1.
[2] Ps. lxviii. 6, Septuagint.

[3] *Qui nullâ seminis conditione natus est.*
[4] Rom. vi. 9.

of His resurrection, just as it had none upon the nature of His death, so as to make it different from ours. His death was not the less real because of His not having been begotten by an earthly father; just as the difference between the mode of the origination of the body of the first man, who was formed immediately from the dust of the earth, and of our bodies, which we derive from our parents, made no such difference as that his death should be of another kind than ours. As, therefore, difference in the mode of birth does not make any difference in the nature of death, neither does it make any difference in the nature of resurrection.

4. But lest the men who doubt this should, with similar scepticism, refuse to accept as true what is written concerning the first man's creation, let them inquire or observe, if they can at least believe this, how numerous are the species of animals which are born from the earth without deriving their life from parents, but which by ordinary procreation reproduce offspring like themselves, and in which, notwithstanding the different mode of origination, the nature of the parents born from the earth and of the offspring born from them is the same; for they live alike and they die alike, although born in different ways. There is therefore no absurdity in the statement that bodies dissimilar in their origination are alike in their resurrection. But men of this kind, not being competent to discern in what respect any diversity between things affects or does not affect them, so soon as they discover any unlikeness between things in their original formation, contend that in all that follows the same unlikeness must still exist. Such men may as reasonably suppose that oil made from fat should not float on the surface in water as olive oil does, because the origin of the two oils is so different, the one being from the fruit of a tree, the other from the flesh of an animal.

5. Again, as to the alleged difference in regard to the resurrection of Christ's body and of ours, that His was raised on the third day not dissolved by decay and corruption, whereas ours shall be fashioned again after a long time, and out of the mass into which undistinguished they shall have been resolved, — both of these things are impossible for man to do, but to divine power both are most easy. For as the glance of the eye does not come more quickly to objects which are at hand, and more slowly to objects more remote, but darts to either distance with equal swiftness, so, when the resurrection of the dead is accomplished "in the twinkling of an eye,"[1] it is as easy for the omnipotence of God and for the ineffable expression of His will[2] to raise again bodies which have by long lapse of time been dissolved, as to raise those which have recently fallen under the stroke of death. These things are to some men incredible because they transcend their experience, although all nature is full of wonders so numerous, that they do not seem to us to be wonderful, and are therefore accounted unworthy of attentive study or investigation, not because our faculties can easily comprehend them, but because we are so accustomed to see them. For myself, and for all who along with me labour to understand the invisible things of God by means of the things which are made,[3] I may say that we are filled not less, perhaps even more, with wonder by the fact, that in one grain of seed, so insignificant, there lies bound up as it were all that we praise in the stately tree, than by the fact that the bosom of this earth, so vast, shall restore entire and perfect to the future resurrection all those elements of human bodies which it is now receiving when they are dissolved.

6. Again, what contradiction is there between the fact that Christ partook of food after His resurrection, and the doctrine that in the promised resurrection-state there shall be no need of food, when we read that angels also have partaken of food of the same kind and in the same way, not in empty and illusive simulation, but in unquestionable reality; not, however, under the pressure of necessity, but in the free exercise of their power? For water is absorbed in one way by the thirsting earth, in another way by the glowing sunbeams; in the former we see the effect of poverty, in the latter of power. Now the body of that future resurrection-state shall be imperfect in its felicity if it be incapable of taking food; imperfect, also, if, on the other hand, it be dependent on food. I might here enter on a fuller discussion concerning the changes possible in the qualities of bodies, and the dominion which belongs to higher bodies over those which are of inferior nature; but I have resolved to make my reply short, and I write this for minds so endowed that the simple suggestion of the truth is enough for them.

7. Let him who proposed these questions know by all means that Christ did, after His resurrection, show the scars of His wounds, not the wounds themselves, to disciples who doubted; for whose sake, also, it pleased Him to take food and drink more than once, lest they should suppose that His body was not real, but that He was a spirit, appearing to them as a phantom, and not a substantial form. These scars would indeed have been mere illusive appearances if no wounds had gone before; yet even the scars would not have remained if He had willed it otherwise. But it pleased Him to retain them

---

[1] 1 Cor. xv. 52.
[2] *Ineffabili nutui.*

[3] Rom. i. 20.

with a definite purpose, namely, that to those whom He was building up in faith unfeigned He might show that one body had not been substituted for another, but that the body which they had seen nailed to the cross had risen again. What reason is there, then, for saying, " If He did this to convince the doubting, He practised a deception"? Suppose that a brave man, who had received many wounds in confronting the enemy when fighting for his country, were to say to a physician of extraordinary skill, who was able so to heal these wounds as to leave not a scar visible, that he would prefer to be healed in such a way that the traces of the wounds should remain on his body as tokens of the honours he had won, would you, in such a case, say that the physician practised deception, because, though he might by his art make the scars wholly disappear, he did by the same art, for a definite reason, rather cause them to continue as they were? The only ground upon which the scars could be proved to be a deception would be, as I have already said, if no wounds had been healed in the places where they were seen.

8. QUESTION II. Concerning the epoch of the Christian religion, they have advanced, moreover, some other things, which they might call a selection of the more weighty arguments of Porphyry against the Christians : " If Christ," they say, " declares Himself to be the Way of salvation, the Grace and the Truth, and affirms that in Him alone, and only to souls believing in Him, is the way of return to God,[1] what has become of men who lived in the many centuries before Christ came? To pass over the time," he adds, " which preceded the founding of the kingdom of Latium, let us take the beginning of that power as if it were the beginning of the human race. In Latium itself gods were worshipped before Alba was built ; in Alba, also, religious rites and forms of worship in the temples were maintained. Rome itself was for a period of not less duration, even for a long succession of centuries, unacquainted with Christian doctrine. What, then, has become of such an innumerable multitude of souls, who were in no wise blameworthy, seeing that He in whom alone saving faith can be exercised had not yet favoured men with His advent? The whole world, moreover, was not less zealous than Rome itself in the worship practised in the temples of the gods. Why, then," he asks, " did He who is called the Saviour withhold Himself for so many centuries of the world? And let it not be said," he adds, " that provision had been made for the human race by the old Jewish law. It was only after a long time that the Jewish law appeared and flourished within the narrow limits of Syria, and

after that, it gradually crept onwards to the coasts of Italy ; but this was not earlier than the end of the reign of Caius, or, at the earliest, while he was on the throne. What, then, became of the souls of men in Rome and Latium who lived before the time of the Cæsars, and were destitute of the grace of Christ, because He had not then come?"

9. To these statements we answer by requiring those who make them to tell us, in the first place, whether the sacred rites, which we know to have been introduced into the worship of their gods at times which can be ascertained, were or were not profitable to men. If they say that these were of no service for the salvation of men, they unite with us in putting them down, and confess that they were useless. We indeed prove that they were baneful ; but it is an important concession that by them it is at least admitted that they were useless. If, on the other hand, they defend these rites, and maintain that they were wise and profitable institutions, what, I ask, has become of those who died before these were instituted? for they were defrauded of the saving and profitable efficacy which these possessed. If, however, it be said that they could be cleansed from guilt equally well in another way, why did not the same way continue in force for their posterity? What use was there for instituting novelties in worship.

10. If, in answer to this, they say that the gods themselves have indeed always existed, and were in all places alike powerful to give liberty to their worshippers, but were pleased to regulate the circumstances of time, place, and manner in which they were to be served, according to the variety found among things temporal and terrestrial, in such a way as they knew to be most suitable to certain ages and countries, why do they urge against the Christian religion this question, which, if it be asked in regard to their own gods, they either cannot themselves answer, or, if they can, must do so in such a way as to answer for our religion not less than their own? For what could they say but that the difference between sacraments which are adapted to different times and places is of no importance, if only that which is worshipped in them all be holy, just as the difference between sounds of words belonging to different languages and adapted to different hearers is of no importance, if only that which is spoken be true ; although in this respect there is a difference, that men can, by agreement among themselves, arrange as to the sounds of language by which they may communicate their thoughts to one another, but that those who have discerned what is right have been guided only by the will of God in regard to the sacred rites which were agreeable to the Divine Being. This divine will has never been

---

wanting to the justice and piety of mortals for their salvation; and whatever varieties of worship there may have been in different nations bound together by one and the same religion, the most important thing to observe was this: how far, on the one hand, human infirmity was thereby encouraged to effort, or borne with, while, on the other hand, the divine authority was not assailed.

11. Wherefore, since we affirm that Christ is the Word of God, by whom all things were made, and is the Son, because He is the Word, not a word uttered and belonging to the past but abides unchangeably with the unchangeable Father, Himself unchangeable, under whose rule the whole universe, spiritual and material, is ordered in the way best adapted to different times and places, and that He has perfect wisdom and knowledge as to what should be done, and when and where everything should be done in the controlling and ordering of the universe, — most certainly, both before He gave being to the Hebrew nation, by which He was pleased, through sacraments suited to the time, to prefigure the manifestation of Himself in His advent, and during the time of the Jewish commonwealth, and, after that, when He manifested Himself in the likeness of mortals to mortal men in the body which He received from the Virgin, and thenceforward even to our day, in which He is fulfilling all which He predicted of old by the prophets, and from this present time on to the end of the world, when He shall separate the holy from the wicked, and give to every man his due recompense, — in all these successive ages He is the same Son of God, co-eternal with the Father, and the unchangeable Wisdom by whom universal nature was called into existence, and by participation in whom every rational soul is made blessed.

12. Therefore, from the beginning of the human race, whosoever believed in Him, and in any way knew Him, and lived in a pious and just manner according to His precepts, was undoubtedly saved by Him, in whatever time and place he may have lived. For as we believe in Him both as dwelling with the Father and as having come in the flesh, so the men of the former ages believed in Him both as dwelling with the Father and as destined to come in the flesh. And the nature of faith is not changed, nor is the salvation made different, in our age, by the fact that, in consequence of the difference between the two epochs, that which was then foretold as future is now proclaimed as past. Moreover, we are not under necessity to suppose different things and different kinds of salvation to be signified, when the self-same thing is by different sacred words and rites of worship announced in the one case as fulfilled, in the other as future. As to the manner and time, however, in which anything that pertains to the one salvation common to all believers and pious persons is brought to pass, let us ascribe wisdom to God, and for our part exercise submission to His will. Wherefore the true religion, although formerly set forth and practised under other names and with other symbolical rites than it now has, and formerly more obscurely revealed and known to fewer persons than now in the time of clearer light and wider diffusion, is one and the same in both periods.

13. Moreover, we do not raise any objection to their religion on the ground of the difference between the institutions appointed by Numa Pompilius for the worship of the gods by the Romans, and those which were up till that time practised in Rome or in other parts of Italy; nor on the fact that in the age of Pythagoras that system of philosophy became generally adopted which up to that time had no existence, or lay concealed, perhaps, among a very small number whose views were the same, but whose religious practice and worship was different: the question upon which we join issue with them is, whether these gods were true gods, or worthy of worship, and whether that philosophy was fitted to promote the salvation of the souls of men. This is what we insist upon discussing; and in discussing it we pluck up their sophistries by the root. Let them, therefore, desist from bringing against us objections which are of equal force against every sect, and against religion of every name. For since, as they admit, the ages of the world do not roll on under the dominion of chance, but are controlled by divine Providence, what may be fitting and expedient in each successive age transcends the range of human understanding, and is determined by the same wisdom by which Providence cares for the universe.

14. For if they assert that the reason why the doctrine of Pythagoras has not prevailed always and universally is, that Pythagoras was but a man, and had not power to secure this, can they also affirm that in the age and in the countries in which his philosophy flourished, all who had the opportunity of hearing him were found willing to believe and follow him? And therefore it is the more certain that, if Pythagoras had possessed the power of publishing his doctrines where he pleased and when he pleased, and if he had also possessed along with that power a perfect foreknowledge of events, he would have presented himself only at those places and times in which he foreknew that men would believe his teaching. Wherefore, since they do not object to Christ on the ground of His doctrine not being universally embraced, — for they feel that this would be a futile objection if alleged either

against the teaching of philosophers or against the majesty of their own gods, — what answer, I ask, could they make, if, leaving out of view that depth of the wisdom and knowledge of God within which it may be that some other divine purpose lies much more deeply hidden, and without prejudging the other reasons possibly existing, which are fit subjects for patient study by the wise, we confine ourselves, for the sake of brevity in this discussion, to the statement of this one position, that it pleased Christ to appoint the time in which He would appear and the persons among whom His doctrine was to be proclaimed, according to His knowledge of the times and places in which men would believe on Him?[1] For He foreknew, regarding those ages and places in which His gospel has not been preached, that in them the gospel, if preached, would meet with such treatment from all, without exception, as it met with, not indeed from all, but from many, at the time of His personal presence on earth, who would not believe in Him, even though men were raised from the dead by Him ; and such as we see it meet with in our day from many who, although the predictions of the prophets concerning Him are so manifestly fulfilled, still refuse to believe, and, misguided by the perverse subtlety of the human heart, rather resist than yield to divine authority, even when this is so clear and manifest, so glorious and so gloriously published abroad. So long as the mind of man is limited in capacity and in strength, it is his duty to yield to divine truth. Why, then, should we wonder if Christ knew that the world was so full of unbelievers in the former ages, that He righteously refused to manifest Himself or to be preached to those of whom He foreknew that they would not believe either His words or His miracles? For it is not incredible that all may have been then such as, to our amazement, so many have been from the time of His advent to the present time, and even now are.

15. And yet, from the beginning of the human race, He never ceased to speak by His prophets, at one time more obscurely, at another time more plainly, as seemed to divine wisdom best adapted to the time ; nor were there ever wanting men who believed in Him, from Adam to Moses, and among the people of Israel itself, which was by a special mysterious appointment a prophetic nation, and among other nations before He came in the flesh. For seeing that in the sacred Hebrew books some are mentioned, even from Abraham's time, not belonging to his natural posterity nor to the people of Israel, and not proselytes added to that people, who were nevertheless partakers of this holy mystery,[2] why may we not believe that in other nations also, here and there, some more were found, although we do not read their names in these authoritative records? Thus the salvation provided by this religion, by which alone, as alone true, true salvation is truly promised, was never wanting to any one who was worthy of it, and he to whom it was wanting was not worthy of it.[3] And from the beginning of the human family, even to the end of time, it is preached, to some for their advantage, to some for their condemnation. Accordingly, those to whom it has not been preached at all are those who were foreknown as persons who would not believe ; those to whom, notwithstanding the certainty that they would not believe, the salvation has been proclaimed are set forth as an example of the class of unbelievers ; and those to whom, as persons who would believe, the truth is proclaimed are being prepared for the kingdom of heaven and for the society of the holy angels.

16. QUESTION III. Let us now look to the question which comes next in order. "They find fault," he says, "with the sacred ceremonies, the sacrificial victims, the burning of incense, and all the other parts of worship in our temples ; and yet the same kind of worship had its origin in antiquity with themselves, or from the God whom they worship, for He is represented by them as having been in need of the first-fruits."

17. This question is obviously founded upon the passage in our Scriptures in which it is written that Cain brought to God a gift from the fruits of the earth, but Abel brought a gift from the firstlings of the flock.[4] Our reply, therefore, is, that from this passage the more suitable inference to be drawn is, how ancient is the ordinance of sacrifice which the infallible and sacred

---

[1] Augustin, having been informed by Hilary (*Ep.* 219) that this passage was quoted by Semipelagians in defence of their error, made the following remark on it in his work *De Praedestinatione Sanctorum*, c. ix.: " Do you not observe that my design in this sentence was, without excluding the secret counsel of God and any other causes, to say, in reference to Christ's foreknowledge, what seemed sufficient to reduce to silence the unbelief of the Pagans by whom the objection had been raised? For what is more certain than this, that Christ foreknew who would believe in Him, and in what time and place they would live? But I did not deem it necessary, in that connection, to investigate and discuss the question as to this faith in Christ preached to them, whether they would have it of themselves or would receive it from God — in other words, whether God merely foreknew, or also predestinated them. The sentence, therefore, ' that it pleased Christ to appoint the time in which He would appear, and the persons among whom His doctrine was to be proclaimed, according to His knowledge of the times and places in which men would believe in Him,' might have been put thus: that it pleased Christ to appoint the time in which He would appear, and the persons among whom His doctrine was to be proclaimed, according to His knowledge of the times and places in which those would be found who had been chosen in Him before the foundation of the world."

[2] *Sacramenti.*

[3] On these words Augustin remarks in his *Retractations*, Book II. ch. xxxi.: "This I said, not meaning that any one could be worthy through his own merit, but in the same sense as the apostle said, ' Not of works, but of Him that calleth ; it was said unto her, " The elder shall serve the younger "' (Rom. ix. 11, 12), — a calling which he affirms to pertain to the purpose of God. For which reason he says, ' Not according to our works, but according to His own purpose and grace ' (2 Tim. i. 9) ; and again, ' We know that all things work together for good to 'them that love God, to them that are called according to His purpose' (Rom. viii. 28). Of which calling he says, ' That our God would count you worthy of this calling ' (2 Thess. i. 11)."

[4] Gen. iv. 3, 4.

writings declare to be due to no other than to the one true God; not because God needs our offerings, seeing that, in the same Scriptures, it is most clearly written, "I said unto the Lord, Thou art my Lord, for Thou hast no need of my good,"[1] but because, even in the acceptance or rejection or appropriation of these offerings, He considers the advantage of men, and of them alone. For in worshipping God we do good to ourselves, not to Him. When, therefore, He gives an inspired revelation, and teaches how He is to be worshipped, He does this not only from no sense of need on His part, but from a regard to our highest advantage. For all such sacrifices are significant, being symbols of certain things by which we ought to be roused to search or know or recollect the things which they symbolize. To discuss this subject satisfactorily would demand of us something more than the short discourse in which we have resolved to give our reply at this time, more particularly because in other treatises we have spoken of it fully.[2] Those also who have before us expounded the divine oracles, have spoken largely of the symbols of the sacrifices of the Old Testament as shadows and figures of things then future.

18. With all our desire, however, to be brief, this one thing we must by no means omit to remark, that the false gods, that is to say, the demons, which are lying angels, would never have required a temple, priesthood, sacrifice, and the other things connected with these from their worshippers, whom they deceive, had they not known that these things were due to the one true God. When, therefore, these things are presented to God according to His inspiration and teaching, it is true religion; but when they are given to demons in compliance with their impious pride, it is baneful superstition. Accordingly, those who know the Christian Scriptures of both the Old and the New Testaments do not blame the profane rites of Pagans on the mere ground of their building temples, appointing priests, and offering sacrifices, but on the ground of their doing all this for idols and demons. As to idols, indeed, who entertains a doubt as to their being wholly devoid of perception? And yet, when they are placed in these temples and set on high upon thrones of honour, that they may be waited upon by suppliants and worshippers praying and offering sacrifices, even these idols, though devoid both of feeling and of life, do, by the mere image of the members and senses of beings endowed with life, so affect weak minds, that they appear to live and breathe, especially under the added influence of the profound veneration with which the multitude freely renders such costly service.

19. To these morbid and pernicious affections of the mind divine Scripture applies a remedy, by repeating, with the impressiveness of wholesome admonition, a familiar fact, in the words, "Eyes have they, but they see not; they have ears, but they hear not,"[3] etc. For these words, by reason of their being so plain, and commending themselves to all people as true, are the more effective in striking salutary shame into those who, when they present divine worship before such images with religious fear, and look upon their likeness to living beings while they are venerating and worshipping them, and utter petitions, offer sacrifices, and perform vows before them as if present, are so completely overcome, that they do not presume to think of them as devoid of perception. Lest, moreover, these worshippers should think that our Scriptures intend only to declare that such affections of the human heart spring naturally from the worship of idols, it is written in the plainest terms, "All the gods of the nations are devils."[4] And therefore, also, the teaching of the apostles not only declares, as we read in John, "Little children, keep yourselves from idols,"[5] but also, in the words of Paul, "What say I then? that the idol is anything, or that which is offered in sacrifice to idols is anything? But I say, that the things which the Gentiles sacrifice they sacrifice to devils, and not to God; and I would not that ye should have fellowship with devils."[6] From which it may be clearly understood, that what is condemned in heathen superstitions by the true religion is not the mere offering of sacrifices (for the ancient saints offered these to the true God), but the offering of sacrifices to false gods and to impious demons. For as the truth counsels men to seek the fellowship of the holy angels, in like manner impiety turns men aside to the fellowship of the wicked angels, for whose associates everlasting fire is prepared, as the eternal kingdom is prepared for the associates of the holy angels.

20. The heathen find a plea for their profane rites and their idols in the fact that they interpret with ingenuity what is signified by each of them, but the plea is of no avail. For all this interpretation relates to the creature, not to the Creator, to whom alone is due that religious service which is in the Greek language distinguished by the word λατρεία. Neither do we say that the earth, the seas, the heaven, the sun, the moon, the stars, and any other celestial influences which may be beyond our ken are demons; but since all created things are divided into material and immaterial, the latter of which we also call spir-

---

[1] Ps. xvi. 2: ὅτι τῶν ἀγαθῶν μου οὐ χρείαν ἔχεις, LXX.
[2] E.g., in the reply to Faustus, Book xxii.
[3] Ps. cxv. 5, 6.
[4] Ps. xcvi. 5: δαιμόνια, LXX.
[5] 1 John v. 21.
[6] 1 Cor. x. 19, 20.

itual, it is manifest that what is done by us under the power of piety and religion proceeds from the faculty of our souls known as the will, which belongs to the spiritual creation, and is therefore to be preferred to all that is material. Whence it is inferred that sacrifice must not be offered to anything material. There remains, therefore, the spiritual part of creation, which is either pious or impious, — the pious consisting of men and angels who are righteous, and who duly serve God; the impious consisting of wicked men and angels, whom we also call devils. Now, that sacrifice must not be offered to a spiritual creature, though righteous, is obvious from this consideration, that the more pious and submissive to God any creature is, the less does he presume to aspire to that honour which he knows to be due to God alone. How much worse, therefore, is it to sacrifice to devils, that is, to a wicked spiritual creature, which, dwelling in this comparatively dark heaven nearest to earth, as in the prison assigned to him in the air, is doomed to eternal punishment. Wherefore, even when men say that they are offering sacrifices to the higher celestial powers, which are not devils, and imagine that the only difference between us and them is in a name, because they call them gods and we call them angels, the only beings which really present themselves to these men, who are given over to be the sport of manifold deceptions, are the devils who find delight and, in a sense, nourishment in the errors of mankind. For the holy angels do not approve of any sacrifice except what is offered, agreeably to the teaching of true wisdom and true religion, unto the one true God, whom in holy fellowship they serve. Therefore, as impious presumption, whether in men or in angels, commands or covets the rendering to itself of those honours which belong to God, so, on the other hand, pious humility, whether in men or in holy angels, declines these honours when offered, and declares to whom alone they are due, of which most notable examples are conspicuously set forth in our sacred books.

21. In the sacrifices appointed by the divine oracles there has been a diversity of institution corresponding to the age in which they were observed. Some sacrifices were offered before the actual manifestation of that new covenant, the benefits of which are provided by the one true offering of the one Priest, namely, by the shed blood of Christ; and another sacrifice, adapted to this manifestation, and offered in the present age by us who are called Christians after the name of Him who has been revealed, is set before us not only in the gospels, but also in the prophetic books. For a change, not of the God who is worshipped, nor of the religion itself, but of sacrifices and of sacraments, would seem to be proclaimed without warrant now, if it had not been foretold in the earlier dispensation. For just as when the same man brings to God in the morning one kind of offering, and in the evening another, according to the time of day, he does not thereby change either his God or his religion, any more than he changes the nature of a salutation who uses one form of salutation in the morning and another in the evening: so, in the complete cycle of the ages, when one kind of offering is known to have been made by the ancient saints, and another is presented by the saints in our time, this only shows that these sacred mysteries are celebrated not according to human presumption, but by divine authority, in the manner best adapted to the times. There is here no change either in the Deity or in the religion.

22. QUESTION IV. Let us, in the next place, consider what he has laid down concerning the proportion between sin and punishment when, misrepresenting the gospel, he says: "Christ threatens eternal punishment to those who do not believe in Him;"[1] and yet He says in another place, "With what measure ye mete, it shall be measured to you again."[2] "Here," he remarks, "is something sufficiently absurd and contradictory; for if He is to award punishment according to measure, and all measure is limited by the end of time, what mean these threats of eternal punishment?"

23. It is difficult to believe that this question has been put in the form of objection by one claiming to be in any sense a philosopher; for he says, "All measure is limited by time," as if men were accustomed to no other measures than measures of time, such as hours and days and years, or such as are referred to when we say that the time of a short syllable is one-half of that of a long syllable.[3] For I suppose that bushels and firkins, urns and amphoræ, are not measures of time. How, then, is all measure limited by time? Do not the heathen themselves affirm that the sun is eternal? And yet they presume to calculate and pronounce on the basis of geometrical measurements what is the proportion between it and the earth. Whether this calculation be within or beyond their power, it is certain, notwithstanding, that it has a disc of definite dimensions. For if they do ascertain how large it is, they know its dimensions, and if they do not succeed in their investigation, they do not know these; but the fact that men cannot discover them is no proof that they do not exist. It is possible, therefore, for something to be eternal, and nevertheless to have a definite

---

[1] John iii. 18.
[2] Matt. vii. 2.
[3] " Longam syllabam esse duorum temporum brevem unius etiam pueri sciunt." — Quintil. ix. 4, 47.

measure of its proportions. In this I have been speaking upon the assumption of their own view as to the eternal duration of the sun, in order that they may be convinced by one of their own tenets, and obliged to admit that something may be eternal and at the same time measurable. And therefore let them not think that the threatening of Christ concerning eternal punishment is not to be believed because of His also saying, " In what measure ye mete, it shall be measured unto you."

24. For if He had said, " That which you have measured shall be measured unto you," even in that case it would not have been necessary to take the clauses as referring to something which was in all respects the same. For we may correctly say, That which you have planted you shall reap, although men plant not fruit but trees, and reap not trees but fruit. We say it, however, with reference to the kind of tree ; for a man does not plant a fig-tree, and expect to gather nuts from it. In like manner it might be said, What you have done you shall suffer ; not meaning that if one has committed adultery, for example, he shall suffer the same, but that what he has in that crime done to the law, the law shall do unto him, i.e. forasmuch as he has removed from his life the law which prohibits such things, the law shall requite him by removing him from that human life over which it presides.

Again, if He had said, " As much as ye shall have measured, so much shall be measured unto you," even from this statement it would not necessarily follow that we must understand punishments to be in every particular equal to the sins punished. Barley and wheat, for example, are not equal in quality, and yet it might be said, " As much as ye shall have measured, so much shall be measured unto you," meaning for so much wheat so much barley. Or if the matter in question were pain, it might be said, " As great pain shall be inflicted on you as you have inflicted on others ; " this might mean that the pain should be in severity equal, but in time more protracted, and therefore by its continuance greater. For suppose I were to say of two lamps, " The flame of this one was as hot as the flame of the other," this would not be false, although, perchance, one of them was earlier extinguished than the other. Wherefore, if things are equally great in one respect, but not in another, the fact that they are not alike in all respects does not invalidate the statement that in one respect, as admitted, they are equally great.

25. Seeing, however, that the words of Christ were these, " In what measure ye mete, it shall be measured unto you," and that beyond all question the measure in which anything is meas-

ured is one thing, and that which is measured in it is another, it is obviously possible that with the same measure with which men have measured, say, a bushel of wheat, there may be measured to them thousands of bushels, so that with no difference in the measure there may be all that difference in the quantity, not to speak of the difference of quality which might be in the things measured ; for it is not only possible that with the same measure with which one has measured barley to others, wheat may be measured to him, but, moreover, with the same measure with which he has measured grain, gold may be measured to him, and of the grain there may have been one bushel, while there may be very many of the gold. Thus, although there is a difference both in kind and quantity, it may be nevertheless truly said in reference to things which are thus unlike : " In the measure in which he measured to others it is measured unto him."

The reason, moreover, why Christ uttered this saying is sufficiently plain from the immediately preceding context. " Judge not," He said, "that ye be not judged ; for in the judgment in which ye judge ye shall be judged." Does this mean that if they have judged any one with injustice they shall themselves be unjustly judged? Of course not ; for there is no unrighteousness with God. But it is thus expressed, " In the judgment in which ye judge ye shall be judged," as if it were said, In the will in which ye have dealt kindly with others ye shall be set at liberty, or in the will in which ye have done evil to others ye shall be punished. As if any one, for example, using his eyes for the gratification of base desires, were ordered to be made blind, this would be a just sentence for him to hear, " In those eyes by which thou hast sinned, in them hast thou deserved to be punished." For every one uses the judgment of his own mind, according as it is good or evil, for doing good or for doing evil. Wherefore it is not unjust that he be judged in that in which he judges, that is to say, that he suffer the penalty in the mind's faculty of judgment when he is made to endure those evils which are the consequences of the sinful judgment of his mind.

26. For while other torments which are prepared to be hereafter inflicted are visible, — torments occasioned by the same central cause, namely, a depraved will, — it is also the fact that within the mind itself, in which the appetite of the will is the measure of all human actions, sin is followed immediately by punishment, which is for the most part increased in proportion to the greater blindness of one by whom it is not felt. Therefore when He had said, " With [or rather, as Augustin renders it, In] what judgment ye judge, ye shall be judged," He went on to add, " And in what measure ye mete, it shall be meas-

ured unto you." A good man, that is to say, will measure out good actions in his own will, and in the same shall blessedness be measured unto him ; and in like manner, a bad man will measure out bad actions in his own will, and in the same shall misery be meted out to him ; for in whatsoever any one is good when his will aims at what is good, in the same he is evil when his will aims at what is evil. And therefore it is also in this that he is made to experience bliss or misery, viz. in the feeling experienced by his own will, which is the measure both of all actions and of the recompenses of actions. For we measure actions, whether good or bad, by the quality of the volitions which produce them, not by the length of time which they occupy. Were it otherwise, it would be regarded a greater crime to fell a tree than to kill a man. For the former takes a long time and many strokes, the latter may be done with one blow in a moment of time ; and yet, if a man were punished with no more than transportation for life for this great crime committed in a moment, it would be said that he had been treated with more clemency than he deserved, although, in regard to the duration of time, the protracted punishment is not in any way to be compared with the sudden act of murder. Where, then, is anything contradictory in the sentence objected to, if the punishments shall be equally protracted or even alike eternal, but differing in comparative gentleness and severity? The duration is the same ; the pain inflicted is different in degree, because that which constitutes the measure of the sins themselves is found not in the length of time which they occupy, but in the will of those who commit them.

27. Certainly the will itself endures the punishment, whether pain be inflicted on the mind or on the body ; so that the same thing which is gratified by the sin is smitten by the penalty, and so that he who judgeth without mercy is judged without mercy ; for in this sentence also the standard of measure is the same only in this point, that what he did not give to others is denied to him, and therefore the judgment passed on him shall be eternal, although the judgment pronounced by him cannot be eternal. It is therefore in the sinner's own measure that punishments which are eternal are measured out to him, though the sins thus punished were not eternal ; for as his wish was to have an eternal enjoyment of sin, so the award which he finds is an eternal endurance of suffering.

The brevity which I study in this reply precludes me from collecting all, or at least as many as I could, of the statements contained in our sacred books as to sin and the punishment of sin, and deducing from these one indisputable

proposition on the subject ; and perhaps, even if I obtained the necessary leisure, I might not possess abilities competent to the task. Nevertheless, I think that in the meantime I have proved that there is no contradiction between the eternity of punishment and the principle that sins shall be recompensed in the same measure in which men have committed them.

28. QUESTION V. The objector who has brought forward these questions from Porphyry has added this one in the next place : Will you have the goodness to instruct me as to whether Solomon said truly or not that God has no Son?

29. The answer is brief : Solomon not only did not say this, but, on the contrary, expressly said that God hath a Son. For in one of his writings Wisdom saith : "Before the mountains were settled, before the hills was I brought forth."[1] And what is Christ but the Wisdom of God? Again, in another place in the book of Proverbs, he says : "God hath taught me wisdom, and I have learned the knowledge of the holy.[2] Who hath ascended up into heaven and descended? who hath gathered the winds in His fists? who hath bound the waters in a garment? who hath established all the ends of the earth? What is His name, and what is His Son's name?"[3] Of the two questions concluding this quotation, the one referred to the Father, namely, "What is His name?" — with allusion to the foregoing words, "God hath taught me wisdom," — the other evidently to the Son, since he says, "or what is His Son's name?" — with allusion to the other statements, which are more properly understood as pertaining to the Son, viz. "Who hath ascended up into heaven and descended?" — a question brought to remembrance by the words of Paul : "He that descended is the same also that ascended up far above all heavens ; "[4] — "Who hath gathered the winds in His fists?" i.e. the souls of believers in a hidden and secret place, to whom, accordingly, it is said, "Ye are dead, and your life is hid with Christ in God ; "[5] — "Who hath bound the waters in a garment?"[6] whence it could be said, "As many of you as have been baptized into Christ have put on Christ ; "[7] — "Who hath established all the ends of the earth?" the same who said to His disciples, "Ye shall be witnesses unto Me, both in Jerusalem, and in all Judea, and in Samaria, and unto the uttermost part of the earth."[8]

30. QUESTION VI. The last question proposed is concerning Jonah, and it is put as if it were

---

[1] Prov. viii. 25: πρὸ δὲ πάντων βουνῶν γεννᾷ με, LXX.
[2] According to LXX.
[3] Prov. xxx. 3, 4.
[4] Eph. iv. 10.
[5] Col. iii. 3.
[6] Augustin's words are : quis convertit aquam in vestimento ? from the LXX. : τίς συνεστρεψεν ὕδωρ ἐν ἱματίῳ.
[7] Gal. iii. 27.
[8] Acts i. 8.

not from Porphyry, but as being a standing subject of ridicule among the Pagans; for his words are: " In the next place, what are we to believe concerning Jonah, who is said to have been three days in a whale's belly? The thing is utterly improbable and incredible, that a man swallowed with his clothes on should have existed in the inside of a fish. If, however, the story is figurative, be pleased to explain it. Again, what is meant by the story that a gourd sprang up above the head of Jonah after he was vomited by the fish? What was the cause of this gourd's growth?" Questions such as these I have seen discussed by Pagans amidst loud laughter, and with great scorn.

31. To this I reply, that either all the miracles wrought by divine power may be treated as incredible, or there is no reason why the story of this miracle should not be believed. The resurrection of Christ Himself upon the third day would not be believed by us, if the Christian faith was afraid to encounter Pagan ridicule. Since, however, our friend did not on this ground ask whether it is to be believed that Lazarus was raised on the fourth day, or that Christ rose on the third day, I am much surprised that he reckoned what was done with Jonah to be incredible; unless, perchance, he thinks it easier for a dead man to be raised in life from his sepulchre, than for a living man to be kept in life in the spacious belly of a sea monster. For without mentioning the great size of sea monsters which is reported to us by those who have knowledge of them, let me ask how many men could be contained in the belly which was fenced round with those huge ribs which are fixed in a public place in Carthage, and are well known to all men there? Who can be at a loss to conjecture how wide an entrance must have been given by the opening of the mouth which was the gateway of that vast cavern? unless, perchance, as our friend stated it, the clothing of Jonah stood in the way of his being swallowed without injury, as if he had required to squeeze himself through a narrow passage, instead of being, as was the case, thrown headlong through the air, and so caught by the sea monster as to be received into its belly before he was wounded by its teeth. At the same time, the Scripture does not say whether he had his clothes on or not when he was cast down into that cavern, so that it may without contradiction be understood that he made that swift descent unclothed, if perchance it was necessary that his garment should be taken from him, as the shell is taken from an egg, to make him more easily swallowed. For men are as much concerned about the raiment of this prophet as would be reasonable if it were stated that he had crept through a very small window, or had been going into a bath;

and yet, even though it were necessary in such circumstances to enter without parting with one's clothes, this would be only inconvenient, not miraculous.

32. But perhaps our objectors find it impossible to believe in regard to this divine miracle that the heated moist air of the belly, whereby food is dissolved, could be so moderated in temperature as to preserve the life of a man. If so, with how much greater force might they pronounce it incredible that the three young men cast into the furnace by the impious king walked unharmed in the midst of the flames! If, therefore, these objectors refuse to believe any narrative of a divine miracle, they must be refuted by another line of argument. For it is incumbent on them in that case not to single out some one to be objected to, and called in question as incredible, but to denounce as incredible all narratives in which miracles of the same kind or more remarkable are recorded. And yet, if this which is written concerning Jonah were said to have been done by Apuleius of Madaura or Apollonius of Tyana, by whom they boast, though unsupported by reliable testimony, that many wonders were performed (albeit even the devils do some works like those done by the holy angels, not in truth, but in appearance, not by wisdom, but manifestly by subtlety), — if, I say, any such event were narrated in connection with these men to whom they give the flattering name of magicians or philosophers, we should hear from their mouths sounds not of derision, but of triumph. Be it so, then; let them laugh at our Scriptures; let them laugh as much as they can, when they see themselves daily becoming fewer in number, while some are removed by death, and others by their embracing the Christian faith, and when all those things are being fulfilled which were predicted by the prophets who long ago laughed at them, and said that they would fight and bark against the truth in vain, and would gradually come over to our side; and who not only transmitted these statements to us, their descendants, for our learning, but promised that they should be fulfilled in our experience.

33. It is neither unreasonable nor unprofitable to inquire what these miracles signify, so that, after their significance has been explained, men may believe not only that they really occurred, but also that they have been recorded, because of their possessing symbolical meaning. Let him, therefore, who proposes to inquire why the prophet Jonah was three days in the capacious belly of a sea monster, begin by dismissing doubts as to the fact itself; for this did actually occur, and did not occur in vain. For if figures which are expressed in words only, and not in actions, aid our faith, how much more should our

faith be helped by figures expressed not only in words, but also in actions! Now men are wont to speak by words; but divine power speaks by actions as well as by words. And as words which are new or somewhat unfamiliar lend brilliancy to a human discourse when they are scattered through it in a moderate and judicious manner, so the eloquence of divine revelation receives, so to speak, additional lustre from actions which are at once marvellous in themselves and skilfully designed to impart spiritual instruction.

34. As to the question, What was prefigured by the sea monster restoring alive on the third day the prophet whom it swallowed? why is this asked of us, when Christ Himself has given the answer, saying, "An evil and adulterous generation seeketh after a sign, and there shall no sign be given it but the sign of the prophet Jonas: for as Jonas was three days and three nights in the whale's belly, so must the Son of man be three days and three nights in the heart of the earth"[1]? In regard to the three days in which the Lord Christ was under the power of death, it would take long to explain how they are reckoned to be three whole days, that is, days along with their nights, because of the whole of the first day and of the third day being understood as represented on the part of each; moreover, this has been already stated very often in other discourses. As, therefore, Jonah passed from the ship to the belly of the whale, so Christ passed from the cross to the sepulchre, or into the abyss of death. And as Jonah suffered this for the sake of those who were endangered by the storm, so Christ suffered for the sake of those who are tossed on the waves of this world. And as the command was given at first that the word of God should be preached to the Ninevites by Jonah, but the preaching of Jonah did not come to them until after the whale had vomited him forth, so prophetic teaching was addressed early to the Gentiles, but did not actually come to the Gentiles until after the resurrection of Christ from the grave.

35. In the next place, as to Jonah's building for himself a booth, and sitting down over against Nineveh, waiting to see what would befall the city, the prophet was here in his own person the symbol of another fact. He prefigured the carnal people of Israel. For he also was grieved at the salvation of the Ninevites, that is, at the redemption and deliverance of the Gentiles, from among whom Christ came to call, not righteous men, but sinners to repentance.[2] Wherefore the shadow of that gourd over his head prefigured the promises of the Old Testament, or rather the privileges already enjoyed in it, in which there was, as the apostle says, "a shadow of things to come,"[3] furnishing, as it were, a refuge from the heat of temporal calamities in the land of promise. Moreover, in that morning-worm,[4] which by its gnawing tooth made the gourd wither away, Christ Himself is again prefigured, forasmuch as, by the publication of the gospel from His mouth, all those things which flourished among the Israelites for a time, or with a shadowy symbolical meaning in that earlier dispensation, are now deprived of their significance, and have withered away. And now that nation, having lost the kingdom, the priesthood, and the sacrifices formerly established in Jerusalem, all which privileges were a shadow of things to come, is burned with grievous heat of tribulation in its condition of dispersion and captivity, as Jonah was, according to the history, scorched with the heat of the sun, and is overwhelmed with sorrow; and notwithstanding, the salvation of the Gentiles and of the penitent is of more importance in the sight of God than this sorrow of Israel and the "shadow" of which the Jewish nation was so glad.

36. Again, let the Pagans laugh, and let them treat with proud and senseless ridicule Christ the Worm and this interpretation of the prophetic symbol, provided that He gradually and surely, nevertheless, consume them. For concerning all such Isaiah prophesies, when by him God says to us, "Hearken unto me, ye that know righteousness, the people in whose heart is my law; fear ye not the reproach of men, neither be ye afraid of their revilings: for the moth shall eat them up as a garment, and the worm shall eat them like wool; but my righteousness shall be for ever."[5] Let us therefore acknowledge Christ to be the morning-worm, because, moreover, in that psalm which bears the title, "Upon the hind of the morning,"[6] He has been pleased to call Himself by this very name: "I am," He says, "a worm, and no man, a reproach of men, and despised of the people." This reproach is one of those reproaches which we are commanded not to fear in the words of Isaiah, "Fear ye not the reproach of men." By that Worm, as by a moth, they are being consumed who under the tooth of His gospel are made to wonder daily at the diminution of their numbers, which is caused by desertion from their party. Let us therefore acknowledge this symbol of Christ; and because of the salvation of God, let us bear patiently the reproaches of men. He is a Worm because of the lowliness of the flesh which He assumed — perhaps, also, because of His being born of a virgin; for the worm is generally not begotten, but spontaneously origi-

---

[1] Matt. xii. 39, 40.
[2] Luke v. 32.
[3] Col. ii. 17.
[4] Vermis matutinus.
[5] Isa. li. 7, 8.
[6] Ps. xxii. The title in the LXX. is, "ὑπὲρ τῆς ἀντιληψέως τῆς ἑωθινῆς," which Augustin translates, "pro susceptione matutina."

nated in flesh or any vegetable product [sine concubitu nascitur]. He is the *morning*-worm, because He rose from the grave before the dawn of day. That gourd might, of course, have withered without any worm at its root; and finally, if God regarded the worm as necessary for this work, what need was there to add the epithet *morning*-worm, if not to secure that He should be recognised as the Worm who in the psalm, "pro susceptione matutina," sings, "I am a worm, and no man"?

37. What, then, could be more palpable than the fulfilment of this prophecy in the accomplishment of the things foretold? That Worm was indeed despised when He hung upon the cross, as is written in the same psalm: "They shoot out the lip, they shake the head, saying, He trusted in the Lord that he would deliver him; let him deliver him, seeing he delighted in him;"[1] and again, when this was fulfilled which the psalm foretold, "They pierced my hands and my feet. They have told all my bones: they look and stare upon me. They part my garments among them, and cast lots upon my vesture,"[2] — circumstances which are in that ancient book described when future by the prophet with as great plainness as they are now recorded in the gospel history after their occurrence. But if in His humiliation that Worm was despised, is He to be still despised when we behold the accomplishment of those things which are predicted in the latter part of the same psalm: "All the ends of the world shall remember, and turn unto the Lord; and all the kindreds of the nations shall worship in His presence. For the kingdom is the Lord's; and He shall govern among the nations"?[3] Thus the Ninevites "remembered, and turned unto the Lord." The salvation granted to the Gentiles on their repentance, which was thus so long before prefigured, Israel then, as represented by Jonah, regarded with grief, as now their nation grieves, bereft of their shadow, and vexed with the heat of their tribulations. Any one is at liberty to open up with a different interpretation, if only it be in harmony with the rule of faith, all the other particulars which are hidden in the symbolical history of the prophet Jonah; but it is obvious that it is not lawful to interpret the three days which he passed in the belly of the whale otherwise than as it has been revealed by the heavenly Master Himself in the gospel, as quoted above.

38. I have answered to the best of my power the questions proposed; but let him who proposed them become now a Christian at once, lest, if he delay until he has finished the discussion of all difficulties connected with the sacred books, he come to the end of this life before he pass from death to life. For it is reasonable that he inquire as to the resurrection of the dead before he is admitted to the Christian sacraments. Perhaps he ought also to be allowed to insist on preliminary discussion of the question proposed concerning Christ — why He came so late in the world's history, and of a few great questions besides, to which all others are subordinate. But to think of finishing all such questions as those concerning the words, "In what measure ye mete, it shall be measured unto you," and concerning Jonah, before he becomes a Christian, is to betray great unmindfulness of man's limited capacities, and of the shortness of the life which remains to him. For there are innumerable questions the solution of which is not to be demanded before we believe, lest life be finished by us in unbelief. When, however, the Christian faith has been thoroughly received, these questions behove to be studied with the utmost diligence for the pious satisfaction of the minds of believers. Whatever is discovered by such study ought to be imparted to others without vain self-complacency; if anything still remain hidden, we must bear with patience an imperfection of knowledge which is not prejudicial to salvation.

LETTER CIII.

(A.D. 409.)

TO MY LORD AND BROTHER, AUGUSTIN, RIGHTLY AND JUSTLY WORTHY OF ESTEEM AND OF ALL POSSIBLE HONOUR, NECTARIUS SENDS GREETING IN THE LORD.

1. In reading the letter of your Excellency, in which you have overthrown the worship of idols and the ritual of their temples,[4] I seemed to myself to hear the voice of a philosopher, — not of such a philosopher as the academician of whom they say, that having neither new doctrine to propound nor earlier statements of his own to defend, he was wont to sit in gloomy corners on the ground absorbed in some deep reverie, with his knees drawn back to his forehead, and his head buried between them, contriving how he might as a detractor assail the discoveries or cavil at the statements by which others had earned renown; nay, the form which rose under the spell of your eloquence and stood before my eyes was rather that of the great statesman Cicero, who, having been crowned with laurels for saving the lives of many of his countrymen, carried the trophies won in his forensic victories into the wondering schools of Greek philosophy, when, as one pausing for

---

[1] Ps. xxii. 7, 8.
[2] Ps. xxii. 16-18.
[3] Ps. xxii. 27, 28.

[4] Letter XCI. p. 376.

breath, he laid down the trumpet of sonorous voice and language which he had blown with blast of just indignation against those who had broken the laws and conspired against the life of the republic, and, adopting the fashion of the Grecian mantle, unfastened and threw back over his shoulders the toga's ample folds.

2. I therefore listened with pleasure when you urged us to the worship and religion of the only supreme God; and when you counselled us to look to our heavenly fatherland, I received the exhortation with joy. For you were obviously speaking to me not of any city confined by encircling ramparts, nor of that commonwealth on this earth which the writings of philosophers have mentioned and declared to have all mankind as its citizens, but of that City which is inhabited and possessed by the great God, and by the spirits which have earned this recompense from Him, to which, by diverse roads and pathways, all religions aspire,—the City which we are not able in language to describe, but which perhaps we might by thinking apprehend. But while this City ought therefore to be, above all others, desired and loved, I am nevertheless of opinion that we are bound not to prove unfaithful to our own native land,—the land which first imparted to us the enjoyment of the light of day, in which we were nursed and educated, and (to pass to what is specially relevant in this case) the land by rendering services to which men obtain a home prepared for them in heaven after the death of the body; for, in the opinion of the most learned, promotion to that celestial City is granted to those men who have deserved well of the cities which gave them birth, and a higher experience of fellowship with God is the portion of those who are proved to have contributed by their counsels or by their labours to the welfare of their native land.

As to the remark which you were pleased wittily to make regarding our town, that it has been made conspicuous not so much by the achievements of warriors as by the conflagrations of incendiaries, and that it has produced thorns rather than flowers, this is not the severest reproof that might have been given, for we know that flowers are for the most part borne on thorny bushes. For who does not know that even roses grow on briars, and that in the bearded heads of grain the ears are guarded by spikes, and that, in general, pleasant and painful things are found blended together?

3. The last statement in your Excellency's letter was, that neither capital punishment nor bloodshed is demanded in order to compensate for the wrong done to the Church, but that the offenders must be deprived of the possessions which they most fear to lose. But in my deliberate judgment, though, of course, I may be mistaken, it is a more grievous thing to be deprived of one's property than to be deprived of life. For, as you know, it is an observation frequently recurring in the whole range of literature, that death terminates the experience of all evils, but that a life of indigence only confers upon us an eternity of wretchedness; for it is worse to live miserably than to put an end to our miseries by death. This fact, also, is declared by the whole nature and method of your work, in which you support the poor, minister healing to the diseased, and apply remedies to the bodies of those who are in pain, and, in short, make it your business to prevent the afflicted from feeling the protracted continuance of their sufferings.

Again, as to the degree of demerit in the faults of some as compared with others, it is of no importance what the quality of the fault may seem to be in a case in which forgiveness is craved. For, in the first place, if penitence procures forgiveness and expiates the crime — and surely he is penitent who begs pardon and humbly embraces the feet of the party whom he has offended — and if, moreover, as is the opinion of some philosophers, all faults are alike, pardon ought to be bestowed upon all without distinction. One of our citizens may have spoken somewhat rudely: this was a fault; another may have perpetrated an insult or an injury: this was equally a fault; another may have violently taken what was not his own: this is reckoned a crime; another may have attacked buildings devoted to secular or to sacred purposes: he ought not to be for this crime placed beyond the reach of pardon. Finally, there would be no occasion for pardon if there were no foregoing faults.

4. Having now replied to your letter, not as the letter deserved, but to the best of my ability, such as it is, I beg and implore you (oh that I were in your presence, that you might also see my tears!) to consider again and again who you are, what is your professed character, and what is the business to which your life is devoted. Reflect upon the appearance presented by a town from which men doomed to torture are dragged forth; think of the lamentations of mothers and wives, of sons and of fathers; think of the shame felt by those who may return, set at liberty indeed, but having undergone the torture; think what sorrow and groaning the sight of their wounds and scars must renew. And when you have pondered all these things, first think of God, and think of your good name among men; or rather think of what friendly charity and the bonds of common humanity require at your hands, and seek to be praised not by punishing but by pardoning the offenders. And such things may indeed be said regarding your treatment of those whom actual guilt con-

demns on their own confession : to these persons you have, out of regard to your religion, granted pardon ; and for this I shall always praise you. But now it is scarcely possible to express the greatness of that cruelty which pursues the innocent, and summons those to stand trial on a capital charge of whom it is certain that they had no share in the crimes alleged. If it so happen that they are acquitted, consider, I beseech you, with what ill-will their acquittal must be regarded by their accusers who of their own accord dismissed the guilty from the bar, but let the innocent go only when they were defeated in their attempts against them.

May the supreme God be your keeper, and preserve you as a bulwark of His religion and an ornament to our country.

LETTER CIV.

(A.D. 409.)

TO NECTARIUS, MY NOBLE LORD AND BROTHER, JUSTLY WORTHY OF ALL HONOUR AND ESTEEM, AUGUSTIN SENDS GREETING IN THE LORD.

CHAP. I. — 1. I have read the letter which you kindly sent in answer to mine. Your reply comes at a very long interval after the time when I despatched my letter to you. For I had written an answer to you[1] when my holy brother and colleague Possidius was still with us, before he had entered on his voyage ; but the letter which you have been pleased to entrust to him for me I received on March 27th, about eight months after I had written to you. The reason why my communication was so late in reaching you, or yours so late in being sent to me, I do not know. Perhaps your prudence has only now dictated the reply which your pride formerly disdained. If this be the explanation, I wonder what has occasioned the change. Have you perchance heard some report, which is as yet unknown to us, that my brother Possidius had obtained authority for proceedings of greater severity against your citizens, whom — you must excuse me for saying this — he loves in a way more likely to promote their welfare than you do yourself ? For your letter shows that you apprehended something of this kind when you charge me to set before my eyes " the appearance presented by a town from which men doomed to torture are dragged forth," and to " think of the lamentations of mothers and wives, of sons and of fathers ; of the shame felt by those who may return, set at liberty indeed, but having undergone the torture ; and of the sorrow and groaning which the sight of their wounds and scars must renew."[2] Far be it from us to demand

the infliction, either by ourselves or by any one, of such hardships upon any of our enemies ! But, as I have said, if report has brought any such measures of severity to your ears, give us a more clear and particular account of the things reported, that we may know either what to do in order to prevent these things from being done, or what answer we must make in order to disabuse the minds of those who believe the rumour.

2. Examine more carefully my letter, to which you have so reluctantly sent a reply, for I have in it made my views sufficiently plain ; but through not remembering, as I suppose, what I had written, you have in your reply made reference to sentiments widely differing from mine, and wholly unlike them. For, as if quoting from memory what I had written, you have inserted in your letter what I never said at all in mine. You say that the concluding sentence of my letter was, " that neither capital punishment nor bloodshed is demanded in order to compensate for the wrong done to the Church, but that the offenders must be deprived of that which they most fear to lose ; " and then, in showing how great a calamity this imports, you add and connect with my words that you " deliberately judge — though you may perhaps be mistaken — that it is a more grievous thing to be deprived of one's possessions than to be deprived of life." And in order to expound more clearly the kind of possessions to which you refer, you go on to say that it must be known to me, " as an observation frequently recurring in the whole range of literature, that death terminates the experience of all evils, but that a life of indigence only confers upon us an eternity of wretchedness." From which you have drawn the conclusion that it is " worse to live miserably than to put an end to our miseries by death."

3. Now I for my part do not recollect reading anywhere — either in our [Christian] literature, to which I confess that I was later of applying my mind than I could now wish that I had been, or in your [Pagan] literature, which I studied from my childhood — that " a life of indigence only confers upon us an eternity of wretchedness." For the poverty of the industrious is never in itself a crime ; nay, it is to some extent a means of withdrawing and restraining men from sin. And therefore the circumstance that a man has lived in poverty here is no ground for apprehending that this shall procure for him after this brief life " an eternity of wretchedness ; " and in this life which we spend on earth it is utterly impossible for any misery to be eternal, seeing that this life cannot be eternal, nay, is not of long duration even in those who attain to the most advanced old age. In the writings referred to, I for my part have read, not that in this life — as you think, and as you allege that these writ-

---

[1] Letter XCI. p. 376.
[2] Letter CIII. p. 426.

ings frequently affirm — there can be an eternity of wretchedness, but rather that this life itself which we here enjoy is short. Some, indeed, but not all, of your authors have said that death is the end of all evils : that is indeed the opinion of the Epicureans, and of such others as believe the soul to be mortal. But those philosophers whom Cicero designates " consulares " in a certain sense, because he attaches great weight to their authority, are of opinion that when our last hour on earth comes the soul is not annihilated, but removes from its tenement, and continues in existence for a state of blessedness or of misery, according to that which a man's actions, whether good or bad, claim as their due recompense. This agrees with the teaching of our sacred writings, with which I wish that I were more fully conversant. Death is therefore the end of all evils — but only in the case of those whose life is pure, religious, upright, and blameless ; not in the case of those who, inflamed with passionate desire for the trifles and vanities of time, are proved to be miserable by the utter perversion of their desires, though meanwhile they esteem themselves happy, and are after death compelled not only to accept as their lot, but to realize in their experience far greater miseries.

4. These sentiments, therefore, being frequently expressed both in some of your own authors, whom you deem worthy of greater esteem, and in all our Scriptures, be it yours, O worthy lover of the country which is on earth your fatherland, to dread on behalf of your countrymen a life of luxurious indulgence rather than a life of indigence ; or if you fear a life of indigence, warn them that the poverty which is to be more studiously shunned is that of the man who, though surrounded with abundance of worldly possessions, is, through the insatiable eagerness wherewith he covets these, kept always in a state of want, which, to use the words of your own authors, neither plenty nor scarcity can relieve. In the letter, however, to which you reply, I did not say that those of your citizens who are enemies to the Church were to be corrected by being reduced to that extremity of indigence in which the necessaries of life are wanting, and to which succour is brought by that compassion of which you have thought it incumbent on you to point out to me that it is professed by us in the whole plan of those labours wherein we " support the poor, minister healing to the diseased, and apply remedies to the bodies of those who are in pain ; " albeit, even such extremity of want as this would be more profitable than abundance of all things, if abused to the gratification of evil passions. But far be it from me to think that those about whom we are treating should be reduced to such destitution by the measures of coercion proposed.

CHAP. II.— 5. Though you did not consider it worth while to read my letter over when it was to be answered, perhaps you have at least so far esteemed it as to preserve it, in order to its being brought to you when you at any time might desire it and call for it ; if this be the case, look over it again, and mark carefully my words : you will assuredly find in it one thing to which, in my opinion, you must admit that you have made no reply. For in that letter occur the words which I now quote : " We do not desire to gratify our anger by vindictive retribution for the past, but we are concerned to make provision in a truly merciful spirit for the future. Now wicked men have something in respect to which they may be punished, and that by Christians, in a merciful way, and so as to promote their own profit and well-being. For they have these three things — life and health of the body, the means of supporting that life, and the means and opportunities of living a wicked life. Let the two former remain untouched in the possession of those who repent of their crime ; this we desire, and this we spare no pains to secure. But as to the third, if it please God to deal with it as a decaying or diseased part, which must be removed with the pruning-knife, He will in such punishment prove the greatness of his compassion." [1] If you had read over these words of mine again, when you were pleased to write your reply, you would have looked upon it rather as an unkind insinuation than as a necessary duty to address to me a petition not only for deliverance from death, but also for exemption from torture, on behalf of those regarding whom I said that we wished to leave unimpaired their possession of bodily life and health. Neither was there any ground for your apprehending our inflicting a life of indigence and of dependence upon others for daily bread on those regarding whom I had said that we desired to secure to them the second of the possessions named above, viz. the means of supporting life. But as to their third possession, viz. the means and opportunities of living wickedly, that is to say — passing over other things — their silver with which they constructed those images of their false gods, in whose protection or adoration or unhallowed worship an attempt was made even to destroy the church of God by fire, and the provision made for relieving the poverty of very pious persons was given up to become the spoil of a wretched mob, and blood was freely shed — why, I ask, does your patriotic heart dread the stroke which shall cut this away, in order to prevent a fatal boldness from being in everything fostered and confirmed by impunity? This I beg you to discuss fully, and to show me in well-considered

---

[1] Letter CXI. 9, p. 379.

arguments what wrong there is in this ; mark carefully what I say, lest under the form of a petition in regard to what I am saying you appear to bring against us an indirect accusation.

6. Let your countrymen be well reported of for their virtuous manners, not for their superfluous wealth ; we do not wish them to be reduced through coercive measures on our account to the plough of Quintius [Cincinnatus], or to the hearth of Fabricius. Yet by such extreme poverty these statesmen of the Roman republic not only did not incur the contempt of their fellow-citizens, but were on that very account peculiarly dear to them, and esteemed the more qualified to administer the resources of their country. We neither desire nor endeavour to reduce the estates of your rich men, so that in their possession should remain no more than ten pounds of silver, as was the case with Ruffinus, who twice held the consulship, which amount the stern censorship of that time laudably required to be still further reduced as culpably large. So much are we influenced by the prevailing sentiments of a degenerate age in dealing more tenderly with minds that are very feeble, that to Christian clemency the measure which seemed just to the censors of that time appears unduly severe ; yet you see how great is the difference between the two cases, the question being in the one, whether the mere fact of possessing ten pounds of silver should be dealt with as a punishable crime, and in the other, whether any one, after committing other very great crimes, should be permitted to retain the sum aforesaid in his possession ; we only ask that what in those days was itself a crime be in our days made the punishment of crime. There is, however, one thing which can be done, and ought to be done, in order that, on the one hand, severity may not be pushed even so far as I have mentioned, and that, on the other, men may not, presuming on impunity, run into excess of exultation and rioting, and thus furnish to other unhappy men an example by following which they would become liable to the severest and most unheard of punishments. Let this at least be granted by you, that those who attempt with fire and sword to destroy what are necessaries to us be made afraid of losing those luxuries of which they have a pernicious abundance. Permit us also to confer upon our enemies this benefit, that we prevent them, by their fears about that which it would do them no harm to forfeit, from attempting to that which would bring harm to themselves. For this is to be termed prudent prevention, not punishment of crime ; this is not to impose penalties, but to protect men from becoming liable to penalties.

7. When any one uses measures involving the infliction of some pain, in order to prevent an inconsiderate person from incurring the most dreadful punishments by becoming accustomed to crimes which yield him no advantage, he is like one who pulls a boy's hair in order to prevent him from provoking serpents by clapping his hands at them ; in both cases, while the acting of love is vexatious to its object, no member of the body is injured, whereas safety and life are endangered by that from which the person is deterred. We confer a benefit upon others, not in every case in which we do what is requested, but when we do that which is not hurtful to our petitioners. For in most cases we serve others best by not giving, and would injure them by giving, what they desire. Hence the proverb, " Do not put a sword in a child's hand." " Nay," says Cicero, " refuse it even to your only son. For the more we love any one, the more are we bound to avoid entrusting to him things which are the occasion of very dangerous faults." He was referring to riches, if I am not mistaken, when he made these observations. Wherefore it is for the most part an advantage to themselves when certain things are removed from persons in whose keeping it is hazardous to leave them, lest they abuse them. When surgeons see that a gangrene must be cut away or cauterized, they often, out of compassion, turn a deaf ear to many cries. If we had been indulgently forgiven by our parents and teachers in our tender years on every occasion on which, being found in a fault, we begged to be let off, which of us would not have grown up intolerable ? which of us would have learned any useful thing ? Such punishments are administered by wise care, not by wanton cruelty. Do not, I beseech you, in this matter think only how to accomplish that which you are requested by your countrymen to do, but carefully consider the matter in all its bearings. If you overlook the past, which cannot now be undone, consider the future ; wisely give heed, not to the desire, but to the real interests of the petitioners who have applied to you. We are convicted of unfaithfulness towards those whom we profess to love, if our only care is lest, by refusing to do what they ask of us, their love towards us be diminished. And what becomes of that virtue which even your own literature commends, in the ruler of his country who studies not so much the wishes as the welfare of his people ?

CHAP. 3. — 8. You say " it is of no importance what the quality of the fault may be in any case in which forgiveness is craved." In this you would state the truth if the matter in question were the punishment and not the correction of men. Far be it from a Christian heart to be carried away by the lust of revenge to inflict punishment on any one. Far be it from a Christian, when forgiving any one his fault, to do otherwise than either anticipate or at least promptly answer the petition of him who asks forgiveness ; but let his purpose in doing this be, that he may overcome the temptation to hate the man who has offended him, and to render evil for evil, and to be inflamed with rage prompting him, if not to do an injury, at least to desire to see the infliction of the penalties appointed by law ; let it not be that he may relieve himself from considering the offender's interest, exercising foresight on his behalf, and restraining him from evil actions. For it is possible, on the one hand, that, moved by more vehement hostility, one may neglect the correction of a man whom he hates bitterly, and, on the other hand, that by correction involving the infliction of some pain one may secure the improvement of another whom he dearly loves.

9. I grant that, as you write, "penitence procures forgiveness, and blots out the offence," but it is that penitence which is practised under the influence of the true religion, and which has regard to the future judgment of God ; not that penitence which is for the time professed or pretended before men, not to secure the cleansing of the soul for ever from the fault, but only to deliver from present apprehension of pain the life which is so soon to perish. This is the reason why in the case of some Christians who confessed their fault, and asked forgiveness for having been involved in the guilt of that crime, — either by their not protecting the church when in danger of being burned, or by their appropriating a portion of the property which the miscreants carried off, — we believed that the pain of repentance had borne fruit, and considered it sufficient for their correction, because in their hearts is found that faith by which they could realize what they ought to fear from the judgment of God for their sin. But how can there be any healing virtue in the repentance of those who not only fail to acknowledge, but even persist in mocking and blaspheming Him who is the fountain of forgiveness? At the same time, towards these men we do not cherish any feeling of enmity in our hearts, which are naked and opened unto the eyes of Him whose judgment both in this life and in the life to come we dread, and in whose help we place our hope. But we think that we are even taking measures for the benefit of these men, if, seeing that they do not fear God, we inspire fear in them by doing something whereby their folly is chastened, while their real interests suffer no wrong. We thus prevent that God whom they despise from being more grievously provoked by their greater crimes, to which they would be emboldened by a disastrous assurance of impunity, and we prevent their assurance of impunity from being set forth with even more mischievous effect as an

encouragement to others to imitate their example. In fine, on behalf of those for whom you make intercession to us, we intercede before God, beseeching Him to turn them to Himself, and to teach them the exercise of genuine and salutary repentance, purifying their hearts by faith.

10. Behold, then, how we love those men against whom you suppose us to be full of anger, —loving them, you must permit me to say, with a love more prudent and profitable than you yourself cherish towards them ; for we plead on their behalf that they may escape much greater afflictions, and obtain much greater blessings. If you also loved these men, not in the mere earthly affections of men, but with that love which is the heavenly gift of God, and if you were sincere in writing to me that you gave ear with pleasure to me when I was recommending to you the worship and religion of the Supreme God, you would not only wish for your countrymen the blessings which we seek on their behalf, but you would yourself by your example lead them to their possession. Thus would the whole business of your interceding with us be concluded with abundant and most reasonable joy. Thus would your title to that heavenly fatherland, in regard to which you say that you welcomed my counsel that you should fix your eye upon it, be earned by a true and pious exercise of your love for the country which gave you birth, when seeking to make sure to your fellow-citizens, not the vain dream of temporal happiness, nor a most perilous exemption from the due punishment of their faults, but the gracious gift of eternal blessedness.

11. You have here a frank avowal of the thoughts and desires of my heart in this matter. As to what lies concealed in the counsels of God, I confess it is unknown to me ; I am but a man ; but whatever it be, His counsel stands most sure, and incomparably excels in equity and in wisdom all that can be conceived by the minds of men. With truth is it said in our books, "There are many devices in a man's heart ; but the counsel of the Lord, that shall stand."[1] Wherefore, as to what time may bring forth, as to what may arise to simplify or complicate our procedure, in short, as to what desire may suddenly be awakened by the fear of losing or the hope of retaining present possessions ; whether God shall show Himself so displeased by what they have done that they shall be punished with the more weighty and severe sentence of a disastrous impunity, or shall appoint that they shall be compassionately corrected in the manner which we propose, or shall avert whatever terrible doom was being prepared for them, and convert it into

[1] Prov. xix. 21.

joy by some more stern but more salutary correction, leading to their turning unfeignedly to seek mercy not from men but from Himself, — all this He knoweth; we know not. Why, then, should your Excellency and I be spending toil in vain over this matter before the time? Let us for a little while lay aside a care the hour of which has not yet come, and, if you please, let us occupy ourselves with that which is always pressing. For there is no time at which it is not both suitable and necessary for us to consider in what way we can please God; because for a man to attain completely in this life to such perfection that no sin whatever shall remain in him is either impossible or (if perchance any attain to it) extremely difficult: wherefore without delay we ought to flee at once to the grace of Him to whom we may address with perfect truth the words which were addressed to some illustrious man by a poet, who declared that he had borrowed the lines from a Cumæan oracle, or ode of prophetic inspiration: "With thee as our leader, the obliteration of all remaining traces of our sin shall deliver the earth from perpetual alarm."[1] For with Him as our leader, all sins are blotted out and forgiven; and by His way we are brought to that heavenly fatherland, the thought of which as a dwelling-place pleased you greatly when I was to the utmost of my power commending it to your affection and desire.

CHAP. IV. — 12. But since you said that all religions by diverse roads and pathways aspire to that one dwelling-place, I fear lest, perchance, while supposing that the way in which you are now found tends thither, you should be somewhat reluctant to embrace the way which alone leads men to heaven. Observing, however, more carefully the word which you used, I think that it is not presumptuous for me to expound its meaning somewhat differently; for you did not say that all religions by diverse roads and pathways reach heaven, or reveal, or find, or enter, or secure that blessed land, but by saying in a phrase deliberately weighed and chosen that all religions aspire to it, you have indicated, not the fruition, but the desire of heaven as common to all religions. You have in these words neither shut out the one religion which is true, nor admitted other religions which are false; for certainly the way which brings us to the goal aspires thitherward, but not every way which aspires thitherward brings us to the place wherein all who are brought thither are unquestionably blest. Now we all wish, that is, we aspire, to be blest; but we cannot all achieve what we wish, that is, we do not all obtain what we aspire to. That man, therefore, obtains heaven who walks in the way which not only aspires thitherward, but actually brings him thither, separating himself from others who keep to the ways which aspire heavenward without finally reaching heaven. For there would be no wandering if men were content to aspire to nothing, or if the truth which men aspire to were obtained. If, however, in using the expression "diverse ways," you meant me not to understand contrary ways, but different ways, in the sense in which we speak of diverse precepts, which all tend to build up a holy life, — one enjoining chastity, another patience or faith or mercy, and the like, — in roads and pathways which are only in this sense diverse, that country is not only aspired unto but actually found. For in Holy Scripture we read both of ways and of a way, — of ways, e.g. in the words, "I will teach transgressors Thy ways, and sinners shall be converted unto Thee;"[2] of a way, e.g. in the prayer, "Teach me Thy way, O Lord; I will walk in Thy truth."[3] Those ways and this way are not different; but in one way are comprehended all those of which in another place the Holy Scripture saith, "All the ways of the Lord are mercy and truth."[4] The careful study of these ways furnishes theme for a long discourse, and for most delightful meditation; but this I shall defer to another time if it be required.

13. In the meantime, however, — and this, I think, may suffice in the present reply to your Excellency, — seeing that Christ has said, "I am the way,"[5] it is in Him that mercy and truth are to be sought: if we seek these in any other way, we must go astray, following a path which aspires to the true goal, but does not lead men thither. For example, if we resolved to follow the way indicated in the maxim which you mentioned, "All sins are alike,"[6] would it not lead us into hopeless exile from that fatherland of truth and blessedness? For could anything more absurd and senseless be said, than that the man who has laughed too rudely, and the man who has furiously set his city on fire, should be judged as having committed equal crimes? This opinion, which is not one of many diverse ways leading to the heavenly dwelling-place, but a perverse way leading inevitably to most fatal error, you have judged it necessary to quote from certain philosophers, not because you concurred in the sentiment, but because it might help your plea for your fellow-citizens — that we might forgive those whose rage set our church in flames on the same terms as we would forgive those who may have assailed us with some insolent reproach.

14. But reconsider with me the reasoning by which you supported your position. You say,

1 Virgil, *Ecl.* iv. 5.

2 Ps. li. 13.
3 Ps. lxxxvi. 11.
4 Ps. xxv. 10.
5 John xiv. 6.
6 Letter CIII. § 3, p. 426.

"If, as is the opinion of some philosophers, all faults are alike, pardon ought to be bestowed upon all without distinction." Thereafter, labouring apparently to prove that all faults are alike, you go on to say, "One of our citizens may have spoken somewhat rudely: this was a fault; another may have perpetrated an insult or an injury: this was equally a fault." This is not teaching truth, but advancing, without any evidence in its support, a perversion of truth. For to your statement, "this was equally a fault," we at once give direct contradiction. You demand, perhaps, proof; but I reply, What proof have you given of your statement? Are we to hear as evidence your next sentence, "Another may have violently taken away what was not his own: this is reckoned a misdemeanour"? Here you own yourself to be ashamed of the maxim which you quoted; you had not the assurance to say that this was equally a fault, but you say "it is reckoned a misdemeanour." But the question here is not whether this also is reckoned a misdemeanour, but whether this offence and the others which you mentioned are faults equal in demerit, unless, of course, they are to be pronounced equal because they are both offences; in which case the mouse and the elephant must be pronounced equal because they are both animals, and the fly and the eagle because they both have wings.

15. You go still further, and make this proposition: "Another may have attacked buildings devoted to secular or to sacred purposes: he ought not for this crime to be placed beyond the reach of pardon." In this sentence you have indeed come to the most flagrant crime of your fellow-citizens, in speaking of injury done to sacred buildings; but even you have not affirmed that this is a crime equal only to the utterance of an insolent word. You have contented yourself with asking, on behalf of those who were guilty of this, that forgiveness which is rightly asked from Christians on the ground of their overflowing compassion, not on the ground of an alleged equality of all offences. I have already quoted a sentence of Scripture, "All the ways of the Lord are mercy and truth." They shall therefore find mercy if they do not hate truth. This mercy is granted, not as if it were due on the ground of the faults of all being only equal to the fault of those who have uttered rude words, but because the law of Christ claims pardon for those who are penitent, however inhuman and impious their crime may have been. I beg you, esteemed sir, not to propound these paradoxes of the Stoics as rules of conduct for your son Paradoxus, whom we wish to see grow up in piety and in prosperity, to your satisfaction. For what could be worse for himself, yea, what more dangerous for yourself, than that your ingenuous boy should imbibe an error which would make the guilt, I shall not say of parricide, but of insolence to his father, equal only to that of some rude word inconsiderately spoken to a stranger?

16. You are wise, therefore, to insist, when pleading with us for your countrymen on the compassion of Christians, not on the stern doctrines of the Stoical philosophy, which in no wise help, but much rather hinder, the cause which you have undertaken to support. For a merciful disposition, which we must have if it be possible for us to be moved either by your intercession or by their entreaties, is pronounced by the Stoics to be an unworthy weakness, and they expel it utterly from the mind of the wise man, whose perfection, in their opinion, is to be as impassive and inflexible as iron. With more reason, therefore, might it have occurred to you to quote from your own Cicero that sentence in which, praising Cæsar, he says, "Of all your virtues, none is more worthy of admiration, none more graceful, than your clemency." [1] How much more ought this merciful disposition to prevail in the churches which follow Him who said, "I am the way," and which learn from His word, "All the ways of the Lord are mercy and truth"! Fear not, then, that we will try to bring innocent persons to death, when in truth we do not even wish the guilty to experience the punishment which they deserve, being moved by that mercy which, joined with truth, we love in Christ. But the man who, from fear of painfully crossing the will of the guilty, spares and indulges vices which must thereby gather more strength, is less merciful than the man who, lest he should hear his little boy crying, will not take from him a dangerous knife, and is unmoved by fear of the wounds or death which he may have to bewail as the consequence of his weakness. Reserve, therefore, until the proper time the work of interceding with us for those men, in loving whom (excuse my saying so) you not only do not go beyond us, but are even hitherto refusing to follow our steps; and write rather in your reply what influences you to shun the way which we follow, and in which we beseech you to go along with us towards that fatherland above, in which we rejoice to know that you take great delight.

17. As to those who are by birth your fellow-citizens, you have said indeed that some of them, though not all, were innocent; but, as you must see if you read over again my other letter, you have not made out a defence for them. When, in answer to your remark that you wished to leave your country flourishing, I said that we had felt thorns rather than found flowers in your countrymen, you thought that I wrote in jest. As if, forsooth, in the midst of evils of such

---

[1] *Oratio pro Q. Ligario.*

magnitude we were in a mood for mirth. Certainly not. While the smoke was ascending from the ruins of our church consumed by fire, were we likely to joke on the subject? Although, indeed, none in your city appeared in my opinion innocent, but those who were absent, or were sufferers, or were destitute both of strength and of authority to prevent the tumult, I nevertheless distinguished in my reply those whose guilt was greater from those who were less to blame, and stated that there was a difference between the cases of those who were moved by fear of offending powerful enemies of the Church, and of those who desired these outrages to be committed ; also between those who committed them and those who instigated others to their commission ; resolving, however, not to institute inquiry in regard to the instigators, because these, perhaps, could not be ascertained without recourse to the use of tortures, from which we shrink with abhorrence, as utterly inconsistent with our aims. Your friends the Stoics, who hold that all faults are alike, must, however, if they were the judges, pronounce them all equally guilty ; and if to this opinion they join that inflexible sternness wherewith they disparage clemency as a vice, their sentence would necessarily be, not that all should be pardoned alike, but that all should be punished alike. Dismiss, therefore, these philosophers altogether from the position of advocates in this case, and rather desire that we may act as Christians, so that, as we desire, we may gain in Christ those whom we forgive, and may not spare them by such indulgence as would be ruinous to themselves. May God, whose ways are mercy and truth, be pleased to enrich you with true felicity !

LETTER CXI.

(NOVEMBER, A.D. 409.)

TO VICTORIANUS, HIS BELOVED LORD AND MOST LONGED-FOR BROTHER AND FELLOW-PRESBYTER, AUGUSTIN SENDS GREETING IN THE LORD.

1. My heart has been filled with great sorrow by your letter. You asked me to discuss certain things at great length in my reply ; but such calamities as you narrate claim rather many groans and tears than prolix treatises. The whole world, indeed, is afflicted with such portentous misfortunes, that there is scarcely any place where such things as you describe are not being committed and complained of. A short time ago some brethren were massacred by the barbarians even in those deserts of Egypt in which, in order to perfect security, they had chosen places remote from all disturbance as the sites of their monasteries. I suppose, moreover,

that the outrages which they have perpetrated in the regions of Italy and Gaul are known to you also ; and now similar events begin to be announced to us from many provinces of Spain, which for long seemed exempt from these evils. But why go to a distance for examples? Behold ! in our own county of Hippo, which the barbarians have not yet touched, the ravages of the Donatist clergy and Circumcelliones make such havoc in our churches, that perhaps the cruelties of barbarians would be light in comparison. For what barbarian could ever have devised what these have done, viz. casting lime and vinegar into the eyes of our clergymen, besides atrociously beating and wounding every part of their bodies? They also sometimes plunder and burn houses, rob granaries, and pour out oil and wine ; and by threatening to do this to all others in the district, they compel many even to be re-baptized. Only yesterday, tidings came to me of forty-eight souls in one place having submitted, under fear of such things, to be re-baptized.

2. These things should make us weep, but not wonder ; and we ought to cry unto God that not for our merit, but according to His mercy, He may deliver us from so great evils. For what else was to be expected by the human race, seeing that these things were so long ago foretold both by the prophets and in the Gospels? We ought not, therefore, to be so inconsistent as to believe these Scriptures when they are read by us, and to complain when they are fulfilled ; rather, surely, ought even those who had refused to believe when they read or heard these things in Scripture to become believers now when they behold the word fulfilled ; so that under this great pressure, as it were, in the olive-press of the Lord our God, although there be the dregs of unbelieving murmurs and blasphemies, there is also a steady outflowing of pure oil in the confessions and prayers of believers. For unto those men who incessantly reproach the Christian faith, impiously saying that the human race did not suffer such grievous calamities before the Christian doctrine was promulgated throughout the world, it is easy to find a reply in the Lord's own words in the gospel, " That servant which knew not his lord's will, and did commit things worthy of stripes, shall be beaten with few stripes ; but the servant which knew his lord's will, and prepared not himself, neither did according to his will, shall be beaten with many stripes." [1] What is there to excite surprise, if, in the Christian dispensation, the world, like that servant, knowing the will of the Lord, and refusing to do it, is beaten with many stripes? These men remark the rapidity with which the

---

[1] Luke xii. 47, 48.

gospel is proclaimed : they do not remark the perversity with which by many it is despised. But the meek and pious servants of God, who have to bear a double portion of temporal calamities, since they suffer both at the hands of wicked men and along with them, have also consolations peculiarly their own, and the hope of the world to come ; for which reason the apostle says, "The sufferings of this present time are not worthy to be compared with the glory which shall hereafter be revealed in us." [1]

3. Wherefore, my beloved, even when you meet those whose words you say you cannot bear, because they say, "If we have deserved these things for our sins, how comes it that the servants of God are cut off not less than ourselves by the sword of the barbarians, and the handmaids of God are led away into captivity?" — answer them humbly, truly, and piously in such words as these : However carefully we keep the way of righteousness, and yield obedience to our Lord, can we be better than those three men who were cast into the fiery furnace for keeping the law of God? And yet, read what Azarias, one of those three, said, opening his lips in the midst of the fire : "Blessed art Thou, O Lord God of our fathers : Thy name is worthy to be praised and glorified for evermore ; for Thou art righteous in all the things that Thou hast done to us ; yea, true are all Thy works : Thy ways are right, and all Thy judgments truth. In all the things which Thou hast brought upon us, and upon the holy city of our fathers, even Jerusalem, Thou hast executed true judgment ; for according to truth and judgment didst Thou bring all these things upon us because of our sins. For we have sinned and committed iniquity, departing from Thee. In all things have we trespassed, and not obeyed Thy commandments, nor kept them, neither done as Thou hast commanded us, that it might go well with us. Wherefore all that Thou hast brought upon us, and everything that Thou hast done to us, Thou hast done in true judgment. And Thou didst deliver us into the hands of lawless enemies, most hateful forsakers of God, and to an unjust king, and the most wicked in all the world. And now we cannot open our mouths : we are become a shame and reproach to Thy servants, and to them that worship Thee. Yet deliver us not up wholly, for Thy name's sake, neither disannul Thou Thy covenant ; and cause not Thy mercy to depart from us, for Thy beloved Abraham's sake, for Thy servant Isaac's sake, and for Thy holy Israel's sake, to whom Thou hast spoken, and promised that Thou wouldst multiply their seed as the stars of heaven, and as the sand that lieth upon the sea-shore. For we, O

Lord, are become less than any nation, and be kept under this day in all the world because of our sins." [2] Here, my brother, thou mayest surely see how men such as they, men of holiness, men of courage in the midst of tribulation, — from which, however, they were delivered, the flame itself fearing to consume them, — were not silent about their sins, but confessed them, knowing that because of these sins they were deservedly and justly brought low.

4. Nay, can we be better men than Daniel himself, concerning whom God, speaking to the prince of Tyre, says by the prophet Ezekiel, "Art thou wiser than Daniel?" [3] who also is placed among the three righteous men to whom alone God saith that He would grant deliverance, — pointing, doubtless, in them to three representative righteous men, — declaring that he would deliver only Noah, Daniel, and Job, and that they should save along with themselves neither son nor daughter, but only their own souls? [4] Nevertheless, read also the prayer of Daniel, and see how, when in captivity, he confesses not only the sins of his people, but his own also, and acknowledges that because of these the justice of God has visited them with the punishment of captivity and with reproach. For it is thus written : "And I set my face unto the Lord God, to seek by prayer and supplications, with fasting, and sackcloth, and ashes : and I prayed unto the Lord my God, and made my confession, and said : O Lord, the great and dreadful God, keeping the covenant and mercy to them that love Him, and to them that keep His commandments ; we have sinned, and have committed iniquity, and have done wickedly, and have rebelled, even by departing from Thy precepts and from Thy judgments : neither have we hearkened unto Thy servants the prophets, which spake in Thy name to our kings, our princes, and our fathers, and to all the people of the land. O Lord, righteousness belongeth unto Thee, but unto us confusion of faces, as at this day ; to the men of Judah, and to the inhabitants of Jerusalem, and unto all Israel, that are near, and that are far off, through all the countries whither Thou hast driven them, because of their trespass that they have trespassed against Thee. O Lord, to us belongeth confusion of face, to our kings, to our princes, and to our fathers, because we have sinned against Thee. To the Lord our God belong mercies and forgivenesses, though we have rebelled against Him ; neither have we obeyed the voice of the Lord, to walk in His laws which He set before us by His servants the prophets. Yea, all Israel have transgressed Thy law, even by departing, that they might not obey Thy voice ; therefore the

---

[2] Song of the Three Holy Children, vers. 3-14.
[3] Ezek. xxviii. 3.
[4] Ezek. xiv. 14, 18, 20.

[1] Rom. viii. 18.

curse is poured upon us, and the oath that is written in the law of Moses the servant of God, because we have sinned against them. And He hath confirmed His words which He spake against us, and against our judges that judged us, by bringing upon us a great evil; for under the whole heaven hath not been done as hath been done upon Jerusalem. As it is written in the law of Moses, all this evil is come upon us: yet made we not our prayer before the Lord our God, that we might turn from our iniquities and understand Thy truth. Therefore hath the Lord watched upon the evil, and brought it upon us; for the Lord our God is righteous in all His works which He doeth; for we obeyed not His voice. And now, O Lord our God, that hast brought Thy people forth out of the land of Egypt with a mighty hand, and hast gotten Thee renown as at this day; we have sinned, we have done wickedly. O Lord, according to all Thy righteousness, I beseech Thee, let Thine anger and Thy fury be turned away from Thy city Jerusalem, Thy holy mountain, because, for our sins, and for the iniquities of our fathers, Jerusalem and Thy people are become a reproach to all that are about us. Now, therefore, O our God, hear the prayer of Thy servant, and His supplications, and cause Thy face to shine upon Thy sanctuary which is desolate, for the Lord's sake. O my God, incline Thine ear, and hear; open Thine eyes, and behold our desolations, and the city which is called by Thy name; for we do not present our supplications before Thee for our righteousnesses, but for Thy great mercies. O Lord, hear; O Lord, forgive; O Lord, hearken and do: defer not, for Thine own sake, O my God; for Thy city and Thy people are called by Thy name. And while I was speaking, and praying, and confessing my sin, and the sin of my people . . . "[1] Observe how he spoke first of his own sins, and then of the sins of his people. And he extols the righteousness of God, and gives praise to God for this, that He visits even His saints with the rod, not unjustly, but because of their sins. If, therefore, this be the language of men who by reason of their eminent sanctity found even encompassing flames and lions harmless, what language would befit men standing on a level so low as we occupy, seeing that, whatever righteousness we may seem to practise, we are very far from being worthy of comparison with them?

5. Lest, however, any one should think that those servants of God, whose death at the hand of barbarians you relate, ought to have been delivered from them in the same manner as the three young men were delivered from the fire, and Daniel from the lions, let such an one know

that these miracles were performed in order that the kings by whom they were delivered to these punishments might believe that they worshipped the true God. For in His hidden counsel and mercy God was in this manner making provision for the salvation of these kings. It pleased Him, however, to make no such provision in the case of Antiochus the king, who cruelly put the Maccabees to death; but He punished the heart of the obdurate king with sharper severity through their most glorious sufferings. Yet read what was said by even one of them — the sixth who suffered: "After him they brought also the sixth, who, being ready to die, said, 'Be not deceived without cause; for we suffer these things for ourselves, having sinned against God: therefore marvellous things are done unto us; but think not thou that takest in hand to strive against God and His law that thou shalt escape unpunished.'"[2] You see how these also are wise in the exercise of humility and sincerity, confessing that they are chastened because of their sins by the Lord, of whom it is written: "Whom the Lord loveth He correcteth,"[3] and "He scourgeth every son whom He receiveth;"[4] wherefore the Apostle says also, "If we would judge ourselves, we should not be judged; but when we are judged, we are chastened of the Lord, that we should not be condemned with the world."[5]

6. These things read faithfully, and proclaim faithfully; and to the utmost of your power beware, and teach others that they must beware, of murmuring against God in these trials and tribulations. You tell me that good, faithful, and holy servants of God have been cut off by the sword of the barbarians. But what matters it whether it is by sickness or by sword that they have been set free from the body? The Lord is careful as to the character with which His servants go from this world — not as to the mere circumstances of their departure, excepting this, that lingering weakness involves more suffering than a sudden death; and yet we read of this same protracted and dreadful weakness as the lot of that Job to whose righteousness God Himself, who cannot be deceived, bears such testimony.

7. Most calamitous, and much to be bewailed, is the captivity of chaste and holy women; but their God is not in the power of their captors, nor does He forsake those captives whom He knows indeed to be His own. For those holy men, the record of whose sufferings and confessions I have quoted from the Holy Scriptures, being held in captivity by enemies who had car-

---

[1] Dan. ix. 3-20.

[2] 2 Macc. vii. 18, 19.
[3] Prov. iii. 12.
[4] Heb. xii. 6.
[5] 1 Cor. xi. 31, 32.

ried them away, uttered those words, which, preserved in writing, we can read for ourselves, in order to make us understand that servants of God, even when they are in captivity, are not forsaken by their Lord. Nay, more, do we know what wonders of power and grace the almighty and merciful God may please to accomplish by means of these captive women even in the land of the barbarians? Be that as it may, cease not to intercede with groanings on their behalf before God, and to seek, so far as your power and His providence permits you, to do for them whetever can be done, and to give them whatever consolation can be given, as time and opportunity may be granted. A few years ago, a nun, a grand-daughter of Bishop Severus, was carried off by barbarians from the neighbourhood of Sitifa, and was by the marvellous mercy of God restored with great honour to her parents. For at the very time when the maiden entered the house of her barbarian captors, it became the scene of much distress through the sudden illness of its owners, all the barbarians — three brothers, if I mistake not, or more — being attacked with most dangerous disease. Their mother observed that the maiden was dedicated to God, and believed that by her prayers her sons might be delivered from the danger of death, which was imminent. She begged her to intercede for them, promising that if they were healed she should be restored to her parents. She fasted and prayed, and straightway was heard; for, as the result showed, the event had been appointed that this might take place. They therefore, having recovered health by this unexpected favour from God, regarded her with admiration and respect, and fulfilled the promise which their mother had made.

8. Pray, therefore, to God for them, and beseech Him to enable them to say such things as the holy Azariah, whom we have mentioned, poured forth along with other expressions in his prayer and confession before God. For in the land of their captivity these women are in circumstances similar to those of the three Hebrew youths in that land in which they could not sacrifice to the Lord their God in the manner prescribed: they cannot either bring an oblation to the altar of God, or find a priest by whom their oblation may be presented to God. May God therefore grant them grace to say to Him what Azariah said in the following sentences of his prayer: "Neither is there at this time prince, or prophet, or leader, or burnt-offering, or sacrifice, or oblation, or incense, or place to sacrifice before Thee, and to find mercy: nevertheless, in a contrite heart and humble spirit let us be accepted. Like as in the burnt-offerings of rams and bullocks, and like as in ten thousands of fat lambs, so let our sacrifice be in Thy sight this day. And grant that we may wholly go after Thee; for they shall not be confounded that put their trust in Thee. And now we follow Thee with all our heart: we fear Thee and seek Thy face. Put us not to shame, but deal with us after Thy loving-kindness, and according to the multitude of Thy mercies. Deliver us also according to Thy marvellous works, and give glory to Thy name, O Lord; and let all them that do Thy servants hurt be ashamed: and let them be confounded in all their power and might, and let their strength be broken: and let them know that Thou art Lord, the only God, and glorious over the whole world."[1]

9. When His servants use these words, and pray fervently to God, He will stand by them, as He has been wont ever to stand by His own, and will either not permit their chaste bodies to suffer any wrong from the lust of their enemies, or if He permit this, He will not lay sin to their charge in the matter. For when the soul is not defiled by any impurity of consent to such wrong, the body also is thereby protected from all participation in the guilt; and in so far as nothing was committed or permitted by lust on the part of her who suffers, the whole blame lies with him who did the wrong, and all the violence done to the sufferer will be regarded not as implying the baseness of wanton compliance, but as a wound blamelessly endured. For such is the worth of unblemished purity in the soul, that while it remains intact, the body also retains its purity unsullied, even although by violence its members may be overpowered.

I beg your Charity to be satisfied with this letter, which is very long considering my other work (although too short to meet your wishes), and is somewhat hurriedly written, because the bearer is in haste to be gone. The Lord will furnish you with much more abundant consolation if you read attentively His holy word.

LETTER CXV.

(A.D. 410.)

TO FORTUNATUS, MY COLLEAGUE IN THE PRIESTHOOD, MY LORD MOST BLESSED, AND MY BROTHER BELOVED WITH PROFOUND ESTEEM, AND TO THE BRETHREN WHO ARE WITH THEE, AUGUSTIN SENDS GREETING IN THE LORD.

Your Holiness is well acquainted with Faventius, a tenant on the estate of the Paratian forest. He, apprehending some injury or other at the hands of the owner of that estate, took refuge in the church at Hippo, and was there, as fugitives are wont to do, waiting till he could get the matter settled through my mediation. Becoming every day, as often happens, less and

---

[1] Song of the Three Children, vers. 15-22.

less alarmed, and in fact completely off his guard, as if his adversary had desisted from his enmity, he was, when leaving the house of a friend after supper, suddenly carried off by one Florentinus, an officer of the Count, who used in this act of violence a band of armed men sufficient for the purpose. When this was made known to me, and as yet it was unknown by whose orders or by whose hands he had been carried off, though suspicion naturally fell on the man from whose apprehended injury he had claimed the protection of the Church, I at once communicated with the tribune who is in command of the coast-guard. He sent out soldiers, but no one could be found. But in the morning we learned in what house he had passed the night, and also that he had left it after cockcrowing, with the man who had him in custody. I sent also to the place to which it was reported that he had been removed : there the officer above-named was found, but refused to allow the presbyter whom I had sent to have even a sight of his prisoner. On the following day I sent a letter requesting that he should be allowed the privilege which the Emperor appointed in cases such as his, namely, that persons summoned to appear to be tried should in the municipal court be interrogated whether they desired to spend thirty days under adequate surveillance in the town, in order to arrange their affairs, or find funds for the expense of their trial, my expectation being that within that period of time we might perhaps bring his matters to some amicable settlement. Already, however, he had gone farther under charge of the officer Florentinus ; but my fear is, lest perchance, if he be brought before the tribunal of the magistrate,[1] he suffer some injustice. For although the integrity of that judge is widely famed as incorruptible, Faventius has for his adversary a man of very great wealth. To secure that money may not prevail in that court, I beg your Holiness, my beloved lord and venerable brother, to have the kindness to give the accompanying letter to the honourable magistrate, a man very much beloved by us, and to read this letter also to him ; for I have not thought it necessary to write twice the same statement of the case. I trust that he will delay the hearing of the case, because I do not know whether the man is innocent or guilty. I trust also that he will not overlook the fact that the laws have been violated in his having been suddenly carried off, without being brought, as was enacted by the Emperor, before the municipal court, in order to his being asked whether he wished to accept the benefit of the delay of thirty days, so that in this way we may get the affair settled between him and his adversary.

[1] Consularis.

LETTER CXVI.

(ENCLOSED IN THE FOREGOING LETTER.)

TO GENEROSUS, MY NOBLE AND JUSTLY DISTINGUISHED LORD, MY HONOURED AND MUCH-LOVED SON, AUGUSTIN SENDS GREETING IN THE LORD.

Although the praises and favourable report of your administration and your own illustrious good name always give me the greatest pleasure, because of the love which we feel due to your merit and to your benevolence, on no occasion have I hitherto been burdensome to your Excellency as an intercessor requesting any favour from you, my much-loved lord and justly-honoured son. When, however, your Excellency has learned from the letters which I have sent to my venerable brother and colleague, Fortunatus, what has occurred in the town in which I serve the Church of God, your kind heart will at once perceive the necessity under which I have been constrained to trespass by this petition on your time, already fully occupied. I am perfectly assured that, cherishing towards us the feeling which, in the name of Christ, we are fully warranted to expect, you will act in this matter as becomes not only an upright, but also a Christian magistrate.

LETTER CXVII.

(A.D. 410.)

FROM DIOSCORUS TO AUGUSTIN.

To you, who esteem the substance, not the style of expression, as important, any formal preamble to this letter would be not only unnecessary, but irksome. Therefore, without further preface, I beg your attention. The aged Alypius had often promised, in answer to my request, that he would, with your help, furnish a reply to a very few brief questions of mine in regard to the Dialogues of Cicero ; and as he is said to be at present in Mauritania, I ask and earnestly entreat you to condescend to give, without his assistance, those answers which, even had your brother been present, it would doubtless have fallen to you to furnish. What I require is not money, it is not gold ; though, if you possessed these, you would, I am sure, be willing to give them to me for any fit object. This request of mine you can grant without effort, by merely speaking. I might importune you at a greater length, and through many of your dear friends ; but I know your disposition, that you do not desire to be solicited, but show kindness readily to all, if only there be nothing improper in the thing requested : and there is absolutely nothing improper in what I ask. Be this, however, as it may, I beg you to do me this kindness, for I am on the point of embarking on a voyage. You know how very painful it is to me to be burdensome to any one, and much more to one of your frank disposition ; but God alone knows how irresistible is the pressure of the necessity under which I have made this application. For, taking leave of you, and committing myself to divine protection, I am about to undertake a voyage ; and you know the ways of men, how prone they are to censure, and you see how any one will be regarded as illiterate and stupid who, when questions are addressed to him, can return no answer. Therefore, I implore you, answer all my queries without delay. Send me not away downcast. I ask this that so I may see my parents ; for on this one errand I have sent Cerdo to you, and I now delay only till he return. My brother Zenobius has been appointed imperial remembrancer,[1] and has sent me a free pass for my journey, with provisions. If I am not worthy of your reply, let at least the fear of my forfeiting these provisions by delay move you to give answers to my little questions.[2]

May the most high God spare you long to us in health ! Papas salutes your excellency most cordially.

LETTER CXVIII.

(A.D. 410.)

AUGUSTIN TO DIOSCORUS.

CHAP. I.—1. You have sent suddenly upon me a countless multitude of questions, by which you must have purposed to blockade me on every side, or rather bury me completely, even if you were under the impression that I was otherwise unoccupied and at leisure ; for how could I, even though wholly at leisure, furnish the solution of so many questions to one in such haste as you are, and, in fact, as you write, on the eve of a journey? I would, indeed, be prevented by the mere number of the questions to be resolved, even if their solution were easy. But they are so perplexingly intricate, and so hard, that even if they were few in number, and engaging me when otherwise wholly at leisure, they would, by the mere time required, exhaust my powers of application, and wear out my strength. I would, however, fain snatch you forcibly away from the midst of those inquiries in which you so much delight, and fix you down among the cares which engage my attention, in order that you may either learn not to be unprofitably curious, or desist from presuming to

impose the task of feeding and fostering your curiosity upon men among whose cares one of the greatest is to repress and curb those who are too inquisitive. For if time and pains are devoted to writing anything to you, how much better and more profitably are these employed in endeavours to cut off those vain and treacherous passions (which are to be guarded against with a caution proportioned to the ease with which they impose upon us, by their being disguised and cloaked under the semblance of virtue and the name of liberal studies), rather than in causing them to be, by our service, or rather obsequiousness, so to speak, roused to a more vehement assertion of the despotism under which they so oppress your excellent spirit.

2. For tell me what good purpose is served by the many Dialogues which you have read, if they have in no way helped you towards the discovery and attainment of the end of all your actions? For by your letter you indicate plainly enough what you have proposed to yourself as the end to be attained by all this most ardent study of yours, which is at once useless to yourself and troublesome to me. For when you were in your letter using every means to persuade me to answer the questions which you sent, you wrote these words : " I might importune you at greater length, and through many of your dear friends ; but I know your disposition, that you do not desire to be solicited, but show kindness readily to all, if only there be nothing improper in the thing requested : and there is absolutely nothing improper in what I ask. Be this, however, as it may, I beg you to do me this kindness, for I am on the point of embarking on a voyage." In these words of your letter you are indeed right in your opinion as to myself, that I am desirous of showing kindness to all, if only there be nothing improper in the request made ; but it is not my opinion that there is nothing improper in what you ask. For when I consider how a bishop is distracted and overwrought by the cares of his office clamouring on every side, it does not seem to me proper for him suddenly, as if deaf, to withdraw himself from all these, and devote himself to the work of expounding to a single student some unimportant questions in the Dialogues of Cicero. The impropriety of this you yourself apprehend, although, carried away with zeal in the pursuit of your studies, you will by no means give heed to it. For what other construction can I put on the fact that, after saying that in this matter there is absolutely nothing improper, you have immediately subjoined : " Be this, however, as it may, I beg you to do me this kindness, for I am on the point of embarking on a voyage "? For this intimates that in your view, at least, there is no impropriety in your request, but that whatever impro-

---

[1] This officer, " magister memoriæ," was a private secretary of the emperor, and had, among other privileges of his office, the right of granting liberty to private individuals to travel by the imperial conveyances along the great highways connecting Rome with the remotest boundaries of the provinces. See Suetonius, *Vita Augusti*, chap. xlix., and Pliny, *Letters*, Books x.-xiv., and *Codex Justiniani*, Book xii. Title 51.

[2] We conjecture from the context that this expresses the force of the obscure words, " saltem timeantur annonæ."

priety may be in it, you nevertheless ask me to do what you ask, because you are about to go on a voyage. Now what is the force of this supplementary plea — "I am on the point of embarking on a voyage"? Do you mean that, unless you were in these circumstances, I ought not to do you service in which anything improper may be involved? You think, forsooth, that the impropriety can be washed away by salt water. But even were it so, my share at least of the fault would remain unexpiated, because I do not propose undertaking a voyage.

3. You write, further, that I know how very painful it is to you to be burdensome to any one, and you solemnly protest that God alone knows how irresistible is the necessity under which you make the application. When I came to this statement in your letter, I turned my attention eagerly to learn the nature of the necessity; and, behold, you bring it before me in these words: "You know the ways of men, how prone they are to censure, and how any one will be regarded as illiterate and stupid who, when questions are addressed to him, can return no answer." On reading this sentence, I felt a burning desire to reply to your letter; for, by the morbid weakness of mind which this indicated, you pierced my inmost heart, and forced your way into the midst of my cares, so that I could not refuse to minister to your relief, so far as God might enable me — not by devising a solution of your difficulties, but by breaking the connection between your happiness and the wretched support on which it now insecurely hangs, viz. the opinions of men, and fastening it to a hold which is firm and immovable. Do you not, O Dioscorus, remember an ingenious line of your favourite Persius, in which he not only rebukes your folly, but administers to your boyish head, if you have only sense to feel it, a deserved correction, restraining your vanity with the words, "To know is nothing in your eyes unless another knows that you know"?[1] You have, as I said before, read so many Dialogues, and devoted your attention to so many discussions of philosophers — tell me which of them has placed the chief end of his actions in the applause of the vulgar, or in the opinion even of good and wise men? But you, — and what should make you the more ashamed, — you, when on the eve of sailing away from Africa, give evidence of your having made signal progress, forsooth, in your studies here, when you affirm that the only reason why you impose the task of expounding Cicero to you upon bishops, who are already oppressed with work and engrossed with matters of a very different nature, is, that you fear that if, when questioned by men prone to censure, you cannot

answer, you will be regarded by them as illiterate and stupid. O cause well worthy to occupy the hours which bishops devote to study while other men sleep!

4. You seem to me to be prompted to mental effort night and day by no other motive than ambition to be praised by men for your industry and acquisitions in learning. Although I have ever regarded this as fraught with danger to persons who are striving after the true and the right, I am now, by your case, more convinced of the danger than before. For it is due to no other cause than this same pernicious habit that you have failed to see by what motive we might be induced to grant to you what you asked; for as by a perverted judgment you yourself are urged on to acquire a knowledge of the things about which you put questions, from no other motive than that you may receive praise or escape censure from men, you imagine that we, by a like perversity of judgment, are to be influenced by the considerations alleged in your request. Would that, when we declare to you that by your writing such things concerning yourself we are moved, not to grant your request, but to reprove and correct you, we might be able to effect for you also complete emancipation from the influence of a boon so worthless and deceitful as the applause of men! "It is the manner of men," you say, "to be prone to censure." What then? "Any one who can make no reply when questions are addressed to him," you say, "will be regarded as illiterate and stupid." Behold, then, I ask you a question not concerning something in the books of Cicero, whose meaning, perchance, his readers may not be able to find, but concerning your own letter and the meaning of your own words. My question is: Why did you not say, "Any one who can make no reply will be *proved* to be illiterate and stupid," but prefer to say, "He will be *regarded* as illiterate and stupid"? Why, if not for this reason, that you yourself already understand well enough that the person who fails to answer such questions is not in reality, but only in the opinion of some, illiterate and stupid? But I warn you that he who fears to be subjected to the edge of the pruning-hook by the tongues of such men is a sapless log, and is therefore not only regarded as illiterate and stupid, but is actually such, and proved to be so.

5. Perhaps you will say, "But seeing that I am not stupid, and that I am specially earnest in striving not to be stupid, I am reluctant even to be regarded as stupid." And rightly so; but I ask, What is your motive in this reluctance? For in stating why you did not hesitate to burden us with those questions which you wish to have solved and explained, you said that this was the reason, and that this was the end, and an end so

---

[1] "Scire tuum nihil est nisi te scire hoc sciat alter." — Persius, *Sat.* i. 27.

necessary in your estimation that you said it was of overwhelming urgency, — lest, forsooth, if you were posed with these questions and gave no answer, you should be regarded as illiterate and stupid by men prone to censure. Now, I ask, is this [jealousy as to your own reputation] the whole reason why you beg this from us, or is it because of some ulterior object that you are unwilling to be thought illiterate and stupid? If this be the whole reason, you see, as I think, that this one thing [the praise of men] is the end pursued by that vehement zeal of yours, by which, as you admit, a burden is imposed on us. But, from Dioscorus, what can be to us a burden, except that burden which Dioscorus himself unconsciously bears, — a burden which he will begin to feel only when he attempts to rise, — a burden of which I would fain believe that it is not so bound to him as to defy his efforts to shake his shoulders free? And this I say not because these questions engage your studies, but because they are studied by you for such an end. For surely you by this time feel that this end is trivial, unsubstantial, and light as air. It is also apt to produce in the soul what may be likened to a dangerous swelling, beneath which lurk the germs of decay, and by it the eye of the mind becomes suffused, so that it cannot discern the riches of truth. Believe this, my Dioscorus, it is true: so shall I enjoy thee in unfeigned longing for truth, and in that essential dignity of truth by the shadow of which you are turned aside. If I have failed to convince you of this by the method which I have now used, I know no other that I can use. For you do not see it; nor can you possibly see it so long as you build your joys on the crumbling foundation of human applause.

6. If, however, this be not the end aimed at in these actions and by this zeal of yours, but there is some other ulterior reason for your unwillingness to be regarded as illiterate and stupid, I ask what that reason is. If it be to remove impediments to the acquisition of temporal riches, or the obtaining of a wife, or the grasping of honours, and other things of that kind which are flowing past with a headlong current, and dragging to the bottom those who fall into them, it is assuredly not our duty to help you towards that end, nay, rather we ought to turn you away from it. For we do not so forbid your fixing the aim of your studies in the precarious possession of renown as to make you leave, as it were, the waters of the Mincius and enter the Eridanus, into which, perchance, the Mincius would carry you even without yourself making the change. For when the vanity of human applause has failed to satisfy the soul, because it furnishes for its nourishment nothing real and substantial, this same eager desire compels the mind to go on to something else as more rich and productive; and if, nevertheless, this also belong to the things which pass away with time, it is as when one river leads us into another, so that there can be no rest from our miseries so long as the end aimed at in our discharge of duty is placed in that which is unstable. We desire, therefore, that in some firm and immutable good you should fix the home of your most stedfast efforts, and the perfectly secure resting-place of all your good and honourable activity. Is it, perchance, your intention, if you succeed by the breath of propitious fame, or even by spreading your sails for its fitful gusts, in reaching that earthly happiness of which I have spoken, to make it subservient to the acquisition of the other — the sure and true and satisfying good? But to me it does not seem probable — and truth itself forbids the supposition — that it should be reached either by such a circuitous way when it is at hand, or at such cost when it is freely given.

7. Perhaps you think that we ought to turn the praise of men itself to good account as an instrument for making others accessible to counsels regarding that which is good and useful; and perhaps you are anxious lest, if men regard you as illiterate and stupid, they think you unworthy to receive their earnest or patient attention, if you were either exhorting any one to do well, or reproving the malice and wickedness of an evil-doer. If, in proposing these questions, you contemplated this righteous and beneficent end, we have certainly been wronged by your not giving the preference to this in your letter as the consideration by which we might be moved either to grant willingly what you asked, or, if declining your request, to do so on the ground of some other cause which might perchance prevent us, but not on the ground of our being ashamed to accept the position of serving or even not resisting the aspirations of your vanity. For, I pray you, consider how much better and more profitable it is for you to receive from us with far more certainty and with less loss of time those principles of truth by which you can for yourself refute all that is false, and by so doing be prevented from cherishing an opinion so false and contemptible as this — that you are learned and intelligent if you have studied with a zeal in which there is more pride than prudence the worn-out errors of many writers of a bygone age. But this opinion I do not suppose you now to hold, for surely I have not in vain spoken so long to Dioscorus things so manifestly true; and from this, as understood, I proceed with my letter.

CHAP. II. — 8. Wherefore, seeing that you do not consider a man illiterate and stupid merely on the ground of ignorance of these things, but only if he be ignorant of the truth itself, and that, consequently, the opinions of any one who has written or may have written on these subjects are either true, and therefore are already held by you, or false, and therefore you may be content not to know them, and need not be consumed with vain solicitude about knowing the variety of the opinions of other men under the fear of otherwise remaining illiterate and stupid, — seeing, I say, that this is the case, let us now, if you please, consider whether, in the event of other men, who are, as you say, prone to censure, finding you ignorant of these things, and therefore regarding you, though falsely, as an illiterate and stupid person, this mistake of theirs ought to have so much weight with you as to make it not unseemly for you to apply to bishops for instruction in these things. I propose this on the assumption that we now believe you to be seeking this instruction in order that by it you may be helped in recommending the truth to men, and in reclaiming men who, if they supposed you to be illiterate and stupid in regard to those books of Cicero, would regard you as a person from whom they considered it unworthy of them to receive any useful or profitable instruction. Believe me, you are under a mistake.

9. For, in the first place, I do not at all see that, in the countries in which you are so afraid of being esteemed deficient in education and acuteness, there are any persons who will ask you a single question about these matters. Both in this country, to which you came to learn these things, and at Rome, you know by experience how little they are esteemed, and that, in consequence, they are neither taught nor learned ; and throughout all Africa, so far are you from being troubled by any such questioner, that you cannot find any one who will be troubled with your questions, and are compelled by the dearth of such persons to send your questions to bishops to be solved by them : as if, indeed, these bishops, although in their youth, under the influence of the same ardour — let me rather say error — which carries you away, they were at pains to learn these things as matters of great moment, permitted them still to remain in memory now that their heads are white with age and they are burdened with the responsibilities of episcopal office ; or as if, supposing them to desire to retain these things in memory, greater and graver cares would not in spite of their desire banish them from their hearts ; or as if, in the event of some of these things lingering in recollection by the force of long habit, they would not wish rather to bury in utter oblivion what was thus remembered, than to answer senseless questions at a time when, even amidst the comparative leisure enjoyed in the schools and in the lecture-rooms of rhetoricians, they seem to have so lost both voice and vigour that, in order to have in-

struction imparted concerning them, it is deemed necessary to send from Carthage to Hippo, — a place in which all such things are so unwonted and so wholly foreign, that if, in taking the trouble of writing an answer to your question, I wished to look at any passage to discover the order of thought in the context preceding or following the words requiring exposition, I would be utterly unable to find a manuscript of the works of Cicero. However, these teachers of rhetoric in Carthage who have failed to satisfy you in this matter are not only not blamed, but, on the contrary, commended by me, if, as I suppose, they have not forgotten that the scene of these contests was wont to be, not the Roman forum, but the Greek gymnasia. But when you have applied your mind to these gymnasia, and have found even them to be in such things bare and cold, the church of the Christians of Hippo occurred to you as a place where you might lay down your cares, because the bishop now occupying that see at one time took fees for instructing boys in these things. But, on the one hand, I do not wish you to be still a boy, and, on the other hand, it is not becoming for me, either for a fee or as a favour, to be dealing now in childish things. This, therefore, being the case — seeing, that is to say, that these two great cities, Rome and Carthage, the living centres of Latin literature, neither try your patience by asking you such questions as you speak of, nor care patiently to listen to you when you propound them, I am amazed in a degree beyond all expression that a young man of your good sense should be afraid lest you should be afflicted with any questioner on these subjects in the cities of Greece and of the East. You are much more likely to hear jackdaws [1] in Africa than this manner of conversation in those lands.

10. Suppose, however, in the next place, that I am wrong, and that perchance some one should arise putting questions like these, — a phenomenon the more unwelcome because in those parts peculiarly absurd, — are you not much more afraid lest far more readily men arise who, being Greeks, and finding you settled in Greece, and acquainted with the Greek language as your mother tongue, may ask you some things in the original works of their philosophers which Cicero may not have put into his treatises? If this happen, what reply will you make? Will you say that you preferred to learn these things from the books of Latin rather than of Greek authors? By such an answer you will, in the first place, put an affront upon Greece ; and you know how men of that nation resent this. And in the next place, they being now wounded and angry, how

---

[1] *Corniculas.* The lapse of centuries may have introduced into the north of Africa birds unknown in Augustin's time. The translator has seen these birds in Egypt.

readily will you find what you are too anxious to avoid, that they will count you on the one hand stupid, because you preferred to learn the opinions of the Greek philosophers, or, more properly speaking, some isolated and scattered tenets of their philosophy, in Latin dialogues, rather than to study the complete and connected system of their opinions in the Greek originals, — and, on the other hand, illiterate, because, although ignorant of so many things written in your language, you have unsuccessfully laboured to gather some of them together from writings in a foreign tongue. Or will you perhaps reply that you did not despise the Greek writings on these subjects, but that you devoted your attention first to the study of Latin works, and now, proficient in these, are beginning to inquire after Greek learning? If this does not make you blush, to confess that you, being a Greek, have in your boyhood learned Latin, and are now, like a man of some foreign nation,[1] desirous of studying Greek literature, surely you will not blush to own that in the department of Latin literature you are ignorant of some things, of which you may perceive how many versed in Latin learning are equally ignorant, if you will only consider that, although living in the midst of so many learned men in Carthage, you assure me that it is under the pressure of necessity that you impose this burden on me.

11. Finally, suppose that you, being asked all those questions which you have submitted to me, have been able to answer them all. Behold ! you are now spoken of as most learned and most acute ; behold ! now this insignificant breath of Greek laudation raises you to heaven. Be it yours now to remember your responsibilities and the end for which you coveted these praises, namely, that to men who have been easily won to admire you by these trifles, and who are now hanging most affectionately and eagerly on your lips, you may impart some truly important and wholesome instruction ; and I should like to know whether you possess, and can rightly impart to others, that which is truly most important and wholesome. For it is absurd if, after learning many unnecessary things with a view to preparing the ears of men to receive what is necessary, you be found not to possess those necessary things for the reception of which you have by these unnecessary things prepared the way ; it is absurd if, while busying yourself with learning things by which you may win men's attention, you refuse to learn that which may be poured into their minds when their attention is secured. But if you reply that you have already learned this, and say that the truth supremely necessary is Christian doctrine, which I know that you es-

teem above all other things, placing in it alone your hope of everlasting salvation, then surely this does not demand a knowledge of the Dialogues of Cicero, and a collection of the beggarly and divided opinions of other men, in order to your persuading men to give it a hearing. Let your character and manner of life command the attention of those who are to receive any such teaching from you. I would not have you open the way for teaching truth by first teaching what must be afterwards unlearned.

12. For if the knowledge of the discordant and mutually contradictory opinions of others is of any service to him who would obtain an entrance for Christian truth in overthrowing the opposition of error, it is useful only in the way of preventing the assailant of the truth from being at liberty to fix his eye solely on the work of controverting your tenets, while carefully hiding his own from view. For the knowledge of the truth is of itself sufficient both to detect and to subvert all errors, even those which may not have been heard before, if only they are brought forward. If, however, in order to secure not only the demolition of open errors, but also the rooting out of those which lurk in darkness, it is necessary for you to be acquainted with the erroneous opinions which others have advanced, let both eye and ear be wakeful, I beseech you, — look well and listen well whether any of our assailants bring forward a single argument from Anaximenes and from Anaxagoras, when, though the Stoic and Epicurean philosophies were more recent and taught largely, even their ashes are not so warm as that a single spark can be struck out from them against the Christian faith. The din which resounds in the battle-field of controversy now comes from innumerable small companies and cliques of sectaries, some of them easily discomfited, others presuming to make bold resistance, — such as the partisans of Donatus, Maximian, and Manichæus here, or the unruly herds of Arians, Eunomians, Macedonians, and Cataphrygians and other pests which abound in the countries to which you are on your way. If you shrink from the task of acquainting yourself with the errors of all these sects, what occasion have we in defending the Christian religion to inquire after the tenets of Anaximenes, and with idle curiosity to awaken anew controversies which have slept for ages, when already the cavillings and arguments even of some of the heretics who claimed the glory of the Christian name, such as the Marcionites and the Sabellians, and many more, have been put to silence? Nevertheless, if it be necessary, as I have said, to know beforehand some of the opinions which war against the truth, and become thoroughly conversant with these, it is our duty to give a place in such study to the here-

---

[1] *Barbarum.*

tics who call themselves Christians, much rather than to Anaxagoras and Democritus.

CHAP. III. — 13. Again, whoever may put to you the questions which you have propounded to us, let him understand that, under the guidance of deeper erudition and greater wisdom, you are ignorant of things like these. For if Themistocles regarded it as a small matter that he was looked upon as imperfectly educated when he had declined to play on the lyre at a banquet, and at the same time, when, after he had confessed ignorance of this accomplishment, one said, "What, then, do you know?" gave as his reply, "The art of making a small republic great" — are you to hesitate about admitting ignorance in trifles like these, when it is in your power to answer any one who may ask, "What, then, do you know?" — "The secret by which without such knowledge a man may be blessed"? And if you do not yet possess this secret, you act in searching into those other matters with as blind perversity as if, when labouring under some dangerous disease of the body, you eagerly sought after dainties in food and finery in dress, instead of physic and physicians. For this attainment ought not to be put off upon any pretext whatever, and no other knowledge ought, especially in our age, to receive a prior place in your studies. And now see how easily you may have this knowledge if you desire it. He who inquires how he may attain a blessed life is assuredly inquiring after nothing else than this: where is the highest good? in other words, wherein resides man's supreme good, not according to the perverted and hasty opinions of men, but according to the sure and immovable truth? Now its residence is not found by any one except in the body, or in the mind, or in God, or in two of these, or in the three combined. If, then, you have learned that neither the supreme good nor any part whatever of the supreme good is in the body, the remaining alternatives are, that it is in the mind, or in God, or in both combined. And if now you have also learned that what is true of the body in this respect is eqally true of the mind, what now remains but God Himself as the One in whom resides man's supreme good? — not that there are no other goods, but that good is called the supreme good to which all others are related. For every one is blessed when he enjoys that for the sake of which he desires to have all other things, seeing that it is loved for its own sake, and not on account of something else. And the supreme good is said to be there because at this point nothing is found towards which the supreme good can go forth, or to which it is related. In it is the resting-place of desire; in it is assured fruition; in it the most tranquil satisfaction of a will morally perfect.

14. Give me a man who sees at once that the body is not the good of the mind, but that the mind is rather the good of the body : with such a man we would, of course, forbear from inquiring whether the highest good of which we speak, or any part of it, is in the body. For that the mind is better than the body is a truth which it would be utter folly to deny. Equally absurd would it be to deny that that which gives a happy life, or any part of a happy life, is better than that which receives the boon. The mind, therefore, does not receive from the body either the supreme good or any part of the supreme good. Men who do not see this have been blinded by that sweetness of carnal pleasures which they do not discern to be a consequence of imperfect health. Now, perfect health of body shall be the consummation of the immortality of the whole man. For God has endowed the soul with a nature so powerful, that from that consummate fulness of joy which is promised to the saints in the end of time, some portion overflows also upon the lower part of our nature, the body, — not the blessedness which is proper to the part which enjoys and understands, but the plenitude of health, that is, the vigour of incorruption. Men who, as I have said, do not see this war with each other in unsatisfactory debates, each maintaining the view which may please his own fancy, but all placing the supreme good of man in the body, and so stir up crowds of disorderly carnal minds, of whom the Epicureans have flourished in pre-eminent estimation with the unlearned multitude.

15. Give me a man who sees at once, moreover, that when the mind is happy, it is happy not by good which belongs to itself, else it would never be unhappy: and with such a man we would, of course, forbear from inquiring whether that highest and, so to speak, bliss-bestowing good, or any part of it, is in the mind. For when the mind is elated with joy in itself, as if in good which belongs to itself, it is proud. But when the mind perceives itself to be mutable, — a fact which may be learned from this, even though nothing else proved it, that the mind from being foolish may be made wise, — and apprehends that wisdom is unchangeable, it must at the same time apprehend that wisdom is superior to its own nature, and that it finds more abundant and abiding joy in the communications and light of wisdom than in itself. Thus desisting and subsiding from boasting and self-conceit, it strives to cling to God, and to be recruited and reformed by Him who is unchangeable ; whom it now understands to be the Author not only of every species of all things with which it comes in contact, either by the bodily senses or by intellectual faculties, but also of even the very capacity of taking form before any form has been taken, since the formless is defined to

be that which can receive a form. Therefore it feels its own instability more, just in proportion as it clings less to God, whose being is perfect: it discerns also that the perfection of His being is consummate because He is immutable, and therefore neither gains nor loses, but that in itself every change by which it gains capacity for perfect clinging to God is advantageous, but every change by which it loses is pernicious, and further, that all loss tends towards destruction; and although it is not manifest whether any thing is ultimately destroyed, it is manifest to every one that the loss brings destruction so far that the object no longer is what it was. Whence the mind infers that the one reason why things suffer loss, or are liable to suffer loss, is, that they were made out of nothing; so that their property of being, and of permanence, and the arrangement whereby each finds even according to its imperfections its own place in the complex whole, all depend on the goodness and omnipotence of Him whose being is perfect,[1] and who is the Creator able to make out of nothing not only something, but something great; and that the first sin, *i.e.* the first voluntary loss, is rejoicing in its own power: for it rejoices in something less than would be the source of its joy if it rejoiced in the power of God, which is unquestionably greater. Not perceiving this, and looking only to the capacities of the human mind, and the great beauty of its achievements in word and deed, some, who would have been ashamed to place man's supreme good in the body, have, by placing it in the mind, assigned to it unquestionably a lower sphere than that assigned to it by unsophisticated reason. Among Greek philosophers who hold these views, the chief place both in number of adherents and in subtlety of disputation has been held by the Stoics, who have, however, in consequence of their opinion that in nature everything is material, succeeded in turning the mind rather from carnal than material objects.

16. Among those, again, who say that our supreme and only good is to enjoy God, by whom both we ourselves and all things were made, the most eminent have been the Platonists, who not unreasonably judged it to belong to their duty to confute the Stoics and Epicureans — the latter especially, and almost exclusively. The Academic School is identical with the Platonists, as is shown plainly enough by the links of unbroken succession connecting the schools. For if you ask who was the predecessor of Arcesilas, the first who, announcing no doctrine of his own, set himself to the one work of refuting the Stoics and Epicureans, you will find that it was Polemo; ask who preceded Polemo, it was Xen-

ocrates; but Xenocrates was Plato's disciple, and by him appointed his successor in the academy. Wherefore, as to this question concerning the supreme good, if we set aside the representatives of conflicting views, and consider the abstract question, you find at once that two errors confront each other as diametrically opposed — the one declaring the body, and the other declaring the mind to be the seat of the supreme good of men. You find also that truly enlightened reason, by which God is perceived to be our supreme good, is opposed to both of these errors, but does not impart the knowledge of what is true until it has first made men unlearn what is false. If now you consider the question in connection with the advocates of different views, you will find the Epicureans and Stoics most keenly contending with each other, and the Platonists, on the other hand, endeavouring to decide the controversy between them, concealing the truth which they held, and devoting themselves only to prove and overthrow the vain confidence with which the others adhered to error.

17. It was not in the power of the Platonists, however, to be so efficient in supporting the side of reason enlightened by truth, as the others were in supporting their own errors. For from them all there was then withheld that example of divine humility, which, in the fulness of time,[2] was furnished by our Lord Jesus Christ, — that one example before which, even in the mind of the most headstrong and arrogant, all pride bends, breaks, and dies. And therefore the Platonists, not being able by their authority to lead the mass of mankind, blinded by love of earthly things, into faith in things invisible, — although they saw them moved, especially by the arguments of the Epicureans, not only to drink freely the cup of the pleasures of the body to which they were naturally inclined, but even to plead for these, affirming that they constitute man's highest good; although, moreover, they saw that those who were moved to abstinence from these pleasures by the praise of virtue found it easier to regard pleasure as having its true seat in the soul, whence the good actions, concerning which they were able, in some measure, to form an opinion, proceeded, — at the same time, saw that if they attempted to introduce into the minds of men the notion of something divine and supremely immutable, which cannot be reached by any one of the bodily senses, but is apprehensible only by reason, which, nevertheless, surpasses in its nature the mind itself, and were to teach that this is God, set before the human soul to be enjoyed by it when purged from all stains of human desires, in whom alone every longing after happiness

---

[1] *Qui summe est.*

[2] *Opportunissimo tempore.*

finds rest, and in whom alone we ought to find the consummation of all good, — men would not understand them, and would much more readily award the palm to their antagonists, whether Epicureans or Stoics; the result of which would be a thing most disastrous to the human race, namely, that the doctrine, which is true and profitable, would become sullied by the contempt of the uneducated masses. So much in regard to Ethical questions.

18. As to Physics, if the Platonists taught that the originating cause of all natures is immaterial wisdom, and if, on the other hand, the rival sects of philosophers never got above material things, while the beginning of all things was attributed by some to atoms, by others to the four elements, in which fire was of special power in the construction of all things, — who could fail to see to which opinion a favourable verdict would be given, when the great mass of unthinking men are enthralled by material things, and can in no wise comprehend that an immaterial power could form the universe?

19. The department of dialectic questions remains to be discussed; for, as you are aware, all questions in the pursuit of wisdom are classified under three heads, — Ethics, Physics, and Dialectics. When, therefore, the Epicureans said that the senses are never deceived, and, though the Stoics admitted that they sometimes are mistaken, both placed in the senses the standard by which truth is to be comprehended, who would listen to the Platonists when both of these sects opposed them? Who would look upon them as entitled to be esteemed men at all, and much less wise men, if, without hesitation or qualification, they affirmed not only that there is something which cannot be discerned by touch, or smell, or taste, or hearing, or sight, and which cannot be conceived of by any image borrowed from the things with which the senses acquaint us, but that this alone truly exists, and is alone capable of being perceived, because it is alone unchangeable and eternal, but is perceived only by reason, the faculty whereby alone truth, in so far as it can be discovered by us, is found?

20. Seeing, therefore, that the Platonists held opinions which they could not impart to men enthralled by the flesh; seeing also that they were not of such authority among the common people as to persuade them to accept what they ought to believe until the mind should be trained to that condition in which these things can be understood, — they chose to hide their own opinions, and to content themselves with arguing against those who, although they affirmed that the discovery of truth is made through the senses of the body, boasted that they had found the truth. And truly, what occasion have we to inquire as to the nature of their teaching? We

know that it was not divine, nor invested with any divine authority. But this one fact merits our attention, that whereas Plato is in many ways most clearly proved by Cicero to have placed both the supreme good and the causes of things, and the certainty of the processes of reason, in Wisdom, not human, but divine, whence in some way the light of human wisdom is derived — in Wisdom which is wholly immutable, and in Truth always consistent with itself; and whereas we also learn from Cicero that the followers of Plato laboured to overthrow the philosophers known as Epicureans and Stoics, who placed the supreme good, the causes of things, and the certainty of the processes of reason, in the nature either of body or of mind, — the controversy had continued rolling on with successive centuries, so that even at the commencement of the Christian era, when the faith of things invisible and eternal was with saving power preached by means of visible miracles to men, who could neither see nor imagine anything beyond things material, these same Epicureans and Stoics are found in the Acts of the Apostles to have opposed themselves to the blessed Apostle Paul, who was beginning to scatter the seeds of that faith among the Gentiles.

21. By which thing it seems to me to be sufficiently proved that the errors of the Gentiles in ethics, physics, and the mode of seeking truth, errors many and manifold, but conspicuously represented in these two schools of philosophy, continued even down to the Christian era, notwithstanding the fact that the learned assailed them most vehemently, and employed both remarkable skill and abundant labour in subverting them. Yet these errors we see in our time to have been already so completely silenced, that now in our schools of rhetoric the question what their opinions were is scarcely ever mentioned; and these controversies have been now so completely eradicated or suppressed in even the Greek gymnasia, notably fond of discussion, that whenever now any school of error lifts up its head against the truth, i.e. against the Church of Christ, it does not venture to leap into the arena except under the shield of the Christian name. Whence it is obvious that the Platonist school of philosophers felt it necessary, having changed those few things in their opinions which Christian teaching condemned, to submit with pious homage to Christ, the only King who is invincible, and to apprehend the Incarnate Word of God, at whose command the truth which they had even feared to publish was immediately believed.

22. To Him, my Dioscorus, I desire you to submit yourself with unreserved piety, and I wish you to prepare for yourself no other way of seizing and holding the truth than that which

has been prepared by Him who, as God, saw the weakness of our goings. In that way the first part is humility; the second, humility; the third, humility: and this I would continue to repeat as often as you might ask direction, not that there are no other instructions which may be given, but because, unless humility precede, accompany, and follow every good action which we perform, being at once the object which we keep before our eyes, the support to which we cling, and the monitor by which we are restrained, pride wrests wholly from our hand any good work on which we are congratulating ourselves.[1] All other vices are to be apprehended when we are doing wrong; but pride is to be feared even when we do right actions, lest those things which are done in a praiseworthy manner be spoiled by the desire for praise itself. Wherefore, as that most illustrious orator, on being asked what seemed to him the first thing to be observed in the art of eloquence, is said to have replied, Delivery; and when he was asked what was the second thing, replied again, Delivery; and when asked what was the third thing, still gave no other reply than this, Delivery; so if you were to ask me, however often you might repeat the question, what are the instructions of the Christian religion, I would be disposed to answer always and only, "Humility," although, perchance, necessity might constrain me to speak also of other things.

CHAP. IV. — 23. To this most wholesome humility, in which our Lord Jesus Christ is our teacher — having submitted to humiliation that He might instruct us in this — to this humility, I say, the most formidable adversary is a certain kind of most unenlightened knowledge, if I may so call it, in which we congratulate ourselves on knowing what may have been the views of Anaximenes, Anaxagoras, Pythagoras, Democritus, and others of the same kind, imagining that by this we become learned men and scholars, although such attainments are far removed from true learning and erudition. For the man who has learned that God is not extended or diffused through space, either finite or infinite, so as to be greater in one part and less in another, but that He is wholly present everywhere, as the Truth is, of which no one in his senses will affirm that it is partly in one place, partly in another — and the Truth is God Himself — such a man will not be moved by the opinions of any philosopher soever who believes [like Anaximenes]

that the infinite air around us is the true God. What matters it to such a man though he be ignorant what bodily form they speak of, since they speak of a form which is bounded on all sides? What matters it to him whether it was only as an Academician, and merely for the purpose of confuting Anaximenes, who had said that God is a material existence, — for air is material, — that Cicero objected that God must have form and beauty?[2] or himself perceived that truth has immaterial form and beauty, by which the mind itself is moulded, and by which we judge all the deeds of the wise man to be beautiful, and therefore affirmed that God must be of the most perfect beauty, not merely for the purpose of confuting an antagonist, but with profound insight into the fact that nothing is more beautiful than truth itself, which is cognisable by the understanding alone, and is immutable? Moreover, as to the opinion of Anaximenes, who held that the air is generated, and at the same time believed it to be God, it does not in the least move the man who understands that, since the air is certainly not God, there is no likeness between the manner in which the air is generated, that is to say, produced by some cause, and the manner, understood by none except through divine inspiration, in which He was begotten who is the Word of God, God with God. Moreover, who does not see that even in regard to material things he speaks most foolishly in affirming that air is generated, and is at the same time God, while he refuses to give the name of God to that by which the air has been generated, — for it is impossible that it could be generated by no power? Yet once more, his saying that the air is always in motion will have no disturbing influence as proof that the air is God upon the man who knows that all movements of body are of a lower order than movements of the soul, but that even the movements of the soul are infinitely slow compared with His who is supreme and immutable Wisdom.

24. In like manner, if Anaxagoras or any other affirm that the mind is essential truth and wisdom,[3] what call have I to debate with a man about a word? For it is manifest that mind gives being to the order and mode of all things, and that it may be suitably called infinite with respect not to its extension in space, but to its power, the range of which transcends all human thought. Nor [shall I dispute his assertion] that this essential wisdom is formless; for this is a property of material things, that whatever

---

[1] We give the original of this exquisite sentence, both for its intrinsic value, and because it is a good example of that antithetic style of writing which makes the exact and felicitous rendering of Augustin's words into any other language peculiarly difficult: *Nisi humilitas omnia quæcumque bene facimus et præcesserit, et comitetur, et consecuta fuerit, et proposita quam intueamur, et apposita cui adhæreamus, et imposita qua reprimamur, jam nobis de aliquo bono facto gaudentibus totum extorquet de manu superbia.*

[2] The words of Cicero are: "Post, Anaximenes aera Deum statuit, eumque gigni, esseque immensum, et infinitum, et semper in motu: quasi aut aer sine ulla forma Deus esse possit, cum præsertim Deum non modo aliqua sed pulcherrima specie esse deceat; aut non omne quod ortum sit mortalitas consequatur." — *De Natura Deorum*, Book I.

[3] *Ipsam veritatem atque sapientiam.*

bodies are infinite are also formless. Cicero, however, from his desire to confute such opinions, as I suppose, in contending with adversaries who believed in nothing immaterial, denies that anything can be annexed to that which is infinite, because in things material there must be a boundary at the part to which anything is annexed. Therefore he says that Anaxagoras "did not see that motion joined to sensation and to it" (i.e. linked to it in unbroken connection) "is impossible in the infinite" (that is, in a substance which is infinite), as if treating of material substances, to which nothing can be joined except at their boundaries. Moreover, in the succeeding words — "and that sensation of which the whole system of nature is not sensible when struck is an impossibility"[1] — Cicero speaks as if Anaxagoras had said that mind — to which he ascribed the power of ordering and fashioning all things — had sensation such as the soul has by means of the body. For it is manifest that the whole soul has sensation when it feels anything by means of the body; for whatever is perceived by sensation is not concealed from the whole soul. Now, Cicero's design in saying that the whole system of nature must be conscious of every sensation was, that he might, as it were, take from the philosopher that mind which he affirms to be infinite. For how does the whole of nature experience sensation if it be infinite? Bodily sensation begins at some point, and does not pervade the whole of any substance unless it be one in which it can reach an end; but this, of course, cannot be said of that which is infinite. Anaxagoras, however, had not said anything about bodily sensation. The word "whole," moreover, is used differently when we speak of that which is immaterial, because it is understood to be without boundaries in space, so that it may be spoken of as a whole and at the same time as infinite — the former because of its completeness, the latter because of its not being limited by boundaries in space.

25. "Furthermore," says Cicero, "if he will affirm that the mind itself is, so to speak, some kind of animal, there must be some principle from within from which it receives the name 'animal,'" — so that mind, according to Anaxagoras, is a kind of body, and has within it an animating principle, because of which it is called "animal." Observe how he speaks in language which we are accustomed to apply to things corporeal, — animals being in the ordinary sense of the word visible substances, — adapting himself, as I suppose, to the blunted perceptions of those against whom he argues; and yet he has uttered a thing which, if they could awake to perceive it, might suffice to teach them that everything which presents itself to our minds as a living body must be thought of not as itself a soul, but as an animal having a soul. For having said, "There must be something within from which it receives the name animal," he adds, "But what is deeper within than mind?" The mind, therefore, cannot have any inner soul, by possessing which it is an animal; for it is itself that which is innermost. If, then, it is an animal, let it have some external body in relation to which it may be within; for this is what he means by saying, "It is therefore girt round by an exterior body," as if Anaxagoras had said that mind cannot be otherwise than as belonging to some animal. And yet Anaxagoras held the opinion that essential supreme Wisdom is mind, although it is not the peculiar property of any living being, so to speak, since Truth is near to all souls alike that are able to enjoy it. Observe, therefore, how wittily he concludes the argument: "Since this is not the opinion of Anaxagoras" (i.e. seeing that he does not hold that that mind which he calls God is girt about with an external body, through its relation to which it could be an animal), "we must say that mind pure and simple, without the addition of anything" (i.e. of any body) "through which it may exercise sensation, seems to be beyond the range and conceptions of our intelligence."[2]

26. Nothing is more certain than that this lies beyond the range and conception of the intelligence of Stoics and Epicureans, who cannot think of anything which is not material. But by the word "our" intelligence he means "human" intelligence; and he very properly does not say, "it lies beyond our intelligence," but "it seems to lie beyond." For their opinion is, that this lies beyond the understanding of all men, and therefore they think that nothing of the kind can be. But there are some whose intelligence apprehends, in so far as this is given to man, the fact that there is pure and simple Wisdom and Truth, which is the peculiar property of no living being, but which imparts wisdom and truth to all souls alike which are susceptible of its influence. If Anaxagoras perceived the existence of this supreme Wisdom, and apprehended it to be God, and called it Mind, it is not by the mere name of this philosopher — with whom, on account of his place in the remote antiquity of erudition, all raw recruits in literature[3] (to adopt a military phrase) delight to boast an acquaintance — that we are made learned and wise; nor is it even by our having the knowledge through which he knew this truth. For truth ought to be dear to me not

---

[1] The words of Cicero are these: "Nec vidit neque motum sensui junctum et continentem in infinito ullum esse posse, neque sensum omnino quo non tota natura pulsa sentiret." Augustin, quoting probably from memory (see § 9), gives *infinito* as the dative of possession instead of *in infinito*.

[2] Cicero, *de Natura Deorum*, lib. I.
[3] *Litteriones ut militariter loquar*.

merely because it was not unknown to Anaxagoras, but because, even though none of these philosophers had known it, it is the truth.

27. If, therefore, it is unbecoming for us to be elated either by the knowledge of the man who peradventure apprehended the truth, by which knowledge we obtain, as it were, the appearance of learning, or even by the solid possession of the truth itself, whereby we obtain real acquisitions in learning, how much less can the names and tenets of those men who were in error assist us in Christian learning and in making known things obscure? For if we be men, it would be more fitting that we should grieve on account of the errors into which so many famous men fell, if we happen to hear of them, than that we should studiously investigate them, in order that, among men who are ignorant of them, we may enjoy the gratification of a most contemptible conceit of knowledge. For how much better would it be that I should never have heard the name of Democritus, than that I should now with sorrow ponder the fact that a man was highly esteemed in his own age who thought that the gods were images which emanated from solid bodies, but were not solid themselves; and that these, circling this way and that way by their independent motion, and gliding into the minds of men, make the divine power enter into the region of their thoughts, although, certainly, that body from which the image emanated may be rightly judged to surpass the image in excellence and proportion, as it surpasses it in solidity. Hence his opinion wavered, as they say, and oscillated, so that sometimes he said that the deity was some kind of nature from which images emanate, and which nevertheless can be thought of only by means of those images which he pours forth and sends out, that is, which from that nature (which he considered to be something material and eternal, and on this very account divine) were borne as by a kind of evaporation or continuous emanation, and came and entered into our minds, so that we could form the thought of a god or gods. For these philosophers conceive of no cause of thought in our minds, except when images from those bodies which are the object of our thoughts come and enter into our minds; as if, forsooth, there were not many things, yea, more than we can number, which, without any material form, and yet intelligible, are apprehended by those who know how to apprehend such things. Take as an example essential Wisdom and Truth, of which if they can frame no idea, I wonder why they dispute concerning it at all; if, however, they do frame some idea of it in thought, I wish they would tell me either from what body the image of truth comes into their minds, or of what kind it is.

28. Democritus, however, is said to differ here also in his doctrine on physics from Epicurus; for he holds that there is in the concourse of atoms a certain vital and breathing power, by which power (I believe) he affirms that the images themselves (not all images of all things, but images of the gods) are endued with divine attributes, and that the first beginnings of the mind are in those universal elements to which he ascribed divinity, and that the images possess life, inasmuch as they are wont either to benefit or to hurt us. Epicurus, however, does not assume anything in the first beginnings of things but atoms, that is, certain corpuscles, so minute that they cannot be divided or perceived either by sight or by touch; and his doctrine is, that by the fortuitous concourse (clashing) of these atoms, existence is given both to innumerable worlds and to living things, and to the souls which animate them, and to the gods whom, in human form, he has located, not in any world, but outside of the worlds, and in the spaces which separate them; and he will not allow of any object of thought beyond things material. But in order to these becoming an object of thought, he says that from those things which he represents as formed of atoms, images more subtle than those which come to our eyes flow down and enter into the mind. For according to him, the cause of our seeing is to be found in certain images so huge that they embrace the whole outer world. But I suppose that you already understand their opinions regarding these images.

29. I wonder that Democritus was not convinced of the error of his philosophy even by this fact, that such huge images coming into our minds, which are so small (if being, as they affirm, material, the soul is confined within the body's dimensions), could not possibly, in the entirety of their size, come into contact with it. For when a small body is brought into contact with a large one, it cannot in any wise be touched at the same moment by all points of the larger. How, then, are these images at the same moment in their whole extent objects of thought, if they become objects of thought only in so far as, coming and entering into the mind, they touch it, seeing that they cannot in their whole extent either find entrance into so small a body or come in contact with so small a mind? Bear in mind, of course, that I am speaking now after their manner; for I do not hold the mind to be such as they affirm. It is true that Epicurus alone can be assailed with this argument, if Democritus holds that the mind is immaterial; but we may ask him in turn why he did not perceive that it is at once unnecessary and impossible for the mind, being immaterial, to think through the approach and contact of material

images. Both philosophers alike are certainly confuted by the facts of vision; for images so great cannot possibly touch in their entirety eyes so small.

30. Moreover, when the question is put to them, how it comes that one image is seen of a body from which images emanate in countless multitudes, their answer is, that just because the images are emanating and passing in such multitudes, the effect produced by their being crowded and massed together is, that out of the many one is seen. The absurdity of this Cicero exposes by saying that their deity cannot be thought of as eternal, for this very reason, that he is thought of through images which are in countless multitudes flowing forth and passing away. And when they say that the forms of the gods are rendered eternal by the innumerable hosts of atoms supplying constant reinforcements, so that other corpuscles immediately take the place of those which depart from the divine substance, and by the same succession prevent the nature of the gods from being dissolved, Cicero replies, " On this ground all things would be eternal as well as the gods," since there is nothing which has not the same boundless store of atoms by which it may repair its perpetual decays. Again, he asks how their god could be otherwise than afraid of coming to destruction, seeing that he is without a moment's intermission beaten and shaken by an unceasing incursion of atoms, — beaten, inasmuch as he is struck by atoms rushing upon him, and shaken, inasmuch as he is penetrated by atoms rushing through him. Nay, more ; seeing that from himself there emanate continually images (of which we have said enough), what good ground can he have for persuasion of his own immortality? [1]

31. As to all these ravings of the men who entertain such opinions, it is especially deplorable that the mere statement of them does not suffice to secure their rejection without any one controverting them in discussion ; instead of which, the minds of men most gifted with acuteness have accepted the task of copiously refuting opinions which, as soon as they were enunciated, ought to have been rejected with contempt even by the slowest intellects. For even granting that there are atoms, and that these strike and shake each other by clashing together as chance may guide them, is it lawful for us to grant also that atoms thus meeting in fortuitous concourse can so make anything as to fashion its distinctive forms, determine its figure, polish its surface, enliven it with colour, or quicken it by imparting to it a spirit? — all which things every one sees to be accomplished in no other way than by the providence of God, if only he loves to see with the mind rather than with the eye alone, and asks this faculty of intelligent perception from the Author of his being. Nay, more ; we are not at liberty even to grant the existence of atoms themselves, for, without discussing the subtle theories of the learned as to the divisibility of matter, observe how easily the absurdity of atoms may be proved from their own opinions. For they, as is well known, affirm that there is nothing else in nature but bodies and empty space, and the accidents of these, by which I believe that they mean motion and striking, and the forms which result from these. Let them tell us, then, under which category they reckon the images which they suppose to flow from the more solid bodies, but which, if indeed they are bodies, possess so little solidity that they are not discernible except by their contact with the eyes when we see them, and with the mind when we think of them. For the opinion of these philosophers is, that these images can proceed from the material object and come to the eyes or to the mind, which, nevertheless, they affirm to be material. Now, I ask, do these images flow from atoms themselves? If they do, how can these be atoms from which some bodily particles are in this process separated? If they do not, either something can be the object of thought without such images, which they vehemently deny, or we ask, whence have they acquired a knowledge of atoms, seeing that they can in nowise become objects of thought to us? But I blush to have even thus far refuted these opinions, although they did not blush to hold them. When, however, I consider that they have even dared to defend them, I blush not on their account, but for the race of mankind itself whose ears could tolerate such nonsense.

CHAP. V. — 32. Wherefore, seeing that the minds of men are, through the pollution of sin and the lust of the flesh, so blinded that even these monstrous errors could waste in discussion concerning them the leisure of learned men, will you, Dioscorus, or will any man of an observant mind, hesitate to affirm that in no way could better provision have been made for the pursuit of truth by mankind than that a Man, assumed into ineffable and miraculous union by the Truth Himself, and being the manifestation of His Person on the earth, should by perfect teaching and divine acts move men to saving faith in that which could not as yet be intellectually apprehended? To the glory of Him who has done this we give our service ; and we exhort you to believe immoveably and stedfastly in Him through whom it has come to pass that not a select few, but whole peoples, unable to discern these things by reason, do accept them in faith, until, upheld by instruction in saving truth, they

---

[1] Cicero, *de Natura Deorum*, lib. I.

escape from these perplexities into the atmosphere of perfectly pure and simple truth. It becomes us, moreover, to yield submission to His authority all the more unreservedly, when we see that in our day no error dares to lift up itself to rally round it the uninstructed crowd without seeking the shelter of the Christian name, and that of all who, belonging to an earlier age, now remain outside of the Christian name, those alone continue to have in their obscure assemblies a considerable attendance who retain the Scriptures by which, however they may pretend not to see or understand it, the Lord Jesus Christ Himself was prophetically announced. Moreover, those who, though they are not within the Catholic unity and communion, boast of the name of Christians, are compelled to oppose them that believe, and presume to mislead the ignorant by a pretence of appealing to reason, since the Lord came with this remedy above all others, that He enjoined on the nations the duty of faith. But they are compelled, as I have said, to adopt this policy because they feel themselves most miserably overthrown if their authority is compared with the Catholic authority. They attempt, accordingly, to prevail against the firmly-settled authority of the immoveable Church by the name and the promises of a pretended appeal to reason. This kind of effrontery is, we may, say, characteristic of all heretics. But He who is the most merciful Lord of faith has both secured the Church in the citadel of authority by most famous œcumenical Councils and the Apostolic sees themselves, and furnished her with the abundant armour of equally invincible reason by means of a few men of pious erudition and unfeigned spirituality. The perfection of method in training disciples is, that those who are weak be encouraged to the utmost to enter the citadel of authority, in order that when they have been safely placed there, the conflict necessary for their defence may be maintained with the most strenuous use of reason.

33. The Platonists, however, who, amidst the errors of false philosophies assailing them at that time on all sides, rather concealed their own doctrine to be searched for than brought it into the light to be vilified, as they had no divine personage to command faith, began to exhibit and unfold the doctrines of Plato after the name of Christ had become widely known to the wondering and troubled kingdoms of this world. Then flourished at Rome the school of Plotinus, which had as scholars many men of great acuteness and ability. But some of them were corrupted by curious inquiries into magic, and others, recognising in the Lord Jesus Christ the impersonation of that essential and immutable Truth and Wisdom which they were endeavour-

ing to reach, passed into His service. Thus the whole supremacy of authority and light of reason for regenerating and reforming the human race has been made to reside in the one saving Name, and in His one Church.

34. I do not at all regret that I have stated these things at great length in this letter, although perhaps you would have preferred that I had taken another course; for the more progress that you make in the truth, the more will you approve what I have written, and you will then approve of my counsel, though now you do not think it helpful to your studies. At the same time, I have, to the best of my ability, given answers to your questions, — to some of them in this letter, and to almost all the rest by brief annotations on the parchments on which you had sent them. If in these answers you think I have done too little, or done something else than you expected, you do not duly consider, my Dioscorus, to whom you addressed your questions. I have passed without reply all the questions concerning the orator and the books of Cicero *de Oratore*. I would have seemed to myself a contemptible trifler if I had entered on the exposition of these topics. For I might with propriety be questioned on all the other subjects, if any one desired me to handle and expound them, not in connection with the works of Cicero, but by themselves; but in these questions the subjects themselves are not in harmony with my profession now. I would not, however, have done all that I have done in this letter had I not removed from Hippo for a time after the illness under which I laboured when your messenger came to me. Even in these days I have been visited again with interruption of health and with fever, on which account there has been more delay than might otherwise have been in sending these to you. I earnestly beg you to write and let me know how you receive them.

LETTER CXXII.

(A.D. 410.)

TO HIS WELL-BELOVED BRETHREN THE CLERGY, AND TO THE WHOLE PEOPLE [OF HIPPO], AUGUSTIN SENDS GREETING IN THE LORD.

1. In the first place, I beseech you, my friends, and implore you, for Christ's sake, not to let my bodily absence grieve you. For I suppose you do not imagine that I could by any means be separated in spirit and in unfeigned love from you, although perchance it is even a greater grief to me than to you that my weakness unfits me for bearing all the cares which are laid on me by those members of Christ to whose service both fear of Him and love to them constrain me to devote myself. For you know this,

my beloved, that I have never absented myself from you through self-indulgent taking of ease, but only when compelled by such duties as have made it necessary for some of my holy colleagues and brethren to endure, both on the sea and in countries beyond the sea, labours from which I was exempted, not because of reluctance of spirit, but by reason of imperfect bodily health. Wherefore, my dearly-beloved brethren, act so that, as the apostle says, "whether I come and see you, or else be absent, I may hear of your affairs, that ye stand fast in one spirit, with one mind striving together for the faith of the gospel."[1] If any vexation pertaining to time causes you distress, this itself ought the more to remind you how you should occupy your thoughts with that life in which you may live without any burden, escaping not the annoying hardships of this short life, but the dread flames of eternal fire. For if ye strive with so much anxiety, so much earnestness, and so much labour, to save yourselves from falling into some transient sufferings in this world, how solicitous ought you to be to escape everlasting misery! And if the death which puts an end to the labours of time is so feared, how ought we to fear the death which ushers men into eternal pain! And if the short-lived and sordid pleasures of this world are so loved, with how much greater earnestness ought we to seek the pure and infinite joys of the world to come! Meditating upon these things, be not slothful in good works, that ye may come in due season to reap what you have sown.

2. It has been reported to me that you have forgotten your custom of providing raiment for the poor, to which work of charity I exhorted you when I was present with you; and I now exhort you not to allow yourselves to be overcome and made slothful by the tribulation of this world, which you see now visited with such calamities as were foretold by our Lord and Redeemer, who cannot lie. You ought in present circumstances not to be less diligent in works of charity, but rather to be more abundant in these than you were wont to be. For as men betake themselves in greater haste to a place of greater security when they see in the shaking of their walls the ruin of their house impending, so ought Christians, the more that they perceive, from the increasing frequency of their afflictions, that the destruction of this world is at hand, to be the more prompt and active in transferring

to the treasury of heaven the goods which they were proposing to store up on earth, in order that, if any accident common to the lot of men occur, he may rejoice who has escaped from a dwelling doomed to ruin; and if, on the other hand, nothing of this kind happen, he may be exempt from painful solicitude who, die when he may, has committed his possessions to the keeping of the ever-living Lord, to whom he is about to go. Wherefore, my dearly-beloved brethren, let every one of you, according to his ability, of which he himself is the best judge, do with a portion of his substance as ye were wont to do; do it also with a more willing mind than ye were wont; and amid all the vexations of this life bear in your hearts the apostolic exhortation: "The Lord is at hand: be careful for nothing."[2] Let such things be reported to me concerning you as may make me understand that it is not through my presence with you, but from obedience to the precept of God, who is never absent, that you follow that good practice which for many years while I was with you, and for some time after my departure, you observed.

May the Lord preserve you in peace! And, dearly-beloved brethren, pray for us.

LETTER CXXIII.

(A.D. 410.)

[FROM JEROME TO AUGUSTIN.]

There are many who go halting upon both feet, and refuse to bend their heads even when their necks are broken, persisting in adherence to their former errors, even though they have not their former liberty of proclaiming them.

Respectful salutations are sent to you by the holy brethren who are with your humble servant, and especially by your pious and venerable daughters.[3] I beg your Excellency to salute in my name your brethren my lord Alypius and my lord Evodius. Jerusalem is held captive by Nebuchadnezzar, and refuses to listen to the counsels of Jeremiah, preferring to look wistfully towards Egypt, that it may die in Tahpanhes, and perish there in eternal bondage.[4]

---

[1] Phil. i. 27.

[2] Phil. iv. 5, 6.
[3] Paula, Eustochium, and other recluses of Bethlehem.
[4] Two opinions have been advanced as to the signification of this enigmatical allusion to the events recorded in Jeremiah, chap. xlii. Some think that Jerome refers to Rome, then occupied by the Goths. Others find here a reference to the state of the Church at Jerusalem at the time: perhaps under the name of Nebuchadnezzar some heretical bishop is designed.

THIRD DIVISION.

LETTERS WHICH WERE WRITTEN BY AUGUSTIN AFTER THE TIME OF THE CONFERENCE WITH THE DONATISTS AND THE RISE OF THE PELAGIAN HERESY IN AFRICA; I.E., DURING THE LAST TWENTY YEARS OF HIS LIFE (A.D. 411–430).

LETTER CXXIV.

(A.D. 411.)

TO ALBINA, PINIANUS, AND MELANIA,[1] HONOURED IN THE LORD, BELOVED IN HOLINESS AND LONGED FOR IN BROTHERLY AFFECTION, AUGUSTIN SENDS GREETING IN THE LORD.

1. I AM, whether through present infirmity or by natural temperament, very susceptible of cold; nevertheless, it would not be possible for me to suffer greater heat than I have done throughout this exceptionally dreadful winter, having been kept in a fever by distress because I have been unable, I do not say to hasten, but to fly to you (to visit whom it would have been fitting for me to fly across the seas), after you had been settled so near to me, and had come from so remote a land to see me. It may be, also, that you have supposed the rigorous weather of this winter to be the only cause of my suffering this disappointment; I pray you, beloved, give no place to this thought. For what inconvenience, hardship, or even danger, can these heavy rains bring, which I would not have encountered and endured in order to make my way to you, who are such comforters to us in our great calamities, and who, in the midst of a crooked and perverse generation, are lights kindled into vehement flame by the Supreme Light, raised aloft by lowliness of spirit, and deriving more glorious lustre from the glory which you have despised? Moreover, I would have enjoyed participation in the spiritual felicity vouchsafed to my earthly birthplace, in that it has been permitted to have you present, of whom when absent its citizens had heard much — so much, indeed, that although giving charitable credence to the report of what you were by nature and had become by grace, they feared, perchance, to repeat it to others, lest it should be disbelieved.

2. I shall therefore tell you the reason why I have not come, and the trials by which I have been kept back from so great a privilege, that I may obtain not only your forgiveness, but also, through your prayers, the mercy of Him who so works in you that ye live to Him. The congregation of Hippo, whom the Lord has ordained me to serve, is in great measure, and almost wholly, of a constitution so infirm, that the pressure of even a comparatively light affliction might seriously endanger its well-being; at present, however, it is smitten with tribulation so overwhelming, that, even were it strong, it could scarcely survive the imposition of the burden. Moreover, when I returned to it recently, I found it offended to a most dangerous degree by my absence; and you, over whose spiritual strength we rejoice in the Lord, can with healthful taste relish and approve the saying of Paul: "Who is weak, and I am not weak? who is offended, and I burn not?"[2] I feel this especially because there are many here who by disparaging us attempt to excite against us the minds of the others by whom we seem to be loved, in order that they may make room in them for the devil. But when those whose salvation is our care are angry with us, their strong determination to take vengeance on us is only an unreasonable desire for bringing death to themselves, — not the death of the body, but of the soul, in which the fact of death discovers itself mysteriously by the odour of corruption before it is possible for our care to foresee and provide against it.

Doubtless you will readily excuse this anxiety on my part, especially because, if you were displeased and wished to punish me, you could perhaps invent no severer pain than what I already suffer in not seeing you at Thagaste. I trust, however, that, assisted by your prayers, I may be permitted when the present hindrance has been removed with all speed to come to you, in whatsoever part of Africa you may be, if this town in which I labour is not worthy (and I do not presume to pronounce it worthy) to be along with us made joyful by your presence.

---

[1] The name Melania, though now almost as little known to the world at large as the fossil univalve molluscs to which palæontologists have assigned the designation, was in the time of Augustin highly esteemed throughout Christendom. The elder Melania, a lady of rank and affluence, left Rome when it was threatened by Alaric, and spent thirty-seven years in the East, returning to the city in 445 A.D. Her daughter-in-law, Albina, and her grand-daughter, the younger Melania (whose husband was the Pinianus mentioned here and in the two following letters), left Rome with her in 408 A.D., and after spending two years in Sicily, passed over into Africa, and fixed their residence at Thagaste, the native town of St. Augustin. A visit which they paid to him at Hippo was the occasion of the extraordinary proceedings referred to in Letters CXXV. and CXXVI.

[2] 2 Cor. xi. 29.

LETTER CXXV.

(A.D. 411.)

TO ALYPIUS, MY LORD MOST BLESSED AND BROTHER BELOVED WITH ALL REVERENCE, AND MY PARTNER IN THE PRIESTLY OFFICE, AND TO THE BRETHREN WHO ARE WITH HIM, AUGUSTIN AND THE BRETHREN WHO ARE WITH HIM SEND GREETING IN THE LORD.

1. We are deeply grieved, and can by no means regard it as a small matter, that the people of Hippo clamorously said so much to the disparagement of your Holiness; but, my good brother, their clamorous utterance of these things is not so great a cause for grief as the fact that we are, without open accusation, deemed guilty of similar things. For when we are believed to be actuated in retaining God's servants among us, not by love of righteousness, but by love of money, is it not to be desired that persons who believe this concerning us should with their voices avow what is hidden in their hearts, and so obtain, if possible, remedies great in proportion to the disease, rather than silently perish under the venom of these fatal suspicions? Wherefore it ought to be a greater care to us (and for this reason we conferred together before this happened) to provide how men to whom we are commanded to be examples in good works may be convinced that there is no ground for suspicions which they cherish, than to provide how those may be rebuked who in words give definite utterance to their suspicions.

2. Wherefore I am not angry with the pious Albina, nor do I judge her to deserve rebuke; but I think she requires to be cured of such suspicions. It is true that she has not pointed at myself the words to which I refer, but has complained of the people of Hippo, as it were, alleging that their covetousness has been brought to light, and that in desiring to retain among them a man of wealth who was known to despise money, and to give it away freely, they were moved, not by his fitness for the office, but by regard to his ample means; nevertheless, she almost said openly that she had the same suspicion of myself, and not she only, but also her pious son-in-law and daughter, who, on that very day, said the same thing in the apse of the church.[1] In my opinion, it is more necessary that the suspicions of these persons should be removed than that their utterance of them should be rebuked. For where can immunity and rest from such thorns be provided and given to us, if they can sprout forth against us even in the hearts of intimate friends, so pious

and so much beloved by us? It is by the ignorant multitude that such things have been thought concerning you, but I am the victim of similar suspicions from those who are the lights of the Church; you may see, therefore, which of us has the greater cause for grief. It seems to me that both cases call, not for invectives, but for remedial measures; for they are men, and their suspicions are of men, and therefore such things as they suspect, though they may be false, are not incredible. Persons such as these are of course not so foolish as to believe that the people are coveting their money, especially after their experience that the people of Thagaste obtained none of their money, from which it was certain that the people of Hippo would also obtain none. Nay, all the violence of this odium comes against the clergy alone, and especially against the bishops, whose authority is visibly pre-eminent, and who are supposed to use and enjoy as owners and lords the property of the Church. My dear Alypius, let not the weak be encouraged through our example to cherish this pernicious and fatal covetousness. Call to mind what we said to each other before the occurrence of this temptation, which makes the duty all the more urgent. Let us rather by God's help endeavour to have this difficulty removed by friendly conference, and let us not count it sufficient to be guided by our own conscience alone; for this is not one of the cases in which its voice alone is sufficient for our direction. For if we be not unworthy servants of our God, if there live in us a spark of that charity which seeketh not her own, we are bound by all means to provide things honest, not only in the sight of God, but also in the sight of men, lest while drinking untroubled waters in our own conscience, we be chargeable with treading with incautious feet, and so making the Lord's flock drink from a turbid stream.

3. For as to the proposal in your letter that we should discuss together the obligation of an oath which has been extorted by force, I beseech you, let not the method of our discussion involve in obscurity things which are perfectly clear. For if inevitable death were threatened in order to compel a servant of God to swear that he would do something forbidden by laws both human and divine, it would be his duty to prefer death to such an oath, lest he should be guilty of a crime in fulfilling his oath. But in this case, in which the determined clamour of the people, and only this, was forcing the man, not to a crime, but to that which if it were done would be lawfully done; when, moreover, there was indeed apprehension lest some reckless men, such as are mixed with a multitude even of good men, should through love of rioting break out into some wicked deeds of violence, if they found a pretext for disturbance and for plausibly justifiable indignation, but

---

[1] The "absis" was a chapel or recess in the choir, where the bishop was accustomed to stand surrounded by his clergy.

there was no certainty of this fear being realized, —who will affirm that it is lawful to commit a deliberate act of perjury in order to escape from uncertain consequences, involving, I shall not say loss or bodily injury, but even death itself? Regulus had not heard anything from the Holy Scriptures concerning the impiety of perjury, he had never heard of the flying roll of Zechariah,[1] and he confirmed his oath to the Carthaginians, not by the sacraments of Christ, but by the abominations of false gods; and yet in the face of inevitable tortures, and a death of unprecedented horror, he was not moved by fear so as to swear under constraint, but, because he had given his oath, he of his own free will submitted to these, lest he should be guilty of perjury. In that age, also, the Roman censors refused to inscribe in the roll, not of saints inheriting heavenly glory, but of senators received into the curia of Rome, not only men who, through fear of death and of cruel tortures, had chosen rather to commit manifest perjury than to return to merciless enemies, but also one who had believed himself clear of the guilt of perjury, because, after giving his oath, he had under the pretext of alleged necessity violated it by returning; in which we see that those who expelled him from the senate took into consideration, not what he himself had in his mind when he gave his oath, but what those to whom he pledged his word expected from him. Yet they had never read what we sing continually in the Psalm: "He that sweareth to his own hurt, and changeth not."[2] We are wont to speak of these instances of virtue with the highest admiration, although they are found in men who were strangers to the grace and to the name of Christ; and yet do we seriously imagine that the question whether perjury is occasionally lawful is one for an answer to which we should search the divine books, in which, to prevent us from falling into this sin by inconsiderate oaths, this prohibition is written: "Swear not at all"?

4. I by no means dispute the perfect correctness of the maxim, that good faith requires an oath to be kept, not according to the mere words of him who gives it, but according to that which the person giving the oath knows to be the expectation of the person to whom he swears. For it is very difficult to define in words, especially in few words, the promise in regard to which security is exacted from him who gives his oath. They, therefore, are guilty of perjury, who, while adhering to the letter of their promise, disappoint the known expectation of those to whom their oath was given; and they are not guilty of perjury, who, even though

departing from the letter of the promise, fulfil that which was expected of them when they gave their oath. Wherefore, seeing that the people of Hippo desired to have the holy Pinianus, not as a prisoner who had forfeited liberty, but as a much-loved resident in their town, the limits of that which they expected from him, though it could not be adequately embraced in the words of his promise, are nevertheless so obvious that the fact of his being at this moment absent, after giving his oath to remain among them, does not disturb any one who may have heard that he was to leave this place for a definite purpose, and with the intention of returning. Accordingly, he will not be guilty of perjury, nor will he be regarded by them as violating his oath, unless he disappoint their expectation; and he will not disappoint their expectation, unless he either abandon his purpose of residing among them, or at some future time depart from them without intending to return. May God forbid that he should so depart from the holiness and fidelity which he owes to Christ and to the Church! For, not to speak of the dread judgment of God upon perjurers, which you know as well as myself, I am perfectly certain that henceforth we shall have no right to be displeased with any one who may refuse to believe what we attest by an oath, if we are found to think that perjury in such a man as Pinianus is to be not only tolerated without indignation, but actually defended. From this may we be saved by the mercy of Him who delivers from temptation those who put their trust in Him! Let Pinianus, therefore, as you have written in your communication, fulfil the promise by which he bound himself not to depart from Hippo, just as I myself and the other inhabitants of the town do not depart from it, having, of course, full freedom in going and returning at any time; the only difference being, that those who are not bound by any oath to reside here have it also in their power at any time, without being chargeable with perjury, to depart with no purpose of coming back again.

5. As to our clergy and the brethren settled in our monastery, I do not know that it can be proved that they either aided or abetted in the reproaches which were made against you. For when I inquired into this, I was informed that only one from our monastery, a man of Carthage, had taken part in the clamour of the people; and this was not when they were uttering insults against you, but when they were demanding Pinianus as presbyter.

I have annexed to this letter a copy of the promise given to him, taken from the very paper which he subscribed and corrected under my own inspection.

---

[1] Zech. v. 4. Augustin calls it " Zachariæ falx," translating, as the LXX. have done: δρέπανον.
[2] Ps. xv. 4.

LETTER CXXVI.

(A.D. 411.)

TO THE HOLY LADY AND VENERABLE HANDMAID OF GOD, ALBINA, AUGUSTIN SENDS GREETING IN THE LORD.

1. As to the sorrow of your spirit, which you describe as inexpressible, it becomes me to assuage rather than to augment its bitterness, endeavouring if possible to remove your suspicions, instead of increasing the agitation of one so venerable and so devoted to God by giving vent to indignation because of that which I have suffered in this matter. Nothing was done to our holy brother, your son-in-law Pinianus, by the people of Hippo which might justly awaken in him the fear of death, although, perchance, he himself had such fears. Indeed, we also were apprehensive lest some of the reckless characters who are often secretly banded together for mischief in a crowd might break out into bold acts of violence, finding occasion for beginning a riot with some plausible pretext for passionate excitement. Nothing of this nature, however, was either spoken of or attempted by any one, as I have since had opportunity to ascertain; but against my brother Alypius the people did clamorously utter many opprobrious and unworthy reproaches, for which great sin I desire that they may obtain pardon in answer to his prayers. For my own part, after their outcries began, when I had told them how I was precluded by promise from ordaining him against his will, adding that, if they obtained him as their presbyter through my breaking my word, they could not retain me as their bishop, I left the multitude, and returned to my own seat.[1] Thereupon, they being made for a little while to pause and waver by my unexpected reply, like a flame driven back for a moment by the wind, began to be much more warmly excited, imagining that possibly a violation of my promise might be extorted from me, or that, in the event of my abiding by my promise, he might be ordained by another bishop. To all to whom I could address myself, namely, to the more venerable and aged men who had come up to me in the apse, I stated that I could not be moved to break my word, and that in the church committed to my care he could not be ordained by any other bishop except with my consent asked and obtained, in granting which I should be no less guilty of a breach of faith. I said, moreover, that if he were ordained against his own will, the people were only wishing him to depart from us as soon as he was ordained. They did not believe that this was possible. But the crowd having gathered in front of the steps,

and persisting in the same determination with terrible and incessant clamour and shouting, made them irresolute and perplexed. At that time unworthy reproaches were loudly uttered against my brother Alypius: at that time, also, more serious consequences were apprehended by us.

2. But although I was much disturbed by so great a commotion among the people, and such trepidation among the office-bearers of the church, I did not say to that mob anything else than that I could not ordain him against his own will; nor after all that had passed was I influenced to do what I had also promised not to do, namely, to advise him in any way to accept the office of presbyter, which had I been able to persuade him to do, his ordination would have been with his consent. I remained faithful to both the promises which I had made, — not only to the one which I had shortly before intimated to the people, but also to the one in regard to which I was bound, so far as men were concerned, by only one witness. I was faithful, I say, not to an oath, but to my bare promise, even in the face of such danger. It is true that the fears of danger were, as we afterwards ascertained, without foundation; but whatever the danger might be, it was shared by us all alike. The fear was also shared by all; and I myself had thoughts of retiring, being alarmed chiefly for the safety of the building in which we were assembled. But there was reason to apprehend that if I were absent some disaster might be more likely to occur, as the people would then be more exasperated by disappointment, and less restrained by reverential sentiments. Again, if I had gone through the dense mob along with Alypius, I had reason to fear lest some one should dare to lay violent hands on him; if, on the other hand, I had gone without him, what would have been the most natural opinion for men to have formed, if any accident had befallen Alypius, and I appeared to have deserted him in order to hand him over to the power of an infuriated people?

3. In the midst of this excitement and great distress, when, being at our wit's end, we could not, so to speak, take breath, behold our pious son Pinianus, suddenly and quite unexpectedly, sends to me a servant of God, to tell me that he wished to swear to the people, that if he were ordained against his will he would leave Africa altogether, thinking, I believe, that the people, knowing that of course he could not violate his oath, would not continue their outcry, seeing that by perseverance they could gain nothing, but only drive from among us a man whom we ought at least to retain as a neighbour, if he was to be no more. As it seemed to me, however, that it was to be feared that the vehemence of the people's grief would be increased by his

---

[1] *Ad nostra subsellia.*

taking an oath of this kind, I was silent in regard to it; and as he had by the same messenger begged me to come to him, I went without delay. When he had said to me again what he had stated by the messenger, he immediately added to the same oath what he had sent another messenger to·intimate to me while I was hastening towards him, namely, that he would consent to reside in Hippo if no one compelled him to accept against his will the burden of the clerical office. On this, being comforted in my perplexities as by a breath of air when in danger of suffocation, I made no reply, but went with quickened pace to my brother Alypius, and told him what Pinianus had said. But he, being careful, I suppose, lest anything should be done with his sanction by which he thought you might be offended, said, "Let no one ask my opinion on this subject." Having heard this, I hastened to the noisy crowd, and having obtained silence, declared to them what had been promised, along with the proffered guarantee of an oath. The people, however, having no other thought or desire than that he should be their presbyter, did not receive the proposal as I had expected they would, but, after talking in an under-tone among themselves, made the request that to this promise and oath a clause might be added, that if at any time he should be pleased to consent to accept the clerical office, he should do so in no other church than that of Hippo. I reported this to him: without hesitation he agreed to it. I returned to them with his answer; they were filled with joy, and presently demanded the promised oath.

4. I came back to your son-in-law, and found, him at a loss as to the words in which his promise, confirmed by oath, could be expressed, because of various kinds of necessity which might emerge and might make it necessary for him to leave Hippo. He stated at the time what he feared, namely, that a hostile incursion of barbarians might occur, to avoid which it would be necessary to leave the place. The holy Melania wished to add also, as a possible reason for departure, the unhealthiness of the climate; but she was kept from this by his reply. I said, however, that he had brought forward an important reason deserving consideration, and one which, if it occurred, would compel the citizens themselves to abandon the place; but that, if this reason were stated to the people, we might justly fear lest they should regard us as prophesying evil, and, on the other hand, if a pretext for withdrawing from the promise were put under the general name of necessity, it might be thought that the necessity was only covering an intention to deceive. It seemed good to him, therefore, that we should test the feeling of the people in regard to this, and we found the re-

sult exactly as I had expected. For when the words which he had dictated were read by the deacon, and had been received with approbation, as soon as the clause concerning necessity which might hinder the fulfilment of his promise fell upon their ears, there arose at once a shout of remonstrance, and the promise was rejected; and the tumult began to break out again, the people thinking that these negotiations had no other object than to deceive them. When our pious son saw this, he ordered the clause regarding necessity to be struck out, and the people recovered their cheerfulness once more.

5. I would gladly have excused myself on the ground of fatigue, but he would not go to the people unless I accompanied him; so we went together. He told them that he had himself dictated what they had heard from the deacon, that he had confirmed the promise by an oath, and would do the things promised, after which he forthwith rehearsed all in the words which he had dictated. The response of the people was, "Thanks be unto God!" and they begged that all which was written should be subscribed. We dismissed the catechumens, and he adhibited his signature to the document at once. Then we [Alypius and myself] began to be urged, not by the voices of the crowd, but by faithful men of good report as their representatives, that we also as bishops should subscribe the writing. But when I began to do this, the pious Melania protested against it. I wondered why she did this so late, as if we could make his promise and oath void by forbearing from appending our names to it; I obeyed, however, and so my signature remained incomplete, and no one thought it necessary to insist further upon our subscription.

6. I have been at pains to communicate to your Holiness, so far as I thought sufficient, what were the feelings, or rather the remarks, of the people on the following day, when they heard that he had left the town. Whoever, therefore, may have told you anything contradicting what I stated, is either intentionally or through his own mistake misleading you. For I am aware that I passed over some things which seemed to me irrelevant, but I know that I said nothing but the truth. It is therefore true that our holy son Pinianus took his oath in my presence and with my permission, but it is not true that he did it in obedience to any command from me. He himself knows this: it is also known to those servants of God whom he sent to me, the first being the pious Barnabas, the second Timasius, by whom also he sent me the promise of his remaining in Hippo. As for the people themselves, moreover, they were urging him by their cries to accept the office of presbyter. They did not ask for his oath, but they did not

refuse it when offered, because they hoped that if he remained amongst us, there might be produced in him a willingness to consent to ordination, while they feared lest, if ordained against his will, he should, according to his oath, leave Africa. And therefore they also were actuated in their clamorous procedure by regard to God's work (for surely the consecration of a presbyter is a work of God) ; and inasmuch as they did not feel satisfied with his promise of remaining in Hippo, unless it were also promised that, in the event of his at any time accepting the clerical office, he should do it nowhere else than among them, it is perfectly manifest what they hoped for from his dwelling among them, and that they did not abandon their zeal for the work of God.

7. On what ground, then, do you allege that the people did this out of a base desire for money ? In the first place, the people who were so clamorous have nothing whatever of this kind to gain ; for as the people of Thagaste derive from the gifts which you have bestowed on their church no profit but the joy of seeing your good work, it will be the same in the case of the people of Hippo, or of any other place in which you have obeyed or may yet obey the law of your Lord concerning the " mammon of unrighteousness." The people, therefore, in most vehemently insisting upon guiding the procedure of their church in regard to so great a man, did not ask from you a pecuniary advantage, but testified their admiration for your contempt of money. For if in my own case, because they had heard that, despising my patrimony, which consisted of only a few small fields, I had consecrated myself to the liberty of serving God, they loved this disinterestedness, and did not grudge this gift to the church of my birthplace, Thagaste, but, when it had not imposed upon me the clerical office, made me by force, so to speak, their own, how much more ardently might they love in our Pinianus his overcoming and treading under foot with such remarkable decision riches so great and hopes so bright, and a strong natural capacity for enjoying this world ! I indeed seem, in the opinion of many, who compare themselves with themselves, to have rather found than forsaken wealth. For my patrimony can scarcely be considered a twentieth part of the ecclesiastical property which I am now supposed to possess as master. But in whatever church, especially in Africa, our Pinianus might be ordained (I do not say a presbyter, but) a bishop, he would be still in deep poverty compared with his former affluence, even if he were using the church's revenues in the spirit of one lording it over God's heritage. Christian poverty is much more clearly and certainly loved in the case of one in whom there is no room for

suspecting a desire for acquiring an accession to his wealth. It was this admiration which kindled the minds of the people, and roused them to such violence of persevering clamour. Let us therefore not charge them gratuitously with base covetousness, but rather, without imputing unworthy motives, allow them at least to love in others that good thing which they do not themselves possess. For although there may have mixed in the crowd some who are indigent or beggars, who helped to increase the clamour, and were actuated by the hope of some relief to their wants out of your honourable affluence, even this is not, in my opinion, base covetousness.

8. It remains, therefore, that the reproach of disgraceful covetousness must be levelled indirectly at the clergy, and especially at the bishop. For we are supposed to act as lords of the church's property ; we are supposed to enjoy its revenues. In short, whatever money we have received for the church either is still in our possession or has been spent according to our judgment ; and of it we have given nothing to any of the people besides the clergy and the brethren in the monastery, excepting only a very few indigent persons. I do not mean by this to say that the things which were said by you must necessarily have been said specially against us, but that, if said against any others than ourselves, they must have been incredible. What, then, shall we do ? If it be not possible to clear ourselves before enemies, by what means may we at least clear ourselves before you ? The matter is one pertaining to the soul ; it is within us, hidden from the eyes of men, and known to God alone. What, then, remains for us but to call to witness God, to whom it is known ? When, therefore, you harbour these suspicions concerning us, you do not command but absolutely compel us to give our oath, — a much more grievous wrong than the commanding of an oath, which you have thought proper in your letter to censure as highly culpable in me ; you compel us, I say, not by menacing death to the body, as the people of Hippo were supposed to have done, but by menacing death to our good name, which deserves to be regarded by us as more precious than life itself, for the sake of those weak brethren to whom we endeavour in all circumstances to exhibit ourselves as ensamples in good works.

9. We, however, are not indignant against you who compel us to this oath, as you are indignant against the people of Hippo. For you believe, as men judging of other men, things which, though not actually existing in us, might possibly have existed. Your suspicions we must labour not so much to reprove as to remove ; and since our conscience is clear in the sight of God,

we must seek to clear our character in your sight. It may be, as Alypius and I said to each other before this trial occurred, that God will grant that not only you, our much-beloved fellow-members of Christ's body, but even our most implacable enemies, may be thoroughly satisfied that we are not defiled by any love of money in our administration of ecclesiastical affairs. Until this be done (if the Lord, answering our prayer, permit it to be done), hear in the meantime what we are compelled to do, rather than put off for any length of time the healing of your heart. God is my witness that, as for the whole management of those ecclesiastical revenues over which we are supposed to love to exercise lordship, I only bear it as a burden which is imposed on me by love to the brethren and fear of God: I do not love it; nay, if I could, without unfaithfulness to my office, I would desire to be rid of it. God also is my witness that I believe the sentiments of Alypius to be the same as mine in this matter. Nevertheless, on the one hand, the people, and what is worse, the people of Hippo, have hastily done Alypius great wrong by entertaining another opinion of his character; and on the other hand, you who are saints of God and full of unfeigned compassion have, through believing such things concerning us, thought proper to touch and admonish us while nominally censuring the same people of Hippo, who have no part whatever in the guilt of the alleged covetousness. You have desired unquestionably to correct us, and that without hating us (this be far from you!); wherefore I ought not to be angry with you, but to thank you, because it was not possible for you to have combined modesty and freedom more happily than when, instead of stating your sentiments as an offensive accusation against the bishop, you left them to be discovered by indirect inferences.

10. Let not the fact that I have thought it necessary thus to confirm my statements by oath cause you vexation by making you think that you are treated with harshness. There was no harshness or lack of kindly feeling in the apostle towards those to whom he wrote: " Neither used we at any time flattering words, as ye know, nor a cloak of covetousness; God is witness." [1] In the thing which was opened to men's observation he appealed to their own testimony, but in regard to that which was hidden, to whom could he appeal but to God? If, therefore, fear lest the ignorance of men should make them entertain some such thoughts concerning him was reasonably felt even by Paul, whose labours, as all men knew, were such that except in extreme necessity he never took anything for his own benefit from the communities to which he dis-

pensed the grace of Christ, obtaining in all other cases the necessary provision for his support by working with his own hands, how much more pains must be taken to establish confidence in our disinterestedness by us, who are, both in the merit of holiness and in strength of mind, so far behind him, and who are not only unable to do anything by the work of our hands to support ourselves, but also precluded from this, even if we could work, by an accumulation of duties from which I believe that the apostles were exempt! Let the charge, therefore, of most base covetousness be brought no more in this matter against the Christian people — that is, the Church of Christ. For it is more tolerable that this charge be alleged against us, on whom the suspicion, though groundless, might fall without being utterly improbable, than on the people, of whom it is certainly known that they could not either cherish the covetous desire or be reasonably suspected of entertaining it.

11. For persons possessing any faith — and how much more the Christian faith! — to be unfaithful to their oath, I do not say by doing something contrary to it, but by hesitating at all as to its fulfilment, is utterly wrong. What my judgment is on this question I have with sufficient fulness declared in the letter which I sent to my brother Alypius. Your Holiness wrote asking me "whether I or the people of Hippo consider any one under obligation to fulfil an oath which has been extorted by violence." But what is your opinion? Do you think that even if death, which in this case was feared without reason, were certainly imminent, a Christian might use the name of his Lord to confirm a lie, and call his God to be witness to a falsehood? For assuredly a Christian, if urged by the menace of instant death to perjure himself by false testimony, ought to fear the loss of honour more than the loss of life. Hostile armies confront each other in the battle-field with mutual menaces of death, about which there can be no uncertainty; and yet, when they pledge themselves to each other by oath, we praise those who are faithful to their engagement, and we justly abhor those who are unfaithful. Now what was the motive leading them to swear to each other, but the fear on both sides of being killed or taken prisoners? And by this promise even such men hold themselves bound, lest they be guilty of sacrilege and perjury if they did not fulfil the oath extorted by the fear of death or captivity, and broke the promise given in such circumstances: they are more afraid of breaking their oath than of taking a man's life. And do we propose to discuss as a debatable question whether an oath must be fulfilled which has been given under fear of harm by servants of God, who are under pre-eminent obligations to holi-

[1] 1 Thess. ii. 5.

ness, by monks who are running the race towards Christian perfection, by distributing their property according to Christ's command?

12. Tell me, I beseech you, what hardship deserving the name of exile, or transportation, or banishment, is involved in his promise to reside here? I suppose that the office of presbyter is not exile. Would our Pinianus prefer exile to that office? Far be it from us to find such apology for one who is a saint of God and very dear to us: God forbid, I say, that it should be said of him that he preferred exile to the office of presbyter, and preferred to perjure himself rather than submit to exile. This I would say even if it were true that the oath by which he promised to reside among us had been extorted from him; but the fact is that, instead of being extorted in spite of his refusal, it was accepted when he had proffered it himself. It was accepted, moreover, as I have already said, because of the hope, which was encouraged by his remaining here, that he might also consent to comply with our desire that he should accept the clerical office. In fine, whatever opinion may be entertained concerning us or concerning the people of Hippo, the case of those who may have compelled him to take the oath is very different from that of those who may have — I do not say compelled, but at least — counselled him to break the oath. I trust, also, that Pinianus himself will not refuse to consider seriously whether it is worse to swear under the pressure of fear, however great, or, in the absence of all alarm, to commit deliberate perjury.

13. God be thanked that the men of Hippo regard his promise of residence here as kept fully, if only he come with the intention of making this town his home, and in going whithersoever necessity may call him, go with the intention of coming back to us again. For if they were to exact literal fulfilment of the words of the promise, it would be the duty of a servant of God to adhere to every sentence of it rather than forswear himself. But as it would be a crime for them so to bind any one, much more such a man as he is, so they have themselves proved that they had no such unreasonable expectation; for on hearing that he had gone away with the intention of returning, they expressed their satisfaction; and fidelity to an oath requires no more than the performance of what was expected by those to whom it was given. Let me ask, moreover, what is meant by saying that he, in giving the oath with his own lips, mentioned the possibility of necessity preventing his fulfilment of the promise? The truth is, that with his own lips he ordered the qualifying clause to be removed. If he put it in, it would be when he himself spoke to the people; but if he had done so, they assuredly would not have answered, "Thanks be unto God," but would have renewed the protestations which they made when it was read with the qualifying clause by the deacon. And what difference does it really make whether this plea of necessity for departing from the promise was or was not inserted? Nothing more than we have stated above was expected from him; but he who disappoints the known expectation of those to whom his oath is given, cannot but be a perjured person.

14. Wherefore, let his promise be fulfilled, and let the hearts of the weak be healed, lest, on the one hand, those who approve of it be taught by such a conspicuous example to imitate an act of perjury, and lest, on the other hand, those who condemn it have just grounds for saying that none of us is worthy to be believed, not only when we make promises, but even when we give our oath. Let us especially guard against giving occasion in this to the tongues of enemies, which are used by the great Enemy as darts wherewith to slay the weak. But God forbid that we should expect from a man like Pinianus anything else than what the fear of God inspires, and the superior excellence of his own piety approves. As for myself, whom you blame for not interfering to forbid his oath, I admit that I could not bring myself to believe that, in circumstances so disorderly and scandalous, I ought rather to allow the church which I serve to be overthrown, than accept the deliverance which was offered to us by such a man.

LETTER CXXX.

(A.D. 412.)

TO PROBA,[1] A DEVOTED HANDMAID OF GOD, BISHOP AUGUSTIN, A SERVANT OF CHRIST AND OF CHRIST'S SERVANTS, SENDS GREETING IN THE NAME OF THE LORD OF LORDS.

CHAP. I. — 1. Recollecting your request and my promise, that as soon as time and opportunity should be given by Him to whom we pray, I would write you something on the sub-

---

[1] Anicia Faltonia Proba, the widow of Sextus Petronius Probus, belonged to a Roman family of great wealth and noble lineage. Three of her sons held the consulship, two of them together in 395 A.D., and the third in 406 A.D. When Rome was taken by Alaric in 410, Proba and her family were in the city, and narrowly escaped from violence during the six days in which the Goths pillaged the city. About this time one of the sons of Proba died, and very soon after this sad event she resolved to quit Rome, as the return of Alaric was daily apprehended. Having realized her ample fortune, she sailed to Africa, accompanied by her daughter-in-law Juliana (the widow of Anicus Hermogenianus Olybrius), and the daughter of Juliana, Demetrias, the well known *religieuse*, whose taking of the veil in 413 produced so profound an impression throughout the ecclesiastical world. A considerable retinue of widows and younger women, seeking protection under her escort, accompanied the distinguished refugee to Carthage. After paying a large sum to secure the protection of Heraclianus, Count of Africa, she was permitted to establish herself with her community of pious women in Carthage. Her piety led her to seek the friendship and counsel of Augustin. How readily it was given is seen here, and in Letters CXXXI., CL., and CLXXXVIII.

ject of prayer to God, I feel it my duty now to discharge this debt, and in the love of Christ to minister to the satisfaction of your pious desire. I cannot express in words how greatly I rejoiced because of the request, in which I perceived how great is your solicitude about this supremely important matter. For what could be more suitably the business of your widowhood than to continue in supplications night and day, according to the apostle's admonition, "She that is a widow indeed, and desolate, trusteth in God, and continueth in supplications night and day"?[1] It might, indeed, appear wonderful that solicitude about prayer should occupy your heart and claim the first place in it, when you are, so far as this world is concerned, noble and wealthy, and the mother of such an illustrious family, and, although a widow, not desolate, were it not that you wisely understand that in this world and in this life the soul has no sure portion.

2. Wherefore He who inspired you with this thought is assuredly doing what He promised to His disciples when they were grieved, not for themselves, but for the whole human family, and were despairing of the salvation of any one, after they heard from Him that it was easier for a camel to go through the eye of a needle than for a rich man to enter into the kingdom of heaven. He gave them this marvellous and merciful reply: "The things which are impossible with men are possible with God."[2] He, therefore, with whom it is possible to make even the rich enter into the kingdom of heaven, inspired you with that devout anxiety which makes you think it necessary to ask my counsel on the question how you ought to pray. For while He was yet on earth, He brought Zaccheus,[3] though rich, into the kingdom of heaven, and, after being glorified in His resurrection and ascension, He made many who were rich in this present world, and made them more truly rich by extinguishing their desire for riches through His imparting to them His Holy Spirit. For how could you desire so much to pray to God if you did not trust in Him? And how could you trust in Him if you were fixing your trust in uncertain riches, and neglecting the wholesome exhortation of the apostle: "Charge them that are rich in this world that they be not high-minded, nor trust in uncertain riches, but in the living God, who giveth us richly all things to enjoy; that they do good, that they be rich in good works, ready to distribute, willing to communicate, laying up in store for themselves a good foundation, that they may lay hold on eternal life"?[4]

CHAP. II. — 3. It becomes you, therefore, out of love to this true life, to account yourself "desolate" in this world, however great the prosperity of your lot may be. For as that is the true life, in comparison with which the present life, which is much loved, is not worthy to be called life, however happy and prolonged it be, so is it also the true consolation promised by the Lord in the words of Isaiah, "I will give him the true consolation, peace upon peace,"[5] without which consolation men find themselves, in the midst of every mere earthly solace, rather desolate than comforted. For as for riches and high rank, and all other things in which men who are strangers to true felicity imagine that happiness exists, what comfort do they bring, seeing that it is better to be independent of such things than to enjoy abundance of them, because, when possessed, they occasion, through our fear of losing them, more vexation than was caused by the strength of desire with which their possession was coveted? Men are not made good by possessing these so-called good things, but, if men have become good otherwise, they make these things to be really good by using them well. Therefore true comfort is to be found not in them, but rather in those things in which true life is found. For a man can be made blessed only by the same power by which he is made good.

4. It is true, indeed, that good men are seen to be the sources of no small comfort to others in this world. For if we be harassed by poverty, or saddened by bereavement, or disquieted by bodily pain, or pining in exile, or vexed by any kind of calamity, let good men visit us, — men who can not only rejoice with them that rejoice, but also weep with them that weep,[6] and who know how to give profitable counsel, and win us to express our feelings in conversation: the effect is, that rough things become smooth, heavy burdens are lightened, and difficulties vanquished most wonderfully. But this is done in and through them by Him who has made them good by His Spirit. On the other hand, although riches may abound, and no bereavement befal us, and health of body be enjoyed, and we live in our own country in peace and safety, if, at the same time, we have as our neighbours wicked men, among whom there is not one who can be trusted, not one from whom we do not apprehend and experience treachery, deceit, outbursts of anger, dissensions, and snares, — in such a case are not all these other things made bitter and vexatious, so that nothing sweet or pleasant is left in them? Whatever, therefore, be our circumstances in this world, there is nothing truly enjoyable without a friend. But how

[1] 1 Tim. v. 5.
[2] Matt. xix. 21-26.
[3] Luke xix. 9.
[4] 1 Tim. vi. 17-19.

[5] Isa. lvii. 18, 19, in LXX. version.
[6] Rom. xii. 15.

rarely is one found in this life about whose spirit and behaviour as a true friend there may be perfect confidence! For no one is known to another so intimately as he is known to himself, and yet no one is so well known even to himself that he can be sure as to his own conduct on the morrow; wherefore, although many are known by their fruits, and some gladden their neighbours by their good lives, while others grieve their neighbours by their evil lives, yet the minds of men are so unknown and so unstable, that there is the highest wisdom in the exhortation of the apostle: "Judge nothing before the time until the Lord come, who both will bring to light the hidden things of darkness, and will make manifest the counsels of the hearts; and then shall every man have praise of God."[1]

5. In the darkness, then, of this world, in which we are pilgrims absent from the Lord as long as "we walk by faith and not by sight,"[2] the Christian soul ought to feel itself desolate, and continue in prayer, and learn to fix the eye of faith on the word of the divine sacred Scriptures, as "on a light shining in a dark place, until the day dawn, and the day-star arise in our hearts."[3] For the ineffable source from which this lamp borrows its light is the Light which shineth in darkness, but the darkness comprehendeth it not — the Light, in order to seeing which our hearts must be purified by faith; for "blessed are the pure in heart, for they shall see God;"[4] and "we know that when He shall appear, we shall be like Him, for we shall see Him as He is."[5] Then after death shall come the true life, and after desolation the true consolation, that life shall deliver our "souls from death" — that consolation shall deliver our "eyes from tears," and, as follows in the psalm, our feet shall be delivered from falling; for there shall be no temptation there.[6] Moreover, if there be no temptation, there will be no prayer; for there we shall not be waiting for promised blessings, but contemplating the blessings actually bestowed; wherefore he adds, "I will walk before the Lord in the land of the living,"[7] where we shall then be — not in the wilderness of the dead, where we now are: "For ye are dead," says the apostle, "and your life is hid with Christ in God; when Christ, who is our life, shall appear, then shall ye also appear with Him in glory."[8] For that is the true life on which the rich are exhorted to lay hold by being rich in good works; and in it is the true consolation, for want of which, meanwhile, a widow is "desolate" indeed, even though she has sons and grandchildren, and conducts her household piously, entreating all dear to her to put their hope in God: and in the midst of all this, she says in her prayer, "My soul thirsteth for Thee; my flesh longeth in a dry and thirsty land, where no water is;"[9] and this dying life is nothing else than such a land, however numerous our mortal comforts, however pleasant our companions in the pilgrimage, and however great the abundance of our possessions. You know how uncertain all these things are; and even if they were not uncertain, what would they be in comparison with the felicity which is promised in the life to come!

6. In saying these things to you, who, being a widow, rich and noble, and the mother of an illustrious family, have asked from me a discourse on prayer, my aim has been to make you feel that, even while your family are spared to you, and live as you would desire, you are desolate so long as you have not attained to that life in which is the true and abiding consolation, in which shall be fulfilled what is spoken in prophecy: "We are satisfied in the morning with Thy mercy, we rejoice and are glad all our days; we are made glad according to the days wherein Thou hast afflicted us, and the years wherein we have seen evil."[10]

CHAP. III. — 7. Wherefore, until that consolation come, remember, in order to your "continuing in prayers and supplications night and day," that, however great the temporal prosperity may be which flows around you, you are desolate. For the apostle does not ascribe this gift to every widow, but to her who, being a widow indeed, and desolate, "trusteth in God, and continueth in supplication night and day." Observe, however, most vigilantly the warning which follows: "But she that liveth in pleasure is dead while she liveth;"[11] for a person lives in those things which he loves, which he greatly desires, and in which he believes himself to be blessed. Wherefore, what Scripture has said of riches: "If riches increase, set not your heart upon them,"[12] I say to you concerning pleasures: "If pleasures increase, set not your heart upon them." Do not, therefore, think highly of yourself because these things are not wanting, but are yours abundantly, flowing, as it were, from a most copious fountain of earthly felicity. By all means look upon your possession of these things with indifference and contempt, and seek nothing from them beyond health of body. For this is a blessing not to be despised, because of its being necessary to the work of life until "this mortal

---

[1] 1 Cor. iv. 5.
[2] 2 Cor. v. 6, 7.
[3] 2 Pet. i. 19.
[4] Matt. v. 8.
[5] 1 John iii. 2.
[6] Ps. cxvi. 8.
[7] Ps. cxvi. 9. In the LXX., εὐαρεστήσω; in Aug., "placebo."
[8] Col. iii. 3, 4.

[9] Ps. lxiii. 1.
[10] Ps. xc. 14, 15, version of LXX.
[11] 1 Tim. v. 5, 6.
[12] Ps. lxii. 10.

shall have put on immortality "[1] — in other words, the true, perfect, and everlasting health, which is neither reduced by earthly infirmities nor repaired by corruptible gratification, but, enduring with celestial vigour, is animated with a life eternally incorruptible. For the apostle himself says, "Make not provision for the flesh, to fulfil the lusts thereof,"[2] because we must take care of the flesh, but only in so far as is necessary for health; "For no man ever yet hated his own flesh,"[3] as he himself likewise says. Hence, also, he admonished Timothy, who was, as it appears, too severe upon his body, that he should "use a little wine for his stomach's sake, and for his often infirmities."[4]

8. Many holy men and women, using every precaution against those pleasures in which she that liveth, cleaving to them, and dwelling in them as her heart's delight, is dead while she liveth, have cast from them that which is as it were the mother of pleasures, by distributing their wealth among the poor, and so have stored it in the safer keeping of the treasury of heaven. If you are *hindered* from doing this by some consideration of duty to your family, you know yourself what account you can give to God of your use of riches. For no one knoweth what passeth within a man, "but the spirit of the man which is in him."[5] We ought not to judge anything "before the time until the Lord come, who both will bring to light the hidden things of darkness, and will make manifest the counsels of the hearts, and then shall every man have praise of God."[6] It pertains, therefore, to your care as a widow, to see to it that if pleasures increase you do not set your heart upon them, lest that which ought to rise that it may live, die through contact with their corrupting influence. Reckon yourself to be one of those of whom it is written, "Their hearts shall live for ever."[7]

Chap. iv. — 9. You have now heard what manner of person you should be if you would pray; hear, in the next place, what you ought to pray for. This is the subject on which you have thought it most necessary to ask my opinion, because you were disturbed by the words of the apostle: "We know not what we should pray for as we ought;"[8] and you became alarmed lest it should do you more harm to pray otherwise than you ought, than to desist from praying altogether. A short solution of your difficulty may be given thus: "Pray for a happy life." This all men wish to have; for even those whose lives are worst and most abandoned would by no means live thus, unless they thought that in this way they either were made or might be made truly happy. Now what else ought we to pray for than that which both bad and good desire, but which only the good obtain?

Chap. v. — 10. You ask, perchance, What is this happy life? On this question the talents and leisure of many philosophers have been wasted, who, nevertheless, failed in their researches after it just in proportion as they failed to honour Him from whom it proceeds, and were unthankful to Him. In the first place, then, consider whether we should accept the opinion of those philosophers who pronounce that man happy who lives according to his own will. Far be it, surely, from us to believe this; for what if a man's will inclines him to live in wickedness? Is he not proved to be a miserable man in proportion to the facility with which his depraved will is carried out? Even philosophers who were strangers to the worship of God have rejected this sentiment with deserved abhorrence. One of them, a man of the greatest eloquence, says: "Behold, however, others, not philosophers indeed, but men of ready power in disputation, who affirm that all men are happy who live according to their own will. But this is certainly untrue, for to wish that which is unbecoming is itself a most miserable thing; nor is it so miserable a thing to fail in obtaining what you wish as to wish to obtain what you ought not to desire."[9] What is your opinion? Are not these words, by whomsoever they are spoken, derived from the Truth itself? We may therefore here say what the apostle said of a certain Cretan poet[10] whose sentiment had pleased him: "This witness is true."[11]

11. He, therefore, is truly happy who has all that he wishes to have, and wishes to have nothing which he ought not to wish. This being understood, let us now observe what things men may without impropriety wish to have. One desires marriage; another, having become a widower, chooses thereafter to live a life of continence; a third chooses to practise continence though he is married. And although of these three conditions one may be found better than another, we cannot say that any one of the three persons is wishing what he ought not: the same is true of the desire for children as the fruit of marriage, and for life and health to be enjoyed by the children who have been received, — of which desires the latter is one with which widows remaining unmarried are for the most part occupied; for although, refusing a second marriage, they do not now wish to have children, they wish that the children that they have may live in

1 1 Cor. xv. 54.
2 Rom. xiii. 14.
3 Eph. v. 39.
4 1 Tim. v. 23.
5 1 Cor. ii. 11.
6 1 Cor. iv. 5.
7 Ps. xxii. 26.
8 Rom. viii. 26.

9 Cicero Hortensius.
10 Epimenides.
11 Titus i. 13.

health. From all such care those who preserve their virginity intact are free. Nevertheless, all have some dear to them whose temporal welfare they do without impropriety desire. But when men have obtained this health for themselves, and for those whom they love, are we at liberty to say that they are now happy? They have, it is true, something which it is quite becoming to desire; but if they have not other things which are greater, better, and more full both of utility and beauty, they are still far short of possessing a happy life.

CHAP. VI. — 12. Shall we then say, that in addition to this health of body men may desire for themselves and for those dear to them honour and power? By all means, if they desire these in order that by obtaining them they may promote the interest of those who may be their dependants. If they seek these things not for the sake of the things themselves, but for some good thing which may through this means be accomplished, the wish is a proper one; but if it be merely for the empty gratification of pride and arrogance, and for a superfluous and pernicious triumph of vanity, the wish is improper. Wherefore, men do nothing wrong in desiring for themselves and for their kindred the competent portion of necessary things, of which the apostle speaks when he says: "Godliness with a competency [contentment in English version] is great gain; for we brought nothing into this world, and it is certain we can carry nothing out: and having food and raiment, let us be therewith content. But they that will be rich fall into temptation, and a snare, and into many foolish and hurtful lusts, which drown men in destruction and perdition; for the love of money is the root of all evil, which while some coveted after, they have erred from the faith, and pierced themselves through with many sorrows."[1] This competent portion he desires without impropriety who desires it and nothing beyond it; for if his desires go beyond it, he is not desiring it, and therefore his desire is improper. This was desired, and was prayed for by him who said: "Give me neither poverty nor riches: feed me with food convenient for me: lest I be full, and deny Thee, and say, Who is the Lord? or lest I be poor, and steal, and take the name of my God in vain."[2] You see assuredly that this competency is desired not for its own sake, but to secure the health of the body, and such provision of house and clothing as is befitting the man's circumstances, that he may appear as he ought to do among those amongst whom he has to live, so as to retain their respect and discharge the duties of his position.

13. Among all these things, our own welfare and the benefits which friendship bids us ask for others are things to be desired on their own account; but a competency of the necessaries of life is usually sought, if it be sought in the proper way, not on its own account, but for the sake of the two higher benefits. Welfare consists in the possession of life itself, and health and soundness of mind and body. The claims of friendship, moreover, are not to be confined within *too* narrow range, for it embraces all to whom love and kindly affection are due, although the heart goes out to some of these more freely, to others more cautiously; yea, it even extends to our enemies, for whom also we are commanded to pray. There is accordingly no one in the whole human family to whom kindly affection is not due by reason of the bond of a common humanity, although it may not be due on the ground of reciprocal love; Chap. vii. — but in those by whom we are requited with a holy and pure love, we find great and reasonable pleasure.

For these things, therefore, it becomes us to pray: if we have them, that we may keep them; if we have them not, that we may get them.

14. Is this all? Are these the benefits in which exclusively the happy life is found? Or does truth teach us that something else is to be preferred to them all? We know that both the competency of things necessary, and the well-being of ourselves and of our friends, so long as these concern this present world alone, are to be cast aside as dross in comparison with the obtaining of eternal life; for although the body may be in health, the mind cannot be regarded as sound which does not prefer eternal to temporal things; yea, the life which we live in time is wasted, if it be not spent in obtaining that by which we may be worthy of eternal life. Therefore all things which are the objects of useful and becoming desire are unquestionably to be viewed with reference to that one life which is lived with God, and is derived from Him. In so doing, we love ourselves if we love God; and we truly love our neighbours as ourselves, according to the second great commandment, if, so far as is in our power, we persuade them to a similar love of God. We love God, therefore, for what He is in Himself, and ourselves and our neighbours for His sake. Even when living thus, let us not think that we are securely established in that happy life, as if there was nothing more for which we should still pray. For how could we be said to live a happy life now, while that which alone is the object of a well-directed life is still wanting to us?

CHAP. VIII. — 15. Why, then, are our desires scattered over many things, and why, through fear of not praying as we ought, do we ask what we should pray for, and not rather say

[1] 1 Tim. vi. 6-10.
[2] Prov. xxx. 8, 9.

with the Psalmist: "One thing have I desired of the Lord, that will I seek after: that I may dwell in the house of the Lord all the days of my life, to behold the beauty of the Lord, and to inquire in His temple"?[1] For in the house of the Lord "all the days of life" are not days distinguished by their successively coming and passing away: the beginning of one day is not the end of another; but they are all alike unending in that place where the life which is made up of them has itself no end. In order to our obtaining this true blessed life, He who is Himself the True Blessed Life has taught us to pray, not with much speaking, as if our being heard depended upon the fluency with which we express ourselves, seeing that we are praying to One who, as the Lord tells us, "knoweth what things we have need of before we ask Him."[2] Whence it may seem surprising that, although He has forbidden "much speaking," He who knoweth before we ask Him what things we need has nevertheless given us exhortation to prayer in such words as these: "Men ought always to pray and not to faint;" setting before us the case of a widow, who, desiring to have justice done to her against her adversary, did by her persevering entreaties persuade an unjust judge to listen to her, not moved by a regard either to justice or to mercy, but overcome by her wearisome importunity; in order that we might be admonished how much more certainly the Lord God, who is merciful and just, gives ear to us praying continually to Him, when this widow, by her unremitting supplication, prevailed over the indifference of an unjust and wicked judge, and how willingly and benignantly He fulfils the good desires of those whom He knows to have forgiven others their trespasses, when this suppliant, though seeking vengeance upon her adversary, obtained her desire.[3] A similar lesson the Lord gives in the parable of the man to whom a friend in his journey had come, and who, having nothing to set before him, desired to borrow from another friend three loaves (in which, perhaps, there is a figure of the Trinity of persons of one substance), and finding him already along with his household asleep, succeeded by very urgent and importunate entreaties in rousing him up, so that he gave him as many as he needed, being moved rather by a wish to avoid further annoyance than by benevolent thoughts: from which the Lord would have us understand that, if even one who was asleep is constrained to give, even in spite of himself, after being disturbed in his sleep by the person who asks of him, how much more kindly will He give who never sleeps, and who rouses us from sleep that we may ask from Him.[4]

16. With the same design He added: "Ask, and ye shall receive; seek, and ye shall find; knock, and it shall be opened unto you: for every one that asketh receiveth; and he that seeketh findeth; and to him that knocketh it shall be opened. If a son shall ask bread of any of you that is a father, will he give him a stone? or if he ask a fish, will he for a fish give him a serpent? or if he shall ask an egg, will he offer him a scorpion? If ye then, being evil, know how to give good gifts unto your children, how much more shall your heavenly Father give good things to them that ask Him?"[5] We have here what corresponds to those three things which the apostle commends: *faith* is signified by the fish, either on account of the element of water used in baptism, or because it remains unharmed amid the tempestuous waves of this world, — contrasted with which is the serpent, that with poisonous deceit persuaded man to disbelieve God; *hope* is signified by the egg, because the life of the young bird is not yet in it, but is to be — is not seen, but hoped for, because "hope which is seen is not hope,"[6] — contrasted with which is the scorpion, for the man who hopes for eternal life forgets the things which are behind, and reaches forth to the things which are before, for to him it is dangerous to look back; but the scorpion is to be guarded against on account of what it has in its tail, namely, a sharp and venomous sting; *charity* is signified by bread, for "the greatest of these is charity," and bread surpasses all other kinds of food in usefulness, — contrasted with which is a stone, because hard hearts refuse to exercise charity. Whether this be the meaning of these symbols, or some other more suitable be found, it is at least certain that He who knoweth how to give good gifts to His children urges us to "ask and seek and knock."

17. Why this should be done by Him who "before we ask Him knoweth what things we have need of," might perplex our minds, if we did not understand that the Lord our God requires us to ask not that thereby our wish may be intimated to Him, for to Him it cannot be unknown, but in order that by prayer there may be exercised in us by supplications that desire by which we may receive what He prepares to bestow. His gifts are very great, but we are small and straitened in our capacity of receiving. Wherefore it is said to us: "Be ye enlarged, not bearing the yoke along with unbelievers."[7] For, in proportion to the simplicity of our faith, the firmness of our hope, and the ardour of our desire, will we more largely receive of that which is immensely great; which "eye hath not seen,"

---

[1] Ps. xxvii. 4.
[2] Matt. vi. 7, 8.
[3] Luke xviii. 1–8.
[4] Luke xi. 5–8.

[5] Luke xi. 9–13, and Matt. vii. 7–11.
[6] Rom. viii. 24.
[7] 2 Cor. vi. 13, 14.

for it is not colour; which "the ear hath not heard," for it is not sound; and which hath not ascended into the heart of man, for the heart of man must ascend to it.[1]

CHAP. IX. — 18. When we cherish uninterrupted desire along with the exercise of faith and hope and charity, we "pray always." But at certain stated hours and seasons we also use words in prayer to God, that by these signs of things we may admonish ourselves, and may acquaint ourselves with the measure of progress which we have made in this desire, and may more warmly excite ourselves to obtain an increase of its strength. For the effect following upon prayer will be excellent in proportion to the fervour of the desire which precedes its utterance. And therefore, what else is intended by the words of the apostle: "Pray without ceasing,"[2] than, "Desire without intermission, from Him who alone can give it, a happy life, which no life can be but that which is eternal"? This, therefore, let us desire continually from the Lord our God; and thus let us pray continually. But at certain hours we recall our minds from other cares and business, in which desire itself somehow is cooled down, to the business of prayer, admonishing ourselves by the words of our prayer to fix attention upon that which we desire, lest what had begun to lose heat become altogether cold, and be finally extinguished, if the flame be not more frequently fanned. Whence, also, when the same apostle says, "Let your requests be made known unto God,"[3] this is not to be understood as if thereby they become known to God, who certainly knew them before they were uttered, but in this sense, that they are to be made known to ourselves in the presence of God by patient waiting upon Him, not in the presence of men by ostentatious worship. Or perhaps that they may be made known also to the angels that are in the presence of God, that these beings may in some way present them to God, and consult Him concerning them, and may bring to us, either manifestly or secretly, that which, hearkening to His commandment, they may have learned to be His will, and which must be fulfilled by them according to that which they have there learned to be their duty; for the angel said to Tobias:[4] "Now, therefore, when thou didst pray, and Sara thy daughter-in-law, I did bring the remembrance of your prayers before the Holy One."

CHAP. X. — 19. Wherefore it is neither wrong nor unprofitable to spend much time in praying, if there be leisure for this without hindering other good and necessary works to which duty calls us, although even in the doing of these, as I have said, we ought by cherishing holy desire to pray without ceasing. For to spend a long time in prayer is not, as some think, the same thing as to pray "with much speaking." Multiplied words are one thing, long-continued warmth of desire is another. For even of the Lord Himself it is written, that He continued all night in prayer,[5] and that His prayer was more prolonged when He was in an agony;[6] and in this is not an example given to us by Him who is in time an Intercessor such as we need, and who is with the Father eternally the Hearer of prayer?

20. The brethren in Egypt are reported to have very frequent prayers, but these very brief, and, as it were, sudden and ejaculatory, lest the wakeful and aroused attention which is indispensable in prayer should by protracted exercises vanish or lose its keenness. And in this they themselves show plainly enough, that just as this attention is not to be allowed to become exhausted if it cannot continue long, so it is not to be suddenly suspended if it is sustained. Far be it from us either to use "much speaking" in prayer, or to refrain from prolonged prayer, if fervent attention of the soul continue. To use much speaking in prayer is to employ a superfluity of words in asking a necessary thing; but to prolong prayer is to have the heart throbbing with continued pious emotion towards Him to whom we pray. For in most cases prayer consists more in groaning than in speaking, in tears rather than in words. But He setteth our tears in His sight, and our groaning is not hidden from Him who made all things by the word, and does not need human words.

CHAP. XI. — 21. To us, therefore, words are necessary, that by them we may be assisted in considering and observing what we ask, not as means by which we expect that God is to be either informed or moved to compliance. When, therefore, we say: "Hallowed be Thy name," we admonish ourselves to desire that His name, which is always holy, may be also among men esteemed holy, that is to say, not despised; which is an advantage not to God, but to men. When we say: "Thy kingdom come," which shall certainly come whether we wish it or not, we do by these words stir up our own desires for that kingdom, that it may come to us, and that we may be found worthy to reign in it. When we say: "Thy will be done on earth as it is in heaven," we pray for ourselves that He would give us the grace of obedience, that His will may be done by us in the same way as it is done in heavenly places by His angels. When we say: "Give us this day our daily bread," the word "this day" signifies for the present time, in which we ask either for that competency of tem-

[1] 1 Cor. ii. 9.
[2] 1 Thess. v. 17.
[3] Phil. iv. 6.
[4] Tobias xii. 12.
[5] Luke vi. 12.
[6] Luke xxii. 43. English version, "more earnestly."

poral blessings which I have spoken of before ("bread" being used to designate the whole of those blessings, because of its constituting so important a part of them), or the sacrament of believers, which is in this present time necessary, but necessary in order to obtain the felicity not of the present time, but of eternity. When we say: "Forgive us our debts as we forgive our debtors," we remind ourselves both what we should ask, and what we should do in order that we may be worthy to receive what we ask. When we say: "Lead us not into temptation," we admonish ourselves to seek that we may not, through being deprived of God's help, be either ensnared to consent or compelled to yield to temptation. When we say: "Deliver us from evil," we admonish ourselves to consider that we are not yet enjoying that good estate in which we shall experience no evil. And this petition, which stands last in the Lord's Prayer, is so comprehensive that a Christian, in whatsoever affliction he be placed, may in using it give utterance to his groans and find vent for his tears — may begin with this petition, go on with it, and with it conclude his prayer. For it was necessary that by the use of these words the things which they signify should be kept before our memory.

CHAP. XII. — 22. For whatever other words we may say, — whether the desire of the person praying go before the words, and employ them in order to give definite form to its requests, or come after them, and concentrate attention upon them, that it may increase in fervour, — if we pray rightly, and as becomes our wants, we say nothing but what is already contained in the Lord's Prayer. And whoever says in prayer anything which cannot find its place in that gospel prayer, is praying in a way which, if it be not unlawful, is at least not spiritual; and I know not how carnal prayers can be lawful, since it becomes those who are born again by the Spirit to pray in no other way than spiritually. For example, when one prays: "Be Thou glorified among all nations as Thou art glorified among us," and "Let Thy prophets be found faithful,"[1] what else does he ask than, "Hallowed be Thy name"? When one says: "Turn us again, O Lord God of hosts, cause Thy face to shine, and we shall be saved,"[2] what else is he saying than, "Let Thy kingdom come"? When one says: "Order my steps in Thy word, and let not any iniquity have dominion over me,"[3] what else is he saying than, "Thy will be done on earth as it is in heaven"? When one says: "Give me neither poverty nor riches,"[4] what else is this than, "Give us this day our daily

bread"? When one says: "Lord, remember David, and all his compassion,"[5] or, "O Lord, if I have done this, if there be iniquity in my hands, if I have rewarded evil to them that did evil to me,"[6] what else is this than, "Forgive us our debts as we forgive our debtors"? When one says: "Take away from me the lusts of the appetite, and let not sensual desire take hold on me,"[7] what else is this than, "Lead us not into temptation"? When one says: "Deliver me from mine enemies, O my God; defend me from them that rise up against me,"[8] what else is this than, "Deliver us from evil"? And if you go over all the words of holy prayers, you will, I believe, find nothing which cannot be comprised and summed up in the petitions of the Lord's Prayer. Wherefore, in praying, we are free to use different words to any extent, but we must ask the same things; in this we have no choice.

23. These things it is our duty to ask without hesitation for ourselves and for our friends, and for strangers — yea, even for enemies; although in the heart of the person praying, desire for one and for another may arise, differing in nature or in strength according to the more immediate or more remote relationship. But he who says in prayer such words as, "O Lord, multiply my riches;" or, "Give me as much wealth as Thou hast given to this or that man;" or, "Increase my honours, make me eminent for power and fame in this world," or something else of this sort, and who asks merely from a desire for these things, and not in order through them to benefit men agreeably to God's will, I do not think that he will find any part of the Lord's Prayer in connection with which he could fit in these requests. Wherefore let us be ashamed at least to ask these things, if we be not ashamed to desire them. If, however, we are ashamed of even desiring them, but feel ourselves overcome by the desire, how much better would it be to ask to be freed from this plague of desire by Him to whom we say, "Deliver us from evil"!

CHAP. XIII. — 24. You have now, if I am not mistaken, an answer to two questions, — what kind of person you ought to be if you would pray, and what things you should ask in prayer; and the answer has been given not by my teaching, but by His who has condescended to teach us all. A happy life is to be sought after, and this is to be asked from the Lord God. Many different answers have been given by many in discussing wherein true happiness consists; but why should we go to many teachers, or consider many answers to this question? It has been briefly and truly stated in the divine Scriptures,

---

[1] Ecclus. xxxvi. 4, 18.
[2] Ps. lxxx. 7, 19.
[3] Ps. cxix. 133.
[4] Prov. xxx. 8.

[5] Ps. cxxxii. 1 (LXX.).
[6] Ps. vii. 3, 4.
[7] Ecclus. xxiii. 6.
[8] Ps. lix. 1.

" Blessed is the people whose God is the Lord."[1] That we may be numbered among this people, and that we may attain to beholding Him and dwelling for ever with Him, " the end of the commandment is, charity out of a pure heart, and of a good conscience, and of faith unfeigned."[2] In the same three, hope has been placed instead of a good conscience. Faith, hope, and charity, therefore, lead unto God the man who prays, *i.e.* who believes, hopes, and desires, and is guided as to what he should ask from the Lord by studying the Lord's Prayer. Fasting, and abstinence from gratifying carnal desire in other pleasures without injury to health, and especially frequent almsgiving, are a great assistance in prayer ; so that we may be able to say, " In the day of my trouble I sought the Lord, with my hands in the night before Him, and I was not deceived."[3] For how can God, who is a Spirit, and who cannot be touched, be sought with hands in any other sense than by good works?

CHAP. XIV. — 25. Perhaps you may still ask why the apostle said, " We know not what to pray for as we ought,"[4] for it is wholly incredible that either he or those to whom he wrote were ignorant of the Lord's Prayer. He could not say this either rashly or falsely ; what, then, do we suppose to be his reason for the statement? Is it not that vexations and troubles in this world are for the most part profitable either to heal the swelling of pride, or to prove and exercise patience, for which, after such probation and discipline, a greater reward is reserved, or to punish and eradicate some sins ; but we, not knowing what beneficial purpose these may serve, desire to be freed from all tribulation? To this ignorance the apostle showed that even he himself was not a stranger (unless, perhaps, he did it notwithstanding his knowing what to pray for as he ought), when, lest he should be exalted above measure by the greatness of the revelations, there was given unto him a thorn in the flesh, a messenger of Satan to buffet him ; for which thing, not knowing surely what he ought to pray for, he besought the Lord thrice that it might depart from him. At length he received the answer of God, declaring why that which so great a man prayed for was denied, and why it was expedient that it should not be done : " My grace is sufficient for thee ; my strength is made perfect in weakness."[5]

26. Accordingly, we know not what to pray for as we ought in regard to tribulations, which may do us good or harm ; and yet, because they are hard and painful, and against the natural feelings of our weak nature, we pray, with a desire which is common to mankind, that they may be removed from us. But we ought to exercise such submission to the will of the Lord our God, that if He does not remove those vexations, we do not suppose ourselves to be neglected by Him, but rather, in patient endurance of evil, hope to be made partakers of greater good, for so His strength is perfected in our weakness. God has sometimes in anger granted the request of impatient petitioners, as in mercy He denied it to the apostle. For we read what the Israelites asked, and in what manner they asked and obtained their request; but while their desire was granted, their impatience was severely corrected.[6] Again, He gave them, in answer to their request, a king according to their heart, as it is written, not according to His own heart.[7] He granted also what the devil asked, namely, that His servant, who was to be proved, might be tempted.[8] He granted also the request of unclean spirits, when they besought Him that their legion might be sent into the great herd of swine.[9] These things are written to prevent any one from thinking too highly of himself if he has received an answer when he was urgently asking anything which it would be more advantageous for him not to receive, or to prevent him from being cast down and despairing of the divine compassion towards himself if he be not heard, when, perchance, he is asking something by the obtaining of which he might be more grievously afflicted, or might be by the corrupting influences of prosperity wholly destroyed. In regard to such things, therefore, we know not what to pray for as we ought. Accordingly, if anything is ordered in a way contrary to our prayer, we ought, patiently bearing the disappointment, and in everything giving thanks to God, to entertain no doubt whatever that it was right that the will of God and not our will should be done. For of this the Mediator has given us an example, inasmuch as, after He had said, " Father, if it be possible, let this cup pass from me," transforming the human will which was in Him through His incarnation, He immediately added, " Nevertheless, O Father, not as I will but as Thou wilt."[10] Wherefore, not without reason are many made righteous by the obedience of One.[11]

27. But whoever desires from the Lord that " one thing," and seeks after it,[12] asks in certainty and in confidence, and has no fear lest when obtained it be injurious to him, seeing that, without it, anything else which he may have obtained

[1] Ps. cxliv. 15.
[2] 1 Tim. i. 5.
[3] Ps. lxxvii. 2 (LXX.).
[4] Rom. viii. 26.
[5] 2 Cor. xii. 7-9.

[6] Numb. xi.
[7] 1 Sam. viii. 6, 7.
[8] Job i. 12; ii. 6.
[9] Luke viii. 32.
[10] Matt. xxvi. 39.
[11] Rom. v. 19.
[12] Ps. xxvii. 4.

by asking in a right way is of no advantage to him. The thing referred to is the one true and only happy life, in which, immortal and incorruptible in body and spirit, we may contemplate the joy of the Lord for ever. All other things are desired, and are without impropriety prayed for, with a view to this one thing. For whosoever has it shall have all that he wishes, and cannot possibly wish to have anything along with it which would be unbecoming. For in it is the fountain of life, which we must now thirst for in prayer so long as we live in hope, not yet seeing that which we hope for, trusting under the shadow of His wings before whom are all our desires, that we may be abundantly satisfied with the fatness of His house, and made to drink of the river of His pleasures ; because with Him is the fountain of life, and in His light we shall see light,[1] when our desire shall be satisfied with good things, and when there shall be nothing beyond to be sought after with groaning, but all things shall be possessed by us with rejoicing. At the same time, because this blessing is nothing else than the " peace which passeth all understanding,"[2] even when we are asking it in our prayers, we know not what to pray for as we ought. For inasmuch as we cannot present it to our minds as it really is, we do not know it, but whatever image of it may be presented to our minds we reject, disown, and condemn ; we know it is not what we are seeking, although we do not yet know enough to be able to define what we seek.

CHAP. XV. — 28. There is therefore in us a certain learned ignorance, so to speak — an ignorance which we learn from that Spirit of God who helps our infirmities. For after the apostle said, " If we hope for that we see not, then do we with patience wait for it," he added in the same passage, " Likewise the Spirit also helpeth our infirmities : for we know not what we should pray for as we ought, but the Spirit itself maketh intercession for us, with groanings which cannot be uttered. And He that searcheth the hearts knoweth what is in the mind of the Spirit, because He maketh intercession for the saints according to the will of God."[3] This is not to be understood as if it meant that the Holy Spirit of God, who is in the Trinity, God unchangeable, and is one God with the Father and the Son, intercedes for the saints like one who is not a divine person ; for it is said, " He maketh intercession for the saints," because He enables the saints to make intercession, as in another place it is said, " The Lord your God proveth you, that He may know whether ye love Him,"[4] i.e. that He may make you know. He therefore makes the saints intercede with groanings which cannot be uttered, when He inspires them with longings for that great blessing, as yet unknown, for which we patiently wait. For how is that which is desired set forth in language if it be unknown, for if it were utterly unknown it would not be desired ; and on the other hand, if it were seen, it would not be desired nor sought for with groanings ?

CHAP. XVI. — 29. Considering all these things, and whatever else the Lord shall have made known to you in this matter, which either does not occur to me or would take too much time to state here, strive in prayer to overcome this world : pray in hope, pray in faith, pray in love, pray earnestly and patiently, pray as a widow belonging to Christ. For although prayer is, as He has taught, the duty of all His members, i.e. of all who believe in Him and are united to His body, a more assiduous attention to prayer is found to be specially enjoined in Scripture upon those who are widows. Two women of the name of Anna are honourably named there, — the one, Elkanah's wife, who was the mother of holy Samuel ; the other, the widow who recognised the Most Holy One when He was yet a babe. The former, though married, prayed with sorrow of mind and brokenness of heart because she had no sons ; and she obtained Samuel, and dedicated him to the Lord, because she vowed to do so when she prayed for him.[5] It is not easy, however, to find to what petition of the Lord's Prayer her petition could be referred, unless it be to the last, " Deliver us from evil," because it was esteemed to be an evil to be married and not to have offspring as the fruit of marriage. Observe, however, what is written concerning the other Anna, the widow : she " departed not from the temple, but served God with fastings and prayers night and day."[6] In like manner, the apostle said in words already quoted, " She that is a widow indeed, and desolate, trusteth in God and continueth in supplications and prayers night and day ; "[7] and the Lord, when exhorting men to pray always and not to faint, made mention of a widow, who, by persevering importunity, persuaded a judge to attend to her cause, though he was an unjust and wicked man, and one who neither feared God nor regarded man. How incumbent it is on widows to go beyond others in devoting time to prayer may be plainly enough seen from the fact that from among them are taken the examples set forth as an exhortation to all to earnestness in prayer.

30. Now what makes this work specially suitable to widows but their bereaved and desolate

---

[1] Ps. xxxvi. 8-10.
[2] Phil. iv. 7.
[3] Rom. viii. 25-27.
[4] Deut. xii. 3.

[5] 1 Sam. i.
[6] Luke ii. 36, 37.
[7] 1 Tim. v. 5.

condition? Whosoever, then, understands that he is in this world bereaved and desolate as long as he is a pilgrim absent from his Lord, is careful to commit his widowhood, so to speak, to his God as his shield in continual and most fervent prayer. Pray, therefore, as a widow of Christ, not yet seeing Him whose help you implore. And though you are very wealthy, pray as a poor person, for you have not yet the true riches of the world to come, in which you have no loss to fear. Though you have sons and grandchildren, and a large household, still pray, as I said already, as one who is desolate, for we have no certainty in regard to all temporal blessings that they shall abide for our consolation even to the end of this present life. If you seek and relish the things that are above, you desire things everlasting and sure ; and as long as you do not yet possess them, you ought to regard yourself as desolate, even though all your family are spared to you, and live as you desire. And if you thus act, assuredly your example will be followed by your most devout daughter-in-law,[1] and the other holy widows and virgins that are settled in peace under your care ; for the more pious the manner in which you order your house, the more are you bound to persevere fervently in prayer, not engaging yourselves with the affairs of this world further than is demanded in the interests of religion.

31. By all means remember to pray earnestly for me. I would not have you yield such deference to the office fraught with perils which I bear, as to refrain from giving the assistance which I know myself to need. Prayer was made by the household of Christ for Peter and for Paul. I rejoice that you are in His household ; and I need, incomparably more than Peter and Paul did, the help of the prayers of the brethren. Emulate each other in prayer with a holy rivalry, with one heart, for you wrestle not against each other, but against the devil, who is the common enemy of all the saints. " By fasting, by vigils, and all mortification of the body, prayer is greatly helped." [2] Let each one do what she can ; what one cannot herself do, she does by another who can do it, if she loves in another that which personal inability alone hinders her from doing ; wherefore let her who can do less not keep back the one who can do more, and let her who can do more not urge unduly her who can do less. For your conscience is responsible to God ; to each other owe nothing but mutual love. May the Lord, who is able to do above what we ask or think, give ear to your prayers.[3]

LETTER CXXXI.

(A.D. 412.)

TO HIS MOST EXCELLENT DAUGHTER, THE NOBLE AND DESERVEDLY ILLUSTRIOUS LADY PROBA, AUGUSTIN SENDS GREETING IN THE LORD.

You speak the truth when you say that the soul, having its abode in a corruptible body, is restrained by this measure of contact with the earth, and is somehow so bent and crushed by this burden that its desires and thoughts go more easily downwards to many things than upwards to one. For Holy Scripture says the same : " The corruptible body presseth down the soul, and the earthly tabernacle weigheth down the mind that museth upon many things." [4] But our Saviour, who by His healing word raised up the woman in the gospel that had been eighteen years bowed down [5] (whose case was, perchance, a figure of spiritual infirmity), came for this purpose, that Christians might not hear in vain the call, " Lift up your hearts," and might truly reply, " We lift them up to the Lord." Looking to this, you do well to regard the evils of this world as easy to bear because of the hope of the world to come. For thus, by being rightly used, these evils become a blessing, because, while they do not increase our desires for this world, they exercise our patience ; as to which the apostle says, " We know that all things work together for good to them that love God : " [6] all things, he saith — not only, therefore, those which are desired because pleasant, but also those which are shunned because painful ; since we receive the former without being carried away by them, and bear the latter without being crushed by them, and in all give thanks, according to the divine command, to Him of whom we say, " I will bless the Lord at all times ; His praise shall continually be in my mouth," [7] and, " It is good for me that Thou hast humbled me, that I might learn Thy statutes." [8] The truth is, most noble lady, that if the calm of this treacherous prosperity were always smiling upon us, the soul of man would never make for the haven of true and certain safety. Wherefore, in returning the respectful salutation due to your Excellency, and expressing my gratitude for your most pious care for my welfare, I ask of the Lord that He may grant to you the rewards of the life to come, and consolation in the present life ; and I commend myself to the love and prayers of all of you in whose hearts Christ dwells by faith.

(*In another hand.*) May the true and faithful God truly comfort your heart and preserve

---

[1] Juliana, the mother of Demetrias.
[2] Tobit xii. 8.
[3] Eph. iii. 20.

[4] Wisd. ix. 15.
[5] Luke xiii. 11-13.
[6] Rom. viii. 28.
[7] Ps. xxxiv. 1.
[8] Ps. cxix. 71 (LXX.).

your health, my most excellent daughter and noble lady, deservedly illustrious.

LETTER CXXXII.

(A.D. 412.)

TO VOLUSIANUS, MY NOBLE LORD AND MOST JUSTLY DISTINGUISHED SON, BISHOP AUGUSTIN SENDS GREETING IN THE LORD.

In my desire for your welfare, both in this world and in Christ, I am perhaps not even surpassed by the prayers of your pious mother. Wherefore, in reciprocating your salutation with the respect due to your worth, I beg to exhort you, as earnestly as I can, not to grudge to devote attention to the study of the Writings which are truly and unquestionably holy. For they are genuine and solid truth, not winning their way to the mind by artificial eloquence, nor giving forth with flattering voice a vain and uncertain sound. They deeply interest the man who is hungering not for words but for things; and they cause great alarm at first in him whom they are to render safe from fear. I exhort you especially to read the writings of the apostles, for from them you will receive a stimulus to acquaint yourself with the prophets, whose testimonies the apostles use. If in your reading or meditation on what you have read any question arises to the solution of which I may appear necessary, write to me, that I may write in reply. For, with the Lord helping me, I may perhaps be more able to serve you in this way than by personally conversing with you on such subjects, partly because, through the difference in our occupations, it does not happen that you have leisure at the same times as I might have it, but especially because of the irrepressible intrusion of those who are for the most part not adapted to such discussions, and take more pleasure in a war of words than in the clear light of knowledge; whereas, whatever is written stands always at the service of the reader when he has leisure, and there can be nothing burdensome in the society of that which is taken up or laid aside at your own pleasure.

LETTER CXXXIII.

(A.D. 412.)

TO MARCELLINUS,[1] MY NOBLE LORD, JUSTLY DISTINGUISHED, MY SON VERY MUCH BELOVED, AUGUSTIN SENDS GREETING IN THE LORD.

1. I have learned that the Circumcelliones and clergy of the Donatist faction belonging to the district of Hippo, whom the guardians of public order had brought to trial for their deeds, have been examined by your Excellency, and that the most of them have confessed their share in the violent death which the presbyter Restitutus suffered at their hands, and in the beating of Innocentius, another Catholic presbyter, as well as in digging out the eye and cutting off the finger of the said Innocentius. This news has plunged me into the deepest anxiety, lest perchance your Excellency should judge them worthy, according to the laws, of punishment not less severe than suffering in their own persons the same injuries as they have inflicted on others. Wherefore I write this letter to implore you by your faith in Christ, and by the mercy of Christ the Lord Himself, by no means to do this or permit it to be done. For although we might silently pass over the execution of criminals who may be regarded as brought up for trial not upon an accusation of ours, but by an indictment presented by those to whose vigilance the preservation of the public peace is entrusted, we do not wish to have the sufferings of the servants of God avenged by the infliction of precisely similar injuries in the way of retaliation. Not, of course, that we object to the removal from these wicked men of the liberty to perpetrate further crimes; but our desire is rather that justice be satisfied without the taking of their lives or the maiming of their bodies in any part, and that, by such coercive measures as may be in accordance with the laws, they be turned from their insane frenzy to the quietness of men in their sound judgment, or compelled to give up mischievous violence and betake themselves to some useful labour. This is indeed called a penal sentence; but who does not see that when a restraint is put upon the boldness of savage violence, and the remedies fitted to produce repentance are not withdrawn, this discipline should be called a benefit rather than vindictive punishment?

2. Fulfil, Christian judge, the duty of an affectionate father; let your indignation against their crimes be tempered by considerations of humanity; be not provoked by the atrocity of their sinful deeds to gratify the passion of revenge, but rather be moved by the wounds which these deeds have inflicted on their own souls to exercise a desire to heal them. Do not lose now that fatherly care which you maintained when prosecuting the examination, in doing which you extracted the confession of such horrid crimes,

---

[1] Marcellinus was commissioned by the Emperor Honorius to convene a conference of Catholic and Donatist bishops, with a view to the final peaceful settlement of their differences. He accordingly summoned both parties to a conference, held in the summer of 411, in which he pronounced the Catholic party to have completely gained their cause in argument. He proceeded to carry out with considerable rigour the laws passed for the repression of the Donatist schism, and thus becoming obnoxious to that faction, fell at length a victim to their revenge when a turn of fortune favoured their plots against his life. The honour of a place among the martyrs of the early Church has been assigned to him. His character may be learned from Letters CXXXVI., CXXXVIII., CXXXIX., and CXLIII., and particularly from the beautiful tribute to his worth given in Letter CLI., in which the circumstances of his death are recorded.

not by stretching them on the rack, not by furrowing their flesh with iron claws,[1] not by scorching them with flames, but by beating them with rods, — a mode of correction used by schoolmasters,[2] and by parents themselves in chastising children, and often also by bishops in the sentences awarded by them. Do not, therefore, now punish with extreme severity the crimes which you searched out with lenity. The necessity for harshness is greater in the investigation than in the infliction of punishment; for even the gentlest men use diligence and stringency in searching out a hidden crime, that they may find to whom they may show mercy. Wherefore it is generally necessary to use more rigour in making inquisition, so that when the crime has been brought to light, there may be scope for displaying clemency. For all good works love to be set in the light, not in order to obtain glory from men, but, as the Lord saith, "that they seeing your good works may glorify your Father who is in heaven."[3] And, for the same reason, the apostle was not satisfied with merely exhorting us to practise moderation, but also commands us to make it known: "Let your moderation," he says, "be known unto all men;"[4] and in another place, "Showing all meekness unto all men."[5] Hence, also, that most signal forbearance of the holy David, when he mercifully spared his enemy when delivered into his hand,[6] would not have been so conspicuous had not his power to act otherwise been manifest. Therefore let not the power of executing vengeance inspire you with harshness, seeing that the necessity of examining the criminals did not make you lay aside your clemency. Do not call for the executioner now when the crime has been found out, after having forborne from calling in the tormentor when you were finding it out.

3. In fine, you have been sent hither for the benefit of the Church. I solemnly declare that what I recommend is expedient in the interests of the Catholic Church, or, that I may not seem to pass beyond the boundaries of my own charge, I protest that it is for the good of the Church belonging to the diocese of Hippo. If you do not hearken to me asking this favour as a friend, hearken to me offering this counsel as a bishop; although, indeed, it would not be presumption for me to say — since I am addressing a Christian, and especially in such a case as this — that it becomes you to hearken to me as a bishop commanding with authority, my noble and justly distinguished lord and much-loved son. I am aware that the principal charge of law cases connected with the affairs of the Church has been devolved on your Excellency, but as I believe that this particular case belongs to the very illustrious and honourable proconsul, I have written a letter[7] to him also, which I beg you not to refuse to give to him, or, if necessary, recommend to his attention; and I entreat you both not to resent our intercession, or counsel, or anxiety, as officious. And let not the sufferings of Catholic servants of God, which ought to be useful in the spiritual upbuilding of the weak, be sullied by the retaliation of injuries on those who did them wrong, but rather, tempering the rigour of justice, let it be your care as sons of the Church to commend both your own faith and your Mother's clemency.

May almighty God enrich your Excellency with all good things, my noble and justly distinguished lord and dearly beloved son!

LETTER CXXXV.

(A.D. 412.)

TO BISHOP AUGUSTIN, MY LORD TRULY HOLY, AND FATHER JUSTLY REVERED, VOLUSIANUS SENDS GREETING.

1. O man who art a pattern of goodness and uprightness, you ask me to apply to you for instruction in regard to some of the obscure passages which occur in my reading. I accept at your command the favour of this kindness, and willingly offer myself to be taught by you, acknowledging the authority of the ancient proverb, "We are never too old to learn." With good reason the author of this proverb has not restricted by any limits or end our pursuit of wisdom; for truth,[8] secluded in its original principles, is never so disclosed to those who approach it as to be wholly revealed to their knowledge. It seems to me, therefore, my lord truly holy, and father justly revered, worth while to communicate to you the substance of a conversation which recently took place among us. I was present at a gathering of friends, and a great many opinions were brought forward there, such as the disposition and studies of each suggested. Our discourse was chiefly, however, on the department of rhetoric which treats of proper arrangement.[9] I speak to one familiar with the subject, for you were not long ago a teacher of these things. Upon this followed a discussion

---

[1] Compare "ungulis sulcantibus latera." *Codex Justin,* ix. 18. 7.
[2] *Magistris artium liberalium;* doubtless the name of Master of Arts was originally connected with the office and work of teaching, instead of being a mere honorary title.
[3] Matt. v. 16.
[4] Phil. iv. 5.
[5] Titus iii. 2.
[6] 1 Sam. xxiv. 7.

[7] This letter, No. CXXXIV., is addressed to Apringius, and in somewhat similar terms, but at greater length, urges the same request.
[8] We read here "*veritas,*" instead of "*virtus.*"
[9] "*Partitio,*" defined thus by Quintilian, vii. 1: "Sit igitur *divisio* rerum plurium in singulas — *partitio,* singularum in partes discretas ordo et recta quædam locatio."

regarding "invention" in rhetoric, its nature, what boldness it requires, how great the labour involved in methodical arrangement, what is the charm of metaphors, and the beauty of illustrations, and the power of applying epithets suitable to the character and nature of the subject in hand. Others extolled with partiality the poet's art. This part also of eloquence is not left unnoticed or unhonoured by you. We may appropriately apply to you that line of the poet: "The ivy is intertwined with the laurels which reward your victory."[1] We spoke, accordingly, of the embellishments which skilful arrangement adds to a poem, of the beauty of metaphors, and of the sublimity of well-chosen comparisons; then we spoke of smooth and flowing versification, and, if I may use the expression, the harmonious variation of the pauses in the lines.[2] The conversation turned next to a subject with which you are very familiar, namely, that philosophy which you were wont yourself to cherish, after the manner of Aristotle and Isocrates. We asked what had been achieved by the philosopher of the Lyceum, by the varied and incessant doubtings of the Academy, by the debater of the Porch, by the discoveries of natural philosophers, by the self-indulgence of the Epicureans; and what had been the result of their boundless zeal in disputation with each other, and how truth was more than ever unknown by them after they assumed that its knowledge was attainable.

2. While our conversation continues on these topics, one of the large company says: "Who among us is so thoroughly acquainted with the wisdom taught by Christianity as to be able to resolve the doubts by which I am entangled, and to give firmness to my hesitating acceptance of its teaching by arguments in which truth or probability may claim my belief?" We are all dumb with amazement. Then, of his own accord, he breaks forth in these words: "I wonder whether the Lord and Ruler of the world did indeed fill the womb of a virgin; — did His mother endure the protracted fatigues of ten months, and, being yet a virgin, in due season bring forth her child, and continue even after that with her virginity intact?" To this he adds other statements: "Within the small body of a crying infant He is concealed whom the universe scarcely can contain; He bears the years of childhood, He grows up, He is established in the vigour of manhood; this Governor is so long an exile from His own dwelling-place, and the care of the whole world is transferred to one body of insignificant dimensions. Moreover, He falls asleep, takes food to support Him, is subject to all the sensations of mortal men. Nor

did the proofs of so great majesty shine forth with adequate fulness of evidence; for the casting out of devils, the curing of the sick, and the restoration of the dead to life are, if you consider others who have wrought these wonders, but small works for God to do." We prevent him from continuing such questions, and the meeting having broken up, we referred the matter to the valuable decision of experience beyond our own, lest, by too rashly intruding into hidden things, the error, innocent thus far, should become blameworthy.

You have heard, O man worthy of all honour, the confession of our ignorance; you perceive what is requested at your hands. Your reputation is interested in our obtaining an answer to these questions. Ignorance may, without harm to religion, be tolerated in other priests; but when we come to Bishop Augustin, whatever we find unknown to him is no part of the Christian system. May the Supreme God protect your venerable Grace, my lord truly holy and justly revered!

LETTER CXXXVI.

(A.D. 412.)

TO AUGUSTIN, MY LORD MOST VENERABLE, AND FATHER SINGULARLY WORTHY OF ALL POSSIBLE SERVICE FROM ME, I, MARCELLINUS, SEND GREETING.

1. The noble Volusianus read to me the letter of your Holiness, and, at my urgent solicitation, he read to many more the sentences which had won my admiration, for, like everything else coming from your pen, they were worthy of admiration. Breathing as it did a humble spirit, and rich in the grace of divine eloquence, it succeeded easily in pleasing the reader.. What especially pleased me was your strenuous effort to establish and hold up the steps of one who is somewhat hesitating, by counselling him to form a good resolution. For I have every day some discussion with the same man, so far as my abilities, or rather my lack of talent, may enable me. Moved by the earnest entreaties of his pious mother, I am at pains to visit him frequently, and he is so good as to return my visits from time to time. But on receiving this letter from your venerable Eminence, though he is kept back from firm faith in the true God by the influence of a class of persons who abound in this city, he was so moved, that, as he himself tells me, he was prevented only by the fear of undue prolixity in his letter from unfolding to you every possible difficulty in regard to the Christian faith. Some things, however, he has very earnestly asked you to explain, expressing himself in a polished and accurate style, and

---

[1] Virgil, *Bucol.* Ecl. 8, line 13.
[2] *Cæsurarum modulata variatio.*

with the perspicuity and brilliancy of Roman eloquence, such as you will yourself deem worthy of approbation. The question which he has submitted to you is indeed worn threadbare in controversy, and the craftiness which, from the same quarter, assails with reproaches the Lord's incarnation is well known. But as I am confident that whatever you write in reply will be of use to a very large number, I would approach you with the request, that even in this question you would condescend to give a thoroughly guarded answer to their false statement that in His works the Lord performed nothing beyond what other men have been able to do. They are accustomed to bring forward their Apollonius and Apuleius, and other men who professed magical arts, whose miracles they maintained to have been greater than the Lord's.

2. The noble Volusianus aforesaid declared also in the presence of a number, that there were many other things which might not unreasonably be added to the question which he has sent, were it not that, as I have already stated, brevity had been specially studied by him in his letter. Although, however, he forbore from writing them, he did not pass them over in silence. For he is wont to say that, even if a reasonable account of the Lord's incarnation were now given to him, it would still be very difficult to give a satisfactory reason why this God, who is affirmed to be the God also of the Old Testament, is pleased with new sacrifices after having rejected the ancient sacrifices. For he alleges that nothing could be corrected but that which is proved to have been previously not rightly done; or that what has once been done rightly ought not to be altered in the very least. That which has been rightly done, he said, cannot be changed without wrong, especially because the variation might bring upon the Deity the reproach of inconstancy. Another objection which he stated was, that the Christian doctrine and preaching were in no way consistent with the duties and rights of citizens; because, to quote an instance frequently alleged, among its precepts we find, "Recompense to no man evil for evil," [1] and, "Whosoever shall smite thee on one cheek, turn to him the other also; and if any man take away thy coat, let him have thy cloak also; and whosoever shall compel thee to go a mile, go with him twain;" [2] — all which he affirms to be contrary to the duties and rights of citizens. For who would submit to have anything taken from him by an enemy, or forbear from retaliating the evils of war upon an invader who ravaged a Roman province? The other precepts, as your Eminence understands, are open to similar objections. Volusianus thinks

that all these difficulties may be added to the question formerly stated, especially because it is manifest (though he is silent on this point) that very great calamities have befallen the commonwealth under the government of emperors observing, for the most part, the Christian religion. [3]

3. Wherefore, as your Grace condescends along with me to acknowledge, it is important that all these difficulties be met by a full, thorough, and luminous reply (since the welcome answer of your Holiness will doubtless be put into many hands); especially because, while this discussion was going on, a distinguished lord and proprietor in the region of Hippo was present, who ironically said some flattering things concerning your Holiness, and affirmed that he had been by no means satisfied when he inquired into these matters himself.

I, therefore, not unmindful of your promise, but insisting on its fulfilment, beseech you to write, on the questions submitted, treatises which will be of incredible service to the Church, especially at the present time.

LETTER CXXXVII.

(A.D. 412.)

TO MY MOST EXCELLENT SON, THE NOBLE AND JUSTLY DISTINGUISHED LORD VOLUSIANUS, AUGUSTIN SENDS GREETING IN THE LORD.

CHAP. I. — 1. I have read your letter, containing an abstract of a notable conversation given with praiseworthy conciseness. I feel bound to reply to it, and to forbear from alleging any excuse for delay; for it happens opportunely that I have a short time of leisure from occupation with the affairs of other persons. I have also put off in the meantime dictating to my amanuensis certain things to which I had purposed to devote this leisure, for I think it would be a grievous injustice to delay answering questions which I had myself exhorted the questioner to propound. For which of us who are administering, as we are able, the grace of Christ would wish to see you instructed in Christian doctrine only so far as might suffice to secure to yourself salvation — not salvation in this present life, which, as the word of God is careful to remind us, is but a vapor appearing for a little while and then vanishing away, but that salvation in order to the obtaining and eternal possession of which we are Christians? It seems to us too little that you should receive only so much instruction as suffices to your own deliverance. For your gifted mind, and your singularly able and lucid power of speaking, ought to be of

---

[1] Rom. xii. 17.
[2] Matt. v. 39-41.

service to all others around you, against whom, whether slowness or perversity be the cause, it is necessary to defend in a competent way the dispensation of such abounding grace, which small minds in their arrogance despise, boasting that they can do very great things, while in fact they can do nothing to cure or even to curb their own vices.

2. You ask: "Whether the Lord and Ruler of the world did indeed fill the womb of a virgin? did His mother endure the protracted fatigues of ten months, and, being yet a virgin, in due season bring forth her child, and continue even after that with her virginity intact? Was He whom the universe is supposed to be scarcely able to contain concealed within the small body of a crying infant? did He bear the years of childhood, and grow up and become established in the vigour of manhood? Was this Governor so long an exile from His own dwelling-place, and was the care of the whole world transferred to a body of such insignificant dimensions? Did He sleep, did He take food as nourishment, and was He subject to all the sensations of mortal men?" You go on to say that "the proofs of His great majesty do not shine forth with any adequate fulness of evidence; for the casting out of devils, the curing of the sick, and the restoration of the dead are, if we consider others who have performed these wonders, but small works for God to do."[1] This question, you say, was introduced in a certain meeting of friends by one of the company, but that the rest of you prevented him from bringing forward any further questions, and, breaking up the meeting, deferred the consideration of the matter till you should have the benefit of experience beyond your own, lest, by too rashly intruding into hidden things, the error, innocent thus far, should become blameworthy.

3. Thereupon you appeal to me, and request me to observe what is desired from me after this confession of your ignorance. You add, that my reputation is concerned in your obtaining an answer to these questions, because, though ignorance is tolerated without injury to religion in other priests, when an inquiry is addressed to me, who am a bishop, whatever is not known to me must be no part of the Christian system.

I begin, therefore, by requesting you to lay aside the opinion which you have too easily formed concerning me, and dismiss those sentiments, though they are gratifying evidences of your goodwill, and believe my testimony rather than any other's regarding myself, if you reciprocate my affection. For such is the depth of the Christian Scriptures, that even if I were at-

tempting to study them and nothing else from early boyhood to decrepit old age, with the utmost leisure, the most unwearied zeal, and talents greater than I have, I would be still daily making progress in discovering their treasures; not that there is so great difficulty in coming through them to know the things necessary to salvation, but when any one has accepted these truths with the faith that is indispensable as the foundation of a life of piety and uprightness, so many things which are veiled under manifold shadows of mystery remain to be inquired into by those who are advancing in the study, and so great is the depth of wisdom not only in the words in which these have been expressed, but also in the things themselves, that the experience of the oldest, the ablest, and the most zealous students of Scripture illustrates what Scripture itself has said: "When a man hath done, then he beginneth."[2]

CHAP. II. — 4. But why say more as to this? I must rather address myself to the question which you propose. In the first place, I wish you to understand that the Christian doctrine does not hold that the Godhead was so blended with the human nature in which He was born of the virgin that He either relinquished or lost the administration of the universe, or transferred it to that body as a small and limited material substance. Such an opinion is held only by men who are incapable of conceiving of anything but material substances — whether more dense, like water and earth, or more subtle, like air and light; but all alike distinguished by this condition, that none of them can be in its entirety everywhere, because, by reason of its many parts, it cannot but have one part here, another there, and however great or small the body may be, it must occupy some place, and so fill it that in its entirety it is in no one part of the space occupied. And hence it is the distinctive property of material bodies that they can be condensed and rarefied, contracted and dilated, crushed into small fragments and enlarged to great masses. The nature of the soul is very far different from that of the body; and how much more different must be the nature of God, who is the Creator of both soul and body! God is not said to fill the world in the same way as water, air, and even light occupy space, so that with a greater or smaller part of Himself He occupies a greater or smaller part of the world. He is able to be everywhere present in the entirety of His being: He cannot be confined in any place: He can come without leaving the place where He was: He can depart without forsaking the place to which He had come.

[1] Letter CXXXV. sec. 2, p. 472.

[2] Ecclus. xviii. 6.

5. The mind of man wonders at this, and because it cannot comprehend it, refuses, perhaps, to believe it. Let it, however, not go on to wonder incredulously at the attributes of the Deity without first wondering in like manner at the mysteries within itself; [1] let it, if possible, raise itself for a little above the body, and above those things which it is accustomed to perceive by the bodily organs, and let it contemplate what that is which uses the body as its instrument. Perhaps it cannot do this, for it requires, as one has said, great power of mind to call the mind aside from the senses, and to lead thought away from its wonted track. [2] Let the mind, then, examine the bodily senses in this somewhat unusual manner, and with the utmost attention. There are five distinct bodily senses, which cannot exist either without the body or without the soul; because perception by the senses is possible, on the one hand, only while a man lives, and the body receives life from the soul; and on the other hand, only by the instrumentality of the bodily vessels and organs, through which we exercise sight, hearing, and the three other senses. Let the reasoning soul concentrate attention upon this subject, and consider the senses of the body not by these senses themselves, but by its own intelligence and reason. A man cannot, of course, perceive by these senses unless he lives; but up to the time when soul and body are separated by death, he lives in the body. How, then, does his soul, which lives nowhere else than in his body, perceive things which are beyond the surface of that body? Are not the stars in heaven very remote from his body? and yet does he not see the sun yonder? and is not seeing an exercise of the bodily senses — nay, is it not the noblest of them all? What, then? Does he live in heaven as well as in his body, because he perceives by one of his senses what is in heaven, and perception by sense cannot be in a place where there is no life of the person perceiving? Or does he perceive even where he is not living — because while he lives only in his own body, his perceptive sense is active also in those places which, outside of his body and remote from it, contain the objects with which he is in contact by sight? Do you see how great a mystery there is even in a sense so open to our observation as that which we call sight? Consider hearing also, and say whether the soul diffuses itself in some way abroad beyond the body. For how do we say, "Some one knocks at the door," unless we exercise the sense of hearing at the place where the knock is sounding? In this case also, therefore, we live beyond the limits of our bodies. Or can we perceive by sense in a place in which we are not living? But we know that sense cannot be in exercise where life is not.

6. The other three senses are exercised through immediate contact with their own organs. Perhaps this may be reasonably disputed in regard to the sense of smell; but there is no controversy as to the senses of taste and touch, that we perceive nowhere else than by contact with our bodily organism the things which we taste and touch. Let these three senses, therefore, be set aside from present consideration. The senses of sight and hearing present to us a wonderful question, requiring us to explain either how the soul can perceive by these senses in a place where it does not live, or how it can live in a place where it is not. For it is not anywhere but in its own body, and yet it perceives by these senses in places beyond that body. For in whatever place the soul sees anything, in that place it is exercising the faculty of perception, because seeing is an act of perception; and in whatever place the soul hears anything, in that place it is exercising the faculty of perception, because hearing is an act of perception. Wherefore the soul is either living in that place where it sees or hears, and consequently is itself in that place, or it exercises perception in a place where it is not living, or it is living in a place and yet at the same moment is not there. All these things are astonishing; not one of them can be stated without seeming absurdity; and we are speaking only of senses which are mortal. What, then, is the soul itself which is beyond the bodily senses, that is to say, which resides in the understanding whereby it considers these mysteries? For it is not by means of the senses that it forms a judgment concerning the senses themselves. And do we suppose that something incredible is told us regarding the omnipotence of God, when it is affirmed that the Word of God, by whom all things were made, did so assume a body from the Virgin, and manifest Himself with mortal senses, as neither to destroy His own immortality, nor to change His eternity, nor to diminish His power, nor to relinquish the government of the world, nor to withdraw from the bosom of the Father, that is, from the secret place where He is with Him and in Him?

7. Understand the nature of the Word of God, by whom all things were made, to be such that you cannot think of any part of the Word as passing, and, from being future, becoming past. He remains as He is, and He is everywhere in His entirety. He comes when He is manifested, and departs when He is concealed. But whether concealed or manifested, He is present with us as light is present to the eyes both of the seeing and of the blind; but it is felt to be present by the man who sees, and absent by him who is blind. In like manner, the sound of the voice

[1] We follow the reading of nine MSS., *mirata*, instead of that of the text, *ingrata*.
[2] Cicero, *Quæst. Tuscul. i.*

is near alike to the hearing and to the deaf, but it makes its presence known to the former and is hidden from the latter. But what is more wonderful than what happens in connection with the sound of our voices and our words, a thing, forsooth, which passes away in a moment? For when we speak, there is no place for even the next syllable till after the preceding one has ceased to sound; nevertheless, if one hearer be present, he hears the whole of what we say, and if two hearers be present, both hear the same, and to each of them it is the whole; and if a multitude listen in silence, they do not break up the sounds like loaves of bread, to be distributed among them individually, but all that is uttered is imparted to all and to each in its entirety. Consider this, and say if it is not more incredible that the abiding Word of God should not accomplish in the universe what the passing word of man accomplishes in the ears of listeners, namely, that as the word of man is present in its entirety to each and all of the hearers, so the Word of God should be present in the entirety of His being at the same moment everywhere.

8. There is, therefore, no reason to fear in regard to the small body of the Lord in His infancy, lest in it the Godhead should seem to have been straitened. For it is not in vast size but in power that God is great: He has in His providence given to ants and to bees senses superior to those given to asses and camels; He forms the huge proportions of the fig-tree[1] from one of the minutest seeds, although many smaller plants spring from much larger seeds; He also has furnished the small pupil of the eye with the power which, by one glance, sweeps over almost the half of heaven in a moment; He diffuses the whole fivefold system of the nerves over the body from one centre and point in the brain; He dispenses vital motion throughout the whole body from the heart, a member comparatively small; and by these and other similar things, He, who in small things is great, mysteriously produces that which is great from things which are exceedingly little. Such is the greatness of His power that He is conscious of no difficulty in that which is difficult. It was this same power which originated, not from without, but from within, the conception of a child in the Virgin's womb: this same power associated with Himself a human soul, and through it also a human body — in short, the whole human nature to be elevated by its union with Him — without His being thereby lowered in any degree; justly assuming from it the name of humanity, while amply giving to it the name of Godhead. The body of the infant Jesus was

brought forth from the womb of His mother, still a virgin, by the same power which afterwards introduced His body when He was a man through the closed door into the upper chamber.[2] Here, if the reason of the event is sought out, it will no longer be a miracle; if an example of a precisely similar event is demanded, it will no longer be unique.[3] Let us grant that God can do something which we must admit to be beyond our comprehension. In such wonders the whole explanation of the work is the power of Him by whom it is wrought.

CHAP. III. — 9. The fact that He took rest in sleep, and was nourished by food, and experienced all the feelings of humanity, is the evidence to men of the reality of that human nature which He assumed but did not destroy. Behold, this was the fact; and yet some heretics, by a perverted admiration and praise of His power, have refused altogether to acknowledge the reality of His human nature, in which is the guarantee of all that grace by which He saves those who believe in Him, containing deep treasures of wisdom and knowledge, and imparting faith to the minds which He raises to the eternal contemplation of unchangeable truth. What if the Almighty had created the human nature of Christ not by causing Him to be born of a mother, but by some other way, and had presented Him suddenly to the eyes of mankind? What if the Lord had not passed through the stages of progress from infancy to manhood, and had taken neither food nor sleep? Would not this have confirmed the erroneous impression above re-

---

[1] See Pliny, *Nat. Hist.* Book vii. 2: "In India sub una ficu turmæ conduntur equitum." See also Book xii. c. 5.

[2] John xx. 26.

[3] This sentence having been misunderstood by Bishop Evodius, who quotes and comments upon it in Letter CLXI., Augustin, in replying in Letter CLXII., writes a few sentences, which, as the letters then exchanged with Evodius have been omitted in this selection, we here insert: — " Our sense of wonder is excited when either the reason of a thing is hidden from us, or the thing itself is extraordinary, that is, either unique or rare. It was in reference to the former cause of wonder, namely, the reason of a thing being undiscovered, that, when answering those who declare it to be incredible that Christ was born of a virgin, and that she remained a virgin notwithstanding, I said in the letter which you refer to as read by you, 'If the reason of this event is sought out, it will be no longer a miracle,' for I said this not because the event was without a reason, but because the reason of it is hidden from those to whom it has pleased God that it should be a miracle. . . . For all the works of God, both ordinary and extraordinary, proceed from causes and reasons which are right and faultless. When the causes and reasons of any of His operations are hidden from us, we are filled with wonder; but when the causes and reasons of events are seen by us, we say that they take place in ordinary course and in harmony with our experience, and that they are not to be wondered at since they occur, because they are only what reason required to be done. . . . As to the latter cause of wonder, namely, that an event is unusual, we have an example of this when we read concerning the Lord that He marvelled at the faith of the centurion: for the reason of no event whatever could be concealed from Him, but His wonder has been recorded here for the commendation of one whose equal had not appeared among the Jews, and accordingly the Lord's wondering is sufficiently explained by His words: 'I have not found so great faith, no, not in Israel' (Luke vii. 9). As to examples of events similar to the miraculous birth of Christ, you are wholly mistaken in supposing that you have found such in the production of a worm upon an apple, and other examples which you mention. For instances of a certain degree of resemblance, more or less remote, have been with considerable ingenuity alleged: but Christ alone was born of a virgin; whence you may understand why I said that this was an event without parallel, adding in the letter already referred to the words: ' If an example of a precisely similar event is demanded, it will no longer be unique'" (Letter CLXII. secs. 6, 7).

ferred to, and have made it impossible to believe at all that He had taken to Himself true human nature ; and, while leaving what was marvellous, would eliminate the element of mercy from His actions? But now He has so appeared as the Mediator between God and men, that, uniting the two natures in one person, He both exalted what was ordinary by what was extraordinary, and tempered what was extraordinary by what was ordinary in Himself.

10. But where in all the varied movements of creation is there any work of God which is not wonderful, were it not that through familiarity these wonders have become small in our esteem? Nay, how many common things are trodden under foot, which, if examined carefully, awaken our astonishment ! Take, for example, the properties of seeds : who can either comprehend or declare the variety of species, the vitality, vigour, and secret power by which they from within small compass evolve great things? Now the human body and soul which He took to Himself was created without seed by Him who in the natural world created originally seeds from no pre-existent seeds. In the body which thus became His, He who, without any liability to change in Himself, has woven according to His counsel the vicissitudes of all past centuries, became subject to the succession of seasons and the ordinary stages of the life of man. For His body, as it began to exist at a point of time, became developed with the lapse of time. But the Word of God, who was in the beginning, and to whom the ages of time owe their existence, did not bow to time as bringing round the event of His incarnation apart from His consent, but chose the point of time at which He freely took our nature to Himself. The human nature was brought into union with the divine; God did not withdraw from Himself.[1]

11. Some insist upon being furnished with an explanation of the manner in which the Godhead was so united with a human soul and body as to constitute the one person of Christ, when it was necessary that this should be done once in the world's history, with as much boldness as if they were themselves able to furnish an explanation of the manner in which the soul is so united to the body as to constitute the one person of a man, an event which is occurring every day. For just as the soul is united to the body in one person so as to constitute man, in the same way is God united to man in one person so as to constitute Christ. In the former personality there is a combination of soul and body ; in the latter there is a combination of the Godhead and man. Let my reader, however, guard against borrowing his idea of the combination from the properties of material bodies, by which two fluids when combined are so mixed that neither preserves its original character ; although even among material bodies there are exceptions, such as light, which sustains no change when combined with the atmosphere. In the person of man, therefore, there is a combination of soul and body ; in the person of Christ there is a combination of the Godhead with man ; for when the Word of God was united to a soul having a body, He took into union with Himself both the soul and the body. The former event takes place daily in the beginning of life in individuals of the human race ; the latter took place once for the salvation of men. And yet of the two events, the combination of two immaterial substances ought to be more easily believed than a combination in which the one is immaterial and the other material. For if the soul is not mistaken in regard to its own nature, it understands itself to be immaterial. Much more certainly does this attribute belong to the Word of God ; and consequently the combination of the Word with the human soul is a combination which ought to be much more credible than that of soul and body. The latter is realized by us in ourselves ; the former we are commanded to believe to have been realized in Christ. But if both of them were alike foreign to our experience, and we were enjoined to believe that both had taken place, which of the two would we more readily believe to have occurred? Would we not admit that two immaterial substances could be more easily combined than one immaterial and one material ; unless, perhaps, it be unsuitable to use the word combination in connection with these things, because of the difference between their nature and that of material substances, both in themselves and as known to us?

12. Wherefore the Word of God, who is also the Son of God, co-eternal with the Father, the Power and the Wisdom of God,[2] mightily pervading and harmoniously ordering all things, from the highest limit of the intelligent to the lowest limit of the material creation,[3] revealed and concealed, nowhere confined, nowhere divided, nowhere distended, but without dimensions, everywhere present in His entirety, — this Word of God, I say, took to Himself, in a manner entirely different from that in which He is present to other creatures, the soul and body of a man, and made, by the union of Himself therewith, the one person Jesus Christ, Mediator between God and men,[4] in His Deity equal with the Father, in His flesh, i.e. in His human nature, inferior to the Father, — unchangeably immortal in respect of the divine nature, in which He is equal with

---

[1] *Homo quippe Deo accessit, non Deus a se recessit.*

[2] 1 Cor. i. 24.
[3] Wisd. viii. 1.
[4] 1 Tim. ii. 5.

the Father, and yet changeable and mortal in respect of the infirmity which was His through participation with our nature.

In this Christ there came to men, at the time which He knew to be most fitting, and which He had fixed before the world began, the *instruction* and the *help* necessary to the obtaining of eternal salvation. *Instruction* came by Him, because those truths which had been, for men's advantage, spoken before that time on earth not only by the holy prophets, all whose words were true, but also by philosophers and even poets and authors in every department of literature (for beyond question they mixed much truth with what was false), might by the actual presentation of His authority in human nature be confirmed as true for the sake of those who could not perceive and distinguish them in the light of essential Truth, which Truth was, even before He assumed human nature, present to all who were capable of receiving truth. Moreover, by the fact of His incarnation, He taught this above all other things for our benefit, — that whereas men longing after the Divine Being supposed, from pride rather than piety, that they must approach Him not directly, but through heavenly powers which they regarded as gods, and through various forbidden rites which were holy but profane, — in which worship devils succeed, through the bond which pride forms between mankind and them, in taking the place of holy angels, — now men might understand that the God whom they were regarding as far removed, and whom they approached not directly but through mediating powers, is actually so very near to the pious longings of men after Him, that He has condescended to take a human soul and body into such union with Himself that this complete man is joined to Him in the same way as the body is joined to the soul in man, excepting that whereas both body and soul have a common progressive development, He does not participate in this growth, because it implies mutability, a property which God cannot assume. Again, in this Christ the *help* necessary to salvation was brought to men, for without the grace of that faith which is from Him, no one can either subdue vicious desires, or be cleansed by pardon from the guilt of any power of sinful desire which he may not have wholly vanquished. As to the effects produced by His instruction, is there now even an imbecile, however weak, or a silly woman, however low, that does not believe in the immortality of the soul and the reality of a life after death? Yet these are truths which, when Pherecydes [1] the Assyrian for the first time maintained them in discussion among the Greeks

of old, moved Pythagoras of Samos so deeply by their novelty, as to make him turn from the exercises of the athlete to the studies of the philosopher. But now what Virgil said we all behold: "The balsam of Assyria grows everywhere." [2] And as to the help given through the grace of Christ, in Him truly are the words of the same poet fulfilled: "With Thee as our leader, the obliteration of all the traces of our sin which remain shall deliver the earth from perpetual alarm." [3]

CHAP. IV. — 13. "But," they say, "the proofs of so great majesty did not shine forth with adequate fulness of evidence; for the casting out of devils, the healing of the sick, and the restoration of the dead to life are but small works for God to do, if the others who have wrought similar wonders be borne in mind." [4] We ourselves admit that the prophets wrought some miracles like those performed by Christ. For among these miracles what is more wonderful than the raising of the dead? Yet both Elijah and Elisha did this. [5] As to the miracles of magicians, and the question whether they also raised the dead, let those pronounce an opinion who strive, not as accusers, but as panegyrists, to prove Apuleius guilty of those charges of practising magical arts from which he himself takes abundant pains to defend his reputation. We read that the magicians of Egypt, the most skilled in these arts, were vanquished by Moses, the servant of God, when they were working wonderfully by impious enchantments, and he, by simply calling upon God in prayer, overthrew all their machinations. [6] But this Moses himself and all the other true prophets prophesied concerning the Lord Christ, and gave to Him great glory; they predicted that He would come not as One merely equal or superior to them in the same power of working miracles, but as One who was truly God the Lord of all, and who became man for the benefit of men. He was pleased to do also some miracles, such as they had done, to prevent the incongruity of His not doing in person such things as He had done by them. Nevertheless, He was to do also some things peculiar to Himself, namely, to be born of a virgin, to rise from the dead, to ascend to heaven. I know not what greater things he can look for who thinks these too little for God to do.

14. For I think that such signs of divine power are demanded by these objectors as were not suitable for Him to do when wearing the nature of men. The Word was in the beginning, and the Word was with God, and the Word was God, and by Him all things were made. [7] Now,

---

[1] Pherecydes, a native not of Assyria, but of Syros, one of the Cyclades, was a disciple of Pittacus of Mitylene, and teacher of Pythagoras. He flourished B.C. 544.

[2] "Assyrium vulgo nascetur amomum." — Eclogue iv.
[3] *Ibid.*
[4] Letter CXXXV. sec. 2, p. 472.
[5] 1 Kings xvii. 22; 2 Kings iv. 35.
[6] Ex. vii., viii.
[7] John i. 1.

when the Word became flesh, was it necessary for Him to create another world, that we might believe Him to be the person by whom the world was made? But within this world it would have been impossible to make another greater than itself, or equal to it. If, however, He were to make a world inferior to that which now exists, this, too, would be considered too small a work to prove His deity. Wherefore, since it was not necessary that He should make a new world, He made new things in the world. For that a man should be born of a virgin, and raised from the dead to eternal life, and exalted above the heavens, is perchance a work involving a greater exertion of power than the creating of a world. Here, probably, objectors may answer that they do not believe that these things took place. What, then, can be done for men who despise smaller evidences as inadequate, and reject greater evidences as incredible? That life has been restored to the dead is believed, because it has been accomplished by others, and is too small a work to prove him who performs it to be God: that a true body was created in a virgin, and being raised from death to eternal life, was taken up to heaven, is not believed, because no one else has done this, and it is what God alone could do. On this principle every man is to accept with equanimity whatever he thinks easy for himself not indeed to do, but to conceive, and is to reject as false and fictitious whatever goes beyond that limit. I beseech you, do not be like these men.

15. These topics are elsewhere more amply discussed, and in fundamental questions of doctrine every intricate point has been opened up by thorough investigation and debate; but faith gives the understanding access to these things, unbelief closes the door. What man might not be moved to faith in the doctrine of Christ by such a remarkable chain of events from the beginning, and by the manner in which the epochs of the world are linked together, so that our faith in regard to present things is assisted by what happened in the past, and the record of earlier and ancient things is attested by later and more recent events? One is chosen from among the Chaldeans, a man endowed with most eminent piety and faith, that to him may be given divine promises, appointed to be fulfilled in the last times of the world, after the lapse of so many centuries; and it is foretold that in his seed shall all the nations of the earth be blessed.[1] This man, worshipping the one true God, the Creator of the universe, begets in his old age a son, when sterility and advanced years had made his wife give up all expectation of becoming a mother. The descendants of this son become a very numerous tribe, being increased in Egypt, to which place they had been removed from the East, by Divine Providence multiplying as time went on both the promises given and the works wrought on their behalf. From Egypt they come forth a mighty nation, being brought out with terrible signs and wonders; and the wicked nations of the promised land being driven out from before them, they are brought into it and settled there, and exalted to the position of a kingdom. Thereafter, frequently provoking by prevailing sin and idolatrous impieties the true God, who had bestowed on them so many benefits, and experiencing alternately the chastisements of calamity and the consolations of restored prosperity, the history of the nation is brought down to the incarnation and the manifestation of Christ. Predictions that this Christ, being the Word of God, the Son of God, and God Himself, was to become incarnate, to die, to rise again, to ascend into heaven, to have multitudes of all nations through the power of His name surrendering themselves to Him, and that by Him pardon of sins and eternal salvation would be given to all who believe in Him, — these predictions, I say, have been published by all the promises given to that nation, by all the prophecies, the institution of the priesthood, the sacrifices, the temple, and, in short, by all their sacred mysteries.

16. Accordingly Christ comes: in His birth, life, words, deeds, sufferings, death, resurrection, ascension, all which the prophets had foretold is fulfilled.[2] He sends the Holy Spirit; fills with this Spirit the believers when they are assembled in one house, and expecting with prayer and ardent desire this promised gift. Being thus filled with the Holy Spirit, they speak immediately in the tongues of all nations, they boldly confute errors, they preach the truth that is most profitable for mankind, they exhort men to repent of their past blameworthy lives, and promise pardon by the free grace of God. Signs and miracles suitable for confirmation follow their preaching of piety and of the true religion. The cruel enmity of unbelief is stirred up against them; they bear predicted trials, they hope for promised blessings, and teach that which they had been commanded to make known. Few in number at first, they become scattered like seed throughout the world; they convert nations with wondrous facility; they grow in number in the midst of enemies; they become increased by persecutions; and, under the severity of hardships, instead of being straitened, they extend their influence to the utmost boundaries of the earth. From being very ignorant, despised, and few, they become enlightened, distinguished, and nu-

---

[1] Gen. xii.

[2] Matt. i. 22.

merous, men of illustrious talents and of polished eloquence ; they also bring under the yoke of Christ, and attract to the work of preaching the way of holiness and salvation, the marvellous attainments of men remarkable for genius, eloquence, and erudition. Amid alternations of adversity and prosperity, they watchfully practise patience and self-control ; and when the world's day is drawing near its close, and the approaching consummation is heralded by the calamities which exhaust its energies, they, seeing in this the fulfilment of prophecy, only expect with increased confidence the everlasting blessedness of the heavenly city. Moreover, amidst all these changes, the unbelief of the heathen nations continues to rage against the Church of Christ ; she gains the victory by patient endurance, and by the maintenance of unshaken faith in the face of the cruelties of her adversaries. The sacrifice of Him in whom the truth, long veiled under mystic promises, is revealed, having been offered, those sacrifices by which it was prefigured are finally abolished by the utter destruction of the Jewish temple. The Jewish nation, itself rejected because of unbelief, being now rooted out from its own land, is dispersed to every region of the world, in order that it may carry everywhere the Holy Scriptures, and that in this way our adversaries themselves may bring before mankind the testimony furnished by the prophecies concerning Christ and His Church, thus precluding the possibility of the supposition that these predictions were forged by us to suit the time ; in which prophecies, also, the unbelief of these very Jews is foretold. The temples, images, and impious worship of the heathen divinities are overthrown gradually and in succession, according to the prophetic intimations. Heresies bud forth against the name of Christ, though veiling themselves under His name, as had been foretold, by which the doctrine of the holy religion is tested and developed. All these things are now seen to be accomplished, in exact fulfilment of the predictions which we read in Scripture ; and from these important and numerous instances of fulfilled prophecy, the fulfilment of the predictions which remain is confidently expected. Where, then, is the mind, having aspirations after eternity, and moved by the shortness of this present life, which can resist the clearness and perfection of these evidences of the divine origin of our faith?

CHAP. V. — 17. What discourses or writings of philosophers, what laws of any commonwealth in any land or age, are worthy for a moment to be compared with the two commandments on which Christ saith that all the law and the prophets hang : "Thou shalt love the Lord thy God with all thy heart, and with all thy soul, and with all thy mind, and thou shalt love thy neighbour

as thyself"?[1] All philosophy is here, — physics, ethics, logic : the *first*, because in God the Creator are all the causes of all existences in nature ; the *second*, because a good and honest life is not produced in any other way than by loving, in the manner in which they should be loved, the proper objects of our love, namely, God and our neighbour ; and the *third*, because God alone is the Truth and the Light of the rational soul. Here also is security for the welfare and renown of a commonwealth ; for no state is perfectly established and preserved otherwise than on the foundation and by the bond of faith and of firm concord, when the highest and truest common good, namely, God, is loved by all, and men love each other in Him without dissimulation, because they love one another for His sake from whom they cannot disguise the real character of their love.

18. Consider, moreover, the style in which Sacred Scripture is composed, — how accessible it is to all men, though its deeper mysteries are penetrable to very few. The plain truths which it contains it declares in the artless language of familiar friendship to the hearts both of the unlearned and of the learned ; but even the truths which it veils in symbols it does not set forth in stiff and stately sentences, which a mind somewhat sluggish and uneducated might shrink from approaching, as a poor man shrinks from the presence of the rich ; but, by the condescension of its style, it invites all not only to be fed with the truth which is plain, but also to be exercised by the truth which is concealed, having both in its simple and in its obscure portions the same truth. Lest what is easily understood should beget satiety in the reader, the same truth being in another place more obscurely expressed becomes again desired, and, being desired, is somehow invested with a new attractiveness, and thus is received with pleasure into the heart. By these means wayward minds are corrected, weak minds are nourished, and strong minds are filled with pleasure, in such a way as is profitable to all. This doctrine has no enemy but the man who, being in error, is ignorant of its incomparable usefulness, or, being spiritually diseased, is averse to its healing power.

19. You see what a long letter I have written. If, therefore, anything perplexes you, and you regard it of sufficient importance to be discussed between us, let not yourself be straitened by keeping within the bounds of ordinary letters ; for you know as well as any one what long letters the ancients wrote when they were treating of any subject which they were not able briefly to explain. And even if the custom of authors in other departments of literature had been differ-

---

[1] Matt. xxii. 37-39.

ent, the authority of Christian writers, whose example has a worthier claim upon our imitation, might be set before us. Observe, therefore, the length of the apostolic epistles, and of the commentaries written on these divine oracles, and do not hesitate either to ask many questions if you have many difficulties, or to handle more fully the questions which you propound, in order that, in so far as it can be achieved with such abilities as we possess, there may remain no cloud of doubt to obscure the light of truth.

20. For I am aware that your Excellency has to encounter the most determined opposition from certain persons, who think, or would have others think, that Christian doctrine is incompatible with the welfare of the commonwealth, because they wish to see the commonwealth established not by the stedfast practice of virtue, but by granting impunity to vice. But with God the crimes in which many are banded together do not pass unavenged, as is often the case with a king, or any other magistrate who is only a man. Moreover, His mercy and grace, published to men by Christ, who is Himself man, and imparted to man by the same Christ, who is also God and the Son of God, never fail those who live by faith in Him and piously worship Him, in adversity patiently and bravely bearing the trials of this life, in prosperity using with self-control and with compassion for others the good things of this life; destined to receive, for faithfulness in both conditions, an eternal recompense in that divine and heavenly city in which there shall be no longer calamity to be painfully endured, nor inordinate desire to be with laborious care controlled, where our only work shall be to preserve, without any difficulty and with perfect liberty, our love to God and to our neighbour.

May the infinitely compassionate omnipotence of God preserve you in safety and increase your happiness, my noble and distinguished Lord, and my most excellent son. With profound respect, as is due to your worth, I salute your pious and most truly venerable mother, whose prayers on your behalf may God hear! My pious brother and fellow bishop, Possidius, warmly salutes your Grace.

LETTER CXXXVIII.

(A.D. 412.)

TO MARCELLINUS, MY NOBLE AND JUSTLY FAMOUS LORD, MY SON MOST BELOVED AND LONGED FOR, AUGUSTIN SENDS GREETING IN THE LORD.

CHAP. I. — 1. In writing to the illustrious and most eloquent Volusianus, whom we both sincerely love, I thought it right to confine myself to answering the questions which he thought proper himself to state; but as to the questions which you have submitted to me in your letter for discussion and solution, as suggested or proposed either by Volusianus himself or by others, it is fitting that such reply to these as I may be able to give should be addressed to you. I shall attempt this, not in the manner in which it would require to be done in a formal treatise, but in the manner which is suitable to the conversational familiarity of a letter, in order that, if you, who know their state of mind by daily discussions, think it expedient, this letter also may be read to your friends. But if this communication be not adapted to them, because of their not being prepared by the piety of faith to give ear to it, let what you consider adapted to them be in the first place prepared between ourselves, and afterwards let what may have been thus prepared be communicated to them. For there are many things from which their minds may in the meantime shrink and recoil, which they may perhaps by and by be persuaded to accept as true, either by the use of more copious and skilful arguments, or by an appeal to authority which, in their opinion, may not without impropriety be resisted.

2. In your letter you state that some are perplexed by the question, "Why this God, who is proved to be the God also of the Old Testament, is pleased with new sacrifices after having rejected the ancient ones. For they allege that nothing can be corrected but that which is proved to have been previously not rightly done, or that what has once been done rightly ought not to be altered in the very least: that which has been rightly done, they say, cannot be changed without wrong." [1] I quote these words from your letter. Were I disposed to give a copious reply to this objection, time would fail me long before I had exhausted the instances in which the processes of nature itself and the works of men undergo changes according to the circumstances of the time, while, at the same time, there is nothing mutable in the plan or principle by which these changes are regulated. Of these I may mention a few, that, stimulated by them, your wakeful observation may run, as it were, from them to many more of the same kind. Does not summer follow winter, the temperature gradually increasing in warmth? Do not night and day in turn succeed each other? How often do our own lives experience changes! Boyhood departing, never to return, gives place to youth; manhood, destined itself to continue only for a season, takes in turn the place of youth; and old age, closing the term of manhood, is itself closed by death.[2] All these things are changed, but the plan of Divine Providence

---

[1] Letter CXXXVI. sec. 2, p. 473.
[2] Augustin's four stages of human life are: *Pueritia, adolescentia, juventus, senectus.*

which appoints these successive changes is not changed. I suppose, also, that the principles of agriculture are not changed when the farmer appoints a different work to be done in summer from that which he had ordered in winter. He who rises in the morning, after resting by night, is not supposed to have changed the plan of his life. The schoolmaster gives to the adult different tasks from those which he was accustomed to prescribe to the scholar in his boyhood; his teaching, consistent throughout, changes the instruction when the lesson is changed, without itself being changed.

3. The eminent physician of our own times, Vindicianus, being consulted by an invalid, prescribed for his disease what seemed to him a suitable remedy at that time; health was restored by its use. Some years afterwards, finding himself troubled again with the same disorder, the patient supposed that the same remedy should be applied; but its application made his illness worse. In astonishment, he again returns to the physician, and tells him what had happened; whereupon he, being a man of very quick penetration, answered: "The reason of your having been harmed by this application is, that I did not order it;" upon which all who heard the remark and did not know the man supposed that he was trusting not in the art of medicine, but in some forbidden supernatural power. When he was afterwards questioned by some who were amazed at his words, he explained what they had not understood, namely, that he would not have prescribed the same remedy to the patient at the age which he had now attained. While, therefore, the principle and methods of art remain unchanged, the change which, in accordance with them, may be made necessary by the difference of times is very great.

4. To say, then, that what has once been done rightly must in no respect whatever be changed, is to affirm what is not true. For if the circumstances of time which occasioned anything be changed, true reason in almost all cases demands that what had been in the former circumstances rightly done, be now so altered that, although they say that it is not rightly done if it be changed, truth, on the contrary, protests that it is not rightly done unless it be changed; because, at both times, it will be rightly done if the difference be regulated according to the difference in the times. For just as in the cases of different persons it may happen that, at the same moment, one man may do with impunity what another man may not, because of a difference not in the thing done but in the person who does it, so in the case of one and the same person at different times, that which was duty formerly is not duty now, not because the per-

son is different from his former self, but because the time at which he does it is different.

5. The wide range opened up by this question may be seen by any one who is competent and careful to observe the contrast between the beautiful and the suitable, examples of which are scattered, we may say, throughout the universe. For the beautiful, to which the ugly and deformed is opposed, is estimated and praised according to what it is in itself. But the suitable, to which the incongruous is opposed, depends on something else to which it is bound, and is estimated not according to what it is in itself, but according to that with which it is connected: the contrast, also, between becoming and unbecoming is either the same, or at least regarded as the same. Now apply what we have said to the subject in hand. The divine institution of sacrifice was suitable in the former dispensation, but is not suitable now. For the change suitable to the present age has been enjoined by God, who knows infinitely better than man what is fitting for every age, and who is, whether He give or add, abolish or curtail, increase or diminish, the unchangeable Governor as He is the unchangeable Creator of mutable things, ordering all events in His providence until the beauty of the completed course of time, the component parts of which are the dispensations adapted to each successive age, shall be finished, like the grand melody of some ineffably wise master of song, and those pass into the eternal immediate contemplation of God who here, though it is a time of faith, not of sight, are acceptably worshipping Him.

6. They are mistaken, moreover, who think that God appoints these ordinances for His own advantage or pleasure; and no wonder that, being thus mistaken, they are perplexed, as if it was from a changing mood that He ordered one thing to be offered to Him in a former age, and something else now. But this is not the case. God enjoins nothing for His own advantage, but for the benefit of those to whom the injunction is given. Wherefore He is truly Lord, for He does not need His servants, but His servants stand in need of Him. In those same Old Testament Scriptures, and in the age in which sacrifices were still being offered that are now abrogated, it is said: "I said unto the Lord, Thou art my God, for Thou dost not need my good things."[1] Wherefore God did not stand in need of those sacrifices, nor does He ever need anything; but there are certain acts, symbolical of these divine gifts, whereby the soul receives either present grace or eternal glory, in the celebration and practice of which, pious exercises, serviceable not to God but to ourselves, are performed.

---

[1] Ps. xvi. 2. ὅτι τῶν ἀγαθῶν μου οὐ χρείαν ἔχεις, LXX.; *quoniam bonorum meorum non eges*, AUG.

7. It would, however, take too long to discuss with adequate fulness the differences between the symbolical actions of former and present times, which, because of their pertaining to divine things, are called sacraments.[1] For as the man is not fickle who does one thing in the morning and another in the evening, one thing this month and another in the next, one thing this year and another next year, so there is no variableness with God, though in the former period of the world's history He enjoined one kind of offerings, and in the latter period another, therein ordering the symbolical actions pertaining to the blessed doctrine of true religion in harmony with the changes of successive epochs without any change in Himself. For in order to let those whom these things perplex understand that the change was already in the divine counsel, and that, when the new ordinances were appointed, it was not because the old had suddenly lost the divine approbation through inconstancy in His will, but that this had been already fixed and determined by the wisdom of that God to whom, in reference to much greater changes, these words are spoken in Scripture: "Thou shalt change them, and they shall be changed; but Thou art the same,"[2]—it is necessary to convince them that this exchange of the sacraments of the Old Testament for those of the New had been predicted by the voices of the prophets. For thus they will see, if they can see anything, that what is new in time is not new in relation to Him who has appointed the times, and who possesses, without succession of time, all those things which He assigns according to their variety to the several ages. For in the psalm from which I have quoted above the words: "I said unto the Lord, Thou art my God, for Thou dost not need my good things," in proof that God does not need our sacrifices, it is added shortly after by the Psalmist in Christ's name: "I will not gather their assemblies of blood;"[3] that is, for the offering of animals from their flocks, for which the Jewish assemblies were wont to be gathered together; and in another place he says: "I will take no bullock out of thy house, nor he-goat from thy folds;"[4] and another prophet says: "Behold, the days come, saith the Lord, that I will make a new covenant with the house of Israel, and with the house of Judah: not according to the covenant that I made with their fathers in the day when I took them by the hand to bring them out of the land of Egypt."[5] There are, besides these, many other testimonies on this subject in which it was foretold that God would do as He has done; but it would take too long to mention them.

8. If it is now established that that which was for one age rightly ordained may be in another age rightly changed,—the alteration indicating a change in the work, not in the plan, of Him who makes the change, the plan being framed by His reasoning faculty, to which, unconditioned by succession in time, those things are simultaneously present which cannot be actually done at the same time because the ages succeed each other,—one might perhaps at this point expect to hear from me the causes of the change in question. You know how long it would take to discuss these fully. The matter may be stated summarily, but sufficiently for a man of shrewd judgment, in these words: It was fitting that Christ's future coming should be foretold by some sacraments, and that after His coming other sacraments should proclaim this; just as the difference in the facts has compelled us to change the words used by us in speaking of the advent as future or past: to be foretold is one thing, to be proclaimed is another, and to be about to come is one thing, to have come is another.

CHAP. II. — 9. Let us now observe, in the second place, what follows in your letter.[6] You have added that they said that the Christian doctrine and preaching were in no way consistent with the duties and rights of citizens, because among its precepts we find: "Recompense to no man evil for evil,"[7] and, "Whosoever shall smite thee on one cheek, turn to him the other also; and if any man take away thy coat, let him have thy cloak also; and whosoever will compel thee to go a mile with him, go with him twain,"[8]—all which are affirmed to be contrary to the duties and rights of citizens; for who would submit to have anything taken from him by an enemy, or forbear from retaliating the evils of war upon an invader who ravaged a Roman province? To these and similar statements of persons speaking slightingly, or perhaps I should rather say speaking as inquirers regarding the truth, I might have given a more elaborate answer, were it not that the persons with whom the discussion is carried on are men of liberal education. In addressing such, why should we prolong the debate, and not rather begin by inquiring for ourselves how it was possible that the Republic of Rome was governed and aggrandized from insignificance and poverty to greatness and opulence by men who, when they had suffered wrong, would rather pardon than punish the offender;[9]

---

[1] Observe Augustin's definition of the word *sacramentum* as used by him: "cum ad res divinas pertinent sacramenta appellantur."
[2] Ps. cii. 26, 27.
[3] Ps. xvi. 3. οὐ μὴ συναγάγω τὰς συναγωγὰς αὐτων ἐξ αἱμάτων, LXX.
[4] Ps. l. 9.
[5] Jer. xxxi. 32.
[6] Letter CXXXVI. sec. 2, p. 473.
[7] Rom. xii. 17.
[8] Matt. v. 39–41.
[9] "Accepta injuria ignoscere quam persequi malebant." — Sallust, *Catilina*, c. 9.

or how Cicero, addressing Cæsar, the greatest statesman of his time, said, in praising his character, that he was wont to forget nothing but the wrongs which were done to him?[1] For in this Cicero spoke either praise or flattery: if he spoke praise, it was because he knew Cæsar to be such as he affirmed; if he spoke flattery, he showed that the chief magistrate of a commonwealth ought to do such things as he falsely commended in Cæsar. But what is "not rendering evil for evil," but refraining from the passion of revenge — in other words, choosing, when one has suffered wrong, to pardon rather than to punish the offender, and to forget nothing but the wrongs done to us?

10. When these things are read in their own authors, they are received with loud applause; they are regarded as the record and recommendation of virtues in the practice of which the Republic deserved to hold sway over so many nations, because its citizens preferred to pardon rather than punish those who wronged them. But when the precept, "Render to no man evil for evil," is read as given by divine authority, and when, from the pulpits in our churches, this wholesome counsel is published in the midst of our congregations, or, as we might say, in places of instruction open to all, of both sexes and of all ages and ranks, our religion is accused as an enemy to the Republic! Yet, were our religion listened to as it deserves, it would establish, consecrate, strengthen, and enlarge the commonwealth in a way beyond all that Romulus, Numa, Brutus, and all the other men of renown in Roman history achieved. For what is a republic but a commonwealth? Therefore its interests are common to all; they are the interests of the State. Now what is a State but a multitude of men bound together by some bond of concord? In one of their own authors we read: "What was a scattered and unsettled multitude had by concord become in a short time a State." But what exhortations to concord have they ever appointed to be read in their temples? So far from this, they were unhappily compelled to devise how they might worship without giving offence to any of their gods, who were all at such variance among themselves, that, had their worshippers imitated their quarrelling, the State must have fallen to pieces for want of the bond of concord, as it soon afterwards began to do through civil wars, when the morals of the people were changed and corrupted.

11. But who, even though he be a stranger to our religion, is so deaf as not to know how many precepts enjoining concord, not invented by the discussions of men, but written with the authority of God, are continually read in the churches of Christ? For this is the tendency even of those precepts which they are much more willing to debate than to follow: "That to him who smites us on one cheek we should offer the other to be smitten; to him who would take away our coat we should give our cloak also; and that with him who compels us to go one mile we should go twain." For these things are done only that a wicked man may be overcome by kindness, or rather that the evil which is in the wicked man may be overcome by good, and that the man may be delivered from the evil — not from any evil that is external and foreign to himself, but from that which is within and is his own, under which he suffers loss more severe and fatal than could be inflicted by the cruelty of any enemy from without. He, therefore, who is overcoming evil by good, submits patiently to the loss of temporal advantages, that he may show how those things, through excessive love of which the other is made wicked, deserve to be despised when compared with faith and righteousness; in order that so the injurious person may learn from him whom he wronged what is the true nature of the things for the sake of which he committed the wrong, and may be won back with sorrow for his sin to that concord, than which nothing is more serviceable to the State, being overcome not by the strength of one passionately resenting, but by the good-nature of one patiently bearing wrong. For then it is rightly done when it seems that it will benefit him for whose sake it is done, by producing in him amendment of his ways and concord with others. At all events, it is to be done with this intention, even though the result may be different from what was expected, and the man, with a view to whose correction and conciliation this healing and salutary medicine, so to speak, was employed, refuses to be corrected and reconciled.

12. Moreover, if we pay attention to the words of the precept, and consider ourselves under bondage to the literal interpretation, the right cheek is not to be presented by us if the left has been smitten. "Whosoever," it is said, "shall smite thee on thy right cheek, turn to him the other also;"[2] but the left cheek is more liable to be smitten, because it is easier for the right hand of the assailant to smite it than the other. But the words are commonly understood as if our Lord had said: If any one has acted injuriously to thee in respect of the higher possessions which thou hast, offer to him also the inferior possessions, lest, being more concerned about revenge than about forbearance, thou shouldst despise eternal things in comparison with temporal things, whereas temporal things

---

[1] "Oblivisci soles nihil nisi injurias." — Cicero, *pro Ligario,* c. 12.

[2] Matt. v. 39.

ought to be despised in comparison with eternal things, as the left is in comparison with the right. This has been always the aim of the holy martyrs; for final vengeance is righteously demanded only when there remains no room for amendment, namely, in the last great judgment. But meanwhile we must be on our guard, lest, through desire for revenge, we lose patience itself, — a virtue which is of more value than all which an enemy can, in spite of our resistance, take away from us. For another evangelist, in recording the same precept, makes no mention of the right cheek, but names merely the one and the other;[1] so that, while the duty may be somewhat more distinctly learned from Matthew's gospel, he simply commends the same exercise of patience. Wherefore a righteous and pious man ought to be prepared to endure with patience injury from those whom he desires to make good, so that the number of good men may be increased, instead of himself being added, by retaliation of injury, to the number of wicked men.

13. In fine, that these precepts pertain rather to the inward disposition of the heart than to the actions which are done in the sight of men, requiring us, in the inmost heart, to cherish patience along with benevolence, but in the outward action to do that which seems most likely to benefit those whose good we ought to seek, is manifest from the fact that our Lord Jesus Himself, our perfect example of patience, when He was smitten on the face, answered: "If I have spoken evil, bear witness of the evil, but if not, why smitest thou me?"[2] If we look only to the words, He did not in this obey His own precept, for He did not present the other side of his face to him who had smitten Him, but, on the contrary, prevented him who had done the wrong from adding thereto; and yet He had come prepared not only to be smitten on the face, but even to be slain upon the cross for those at whose hands He suffered crucifixion, and for whom, when hanging on the cross, He prayed, "Father, forgive them, they know not what they do!"[3] In like manner, the Apostle Paul seems to have failed to obey the precept of his Lord and Master, when he, being smitten on the face as He had been, said to the chief priest: "God shall smite thee, thou whited wall, for sittest thou to judge me after the law, and commandest me to be smitten contrary to the law?"[?] And when it was said by them that stood near, "Revilest thou God's high priest?" he took pains sarcastically to indicate what his words meant, that those of them who were discerning might understand that now the whited wall, i.e. the hypocrisy of the Jewish priesthood, was appointed to be thrown down by the coming of Christ; for He said: "I wist not, brethren, that he was the high priest, for it is written, Thou shalt not speak evil of the ruler of thy people;"[4] although it is perfectly certain that he who had grown up in that nation, and had been in that place trained in the law, could not but know that his judge was the chief priest, and could not, by professing ignorance on this point, impose upon those to whom he was so well known.

14. These precepts concerning patience ought to be always retained in the habitual discipline of the heart, and the benevolence which prevents the recompensing of evil for evil must be always fully cherished in the disposition. At the same time, many things must be done in correcting with a certain benevolent severity, even against their own wishes, men whose welfare rather than their wishes it is our duty to consult; and the Christian Scriptures have most unambiguously commended this virtue in a magistrate.[?] For in the correction of a son, even with some sternness, there is assuredly no diminution of a father's love; yet, in the correction, that is done which is received with reluctance and pain by one whom it seems necessary to heal by pain. And on this principle, if the commonwealth observe the precepts of the Christian religion, even its wars themselves will not be carried on without the benevolent design that, after the resisting nations have been conquered, provision may be more easily made for enjoying in peace the mutual bond of piety and justice. For the person from whom is taken away the freedom which he abuses in doing wrong is vanquished with benefit to himself; since nothing is more truly a misfortune than that good fortune of offenders, by which pernicious impunity is maintained, and the evil disposition, like an enemy within the man, is strengthened. But the perverse and froward hearts of men think human affairs are prosperous when men are concerned about magnificent mansions, and indifferent to the ruin of souls; when mighty theatres are built up, and the foundations of virtue are undermined; when the madness of extravagance is highly esteemed, and works of mercy are scorned; when, out of the wealth and affluence of rich men, luxurious provision is made for actors, and the poor are grudged the necessaries of life; when that God who, by the public declarations of His doctrine, protests against public vice, is blasphemed by impious communities, which demand gods of such character that even those theatrical representations which bring disgrace to both body

---

[1] Luke vi. 29.
[2] John xviii. 23.
[3] Luke xxiii. 34.

[4] Acts xxiii. 3–5.

and soul are fitly performed in honour of them. If God permit these things to prevail, He is in that permission showing more grievous displeasure : if He leave these crimes unpunished, such impunity is a more terrible judgment. When, on the other hand, He overthrows the props of vice, and reduces to poverty those lusts which were nursed by plenty, He afflicts in mercy. And in mercy, also, if such a thing were possible, even wars might be waged by the good, in order that, by bringing under the yoke the unbridled lusts of men, those vices might be abolished which ought, under a just government, to be either extirpated or suppressed.

15. For if the Christian religion condemned wars of every kind, the command given in the gospel to soldiers asking counsel as to salvation would rather be to cast away their arms, and withdraw themselves wholly from military service ; whereas the word spoken to such was, " Do violence to no man, neither accuse any falsely, and be content with your wages," [1] — the command to be content with their wages manifestly implying no prohibition to continue in the service. Wherefore, let those who say that the doctrine of Christ is incompatible with the State's well-being, give us an army composed of soldiers such as the doctrine of Christ requires them to be ; let them give us such subjects, such husbands and wives, such parents and children, such masters and servants, such kings, such judges — in fine, even such taxpayers and tax-gatherers, as the Christian religion has taught that men should be, and then let them dare to say that it is adverse to the State's well-being ; yea, rather, let them no longer hesitate to confess that this doctrine, if it were obeyed, would be the salvation of the commonwealth.

CHAP. III — 16. But what am I to answer to the assertion made that many calamities have befallen the Roman Empire through some Christian emperors? This sweeping accusation is a calumny. For if they would more clearly quote some indisputable facts in support of it from the history of past emperors, I also could mention similar, perhaps even greater calamities in the reigns of other emperors who were not Christians ; so that men may understand that these were either faults in the men, not in their religion, or were due not to the emperors themselves, but to others without whom emperors can do nothing. As to the date of the commencement of the downfall of the Roman Republic, there is ample evidence ; their own literature speaks plainly as to this. Long before the name of Christ had shone abroad on the earth, this was said of Rome : " O venal city, and doomed to perish

speedily, if only it could find a purchaser ! " [2] In his book on the Catilinarian conspiracy, which was before the coming of Christ, the same most illustrious Roman historian declares plainly the time when the army of the Roman people began to be wanton and drunken ; to set a high value on statues, paintings, and embossed vases ; to take these by violence both from individuals and from the State ; to rob temples and pollute everything, sacred and profane. When, therefore, the avarice and grasping violence of the corrupt and abandoned manners of the time spared neither men nor those whom they esteemed as gods, the famous honour and safety of the commonwealth began to decline. What progress the worst vices made from that time forward, and with how great mischief to the interests of mankind the wickedness of the Empire went on, it would take too long to rehearse. Let them hear their own satirist speaking playfully yet truly thus : —

" Once poor, and therefore chaste, in former times
Our matrons were   no luxury found room
In low-roofed houses and bare walls of loam ;
Their hands with labour burdened while 'tis light,
A frugal sleep supplied the quiet night ;
While, pinched with want, their hunger held them strait,
When Hannibal was hovering at the gate ;
But wanton now, and lolling at our ease,
We suffer all the inveterate ills of peace
And wasteful riot, whose destructive charms
Revenge the vanquished world of our victorious arms.
No crime, no lustful postures are unknown,
Since poverty, our guardian-god, is gone." [3]

Why, then, do you expect me to multiply examples of the evils which were brought in by wickedness uplifted by prosperity, seeing that among themselves, those who observed events with somewhat closer attention discerned that Rome had more reason to regret the departure of its poverty than of its opulence ; because in its poverty the integrity of its virtue was secured, but through its opulence, dire corruption, more terrible than any invader, had taken violent possession not of the walls of the city, but of the mind of the State?

17. Thanks be unto the Lord our God, who has sent unto us unprecedented help in resisting these evils. For whither might not men have been carried away by that flood of the appalling wickedness of the human race, whom would it have spared, and in what depths would it not have engulfed its victims, had not the cross of Christ, resting on such a solid rock of authority (so to speak), been planted too high and too strong for the flood to sweep it away? so that by laying hold of its strength we may become stedfast, and not be carried off our feet and overwhelmed in the mighty whirlpool of the

---

[1] Luke iii. 14.

[2] Sallust, *Bell. Jugurth.*
[3] Juvenal, vi. 277-295 (Dryden's translation).

evil counsels and evil impulses of this world. For when the empire was sinking in the vile abyss of utterly depraved manners, and of the effete ancient religion, it was signally important that heavenly authority should come to the rescue, persuading men to the practice of voluntary poverty, continence, benevolence, justice, and concord among themselves, as well as true piety towards God, and all the other bright and sterling virtues of life, — not only with a view to the spending of this present life in the most honourable way, nor only with a view to secure the most perfect bond of concord in the earthly commonwealth, but also in order to the obtaining of eternal salvation, and a place in the divine and celestial republic of a people which shall endure for ever — a republic to the citizenship of which faith, hope, and charity admit us; so that, while absent from it on our pilgrimage here, we may patiently tolerate, if we cannot correct, those who desire, by leaving vices unpunished, to give stability to that republic which the early Romans founded and enlarged by their virtues, when, though they had not the true piety towards the true God which could bring them, by a religion of saving power, to the commonwealth which is eternal, they did nevertheless observe a certain integrity of its own kind, which might suffice for founding, enlarging, and preserving an earthly commonwealth. For in the most opulent and illustrious Empire of Rome, God has shown how great is the influence of even civil virtues without true religion, in order that it might be understood that, when this is added to such virtues, men are made citizens of another commonwealth, of which the king is Truth, the law is Love, and the duration is Eternity.

CHAP. IV. — 18. Who can help feeling that there is something simply ridiculous in their attempt to compare with Christ, or rather to put in a higher place, Apollonius and Apuleius, and others who were most skilful in magical arts? Yet this is to be tolerated with less impatience, because they bring into comparison with Him these men rather than their own gods; for Apollonius was, as we must admit, a much worthier character than that author and perpetrator of innumerable gross acts of immorality whom they call Jupiter. "These legends about our gods," they reply, "are fables." Why, then, do they go on praising that luxurious, licentious, and manifestly profane prosperity of the Republic, which invented these infamous crimes of the gods, and not only left them to reach the ears of men as fables, but also exhibited them to the eyes of men in the theatres; in which, more numerous than their deities were the crimes which the gods themselves were well pleased to see openly perpetrated in their honour, whereas

they should have punished their worshippers for even tolerating such spectacles? "But," they reply, "those are not the gods themselves whose worship is celebrated according to the lying invention of such fables." Who, then, are they who are propitiated by the practising in worship of such abominations? Because, forsooth, Christianity has exposed the perversity and chicanery of those devils, by whose power also magical arts deceive the minds of men, and because it has made this patent to the world, and, having brought out the distinction between the holy angels and these malignant adversaries, has warned men to be on their guard against them, showing them also how this may be done, — it is called an enemy to the Republic, as if, even though temporal prosperity could be secured by their aid, any amount of adversity would not be preferable to the prosperity obtained through such means. And yet it pleased God to prevent men from being perplexed in this matter; for in the age of the comparative darkness of the Old Testament, in which is the covering of the New Testament, He distinguished the first nation which worshipped the true God and despised false gods by such remarkable prosperity in this world, that any one may perceive from their case that prosperity is not at the disposal of devils, but only of Him whom angels serve and devils fear.

19. Apuleius (of whom I choose rather to speak, because, as our own countryman, he is better known to us Africans), though born in a place of some note,[1] and a man of superior education and great eloquence, never succeeded, with all his magical arts, in reaching, I do not say the supreme power, but even any subordinate office as a magistrate in the Empire. Does it seem probable that he, as a philosopher, voluntarily despised these things, who, being priest of a province, was so ambitious of greatness that he gave spectacles of gladiatorial combats, provided the dresses worn by those who fought with wild beasts in the circus, and, in order to get a statue of himself erected in the town of Coea, the birthplace of his wife, appealed to law against the opposition made by some of the citizens to the proposal, and then, to prevent this from being forgotten by posterity, published the speech delivered by him on that occasion? So far, therefore, as concerns worldly prosperity, that magician did his utmost in order to success; whence it is manifest that he failed not because he was not wishful, but because he was not able to do more. At the same time we admit that he defended himself with brilliant eloquence against some who imputed to him the crime of practising magical arts; which makes me wonder

---

[1] Madaura.

at his panegyrists, who, in affirming that by these arts he wrought some miracles, attempt to bring evidence contradicting his own defence of himself from the charge. Let them, however, examine whether, indeed, they are bringing true testimony, and he was guilty of pleading what he knew to be false. Those who pursue magical arts only with a view to worldly prosperity or from an accursed curiosity, and those also who, though innocent of such arts, nevertheless praise them with a dangerous admiration, I would exhort to give heed, if they be wise, and to observe how, without any such arts, the position of a shepherd was exchanged for the dignity of the kingly office by David, of whom Scripture has faithfully recorded both the sinful and the meritorious actions, in order that we might know both how to avoid offending God, and how, when He has been offended, His wrath may be appeased.

20. As to those miracles, however, which are performed in order to excite the wonder of men, they do greatly err who compare heathen magicians with the holy prophets, who completely eclipse them by the fame of their great miracles. How much more do they err if they compare them with Christ, of whom the prophets, so incomparably superior to magicians of every name, foretold that He would come both in the human nature, which he took in being born of the Virgin, and in the divine nature, in which He is never separated from the Father!

I see that I have written a very long letter, and yet have not said all concerning Christ which might meet the case either of those who from sluggishness of intellect are unable to comprehend divine things, or of those who, though endowed with acuteness, are kept back from discerning truth through their love of contradiction and the prepossession of their minds in favour of long-cherished error. Howbeit, take note of anything which influences them against our doctrine, and write to me again, so that, if the Lord help us, we may, by letters or by treatises, furnish an answer to all their objections. May you, by the grace and mercy of the Lord, be happy in Him, my noble and justly distinguished lord, my son dearly beloved and longed for!

LETTER CXXXIX.

(A.D. 412.)

TO MARCELLINUS, MY LORD JUSTLY DISTINGUISHED, MY SON VERY MUCH BELOVED AND LONGED FOR, AUGUSTIN SENDS GREETING IN THE LORD.

1. The Acts [1] which your Excellency promised to send I am eagerly expecting, and I am longing to have them read as soon as possible in the church at Hippo, and also, if it can be done, in all the churches established within the diocese, that all may hear and become thoroughly familiar with the men who have confessed their crimes, not because the fear of God subdued them to repentance, but because the rigour of their judges broke through the hardness of their most cruel hearts, — some of them confessing to the murder of one presbyter [Restitutus], and the blinding and maiming of another [Innocentius]; others not daring to deny that they might have known of these outrages, although they say that they disapproved of them, and persisting in the impiety of schism in fellowship with such a multitude of atrocious villains, while deserting the peace of the Catholic Church on the pretext of unwillingness to be polluted by other men's crimes; others declaring that they will not forsake the schismatics, even though the certainty of Catholic truth and the perversity of the Donatists have been demonstrated to them. The work, which it has pleased God to entrust to your diligence, is of great importance. My heart's desire is, that many similar Donatist cases may be tried and decided by you as these have been, and that in this way the crimes and the insane obstinacy of these men may be often brought to light; and that the Acts recording these proceedings may be published, and brought to the knowledge of all men.

As to the statement in your Excellency's letter, that you are uncertain whether you ought to command the said Acts to be published in Theoprepia, [2] my reply is, Let this be done, if a large multitude of hearers can be gathered there; if this be not the case, some other place of more general resort must be provided; it must not, however, be omitted on any account.

2. As to the punishment of these men, I beseech you to make it something less severe than sentence of death, although they have, by their own confession, been guilty of such grievous crimes. I ask this out of a regard both for our own consciences and for the testimony thereby given to Catholic clemency. For this is the special advantage secured to us by their confession, that the Catholic Church has found an opportunity of maintaining and exhibiting forbearance towards her most violent enemies; since in a case where such cruelty was practised, any punishment short of death will be seen by all men to proceed from great leniency. And although such treatment appears to some of our communion, whose minds are agitated by these atrocities, to be less than the crimes deserve, and to have somewhat the aspect of weakness and dereliction of duty, nevertheless, when the feelings, which are wont to be immoderately ex-

---

[1] *Gesta* — records of judicial procedure.

[2] This is supposed to be the name of a Donatist church in Carthage.

cited while such events are recent, have subsided after a time, the kindness shown to the guilty will shine with most conspicuous brightness, and men will take much more pleasure in reading these Acts and showing them to others, my lord justly distinguished, and son very much beloved and longed for.

My holy brother and co-bishop Boniface is on the spot, and I have forwarded by the deacon Peregrinus, who travelled along with him, a letter of instructions; accept these as representing me. And whatever may seem in your joint opinion to be for the Church's interest, let it be done with the help of the Lord, who is able in the midst of so great evils graciously to succour you. One of their bishops, Macrobius, is at present going round in all directions, followed by bands of wretched men and women, and has opened for himself the [Donatist] churches which fear, however slight, had moved their owners to close for a time. By the presence, however, of one whom I have commended and again heartily commend to your love, namely, Spondeus, the deputy of the illustrious Celer, their presumption was indeed somewhat checked; but now, since his departure to Carthage, Macrobius has opened the Donatist churches even within his property, and is gathering congregations for worship in them. In his company, moreover, is Donatus, a deacon, rebaptized by them even when he was a tenant of lands belonging to the Church, who was implicated as a ringleader in the outrage [on Innocentius]. When this man is his associate, who can tell what kind of followers may be in his retinue? If the sentence on these men is to be pronounced by the Proconsul,[1] or by both of you together, and if he perchance insist upon inflicting capital punishment, although he is a Christian and, so far as we have had opportunity of observing, not disposed to such severity — if, I say, his determination make it necessary, order those letters of mine, which I deemed it my duty to address to you severally on this subject,[2] to be brought before you while the trial is still going on; for I am accustomed to hear that it is in the power of the judge to mitigate the sentence, and inflict a milder penalty than the law prescribes. If, however, notwithstanding these letters from me, he refuse to grant this request, let him at least allow that the men be remanded for a time; and we will endeavour to obtain this concession from the clemency of the Emperors, so that the sufferings of the martyrs, which ought to shed bright glory on the Church, may not be tarnished by the blood of their enemies; for I know that in the case of the clergy in the val-

ley of Anaunia,[3] who were slain by the Pagans, and are now honoured as martyrs, the Emperor granted readily a petition that the murderers, who had been discovered and imprisoned, might not be visited with a capital punishment.

3. As to the books concerning the baptism of infants, of which I had sent the original manuscript to your Excellency, I have forgotten for what reason I received them again from you; unless, perhaps, it was that, after examining them, I found them faulty, and wished to make some corrections, which, by reason of extraordinary hindrances, I have not yet been able to overtake. I must also confess that the letter intended to be addressed to you and added to these books, and which I had begun to dictate when I was with you, is still unfinished, little having been added to it since that time. If, however, I could set before you a statement of the toil which it is absolutely necessary for me to devote, both by day and by night, to other duties, you would deeply sympathize with me, and would be astonished at the amount of business not admitting of delay which distracts my mind and hinders me from accomplishing those things to which you urge me in entreaties and admonitions, addressed to one most willing to oblige you, and inexpressibly grieved that it is beyond his power; for when I obtain a little leisure from the urgent necessary business of those men, who so press me into their service[4] that I am neither able to escape them nor at liberty to neglect them, there are always subjects to which I must, in dictating to my amanuenses, give the first place, because they are so connected with the present hour as not to admit of being postponed. Of such things one instance was the abridgement of the proceedings at our Conference,[5] a work involving much labour, but necessary, because I saw that no one would attempt the perusal of such a mass of writing; another was a letter to the Donatist laity[6] concerning the said Conference, a document which I have just completed, after labouring at it for several nights; another was the composition of two long letters,[7] one addressed to yourself, my beloved friend, the other to the illustrious Volusianus, which I suppose you both have received; another is a book, with which I am occupied at present, addressed to our friend Honoratus,[8] in regard to five questions proposed by him in a letter to me, and you see that to him I was unquestionably in duty bound to send a prompt

[1] Apringius. See note, p. 471.
[2] Letters CXXXIII. and CXXXIV.

[3] Anaunia, a valley not far from Trent, destined to be so famous for the Council held there. In the month of May, 397 A.D., Martyrius, Sisinnius, and Alexander were killed there by the heathen.
[4] Angariant. See Matt. v. 41.
[5] The Conference presided over by this Marcellinus at Carthage, in the preceding year.
[6] Letter CXLI.
[7] Letters CXXXVII. and CXXXVIII.
[8] Letter CXL.

reply. For love deals with her sons as a nurse does with children, devoting her attention to them not in the order of the love felt for each, but according to the urgency of each case; she gives a preference to the weaker, because she desires to impart to them such strength as is possessed by the stronger, whom she passes by meanwhile not because of her slighting them, but because her mind is at rest in regard to them. Emergencies of this kind, compelling me to employ my amanuenses in writing on subjects which prevent me from using their pens in work much more congenial to the ardent desires of my heart, can never fail to occur, because I have difficulty in obtaining even a very little leisure, amidst the accumulation of business into which, in spite of my own inclinations, I am dragged by other men's wishes or necessities; and what I am to do, I really do not know.

4. You have heard the burdens, for my deliverance from which I wish you to join your prayers with mine; but at the same time I do not wish you to desist from admonishing me, as you do, with such importunity and frequency; your words are not without some effect. I commend at the same time to your Excellency a church planted in Numidia, on behalf of which, in its present necessities, my holy brother and co-bishop Delphinus has been sent by my brethren and co-bishops who share the toils and the dangers of their work in that region. I write no more on this matter, because you will hear all from his own lips when he comes to you. All other necessary particulars you will find in the letters of instruction, which are sent by me to the presbyter either now or by the deacon Peregrinus, so that I need not again repeat them.

May your heart be ever strong in Christ, my lord justly distinguished, and son very much beloved and longed for!

I commend to your Excellency our son Ruffinus, the Provost [1] of Cirta.

LETTER CXLIII.

(A.D. 412.)

TO MARCELLINUS, MY NOBLE LORD, JUSTLY DISTINGUISHED, MY SON VERY MUCH BELOVED, AUGUSTIN SENDS GREETING IN THE LORD.

1. Desiring to reply to the letter which I received from you through our holy brother, my co-bishop Boniface, I have sought for it, but have not found it. I have recalled to mind, however, that you asked me in that letter how the magicians of Pharaoh could, after all the water of Egypt had been turned into blood, find any with which to imitate the miracle.

There are two ways in which the question is commonly answered: either that it was possible for water to have been brought from the sea, or, which is more credible, that these plagues were not inflicted on the district in which the children of Israel were; for the clear, express statements to this effect in some parts of that scriptural narrative entitle us to assume this in places where the statement is omitted.

2. In your other letter, brought to me by the presbyter Urbanus, a question is proposed, taken from a passage not in the Divine Scriptures, but in one of my own books, namely, that which I wrote on *Free Will*. On questions of this kind, however, I do not bestow much labour; because, even if the statement objected to does not admit of unanswerable vindication, it is mine only; it is not an utterance of that Author whose words it is impiety to reject, even when, through our misapprehension of their meaning, the interpretation which we put on them deserves to be rejected. I freely confess, accordingly, that I endeavour to be one of those who write because they have made some progress, and who, by means of writing, make further progress. If, therefore, through inadvertence or want of knowledge, anything has been stated by me which may with good reason be condemned, not only by others who are able to discover this, but also by myself (for if I am making progress, I ought, at least after it has been pointed out, to see it), such a mistake is not to be regarded with surprise or grief, but rather forgiven, and made the occasion of congratulating me, not, of course, on having erred, but on having renounced an error. For there is an extravagant perversity in the self-love of the man who desires other men to be in error, that the fact of his having erred may not be discovered. How much better and more profitable is it that in the points in which he has erred others should not err, so that he may be delivered from his error by their advice, or, if he refuse this, may at least have no followers in his error. For, if God permit me, as I desire, to gather together and point out, in a work devoted to this express purpose, all the things which most justly displease me in my books, men will then see how far I am from being a partial judge in my own case.

3. As for you, however, who love me warmly, if, in opposing those by whom, whether through malice or ignorance or superior intelligence, I am censured, you maintain the position that I have nowhere in my writings made a mistake, you labour in a hopeless enterprise — you have undertaken a bad cause, in which, even if I myself were judge, you must be easily worsted; for it is no pleasure to me that my dearest friends should think me to be such as I am not, since assuredly they love not me, but instead of me

---

[1] *Principalis.*

another under my name, if they love not what I am, but what I am not; for in so far as they know me, or believe what is true concerning me, I am loved by them; but in so far as they ascribe to me what they do not know to be in me, they love another person, such as they suppose me to be. Cicero, the prince of Roman orators, says of some one, "He never uttered a word which he would wish to recall." This commendation, though it seems to be the highest possible, is nevertheless more likely to be true of a consummate fool than of a man perfectly wise; for it is true of idiots,[1] that the more absurd and foolish they are, and the more their opinions diverge from those universally held, the more likely are they to utter no word which they will wish to recall; for to regret an evil, or foolish, or ill-timed word is characteristic of a wise man. If, however, the words quoted are taken in a good sense, as intended to make us believe that some one was such that, by reason of his speaking all things wisely, he never uttered any word which he would wish to recall, — this we are, in accordance with sound piety, to believe rather concerning men of God, who spoke as they were moved by the Holy Ghost, than concerning the man whom Cicero commends. For my part, so far am I from this excellence, that if I have uttered no word which I would wish to recall, it must be because I resemble more the idiot than the wise man. The man whose writings are most worthy of the highest authority is he who has uttered no word, I do not say which it would be his desire, but which it would be his duty to recall. Let him that has not attained to this occupy the second rank through his humility, since he cannot take the first rank through his wisdom. Since he has been unable, with all his care, to exclude every expression whose use may be justly regretted, let him acknowledge his regret for anything which, as he may now have discovered, ought not to have been said.

4. Since, therefore, the words spoken by me which I would if I could recall, are not, as my very dear friends suppose, few or none, but perhaps even more than my enemies imagine, I am not gratified by such commendation as Cicero's sentence, "He never uttered a word which he would wish to recall," but I am deeply distressed by the saying of Horace, "The word once uttered cannot be recalled."[2] This is the reason why I keep beside me, longer than you wish or patiently bear, the books which I have written on difficult and important questions on the book of Genesis and the doctrine of the Trinity, hoping that, if it be impossible to avoid having some things which may deservedly be found fault with, the number of these may at least be smaller than it might

have been, if, through impatient haste, the works had been published without due deliberation; for you, as your letters indicate (our holy brother and co-bishop Florentius having written me to this effect), are urgent for the publication of these works now, in order that they may be defended in my own lifetime by myself, when, perhaps, they may begin to be assailed in some particulars, either through the cavilling of enemies or the misapprehensions of friends. You say this doubtless because you think there is nothing in them which might with justice be censured, otherwise you would not exhort me to publish the books, but rather to revise them more carefully. But I fix my eye rather on those who are true judges, sternly impartial, between whom and myself I wish, in the first place, to make sure of my ground, so that the only faults coming to be censured by them may be those which it was impossible for me to observe, though using the most diligent scrutiny.

5. Notwithstanding what I have just said, I am prepared to defend the sentence in the third book of my treatise on *Free Will*, in which, discoursing on the rational substance, I have expressed my opinion in these words: "The soul, appointed to occupy a body inferior in nature to itself after the entrance of sin, governs its own body, not absolutely according to its free will, but only in so far as the laws of the universe permit." I bespeak the particular attention of those who think that I have here fixed and defined, as ascertained concerning the human soul, either that it comes by propagation from the parents, or that it has, through sins committed in a higher celestial life, incurred the penalty of being shut up in a corruptible body. Let them, I say, observe that the words in question have been so carefully weighed by me, that while they hold fast what I regard as certain, namely, that after the sin of the first man, all other men have been born and continue to be born in that sinful flesh, for the healing of which "the likeness of sinful flesh"[3] came in the person of the Lord, they are also so chosen as not to pronounce upon any one of those four opinions which I have in the sequel expounded and distinguished — not attempting to establish any one of them as preferable to the others, but disposing in the meantime of the matter under discussion, and reserving the consideration of these opinions, so that whichever of them may be true, praise should unhesitatingly be given to God.

6. For whether all souls are derived by propagation from the first, or are in the case of each individual specially created, or being created apart from the body are sent into it, or introduce themselves into it of their own accord, without doubt

[1] *Quos vulgo moriones vocant.*
[2] *Nescit vox missa reverti.*

[3] Rom. viii. 3.

this creature endowed with reason, namely, the human soul — appointed to occupy an inferior, that is, an earthly body — after the entrance of sin, does not govern its own body absolutely according to its free will.[1] For I did not say, "after his sin," or "after he sinned," but after the entrance of sin, that whatever might afterwards, if possible, be determined by reason as to the question whether the sin was his own or the sin of the first parent of mankind, it might be perceived that in saying that "the soul, appointed, after the entrance of sin, to occupy an inferior body, does not govern its body absolutely according to its own free will," I stated what is true; for "the flesh lusteth against the spirit,[2] and in this we groan, being burdened,"[3] and "the corruptible body weighs down the soul,"[4] — in short, who can enumerate all the evils arising from the infirmity of the flesh, which shall assuredly cease when "this corruptible shall have put on incorruption," so that "that which is mortal shall be swallowed up of life"?[5] In that future condition, therefore, the soul shall govern its spiritual body with absolute freedom of will; but in the meantime its freedom is not absolute, but conditioned by the laws of the universe, according to which it is fixed, that bodies having experienced birth experience death, and having grown to maturity decline in old age. For the soul of the first man did, before the entrance of sin, govern his body with perfect freedom of will, although that body was not yet spiritual, but animal; but after the entrance of sin, that is, after sin had been committed in that flesh from which sinful flesh was thenceforward to be propagated, the reasonable soul is so appointed to occupy an inferior body, that it does not govern its body wtih absolute freedom of will. That infant children, even before they have committed any sin of their own, are partakers of sinful flesh, is, in my opinion, proved by their requiring to have it healed in them also, by the application in their baptism of the remedy provided in Him who came in the likeness of sinful flesh. But even those who do not acquiesce in this view have no just ground for taking offence at the sentence quoted from my book; for it is certain, if I am not mistaken, that even if the infirmity be the consequence not of sin, but of nature, it was at all events only after the entrance of sin that bodies having this infirmity began to be produced; for Adam was not created thus, and he did not beget any offspring before he sinned.

7. Let my critics, therefore, seek other passages to censure, not only in my other more hastily published works, but also in these books of mine on *Free Will*. For I by no means deny that they may in this search discover opportunities of conferring a benefit on me; for if the books, having passed into so many hands, cannot now be corrected, I myself may, being still alive. Those words, however, so carefully selected by me to avoid committing myself to any one of the four opinions or theories regarding the soul's origin, are liable to censure only from those who think that my hesitation as to any definite view in a matter so obscure is blameworthy; against whom I do not defend myself by saying that I think it right to pronounce no opinion whatever on the subject, seeing that I have no doubt either that the soul is immortal — not in the same sense in which God is immortal, who alone hath immortality,[6] but in a certain way peculiar to itself — or that the soul is a creature and not a part of the substance of the Creator, or as to any other thing which I regard as most certain concerning its nature. But seeing that the obscurity of this most mysterious subject, the origin of the soul, compels me to do as I have done, let them rather stretch out a friendly hand to me, confessing my ignorance, and desiring to know whatever is the truth on the subject; and let them, if they can, teach or demonstrate to me what they may either have learned by the exercise of sound reason, or have believed on indisputably plain testimony of the divine oracles. For if reason be found contradicting the authority of Divine Scriptures, it only deceives by a semblance of truth, however acute it be, for its deductions cannot in that case be true. On the other hand, if, against the most manifest and reliable testimony of reason, anything be set up claiming to have the authority of the Holy Scriptures, he who does this does it through a misapprehension of what he has read, and is setting up against the truth not the real meaning of Scripture, which he has failed to discover, but an opinion of his own; he alleges not what he has found in the Scriptures, but what he has found in himself as their interpreter.

8. Let me give an example, to which I solicit your earnest attention. In a passage near the end of Ecclesiastes, where the author is speaking of man's dissolution through death separating the soul from the body, it is written, "Then shall the dust return to the earth as it was, and the spirit shall return unto God who gave it."[7] A statement having the authority on which this one is based is true beyond all dispute, and is not intended to deceive any one; yet if any one wishes to put upon it such an interpretation as may help him in attempting to support the theory of the propagation of souls, according to

---

[1] The text being here obscure, we have followed the MSS., which omit the words, "interim quod constat peccatum primi hominis."
[2] Gal. v. 17.
[3] 2 Cor. v. 4.
[4] Wisd. ix. 15.
[5] 1 Cor. xv. 53.

[6] 1 Tim. vi. 16.
[7] Eccles. xii. 7.

which all other souls are derived from that one which God gave to the first man, what is there said concerning the body under the name of " dust " (for obviously nothing else than body and soul are to be understood by " dust " and " spirit " in this passage) seems to favour his view ; for he may affirm that the soul is said to return to God because of its being derived from the original stock of that soul which God gave to the first man, in the same way as the body is said to return to the dust because of its being derived from the original stock of that body which was made of dust in the first man, and therefore may argue that, from what we know perfectly as to the body, we ought to believe what is hidden from our observation as to the soul ; for there is no difference of opinion as to the original stock of the body, but there is as to the original stock of the soul. In the text thus brought forward as a proof, statements are made concerning both, as if the manner of the return of each to its original was precisely similar in both, — the body, on the one hand, returning to the earth as it was, for thence was it taken when the first man was formed ; the soul, on the other hand, returning to God, for He gave it when He breathed into the nostrils of the man whom He had formed the breath of life, and he became a living soul,[1] so that thenceforward the propagation of each part should go on from the corresponding part in the parent.

9. If, however, the true account of the soul's origin be, that God gives to each individual man a soul, not propagated from that first soul, but created in some other way, the statement that the " spirit returns to God who gave it," is equally consistent with this view. The two other opinions regarding the soul's origin are, then, the only ones which seem to be excluded by this text. For in the first place, as to the opinion that every man's soul is made separately within him at the time of his creation, it is supposed that, if this were the case, the soul should have been spoken of as returning, not to God who gave it, but to God who made it ; for the word " gave " seems to imply that that which could be given had already a separate existence. The words " returneth to God " are further insisted upon by some, who say, How could it return to a place where it had never been before ? Accordingly they maintain that, if the soul is to be believed to have never been with God before, the words should have been " it goes," or " goes on," or " goes away," rather than it " returns " to God. In like manner, as to the opinion that each soul glides of its own accord into its body, it is not easy to explain how this theory is reconcilable with the statement that God gave it.

The words of this scriptural passage are consequently somewhat adverse to these two opinions, namely, the one which supposes each soul to be created in its own body, and the one which supposes each soul to introduce itself into its own body spontaneously. But there is no difficulty in showing that the words are consistent with either of the other two opinions, namely, that all souls are derived by propagation from the one first created, or that, having been created and kept in readiness with God, they are given to each body as required.

10. Nevertheless, even if the theory that each soul is created in its own body may not be wholly excluded by this text, — for if its advocates affirm that God is here said to have given the spirit (or the soul) in the same way as He is said to have given us eyes, ears, hands, or other such members, which were not made elsewhere by Him, and kept in store that He might give them, i.e. add and join them to our bodies, but are made by Him in that body to which He is said to have given them, — I do not see what could be said in reply, unless, perchance, the opinion could be refuted, either by other passages of Scripture, or by valid reasoning. In like manner, those who think that each soul flows of its own accord into its body take the words " God gave it " in the sense in which it is said, " He gave them up to uncleanness, through the lusts of their own hearts."[2] Only one word, therefore, remains apparently irreconcilable with the theory that each soul is made in its own body, namely, the word " returneth," in the expression " returneth to God ; " for in what sense can the soul return to Him with whom it has not formerly been ? By this one word alone are the supporters of this one of the four opinions embarrassed. And yet I do not think that this opinion ought to be held as refuted by this one word, for it may be possible to show that in the ordinary style of scriptural language it may be quite correct to use the word " return," as signifying the spirit created by God returns to Him not because of its having been with Him before its union with the body, but because of its having received being from His creative power.

11. I have written these things in order to show that whoever is disposed to maintain and vindicate any one of these four theories of the soul's origin, must bring forward, either from the Scriptures received into ecclesiastical authority, passages which do not admit of any other interpretation, — as the statement that God made man, — or reasonings founded on premises so obviously true that to call them in question would be madness, such as the statement that

---

[1] Gen. ii. 7.   [2] Rom. i. 24.

none but the living are capable of knowledge or of error; for a statement like this does not require the authority of Scripture to prove its truth, as if the common sense of mankind did not of itself announce its truth with such transparent cogency of reason, that whoever contradicts it must be held to be hopelessly mad. If any one is able to produce such arguments in discussing the very obscure question of the soul's origin, let him help me in my ignorance; but if he cannot do this, let him forbear from blaming my hesitation on the question.

12. As to the virginity of the Holy Mary, if what I have written on this subject does not suffice to prove that it was possible, we must refuse to believe every record of anything miraculous having taken place in the body of any. If, however, the objection to believing this miracle is, that it happened only once, ask the friend who is still perplexed by this, whether instances may not be quoted from secular literature of events which were, like this one, unique, and which, nevertheless, are believed, not merely as fables are believed by the simple, but with that faith with which the history of facts is received — ask him, I beseech you, this question. For if he says that nothing of this kind is to be found in these writings, he ought to have such instances pointed out to him; if he admits this, the question is decided by his admission.

LETTER CXLIV.

(A.D. 412.)

TO MY HONOURABLE AND JUSTLY ESTEEMED LORDS, THE INHABITANTS OF CIRTA, OF ALL RANKS, BRETHREN DEARLY BELOVED AND LONGED FOR, BISHOP AUGUSTIN SENDS GREETING.

1. If that which greatly distressed me in your town has now been removed; if the obduracy of hearts which resisted most evident and, as we might call it, notorious truth, has by the force of truth been overcome; if the sweetness of peace is relished, and the love which tends to unity is the occasion no longer of pain to eyes diseased, but of light and vigour to eyes restored to health,—this is God's work, not ours; on no account would I ascribe these results to human efforts, even had such a remarkable conversion of your whole community taken place when I was with you, and in connection with my own preaching and exhortations. The operation and the success are His who, by His servants, calls men's attention outwardly by the signs of things, and Himself teaches men inwardly by the things themselves. The fact, however, that whatever praiseworthy change has been wrought among you is to be ascribed not to us, but to Him who

alone doeth wonderful works,[1] is no reason for our being more reluctant to be persuaded to visit you. For we ought to hasten much more readily to see the works of God than our own works, for we ourselves also, if we be of service in any work, owe this not to men but to Him; wherefore the apostle says, "Neither is he that planteth anything, neither he that watereth: but God that giveth the increase."[2]

2. You allude in your letter to a fact which I also remember from classic literature, that by discoursing on the benefits of temperance, Xenocrates suddenly converted Polemo from a dissipated to a sober life, though this man was not only habitually intemperate, but was actually intoxicated at the time. Now although this was, as you have wisely and truthfully apprehended, a case not of conversion to God, but of emancipation from the thraldom of self-indulgence, I would not ascribe even the amount of improvement wrought in him to the work of man, but to the work of God. For even in the body, the lowest part of our nature, all excellent things, such as beauty, vigour, health, and so on, are the work of God, to whom nature owes its creation and perfection; how much more certain, therefore, must it be that no other can impart excellent properties to the soul! For what imagination of human folly could be more full of pride and ingratitude than the notion that, although God alone can give comeliness to the body, it belongs to man to give purity to the soul? It is written in the book of Christian Wisdom, "I perceived that no one can have self-restraint unless God give it to him, and that this is a part of true wisdom to know whose gift it is."[3] If, therefore, Polemo, when he exchanged a life of dissipation for a life of sobriety, had so understood whence the gift came, that, renouncing the superstitions of the heathen, he had rendered worship to the Divine Giver, he would then have become not only temperate, but truly wise and savingly religious, which would have secured to him not merely the practice of virtue in this life, but also the possession of immortality in the life to come. How much less, then, should I presume to take to myself the honour of your conversion, or of that of your people which you have now reported to me, which, when I was neither speaking to you nor even present with you, was accomplished unquestionably by divine power in all in whom it has really taken place. This, therefore, know above all things, meditate on this with devout humility. To God, my brethren, to God give thanks. Fear Him, that ye may not go backward: love Him, that ye may go forward.[4]

---

[1] Ps. lxxii. 18.
[2] 1 Cor. iii. 7.
[3] Wisd. viii. 21.
[4] *Deum timete ne deficiatis, amate ut proficiatis.*

3. If, however, love of men still keeps some secretly alienated from the flock of Christ, while fear of other men constrains them to a feigned reconciliation, I charge all such to consider that before God the conscience of man has no covering, and that they can neither impose on Him as a Witness, nor escape from Him as a Judge. But if, by reason of anxiety as to their own salvation, anything as to the question of the unity of Christ's flock perplex them, let them make this demand upon themselves, — and it seems to me a most just demand, — that in regard to the Catholic Church, *i.e.* the Church spread abroad over the whole world, they believe rather the words of Divine Scripture than the calumnies of human tongues. Moreover, with respect to the schism which has arisen among men (who assuredly, whatsoever they may be, do not frustrate the promises of God to Abraham, "In thy seed shall all the nations of the earth be blessed," [1] — promises believed when brought to their ears as a prophecy, but denied, forsooth, when set before their eyes as an accomplished fact), let them meanwhile ponder this one very brief, but, if I mistake not, unanswerable argument: the question out of which the dispute arose either has or has not been tried before ecclesiastical tribunals beyond the sea; if it has not been tried before these, then no guilt in this matter is chargeable on the whole flock of Christ in the nations beyond the sea, in communion with which we rejoice, and therefore their separation from these guiltless communities is an act of impious schism; if, on the other hand, the question has been tried before the tribunal of these churches, who does not understand and feel, nay, who does not see, that those whose communion is now separated from these churches were the party defeated in the trial? Let them therefore choose to whom they should prefer to give credence, whether to the ecclesiastical judges who decided the question, or to the complaints of the vanquished litigants. Observe wisely how impossible it is for them reasonably to answer this brief and most intelligible dilemma; nevertheless, it were easier to turn Polemo from a life of intemperance, than to drive them out of the madness of inveterate error.

Pardon me, my noble and worthy lords, brethren most dearly beloved and longed for, for writing you a letter more prolix than agreeable, but fitted, as I think, to benefit rather than to flatter you. As to my coming to you, may God fulfil the desire which we both equally cherish! For I cannot express in words, but I am sure you will gladly believe, with what fervour of love I burn to see you.

LETTER CXLV.

(A.D. 412 OR 413.)

TO ANASTASIUS, MY HOLY AND BELOVED LORD AND BROTHER, AUGUSTIN SENDS GREETING IN THE LORD.

1. A most satisfactory opportunity of saluting your genuine worth is furnished by our brethren Lupicinus and Concordialis, honourable servants of God, from whom, even without my writing, you might learn all that is going on among us here. But knowing, as I do, how much you love us in Christ, because of your knowing how warmly your love is reciprocated by us in Him, I was sure that it might have disappointed you if you had seen them, and could not but know that they had come directly from us, and were most intimately united in friendship with us, and yet had received with them no letter from me. Besides this, I am owing you a reply, for I am not aware of having written to you since I received your last letter; so great are the cares by which I am encumbered and distracted, that I know not whether I have written or not before now.

2. We desire eagerly to know how you are, and whether the Lord has given you some rest, so far as in this world He can bestow it; for "if one member be honoured, all the members rejoice with it;" [2] and so it is almost always our experience, that when, in the midst of our anxieties, we turn our thoughts to some of our brethren placed in a condition of comparative rest, we are in no small measure revived, as if in them we ourselves enjoyed a more peaceful and tranquil life. At the same time, when vexatious cares are multiplied in this uncertain life, they compel us to long for the everlasting rest. For this world is more dangerous to us in pleasant than in painful hours, and is to be guarded against more when it allures us to love it than when it warns and constrains us to despise it. For although "all that is in the world" is "the lust of the flesh, and the lust of the eyes, and the pride of life," [3] nevertheless, even in the case of men who prefer to these the things which are spiritual, unseen, and eternal, the sweetness of earthly things insinuates itself into our affections, and accompanies our steps on the path of duty with its seductive allurements. For the violence with which present things acquire sway over our weakness is exactly proportioned to the superior value by which future things command our love. And oh that those who have learned to observe and bewail this may succeed in overcoming and escaping from this power of terrestrial things! Such victory and

---

[1] Gen. xxvi. 4.

[2] 1 Cor. xii. 26.
[3] 1 John ii. 16.

emancipation cannot, without God's grace, be achieved by the human will, which is by no means to be called free so long as it is subject to prevailing and enslaving lusts; "For of whom a man is overcome, of the same is he brought in bondage."[1] And the Son of God has Himself said, "If the Son shall make you free, ye shall be free indeed."[2]

3. The law, therefore, by teaching and commanding what cannot be fulfilled without grace, demonstrates to man his weakness, in order that the weakness thus proved may resort to the Saviour, by whose healing the will may be able to do what in its feebleness it found impossible. So, then, the law brings us to faith, faith obtains the Spirit in fuller measure, the Spirit sheds love abroad in us, and love fulfils the law. For this reason the law is called a "schoolmaster,"[3] under whose threatenings and severity "whosoever shall call upon the name of the Lord shall be delivered."[4] But how shall they call on Him in whom they have not believed?"[5] Wherefore unto them that believe and call on Him the quickening Spirit is given, lest the letter without the Spirit should kill them.[6] But by the Holy Ghost, which is given unto us, the love of God is shed abroad in our hearts,[7] so that the words of the same apostle, "Love is the fulfilling of the law,"[8] are realized. So the law is good to the man who uses it lawfully;[9] and he uses it lawfully who, understanding wherefore it was given, betakes himself, under the pressure of its threatenings, to grace, which sets him free. Whoever unthankfully despises this grace, by which the ungodly are justified, and trusts in his own strength, as if he thereby could fulfil the law, being ignorant of God's righteousness, and going about to establish his own righteousness, is not submitting himself to the righteousness of God;[10] and thus the law becomes to him not a help to pardon, but the bond fastening his guilt to him. Not that the law is evil, but because sin worketh death in such persons by that which is good.[11] For by occasion of the commandment he sins more grievously who, by the commandment, knows how evil are the sins which he commits.

4. In vain, however, does any one think himself to have gained the victory over sin, if, through nothing but fear of punishment, he refrains from sin; because, although the outward action to which an evil desire prompts him is not performed, the evil desire itself within the man is an enemy unsubdued. And who is found innocent in God's sight who is willing to do the sin which is forbidden if you only remove the punishment which is feared? And consequently, even in the volition itself, he is guilty of sin who wishes to do what is unlawful, but refrains from doing it because it cannot be done with impunity; for, so far as he is concerned, he would prefer that there were no righteousness forbidding and punishing sins. And assuredly, if he would prefer that there should be no righteousness, who can doubt that he would if he could abolish it altogether? How, then, can that man be called righteous who is such an enemy to righteousness that, if he had the power, he would abolish its authority, that he might not be subject to its threatenings or its penalties? He, then, is an enemy to righteousness who refrains from sin only through fear of punishment; but he will become the friend of righteousness if through love of it he sin not, for then he will be really afraid to sin. For the man who only fears the flames of hell is afraid not of sinning, but of being burned; but the man who hates sin as much as he hates hell is afraid to sin. This is the "fear of the Lord," which "is pure, enduring for ever."[12] For the fear of punishment has torment, and is not in love; and love, when it is perfect, casts it out.[13]

5. Moreover, every one hates sin just in proportion as he loves righteousness; which he will be enabled to do not through the law putting him in fear by the letter of its prohibitions, but by the Spirit healing him by grace. Then that is done which the apostle enjoins in the admonition, "I speak after the manner of men because of the infirmity of your flesh: for as ye have yielded your members servants to uncleanness and to iniquity unto iniquity, even so now yield your members servants to righteousness unto holiness."[14] For what is the force of the conjunctions "as" and "even so," if it be not this: "As no fear compelled you to sin, but the desire for it, and the pleasure taken in sin, even so let not the fear of punishment drive you to a life of righteousness; but let the pleasure found in righteousness and the love you bear to it draw you to practise it"? And even this is, as it seems to me, a righteousness, so to speak, somewhat mature, but not perfect. For he would not have prefaced the admonition with the words, "I speak after the manner of men because of the infirmity of your flesh," had there not been something else that ought to have been said if they had been by that time able to bear it. For surely more devoted service is due to righteousness

---

1 2 Pet. ii. 19.
2 John viii. 36.
3 Gal. iii. 24.
4 Joel ii. 32.
5 Rom. x. 14.
6 2 Cor. iii. 6.
7 Rom. v. 5.
8 Rom. xiii. 10.
9 1 Tim. i. 8.
10 Rom x. 3.
11 Rom. vii. 13.

12 Ps. xix. 9.
13 1 John iv. 18.
14 Rom. vi. 19.

than men are wont to yield to sin. For pain of body restrains men, if not from the desire of sin, at least from the commission of sinful actions; and we should not easily find any one who would openly commit a sin procuring to him an impure and unlawful gratification, if it was certain that the penalty of torture would immediately follow the crime. But righteousness ought to be so loved that not even bodily sufferings should hinder us from doing its works, but that, even when we are in the hands of cruel enemies, our good works should so shine before men that those who are capable of taking pleasure therein may glorify our Father who is in heaven.[1]

6. Hence it comes that that most devoted lover of righteousness exclaims, "Who shall separate us from the love of Christ? shall tribulation, or distress, or persecution, or famine, or nakedness, or peril, or sword? (As it is written, For Thy sake we are killed all the day long; we are accounted as sheep for the slaughter.) Nay, in all these things we are more than conquerors through Him that loved us. For I am persuaded, that neither death, nor life, nor angels, nor principalities, nor powers, nor things present, nor things to come, nor height, nor depth, nor any other creature, shall be able to separate us from the love of God, which is in Christ Jesus our Lord."[2] Observe how he does not say simply, "Who shall separate us from Christ?" but, indicating that by which we cling to Christ, he says, "Who shall separate us from the love of Christ?" We cling to Christ, then, by love, not by fear of punishment. Again, after having enumerated those things which seem to be sufficiently fierce, but have not sufficient force to effect a separation, he has, in the conclusion, called that the love of God which he had previously spoken of as the love of Christ. And what is this "love of Christ" but love of righteousness? for it is said of Him that He "is made of God unto us wisdom, and righteousness, and sanctification, and redemption: that, according as it is written, He that glorieth, let him glory in the Lord."[3] As, therefore he is superlatively wicked who is not deterred even by the penalty of bodily sufferings from the vile works of sordid pleasure, so is he superlatively righteous who is not restrained even by the fear of bodily sufferings from the holy works of most glorious love.

7. This love of God, which must be maintained by unremitting, devout meditation, "is shed abroad in our hearts by the Holy Ghost, which is given to us,"[4] so that he who glories in it must glory in the Lord. Forasmuch, therefore, as we feel ourselves to be poor and destitute of that love by which the law is most truly fulfilled, we ought not to expect and demand its riches from our own indigence, but to ask, seek, and knock in prayer, that He with whom is "the fountain of life" "may satisfy us abundantly with the fatness of His house, and make us drink of the river of His pleasures,"[5] so that, watered and revived by its full flood, we may not only escape from being swallowed up by sorrow, but may even "glory in tribulations: knowing that tribulation worketh patience; and patience, experience; and experience, hope: and hope maketh not ashamed;" — not that we can do this of ourselves, but "because the love of God is shed abroad in our hearts by the Holy Ghost, which is given to us."[6]

8. It has been a pleasure to me to say, at least by a letter, these things which I could not say when you were present. I write them, not in reference to yourself, for you do not affect high things, but are contented with that which is lowly,[7] but in reference to some who arrogate too much to the human will, imagining that, the law being given, the will is of its own strength sufficient to fulfil that law, though not assisted by any grace imparted by the Holy Spirit, in addition to instruction in the law; and by their reasonings they persuade the wretched and impoverished weakness of man to believe that it is not our duty to pray that we may not enter into temptation. Not that they dare openly to say this; but this is, whether they acknowledge it or not, an inevitable consequence of their doctrine.[8] For wherefore is it said to us, "Watch and pray, that ye enter not into temptation;"[9] and wherefore was it that, when He was teaching us to pray, He prescribed, in accordance with this injunction, the use of the petition "lead us not into temptation,"[10] if this be wholly in the power of the will of man, and does not require the help of divine grace in order to its accomplishment?

Why should I say more? Salute the brethren who are with you, and pray for us, that we may be saved with that salvation of which it is said, "They that are whole need not a physician, but they that are sick: I came not to call the righteous, but sinners."[11] Pray, therefore, for us that we may be righteous, — an attainment wholly beyond a man's reach, unless he know righteousness and be willing to practise it, but one which is immediately realized when he is perfectly willing; but this full consent of his will can

---

[1] Matt. v. 16.
[2] Rom. viii. 35-39.
[3] 1 Cor. i. 30, 31; Jer. ix. 24.
[4] Rom. v. 5.

[5] Ps. xxxvi. 8, 9.
[6] Rom. v. 3-5.
[7] Rom. xii. 16.
[8] The heresy of Pelagius is obviously alluded to here as having begun thus early (A.D. 413) to command attention.
[9] Matt. xxiv. 41.
[10] Matt. vi. 13.
[11] Matt. ix. 12, 13.

never be in him unless he is healed and assisted by the grace of the Spirit.

LETTER CXLVI.

(A.D. 413.)

TO PELAGIUS, MY LORD GREATLY BELOVED, AND BROTHER GREATLY LONGED FOR, AUGUSTIN SENDS GREETING IN THE LORD.

I thank you very much for your consideration in making me glad by a letter from you, and informing me of your welfare. May the Lord recompense you with those blessings by the possession of which you may be good for ever, and may live eternally with Him who is eternal, my lord greatly beloved, and brother greatly longed for. Although I do not acknowledge that anything in me deserves the eulogies which the letter of your Benevolence contains concerning me, nevertheless I cannot but be grateful for the goodwill therein manifested towards one so insignificant, while suggesting at the same time that you should rather pray for me that I may be made by the Lord such as you suppose me already to be.

(*In another hand*) May you enjoy safety and the Lord's favour, and be mindful of us![1]

LETTER CXLVIII.

(A.D. 413.)

A LETTER OF INSTRUCTIONS (COMMONITORIUM) TO THE HOLY BROTHER FORTUNATIANUS.[2]

CHAP. I. — 1. I write this to remind you of the request which I made when I was with you, that you would do me the kindness of visiting our brother, whom we mentioned in conversation, in order to ask him to forgive me, if he has construed as a harsh and unfriendly attack upon himself any statement made by me in a recent letter (which I do not regret having written), affirming that the eyes of this body cannot see God, and never shall see Him. I added immediately the reason why I made this statement, namely, to prevent men from believing that God Himself is corporeal and visible, as occupying a place determined by size and by distance from us (for the eye of this body can see nothing except under these conditions), and to prevent men from understanding the expression "face to face"[3] as if God were limited within the

members of a body. Therefore I do not regret having made this statement, as a protest against our forming such unworthy and profane ideas concerning God as to think that He is not everywhere in His totality, but susceptible of division, and distributed through localities in space; for such are the only objects cognizable through these eyes of ours.

2. But if, while holding no such opinion as this concerning God, but believing Him to be a Spirit, unchangeable, incorporeal, present in His whole Being everywhere, any one thinks that the change on this body of ours (when from being a natural body it shall become a spiritual body) will be so great that in such a body it will be possible for us to see a spiritual substance not susceptible of division according to local distance or dimension, or even confined within the limits of bodily members, but everywhere present in its totality, I wish him to instruct me in this matter, if what he has discovered is true; but if in this opinion he is mistaken, it is far less objectionable to ascribe to the body something that does not belong to it, than to take away from God that which belongs to Him. And even if that opinion be correct, it will not contradict my words in that letter; for I said that the eyes of this body shall not see God, meaning that the eyes of this body of ours can see nothing but bodies which are separated from them by some interval of space, for if there be no interval, even bodies themselves cannot through the eyes be seen by us.

3. Moreover, if our bodies shall be changed into something so different from what they now are as to have eyes by means of which a substance shall be seen which is not diffused through space or confined within limits, having one part in one place, another in another, a smaller in a less space, a greater in a larger, but in its totality spiritually present everywhere, — these bodies shall be something very different from what they are at present, and shall no longer be themselves, and shall be not only freed from mortality, and corruption, and weight, but somehow or other shall be changed into the quality of the mind itself, if they shall be able to see in a manner which shall be then granted to the mind, but which is meanwhile not granted even to the mind itself. For if, when a man's habits are changed, we say he is not the man he was, — if, when our age is changed, we say that the body is not what it was, how much more may we say that the body shall not be the same when it shall have undergone so great a change as not only to have immortal life, but also to have power to see Him who is invisible? Wherefore, if they shall thus see God, it is not with the eyes of this body that He shall be seen, because in this also it shall not be the same body, since it has been

---

[1] Pelagius made use of this letter at the Council of Diospolis, in A.D. 415, which compelled Augustin to vindicate himself in reference to it in his narrative of the proceedings of Pelagius. See *Anti-Pelagian Writings*, vol. i. p. 413.

[2] Fortunatianus, Bishop of Sicqua, was one of the seven bishops selected to represent the Catholics in the Conference of Carthage with the Donatists in 411. He was probably a neighbour of the bishop who had regarded himself as aggrieved by the arguments with which Augustin confuted some extravagant speculations of his.

[3] 1 Cor. xiii. 12.

changed to so great an extent in capacity and power ; and this opinion is, therefore, not contrary to the words of my letter. If, however, the body shall be changed only to this extent, that whereas now it is mortal, then it shall be immortal, and whereas now it weighs down the soul, then, devoid of weight, it shall be most ready for every motion, but unchanged in the faculty of seeing objects which are discerned by their dimensions and distances, it will still be utterly impossible for it to see a substance that is incorporeal and is in its totality present everywhere. Whether, therefore, the former or the latter supposition be correct, in both cases it remains true that the eyes of this body shall not see God ; or if they are to see Him, they shall not be the eyes of *this* body, since after so great a change they shall be the eyes of a body very different from this.

4. But if this brother is able to propound anything better on this subject, I am ready to learn either from himself or from his instructor. If I were saying this ironically, I would also say that I am prepared to learn concerning God that He has a body having members, and is divisible in different localities in space ; which I do not say, because I am not speaking ironically, and I am perfectly certain that God is not in any respect of such a nature ; and I wrote that letter to prevent men from believing Him to be such. In that letter, being carried away by my zeal to warn against error, and writing more freely because I did not name the person whose views I assailed, I was too vehement and not sufficiently guarded, and did not consider as I ought to have done the respect which was due by one brother and bishop to the office of another : this I do not defend, but blame ; this I condemn rather than excuse, and beg that it may be forgiven. I entreat him to remember our old friendship, and forget my recent offence. Let him do that which he is displeased with me for not having done ; let him exhibit in granting pardon the gentleness which I have failed to show in writing that letter. I thus ask, through your kindly mediation, what I had resolved to ask of him in person if I had had an opportunity. I indeed made an effort to obtain an interview with him (a venerable man, worthy of being honoured by us all, writing to request it in my name), but he declined to come, suspecting, I suppose, that, as very often happens among men, some plot was prepared against him. Of my absolute innocence of such guile, I beg you to do your utmost to assure him, which by seeing him personally you can more easily do. State to him with what deep and genuine grief I conversed with you about my having hurt his feelings. Let him know how far I am from slighting him, how much in him I fear God, and am mindful of

our Head in whose body we are brethren. My reason for thinking it better not to go to the place in which he resides was, that we might not make ourselves a laughing-stock to those without the pale of the Church, thereby bringing grief to our friends and shame to ourselves. All this may be satisfactorily arranged through the good offices of your Holiness and Charity ; nay, rather, the satisfactory issue is in the hands of Him who, by the faith which is His gift, dwells in your heart, whom I am confident that our brother does not refuse to honour in you, since he knows Christ experimentally as dwelling in himself.

5. I, at all events, do not know what I could do better in this case than ask pardon from the brother who has complained that he was wounded by the harshness of my letter. He will, I hope, do what he knows to be enjoined on him by Him who, speaking through the apostle, says : " Forgiving one another, if any man have a quarrel against any : even as God in Christ has forgiven you ; " [1] " Be ye therefore followers of God, as dear children ; and walk in love, as Christ also hath loved us." [2] Walking in this love, let us inquire with oneness of heart, and, if possible, with yet greater diligence than hitherto, into the nature of the spiritual body which we shall have after our resurrection. " And if in anything we be diversely minded, God shall reveal even this unto us," [3] if we abide in Him. Now he who dwelleth in love dwelleth in God, for " God is love," [4] — whether as the fountain of love in its ineffable essence, or as the fountain whence He freely gives it to us by His Spirit. If, then, it can be shown that love can at any time become visible to our bodily eyes, then we grant that possibly God shall be so too ; but if love never can become visible, much less can He who is Himself its Fountain or whatever other figurative name more excellent or more appropriate can be employed in speaking of One so great.

CHAP. II. — 6. Some men of great gifts, and very learned in the Holy Scriptures, who have, when an opportunity presented itself, done much by their writings to benefit the Church and promote the instruction of believers, have said that the invisible God is seen in an invisible manner, that is, by that nature which in us also is invisible, namely, a pure mind or heart. The holy Ambrose, when speaking of Christ as the Word, says : " Jesus is seen not by the bodily, but by the spiritual eyes ; " and shortly after he adds : " The Jews saw Him not, for their foolish heart was blinded," [5] showing in this way how Christ is seen. Also, when he was speaking of the

---

[1] Col. iii. 13.
[2] Eph. v. 1, 2.
[3] Phil. iii. 15, 16.
[4] 1 John iv. 16.
[5] Ambrosius, Lib. i. *in Luc.* c. i.

Holy Spirit, he introduced the words of the Lord, saying: "I will pray the Father, and He shall give you another Comforter, that He may abide with you for ever, even the Spirit of truth; whom the world cannot receive, because it seeth Him not, neither knoweth Him;"[1] and adds: "With good reason, therefore, did He show Himself in the body, since in the substance of His Godhead He is not seen. We have seen the Spirit, but in a bodily form: let us see the Father also; but since we cannot see Him, let us hear Him." A little after he says: "Let us hear the Father, then, for the Father is invisible; but the Son also is invisible as regards His Godhead, for 'no man hath seen God at any time;'[2] and since the Son is God, He is certainly not seen in that in which He is God."[3]

7. The holy Jerome also says: "The eye of man cannot see God as He is in His own nature; and this is true not of man only; neither angels, nor thrones, nor powers, nor principalities, nor any name which is named can see God, for no creature can see its Creator." By these words this very learned man sufficiently shows what his opinion was on this subject in regard not only to the present life, but also to that which is to come. For however much the eyes of our body may be changed for the better, they shall only be made equal to the eyes of the angels. Here, however, Jerome has affirmed that the nature of the Creator is invisible even to the angels, and to every creature without exception in heaven. If, however, a question arise on this point, and a doubt is expressed whether we shall not be superior to the angels, the mind of the Lord Himself is plain from the words which He uses in speaking of those who shall rise again to the kingdom: "They shall be equal unto the angels."[4] Whence the same holy Jerome thus expresses himself in another passage: "Man, therefore, cannot see the face of God, but the angels of the least in the Church do always behold the face of God.[5] And now we see as in a mirror darkly, in a riddle, but then face to face;[6] when from being men we shall advance to the rank of angels, and shall be able to say with the apostle, 'We all, with unveiled face, beholding as in a mirror the glory of the Lord, are changed into the same image, from glory to glory, even as by the Spirit of the Lord;'[7] although no creature can see the face of God, according to the essential properties of His nature, and He is, in these cases, seen by the mind, since He is believed to be invisible."[8]

8. In these words of this man of God there are many things deserving our consideration: first, that in accordance with the very clear declaration of the Lord, he also is of opinion that we shall then see the face of God when we shall have advanced to the rank of angels, that is, shall be made equal to the angels, which doubtless shall be at the resurrection of the dead. Next, he has sufficiently explained by the testimony of the apostle, that the face is to be understood not of the outward but of the inward man, when it is said we shall "see face to face;" for the apostle was speaking of the face of the heart when he used the words quoted in this connection by Jerome: "We, with unveiled face, beholding as in a mirror the glory of the Lord, are changed into the same image."[9] If any one doubt this, let him examine the passage again, and notice of what the apostle was speaking, namely, of the veil, which remains on the heart of every one in reading the Old Testament, until he pass over to Christ, that the veil may be removed. For he there says: "We also, with unveiled face, beholding as in a mirror the glory of the Lord," — which face had not been unveiled in the Jews, of whom he says, "the veil is upon their heart," — in order to show that the face unveiled in us when the veil is taken away is the face of the heart. In fine, lest any one, looking on these things with too little care and therefore failing to discern their meaning, should believe that God now is or shall hereafter be visible either to angels or to men, when they shall have been made equal to the angels, he has most plainly expressed his opinion by affirming that "no creature can see the face of God according to the essential properties of His nature," and that "He is, in these cases, seen by the mind, since He is believed to be invisible." From these statements he sufficiently showed that when God has been seen by men through the eyes of the body as if He had a body, He has not been seen as to the essential properties of his nature, in which He is seen by the mind, since He is believed to be invisible — invisible, that is to say, to the bodily perception even of celestial beings, as Jerome had said above, of angels, and powers, and principalities. How much more, then, is He invisible to terrestrial beings!

9. Wherefore, in another place, Jerome says in still plainer terms, it is true not only of the divinity of the Father but equally of that of the Son and of that of the Holy Spirit, forming one nature in the Trinity, that it cannot be seen by the eyes of the flesh, but by the eyes of the mind, of which the Saviour Himself says: "Blessed are the pure in heart, for they shall see God."[10]

1 John xiv. 16, 17.
2 1 John iv. 12.
3 Ambrosius, Lib. ii. *in Luc.* c. iii. v. 22.
4 Luke xx. 36.
5 Matt. xviii. 10.
6 1 Cor. xiii. 12.
7 2 Cor. iii. 18.
8 Hieron. lib. i. *in Isai,* i.

9 2 Cor. iii. 18.
10 Hieron. lib. iii. *in Isa,* i.

What could be more clear than this statement? For if he had merely said that it is impossible for the divinity of the Father, or of the Son, or of the Holy Spirit, to be seen by the eyes of the flesh, and had not added the words, "but only by the eyes of the mind," it might perhaps have been said, that when the body shall have become spiritual it can no longer be called "flesh;" but by adding the words, "but only by the eyes of the mind," he has excluded the vision of God from every sort of body. Lest, however, any one should suppose that he was speaking only of the present state of being, observe that he has subjoined also a testimony of the Lord, quoted with the design of defining the eyes of the mind of which he had spoken; in which testimony a promise is given not of present, but of future vision: "Blessed are the pure in heart, for they *shall* see God."

10. The very blessed Athanasius, also, Bishop of Alexandria, when contending against the Arians, who affirm that the Father alone is invisible, but suppose the Son and the Holy Spirit to be visible, asserted the equal invisibility of all the Persons of the Trinity, proving it by testimonies from Holy Scripture, and arguing with all his wonted care in controversy, labouring earnestly to convince his opponents that God has never been seen, except through His assuming the form of a creature; and that in His essential Deity God is invisible, that is, that the Father, the Son, and the Holy Spirit are invisible, except in so far as the Divine Persons can be known by the mind and the spirit. Gregory, also, a holy Eastern bishop, very plainly says that God, by nature invisible, had, on those occasions on which He was seen by the fathers (as by Moses, with whom He talked face to face), made it possible for Himself to be seen by assuming the form of something material and discernible.[1] Our Ambrose says the same: "That the Father, and the Son, and the Holy Spirit, when visible, are seen under forms assumed by choice, not prescribed by the nature of Deity;"[2] thus clearing the truth of the saying, "No man hath seen God at any time,"[3] which is the word of the Lord Christ Himself, and of that other saying, "Whom no man hath seen, nor can see,"[4] which is the word of the apostle, yea, rather, of Christ by His apostle; as well as vindicating the consistency of those passages of Scripture in which God is related to have been seen, because He is both invisible in the essential nature of His Deity, and able to become

visible when He pleases, by assuming such created form as shall seem good to Him.

CHAP. III. 11. Moreover, if invisibility is a property of the divine nature, as incorruptibility is, that nature shall assuredly not undergo such a change in the future world as to cease to be invisible and become visible; because it shall never be possible for it to cease to be incorruptible and become corruptible, for it is in both attributes alike immutable. The apostle assuredly declared the excellence of the divine nature when he placed these two together, saying, "Now, unto the King of ages, invisible, incorruptible, the only God, be honour and glory for ever and ever."[5] Wherefore I dare not make such a distinction as to say incorruptible, indeed, for ever and ever, but invisible — not for ever and ever, but only in this world. At the same time, since the testimonies which we are next to quote cannot be false, — "Blessed are the pure in heart, for they shall see God,"[6] and, "We know that, when He shall appear, we shall be like Him; for we shall see Him as He is,"[7] — we cannot deny that the sons of God shall see God; but they shall see Him as invisible things are seen, in the manner in which He who appeared in the flesh, visible to men, promised that He would manifest Himself to men, when, speaking in the presence of the disciples and seen by their eyes, He said: "I will love him, and *will* manifest myself to him." In what other manner are invisible things seen than by the eyes of the mind, concerning which, as the instruments of our vision of God, I have shortly before quoted the opinion of Jerome?

12. Hence, also, the statement of the Bishop of Milan, whom I have quoted before, who says that even in the resurrection it is not easy for any but those who have a pure heart to see God, and therefore it is written, "Blessed are the pure in heart, for they shall see God." "How many," he says, "had He already enumerated as blessed, and yet to them He had not promised the power of seeing God;" and he adds this inference, "If, therefore, the pure in heart shall see God, it is obvious that others shall not see Him;" and to prevent our understanding him to refer to those others of whom the Lord had said, "Blessed are the poor, blessed are the meek," he immediately subjoined, "For those that are unworthy shall not see God," intending it to be understood that the unworthy are those who, although they shall rise again, shall not be able to see God, since they shall rise to condemnation, because they refused to purify their hearts through that true faith which "worketh by love."[8] For this reason he goes on to say,

---

[1] See the 49th of the discourses published under the name of Gregory of Nazianzum. M. Dupin has shown that the discourse in question must have been the work of some Latin author.
[2] Ambrose *on Luke*, c. i. 11.
[3] John i. 18.
[4] 1 Tim. vi. 16.

[5] 1 Tim. i. 17.
[6] Matt. v. 8.
[7] 1 John iii. 2.
[8] Gal. v. 6.

"Whosoever has been unwilling to see God cannot see Him." Then, since it occurred to him that, in a sense, even all wicked men have a desire to see God, he immediately explains that he used the words, "Whosoever has been unwilling to see God," because the fact that the wicked do not desire to purify the heart, by which alone God can be seen, shows that they do not desire to see God, and follows up this statement with the words: "God is not seen in space, but in the pure heart; nor is He sought out by the eyes of the body; nor is He defined in form by our faculty of sight; nor grasped by the touch; His voice does not fall on the ear; nor are His goings perceived by the senses."[1] By these words the blessed Ambrose desired to teach the preparation which men ought to make if they wish to see God, viz. to purify the heart by the faith which worketh by love, through the gift of the Holy Spirit, from whom we have received the earnest by which we are taught to desire that vision.[2]

CHAP. IV.— 13. For as to the members of God which the Scripture frequently mentions, lest any one should suppose that we resemble God as to the form and figure of the body, the same Scripture speaks of God as having also wings, which we certainly have not. As then, when we hear of the "wings" of God, we understand the divine protection, so by the "hands" of God we ought to understand His working, — by His "feet," His presence, — by His "eyes," His power of seeing and knowing all things, — by His face, that whereby He reveals Himself to our knowledge; and I believe that any other such expression used in Scripture is to be spiritually understood. In this opinion I am not singular, nor am I the first who has stated it. It is the opinion of all who by any spiritual interpretation of such language in Scripture resist those who are called Anthropomorphites. Not to occupy too much time by quoting largely from the writings of these men, I introduce here one extract from the pious Jerome, in order that our brother may know that, if anything moves him to maintain an opposite opinion, he is bound to carry on the debate with those who preceded me not less than with myself.

14. In the exposition which that most learned student of Scripture has given of the psalm in which occur the words, "Understand, ye brutish among the people: and ye fools, when will ye be wise? He that planted the ear, shall he not hear? or He that formed the eye, doth He not behold?"[3] he says, among other things: "This passage furnishes a strong argument against those who are Anthropomorphites, and say that God has members such as we have. For example,

God is said by them to have eyes, because 'the eyes of the Lord behold all things:' in the same literal manner they take the statements that the hand of the Lord doeth all things, and that Adam 'heard the sound of the feet of the Lord walking in the garden,' and thus they ascribe the infirmities of men to the majesty of God. But I affirm that God is all eye, all hand, all foot: all eye, because He sees all things; all hand, because He worketh all things; all foot, because He is everywhere present. See, therefore, what the Psalmist saith: 'He that planted the ear, shall He not hear? He that formed the eye, doth He not behold?' He doth not say: 'He that planted the ear, has He not an ear? and He that formed the eye, has He not an eye?' But what does he say? 'He that planted the ear, shall He not hear? He that formed the eye, doth He not behold?' The Psalmist has ascribed to God the powers of seeing and hearing, but has not assigned members to Him."[4]

15. I have thought it my duty to quote all these passages from the writings of both Latin and Greek authors who, being in the Catholic Church before our time, have written commentaries on the divine oracles, in order that our brother, if he hold any different opinion from theirs, may know that it becomes him, laying aside all bitterness of controversy, and preserving or reviving fully the gentleness of brotherly love, to investigate with diligent and calm consideration either what he must learn from others, or what others must learn from him. For the reasonings of any men whatsoever, even though they be Catholics, and of high reputation, are not to be treated by us in the same way as the canonical Scriptures are treated. We are at liberty, without doing any violence to the respect which these men deserve, to condemn and reject anything in their writings, if perchance we shall find that they have entertained opinions differing from that which others or we ourselves have, by the divine help, discovered to be the truth. I deal thus with the writings of others, and I wish my intelligent readers to deal thus with mine. In fine, I do by the help of the Lord most stedfastly believe, and, in so far as He enables me, I understand what is taught in all the statements which I have now quoted from the works of the holy and learned Ambrose, Jerome, Athanasius, Gregory, and in any other similar statements in other writers which I have read, but have for the sake of brevity forborne from quoting, namely, that God is not a body, that He has not the members of the human frame, that He is not divisible through space, and that He is unchangeably invisible, and appeared not in His essential nature and substance,

---

[1] Ambrose *on Luke*, i. 11.
[2] 2 Cor. v. 4–8.
[3] Ps. xciv. 8, 9.

[4] Jerome, *in loc.*

but in such visible form as He pleased to those to whom he appeared on the occasions on which Scripture records that He was seen by holy persons with the eyes of the body.

CHAP. V. — 16. As to the spiritual body which we shall have in the resurrection, how great a change for the better it is to undergo, — whether it shall become pure spirit, so that the whole man shall then be a spirit, or shall (as I rather think, but do not yet confidently maintain) become a spiritual body in such a way as to be called spiritual because of a certain ineffable facility in its movements, but at the same time to retain its material substance, which cannot live and feel by itself, but only through the spirit which uses it (for in our present state, in like manner, although the body is spoken of as animated [animal], the nature of the animating principle is different from that of the body), — and whether, if the properties of the body then immortal and incorruptible shall remain unchanged, it shall then in some degree aid the spirit to see visible, i.e. material things, as at present we are unable to see anything of that kind except through the eyes of the body, or our spirit shall then be able, even in its higher state, to know material things without the instrumentality of the body (for God Himself does not know these things through bodily senses), — on these and on many other things which may perplex us in the discussion of this subject, I confess that I have not yet read anywhere anything which I would esteem sufficiently established to deserve to be either learned or taught by men.

17. And for this reason, if our brother will bear patiently any degree whatever of hesitation on my part, let us in the meantime, because of that which is written, "We shall see Him as He is," prepare, so far as with the help of God Himself we are enabled, hearts purified for that vision. Let us at the same time inquire more calmly and carefully concerning the spiritual body, for it may be that God, if He know this to be useful to us, may condescend to show us some definite and clear view on the subject, in accordance with His written word. For if a more careful investigation shall result in the discovery that the change on the body shall be so great that it shall be able to see things that are invisible, such power imparted to the body will not, I think, deprive the mind of the power of seeing, and thus give the outward man a vision of God which is denied to the inward man; as if, in contradiction of the plain words of Scripture, "that God may be all and in all,"[1] God were only beside the man — without him, and not in the man, in his inner being; or as if He, who is everywhere present in his entirety, unlimited in space, is so within man that He can be seen outside only by the outward man, but cannot be seen inside by the inward man. If such opinions are palpably absurd, — for, on the contrary, the saints shall be full of God; they shall not, remaining empty within, be surrounded outside by Him; nor shall they, through being blind within, fail to see Him of whom they are full, and, having eyes only for that which is outside of themselves, behold Him by whom they shall be surrounded, — if, I say, these things are absurd, it remains for us to rest meanwhile certainly assured as to the vision of God by the inward man. But if, by some wondrous change, the body shall be endowed with this power, another new faculty shall be added; the faculty formerly possessed shall not be taken away.

18. It is better, then, that we affirm that concerning which we have no doubt, — that God shall be seen by the inward man, which alone is able, in our present state, to see that love in commendation of which the apostle says, "God is love;"[2] the inward man, which alone is able to see "peace and holiness, without which no man shall see the Lord."[3] For no fleshly eye now sees love, peace, and holiness, and such things; yet all of them are seen, so far as they can be seen, by the eye of the mind, and the purer it is the more clearly it sees; so that we may, without hesitation, believe that we shall see God, whether we succeed or fail in our investigations as to the nature of our future body — although, at the same time, we hold it to be certain that the body shall rise again, immortal and incorruptible, because on this we have the plainest and strongest testimony of Holy Scripture. If, however, our brother affirm now that he has arrived at certain knowledge as to that spiritual body, in regard to which I am only inquiring, he will have just cause to be displeased with me if I shall refuse to listen calmly to his instructions, provided only that he also listen calmly to my questions. Now, however, I entreat you, for Christ's sake, to obtain his forgiveness for me for that harshness in my letter, by which, as I have learned, he was, not without cause, offended; and may you, by God's help, cheer my spirit by your answer.

LETTER CL.

(A.D. 413.)

TO PROBA[4] AND JULIANA, LADIES MOST WORTHY OF HONOUR, DAUGHTERS JUSTLY FAMOUS AND MOST DISTINGUISHED, AUGUSTIN SENDS GREETING IN THE LORD.

You have filled our heart with a joy singularly pleasant, because of the love we bear to you, and

---

[1] 1 Cor. xv. 28.
[2] 1 John iv. 8.
[3] Heb. xii. 14.
[4] See note to Letter CXXX. p. 459.

singularly acceptable, because of the promptitude with which the tidings came to us. For while the consecration of the daughter of your house to a life of virginity is being published by most busy fame in all places where you are known, and that is everywhere, you have outstripped its flight by more sure and reliable information in a letter from yourselves, and have made us rejoice in certain knowledge before we had time to be questioning the truth of any report concerning an event so blessed and remarkable. Who can declare in words, or expound with adequate praises, how incomparably greater is the glory and advantage gained by your family in giving to Christ women consecrated to His service, than in giving to the world men called to the honours of the consulship? For if it be a great and noble thing to leave the mark of an honoured name upon the revolving ages of this world, how much greater and nobler is it to rise above it by unsullied chastity both of heart and of body! Let this maiden, therefore, illustrious in her pedigree, yet more illustrious in her piety, find greater joy in obtaining, through espousals to her divine Lord, a pre-eminent glory in heaven, than she could have had in becoming, through espousal to a human consort, the mother of a line of illustrious men. This daughter of the house of Anicius has acted the more magnanimous part, in choosing rather to bring a blessing on that noble family by forbearing from marriage, than to increase the number of its descendants, preferring to be already, in the purity of her body, like unto the angels, rather than to increase by the fruit of her body the number of mortals. For this is a richer and more fruitful condition of blessedness, not to have a pregnant womb, but to develop the soul's lofty capacities; not to have the breasts flowing with milk, but to have the heart pure as snow; to travail not with the earthly in the pangs of labour, but with the heavenly in persevering prayer. May it be yours, my daughters, most worthy of the honour due to your rank, to enjoy in her that which was lacking to yourselves; may she be stedfast to the end, abiding in the conjugal union that has no end. May many handmaidens follow the example of their mistress; may those who are of humble rank imitate this high-born lady, and may those who possess eminence in this uncertain world aspire to that worthier eminence which humility has given to her. Let the virgins who covet the glory of the Anician family be ambitious rather to emulate its piety; for the former lies beyond their reach, however eagerly they may desire it, but the latter shall be at once in their possession if they seek it with full desire. May the right hand of the Most High protect you, giving you safety and greater happiness, ladies most worthy of honour, and most excellent daughters! In the love of the Lord, and with all becoming respect, we salute the children of your Holiness, and above all the one who is above the rest in holiness. We have received with very great pleasure the gift sent as a souvenir of her taking the veil.[1]

LETTER CLI.

(A.D. 413 OR 414.)

TO CÆCILIANUS,[2] MY LORD JUSTLY RENOWNED, AND SON MOST WORTHY OF THE HONOUR DUE BY ME TO HIS RANK, AUGUSTIN SENDS GREETING IN THE LORD.

1. The remonstrance which you have addressed to me in your letter is gratifying to me in proportion to the love which it manifests. If, therefore, I attempt to clear myself from blame in regard to my silence, the thing which I must attempt is to show that you had no just cause for being displeased with me. But since nothing gives me greater pleasure than that you condescended to take offence at my silence, which I had supposed to be a matter of no moment in the midst of your many cares, I will be pleading against myself if I endeavour thus to clear myself from blame. For if you were wrong in being displeased at me for not writing to you, this must be because of your having such a poor opinion of me that you are absolutely indifferent whether I speak or remain silent. Nay, the displeasure which arises from your being distressed by my silence is not displeasure. I therefore feel not so much grief at my withholding, as joy at your desiring a communication from me. For it is an honour, not a vexation, to me, that I should have a place in the remembrance of an old friend, and a man who is (though you may not say it, yet it is our duty to acknowledge it) of such eminent worth and greatness, holding a position in a foreign country, and burdened with public responsibilities. Pardon me, then, for expressing my gratitude that you did not regard me as a person whose silence it was beneath you to resent. For now I am persuaded, through that benevolence which distinguishes you more even than your high rank, that in the midst of your numerous and important occupations, not of a private nature, but public, involving the interests of all, a letter from me may be esteemed by you not burdensome, but welcome.

2. For when I had received the letter of the holy father Innocentius, venerable for his eminent merits, which was sent to me by the brethren, and which was, by manifest tokens, shown to have been forwarded to me from your Excel-

---

[1] *Velationis apophoretum.*
[2] Cæcilianus was raised in 409 to the office of *præfectus prætorio* under Honorius, and is probably the person to whom Augustin addressed Letter LXXXVI. p. 365, in 405 A.D.

lency, I formed the opinion that the reason why no letter from you accompanied it was that, being engrossed with more important affairs, you were unwilling to be embarrassed by the trouble of correspondence. For it seemed certainly not unreasonable to expect, that when you condescended to send me the writings of a holy man, I should receive along with them some writings of your own. I had therefore made up my mind not to trouble you with a letter from me, unless it was necessary for the purpose of commending to you some one to whom I could not refuse the service of my intercession, a favour which it is our custom to grant to all, — a custom which, though involving much trouble, is not to be altogether condemned. I accordingly did this; recommending to your kindness a friend of mine, from whom I have now received a letter, expressing his thanks, to which I add my own, for your service.

3. If, however, I had formed any unfavourable impression concerning you, especially in regard to the matter of which, though it was not expressly named, a subtle odour, so to speak, pervaded your whole letter, far would it have been from me to write to you any such note in order to ask any favour for myself or another. In that case I would either have been silent, waiting for a time when I would have an opportunity of seeing you personally; or if I considered it my duty to write on the subject, I would have given it the first place in my letter, and would have treated it in such a way as to make it almost impossible for you to show displeasure. For when, notwithstanding remonstrances which, under an anxiety shared by you with us, we addressed to him, — beseeching him vehemently, but in vain, to forbear from piercing our hearts with so great sorrow, and mortally wounding his own conscience by such grievous sin, — he [1] perpetrated his impious, savage, and perfidious crime, I left Carthage immediately and secretly, for this reason, lest the numerous and influential persons who in terror sought refuge from his sword within the church should, imagining that my presence could be of use to them, detain me by their passionate weeping and groaning, so that I would be compelled, in order to secure

[1] From the beginning to the end of this letter, Augustin studiously avoids naming the persons concerned in the perfidious act of judicial murder, in connection with which the suspicion of many had been fastened upon Cæcilianus. The person by whose orders the sentence of death was carried into effect was Count Marinus, the general by whom the attempt of Heraclianus (413 A.D.) to seize the imperial power was defeated, and who afterwards received a commission to pass into Africa and punish those who had been implicated in the revolt of Heraclianus. A commission of this kind opened a wide door for the gratification of private revenge by enemies who did not scruple to bring false accusations against the innocent; and among the victims of such injustice were two brothers who had, by their zeal for the Catholic Church, made themselves obnoxious to the Donatists. The elder of these was Apringius, a magistrate to whom Augustin wrote a letter (the 134th) recommending clemency in punishing the Donatists. The younger was Marcellinus, concerning whom see also note to Letter CXXXIII. p. 470.

the preservation of their bodies, to supplicate a favour from one whom it was impossible for me to rebuke in order to the welfare of his soul, with the severity which his crime deserved. As for their personal safety, I knew that the walls of the church sufficed for their protection. But for myself [if I remained to intercede with him on their behalf], it could only be in circumstances painfully embarrassing, for he would not have tolerated my acting towards him as I was bound to do, and I would have been compelled, moreover, to act in a way which would have been unbecoming in me. At the same time, I was truly sorry for the misfortune of my venerable co-bishop, the ruler of such an important church, who was expected to regard it as his duty, even after this man had been guilty of such infamous treachery, to treat him with submissive deference, in order that the lives of others might be spared. I confess the reason of my departure: it was that I would have been unable to meet with the necessary fortitude so great a calamity.

4. The same considerations which made me then depart would have been the cause of my remaining silent to you, if I believed you to have used your influence with him to avenge such wicked injuries. This is believed in regard to you only by those who do not know how, and how frequently, and in what terms, you expressed your mind to us, when we were with anxious solicitude doing our utmost to secure that, because he was so intimate with you, and you were so constantly visiting him, and so often conversing alone with him, he should all the more carefully guard your good name, and save you from being supposed to have used no endeavour to prevent him from inflicting that mode of death on persons said to be your enemies. This, indeed, is not believed of you by me, nor by my brethren who heard you in conversation, and who saw, both in your words and in every gesture, the evidences of your heart's good-will to those who were put to death. But, I beseech you, forgive those by whom it is believed; for they are men, and in the minds of men there are such lurking places and such depths that, although all suspicious persons deserved to be blamed, they think themselves that they even deserve praise for their prudence. There existed reasons for the conduct imputed to you: we knew that you had suffered very grievous injury from one of those whom he had suddenly ordered to be arrested. His brother, also, in whose person especially he persecuted the Church, was said to have answered you in terms implying as it were some harsh accusation. Both were thought to be looked upon by you with suspicion. When they, after being summoned, had gone away, you still remained in the place, and were engaged, it was

said, in conversation of a more private kind than usual with him [Marinus], and then they were suddenly ordered to be detained. Men talked much of your friendship with him as not recent, but of long standing. The closeness of your intimacy, and the frequency of your private conversations with him, confirmed this report. His power was at that time great. The ease with which false accusations could be made against any one was notorious. It was not a difficult thing to find some person who would upon the promise of his own safety make any statements which he might order to be made. All things at that time made it easy for any man to be brought to death without any examination on the part of him who ordered the execution, if even one witness brought forward what seemed to be an odious and, at the same time, credible accusation.

5. Meanwhile, as it was rumored that the power of the Church might deliver them, we were mocked with false promises, so that not only with the consent, but, as it seemed, at the urgent desire of Marinus, a bishop was sent to the Imperial Court to intercede for them, the promise having been brought to the ear of the bishops that, until some pleading should be heard there on behalf of the prisoners, no examination of their case would be proceeded with. At last, on the day before they were put to death, your Excellency came to us; you gave us encouragement such as you had never before given, that he might grant their lives as a favour to you before your departure [for Rome], because you had solemnly and prudently said to him that all his condescension in admitting you so constantly to familiar and private conversation would bring to you disgrace rather than distinction, and would have the effect, after the death of these men had been a subject of conversation and consultation between you, of making every one say that there could be no doubt what was to be the issue of these conferences. When you informed us that you had said these things to him, you stretched out your hand as you spoke towards the place at which the sacraments of believers are celebrated, and while we listened in amazement, you confirmed the statement that you had used these words with an oath so solemn, that not only then, but even now after the dreadful and unexpected death of the prisoners, it seems to me, recalling to memory your whole demeanour, that it would be an aggravated insult if I were to believe any evil concerning you. You said, moreover, that he was so moved by these words of yours, that he purposed to give the lives of these men to you as a present, in token of friendship, before you set out on your journey.

6. Wherefore, I solemnly assure your Grace, that when on the following day (the day on which the infamous crime thus conceived was consummated) tidings were unexpectedly brought to us that they had been led forth from prison to stand before him as their judge, although we were in some alarm, nevertheless, after reflecting on what you had said to us on the preceding day, and on the fact that the day following was the anniversary of the blessed Cyprian, I supposed that he had even purposely selected a day on which he might not only grant your request, but also might aspire, by giving sudden joy to the whole Church of Christ, to emulate the virtue of so great a martyr, proving himself truly greater in using clemency in sparing life than in possessing power to inflict death. Such were my thoughts, when lo! a messenger burst into our presence, from whom, before we could ask him how their trial was being conducted, we learned that they had been beheaded. For care had been taken to arrange, as the scene of execution, a place immediately adjoining, not appointed for the punishment of criminals, but used for the recreation of the citizens, on which spot he had ordered some to be executed a few days previously, with the design (as is with good reason believed) of avoiding the odium of applying it to this purpose for the first time in the case of these men, whom we hoped to be able to snatch secretly from the Church interposing on their behalf, by thus not only ordering their immediate execution, but also ordering it to take place on the nearest available spot. He therefore made it sufficiently manifest that he did not fear to cause cruel pain to that Mother whose intervention he feared, namely, to the holy Church, among whose faithful children, baptized in her bosom, we knew that he himself was reckoned. Therefore, after the issue of so great a plot, in which so much care had been used in negotiating with us that we were made, even by you also, though unwittingly, almost free from solicitude, and almost sure of their safety on the preceding day, who, judging of the circumstances in the way in which ordinary men would judge of them, could avoid regarding it as beyond question that by you also words were given to us and life taken from them? Pardon, then, as I have said, those who believe these things against you, although we do not believe them, O excellent man.

7. Far be it, however, from my heart and from my practice, however defective in many things, to intercede with you for any one, or ask a favour from you for any one, if I believed you to be responsible for this monstrous wrong, this villanous cruelty. But I frankly confess to you, that if you continue, even after that event, to be on the same footing of intimate friendship with him as you were formerly, you must excuse my claiming freedom to be grieved; for by this you would

compel us to believe much which we would rather disbelieve. It is, however, fitting that, as I do not believe you guilty of the other things laid by some to your charge, I should not believe this either. This friend of yours has, in the unexpected triumph of sudden accession to power, done violence not less to your reputation than to these men's lives. Nor is it my design in this statement to kindle hatred in your mind; in so doing I would belie my own feelings and profession. But I exhort you to a more faithful exercise of love towards him. For the man who so deals with the wicked as to make them repent of their evil doings, is one who knows how to be angry with them, and yet consult for their good; for as bad companions hinder men's welfare by compliance, so good friends help them by opposition to their evil ways. The same weapon with which, in the proud abuse of power, he took away the lives of others, inflicted a much deeper and more serious wound on his own soul; and if he do not remedy this by repentance, using wisely the long-suffering of God, he will be compelled to find it out and feel it when this life is ended. Often, moreover, God in His wisdom permits the life of good men in this world to be taken from them by the wicked, that He may prevent men from believing that to suffer such things is in their case a calamity. For what harm can result from the death of the body to men who are destined to die some time? Or what do those who fear death accomplish by their care but a short postponement of the time at which they die? All the evil to which mortal men are liable comes not from death but from life; and if in dying they have the soul sustained by Christian grace, death is to them not the night of darkness in which a good life ends, but the dawn in which a better life begins.[1]

8. The life and conversation of the elder of the two brothers appeared indeed more conformed to this world than to Christ, although he also had after his marriage corrected to a great extent the faults of his early irreligious years. It may, nevertheless, have been not otherwise than in mercy that our merciful God appointed him to be the companion of his brother in death. But as to that younger brother, he lived religiously, and was eminent as a Christian both in heart and in practice. The report that he would approve himself such when commissioned to serve the Church[2] came before him to Africa, and this good report followed him still when he had come. In his conduct, what innocence! in his friendship, what constancy! in his study of Christian truth, what zeal! in his religion, what sincerity! in his domestic life, what purity! in his official duties, what integrity! What patience he showed to enemies, what affability to friends, what humility to the pious, what charity to all men! How great his promptitude in granting, and his bashfulness in asking a favour! How genuine his satisfaction in the good deeds, and his sorrow over the faults of men! What spotless honour, noble grace, and scrupulous piety shone in him! In rendering assistance, how compassionate he was! in forgiving injuries, how generous! in prayer, how confiding! When well informed on any subject, with what modesty he was wont to communicate useful knowledge! when conscious of ignorance, with what diligence did he endeavour by investigation to overcome the disadvantage! How singular was his contempt for the things of time! how ardent his hope and his desires in regard to the blessings that are eternal! He would have relinquished all secular business and girded himself with the insignia of the Christian warfare, had he not been prevented by his having entered into the married state; for he had not begun to desire better things before the time when, being already involved in these bonds, it would have been, notwithstanding their inferiority, an unlawful thing for him to rend them asunder.

9. One day when they were confined in prison together, his brother said to him: "If I suffer these things as the just punishment of my sins, what ill desert has brought you to the same fate, for we know that your life was most strictly and earnestly Christian?" He replied: "Supposing even that your testimony as to my life were true, do you think that God is bestowing a small favour upon me in appointing that my sins be punished in these sufferings, even though they should end in death, instead of being reserved to meet me in the judgment which is to come?" These words might perhaps lead some to suppose that he was conscious of some secret immoralities. I shall therefore mention what it pleased the Lord God to appoint that I should hear from his lips, and know assuredly, to my own great consolation. Being anxious about this very thing, as human nature is liable to fall into such wickedness, I asked him, when I was alone with him after he was confined in prison, if there was no sin for which he ought to seek reconciliation with God[3] by some more severe and special penance. With characteristic modesty he blushed at the mere mention of my suspicion, groundless though it was, but thanked me most warmly for the warning, and with a grave, modest smile he seized with both hands my right hand, and said: "I swear by the sacraments which are dispensed to me by this hand, that I have neither before

[1] In the original of this sentence there is a characteristic antithesis of phrases: "Non sane mors eorum bonæ vitæ occasus fuit sed melioris occasio."
[2] See note to Letter CXXXIII. p. 470.
[3] *Deum sibi placare.*

nor since my marriage been guilty of immoral self-indulgence." [1]

10. What evil, then, was brought to him by death? Nay, rather, was it not the occasion of the greatest possible good to him, because, in the possession of these gifts, he departed from this life to Christ, in whom alone they are really possessed? I would not mention these things in addressing you if I believed that you would be offended by my praising him. But assuredly, as I do not believe this, neither do I believe that his being put to death was even according to your desire or wish, much less that it was done at your request. You, therefore, with a sincerity proportioned to your innocence in this matter, entertain, doubtless, along with us, the opinion that the man who put him to death inflicted more cruel wrong on his own soul than on the sufferer's body, when, in despite of us, in despite of his own promises, in despite of so many supplications and warnings from you, and finally, in despite of the Church of Christ (and in her of Christ Himself), he consummated his base machinations by putting this man to death. Is the high position of the one worthy to be compared with the lot of the other, prisoner though he was, when the man of power was maddened by anger, while the sufferer in his prison was filled with joy? There is nothing in all the dungeons of this world, nay, not even in hell itself, to surpass the dreadful doom of darkness to which a villian is consigned by remorse of conscience. Even to yourself, what evil did he do? He did not destroy your innocence, although he grievously injured your reputation; which, nevertheless, remains uninjured, both in the estimation of those who know you better than we do, and in our estimation, in whose presence the anxiety which, like us, you felt for the prevention of such a monstrous crime, was expressed with so much visible agitation that we could almost see with our eyes the invisible workings of your heart. Whatever harm, therefore, he has done, he has done to himself alone; he has pierced through his own soul, his own life, his own conscience; in fine, he has by that blind deed of cruelty destroyed even his own good name, a thing which the very worst of men are usually fain to preserve. For to all good men he is odious in proportion to his efforts to obtain, or his satisfaction in receiving, the approbation of the wicked.

11. Could anything prove more clearly that he was not under the necessity which he pretended — alleging that he did this evil action as a good man who had no alternative — than the fact that the proceeding was disapproved of by the person whose orders he dared to plead as his excuse? The pious deacon by whose hand we send this was himself associated with the bishop whom we had sent to intercede for them; let him, therefore, relate to your Excellency how it seemed good to the Emperor not even to give a formal pardon, lest by this the stigma of a crime should be in some degree attached to them, but a mere notice commanding them to be immediately set at liberty from all further annoyance. By a purely gratuitous act of cruelty, and under no pressure of necessity (although, perchance, there may have been other causes which we suspect, but which it is unnecessary to state in writing), he did outrageously vex the Church, — the Church to whose sheltering bosom his brother once, in fear of death, had fled, to be requited for protecting his life by finding him active in counselling the perpetration of this crime, — the Church in which he himself had once, when under the displeasure of an offended patron, sought an asylum which could not be denied to him. If you love this man, show your detestation of his crime; if you do not wish him to come into everlasting punishment, shrink with horror from his society. You are bound to take measures of this kiud, both for your own good name and for his life; for he who loves in this man what God hates, is, in truth, hating not only this man but also his own soul.

12. These things being so, I know your benevolence too well to believe that you were the author of this crime, or an accomplice in its commission, or that with malicious cruelty you deceived us: far be such conduct from your life and conversation! At the same time, I would not wish your friendship to be of such a character as tends to make him, to his own destruction, glory in his crime, and to confirm the suspicions naturally cherished by men concerning you; but rather let it be such as to move him to penitence, and to penitence corresponding in quality and in measure to the remedy demanded for the healing of such dreadful wounds. For the more you are an enemy to his crimes, the more really will you be a friend to the man himself. It will be interesting to us to learn, by your Excellency's reply to this letter, where you were on the day on which the crime was committed, how you received the tidings, and what you did thereafter, and what you said to him and heard from him when you next saw him; for I have not been able to hear anything of you in connection with this affair since my sudden departure on the succeeding day.

13. As to the remark in your letter that you are now compelled to believe that I refuse to visit Carthage for fear lest you should be seen there by me, you rather compel me by these words to state explicitly the reasons of my absence. One reason is, that the labour which

[1] Me nullum esse expertum concubitum præter uxorem.

I am obliged to undergo in that city, and which I could not describe without adding as much again to the length of this letter, is more than I am able now to bear, since, in addition to my infirmities peculiar to myself, which are known to all my more intimate friends, I am burdened with an infirmity common to the human family, namely, the weakness of old age. The other reason is, that, in so far as leisure is granted me from the work imperatively demanded by the Church, which my office specially binds me to serve, I have resolved to devote the time entirely, if the Lord will, to the labour of studies pertaining to ecclesiastical learning; in doing which I think that I may, if it please the mercy of God, be of some service even to future generations.

14. There is, indeed, one thing in you, since you wish to hear the truth, which causes me very great distress: it is that, although qualified by age, as well as by life and character, to do otherwise, you still prefer to be a catechumen; as if it were not possible for believers, by making progress in Christian faith and well-doing, to become so much the more faithful and useful in the administration of public business. For surely the promotion of the welfare of men is the one great end of all your great cares and labours. And, indeed, if this were not to be the issue of your public services, it would be better for you even to sleep both day and night than to sacrifice your rest in order to do work which can contribute nothing to the advantage of your fellow-men. Nor do I entertain the slightest doubt that your Excellency . . .

(*Cætera desunt.*)

LETTER CLVIII.

(A.D. 414.)

TO MY LORD AUGUSTIN, MY BROTHER PARTNER IN THE SACERDOTAL OFFICE, MOST SINCERELY LOVED, WITH PROFOUND RESPECT, AND TO THE BRETHREN WHO ARE WITH HIM, EVODIUS[1] AND THE BRETHREN WHO ARE WITH HIM SEND GREETING IN THE LORD.

1. I urgently beg you to send the reply due to my last letter. Indeed, I would have preferred first to learn what I then asked, and afterwards to put the questions which I now submit to you. Give me your attention while I relate an event in which you will kindly take an interest, and which has made me impatient to lose no time in acquiring, if possible in this life, the knowledge which I desired. I had a certain youth as a

clerk, a son of presbyter Armenus of Melonita, whom, by my humble instrumentality, God rescued when he was becoming already immersed in secular affairs, for he was employed as a shorthand writer by the proconsul's solicitor.[2] He was then, indeed, as boys usually are, prompt and somewhat restless, but as he grew older (for his death occurred in his twenty-second year) a gravity of deportment and circumspect probity of life so adorned him that it is a pleasure to dwell upon his memory. He was, moreover, a clever stenographer,[3] and indefatigable in writing: he had begun also to be earnest in reading, so that he even urged me to do more than my indolence would have chosen, in order to spend hours of the night in reading, for he read aloud to me for a time every night after all was still; and in reading, he would not pass over any sentence unless he understood it, and would go over it a third or even a fourth time, and not leave it until what he wished to know was made clear. I had begun to regard him not as a mere boy and clerk, but as a comparatively intimate and pleasant friend, for his conversation gave me much delight.

2. He desired also to " depart and to be with Christ,"[4] a desire which has been fulfilled. For he was ill for sixteen days in his father's house, and by strength of memory he continually repeated portions of Scripture throughout almost the whole time of his illness. But when he was very near to the end of his life, he sang[5] so as to be heard by all, " My soul longeth for and hastens unto the courts of the Lord,"[6] after which he sang again, " Thou hast anointed my head with oil, and beautiful is Thy cup, overpowering my senses with delight! "[7] In these things he was wholly occupied; in the consolation yielded by them he found satisfaction. At the last, when dissolution was just coming upon him, he began to make the sign of the cross on his forehead, and in finishing this his hand was moving down to his mouth, which also he wished to mark with the same sign, but the inward man (which had been truly renewed day by day)[8] had, ere this was done, forsaken the tabernacle of clay. To myself there has been given so great an ecstasy of joy, that I think that after leaving his own body he has entered into my spirit, and is there imparting to me a certain fulness of light from his presence, for I am conscious of a joy beyond all measure through his deliverance and safety — indeed it is ineffable. For I felt no small anxiety on his

---

[1] Evodius, Bishop of Uzala, was one of Augustin's early friends. He was a native of the same town (Tagaste), and joined Augustin and Alypius in seeking religious retirement after their baptism, in 387 A.D. He was also with them at Ostia when Monica died. (*Confessions*, Book ix. ch. 8 and 12).

[2] *Nam scholastico proconsulis excipiebat.*
[3] *Strenuus in notis.*
[4] *Dissolvi et esse cum Christo.* Phil. i. 23.
[5] *Psallebat.*
[6] Ps. lxxxiv. 2, LXX.
[7] Ps. xxiii. 5, 6, LXX.
[8] 2 Cor. iv. 16.

account, being afraid of the dangers peculiar to his years. For I was at pains to inquire of himself whether perchance he had been defiled by intercourse with woman ; he solemnly assured us that he was free from this stain, by which declaration our joy was still more increased. So he died. We honored his memory by suitable obsequies, such as were due to one so excellent, for we continued during three days to praise the Lord with hymns at his grave, and on the third day we offered the sacraments of redemption.[1]

3. Behold, however, two days thereafter, a certain respectable widow from Figentes, an handmaid from God, who said that she had been twelve years in widowhood, saw the following vision in a dream. She saw a certain deacon, who had died four years ago, preparing a palace, with the assistance of servants and handmaids of God (virgins and widows). It was being so much adorned that the place was refulgent with splendor, and appeared to be wholly made of silver. On her inquiring eagerly for whom this palace was being prepared, the deacon aforesaid answered, " For the young man, the son of the presbyter, who was cut off yesterday." There appeared in the same palace an old man robed in white, who gave orders to two others, also dressed in white, to go, and having raised the body from the grave, to carry it up with them to heaven. And she added, that so soon as the body had been taken up from the grave and carried to heaven, there sprang from the same sepulchre branches of the rose, called from its folded blossoms the virgin rose.

4. I have narrated the event : listen now, if you please, to my question, and teach me what I ask, for the departure of that young man's soul forces such questions from me. While we are in the body, we have an inward faculty of perception which is alert in proportion to the activity of our attention, and is more wakeful and eager the more earnestly attentive we become : and it seems to us probable that even in its highest activity it is retarded by the encumbrance of the body, for who can fully describe all that the mind suffers through the body ! In the midst of the perturbation and annoyance which come from the suggestions, temptations, necessities, and varied afflictions of which the body is the cause, the mind does not surrender its strength, it resists and conquers. Sometimes it is defeated ; nevertheless, mindful of what is its own nature, it becomes, under the stimulating influence of such labours, more active and more wary, and breaks through the meshes of wickedness, and so makes its way to better things. Your Holiness will kindly understand what I mean to say. Therefore, while we are in

this life, we are hindered by such deficiencies, and are nevertheless, as it is written, " more than conquerors through Him that loved us."[2] When we go forth from this body, and escape from every burden, and from sin, with its incessant activity, what are we?

5. In the first place, I ask whether there may not be some kind of body (formed, perchance, of one of the four elements, either air or ether) which does not depart from the incorporeal principle, that is, the substance properly called the soul, when it forsakes this earthly body. For as the soul is in its nature incorporeal, if it be absolutely disembodied by death there is now one soul of all that have left this world. And in that case where would the rich man, who was clothed in purple, and Lazarus, who was full of sores, now be? How, moreover, could they be distinguished according to their respective deserts, so that the one should have suffering and the other have joy, if there were only a single soul made by the combination of all disembodied souls, unless, of course, these things are to be understood in a figurative sense? Be that as it may, there is no question that souls which are held in definite places (as that rich man was in the flame, and that poor man was in Abraham's bosom) are held in bodies. If there are distinct places, there are bodies, and in these bodies the souls reside ; and even although the punishments and rewards are experienced in the conscience, the soul which experiences them is nevertheless in a body. Whatever is the nature of that one soul made up of many souls, it must be possible for it in its unbroken unity to be both grieved and made glad at the same moment, if it is to approve itself to be really a substance consisting of many souls gathered into one. If, however, this soul is called one only in the same way as the incorporeal mind is called one, although it has in it memory, and will, and intellect, and if it be alleged that all these are separate incorporeal causes [or powers], and have their several distinctive offices and work without one impeding another in any way, I think this might be in some measure answered by saying that it must be also possible for some of the souls to be under punishment and some of the souls to enjoy rewards simultaneously in this one substance consisting of many souls gathered into one.

6. Or if this be not so [that is, if there be no such body remaining still in union with the incorporeal principle after it quits this earthly body], what is there to hinder each soul from having, when separated from the solid body which it here inhabits, another body, so that the soul always animates a body of some kind? or in what body

---

[1] *Redemptionis sacramenta obtulimus.*

[2] Rom. viii. 37.

does it pass to any region, if such there be, to which necessity compels it to go? For the angels themselves, if they were not numbered by bodies of some kind which they have, could not be called many, as they are by the Truth Himself when He said in the gospel, "I could pray the Father, and He will presently give me twelve legions of angels." [1] Again it is certain that Samuel was seen in the body when he was raised at the request of Saul; [2] and as to Moses, whose body was buried, it is plain from the gospel narrative that he came in the body to the Lord on the mountain to which He and His disciples had retired. [3] In the Apocrypha, and in the *Mysteries of Moses,* a writing which is wholly devoid of authority, it is indeed said that, at the time when he ascended the mount to die, through the power which his body possessed, there was one body which was committed to the earth, and another which was joined to the angel who accompanied him; but I do not feel myself called upon to give to a sentence in apocryphal writings a preference over the definite statements quoted above. We must therefore give attention to this, and search out, by the help either of the authority of revelation or of the light of reason, the matter about which we are inquiring. But it is alleged that the future resurrection of the body is a proof that the soul was after death absolutely without a body. This is not, however, an unanswerable objection, for the angels, who are like our souls invisible, have at times desired to appear in bodily forms and be seen, and (whatever might be the form of body worthy to be assumed by these spirits) they have appeared, for example, to Abraham [4] and to Tobias. [5] Therefore it is quite possible that the resurrection of the body may, as we assuredly believe, take place, and yet that the soul may be reunited to it without its being found to have been at any moment wholly devoid of some kind of body. Now the body which the soul here occupies consists of the four elements, of which one, namely heat, seems to depart from this body at the same moment as the soul. For there remains after death that which is made of earth, moisture also is not wanting to the body, nor is the element of cold matter gone; heat alone has fled, which perhaps the soul takes along with it if it migrates from place to place. This is all that I say meanwhile concerning the body.

7. It seems to me also, that if the soul while occupying the living body is capable, as I have said, of strenuous mental application, how much more unencumbered, active, vigorous, earnest, resolute, and persevering will it be, how much enlarged in capacity and improved in character, if it has while in this body learned to relish virtue! For after laying aside this body, or rather, after having this cloud swept away, the soul will have come to be free from all disturbing influences, enjoying tranquillity and exempt from temptation, seeing whatever it has longed for, and embracing what it has loved. Then, also, it will be capable of remembering and recognising friends, both those who went before it from this world, and those whom it left here below. Perhaps this may be true. I know not, but I desire to learn. But it would greatly distress me to think that the soul after death passes into a state of torpor, being as it were buried, just as it is during sleep while it is in the body, living only in hope, but having nothing and knowing nothing, especially if in its sleep it be not even stirred by any dreams. This notion causes me very great horror, and seems to indicate that the life of the soul is extinguished at death.

8. This also I would ask: Supposing that the soul be discovered to have such a body as we speak of, does that body lack any of the senses? Of course, if there cannot be imposed upon it any necessity for smelling, tasting, or touching, as I suppose will be the case, these senses will be wanting; but I hesitate as to the senses of sight and hearing. For are not devils said to hear (not, indeed, in all the persons whom they harass, for in regard to these there is a question), even when they appear in bodies of their own? And as to the faculty of sight, how can they pass from one place to another if they have a body but are void of the power of seeing, so as to guide its motions? Do you think that this is not the case with human souls when they go forth from the body, — that they have still a body of some kind, and are not deprived of some at least of the senses proper to this body? Else how can we explain the fact that very many dead persons have been observed by day, or by persons awake and walking abroad during the night, to pass into houses just as they were wont to do in their lifetime? This I have heard not once, but often; and I have also heard it said that in places in which dead bodies are interred, and especially in churches, there are commotions and prayers which are heard for the most part at a certain time of the night. This I remember hearing from more than one: for a certain holy presbyter was an eye-witness of such an apparition, having observed a multitude of such phantoms issuing from the baptistery in bodies full of light, after which he heard their prayers in the midst of the church itself. All such things are either true, and therefore helpful to the inquiry which we are now making, or are mere fables, in which case the fact of their invention

is wonderful; nevertheless I would desire to get some information from the fact that they come and visit men, and are seen otherwise than in dreams.

9. These dreams suggest another question. I do not at this moment concern myself about the mere creations of fancy, which are formed by the emotions of the uneducated. I speak of visitations in sleep, such as the apparition to Joseph [1] in a dream, in the manner experienced in most cases of the kind. In the same manner, therefore, our own friends also who have departed this life before us sometimes come and appear to us in dreams, and speak to us. For I myself remember that Profuturus, and Privatus, and Servilius, holy men who within my recollection were removed by death from our monastery, spoke to me, and that the events of which they spoke came to pass according to their words. Or if it be some other higher spirit that assumes their form and visits our minds, I leave this to the all-seeing eye of Him before whom everything from the highest to the lowest is uncovered. If, therefore, the Lord be pleased to speak through reason to your Holiness on all these questions, I beg you to be so kind as make me partaker of the knowledge which you have received. There is another thing which I have resolved not to omit mentioning, for perhaps it bears upon the matter now under investigation:

10. This same youth, in connection with whom these questions are brought forward, departed this life after having received what may be called a summons [2] at the time when he was dying. For one who had been a companion of his as a student, and reader, and shorthand writer to my dictation, who had died eight months before, was seen by a person in a dream coming towards him. When he was asked by the person who then distinctly saw him why he had come, he said, "I have come to take this friend away;" and so it proved. For in the house itself, also, there appeared to a certain old man, who was almost awake, a man bearing in his hand a laurel branch on which something was written. Nay, more, when this one was seen, it is further reported that after the death of the young man, his father the presbyter had begun to reside along with the aged Theasius in the monastery, in order to find consolation there, but lo! on the third day after his death, the young man is seen entering the monastery, and is asked by one of the brethren in a dream of some kind whether he knew himself to be dead. He replied that he knew he was. The other asked whether he had been welcomed by God. This also he answered with great expressions of joy. And when questioned

as to the reason why he had come, he answered, "I have been sent to summon my father." The person to whom these things were shown awakes, and relates what had passed. It comes to the ear of Bishop Theasius. He, being alarmed, sharply admonished the person who told him, lest the matter should come, as it might easily do, to the ear of the presbyter himself, and he should be disturbed by such tidings. But why prolong the narration? Within about four days from this visitation he was saying (for he had suffered from a moderate feverishness) that he was now out of danger, and that the physician had given up attending him, having assured him that there was no cause whatever for anxiety; but that very day this presbyter expired after he had lain down on his couch. Nor should I forbear mentioning, that on the same day on which the youth died, he asked his father three times to forgive him anything in which he might have offended, and every time that he kissed his father he said to him, "Let us give thanks to God, father," and insisted upon his father saying the words along with him, as if he were exhorting one who was to be his companion in going forth from this world. And in fact only seven days elapsed between the two deaths. What shall we say of things so wonderful? Who shall be a thoroughly reliable teacher as to these mysterious dispensations? To you in the hour of perplexity my agitated heart unburdens itself. The divine appointment of the death of the young man and of his father is beyond all doubt, for two sparrows shall not fall to the ground without the will of our heavenly Father. [3]

11. That the soul cannot exist in absolute separation from a body of some kind is proved in my opinion by the fact that to exist without body belongs to God alone. But I think that the laying aside of so great a burden as the body, in the act of passing from this world, proves that the soul will then be very much more wakeful than it is meanwhile; for then the soul appears, as I think, far more noble when no longer encumbered by so great a hindrance, both in action and in knowledge, and that entire spiritual rest proves it to be free from all causes of disturbance and error, but does not make it languid, and as it were slow, torpid, and embarrassed, inasmuch as it is enough for the soul to enjoy in its fulness the liberty to which it has attained in being freed from the world and the body; for, as you have wisely said, the intellect is satisfied with food, and applies the lips of the spirit to the fountain of life in that condition in which it is happy and blest in the undisputed lordship of its own faculties. For before I quitted the monastery I saw brother Servilius in

---

[1] Matt. i. 20.
[2] *Exhibitus quodammodo pergit.*

[3] Matt. x. 29.

a dream after his decease, and he said that we were labouring to attain by the exercise of reason to an understanding of truth, whereas he and those who were in the same state as he was were always resting in the pure joy of contemplation.

12. I also beg you to explain to me in how many ways the word wisdom is used; as God is wisdom, and a wise mind is wisdom (in which way it is said to be as light); as we read also of the wisdom of Bezaleel, who made the tabernacle or the ointment, and the wisdom of Solomon, or any other wisdom, if there be such, and wherein they differ from each other; and whether the one eternal Wisdom which is with the Father is to be understood as spoken of in these different degrees, as they are called diverse gifts of the Holy Spirit, who divideth to every one severally according as He will. Or, with the exception of that Wisdom alone which was not created, were these created, and have they a distinct existence of their own? or are they effects, and have they received their name from the definition of their work? I am asking a great many questions. May the Lord grant you grace to discover the truth sought, and wisdom sufficient to commit it to writing, and to communicate it without delay to me. I have written in much ignorance, and in a homely style; but since you think it worth while to know that about which I am inquiring, I beseech you in the name of Christ the Lord to correct me where I am mistaken, and teach me what you know that I am desirous to learn.

LETTER CLIX.

(A.D. 415.)

TO EVODIUS, MY LORD MOST BLESSED, MY VENERABLE AND BELOVED BROTHER AND PARTNER IN THE PRIESTLY OFFICE, AND TO THE BRETHREN WHO ARE WITH HIM, AUGUSTIN AND THE BRETHREN WHO ARE WITH HIM SEND GREETING IN THE LORD.

1. Our brother Barbarus, the bearer of this letter, is a servant of God, who has now for a long time been settled at Hippo, and has been an eager and diligent hearer of the word of God. He requested from us this letter to your Holiness, whereby we commend him to you in the Lord, and convey to you through him the salutations which it is our duty to offer. To reply to those letters of your Holiness, in which you have interwoven questions of great difficulty, would be a most laborious task, even for men who are at leisure, and who are endowed with much greater ability in discussing and acuteness in apprehending any subject than we possess. One, indeed, of the two letters in which you ask

many great questions has gone amissing, I know not how, and though long sought for cannot be found; the other, which has been found, contains a very pleasing account of a servant of God, a good and chaste young man, stating how he departed from this life, and by what testimonies, communicated through visions of the brethren, his merits were, as you state, made known to you. Taking occasion from this young man's case, you propose and discuss an extremely obscure question concerning the soul,—whether it is associated when it goes forth from this body with some other kind of body, by means of which it can be carried to or confined in places having material boundaries? The investigation of this question, if indeed it admits of satisfactory investigation by beings such as we are, demands the most diligent care and labour, and therefore a mind absolutely at leisure from such occupations as engross my time. My opinion, however, if you are willing to hear it, summed up in a sentence, is, that I by no means believe that the soul in departing from the body is accompanied by another body of any kind.

2. As to the question how these visions and predictions of future events are produced, let him attempt to explain them who understands by what power we are to account for the great wonders which are wrought in the mind of every man when his thoughts are busy. For we see, and we plainly perceive, that within the mind innumerable images of many objects discernible by the eye or by our other senses are produced, — whether they are produced in regular order or in confusion matters not to us at present: all that we say is, that since such images are beyond all dispute produced, the man who is found able to state by what power and in what way these phenomena of daily and perpetual experience are to be accounted for is the only man who may warrantably venture to conjecture or propound any explanation of these visions, which are of exceedingly rare occurrence. For my part, as I discover more plainly my inability to account for the ordinary facts of our experience, when awake or asleep, throughout the whole course of our lives, the more do I shrink from venturing to explain what is extraordinary. For while I have been dictating this epistle to you, I have been contemplating your person in my mind, — you being, of course, absent all the while, and knowing nothing of my thoughts, — and I have been imagining from my knowledge of what is in you how you will be affected by my words; and I have been unable to apprehend, either by observation or by inquiry, how this process was accomplished in my mind. Of one thing, however, I am certain, that although the mental image was very like something material, it was not produced either by masses of matter or by qualities

of matter. Accept this in the meantime from one writing under pressure of other duties, and in haste. In the twelfth of the books which I have written on Genesis this question is discussed with great care, and that dissertation is enriched with a forest of examples from actual experience or from trustworthy report. How far I have been competent to handle the question, and what I have accomplished in it, you will judge when you have read that work; if indeed the Lord shall be pleased in His kindness to permit me now to publish those books systematically corrected to the best of my ability, and thus to meet the expectation of many brethren, instead of deferring their hope by continuing further the discussion of a subject which has already engaged me for a long time.

3. I will narrate briefly, however, one fact which I commend to your meditation. You know our brother Gennadius, a physician, known to almost every one, and very dear to us, who now lives at Carthage, and was in other years eminent as a medical practitioner at Rome. You know him as a man of religious character and of very great benevolence, actively compassionate and promptly liberal in his care of the poor. Nevertheless, even he, when still a young man, and most zealous in these charitable acts, had sometimes, as he himself told me, doubts as to whether there was any life after death. Forasmuch, therefore, as God would in no wise forsake a man so merciful in his disposition and conduct, there appeared to him in sleep a youth of remarkable appearance and commanding presence, who said to him: "Follow me." Following him, he came to a city where he began to hear on the right hand sounds of a melody so exquisitely sweet as to surpass anything he had ever heard. When he inquired what it was, his guide said: "It is the hymn of the blessed and the holy." What he reported himself to have seen on the left hand escapes my remembrance. He awoke; the dream vanished, and he thought of it as only a dream.

4. On a second night, however, the same youth appeared to Gennadius, and asked whether he recognised him, to which he replied that he knew him well, without the slightest uncertainty. Thereupon he asked Gennadius where he had become acquainted with him. There also his memory failed him not as to the proper reply: he narrated the whole vision, and the hymns of the saints which, under his guidance, he had been taken to hear, with all the readiness natural to recollection of some very recent experience. On this the youth inquired whether it was in sleep or when awake that he had seen what he had just narrated. Gennadius answered: "In sleep." The youth then said: "You remember it well; it is true that you saw these things in sleep, but I would have you know that even now you are seeing in sleep." Hearing this, Gennadius was persuaded of its truth, and in his reply declared that he believed it. Then his teacher went on to say: "Where is your body now?" He answered: "In my bed." "Do you know," said the youth, "that the eyes in this body of yours are now bound and closed, and at rest, and that with these eyes you are seeing nothing?" He answered: "I know it." "What, then," said the youth, "are the eyes with which you see me?" He, unable to discover what to answer to this, was silent. While he hesitated, the youth unfolded to him what he was endeavoring to teach him by these questions, and forthwith said: "As while you are asleep and lying on your bed these eyes of your body are now unemployed and doing nothing, and yet you have eyes with which you behold me, and enjoy this vision, so, after your death, while your bodily eyes shall be wholly inactive, there shall be in you a life by which you shall still live, and a faculty of perception by which you shall still perceive. Beware, therefore, after this of harbouring doubts as to whether the life of man shall continue after death." This believer says that by this means all doubts as to this matter were removed from him. By whom was he taught this but by the merciful, providential care of God?

5. Some one may say that by this narrative I have not solved but complicated the question. Nevertheless, while it is free to every one to believe or disbelieve these statements, every man has his own consciousness at hand as a teacher by whose help he may apply himself to this most profound question. Every day man wakes, and sleeps, and thinks; let any man, therefore, answer whence proceed these things which, while not material bodies, do nevertheless resemble the forms, properties, and motions of material bodies: let him, I say, answer this if he can. But if he cannot do this, why is he in such haste to pronounce a definite opinion on things which occur very rarely, or are beyond the range of his experience, when he is unable to explain matters of daily and perpetual observation? For my part, although I am wholly unable to explain in words how those semblances of material bodies, without any real body, are produced, I may say that I wish that, with the same certainty with which I know that these things are not produced by the body, I could know by what means those things are perceived which are occasionally seen by the spirit, and are supposed to be seen by the bodily senses; or by what distinctive marks we may know the visions of men who have been misguided by delusion, or, most commonly, by impiety, since the examples of such visions closely resembling the visions of pious and holy men are so numerous, that if I wished to quote

them, time, rather than abundance of examples, would fail me.

May you, through the mercy of the Lord, grow in grace, most blessed lord and venerable and beloved brother!

LETTER CLXIII.

(A.D. 414.)

TO BISHOP AUGUSTIN, BISHOP EVODIUS SENDS GREETING.

Some time ago I sent two questions to your Holiness; the first, which was sent, I think, by Jobinus, a servant in the nunnery,[1] related to God and reason, and the second was in regard to the opinion that the body of the Saviour is capable of seeing the substance of the Deity. I now propound a third question: Does the rational soul which our Saviour assumed along with His body fall under any one of the theories commonly advanced in discussions on the origin of souls (if any theory indeed can be with certainty established on the subject), — or does His soul, though rational, belong not to any of the species under which the souls of living creatures are classified, but to another?

I ask also a fourth question: Who are those spirits in reference to whom the Apostle Peter testifies concerning the Lord in these words: "Being put to death in the flesh, but quickened in the spirit, in which also He went and preached to the spirits in prison?" giving us to understand that they were in hell, and that Christ descending into hell, preached the gospel to them all, and by grace delivered them all from darkness and punishment, so that from the time of the resurrection of the Lord judgment is expected, hell having then been completely emptied.

What your Holiness believes in this matter I earnestly desire to know.

LETTER CLXIV.

(A.D. 414.)

TO MY LORD EVODIUS MOST BLESSED, MY BROTHER AND PARTNER IN THE EPISCOPAL OFFICE, AUGUSTIN SENDS GREETING IN THE LORD.

1. The question which you have proposed to me from the epistle of the Apostle Peter is one which, as I think you are aware, is wont to perplex me most seriously, namely, how the words which you have quoted are to be understood on the supposition that they were spoken concerning hell? I therefore refer this question back to yourself, that if either you yourself be able, or can find any other person who is able to do so,

you may remove and terminate my perplexities on the subject. If the Lord grant to me ability to understand the words before you do, and it be in my power to impart what I receive from Him to you, I will not withhold it from a friend so truly loved. In the meantime, I will communicate to you the things in the passage which occasion difficulty to me, that, keeping in view these remarks on the words of the apostle, you may either exercise your own thoughts on them, or consult any one whom you find competent to pronounce an opinion.

2. After having said that "Christ was put to death in the flesh, and quickened in the spirit," the apostle immediately went on to say: "in which also He went and preached unto the spirits in prison; which sometime were unbelieving,[2] when once the long-suffering of God waited in the days of Noah, while the ark was a preparing, wherein few, that is, eight souls were saved by water;" thereafter he added the words: "which baptism also now by a like figure has saved you."[3] This, therefore, is felt by me to be difficult. If the Lord when He died preached in hell to spirits in prison, why were those who continued unbelieving while the ark was a preparing the only ones counted worthy of this favour, namely, the Lord's descending into hell? For in the ages between the time of Noah and the passion of Christ, there died many thousands of so many nations whom He might have found in hell. I do not, of course, speak here of those who in that period of time had believed in God, as, e.g. the prophets and patriarchs of Abraham's line, or, going father back, Noah himself and his house, who had been saved by water (excepting perhaps the one son, who afterwards was rejected), and, in addition to these, all others outside of the posterity of Jacob who were believers in God, such as Job, the citizens of Nineveh, and any others, whether mentioned in Scripture or existing unknown to us in the vast human family at any time. I speak only of those many thousands of men who, ignorant of God and devoted to the worship of devils or of idols, had passed out of this life from the time of Noah to the passion of Christ. How was it that Christ, finding these in hell, did not preach to them, but preached only to those who were unbelieving in the days of Noah when the ark was a preparing? Or if he preached to all, why has Peter mentioned only these, and passed over the innumerable multitude of others?

CHAP. II. 3. — It is established beyond question that the Lord, after He had been put to death in the flesh, "descended into hell;" for it is impossible to gainsay either that utterance of prophecy, "Thou wilt not leave my soul in

---

[1] *Qui servit ancillis Dei.*

[2] *Increduli.*
[3] 1 Pet. iii. 18–21.

hell,"[1] — an utterance which Peter himself expounds in the Acts of the Apostles, lest any one should venture to put upon it another interpretation, — or the words of the same apostle, in which he affirms that the Lord "loosed the pains of hell, in which it was not possible for Him to be holden."[2] Who, therefore, except an infidel, will deny that Christ was in hell? As to the difficulty which is found in reconciling the statement that the pains of hell were loosed by Him, with the fact that He had never begun to be in these pains as in bonds, and did not so loose them as if He had broken off chains by which He had been bound, this is easily removed when we understand that they were loosed in the same way as the snares of huntsmen may be loosed to prevent their holding, not because they have taken hold. It may also be understood as teaching us to believe Him to have loosed those pains which could not possibly hold Him, but which were holding those to whom He had resolved to grant deliverance.

4. But who these were it is presumptuous for us to define. For if we say that all who were found there were then delivered without exception, who will not rejoice if we can prove this? Especially will men rejoice for the sake of some who are intimately known to us by their literary labours, whose eloquence and talent we admire, — not only the poets and orators who in many parts of their writings have held up to contempt and ridicule these same false gods of the nations, and have even occasionally confessed the one true God, although along with the rest they observed superstitious rites, but also those who have uttered the same, not in poetry or rhetoric, but as philosophers : and for the sake of many more of whom we have no literary remains, but in regard to whom we have learned from the writings of these others that their lives were to a certain extent praiseworthy, so that (with the exception of their service of God, in which they erred, worshipping the vanities which had been set up as objects of public worship, and serving the creature rather than the Creator) they may be justly held up as models in all the other virtues of frugality, self-denial, chastity, sobriety, braving of death in their country's defence, and faith kept inviolate not only to fellow-citizens, but also to enemies. All these things, indeed, when they are practised with a view not to the great end of right and true piety, but to the empty pride of human praise and glory, become in a sense worthless and unprofitable ; nevertheless, as indications of a certain disposition of mind, they please us so much that we would desire those in whom they exist, either by special preference or

along with the others, to be freed from the pains of hell, were not the verdict of human feeling different from that of the justice of the Creator.

5. These things being so, if the Saviour delivered all from that place, and, to quote the terms of the question in your letter, "emptied hell, so that now from that time forward the last judgment was to be expected," the following things occasion not unreasonable perplexity on this subject, and are wont to present themselves to me in the meantime when I think on it. First, by what authoritative statements can this opinion be confirmed? For the words of Scripture, that "the pains of hell were loosed" by the death of Christ, do not establish this, seeing that this statement may be understood as referring to Himself, and meaning that he so far loosed (that is, made ineffectual) the pains of hell that He Himself was not held by them, especially since it is added that it was "impossible for Him to be holden of them." Or if any one [objecting to this interpretation] ask the reason why He chose to descend into hell, where those pains were which could not possibly hold Him who was, as Scripture says, "free among the dead,"[3] in whom the prince and captain of death found nothing which deserved punishment, the words that "the pains of hell were loosed" may be understood as referring not to the case of all, but only of some whom He judged worthy of that deliverance ; so that neither is He supposed to have descended thither in vain, without the purpose of bringing benefit to any of those who were there held in prison, nor is it a necessary inference that what divine mercy and justice granted to some must be supposed to have been granted to all.

CHAP. III. 6. As to the first man, the father of mankind, it is agreed by almost the entire Church that the Lord loosed him from that prison ; a tenet which must be believed to have been accepted not without reason, — from whatever source it was handed down to the Church, — although the authority of the canonical Scriptures cannot be brought forward as speaking expressly in its support,[4] though this seems to be the opinion which is more than any other borne out by these words in the book of Wisdom.[5] Some add to this [tradition] that the same favour was bestowed on the holy men of antiquity, — on Abel, Seth, Noah and his house, Abraham, Isaac, Jacob, and the other patriarchs and prophets, they also being loosed from those pains at the time when the Lord descended into hell.

7. But, for my part, I cannot see how Abra-

---

[1] Ps. xvi. 10.
[2] Acts ii. 24, 27, in which the words rendered by Augustin "inferni dolores" are; τὰς ὠδῖνας τοῦ θανάτου.
[3] Ps. lxxxviii. 5.
[4] We give the original of this important sentence : — " De illo quidem primo homine patre generis humani, quod eum inde solverit Ecclesia fere tota consentit : quod eam non inaniter credidisse credendum est, undecumque hoc traditum sit, etiamsi canonicarum Scripturarum hinc expressa non proferatur auctoritas."
[5] Wisd. x. 1, 2.

ham, into whose bosom also the pious beggar in the parable was received, can be understood to have been in these pains; those who are able can perhaps explain this. But I suppose every one must see it to be absurd to imagine that only two, namely, Abraham and Lazarus, were in that bosom of wondrous repose before the Lord descended into hell, and that with reference to these two alone it was said to the rich man, "Between us and you there is a great gulf fixed, so that they which would pass from hence to you cannot, neither can they pass to us that would pass from thence." [1] Moreover, if there were more than two there, who will dare to say that the patriarchs and prophets were not there, to whose righteousness and piety so signal testimony is borne in the word of God? What benefit was conferred in that case on them by Him who loosed the pains of hell, in which they were not held, I do not yet understand, especially as I have not been able to find anywhere in Scripture the name of hell used in a good sense. And if this use of the term is nowhere found in the divine Scriptures, assuredly the bosom of Abraham, that is, the abode of a certain secluded rest, is not to be believed to be a part of hell. Nay, from these words themselves of the great Master, in which He says that Abraham said, "Between us and you there is a great gulf fixed," it is, as I think, sufficiently evident that the bosom of that glorious felicity was not any integral part of hell. For what is that great gulf but a chasm completely separating those places between which it not only is, but is fixed? Wherefore, if sacred Scripture had said, without naming hell and its pains, that Christ when He died went to that bosom of Abraham, I wonder if any one would have dared to say that He " descended into hell."

8. But seeing that plain scriptural testimonies make mention of hell and its pains, no reason can be alleged for believing that He who is the Saviour went thither, except that He might save from its pains; but whether He did save all whom He found held in them, or some whom He judged worthy of that favour, I still ask: that He was, however, in hell, and that He conferred this benefit on persons subjected to these pains, I do not doubt. Wherefore, I have not yet found what benefit He, when He descended into hell, conferred upon those righteous ones who were in Abraham's bosom, from whom I see that, so far as regarded the beatific presence of His Godhead, He never withdrew Himself; since even on that very day on which He died, He promised that the thief should be with Him in paradise at the time when He was about to descend to loose the pains of hell. Most cer-

tainly, therefore, He was, before that time, both in paradise and the bosom of Abraham in His beatific wisdom, and in hell in His condemning power; for since the Godhead is confined by no limits, where is He not present? At the same time, however, so far as regarded the created nature, in assuming which at a certain point of time, He, while continuing to be God, became man — that is to say, so far as regarded His soul, He was in hell: this is plainly declared in these words of Scripture, which were both sent before in prophecy and fully expounded by apostolical interpretation: "Thou wilt not leave my soul in hell." [2]

9. I know that some think that at the death of Christ a resurrection such as is promised to us at the end of the world was granted to the righteous, founding this on the statement in Scripture that, in the earthquake by which at the moment of His death the rocks were rent and the graves were opened, many bodies of the saints arose and were seen with Him in the Holy City after He rose. Certainly, if these did not fall asleep again, their bodies being a second time laid in the grave, it would be necessary to see in what sense Christ can be understood to be " the first begotten from the dead," [3] if so many preceded Him in the resurrection. And if it be said, in answer to this, that the statement is made by anticipation, so that the graves indeed are to be supposed to have been opened by that earthquake at the time when Christ was hanging on the cross, but that the bodies of the saints did not rise then, but only after Christ had risen before them, — although on this hypothesis of anticipation in the narrative, the addition of these words would not hinder us from still believing, on the one hand, that Christ was without doubt " the first begotten from the dead," and on the other, that to these saints permission was given, when He went before them, to rise to an eternal state of incorruption and immortality, — there still remains a difficulty, namely, how in that case Peter could have spoken as he did, saying what was without doubt perfectly true, when he affirmed that in the prophecy quoted above the words, that " His flesh should not see corruption," referred not to David but to Christ, and added concerning David, "He is buried, and his sepulchre is with us to this day," [4] — a statement which would have had no force as an argument unless the body of David was still undisturbed in the sepulchre; for of course the sepulchre might still have been there even had the saint's body been raised up immediately after his death, and had thus not seen corruption. But it seems hard that David should not be

included in this resurrection of the saints, if eternal life was given to them, since it is so frequently, so clearly, and with such honourable mention of his name, declared that Christ was to be of David's seed. Moreover, these words in the Epistle to the Hebrews concerning the ancient believers, "God having provided some better thing for us, that they without us should not be made perfect,"[1] will be endangered, if these believers have been already established in that incorruptible resurrection-state which is promised to us when we are to be made perfect at the end of the world.

Chap. IV. — 10. You perceive, therefore, how intricate is the question why Peter chose to mention, as persons to whom, when shut up in prison, the gospel was preached, those only who were unbelieving in the days of Noah when the ark was a preparing — and also the difficulties which prevent me from pronouncing any definite opinion on the subject. An additional reason for my hesitation is, that after the apostle had said, "Which baptism now by a like figure saves you (not the putting away of the filth of the flesh, but the answer of a good conscience towards God) by the resurrection of Jesus Christ, who is on the right hand of God, having swallowed up death that we might be made heirs of eternal life ; and having gone into heaven, angels, and authorities, and powers being made subject to Him," he added : "Forasmuch then as Christ hath suffered for us in the flesh, arm yourselves likewise with the same mind : for he that hath suffered in the flesh hath ceased from sin ; that he no longer should live the rest of his time in the flesh to the lusts of men, but to the will of God ;" after which he continues : "For the time past of our life may suffice us to have wrought the will of the Gentiles, when we walked in lasciviousness, lusts, excess of wine, revellings, banquetings, and abominable idolatries : wherein they think it strange that ye run not with them to the same excess of riot, speaking evil of you ; who shall give account to Him that is ready to judge the quick and the dead." After these words he subjoins : "For for this cause was the gospel preached also to them that are dead, that they might be judged according to men in the flesh, but live according to God in the Spirit."[2]

11. Who can be otherwise than perplexed by words so profound as these? He saith, "The gospel was preached to the dead ;" and if by the "dead" we understand persons who have departed from the body, I suppose he must mean those described above as "unbelieving in the days of Noah," or certainly all those whom Christ found in hell. What, then, is meant by the words, "That they might be judged according

to men in the flesh, but live according to God in the spirit"? For how can they be judged in the flesh, which if they be in hell they no longer have, and which if they have been loosed from the pains of hell they have not yet resumed? For even if " hell was," as you put in your question, " emptied," it is not to be believed that all who were then there have risen again in the flesh, or those who, arising, again appeared with the Lord resumed the flesh for this purpose, that they might be in it judged according to men ; but how this could be taken as true in the case of those who were unbelieving in the days of Noah I do not see, for Scripture does not affirm that they were made to live in the flesh, nor can it be believed that the end for which they were loosed from the pains of hell was that they who were delivered from these might resume their flesh in order to suffer punishment. What, then, is meant by the words, "That they might be judged according to men in the flesh, but live according to God in the spirit?" Can it mean that to those whom Christ found in hell this was granted, that by the gospel they were quickened in the spirit, although at the future resurrection they must be judged in the flesh, that they may pass, through some punishment in the flesh, into the kingdom of God? If this be what is meant, why were only the unbelievers of the time of Noah (and not also all others whom Christ found in hell when He went thither) quickened in spirit by the preaching of the gospel, to be afterwards judged in the flesh with a punishment of limited duration? But if we take this as applying to all, the question still remains why Peter mentioned none but those who were unbelieving in the days of Noah.

12. I find, moreover, a difficulty in the reason alleged by those who attempt to give an explanation of this matter. They say that all those who were found in hell when Christ descended thither had never heard the gospel, and that that place of punishment or imprisonment was emptied of all these, because the gospel was not published to the whole world in their lifetime, and they had sufficient excuse for not believing that which had never been proclaimed to them ; but that thenceforth, men despising the gospel when it was in all nations fully published and spread abroad would be inexcusable, and therefore after the prison was then emptied there still remains a just judgment, in which those who are contumacious and unbelieving shall be punished even with eternal fire. Those who hold this opinion do not consider that the same excuse is available for all those who have, even after Christ's resurrection, departed this life before the gospel came to them. For even after the Lord came back from hell, it was not the case that no one was from that time forward permitted

[1] Heb. xi. 40.
[2] 1 Pet. iv. 1, 6.

to go to hell without having heard the gospel, seeing that multitudes throughout the world died before the proclamation of its tidings came to them, all of whom are entitled to plead the excuse which is alleged to have been taken away from those of whom it is said, that because they had not before heard the gospel, the Lord when He descended into hell proclaimed it to them.

13. This objection may perhaps be met by saying that those also who since the Lord's resurrection have died or are now dying without the gospel having been proclaimed to them, may have heard it or may now hear it where they are, in hell, so that there they may believe what ought to be believed concerning the truth of Christ, and may also have that pardon and salvation which those to whom Christ preached obtained ; for the fact that Christ ascended again from hell is no reason why the report concerning Him should have perished from recollection there, for from this earth also He has gone ascending into heaven, and yet by the publication of His gospel those who believe in Him shall be saved ; moreover, He was exalted, and received a name that is above every name, for this end, that in His name every knee should bow, not only of things in heaven and on earth, but also of things under the earth.[1] But if we accept this opinion, according to which we are warranted in supposing that men who did not believe while they were in life can in hell believe in Christ, who can bear the contradictions both of reason and faith which must follow ? In the first place, if this were true, we should seem to have no reason for mourning over those who have departed from the body without that grace, and there would be no ground for being solicitous and using urgent exhortation that men would accept the grace of God before they die, lest they should be punished with eternal death. If, again, it be alleged that in hell those only believe to no purpose and in vain who refused to accept here on earth the gospel preached to them, but that believing will profit those who never despised a gospel which they never had it in their power to hear, another still more absurd consequence is involved, namely, that forasmuch as all men shall certainly die, and ought to come to hell wholly free from the guilt of having despised the gospel, since otherwise it can be of no use to them to believe it when they come there, the gospel ought not to be preached on earth, — a sentiment not less foolish than profane.

CHAP. V. — 14. Wherefore let us most firmly hold that which faith, resting on authority established beyond all question, maintains : "that Christ died according to the Scriptures," and that "He was buried," and that "He rose again the third day according to the Scriptures," and all other things which have been written concerning Him in records fully demonstrated to be true. Among these doctrines we include the doctrine that He was in hell, and, having loosed the pains of hell, in which it was impossible for Him to be holden, from which also He is with good ground believed to have loosed and delivered whom He would, He took again to Himself that body which He had left on the cross, and which had been laid in the tomb. These things, I say, let us firmly hold ; but as to the question propounded by you from the words of the Apostle Peter, since you now perceive the difficulties which I find in it, and since other difficulties may possibly be found if the subject be more carefully studied, let us continue to investigate it, whether by applying our own thoughts to the subject, or by asking the opinion of any one whom it may be becoming and possible to consult.

15. Consider, however, I pray you, whether all that the Apostle Peter says concerning spirits shut up in prison, who were unbelieving in the days of Noah, may not after all have been written without any reference to hell, but rather to those times the typical character of which he has transferred to the present time. For that transaction had been typical of future events, so that those who do not believe the gospel in our age, when the Church is being built up in all nations, may be understood to be like those who did not believe in that age while the ark was a preparing ; also, that those who have believed and are saved by baptism may be compared to those who at that time, being in the ark, were saved by water ; wherefore he says, "So baptism by a like figure saves you." Let us therefore interpret the rest of the statements concerning them that believed not so as to harmonise with the analogy of the figure, and refuse to entertain the thought that the gospel was once preached, or is even to this hour being preached in hell in order to make men believe and be delivered from its pains, as if a Church had been established there as well as on earth.

16. Those who have inferred from the words, "He preached to the spirits in prison," that Peter held the opinion which perplexes you, seem to me to have been drawn to this interpretation by imagining that the term "spirits" could not be applied to designate souls which were at that time still in the bodies of men, and which, being shut up in the darkness of ignorance, were, so to speak, "in prison," — a prison such as that from which the Psalmist sought deliverance in the prayer, "Bring my soul out of prison, that I may praise Thy name ;"[2] which is in another

---

[1] *Infernorum.* Phil. ii. 9.

[2] Ps. cxlii. 7.

place called the "shadow of death,"[1] from which deliverance was granted, not certainly in hell, but in this world, to those of whom it is written, "They that dwell in the land of the shadow of death, upon them hath the light shined."[2]   But to the men of Noah's time the gospel was preached in vain, because they believed not when God's long suffering waited for them during the many years in which the ark was being built (for the building of the ark was itself in a certain sense a preaching of mercy) ; even as now men similar to them are unbelieving, who, to use the same figure, are shut up in the darkness of ignorance as in a prison, beholding in vain the Church which is being built up throughout the world, while judgment is impending, as the flood was by which at that time all the unbelieving perished ; for the Lord says : "As it was in the days of Noah, so shall it be also in the days of the Son of man ; they did eat, they drank, they married wives, they were given in marriage, until the day that Noah entered into the ark, and the flood came and destroyed them all."[3] But because that transaction was also a type of a future event, that flood was a type both of baptism to believers and of destruction to unbelievers, as in that figure in which, not by a transaction but by words, two things are predicted concerning Christ, when He is represented in Scripture as a stone which was destined to be both to unbelievers a stone of stumbling, and to believers a foundation-stone.[4] Occasionally, however, also in the same figure, whether it be in the form of a typical event or of a parable, two things are used to represent one, as believers were represented both by the timbers of which the ark was built and by the eight souls saved in the ark, and as in the gospel similitude of the sheepfold Christ is both the shepherd and the door.[5]

CHAP. VI. 17. And let it not be regarded as an objection to the interpretation now given, that the Apostle Peter says that Christ Himself preached to men shut up in prison who were unbelieving in the days of Noah, as if we must consider this interpretation inconsistent with the fact that at that time Christ had not come. For although he had not yet come in the flesh, as He came when afterwards He "showed Himself upon earth, and conversed with men,"[6] nevertheless he certainly came often to this earth, from the beginning of the human race, whether to rebuke the wicked, as Cain, and before that, Adam and his wife, when they sinned, or to comfort the good, or to admonish both,

so that some should to their salvation believe, others should to their condemnation refuse to believe, — coming then not in the flesh but in the spirit, speaking by suitable manifestations of Himself to such persons and in such manner as seemed good to Him. As to this expression, "He came in the spirit," surely He, as the Son of God, is a Spirit in the essence of His Deity, for that is not corporeal ; but what is at any time done by the Son without the Holy Spirit, or without the Father, seeing that all the works of the Trinity are inseparable?

18. The words of Scripture which are under consideration seem to me of themselves to make this sufficiently plain to those who carefully attend to them : "For Christ hath died once for our sins, the Just for the unjust, that He might bring us to God ; being put to death in the flesh, but quickened in the spirit : in which also He came and preached unto the spirits in prison, who sometime were unbelieving, when the long-suffering of God waited in the days of Noah, while the ark was a preparing." The order of the words is now, I suppose, carefully noted by you : "Christ being put to death in the flesh, but quickened in the spirit ;" in which spirit He came and preached also to those spirits who had once in the days of Noah refused to believe His word ; since before He came in the flesh to die for us, which He did once, He often came in the spirit, to whom He would, by visions instructing them as He would, coming to them assuredly in the same spirit in which He was quickened when He was put to death in the flesh in His passion. Now what does His being quickened in the spirit mean if not this, that the same flesh in which alone He had experienced death rose from the dead by the quickening spirit?

CHAP. VII. 19. For who will dare to say that Jesus was put to death in His soul, i.e. in the spirit which belonged to Him as man, since the only death which the soul can experience is sin, from which He was absolutely free when for us He was put to death in the flesh? For if the souls of all men are derived from that one which the breath of God gave to the first man, by whom "sin entered into the world, and death by sin, and so death passed upon all men,"[7] either the soul of Christ is not derived from the same source as other souls, because He had absolutely no sin, either original or personal, on account of which death could be supposed to be merited by Him, since He paid on our behalf that which was not on His own account due by Him, in whom the prince of this world, who had the power of death, found nothing[8] — and there is nothing unreasonable in the supposition that

1 Ps. cvii. 14.
2 Isa. ix. 2.
3 Luke xvii. 26, 27.
4 Ps. cxviii. 22; Isa. viii. 14, xxviii. 16; Dan ii. 34, 45; Matt. xxi. 44; Luke xx. 17; Acts iv. 11; Rom. ix. 33, etc.
5 John x. 1, 2.
6 Baruch iii. 37.

7 Rom. v. 12.
8 John xiv. 30.

He who created a soul for the first man should create a soul for Himself; or if the soul of Christ be derived from Adam's soul, He, in assuming it to Himself, cleansed it so that when He came into this world He was born of the Virgin perfectly free from sin either actual or transmitted. If, however, the souls of men are not derived from that one soul, and it is only by the flesh that original sin is transmitted from Adam, the Son of God created a soul for Himself, as He creates souls for all other men, but He united it not to sinful flesh, but to the "likeness of sinful flesh."[1] For He took, indeed, from the Virgin the true substance of flesh ; not, however, "sinful flesh," for it was neither begotten nor conceived through carnal concupiscence, but mortal, and capable of change in the successive stages of life, as being like unto sinful flesh in all points, sin excepted.

20. Therefore, whatever be the true theory concerning the origin of souls, — and on this I feel it would be rash for me to pronounce, meanwhile, any opinion beyond utterly rejecting the theory which affirms that each soul is thrust into the body which it inhabits as into a prison, where it expiates some former actions of its own of which I know nothing, — it is certain, regarding the soul of Christ, not only that it is, according to the nature of all souls, immortal, but also that it was neither put to death by sin nor punished by condemnation, the only two ways in which death can be understood as experienced by the soul ; and therefore it could not be said of Christ that with reference to the soul He was "quickened in the spirit." For He was quickened in that in which He had been put to death ; this, therefore, is spoken with reference to His flesh, for His flesh received life again when the soul returned to it, as it also had died when the soul departed. He was therefore said to be "put to death in the flesh," because He experienced death only in the flesh, but "quickened in the spirit," because by the operation of that Spirit in which He was wont to come and preach to whom He would, that same flesh in which He came to men was quickened and rose from the grave.

21. Wherefore, passing now to the words which we find farther on concerning unbelievers, "Who shall give account to Him who is ready to judge the quick and the dead," there is no necessity for our understanding the "dead" here to be those who have departed from the body. For it may be that the apostle intended by the word "dead" to denote unbelievers, as being spiritually dead, like those of whom it was said, "Let the dead bury their dead,"[2] and by the word "living" to denote those who believe in Him, having not heard in vain the call, "Awake, thou that sleepest, and arise from the dead, and Christ shall give thee light ; "[3] of whom also the Lord said : "The hour is coming, and now is, when the dead shall hear the voice of the Son of God, and they that hear shall live."[4] On the same principle of interpretation, also, there is nothing compelling us to understand the immediately succeeding words of Peter — " For for this cause was the gospel preached also to them that are dead, that they might be judged according to men in the flesh, but live according to God in the spirit "[5] — as describing what has been done in hell. "For for this cause has the gospel been preached " in this life "to the dead," that is, to the unbelieving wicked, " that " when they believed " they might be judged according to men in the flesh," — that is, by means of various afflictions and by the death of the body itself; for which reason the same apostle says in another place : "The time is come that judgment must begin at the house of God,"[6] — "but live according to God in the spirit," since in that same spirit they had been dead while they were held prisoners in the death of unbelief and wickedness.

22. If this exposition of the words of Peter offend any one, or, without offending, at least fail to satisfy any one, let him attempt to interpret them on the supposition that they refer to hell : and if he succeed in solving my difficulties which I have mentioned above, so as to remove the perplexity which they occasion, let him communicate his interpretation to me ; and if this were done, the words might possibly have been intended to be understood in both ways, but the view which I have propounded is not thereby shown to be false.

I wrote and sent by the deacon Asellus a letter, which I suppose you have received, giving such answers as I could to the questions which you sent before, excepting the one concerning the vision of God by the bodily senses, on which a larger treatise must be attempted. In your last note, to which this is a reply, you propounded two questions concerning certain words of the Apostle Peter, and concerning the soul of the Lord, both of which I have discussed, — the former more fully, the latter briefly.[7] I beg you not to grudge the trouble of sending me another copy of the letter containing the question whether it is possible for the substance of the Deity to be seen in a bodily form as limited to place ; for it has, I know not how, gone amissing here, and though long sought for, has not been found.

---

[1] Rom. viii. 3.
[2] Matt. viii. 22.
[3] Eph. v. 14.
[4] John v. 25.
[5] 1 Pet. iv. 6.
[6] 1 Pet iv. 17.
[7] See paragraphs 19 and 20.

LETTER CLXV.

(A.D. 410.[1])

TO MY TRULY PIOUS LORDS MARCELLINUS[2] AND ANAPSYCHIA, SONS WORTHY OF BEING ESTEEMED WITH ALL THE LOVE DUE TO THEIR POSITION, JEROME SENDS GREETING IN CHRIST.

CHAP. I. — 1. At last I have received your joint letter from Africa, and I do not regret the importunity with which, though you were silent, I persevered in sending letters to you, that I might obtain a reply, and learn, not through report from others, but from your own most welcome statement, that you are in health. I have not forgotten the brief query, or rather the very important theological[3] question, which you propounded in regard to the origin of the soul,— does it descend from heaven, as the philosopher Pythagoras and all the Platonists and Origen think? or is it part of the essence of the Deity, as the Stoics, Manichæus, and the Priscillianists of Spain imagine? or are souls kept in a divine treasure-house wherein they were stored of old, as some ecclesiastics, foolishly misled, believe? or are they daily created by God and sent into bodies, according to what is written in the gospel, "My Father worketh hitherto, and I work"?[4] or are souls really produced, as Tertullian, Apollinaris, and the majority of the Western divines conjecture, by propagation, so that as the body is the offspring of body, the soul is the offspring of soul, and exists on conditions similar to those regulating the existence of the inferior animals."[5] I know that I have published my opinion on this question in my brief writings against Ruffinus, in reply to a treatise addressed by him to Anastasius, of holy memory, bishop of the Roman Church, in which, while attempting to impose upon the simplicity of his readers by a slippery and artful, yet withal foolish confession, he exposed to contempt his own faith, or, rather, his own perfidy. These books are, I think, in the possession of your holy kinsman Oceanus, for they were published long ago to meet the calumnies contained in numerous writings of Ruffinus. Be this as it may, you have in Africa that holy man and learned bishop Augustin, who will be able to teach you on this subject *viva voce*, as the saying is, and expound to you his opinion, or, I should rather say, my own opinion stated in his words.

CHAP. II. — 2. I have long wished to begin the volume of Ezekiel, and fulfil a promise frequently made to studious readers; but at the time when I had just begun to dictate the proposed exposition, my mind was so much agitated by the devastation of the western provinces of the empire, and especially by the sack of Rome itself by the barbarians, that, to use a common proverbial phrase, I scarcely knew my own name; and for a long while I was silent, knowing that it was a time for tears. Moreover when I had, in the course of this year, prepared three books of the *Commentary*, a sudden furious invasion of the barbarous tribes mentioned by your Virgil as "the widely roaming Barcæi,"[6] and by sacred Scripture in the words concerning Ishmael, "He shall dwell in the presence of his brethren,"[7] swept over the whole of Egypt, Palestine, Phenice, and Syria, carrying all before them with the vehemence of a mighty torrent, so that it was only with the greatest difficulty that we were enabled, by the mercy of Christ, to escape their hands. But if, as a famous orator has said, "Laws are silent amid the clash of arms,"[8] how much more may this be said of scriptural studies, which demand a multitude of books and silence, together with uninterrupted diligence of amanuenses, and especially the enjoyment of tranquillity and leisure by those who dictate! I have accordingly sent two books to my holy daughter Fabiola, of which, if you wish copies, you may borrow them from her. Through lack of time I have been unable to transcribe others; when you have read these, and have seen the portico, as it were, you may easily conjecture what the house itself is designed to be. But I trust in the mercy of God, who has helped me in the very difficult commencement of the foresaid work, that He will help me also in the predictions concerning the wars of Gog and Magog, which occupy the last division but one of the prophecy,[9] and in the concluding portion itself, describing the building, the details, and the proportions of that most holy and mysterious temple.[10]

CHAP. III. — 3. Our holy brother Oceanus, to whom you desire to be mentioned, is a man of such gifts and character, and so profoundly learned in the law of the Lord, that he may probably give you instruction without any request of mine, and can impart to you on all scriptural questions the opinion which, according to the measure of our joint abilities, we have formed.

May Christ, our almighty God, keep you, my truly pious lords, in safety and prosperity to a good old age!

---

[1] In assigning this place to Jerome's letter to Marcellinus and Anapsychia, the Benedictine editors have departed from the chronological sequence in order to place it in immediate juxtaposition to Letter CLXVI., written by Augustin to Jerome some years later on the subject mentioned in sec. 1.
[2] See note on Marcellinus in Letter CXXXIII. p. 470.
[3] *Ecclesiastica.*
[4] John v. 17.
[5] *Et simili cum brutis animantibus conditione subsistat.*

[6] "Lateque vagantes Barcæi." — Virg. *Æneid*, iv. 43.
[7] Gen. xvi. 12.
[8] Cicero *pro Milone :* "Leges inter arma silent."
[9] Ezek. ch. xxxviii.-xxxix.
[10] *Ibid.* ch. xl.-xliii

LETTER CLXVI.

(A.D. 415.)

A TREATISE ON THE ORIGIN OF THE HUMAN SOUL, ADDRESSED TO JEROME.[1]

CHAP. I. — 1. Unto our God, who hath called us unto His kingdom and glory,[2] I have prayed, and pray now, that what I write to you, holy brother Jerome, asking your opinion in regard to things of which I am ignorant, may by His good pleasure be profitable to us both. For although in addressing you I consult one much older than myself, nevertheless I also am becoming old ; but I cannot think that it is at any time of life too late to learn what we need to know, because, although it is more fitting that old men should be teachers than learners, it is nevertheless more fitting for them to learn than to continue ignorant of that which they should teach to others. I assure you that, amid the many disadvantages which I have to submit to in studying very difficult questions, there is none which grieves me more than the circumstance of separation from your Charity by a distance so great that I can scarcely send a letter to you, and scarcely receive one from you, even at intervals, not of days nor of months, but of several years ; whereas my desire would be, if it were possible, to have you daily beside me, as one with whom I could converse on any theme. Nevertheless, although I have not been able to do all that I wished, I am not the less bound to do all that I can.

2. Behold, a religious young man has come to me, by name Orosius, who is in the bond of Catholic peace a brother, in point of age a son, and in honour a fellow presbyter, — a man of quick understanding, ready speech, and burning zeal, desiring to be in the Lord's house a vessel rendering useful service in refuting those false and pernicious doctrines, through which the souls of men in Spain have suffered much more grievous wounds than have been inflicted on their bodies by the sword of barbarians. For from the remote western coast of Spain he has come with eager haste to us, having been prompted to do this by the report that from me he could learn whatever he wished on the subjects on which he desired information. Nor has his coming been altogether in vain. In the first place, he has learned not to believe all that report affirmed of me : in the next place, I have taught him all that I could, and, as for the things in which I could not teach him, I have told him from whom he may learn them, and have exhorted him to go on to you. As he received this counsel or rather injunction of mine with pleasure, and with intention to comply with it, I asked him to visit us on his way home to his own country when he comes from you. On receiving his promise to this effect, I believed that the Lord had granted me an opportunity of writing to you regarding certain things which I wish through you to learn. For I was seeking some one whom I might send to you, and it was not easy to fall in with one qualified both by trustworthiness in performing and by alacrity in undertaking the work, as well as by experience in travelling. Therefore, when I became acquainted with this young man, I could not doubt that he was exactly such a person as I was asking from the Lord.

CHAP. II. — 3. Allow me, therefore, to bring before you a subject which I beseech you not to refuse to open up and discuss with me. Many are perplexed by questions concerning the soul, and I confess that I myself am of this number. I shall in this letter, in the first place, state explicitly the things regarding the soul which I most assuredly believe, and shall, in the next place, bring forward the things regarding which I am still desirous of explanation.

The soul of man is in a sense proper to itself immortal. It is not absolutely immortal, as God is, of whom it is written that He "alone hath immortality,"[3] for Holy Scripture makes mention of deaths to which the soul is liable — as in the saying, " Let the dead bury their dead ; "[4] but because when alienated from the life of God it so dies as not wholly to cease from living in its own nature, it is found to be from a certain cause mortal, yet so as to be not without reason called at the same time immortal.

The soul is not a part of God. For if it were, it would be absolutely immutable and incorruptible, in which case it could neither go downward to be worse, nor go onward to be better ; nor could it either begin to have anything in itself which it had not before, or cease to have any-

---

[1] The following passage from the *Retractations of Augustin* (Book ii. ch. xlv.) is quoted by the Benedictine Fathers as a preface to this letter and the one immediately succeeding: — "I wrote also two books to Presbyter Jerome, the recluse of Bethlehem [sedentem in Bethlehem]: the one on the origin of the human soul, the other on the sentence of the Apostle James, 'Whosoever shall keep the whole law and offend in one point, he is guilty of all' (Jas. ii. 10), asking his opinion on both subjects. In the former letter I did not give any answer of my own to the question which I proposed; in the latter I did not keep back what seemed to me the best way to solve the question, but asked whether the same solution commended itself to his judgment. He wrote in return, expressing approbation of my submitting the questions to him, but saying that he had not leisure to send me a reply. So long as he lived, therefore, I refused to give these books to the world, lest he should perhaps at any time reply to them, in which case I would have rather published them along with his answer. After his decease, however, I published them, — the former, in order to admonish any who read it, either to forbear altogether from inquiring into the manner in which a soul is given to infants at the time of birth, or, at all events, in a matter so involved in obscurity, to accept only such a solution of the question as does not contradict the clearest truths which the Catholic faith confesses in regard to original sin in infants, as undoubtedly doomed to perdition unless they be regenerated in Christ; the latter in order that what seemed to us the true answer to the question therein discussed might be known. The work begins with the words, 'Deum nostrum qui nos vocavit.'"
[2] 1 Thess. ii. 12.
[3] 1 Tim. vi. 16.
[4] Matt. viii. 22.

thing which it had within the sphere of its own experience. But how different the actual facts of the case are is a point requiring no evidence from without, it is acknowledged by every one who consults his own consciousness. In vain, moreover, is it pleaded by those who affirm that the soul is a part of God, that the corruption and baseness which we see in the worst of men, and the weakness and blemishes which we see in all men, come to it not from the soul itself, but from the body; for what matters it whence the infirmity originates in that which, if it were indeed immutable, could not, from any quarter whatever, be made infirm? For that which is truly immutable and incorruptible is not liable to mutation or corruption by any influence whatever from without, else the invulnerability which the fable ascribed to the flesh of Achilles would be nothing peculiar to him, but the property of every man, so long as no accident befell him. That which is liable to be changed in any manner, by any cause, or in any part whatever, is therefore not by nature immutable; but it were impiety to think of God as otherwise than truly and supremely immutable: therefore the soul is not a part of God.

4. That the soul is immaterial is a fact of which I avow myself to be fully persuaded, although men of slow understanding are hard to be convinced that it is so. To secure myself, however, from either unnecessarily causing to others or unreasonably bringing upon myself a controversy about an expression, let me say that, since the thing itself is beyond question, it is needless to contend about mere terms. If matter be used as a term denoting everything which in any form has a separate existence, whether it be called an essence, or a substance, or by another name, the soul is material. Again, if you choose to apply the epithet immaterial only to that nature which is supremely immutable and is everywhere present in its entirety, the soul is material, for it is not at all endowed with such qualities. But if matter be used to designate nothing but that which, whether at rest or in motion, has some length, breadth, and height, so that with a greater part of itself it occupies a greater part of space, and with a smaller part a smaller space, and is in every part of it less than the whole, then the soul is not material. For it pervades the whole body which it animates, not by a local distribution of parts, but by a certain vital influence, being at the same moment present in its entirety in all parts of the body, and not less in smaller parts and greater in larger parts, but here with more energy and there with less energy, it is in its entirety present both in the whole body and in every part of it. For even that which the mind perceives in only a part of the body is nevertheless not otherwise perceived than by the whole mind; for when any part of the living flesh is touched by a fine-pointed instrument, although the place affected is not only not the whole body, but scarcely discernible in its surface, the contact does not escape the entire mind, and yet the contact is felt not over the whole body, but only at the one point where it takes place. How comes it, then, that what takes place in only a part of the body is immediately known to the whole mind, unless the whole mind is present at that part, and at the same time not deserting all the other parts of the body in order to be present in its entirety at this one? For all the other parts of the body in which no such contact takes place are still living by the soul being present with them. And if a similar contact takes place in the other parts, and the contact occur in both parts simultaneously, it would in both cases alike be known at the same moment, to the whole mind. Now this presence of the mind in all parts of the body at the same moment, so that in every part of the body the whole mind is at the same moment present, would be impossible if it were distributed over these parts in the same way as we see matter distributed in space, occupying less space with a smaller portion of itself, and greater space with a greater portion. If, therefore, mind is to be called material, it is not material in the same sense as earth, water, air, and ether are material. For all things composed of these elements are larger in larger places, or smaller in smaller places, and none of them is in its entirety present at any part of itself, but the dimensions of the material substances are according to the dimensions of the space occupied. Whence it is perceived that the soul, whether it be termed material or immaterial, has a certain nature of its own, created from a substance superior to the elements of this world,—a substance which cannot be truly conceived of by any representation of the material images perceived by the bodily senses, but which is apprehended by the understanding and discovered to our consciousness by its living energy. These things I am stating, not with the view of teaching you what you already know, but in order that I may declare explicitly what I hold as indisputably certain concerning the soul, lest any one should think, when I come to state the questions to which I desire answers, that I hold none of the doctrines which we have learned from science or from revelation concerning the soul.

5. I am, moreover, fully persuaded that the soul has fallen into sin, not through the fault of God, nor through any necessity either in the divine nature or in its own, but by its own free will; and that it can be delivered from the body of this death neither by the strength of its own will, as if that were in itself sufficient to achieve

this, nor by the death of the body itself, but only by the grace of God through our Lord Jesus Christ;[1] and that there is not one soul in the human family to whose salvation the one Mediator between God and men, the man Christ Jesus, is not absolutely necessary. Every soul, moreover, which may at any age whatsoever depart from this life without the grace of the Mediator and the sacrament of this grace, departs to future punishment, and shall receive again its own body at the last judgment as a partner in punishment. But if the soul after its natural generation, which was derived from Adam, be regenerated in Christ, it belongs to His fellowship,[2] and shall not only have rest after the death of the body, but also receive again its own body as a partner in glory. These are truths concerning the soul which I hold most firmly.

CHAP. III.—6. Permit me now, therefore, to bring before you the question which I desire to have solved, and do not reject me; so may He not reject you who condescended to be rejected for our sakes!

I ask where can the soul, even of an infant snatched away by death, have contracted the guilt which, unless the grace of Christ has come to the rescue by that sacrament of baptism which is administered even to infants, involves it in condemnation? I know you are not one of those who have begun of late to utter certain new and absurd opinions, alleging that there is no guilt derived from Adam which is removed by baptism in the case of infants. If I knew that you held this view, or, rather, if I did not know that you reject it, I would certainly neither address this question to you, nor think that it ought to be put to you at all. Since, however, we hold on this subject the opinion consonant with the immoveable Catholic faith, which you have yourself expressed when, refuting the absurd sayings of Jovinian, you have quoted this sentence from the book of Job: "In thy sight no one is clean, not even the infant, whose time of life on earth is a single day,"[3] adding, "for we are held guilty in the similitude of Adam's transgression,"[4]—an opinion which your book on Jonah's prophecy declares in a notable and lucid manner, where you affirm that the little children of Nineveh were justly compelled to fast along with the people, because merely of their original sin,[5]—it is not unsuitable that I should address to you the question—where has the soul contracted the guilt from which, even at that age, it must be delivered by the sacrament of Christian grace?

7. Some years ago, when I wrote certain books concerning *Free Will*, which have gone forth into the hands of many, and are now in the possession of very many readers, after referring to these four opinions as to the manner of the soul's incarnation,—(1) that all other souls are derived from the one which was given to the first man; (2) that for each individual a new soul is made; (3) that souls already in existence somewhere are sent by divine act into the bodies; or (4) glide into them of their own accord,—I thought that it was necessary to treat them in such a way that, whichever of them might be true, the decision should not hinder the object which I had in view when contending with all my might against those who attempt to lay upon God the blame of a nature endowed with its own principle of evil, namely, the Manichæans;[6] for at that time I had not heard of the Priscillianists, who utter blasphemies not very dissimilar to these. As to the fifth opinion, namely, that the soul is a part of God,—an opinion which, in order to omit none, you have mentioned along with the rest in your letter to Marcellinus (a man of pious memory and very dear to us in the grace of Christ), who had consulted you on this question,[7]—I did not add it to the others for two reasons,—first, because, in examining this opinion, we discuss not the incarnation of the soul, but its nature; secondly, because this is the view held by those against whom I was arguing, and the main design of my argument was to prove that the blameless and inviolable nature of the Creator has nothing to do with the faults and blemishes of the creature, while they, on their part, maintained that the substance of the good God itself is, in so far as it is led captive, corrupted and oppressed and brought under a necessity of sinning by the substance of evil, to which they ascribe a proper dominion and principalities. Leaving, therefore, out of the question this heretical error, I desire to know which of the other four opinions we ought to choose. For whichever of them may justly claim our preference, far be it from us to assail this article of faith, about which we have no uncertainty, that every soul, even the soul of an infant, requires to be delivered from the binding guilt of sin, and that there is no deliverance except through Jesus Christ and Him crucified.

CHAP. IV—8. To avoid prolixity, therefore, let me refer to the opinion which you, I believe, entertain, viz. that God even now makes each soul for each individual at the time of birth. To meet the objection to this view which might be taken from the fact that God finished the whole work of creation on the sixth day and rested on the seventh day, you quote the testimony of the

---

[1] Rom. vii. 24, 25.
[2] We read *pertinere*, not *pertinens*.
[3] Job xiv. 4, 5, according to LXX.
[4] Jerome *against Jovinian*, Book ii.
[5] Jerome *on Jonah*, ch. iii.

[6] *De Libero Arbitrio*, iii. 21.
[7] Letter CLXV.

words in the gospel, " My Father worketh hither-to, and I work." [1] This you have written in your letter to Marcellinus, in which letter, moreover, you have most kindly condescended to mention my name, saying that he had me here in Africa, who could more easily explain to him the opinion held by you.[2] But had I been able to do this, he would not have applied for instruction to you, who were so remote from him, though perhaps he did not write from Africa to you. For I know not when he wrote it ; I only know that he knew well my hesitation to embrace any definite view on this subject, for which reason he preferred to write to you without consulting me. Yet, even if he had consulted me, I would rather have encouraged him to write to you, and would have expressed my gratitude for the benefit which might have been conferred on us all, had you not preferred to send a brief note, instead of a full reply, doing this, I suppose, to save yourself from unnecessary expenditure of effort in a place where I, whom you supposed to be thoroughly acquainted with the subject of his inquiries, was at hand. Behold, I am willing that the opinion which you hold should be also mine ; but I assure you that as yet I have not embraced it.

9. You have sent to me scholars, to whom you wish me to impart what I have not yet learned myself. Teach me, therefore, what I am to teach them ; for many urge me vehemently to be a teacher on this subject, and to them I confess that of this, as well as of many other things, I am ignorant, and perhaps, though they maintain a respectful demeanour in my presence, they say among themselves : " Art thou a master in Israel, and knowest not these things ? " [3] — a rebuke which the Lord gave to one who belonged to the class of men who delighted in being called Rabbi ; which was also the reason of his coming by night to the true Teacher, because perchance he, who had been accustomed to teach, blushed to take the learner's place. But, for my own part, it gives me much more pleasure to hear instruction from another, than to be myself listened to as a teacher. For I remember what He said to those whom, above all men, He had chosen : " But be not ye called Rabbi, for one is your master, even Christ." [4] Nor was it any other teacher who taught Moses by Jethro,[5] Cornelius by Peter the earlier apostle,[6] and Peter himself by Paul the later apostle ; [7] for by whomsoever truth is spoken, it is spoken by the gift of Him who is the Truth. What if the reason of our still being ignorant of these things, and of our having failed to discover them, even after praying, reading, thinking, and reasoning, be this : that full proof may be made not only of the love with which we give instruction to the ignorant, but also of the humility with which we receive instruction from the learned ?

10. Teach me, therefore, I beseech you, what I may teach to others ; teach me what I ought to hold as my own opinion ; and tell me this : if souls are from day to day made for each individual separately at birth, where, in the case of infant children, is sin committed by these souls, so that they require the remission of sin in the sacrament of Christ, because of sinning in Adam from whom the sinful flesh has been derived ? or if they do not sin, how is it compatible with the justice of the Creator, that, because of their being united to mortal members derived from another, they are so brought under the bond of the sin of that other, that unless they be rescued by the Church, perdition overtakes them, although it is not in their own power to secure that they be rescued by the grace of baptism ? Where, therefore, is the justice of the condemnation of so many thousands of souls, which in the deaths of infant children leave this world without the benefit of the Christian sacrament, if being newly created they have, not through any preceding sin of their own, but by the will of the Creator, become severally united to the individual bodies to animate which they were created and bestowed by Him, who certainly knew that every one of them was destined, not through any fault of its own, to leave the body without receiving the baptism of Christ ? Seeing, therefore, that we may not say concerning God either that He compels them to become sinners, or that He punishes innocent souls — and seeing that, on the other hand, it is not lawful for us to deny that nothing else than perdition is the doom of the souls, even of little children, which have departed from the body without the sacrament of Christ, tell me, I implore you, where anything can be found to support the opinion that souls are not all derived from that one soul of the first man, but are each created separately for each individual, as Adam's soul was made for him.

CHAP. V. — 11. As for some other objections which are advanced against this opinion, I think that I could easily dispose of them. For example, some think that they urge a conclusive argument against this opinion when they ask, how God finished all His works on the sixth day and rested on the seventh day,[8] if He is still creating new souls. If we meet them with the quotation from the gospel (given by you in

---

[1] John v. 17.
[2] See Letter CLXV., p. 522.
[3] John iii. 10.
[4] Matt. xxiii. 8.
[5] Ex. xviii. 14-25.
[6] Acts x. 25-48.
[7] Gal. ii. 11-21.

[8] Gen. ii. 2.

the letter to Marcellinus already mentioned), "My Father worketh hitherto," they answer that He "worketh" in maintaining those natures which He has created, not in creating new natures; otherwise, this statement would contradict the words of Scripture in Genesis, where it is most plainly declared that God finished all His works. Moreover, the words of Scripture, that He rested, are unquestionably to be understood of His resting from creating new creatures, not from governing those which He had created; for at that time He made things which previously did not exist, and from making these He rested because He had finished all the creatures which before they existed He saw necessary to be created, so that thenceforward He did not create and make things which previously did not exist, but made and fashioned out of things already existing whatever He did make. Thus the statements, "He rested from His works," and, "He worketh hitherto," are both true, for the gospel could not contradict Genesis.

12. When, however, these things are brought forward by persons who advance them as conclusive against the opinion that God now creates new souls as He created the soul of the first man, and who hold either that He forms them from that one soul which existed before He rested from creation, or that He now sends them forth into bodies from some reservoir or storehouse of souls which He then created, it is easy to turn aside their argument by answering, that even in the six days God formed many things out of those natures which He had already created,—as, for example, the birds and fishes were formed from the waters, and the trees, the grass, and the animals from the earth,—and yet it is undeniable that He was then making things which did not exist before. For there existed previously no bird, no fish, no tree, no animal, and it is clearly understood that He rested from creating those things which previously were not, and were then created, that is to say, He ceased in this sense, that, after that, nothing was made by Him which did not already exist. But if, rejecting the opinions of all who believe either that God sends forth into men souls existing already in some incomprehensible reservoir, or that He makes souls emanate like drops of dew from Himself as particles of His own substance, or that He brings them forth from that one soul of the first man, or that He binds them in the fetters of the bodily members because of sins committed in a prior state of existence,—if, I say, rejecting these, we affirm that for each individual He creates separately a new soul when he is born, we do not herein affirm that He makes anything which He had not already made. For He had already made man after His own image on the sixth day; and this work of His is un-

questionably to be understood with reference to the rational soul of man. The same work He still does, not in creating what did not exist, but in multiplying what already existed. Wherefore it is true, on the one hand, that He rested from creating things which previously did not exist, and equally true, on the other hand, that He continues still to work, not only in governing what He has made, but also in making (not anything which did not previously exist, but) a larger number of those creatures which He had already made. Wherefore, either by such an explanation, or by any other which may seem better, we escape from the objection advanced by those who would make the fact that God rested from His works a conclusive argument against our believing that new souls are still being daily created, not from the first soul, but in the same manner as it was made.

13. Again, as for another objection, stated in the question, "Wherefore does He create souls for those whom He knows to be destined to an early death?" we may reply, that by the death of the children the sins of the parents are either reproved or chastised. We may, moreover, with all propriety, leave these things to the disposal of the Lord of all, for we know that he appoints to the succession of events in time, and therefore to the births and deaths of living creatures as included in these, a course which is consummate in beauty and perfect in the arrangement of all its parts; whereas we are not capable of perceiving those things by the perception of which, if it were attainable, we should be soothed with an ineffable, tranquil joy. For not in vain has the prophet, taught by divine inspiration, declared concerning God, "He bringeth forth in measured harmonies the course of time." [1] For which reason music, the science or capacity of correct harmony, has been given also by the kindness of God to mortals having reasonable souls, with a view to keep them in mind of this great truth. For if a man, when composing a song which is to suit a particular melody, knows how to distribute the length of time allowed to each word so as to make the song flow and pass on in most beautiful adaptation to the ever-changing notes of the melody, how much more shall God, whose wisdom is to be esteemed as infinitely transcending human arts, make infallible provision that not one of the spaces of time alloted to natures that are born and die — spaces which are like the words and syllables of the successive epochs of the course of time — shall have, in what we may call the sublime psalm of the vicissitudes of this world, a duration either more brief or more protracted than the fore-

---

[1] Isa. xl. 26; translated by Augustin, "Qui profert numerose sæculam."

known and predetermined harmony requires! For when I may speak thus with reference even to the leaves of every tree, and the number of the hairs upon our heads, how much more may I say it regarding the birth and death of men, seeing that every man's life on earth continues for a time, which is neither longer nor shorter than God knows to be in harmony with the plan according to which He rules the universe.

14. As to the assertion that everything which has begun to exist in time is incapable of immortality, because all things which are born die, and all things which have grown decay through age, and the opinion which they affirm to follow necessarily from this, viz. that the soul of man must owe its immortality to its having been created before time began, this does not disturb my faith; for, passing over other examples, which conclusively dispose of this assertion, I need only refer to the body of Christ, which now "dieth no more; death shall have no more dominion over it." [1]

15. Moreover, as to your remark in your book against Ruffinus, that some bring forward as against this opinion [that souls are created for each individual separately at birth] the objection that it seems unworthy of God that He should give souls to the offspring of adulterers, and who accordingly attempt to build on this a theory that souls may possibly be incarcerated, as it were, in such bodies, to suffer for the deeds of a life spent in some prior state of being, [2] — this objection does not disturb me, as many things by which it may be answered occur to me when I consider it. The answer which you yourself have given, saying, that in the case of stolen wheat, there is no fault in the grain, but only in him who stole it, and that the earth is not under obligation to refuse to cherish the seed because the sower may have cast it in with a hand defiled by dishonesty, is a most felicitous illustration. But even before I had read it, I felt that to me the objection drawn from the offspring of adulterers caused no serious difficulty when I took a general view of the fact that God brings many good things to light, even out of our evils and our sins. Now, the creation of any living creature compels every one who considers it with piety and wisdom to give to the Creator praise which words cannot express; and if this praise is called forth by the creation of any living creature whatsoever, how much more is it called forth by the creation of a man! If, therefore, the cause of any act of creative power be sought for, no shorter or better reply can be given than that every creature of God is good. And [so far from such an act being unworthy of God] what is more worthy of Him than that He, being good, should make those good things which no one else than God alone can make?

CHAP. VI. — 16. These things, and others which I can advance, I am accustomed to state, as well as I can, against those who attempt to overthrow by such objections the opinion that souls are made for each individual, as the first man's soul was made for him.

But when we come to the penal sufferings of infants, I am embarrassed, believe me, by great difficulties, and am wholly at a loss to find an answer by which they are solved; and I speak here not only of those punishments in the life to come, which are involved in that perdition to which they must be drawn down if they depart from the body without the sacrament of Christian grace, but also of the sufferings which are to our sorrow endured by them before our eyes in this present life, and which are so various, that time rather than examples would fail me if I were to attempt to enumerate them. They are liable to wasting disease, to racking pain, to the agonies of thirst and hunger, to feebleness of limbs, to privation of bodily senses, and to vexing assaults of unclean spirits. Surely it is incumbent on us to show how it is compatible with justice that infants suffer all these things without any evil of their own as the procuring cause. For it would be impious to say, either that these things take place without God's knowledge, or that He cannot resist those who cause them, or that He unrighteously does these things, or permits them to be done. We are warranted in saying that irrational animals are given by God to serve creatures possessing a higher nature, even though they be wicked, as we see most plainly in the gospel that the swine of the Gadarenes were given to the legion of devils at their request; but could we ever be warranted in saying this of men? Certainly not. Man is, indeed, an animal, but an animal endowed with reason, though mortal. In his members dwells a reasonable soul, which in these severe afflictions is enduring a penalty. Now God is good, God is just, God is omnipotent — none but a madman would doubt that he is so; let the great sufferings, therefore, which infant children experience be accounted for by some reason compatible with justice. When older people suffer such trials, we are accustomed, certainly, to say, either that their worth is being proved, as in Job's case, or that their wickedness is being punished, as in Herod's; and from some examples, which it has pleased God to make perfectly clear, men are enabled to conjecture the nature of others which are more obscure; but this is in regard to persons of mature age. Tell me, therefore, what we must answer in regard to infant children; is it true that, although they

---

[1] Rom. vi. 9.
[2] Hieron. *Adv. Ruffin.* lib. iii.

suffer so great punishments, there are no sins in them deserving to be punished? for, of course, there is not in them at that age any righteousness requiring to be put to the proof.

17. What shall I say, moreover, as to the [difficulty which besets the theory of the creation of each soul separately at the birth of the individual in connection with the] diversity of talent in different souls, and especially the absolute privation of reason in some? This is, indeed, not apparent in the first stages of infancy, but being developed continuously from the beginning of life, it becomes manifest in children, of whom some are so slow and defective in memory that they cannot learn even the letters of the alphabet, and some (commonly called idiots) so imbecile that they differ very little from the beasts of the field. Perhaps I am told, in answer to this, that the bodies are the cause of these imperfections. But surely the opinion which we wish to see vindicated from objection does not require us to affirm that the soul chose for itself the body which so impairs it, and, being deceived in the choice, committed a blunder; or that the soul, when it was compelled, as a necessary consequence of being born, to enter into some body, was hindered from finding another by crowds of souls occupying the other bodies before it came, so that, like a man who takes whatever seat may remain vacant for him in a theatre, the soul was guided in taking possession of the imperfect body not by its choice, but by its circumstances. We, of course, cannot say and ought not to believe such things. Tell us, therefore, what we ought to believe and to say in order to vindicate from this difficulty the theory that for each individual body a new soul is specially created.

CHAP. VII.—18. In my books on *Free Will*, already referred to, I have said something, not in regard to the variety of capacities in different souls, but, at least, in regard to the pains which infant children suffer in this life. The nature of the opinion which I there expressed, and the reason why it is insufficient for the purposes of our present inquiry, I will now submit to you, and will put into this letter a copy of the passage in the third book to which I refer. It is as follows:—"In connection with the bodily sufferings experienced by the little children who, by reason of their tender age, have no sins — if the souls which animate them did not exist before they were born into the human family — a more grievous and, as it were, compassionate complaint is very commonly made in the remark, 'What evil have they done that they should suffer these things?' as if there could be a meritorious innocence in any one before the time at which it is possible for him to do anything wrong! Moreover, if God accomplishes, in any

measure, the correction of the parents when they are chastised by the sufferings or by the death of the children that are dear to them, is there any reason why these things should not take place, seeing that, after they are passed, they will be, to those who experienced them, as if they had never been, while the persons on whose account they were inflicted will either become better, being moved by the rod of temporal afflictions to choose a better mode of life, or be left without excuse under the punishment awarded at the coming judgment, if, notwithstanding the sorrows of this life, they have refused to turn their desires towards eternal life? Moreover, who knows what may be given to the little children by means of whose sufferings the parents have their obdurate hearts subdued, or their faith exercised, or their compassion proved? Who knows what good recompense God may, in the secret of his judgments, reserve for these little ones? For although they have done no righteous action, nevertheless, being free from any transgression of their own, they have suffered these trials. It is certainly not without reason that the Church exalts to the honourable rank of martyrs those children who were slain when Herod sought our Lord Jesus Christ to put Him to death." [1]

19. These things I wrote at that time when I was endeavouring to defend the opinion which is now under discussion. For, as I mentioned shortly before, I was labouring to prove that whichever of these four opinions regarding the soul's incarnation may be found true, the substance of the Creator is absolutely free from blame, and is completely removed from all share in our sins. And, therefore, whichever of these opinions might come to be established or demolished by the truth, this had no bearing on the object aimed at in the work which I was then attempting, seeing that whichever opinion might win the victory over all the rest, after they had been examined in a more thorough discussion, this would take place without causing me any disquietude, because my object then was to prove that, even admitting all these opinions, the doctrine maintained by me remained unshaken. But now my object is, by the force of sound reasoning, to select, if possible, one opinion out of the four; and, therefore, when I carefully consider the words now quoted from that book, I do not see that the arguments there used in defending the opinion which we are now discussing are valid and conclusive.

20. For what may be called the chief prop of my defence is in the sentence, "Moreover, who knows what may be given to the little children, by means of whose sufferings the parents have

---

[1] *De Libero Arbitrio*, lib. iii. ch. 23, n. 67.

their obdurate hearts subdued, or their faith exercised, or their compassion proved? Who knows what good recompense God may, in the secret of His judgments, reserve for these little ones?" I see that this is not an unwarranted conjecture in the case of infants who, in any way, suffer (though they know it not) for the sake of Christ and in the cause of true religion, and of infants who have already been made partakers of the sacrament of Christ; because, apart from union to the one Mediator, they cannot be delivered from condemnation, and so put in a position in which it is even possible that a recompense could be made to them for the evils which, in diverse afflictions, they have endured in this world. But since the question cannot be fully solved, unless the answer include also the case of those who, without having received the sacrament of Christian fellowship, die in infancy after enduring the most painful sufferings, what recompense can be conceived of in their case, seeing that, besides all that they suffer in this life, perdition awaits them in the life to come? As to the baptism of infants, I have, in the same book, given an answer, not, indeed, fully, but so far as seemed necessary for the work which then occupied me, proving that it profits children, even though they do not know what it is, and have, as yet, no faith of their own; but on the subject of the perdition of those infants who depart from this life without baptism, I did not think it necessary to say anything then, because the question under discussion was different from that with which we are now engaged.

21. If, however, we pass over and make no account of those sufferings which are of brief continuance, and which, when endured, are not to be repeated, we certainly cannot, in like manner, make no account of the fact that "by one man death came, and by one man came also the resurrection of the dead; for as in Adam all die, even so in Christ shall all be made alive."[1] For, according to this apostolical, divine, and perspicuous declaration, it is sufficiently plain that no one goes to death otherwise than through Adam, and that no one goes to life eternal otherwise than through Christ. For this is the force of *all* in the two parts of the sentence; as all men, by their first, that is, their natrual birth, belong to Adam, even so all men, whoever they be, who come to Christ come to the second, that is, the spiritual birth. For this reason, therefore, the word *all* is used in both clauses, because as all who die do not die otherwise than in Adam, so all who shall be made alive shall not be made alive otherwise than in Christ. Wherefore whosoever tells us that any man can be made alive in the resurrection of the dead otherwise than

in Christ, he is to be detested as a pestilent enemy to the common faith. Likewise, whosoever says that those children who depart out of this life without partaking of that sacrament shall be made alive in Christ, certainly contradicts the apostolic declaration, and condemns the universal Church, in which it is the practice to lose no time and run in haste to administer baptism to infant children, because it is believed, as an indubitable truth, that otherwise they cannot be made alive in Christ. Now he that is not made alive in Christ must necessarily remain under the condemnation, of which the apostle says, that "by the offence of one judgment came upon all men to condemnation."[2] That infants are born under the guilt of this offence is believed by the whole Church. It is also a doctrine which you have most faithfully set forth, both in your treatise against Jovinian and your exposition of Jonah, as I mentioned above, and, if I am not mistaken, in other parts of your works which I have not read or have at present forgotten. I therefore ask, what is the ground of this condemnation of unbaptized infants? For if new souls are made for men, individually, at their birth, I do not see, on the one hand, that they could have any sin while yet in infancy, nor do I believe, on the other hand, that God condemns any soul which He sees to have no sin.

CHAP. VIII. — 22. Are we perchance to say, in answer to this, that in the infant the body alone is the cause of sin; but that for each body a new soul is made, and that if this soul live according to the precepts of God, by the help of the grace of Christ, the reward of being made incorruptible may be secured for the body itself, when subdued and kept under the yoke; and that inasmuch as the soul of an infant cannot yet do this, unless it receive the sacrament of Christ, that which could not yet be obtained for the body by the holiness of the soul is obtained for it by the grace of this sacrament; but if the soul of an infant depart without the sacrament, it shall itself dwell in life eternal, from which it could not be separated, as it had no sin, while, however, the body which it occupied shall not rise again in Christ, because the sacrament had not been received before its death?

23. This opinion I have never heard or read anywhere. I have, however, certainly heard and believed the statement which led me to speak thus, namely, "The hour is coming, in the which all that are in the graves shall hear His voice, and shall come forth; they that have done good, unto the resurrection of life,"—the resurrection, namely, of which it is said that "by one man came the resurrection of the dead," and in which "all shall be made alive in Christ,"—"and they

---

[1] 1 Cor. xv. 21, 22.

[2] Rom. v. 18.

that have done evil, unto the resurrection of damnation."[1] Now, what is to be understood regarding infants which, before they could do good or evil, have quitted the body without baptism? Nothing is said here concerning them. But if the bodies of these infants shall not rise again, because they have never done either good or evil, the bodies of the infants that have died after receiving the grace of baptism shall also have no resurrection, because they also were not in this life able to do good or evil. If, however, these are to rise among the saints, *i.e.* among those who have done good, among whom shall the others rise again but among those who have done evil — unless we are to believe that some human souls shall not receive, either in the resurrection of life, or in the resurrection of damnation, the bodies which they lost in death? This opinion, however, is condemned, even before it is formally refuted, by its absolute novelty; and besides this, who could bear to think that those who run with their infant children to have them baptized, are prompted to do so by a regard for their bodies, not for their souls? The blessed Cyprian, indeed, said, in order to correct those who thought that an infant should not be baptized before the eighth day, that it was not the body but the soul which behoved to be saved from perdition — in which statement he was not inventing any new doctrine, but preserving the firmly established faith of the Church; and he, along with some of his colleagues in the episcopal office, held that a child may be properly baptized immediately after its birth.[2]

24. Let every man, however, believe anything which commends itself to his own judgment, even though it run counter to some opinion of Cyprian, who may not have seen in the matter what should have been seen. But let no man believe anything which runs counter to the perfectly unambiguous apostolical declaration, that by the offence of one all are brought into condemnation, and that from this condemnation nothing sets men free but the grace of God through our Lord Jesus Christ, in whom alone life is given to all who are made alive. And let no man believe anything which runs counter to the firmly grounded practice of the Church, in which, if the sole reason for hastening the administration of baptism were to save the children, the dead as well as the living would be brought to be baptized.

25. These things being so, it is necessary still to investigate and to make known the reason why, if souls are created new for every individual at his birth, those who die in infancy without the sacrament of Christ are doomed to perdition;

for that they are doomed to this if they so depart from the body is testified both by Holy Scripture and by the holy Church. Wherefore, as to that opinion of yours concerning the creation of new souls, if it does not contradict this firmly grounded article of faith, let it be mine also; but if it does, let it be no longer yours.

26. Let it not be said to me that we ought to receive as supporting this opinion the words of Scripture in Zechariah, "He formeth the spirit of man within him,"[3] and in the book of Psalms, "He formeth their hearts severally."[4] We must seek for the strongest and most indisputable proof, that we may not be compelled to believe that God is a judge who condemns any soul which has no fault. For to create signifies either as much or, probably, more than to form [*fingere*]; nevertheless it is written, "Create in me a clean heart, O God,"[5] and yet it cannot be supposed that a soul here expresses a desire to be made before it has begun to exist. Therefore, as it is a soul already existing which is created by being renewed in righteousness, so it is a soul already existing which is formed by the moulding power of doctrine. Nor is your opinion, which I would willingly make my own, supported by that sentence in Ecclesiastes, "Then shall the dust return to the earth as it was: and the spirit shall return to God who gave it."[6] Nay, it rather favours those who think that all souls are derived from one; for they say that, as the dust returns to the earth as it was, and yet the body of which this is said returns not to the man from whom it was derived, but to the earth from which the first man was made, the spirit in like manner, though derived from the spirit of the first man, does not return to him but to the Lord, by whom it was given to our first parent. Since, however, the testimony of this passage in their favour is not so decisive as to make it appear altogether opposed to the opinion which I shall gladly see vindicated, I thought proper to submit these remarks on it to your judgment, to prevent you from endeavouring to deliver me from my perplexities by quoting passages such as these. For although no man's wishes can make that true which is not true, nevertheless, were this possible, I would wish that this opinion should be true, as I do wish that, if it is true, it should be most clearly and unanswerably vindicated by you.

CHAP. IX. — 27. The same difficulty attends those also who hold that souls already existing elsewhere, and prepared from the beginning of the works of God, are sent by Him into bodies. For to these persons also the same question may

[1] John v. 29.
[2] Cyprian's Letters (LIX., *Ad Fidum*).
[3] Zech. xii. 1.
[4] Ps. xxxiii. 15 (LXX.).
[5] Ps. li. 10.
[6] Eccles. xii. 7.

be put: If these souls, being without any fault, go obediently to the bodies to which they are sent, why are they subjected to punishment in the case of infants, if they come without being baptized to the end of this life? The same difficulty unquestionably attaches to both opinions. Those who affirm that each soul is, according to the deserts of its actions in an earlier state of being, united to the body alloted to it in this life, imagine that they escape more easily from this difficulty. For they think that to "die in Adam" means to suffer punishment in that flesh which is derived from Adam, from which condition of guilt the grace of Christ, they say, delivers the young as well as the old. So far, indeed, they teach what is right, and true, and excellent, when they say that the grace of Christ delivers the young as well as the old from the guilt of sins. But that souls sin in another earlier life, and that for their sins in that state of being they are cast down into bodies as prisons, I do not believe: I reject and protest against such an opinion. I do this, in the first place, because they affirm that this is accomplished by means of some incomprehensible revolutions, so that after I know not how many cycles the soul must return again to the same burden of corruptible flesh and to the endurance of punishment, — than which opinion I do not know that anything more horrible could be conceived. In the next place, who is the righteous man gone from the earth about whom we should not (if what they say is true) feel afraid lest, sinning in Abraham's bosom, he should be cast down into the flames which tormented the rich man in the parable?[1] For why may the soul not sin after leaving the body, if it can sin before entering it? Finally, to have sinned in Adam (in regard to which the apostle says that in him all have sinned) is one thing, but it is a wholly different thing to have sinned, I know not where, outside of Adam, and then because of this to be thrust into Adam — that is, into the body, which is derived from Adam, as into a prison-house. As to the other opinion mentioned above, that all souls are derived from one, I will not begin to discuss it unless I am under necessity to do so; and my desire is, that if the opinion which we are now discussing is true, it may be so vindicated by you that there shall be no longer any necessity for examining the other.

28. Although, however, I desire and ask, and with fervent prayers wish and hope, that by you the Lord may remove my ignorance on this subject, if, after all, I am found unworthy to obtain this, I will beg the grace of patience from the Lord our God, in whom we have such faith, that even if there be some things which He does not

open to us when we knock, we know it would be wrong to murmur in the least against Him. I remember what He said to the apostles themselves: "I have yet many things to say unto you, but ye cannot bear them now."[2] Among these things, so far at least as I am concerned, let me still reckon this, and let me guard against being angry that I am deemed unworthy to possess this knowledge, lest by such anger I be all the more clearly proved to be unworthy. I am equally ignorant of many other things, yea, of more than I could name or even number; and of this I would be more patiently ignorant, were it not that I fear lest some one of these opinions, involving the contradiction of truth which we most assuredly believe, should insinuate itself into the minds of the unwary. Meanwhile, though I do not yet know which of these opinions is to be preferred, this one thing I profess as my deliberate conviction, that the opinion which is true does not conflict with that most firm and well grounded article in the faith of the Church of Christ, that infant children, even when they are newly born, can be delivered from perdition in no other way than through the grace of Christ's name, which He has given in His sacraments.

LETTER CLXVII.

(A.D. 415.)

FROM AUGUSTIN TO JEROME ON JAMES II. 10.

CHAP. I. — 1. My brother Jerome, esteemed worthy to be honoured in Christ by me, when I wrote to you propounding this question concerning the human soul, — if a new soul be now created for each individual at birth, whence do souls contract the bond of guilt which we assuredly believe to be removed by the sacrament of the grace of Christ, when administered even to new-born children? — as the letter on that subject grew to the size of a considerable volume, I was unwilling to impose the burden of any other question at that time; but there is a subject which has a much stronger claim on my attention, as it presses more seriously on my mind. I therefore ask you, and in God's name beseech you, to do something which will, I believe, be of great service to many, namely, to explain to me (or to direct me to any work in which you or any other commentator has already expounded) the sense in which we are to understand these words in the Epistle of James, "Whosoever shall keep the whole law, and yet offend in one point, he is guilty of all."[3] This subject is of such importance that I very greatly

---

[1] Luke xvi. 22, 23.

[2] John xvi. 12.
[3] Jas. ii. 10.

regret that I did not write to you in regard to it long ago.

2. For whereas in the question which I thought it neccessary to submit to you concerning the soul, our inquiries were engaged with the investigation of a life wholly past and sunk out of sight in oblivion, in this question we study this present life, and how it must be spent if we would attain to eternal life. As an apt illustration of this remark let me quote an entertaining anecdote. A man had fallen into a well where the quantity of water was sufficient to break his fall and save him from death, but not deep enough to cover his mouth and deprive him of speech. Another man approached, and on seeing him cries out in surprise : " How did you fall in here ? " He answers : " I beseech you to plan how you can get me out of this, rather than ask how I fell in." So, since we admit and hold as an article of the Catholic faith, that the soul of even a little infant requires to be delivered out of the guilt of sin, as out of a pit, by the grace of Christ, it is sufficient for the soul of such a one that we know the way in which it is saved, even though we should never know the way in which it came into that wretched condition. But I thought it our duty to inquire into this subject, lest we should incautiously hold any one of those opinions concerning the manner of the soul's becoming united with the body which might contradict the doctrine that the souls of little children require to be delivered, by denying that they are subject to the bond of guilt. This, then, being very firmly held by us, that the soul of every infant needs to be freed from the guilt of sin, and can be freed in no other way except by the grace of God through Jesus Christ our Lord, if we can ascertain the cause and origin of the evil itself, we are better prepared and equipped for resisting adversaries whose empty talk I call not reasoning but quibbling ; if, however, we cannot ascertain the cause, the fact that the origin of this misery is hid from us is no reason for our being slothful in the work which compassion demands from us. In our conflict, however, with those who appear to themselves to know what they do not know, we have an additional strength and safety in not being ignorant of our ignorance on this subject. For there are some things which it is evil not to know ; there are other things which cannot be known, or are not necessary to be known, or have no bearing on the life which we seek to obtain ; but the question which I now submit to you from the writings of the Apostle James is intimately connected with the course of conduct in which we live, and in which, with a view to life eternal, we endeavour to please God.

3. How, then, I beseech you, are we to understand the words : " Whosoever shall keep the whole law, and yet offend in one point, he is guilty of all " ? Does this affirm that the person who shall have committed theft, nay, who even shall have said to the rich man, " Sit thou here," and to the poor man, " Stand thou there," is guilty of homicide, and adultery, and sacrilege? And if he is not so, how can it be said that a person who has offended in one point has become guilty of all? Or are the things which the apostle said concerning the rich man and the poor man not to be reckoned among those things in one of which if any man offend he becomes guilty of all? But we must remember whence that sentence is taken, and what goes before it, and in what connection it occurs. " My brethren," he says, " have not the faith of our Lord Jesus Christ, the Lord of Glory, with respect of persons. For if there come into your assembly a man with a gold ring, in goodly apparel, and there come in also a poor man in vile raiment ; and ye have respect to him that weareth the gay clothing, and say unto him, Sit thou here in a good place ; and say to the poor, Stand thou there, or sit here under my footstool ; are ye not then partial in yourselves, and are become judges of evil thoughts? Hearken, my beloved brethren, Hath not God chosen the poor of this world, rich in faith, and heirs of the kindgom which He hath promised to them that love Him? But ye have despised the poor," [1] — inasmuch as you have said to the poor man, " Stand thou there," when you would have said to a man with a gold ring, " Sit thou here in a good place." And then there follows a passage explaining and enlarging upon that same conclusion : " Do not rich men oppress you by their power, and draw you before the judgment-seats? Do not they blaspheme that worthy name by the which ye are called? If ye fulfil the royal law according to the Scripture, Thou shalt love thy neighbour as thyself, ye do well : but if ye have respect to persons, ye commit sin, and are convinced of the law as transgressors." [2] See how the apostle calls those transgressors of the law who say to the rich man, " Sit here," and to the poor, " Stand there." See how, lest they should think it a trifling sin to transgress the law in this one thing, he goes on to add : " Whosoever shall keep the whole law, and yet offend in one point, he is guilty óf all. For He that said, Do not commit adultery, said also, Do not kill. Now if thou do not kill, yet, if thou commit adultery, thou art become a transgressor of the law," according to that which he had said : " Ye are convinced of the law as transgressors." Since these things are so, it seems to follow, unless it can be shown that we are to understand it in some other way,

---

[1] Jas. ii. 1-6.
[2] Jas. ii. 6-9.

that he who says to the rich man, "Sit here," and to the poor, "Stand there," not treating the one with the same respect as the other, is to be judged guilty as an idolater, and a blasphemer, and an adulterer, and a murderer — in short, — not to enumerate all, which would be tedious, — as guilty of all crimes, since, offending in one, he is guilty of all."

CHAP. II. — 4. But has he who has one virtue all virtues? and has he no virtues who lacks one? If this be true, the sentence of the apostle is thereby confirmed. But what I desire is to have the sentence explained, not confirmed, since of itself it stands more sure in our esteem than all the authority of philosophers could make it. And even if what has just been said concerning virtues and vices were true, it would not follow that therefore all sins are equal. For as to the inseparable co-existence of the virtues, this is a doctrine in regard to which, if I remember rightly, what, indeed, I have almost forgotten (though perhaps I am mistaken), all philosophers who affirm that virtues are essential to the right conduct of life are agreed. The doctrine of the equality of sins, however, the Stoics alone dared to maintain in opposition to the unanimous sentiments of mankind: an absurd tenet, which in writing against Jovinianus (a Stoic in this opinion, but an Epicurean in following after and defending pleasure) you have most clearly refuted from the Holy Scriptures.[1] In that most delightful and noble dissertation you have made it abundantly plain that it has not been the doctrine of our authors, or rather of the Truth Himself, who has spoken through them, that all sins are equal. I shall now do my utmost in endeavouring, with the help of God, to show how it can be that, although the doctrine of philosophers concerning virtues is true, we are nevertheless not compelled to admit the Stoics' doctrine that all sins are equal. If I succeed, I will look for your approbation, and in whatever respect I come short, I beg you to supply my deficiencies.

5. Those who maintain that he who has one virtue has all, and that he who lacks one lacks all, reason correctly from the fact that prudence cannot be cowardly, nor unjust, nor intemperate; for if it were any of these it would no longer be prudence. Moreover, if it be prudence only when it is brave, and just, and temperate, assuredly wherever it exists it must have the other virtues along with it. In like manner, also, courage cannot be imprudent, or intemperate, or unjust; temperance must of necessity be prudent, brave, and just; and justice does not exist unless it be prudent, brave, and temperate. Thus, wherever any one of these virtues truly exists, the others likewise exist; and where some are absent, that which may appear in some measure to resemble virtue is not really present.

6. There are, as you know, some vices opposed to virtues by a palpable contrast, as imprudence is the opposite of prudence. But there are some vices opposed to virtues simply because they are vices which, nevertheless, by a deceitful appearance resemble virtues; as, for example, in the relation, not of imprudence, but of craftiness to the said virtue of prudence. I speak here of that craftiness[2] which is wont to be understood and spoken of in connection with the evilly disposed, not in the sense in which the word is usually employed in our Scriptures, where it is often used in a good sense, as, "Be crafty as serpents,"[3] and again, to give craftiness to the simple."[4] It is true that among heathen writers one of the most accomplished of Latin authors, speaking of Catiline, has said: "Nor was there lacking on his part craftiness to guard against danger,"[5] using "craftiness" (astutia) in a good sense; but the use of the word in this sense is among them very rare, among us very common. So also in regard to the virtues classed under temperance. Extravagance is most manifestly opposite to the virtue of frugality; but that which the common people are wont to call niggardliness is indeed a vice, yet one which, not in its nature, but by a very deceitful similarity of appearance, usurps the name of frugality. In the same manner injustice is by a palpable contrast opposed to justice; but the desire of avenging oneself is wont often to be a counterfeit of justice, but it is a vice. There is an obvious contrariety between courage and cowardice; but hardihood, though differing from courage in nature, deceives us by its resemblance to that virtue. Firmness is a part of virtue; fickleness is a vice far removed from and undoubtedly opposed to it; but obstinacy lays claim to the name of firmness, yet is wholly different, because firmness is a virtue, and obstinacy is a vice.

7. To avoid the necessity of again going over the same ground, let us take one case as an example, from which all others may be understood. Catiline, as those who have written concerning him had means of knowing, was capable of enduring cold, thirst, hunger, and patient in fastings, cold, and watchings beyond what any one could believe, and thus he appeared, both to himself and to his followers, a man endowed with great courage.[6] But this courage was not prudent, for he chose the evil instead of the

---

[1] Jerome, *Contra Jovinianum*, lib. ii.

[2] *Astutia.*
[3] Matt. x. 16.
[4] Prov. i. 4.
[5] Sallust, *De Bello Catilinario.*
[6] *Ibid.*

good; was not temperate, for his life was disgraced by the lowest dissipation; was not just, for he conspired against his country; and therefore it was not courage, but hardihood usurping the name of courage to deceive fools; for if it had been courage, it would not have been a vice but a virtue, and if it had been a virtue, it would never have been abandoned by the other virtues, its inseparable companions.

8. On this account, when it is asked also concerning vices, whether where one exists all in like manner exist, or where one does not exist none exist, it would be a difficult matter to show this, because two vices are wont to be opposed to one virtue, one that is evidently opposed, and another that bears an apparent likeness. Hence the hardihood of Catiline is the more easily seen not to have been courage, since it had not along with it other virtues; but it may be difficult to convince men that his hardihood was cowardice, since he was in the habit of enduring and patiently submitting to the severest hardships to a degree almost incredible. But perhaps, on examining the matter more closely, this hardihood itself is seen to be cowardice, because he shrunk from the toil of those liberal studies by which true courage is acquired. Nevertheless, as there are rash men who are not guilty of cowardice, and there are cowardly men who are not guilty of rashness, and since in both there is vice, for the truly brave man neither ventures rashly nor fears without reason, we are forced to admit that vices are more numerous than virtues.

9. Accordingly, it happens sometimes that one vice is supplanted by another, as the love of money by the love of praise. Occasionally, one vice quits the field that more may take its place, as in the case of the drunkard, who, after becoming temperate in the use of drink, may come under the power of niggardliness and ambition. It is possible, therefore, that vices may give place to vices, not to virtues, as their successors, and thus they are more numerous. When one virtue, however, has entered, there will infallibly be (since it brings all the other virtues along with it) a retreat of all vices whatsoever that were in the man; for all vices were not in him, but at one time so many, at another a greater or smaller number might occupy their place.

CHAP. III. — 10. We must inquire more carefully whether these things are so; for the statement that " he who has one virtue has all, and that all virtues are awanting to him who lacks one," is not given by inspiration, but is the view held by many men, ingenious, indeed, and studious, but still men. But I must avow that, in the case — I shall not say of one of those from whose name the word virtue is said to be de-

rived,[1] but even of a woman who is faithful to her husband, and who is so from a regard to the commandments and promises of God, and, first of all, is faithful to Him, I do not know how I could say of her that she is unchaste, or that chastity is no virtue or a trifling one. I should feel the same in regard to a husband who is faithful to his wife; and yet there are many such, none of whom I could affirm to be without any sins, and doubtless the sin which is in them, whatever it be, proceeds from some vice. Whence it follows that though conjugal fidelity in religious men and women is undoubtedly a virtue, for it is neither a nonentity nor a vice, yet it does not bring along with it all virtues, for if all virtues were there, there would be no vice, and if there were no vice, there would be no sin; but where is the man who is altogether without sin? Where, therefore, is the man who is without any vice, that is, fuel or root, as it were, of sin, when he who reclined on the breast of the Lord says, " If we say that we have no sin, we deceive ourselves, and the truth is not in us "?[2] It is not necessary for us to urge this at greater length in writing to you, but I make the statement for the sake of others who perhaps shall read this. For you, indeed, in that same splendid work against Jovinianus, have carefully proved this from the Holy Scriptures; in which work also you have quoted the words, " in many things we all offend,"[3] from this very epistle in which occur the words whose meaning we are now investigating. For though it is an apostle of Christ who is speaking, he does not say, " ye offend," but, " we offend;" and although in the passage under consideration he says, " Whosoever shall keep the whole law, and yet offend in one point, he is guilty of all,"[4] in the words just quoted he affirms that we offend not in one thing but in *many*, and not that some offend but that we *all* offend.

11. Far be it, however, from any believer to think that so many thousands of the servants of Christ, who, lest they should deceive themselves, and the truth should not be in them, sincerely confess themselves to have sin, are altogether without virtue! For wisdom is a great virtue, and wisdom herself has said to man, " Behold the fear of the Lord, that is wisdom."[5] Far be it from us, then, to say that so many and so great believing and pious men have not the fear of the Lord, which the Greeks call εὐσέβεια, or more literally and fully, θεοσέβεια. And what is the fear of the Lord but His worship? and whence is He truly worshipped except from love? Love, then, out of a pure heart, and a

---

[1] *Virum a quo denominata dicitur virtus.*
[2] 1 John i. 8.
[3] Jas. iii. 2.
[4] Jas. ii. 10.
[5] Job xxviii. 28, Sept. ver.

good conscience, and faith unfeigned, is the great and true virtue, because it is "the end of the commandment."[1] Deservedly is love said to be "strong as death,"[2] because, like death, it is vanquished by none; or because the measure of love in this life is even unto death, as the Lord says, "Greater love hath no man than this, that a man lay down his life for his friends;"[3] or, rather, because, as death forcibly separates the soul from the senses of the body, so love separates it from fleshly lusts. Knowledge, when it is of the right kind, is the handmaid to love, for without love "knowledge puffeth up,"[4] but where love, by edifying, has filled the heart, there knowledge will find nothing empty which it can puff up. Moreover, Job has shown what is that useful knowledge by defining it where, after saying, "The fear of the Lord, that is wisdom," he adds, "and to depart from evil, that is understanding."[5] Why do we not then say that the man who has this virtue has all virtues, since "love is the fulfilling of the law?"[6] Is it not true that, the more love exists in a man the more he is endowed with virtue, and the less love he has the less virtue is in him, for love is itself virtue; and the less virtue there is in a man so much the more vice will there be in him? Therefore, where love is full and perfect, no vice will remain.

12. The Stoics, therefore, appear to me to be mistaken in refusing to admit that a man who is advancing in wisdom has any wisdom at all, and in affirming that he alone has it who has become altogether perfect in wisdom. They do not, indeed, deny that he has made progress, but they say that he is in no degree entitled to be called wise, unless, by emerging, so to speak, from the depths, he suddenly springs forth into the free air of wisdom. For, as it matters not when a man is drowning whether the depth of water above him be many stadia or only the breadth of a hand or finger, so they say in regard to the progress of those who are advancing towards wisdom, that they are like men rising from the bottom of a whirlpool towards the air, but that unless they by their progress, so escape as to emerge wholly from folly as from an overwhelming flood, they have not virtue and are not wise; but that, when they have so escaped, they immediately have wisdom in perfection, and not a vestige of folly whence any sin could be originated remains.

12. This simile, in which folly is compared to water and wisdom to air, so that the mind emerging, as it were, from the stifling influence

of folly breathes suddenly the free air of wisdom, does not appear to me to harmonize sufficiently with the authoritative statement of our Scriptures; a better simile, so far, at least, as illustration of spiritual things can be borrowed from material things, is that which compares vice or folly to darkness, and virtue or wisdom to light. The way to wisdom is therefore not like that of a man rising from the water into the air, in which, in the moment of rising above the surface of the water, he suddenly breathes freely, but, like that of a man proceeding from darkness into light, on whom more light gradually shines as he advances. So long, therefore, as this is not fully accomplished, we speak of the man as of one going from the dark recesses of a vast cavern towards its entrance, who is more and more influenced by the proximity of the light as he comes nearer to the entrance of the cavern; so that whatever light he has proceeds from the light to which he is advancing, and whatever darkness still remains in him proceeds from the darkness out of which he is emerging. Therefore it is true that in the sight of God "shall no man living be justified,"[7] and yet that "the just shall live by his faith."[8] On the one hand, "the saints are clothed with righteousness,"[9] one more, another less; on the other hand, no one lives here wholly without sin — one sins more, another less, and the best is the man who sins least.

CHAP. IV. — 14. But why have I, as if forgetting to whom I address myself, assumed the tone of a teacher in stating the question regarding which I wish to be instructed by you? Nevertheless, as I had resolved to submit to your examination my opinion regarding the equality of sins (a subject involving a question closely bearing on the matter on which I was writing), let me now at last bring my statement to a conclusion. Even though it were true that he who has one virtue has all virtues, and that he who lacks one virtue has none, this would not involve the consequence that all sins are equal; for although it is true that where there is no virtue there is nothing right, it by no means follows that among bad actions one cannot be worse than another, or that divergence from that which is right does not admit of degrees. I think, however, that it is more agreeable to truth and consistent with the Holy Scriptures to say, that what is true of the members of the body is true of the different dispositions of the soul (which, though not seen occupying different places, are by their distinctive workings perceived as plainly as the members of the body), namely, that as in the same body one member is more fully

---

[1] 1 Tim. i. 5.
[2] Song of Sol. viii. 6.
[3] John xv. 13.
[4] 1 Cor. viii. 1.
[5] Job xxviii. 28.
[6] Rom. xiii. 10.

[7] Ps. cxliii. 2.
[8] Hab. ii. 4.
[9] Job xxix. 14.

shone upon by the light, another is less shone upon, and a third is altogether without light, and remains in the dark under some impervious covering, something similar takes place in regard to the various dispositions of the soul. If this be so, then according to the manner in which every man is shone upon by the light of holy love, he may be said to have one virtue and to lack another virtue, or to have one virtue in larger and another in smaller measure. For in reference to that love which is the fear of God, we may correctly say both that it is greater in one man than in another, and that there is some of it in one man, and none of it in another; we may also correctly say as to an individual that he has greater chastity than patience, and that he has either virtue in a higher degree than he had yesterday, if he is making progress, or that he still lacks self-control, but possesses, at the same time, a large measure of compassion.

15. To sum up generally and briefly the view which, so far as relates to holy living, I entertain concerning virtue, — virtue is the love with which that which ought to be loved is loved. This is in some greater, in others less, and there are men in whom it does not exist at all; but in the absolute fulness which admits of no increase, it exists in no man while living on this earth; so long, however, as it admits of being increased there can be no doubt that, in so far as it is less than it ought to be, the shortcoming proceeds from vice. Because of this vice there is "not a just man upon earth that doeth good and sinneth not;"[1] because of this vice, "in God's sight shall no man living be justified."[2] On account of this vice, "if we say that we have no sin, we deceive ourselves, and the truth is not in us."[3] On account of this also, whatever progress we may have made, we must say, "Forgive us our debts,"[4] although all debts in word, deed, and thought were washed away in baptism. He, then, who sees aright, sees whence, and when, and where, and where he must hope for that perfection to which nothing can be added. Moreover, if there had been no commandments, there would have been no means whereby a man might certainly examine himself and see from what things he ought to turn aside, whither he should aspire, and in what things he should find occasion for thanksgiving or for prayer. Great, therefore, is the benefit of commandments, if to free will so much liberty be granted that the grace of God may be more abundantly honoured.

CHAP. V. — 16. If these things be so, how shall a man who shall keep the whole law, and yet offend in one point, be guilty of all? May

it not be, that since the fulfilling of the law is that love wherewith we love God and our neighbour, on which commandments of love "hang all the law and the prophets,"[5] he is justly held to be guilty of all who violates that on which all hang? Now, no one sins without violating this love; "for this, thou shalt not commit adultery; thou shalt do no murder; thou shalt not steal; thou shalt not covet; and if there be any other commandment, it is briefly comprehended in this saying, Thou shalt love thy neighbour as thyself. Love worketh no ill to his neighbour: therefore love is the fulfilling of the law."[6] No one, however, loves his neighbour who does not out of his love to God do all in his power to bring his neighbour also, whom he loves as himself, to love God, whom if he does not love, he neither loves himself nor his neighbour. Hence it is true that if a man shall keep the whole law, and yet offend in one point, he becomes guilty of all, because he does what is contrary to the love on which hangs the whole law. A man, therefore, becomes guilty of all by doing what is contrary to that on which all hang.

17. Why, then, may not all sins be said to be equal? May not the reason be, that the transgression of the law of love is greater in him who commits a more grievous sin, and is less in him who commits a less grievous sin? And in the mere fact of his committing any sin whatever, he becomes guilty of all; but in committing a more grievous sin, or in sinning in more respects than one, he becomes more guilty; committing a less grievous sin, or sinning in fewer respects, he becomes less guilty, — his guilt being thus so much the greater the more he has sinned, the less the less he has sinned. Nevertheless, even though it be only in one point that he offend, he is guilty of all, because he violates that love on which all hang. If these things be true, an explanation is by this means found, clearing up that saying of the man of apostolic grace, "In many things we offend all."[7] For we all offend, but one more grievously, another more slightly, according as each may have committed a more grievous or a less grievous sin; every one being great in the practice of sin in proportion as he is deficient in loving God and his neighbour, and, on the other hand, decreasing in the practice of sin in proportion as he increases in the love of God and of his neighbour. The more, therefore, that a man is deficient in love, the more is he full of sin. And perfection in love is reached when nothing of sinful infirmity remains in us.

18. Nor, indeed, in my opinion, are we to esteem it a trifling sin " to have the faith of our

---

[1] Eccles. v. 7.
[2] Ps. cxliii. 2.
[3] 1 John i. 8.
[4] Matt. vi. 12.

[5] Matt. xxii. 40.
[6] Rom. xiii. 9, 10.
[7] Jas. iii. 2.

Lord Jesus Christ with respect of persons," if we take the difference between sitting and standing, of which mention is made in the context, to refer to ecclesiastical honours; for who can bear to see a rich man chosen to a place of honour in the Church, while a poor man, of superior qualifications and of greater holiness, is despised? If, however, the apostle speaks there of our daily assemblies, who does not offend in the matter? At the same time, only those really offend here who cherish in their hearts the opinion that a man's worth is to be estimated according to his wealth; for this seems to be the meaning of the expression, "Are ye not then partial in yourselves, and are become judges of evil thoughts?"

19. The law of liberty, therefore, the law of love, is that of which he says: "If ye fulfil the royal law according to the Scripture, Thou shalt love thy neighbour as thyself, ye do well: but if ye have respect to persons, ye commit sin, and are convinced of the law as transgressors.[1] And then (after the difficult sentence, "Whosoever shall keep the whole law, and yet offend in one point, he is guilty of all," concerning which I have with sufficient fulness stated my opinion), making mention of the same law of liberty, he says: "So speak ye, and so do, as they that shall be judged by the law of liberty." And as he knew by experience what he had said a little before, "in many things we offend all," he suggests a sovereign remedy, to be applied, as it were day by day, to those less serious but real wounds which the soul suffers day by day, for he says: "He shall have judgment without mercy that hath showed no mercy."[2] For with the same purpose the Lord says: "Forgive, and ye shall be forgiven: give, and it shall be given unto you."[3] After which the apostle says: "But mercy rejoiceth over judgment:" it is not said that mercy prevails over judgment, for it is not an adversary of judgment, but it "rejoiceth" over judgment, because a greater number are gathered in by mercy; but they are those who have shown mercy, for, "Blessed are the merciful, for God shall have mercy on them."[4]

20. It is, therefore, by all means just that they be forgiven, because they have forgiven others, and that what they need be given to them, because they have given to others. For God uses mercy when He judgeth, and uses judgment when He showeth mercy. Hence the Psalmist says: "I will sing of mercy and of judgment unto Thee, O Lord."[5] For if any man, thinking himself too righteous to require mercy, presumes, as if he had no reason for anxiety, to wait for judgment without mercy, he provokes that most righteous indignation through fear of which the Psalmist said: "Enter not into judgment with Thy servant."[6] For this reason the Lord says to a disobedient people: "Wherefore will ye contend with me in judgment?[7] For when the righteous King shall sit upon His throne, who shall boast that he has a pure heart, or who shall boast that he is clean from sin? What hope is there then unless mercy shall "rejoice over" judgment? But this it will do only in the case of those who have showed mercy, saying with sincerity, "Forgive us our debts, as we forgive our debtors," and who have given without murmuring, for "the Lord loveth a cheerful giver."[8] To conclude, St. James is led to speak thus concerning works of mercy in this passage, in order that he may console those whom the statements immediately foregoing might have greatly alarmed, his purpose being to admonish us how those daily sins from which our life is never free here below may also be expiated by daily remedies; lest any man, becoming guilty of all when he offends in even one point, be brought, by offending in many points (since "in many things we all offend"), to appear before the bar of the Supreme Judge under the enormous amount of guilt which has accumulated by degrees, and find at that tribunal no mercy, because he showed no mercy to others, instead of rather meriting the forgiveness of his own sins, and the enjoyment of the gifts promised in Scripture, by his extending forgiveness and bounty to others.

21. I have written at great length, which may perhaps have been tedious to you, as you, although approving of the statements now made, do not expect to be addressed as if you were but learning truths which you have been accustomed to teach to others. If, however, there be anything in these statements — not in the style of language in which they are expounded, for I am not much concerned as to mere phrases, but in the substance of the statements — which your erudite judgment condemns, I beseech you to point this out to me in your reply, and do not hesitate to correct my error. For I pity the man who, in view of the unwearied labour and sacred character of your studies, does not on account of them both render to you the honour which you deserve, and give thanks unto our Lord God by whose grace you are what you are. Wherefore, since I ought to be more willing to learn from any teacher the things of which to my disadvantage I am ignorant, than prompt to teach any others what I know, with how much greater reason do I claim the payment of

---

[1] Jas. ii. 8, 9.
[2] Jas. ii. 13.
[3] Luke vi. 37, 38.
[4] Matt. v. 7.
[5] Ps. ci. 1.
[6] Ps. cxliii. 2,
[7] Jer. ii. 28, LXX.
[8] 2 Cor. ix. 7.

this debt of love from you, by whose learning ecclesiastical literature in the Latin tongue has been, in the Lord's name, and by His help, advanced to an extent which had been previously unattainable. Especially, however, I ask attention to the sentence: "Whosoever shall keep the whole law, and offend in one point, is guilty of all." If you know any better way, my beloved brother, in which it can be explained, I beseech you by the Lord to favour us by communicating to us your exposition.

LETTER CLXIX.

(A.D. 415.)

BISHOP AUGUSTIN TO BISHOP EVODIUS.

CHAP. I. — 1. If acquaintance with the treatises which specially occupy me, and from which I am unwilling to be turned aside to anything else, is so highly valued by your Holiness, let some one be sent to copy them for you. For I have now finished several of those which had been commenced by me this year before Easter, near the beginning of Lent. For, to the three books on the *City of God*, in opposition to its enemies, the worshippers of demons, I have added two others, and in these five books I think enough has been said to answer those who maintain that the [heathen] gods must be worshipped in order to secure prosperity in this present life, and who are hostile to the Christian name from an idea that that prosperity is hindered by us. In the sequel I must, as I promised in the first book,[1] answer those who think that the worship of their gods is the only way to obtain that life after death with a view to obtain which we are Christians. I have dictated also, in volumes of considerable size, expositions of three Psalms, the 68th, the 72d, and the 78th. Commentaries on the other Psalms — not yet dictated, nor even entered on — are eagerly expected and demanded from me. From these studies I am unwilling to be called away and hindered by any questions thrusting themselves upon me from another quarter; yea, so unwilling, that I do not wish to turn at present even to the books on the Trinity, which I have long had on hand and have not yet completed, because they require a great amount of labour, and I believe that they are of a nature to be understood only by few; on which account they claim my attention less urgently than writings which may, I hope, be useful to very many.

2. For the words, "He that is ignorant shall be ignored,"[2] were not used by the apostle in reference to this subject, as your letter affirms; as if this punishment were to be inflicted on the

man who is not able to discern by the exercise of his intellect the ineffable unity of the Trinity, in the same way as the unity of memory, understanding, and will in the soul of man is discerned. The apostle said these words with a wholly different design. Consult the passage and you will see that he was speaking of those things which might be for the edification of the many in faith and holiness, not of those which might with difficulty be comprehended by the few, and by them only in the small degree in which the comprehension of so great a subject is attainable in this life. The positions laid down by him were, — that prophesying was to be preferred to speaking with tongues; that these gifts should not be exercised in a disorderly manner, as if the spirit of prophecy compelled them to speak even against their will; that women should keep silence in the Church; and that all things should be done decently and in order. While treating of these things he says: "If any man think himself to be a prophet, or spiritual, let him know the things which I write to you, for they are the commands of the Lord. If any man be ignorant, he shall be ignored;" intending by these words to restrain and call to order persons who were specially ready to cause disorder in the Church, because they imagined themselves to excel in spiritual gifts, although they were disturbing everything by their presumptuous conduct. "If any man think himself to be a prophet, or spiritual, let him know," he says, "the things which I write to you, for they are the commands of the Lord." If any man thinks himself to be, and in reality is not, a prophet, for he who is a prophet undoubtedly knows and does not need admonition and exhortation, because "he judgeth all things, and is himself judged of no man."[3] Those persons, therefore, caused confusion and trouble in the Church who thought themselves to be in the Church what they were not. He teaches these to know the commandments of the Lord, for he is not a "God of confusion, but of peace."[4] But "if any one is ignorant, he shall be ignored," that is to say, he shall be rejected; for God is not ignorant — so far as mere knowledge is concerned — in regard to the persons to whom He shall one day say, "I know you not,"[5] but their rejection is signified by this expression.

3. Moreover, since the Lord says, "Blessed are the pure in heart, for they shall see God,"[6] and that sight is promised to us as the highest reward at the last, we have no reason to fear lest, if we are now unable to see clearly those things which we believe concerning the nature of God,

---

[1] *De Civitate Dei*, lib. I. ch. xxxvi.
[2] 1 Cor. xiv. 38.
[3] 1 Cor. ii. 15.
[4] 1 Cor. xiv. 33.
[5] Luke xiii. 27.
[6] Matt. v. 8.

this defective apprehension should bring us under the sentence, "He that is ignorant shall be ignored." For when "in the wisdom of God the world by wisdom knew not God, it pleased God by the foolishness of preaching to save those who believed." This foolishness of preaching and "foolishness of God which is wiser than man"[1] draws many to salvation, in such a way that not only those who are as yet incapable of perceiving with clear intelligence the nature of God which in faith they hold, but even those who have not yet so learned the nature of their own soul as to distinguish between its incorporeal essence and the body as a whole with the same certainty with which they perceive that they live, understand, and will, are not on this account shut out from that salvation which that foolishness of preaching bestows on believers.

4. For if Christ died for those only who with clear intelligence can discern these things, our labour in the Church is almost spent in vain. But if, as is the fact, crowds of common people, possessing no great strength of intellect, run to the Physician in the exercise of faith, with the result of being healed by Christ and Him crucified, that "where sin has abounded, grace may much more abound,"[2] it comes in wondrous ways to pass, through the depths of the riches of the wisdom and knowledge of God and His unsearchable judgments, that, on the one hand, some who do discern between the material and the spiritual in their own nature, while pluming themselves on this attainment, and despising that foolishness of preaching by which those who believe are saved, wander far from the only path which leads to eternal life; and, on the other hand, because not one perishes for whom Christ died,[3] many glorying in the cross of Christ, and not withdrawing from that same path, attain, notwithstanding their ignorance of those things which some with most profound subtlety investigate, unto that eternity, truth, and love, — that is, unto that enduring, clear, and full felicity, — in which to those who abide, and see, and love, all things are plain.

CHAP. II. — 5. Therefore let us with stedfast piety believe in one God, the Father, and the Son, and the Holy Spirit; let us at the same time believe that the Son is not [the person] who is the Father, and the Father is not [the person] who is the Son, and neither the Father nor the Son is [the person] who is the Spirit of both the Father and the Son. Let it not be supposed that in this Trinity there is any separation in respect of time or place, but that these Three are equal and co-eternal, and absolutely of one nature: and that the creatures have been made, not some by the Father, and some by the Son, and some by the Holy Spirit, but that each and all that have been or are now being created subsist in the Trinity as their Creator; and that no one is saved by the Father without the Son and the Holy Spirit, or by the Son without the Father and the Holy Spirit, or by the Holy Spirit without the Father and the Son, — but by the Father, the Son, and the Holy Spirit, the only one, true, and truly immortal (that is, absolutely unchangeable) God. At the same time, we believe that many things are stated in Scripture separately concerning each of the Three, in order to teach us that, though they are an inseparable Trinity, yet they are a Trinity. For, just as when their names are pronounced in human language they cannot be named simultaneously, although their existence in inseparable union is at every moment simultaneous, even so in some places of Scripture also, they are by certain created things presented to us distinctively and in mutual relation to each other: for example, [at the baptism of Christ] the Father is heard in the voice which said, "Thou art my Son;" the Son is seen in the human nature which, in being born of the Virgin, He assumed; the Holy Spirit is seen in the bodily form of a dove,[4] — these things presenting the Three to our apprehension separately, indeed, but in no wise separated.

6. To present this in a form which the intellect may apprehend, we borrow an illustration from the Memory, the Understanding, and the Will. For although we can speak of each of these faculties severally in its own order, and at a separate time, we neither exercise nor even mention any one of them without the other two. It must not, however, be supposed, from our using this comparison between these three faculties and the Trinity, that the things compared agree in every particular, for where, in any process of reasoning, can we find an illustration in which the correspondence between the things compared is so exact that it admits of application in every point to that which it is intended to illustrate? In the first place, therefore, the similarity is found to be imperfect in this respect, that whereas memory, understanding, and will are not the soul, but only exist in the soul, the Trinity does not exist in God, but is God. In the Trinity, therefore, there is manifested a singleness [*simplicitas*] commanding our astonishment, because in this Trinity it is not one thing to exist, and another thing to understand, or do anything else which is attributed to the nature of God; but in the soul it is one thing that it exists, and another thing that it understands, for even when it is not using the understand-

---

[1] 1 Cor. i. 21, 25.
[2] Rom. v. 20.
[3] John xvii. 12.

[4] Luke iii. 22.

ing it still exists. In the second place, who would dare to say that the Father does not understand by Himself but by the Son, as memory does not understand by itself but by the understanding, or, to speak more correctly, the soul in which these faculties are understands by no other faculty than by the understanding, as it remembers only by memory, and exercises volition only by the will? The point, therefore, to which the illustration is intended to apply is this, — that, whatever be the manner in which we understand, in regard to these three faculties in the soul, that when the several names by which they are severally represented are uttered, the utterance of each separate name is nevertheless accomplished only in the combined operation of all the three, since it is by an act of memory and of understanding and of will that it is spoken, — it is in the same manner that we understand, in regard to the Father, the Son, and the Holy Spirit, that no created thing which may at any time be employed to present only one of the Three to our minds is produced otherwise than by the simultaneous, because essentially inseparable, operation of the Trinity; and that, consequently, neither the voice of the Father, nor the body and soul of the Son, nor the dove of the Holy Spirit, was produced in any other way than by the combined operation of the Trinity.

7. Moreover, that sound of a voice was certainly not made indissolubly one with the person of the Father, for so soon as it was uttered it ceased to be. Neither was that form of a dove made indissolubly one with the person of the Holy Spirit, for it also, like the bright cloud which covered the Saviour and His three disciples on the mount,[1] or rather like the tongues of flame which once represented the same Holy Spirit, ceased to exist as soon as it had served its purpose as a symbol. But it was otherwise with the body and soul in which the Son of God was manifested: seeing that the deliverance of men was the object for which all these things were done, the human nature in which He appeared was, in a way marvellous and unique, assumed into real union with the person of the Word of God, that is, of the only Son of God, — the Word remaining unchangeably in His own nature, wherein it is not conceivable that there should be composite elements in union with which any mere semblance of a human soul could subsist. We read, indeed, that "the Spirit of wisdom is manifold;"[2] but it is as properly termed simple. Manifold it is, indeed, because there are many things which it possesses; but simple, because it is not a different thing from what it possesses, as the Son is said to have life in Himself, and yet He is Himself that life. The human nature came to the Word; the Word did not come, with susceptibility of change, into the human nature;[3] and therefore, in His union to the human nature which He has assumed, He is still properly called the Son of God; for which reason the same person is the Son of God immutable and co-eternal with the Father, and the Son of God who was laid in the grave, — the former being true of Him only as the Word, the latter true of Him only as a man.

8. Wherefore it behoves us, in reading any statements made concerning the Son of God, to observe in reference to which of these two natures they are spoken. For by His assumption of the soul and body of a man, no increase was made in the number of Persons: the Trinity remained as before. For just as in every man, with the exception of that one whom alone He assumed into personal union, the soul and body constitute one person, so in Christ the Word and His human soul and body constitute one person. And as the name philosopher, for example, is given to a man certainly with reference only to his soul, and yet it is nothing absurd, but only a most suitable and ordinary use of language, for us to say the philosopher was killed, the philosopher died, the philosopher was buried, although all these events befell him in his body, not in that part of him in which he was a philosopher; in like manner the name of God, or Son of God, or Lord of Glory, or any other such name, is given to Christ as the Word, and it is, nevertheless, correct to say that God was crucified, seeing that there is no question that He suffered this death in his human nature, not in that in which He is the Lord of Glory.[4]

9. As for the sound of the voice, however, and the bodily form of a dove, and the cloven tongues which sat upon each of them, these, like the terrible wonders wrought at Sinai,[5] and like the pillar of cloud by day and of fire by night,[6] were produced only as symbols, and vanished when this purpose had been served. The thing which we must especially guard against in connection with them is, lest any one should believe that the nature of God — whether of the Father, or of the Son, or of the Holy Spirit — is susceptible of change or transformation. And we must not be disturbed by the fact that the sign sometimes receives the name of the thing signified, as when the Holy Spirit is said to have descended in a bodily form as a dove and abode upon Him; for in like manner the smitten rock is called Christ,[7] because it was a symbol of Christ.

[1] Matt. xvii. 5.
[2] Wisd. vii. 22.

[3] Homo autem Verbo accessit, non Verbum in hominem convertibiliter accessit.
[4] 1 Cor. ii. 8.
[5] Ex. xix. 18.
[6] Ex. xiii. 21.
[7] 1 Cor. x. 4.

CHAP. III. — 10. I wonder, however, that, although you believe it possible for the sound of the voice which said, "Thou art my Son," to have been produced through a divine act, without the intermediate agency of a soul, by something the nature of which was corporeal, you nevertheless do not believe that a bodily form and movements exactly resembling those of any real living creature whatsoever could be produced in the same way, namely, through a divine act, without the intermediate agency of a spirit imparting life. For if inanimate matter obeys God without the instrumentality of an animating spirit, so as to emit sounds such as are wont to be emited by animated bodies, in order to bring to the human ear words articulately spoken, why should it not obey Him, so as to present to the human eye the figure and motions of a bird, by the same power of the Creator without the instrumentality of any animating spirit? The objects of both sight and hearing — the sound which strikes the ear and the appearance which meets the eye, the articulations of the voice and the outlines of the members, every audible and visible motion — are both alike produced from matter contiguous to us; is it, then, granted to the sense of hearing, and not to the sense of sight, to tell us regarding the body which is perceived by this bodily sense, both that it is a true body, and that it is nothing beyond what the bodily sense perceives it to be? For in every living creature the soul is, of course, not perceived by any bodily sense. We do not, therefore, need to inquire how the bodily form of the dove appeared to the eye, just as we do not need to inquire how the voice of a bodily form capable of speech was made to fall upon the ear. For if it was possible to dispense with the intermediate agency of a soul in the case in which a voice, not something like a voice, is said to have been produced, how much more easily was it possible in the case in which it is said that the Spirit descended "*like* a dove," a phrase which signifies that a mere bodily form was exhibited to the eye, and does not affirm that a real living creature was seen! In like manner, it is said that on the day of Pentecost, "suddenly there came a sound from heaven as of a mighty rushing wind, and there appeared to them cloven tongues like as of fire," [1] in which something like wind and like fire, *i.e.* resembling these common and familiar natural phenomena, is said to have been perceived, but it does not seem to be indicated that these common and familiar natural phenomena were actually produced.

11. If, however, more subtle reasoning or more thorough investigation of the matter result in demonstrating that that which is naturally destitute of motion both in time and in space [*i.e.* matter] cannot be moved otherwise than through the intermediate agency of that which is capable of motion only in time, not in space [*i.e.* spirit], it will follow from this that all those things must have been done by the instrumentality of a living creature, as things are done by angels, on which subject a more elaborate discussion would be tedious, and is not necessary. To this it must be added, that there are visions which appear to the spirit as plainly as to the senses of the body, not only in sleep or delirium, but also to persons of sound mind in their waking hours, — visions which are due not to the deceitfulness of devils mocking men, but to some spiritual revelation accomplished by means of immaterial forms resembling bodies, and which cannot by any means be distinguished from real objects, unless they are by divine assistance more fully revealed and discriminated by the mind's intelligence, which is done sometimes (but with difficulty) at the time, but for the most part after they have disappeared. This being the case in regard to these visions which, whether their nature be really material, or material only in appearance but really spiritual, seem to manifest themselves to our spirit as if they were perceived by the bodily senses, we ought not, when these things are recorded in sacred Scripture, to conclude hastily to which of these two classes they are to be referred, or whether, if they belong to the former, they are produced by the intermediate agency of a spirit; while, at the same time, as to the invisible and immutable nature of the Creator, that is, of the supreme and ineffable Trinity, we either simply, without any doubt, believe, or, in addition to this, with some degree of intellectual apprehension, understand that it is wholly removed and separated both from the senses of fleshly mortals, and from all susceptibility of being changed either for the worse or for the better, or to anything whatever of a variable nature.

CHAP. IV. — 12. These things I send you in reference to two of your questions, — the one concerning the Trinity, and the other concerning the dove in which the Holy Spirit, not in His own nature, but in a symbolical form, was manifested, as also the Son of God, not in His eternal Sonship (of which the Father said: "Before the morning star I have begotten Thee " [2]), but in that human nature which He assumed from the Virgin's womb, was crucified by the Jews: observe that to you who are at leisure I have been able, notwithstanding immense pressure of business, to write so much. I have not, however, deemed it necessary to discuss everything which you have brought forward in your

---

[1] Acts ii. 2, 3.

[2] Ps. cx. 3, LXX.

letter; but on these two questions which you wished me to solve, I think I have written as much as is exacted by Christian charity, though I may not have satisfied your vehement desire.

13. Besides the two books added to the first three in the *City of God*, and the exposition of three psalms, as above mentioned,[1] I have also written a treatise to the holy presbyter Jerome concerning the origin of the soul,[2] asking him, in regard to the opinion which, in writing to Marcellinus of pious memory, he avowed as his own, that a new soul is made for each individual at birth, how this can be maintained without overthrowing that most surely established article of the Church's faith, according to which we firmly believe that all die in Adam,[3] and are brought down under condemnation unless they be delivered by the grace of Christ, which, by means of His sacrament, works even in infants. I have, moreover, written to the same person to inquire his opinion as to the sense in which the words of James, "Whosoever shall keep the whole law, and yet offend in one point, he is guilty of all," are to be understood.[4] In this letter I have also stated my own opinion: in the other, concerning the origin of the soul, I have only asked what was his opinion, submitting the matter to his judgment, and at the same time discussing it to some extent. I wrote these to Jerome because I did not wish to lose an opportunity of correspondence afforded by a certain very pious and studious young presbyter, Orosius, who, prompted only by burning zeal in regard to the Holy Scriptures, came to us from the remotest part of Spain, namely, from the shore of the ocean, and whom I persuaded to go on from us to Jerome. In answer to certain questions of the same Orosius, as to things which troubled him in reference to the heresy of the Priscillianists, and some opinions of Origen which the Church has not accepted, I have written a treatise of moderate size with as much brevity and clearness as was in my power. I have also written a considerable book against the heresy of Pelagius,[5] being constrained to do this by some brethren whom he had persuaded to adopt his fatal error, denying the grace of Christ. If you wish to have all these, send some one to copy them all for you. Allow me, however, to be free from distraction in studying and dictating to my clerks those things which, being urgently required by many, claim in my opinion precedence over your questions, which are of interest to very few.

LETTER CLXXII.

(A.D. 416.)

TO AUGUSTIN, MY TRULY PIOUS LORD AND FATHER, WORTHY OF MY UTMOST AFFECTION AND VENERATION, JEROME SENDS GREETING IN CHRIST.

1. That honourable man, my brother, and your Excellency's son, the presbyter Orosius, I have, both on his own account and in obedience to your request, made welcome. But a most trying time has come upon us,[6] in which I have found it better for me to hold my peace than to speak, so that our studies have ceased, lest what Appius calls "the eloquence of dogs" should be provoked into exercise.[7] For this reason I have not been able at the present time to give to those two books dedicated to my name — books of profound erudition, and brilliant with every charm of splendid eloquence — the answer which I would otherwise have given; not that I think anything said in them demands correction, but because I am mindful of the words of the blessed apostle in regard to the variety of men's judgments, "Let every man be fully persuaded in his own mind."[8] Certainly, whatever can be said on the topics there discussed, and whatever can be drawn by commanding genius from the fountain of sacred Scripture regarding them, has been in these letters stated in your positions, and illustrated by your arguments. But I beg your Reverence to allow me for a little to praise your genius. For in any discussion between us, the object aimed at by both of us is advancement in learning. But our rivals, and especially heretics, if they see different opinions maintained by us, will assail us with the calumny that our differences are due to mutual jealousy. For my part, however, I am resolved to love you, to look up to you, to reverence and admire you, and to defend your opinions as my own. I have also in a dialogue, which I recently published, made allusion to your Blessedness in suitable terms. Be it ours, therefore, rather to rid the Church of that most pernicious heresy which always feigns repentance, in order that it may have liberty to teach in our churches, and may not be expelled and extinguished, as it would be if it disclosed its real character in the light of day.

2. Your pious and venerable daughters, Eusto-

---

[1] Par. 1, p. 539.
[2] Letter CLXVI.
[3] 1 Cor. xv. 22.
[4] Letter CLXVII.
[5] The work on *Nature and Grace*, addressed to Timasius and Jacobus — translated in the fourth volume of this series, *Antipelagian Writings*, i. 233.

[6] The allusion is probably to the acquittal of Pelagius in 415 by the Council of Diospolis (or Lydda, a place between Joppa and Jerusalem). Augustin viewed this Council's decisions more favourably than Jerome, who denounces it without measure as a pitiful assembly, which allowed itself to be imposed upon by the evasions and feigned recantation of Pelagius; to this he makes reference in the concluding sentence of this paragraph.
[7] We adopt here the reading found in Letter CCII. *bis*, sec. 3, where this sentence is quoted by Augustin in writing to Optatus, and we have "*ne* (instead of *et*) juxta Appium canina facundia exerceretur." On the phrase "canina facundia," see Lactantius, book vi. ch. 18.
[8] Rom. xiv. 5. Translated by Jerome: "Unusquisque in suo sensu abundet."

chium and Paula, continue to walk worthy of their own birth and of your counsels, and they send special salutations to your Blessedness: in which they are joined by the whole brotherhood of those who with us labour to serve the Lord our Saviour. As for the holy presbyter Firmus, we sent him last year to go on business of Eustochium and Paula, first to Ravenna, and afterwards to Africa and Sicily, and we suppose that he is now detained somewhere in Africa. I beseech you to present my respectful salutations to the saints who are associated with you. I have also sent to your care a letter from me to the holy presbyter Firmus; if it reaches you, I beg you to take the trouble of forwarding it to him. May Christ the Lord keep you in safety, and mindful of me, my truly pious lord and most blessed father.

(*As a postscript.*) We suffer in this province from a grievous scarcity of clerks acquainted with the Latin language; this is the reason why we are not able to comply with your instructions, especially in regard to that version of the Septuagint which is furnished with distinctive asterisks and obelisks;[1] for we have lost, through some one's dishonesty, the most of the results of our earlier labour.

LETTER CLXXIII.

(A.D. 416.)

TO DONATUS, A PRESBYTER OF THE DONATIST PARTY, AUGUSTIN, A BISHOP OF THE CATHOLIC CHURCH, SENDS GREETING.

1. If you could see the sorrow of my heart and my concern for your salvation, you would perhaps take pity on your own soul, doing that which is pleasing to God, by giving heed to the word which is not ours but His; and would no longer give to His Scripture only a place in your memory, while shutting it out from your heart. You are angry because you are being drawn to salvation, although you have drawn so many of our fellow Christians to destruction. For what did we order beyond this, that you should be arrested, brought before the authorities, and guarded, in order to prevent you from perishing? As to your having sustained bodily injury, you have yourself to blame for this, as you would not use the horse which was immediately brought to you, and then dashed yourself violently to the ground; for, as you well know, your companion, who was brought along with you, arrived uninjured, not having done any harm to himself as you did.

2. You think, however, that even what we

have done to you should not have been done, because, in your opinion, no man should be compelled to that which is good. Mark, therefore, the words of the apostle: "If a man desire the office of a bishop, he desireth a good work," and yet, in order to make the office of a bishop be accepted by many men, they are seized against their will,[2] subjected to importunate persuasion, shut up and detained in custody, and made to suffer so many things which they dislike, until a willingness to undertake the good work is found in them. How much more, then, is it fitting that you should be drawn forcibly away from a pernicious error, in which you are enemies to your own souls, and brought to acquaint yourselves with the truth, or to choose it when known, not only in order to your holding in a safe and advantageous way the honour belonging to your office, but also in order to preserve you from perishing miserably! You say that God has given us free will, and that therefore no man should be compelled even to good. Why, then, are those whom I have above referred to compelled to that which is good? Take heed, therefore, to something which you do not wish to consider. The aim towards which a good will compassionately devotes its efforts is to secure that a bad will be rightly directed. For who does not know that a man is not condemned on any other ground than because his bad will deserved it, and that no man is saved who has not a good will? Nevertheless, it does not follow from this that those who are loved should be cruelly left to yield themselves with impunity to their bad will; but in so far as power is given, they ought to be both prevented from evil and compelled to good.

3. For if a bad will ought to be always left to its own freedom, why were the disobedient and murmuring Israelites restrained from evil by such severe chastisements, and compelled to come into the land of promise? If a bad will ought always to be left to its own freedom, why was Paul not left to the free use of that most perverted will with which he persecuted the Church? Why was he thrown to the ground that he might be blinded, and struck blind that he might be changed, and changed that he might be sent as an apostle, and sent that he might suffer for the truth's sake such wrongs as he had inflicted on others when he was in error? If a bad will ought always to be left to its own freedom, why is a father instructed in Holy Scripture not only to correct an obstinate son by words of rebuke, but also to beat his sides, in order that, being compelled and subdued, he may be guided to good conduct?[3] For which reason Solomon

---

[1] Jerome probably alludes here to Augustin's request in Letter LXXI., sec. 3, 4; *Letters*, pp. 326, 327.

[2] An example is furnished in the case of Castorius, Letter LXIX.; *Letters*, p. 326.

[3] Eccles. xxx. 12.

also says: "Thou shalt beat him with the rod, and shalt deliver his soul from hell."[1] If a bad will ought always to be left to its own freedom, why are negligent pastors reproved? and why is it said to them, "Ye have not brought back the wandering sheep, ye have not sought the perishing"?[2] You also are sheep belonging to Christ, you bear the Lord's mark in the sacrament which you have received, but you are wandering and perishing. Let us not, therefore, incur your displeasure because we bring back the wandering and seek the perishing; for it is better for us to obey the will of the Lord, who charges us to compel you to return to His fold, than to yield consent to the will of the wandering sheep, so as to leave you to perish. Say not, therefore, what I hear that you are constantly saying, "I wish thus to wander; I wish thus to perish;" for it is better that we should so far as is in our power absolutely refuse to allow you to wander and perish.

4. When you threw yourself the other day into a well, in order to bring death upon yourself, you did so no doubt with your free will. But how cruel the servants of God would have been if they had left you to the fruits of this bad will, and had not delivered you from that death! Who would not have justly blamed them? Who would not have justly denounced them as inhuman? And yet you, with your own free will, threw yourself into the water that you might be drowned. They took you against your will out of the water, that you might not be drowned. You acted according to your own will, but with a view to your destruction; they dealt with you against your will, but in order to your preservation. If, therefore, mere bodily safety behoves to be so guarded that it is the duty of those who love their neighbour to preserve him even against his own will from harm, how much more is this duty binding in regard to that spiritual health in the loss of which the consequence to be dreaded is eternal death! At the same time let me remark, that in that death which you wished to bring upon yourself you would have died not for time only but for eternity, because even though force had been used to compel you — not to accept salvation, not to enter into the peace of the Church, the unity of Christ's body, the holy indivisible charity, but — to suffer some evil things, it would not have been lawful for you to take away your own life.

5. Consider the divine Scriptures, and examine them to the utmost of your ability, and see whether this was ever done by any one of the just and faithful, though subjected to the most grievous evils by persons who were endeavouring to drive them, not to eternal life, to which you are being compelled by us, but to eternal death. I have heard that you say that the Apostle Paul intimated the lawfulness of suicide, when he said, "Though I give my body to be burned,"[3] supposing that because he was there enumerating all the good things which are of no avail without charity, such as the tongues of men and of angels, and all mysteries, and all knowledge, and all prophecy, and the distribution of one's goods to the poor, he intended to include among these good things the act of bringing death upon oneself. But observe carefully and learn in what sense Scripture says that any man may give his body to be burned. Certainly not that any man may throw himself into the fire when he is harassed by a pursuing enemy, but that, when he is compelled to choose between doing wrong and suffering wrong, he should refuse to do wrong rather than to suffer wrong, and so give his body into the power of the executioner, as those three men did who were being compelled to worship the golden image, while he who was compelling them threatened them with the burning fiery furnace if they did not obey. They refused to worship the image: they did not cast themselves into the fire, and yet of them it is written that they "yielded their bodies, that they might not serve nor worship any god except their own God."[4] This is the sense in which the apostle said, "If I give my body to be burned."

6. Mark also what follows: — "If I have not charity, it profiteth me nothing." To that charity you are called; by that charity you are prevented from perishing: and yet you think, forsooth, that to throw yourself headlong to destruction, by your own act, will profit you in some measure, although, even if you suffered death at the hands of another, while you remain an enemy to charity it would profit you nothing. Nay, more, being in a state of exclusion from the Church, and severed from the body of unity and the bond of charity, you would be punished with eternal misery even though you were burned alive for Christ's name; for this is the apostle's declaration, "Though I give my body to be burned, and have not charity, it profiteth me nothing." Bring your mind back, therefore, to rational reflection and sober thought; consider carefully whether it is to error and to impiety that you are being called, and, if you still think so, submit patiently to any hardship for the truth's sake. If, however, the fact rather be that you are living in error and in impiety, and that in the Church to which you are called truth and piety are found, because there is Christian unity and the love (*charitas*) of the Holy Spirit, why

do you labour any longer to be an enemy to yourself?

7. For this end the mercy of the Lord appointed that both we and your bishops met at Carthage in a conference which had repeated meetings, and was largely attended, and reasoned together in the most orderly manner in regard to the grounds of our separation from each other. The proceedings of that conference were written down; our signatures are attached to the record: read it, or allow others to read it to you, and then choose which party you prefer. I have heard that you have said that you could to some extent discuss the statements in that record with us if we would omit these words of your bishops: "No case forecloses the investigation of another case, and no person compromises the position of another person." You wish us to leave out these words, in which, although they knew it not, the truth itself spoke by them. You will say, indeed, that here they made a mistake, and fell through want of consideration into a false opinion. But we affirm that here they said what was true, and we prove this very easily by a reference to yourself. For if in regard to these bishops of your own, chosen by the whole party of Donatus on the understanding that they should act as representatives, and that all the rest should regard whatever they did as acceptable and satisfactory, you nevertheless refuse to allow them to compromise your position by what you think to have been a rash and mistaken utterance on their part, in this refusal you confirm the truth of their saying: "No case forecloses the investigation of another case, and no person compromises the position of another person." And at the same time you ought to acknowledge, that if you refuse to allow the conjoint authority of so many of your bishops represented in these seven to compromise Donatus, presbyter in Mutugenna, it is incomparably less reasonable that one person, Cæcilianus, even had some evil been found in him, should compromise the position of the whole unity of Christ, the Church, which is not shut up within the one village of Mutugenna, but spread abroad throughout the entire world.

8. But, behold, we do what you have desired; we treat with you as if your bishops had not said: "No case forecloses the investigation of another case, and no person compromises the position of another person." Discover, if you can, what they ought, rather than this, to have said in reply, when there was alleged against them the case and the person of Primianus,[1] who, notwithstanding his joining the rest of the bishops in passing sentence of condemnation on those who had passed sentence of condemnation upon him, nevertheless received back into their former honours those whom he had condemned and denounced, and chose to acknowledge and accept rather than despise and repudiate the baptism administered by these men while they were "dead" (for of them it was said in the notable decree [of the Council of Bagai], that "the shores were full of dead men"), and by so doing swept away the argument which you are accustomed to rest on a perverse interpretation of the words: "Qui baptizatur a mortuo quid ei prodest lavacrum ejus?"[2] If, therefore, your bishops had not said: "No case forecloses the investigation of another case, and no person compromises the position of another person," they would have been compelled to plead guilty in the case of Primianus; but, in saying this, they declared the Catholic Church to be, as we mentioned, not guilty in the case of Cæcilianus.

9. However, read all the rest and examine it well. Mark whether they have succeeded in proving any charge of evil brought against Cæcilianus himself, through whose person they attempted to compromise the position of the Church. Mark whether they have not rather brought forward much that was in his favour, and confirmed the evidence that his case was a good one, by a number of extracts which, to the prejudice of their own case, they produced and read. Read these or let them be read to you. Consider the whole matter, ponder it carefully, and choose which you should follow: whether you should, in the peace of Christ, in the unity of the Catholic Church, in the love of the brethren, be partaker of our joy, or, in the cause of wicked discord, the Donatist faction and impious schism, continue to suffer the annoyance caused to you by the measures which out of love to you we are compelled to take.

10. I hear that you have remarked and often quote the fact recorded in the gospels, that the seventy disciples went back from the Lord, and that they had been left to their own choice in this wicked and impious desertion, and that to the twelve who alone remained the Lord said, "Will ye also go away?"[3] But you have neglected to remark, that at that time the Church was only beginning to burst into life from the recently planted seed, and that there was not yet fulfilled in her the prophecy: "All kings shall fall down before Him; yea, all nations shall serve

---

[1] Primianus, Donatist bishop in Carthage, was in 393 deposed by a factious clique of bishops, who appointed Maximianus in his place. The other Donatist bishops, however, assembled in the following year at Bagai in Numidia, and, reversing the decision of their co-bishops deposed them in turn, and passed a sentence to which, as stated in the text, they did not inexorably adhere. The matter is referred to in Letter XLIII. p. 276.

[2] Ecclus. xxxiv. 25, translated, accurately enough, in our English version: "He that washeth himself after touching a dead body, if he touch it again, what availeth his washing?" The Donatist, in quoting the passage to support their practice of re-baptizing Catholics, omitted the clause, "et iterum tangit mortuum," and translated the sentence thus: "He that is baptized by one who is dead, what availeth his baptism?" It would be difficult to quote from the annals of controversy a more flagrant example of ignorant ingenuity in the wresting of words to serve a purpose.

[3] John vi. 67.

Him;"[1] and it is in proportion to the more enlarged accomplishment of this prophecy that the Church wields greater power, so that she may not only invite, but even compel men to embrace what is good. This our Lord intended then to illustrate, for although He had great power, He chose rather to manifest His humility. This also He taught, with sufficient plainness, in the parable of the Feast, in which the master of the house, after He had sent a message to the invited guests, and they had refused to come, said to his servants: "Go out quickly into the streets and lanes of the city, and bring in hither the poor, and the maimed, and the halt, and the blind. And the servant said, Lord, it is done as thou hast commanded, and yet there is room. And the Lord said unto the servant, Go out into the highways and hedges, and compel them to come in, that my house may be filled."[2] Mark, now, how it was said in regard to those who came first, "bring them in;" it was not said, "compel them to come in," — by which was signified the incipient condition of the Church, when it was only growing towards the position in which it would have strength to compel men to come in. Accordingly, because it was right that when the Church had been strengthened, both in power and in extent, men should be compelled to come in to the feast of everlasting salvation, it was afterwards added in the parable, "The servant said, Lord, it is done as thou hast commanded, and yet there is room. And the Lord said unto the servants, Go out into the highways and hedges, and compel them to come in." Wherefore, if you were walking peaceably, absent from this feast of everlasting salvation and of the holy unity of the Church, we should find you, as it were, in the "highways;" but since, by multiplied injuries and cruelties, which you perpetrate on our people, you are, as it were, full of thorns and roughness, we find you as it were in the "hedges," and we compel you to come in. The sheep which is compelled is driven whither it would not wish to go, but after it has entered, it feeds of its own accord in the pastures to which it was brought. Wherefore restrain your perverse and rebellious spirit, that in the true Church of Christ you may find the feast of salvation.

LETTER CLXXX.

(A.D. 416.)

TO OCEANUS, HIS DESERVEDLY BELOVED LORD AND BROTHER, HONOURED AMONG THE MEMBERS OF CHRIST, AUGUSTIN SENDS GREETING.

1. I received two letters from you at the same time, in one of which you mention a third, and state that you had sent it before the others. This letter I do not remember having received, or, rather, I think I may say the testimony of my memory is, that I did not receive it; but in regard to those which I have received, I return you many thanks for your kindness to me. To these I would have returned an immediate answer, had I not been hurried away by a constant succession of other matters urgently demanding attention. Having now found a moment's leisure from these, I have chosen rather to send some reply, however imperfect, than continue towards a friend so true and kind a protracted silence, and become more annoying to you by saying nothing than by saying too much.

2. I already knew the opinion of the holy Jerome as to the origin of souls, and had read the words which in your letter you have quoted from his book. The difficulty which perplexes some in regard to this question, "How God can justly bestow souls on the offspring of persons guilty of adultery?" does not embarrass me, seeing that not even their own sins, much less the sins of their parents, can prove prejudicial to persons of virtuous lives, converted to God, and living in faith and piety. The really difficult question is, if it be true that a new soul created out of nothing is imparted to each child at its birth, how can it be that the innumerable souls of those little ones, in regard to whom God knew with certainty that before attaining the age of reason, and before being able to know or understand what is right or wrong, they were to leave the body without being baptized, are justly given over to eternal death by Him with whom "there is no unrighteousness!"[3] It is unnecessary to say more on this subject, since you know what I intend, or rather what I do not at present intend to say. I think what I have said is enough for a wise man. If, however, you have either read, or heard from the lips of Jerome, or received from the Lord when meditating on this difficult question, anything by which it can be solved, impart it to me, I beseech you, that I may acknowledge myself under yet greater obligation to you.

3. As to the question whether lying is in any case justifiable and expedient, it has appeared to you that it ought to be solved by the example of our Lord's saying, concerning the day and hour of the end of the world, "Neither doth the Son know it."[4] When I read this, I was charmed with it as an effort of your ingenuity; but I am by no means of opinion that a figurative mode of expression can be rightly termed a falsehood. For it is no falsehood to call a day joyous because it renders men joyous, or a lupine harsh because by its bitter flavour it imparts harshness

---

[1] Ps. lxxii. 11.
[2] Luke xiv. 21-23.

[3] Rom. ix. 14.
[4] Mark xiii. 32.

to the countenance of him who tastes it, or to say that God knows something when He makes man know it (an instance quoted by yourself in these words of God to Abraham, " Now I know that thou fearest God ").[1] These are by no means false statements, as you yourself readily see. Accordingly, when the blessed Hilary explained this obscure statement of the Lord, by means of this obscure kind of figurative language, saying that we ought to understand Christ to affirm in these words that He knew not that day with no other meaning than that He, by concealing it, caused others not to know it, he did not by this explanation of the statement apologize for it as an excusable falsehood, but he showed that it was not a falsehood, as is proved by comparing it not only with these common figures of speech, but also with the metaphor, a mode of expression very familiar to all in daily conversation. For who will charge the man who says that harvest fields *wave* and children *bloom* with speaking falsely, because he sees not in these things the waves and the flowers to which these words are literally applied?

4. Moreover, a man of your talent and learning easily perceives how different from these metaphorical expressions is the statement of the apostle, " When I saw that they walked not uprightly, according to the truth of the gospel, I said unto Peter before them all, If thou, being a Jew, livest after the manner of the Gentiles, and not as do the Jews, why compellest thou the Gentiles to live as do the Jews ? "[2] Here there is no obscurity of figurative language ; these are literal words of a plain statement. Surely, in addressing persons " of whom he travailed in birth till Christ should be formed in them,"[3] and to whom, in solemnly calling God to confirm his words, he said : " The things which I write unto you, behold, before God, I lie not,"[4] the great teacher of the Gentiles affirmed in the words above quoted either what was true or what was false ; if he said what was false, which God forbid, you see the consequences which would follow ; and Paul's own assertion of his veracity, together with the example of wondrous humility in the Apostle Peter, may warn you to recoil from such thoughts.[5]

5. But why say more? This question the venerable Father Jerome and I have discussed fully in letters[6] which we exchanged, and in

his latest work, published under the name of *Critobulus*, against Pelagius,[7] he has maintained the same opinion concerning that transaction and the words of the apostle which, in accordance with the views of the blessed Cyprian,[8] I myself have held. In regard to the question as to the origin of souls, I think there is reasonable ground for inquiry, not as to the giving of souls to the offspring of adulterous parents, but as to the condemnation (which God forbid) of those who are innocent. If you have learned anything from a man of such character and eminence as Jerome which might form a satisfactory answer to those in perplexity on this subject, I pray you not to refuse to communicate it to me. In your correspondence, you have approved yourself so learned and so affable that it is a privilege to hold intercourse with you by letter. I ask you not to delay to send a certain book by the same man of God, which the presbyter Orosius brought and gave to you to copy, in which the resurrection of the body is treated of by him in a manner said to merit distinguished praise. We have not asked it earlier, because we knew that you had both to copy and to revise it ; but for both of these we think we have now given you ample time.

Live to God, and be mindful of us.

[For translation of Letter CLXXXV. to Count Boniface, containing an exhaustive history of the Donatist schism, see *Anti-Donatist Writings*.

LETTER CLXXXVIII.

(A.D. 416.)

TO THE LADY JULIANA, WORTHY TO BE HONOURED IN CHRIST WITH THE SERVICE DUE TO HER RANK, OUR DAUGHTER DESERVEDLY DISTINGUISHED, ALYPIUS AND AUGUSTIN SEND GREETING IN THE LORD.

CHAP. I. — 1. Lady, worthy to be honoured in Christ with the service due to your rank, and daughter deservedly distinguished, it was very pleasant and agreeable to us that your letter reached us when together at Hippo, so that we might send this joint reply to you, to express our joy in hearing of your welfare, and with sincere reciprocation of your love to let you know of our welfare, in which we are sure that you take an affectionate interest. We are well aware that you are not ignorant how great Christian affection we consider due to you, and how much, both before God and among men, we are interested in you. For though we knew you, at first by letter, afterwards by personal intercourse, to be pious and Catholic, that is, true members

---

[1] Gen. xxii. 12.
[2] Gal. ii. 14.
[3] Gal. iv. 19.
[4] Gal. i. 20.
[5] We have left the word *ambo* in " ambo ista exhorrescas " untranslated. Critics are agreed that a few words of the original are probably wanting here, only one alternative of the dilemma being stated by St. Augustin in the text.
[6] In Letters XXVIII., XL., LXXV., and LXXXII., translated in *Letters*, pp. 251, 272, 333, 349.

[7] *Adversus Pelagium*, book i.
[8] *Letters* of Cyprian, LXXI.

of the body of Christ, nevertheless, our humble ministry also was of use to you, for when you had received the word of God from us, "you received it," as says the apostle, "not as the word of men, but as it is in truth the word of God." [1] Through the grace and mercy of the Saviour, so great was the fruit arising from this ministry of ours in your family, that when preparations for her marriage [2] were already completed, the holy Demetrias preferred the spiritual embrace of that Husband who is fairer than the sons of men, and in espousing themselves to whom virgins retain their virginity, and gain more abundant spiritual fruitfulness. We should not, however, yet have known how this exhortation of ours had been received by the faithful and noble maiden, as we departed shortly before she took on her the vow of chastity, had we not learned from the joyful announcement and reliable testimony of your letter, that this great gift of God, planted and watered indeed by means of His servants, but owing its increase to Himself, had been granted to us as labourers in His vineyard.

2. Since these things are so, no one may charge us with presuming, if, on the ground of this closer spiritual relation, we manifest our solicitude for your welfare by warning you to avoid opinions opposed to the grace of God. For though the apostle commands us in preaching the word to be "instant in season and out of season," [3] yet we do not reckon you among the number of those to whom a word or a letter from us exhorting you carefully to avoid what is inconsistent with sound doctrine would seem "out of season." Hence it was that you received our admonition in so kindly a manner, that, in the letter to which we are now replying, you say, "I thank you heartily for the pious advice which your Reverence gave me, not to lend an ear to those men who, by their mischievous writings, often corrupt our holy faith."

3. In this letter you go on to say, "But your Reverence knows that I and my household are entirely separated from persons of this description; and all our family follow so strictly the Catholic faith as never at any time to have wandered from it, or fallen into any heresy, — I speak not of the heresy of sects who have erred in a measure hardly admiting of expiation, but of those whose errors seem to be trivial." This statement renders it more and more necessary for us, in writing to you, not to pass over in silence the conduct of those who are attempting to corrupt even those who are sound in the faith. We consider your house to be no insignificant

Church of Christ, nor indeed is the error of those men trivial who think that we have of ourselves whatever righteousness, temperance, piety, chastity is in us, on the ground that God has so formed us, that beyond the revelation which He has given He imparts to us no further aid for performing by our own choice those things which by study we have ascertained to be our duty; declaring nature and knowledge to be the grace of God, and the only aid for living righteously and justly. For the possession, indeed, of a will inclined to what is good, whence proceed the life of uprightness and that love which so far excels all other gifts that God Himself is said to be love, and by which alone is fulfilled in us as far as we fulfil them, the divine law and council, — for the possession, I say, of such a will, they hold that we are not indebted to the aid of God, but affirm that we ourselves of our own will are sufficient for these things. Let it not appear to you a trifling error that men should wish to profess themselves Christians, and yet be unwilling to hear the apostle of Christ, who, having said, "The love of God is shed abroad in our hearts," lest any one should think that he had this love through his own free will, immediately subjoined, "by the Holy Spirit who is given unto us." [4] Understand, then, how greatly and how fatally that man errs who does not acknowledge that this is the "great gift of the Saviour," [5] who, when He ascended on high, "led captivity captive, and gave gifts unto men." [6]

CHAP. II. — 4. How, then, could we so far conceal our true feelings as not to warn you, in whom we feel so deep an interest, to beware of such doctrines, after we had read a certain book addressed to the holy Demetrias? Whether this book has reached you, [7] and who is its author, we are desirous to hear in your answer to this. In this book, were it lawful for such a one to read it, a virgin of Christ would read that her holiness and all her spiritual riches are to spring from no other source than herself, and thus, before she attains to the perfection of blessedness, she would learn, — which may God forbid ! — to be ungrateful to God. For the words addressed to her in the said book are these: — "You have here, then, those things on account of which you are deservedly, nay more, more especially to be preferred before others; for your earthly rank and wealth are understood to be derived from your relatives, not from yourself, but your spiritual riches no one can have conferred on you but yourself; for these, then, you are justly to be praised, for these you are de-

---

[1] 1 Thess. ii. 13.
[2] In a letter of Jerome (the eighth) addressed to Demetrias, we have a very graphic narrative of the manner in which Demetrias formed and carried into effect the vow for which she is here commended.
[3] 2 Tim. iii. 2.

[4] Rom. v. 5.
[5] Eph. iv. 7.
[6] Ps. lxviii. 18.
[7] In the end of this letter, Augustin distinctly ascribes to Pelagius the authorship of the letter to Demetrias, as also in his work on *The Grace of Christ*, ch. xxii.

servedly to be preferred to others, for they can exist only from yourself, and in yourself." [1]

5. You see, doubtless, how dangerous is the doctrine in these words, against which you must be on your guard. For the affirmation, indeed, that these spiritual riches can exist only in yourself, is very well and truly said: that evidently is food; but the affirmation that they cannot exist except from you is unmixed poison. Far be it from any virgin of Christ willingly to listen to statements like these. Every virgin of Christ understands the innate poverty of the human heart, and therefore declines to have it adorned otherwise than by the gifts of her Spouse. Let her rather listen to the apostle when he says: "I have espoused you to one husband, that I may present you as a chaste virgin to Christ. But I fear, lest by any means, as the serpent beguiled Eve through his subtilty, so your minds should be corrupted from the simplicity that is in Christ." [2] And therefore in regard to these spiritual riches let her listen, not to him who says: "No one can confer them on you except yourself, and they cannot exist except from you and in you;" but to him who says: "We have this treasure in earthen vessels, that the excellency of the power may be of God, and not of us." [3]

6. In regard to that sacred virginal chastity, also, which does not belong to her from herself, but is the gift of God, bestowed, however, on her who is believing and willing, let her hear the same truthful and pious teacher, who when he treats of this subject says: "I would that all men were even as I myself: but every man hath his proper gift of God, one after this manner, and another after that." [4] Let her hear also Him who is the only Spouse, not only of herself, but of the whole Church, thus speaking of this chastity and purity: "All cannot receive this saying, save they to whom it is given;" [5] that she may understand that for her possession of this so great and excellent gift, she ought rather to render thanks to our God and Lord, than to listen to the words of any one who says that she possessed it from herself, — words which we may not designate as those of a flatterer seeking to please, lest we seem to judge rashly concerning the hidden thoughts of men, but which are assuredly those of a misguided eulogist. For "every good gift and every perfect gift," as the Apostle James says, "is from above, and cometh down from the Father of Lights;" [6] from this source, therefore, cometh this holy virginity, in which you who approve of it, and rejoice in it, have

been excelled by your daughter, who, coming after you in birth, has gone before you in conduct; descended from you in lineage, has risen above you in honour; following you in age, has gone beyond you in holiness; in whom also that begins to be yours which could not be in your own person. For she did not contract an earthly marriage, that she might be, not for herself only, but also for you, spiritually enriched, in a higher degree than yourself, since you, even with this addition, are inferior to her, because you contracted the marriage of which she is the offspring. These things are gifts of God, and are yours, indeed, but are not from yourselves; for you have this treasure in earthly bodies, which are still frail as the vessels of the potter, that the excellency of the power may be of God, and not of you. And be not surprised because we say that these things are yours, and not from you, for we speak of "daily bread" as ours, but yet add, [7] "give it to us," lest it should be thought that it was from ourselves.

7. Wherefore obey the precept of Scripture, "Pray without ceasing. In everything give thanks;" [8] for you pray in order that you may have constantly and increasingly these gifts, you render thanks because you have them not of yourself. For who separates you from that mass of death and perdition derived from Adam? Is it not He "who came to seek and to save that which was lost?" [9] Was, then, a man, indeed, on hearing the apostle's question, "Who maketh thee to differ?" to reply, "My own good will, my faith, my righteousness," and to disregard what immediately follows? "What hast thou that thou didst not receive? Now, if thou didst receive it, why dost thou glory as if thou hadst not received it?" [10] We are unwilling, then, yea, utterly unwilling, that a consecrated virgin, when she hears or reads these words: "Your spiritual riches no one can have conferred on you; for these you are justly to be praised, for these you are deservedly to be preferred to others, for they can exist only from yourself, and in yourself," should thus boast of her riches as if she had not received them. Let her say, indeed, "In me are Thy vows, O God, I will render praises unto Thee;" [11] but since they are in her, not from her, let her remember also to say, "Lord, by Thy will Thou hast furnished strength to my beauty," [12] because, though it be from her, inasmuch as it is the acting of her own will, without which we cannot do what is good, yet we are not to say, as he said, that it is "only from her." For our own will, unless it be aided by the grace

---

[1] *Epistle to Demetrias,* ch. xi.
[2] 2 Cor. xi. 2, 3.
[3] 2 Cor. iv. 7.
[4] 1 Cor. iv. 7.
[5] Matt. xix. 11.
[6] Jas. i. 17.

[7] Luke xi. 3.
[8] 1 Thess. v. 17, 18.
[9] Luke xix. 10.
[10] 1 Cor. iv. 7.
[11] Ps. lvi. 12.
[12] Ps. xxx. 7, LXX.

of God, cannot alone be even in name good will, for, says the apostle, "it is God who worketh in us, both to will, and to do according to good will," [1] — not, as these persons think, merely by revealing knowledge, that we may know what we ought to do, but also by inspiring Christian love, that we may also by choice perform the things which by study we have learned.

8. For doubtless the value of the gift of continence was known to him who said, "I perceived that no man can be continent unless God bestowed the gift." He not only knew then how great a benefit it was, and how eagerly it ought to be coveted, but also that, unless God gave it, it could not exist; for wisdom had taught him this, for he says, "This also was a point of wisdom, to know whose gift it was;" and the knowledge did not suffice him, but he says, "I went to the Lord and made my supplication to Him." [2] God then aids us in this matter, not only by making us know what is to be done, but also by making us do through love what we already know through learning. No one, therefore, can possess, not only knowledge, but also continence, unless God give it to him. Whence it was that when he had knowledge he prayed that he might have continence, that it might be in him, because he knew that it was not from him; or if on account of the freedom of his will it was in a certain sense from himself, yet it was not from himself alone, because no one can be continent unless God bestow on him the gift. But he whose opinions I am censuring, in speaking of spiritual riches, among which is doubtless that bright and beautiful gift of continence, does not say that they may exist in you, and from yourself, but says that they can exist *only* from you, and in you, in such a way that, as a virgin of Christ has these things nowhere else than in herself, so it can be believed possible for her to have them from no other source than from herself, and in this way (which may a merciful God avert from her heart!) she shall so boast as if she had not received them!

CHAP. III. — 9. We indeed hold such an opinion concerning the training of this holy virgin, and the Christian humility in which she was nourished and brought up, as to be assured that when she read these words, if she did read them, she would break out into lamentations, and humbly smite her breast, and perhaps burst into tears, and pray in faith to the Lord to whose service she was dedicated and by whom she was sanctified, pleading with Him that these were not her own words, but another's, and asking that her faith might not be such as to believe that she had anything whereof to glory in her-

self and not in the Lord. For her glory is in herself, not in the words of another, as the apostle says: "Let every man prove his own work, and then shall he have glory (rejoicing) in himself alone, and not in another." [3] But God forbid that her glory should be in herself, and not in Him to whom the Psalmist says, "Thou art my glory, and the lifter up of mine head." [4] For her glory is then profitably in herself, when God, who is in her, is Himself her glory, from whom she has every good, by which she is good, and shall have all things by which she shall be made better, in as far as she may become better in this life, and by which she shall be made perfect when rendered so by divine grace, not by human praise. "For her soul shall be praised in the Lord," [5] "who satisfieth her desire with good things," [6] because He Himself has inspired this desire, that His virgin should not boast of any good, as if she had not received it.

10. Inform us, then, in reply to this letter, whether we have judged truly in supposing these to be your daughter's sentiments. For we know well that you and all your family are, and have been, worshippers of the indivisible Trinity. But human error insinuates itself in other forms than in erroneous opinions concerning the indivisible Trinity. There are other subjects also, in regard to which men fall into very dangerous errors. As, for example, that of which we have spoken in this letter at greater length, perhaps, than might have sufficed to a person of your stedfast and pure wisdom. And yet we know not to whom, except to God, and therefore to the Trinity, wrong is done by the man who denies that the good that comes from God is from God; which evil may God avert from you, as we believe He does! May God altogether forbid that the book out of which we have thought it our duty to extract some words, that they might be more easily understood, should produce any such impression, we do not say on your mind, or on that of the holy virgin your daughter, but on the mind of the least deserving of your male or female servants.

11. But if you study more carefully even those words in which the writer appears to speak in favour of grace or the aid of God, you will find them so ambiguous that they may have reference either to nature or to knowledge, or to forgiveness of sins. For even in regard to that which they are forced to acknowledge, that we ought to pray that we may not enter into temptation, they may consider that the words mean that we are so far helped to it that, by our praying and knocking, the knowledge of the truth

---

[1] Phil. ii. 13.
[2] Wisd. viii. 21.

[3] Gal. vi. 4.
[4] Ps. iii. 3.
[5] Ps. xxxiv. 2.
[6] Ps. ciii. 5.

is so revealed to us that we may learn what it is our duty to do, not so far as that our will receives strength, whereby we may do that which we learn to be our duty; and as to their saying that it is by the grace or help of God that the Lord Christ has been set before us as an example of holy living, they interpret this so as to teach the same doctrine, affirming, namely, that we learn by His example how we ought to live, but denying that we are so aided as to do through love what we know by learning.

12. Find in this book, if you can, anything in which, excepting nature and the freedom of the will (which pertains to the same nature), and the remission of sin and the revealing of doctrine, any such aid of God is acknowledged as that which he acknowledges who said: "When I perceived that no man can be continent unless God bestow the gift, and that this also is a point of wisdom to know whose gift it is, I went to the Lord, and made my supplication to Him."[1] For he did not desire to receive, in answer to his prayer, the nature in which he was made; nor was he solicitous to obtain the natural freedom of the will with which he was made; nor did he crave the remission of sins, seeing that he prayed rather for continence, that he might not sin; nor did he desire to know what he ought to do, seeing that he already confessed that he knew whose gift this continence was; but he wished to receive from the Spirit of wisdom such strength of will, such ardour of love, as should suffice for fully practising the great virtue of continence. If, therefore, you succeed in finding any such statement in that book, we will heartily thank you if, in your answer, you deign to inform us of it.

13. It is impossible for us to tell how greatly we desire to find in the writings of these men, whose works are read by very many for their pungency and eloquence, the open confession of that grace which the apostle vehemently commends, who says that "God has given to every man the measure of faith,"[2] "without which it is impossible to please God,"[3] "by which the just live,"[4] "which worketh by love,"[5] before which and without which no works of any man are in any respect to be reckoned good, since "whatsoever is not of faith is sin."[6] He affirms that God distributes to every man,[7] and that we receive divine assistance to live piously and justly, not only by the revelation of that knowledge which without charity "puffeth up,"[8] but by our being inspired with that "love which is the ful-

filling of the law,"[9] and which so edifies our heart that knowledge does not puff it up. But hitherto I have failed to find any such statements in the writings of these men.

14. But especially we should wish that these sentiments should be found in that book from which we have quoted the words in which the author, praising a virgin of Christ as if no one except herself could confer on her spiritual riches, and as if these could not exist except from herself, does not wish her to glory in the Lord, but to glory as if she had not received them. In this book, though it contain neither his name nor your own honoured name, he nevertheless mentions that a request had been made to him by the mother of the virgin to write to her. In a certain epistle of his, however, to which he openly attaches his name, and does not conceal the name of the sacred virgin, the same Pelagius says that he had written to her, and endeavours to prove, by appealing to the said work, that he most openly confessed the grace of God, which he is alleged to have passed over in silence, or denied. But we beg you to condescend to inform us, in your reply, whether that be the very book in which he has inserted these words about spiritual riches, and whether it has reached your Holiness.

LETTER CLXXXIX.

(A.D. 418.)

TO BONIFACE,[10] MY NOBLE LORD AND JUSTLY DISTINGUISHED AND HONOURABLE SON, AUGUSTIN SENDS GREETING IN THE LORD.

1. I had already written a reply to your Charity, but while I was waiting for an opportunity of forwarding the letter, my beloved son Faustus arrived here on his way to your Excellency. After he had received the letter which I had intended to be carried by him to your Benevolence, he stated to me that you were very desirous that I should write you something which might build

---

[1] Wisd. viii. 21.
[2] Rom. xii. 3.
[3] Heb. xi. 6.
[4] Rom. i. 17.
[5] Gal. v. 6.
[6] Rom. xiv. 23.
[7] Rom. xii. 3.
[8] 1 Cor. viii. 1.

[9] Rom. xiii. 10.
[10] Count Boniface, to whom St. Augustin also addressed Letters CLXXXV. and CCXX., was governor of the province of Africa under Placidia, who for twenty-five years ruled the empire in the name of her son Valentinian. By his perfidious rival Aetius, Boniface was persuaded to disobey the order of Placidia, when, under the instigation of Aetius himself, she recalled him from the government of Africa. The necessity of powerful allies in order to maintain his position led him to invite the Vandals to pass from Spain into Africa. They came, under Genseric, and the fertile provinces of Northern Africa fell an easy prey to their invading armies. When the treachery of Aetius was discovered, Placidia received Boniface again into favour, and he devoted all his military talents to the task of expelling the barbarians whom his own invitation had made masters of North Africa. But it was now too late to wrest this Roman province from the Vandals; defeated in a great battle, Boniface was compelled in 430 to retire into Hippo Regius, where he succeeded in resisting the besieging army for fourteen months. It was during this siege, and after it had continued three months, that Augustin died. Reinforced by troops from Constantinople, Boniface fought one more desperate but unsuccessful battle, after which he left Hippo in the hands of Genseric, and returned by order of Placidia to Italy For fuller particulars of his history, see Gibbon's *History of the Decline and Fall of the Roman Empire*, ch. xxxiii.

you up unto the eternal salvation of which you have hope in Christ Jesus our Lord. And, although I was busily occupied at the time, he insisted, with an earnestness corresponding to the love which, as you know, he bears to you, that I should do this without delay. To meet his convenience, therefore, as he was in haste to depart, I thought it better to write, though necessarily without much time for reflection, rather than put off the gratification of your pious desire, my noble lord and justly distinguished and honourable son.

2. All is contained in these brief sentences: "Love the Lord thy God with all thy heart, and with all thy soul, and with all thy strength: and love thy neighbour as thyself;"[1] for these are the words in which the Lord, when on earth, gave an epitome of religion, saying in the gospel, "On these two commandments hang all the law and the prophets." Daily advance, then, in this love, both by praying and by well-doing, that through the help of Him, who enjoined it on you, and whose gift it is, it may be nourished and increased, until, being perfected, it render you perfect. "For this is the love which," as the apostle says, "is shed abroad in our hearts by the Holy Ghost, which is given unto us."[2] This is "the fulfilling of the law;"[3] this is the same love by which faith works, of which he says again, "Neither circumcision availeth anything, nor uncircumcision; but faith, which worketh by love."[4]

3. In this love, then, all our holy fathers, patriarchs, prophets, and apostles pleased God. In this all true martyrs contended against the devil even to the shedding of blood, and because in them it neither waxed cold nor failed, they became conquerors. In this all true believers daily make progress, seeking to acquire not an earthly kingdom, but the kingdom of heaven; not a temporal, but an eternal inheritance; not gold and silver, but the incorruptible riches of the angels; not the good things of this life, which are enjoyed with trembling, and which no one can take with him when he dies, but the vision of God, whose grace and power of imparting felicity transcend all beauty of form in bodies not only on earth but also in heaven, transcend all spiritual loveliness in men, however just and holy, transcend all the glory of the angels and powers of the world above, transcend not only all that language can express, but all that thought can imagine concerning Him. And let us not despair of the fulfilment of such a great promise because it is exceeding great, but rather believe that we shall receive it because He who has

promised it is exceeding great, as the blessed Apostle John says: "Now are we the sons of God; and it doth not yet appear what we shall be: but we know that, when He shall appear, we shall be like Him; for we shall see Him as He is."[5]

4. Do not think that it is impossible for any one to please God while engaged in active military service. Among such persons was the holy David, to whom God gave so great a testimony; among them also were many righteous men of that time; among them was also that centurion who said to the Lord: "I am not worthy that Thou shouldest come under my roof, but speak the word only, and my servant shall be healed: for I am a man under authority, having soldiers under me: and I say to this man, Go, and he goeth; and to another, Come, and he cometh; and to my servant, Do this, and he doeth it;" and concerning whom the Lord said: "Verily, I say unto you, I have not found so great faith, no, not in Israel."[6] Among them was that Cornelius to whom an angel said: "Cornelius, thine alms are accepted, and thy prayers are heard,"[7] when he directed him to send to the blessed Apostle Peter, and to hear from him what he ought to do, to which apostle he sent a devout soldier, requesting him to come to him. Among them were also the soldiers who, when they had come to be baptized by John, — the sacred forerunner of the Lord, and the friend of the Bridegroom, of whom the Lord says: "Among them that are born of women there hath not arisen a greater than John the Baptist,"[8] — and had inquired of him what they should do, received the answer, "Do violence to no man, neither accuse any falsely; and be content with your wages."[9] Certainly he did not prohibit them to serve as soldiers when he commanded them to be content with their pay for the service.

5. They occupy indeed a higher place before God who, abandoning all these secular employments, serve Him with the strictest chastity; but "every one," as the apostle says, "hath his proper gift of God, one after this manner, and another after that."[10] Some, then, in praying for you, fight against your invisible enemies; you, in fighting for them, contend against the barbarians, their visible enemies. Would that one faith existed in all, for then there would be less weary struggling, and the devil with his angels would be more easily conquered; but since it is necessary in this life that the citizens of the kingdom of heaven should be subjected to temptations among erring and impious men, that they

---

[1] Matt. xxii. 37-40.
[2] Rom. v. 5.
[3] Rom. xiii. 10.
[4] Gal. v. 6.

[5] John iii. 2.
[6] Matt. viii. 8-10.
[7] Acts x. 4.
[8] Matt. xi. 11.
[9] Luke iii. 14.
[10] 1 Cor. vii. 7.

may be exercised, and "tried as gold in the furnace," [1] we ought not before the appointed time to desire to live with those alone who are holy and righteous, so that, by patience, we may deserve to receive this blessedness in its proper time.

6. Think, then, of this first of all, when you are arming for the battle, that even your bodily strength is a gift of God; for, considering this, you will not employ the gift of God against God. For, when faith is pledged, it is to be kept even with the enemy against whom the war is waged, how much more with the friend for whom the battle is fought! Peace should be the object of your desire; war should be waged only as a necessity, and waged only that God may by it deliver men from the necessity and preserve them in peace. For peace is not sought in order to the kindling of war, but war is waged in order that peace may be obtained. Therefore, even in waging war, cherish the spirit of a peacemaker, that, by conquering those whom you attack, you may lead them back to the advantages of peace; for our Lord says: "Blessed are the peacemakers; for they shall be called the children of God." [2] If, however, peace among men be so sweet as procuring temporal safety, how much sweeter is that peace with God which procures for men the eternal felicity of the angels! Let necessity, therefore, and not your will, slay the enemy who fights against you. As violence is used towards him who rebels and resists, so mercy is due to the vanquished or the captive, especially in the case in which future troubling of the peace is not to be feared.

7. Let the manner of your life be adorned by chastity, sobriety, and moderation; for it is exceedingly disgraceful that lust should subdue him whom man finds invincible, and that wine should overpower him whom the sword assails in vain. As to worldly riches, if you do not possess them, let them not be sought after on earth by doing evil; and if you possess them, let them by good works be laid up in heaven. The manly and Christian spirit ought neither to be elated by the accession, nor crushed by the loss of this world's treasures. Let us rather think of what the Lord says: "Where your treasure is, there will your heart be also;" [3] and certainly, when we hear the exhortation to lift up our hearts, it is our duty to give unfeignedly the response which you know that we are accustomed to give. [4]

8. In these things, indeed, I know that you are very careful, and the good report which I hear of you fills me with great delight, and moves me to congratulate you on account of it in the Lord. This letter, therefore, may serve rather as a mirror in which you may see what you are, than as a directory from which to learn what you ought to be: nevertheless, whatever you may discover, either from this letter or from the Holy Scriptures, to be still wanting to you in regard to a holy life, persevere in urgently seeking it both by effort and by prayer; and for the things which you have, give thanks to God as the Fountain of goodness, whence you have received them; in every good action let the glory be given to God, and humility be exercised by you, for, as it is written, "Every good gift and every perfect gift is from above, and cometh down from the Father of lights." [5] But however much you may advance in the love of God and of your neighbour, and in true piety, do not imagine, as long as you are in this life, that you are without sin, for concerning this we read in Holy Scripture: "Is not the life of man upon earth a life of temptation?" [6] Wherefore, since always, as long as you are in this body, it is necessary for you to say in prayer, as the Lord taught us: "Forgive us our debts, as we forgive our debtors," [7] remember quickly to forgive, if any one shall do you wrong and shall ask pardon from you, that you may be able to pray sincerely, and may prevail in seeking pardon for your own sins.

These things, my beloved friend, I have written to you in haste, as the anxiety of the bearer to depart urged me not to detain him; but I thank God that I have in some measure complied with your pious wish. May the mercy of God ever protect you, my noble lord and justly distinguished son.

LETTER CXCI.

(A.D. 418.)

TO MY VENERABLE LORD AND PIOUS BROTHER AND CO-PRESBYTER SIXTUS, [8] WORTHY OF BEING RECEIVED IN THE LOVE OF CHRIST, AUGUSTIN SENDS GREETING IN THE LORD.

1. Since the arrival of the letter which, in my absence, your Grace forwarded by our holy brother the presbyter Firmus, and which I read on my return to Hippo, but not until after the bearer had departed, the present is my first opportunity

---

[1] Wisd. iii. 6.
[2] Matt. v. 9.
[3] Matt. vi. 21.
[4] The allusion is evidently to the ancient formulary in public worship, first mentioned by Cyprian in his treatise on the Lord's Prayer. To the presbyter's exhortation, "Sursum corda!" the people responded, "Habemus ad Dominum." For an account of this formulary and a most beautiful exposition of it, quoted from Cyril of Jerusalem, see Riddle's *Christian Antiquities*, book IV. ch. i. sec. 2.

[5] Jas. i. 17.
[6] Job. vii. 1, LXX.
[7] Matt. vi. 12.
[8] Sixtus, afterwards Sixtus III., Bishop of Rome, the immediate successor of Cælestine, to whom the next letter is addressed. His name is the forty-third in the list of Popes, and he was in office from 432 to 440 A.D. The 194th letter of Augustin was addressed to the same Sixtus, and is a very elaborate dissertation on Pelagianism. It is omitted from this selection as being rather a theological treatise than a letter.

of sending to you any reply, and it is with great pleasure that I entrust it to our very dearly beloved son, the acolyte Albinus. Your letter, addressed to Alypius and myself jointly, came at a time when we were not together, and this is the reason why you will now receive a letter from each of us, instead of one from both, in reply. For the bearer of this letter has just gone, meanwhile, from me to visit my venerable brother and co-bishop Alypius, who will write a reply for himself to your Holiness, and he has carried with him your letter, which I had already perused. As to the great joy with which that letter filled my heart, why should a man attempt to say what it is impossible to express? Indeed, I do not think that you yourself have any adequate idea of the amount of good done by your sending that letter to us; but take our word for it, for as you bear witness to your feelings, so do we bear witness to ours, declaring how profoundly we have been moved by the perfectly transparent soundness of the views declared in that letter. For if, when you sent a very short letter on the same subject to the most blessed aged Aurelius, by the acolyte Leo, we transcribed it with joyful alacrity, and read it with enthusiastic interest to all who were within our reach, as an exposition of your sentiments, both in regard to that most fatal dogma [of Pelagius], and in regard to the grace of God freely given by Him to small and great, to which that dogma is diametrically opposed; how great, think you, is the joy with which we have read this more extended statement in your writing, how great the zeal with which we take care that it be read by all to whom we have been able already or may yet be able to make it known! For what could be read or heard with greater satisfaction than so clear a defence of the grace of God against its enemies, from the mouth of one who was before this proudly claimed by these enemies as a mighty supporter of their cause?[1] Or is there anything for which we ought to give more abundant thanksgivings to God, than that His grace is so ably defended by those to whom it is given, against those to whom it is not given, or by whom, when given, it is not accepted, because in the secret and just judgment of God the disposition to accept it is not given to them?

2. Wherefore, my venerable lord, and holy brother worthy of being received in the love of Christ, although you render a most excellent service when you thus write on this subject to brethren before whom the adversaries are wont to boast themselves of your being their friend, nevertheless, there remains upon you the yet greater duty of seeing not only that those be punished with wholesome severity who dare to prate more openly their declaration of that error, most dangerously hostile to the Christian name, but also that with pastoral vigilance, on behalf of the weaker and simpler sheep of the Lord, most strenuous precautions be used against those who more covertly, indeed, and timidly, but perseveringly, and in whispers, as it were, teach this error, "creeping into houses," as the apostle says, and doing with practised impiety all those other things which are mentioned immediately afterwards in that passage.[2] Nor ought those to be overlooked who under the restraint of fear hide their sentiments under the most profound silence, yet have not ceased to cherish the same perverse opinions as before. For some of their party might be known to you before that pestilence was denounced by the most explicit condemnation of the apostolic see, whom you perceive to have now become suddenly silent; nor can it be ascertained whether they have been really cured of it, otherwise than through their not only forbearing from the utterance of these false dogmas, but also defending the truths which are opposed to their former errors with the same zeal as they used to show on the other side. These are, however, to be more gently dealt with; for what need is there for causing further terror to those whom their silence itself proves to be sufficiently terrified already? At the same time, though they should not be frightened, they should be taught; and in my opinion they may more easily, while their fear of severity assists the teacher of the truth, be so taught that by the Lord's help, after they have learned to understand and love His grace, they may speak out as antagonists of the error which meanwhile they dare not confess.

LETTER CXCII.

(A.D. 418.)

TO MY VENERABLE LORD AND HIGHLY ESTEEMED AND HOLY BROTHER, CÆLESTINE,[3] AUGUSTIN SENDS GREETING IN THE LORD.

1. I was at a considerable distance from home when the letter of your Holiness addressed to me at Hippo arrived by the hands of the clerk Projectus. When I had returned home, and, having read your letter, felt myself to be owing you a reply, I was still waiting for some means of communicating with you, when, lo! a most desirable opportunity presented itself in the departure of our very dear brother the acolyte Albinus, who leaves us immediately. Rejoicing, therefore, in your health, which is most earnestly desired by me, I return to your Holiness the salutation which I was owing. But I always owe

---

[1] Sixtus had been not without reason reckoned as a sympathiser with Pelagius, until their views were finally condemned in this year 418 by Zosimus.

[2] 2 Tim. iii. 6.

[3] Cælestine, who was at the date of this letter a deacon in Rome, was raised in 423 to succeed Boniface as Bishop of Rome; he stands forty-second in the list of the Popes. Letter CCIX. is addressed to him.

you love, the only debt which, even when it has been paid, holds him who has paid it a debtor still. For it is given when it is paid, but it is owing even after it has been given, for there is no time at which it ceases to be due. Nor when it is given is it lost, but it is rather multiplied by giving it; for in possessing it, not in parting with it, it is given. And since it cannot be given unless it is possessed, so neither can it be possessed unless it is given; nay, at the very time when it is given by a man it increases in that man, and, according to the number of persons to whom it is given, the amount of it which is gained becomes greater. Moreover, how can that be denied to friends which is due even to enemies? To enemies, however, this debt is paid with caution, whereas to friends it is repaid with confidence. Nevertheless, it uses every effort to secure that it receives back what it gives, even in the case of those to whom it renders good for evil. For we wish to have as a friend the man whom, as an enemy, we truly love, for we do not sincerely love him unless we wish him to be good, which he cannot be until he be delivered from the sin of cherished enmities.

2. Love, therefore, is not paid away in the same manner as money; for, whereas money is diminished by paying it away, love is increased by paying it away. They differ also in this, — that we give evidence of greater goodwill to the man to whom we may have given money if we do not seek to have it returned; but no one can be a true donor of love unless he lovingly insist on its repayment. For money, when it is received, accrues to him to whom it is given, but forsakes him by whom it is given; love, on the contrary, even when it is not repaid, nevertheless increases with the man who insists on its repayment by the person whom he loves; and not only so, but the person by whom it is returned to him does not begin to possess it till he pays it back again.

Wherefore, my lord and brother, I willingly give to you, and joyfully receive from you, the love which we owe to each other. The love which I receive I still claim, and the love which I give I still owe. For we ought to obey with docility the precept of the One Master, whose disciples we both profess to be, when He says to us by His apostle : " Owe no man anything, but to love one another." [1]

LETTER CXCV.

(A.D. 418.)

TO HIS HOLY LORD AND MOST BLESSED FATHER,[2] AUGUSTIN, JEROME SENDS GREETING.

At all times I have esteemed your Blessedness with becoming reverence and honour, and have

[1] Rom. xiii. 8.
[2] *Papa.*

loved the Lord and Saviour dwelling in you. But now we add, if possible, something to that which has already reached a climax, and we heap up what was already full, so that we do not suffer a single hour to pass without the mention of your name, because you have, with the ardour of unshaken faith, stood your ground against opposing storms, and preferred, so far as this was in your power, to be delivered from Sodom, though you should come forth alone, rather than linger behind with those who are doomed to perish. Your wisdom apprehends what I mean to say. Go on and prosper ! You are renowned throughout the whole world ; Catholics revere and look up to you as the restorer of the ancient faith, and — which is a token of yet more illustrious glory — all heretics abhor you. They persecute me also with equal hatred, seeking by imprecation to take away the life which they cannot reach with the sword. May the mercy of Christ the Lord preserve you in safety and mindful of me, my venerable lord and most blessed father.[3]

LETTER CCI.

(A.D. 419.)

THE EMPERORS HONORIUS AUGUSTUS AND THEODOSIUS AUGUSTUS TO BISHOP AURELIUS SEND GREETING.

1. It had been indeed long ago decreed that Pelagius and Celestius, the authors of an execrable heresy, should, as pestilent corruptors of the Catholic truth, be expelled from the city of Rome, lest they should, by their baneful influence, pervert the minds of the ignorant. In this our clemency followed up the judgment of your Holiness, according to which it is beyond all question that they were unanimously condemned after an impartial examination of their opinions. Their obstinate persistence in the offence having, however, made it necessary to issue the decree a second time, we have enacted further by a recent edict, that if any one. knowing that they are concealing themselves in any part of the provinces, shall delay either to drive them out or to inform on them, he, as an accomplice, shall be liable to the punishment prescribed.

2. To secure, however, the combined efforts of the Christian zeal of all men for the destruction of this preposterous heresy, it will be proper, most dearly beloved father, that the authority of

[3] In two MSS. this letter has, as a postscript, the letter already translated as CXXIII.; see page 451. The reason for that letter being supposed to belong to the year 410 is the interpretation which some put upon one of its obscure sentences as alluding to the fall of Rome in that year. If, however, the sentence in question referred to the ecclesiastical difficulties disturbing Jerusalem and all the East in connection with the Pelagian controversy, there is nothing to forbid the conjecture which its place in the MSS. aforesaid suggests, namely, that it was sent at the same time as this letter, with which in them it stands connected.

your Holiness be applied to the correction of certain bishops, who either support the evil reasonings of these men by their silent consent, or abstain from assailing them with open opposition. Let your Reverence, then, by suitable writings, cause all bishops to be admonished (as soon as they shall know, by the order of your Holiness, that this order is laid upon them) that whoever shall, through impious obstinacy, neglect to vindicate the purity of their doctrine by subscribing the condemnation of the persons before mentioned, shall, after being punished by the loss of their episcopal office, be cut off by excommunication and banished for life from their sees. For as, by a sincere confession of the truth, we ourselves, in obedience to the Council of Nice, worship God as the Creator of all things, and as the Fountain of our imperial sovereignty, your Holiness will not suffer the members of this odious sect, inventing, to the injury of religion, notions new and strange, to hide in writings privately circulated an error condemned by public authority. For, most beloved and loving father, the guilt of heresy is in no degree less grievous in those who either by dissimulation lend the error their secret support, or by abstaining from denouncing it extend to it a fatal approbation.

(*In another hand.*) May the Divinity preserve you in safety for many years!

Given at Ravenna, on the 9th day of June, in the Consulship of Monaxius and Plinta.

A letter, in the same terms, was also sent to the holy Bishop Augustin.

LETTER CCII.

(A.D. 419.)

TO THE BISHOPS ALYPIUS AND AUGUSTIN, MY LORDS TRULY HOLY, AND DESERVEDLY LOVED AND REVERENCED, JEROME SENDS GREETING IN CHRIST.[1]

CHAP. I. — I. The holy presbyter Innocentius, who is the bearer of this letter, did not last year take with him a letter from me to your Eminences, as he had no expectation of returning to Africa. We thank God, however, that it so happened, as it afforded you an opportunity of overcoming [evil with good in requiting] our silence by your letter. Every opportunity of writing to you, revered fathers, is most acceptable to me. I call God to witness that, if it were possible, I would take the wings of a dove and fly to be folded in your embrace. Loving you, indeed, as I have always done, from a deep sense of your worth, but now especially because your co-operation and your leadership have succeeded in strangling the heresy of Celestius, a heresy which has so poisoned the hearts of many,

that, though they felt they were vanquished and condemned, yet they did not lay aside their venomous sentiments, and, as the only thing that remained in their power, hated us by whom they imagined that they had lost the liberty of teaching heretical doctrines.

CHAP. II. — 2. As to your inquiry whether I have written in opposition to the books of Annianus, this pretended deacon[2] of Celedæ, who is amply provided for in order that he may furnish frivolous accounts of the blasphemies of others, know that I received these books, sent in loose sheets by our holy brother, the presbyter Eusebius, not long ago. Since then I have suffered so much through the attacks of disease, and through the falling asleep of your distinguished and holy daughter Eustochium, that I almost thought of passing over these writings with silent contempt. For he flounders from beginning to end in the same mud, and, with the exception of some jingling phrases which are not original, says nothing he had not said before. Nevertheless, I have gained much in the fact, that in attempting to answer my letter he has declared his opinions with less reserve, and has published to all men his blasphemies; for every error which he disowned in the wretched synod of Diospolis he in this treatise openly avows. It is indeed no great thing to answer his superlatively silly puerilities, but if the Lord spare me, and I have a sufficient staff of amanuenses, I will in a few brief lucubrations answer him, not to refute a defunct heresy, but to silence his ignorance and blasphemy by arguments: and this your Holiness could do better than I, as you would relieve me from the necessity of praising my own works in writing to the heretic. Our holy daughters Albina and Melania, and our son Pinianus, salute you cordially. I give to our holy presbyter Innocentius this short letter to convey to you from the holy place Bethlehem. Your niece Paula piteously entreats you to remember her, and salutes you warmly. May the mercy of our Lord Jesus Christ preserve you safe and mindful of me, my lords truly holy, and fathers deservedly loved and reverenced.

LETTER CCIII.

(A.D. 420.)

TO MY NOBLE LORD AND MOST EXCELLENT AND LOVING SON, LARGUS, AUGUSTIN SENDS GREETING IN THE LORD.

I received the letter of your Excellency, in which you ask me to write to you. This assuredly you would not have done unless you had esteemed acceptable and pleasant that which you suppose me capable of writing to you. In

---

[1] [The last letter of Jerome, who died at Bethlehem, 419.]

[2] *Pseudodiaconus.*

other words, I assume that, having desired the vanities of this life when you had not tried them, now, after the trial has been made, you despise them, because in them the pleasure is deceitful, the labour fruitless, the anxiety perpetual, the elevation dangerous. Men seek them at first through imprudence, and give them up at last with disappointment and remorse. This is true of all the things which, in the cares of this mortal life, are coveted with more eagerness than wisdom by the uneasy solicitude of the men of the world. But it is wholly otherwise with the hope of the pious: very different is the fruit of their labours, very different the reward of their dangers. Fear and grief, and labour and danger are unavoidable, so long as we live in this world; but the great question is, for what cause, with what expectation, with what aim a man endures these things. When, indeed, I contemplate the lovers of this world, I know not at what time wisdom can most opportunely attempt their moral improvement; for when they have apparent prosperity, they reject disdainfully her salutary admonitions, and regard them as old wives' fables; when, again, they are in adversity, they think rather of escaping merely from present suffering than of obtaining the real remedy by which they may be made whole, and may arrive at that place where they shall be altogether exempt from suffering. Occasionally, however, some open their ears and hearts to the truth, — rarely in prosperity, more frequently in adversity. These are indeed the few, for such it is predicted that they shall be. Among these I desire you to be, because I love you truly, my noble lord and most excellent and loving son. Let this counsel be my answer to your letter, because though I am unwilling that you should henceforth suffer such things as you have endured, yet I would grieve still more if you were found to have suffered these things without any change for the better in your life.

LETTER CCVIII.

(A.D. 423.)

TO THE LADY FELICIA, HIS DAUGHTER IN THE FAITH, AND WORTHY OF HONOUR AMONG THE MEMBERS OF CHRIST, AUGUSTIN SENDS GREETING IN THE LORD.

1. I do not doubt, when I consider both your faith and the weakness or wickedness of others, that your mind has been disturbed, for even a holy apostle, full of compassionate love, confesses a similiar experience, saying, "Who is weak, and I am not weak? who is offended, and I burn not?"[1] Wherefore, as I myself share your pain, and am solicitous for your welfare in Christ, I have thought it my duty to address this letter, partly consolatory, partly hortatory, to your Holiness, because in the body of our Lord Jesus Christ, in which all His members are one, you are very closely related to us, being loved as an honourable member in that body, and partaking with us of life in His Holy Spirit.

2. I exhort you, therefore, not to be too much troubled by those offences which for this very reason were foretold as destined to come, that when they came we might remember that they had been foretold, and not be greatly disconcerted by them. For the Lord Himself in His gospel foretold them, saying, "Woe unto the world because of offences! for it must needs be that offences come; but woe unto that man by whom the offence cometh!"[2] These are the men of whom the apostle said, "They seek their own, not the things that are Jesus Christ's."[3] There are, therefore, some who hold the honourable office of shepherds in order that they may provide for the flock of Christ; others occupy that position that they may enjoy the temporal honours and secular advantages connected with the office. It must needs happen that these two kinds of pastors, some dying, others succeeding them, should continue in the Catholic Church even to the end of time, and the judgment of the Lord. If, then, in the times of the apostles there were men such that Paul, grieved by their conduct, enumerates among his trials, "perils among false brethren,"[4] and yet he did not haughtily cast them out, but patiently bore with them, how much more must such arise in our times, since the Lord most plainly says concerning this age which is drawing to a close, "that because iniquity shall abound the love of many shall wax cold."[5] The word which follows, however, ought to console and exhort us, for He adds, "He that shall endure to the end, the same shall be saved."

3. Moreover, as there are good shepherds and bad shepherds, so also in flocks there are good and bad. The good are represented by the name of sheep, but the bad are called goats: they feed, nevertheless, side by side in the same pastures, until the Chief Shepherd, who is called the One Shepherd, shall come and separate them one from another according to His promise, "as a shepherd divideth the sheep from the goats." On us He has laid the duty of gathering the flock; to Himself He has reserved the work of final separation, because it pertains properly to Him who cannot err. For those presumptuous servants, who have lightly ventured to separate before the time which the Lord has reserved in His own hand, have, instead of

[1] 2 Cor. xi. 29.
[2] Matt. xviii. 7.
[3] Phil. ii. 21.
[4] 1 Cor. xi. 26.
[5] Matt. xxiv. 12, 13.

separating others, only been separated themselves from Catholic unity; for how could those have a clean flock who have by schism become unclean?

4. In order, therefore, that we may remain in the unity of the faith, and not, stumbling at the offences occasioned by the chaff, desert the threshing-floor of the Lord, but rather remain as wheat till the final winnowing,[1] and by the love which imparts stability to us bear with the beaten straw, our great Shepherd in the gospel admonishes us concerning the good shepherds, that we should not, on account of their good works, place our hope in them, but glorify our heavenly Father for making them such; and concerning the bad shepherds (whom He designed to point out under the name of Scribes and Pharisees), He reminds us that they teach that which is good though they do that which is evil.[1]

5. Concerning the good shepherds He thus speaks: "Ye are the light of the world. A city that is set on an hill cannot be hid. Neither do men light a candle, and put it under a bushel, but on a candlestick; and it giveth light unto all that are in the house. Let your light so shine before men, that they may see your good works, and glorify your Father who is in heaven."[2] Concerning the bad shepherds He admonishes the sheep in these words: "The Scribes and the Pharisees sit in Moses' seat: all, therefore, whatsoever they bid you observe, that observe and do; but do not ye after their works: for they say, and do not."[3] When these are listened to, the sheep of Christ, even through evil teachers, hear His voice, and do not forsake the unity of His flock, because the good which they hear them teach belongs not to the shepherds but to Him, and therefore the sheep are safely fed, since even under bad shepherds they are nourished in the Lord's pastures. They do not, however, imitate the actions of the bad shepherds, because such actions belong not to the world but to the shepherds themselves. In regard, however, to those whom they see to be good shepherds, they not only hear the good things which they teach, but also imitate the good actions which they perform. Of this number was the apostle, who said: "Be ye followers of me, even as I also am of Christ."[4] He was a light kindled by the Eternal Light, the Lord Jesus Christ Himself, and was placed on a candlestick because He gloried in His cross, concerning which he said: "God forbid that I should glory, save in the cross of our Lord Jesus Christ."[5] Moreover, since he sought not his

own things, but the things which are Jesus Christ's, whilst he exhorts to the imitation of his own life those whom he had "begotten through the gospel,"[6] he yet severely reproved those who, by the names of apostles, introduced schisms, and he chides those who said, "I am of Paul; was Paul crucified for you? or were ye baptized in the name of Paul?"[7]

6. Hence we understand both that the good shepherds are those who seek not their own, but the things of Jesus Christ, and that the good sheep, though imitating the works of the good shepherds by whose ministry they have been gathered together, do not place their hope in them, but rather in the Lord, by whose blood they are redeemed; so that when they may happen to be placed under bad shepherds, preaching Christ's doctrine and doing their own evil works, they will do what they teach, but will not do what they do, and will not, on account of these sons of wickedness, forsake the pastures of the one true Church. For there are both good and bad in the Catholic Church, which, unlike the Donatist sect, is extended and spread abroad, not in Africa only, but through all nations; as the apostle expresses it, "bringing forth fruit, and increasing in the whole world."[8] But those who are separated from the Church, as long as they are opposed to it cannot be good; although an apparently praiseworthy conversation seems to prove some of them to be good, their separation from the Church itself renders them bad, according to the saying of the Lord: "He that is not with me is against me; and he that gathereth not with me scattereth."[9]

7. Therefore, my daughter, worthy of all welcome and honour among the members of Christ, I exhort you to hold faithfully that which the Lord has committed to you, and love with all your heart Him and His Church who suffered you not, by joining yourself with the lost, to lose the recompense of your virginity, or perish with them. For if you should depart out of this world separated from the unity of the body of Christ, it will avail you nothing to have preserved inviolate your virginity. But God, who is rich in mercy, has done in regard to you that which is written in the gospel: when the invited guests excused themselves to the master of the feast, he said to the servants, "Go ye, therefore, into the highways and hedges, and as many as ye shall find compel them to come in."[10] Although, however, you owe sincerest affection to those good servants of His through whose instrumentality you were compelled to come in, yet it is your duty,

---

[1] Matt. iii. 12.
[2] Matt. v. 14, 15, 16.
[3] Matt. xxiii. 2, 3.
[4] 1 Cor. xi. 1.
[5] Gal. vi. 14.

[6] 1 Cor. iv. 15.
[7] 1 Cor. i. 12, 13.
[8] Col. i. 6 The words " καὶ αὐξανόμενον," here translated by Augustin, are found in some MSS. but omitted in the *Textus Receptus.*
[9] Matt. xii. 30.
[10] Matt. xxii. 9; Luke xiv. 23.

nevertheless, to place your hope on Him who prepared the banquet, by whom also you have been persuaded to come to eternal and blessed life. Committing to Him your heart, your vow, and your sacred virginity, and your faith, hope, and charity, you will not be moved by offences, which shall abound even to the end; but, by the unshaken strength of piety, shall be safe and shall triumph in the Lord, continuing in the unity of His body even to the end. Let me know, by your answer, with what sentiments you regard my anxiety for you, to which I have to the best of my ability given expression in this letter. May the grace and mercy of God ever protect you!

LETTER CCIX.

(A.D. 423.)

TO CÆLESTINE,[1] MY LORD MOST BLESSED, AND HOLY FATHER VENERATED WITH ALL DUE AFFECTION, AUGUSTIN SENDS GREETING IN THE LORD.

1. First of all I congratulate you that our Lord God has, as we have heard, established you in the illustrious chair which you occupy without any division among His people. In the next place, I lay before your Holiness the state of affairs with us, that not only by your prayers, but with your council and aid you may help us. For I write to you at this time under deep affliction, because, while wishing to benefit certain members of Christ in our neighbourhood, I brought on them a great calamity by my want of prudence and caution.

2. Bordering on the district of Hippo, there is a small town,[2] named Fussala: formerly there was no bishop there, but, along with the contiguous district, it was included in the parish of Hippo. That part of the country had few Catholics; the error of the Donatists held under its miserable influence all the other congregations located in the midst of a large population, so that in the town of Fussala itself there was not one Catholic. In the mercy of God, all these places were brought to attach themselves to the unity of the Church; with how much toil, and how many dangers it would take long to tell, — how the presbyters originally appointed by us to gather these people into the fold were robbed, beaten, maimed, deprived of their eyesight, and even put to death; whose sufferings, however, were not useless and unfruitful, seeing that by them the re-establishment of unity was achieved. But as Fussala is forty miles distant from Hippo, and

I saw that in governing its people, and gathering together the remnant, however small, of persons of both sexes, who, not threatening others, but fleeing for their own safety, were scattered here and there, my work would be extended farther than it ought, and that I could not give the attention which I clearly perceived to be necessary, I arranged that a bishop should be ordained and appointed there.

3. With a view to the carrying out of this, I sought for a person who might be suitable to the locality and people, and at the same time acquainted with the Punic language; and I had in my mind a presbyter fitted for the office. Having applied by letter to the holy senior bishop who was then Primate of Numidia, I obtained his consent to come from a great distance to ordain this presbyter. After his coming, when all our minds were intent on an affair of so great consequence, at the last moment, the person whom I believed to be ready to be ordained disappointed us by absolutely refusing to accept the office. Then I myself, who, as the event showed, ought rather to have postponed than precipitated a matter ·so perilous, being unwilling that the very venerable and holy old man, who had come with so much fatigue to us, should return home without accomplishing the business for which he had journeyed so far, offered to the people, without their seeking him, a young man, Antonius, who was then with me. He had been from childhood brought up in a monastery by us, but, beyond officiating as a reader, he had no experience of the labours pertaining to the various degrees of rank in the clerical office. The unhappy people, not knowing what was to follow, submissively trusting me, accepted him on my suggestion. What need I say more? The deed was done; he entered on his office as their bishop.

4. What shall I do? I am unwilling to accuse before your venerable Dignity one whom I brought into the fold, and nourished with care; and I am unwilling to forsake those in seeking whose ingathering to the Church I have travailed, amid fears and anxieties; and how to do justice to both I cannot discover. The matter has come to such a painful crisis, that those who, in compliance with my wishes, had, in the belief that they were consulting their own interests, chosen him for their bishop, are now bringing charges against him before me. When the most serious of these, namely, charges of gross immorality, which were brought forward not by those whose bishop he was, but by certain other individuals, were found to be utterly unsupported by evidence, and he seemed to us fully acquitted of the crimes laid most ungenerously to his charge, he was on this account regarded, both by ourselves and by others, with such sympathy that

---

[1] The successor of Boniface as Bishop of Rome. See note to Letter CXCII. For a summary of the arguments which may be used on both sides in regard to the genuineness of this letter, which is found in only one MS., see Dupin's remarks upon it in his *Ecclesiastical History*, 5th century.

[2] Castellum.

the things complained of by the people of Fussala and the surrounding district, — such as intolerable tyranny and spoliation, and extortion, and oppression of various kinds, — by no means seemed so grievous that for one, or for all of them taken together, we should deem it necessary to deprive him of the office of bishop; it seemed to us enough to insist that he should restore what might be proved to have been taken away unjustly.

5. In fine, we so mixed clemency with severity in our sentence, that while reserving to him his office of bishop, we did not leave altogether unpunished offences which behoved neither to be repeated again by himself, nor held forth to the imitation of others. We therefore, in correcting him, reserved to the young man the rank of his office unimpaired, but at the same time, as a punishment, we took away his power, appointing that he should not any longer rule over those with whom he had dealt in such a manner, that with just resentment they could not submit to his authority, and might perhaps manifest their impatient indignation by breaking forth into some deeds of violence fraught with danger· both to themselves and to him. That this was the state of feeling evidently appeared when the bishops dealt with them concerning Antonius, although at present that conspicuous man Celer, of whose powerful interference against him he complained, possesses no power, either in Africa or elsewhere.

6. But why should I detain you with further particulars? I beseech you to assist us in this laborious matter, blessed lord and holy father, venerated for your piety, and revered with due affection; and command all the documents which have been forwarded to be read aloud to you. Observe in what manner Antonius discharged his duties as bishop; how, when debarred from communion until full restitution should be made to the men of Fussala, he submitted to our sentence, and has now set apart a sum out of which to pay what may after inquiry be deemed just for compensation, in order that the privilege of communion might be restored to him; with what crafty reasoning he prevailed on our aged primate, a most venerable man, to believe all his statements, and to recommend him as altogether blameless to the venerable Pope Boniface. But why should I rehearse all the rest, seeing that the venerable old man aforesaid must have reported the entire matter to your Holiness?

7. In the numerous minutes of procedure in which our judgment regarding him is recorded, I should have feared that we might appear to you to have passed a sentence less severe than we ought to have done, did I not know that you are so prone to mercy that you will deem it your duty to spare not us only, because we

spared him, but also the man himself. But what we did, whether in kindness or laxity, he attempts to turn to account, and use as a legal objection to our sentence. He boldly protests: "Either I ought to sit in my own episcopal chair, or ought not to be a bishop at all," as if he were now sitting in any seat but his own. For, on this very account, those places were set apart and assigned to him in which he had previously been bishop, that he might not be said to be unlawfully translated to another see, contrary to the statutes of the Fathers;[1] or is it to be maintained that one ought to be so rigid an advocate, either for severity or for lenity, as to insist, either that no punishment be inflicted on those who seem not to deserve deposition from the office of bishop, or that the sentence of deposition be pronounced on all who seem to deserve any punishment?

8. There are cases on record, in which the Apostolic See, either pronouncing judgment or confirming the judgment of others, sanctioned decisions by which persons, for certain offences, were neither deposed from their episcopal office nor left altogether unpunished. I shall not bring forward those which occurred at a period very remote from our own time; I shall mention recent instances. Let Priscus, a bishop of the province of Cæsarea, protest boldly: "Either the office of primate should be open to me, as to other bishops, or I ought not to remain a bishop." Let Victor, another bishop of the same province, with whom, when involved in the same sentence as Priscus, no bishop beyond his own diocese holds communion, let him, I say, protest with similar confidence: "Either I ought to have communion everywhere, or I ought not to have it in my own district." Let Laurentius, a third bishop of the same province, speak, and in the precise words of this man he may exclaim: "Either I ought to sit in the chair to which I have been ordained, or I ought not to be a bishop." But who can find fault with these judgments, except one who does not consider that, neither on the one hand ought all offences to be left unpunished, nor on the other ought all to be punished in one way.

9. Since, then, the most blessed Pope Boniface, speaking of Bishop Antonius, has in his epistle, with the vigilant caution becoming a pastor, inserted in his judgment the additional clause, "if he has faithfully narrated the facts of the case to us," receive now the facts of the case, which in his statement to you he passed over in silence, and also the transactions which took place after the letter of that man of blessed memory had been read in Africa, and in the mercy of Christ extend your aid to men implor-

---

[1] Translations from one see to another, now permitted, had been forbidden by the Councils of Nice, Sardis, and Antioch.

ing it more earnestly than he does from whose turbulence they desire to be freed. For either from himself, or at least from very frequent rumours, threats are held out that the courts of justiciary, and the public authorities, and the violence of the military, are to carry into force the decision of the Apostolic See; the effect of which is that these unhappy men, being now Catholic Christians, dread greater evils from a Catholic bishop than those which, when they were heretics, they dreaded from the laws of Catholic emperors. Do not permit these things to be done, I implore you, by the blood of Christ, by the memory of the Apostle Peter, who has warned those placed over Chistian people against violently "lording it over their brethren." [1] I commend to the gracious love of your Holiness the Catholics of Fussala, my children in Christ, and also Bishop Antonius, my son in Christ, for I love both, and I commend both to you. I do not blame the people of Fussala for bringing to your ears their just complaint against me for imposing on them a man whom I had not proved, and who was in age at least not yet established, by whom they have been so afflicted; nor do I wish any wrong done to Antonius, whose evil covetousness I oppose with a determination proportioned to my sincere affection for him. Let your compassion be extended to both, — to them, so that they may not suffer evil; to him, so that he may not do evil; to them, so that they may not hate the Catholic Church, if they find no aid in defence against a Catholic bishop extended to them by Catholic bishops, and especially by the Apostolic See itself; to him, on the other hand, so that he may not involve himself in such grievous wickedness as to alienate from Christ those whom against their will he endeavours to make his own.

10. As for myself, I must acknowledge to your Holiness, that in the danger which threatens both, I am so racked with anxiety and grief that I think of retiring from the responsibilities of the episcopal office, and abandoning myself to demonstrations of sorrow corresponding to the greatness of my error, if I shall see (through the conduct of him in favour of whose election to the bishopric I imprudently gave my vote) the Church of God laid waste, and (which may God forbid) even perish, involving in its destruction the man by whom it was laid waste. Recollecting what the apostle says: "If we would judge ourselves, we should not be judged." [2] I will judge myself, that He may spare me who is hereafter to judge the quick and the dead. If, however, you succeed in restoring the members of Christ in that district from their deadly fear

and grief, and in comforting my old age by the administration of justice tempered with mercy, He who brings deliverance to us through you in this tribulation, and who has established you in the seat which you occupy, shall recompense unto you good for good, both in this life and in that which is to come.

LETTER CCX.

(A.D. 423.)

TO THE MOST BELOVED AND MOST HOLY MOTHER FELICITAS,[3] AND BROTHER RUSTICUS, AND TO THE SISTERS WHO ARE WITH THEM, AUGUSTIN AND THOSE WHO ARE WITH HIM SEND GREETING IN THE LORD.

1. Good is the Lord, and to every place extends His mercy, which comforts us by your love to us in Him. How much He loves those who believe and hope in Him, and who both love Him and love one another, and what blessings He keeps in store for them hereafter, He proves most remarkably in this, that on the unbelieving, the abandoned, and the perverse, whom He threatens with eternal fire, if they persevere in their evil disposition to the end, He does in this life bestow so many benefits, making "His sun to rise on the evil and on the good," "on the just and on the unjust," [4] words in which, for the sake of brevity, some instances are mentioned that many more may be suggested to reflection; for who can reckon up how many gracious benefits the wicked receive in this life from Him whom they despise? Amongst these, this is one of great value, that by the experience of the occasional afflictions, which like a good physician He mingles with the pleasures of this life, He admonishes them, if only they will give heed, to flee from the wrath to come, and while they are in the way, that is, in this life, to agree with the word of God, which they have made an adversary to themselves by their wicked lives. What, then, is not bestowed in mercy on men by the Lord God, since even affliction sent by Him is a blessing? For prosperity is a gift of God when He comforts, adversity a gift of God when He warns; and if He bestows these things, as I have said, even on the wicked, what does He prepare for those who bear with one another? Into this number you rejoice that through His grace you have been gathered, "forbearing one another in love; endeavouring to keep the unity of the Spirit in the bond of peace." [5] For there shall not be awanting occasion for

---

[1] 1 Pet. v. 3.
[2] 1 Cor. xi. 31.

[3] The prioress of the nunnery at Hippo, appointed to that office after the death of the sister of Augustin.
[4] Matt. v. 45.
[5] Eph. iv. 2, 3.

your bearing one with another till God shall have so purified you, that, death being "swallowed up in victory," [1] "God shall be all in all." [2]

2. We ought never, indeed, to take pleasure in quarrels ; but however averse we may be to them, they occasionally either arise from love, or put it to the test. For how difficult is it to find any one willing to be reproved ; and where is the wise man of whom it is said, "Rebuke a wise man, and he will love thee"? [3] But are we on that account not to reprove and find fault with a brother, to prevent him from going down through false security to death? For it is a common and frequent experience, that when a brother is found fault with he is mortified at the time, and resists and contradicts his friend, but afterwards reconsiders the matter in silence alone with God, where he is not afraid of giving offence to men by submitting to correction, but is afraid of offending God by refusing to be reformed, and thenceforward refrains from doing that for which he has been justly reproved ; and in proportion as he hates his sin, he loves the brother whom he feels to have been the enemy of his sin. But if he belong to the number of those of whom it is said, "Reprove not a scorner lest he hate thee," [3] the quarrel does not arise from love on the part of the reproved, but it exercises and tests the love of the reprover ; for he does not return hatred for hatred, but the love which constrains him to find fault endures unmoved, even when he who is found fault with requites it with hatred. But if the reprover renders evil for evil to the man who takes offence at being reproved, he was not worthy to reprove another, but evidently deserves to be himself reproved. Act upon these principles, so that either quarrels may not arise, or, if they do arise, may quickly terminate in peace. Be more earnest to dwell in concord than to vanquish each other in controversy. For as vinegar corrodes a vessel if it remain long in it, so anger corrodes the heart if it is cherished till the morrow. These things, therefore, observe, and the God of peace shall be with you. Pray also unitedly for us, that we may cheerfully practise the good advices which we give to you.

LETTER CCXI.

(A.D. 423.)

IN THIS LETTER AUGUSTIN REBUKES THE NUNS OF THE MONASTERY IN WHICH HIS SISTER HAD BEEN PRIORESS, FOR CERTAIN TURBULENT MANIFESTATIONS OF DISSATISFACTION WITH HER SUCCESSOR, AND LAYS DOWN GENERAL RULES FOR THEIR GUIDANCE. [4]

1. As severity is ready to punish the faults which it may discover, so charity is reluctant to discover the faults which it must punish. This was the reason of my not acceding to your request for a visit from me, at a time when, if I had come, I must have come not to rejoice in your harmony, but to add more vehemence to your strife. For how could I have treated your behaviour with indifference, or have allowed it to pass unpunished, if so great a tumult had arisen among you in my presence, as that which, when I was absent, assailed my ears with the din of your voices, although my eyes did not witness your disorder ? For perhaps your rising against authority would have been even more violent in my presence, since I must have refused the concessions which you demanded, — concessions involving, to your own disadvantage, some most dangerous precedents, subversive of sound discipline ; and I must thus have found you such as I did not desire, and must have myself been found by you such as you did not desire.

2. The apostle, writing to the Corinthians, says : "Moreover, I call God for a record upon my soul, that to spare you I came not as yet to Corinth. Not for that we have dominion over your faith, but are helpers of your joy." [5] I also say the same to you ; to spare you I have not come to you. I have also spared myself, that I might not have sorrow upon sorrow, and have chosen not to see you face to face, but to pour out my heart to God on your behalf, and to plead the cause of your great danger not in words before you, but in tears before God ; entreating Him that He may not turn into grief the joy wherewith I am wont to rejoice in you, and that amid the great offences with which this world everywhere abounds, I may be comforted at times by thinking of your number, your pure affection, your holy conversation, and the abundant grace of God which is given to you, so that you not only have renounced matrimony, but have chosen to dwell with one accord in fellowship under the same roof, that you may have one soul and one heart in God.

3. When I reflect on these good things, these gifts of God in you, my heart, amid the many storms by which it is agitated through evils elsewhere, is wont to find perfect rest. "Ye did run well ; who did hinder you, that ye should not obey the truth? This persuasion cometh not of Him that calleth you." [6] "A little leaven" — [7]

---

[1] 1 Cor. xv. 24.
[2] 1 Cor. xv. 28.
[3] Prov. ix. 8.

[4] This letter is of historical value, as embodying the rules of nunneries belonging to the Augustinian orders. In the end of the first volume of the Benedictine edition of his writings, this rule of monastic life is given, adapted by some later writer to convents of monks.
[5] 2 Cor. i. 23.
[6] Gal. v. 7, 8.
[7] 1 Cor. v. 6.

I am unwilling to complete the sentence, for I rather desire, entreat, and exhort that the leaven itself be transformed into something better, lest it change the whole lump for the worse, as it has already almost done. If, therefore, you have begun to put forth again the buddings of a sound discernment as to your duty, pray that you enter not into temptation, nor fall again into strifes, emulations, animosities, divisions, evil speaking, seditions, whisperings. For we have not laboured as we have done in planting and watering the garden of the Lord among you, that we may reap these thorns from you. If, however, your weakness be still disturbed by turbulence, pray that you may be delivered from this temptation. As for the troublers of your peace, if such there be still among you, they shall, unless they amend their conduct, bear their judgment, whoever they be.

4. Consider how evil a thing it is, that at the very time when we rejoice in the return of the Donatists to our unity, we have to lament internal discord within our monastery. Be stedfast in observing your good vows, and you will not desire to change for another the prioress whose care of the monastery has been for so many years unwearied, under whom also you have both increased in numbers and advanced in age, and who has given you the place in her heart which a mother gives to her own children. All of you when you came to the monastery found her there, either discharging satisfactorily the duties of assistant to the late holy prioress, my sister, or, after her own accession to that office, giving you a welcome to the sisterhood. Under her you spent your noviciate, under her you took the veil, under her your number has been multiplied, and yet you are riotously demanding that she should be replaced by another, whereas, if the proposal to put another in her place had come from us, it would have been seemly for you to have mourned over such a proposal. For she is one whom you know well; to her you came at first, and under her you have for so many years advanced in age and in numbers. No official previously unknown to you has been appointed, excepting the prior; if it be on his account that you seek a change, and if through aversion to him you thus rebel against your mother, why do you not rather petition for his removal? If, however, you recoil from this suggestion, for I know how you reverence and love him in Christ, why do you not all the more for his sake reverence and love her? For the first measures of the recently appointed prior in presiding over you are so hindered by your disorderly behaviour, that he is himself disposed to leave you, rather than be subjected on your account to the dishonour and odium which must arise from the report going abroad, that you

would not have sought another prioress unless you had begun to have him as your prior. May God therefore calm and compose your minds: let not the work of the devil prevail in you, but may the peace of Christ gain the victory in your hearts; and do not rush headlong to death, either through vexation of spirit, because what you desire is refused, or through shame, because of having desired what you ought not to have desired, but rather by repentance resume the conscientious discharge of duty; and imitate not the repentance of Judas the traitor, but the tears of Peter the shepherd.

5. The rules which we lay down to be observed by you as persons settled in a monastery are these:—

First of all, in order to fulfil the end for which you have been gathered into one community, dwell in the house with oneness of spirit, and let your hearts and minds be one in God. Also call not anything the property of any one, but let all things be common property, and let distribution of food and raiment be made to each of you by the prioress,—not equally to all, because you are not all equally strong, but to every one according to her need. For you read in the Acts of the Apostles: "They had all things common: and distribution was made to every man according as he had need."[1] Let those who had any worldly goods when they entered the monastery cheerfully desire that these become common property. Let those who had no worldly goods not ask within the monastery for luxuries which they could not have while they were outside of its walls; nevertheless, let the comforts which the infirmity of any of them may require be given to such, though their poverty before coming in to the monastery may have been such that they could not have procured for themselvs the bare necessaries of life; and let them in such case be careful not to reckon it the chief happiness of their present lot that they have found within the monastery food and raiment, such as was elsewhere beyond their reach.

6. Let them, moreover, not hold their heads high because they are associated on terms of equality with persons whom they durst not have approached in the outer world; but let them rather lift their hearts on high, and not seek after earthly possessions, lest, if the rich be made lowly but the poor puffed up with vanity in our monasteries, these institutions become useful only to the rich, and hurtful to the poor. On the other hand, however, let not those who seemed to hold some position in the world regard with contempt their sisters, who in coming into this sacred fellowship have left a condition of poverty; let them be careful to glory rather in

---

[1] Acts iv. 32, 35.

the fellowship of their poor sisters, than in the rank of their wealthy parents. And let them not lift themselves up above the rest because of their having, perchance, contributed something from their own resources to the maintenance of the community, lest they find in their riches more occasion for pride, because they divide them with others in a monastery, than they might have found if they had spent them in their own enjoyment in the world. For every other kind of sin finds scope in evil works, so that by it they are done, but pride lurks even in good works, so that by it they are undone ; and what avails it to lavish money on the poor, and become poor oneself, if the unhappy soul is rendered more proud by despising riches than it had been by possessing them? Live, then, all of you, in unanimity and concord, and in each other give honour to that God whose temples you have been made.

7. Be regular (*instate*) in prayers at the appointed hours and times. In the oratory let no one do anything else than the duty for which the place was made, and from which it has received its name ; so that if any of you, having leisure, wish to pray at other hours than those appointed, they may not be hindered by others using the place for any other purpose. In the psalms and hymns used in your prayers to God, let that be pondered in the heart which is uttered by the voice ; chant nothing but what you find prescribed to be chanted ; whatever is not so prescribed is not to be chanted.

8. Keep the flesh under by fastings and by abstinence from meat and drink, so far as health allows. When any one is not able to fast, let her not, unless she be ill, take any nourishment except at the customary hour of repast. From the time of your coming to table until you rise from it, listen without noise and wrangling to whatever may be in course read to you ; let not your mouths alone be exercised in receiving food, let your ears be also occupied in receiving the word of God.

9. If those who are weak in consequence of their early training are treated somewhat differently in regard to food, this ought not to be vexatious or seem unjust to others whom a different training has made more robust. And let them not esteem these weaker ones more favoured than themselves, because they receive a fare somewhat less frugal than their own, but rather congratulate themselves on enjoying a vigour of constitution which the others do not possess. And if to those who have entered the monastery after a more delicate upbringing at home, there be given any food, clothing, couch, or covering which to others who are stronger, and in that respect more favourably circumstanced, is not given, the sisters to whom these indulgences are not given ought to consider how great a descent

the others have made from their style of living in the world to that which they now have, although they may not have been able to come altogether down to the severe simplicity of others who have a more hardy constitution. And when those who were originally more wealthy see others receiving — not as mark of higher honour, but out of consideration for infirmity — more largely than they do themselves, they ought not to be disturbed by fear of any such detestable perversion of monastic discipline as this, that the poor are to be trained to luxury in a monastery in which the wealthy are, so far as they can bear it, trained to hardships. For, of course, as those who are ill must take less food, otherwise they would increase their disease, so after illness, those who are convalescent must, in order to their more rapid recovery, be so nursed — even though they may have come from the lowest poverty to the monastery — as if their recent illness had conferred on them the same claim for special treatment as their former style of living confers upon those who, before entering the monastery, were rich. So soon, however, as they regain their wonted health, let them return to their own happier mode of living, which, as involving fewer wants, is more suitable for those who are servants of God ; and let not inclination detain them when they are strong in that amount of ease to which necessity had raised them when they were weak. Let those regard themselves as truly richer who are endowed with greater strength to bear hardships. For it is better to have fewer wants than to have larger resources.

10. Let your apparel be in no wise conspicuous ; and aspire to please others by your behaviour rather than by your attire. Let your head-dresses not be so thin as to let the nets below them be seen. Let your hair be worn wholly covered, and let it neither be carelessly dishevelled nor too scrupulously arranged when you go beyond the monastery. When you go anywhere, walk together ; when you come to the place to which you were going, stand together. In walking, in standing, in deportment, and in all your movements let nothing be done which might attract the improper desires of any one, but rather let all be in keeping with your sacred character. Though a passing glance be directed towards any man, let your eyes look fixedly at none ; for when you are walking you are not forbidden to see men, but you must neither let your desires go out to them, nor wish to be the objects of desire on their part. For it is not only by touch that a woman awakens in any man or cherishes towards him such desire, this may be done by inward feelings and by looks. And say not that you have chaste minds though you may have wanton eyes, for a wanton eye is the

index of a wanton heart. And when wanton hearts exchange signals with each other in looks, though the tongue is silent, and are, by the force of sensual passion, pleased by the reciprocation of inflamed desire, their purity of character is gone, though their bodies are not defiled by any act of uncleanness. Nor let her who fixes her eyes upon one of the other sex, and takes pleasure in his eye being fixed on her, imagine that the act is not observed by others; she is seen assuredly by those by whom she supposes herself not to be remarked. But even though she should elude notice, and be seen by no human eye, what shall she do with that Witness above us from whom nothing can be concealed? Is He to be regarded as not seeing because His eye rests on all things with a long-suffering proportioned to His wisdom? Let every holy woman guard herself from desiring sinfully to please man by cherishing a fear of displeasing God; let her check the desire of sinfully looking upon man by remembering that God's eye is looking upon all things. For in this very matter we are exhorted to cherish fear of God by the words of Scripture: — "He that looks with a fixed eye is an abomination to the Lord."[1] When, therefore, you are together in the church, or in any other place where men also are present, guard your chastity by watching over one another, and God, who dwelleth in you, will thus guard you by means of yourselves.

11. And if you perceive in any one of your number this frowardness of eye, warn her at once, so that the evil which has begun may not go on, but be checked immediately. But if, after this admonition, you see her repeat the offence, or do the same thing on any other subsequent day, whoever may have had the opportunity of seeing this must now report her as one who has been wounded and requires to be healed, but not without pointing her out to another, and perhaps a third sister, so that she may be convicted by the testimony of two or three witnesses,[2] and may be reprimanded with necessary severity. And do not think that in thus informing upon one another you are guilty of malevolence. For the truth rather is, that you are not guiltless if by keeping silence you allow sisters to perish, whom you may correct by giving information of their faults. For if your sister had a wound on her person which she wished to conceal through fear of the surgeon's lance, would it not be cruel if you kept silence about it, and true compassion if you made it known? How much more, then, are you bound to make known her sin, that she may not suffer more fatally from a neglected spiritual wound. But before she is pointed out to others as wit-

nesses by whom she may be convicted if she deny the charge, the offender ought to be brought before the prioress, if after admonition she has refused to be corrected, so that by her being in this way more privately rebuked, the fault which she has committed may not become known to all the others. If, however, she then deny the charge, then others must be employed to observe her conduct after the denial, so that now before the whole sisterhood she may not be accused by one witness, but convicted by two or three. When convicted of the fault, it is her duty to submit to the corrective discipline which may be appointed by the prioress or the prior. If she refuse to submit to this, and does not go away from you of her own accord, let her be expelled from your society. For this is not done cruelly but mercifully, to protect very many from perishing through infection of the plague with which one has been stricken. Moreover, what I have now said in regard to abstaining from wanton looks should be carefully observed, with due love for the persons and hatred of the sin, in observing, forbidding, reporting, proving, and punishing of all other faults. But if any one among you has gone on into so great sin as to receive secretly from any man letters or gifts of any description, let her be pardoned and prayed for if she confess this of her own accord. If, however, she is found out and is convicted of such conduct, let her be more severely punished, according to the sentence of the prioress, or of the prior, or even of the bishop.

12. Keep your clothes in one place, under the care of one or two, or as many as may be required to shake them so as to keep them from being injured by moths; and as your food is supplied from one storeroom, let your clothes be provided from one wardrobe. And whatever may be brought out to you as wearing apparel suitable for the season, regard it, if possible, as a matter of no importance whether each of you receives the very same article of clothing which she had formerly laid aside, or one receive what another formerly wore, provided only that what is necessary be denied to no one. But if contentions and murmurings are occasioned among you by this, and some one of you complains that she has received some article of dress inferior to that which she formerly wore, and thinks it beneath her to be so clothed as her other sister was, by this prove your own selves, and judge how far deficient you must be in the inner holy dress of the heart, when you quarrel with each other about the clothing of the body. Nevertheless, if your infirmity is indulged by the concession that you are to receive again the identical article which you had laid aside, let whatever you put past be nevertheless, kept in one place, and in charge of the ordinary keep-

---

[1] Prov. xxvii. 20, LXX. βδέλυγμα κυρίῳ στηρίζων ὀφθαλμὸν.
[2] Matt. xviii. 16.

ers of the wardrobe; it being, of course, understood that no one is to work in making any article of clothing or for the couch, or any girdle, veil, or head-dress, for her own private comfort, but that all your works be done for the common good of all, with greater zeal and more cheerful perseverance than if you were each working for your individual interest. For the love concerning which it is written, "Charity seeketh not her own,"[1] is to be understood as that which prefers the common good to personal advantage, not personal advantage to the common good. Therefore the more fully that you give to the common good a preference above your personal and private interests, the more fully will you be sensible of progress in securing that, in regard to all those things which supply wants destined soon to pass away, the charity which abides may hold a conspicuous and influential place. An obvious corollary from these rules is, that when persons of either sex bring to their own daughters in the monastery, or to inmates belonging to them by any other relationship, presents of clothing or of other articles which are to be regarded as necessary, such gifts are not to be received privately, but must be under the control of the prioress, that, being added to the common stock, they may be placed at the service of any inmate to whom they may be necessary. If any one conceal any gift bestowed on her, let sentence be passed on her as guilty of theft.

13. Let your clothes be washed, whether by yourselves or by washerwomen, at such intervals as are approved by the prioress, lest the indulgence of undue solicitude about spotless raiment produce inward stains upon your souls. Let the washing of the body and the use of baths be not constant, but at the usual interval assigned to it, *i.e.* once in a month. In the case, however, of illness rendering necessary the washing of the person, let it not be unduly delayed; let it be done on the physician's recommendation without complaint; and even though the patient be reluctant, she must do at the order of the prioress what health demands. If, however, a patient desires the bath, and it happen to be not for her good, her desire must not be yielded to, for sometimes it is supposed to be beneficial because it gives pleasure, although in reality it may be doing harm. Finally, if a handmaid of God suffers from any hidden pain of body, let her statement as to her suffering be believed without hesitation; but if there be any uncertainty whether that which she finds agreeable be really of use in curing her pain, let the physician be consulted. To the baths, or to any place whither it may be necessary to go, let no fewer

than three go at any time. Moreover, the sister requiring to go anywhere is not to go with those whom she may choose herself, but with those whom the prioress may order. The care of the sick, and of those who require attention as convalescents, and of those who, without any feverish symptoms, are labouring under debility, ought to be committed to some one of your number, who shall procure for them from the storeroom what she shall see to be necessary for each. Moreover, let those who have charge, whether in the storeroom, or in the wardrobe, or in the library, render service to their sisters without murmuring. Let manuscripts be applied for at a fixed hour every day, and let none who ask them at other hours receive them. But at whatever time clothes and shoes may be required by one in need of these, let not those in charge of this department delay supplying the want.

14. Quarrels should be unknown among you, or at least, if they arise, they should as quickly as possible be ended, lest anger grow into hatred, and convert "a mote into a beam,"[2] and make the soul chargeable with murder. For the saying of Scripture: "He that hateth his brother is a murderer,"[3] does not concern men only, but women also are bound by this law through its being enjoined on the other sex, which was prior in the order of creation. Let her, whoever she be, that shall have injured another by taunt or abusive language, or false accusation, remember to remedy the wrong by apology as promptly as possible, and let her who was injured grant forgiveness without further disputation. If the injury has been mutual, the duty of both parties will be mutual forgiveness, because of your prayers, which, as they are more frequent, ought to be all the more sacred in your esteem. But the sister who is prompt in asking another whom she confesses that she has wronged to grant her forgiveness is, though she may be more frequently betrayed by a hasty temper, better than another who, though less irascible, is with more difficulty persuaded to ask forgiveness. Let not her who refuses to forgive her sister expect to receive answers to prayer: as for any sister who never will ask forgiveness, or does not do it from the heart, it is no advantage to such an one to be in a monastery, even though, perchance, she may not be expelled. Wherefore abstain from hard words; but if they have escaped your lips, be not slow to bring words of healing from the same lips by which the wounds were inflicted. When, however, the necessity of discipline compels you to use hard words in restraining the younger inmates, even though you feel that in these you have gone too far, it is not imperative on you to ask their forgiveness, lest

---

[1] 1 Cor. xiii. 5.

[2] Matt. vii. 3.
[3] 1 John iii. 15.

while undue humility is observed by you towards those who ought to be subject to you, the authority necessary for governing them be impaired ; but pardon must nevertheless be sought from the Lord of all, who knows with what goodwill you love even those whom you reprove it may be with undue severity. The love which you bear to each other must be not carnal, but spiritual : for those things which are practised by immodest women in shameful frolic and sporting with one another ought not even to be done by those of your sex who are married, or are intending to marry, and much more ought not to be done by widows or chaste virgins dedicated to be handmaids of Christ by a holy vow.

15. Obey the prioress as a mother, giving her all due honour, that God may not be offended by your forgetting what you owe to her : still more is it incumbent on you to obey the presbyter who has charge of you all. To the prioress most specially belongs the responsibility of seeing that all these rules be observed, and that if any rule has been neglected, the offence be not passed over, but carefully corrected and punished ; it being, of course, open to her to refer to the presbyter any matter that goes beyond her province or power. But let her count herself happy not in exercising the power which rules, but in practising the love which serves. In honour in the sight of men let her be raised above you, but in fear in the sight of God let her be as it were beneath your feet. Let her show herself before all a " pattern of good works." [1] Let her " warn the unruly, comfort the feeble-minded, support the weak, be patient toward all." [2] Let her cheerfully observe and cautiously impose rules. And, though both are necessary, let her be more anxious to be loved than to be feared by you ; always reflecting that for you she must give account to God. For this reason yield obedience to her out of compassion not for yourselves only but also for her, because, as she occupies a higher position among you, her danger is proportionately greater than your own.

16. The Lord grant that you may yield loving submission to all these rules, as persons enamoured of spiritual beauty, and diffusing a sweet savour of Christ by means of a good conversation, not as bondwomen under the law, but as established in freedom under grace. That you may, however, examine yourselves by this treatise as by a mirror, and may not through forgetfulness neglect anything, let it be read over by you once a week ; and in so far as you find yourselves practising the things written here, give thanks for this to God, the Giver of all good ; in so far, however, as any of you finds

herself to be in some particular defective, let her lament the past and be on her guard in the time to come, praying both that her debt may be forgiven, and that she may not be led into temptation.

LETTER CCXII.

(A.D. 423.)

TO QUINTILIANUS, MY LORD MOST BLESSED AND BROTHER AND FELLOW BISHOP DESERVEDLY VENERABLE, AUGUSTIN SENDS GREETING.

Venerable father, I commend to you in the love of Christ these honourable servants of God and precious members of Christ, Galla, a widow (who has taken on herself sacred vows), and her daughter Simplicia, a consecrated virgin, who is subject to her mother by reason of her age, but above her by reason of her holiness. We have nourished them as far as we have been able with the word of God ; and by this epistle, as if it were with my own hand, I commit them to you, to be comforted and aided in every way which their interest or necessity requires. This duty your Holiness would doubtless have undertaken without any recommendation from me ; for if it is our duty on account of the Jerusalem above, of which we are all citizens, and in which they desire to have a place of distinguished holiness, to cherish towards them not only the affection due to fellow-citizens, but even brotherly love, how much stronger is their claim on you, who reside in the same country in this earth in which these ladies, for the love of Christ, renounced the distinctions of this world ! I also ask you to condescend to receive with the same love with which I have offered it my official salutation, and to remember me in your prayers. These ladies carry with them relics of the most blessed and glorious martyr Stephen : your Holiness knows how to give due honour to these, as we have done.[3]

LETTER CCXIII.

(SEPTEMBER 26TH, A.D. 426.)

RECORD, PREPARED BY ST. AUGUSTIN, OF THE PROCEEDINGS ON THE OCCASION OF HIS DESIGNATING ERACLIUS TO SUCCEED HIM IN THE EPISCOPAL CHAIR, AND TO RELIEVE HIM MEANWHILE IN HIS OLD AGE OF A PART OF HIS RESPONSIBILITIES.

In the Church of Peace in the district of Hippo Regius, on the 26th day of September in the year of the twelfth consulship of the most renowned Theodosius, and of the second consulship of Valentinian Augustus : [4]

---

[1] Titus ii. 7.
[2] 1 Thess. v. 14.

[3] A memorial chapel for the reception of relics of Saint Stephen had been built at Hippo. — See *City of God*, book XXII.
[4] A.D. 426.

— Bishop Augustin having taken his seat along with his fellow bishops Religianus and Martinianus, there being present Saturninus, Leporius, Barnabas, Fortunatianus, Rusticus, Lazarus, and Eraclius, — presbyters, — while the clergy and a large congregation of laymen stood by, — Bishop Augustin said: —

"The business which I brought before you yesterday, my beloved, as one in connection with which I wished you to attend, as I see you have done in greater numbers than usual, must be at once disposed of. For while your minds are anxiously preoccupied with it, you would scarcely listen to me if I were to speak of any other subject. We all are mortal, and the day which shall be the last of life on earth is to every man at all times uncertain; but in infancy there is hope of entering on boyhood, and so our hope goes on, looking forward from boyhood to youth, from youth to manhood, and from manhood to old age: whether these hopes may be realized or not is uncertain, but there is in each case something which may be hoped for. But old age has no other period of this life to look forward to with expectation: how long old age may in any case be prolonged is uncertain, but it is certain that no other age destined to take its place lies beyond. I came to this town — for such was the will of God — when I was in the prime of life. I was young then, but now I am old. I know that churches are wont to be disturbed after the decease of their bishops by ambitious or contentious parties, and I feel it to be my duty to take measures to prevent this community from suffering, in connection with my decease, that which I have often observed and lamented elsewhere. You are aware, my beloved, that I recently visited the Church of Milevi; for certain brethren, and especially the servants of God there, requested me to come, because some disturbance was apprehended after the death of my brother and fellow bishop Severus, of blessed memory. I went accordingly, and the Lord was in mercy pleased so to help us that they harmoniously accepted as bishop the person designated by their former bishop in his lifetime; for when this designation had become known to them, they willingly acquiesced in the choice which he had made. An omission, however, had occurred by which some were dissatisfied; for brother Severus, believing that it might be sufficient for him to mention to the clergy the name of his successor, did not speak of the matter to the people, which gave rise to dissatisfaction in the minds of some. But why should I say more? By the good pleasure of God, the dissatisfaction was removed, joy took its place in the minds of all, and he was or-dained as bishop whom Severus had proposed. To obviate all such occasion of complaint in this case, I now intimate to all here my desire, which I believe to be also the will of God: I wish to have for my successor the presbyter Eraclius."

The people shouted, "To God be thanks! To Christ be praise" (this was repeated twenty-three times). "O Christ, hear us; may Augustin live long!" (repeated sixteen times). "We will have thee as our father, thee as our bishop" (repeated eight times).

2. *Silence having been obtained, Bishop Augustin said: —*

"It is unnecessary for me to say anything in praise of Eraclius; I esteem his wisdom and spare his modesty; it is enough that you know him: and I declare that I desire in regard to him what I know you also to desire, and if I had not known it before, I would have had proof of it to-day. This, therefore, I desire; this I ask from the Lord our God in prayers, the warmth of which is not abated by the chill of age; this I exhort, admonish, and entreat you also to pray for along with me, — that God may confirm that which He has wrought in us [1] by blending and fusing together the minds of all in the peace of Christ. May He who has sent him to me preserve him! preserve him safe, preserve him blameless, that as he gives me joy while I live, he may fill my place when I die.

"The notaries of the church are, as you observe, recording what I say, and recording what you say; both my address and your acclamations are not allowed to fall to the ground. To speak more plainly, we are making up an ecclesiastical record of this day's proceedings; for I wish them to be in this way confirmed so far as pertains to men."

The people shouted thirty-six times, "To God be thanks! To Christ be praise!" "O Christ, hear us; may Augustin live long!" was said thirteen times. "Thee, our father! thee, our bishop!" was said eight times. "He is worthy and just," was said twenty times. "Well deserving, well worthy!" was said five times. "He is worthy and just!" was said six times.

3. *Silence having been obtained, Bishop Augustin said: —*

"It is my wish, as I was just now saying, that my desire and your desire be confirmed, so far as pertains to men, by being placed on an ecclesiastical record; but so far as pertains to the will of the Almighty, let us all pray, as I said

[1] Ps. lxviii. 28.

before, that God would confirm that which He has wrought in us."

The people shouted, saying sixteen times, "We give thanks for your decision:" then twelve times, "Agreed! Agreed!" and then six times, "Thee, our father! Eraclius, our bishop!"

4. *Silence having been obtained, Bishop Augustin said:—*

"I approve of that of which you also express your approval;[1] but I do not wish that to be done in regard to him which was done in my own case. What was done many of you know; in fact, all of you, excepting only those who at that time were not born, or had not attained to the years of understanding. When my father and bishop, the aged Valerius, of blessed memory, was still living, I was ordained bishop and occupied the episcopal see along with him, which I did not know to have been forbidden by the Council of Nice; and he was equally ignorant of the prohibition. I do not wish to have my son here exposed to the same censure as was incurred in my own case."

The people shouted, saying thirteen times, "To God be thanks! To Christ be praise!"

5. *Silence having been obtained, Bishop Augustin said:—*

"He shall be as he now is, a presbyter, meanwhile; but afterwards, at such time as may please God, your bishop. But now I will assuredly begin to do, as the compassion of Christ may enable me, what I have not hitherto done. You know what for several years I would have done, had you permitted me. It was agreed between you and me that no one should intrude on me for five days of each week, that I might discharge the duty in the study of Scripture which my brethren and fathers the co-bishops were pleased to assign to me in the two councils of Numidia and Carthage. The agreement was duly recorded, you gave your consent, you signified it by acclamations. The record of your consent and of your acclamations, was read aloud to you. For a short time the agreement was observed by you; afterwards, it was violated without consideration, and I am not permitted to have leisure for the work which I wish to do: forenoon and afternoon alike, I am involved in the affairs of other people demanding my attention. I now beseech you, and solemnly engage you, for Christ's sake, to suffer me to devolve the burden of this part of my labours on this young man, I mean on Eraclius,

[1] Referring to their last words, giving to Eraclius the title of bishop

the presbyter, whom to-day I designate in the name of Christ as my successor in the office of bishop."

The people shouted, saying twenty-six times, "We give thanks for your decision."

6. *Silence having been obtained, Bishop Augustin said:—*

"I give thanks before the Lord our God for your love and your goodwill; yes, I give thanks to God for these. Wherefore, henceforth, my brethren, let everything which was wont to be brought by you to me be brought to him. In any case in which he may think my advice necessary, I will not refuse it; far be it from me to withdraw this: nevertheless, let everything be brought to him which used to be brought to me. Let Eraclius himself, if in any case, perchance, he be at a loss as to what should be done, either consult me, or claim an assistant in me, whom he has known as a father. By this arrangement you will, on the one hand, suffer no disadvantage, and I will at length, for the brief space during which God may prolong my life, devote the remainder of my days, be they few or many, not to idleness nor to the indulgence of a love of ease, but, so far as Eraclius kindly gives me leave, to the study of the sacred Scriptures: this also will be of service to him, and through him to you likewise. Let no one therefore grudge me this leisure, for I claim it only in order to do important work.

"I see that I have now transacted with you all the business necessary in the matter for which I called you together. The last thing I have to ask is, that as many of you as are able be pleased to subscribe your names to this record. At this point I require a response from you. Let me have it: show your assent by some acclamations."

The people shouted, saying twenty-five times, "Agreed! agreed!" then twenty-eight times, "It is worthy, it is just!" then fourteen times, "Agreed! agreed!" then twenty-five times, "He has long been worthy, he has long been deserving!" then thirteen times, "We give thanks for your decision!" then eighteen times, "O Christ, hear us; preserve Eraclius!"

7. *Silence having been obtained, Bishop Augustin said:—*

"It is well that we are able to transact around His sacrifice those things which belong to God; and in this hour appointed for our supplications, I especially exhort you, beloved, to suspend all your occupations and business, and pour out before the Lord your petitions for this church, and for me, and for the presbyter Eraclius."

LETTER CCXVIII.

(A.D. 426.)

TO PALATINUS, MY WELL-BELOVED LORD AND SON, MOST TENDERLY LONGED FOR, AUGUSTIN SENDS GREETING.

1. Your life of eminent fortitude and fruitfulness towards the Lord our God has brought to us great joy. For "you have made choice of instruction from your youth upwards, that you may still find wisdom even to grey hairs;"[1] for "wisdom is the grey hair unto men, and an unspotted life is old age;"[2] which may the Lord, who knoweth how to give good gifts unto His children, give to you asking, seeking, knocking.[3] Although you have many counsellors and many counsels to direct you in the path which leads to eternal glory, and although, above all, you have the grace of Christ, which has so effectually spoken in saving power in your heart, nevertheless we also, as in duty bound by the love which we owe to you, offer to you, in hereby reciprocating your salutation, some words of counsel, designed not to awaken you as one hindered by sloth or sleep, but to stimulate and quicken you in the race which you are already running.

2. You require wisdom, my son, for stedfastness in this race, as it was under the influence of wisdom that you entered on it at first. Let this then be "a part of your wisdom, to know whose gift it is."[4] "Commit thy way unto the Lord; trust also in Him, and He shall bring it to pass: and He shall bring forth thy righteousness as the light, and thy judgment as the noonday."[5] "He will make straight thy path, and guide thy steps in peace."[6] As you despised your prospects of greatness in this world, lest you should glory in the abundance of riches which you had begun to covet after the manner of the children of this world, so now, in taking up the yoke of the Lord and His burden, let not your confidence be in your own strength; so shall "His yoke be easy, and His burden light."[7] For in the book of Psalms those are alike censured "who trust in their strength," and "who boast themselves in the multitude of their riches."[8] Therefore, as formerly you did not seek glory in riches, but most wisely despised that which you had begun to desire, so now be on your guard against insidious temptation to trust in your strength; for you are but man, and "cursed is every one that trusteth in man."[9]

But by all means trust in God with your whole heart, and He will Himself be your strength, wherein you may trust with piety and thankfulness, and to Him you may say with humility and boldness, "I will love thee, O Lord, my strength;"[10] because even the love of God, which, when it is perfect, "casteth out fear,"[11] is shed abroad in our hearts, not by our strength, that is, by any human power, but, as the apostle says, "by the Holy Ghost, which is given unto us."[12]

3. "Watch, therefore, and pray that you enter not into temptation."[13] Such prayer is indeed in itself an admonition to you that you need the help of the Lord, and that you ought not to rest upon yourself your hope of living well. For now you pray, not that you may obtain the riches and honours of this present world, or any unsubstantial human possession, but that you may not enter into temptation, a thing which would not be asked in prayer if a man could accomplish it for himself by his own will. Wherefore we would not pray that we may not enter into temptation if our own will sufficed for our protection; and yet if the will to avoid temptation were wanting to us, we could not so pray. It may, therefore, be present with us to will,[14] when we have through his own gift been made wise, but we must pray that we may be able to perform that which we have so willed. In the fact that you have begun to exercise this true wisdom, you have reason to give thanks. "For what have you which you have not received? But if you have received it, beware that you boast not as if you had not received it,"[15] that is, as if you could have had it of yourself. Knowing, however, whence you have received it, ask Him by whose gift it was begun to grant that it may be perfected. "Work out your own salvation with fear and trembling: for it is God that worketh in you, both to will and to do, of His good pleasure;"[16] for "the will is prepared by God,"[17] and "the steps of a good man are ordered by the Lord, and He delighteth in his way."[18] Holy meditation on these things will preserve you, so that your wisdom shall be piety, that is, that by God's gift you shall be good, and not ungrateful for the grace of Christ.

4. Your parents, unfeignedly rejoicing with you in the better hope which in the Lord you have begun to cherish, are longing earnestly for your presence. But whether you be absent from us or present with us in the body, we desire to have you with us in the one Spirit by whom love

---

[1] Ecclus. vi. 18.
[2] Wisd. iv. 9.
[3] Matt. vii. 11.
[4] Wisd. viii. 20.
[5] Ps. xxxvii. 5, 6.
[6] Prov. iv. 27, LXX.
[7] Matt. xi. 30
[8] Ps. xlix. 6, LXX.
[9] Jer. xvii. 5.

[10] Ps. xviii. 1.
[11] 1 John iv. 18.
[12] Rom. v. 5.
[13] Mark xiv. 38.
[14] Rom. vii. 18.
[15] 1 Cor. iv. 7.
[16] Phil. ii. 12, 13.
[17] Prov. viii. 35, LXX.
[18] Ps. xxxvii. 23.

is shed abroad in our hearts, so that, in whatever place our bodies may sojourn, our spirits may be in no degree sundered from each other.

We have most thankfully received the cloaks of goat's-hair cloth [1] which you sent to us, in which gift you have yourself anticipated me in admonition as to the duty of being often engaged in prayer, and of practising humility in our supplications.

LETTER CCXIX.

(A.D. 426.)

TO PROCULUS AND CYLINUS, BRETHREN MOST BELOVED AND HONOURABLE, AND PARTNERS IN THE SACERDOTAL OFFICE, AUGUSTIN, FLORENTIUS, AND SECUNDINUS SEND GREETING IN THE LORD.

1. When our son Leporius, whom for his obstinacy in error you had justly and fitly rebuked, came to us after he had been expelled by you, we received him as one afflicted for his good, whom we should, if possible, deliver from error and restore to spiritual health. For, as you obeyed in regard to him the apostolic precept, "Warn the unruly," so it was our part to obey the precept immediately annexed, "Comfort the feeble-minded, and support the weak." [2] His error was indeed not unimportant, seeing that he neither approved what is right nor perceived what is true in some things relating to the only-begotten Son of God, of whom it is written that, "In the beginning was the Word, and the Word was with God, and the Word was God," but that when the fulness of time had come, "the Word was made flesh, and dwelt among us;" [3] for he denied that God became man, regarding it as a doctrine from which it must follow necessarily that the divine substance in which He is equal to the Father suffered some unworthy change or corruption, and not seeing that he was thus introducing into the Trinity a fourth person, which is utterly contrary to the sound doctrine of the Creed and of Catholic truth. Since, however, dearly beloved and honourable brethren, he had as a fallible man "been overtaken" in this error, we did our utmost, the Lord helping us, to instruct him "in the spirit of meekness," especially remembering that when the "chosen vessel" gave this command to which we refer, he added, "Considering thyself, lest thou also be tempted," — lest some, perchance, should so rejoice in the measure of spiritual progress as to imagine that they could no longer be tempted like other men, — and joined with it the salutary and peace-promoting sentence, "Bear ye one another's burdens, and so fulfil the law of Christ. For if a man think himself to be something, when he is nothing, he deceiveth himself." [4]

2. This restoration of Leporius we could perhaps in nowise have accomplished, had you not previously censured and punished those things in him which required correction. So then the same Lord, our Divine Physician, using His own instruments and servants, has by you wounded him when he was proud, and by us healed him when he was penitent, according to his own saying, "I wound, and I heal." [5] The same Divine Ruler and Overseer of His own house has by you thrown down what was defective in the building, and has by us replaced with a well-ordered structure what he had removed. The same Divine Husbandman has in His careful diligence by you rooted up what was barren and noxious in His field, and by us planted what is useful and fruitful. Let us not, therefore, ascribe glory to ourselves, but to the mercy of Him in whose hand both we and all our words are. And as we humbly praise the work which you have done as His ministers in the case of our son aforesaid, so do you rejoice with holy joy in the work performed by us. Receive, then, with the love of fathers and of brethren, him whom we have with merciful severity corrected. For although one part of the work was done by you and another part by us, both parts, being indispensable to our brother's salvation, were done by the same love. The same God was therefore working in both, for "God is love." [6]

3. Wherefore, as he has been welcomed into fellowship by us on the ground of his repentance, let him be welcomed by you on the ground of his letter, [7] to which letter we have thought it right to adhibit our signatures attesting its genuiness. We have not the least doubt that you, in the exercise of Christian love, will not only hear with pleasure of his amendment, but also make it known to those to whom his error was a stumbling-block. For those who came with him to us have also been corrected and restored along with him, as is declared by their signatures, which have been adhibited to the letter in our presence. It remains only that you, being made joyful by the salvation of a brother, condescend to make us joyful in our turn by sending a reply to our communication. Farewell in the Lord, most beloved and honourable brethren; such is our desire on your behalf: remember us.

---

[1] Cilicia.
[2] 1 Thess. v. 14.
[3] John i. 1, 14.

[4] Gal. vi. 1, 3.
[5] Deut. xxxii. 39.
[6] 1 John iv. 8, 16.
[7] A formal written retractation of his errors, called elsewhere "emendationis libellum."

LETTER CCXX.

(A.D. 427.)

TO MY LORD BONIFACE,[1] MY SON COMMENDED TO THE GUARDIANSHIP AND GUIDANCE OF DIVINE MERCY, FOR PRESENT AND ETERNAL SALVATION, AUGUSTIN SENDS GREETING.

1. Never could I have found a more trustworthy man, nor one who could have more ready access to your ear when bearing a letter from me, than this servant and minister of Christ, the deacon Paulus, a man very dear to both of us, whom the Lord has now brought to me in order that I may have the opportunity of addressing you, not in reference to your power and the honour which you hold in this evil world, nor in reference to the preservation of your corruptible and mortal body, — because this also is destined to pass away, and how soon no one can tell, — but in reference to that salvation which has been promised to us by Christ, who was here on earth despised and crucified in order that He might teach us rather to despise than to desire the good things of this world, and to set our affections and our hope on that world which He has revealed by His resurrection. For He has risen from the dead, and now " dieth no more ; death hath no more dominion over Him." [2]

2. I know that you have no lack of friends, who love you so far as life in this world is concerned, and who in regard to it give you counsels, sometimes useful, sometimes the reverse ; for they are men, and therefore, though they use their wisdom to the best of their ability in regard to what is present, they know not what may happen on the morrow. But it is not easy for any one to give you counsel in reference to God, to prevent the perdition of your soul, not because you lack friends who would do this, but because it is difficult for them to find an opportunity of speaking with you on these subjects. For I myself have often longed for this, and never found place or time in which I might deal with you as I ought to deal with a man whom I ardently love in Christ. You know besides in what state you found me at Hippo, when you did me the honor to come to visit me, — how I was scarcely able to speak, being prostrated by bodily weakness. Now, then, my son, hear me when I have this opportunity of addressing you at least by a letter, — a rare opportunity, for it was not in my power to send such communication to you in the midst of your dangers, both because I apprehended danger to the bearer, and because I was afraid lest my letter should reach persons into whose hands I was unwilling that it should fall. Wherefore I beg you to forgive me if you think that I have been more afraid than I should have been ; however this may be, I have stated what I feared.

3. Hear me, therefore ; nay, rather hear the Lord our God speaking by me, His feeble servant. Call to remembrance what manner of man you were while your former wife, of hallowed memory, still lived, and how under the stroke of her death, while that event was yet recent, the vanity of this world made you recoil from it, and how you earnestly desired to enter the service of God. We know and we can testify what you said as to your state of mind and your desires when you conversed with us at Tubunæ. My brother Alypius and I were alone with you. [I beseech you, then, to call to remembrance that conversation], for I do not think that the worldly cares with which you are now engrossed can have such power over you as to have effaced this wholly from your memory. You were then desirous to abandon all the public business in which you were engaged, and to withdraw into sacred retirement, and live like the servants of God who have embraced a monastic life. And what was it that prevented you from acting according to these desires? Was it not that you were influenced by considering, on our representation of the matter, how much service the work which then occupied you might render to the churches of Christ if you pursued it with this single aim, that they, protected from all disturbance by barbarian hordes, might live " a quiet and peaceable life," as the apostle says, " in all godliness and honesty ; " [3] resolving at the same time for your own part to seek no more from this world than would suffice for the support of yourself and those dependent on you, wearing as your girdle the cincture of a perfectly chaste self-restraint, and having underneath the accoutrements of the soldier the surer and stronger defence of spiritual armour.

4. At the very time when we were full of joy that you had formed this resolution, you embarked on a voyage and you married a second wife. Your embarkation was an act of the obedience due, as the apostle has taught us, to the " higher powers ; " [4] but you would not have married again had you not, abandoning the continence to which you had devoted yourself, been overcome by concupiscence. When I learned this, I was, I must confess it, dumb with amazement ; but, in my sorrow, I was in some degree comforted by hearing that you refused to marry her unless she became a Catholic before the marriage, and yet the heresy of those who refuse to believe in the true Son of God has so prevailed in your house, that by these heretics your daughter was baptized. Now, if the report be true (would

1 See note to Letter CLXXXIX, p. 552.
2 Rom. vi. 9.
3 1 Tim. ii. 2.
4 Rom. xiii. 1.

to God that it were false !) that even some who were dedicated to God as His handmaids have been by these heretics re-baptized, with what floods of tears ought this great calamity to be bewailed by us ! Men are saying, moreover, — perhaps it is an unfounded slander, — that one wife does not satisfy your passions, and that you have been defiled by consorting with some other women as concubines.

5. What shall I say regarding these evils — so patent to all, and so great in magnitude as well as number — of which you have been, directly or indirectly, the cause since the time of your being married? You are a Christian, you have a conscience, you fear God ; consider, then, for yourself some things which I prefer to leave unsaid, and you will find for how great evils you ought to do penance ; and I believe that it is to afford you an opportunity of doing this in the way in which it ought to be done, that the Lord is now sparing you and delivering you from all dangers. But if you will listen to the counsel of Scripture, I pray you, "make no tarrying to turn to the Lord, and put not off from day to day."[1] You allege, indeed, that you have good reason for what you have done, and that I cannot be a judge of the sufficiency of that reason, because I cannot hear both sides of the question ;[2] but, whatever be your reason, the nature of which it is not necessary at present either to investigate or to discuss, can you, in the presence of God, affirm that you would ever have come into the embarrassments of your present position had you not loved the good things of this world, which, being a servant of God, such as we knew you to be formerly, it was your duty to have utterly despised and esteemed as of no value, — accepting, indeed, what was offered to you, that you might devote it to pious uses, but not so coveting that which was denied to you, or was entrusted to your care, as to be brought on its account into the difficulties of your present position, in which, while good is loved, evil things are perpetrated, — few, indeed, by you, but many because of you, and while things are dreaded which, if hurtful, are so only for a short time, things are done which are really hurtful for eternity?

6. To mention one of these things, — who can help seeing that many persons follow you for the purpose of defending your power or safety, who, although they may be all faithful to you, and no treachery is to be apprehended from any of them, are desirous of obtaining through you certain advantages which they also covet, not with a godly desire, but from worldly motives? And in this way you, whose duty it is to curb and check your own passions, are forced

to satisfy those of others. To accomplish this, many things which are displeasing to God must be done ; and yet, after all, these passions are not thus satisfied, for they are more easily mortified finally in those who love God, than satisfied even for a time in those who love the world. Therefore the Divine Scripture says : " Love not the world, nor the things that are in the world. If any man love the world, the love of the Father is not in him. For all that is in the world, the lust of the flesh, and the lust of the eyes, and pride of life, is not of the Father, but is of the world. And the world passeth away, and the lust thereof: but he that doeth the will of God abideth for ever, as God abideth for ever."[3] Associated, therefore, as you are with such multitudes of armed men, whose passions must be humoured, and whose cruelty is dreaded, how can the desires of these men who love the world ever be, I do not say satiated, but even partially gratified by you, in your anxiety to prevent still greater wide-spread evils, unless you do that which God forbids, and in so doing become obnoxious to threatened judgment? So complete has been the havoc wrought in order to indulge their passions, that it would be difficult now to find anything for the plunderer to carry away.

7. But what shall I say of the devastation of Africa at this hour by hordes of African barbarians, to whom no resistance is offered, while you are engrossed with such embarrassments in your own circumstances, and are taking no measures for averting this calamity? Who would ever have believed, who would have feared, after Boniface had become a Count of the Empire and of Africa, and had been placed in command in Africa with so large an army and so great authority, that the same man who formerly, as Tribune, kept all these barbarous tribes in peace, by storming their strongholds, and menacing them with his small band of brave confederates, should now have suffered the barbarians to be so bold, to encroach so far, to destroy and plunder so much, and to turn into deserts such vast regions once densely peopled? Where were any found that did not predict that, as soon as you obtained the authority of Count, the African hordes would be not only checked, but made tributaries to the Roman Empire? And now, how completely the event has disappointed men's hopes you yourself perceive ; in fact, I need say nothing more on this subject, because your own reflection must suggest much more than I can put in words.

8. Perhaps you defend yourself by replying that the blame here ought rather to rest on persons who have injured you, and, instead of justly

requiting the services rendered by you in your office, have returned evil for good. These matters I am not able to examine and judge. I beseech you rather to contemplate and inquire into the matter, in which you know that you have to do not with men at all, but with God; living in Christ as a believer, you are bound to fear lest you offend Him. For my attention is more engaged by higher causes, believing that men ought to ascribe Africa's great calamities to their own sins. Nevertheless, I would not wish you to belong to the number of those wicked and unjust men whom God uses as instruments in inflicting temporal punishments on whom He pleases; for He who justly employs their malice to inflict temporal judgments on others, reserves eternal punishments for the unjust themselves if they be not reformed. Be it yours to fix your thoughts on God, and to look to Christ, who has conferred on you so great blessings and endured for you so great sufferings. Those who desire to belong to His kingdom, and to live for ever happily with Him and under Him, love even their enemies, do good to them that hate them, and pray for those from whom they suffer persecution;[1] and if, at any time, in the way of discipline they use irksome severity, yet they never lay aside the sincerest love. If these benefits, though earthly and transitory, are conferred on you by the Roman Empire, — for that empire itself is earthly, not heavenly, and cannot bestow what it has not in its power, — if, I say, benefits are conferred on you, return not evil for good; and if evil be inflicted on you, return not evil for evil. Which of these two has happened in your case I am unwilling to discuss, I am unable to judge. I speak to a Christian — return not either evil for good, nor evil for evil.

9. You say to me, perhaps: In circumstances so difficult, what do you wish me to do? If you ask counsel of me in a worldly point of view how your safety in this transitory life may be secured, and the power and wealth belonging to you at present may be preserved or even increased, I know not what to answer you, for any counsel regarding things so uncertain as these must partake of the uncertainty inherent in them. But if you consult me regarding your relation to God and the salvation of your soul, and if you fear the word of truth which says: "What is a man profited, if he shall gain the whole world, and lose his own soul?"[2] I have a plain answer to give. I am prepared with advice to which you may well give heed. But what need is there for my saying anything else than what I have already said. "Love not the world, neither the things that are in the world. If any man love the world, the love of the Father is not in him. For all that

is in the world, the lust of the flesh, and the lust of the eyes, and the pride of life, is not of the Father, but is of the world. And the world passeth away, and the lust thereof: but he that doeth the will of God abideth forever."[3] Here is counsel! Seize it and act on it. Show that you are a brave man. Vanquish the desires with which the world is loved. Do penance for the evils of your past life, when, vanquished by your passions, you were drawn away by sinful desires. If you receive this counsel, and hold it fast, and act on it, you will both attain to those blessings which are certain, and occupy yourself in the midst of these uncertain things without forfeiting the salvation of your soul.

10. But perhaps you again ask of me how you can do these things, entangled as you are with so great worldly difficulties. Pray earnestly, and say to God, in the words of the Psalm: "Bring Thou me out of my distresses,"[4] for these distresses terminate when the passions in which they originate are vanquished. He who has heard your prayer and ours on your behalf, that you might be delivered from the numerous and great dangers of visible wars in which the body is exposed to the danger of losing the life which sooner or later must end, but in which the soul perishes not unless it be held captive by evil passions, — He, I say, will hear your prayer that you may, in an invisible and spiritual conflict, overcome your inward and invisible enemies, that is to say, your passions themselves, and may so use the world, as not abusing it, so that with its good things you may do good, not become bad through possessing them. Because these things are in themselves good, and are not given to men except by Him who has power over all things in heaven and earth. Lest these gifts of His should be reckoned bad, they are given also to the good; at the same time, lest they should be reckoned great, or the supreme good, they are given also to the bad. Further, these things are taken away from the good for their trial, and from the bad for their punishment.

11. For who is so ignorant, who so foolish, as not to see that the health of this mortal body, and the strength of its corruptible members, and victory over men who are our enemies, and temporal honours and power, and all other mere earthly advantages are given both to the good and to the bad, and are taken away both from the good and from the bad alike? But the salvation of the soul, along with immortality of the body, and the power of righteousness, and victory over hostile passions, and glory, and honour, and everlasting peace, are not given except to the good. Therefore love these things, covet

---

[1] Matt. v. 44.
[2] Matt. xvi. 26.
[3] 1 John ii. 15-17.
[4] Ps. xxv. 17.

these things, and seek them by every means in your power. With a view to acquire and retain these things, give alms, pour forth prayers, practise fasting as far as you can without injury to your body. But do not love these earthly goods, how much soever they may abound to you. So use them as to do many good things by them, but not one evil thing for their sake. For all such things will perish; but good works, yea, even those good works which are performed by means of the perishable good things of this world, shall never perish.

12. If you had not now a wife, I would say to you what we said at Tubunæ, that you should live in the holy state of continence, and would add that you should now do what we prevented you from doing at that time, namely, withdraw yourself so far as might be possible without prejudice to the public welfare from the labours of military service, and take to yourself the leisure which you then desired for that life in the society of the saints in which the soldiers of Christ fight in silence, not to kill men, but to "wrestle against principalities and powers, and spiritual wickedness,"[1] that is, the devil and his angels. For the saints gain their victories over enemies whom they cannot see, and yet they gain the victory over these unseen enemies by gaining the victory over things which are the objects of sense. I am, however, prevented from exhorting you to that mode of life by your having a wife, since without her consent it is not lawful for you to live under a vow of continence; because, although you did wrong in marrying again after the declaration which you made at Tubunæ, she, being not aware of this, became your wife innocently and without restrictions. Would that you could persuade her to agree to a vow of continence, that you might without hindrance render to God what you know to be due to Him! If, however, you cannot make this agreement with her, guard carefully by all means conjugal chastity, and pray to God, who will deliver you out of difficulties, that you may at some future time be able to do what is meanwhile impossible. This, however, does not affect your obligation to love God and not to love the world, to hold the faith stedfastly even in the cares of war, if you must still be engaged in them, and to seek peace; to make the good things of this world serviceable in good works, and not to do what is evil in labouring to obtain these earthly good things, — in all these duties your wife is not, or, if she is, ought not to be, a hindrance to you.

These things I have written, my dearly beloved son, at the bidding of the love with which I love you with regard not to this world, but to God; and because, mindful of the words of Scripture, "Reprove a wise man, and he will love thee; reprove a fool, and he will hate thee more,"[2] I was bound to think of you as certainly not a fool but a wise man.

LETTER CCXXVII.

(A.D. 428 or 429.)

TO THE AGED ALYPIUS, AUGUSTIN SENDS GREETING.

Brother Paulus has arrived here safely: he reports that the pains devoted to the business which engaged him have been rewarded with success; the Lord will grant that with these his trouble in that matter may terminate. He salutes you warmly, and tells us tidings concerning Gabinianus which give us joy, namely, that having by God's mercy obtained a prosperous issue in his case, he is now not only in name a Christian, but in sincerity a very excellent convert to the faith, and was baptized recently at Easter, having both in his heart and on his lips the grace which he received. How much I long for him I can never express; but you know that I love him.

The president of the medical faculty,[3] Dioscorus, has also professed the Christian faith, having obtained grace at the same time. Hear the manner of his conversion, for his stubborn neck and his bold tongue could not be subdued without some miracle. His daughter, the only comfort of his life, was sick, and her sickness became so serious that her life was, according even to her father's own admission, despaired of. It is reported, and the truth of the report is beyond question, for even before brother Paul's return the fact was mentioned to me by Count Peregrinus, a most respectable and truly Christian man, who was baptized at the same time with Dioscorus and Gabinianus, — it is reported, I say, that the old man, feeling himself at last constrained to implore the compassion of Christ, bound himself by a vow that he would become a Christian if he saw her restored to health. She recovered, but he perfidiously drew back from fulfilling his vow. Nevertheless the hand of the Lord was still stretched forth, for suddenly he is smitten with blindness, and immediately the cause of this calamity was impressed upon his mind. He confessed his fault aloud, and vowed again that if his sight were given back he would perform what he had vowed. He recovered his sight, fulfilled his vow, and still the hand of God was stretched forth. He had not committed the Creed to memory, or perhaps had refused to commit it, and had excused himself on the plea of inability. God had seen this. Immediately

---

[1] Eph. vi. 12.

[2] Prov. ix. 8.
[3] *Archiater.*

after all the ceremonies of his reception he is seized with paralysis, affecting many, indeed almost all his members, and even his tongue. Then, being warned by a dream, he confesses in writing that it had been told to him that this had happened because he had not repeated the Creed. After that confession the use of all his members was restored to him, except the tongue alone; nevertheless he, being still under this affliction, made manifest by writing that he had, notwithstanding, learned the Creed, and still retained it in his memory; and so that frivolous loquacity which, as you know, blemished his natural kindliness, and made him, when he mocked Christians, exceedingly profane, was altogether destroyed in him, What shall I say, but, "Let us sing a hymn to the Lord, and highly exalt Him for ever! Amen."

LETTER CCXXVIII.

(A.D. 428 or 429.)

TO HIS HOLY BROTHER AND CO-BISHOP HONO-RATUS,[1] AUGUSTIN SENDS GREETING IN THE LORD.

1. I thought that by sending to your Grace a copy of the letter which I wrote to our brother and co-bishop Quodvultdeus,[2] I had earned exemption from the burden which you have imposed upon me, by asking my advice as to what you ought to do in the midst of the dangers which have befallen us in these times. For although I wrote briefly, I think that I did not pass over anything that was necessary either to be said by me or heard by my questioner in correspondence on the subject: for I said that, on the one hand, those who desire to remove, if they can, to fortified places are not to be forbidden to do so; and, on the other hand, we ought not to break the ties by which the love of Christ has bound us as ministers not to forsake the churches which it is our duty to serve. The words which I used in the letter referred to were: "Therefore, however small may be the congregation of God's people among whom we are, if our ministry is so necessary to them that it is a clear duty not to withdraw it from them, it remains for us to say to the Lord, 'Be Thou to us a God of defence, and a strong fortress.'"[3]

2. But this counsel does not commend itself to you, because, as you say in your letter, it does not become us to endeavour to act in opposition to the precept or example of the Lord, admonishing us that we should flee from one city to another. We remember, indeed, the words of the Lord, "When they persecute you in one city, flee to another;"[4] but who can believe that the Lrod wished this to be done in cases in which the flocks which He purchased with His own blood are by the desertion of their pastors left without that necessary ministry which is indispensable to their life? Did Christ do this Himself, when, carried by His parents, He fled into Egypt in His infancy? No; for He had not then gathered churches which we could affirm to have been deserted by Him. Or, when the Apostle Paul was "let down in a basket through a window," to prevent his enemies from seizing him, and so escaped their hands,[5] was the church in Damascus deprived of the necessary labours of Christ's servants? Was not all the service that was requisite supplied after his departure by other brethren settled in that city? For the apostle had done this at their request, in order that he might preserve for the Church's good his life, which the persecutor on that occasion specially sought to destroy. Let those, therefore, who are servants of Christ, His ministers in word and sacrament, do what he has commanded or permitted. When any of them is specially sought for by persecutors, let him by all means flee from one city to another, provided that the Church is not hereby deserted, but that others who are not specially sought after remain to supply spiritual food to their fellow-servants, whom they know to be unable otherwise to maintain spiritual life. When, however, the danger of all, bishops, clergy, and laity, is alike, let not those who depend upon the aid of others be deserted by those on whom they depend. In that case, either let all remove together to fortified places, or let those who must remain be not deserted by those through whom in things pertaining to the Church their necessities must be provided for; and so let them share life in common, or share in common that which the Father of their family appoints them to suffer.

3. But if it shall happen that all suffer, whether some suffer less, and others more, or all suffer equally, it is easy to see who among them are suffering for the sake of others: they are obviously those who, although they might have freed themselves from such evils by flight, have chosen to remain rather than abandon others to whom they are necessary. By such conduct especially is proved the love commended by the Apostle John in the words: "Christ laid down His life for us: and we ought to lay down our lives for the brethren."[6] For those who betake themselves to flight, or are prevented from doing so only by circumstances thwarting their design, if they be seized and made to suffer, endure this suffering only for themselves, not for their breth-

---

[1] Bishop of Thiaba in Mauritania.
[2] This letter is not extant.
[3] Ps. xxxi. 3, LXX.

[4] Matt. x. 23.
[5] 2 Cor xi. 33.
[6] 1 John iii. 16.

ren; but those who are involved in suffering because of their resolving not to abandon others, whose Christian welfare depended on them, are unquestionably "laying down their lives for the brethren."

4. For this reason, the saying which we have heard attributed to a certain bishop, namely: "If the Lord has commanded us to flee, in those persecutions in which we may reap the fruit of martyrdom, how much more ought we to escape by flight, if we can, from barren sufferings inflicted by the hostile incursions of barbarians!" is a saying true and worthy of acceptation, but applicable only to those who are not confined by the obligations of ecclesiastical office. For the man who, having it in his power to escape from the violence of the enemy, chooses not to flee from it, lest in so doing he should abandon the ministry of Christ, without which men can neither become Christians nor live as such, assuredly finds a greater reward of his love, than the man who, fleeing not for his brethren's sake but for his own, is seized by persecutors, and, refusing to deny Christ, suffers martyrdom.

5. What, then, shall we say to the position which you thus state in your former epistle:— "I do not see what good we can do to ourselves or to the people by continuing to remain in the churches, except to see before our eyes men slain, women outraged, churches burned, ourselves expiring amid torments applied in order to extort from us what we do not possess"? God is powerful to hear the prayers of His children, and to avert those things which they fear; and we ought not, on account of evils that are uncertain, to make up our minds absolutely to the desertion of that ministry, without which the people must certainly suffer ruin, not in the affairs of this life, but of that other life which ought to be cared for with incomparably greater diligence and solicitude. For if those evils which are apprehended, as possibly visiting the places in which we are, were certain, all those for whose sake it was our duty to remain would take flight before us, and would thus exempt us from the neccessity of remaining; for no one says that ministers are under obligation to remain in any place where none remain to whom their ministry is necessary. In this way some holy bishops fled from Spain when their congregations had, before their flight, been annihilated, the members having either fled, or died by the sword, or perished in the siege of their towns, or gone into captivity: but many more of the bishops of that country remained in the midst of these abounding dangers, because those for whose sakes they remained were still remaining there. And if some have abandoned their flocks, this is what we say ought not to be done, for they were not taught to do so by divine author-

ity, but were, through human infirmity, either deceived by an error or overcome by fear.

6. [We maintain, as one alternative, that they were deceived by an error,] for why do they think that indiscriminate compliance must be given to the precept in which they read of fleeing from one city to another, and not shrink with abhorrence from the character of the "hireling," who "seeth the wolf coming, and fleeth, because he careth not for the sheep"?[1] Why do they not honour equally both of these true sayings of the Lord, the one in which flight is permitted or enjoined, the other in which it is rebuked and censured, by taking pains so to understand them as to find that they are, as is indeed the case, not opposed to each other? And how is their reconciliation to be found, unless that which I have above proved be borne in mind, that under pressure of persecution we who are ministers of Christ ought to flee from the places in which we are only in one or other of two cases, namely, either that there is no congregation to which we may minister, or that there is a congregation, but that the ministry necessary for it can be supplied by others who have not the same reason for flight as makes it imperative on us? Of which we have one example, as already mentioned, in the Apostle Paul escaping by being let down from the wall in a basket, when he was personally sought by the persecutor, there being others on the spot who had not the same necessity for flight, whose remaining would prevent the Church from being destitute of the service of ministers. Another example we have in the holy Athanasius, Bishop of Alexandria, who fled when the Emperor Constantius wished to seize him specially, the Catholic people who remained in Alexandria not being abandoned by the other servants of God. But when the people remain and the servants of God flee, and their service is withdrawn, what is this but the guilty flight of the "hireling" who careth not for the sheep? For the wolf will come,—not man, but the devil, who has very often perverted to apostasy believers to whom the daily ministry of the Lord's body was wanting; and so, not "through thy knowledge," but through thine ignorance, "shall the weak brother perish for whom Christ died."[2]

7. As for those, however, who flee not because they are deceived by an error, but because they have been overcome by fear, why do they not rather, by the compassion and help of the Lord bestowed on them, bravely fight against their fear, lest evils incomparably heavier and much more to be dreaded befall them? This victory over fear is won wherever the flame of the love of God, without the smoke of worldliness, burns

[1] John x. 12, 13.
[2] 1 Cor. viii. 9, 11.

in the heart. For love says, "Who is weak, and I am not weak? who is offended, and I burn not?"[1] But love is from God. Let us, therefore, beseech Him who requires it of us to bestow it on us, and under its influence let us fear more lest the sheep of Christ should be slaughtered by the sword of spiritual wickedness reaching the heart, than lest they should fall under the sword that can only harm that body in which men are destined at any rate, at some time, and in some way or other, to die. Let us fear more lest the purity of faith should perish through the taint of corruption in the inner man, than lest our women should be subjected by violence to outrage; for if chastity is preserved in the spirit, it is not destroyed by such violence, since it is not destroyed even in the body when there is no base consent of the sufferer to the sin, but only a submission without the consent of the will to that which another does. Let us fear more lest the spark of life in "living stones" be quenched through our absence, than lest the stones and timbers of our earthly buildings be burned in our presence. Let us fear more lest the members of Christ's body should die for want of spiritual food, than lest the members of our own bodies, being overpowered by the violence of enemies, should be racked with torture. Not because these are things which we ought not to avoid when this is in our power, but because we ought to prefer to suffer them when they cannot be avoided without impiety, unless, perchance, any one be found to maintain that that servant is not guilty of impiety who withdraws the service necessary to piety at the very time when it is peculiarly necessary.

8. Do we forget how, when these dangers have reached their extremity, and there is no possibility of escaping from them by flight, an extraordinary crowd of persons, of both sexes and of all ages, is wont to assemble in the church, — some urgently asking baptism, others reconciliation, others even the doing of penance, and all calling for consolation and strengthening through the administration of sacraments? If the ministers of God be not at their posts at such a time, how great perdition overtakes those who depart from this life either not regenerated or not loosed from their sins![2] How deep also is the sorrow of their believing kindred, who shall not have these lost ones with them in the blissful rest of eternal life! In fine, how loud are the cries of all, and the indignant imprecations of not a few, because of the want of ordinances and the absence of those who should have dispensed them! See what the fear of temporal calamities may effect, and of how great a multitude of eternal calamities it may be the

procuring cause. But if the ministers be at their posts, through the strength which God bestows upon them, all are aided, — some are baptized, others reconciled to the Church. None are defrauded of the communion of the Lord's body; all are consoled, edified, and exhorted to ask of God, who is able to do so, to avert all things which are feared, — prepared for both alternatives, so that "if the cup may not pass" from them, His will may be done[3] who cannot will anything that is evil.

9. Assuredly you now see (what, according to your letter, you did not see before) how great advantage the Christian people may obtain if, in the presence of calamity, the presence of the servants of Christ be not withdrawn from them. You see, also, how much harm is done by their absence, when "they seek their own, not the things that are Jesus Christ's,"[4] and are destitute of that charity of which it is said, "it seeketh not her own,"[5] and fail to imitate him who said, "I seek not mine own profit, but the profit of many, that they may be saved,"[6] and who, moreover, would not have fled from the insidious attacks of the imperial persecutor, had he not wished to save himself for the sake of others to whom he was necessary; on which account he says, "I am in a strait betwixt two, having a desire to depart, and to be with Christ; which is far better: nevertheless to abide in the flesh is more needful for you."[7]

10. Here, perhaps, some one may say that the servants of God ought to save their lives by flight when such evils are impending, in order that they may reserve themselves for the benefit of the Church in more peaceful times. This is rightly done by some, when others are not wanting by whom the service of the Church may be supplied, and the work is not deserted by all, as we have stated above that Athanasius did; for the whole Catholic world knows how necessary it was to the Church that he should do so, and how useful was the prolonged life of the man who by his word and loving service defended her against the Arian heretics. But this ought by no means to be done when the danger is common to all; and the thing to be dreaded above all is, lest any one should be supposed to do this not from a desire to secure the welfare of others, but from fear of losing his own life, and should therefore do more harm by the example of deserting the post of duty than all the good that he could do by the preservation of his life for future service. Finally, observe how the holy David acquiesced in the urgent petition of his people, that he should

[1] 2 Cor. xi. 29.
[2] Ligati.

[3] Matt. xxvi. 42.
[4] Phil. ii. 21.
[5] 1 Cor. xiii. 5.
[6] 1 Cor. x. 33.
[7] Phil. i. 23, 24.

not expose himself to the dangers of battle, and, as it is said in the narrative, " quench the light of Israel," [1] but was not himself the first to propose it ; for had he been so, he would have made many imitate the cowardice which they might have attributed to him, supposing that he had been prompted to this not through regard to the advantage of others, but under the agitation of fear as to his own life.

11. Another question which we must not regard as unworthy of notice is suggested here. For if the interests of the Church are not to be lost sight of, and if these make it necessary that when any great calamity is impending some ministers should flee, in order that they may survive to minister to those whom they may find remaining after the calamity is passed, — the question arises, what is to be done when it appears that, unless some flee, all must perish together ? what if the fury of the destroyer were so restricted as to attack none but the ministers of the Church ? What shall we reply ? Is the Church to be deprived of the service of her ministers because of fleeing from their work through fear lest she should be more unhappily deprived of their service because of their dying in the midst of their work ? Of course, if the laity are exempted from the persecution, it is in their power to shelter and conceal their bishops and clergy in some way, as He shall help them under whose dominion all things are, and who, by His wondrous power, can preserve even one who does not flee from danger. But the reason for our inquiring what is the path of our duty in such circumstances is, that we may not be chargeable with tempting the Lord by expecting divine miraculous interposition on every occasion.

There is, indeed, a difference in the severity of the tempest of calamity when the danger is common to both laity and clergy, as the perils of stormy weather are common to both merchants and sailors on board of the same ship. But far be it from us to esteem this ship of ours so lightly as to admit that it would be right for the crew, and especially for the pilot, to abandon her in the hour of peril, although they might have it in their power to escape by leaping into a small boat, or even swimming ashore. For in the case of those in regard to whom we fear lest through our deserting our work they should perish, the evil which we fear is not temporal death, which is sure to come at one time or other, but eternal death, which may come or may not come, according as we neglect or adopt measures whereby it may be averted. Moreover, when the lives of both laity and clergy are exposed to common danger, what reason have

we for thinking that in every place which the enemy may invade all the clergy are likely to be put to death, and not that all the laity shall also die, in which event the clergy, and those to whom they are necessary, would pass from this life at the same time ? Or why may we not hope that, as some of the laity are likely to survive, some of the clergy may also be spared, by whom the necessary ordinances may be dispensed to them ?

12. Oh that in such circumstances the question debated among the servants of God were which of their number should remain, that the Church might not be left destitute by all fleeing from danger, and which of their number should flee, that the Church might not left destitute by all perishing in the danger. Such a contest will arise among the brethren who are all alike glowing with love and satisfying the claims of love. And if it were in any case impossible otherwise to terminate the debate, it appears to me that the persons who are to remain and who are to flee should be chosen by lot. For those who say that they, in preference to others, ought to flee, will appear to be chargeable either with cowardice, as persons unwilling to face impending danger, or with arrogance, as esteeming their own lives more necessary to be preserved for the good of the Church than those of other men. Again, perhaps, those who are better will be first to choose to lay down their lives for the brethren ; and so preservation by flight will be given to men whose life is less valuable because their skill in counselling and ruling the Church is less ; yet these, if they be pious and wise, will resist the desires of men in regard to whom they see, on the one hand, that it is more important for the Church that they should live, and on the other hand, that they would rather lose their lives than flee from danger. In this case, as it is written, " the lot causeth contentions to cease, and parteth between the mighty ; " [2] for, in difficulties of this kind, God judges better than men, whether it please Him to call the better among His servants to the reward of suffering, and to spare the weak, or to make the weak stronger to endure trials, and then to withdraw them from this life, as persons whose lives could not be so serviceable to the Church as the lives of the others who are stronger than they. If such an appeal to the lot be made, it will be, I admit, an unusual proceeding, but if it is done in any case, who will dare to find fault with it ? Who but the ignorant or the prejudiced will hesitate to praise with the approbation which it deserves ? If, however, the use of the lot is not adopted because there is no precedent for such an appeal, let it by all means be secured that the Church

---

[1] 2 Sam. xxi. 17.

[2] Prov. xviii. 18.

be not, through the flight of any one, left destitute of that ministry which is more especially necessary and due to her in the midst of such great dangers. Let no one hold himself in such esteem because of apparent superiority in any grace as to say that he is more worthy of life than others, and therefore more entitled to seek safety in flight. For whoever thinks this is too self-satisfied, and whoever utters this must make all dissatisfied with him.

13. There are some who think that bishops and clergy may, by not fleeing but remaining in such dangers, cause the people to be misled, because, when they see those who are set over them remaining, this makes them not flee from danger. It is easy for them, however, to obviate this objection, and the reproach of misleading others, by addressing their congregations, and saying: "Let not the fact that we are not fleeing from this place be the occasion of misleading you, for we remain here not for our own sakes but for yours, that we may continue to minister to you whatever we know to be necessary to your salvation, which is in Christ; therefore, if you choose to flee, you thereby set us also at liberty from the obligations by which we are bound to remain." This, I think, ought to be said, when it seems to be truly advantageous to remove to places of greater security. If, after such words have been spoken in their hearing, either all or some shall say: "We are at His disposal from whose anger none can escape whithersoever they may go, and whose mercy may be found wherever their lot is cast by those who, whether hindered by known insuperable difficulties, or unwilling to toil after unknown refuges, in which perils may be only changed not finished, prefer not to go away elsewhere," — most assuredly those who thus resolve to remain ought not to be left destitute of the service of Christian ministers. If, on the other hand, after hearing their bishops and clergy speak as above, the people prefer to leave the place, to remain behind them is not now the duty of those who were only remaining for their sakes, because none are left there on whose account it would still be their duty to remain.

14. Whoever, therefore, flees from danger in circumstances in which the Church is not deprived, through his flight, of necessary service, is doing that which the Lord has commanded or permitted. But the minister who flees when the consequence of his flight is the withdrawal from Christ's flock of that nourishment by which its spiritual life is sustained, is an "hireling who seeth the wolf coming, and fleeth because he careth not for the sheep."

With love, which I know to be sincere, I have now written what I believe to be true on this question, because you asked my opinion, my dearly beloved brother; but I have not enjoined you to follow my advice, if you can find any better than mine. Be that as it may, we cannot find anything better for us to do in these dangers than continually beseech the Lord our God to have compassion on us. And as to the matter about which I have written, namely, that ministers should not desert the churches of God, some wise and holy men have by the gift of God been enabled both to will and to do this thing, and have not in the least degree faltered in the determined prosecution of their purpose, even though exposed to the attacks of slanderers.

LETTER CCXXIX.

(A.D. 429.)

TO DARIUS,[1] HIS DESERVEDLY ILLUSTRIOUS AND VERY POWERFUL LORD AND DEAR SON IN CHRIST, AUGUSTIN SENDS GREETING IN THE LORD.

1. Your character and rank I have learned from my holy brothers and co-bishops, Urbanus and Novatus. The former of these became acquainted with you near Carthage, in the town of Hilari, and more recently in the town of Sicca; the latter at Sitifis. Through them it has come to pass that I cannot regard you as unknown to me. For though my bodily weakness and the chill of age do not permit me to converse with you personally, it cannot on this account be said that I have not seen you; for the conversation of Urbanus, when he kindly visited me, and the letters of Novatus, so described to me the features, not of your face but of your mind, that I have seen you, and have seen you with all the more pleasure, because I have seen not the outward appearance but the inner man. These features of your character are joyfully seen both by us, and through the mercy of God by yourself also, as in a mirror in the holy Gospel, in which it is written in words uttered by Him who is truth: "Blessed are the peacemakers: for they shall be called the children of God."[2]

2. Those warriors are indeed great and worthy of singular honour, not only for their consummate bravery, but also (which is a higher praise) for their eminent fidelity, by whose labours and dangers, along with the blessing of divine protection and aid, enemies previously unsubdued are conquered, and peace obtained for the State, and the provinces reduced to subjection. But it is a higher glory still to stay war itself with a word, than to slay men with the sword, and to

---

[1] This Darius was an officer of distinction in the service of the Empress Placidia, and was the instrument of effecting a reconciliation between her and Count Boniface. He was also successful in obtaining a truce with the Vandals, on which Augustin congratulates him in this letter.
[2] Matt. v. 9.

procure or maintain peace by peace, not by war. For those who fight, if they are good men, doubtless seek for peace; nevertheless it is through blood. Your mission, however, is to prevent the shedding of blood. Yours, therefore, is the privilege of averting that calamity which others are under the necessity of producing. Therefore, my deservedly illustrious and very powerful lord and very dear son in Christ, rejoice in this singularly great and real blessing vouchsafed to you, and enjoy it in God, to whom you owe that you are what you are, and that you undertook the accomplishment of such a work. May God "strengthen that which He hath wrought for us through you." [1] Accept this our salutation, and deign to reply. From the letter of my brother Novatus, I see that he has taken pains that your learned Excellency should become acquainted with me also through my works. If, then, you have read what he has given you, I also shall have become known to your inward perception. As far as I can judge, they will not greatly displease you if you have read them in a loving rather than a critical spirit. It is not much to ask, but it will be a great favour, if for this letter and my works you send us one letter in reply. I salute with due affection the pledge of peace,[2] which through the favour of our Lord and God you have happily received.

LETTER CCXXXI.

(A.D. 429.)

TO DARIUS, HIS SON, AND A MEMBER OF CHRIST, AUGUSTIN, A SERVANT OF CHRIST AND OF THE MEMBERS OF CHRIST, SENDS GREETING IN THE LORD.

1. You requested an answer from me as a proof that I had gladly received your letter.[3] Behold, then, I write again; and yet I cannot express the pleasure I felt, either by this answer or by any other, whether I write briefly or at the utmost length, for neither by few words nor by many is it possible for me to express to you what words can never express. I, indeed, am not eloquent, though ready in speech; but I could by no means allow any man, however eloquent, even though he could see as well into my mind as I do myself, to do that which is beyond my own power, viz. to describe in a letter, however able and however long, the effect which your epistle had on my mind. It remains, then,

for me so to express to you what you wished to know, that you may understand as being in my words that which they do not express. What, then, shall I say? That I was delighted with your letter, exceedingly delighted; — the repetition of this word is not a mere repetition, but, as it were, a perpetual affirmation; because it was impossible to be always saying it, therefore it has been at least once repeated, for in this way perhaps my feelings may be expressed.

2. If some one inquire here what after all delighted me so exceedingly in your letter, — "Was it its eloquence?" I will answer, No; and he, perhaps, will reply, "Was it, then, the praises bestowed on yourself?" but again I will reply, No; and I shall reply thus not because these things are not in that letter, for the eloquence in it is so great that it is very clearly evident that you are naturally endowed with the highest talents, and that you have been most carefully educated; and your letter is undeniably full of my praises. Some one then may say, "Do not these things delight you?" Yes, truly, for "my heart is not," as the poet says, "of horn," [4] so that I should either not observe these things or observe them without delight. These things do delight; but what have these things to do with that with which I said I was highly delighted? Your eloquence delights me since it is at once genial in sentiment and dignified in expression; and though assuredly I am not delighted with all sorts of praise from all sorts of persons, but only with such praises as you have thought me worthy of, and only coming from those who are such as you are — that is, from persons who, for Christ's sake, love His servants, I cannot deny that I am delighted with the praises bestowed upon me in your letter.

3. Thoughtful and experienced men will be at no loss as to the opinion which they should form of Themistocles (if I remember the name rightly), who, having refused at a banquet to play on the lyre, a thing which the distinguished and learned men of Greece were accustomed to do, and having been on that account regarded as uneducated, was asked, when he expressed his contempt for that sort of amusement, "What, then, does it delight you to hear?" and is reported to have answered: "My own praises." Thoughtful and experienced men will readily see with what design and in what sense these words must have been used by him, or must be understood by them, if they are to believe that he uttered them; for he was in the affairs of this world a most remarkable man, as may be illustrated by the answer which he gave when he was further pressed with the question: "What, then, do you know?" "I know," he replied,

---

[1] Ps. lxviii. 29.
[2] Verimodus, the son of Darius.
[3] Referring to Darius' reply (Letter CCXXX.) to the foregoing Letter (CCXXIX.). In it, Darius, after reciprocating in the warmest manner every expression of admiration and esteem, expresses his hope that the peace concluded with the Vandals may be permanent, entreats Augustin to pray for him (alluding to the letter said to have been written by Abgaris, king of Edessa, to our Saviour), and asks him to send a copy of his *Confessions* along with his reply to this communication.

[4] Persius, *Sat.* i. line 47. "Cornea."

"how to make a small republic great." As to the thirst for praise spoken of by Ennius in the words : "All men greatly desire to be praised," I am of opinion that it is partly to be approved of, partly guarded against. For as, on the one hand, we should vehemently desire the truth, which is undoubtedly to be eagerly sought after as alone worthy of praise, even though it be not praised : so, on the other hand, we must carefully shun the vanity which readily insinuates itself along with praise from men : and this vanity is present in the mind when either the things which are worthy of praise are not reckoned worth having unless the man be praised for them by his fellow-men, or things on account of possessing which any man wishes to be much praised are deserving either of small praise, or it may be of severe censure. Hence Horace, a more careful observer than Ennius, says : "Is fame your passion? Wisdom's powerful charm if thrice read over shall its power disarm."[1]

4. Thus the poet thought that the malady arising from the love of human praise, which was thoroughly attacked with his satire, was to be charmed away by words of healing power. The great Teacher has accordingly taught us by His apostle, that we ought not to do good with a view to be praised by men, that is, we ought not to make the praises of men the motive for our well-doing ; and yet, for the sake of men themselves, He teaches us to seek their approbation. For when good men are praised, the praise does not benefit those on whom it is bestowed, but those who bestowed it. For to the good, so far as they are themselves concerned, it is enough that they are good ; but those are to be congratulated whose interest is to imitate the good when the good are praised by them, since they thus show that the persons whom they sincerely praise are persons whose conduct they appreciate. The apostle says in a certain place, "If I yet pleased men, I should not be the servant of Christ ; "[2] and the same apostle says in another place, " I please all men in all things," and adds the reason, " Not seeking mine own profit, but the profit of many, that they may be saved."[3] Behold what he sought in the praise of men, as it is declared in these words : " Finally, my brethren, whatsoever things are true, whatsoever things are honest, whatsoever things are just, whatsoever things are pure, whatsoever things are lovely, whatsoever things are of good report ; if there be any virtue, and if there be any praise, think on these things. Those things, which ye have both learned, and received, and heard, and seen in me, do : and the God of peace shall be with you."[4] All the other things which

I have named above, he summed up under the name of Virtue, saying, " If there be any virtue ; " but the definition which he subjoined, " Whatsoever things are of good report," he followed up by another suitable word, " If there be any praise." What the apostle says, then, in the first of these passages, " If I yet pleased men, I should not be the servant of Christ," is to be understood as if he said, If the good things which I do were done by me with human praise as my motive, if I were puffed up with the love of praise, I should not be the servant of Christ. The apostle, then, wished to please all men, and rejoiced in pleasing them, not that he might himself be inflated with their praises, but that he being praised might build them up in Christ. Why, then, should it not delight me to be praised by you, since you are too good a man to speak insincerely, and you bestow your praise on things which you love, and which it is profitable and wholesome to love, even though they be not in me ? This, moreover, does not benefit you alone, but also me. For if they are not in me, it is good for me that I am put to the blush, and am made to burn with desire to possess them. And in regard to anything in your praise which I recognise as in my possession, I rejoice that I possess it, and that such things are loved by you, and that I am loved for their sake. And in regard to those things which I do not recognise as belonging to me, I not only desire to obtain them, that I may possess them for myself, but also that those who love me sincerely may not always be mistaken in praising me for them.

5. Behold how many things I have said, and still I have not yet spoken of that in your letter which delighted me more than your eloquence, and far more than the praises you bestowed on me. What do you think, O excellent man, that this can be ? It is that I have acquired the friendship of so distinguished a man as you are, and that without having even seen you ; if, indeed, I ought to speak of one as unseen whose soul I have seen in his own letters, though I have not seen his body. In which letters I rest my opinion concerning you on my own knowledge, and not, as formerly, on the testimony of my brethren. For what your character was I had already heard, but how you stood affected to me I knew not until now. From this, your friendship to me, I doubt not that even the praises bestowed on me, which give me pleasure for a reason about which I have already said enough, will much more abundantly benefit the Church of Christ, since the fact that you possess, and study, and love, and commend my labours in defence of the gospel against the remnant of impious idolaters, secures for me a wider influence in these writings in proportion to the high position which you occupy ; for, illustrious your-

---

[1] Horace, Book I. *Ep.* i. lines 36-37. Francis' translation.
[2] Gal. i. 10.
[3] 1 Cor. x. 33.
[4] Phil. iv. 8-9.

self, you insensibly shed a lustre upon them. You, being celebrated, give celebrity to them, and wherever you shall see that the circulation of them might do good, you will not suffer them to remain altogether unknown. If you ask me how I know this, my reply is, that such is the impression concerning you produced on me by reading your letters. Herein you will now see how great delight your letter could impart to me, for if your opinion of me be favourable, you are aware how great delight is given to me by gain to the cause of Christ. Moreover, when you tell me concerning yourself that, although, as you say, you belong to a family which not for one or two generations, but even to remote ancestors, has been known as able to accept the doctrine of Christ, you have nevertheless been aided by my writings against the Gentile rites so to understand these as you never had done before, can I esteem it a small matter how great benefit our writings, commended and circulated by you, may confer upon others, and to how many and how illustrious persons your testimony may bring them, and how easily and profitably through these persons they may reach others? Or, reflecting on this, can the joy diffused in my heart be small or moderate in degree?

6. Since, then, I cannot in words express how great delight I have received from your letter, I have spoken of the reason why it delighted me, and may that which I am unable adequately to utter on this subject I leave to you to conjecture. Accept, then, my son — accept, O excellent man, Christian not by outward profession merely, but by Christian love — accept, I say, the books containing my " Confessions," which you desired to have. In these behold me, that you may not praise me beyond what I am; in these believe what is said of me, not by others, but by myself; in these contemplate me, and see what I have been in myself, by myself; and if anything in me please you, join me, because of it, in praising Him to whom, and not to myself, I desire praise to be given. For " He hath made us, and not we ourselves ; " [1] indeed, we had destroyed ourselves, but He who made us has made us anew. When, however, you find me in these books, pray for me that I may not fail, but be perfected. Pray, my son ; pray. I feel what I say ; I know what I ask. Let it not seem to you a thing unbecoming, and, as it were, beyond your merits. You will defraud me of a great help if you do not do so. Let not only you yourself, but all also who by your testimony shall come to love me, pray for me. Tell them that I have entreated this, and if you think highly of us, consider that we command what we have asked ; in any case,

whether as granting a request or obeying a command, pray for us. Read the Divine Scriptures, and you will find that the apostles themselves, the leaders of Christ's flock, requested this from their sons, or enjoined it on their hearers. I certainly, since you ask it of me, will do this for you as far as I can. He sees this who is the Hearer of prayer, and who saw that I prayed for you before you asked me ; but let this proof of love be reciprocated by you. We are placed over you ; you are the flock of God. Consider and see that our dangers are greater than yours, and pray for us, for this becomes both us and you, that we may give a good account of you to the Chief Shepherd and Head over us all, and may escape both from the trials of this world and its allurements, which are still more dangerous, except when the peace of this world has the effect for which the apostle has directed us to pray, " That we may lead a quiet and peaceable life in all godliness and honesty." [2] For if godliness and honesty be wanting, what is a quiet and peaceful exemption from the evils of the world but an occasion either of inviting men to enter, or assisting men to follow, a course of self-indulgence and perdition? Do you, then, ask for us what we ask for you, that we may lead a quiet and peaceable life in all godliness and honesty. Let us ask this for each other wherever you are and wherever we are, for He whose we are is everywhere present.

7. I have sent you also other books which you did not ask, that I might not rigidly restrict myself to what you asked : — my works on *Faith in Things Unseen*, on *Patience*, on *Continence*, on *Providence*, and a large work on *Faith, Hope, and Charity*. If, while you are in Africa, you shall read all these, either send your opinion of them to me, or let it be sent to some place whence it may be sent us by my lord and brother Aurelius, though wherever you shall be we hope to have letters from you ; and do you expect letters from us as long as we are able. I most gratefully received the things you sent to me, in which you deigned to aid me both in regard to my bodily health,[3] since you desire me to be free from the hindrance of sickness in devoting my time to God, and in regard to my library, that I may have the means to procure new books and repair the old. May God recompense you, both in the present life and in that to come, with those favours which He has prepared for such as He has willed you to be. I request you now to salute again for me, as before, the pledge of peace entrusted to you, very dear to both of us.

---

[1] Ps. c. 3.

[2] 1 Tim. ii. 2.
[3] The reference is to some medicines sent by Darius, and mentioned by him in the end of his letters.

FOURTH DIVISION.

[Hitherto the order followed in the arrangement of the letters has been the chronological. It being impossible to ascertain definitely the date of composition of thirty-nine of the letters, these have been placed by the Benedictine editors in the fourth division, and in it they are arranged under two principal divisions, the first embracing some controversial letters, and the second a number of those which were occasioned either by Augustin's interest in the welfare of individuals, or by the claims of official duty.]

LETTER CCXXXII.

TO THE PEOPLE OF MADAURA, MY LORDS WORTHY OF PRAISE, AND BRETHREN MOST BELOVED, AUGUSTIN SENDS GREETING, IN REPLY TO THE LETTER RECEIVED BY THE HANDS OF BROTHER FLORENTINUS.

1. IF, perchance, such a letter as I have received was sent to me by those among you who are Catholic Christians, the only thing at which I am surprised is, that it was sent in the name of the municipality, and not in their own name. If, however, it has pleased all or almost all of your men of rank to send a letter to me, I am surprised at the title "Father" and the "salutation in the Lord" addressed to me by you, of whom I know certainly, and with much regret, that you regard with superstitious veneration those idols against which your temples are more easily shut than your hearts; or, I should rather say, those idols which are not more truly shut up in your temples than in your hearts.[1] Can it be that you are at last, after wise reflection, seriously thinking of that salvation which is in the Lord, in whose name you have chosen to salute me? For if it be not so, I ask you, my lords worthy of all praise, and brethren most beloved, in what have I injured, in what have I offended your benevolence, that you should think it right to treat me with ridicule rather than with respect in the salutation prefixed to your letter?

2. For when I read the words, "To Father Augustin, eternal salvation in the Lord," I was suddenly elated with such fulness of hope, that I believed you either already converted to the Lord Himself, and to that eternal salvation of which He is the author, or desirous, through our ministry, to be so converted. But when I read the rest of the letter my heart was chilled. I inquired, however, from the bearer of the letter, whether you were already Christians or were desirous to be so. After I learned from his answer that you were in no way changed, I was deeply grieved that you thought it right not only to reject the name of Christ, to whom you already see the whole world submitting, but even to insult His name in my person; for I could not think of any other Lord than Christ the Lord in whom a bishop could be addressed by you as a father, and if there had been any doubt as to the meaning to be attached to your words, it would have been removed by the closing sentence of your letter, where you say plainly, "We desire that, for many years, your lordship may always, in the midst of your clergy, be glad in God and His Christ." After reading and pondering all these things, what could I (or, indeed, could any man) think but that these words were written either as the genuine expression of the mind of the writers, or with an intention to deceive? If you write these things as the genuine expression of your mind, who has barred your way to the truth? Who has strewn it with thorns? What enemy has placed masses of rock across your path? In fine, if you are desiring to come in, who has shut the door of our places of worship against you, so that you are unwilling to enjoy the same salvation with us in the same Lord in whose name you salute us? But if you write these things deceitfully and mockingly, do you, then, in the very act of imposing on me the care of your affairs, presume to insult, with the language of feigned adulation, the name of Him through whom alone I can do anything, instead of honouring Him with the veneration which is due to Him?

3. Be assured, dearest brethren, that it is with inexpressible trembling of heart on your account that I write this letter to you, for I know how much greater in the judgment of God must be your guilt and your doom if I shall have said these things to you in vain. In regard to everything in the history of the human race which our forefathers observed and handed down to us, and not less in regard to everything connected with the seeking and holding of true religion which we now see and put on record for those who come after us, the Divine Scriptures have not been silent; so far from this, all things come to pass exactly according to the predictions of Scripture. You cannot deny that you see the Jewish people torn from the abodes of their ancestry, dispersed and scattered over almost every country: now, the origin of that people, their gradual increase, their losing of the kingdom,

---

[1] Reference is here made to the laws of Honorius against idolatry, passed in A.D. 399. See below in sec. 3.

their dispersion through all the world, have happened exactly as foretold. You cannot deny that you see that the word of the Lord, and the law coming forth from that people through Christ, who was miraculously born among their nation, has taken and retained possession of the faith of all nations : now we read of all these announced beforehand as we see them. You cannot deny that you see what we call heresies and schisms, that is, many cut off from the root of the Christian society, which by means of the Apostolic Sees, and the successions of bishops, is spread abroad in an indisputably world-wide diffusion, claiming the name of Christians, and as withering branches boasting of the mere appearance of being derived from the true vine : all this has been foreseen, predicted, and described in Scripture. You cannot deny that you see some temples of the idols fallen into ruin through neglect, others thrown down by violence, others closed, and some applied to other purposes ; you see the idols themselves either broken to pieces, or burnt, or shut up, or destroyed, and the same powers of this world, who in defence of idols persecuted Christians, now vanquished and subdued by Christians, who did not fight for the truth but died for it, and directing their attacks and their laws against the very idols in defence of which they put Christians to death, and the highest dignitary of the noblest empire laying aside his crown and kneeling as a suppliant at the tomb of the fisherman Peter.

4. The Divine Scriptures, which have now come into the hands of all, testified long before that all these things would come to pass. We rejoice that all these things have happened, with a faith which is strong in proportion to the discovery thereby made of the greatness of the authority with which they are declared in the sacred Scriptures. Seeing, then, that all these things have come to pass as foretold, are we, I ask, to suppose that the judgment of God, which we read of in the same Scriptures as appointed to separate finally between the believing and the unbelieving, is the only event in regard to which the prophecy is to fail? Yea, certainly, as all these events have come, it shall also come. Nor shall there be a man of our time who shall be able in that day to plead anything in defence of his unbelief. For the name of Christ is on the lips of every man : it is invoked by the just man in doing justice, by the perjurer in the act of deceiving, by the king to confirm his rule, by the soldier to nerve himself for battle, by the husband to establish his authority, by the wife to confess her submission, by the father to enforce his command, by the son to declare his obedience, by the master in supporting his right to govern, by the slave in performing his duty, by the humble in quickening piety,

by the proud in stimulating ambition, by the rich man when he gives, and by the poor when he receives an alms, by the drunkard at his wine-cup, by the beggar at the gate, by the good man in keeping his word, by the wicked man in violating his promises : all frequently use the name of Christ, the Christian with genuine reverence, the Pagan with feigned respect ; and they shall undoubtedly give to that same Being whom they invoke an account both of the spirit and of the language in which they repeat His name.

5. There is One invisible, from whom, as the Creator and First Cause, all things seen by us derive their being : He is supreme, eternal, unchangeable, and comprehensible by none save Himself alone. There is One by whom the supreme Majesty utters and reveals Himself, namely, the Word, not inferior to Him by whom it is begotten and uttered, by which Word He who begets it is manifested. There is One who is holiness, the sanctifier of all that becomes holy, who is the inseparable and undivided mutual communion between this unchangeable Word by whom that First Cause is revealed, and that First Cause who reveals Himself by the Word which is His equal. But who is able with perfectly calm and pure mind to contemplate this whole Essence (whom I have endeavoured to describe without giving His name, instead of giving His name without describing Him), and to draw blessedness from that contemplation, and by sinking, as it were, in the rapture of such meditation, to become oblivious of self, and to press on to that the sight of which is beyond our sphere of perception ; in other words, to be clothed with immortality, and obtain that eternal salvation which you were pleased to desire on my behalf in your greeting? Who, I say, is able to do this but the man who, confessing his sins, shall have levelled with the dust all the vain risings of pride, and prostrated himself in meekness and humility to receive God as his Teacher?

6. Since, therefore, it is necessary that we be first brought down from vain self-sufficiency to lowliness of spirit, that rising thence we may attain to real exaltation, it was not possible that this spirit could be produced in us by any method at once more glorious and more gentle (subduing our haughtiness by persuasion instead of violence) than that the Word by whom the Father reveals Himself to angels, who is His Power and Wisdom, who could not be discerned by the human heart so long as it was blinded by love for the things which are seen, should condescend to assume our nature, and so to exercise and manifest His personality when incarnate as to make men more afraid of being elated by the pride of man, than of being brought low after the example of God. Therefore the Christ who is preached throughout the whole world is not

Christ adorned with an earthly crown, nor Christ rich in earthly treasures, nor Christ illustrious for earthly prosperity, but Christ crucified. This was ridiculed, at first, by whole nations of proud men, and is still ridiculed by a remnant among the nations, but it was the object of faith at first to a few and now to whole nations, because when Christ crucified was preached at that time, notwithstanding the ridicule of the nations, to the few who believed, the lame received power to walk, the dumb to speak, the deaf to hear, the blind to see, and the dead were restored to life. Thus, at length, the pride of this world was convinced that, even among the things of this world, there is nothing more powerful than the humility of God,[1] so that beneath the shield of a divine example that humility, which it is most profitable for men to practise, might find defence against the contemptuous assaults of pride.

7. O men of Madaura, my brethren, nay, my fathers,[2] I beseech you to awake at last: this opportunity of writing to you God has given to me. So far as I could, I rendered my service and help in the business of brother Florentinus, by whom, as God willed it, you wrote to me; but the business was of such a nature, that even without my assistance it might have been easily transacted, for almost all the men of his family, who reside at Hippo, know Florentinus, and deeply regret his bereavement. But the letter was sent by you to me, that, having occasion to reply, it might not seem presumptuous on my part, when the opportunity was afforded me by yourselves, to say something concerning Christ to the worshippers of idols. But I beseech you, if you have not taken His name in vain in that epistle, suffer not these things which I write to you to be in vain; but if in using His name you wished to mock me, fear Him whom the world formerly in its pride scorned as a condemned criminal, and whom the same world now, subjected to His sway, awaits as its Judge. For the desire of my heart for you, expressed as far as in my power by this letter, shall witness against you at the judgment-seat of Him who shall establish for ever those who believe in Him and confound the unbelieving. May the one true God deliver you wholly from the vanity of this world, and turn you to Himself, my lords worthy of all praise and brethren most beloved.

LETTER CCXXXVII.

This letter was addressed to Ceretius, a bishop, who had sent to Augustin certain apocryphal writings, on which the Spanish heretical sect called Priscillianists[3] founded some of their doctrines.

Ceretius had especially directed his attention to a hymn which they alleged to have been composed by the Lord Jesus Christ, and given by Him to His disciples on that night on which He was betrayed, when they sang an "hymn" before going out to the Mount of Olives. The length of the letter precludes its insertion here, but we believe it will interest many to read the few lines of this otherwise long-forgotten hymn, which Augustin has here preserved. They are as follows: —

> " Salvare volo et salvari volo;
> Solvere volo et solvi volo;
> Ornare volo et ornari volo;
> Generari volo;
> Cantare volo, saltate cuncti:
> Plangere volo, tundite vos omnes:
> Lucerna sum tibi, ille qui me vides;
> Janua sum tibi, quicunque me pulsas;
> Qui vides quod ago, tace opera mea;
> Verbo illusi cuncta et non sum illusus in totum."

The reader who ponders these extracts, and remembers the occasion on which the hymn is alleged to have been composed, will agree with us that Augustin employs a very unnecessary fulness of argument in devoting several paragraphs to demolish the claims advanced on its behalf as a revelation more profound and sacred than anything contained in the canonical Scriptures. Augustin also brings against the Priscillianists the charge of justifying perjury when it might be of service in concealing their real opinions, and quotes a line in which, as he had heard from some who once belonged to that sect, the lawfulness of such deceitful conduct was taught: —

> " Jura, perjura, secretum prodere noli."

LETTER CCXLV.

TO POSSIDIUS,[4] MY MOST BELOVED LORD AND VENERABLE BROTHER IN THE SACERDOTAL OFFICE, AND TO THE BRETHREN WHO ARE WITH HIM, AUGUSTIN AND THE BRETHREN WHO ARE WITH HIM SEND GREETING IN THE LORD.

1. It requires more consideration to decide what to do with those who refuse to obey you, than to discover how to show them that things which they do are unlawful. Meanwhile, however, the letter of your Holiness has come upon me when I am exceedingly pressed with business, and the very hasty departure of the bearer has made it necessary for me to write you in reply, but has not given me time to answer as I ought to have done in regard to the matters on which you have consulted me. Let me say,

---

[1] 1 Cor. i. 23-25.
[2] Referring to his birth at Tagaste (not far distant from Madaura), and to Madaura as the scene of the studies of his boyhood.
[3] See p. 268, note 6.

[4] Possidius, a disciple of Augustin, spoken of in Letter CI. sec. 1, p. 412, was the Bishop of Calama who made the narrow escape recorded in Letter XCI. sec. 8, p. 379. He was for forty years an intimate friend of Augustin, was with him at his death, and wrote his biography.

however, in regard to ornaments of gold and costly dress, that I would not have you come to a precipitate decision in the way of forbidding their use, except in the case of those who, neither being married nor intending to marry, are bound to consider only how they may please God. But those who belong to the world have also to consider how they may in these things please their wives if they be husbands, their husbands if they be wives;[1] with this limitation, that it is not becoming even in married women to uncover their hair, since the apostle commands women to keep their heads covered.[2] As to the use of pigments by women in colouring the face, in order to have a ruddier or a fairer complexion, this is a dishonest artifice, by which I am sure that even their own husbands do not wish to be deceived; and it is only for their own husbands that women ought to be permitted to adorn themselves, according to the toleration, not the injunction, of Scripture. For the true adorning, especially of Christian men and women, consists not only in the absence of all deceitful painting of the complexion, but in the possession not of magnificent golden ornaments or rich apparel, but of a blameless life.

2. As for the accursed superstition of wearing amulets (among which the ear-rings worn by men at the top of the ear on one side are to be reckoned), it is practised with the view not of pleasing men, but of doing homage to devils. But who can expect to find in Scripture express prohibition of every form of wicked superstition, seeing that the apostle says generally, "I would not that ye should have fellowship with devils,"[3] and again, "What concord hath Christ with Belial?"[4] unless, perchance, the fact that he named Belial, while he forbade in general terms fellowship with devils, leaves it open for Christians to sacrifice to Neptune, because we nowhere read an express prohibition of the worship of Neptune! Meanwhile, let those unhappy people be admonished that, if they persist in disobedience to salutary precepts, they must at least forbear from defending their impieties, and thereby involving themselves in greater guilt. But why should we argue at all with them if they are afraid to take off their ear-rings, and are not afraid to receive the body of Christ while wearing the badge of the devil?

As to ordaining a man who was baptized in the Donatist sect, I cannot take the responsibility of recommending you to do this; it is one thing for you to do it if you are left without alternative, it is another thing for me to advise that you should do it.

1 1 Cor. vii. 32–34.
2 1 Cor. xi. 5–13.
3 1 Cor. x. 20.
4 2 Cor. vi. 15.

LETTER CCXLVI.

TO LAMPADIUS, AUGUSTIN SENDS GREETING.

1. On the subject of Fate and Fortune, by which, as I perceived when I was with you, and as I now know in a more gratifying and more reliable way by your own letter, your mind is seriously disturbed, I ought to write you a considerable volume; the Lord will enable me to explain it in the manner which He knows to be best fitted to preserve your faith. For it is no small evil that when men embrace perverse opinions they are not only drawn by the allurement of pleasure to commit sin, but are also turned aside to vindicate their sin rather than seek to have it healed by acknowledging that they have done wrong.

2. Let me, therefore, briefly remind you of one thing bearing on the question which you certainly know, that all laws and all means of discipline, commendations, censures, exhortations, threatenings, rewards, punishments, and all other things by which mankind are managed and ruled, are utterly subverted and overthrown, and found to be absolutely devoid of justice, unless the will is the cause of the sins which a man commits. How much more legitimate and right, therefore, is it for us to reject the absurdities of astrologers [*mathematici*], than to submit to the alternative necessity of condemning and rejecting the laws proceeding from divine authority, or even the means needful for governing our own families. In this the astrologers themselves ignore their own doctrine as to Fate and Fortune, for when any one of them, after selling to moneyed simpletons his silly prognostications of Fate, calls back his thoughts from the ivory tablets to the management and care of his own house, he reproves his wife, not with words only, but with blows, if he finds her, I do not say jesting rather forwardly, but even looking too much out of the window. Nevertheless, if she were to expostulate in such a case, saying: "Why beat *me?* beat Venus, rather, if you can, since it is under that planet's influence that I am compelled to do what you complain of," — he would certainly apply his energies not to invent some of the absurd jargon by which he cajoles the public, but to inflict some of the just correction by which he maintains his authority at home.

3. When, therefore, any one, upon being reproved, affirms that Fate is the cause of the action, and insists that therefore he is not to be blamed, because he says that under the compulsion of Fate he did the action which is censured, let him come back to apply this to his own case, let him observe this principle in managing his own affairs: let him not chastise a dishonest servant; let him not complain of a disrespectful son; let him not utter threats against

a mischievous neighbour. For in doing which of these things would he act justly, if all from whom he suffers such wrong are impelled to commit it by Fate, not by any fault of their own? If, however, from the right inherent in himself, and the duty incumbent on him as the head of a family towards all whom for the time he has under his control, he exhorts them to do good, deters them from doing evil, commands them to obey his will, honours those who yield implicit obedience, inflicts punishment on those who set him at naught, gives thanks to those who do him good, and hates those who are ungrateful, — shall I wait to prove the absurdity of the astrologer's calculations of Fate, when I find him proclaiming, not by words but by deeds, things so conclusive against his pretensions that he seems to destroy almost with his own hands every hair on the heads of the astrologers?

If your eager desire is not satisfied with these few sentences, and demands a book which will take longer time to read on this subject, you must wait patiently until I get some respite from other duties; and you must pray to God that He may be pleased to allow both leisure and capacity to write, so as to set your mind at rest on this matter. I will, however, do this with more willing readiness, if your Charity does not grudge to remind me of it by frequent letters, and to show me in your reply what you think of this letter.

LETTER CCL.

TO HIS BELOVED LORD AND VENERABLE BROTHER AND PARTNER IN THE PRIESTLY OFFICE, AUXILIUS,[1] AUGUSTIN SENDS GREETING IN THE LORD.

1. Our son Classicianus, a man of rank, has addressed to me a letter complaining bitterly that he has suffered excommunication wrongfully at the hand of your Holiness. His account of the matter is, that he came to the church with a small escort suitable to his official authority, and begged of you that you would not, to the detriment of their own spiritual welfare, extend the privilege of the sanctuary to men who, after violating an oath which they had taken on the Gospel, were seeking in the house of faith itself assistance and protection in their crime of breaking faith; that thereafter the men themselves, reflecting on the sin which they had committed, went forth from the church, not under violent compulsion, but of their own accord; and that because of this transaction your Holiness was so displeased with him, that with the usual forms of ecclesiastical procedure you smote him and all his household with a sentence of excommunication.

On reading this letter from him, being very much troubled, the thoughts of my heart being agitated like the waves of a stormy sea, I felt it impossible to forbear from writing to you, to beg that if you have thoroughly examined your judgment in this matter, and have proved it by irrefragable reasoning or Scripture testimonies, you will have the kindness to teach me also the grounds on which it is just that a son should be anathematized for the sin of his father, or a wife for the sin of her husband, or a servant for the sin of his master, or how it is just that even the child as yet unborn should lie under an anathema, and be debarred, even though death were imminent, from the deliverance provided in the laver of regeneration, if he happen to be born in a family at the time when the whole household is under the ban of excommunication. For this is not one of those judgments merely affecting the body, in which, as we read in Scripture, some despisers of God were slain with all their households, though these had not been sharers in their impiety. In those cases, indeed, as a warning to the survivors, death was inflicted on *bodies* which, as mortal, were destined at some time to die; but a spiritual judgment, founded on what is written, "That which ye shall bind on earth shall be bound in heaven,"[2] — is binding on *souls*, concerning which it is said, "As the soul of the father is mine, so also the soul of the son is mine: the soul that sinneth it shall die."[3]

2. It may be that you have heard that other priests of great reputation have in some cases included the household of a transgressor in the anathema pronounced on him; but these could, perchance, if they were required, give a good reason for so doing. For my own part, although I have been most grievously troubled by the cruel excesses with which some men have vexed the Church, I have never ventured to do as you have done, for this reason, that if any one were to challenge me to justify such an act, I could give no satisfactory reply. But if, perchance, the Lord has revealed to you that it may be justly done, I by no means despise your youth and your inexperience, as having been but recently elevated to high office in the Church. Behold, though far advanced in life, I am ready to learn from one who is but young; and notwithstanding the number of years for which I have been a bishop, I am ready to learn from one who has not yet been a twelvemonth in the same office, if he undertakes to teach me how we can justify our conduct, either before men or before God, if we inflict a spiritual punishment on innocent souls because of another person's crime, in which they are not involved in the same way as they are involved in the original sin of Adam,

---

[1] Probably the Bishop of Nurco, named Auxilius, who was present at the conference in Carthage in 411.

[2] Matt. xvi. 19.
[3] Ezek. xviii. 14.

in whom "all have sinned." For although the son of Classicianus derived through his father, from our first parent, guilt which behoved to be washed away by the sacred waters of baptism, who hesitates for a moment to say that he is in no way responsible for any sin which his father may have committed, since he was born, without his participation? What shall I say of his wife? What of so many souls in the entire household?—of which if even one, in consequence of the severity which included the whole household in the excommunication, should perish through departing from the body without baptism, the loss thus occasioned would be an incomparably greater calamity than the bodily death of an innumerable multitude, even though they were innocent men, dragged from the courts of the sanctuary and murdered. If, therefore, you are able to give a good reason for this, I trust that you will in your reply communicate it to me, that I also may be able to do the same; but if you cannot, what right have you to do, under the promptings of inconsiderate excitement, an act for which, if you were asked to give a satisfactory reason, you could find none?

3 What I have said hitherto applies to the case even on the supposition that our son Classicianus has done something which might appear to demand most righteously at your hands the punishment of excommunication. But if the letter which he sent to me contained the truth, there was no reason why even he himself (even though his household had been exempted from the stroke) should have been so punished. As to this, however, I do not interfere with your Holiness; I only beseech you to pardon him when he asks forgiveness, if he acknowledges his fault; and if, on the other hand, you, upon reflection, acknowledge that he did nothing wrong, since in fact the right rather lay on his side who earnestly demanded that in the house of faith, faith should be sacredly kept, and that it should not be broken in the place where the sinfulness of such breach of faith is taught from day to day, do, in this event, what a man of piety ought to do,—that is to say, if to you as a man anything has happened such as was confessed by one who was truly a man of God in the words of the psalm, "Mine eye was discomposed by anger," [1] fail not to cry to the Lord, as he did, "Have pity on me, O Lord, for I am weak," [2] so that He may stretch forth His right hand to you, rebuking the storm of your passion, and making your mind calm that you may see and may perform what is just; for, as it is written, "the wrath of man worketh not the right-

eousness of God." [3] And think not that, because we are bishops, it is impossible for unjust passionate resentment to gain secretly upon us; let us rather remember that, because we are men, our life in the midst of temptation's snares is beset with the greatest possible dangers. Cancel, therefore, the ecclesiastical sentence which, perhaps under the influence of unusual excitement, you have passed; and let the mutual love which, even from the time when you were a catechumen, has united him and you, be restored again; let strife be banished and peace invited to return, lest this man who is your friend be lost to you, and the devil who is your enemy rejoice over you both. Mighty is the mercy of our God; it may be that His compassion shall hear even my prayer, imploring of Him that my sorrow on your account may not be increased, but that rather what I have begun to suffer may be removed; and may your youth, not despising my old age, be encouraged and made full of joy by His grace! Farewell!

[Annexed to this letter is a fragment of a letter written at the same time to Classicianus; it is as follows:—

To restrain those who for the offence of one soul bind a transgressor's entire household, that is, a large number of souls, under one sentence of excommunication, and especially to prevent any one from departing this life unbaptized in consequence of such an anathema,—also to decide the question whether persons ought not to be driven forth even from a church, who seek a refuge there in order that they may break the faith pledged to sureties, I desire with the Lord's help to use the necessary measures in our Council, and, if it be necessary, to write to the Apostolic See; that, by a unanimous authoritative decision of all, we may have the course which ought to be followed in these cases determined and established. One thing I say deliberately as an unquestionable truth, that if any believer has been wrongfully excommunicated, the sentence will do harm rather to him who pronounces it than to him who suffers this wrong. For it is by the Holy Spirit dwelling in holy persons that any one is loosed or bound, and He inflicts unmerited punishment upon no one; for by Him the love which worketh not evil is shed abroad in our hearts. [4]]

---

[1] Ps. vi. 8, LXX.
[2] Ps. vi. 3.

[3] Jas. i. 20.
[4] This noble vindication of Christian liberty merits quotation in the original:—"Illud plane non temere dixerim, quod si quisquam fidelium fuerit anathematus injuste, ei potius oberit qui faciet quam ei qui hanc patietur injuriam. Spiritus enim sanctus habitans in sanctis, per quem quisque ligatur aut solvitur, immeritam nulli pœnam ingerit: per eum quippe diffunditur charitas in cordibus nostris quæ non agit perperam."

LETTER CCLIV.

TO BENENATUS, MY MOST BLESSED LORD, MY ES-
TEEMED AND AMIABLE BROTHER AND PARTNER
IN THE PRIESTLY OFFICE, AND TO THE BRETH-
REN WHO ARE WITH HIM, AUGUSTIN AND THE
BRETHREN WHO ARE WITH HIM SEND GREETING
IN THE LORD.

The maiden[1] about whom your Holiness wrote
to me is at present disposed to think, that if she
were of full age she would refuse every proposal
of marriage. She is, however, so young, that
even if she were disposed to marriage, she ought
not yet to be either given or betrothed to any
one. Besides this, my lord Benenatus, brother
revered and beloved, it must be remembered
that God takes her under guardianship in His
Church with the design of protecting her against
wicked men; placing her, therefore, under my
care not so as that she can be given by me to
whomsoever I might choose, but so as that she
cannot be taken away against my will by any
person who would be an unsuitable partner.
The proposal which you have been pleased to
mention is one which, if she were disposed and
prepared to marry, would not displease me; but
whether she will marry any one, — although for
my own part, I would much prefer that she carried out what she now talks of, — I do not in the
meantime know, for she is at an age in which her
declaration that she wishes to be a nun is to be
received rather as the flippant utterance of one
talking heedlessly, than as the deliberate promise of one making a solemn vow. Moreover,
she has an aunt by the mother's side married to
our honourable brother Felix, with whom I have
conferred in regard to this matter, — for I neither could, nor indeed should have avoided consulting him, — and he has not been reluctant to
entertain the proposal, but has, on the contrary,
expressed his satisfaction; but he expressed not
unreasonably his regret that nothing had been
written to him on the subject, although his relationship entitled him to be apprised of it. For,
perhaps, the mother of the maiden will also
come forward, though in the meantime she does
not make herself known, and to a mother's
wishes in regard to the giving away of a daughter, nature gives in my opinion the precedence
above all others, unless the maiden herself be

already old enough to have legitimately a
stronger claim to choose for herself what she
pleases. I wish your Honour also to understand, that if the final and entire authority in the
matter of her marriage were committed to me,
and she herself, being of age and willing to
marry, were to entrust herself to me under God
as my Judge to give her to whomsoever I thought
best, — I declare, and I declare the truth, in saying that the proposal which you mention pleases
me meanwhile, but because of God being my
Judge I cannot pledge myself to reject on her
behalf a better offer if it were made; but whether
any such proposal shall at any future time be
made is wholly uncertain. Your Holiness perceives, therefore, how many important considerations concur to make it impossible for her to
be, in the meantime, definitely promised to any
one.

LETTER CCLXIII.

TO THE EMINENTLY RELIGIOUS LADY AND HOLY
DAUGHTER SAPIDA, AUGUSTIN SENDS GREETING
IN THE LORD.

1. The gift prepared by the just and pious industry of your own hands, and kindly presented
by you to me, I have accepted, lest I should increase the grief of one who needs, as I perceive,
much rather to be comforted by me; especially
because you expressed yourself as esteeming it
no small consolation to you if I would wear this
tunic, which you had made for that holy servant
of God your brother, since he, having departed
from the land of the dying, is raised above the
need of the things which perish in the using. I
have, therefore, complied with your desire, and
whatever be the kind and degree of consolation
which you may feel this to yield, I have not refused it to your affection for your brother.[2] The
tunic which you sent I have accordingly ac-

---

[1] The maiden referred to was an orphan whom a magistrate (*vir spectabilis*) had requested Augustin to bring up as a ward of the Church. Four letters written by him concerning her have been preserved, viz. the 252d, in which he intimates to Felix that he can decide nothing in regard to her without consulting the friend by whom she had been placed under his guardianship; the 253d, expressing to Benenatus his surprise that he should propose for her a marriage which would not strengthen the Church; the 254th, addressed also to Benenatus, in which we have translated as a specimen of the series; and the 255th, in which, writing to Rusticus, a Pagan who had sought her hand for his son, Augustin bluntly denies his request, referring him for the grounds of the refusal to his correspondence with Benenatus.

Two Catholic bishops named Benenatus attended the conference with the Donatists at Carthage in 412; the one who belonged to Hospsti, in Numidia, is supposed to be Augustin's correspondent.

[2] The hesitation which Augustin here indicates in regard to accepting this gift may be understood from the following sentences of one of his sermons: — "Let no one give me a present of clothing, whether linen, or tunic, or any other article of dress, except as a gift to be used in common by my brethren and myself. I will accept nothing for myself which is not to be of service to our community, because I do not wish to have anything which does not equally belong to all the rest. Wherefore I request you, my brethren, to offer me no gift of apparel which may not be worn by the others as suitably as by me. A gift of costly raiment, for example, may sometimes be presented to me as becoming apparel for a bishop to wear; but it is not becoming for Augustin, who is poor, and who is the son of poor parents. Would you have men say that in the Church I found means to obtain richer clothing than I could have had in my father's house, or in the pursuit of secular employment? That would be a shame to me! The clothing worn by me must be such that I can give it to my brethren if they require it. I do not wish anything which would not be suitable for a presbyter, a deacon, or a sub-deacon, for I receive everything in common with them. If gifts of more costly apparel be given to me, I shall sell them, as has been my custom hitherto, in order that, if the dress be not available for all, the money realized by the sale may be a common benefit. I sell them accordingly, and distribute their price among the poor. Wherefore, if any wish me to wear articles of clothing presented to me as gifts, let them give such clothing as shall not make me blush when I use it. For I assure you that a costly dress makes me blush, because it is not in harmony with my profession, or with such exhortations as I now give to you, and ill becomes one whose frame is bent, and whose locks are whitened, as you see, by age." — *Sermon* 356, Bened. edition, vol. v. col. 1389, quoted by Tillemont, xiii. p. 222.

cepted, and have already begun to wear it before writing this to you. Be therefore of good cheer; but apply yourself, I beseech you, to far better and far greater consolations, in order that the cloud which, through human weakness, gathers darkness closely round your heart, may be dissipated by the words of divine authority; and, at all times, so live that you may live with your brother, since he has so died that he lives still.

2. It is indeed a cause for tears that your brother, who loved you, and who honoured you especially for your pious life, and your profession as a consecrated virgin, is no more before your eyes, as hitherto, going in and out in the assiduous discharge of his ecclesiastical duties as a deacon of the church of Carthage, and that you shall no more hear from his lips the honourable testimony which, with kindly, pious, and becoming affection, he was wont to render to the holiness of a sister so dear to him. When these things are pondered, and are regretfully desired [1] with all the vehemence of long-cherished affection, the heart is pierced, and, like blood from the pierced heart, tears flow apace. But let your heart rise heavenward, and your eyes will cease to weep.[2] The things over the loss of which you mourn have indeed passed away, for they were in their nature temporary, but their loss does not involve the annihilation of that love with which Timotheus loved [his sister] Sapida, and loves her still: it abides in its own treasury, and is hidden with Christ in God. Does the miser lose his gold when he stores it in a secret place? Does he not then become, so far as lies in his power, more confidently assured that the gold is in his possession when he keeps it in some safer hiding-place, where it is hidden even from his eyes? Earthly covetousness believes that it has found a safer guardianship for its loved treasures when it no longer sees them; and shall heavenly love sorrow as if it had lost for ever that which it has only sent before it to the garner of the upper world? O Sapida, give yourself wholly to your high calling, and set your affections[3] on things above, where, at the right hand of God, Christ sitteth, who condescended for us to die, that we, though we were dead, might live, and to secure that no man should fear death as if it were destined to destroy him, and that no one of those for whom the Life died should after death be mourned for as if he had lost life. Take to yourself these and other similar divine consolations, before which human sorrow may blush and flee away.

3. There is nothing in the sorrow of mortals over their dearly beloved dead which merits displeasure; but the sorrow of believers ought not to be prolonged. If, therefore, you have been grieved till now, let this grief suffice, and sorrow not as do the heathen, "who have no hope."[4] For when the Apostle Paul said this, he did not prohibit sorrow altogether, but only such sorrow as the heathen manifest who have no hope. For even Martha and Mary, pious sisters, and believers, wept for their brother Lazarus, of whom they knew that he would rise again, though they knew not that he was at that time to be restored to life; and the Lord Himself wept for that same Lazarus, whom He was going to bring back from death;[5] wherein doubtless He by His example permitted, though He did not by any precept enjoin, the shedding of tears over the graves even of those regarding whom we believe that they shall rise again to the true life. Nor is it without good reason that Scripture saith in the book of Ecclesiasticus: "Let tears fall down over the dead, and begin to lament as if thou hadst suffered great harm thyself;" but adds, a little further on, this counsel, "and then comfort thyself for thy heaviness. For of heaviness cometh death, and the heaviness of the heart breaketh strength."[6]

4. Your brother, my daughter, is alive as to the soul, is asleep as to the body: "Shall not he who sleeps also rise again from sleep?"[7] God, who has already received his spirit, shall again give back to him his body, which He did not take away to annihilate, but only took aside to restore. There is therefore no reason for protracted sorrow, since there is a much stronger reason for everlasting joy. For even the mortal part of your brother, which has been buried in the earth, shall not be for ever lost to you;—that part in which he was visibly present with you, through which also he addressed you and conversed with you, by which he spoke with a voice not less thoroughly known to your ear than was his countenance when presented to your eyes, so that, wherever the sound of his voice was heard, even though he was not seen, he used to be at once recognised by you. These things are indeed withdrawn so as to be no longer perceived by the senses of the living, that the absence of the dead may make surviving friends mourn for them. But seeing that even the bodies of the dead shall not perish (as not even a hair of the head shall perish),[8] but shall, after being laid aside for a time, be received again never more to be laid aside, but fixed finally in the higher condition of existence into which they shall have

[1] For *requiritur* the Benedictine editors suggest *recurrit*, as a conjectural emendation of the text. We propose, and adopt in the translation, a simpler and perhaps more probable alteration, and read *requiruntur*.

[2] *Sursum sit cor et sicci erunt oculi.*

[3] In the Latin word *sapere* here employed, there is an allusion to her name (Sapida), which she has with a view to this repeated immediately before.

[4] 1 Thess. iv. 12.
[5] John xi. 19-35.
[6] Ecclus. xxxviii. 16-18.
[7] Ps. xli. 8, LXX.
[8] Luke xxi. 18.

been changed, certainly there is more cause for thankfulness in the sure hope for an immeasurable eternity, than for sorrow in the transient experience of a very short span of time. This hope the heathen do not possess, because they know not the Scriptures nor the power of God,[1] who is able to restore what was lost, to quicken what was dead, to renew what has been subjected to corruption, to re-unite things which have been severed from each other, and to preserve thenceforward for evermore what was originally corruptible and shortlived. These things He has promised, who has, by the fulfilment of other promises, given our faith good ground to believe that these also shall be fulfilled. Let your faith often discourse now to you on these things, because your hope shall not be disappointed, though your love may be now for a season interrupted in its exercise ; ponder these things ; in them find more solid and abundant consolation. For if the fact that I now wear (because he could not) the garment which you had woven for your brother yields some comfort to you, how much more full and satisfactory the comfort which you should find in considering that he for whom this was prepared, and who then did not require an imperishable garment, shall be clothed with incorruption and immortality !

[1] Matt. xxii. 29.

LETTER CCLXIX.

TO NOBILIUS, MY MOST BLESSED AND VENERABLE BROTHER AND PARTNER IN THE PRIESTLY OFFICE, AUGUSTIN SENDS GREETING.

So important is the solemnity at which your brotherly affection invites me to be present, that my heart's desire would carry my poor body to you, were it not that infirmity renders this impossible. I might have come if it had not been winter ; I might have braved the winter if I had been young : for in the latter case the warmth of youth would have borne uncomplainingly the cold of the season ; in the former case the warmth of summer would have met with gentleness the chill languor of old age. For the present, my lord most blessed, my holy and venerable partner in the priestly office, I cannot undertake in winter so long a journey, carrying with me as I must the frigid feebleness of very many years. I reciprocate the salutation due to your worth, on behalf of my own welfare I ask an interest in your prayers, and I myself beseech the Lord God to grant that the prosperity of peace may follow the dedication of so great an edifice to His sacred service.[2]

[2] This letter, probably one of the latest from the pen of Augustin, is the last of his letters in the Benedictine edition; the only remaining one, the 270th, was not written by Augustin, but addressed to him by an unknown correspondent.

INDEXES

THE CONFESSIONS OF ST. AUGUSTIN.

INDEX OF SUBJECTS.

THE CONFESSIONS OF ST. AUGUSTIN.

INDEX OF TEXTS.

LETTERS OF ST. AUGUSTIN.

INDEX OF SUBJECTS.

LETTERS OF ST. AUGUSTIN.

INDEX OF TEXTS.

LETTERS OF ST. AUGUSTIN.

INDEX OF AUTHORS QUOTED.

INDEX

EXHIBITING THE ORDER ACCORDING TO WHICH THE LETTERS TRANSLATED IN THESE VOLUMES ARE QUOTED WHEN REFERRED TO BY ANY AUTHOR (*e.g.* TILLEMONT, PAREUS, ETC.) PRIOR TO THE GENERAL RECEPTION OF THE BENEDICTINE AS THE STANDARD EDITION IN THE BEGINNING OF LAST CENTURY. THE NUMBER IN THE BENEDICTINE EDITION IS PLACED OPPOSITE THE EARLIER NUMBER OF EACH LETTER.

LETTERS OF ST. AUGUSTIN.